Lecture Notes in Computer Science 5168

Commenced Publication in 1973
Founding and Former Series Editors:
Gerhard Goos, Juris Hartmanis, and Jan van Leeuwen

Editorial Board

David Hutchison
  Lancaster University, UK
Takeo Kanade
  Carnegie Mellon University, Pittsburgh, PA, USA
Josef Kittler
  University of Surrey, Guildford, UK
Jon M. Kleinberg
  Cornell University, Ithaca, NY, USA
Alfred Kobsa
  University of California, Irvine, CA, USA
Friedemann Mattern
  ETH Zurich, Switzerland
John C. Mitchell
  Stanford University, CA, USA
Moni Naor
  Weizmann Institute of Science, Rehovot, Israel
Oscar Nierstrasz
  University of Bern, Switzerland
C. Pandu Rangan
  Indian Institute of Technology, Madras, India
Bernhard Steffen
  University of Dortmund, Germany
Madhu Sudan
  Massachusetts Institute of Technology, MA, USA
Demetri Terzopoulos
  University of California, Los Angeles, CA, USA
Doug Tygar
  University of California, Berkeley, CA, USA
Gerhard Weikum
  Max-Planck Institute of Computer Science, Saarbruecken, Germany

Emilio Luque   Tomàs Margalef
Domingo Benítez (Eds.)

Euro-Par 2008
Parallel Processing

14th International Euro-Par Conference
Las Palmas de Gran Canaria, Spain, August 26-29, 2008
Proceedings

Volume Editors

Emilio Luque
Tomàs Margalef
Universidad Autónoma de Barcelona (UAB)
Departamento de Arquitectura de Computadores y Sistemas Operativos
08193 Barcelona, Spain
E-mail: emilio.luque@uab.es, tomas.margalef@uab.cat

Domingo Benítez
Universidad de Las Palmas de Gran Canaria
Departamento de Informática y Sistemas
35001 Las Palmas de Gran Canaria, Spain
E-mail: dbenitez@dis.ulpgc.es

Library of Congress Control Number: 2008933375

CR Subject Classification (1998): C.2.4, D.1.3, D.3.2, H.2.4, C.4

LNCS Sublibrary: SL 1 – Theoretical Computer Science and General Issues

ISSN	0302-9743
ISBN-10	3-540-85450-9 Springer Berlin Heidelberg New York
ISBN-13	978-3-540-85450-0 Springer Berlin Heidelberg New York

This work is subject to copyright. All rights are reserved, whether the whole or part of the material is concerned, specifically the rights of translation, reprinting, re-use of illustrations, recitation, broadcasting, reproduction on microfilms or in any other way, and storage in data banks. Duplication of this publication or parts thereof is permitted only under the provisions of the German Copyright Law of September 9, 1965, in its current version, and permission for use must always be obtained from Springer. Violations are liable to prosecution under the German Copyright Law.

Springer is a part of Springer Science+Business Media

springer.com

© Springer-Verlag Berlin Heidelberg 2008
Printed in Germany

Typesetting: Camera-ready by author, data conversion by Scientific Publishing Services, Chennai, India
Printed on acid-free paper   SPIN: 12455478   06/3180   5 4 3 2 1 0

Preface

Euro-Par is an annual series of international conferences dedicated to the promotion and advancement of all aspects of parallel computing. The major themes can be divided into the broad categories of theory, high-performance, cluster and grid, and distributed and mobile computing. These four categories comprise 14 topics that focus on particular issues of the mentioned categories.

The objective of Euro-Par is to provide a forum within which to promote the development of parallel computing both as an industrial technique and an academic discipline, extending the frontier of both the state of the art and the state of practice. The main audience for and participants in Euro-Par are seen as researchers in academic departments, government laboratories and industrial organizations.

Previous Euro-Par conferences took place in Stockholm, Lyon, Passau, Southampton, Tolouse, Munich, Manchester, Padderborn, Klagenfurt, Pisa, Lisbon, Dresden and Rennes. Next year the conference will take place in Delft.

Euro-Par 2008 was the 14th conference in the Euro-Par series. It was jointly co-organized by the Computer Architecture and Operating Systems Department of the Universitat Autònoma of Barcelona and the University Institute for Intelligent Systems and Numerical Applications in Engineering of the Universidad de Las Palmas de Gran Canaria, at the Tafira Campus of Universidad de Las Palmas de Gran Canaria.

In this edition, nine workshops were held in conjunction with the main track of the conference. These workshops were the CoreGrid symposium, the Third Workshop on Virtualization in High-Performance Cluster and Grid Computing, the Unicore Summit 2008, the Second Workshop on Highly Parallel Processing on a Chip, the 5th International Workshop on Grid Economics and Business Models, the Workshop on Productivity and Performance Tools for HPC Application Development, the Real-time Online Interactive Applications on the Grid and the Abstractions for Distributed Systems Workshops and the Workshop on Secure, Trusted, Manageable and Controllable Grid Services.

As mentioned, the conference was organized in 14 topics. Each topic was supervised by a committee of four persons: a Global Chair, a Local Chair and two Vice-Chairs. Certain topics with a high number of submissions were managed by a larger committee with more vice-chairs. The call for papers attracted a total of 264 submissions, representing 36 countries (based on the corresponding author's country). A total number of 1,013 review reports were collected which makes an average of 3.84 review reports per paper. Four papers were selected for a Best Paper session and 85 papers were accepted as regular papers to be presented in the conference and included in the proceedings of the conference, representing 25 countries. The principal contributors by country were Spain with 22 accepted papers, France with 15 accepted papers, and Germany and the USA with 9 accepted papers each.

The conference was made possible due to the support of many individuals and organizations. A number of institutional and industrial sponsors contributed toward the organization of the conference. Their names and logos appear on the Euro-Par 2008 website http://www.caos.uab.es/europar2008/.

Special thanks are due to the authors of all the submitted papers, the members of the topic committees and all the reviewers in all topics, for their contributions to the success of the conference.

We are grateful to the members of the Euro-Par Steering Committee for their support. In particular, Anne-Marie Kermarrec and Luc Bougé, co-organizers of Euro-Par 2007, never failed to give us their prompt advice regarding all the organizational details. We owe special thanks to Christian Lengauer, Chairman of the Steering Committee, who was always available for sharing with us his experience in the organization of Euro-Par.

We are grateful to Springer for publishing these proceedings. In particular to Alfred Hofmann, and also especially to Anna Kramer and Christine Guenther, for their permanent availability and willingness to solve the difficulties that arose in the preparation of the proceedings.

It was our pleasure and honour to host Euro-Par 2008 at Universidad de Las Palmas de Gran Canaria. We hope all the participants enjoyed the technical program and the social events organized during the conference.

August 2008

Emilio Luque
Tomàs Margalef
Domingo Benítez

Organization

Euro-Par Steering Committee

Chair

Christian Lengauer   University of Passau, Germany

Vice-Chair

Luc Bougé   ENS Cachan, France

European Representatives

José Cunha	New University of Lisbon, Portugal
Marco Danelutto	University of Pisa, Italy
Rainer Feldmann	University of Paderborn, Germany
Christos Kaklamanis	Computer Technology Institute, Greece
Anne-Marie Kermarrec	IRISA, Rennes, France
Paul Kelly	Imperial College, UK
Harald Kosch	University of Klagenfurt, Austria
Thomas Ludwig	University of Heidelberg, Germany
Emilio Luque	Autonomous University of Barcelona, Spain
Luc Moreau	University of Southampton, UK
Wolfgang Nagel	Dresden University of Technology, Germany
Rizos Sakellariou	University of Manchester, UK

Non-European Representatives

Jack Dongarra	University of Tennessee at Knoxville, USA
Shinji Tomita	Kyoto University, Japan

Honorary Members

Ron Perrott	Queen's University Belfast, UK
Karl Dieter Reinartz	University of Erlangen-Nuremberg, Germany

Observers

Domingo Benítez   University of Las Palmas, Gran Canaria, Spain
Henk Sips   Delft University of Technology, The Netherlands

Euro-Par 2008 Local Organization

Conference Co-chairs

Emilio Luque	UAB	General Chair
Domingo Benítez	ULPGC	Vice-Chair
Tomàs Margalef	UAB	Vice-Chair

Local Organization Committee

Eduardo César (UAB)
Ana Cortés (UAB)
Daniel Franco (UAB)
Elisa Heymann (UAB)
Anna Morajko (UAB)
Juan Carlos Moure (UAB)
Dolores Rexachs (UAB)
Miquel Àngel Senar (UAB)
Joan Sorribes (UAB)
Remo Suppi (UAB)

Web and Technical Support

Daniel Ruiz (UAB)
Javier Navarro (UAB)

Euro-Par 2008 Program Committee

Topic 1: Support Tools and Environments

Global Chair
Marios Dikaiakos   University of Cyprus, Cyprus

Local Chair
Joao Lourenço   Universidade Nova de Lisboa, Portugal

Vice-Chairs
Omer Rana   Cardiff University, UK
Shmuel Ur   IBM Research Labs, Israel

Topic 2: Performance Prediction and Evaluation

Global Chair
Michael Gernt   Technische Universität München, Germany

Local Chair
Francisco Almeida   Universidad La Laguna, Spain

Vice-Chairs
Adolfy Hoise   Los Alamos National Lab, USA
Martin Schulz   Lawrence Livermore National Lab, USA

Topic 3: Scheduling and Load Balancing

Global Chair
Dieter Kranzlmüller   University of Linz, Austria

Local Chair
Francisco Fernández-Rivera   Universidad de Santiago de Compostela, Spain

Vice-Chairs
Uwe Schwiegelshohn   University of Dortmund, Germany
Yves Robert   Ecole Normal Supérieur Lyon, France

Topic 4: High-Performance Architectures and Compilers

Global Chair
Koen de Bosschere   Ghent University, Belgium

Local Chair
Luis Piñuel   Universidad Complutense, Spain

Vice-Chairs
Ayal Zaks   IBM Research Labs, Israel
Michael C. Huang   University of Rochester, USA

Topic 5: Parallel and Distributed Databases

Global Chair
Doménico Talia   University of Calabria, Italy

Local Chair
Josep Lluis Larriba-Pey   Universitat Politècnica de Catalunya, Spain

Vice-Chairs
Hillol Kargupta   University of Maryland, USA
Esther Pacitti   Université de Nantes, France

Topic 6: Grid and Cluster Computing

Global Chair
Marco Danelutto — University of Pisa, Italy

Local Chair
Juan Touriño — Universidad de La Coruña, Spain

Vice-Chairs
Mark Baker — University of Reading, UK
Rajkumar Buyya — The University of Melbourne, Australia
Paraskevi Fragopoulou — FORTH, Greece
Christian Perez — IRISA/INRIA, France
Erich Schikuta — University of Vienna, Austria

Topic 7: Peer-to-Peer Computing

Global Chair
Dick Epema — Delft University, The Netherlands

Local Chair
Josep Jorba — Universitat Oberta de Catalunya, Spain

Vice-Chairs
Alberto Montresor — University of Trento, Italy
Mark Jelasity — Szeged University, Hungary

Topic 8: Distributed Systems and Algorithms

Global Chair
Marc Shapiro — INRIA, France

Local Chair

Elsa Macías — Universidad de Las Palmas de Gran Canaria, Spain

Vice-Chairs
Thomas Ludwig — University of Trento, Italy
Mark Jelasity — Heidelberg University, Germany
Casiano Rodríguez León — La Laguna University, Spain
Gabriel Antoniu — IRISA/INRIA, France
Roy Friedman — Technion, Israel
Manuel Costa — Microsoft Research Cambridge, USA

Topic 9: Parallel and Distributed Programming

Global Chair
J. Nelson Amaral — University of Alberta, Canada

Local Chair
Joaquim Gabarró — Universitat Politècnica de Catalunya, Spain

Vice-Chairs
Luc Bougé — École Normale Supérieure de Cachan, France
Marcelo Cintra — The University of Edinburgh, UK
Marc Feeley — Université de Montréal, Canada
Vivek Sarkar — Rice University, USA
Paul Kelly — Imperial College, UK

Topic 10: Parallel Numerical Algorithms

Global Chair
Hans-Joachim Bungartz — Technische Universität München, Germany

Local Chair
Javier Bruguera — Universidad de Santiago de Compostela, Spain

Vice-Chairs
Peter Arbenz — ETH Zürich, Switzerland
Bruce Hendrickson — Sandia National Labs, USA

Topic 11: Distributed and High-Performance Multimedia

Global Chair
Frank Seinstra — Vrije Universiteit Amsterdam, The Netherlands

Local Chair
Nicolás Guil — Universidad de Málaga, Spain

Vice-Chairs
Zoltan Juhasz — University of Pannonia, Hungary
Simon Wilson — Trinity College Dublin, Ireland

Topic 12: Theory and Algorithms for Parallel Computation

Global Chair
Geppino Pucci — Università di Padova, Italy

Local Chair
Coromoto León — La Laguna University, Spain

XII   Organization

Vice-Chairs
Ioannis Caragiannis   University of Patras, Greece
Kieran T. Herley   University College Cork, Ireland

Topic 13: High-Performance Networks

Global Chair
Tor Skeie   Simula, Norway

Local Chair
Daniel Ortega   HP Labs, Spain

Vice-Chairs
Raimir Holanda-Filho   University of Fortaleza, Brazil
José Flich   Technical University of Valencia, Spain

Topic 14: Mobile and Ubiquitous Computing

Global Chair
Eric Fleury   ENS Lyon / INRIA ARES, France

Local Chair
Alvaro Suárez   Universidad de Las Palmas de Gran Canaria, Spain

Vice-Chairs
Artur Ziviani   LNCC, Brazil
Martin May   ETH Zürich, Switzerland
Pedro Merino Gomez   Universidad de Málaga, Spain
Jorge Garcia Vidal   Universitat Politècnica de Catalunya, Spain
Marcelo Dias de Amorim   Université Pierre & Marie Curie, France
Ryuji Wakikawa   Keio University, Japan
Gregor Schiele   University of Mannheim, Germany
Pedro Marron   University of Bonn, Germany

Euro-Par 2008 Referees

Jesus Alastruey
Julio Albín
Carl Albing
Marco Aldinucci
Rob Allan
Francisco Almeida
Jose Amaral
Stergios Anastasiadis
Artur Andrzejak
Elisardo Antelo

Peter Arbenz
Alvaro Arenas
Manuel Arenaz
Eduardo Argollo
Francisco Argüello
Joan Arnedo-Moreno
Stefano Arteconi
Rafael Asenjo
David Atienza
Michael Bader

José Badía-Contelles
Tongxin Bai
Mark Baker
Andoena Balla
Kevin Barker
Anne Benoit
Peter Paul Beran
Marco Biazzini
Marina Biberstein
Angelos Bilas
Vicente Blanco
Jon Blower
Rich Boakes
François Bodin
Montserrat Boo
Nikolay Borissov
Jose Bosque
Miguel Bote-Lorenzo
Luc Bougé
Hinde Bouziane
Francisco Brasileiro
David Breitgand
Greg Bronevetsky
Javier Bruguera
Zoran Budimlić
Shay Bushinsky
Alfredo Buttari
Rajkumar Buyya
José Cabaleiro
Alejandro Calderon
Mario Cannataro
Junwei Cao
Ioannis Caragiannis
Josep Carmona
Eddy Caron
Damiano Carra
Jesus Carretero
Henri Casanova
Roberto Cascella
Claris Castillo
Fernando Castro
Jose Cela
John Chandy
Pedro Chaparro Monferrer
Daniel Chaver
Andy Cheadle
Lei Chen

Marcelo Cintra
Thomas Clausen
Jose Claver
Ben Clifford
Albert Cohen
Murray Cole
Peter Collingbourne
Carmela Comito
Antonio Congiusta
Fernando Cores
Jay Cornwall
Toni Cortes
Alan L. Cox
Loïc Cudennec
Javier Cuenca
Matthew Curtis-Maury
Erik D'Hollander
Marco Danelutto
Anwitaman Datta
Kei Davis
Francisco de Sande
Bjorn De Sutter
Koen DeBosschere
Ewa Deelman
Roman Dementiev
Ludovic Denoyer
Veerle Desmet
Marcelo Dias de Amorim
Ivan Diaz
Marios Dikaiakos
David Dominguez-Sal
Fanpeng Dong
Jim Dowling
Vitor Duarte
Lieven Eeckhout
Wael El Essawy
Ali El-Moursy
Dick Epema
Stijn Eyerman
Thomas Fahringer
Ayose Falcón
Joel Falcou
Paolo Faraboschi
Zoltan Farkas
Dror G. Feitelson
Alan Fekete
Christian Fensch

Alvaro Fernandes
Juan Fernández
Roger Ferrer
Tony Field
Steve Fisher
Sergio Flesca
Eric Fleury
Jose Flich
Michail Flouris
Pierfrancesco Foglia
Vivi Fragopoulou
Bjoern Franke
Leonor Frias
Roy Friedman
Filippo Furfaro
Joaquim Gabarró
Jorge Garcia
Patricio Garcia
Alok Garg
Anurag Garg
Rahul Garg
Matthias Gauger
Chryssis Georgiou
Michael Gerndt
Ali Ghodsi
Domingo Gimenez
Harald Gjermundrod
Maayan Goldstein
Antonio Tadeu Gomes
Cecilia Gomes
Jose Gómez
Sergio Gómez-Villamor
Evelio González
Patricia González
Anastasios Gounaris
Maria Gradinariu
Christian Grimme
Crina Grosan
Mat Grove
Michael Gschwind
Xiaoming Gu
Nicolas Guil
Rajiv Gupta
Jens Gustedt
Houssam Haitof
Irfan Haq
Xin He

Yuxiong He
Andre Heilper
Bruce Hendrickson
Dora Heras
Kieran Herley
Maurice Herlihy
José Herrero
Adolfy Hoisie
Raimir Holanda
JoAnne Holliday
Jeffrey Hollingsworth
Peter Honeyman
Javier Hormigo
Hemayet Hossain
Lee Howes
Michael Huang
Kevin Huck
Thomas Huckle
Yannis Ioannidis
Latchesar Ionkov
Kashif Iqbal
Mustafa Jarrar
Emmanuel Jeannot
Yvon Jegou
Mark Jelasity
Gian Paolo Jesi
Daniel Jiménez-González
Josep Jorba
Zoltan Juhasz
Roy Kalawsky
Hillol Kargupta
Nicholas Karonis
Asterios Katsifodimos
Stefanos Kaxiras
Paul Kelly
Kirk Kelsey
Darren Kerbyson
Ramin Khalili
Akram Khan
Peter Kilpatrick
Akihiro Kishimoto
Tobias Klug
Charles Koelbel
Derrick Kondo
Harald Kosch
Dieter Kranzlmüller
Christof Kraus

Gary Kumfert
Jan Kwiatkowski
Renaud Lachaized
Rahim Lakhoo
Michael Lang
Josep Lluis Larriba-Pey
Daniel Lázaro
Adrien Lebre
Benjamin Lee
Yih-Jiun Lee
Laurent Lefevre
Arnaud Legrand
Coromoto Leon
Joachim Lepping
Clement Leung
Xin Li
Weiguo Liu
Anton Lokhmotov
Pedro Lopez
Frederic Loulergue
Antonio Loureiro
João Lourenço
David Lowenthal
Paul Lu
Claudio Lucchese
Thomas Ludwig
Mikel Lujan
Jesus Luna
Ignacio M. Llorente
Steve MacDonald
Werner Mach
Elsa Macías López
Jonas Maebe
Anirban Mandal
Jürgen Mangler
Costa Manuel
Michael Manzke
Virendra Marathe
Loris Marchal
Joan Manuel Marquès
Rui Marques
Pedro Marron
María Martín
Diego Martínez
José Martinez
Norbert Martínez-Bazán

Xavier Martorell
David Masip
Carlo Mastroianni
Tim Mattson
John May
Martin May
Pedro Medeiros
Miriam Mehl
René Meier
Hein Meling
Jean-Marc Menaud
Celso Mendes
Romero Mendes
David Meredith
Pedro Merino
Ningfang Mi
Bernd Mohr
Sébastien Monnet
Teresa Monreal
Miguel Monteiro
Rubén S. Montero
Alberto Montresor
Jose Moreira
Andrew Morton
Achour Mostefaoui
Gregory Mounié
J. Carlos Mouriño
Anelise Munaretto
Ralf-Peter Mundani
Francesc Muñoz
Victor Muntés-Mulero
Richard Murphy
Gayathri Nadarajan
Wolfgang Nagel
Thomas Naughton
Antonio Nebro
Zsolt Nemeth
Dirk Neumann
Robert Niewiadomski
Yarden Nir
Morioyshi Ohara
Katzalin Olcoz
Rui Carlos Oliveira
Hong Ong
Salvatore Orlando
Daniel Ortega

Michael Ott
Yuki Oyabu
Esther Pacitti
Scott Pakin
George Pallis
Alexander Papaspyrou
Manish Parashar
Inmaculada Pardines
Hervé Paulino
Tomás Pena
Christian Perez
Maria Perez-Hernandez
Jordi Petit
Frédéric Pétrot
Juan Pichel
Jean-Francois Pineau
Luis Piñuel
Rosario Piro
Oscar Plata
Javier Poncela González
Nuno Preguica
Manuel Prieto Matias
Thierry Priol
Radu Prodan
Geppino Pucci
Dan Quinlan
Martin Quinson
Enrique Quintana Orti
Ramakrishnan Rajamony
Omer Rana
M. Wasiur Rashid
Lawrence Rauchwerger
Orna Raz
Peter Reichl
Sven-Arne Reinemo
Francisco Rivera
Yves Robert
Ricardo Rocha
Casiano Rodriguez
Thomas Ropars
Barry Rountree
Mema Roussopoulos
Vicente Ruiz
Sean Rul
Francis Russell
Matthew Sackman
Ponnuswamy Sadayappan

Rizos Sakellariou
Jose Sancho
Peter Sanders
Adián Santos
Vijay Saraswat
Vivek Sarkar
Olga Saukh
Robert Sauter
Yanos Sazeides
Maraike Schellmann
Gregor Schiele
Erich Schikuta
Lars Schley
Peter Schulthess
Martin Schulz
Uwe Schwiegelshohn
Frank Seinstra
Frank Olaf Sem-Jacobsen
Natalia Seoane
Aamir Shafi
Marc Shapiro
Onn Shehory
Moran Shochat
Arrvindh Shriraman
Gheorghe Cosmin Silaghi
Luis Silva
David E. Singh
Karan Singh
Richard Sinnott
Fabrizio Sivestri
Tor Skeie
Garry Smith
João Sobral
Julien Sopena
Konrad Stark
Per Stenstrom
Alan Stewart
Heinz Stockinger
Kurt Stockinger
Mario Strasser
Nicholas Stylianides
Alvaro Suárez-Sarmiento
Frederic Suter
Pierre Sutra
Thomas Sødring
Guillermo Taboada
Domenico Talia

Jie Tao
Olivier Tardieu
Christian Tenllado
Neophytos Theodorou
William Thies
Ricardo Torlone
Juan Touriño
Liem Tran
Guy Tremblay
Phil Trinder
Carsten Trinitis
Paolo Trunfio
Kagan Tumer
Shmuel Ur
Patrick Valduriez
Rob van Nieuwpoort
Hans Vandierendonck
Pierangelo Veltri
Javier Verdu
Xavier Vilajosana
Elisabeth Vinek
Christof Voemel
Gregor von Laszewski
Spyros Voulgaris

Frédéric Wagner
Franck Wajsburt
Ryuji Wakikawa
Max Walter
Helmut Wanek
Cho-Li Wang
John Watt
Josef Weidendorfer
Adam Welc
Marcus Wittberger
Christoph Witzany
Felix Wolf
Ran Wolff
Fatos Xhafa
Wei Xing
Elad Yom-Tov
Ayal Zaks
Demetrios Zeinalipour-Yazti
Hongzhou Zhao
Yongkang Zhu
Eugenio Zimeo
Stefan Zimmer
Artur Ziviani
Aviad Zlotnick

Table of Contents

Topic 1: Support Tools and Environments

Introduction... 1
    Marios Dikaiakos, Omer Rana, Shmuel Ur, and Joao Lourenço (Topic Chairs)

Clock Synchronization in Cell BE Traces........................ 3
    Marina Biberstein, Yuval Harel, and Andre Heilper

DGSim: Comparing Grid Resource Management Architectures through Trace-Based Simulation.. 13
    Alexandru Iosup, Ozan Sonmez, and Dick Epema

Supporting Parameter Sweep Applications with Synthesized Grid Services.. 26
    Jürgen Hofer and Thomas Fahringer

A P2P Approach to Resource Discovery in On-Line Monitoring of Grid Workflows.. 37
    Bartłomiej Łabno, Marian Bubak, and Bartosz Baliś

Transparent Mobile Middleware Integration for Java and .NET Development Environments...................................... 47
    Edgar Marques, Luís Veiga, and Paulo Ferreira

Providing Non-stop Service for Message-Passing Based Parallel Applications with RADIC....................................... 58
    Guna Santos, Angelo Duarte, Dolores Rexachs, and Emilio Luque

On-Line Performance Modeling for MPI Applications............. 68
    Oleg Morajko, Anna Morajko, Tomàs Margalef, and Emilio Luque

MPC: A Unified Parallel Runtime for Clusters of NUMA Machines..... 78
    Marc Pérache, Hervé Jourdren, and Raymond Namyst

Topic 2: Performance Prediction and Evaluation

Introduction.. 89
    Francisco Almeida, Michael Gerndt, Adolfy Hoisie, and Martin Schulz (Topic Chairs)

Directory-Based Metadata Optimizations for Small Files in PVFS...... 90
    Michael Kuhn, Julian Kunkel, and Thomas Ludwig

Caspian: A Tunable Performance Model for Multi-core Systems 100
    Abbas Eslami Kiasari, Hamid Sarbazi-Azad, and Shaahin Hessabi

Performance Model for Parallel Mathematical Libraries Based on
Historical Knowledgebase 110
    I. Salawdeh, E. César, A. Morajko, T. Margalef, and E. Luque

A Performance Model of Dense Matrix Operations on Many-Core
Architectures 120
    *Guoping Long, Dongrui Fan, Junchao Zhang, Fenglong Song,
    Nan Yuan, and Wei Lin*

Empirical Analysis of a Large-Scale Hierarchical Storage System 130
    *Weikuan Yu, H. Sarp Oral, R. Shane Canon,
    Jeffrey S. Vetter, and Ramanan Sankaran*

To Snoop or Not to Snoop: Evaluation of Fine-Grain and Coarse-Grain
Snoop Filtering Techniques. 141
    *Jessica Young, Srihari Makineni, Ravishankar Iyer,
    Don Newell, and Adrian Moga*

Performance Implications of Cache Affinity on Multicore Processors 151
    Vahid Kazempour, Alexandra Fedorova, and Pouya Alagheband

Observing Performance Dynamics Using Parallel Profile Snapshots 162
    Alan Morris, Wyatt Spear, Allen D. Malony, and Sameer Shende

Event Tracing and Visualization for Cell Broadband Engine Systems . . . 172
    Daniel Hackenberg, Holger Brunst, and Wolfgang E. Nagel

Evaluating Heterogeneous Memory Model by Realistic Trace-Driven
Hardware/Software Co-simulation 182
    Wei Wang, Qigang Wang, Wei Wei, and Dong Liu

Mapping Heterogeneous Distributed Applications on Clusters 192
    *Sylvain Jubertie, Emmanuel Melin, Jérémie Vautard, and
    Arnaud Lallouet*

Neural Network-Based Load Prediction for Highly Dynamic Distributed
Online Games 202
    Vlad Nae, Radu Prodan, and Thomas Fahringer

Bottleneck Detection in Parallel File Systems with Trace-Based
Performance Monitoring 212
    Julian M. Kunkel and Thomas Ludwig

Topic 3: Scheduling and Load Balancing

Introduction. 222
    *Dieter Kranzlmueller, Uwe Schwiegelshohn, Yves Robert, and
    Francisco F. Rivera (Topic Chairs)*

Dynamic Grid Scheduling Using Job Runtime Requirements and
Variable Resource Availability 223
   Sam Verboven, Peter Hellinckx, Jan Broeckhove, and Frans Arickx

Enhancing Prediction on Non-dedicated Clusters 233
   *J.Ll. Lérida, F. Solsona, F. Giné, J.R. García, M. Hanzich, and
P. Hernández*

Co-allocation with Communication Considerations in Multi-cluster
Systems 243
   John Ngubiri and Mario van Vliet

Fine-Grained Task Scheduling Using Adaptive Data Structures 253
   Ralf Hoffmann and Thomas Rauber

Exploration of the Influence of Program Inputs on CMP
Co-scheduling 263
   Yunlian Jiang and Xipeng Shen

Integrating Dynamic Memory Placement with Adaptive Load-Balancing
for Parallel Codes on NUMA Multiprocessors 274
   Paul Slavin and Len Freeman

Guest-Aware Priority-Based Virtual Machine Scheduling for Highly
Consolidated Server 285
   *Dongsung Kim, Hwanju Kim, Myeongjae Jeon, Euiseong Seo, and
Joonwon Lee*

Dynamic Pipeline Mapping (DPM).................................... 295
   *A. Moreno, E. César, A. Guevara, J. Sorribes, T. Margalef, and
E. Luque*

Formal Model and Scheduling Heuristics for the Replica Migration
Problem 305
   *Nikos Tziritas, Thanasis Loukopoulos, Petros Lampsas, and
Spyros Lalis*

Topic 4: High Performance Architectures and Compilers

Introduction.. 315
   *Koen de Bosschere, Ayal Zaks, Michael C. Huang, and Luis Piñuel
(Topic Chairs)*

Reducing the Number of Bits in the BTB to Attack the Branch
Predictor Hot-Spot 317
   N. Tomás, J. Sahuquillo, S. Petit, and P. López

Low-Cost Adaptive Data Prefetching 327
    Luis M. Ramos, José Luis Briz, Pablo E. Ibáñez, and Víctor Viñals

Stream Scheduling: A Framework to Manage Bulk Operations in
Memory Hierarchies 337
    Abhishek Das and William J. Dally

Interprocedural Speculative Optimization of Memory Accesses to
Global Variables 350
    Lars Gesellensetter and Sabine Glesner

Efficiently Building the Gated Single Assignment Form in Codes with
Pointers in Modern Optimizing Compilers 360
    Manuel Arenaz, Pedro Amoedo, and Juan Touriño

Inter-Block Scoreboard Scheduling in a JIT Compiler for VLIW
Processors 370
    Benoît Dupont de Dinechin

Global Tiling for Communication Minimal Parallelization on
Distributed Memory Systems 382
    Lei Liu, Li Chen, ChengYong Wu, and Xiao-bing Feng

Topic 5: Parallel and Distributed Databases

Introduction 392
    Domenico Talia, Josep Lluis Larriba-Pey, Hillol Kargupta, and Esther Pacitti (Topic Chairs)

Reducing Transaction Abort Rates with Prioritized Atomic Multicast
Protocols 394
    Emili Miedes, Francesc D. Muñoz-Escoí, and Hendrik Decker

Fault-Tolerant Partial Replication in Large-Scale Database Systems 404
    Pierre Sutra and Marc Shapiro

Exploiting Hybrid Parallelism in Web Search Engines 414
    Carolina Bonacic, Carlos Garcia, Mauricio Marin, Manuel Prieto, and Francisco Tirado

Complex Queries for Moving Object Databases in DHT-Based
Systems 424
    Cecilia Hernández, M. Andrea Rodríguez, and Mauricio Marin

Scheduling Intersection Queries in Term Partitioned Inverted Files 434
    Mauricio Marin, Carlos Gomez-Pantoja, Senen Gonzalez, and Veronica Gil-Costa

Topic 6: Grid and Cluster Computing

Introduction.. 444
    Marco Danelutto, Juan Touriño, Mark Baker, Rajkumar Buyya,
    Paraskevi Fragopoulou, Christian Perez, and Erich Schikuta
    (Topic Chairs)

Integration of GRID Superscalar and GridWay Metascheduler with the
DRMAA OGF Standard... 445
    R.M. Badia, D. Du, E. Huedo, A. Kokossis, I.M. Llorente,
    R.S. Montero, M. de Palol, R. Sirvent, and C. Vázquez

Building Hierarchical Grid Storage Using the GFARM Global File
System and the JUXMEM Grid Data-Sharing Service 456
    Gabriel Antoniu, Loïc Cudennec, Majd Ghareeb, and Osamu Tatebe

Enhancing Grids for Massively Multiplayer Online Computer Games ... 466
    Sergei Gorlatch, Frank Glinka, Alexander Ploss, Jens Müller-Iden,
    Radu Prodan, Vlad Nae, and Thomas Fahringer

Spectral Clustering Scheduling Techniques for Tasks with Strict QoS
Requirements.. 478
    Nikos Doulamis, Panagiotis Kokkinos, and Emmanouel Varvarigos

QoS-Oriented Reputation-Aware Query Scheduling in Data Grids....... 489
    Rogério Luís de Carvalho Costa and Pedro Furtado

Flying Low: Simple Leases with Workspace Pilot.................... 499
    Timothy Freeman and Katarzyna Keahey

Self-configuring Resource Discovery on a Hypercube Grid Overlay.... 510
    Antonia Gallardo, Luis Díaz de Cerio, and Kana Sanjeevan

Auction Protocols for Resource Allocations in Ad-Hoc Grids 520
    Behnaz Pourebrahimi and Koen Bertels

GrAMoS: A Flexible Service for WS-Agreement Monitoring in Grid
Environments 534
    Glauber Scorsatto and Alba Cristina Magalhaes Alves de Melo

Scalability of Grid Simulators: An Evaluation..................... 544
    Wim Depoorter, Nils De Moor, Kurt Vanmechelen, and
    Jan Broeckhove

Performance Evaluation of Data Management Layer by Data Sharing
Patterns for Grid RPC Applications................................ 554
    Yoshihiro Nakajima, Yoshiaki Aida, Mitsuhisa Sato, and
    Osamu Tatebe

The Impact of Clustering on Token-Based Mutual Exclusion
Algorithms 565
 Julien Sopena, Luciana Arantes, Fabrice Legond-Aubry, and
 Pierre Sens

Reducing Kernel Development Complexity in Distributed
Environments 576
 Adrien Lèbre, Renaud Lottiaux, Erich Focht, and Christine Morin

A Twofold Distributed Game-Tree Search Approach Using
Interconnected Clusters 587
 Kai Himstedt, Ulf Lorenz, and Dietmar P.F. Möller

Topic 7: Peer-to-Peer Computing

Introduction 599
 Dick Epema, Márk Jelasity, Josep Jorba, and Alberto Montresor
 (Topic Chairs)

Scalable Byzantine Fault Tolerant Public Key Authentication for
Peer-to-Peer Networks 601
 Ruichuan Chen, Wenjia Guo, Liyong Tang, Jianbin Hu, and
 Zhong Chen

Secure Forwarding in DHTs – Is Redundancy the Key to
Robustness? 611
 Marc Sànchez-Artigas, Pedro García-López, and
 Antonio G. Skarmeta

P2P Evolutionary Algorithms: A Suitable Approach for Tackling Large
Instances in Hard Optimization Problems 622
 J.L.J. Laredo, A.E. Eiben, M. van Steen, P.A. Castillo,
 A.M. Mora, and J.J. Merelo

Efficient Processing of Continuous Join Queries Using Distributed Hash
Tables 632
 Wenceslao Palma, Reza Akbarinia, Esther Pacitti, and
 Patrick Valduriez

Topic 8: Distributed Systems and Algorithms

Introduction 642
 Elsa María Macías López and Marc Shapiro (Topic Chairs)

Automatic Prefetching with Binary Code Rewriting in Object-Based
DSMs 643
 Jean Christophe Beyler, Michael Klemm, Michael Philippsen, and
 Philippe Clauss

A PGAS-Based Algorithm for the Longest Common Subsequence
Problem 654
   M. Bakhouya, O. Serres, and T. El-Ghazawi

Data Mining Algorithms on the Cell Broadband Engine............... 665
   Rubing Duan and Alfred Strey

Efficient Management of Complex Striped Files in Active Storage 676
   Juan Piernas and Jarek Nieplocha

Topic 9: Parallel and Distributed Programming

Introduction... 686
   José Nelson Amaral and Joaquim Gabarró (Topic Chairs)

Improving the Performance of Multiple Conjugate Gradient Solvers by
Exploiting Overlap 688
   José Carlos Sancho and Darren J. Kerbyson

A Software Component Model with Spatial and Temporal Compositions
for Grid Infrastructures 698
   Hinde Lilia Bouziane, Christian Pérez, and Thierry Priol

A Design Pattern for Component Oriented Development of Agent
Based Multithreaded Applications 709
   A.L. Rodríguez, P.E. López-de-Teruel, A. Ruiz,
   G. García-Mateos, and L. Fernández

Advanced Concurrency Control for Transactional Memory Using
Transaction Commit Rate....................................... 719
   Mohammad Ansari, Christos Kotselidis, Kim Jarvis, Mikel Luján,
   Chris Kirkham, and Ian Watson

Meta-programming Applied to Automatic SMP Parallelization of
Linear Algebra Code 729
   Joel Falcou, Jocelyn Sérot, Lucien Pech, and Jean-Thierry Lapresté

Solving Dense Linear Systems on Graphics Processors 739
   Sergio Barrachina, Maribel Castillo, Francisco D. Igual,
   Rafael Mayo, and Enrique S. Quintana-Ortí

Radioastronomy Image Synthesis on the Cell/B.E. 749
   Ana Lucia Varbanescu, Alexander S. van Amesfoort, Tim Cornwell,
   Andrew Mattingly, Bruce G. Elmegreen, Rob van Nieuwpoort,
   Ger van Diepen, and Henk Sips

Parallel Lattice Boltzmann Flow Simulation on Emerging Multi-core
Platforms 763
    Liu Peng, Ken-ichi Nomura, Takehiro Oyakawa, Rajiv K. Kalia,
    Aiichiro Nakano, and Priya Vashishta

Topic 10: Parallel Numerical Algorithms

Introduction 778
    H.-J. Bungartz, J.D. Bruguera, P. Arbenz, and B.A. Hendrickson
    (Topic Chairs)

Parallel Algorithms for Triangular Periodic Sylvester-Type Matrix
Equations 780
    Per Andersson, Robert Granat, Isak Jonsson, and Bo Kågström

A Parallel Sparse Linear Solver for Nearest-Neighbor Tight-Binding
Problems 790
    Mathieu Luisier, Gerhard Klimeck, Andreas Schenk,
    Wolfgang Fichtner, and Timothy B. Boykin

Exploiting the Locality Properties of Peano Curves for Parallel Matrix
Multiplication 801
    Michael Bader

Systematic Parallelization of Medical Image Reconstruction for
Graphics Hardware 811
    Maraike Schellmann, Jürgen Vörding, and Sergei Gorlatch

Load-Balancing for a Block-Based Parallel Adaptive 4D Vlasov
Solver 822
    Olivier Hoenen and Eric Violard

A Parallel Sensor Scheduling Technique for Fault Detection in
Distributed Parameter Systems 833
    Maciej Patan

Topic 11: Distributed and High-Performance Multimedia

Introduction 844
    Frank Seinstra, Nicolás Guil, Zoltan Juhasz, and Simon Wilson
    (Topic Chairs)

On a Novel Dynamic Parallel Hardware Architecture for Lifting-Based
DWT 846
    Sami Khanfir and Mohamed Jemni

Analytical Evaluation of Clients' Failures in a LVoD Architecture Based
on P2P and Multicast Paradigms 856
  Rodrigo Godoi, Xiaoyuan Yang, and Porfidio Hernández

A Search Engine Index for Multimedia Content 866
  Mauricio Marin, Veronica Gil-Costa, and Carolina Bonacic

Topic 12: Theory and Algorithms for Parallel Computation

Introduction.. 876
  *Geppino Pucci, Coromoto Leon, Ioannis Caragiannis, and
  Kieran T. Herley (Topic Chairs)*

Bi-objective Approximation Scheme for Makespan and Reliability
Optimization on Uniform Parallel Machines 877
  Emmanuel Jeannot, Erik Saule, and Denis Trystram

Deque-Free Work-Optimal Parallel STL Algorithms 887
  *Daouda Traoré, Jean-Louis Roch, Nicolas Maillard,
  Thierry Gautier, and Julien Bernard*

Topic 13: High-Performance Networks

Introduction.. 898
  *Tor Skeie, Daniel Ortega, José Flich, and Raimir Holanda
  (Topic Chairs)*

Reducing Packet Dropping in a Bufferless NoC (Best Paper Award) 899
  Crispín Gómez, María E. Gómez, Pedro López, and José Duato

A Communication-Aware Topological Mapping Technique for NoCs 910
  Rafael Tornero, Juan M. Orduña, Maurizio Palesi, and José Duato

Approximating the Traffic Grooming Problem with Respect to ADMs
and OADMs (Extended Abstract)....................................... 920
  *Michele Flammini, Gianpiero Monaco, Luca Moscardelli,
  Mordechai Shalom, and Shmuel Zaks*

On the Influence of the Packet Marking and Injection Control Schemes
in Congestion Management for MINs 930
  *Joan-LLuís Ferrer, Elvira Baydal, Antonio Robles,
  Pedro López, and José Duato*

Deadlock-Free Dynamic Network Reconfiguration Based on Close
Up*/Down* Graphs 940
  *Antonio Robles-Gómez, Aurelio Bermúdez, Rafael Casado, and
  Åshild Grønstad Solheim*

HITP: A Transmission Protocol for Scalable High-Performance
Distributed Storage 950
    P. Giacomin, A. Bassi, F.J. Seinstra, T. Kielmann, and H.E. Bal

Author Index... 961

Topic 1: Support Tools and Environments

Marios Dikaiakos[*], Omer Rana[*], Shmuel Ur[*], and Joao Lourenço[*]

The spread of systems that provide parallelism either "in-the-large" (grid infrastructures, clusters) or "in-the-small" (multi-core chips), creates new opportunities for exploiting parallelism in a wider spectrum of application domains. However, the increasing complexity of parallel and distributed platforms renders the programming, the use, and the management of these systems a costly endeavor that requires advanced expertise and skills. Therefore, there is an increasing need for powerful support tools and environments that will help end-users, application programmers, software engineers and system administrators to manage the increasing complexity of parallel and distributed platforms.

This topic aims at bringing together tool designers, developers, and users in order to share novel ideas, concepts, and products in the field of Support Tools and Environments. The Program Committee sought high-quality contributions with solid foundations and experimental validations on real systems, and encouraged the submission of new ideas on tools for parallel programming as well as tools for clusters and grids with possibly large numbers of nodes and some degree of heterogeneity.

This year, twenty-one papers were submitted to Topic 1 and eight papers were accepted. The accepted papers cover a wide range of interests and contributions:

- Two papers examine aspects of runtime environments in the context of clusters and parallel supercomputers. In particular, the paper titled "MPC: a unified parallel runtime for clusters of NUMA machines" introduces a runtime environment, which aims at providing programmers with an efficient system for existing MPI, POSIX Thread or hybrid MPI+Thread applications that run on top of clusters with multi-core nodes. The paper titled "Providing non-stop service for message-passing based parallel applications with RADIC" introduces a software layer that performs fault-masking and provides fault-tolerance support to message-passing systems.
- Three papers discuss tools for grids: the paper titled "DGSim: Comparing Grid Resource Management Architectures Through Trace-Based Simulation" describes the design and implementation of a framework for simulating grid resource management architectures, whereas the paper on "Supporting Parameter Sweep Applications with Synthesized Grid Services" introduces a tool to support the deployment of an important class of applications (parameter sweep) over service-oriented grids. Finally, the paper titled "A P2P Approach to Resource Discovery in On-line Monitoring of Grid Workflows" examines the use of structured P2P technologies for the development of Grid monitoring systems.

---

[*] Topic chairs.

- Two papers focus on performance analysis. In particular, the paper titled "Clock Synchronization in Cell BE Traces" presents an algorithm that can be used to assign consistent time-stamps to the trace records collected from a heterogeneous multi-core processor, thus enabling the trace analysis for the performance evaluation of parallel workloads. The paper titled "On-Line Performance Modeling for MPI Applications" introduces an online performance modeling technique that supports the automated, runtime discovery of causal execution flows composed of communication and computational activities in message-passing programs.
- Last, but not least, the paper "Transparent mobile middleware integration for Java and .NET development environments" presents an automatic code-generation tool that supports the transparent integration of applications on mobile middleware, facilitating the development of distributed applications on resource constrained mobile devices.

Clock Synchronization in Cell BE Traces

Marina Biberstein, Yuval Harel, and Andre Heilper

IBM Haifa Research Lab
Haifa University Campus
Haifa 31905, Israel
{biberstein,harely,heilper}@il.ibm.com

Abstract. Cell BE is a heterogeneous multicore processor that has been developed as a means for efficient execution of parallel and vectorizable applications with high computation and memory requirements. The transition to multicores introduces the challenge of providing tools that help programmers tune their code running on these architectures. Tracing tools, in particular, often help locate performance problems related to thread and process communication.

A major impediment to implementing tracing on Cell is the absence of a common clock that can be accessed at low cost from all cores. The OS clock is costly to access from the auxiliary cores and the hardware timers cannot be simultaneously set on all the cores. In this paper, we describe an offline trace analysis that assigns wall-clock time to trace records based on their thread-local time stamps and event order. Our experiments on several Cell SDK workloads show that the indeterminism in assigning the wall-clock time is low, on average 20–40 clock ticks (1.4–2.8 μs for 14.8 MHz clock). We also show how various practical problems, such as the imprecision of time measurement, can be overcome.

1 Introduction

The Cell BE [1] has been developed as a power-efficient processor for running highly parallel and vectorizable workloads. A heterogeneous multicore, it has one 64-bit Power Architecture core, known as the *Power Processor Element* (PPE), and eight specialized single-instruction multiple-data (SIMD) co-processors called *Synergistic Processor Elements* (SPEs). The SPEs operate from a local store, containing both the code and the data, and communicate with the main memory using the *Direct Memory Access* (DMA). Additional channels of communication between threads executing on different cores include mailboxes and mutual exclusion routines.

Tracing tools are a popular answer to performance and correctness problems encountered by parallel programs. When implementing trace collection and visualization on Cell [2], one of the major obstacles we encountered was the lack of a wallclock, i.e., a clock efficiently accessible from all the cores. The hardware provides a 64-bit *timebase* register on the PPE and 32-bit *decrementer* registers on the SPEs, which are modified all at the same rate; unfortunately, there is no way to set all these registers simultaneously.

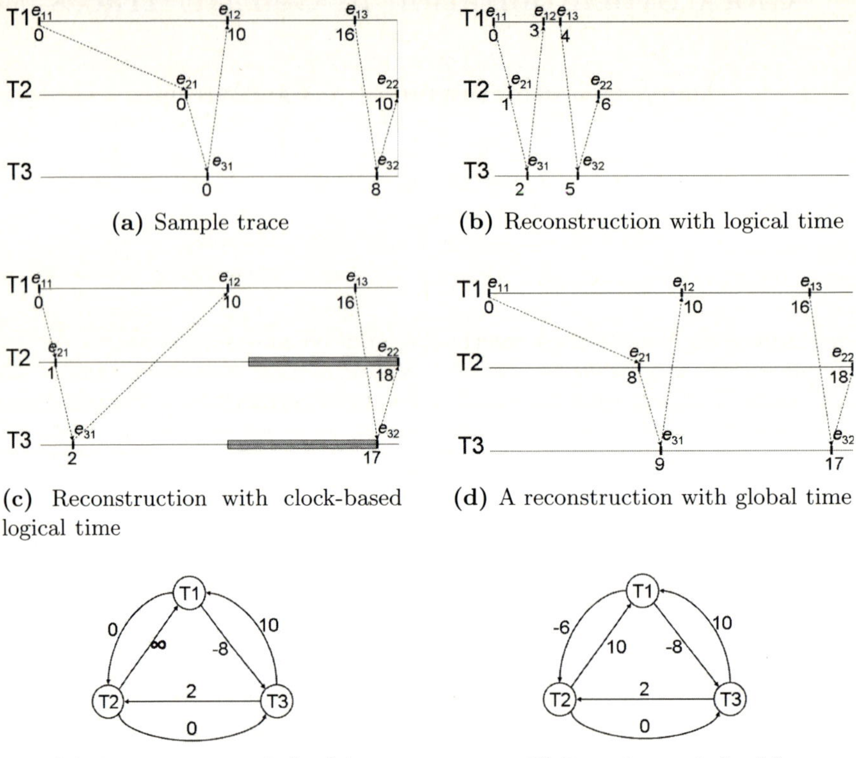

Fig. 1. A parallel execution example

Figure 1(a) provides an example of a multi-threaded execution and its trace in the absence of a wall clock. There are three threads in this example, marked T_1, T_2, and T_3. Each of the threads executes several traced events, marked $e_{11}, \ldots, e_{32}$. The trace record of an event identifies the executing thread, the timestamp based on the thread's clock (shown in the figure below each event), and the event's happened-before relationship with events in other threads (shown in the figure with dotted arrows). The information missing from the trace is the relative shift of the threads' clocks, which is required to determine how much time elapsed between events in different threads, e.g., e_{11} and e_{21}. This information is critical for performance analysis and visualization of the trace.

In this paper, we present an algorithm for post-processing the trace and establishing a wall-clock time that is consistent with the original trace, i.e., that preserves both the event precedence and the relative timing of events within each thread. Such wall-clock time for our example is illustrated by Figure 1(d). The algorithm can determine the precision it achieves on the given input. We also discuss technical details of implementing this algorithm for Cell and illustrate its precision on traces collected on several important Cell workloads.

The paper is organized as follows. Section 2 discusses related work. In Section 3 we describe the wall-clock time algorithm. In Section 4 we show how this algorithm can be applied to Cell traces collected by PDT. Section 5 shows the results of algorithm execution on several publicly available benchmarks. Section 6 wraps up with conclusions and future work.

2 Related Work

The problem of clock synchronization is long familiar in the context of debugging parallel programs. Lamport [3] proposed an algorithm for construction of *logical time* based on happened-before relationships between events in different threads. This algorithm is only concerned with reconstructing a possible event order; the thread-local timestamps are not even part of its input. The result of the execution of this algorithm on our sample trace is shown in Figure 1(b), with the corresponding logical time marked below each event. While logical time and its variants such as vector time [4] found a wealth of applications, from distributed debugging to coherency protocols [5], they are clearly inapplicable to the performance analysis.

Lamport [3] also offers a variant of the logical time algorithm that aims to preserve, to some extent, the timing of the traced execution. It bumps the logical timestamps enough to avoid shrinking the interval between the event and its predecessor in the same thread. The objective of this algorithm is to compensate for clock drift and small imprecision in clock synchronization. It does not cope well with clocks that are not synchronized at all. Figure 1(c) shows the algorithm's output on input from Fig. 1(a). Since e_{21} is timed too early, the interval between e_{11} and e_{21} takes one time unit instead of eight, and the interval between e_{21} and e_{22} is correspondingly longer; thus even interval durations within the thread are not preserved.

Another common means for clock synchronization is the Network Time Protocol (NTP) [6]. This protocol solves both clock offset and clock drift problems, the latter of which is irrelevant in the Cell context. There were several reasons that made the adoption of an NTP-style solution impractical. The SPEs would have to monitor some communication channel for the arrival of time data from the PPE, introducing the tradeoff between low precision and high overhead. Additionally, because of the SPE context switches, which affect the clock offsets, each client clock may run only for a relatively short time between resets, and will not be aware of its own resets, again forcing the synchronizer to increase overhead to achieve reasonable precision. Other approaches, like [7], use the constraints to set up an over-determined set of equations, then compute a least-squares optimal solution, which may not prevent inconsistent time sequences.

The all-pairs shortest path computation, referenced below, is a classical graph problem (seee, for example, Section 2.6 of [8]). The graphs that arise in the context of clock synchronization tend to be dense, making the Floyd-Warshall algorithm preferable over Johnson.

3 Clock Synchronization Algorithm

We define our system as composed of one or more threads of control, each thread a sequence of events. We are not concerned with the semantics of the events; for example, they might be communication notifications, system calls, or application stages.

Definition 1. *The* trace *is a tuple* $(E, \text{tid}, \leq, \text{ttime})$, *where:*

- E *is the set of events*
- $\text{tid}: E \to \mathbb{N}$ *is a function that matches each event with its thread id.*
- $\leq$ *is a happened-before relation over E: $e_1 \leq e_2$ implies the e_1 occured not later than e_2.*
- $\text{ttime}: E \to \mathbb{R}$ *is a function that matches each event to its thread-local timestamp. We assume that the clocks advance at the same rate for all the threads. We also assume, w.l.o.g., that the clocks are incrementing:*

$$\text{tid}(e_1) = \text{tid}(e_2), e_1 \leq e_2 \implies \text{ttime}(e_1) \leq \text{ttime}(e_2). \tag{1}$$

This definition of trace leaves a lot of freedom in implementing the tracing. The tracer may allocate a buffer per thread or use the same buffer for all threads and place a thread id field into the event record. Similarly, the order between events may be inferred from the events' semantics, as in [3], or from the event order in the shared buffer, as in [2].

Our goal is to define a global time function that is consistent with thread-local time (within a thread, time between events according to global time is the same as according to thread-local time) and the event order (an event's global time is no less than the global time of any of its predecessors):

Definition 2. *Given a trace $(E, \text{tid}, \leq, \text{ttime})$, global time is a function* $\text{gtime}: E \to \mathbb{R}$ *such that for every two events $e_1, e_2 \in E$*

$$\text{tid}(e_1) = \text{tid}(e_2) \implies \text{gtime}(e_1) - \text{gtime}(e_2) = \text{ttime}(e_1) - \text{ttime}(e_2) \tag{2}$$

$$e_1 \leq e_2 \implies \text{gtime}(e_1) \leq \text{gtime}(e_2) \tag{3}$$

Lemma 1. gtime *is fully defined by a single value per thread,* $\{g_t\}_{t \in \text{tid}(E)}$:

$$\forall e \in E: \text{gtime}(e) = g_{\text{tid}(e)} + \text{ttime}(e). \tag{4}$$

Proof. Let $e_1, e_2 \in E$ and assume $\text{tid}(e_1) = \text{tid}(e_2) = t$. Let $g_t = \text{gtime}(e_1) - \text{ttime}(e_1)$. Then

$$\text{gtime}(e_2) = \text{gtime}(e_1) + \text{ttime}(e_2) - \text{ttime}(e_1) = g_t + \text{ttime}(e_2).$$

□

Example 1. In Fig. 1(a), if e_{21} is assigned global time 8, then, according to (2), $\text{gtime}(e_{22}) = 8 + (10 - 0) = 18$.

Next we note that any pair of events from different threads with a known order between them imposes a constraint on the difference of their respective g_ts.

Example 2. In the scenario depicted in Fig. 1(a), the event e_{11} is known to have preceded e_{21}. If we choose $g_1 \leq g_2$, this guarantees that $\texttt{gtime}(e_1) \leq \texttt{gtime}(e_2)$, i.e., (3) is satisfied with respect to e_{11} and e_{21}. If, on the other hand, we select $g_1 > g_2$, then $\texttt{gtime}(e_1) > \texttt{gtime}(e_2)$, contradicting the event order.

Lemma 2. *A function* $\texttt{gtime} : E \to \mathbb{R}$ *is a global time function if and only if it is of the form* (4) *and*

$$\forall e_1, e_2 \in E, e_1 \leq e_2 : g_{\texttt{tid}(e_1)} - g_{\texttt{tid}(e_2)} \leq \texttt{ttime}(e_2) - \texttt{ttime}(e_1). \quad (5)$$

Proof. According to Lemma 1, global time function must be of form (4), and (4) substituted into (3) gives (5). Conversely, (4) implies (2), and (4) together with (5) gives (3). □

Note that (5) defines a huge set of up to $|E|^2$ constraints, making it difficult to collect and use them. Our next step is to find a way to summarize these constraints.

Definition 3. *Let* e_1, e_2 *be two events. We say that* e_1 *is an* **immediate predecessor** *of* e_2, *denoted* $e_1 \prec e_2$, *if* e_1 *precedes* e_2 *and there is no event e between them:* $\nexists e : e_1 < e < e_2$.

Definition 4. *Let* $(E, \texttt{tid}, \leq, \texttt{ttime})$ *be a trace. For* $t_1, t_2 \in \texttt{tid}(E)$, *let*

$$L(t_1, t_2) = \{(e_1, e_2) | \texttt{tid}(e_1) = t_1, \texttt{tid}(e_2) = t_2, e_1 \prec e_2\}.$$

The **constraints graph** *for this trace is defined as the weighted clique*

$$G = (\texttt{tid}(E), \texttt{tid}(E) \times \texttt{tid}(E), w : \texttt{tid}(E) \times \texttt{tid}(E) \to \mathbb{R}),$$

$$w(t_1, t_2) = \min\{\texttt{ttime}(e_2) - \texttt{ttime}(e_1) | (e_1, e_2) \in L(t_1, t_2)\} \quad (6)$$

In other words, in the constraints graph, the weight of an edge (s, t) is the best bound on $g_s - g_t$ that we can derive using (5) from all event pairs related by $\prec$. We assume $\min(\emptyset) = \infty$.

Example 3. In the trace in Fig. 1(a), the order $\leq$ is linear, so G can be constructed in $O(|E|)$ steps. Figure 1(e) shows the constraints graph for this trace. Note that the constraints graph doesn't contain an explicit bound on the value of $g_2 - g_1$. However, it does contain an implicit constraint: $g_2 - g_1 = (g_2 - g_3) + (g_3 - g_1) \leq w(2, 3) + w(3, 1) = 10$. Similarly, while the explicit bound on $g_1 - g_2$ is $w(1, 2) = 0$, we also have $g_1 - g_2 = (g_1 - g_3) + (g_3 - g_2) \leq w(1, 3) + w(3, 2) = -6$.

To find the tightest bound on $g_s - g_t$, taking into account both explicit and implicit ones, we define

Definition 5. *Let $(E, \mathtt{tid}, \leq, \mathtt{ttime})$ be a trace and $G = (\mathtt{tid}(E), \mathtt{tid}(E) \times \mathtt{tid}(E), w)$ the corresponding constraints graph. The* **bounds graph** *is a clique $\bar{G} = (\mathtt{tid}(E), \mathtt{tid}(E) \times \mathtt{tid}(E), \bar{w})$, where $\bar{w}(s, t)$ is the weight of the shortest path between s and t in G (zero if $s = t$).*

The bounds graph can be computed using the Floyd-Warshall algorithm in $O(|\mathtt{tid}(E)|^3)$. We now show that the bounds graph indeed summarizes (5).

Lemma 3. *A function $\mathtt{gtime} : E \to \mathbb{R}$ is a global time function if and only if it satisfies (4) and*

$$\forall t_1, t_2 \in \mathtt{tid}(E) : g_{t_1} - g_{t_2} \leq \bar{w}(t_1, t_2). \tag{7}$$

Proof. It suffices to show that (5) $\Leftrightarrow$ (7). Assume that (5) holds and (7) does not, i.e.,

$$\exists t, t' \in \mathtt{tid}(E) : g_t - g_{t'} > \bar{w}(t, t'). \tag{8}$$

Since $\bar{w}(t, t')$ is defined as the weight of the shortest path between t and t' in G, there must exist a sequence of threads $t = t_0, t_1, \ldots, t_n = t'$ such that $\bar{w}(t, t') = w(t_0, t_1) + \ldots + w(t_{n-1}, t_n)$. According to (6), for every i, there exists a pair of events e_i, e'_i such that $\mathtt{tid}(e_i) = t_i$, $\mathtt{tid}(e'_i) = t_{i+1}$, and $w(t_i, t_{i+1}) = \mathtt{ttime}(e'_i) - \mathtt{ttime}(e_i)$. Substituting into (8),

$$g_t - g_{t'} > \bar{w}(t, t') = \sum_{i=0}^{n-1} w(t_i, t_{i+1}) = \sum_{i=0}^{n-1} (\mathtt{ttime}(e'_i) - \mathtt{ttime}(e_i)) \overset{(5)}{\geq} \sum_{i=0}^{n-1} (g_{t_i} - g_{t_{i+1}}) = g_t - g_{t'}.$$

Conversely, assume that (7) holds, and let e, e' be any two events such that $e \leq e'$. Then there exists a sequence of events $e = e_0, e_1, \ldots, e_n = e'$ such that for any i, $e_i \prec e_{i+1}$. Let $t_i = \mathtt{tid}(e_i)$. Then

$$g_{t_0} - g_{t_n} = \sum_{i=0}^{n-1}(g_i - g_{i+1}) \overset{(7)}{\leq} \sum_{i=0}^{n-1} \bar{w}(t_i, t_{i+1}) \leq \sum_{i=0}^{n-1} w(t_i, t_{i+1}) \leq$$

$$\leq \sum_{i=0}^{n-1}(\mathtt{ttime}(e_{i+1}) - \mathtt{ttime}(e_i)) = \mathtt{ttime}(e') - \mathtt{ttime}(e).$$

□

Example 4. Figure 1(f) shows the bounds graph corresponding to the trace in Fig. 1(a).

Having now summarized all the constraints imposed by the trace, we are ready to costruct some global time functions.

Lemma 4. *Let $\tau \in \mathtt{tid}(E)$ be a thread, and let α be a parameter, $0 \leq \alpha \leq 1$. For every thread t, define*

$$g_t = \alpha \bar{w}(t, \tau) - (1 - \alpha)\bar{w}(\tau, t). \tag{9}$$

Then the function $\mathtt{gtime}(e) = g_{\mathtt{tid}(e)} + \mathtt{ttime}(e)$ is a global time function.

Proof. We will use two obvious facts, both following from $\bar{w}$'s definition as the shortest path:

$$\forall i, j, k \in \mathtt{tid}(E) \quad \bar{w}(i,j) \leq \bar{w}(i,k) + \bar{w}(k,j) \tag{10}$$
$$\forall i, j \in \mathtt{tid}(E) \quad 0 = \bar{w}(i,i) \leq \bar{w}(i,j) + \bar{w}(j,i) \tag{11}$$

It suffices to show that for g_ts defined as in (9), (7) holds.

$$g_i - g_j \stackrel{(9)}{=} \alpha(\bar{w}(i,\tau) - \bar{w}(j,\tau)) - (1-\alpha)(\bar{w}(\tau,i) - \bar{w}(\tau,j)) \stackrel{(10)}{\leq}$$
$$\stackrel{(10)}{\leq} \alpha \bar{w}(i,j) - (1-\alpha)\bar{w}(j,i) \stackrel{(11)}{\leq} \alpha \bar{w}(i,j) + (1-\alpha)\bar{w}(i,j) = \bar{w}(i,j)$$

Note, by the way, that the inequalities above turn into equalities for $\alpha = 1, j = \tau$. Therefore the bounds imposed by $\bar{w}$ are tight. □

Example 5. The global time in Fig. 1(a) is obtained using $\tau = T_1, \alpha = \frac{1}{2}$.

Summing up, given a trace $(E, \mathtt{tid}, \leq, \mathtt{ttime})$, the algorithm performs the following steps:

- Build the constraints graph. The complexity of this step depends on $\leq$'s definition; for a linear order it's $O(|E|)$.
- Build the bounds graph. This can be done in $O(|\mathtt{tid}(E)|^3)$.
- Choose τ and α and build $\mathtt{gtime}$ according to (9). This takes $O(|\mathtt{tid}(E)|)$ steps.

4 Implementation Aspects

In this section, we discuss the application of the clock synchronization algorithm to traces collected on Cell; the issues we encountered; and the solutions that were adopted.

The PDT [2] events correspond to method calls in PDT-instrumented libraries. Such instrumentation is available, for example, for libraries that handle communications between the cores via mailboxes and communication between the cores and main memory through the DMA. In addition, certain events are monitored to provide enough information for trace post-processing. In particular, PDT traces all the context switch events on the SPEs.

Events monitored by the PDT can rarely be used to establish inter-event order based on the event semantics, as in [3]. To improve the precision of time computation, the PDT forces global ordering of all traced events. All the events are written into a single buffer in the order of their arrival.

Context switches pose a problem to the algorithm because the decrementer register value is restored when a thread resumes. Our solution was to treat each live interval (a thread execution from one context switch to the next) as a "thread" in terms of the clock synchronization algorithm. This solution has the drawback of less events (and hence less constraints) generated for each "thread",

Table 1. Clock synchronization precision by benchmark

Name	Max error	Max error (SPEs)	Av. error	Av. error (SPEs)
BlackScholes	63	63	39	33
FFT16M	24	18	20	12
JuliaSet	34	19	27	12
Matrix_mul	33	11	31	8

but it still gives better precision than the alternatives. However, the PPE threads are all treated as one, since they use the same clock.

Another issue is possible imprecision in collecting timestamps and event order information. For example, if the timestamp precision is $\pm\delta$, then constraint (3) becomes less tight:

$$g_{\texttt{tid}(e_1)} + \texttt{ttime}(e_1) - \delta \leq g_{\texttt{tid}(e_2)} + \texttt{ttime}(e_2) + \delta. \quad (12)$$

In most practical situations, however, the value of δ is not known and cannot be taken into account when the constraints are computed. Consequently, constraints graph may contain negative-weight cycles of weight up to -2δ, and the all-pairs shortest path computation would fail.

One solution to this problem lies with the tracer, which can take measures to reduce the δ. In particular, the PDT event timestamp corresponds to the time event was written into the buffer rather than when it occurred. This difference is very small, but significant for the algorithm, since it prevents negative-weight cycles. Once we adopted this approach, we no longer saw negative cycles in any PDT-generated traces since this approach was adopted. Another solution is based on the observation that if a negative cycle of weight $-d$ is discovered, then $\delta \geq d/2$, and all the constraints should be made less tight as in (12). This can be done efficiently by setting $w(i,j) \leftarrow w(i,j) + \frac{d}{2}$. This step can be repeated until no negative cycles remain, generating in the process an estimate for δ.

5 Experimental Results

To estimate the practical applicability of the clock synchronization algorithm, we ran it on traces generated by several workloads from Cell SDK 3.0 [9]: BlackScholes, FFT16M, JuliaSet and Matrix_Mul. All the workloads executed on a IBM QS20 BladeCenter running two Cell BE Processors at 3.2GHz, under Fedora 7 Linux. The PDT was configured to trace all stalling events, such as waiting for a mailbox or DMA transfer to arrive. Non-stalling events, such as asynchronously issuing a DMA request, were not traced. The workloads were configured to utilize all the 16 SPUs on the blade.

Let s and t be two threads. According to (7), $-\bar{w}(t,s) \leq g_s - g_t \leq \bar{w}(s,t)$. Thus $\bar{w}(s,t) + \bar{w}(t,s)$ is an upper bound on the possible shift of the time scales of s and t for any global time on a trace. Table 1 aggregates these timing error bounds, measured in ticks, over trace pairs. The first column shows the maximum timing error for all thread pairs; the second column lists the maximum error over all SPE-SPE thread pairs; the third column contains the average timing error for SPE-PPE thread pairs; and the fourth column shows the average timing error for SPE-SPE thread pairs.

As Table 1 shows, the algorithm generated high-precision results for these benchmarks, with the max error ranging from 63 ticks for BlackScholes to 33 ticks for Matrix_mul, and the average error about two thirds of that. For a 14.8 MHz clock, this translates into 1.4–2.8 μs average error bounds. For all those benchmarks, most of the work is done on the SPEs, with the PPE largely responsible for intialization and coordination of the SPE threads. Since the events on the SPEs are much more dense, it is not surprising that the errors in the relative timing of SPE events are typically smaller. The most dramatic drop is observed on Matrix_mul, where the error is limited by 33 for all the events, but falls to 11 when only SPU events are considered. Given this pattern, we recommend selecting the global time function defined by (9) in which τ is the PPE "thread" and $\alpha = \frac{1}{2}$, cutting the SPE-PPE error estimate by half.

We also conducted an experiment to check how the instrumentation level affects clock synchronization precision, by fixing a benchmark (FFT16M) and running it with different levels of instrumentation. The full instrumentation, which traces all (stalling and non-stalling) communications, naturally gave the best precision (maximal error bound of 20 ticks, 11 ticks if restricted to SPE events). The basic instrumentation, which only traces thread start and end for SPE threads, gave the worst precision, 17,590 ticks. For a more interesting example of algorithm behavior on sparse traces, we configured the PDT to trace only stalls occurring in FFT's outer loop. This generated 88 events per SPE, with the average of 1,993,360 ticks between events. However, the maximal error bound on this trace was 53 ticks. This result can be understood if we take into account that this instrumentation level generates bursts of several temporally close events per thread, and that the bursts come at approximately the same time across threads, due to phase synchronization.

6 Conclusions

The absence of wall-clock timestamps in the trace is a severe limitation on the trace visualization and usage. In this paper, we showed how this problem can be solved during trace post-processing. We presented an algorithm for estimating the wall-clock time based on thread-local time and partial event ordering. The algorithm is linear in the size of the partial order relation between the events, and cubical in the number of threads. We have shown how to estimate the precision that the algorithm provides on a particular trace, and how it can recover from minor imprecision in time measurements and event ordering. The algorithm was used on several workloads from the Cell SDK 3.0, traced with different instrumentation levels, and showed good precision results. It's significant to note that the algorithm is by definition precise enough to preserve important properties of the input trace, namely, intra-thread timing and inter-thread event order. The algorithm is used in the Trace Analyzer tool, publicly available as part of the Visual Performance Analyzer [10]. We also apply it to traces from other multicores.

There are several important directions for future research. Our algorithm does not handle the clock drift. Since the algorithm depends on the distribution of events in the trace, it may be possible to improve the precision of the algorithm on sparse traces by allowing the tracer to generate a small number of extra events on each core; how to achieve this in an optimal way remains a topic for further research. Another requirement that the time synchronization algorithm imposes on the tracer tool is the preservation of enough event order data. Currently the PDT achieves this by sharing the same buffer for all the events. Using different buffers for different cores or accumulating several events on core before flushing them to the global buffer can reduce the tracing overhead. It remains to be seen how to optimally balance overhead reduction with clock precision.

Acknowledgements

We thank Ayal Zaks, Bilha Mendelson, Javier Turek, Orit Edelstein, Uzi Shvadron, and Yehuda Naveh for the many interesting discussions of the topic. We are also very grateful to the referees for the helpful suggestions.

References

1. Chen, T., Raghavan, R., Dale, J., Iwata, E.: Cell Broadband Engine architecture and its first implementation,
   http://www.ibm.com/developerworks/power/library/pa-cellperf/
2. Biberstein, M., Chang, M.S., Mendelson, B., Shvadron, U., Turek, J.: Trace-based performance analysis on Cell BE. In: Proceedings of IEEE International Symposium on Performance Analysis of Systems and Software (ISPASS) (2008)
3. Lamport, L.: Time, clocks, and the ordering of events in a distributed system. Commun. ACM 21(7), 558–565 (1978)
4. Mattern, F.: Virtual time and global states of distributed systems. In: Parallel and Distributed Algorithms: Proceedings of the International Workshop on Parallel and Distributed Algorithms (1988)
5. Williams, C., Reynolds, P.F., de Supinski, B.R.: Delta coherence protocols. IEEE Concurrency 8(3), 23–29 (2000)
6. Mills, D.L.: Internet time synchronization: The network time protocol. In: Yang, Z., Marsland, T.A. (eds.) Global States and Time in Distributed Systems. IEEE Computer Society Press, Los Alamitos (1994)
7. Maillet, E., Tron, C.: On efficiently implementing global time for performance evaluation on multiprocessor systems. Journal of Parallel and Distributed Computing 28(1), 84–93 (1995)
8. Cormen, T.H., Leiserson, C.E., Rivest, R.L., Stein, C.: Introduction to Algorithms, 2nd edn. MIT Press, Cambridge (2001)
9. IBM: Cell BE SDK 3.0,
   http://-www.ibm.com/developerworks/power/cellpkgdownloads.html
10. IBM: Visual Performance Analyzer, http://www.alphaworks.ibm.com/tech/vpa

The job scheduling model Each cluster contains one or more scheduling queues. From each queue, the queue's *job selection policy* extracts an eligible set of jobs to be scheduled; the eligible set can be ordered by tagging the extracted jobs. The eligible set is scheduled on the local resources using the queue's *job scheduling policy*. The events which trigger the job selection and the job scheduling policies are dependent on the simulated setup, that is, they can be set by the user. A DGSIM user can easily modify or re-implement the selection and the scheduling policies at various levels of the GRM architecture, using the Python scripting language. DGSIM already provides seven selection policies, and over ten scheduling policies, including FCFS, two FCFS/backfilling variants, and eight scheduling policies for bags-of-tasks [15]. While we have not experimented with with several queues at the same cluster, e.g., to simulate a cluster with per-VO queues, the DGSIM user can implement such a setup and use the workload model's user/VO characteristics to set the arrival queue of a job, and prioritizing the treatment of queues.

The information model deals with the accuracy and the timeliness of the information in an inter-operated (distributed) grid. A scheduling policy that deals with a job needs pieces of information that may be unavailable, inaccurate, or unknown in a realistic setting: the job's amount of work to be computed, a remote cluster's dynamic status, and even the remote cluster's static resource characteristics. Information inaccuracy can be the result of predictions; the DGSIM implementation currently provides over ten predictors widely used in large-scale distributed systems [16].

3.3 Grid Dynamics and Grid Evolution

We have already argued that grids change over time. We identify two types of change: over the short term, determined by dynamic resource availability (e.g., processors failing), and over the long term, determined by static resource availability (e.g., the addition of a new cluster to a grid, or of new processors to its clusters). We call the former *grid dynamics*, and the latter *grid evolution*. Only one of the surveyed grid simulators considers grid dynamics, i.e., GSSIM [6]; none of them considers grid evolution. Moreover, in comparison with GSSIM, our grid dynamics model also considers the concept of correlated failures, that is, of failures that affect several resources at the same time; this phenomenon is common in and important for the performance of both clusters and cluster-based grids [17,18].

The grid dynamics model considered by DGSIM describes the changes in resource availability status, and includes the following aspects: the clusters where a change occurs, the number of resources involved in the change, the time when the change occurs, and the time until the next status change for the same resource(s). DGSIM currently implements the realistic grid dynamics model proposed in [18].

The grid evolution model The grid evolution phenomenon is depicted in Figure 3: in less than three years, the WLCG has grown from 100 to 300 clusters; during the same period, the median cluster size has increased by just 20% (not shown). To account for grid evolution, we have designed a generator that for a grid system outputs the topology and resources for a time frame that spans from "present" to "far-future". A researcher can opt to perform simulations only for the present grid system, or for several sizes up to the far-future.

3.4 Grid Workload Generator

One of the most important problems when performing simulations of computer systems is setting the input workload. The experiment results may not be meaningful when using unrealistic workload models. To assess the behavior of a resource management component, workloads that incur the same average system load but have very different characteristics need to be generated. Moreover, it is sometimes useful to have some overlap of the characteristics of the generated input, to put in evidence the impact of the non-overlapping characteristics; then, only the values of some of the model parameters can be changed.

Realistic workload models DGSIM currently supports two realistic workload models: the Lublin-Feitelson (LF) model for jobs in parallel supercomputers and clusters [19] and a model for bags-of-tasks in grids [20]. The LF model considers for a job its parallelism, its runtime, and their correlation, and for the whole workload the arrival patterns (i.e., daily cycle, peak hours); this model has been validated using four long-term traces from parallel production environments and used by numerous grid researchers [21,22]. The model for bags-of-tasks in grids considers, in addition to the LF model, the individual users and the grouping of jobs in bags-of-tasks; this model has been validated using seven long-term grid traces, including five from the Grid Workloads Archive (GWA) [23].

Iterative workload generation The realistic grid workload models are complex, that is, they have many parameters and correlations between parameters. Generating a workload with a desired load from a complex model is difficult, especially when only some of the model parameters can be changed. To this end, we have developed an Iterative grid Workload Generation algorithm (IWG). The IWG algorithm takes as input a description of the target system (S), the target load (L), the maximum deviation from the target load ϵ, the workload model, and the fixed parameters of the model. It outputs a workload generated with the model such that the workload incurs on the target system the target load (taking into account ϵ). To achieve this, the algorithm tries to iteratively change (increase or decrease) the value of a non-fixed parameter, e.g., the job inter-arrival rate. The algorithm quits after a fixed number of iterations.

3.5 Simulator Validation

Arguably the crux of developing a simulator is its validation. According to Sargent, "a model is considered valid for a set of experimental conditions if the model's accuracy is within its acceptable range, which is the amount of accuracy required for the model's intended purpose" [24]. Thus, a simulator validated for one experiment may not be valid for another. However, our results show evidence that DGSIM gives valid results in many settings. The simulation results in Section 4.1 are very similar to real system behavior. The results in Section 4.2 lead to a reasonable distinction between architectures belonging to three classes (i.e., independent clusters, centralized grid schedulers, and decentralized grid schedulers). We have also performed several other validation tests, including the functional validation of the simulator through operational graphics [24] for several selected scenarios, and a comparison of simulated and real-environment performance for co-allocated workloads on the DAS-3 multi-cluster grid.

4 Experiments Using DGSim

We have already used DGSim in a variety of experiments. In this section we present a summary of these experiments, with the purpose of demonstrating the usefulness of our framework. For each experiment we describe the problem and the setup; for more details we refer to [18,22].

4.1 Performance Evaluation Using Real Workload Traces

Summary. Using DGSim, we have assessed the behavior of five grid resource management architectures under real load [22].

Setup. For this experiment, we have simulated the inter-operation of the DAS-2 and Grid'5000 grids, so that together they constitute a system with 20 clusters and over 3000 resources. The input workload was a contiguous subset of 12 months from the real grid traces taken from DAS-2 and Grid'5000, starting from 01/11/2005 [23]. Figures 4 and 5 show the configuration files for the environment

```
ID    Cluster        NProcs
c01   DAS/fs0        144
...
c06   G5K/site1/c1   128
c07   G5K/site1/c2   128
...
```

Fig. 4. The configuration file for the environment setup

```
Sim       PlugIn
cern      sim_cern.py
condor    sim_condor.py
DMM       sim_dmm.py
fcondor   sim_fcondor.py
koala     sim_koala.py
```

Fig. 5. The configuration file for the simulator setup

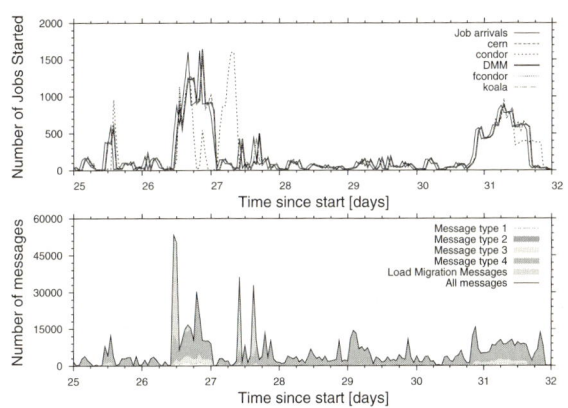

Fig. 6. System operation over time: (*top*) comparison of the number of jobs started by five grid resource management architectures. (*bottom*) the number of messages for DMM, per message type.

```
experiment.ID = E2-1D
scenario.SimTypes = DMM,sep-c,cern,condor,fcondor,koala
scenario.Loads = 10,30,50,60,70,80,90,95,98
scenario.TracesBaseDir = K:\EuroPar08\traces\10x\
scenario.BaseOutputDir = K:\EuroPar08\results\
...
```

Fig. 7. The configuration file for the second experiment

and for the simulator setup, respectively. Figure 6 depicts a comparative display of the number of jobs started by each of the five architectures over time. At the middle of days 26 and 27 the number of jobs submitted to one of the clusters surges, and DMM and fcondor start migrating load across clusters (the bottom row depicts the messages of DMM). This demonstrates how using DGSIM's automated analysis features, including graphing, facilitates understanding the causes of the performance variations across various grid configurations.

4.2 Performance Evaluation Using Realistic Workload Traces

Summary. Using DGSIM, we have assessed the performance of six grid resource management architectures under realistic load from 10% to 98% [22].

Setup. Similarly to the previous experiment, we have simulated the interoperation of the DAS-2 and Grid'5000 grids. First, the workloads are generated using the LF model with the parameter values extracted automatically from the grid traces present in the GWA [23]. Then, the experiment is run automatically; in particular, all the configuration files (540, that is, 6 architectures × 9 loads × 10 repetitions of each simulation for statistical soundness) are automatically generated. Finally, the results (over 20GB of data) are automatically analyzed to produce more than 20 common performance metrics. Throughout the process the tools use the same experiment configuration file, depicted in Figure 7. This configuration file specifies, among others, the experiment unique identifier (tag experiment.ID), the six simulated architectures (tag scenario.SimTypes), the nine loads under which the simulated system will operate (tag scenario.Loads), and the input and output base directories (tags scenario.TracesBaseDir and scenario.BaseOutputDir, respectively; the last part of the scenario.TracesBaseDir tag (10x) shows that there are 10 sets of traces in the input directory, one for each experiment repetition).

5 Related Work

In this section we survey several approaches to simulation of grid computing systems. We assess the relative merits of the surveyed approaches according to the requirements described in Section 2. Table 1 summarizes our survey; other simulators we have reviewed [21,30,31,32,33] may improve marginally on this body of knowledge. All the surveyed simulators have a discrete model representation, that is, the simulation model changes state only at discrete points

Table 1. A summary of simulators in grid computing research. The metrics M1-5 are evaluated for the largest reported set of experiments. Acronyms: T – from trace, M – from model, D – dynamic, G – generate until reaching the user-specified goal. The sign '-' shows that the feature must be implemented by the user, that the default values are tightly-coupled with the simulator, or that for the columns under the header "Performance" the value was not made public.

Simulator	Distinctive Feature	Experimental Setup			Experiment Support			Performance					
		a	b	c	a	b	c	M2 scen.	M3 sim.	M4 proc.	M4 sites	M5 jobs	M5 load
BeoSim [3]	co-allocation	-	-	M	-	+	+	350	20k	100	5	4M	-
ChicSim [2]	data replication	-	-	M	-	-	-	12	72	-	30	6k	-
CSim/Grid [25]	co-allocation	-	-	M	-	+	-	100	4k	200	4	-	70%
GangSim [5]	usage SLAs	-	-	T	-	+	+	10	100	300	20	1k	-
GridSim [1, 26, 27]	economic SLAs	-	-	TM	-	-	-	100	100	10k	15	5k	-
GSSIM [6]	automation	TMD	M	M	-	-	-	1	1	4	1	10	-
MONARC [28]	CERN	-	-	M	-	-	+	100	100	2k	5	5k	-
OptorSim [4]	data replication	-	-	-	-	-	+	50	0	-	20	10k	-
SimGrid [15, 29, 7]	batch&DAG jobs	TMD	-	TM	-	+	-	100	10k	300	-	4k	-
DGSim	see Section 3	TMD	TM	TMG	+	+	+	100	6k	3k	20	1.4M	300%

in simulation time[3]. With the exception of GangSim and MONARC, which are discrete time-stepped simulators, all the surveyed simulators are discrete event simulators. To speed-up the simulation, DGSim can run on clusters and grids to execute multiple individual simulations in parallel, while MONARC and SimGrid use multi-threading to speed-up individual simulations. Compared to the previous simulation tools, DGSim focuses more on the simulation process, with richer grid system and workload generation, and support for large numbers of individual and grouped simulations. This is particularly visible in the size of the reported experiments: DGSim can use workloads orders of magnitude larger than the other simulators (with the exception of BeoSim), on similarly sized simulated environments; BeoSim can work with a workload of similar size, but on a system that is an order of magnitude smaller. We did not have enough data to calculate the values for the metric M1; however, a large part of this value depends on the features listed under the headings "Experimental Setup" and "Experiment Support", where DGSim generally automates the tasks.

6 Conclusion and Future Work

The evolution of today's grids into the technological solution of choice for sharing computing resources depends on the ability of its developers to improve significantly the current grid resource management systems. To accomplish this difficult task, a toolbox in which simulators play a critical role is needed. In this paper we have proposed DGSim, a framework for simulating grid resource management architectures, which focuses on automating and optimizing the overall simulation process, from hypothesis to obtaining simulation results. From the methodological side, DGSim introduces or extends the concepts of grid interoperation, grid resource dynamics, grid evolution, and grid workload model. We

---
[3] For all the terms related to simulation we refer to the textbook of Fujimoto [8].

have presented in this work the design, the reference implementation, and two real cases where DGSim was used.

For the near future, we plan to continue the development of DGSim by extending it with libraries of algorithms and mechanisms for job scheduling, data management, and grid inter-operation. This extension will allow scientists to setup simulations in which these algorithms can be readily compared with alternatives.

References

1. Buyya, R., Murshed, M.M.: GridSim: a toolkit for the modeling and simulation of distributed resource management and scheduling for grid computing. C&C: Practice and Experience 14(13-15), 1175–1220 (2002)
2. Ranganathan, K., Foster, I.T.: Decoupling computation and data scheduling in distributed data-intensive applications. In: HPDC, pp. 352–358. IEEE CS, Los Alamitos (2002)
3. Jones, W.M., Pang, L.W., Stanzione Jr., D.C., Ligon III, W.B.: Job communication characterization and its impact on meta-scheduling co-allocated jobs in a mini-grid. In: IPDPS (2004)
4. Cameron, D.G., Millar, A.P., Nicholson, C., Carvajal-Schiaffino, R., Stockinger, K., Zini, F.: Analysis of scheduling and replica optimisation strategies for data grids using OptorSim. J. Grid Comput. 2(1), 57–69 (2004)
5. Dumitrescu, C., Foster, I.T.: GangSim: a simulator for grid scheduling studies. In: CCGRID, pp. 1151–1158. IEEE CS, Los Alamitos (2005)
6. Kurowski, K., Nabrzyski, J., Oleksiak, A., Weglarz, J.: Grid scheduling simulations with GSSIM. In: SRMPDS (2007)
7. Caron, E., Garonne, V., Tsaregorodtsev, A.: Definition, modelling and simulation of a grid computing scheduling system for high throughput computing. FGCS 23(8), 968–976 (2007)
8. Fujimoto, R.M.: Parallel and Distribution Simulation Systems. John Wiley & Sons, Inc., NY (1999)
9. Law, A.M., Kelton, W.D.: Simulation Modeling and Analysis, 3rd edn. McGraw Hill, NY (2000)
10. Banks, J.S., Carson II, J., Nelson, B.L., Nicol, D.M.: Discrete-Event System Simulation, 3rd edn. Prentice-Hall, Inc., New Jersey (2001)
11. Fishwick, P.: Simulation model design. In: WSC, pp. 209–211. ACM Press, New York (1995)
12. Perumalla, K.S.: Parallel and distributed simulation: traditional techniques and recent advances. In: WSC, pp. 84–95. ACM Press, New York (2006)
13. Iosup, A., Dumitrescu, C., Epema, D.H., Li, H., Wolters, L.: How are real grids used? The analysis of four grid traces and its implications. In: GRID, pp. 262–270. IEEE CS, Los Alamitos (2006)
14. Worldwide LHC Grid Computing (2007), http://lcg.web.cern.ch/LCG/
15. Casanova, H., Legrand, A., Zagorodnov, D., Berman, F.: Heuristics for scheduling parameter sweep applications in grid environments. In: HCW, pp. 349–363 (2000)
16. Sahoo, R.K., et al.: Critical event prediction for proactive management in large-scale computer clusters. In: KDD, pp. 426–435. ACM Press, New York (2003)

17. Zhang, Y., Squillante, M.S., Sivasubramaniam, A., Sahoo, R.K.: Performance implications of failures in large-scale cluster scheduling. In: Feitelson, D.G., Rudolph, L., Schwiegelshohn, U. (eds.) JSSPP 2004. LNCS, vol. 3277, pp. 233–252. Springer, Heidelberg (2004)
18. Iosup, A., Jan, M., Sonmez, O., Epema, D.H.: On the dynamic resource availability in grids. In: GRID, pp. 26–33. IEEE CS, Los Alamitos (2007)
19. Lublin, U., Feitelson, D.G.: The workload on parallel supercomputers: modeling the characteristics of rigid jobs. J. PDC 63(11), 1105–1122 (2003)
20. Iosup, A., Sonmez, O., Anoep, S., Epema, D.H.: The performance of bags-of-tasks in large-scale distributed systems. In: HPDC (2008) (accepted)
21. Casanova, H.: On the harmfulness of redundant batch requests. In: HPDC, pp. 70–79. IEEE CS, Los Alamitos (2006)
22. Iosup, A., Epema, D., Tannenbaum, T., Farrellee, M., Livny, M.: Inter-operating grids through delegated matchmaking. In: SC. ACM Press, New York (2007)
23. The Grid Workloads Archive (2007), http://gwa.ewi.tudelft.nl
24. Sargent, R.G.: Verification and validation of simulation models. In: WSC, pp. 130–143. ACM Press, New York (2005)
25. Bucur, A.I.D., Epema, D.H.J.: Trace-based simulations of processor co-allocation policies in multiclusters. In: HPDC, pp. 70–79. IEEE CS, Los Alamitos (2003)
26. Ranjan, R., Buyya, R., Harwood, A.: A case for cooperative and incentive-based coupling of distributed clusters. In: CLUSTER. IEEE CS, Los Alamitos (2005)
27. Sulistio, A., Poduval, G., Buyya, R., Tham, C.K.: On incorporating differentiated levels of network service into GridSim. FGCS 23(4), 606–615 (2007)
28. Legrand, I., Newman, H.B.: The MONARC toolset for simulating large network-distributed processing systems. In: WSC, pp. 1794–1801 (2000)
29. Legrand, A., Marchal, L., Casanova, H.: Scheduling distributed applications: the simgrid simulation framework. In: CCGRID, pp. 138–145. IEEE CS, Los Alamitos (2003)
30. Takefusa, A., Matsuoka, S., Nakada, H., Aida, K., Nagashima, U.: Overview of a performance evaluation system for global computing scheduling algorithms. In: HPDC. IEEE CS, Los Alamitos (1999)
31. Phatanapherom, S., Uthayopas, P., Kachitvichyanukul, V.: Fast simulation model for grid scheduling using HyperSim. In: WSC, pp. 1494–1500. ACM, New York (2003)
32. He, L., Jarvis, S.A., Spooner, D.P., Bacigalupo, D.A., Tan, G., Nudd, G.R.: Mapping dag-based applications to multiclusters with background workload. In: CCGRID, pp. 855–862 (2005)
33. Ramakrishnan, A., et al.: Scheduling data-intensive workflows onto storage-constrained distributed resources. In: CCGRID, pp. 401–409. IEEE CS, Los Alamitos (2007)

Supporting Parameter Sweep Applications with Synthesized Grid Services

Jürgen Hofer and Thomas Fahringer

Distributed and Parallel Systems Group, University of Innsbruck, Austria
{juergen,tf}@dps.uibk.ac.at

Abstract. Specialized tools already provide support for creation and execution of parameter sweeps. In such applications many tasks perform similar computations for varying input parameters. So far however none of these existing tools integrates well into service-oriented architectures or allows parametric modeling directly at the service interface. We address exactly this gap and demonstrate practical applicability with a concrete system architecture and implementation. Moreover we extend our services with reduction operators well known from parallel programming that perform certain aggregations or selections over the result set from all tasks of a given parameter study. Our efforts are substantial extensions to previous work on the service synthesis tool the 'Otho Toolkit' that allows smooth integration of scientific applications into service-oriented Grids. An experimental evaluation concludes our paper.[1]

1 Introduction

Parameter sweeping applications consist of many tasks that perform same or similar computations for varying input parameters and are quite common in many scientific and engineering domains. Often the individual tasks are independent, i.e. they do not require any inter-task communication, and therefore are easy to parallelize and well-suited for large-scale Grids [5]. We use the following definitions. *Parameters* are the set of input values to solve a particular problem constellation. The *parameter space* is a certain variation of parameters in given ranges to solve a related set of problems. Finally a *parameter sweep* or *parameter study* is the results of running a program with a given parameter space. To maximize practical utility certain technical difficulties have to be addressed. First the individual tasks of the parameter sweep should run on a large variety of Grid resources. Another important aspect is that parameter may not only occur in form of commandline arguments, but also in form of environment variables, input file names, within configuration or even application source-code files. Moreover large parametric experiments produce many results which makes their management and analysis hard and time-consuming. When addressing those issues parameter studies easily become complex, a reason why

---

[1] This work was partially funded by the European Union through the IST FP6-004265 CoreGRID and IST FP6-031688 EGEE-2 projects.

many existing tools are specific to certain environments or applications. The great interest the scientific community has in such tools has motivated us to extend our work in that direction.

In previous work [6,7] we discussed the semi-automatic transformation of legacy applications into service-oriented Grid environments and suggested a mechanism and corresponding tools for synthesis of tailor-made application services. Our focus thereby lies on existing, resource-intensive non-interactive commandline legacy application, shortly denoted by $\mathcal{RLA}$, as typically used in high-performance and Grid computing environments. The synthesized services are called Executor Services $\mathcal{XS}$ and are customized wrapper services tailor-made for a specific application and adapted to a certain Grid resource. They provide a purely functional interface that exposes the application parameters (commandline arguments, arguments located inside input or configuration files, input/output data files) but hides all technical details of the resource allocation and application execution process. The Otho Toolkit is a software system that has proven to be a valuable tool for automatized synthesis of $\mathcal{XS}$ source codes including all required service and application artifacts to build a self contained deployable service package. The Otho Toolkit and the Executor Services it synthesizes are the basis for the research presented subsequently.

Related Work. There are two major research directions so far. The first uses templates, markup languages or source code annotations for modeling the parameter studies and usually provides management tools for execution. Certain existing grid middleware systems such as Condor [10], UNICORE [2] or AppLeS [3] allow to launch pre-existing parameter studies however these tools do not directly support modeling or creation. AppLeS itself is a Grid scheduler which was later on extended with AppLeS Parameter-Sweep Template (APST) targeting parameter studies. Nimrod is a parametric modeling system that uses a declarative language to express a parametric experiment and provides automation of the formulation, running, monitoring and result collating tasks [1]. Its parametrization capabilities are however limited to input files. ZENTURIO [9] is an experiment management tool that can be used for execution of parameter studies on cluster and Grid architectures. It uses a directive-based language for source code instrumentation. Even though it provides a convenient graphical user interface and also a service interface it is not applicable to extend services with integral parameter study capabilities. The second stream of research takes advantage of graphical user interfaces for modeling parameter studies. ILAB [14] enables the creation of parameter study-oriented workflows using an advanced GUI that allows to specify how to create and distribute the parameter files. However their approach is rather static and also its parametrization is limited to input files. Both SEGL [4] and a parameter sweep extension to the P-GRADE portal [8] focus on embedding support for parameter sweeps inside potentially complex workflows. Both approaches are certainly very interesting but have a different focus than our approach as we wanted to make the parameter study support an integral part of our synthesized services such that it can be used from any client without the need for a dedicated GUI or Grid portal system.

2 Parametric Modeling

The parameter space is the variation of input parameters in given ranges to solve a related set of problems. Parametric Modeling then denotes the mechanism for describing and building a parameter space. We designed a formal language and derived from that a syntactical textual rendering. First we define so-called value sets that are abbreviations and allow concise formulation of parameter ranges instead of complete exhaustive enumeration. The syntactical rendering relies on XML-Schema to define a XML-syntax that naturally integrates with current Web service technologies such as SOAP. Then we present the mechanism used to combine the given value sets to build the full parameter space.

2.1 Value Sets

Value set are abbreviations and allow concise formulation of parameter ranges instead of complete taxative enumeration. We distinguish three value-set datatypes: string-set, int-set and real-set. The grammar is defined as follows for $\mathtt{REAL} \in \mathbb{R}$ and $\mathtt{INT} \in \mathbb{N}$.

```
STRING       := '"' CHAR+ '"'
CHAR         := [^"{},:] | "\"" | "\{" | "\}" | "\," | "\:"
SET          := '{' ( INT_SET | STRING_SET |
                      BOOL_SET | ENUM_SET ) '}'
INT_SET      := INT | ( INT_SET, INT_SET) | INT_SEQU
INT_SEQU     := INT_FROM ':' INT_TO [ ':' INT_STRIDE ]
INT_FROM, INT_TO, INT_STRIDE := INT
REAL_SET     := REAL | ( REAL_SET, REAL_SET) | REAL_SEQU
REAL_SEQU    := REAL_FROM ':' REAL_TO [ ':' REAL_STRIDE ]
REAL_FROM, REAL_TO, REAL_STRIDE := REAL
STRING_SET   := STRING | ( STRING, STRING_SET )
STRING       := STRING '+' SET
```

They allow users to define multiple value sets for arguments by enumerating values or the use of special set operators. Argument value sets are defined by the well-defined evaluation function $\Phi(\sigma) \to \psi$ resolving an argument set σ into a finite non-empty list of ordered argument values ψ. Once evaluated all resolved elements $\psi = \{e_1, \ldots, e_{n|n \geq 1}\}$ are ordered and denoted by indexes $0 \ldots n$. Empty sets are disallowed, i.e. $n \geq 1$. For each basic datatype a customised evaluation function is provided returning a list of accordingly typed argument values: integer $\Phi^{\mathcal{I}}$, real $\Phi^{\mathcal{R}}$, string $\Phi^{\mathcal{S}}$, enumeration $\Phi^{\mathcal{E}}$ and boolean $\Phi^{\mathcal{B}}$ functions. For referring to specific elements the function Φ can be indexed, e.g. $\Phi_1(\sigma)$ returns the first element and $\Phi_n(\sigma)$ the last element. The $\diamond$ operator is used to concatenate a string with another string or valid element (e.g. integer sets, etc). For convenience we allow concise numerical set definitions via the special set operator $\Phi(\mathtt{a\!:\!b\!:\!c})$ where a is the start value, b the end value and c specifies the stride that defaults to 1, i.e. $\Phi(\mathtt{from\!:\!to}) \equiv \Phi(\mathtt{from\!:\!to\!:\!1})$. The evaluation function Φ may be applied recursively, quite commonly found e.g. in combination with the string concatenation operator $\diamond$ to build a list of file names. If $\mathcal{V}_\mathcal{E}$ denotes the value set of a certain enumeration datatype $\mathcal{E}$, then $\Phi^{\mathcal{E}}(\psi) = \{e_0, \ldots, e_n\} \land \forall e_i | e_i \in \mathcal{V}_\mathcal{E}$. Subsequent examples show practical use of Φ.

Supporting Parameter Sweep Applications with Synthesized Grid Services   29

$\Phi^\mathcal{I}(\texttt{2,5,17,99}) \equiv \{2, 5, 17, 99\}$
$\Phi^\mathcal{I}(\Phi^\mathcal{I}(\texttt{2:5}), \Phi^\mathcal{I}(\texttt{17,99})) \equiv \{2, 3, 4, 5, 17, 99\}$
$\Phi^\mathcal{I}(\texttt{-4:4:2}) \equiv \{-4, -2, 0, 2, 4\}$
$\Phi^\mathcal{R}(\texttt{0.03:0.05:0.01}) \equiv \{0.03, 0.04, 0.05\}$
$\Phi^\mathcal{S}(\texttt{"mriaa.df3"}, \texttt{"mriab.df3"}, \texttt{"mriac.df3"}) \equiv \{mriaa.df3,\ mriab.df3,\ mriac.df3\ \}$
$\Phi^\mathcal{S}(\texttt{"mria"} \diamond \Phi^\mathcal{S}(\texttt{"a"}, \texttt{"b"}, \texttt{"c"}) \diamond \texttt{".df3"}) \equiv \{mriaa.df3,\ mriab.df3,\ mriac.df3\ \}$
$\Phi^\mathcal{S}(\texttt{"mri"} \diamond \Phi^\mathcal{I}(\texttt{0:3}) \diamond \texttt{".df3"}) \equiv \{mri0.df3, mri1.df3, mri2.df3, mri3.df3\}$

In the first three examples printed above integer sets are defined by enumeration, hierarchical combination, sequential range specification with default stride of one and then a stride length of two. A three item real set is then given in the range [0.03, 0.05]. Finally three string set examples are given that demonstrate also concatenation and inclusion of an integer value set.

2.2 Web Service Interface Syntax

In order to make practical use of the value sets for specification of parameter studies at the service-level a syntactical rendering that integrates well with current Web service technologies such as WSDL and SOAP is required. We use custom XML-Schema datatypes for this purpose. The value sets themselves are not expressed token by token in XML as this would cause exorbitant overheads for marginal benefit. Instead we use a XML string type as wrapper and concise textual syntax for the value sets. The use of valuesets is shown below.

```
<complexType name="ExecutePovrayAnimationRequest">
   <sequence>
      <element name="scenepov"     type="pst:valueset" />
      <element name="frame"        type="pst:valueset" />
      <element name="sceneini"     type="xsd:string"   />
      <element name="width"        type="xsd:int"      />
      <element name="height"       type="xsd:int"      />
      <element name="format"       type="tns:PovrayImageFormat" />
   </sequence>
</complexType>
```

The code snippet contains a XML-Schema type used inside the request message to an Executor Service for the POV-Ray [13] application. The first two arguments namely *scenepov* and *frame* use our custom *pst:valueset* datatype that allows value set specification at this positions.

```
<ExecutePovrayAnimationRequest>
    <scenepov>SS{'MRI_61FA_1.pov', SS{'MRI_FB2E_' + IS{2:6:2} + '.pov'}}</scenepov>
    <frame>IS{1:3}</frame>
    <sceneini>MRI.ini<sceneini>
    <width>1920</width>
    <height>1280</height>
    <format>PNG</format>
</ExecutePovrayAnimationRequest>
```

A possible invocation of the service may contain the XML elements printed above. Both *pstudyset* datatypes specify value sets. The *scenepov* argument contains a string set that contains one terminal string and another string-set that unfolds to three terminal strings therefore has a total length of four strings. The *frame* parameter specifies an integer set that unfolds to the numbers $1, 2, 3$.

2.3 Building the Parameter Space

The crossproduct of all elements in all sets is calculated and used as parameter space for invoking the instances of the specified task. Lets assume we have n value set parameters $P_1, \ldots P_n$. Each parameter P_i has a different set of l^{P_i} argument values $V^{P_i} = v_1^{P_i}, v_2^{P_i}, \ldots, v_{l^{P_i}}^{P_i}$. In order to generate the parameter space PS the cross product of all argument values has to be computed, i.e.

$$PS = P_1 \times P_2 \times \ldots \times P_n = v_1^{P_1}, v_1^{P_2}, \ldots, v_2^{P_1}, v_2^{P_2}, \ldots, v_3^{P_1}, v_3^{P_2}, \ldots$$

which means that the first values of each parameter are combined then the last parameter is assigned the second value and so forth until all values of P_n have been used, then P_n is reset and P_{n-1} is changed to the second value, etc.

pspace = {pstudyset(scenepov) × pstudyset(frame)} = {

{ {MRI_61FA_2.pov, 1, ...} {MRI_61FA_2.pov, 2, ...} {MRI_61FA_3.pov, 1, ...}
 {MRI_FB2E_2.pov, 1, ...} {MRI_FB2E_2.pov, 2, ...} {MRI_FB2E_2.pov, 3, ...}
 {MRI_FB2E_4.pov, 1, ...} {MRI_FB2E_4.pov, 2, ...} {MRI_FB2E_4.pov, 3, ...}
 {MRI_FB2E_6.pov, 1, ...} {MRI_FB2E_6.pov, 2, ...} {MRI_FB2E_6.pov, 3, ...} }

For the POV-Ray example invocation printed in the previous example the parameter space then contains $4 \times 3 = 12$ elements. It is listed above. Each P_i is assigned to a service $\mathcal{XS}_i$ for execution.

3 Reduction Operations

The result space of parameter studies grows in direct proportion with the parameter space and its size and complexity quickly becomes hard to manage and analyze. The parallel computing community developed several shortcut communication patterns between sets of individual processes (scatter and gather, subset and group messages and reduction operations) to ease development and at the same time increase efficiency of parallel programs. In the scatter operation the originator sends a personalized message to a set of nodes. For instance an n-size array is distributed to n nodes such that the first node receives the first element, the second node the second element and so forth. Mapped to our context the building of the parameter space and allocation of n services corresponds to this scatter operation. Each element of the parameter space is used as input parametrization for another service. The reverse is the gather operation which corresponds to the default behavior of our parameter study executor services as described in the previous sections.

We suggest an additional alternative behavior for our services inspired by the idea of reduction operations. After termination of each part of the parameter study n result items are available at each of the n services $\mathcal{XS}_{i \in 1\ldots n}$ as described by the response message of the service interface. An all-to-one reduction operation collects these n data items and combines them through an associative operator into the primary service $\mathcal{XS}_0$. Different reduction operators for combination, aggregation and mathematical operations are possible. Currently available are the following eight operators.

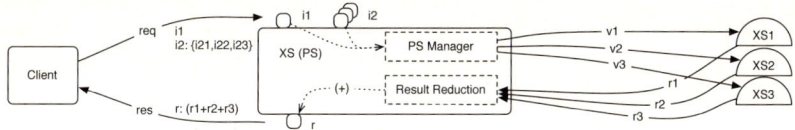

Fig. 1. Result Reduction

```
REDUCTION_SUM        REDUCTION_MIN    REDUCTION_MEAN     REDUCTION_SORTED_ASC
REDUCTION_PRODUCT    REDUCTION_MAX    REDUCTION_MEDIAN   REDUCTION_SORTED_DESC
```

Reduction operations are very helpful to design many parallel algorithms but also to quickly identify maxima or minima as commonly intended when executing large parameter studies. To better illustrate the usage of our reduction operations we use a simple service that calculates the square of each element of a set of integer values. The corresponding request type is shown below. Now assume the valueset `<set>IS{2:8:2}</set>` is sent as part of the as request message. The valueset unfolds to the four elements $2, 4, 6, 8$ and the corresponding squares are returned as part of the response message printed below.

```
<complexType name="SquaresRequest">               <SquaresResponse>
    <sequence>                                        <result>4</result>
        <element name="set" type="pst:valueset" />    <result>16</result>
    </sequence>                                       <result>36</result>
</complexType>                                        <result>64</result>
                                                  </SquaresResponse>
```

Now lets assume the user does not need all result elements, rather is only interested in finding the maximum and perhaps the sum of all values.

```
<complexType name="SumOfSquaresResponse">          <SumOfSquaresResponse>
    <sequence>                                         <max>
        <element name="max" type="pst:reduction_max" />    <value>64</value>
        <element name="sum" type="pst:reduction_sum" />    <index>3</index>
    </sequence>                                        </max>
</complexType>                                         <sum>120</sum>
                                                   </SumOfSquaresResponse>
```

From user perspective this task becomes now trivial by using the two reduction operators as shown above. In the response message type declaration the reduction operators are defined as special datatypes. The response message itself then contains for the example given above a *max* and a *sum* element with the corresponding results. While *sum*, *product*, *mean* and *median* affect all elements the *max* and *min* operator results also contain the index position of the element as users are likely to be interested in which concrete parametrization is associated with the result. The result index position corresponds to the sequence created by unfolding the parameter space as explained in the previous section.

4 Implementation

We used the Otho Toolkit to synthesize a set of executor services ($\mathcal{XS}$). Each set of service replicas was synthesized for three case study applications, namely

Wien2k [12], a material science software performing electronic structure calculations of solids, POV-Ray [13], a high-quality raytracer, as representative for parameter sweep applications and a simple java-based program that calculates the squares of integer values as described in Section 3. We then extended the generated service source codes and integrated the parameter sweep capabilities. Figure 2 illustrates our system architecture. First we updated the $\mathcal{XS}$ interfaces and integrated the valueset parameters. One of the service replicas was determined to be the primary $\mathcal{XS}_{PS}$ and the remaining services became workers denoted by $\mathcal{XS}_{i \in 1...n}$. The primary $\mathcal{XS}_{PS}$ accepts user requests, parses the valueset parameter ranges and creates the parameter space. It then instantiates the *PS manager* component to which it hands over the parameter space. The PS manager creates for each parameter combination a parameter object that contains the parametrization of a certain task. This set is then stored into a repository. Each $\mathcal{XS}_{i \in 1...n}$ regularly contacts the repository and queries for tasks to execute. If a matching task is available it marks it as *active* and starts with the processing. While active each worker updates in regular intervals a timestamp associated with each task in order to identify failures. The repository is implemented as a relational database with a Web service interface. The PS manager uses a separate component the *PS monitor* that regularly checks the PS repository and notifies the manager upon completion. Once all task of the parameter sweep have been finished the PS manager retrieves all results by contacting all worker services $\mathcal{XS}_{i \in 1...n}$. If a response message argument uses of of our reduction operators the primary service $\mathcal{XS}_{PS}$ calculates the result using a generic library. Otherwise the individual results are combined into the result array before being returned to the service requestor.

5 Experiments

In order to assess and evaluate our approach and implementation we conducted a set of experiments on the AustrianGrid [11] infrastructure. We deployed the synthesized and adapted Executor Services ($\mathcal{XS}$) on several Grid sites. The repository was deployed on the Grid site in Innsbruck. We were interested in answering the following questions. (1) What is the communication time complexity of a typical $\mathcal{XS}$ u sage if no parametric modeling is available? (2) Which overheads are introduced if parametric modeling and parameter sweep support at the $\mathcal{XS}$-level is available? (3) How big are those overheads and comparison with

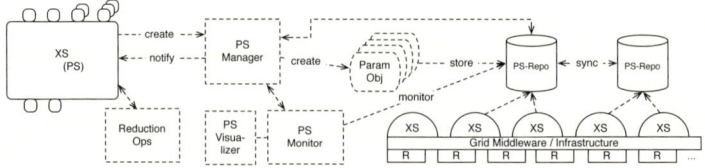

Fig. 2. System Architecture

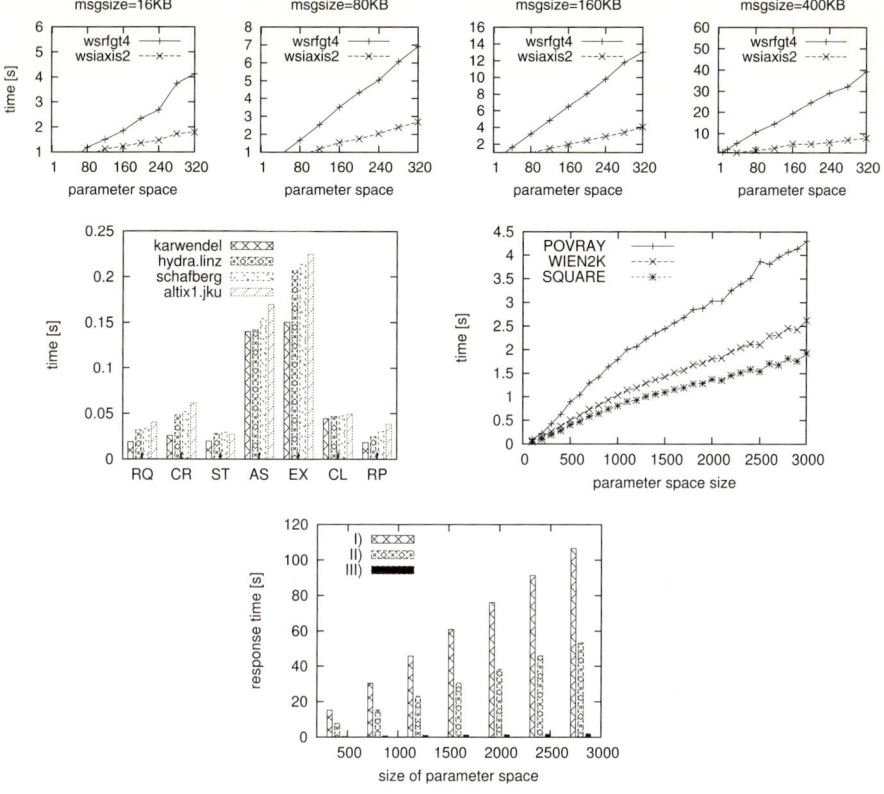

Fig. 3. Experimental Results

how do they compare regarding communication complexity without parameter study support? The first chart in Figure 3 contains the results of the following set of experiments. We executed several parameter studies for the POV-Ray application and varied the size of the parameter space and the size of the request message, i.e. for large parameter values. The chart plots the total response time for all service usages to complete however with the actual execution time excluded. With both growing message size and size of the parameter space the response time increases steadily. If the parameter space contains only a single element $n = 1$ then our experiment runs terminated after 0.027s for 16kB, and 0.046s for 800kB messages. Given a parameter space size $n = 320$ completion already requires 1.79s for 16kB, 3.21s for 120kB and already 14.98s for 800kB messages. This corresponds to a 325fold super-linear increase for 320 messages with 800kB. Clearly the use of parametric modeling to reduce the number of interactions will improve overall system performance dramatically. The additional overheads introduced by the support for parameter studies are directly derived by our system architecture in Figure 2. First the client sends a request to the $\mathcal{XS}$-PS primary service, which creates the PS object and stores it in the

Table 1. PStudy Messaging Overheads Details

scenario	I	II	III	I	II	III
n	200	200	200	2400	2400	2400
request	3807.0	19.0	19.0	45684.0	19.0	19.0
createPS	-	26.4	26.4	-	32.0	32.0
storePS	-	30.5	30.5	-	37.1	37.1
async	-	30.5	30.5	-	37.1	37.1
reduction	-	-	100.7	-	-	1585.8
response	3807.0	3807.0	19.0	45684.0	45684.0	19.0
$\sum$	7614.0	3913.4	226.1	91368.0	45809.2	1730.1

repository. The next overhead category is the time required by $\mathcal{XS}_{i \in 1...n}$ to query the repository for open tasks which we configured to be done on a scheduled interval of 50ms. After the actual program execution all results are collected and aggregated at the primary. Finally the result is sent in a response message to the client. The top-right plot in Figure 3 shows the detailed overheads we measured while running the POV-ray parameter study at $n = 200$ with the master being located at four different Grid sites. In the third set of experiments we focused on the cost of the reduction operation for increasing size of the parameter space n. We used our three pilot applications. The Square application used the `REDUCTION_SUM` operator to build a global sum of the partial results. For Wien2k and POV-Ray we implemented custom application-specific operators, namely a text-file concatenator for Wien2k and a converter of multiple images into a movie using the Unix utility `png2yuv`. The third chart in Figure 3 depicts the experienced overhead of the reduction operations for all three applications for parameter spaces up to $n = 3000$. Finally we created a direct comparison between three cases using the Squares application. For an increasing parameter space size n we plotted the response time in milliseconds measured using the Squares application. In the fourth plot in Figure 3 we compare separate invocations not using parametric modeling, a parameter study with full parameter space combined into a single parametrically modeled argument with and without a reduction operation. The results for $n = 200$ broken down into individual overheads is shown in Figure 3. Given the fact that by using the reduction the total amount of interactions can be cut down to only two messages exchanged between client and master the total experienced response time of the parameter study and reduction case was an order of magnitude smaller than for the combined and again for the case of separate invocations.

6 Conclusion

We suggested a comfortable user-transparent parameter study mechanism directly integrated into Grid applications services for easy use within service-oriented Grid environments. Our parametric modeling approach uses formally defined value sets, a concise textual syntax embedded within the service-interface and a mechanism to automatically build the parameter space. Moreover we introduce reduction operations as shortcut communication patterns well known from parallel computing to our parameter study enabled services. Our prototype implementation is based on the Otho Toolkit, a service synthesis tool for automatic integration of legacy applications into service-oriented Grids. In a set of experiments we evaluated the involved overheads for three pilot applications. We demonstrated that under ideal circumstances efficiency can be greatly increased by using parametric modeling and the reduction operations given that the total amount of necessary message interactions is minimized. Future work goes in two directions. First we plan to improve on the scheduling of the individual tasks as we currently apply a trivial random-based scheme. Second when implementing the prototypes for our applications we noticed that the greatest benefit for users would arise from availability of custom reduction operators. We also want to investigate in this direction possibly providing several new operators that are useful to certain classes of applications.

References

1. Abramson, D., Giddy, J., Kotler, L.: High performance parametric modeling with nimrod/g: Killer application for the global grid? In: Proceedings of the International Parallel and Distributed Processing Symposium (IPDPS 2000), Cancun, Mexico, May 1-5 2000. IEEE Computer Society Press, Los Alamitos (2000)
2. Almond, J., Snelling, D.: Unicore: Uniform access to supercomputing as an element of electronic commerce. Future Generation Computer Systems 15, 539–548 (1999)
3. Casanova, H., Obertelli, G., Berman, F., Wolski, R.: The apples parameter sweep template: User level middleware for the grid. In: Proceedings of the Supercomputing Conference (SC 2002), Dallas, USA. IEEE Computer Society Press, Los Alamitos (2002)
4. Currle-Linde, N., Boes, F., Lindner, P., Pleiss, P., Resch, M.: A management system for complex parameter studies and experiments in grid computing. In: Proceedings of the 16th IASTED International Conference on Parallel and Distributed Computing and Systems, Cambridge, USA, pp. 34–39 (2004)
5. Foster, I., Kesselman, C., Tuecke, S.: The anatomy of the grid: Enabling scalable virtual organizations. Int. Journal of Supercomputer Applications 15(3), 200–222 (2001)
6. Hofer, J., Fahringer, T.: The Otho Toolkit - Synthesizing Tailor-made Scientific Grid Application Wrapper Services. Journal of Multiagent and Grid Systems 3(3) (2007)
7. Hofer, J., Fahringer, T.: Synthesizing Byzantine Fault-Tolerant Grid Application Wrapper Services. In: Proceedings of 8th IEEE International Symposium on Cluster Computing and the Grid (CCGrid 2008), Lyon, France, May 19-22, 2008. IEEE Computer Society Press, Los Alamitos (2008)
8. Kacsuk, P., Farkas, Z., Sipos, G., Toth, A., Hermann, G.: Workflow-level Parameter Study Management in multi-Grid environments by the P-GRADE Grid portal. In: Proceedings of 2nd International Workshop on Grid Computing Environments (GCE), Tampa, Florida (2006)
9. Prodan, R., Fahringer, T.: On using ZENTURIO for Performance and Parameter Studies on Clusters and Grids. In: Proc. of the 11th Euromicro Conf. on Parallel Distributed and Network based Processing (PDP 2003), Genova (February 2003)

10. Thain, D., Tannenbaum, T., Livny, M.: Condor and the grid. In: Berman, F., Fox, G.C., Hey, A.J.G. (eds.) Grid Computing: Making the Global Infrastructure a Reality, pp. 299–335. Wiley, Chichester (2003)
11. AustrianGrid, http://www.austriangrid.at
12. WIEN2k, http://www.wien2k.at
13. POV-Ray, http://www.povray.org
14. Yarrow, M., McCann, K., Biswas, R., van der Wijngaart, R.: An advanced user interface approach for complex parameter study process specification on the information power grid. In: Proceedings of the 1st Workshop on Grid Computing (Grid 2000), Bangalore, India (December 2000)

A P2P Approach to Resource Discovery in On-Line Monitoring of Grid Workflows

Bartłomiej Łabno[1], Marian Bubak[1,2], and Bartosz Baliś[2]

[1] Academic Computer Centre - CYFRONET, Poland
[2] Institute of Computer Science, AGH Poland

Abstract. On-line monitoring of Grid workflows is challenging since workflows are loosely coupled and highly dynamic. An efficient mechanism of automatic resource discovery is needed in order to discover new producers of workflow monitoring data fast. However, currently used Grid information systems are not suitable for this due to insufficient performance characteristics. We propose to associate the monitoring infrastructure with a P2P DHT infrastructure in order to achieve the automatic resource discovery wherein consumers of monitoring data can be notified fast about new producers. In our solution, the consumer of monitoring data can subscribe to any monitoring endpoint and the automatic resource discovery is handled transparently. We evaluate performance of the presented solution, and demonstrated a case study scenario of monitoring of a traffic management workflow.

Keywords: grid computing, monitoring, workflows, resource discovery, peer to peer, distributed hash tables.

1 Introduction

Monitoring of scientific workflows is important for many purposes including status tracking, recording provenance, or performance improvement. Resource discovery is an indispensable phase in Grid monitoring scenarios. A directory service is usually a part of the monitoring infrastructure to serve as an information service [13]. Monitoring producers advertise themselves in the directory service providing information about the monitored resources and endpoint where monitoring data can be acquired. Consumers need to discover the monitoring service endpoint using the name or attributes of the resource to be monitored.

In some cases, on-line monitoring is desirable in order to quickly respond to problems or react to environment changes, as in dynamic rescheduling, for example, wherein computing resources are dynamically re-allocated in response to performance degradations. However, the distributed and dynamic nature of workflows combined with the fully decentralized architecture of the monitoring infrastructure, required in the Grid, makes this task difficult to achieve. As workflow's activities dynamically emerge at unpredictable times and locations, a mechanism of *fast and automatic resource discovery* wherein new producers of workflow monitoring data are automatically discovered and transparently receive subscription requests on behalf of active subscribers, seems to be the key issue to enable on-line monitoring of Grid workflows.

Unfortunately, existing information services used in Grid production infrastructures are not suitable for frequently changing resources. Two factors are responsible for this. First, the high 'put latency' of directory services; second, the lack of efficient notification-based discovery mechanism. The 'put latency' denotes the delay from the registration of a new resource (or information update thereof) in the resource discovery system to the time it can actually be discovered (the information propagation delay). The 'get latency', on the other hand, is the delay needed to retrieve information from a directory service (the response time of a discovery request). While in most approaches the 'get latency' is of greatest concern (to ensure low response times regardless of a growing size of resource database), the low 'put latency' is essential for a fast discovery of changing resources required for on-line monitoring.

Peer-to-peer technologies are increasingly important for distributed systems, such as distributed storage systems [5] or in Grid technologies improving rich media content delivery [8]. The two technologies – the Grid and peer to peer are viewed as complimentary and likely to converge [9]. *Distributed Hash Table* is a special form of a peer-to-peer network and it acts as a hash table which is distributed among all the nodes in the network [14]. Each node keeps a piece of information which is usually a range of keys and associated values. An interface is provided for registering key – value pairs and for retrieving thereof. A DHT network is often structured, i.e. though it is not known in which node of the network a specific key is stored, one is guaranteed to reach this node by routing in no more than $log(n)$ hops [14] (n being the total number of nodes in the P2P network). The same complexity is guaranteed for putting a new key – value pair into the network. As a result, DHT networks can provide excellent performance, high scalability and availability. For example, for the Amazon's Dynamo, a highly available and scalable key-value store, the reported latencies are around $15ms$ for reads and $30ms$ for writes, while the $99.9th$ percentile latencies are around $200ms$ for reads and $300ms$ for writes [7].

The goal of this work is to investigate the peer to peer distributed hash table technologies for supporting the automatic resource discovery in on-line monitoring of Grid workflows. In our approach, essentially, one can subscribe to, e.g., 'all workflow $Wf1$ events', in *any* monitoring service endpoint. The actual automatic resource discovery is performed by means of the P2P DHT infrastructure associated with the monitoring infrastructure. Last but not least, it must be noted that the automatic resource discovery for Grid workflows requires a simple name-based lookup, as opposed to complex, *ad-hoc* content-based lookup featured by full-blown discovery services and required for more complex resource discovery scenarios based on attribute values (e.g. resource matching). Consequently, the DHT infrastructure introduced in the presented solution is not meant to replace the global discovery service but rather support it in some special scenarios where performance is critical.

The remainder of this paper is organized as follows. Section 2 overviews the related works. Section 3 presents the proposed solution for P2P-DHT-based automatic resource discovery. In Section 4, performance evaluation of the prototype monitoring infrastructure with P2P-DHT deployment is presented. Section 5 presents a case-study monitoring of a Coordinated Traffic Management workflow. Finally, Section 6 summarizes the presented work and overviews possible paths for future investigation.

2 Related Work

The goal of this section is to overview existing resource discovery services focusing on those found in large-scale production Grid deployments, and the analysis of their suitability for on-line monitoring of Grid workflows.

Globus *Monitoring and Discovery System* (MDS) [11,12] started as a centralized LDAP server (MDS-1), but the limitations of this solution led to a distributed LDAP architecture in MDS-2. Its successors, MDS-3 and MDS-4, are conceptually similar to MDS-2, but they follow the *Service Oriented Architecture* patterns. MDS-4 allows to acquire the monitoring data from the *Index Services*. Every Index Service aggregates Service Data Elements which describe resources registered to them. A hierarchy can be formed and an upper-level Index Service can aggregate information from the lower-level ones.

Berkeley Database Information Index (BDII) is an information system deployed at over 250 sites in the EGEE project. BDII was made as a replacement for Globus MDS2. It has a hierarchical architecture in which low-level Grid Resource Information Services (GRIS) provide information to site BDII which is in turn combined and exposed by top-level BDIIs. The information is refreshed in a top-down manner, i.e. a top-level BDII scans site BDIIs which obtain information from GRISes. The refresh is done by reloading the entire database and rebuilding indices every 2-3 minutes [2].

iGrid is a grid information service developed within the European GridLab [1]. The project started with Globus MDS and LDAP as a core, however, it has moved to a relational database storage, due to the disadvantages LDAP which is designed for frequent reads but not updates. Also, the deficiencies of LDAP-based queries and overall poor performance caused this. Still, a migration to a DHT in iGrid is planned to improve performance.

R-GMA is a relational implementation of the Grid Monitoring Architecture ([13]), developed within the European DataGrid. It is based on the relational model and it supports SQL as the query interface, though it does not feature a distributed RDBMS [6]. R-GMA has been reported to have performance problems and a relatively low throughput [15].

In general, the described systems have certain common characteristics. First, they are distributed, usually featuring a hierarchical architecture. Second, they are oriented towards high query performance, not update performance. Third, high scalability is achieved usually by using caching of information. Systems not using caching have been shown to display very low throughput of around

1-5 query requests per second [15]. A performance study of a web-service-based information system of the latest generation, MDS4 (Monitoring and Discovery System), has shown that it can sustain a throughput of 10 requests per second (dual 2.4 Xeon with 4GB RAM), regardless of the number of concurrent clients, but for the index size as small as 500 entries [12]. While the larger index sizes were not investigated we can note how throughput degrades with the index size by observing that for the index of size 500 it is twice as big as for the index of size 100 [12].

In summary, the analysis of existing Grid information systems operating on large-scale deployments of production Grids (such as BDII in the EGEE testbed) shows that the realistic update rate is of order of minutes. This is insufficient for the on-line monitoring scenario.

3 The Automatic Resource Discovery Scenario

The common Grid monitoring scenario consists of the following phases: producer advertisement, resource discovery, subscription to monitoring data, and actual transfer of monitoring data. However, it is not sufficient for on-line monitoring of Grid workflows. For example, for a simple monitoring request 'subscribe to all monitoring events for workflow Wf1', the initial resource discovery will reveal only those data sources which monitor workflow activities existing at the time. However, the occurrence of further workflow activities will not be discovered. A notification mechanism is required to notify data consumers about new data sources upon their appearance. This scenario may be called *automatic resource discovery*.

Our goal is to realize the scenario wherein a consumer could subscribe to a workflow monitoring data only once to an arbitrary monitoring service endpoint, and the underlying resource discovery and data transfer will be handled automatically by the monitoring infrastructure itself. The proposed solution architecture is presented in Fig. 1. We assume a fully distributed monitoring system architecture consisting of *Sensors* – producers of monitoring data local to monitored resources, and *Monitors* managing Sensors and exposing interfaces to consumers of monitoring data. In addition, an external P2P Distributed Hash Table infrastructure is associated with the Monitor network to provide global information about Sensors.

The proposed scenario for automatic resource discovery in monitoring of Grid workflows is presented in Fig. 2. Workflow $wf1$ is monitored and its activities appear in various times and locations. The first workflow activity is monitored by Sensor $s1$. The sensor registers to its respective Monitor $m1$. This monitor performs a lookup in the DHT network in order to check if the workflow has already been registered in the monitoring system. If it is not the case (as in the example), $m1$ puts the first entry in the DHT, where the key is the unique workflow ID, and the value is the Monitor $m1$ endpoint. A consumer (tool), in order to request monitoring data for workflow $w1$, needs first to discover *any* Monitor endpoint (from a traditional information service). In this case it

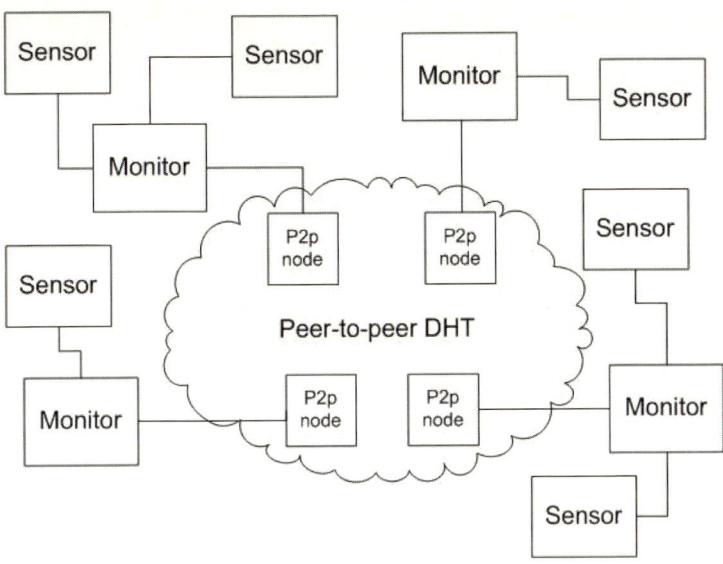

Fig. 1. Architecture of the monitoring system

obtains Monitor's $m0$ endpoint and subscribes in it. From now on, Monitor $m0$ manages the tool's subscription. It looks up the DHT for all producers for workflow $w1$ and forwards them subscription requests on behalf of the tool, and the monitoring data are pushed directly from from producers to the tool (consumer). When a new producer for workflow $w1$ appears at a later time ($m2$), $m0$ automatically detects it and sends it the subscription request. The discovery of new producers could be achieved either by using an external event notification service, or periodically polling the DHT for new entries. The latter solution is shown. Though it is less efficient that the notification-based one, the DHT still offers a sufficient latency to make this solution feasible.

4 Performance Evaluation

In order to study the feasibility of the scenario presented in the previous section, we have made the performance evaluation of our solution. To this end, we have deployed our GEMINI monitoring framework [3] and the Bamboo DHT network[1]. We have used a Core Duo 2 GHz Pentium processor machine with 2 GB RAM running Open SuSe 10.1. In addition, we have used the OpenDHT project infrastructure[2] which is a deployment of Bamboo DHT on the PlanetLab infrastructure[3] distributed all over the world.

---

[1] Bamboo project homepage: http://bamboo-dht.org/
[2] OpenDHT project homepage: http://opendht.org/
[3] PlanetLab project homepage: http://www.planet-lab.org/

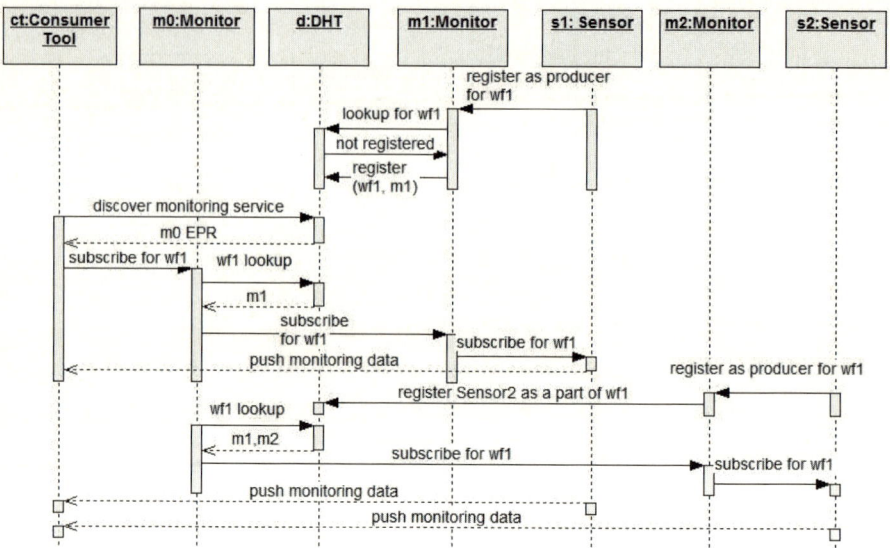

Fig. 2. Scenario of automatic resource discovery and subscription for workflow monitoring data

Test results are presented in Tab. 1 as average operation latencies. The tests performed on one node show that the fastest operation is get; remove is about five times slower while the most time consuming one is put which is about seventeen times longer than the remove operation. While those times are considerably larger on a 247-nodes deployment, they are still satisfactory, around one second each.

Table 1. Average time of operations on the Bamboo DHT network with one node and OpenDHT network with 247 nodes

Network type	Operation	Average time, s
Bamboo DHT with one node	put	0.166
	get	0.002
	remove	0.010
OpenDHT - Bamboo on 247 nodes	put	1.106
	get	0.902
	remove	0.998

The obtained performance characteristics of the tested systems allowed us to perform a model-based performance analysis of the presented solution which revealed that it can accommodate very high workloads. Up to 10 job arrivals per second have been tested which is much more than in the current large-scale production Grids. The **automatic discovery delay** (the time from the arrival

Table 2. Average latency of get operation for different DHT deployments

Operation	System type	Average time, s
get	Bamboo DHT with one node	0.002
	OpenDHT – Bamboo on 247 nodes	0.902

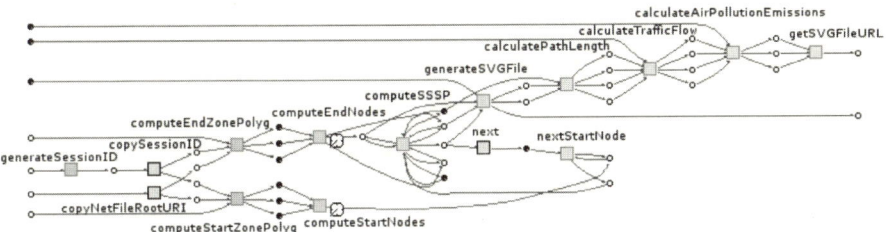

Fig. 3. Coordinated Traffic Management workflow

of a new workflow job until the beginning of the monitoring data transfer) was stable at around $1500ms$, which is perfectly sufficient for on-line monitoring.

5 Case Study: Monitoring of Coordinated Traffic Management Workflow

To demonstrate workflow monitoring, we have chosen the Coordinated Traffic Management (CTM) workflow constructed from application services provided by Softeco Sismat within the K-Wf Grid Project [4]. This application targets the computation of the emission of traffic air pollutants in an urban area and has been developed in tight collaboration with the Urban Mobility Department of the Municipality of Genoa, which provided a monolithic implementation of the model for the pollutant emission calculations, the urban topology network and real urban traffic data. The CTM application workflow has been divided into several different steps in order to allow the semi-automatic composition of services and the definition of a set of ontologies which describe the CTM domain and feed the system with the information needed for the proper selection and execution of services [10].

The main CTM application functionalities are best route, traffic flow and air pollutant emissions calculations. Data graphical representation in SVG format is also supported. For monitoring, a complex use case was used. It consisted of several executable transitions and three control transitions (Fig. 3).

The first activity in the workflow is the generation of a session ID. Next, there are two activities done in parallel – the computation of start and end zone district polygons. Subsequently, node coordinates for start and end are computed, also in parallel. After that, a set of calculations is done for nodes computed in earlier activities. Finally, computations responsible for calculating path length, traffic flow and air pollutants emission follow. Results are also written to the SVG format file, which is done in one of the activities.

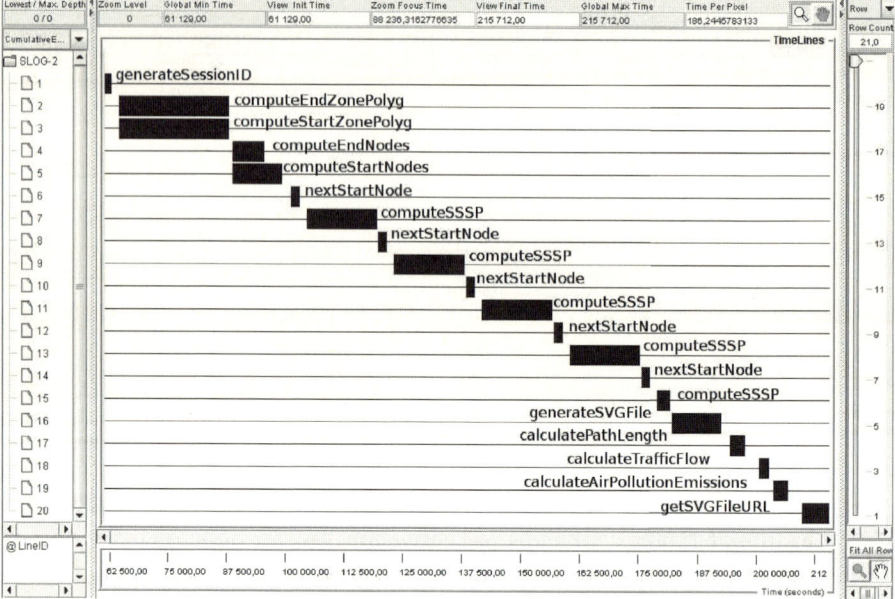

Fig. 4. Monitoring results – global view

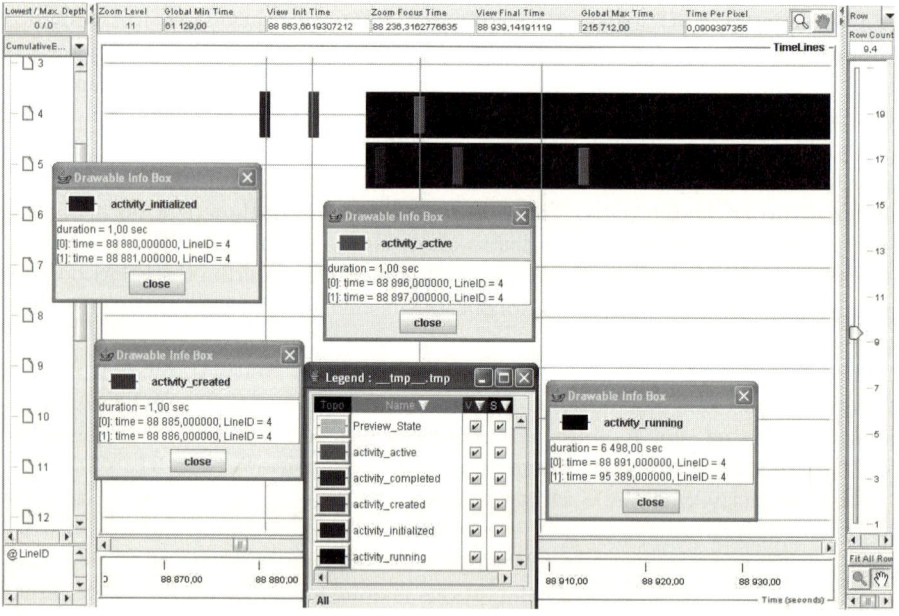

Fig. 5. Monitoring results – detailed local view

During the running of the above scenario monitoring data were acquired by instrumentation of the worklow enactment engine and workflow activities. For each activity, several events were produced: when it was initialized, created, went to the active state, at start and end of the actual running phase, and when it has completed. Each of these events has a precise time of occurrence. Activities such as initialization, creation, activation and completion should be treated as a point in time. The running state is treated as a period of time.

For visualization of the monitoring results, we have used the Jumpshot tool[4]. To this end, events collected from GEMINI were translated to Jumpshot's SLOG-2 format. We can observe how the workflow was executed, how much time each activity has taken, and when it was invoked. Fig. 4 presents a global view showing all activities. However, due to the time scale, only the running periods can be seen. Fig. 5 presents a zoom of a particular diagram section to show more details – individual events can be seen now. Additionally, windows describing individual bars (representing events and periods) are shown.

6 Conclusion

We have presented how P2P DHT systems can be used to achieve on-line monitoring of Grid workflows through automatic resource discovery. The DHT network was used not as a replacement of a global discovery service, but rather as a supporting infrastructure which can improve performance in certain scenarios. Thus, a traditional directory service can be used in our monitoring architecture only to discover any monitoring endpoint, while the subsequent discovery of workflow activities is handled by the monitoring infrastructure associated with the DHT network. In the future, we plan to integrate our solution for monitoring of resources in applications in the context of media and banking solutions in the Gredia project[5].

Acknowledgement. This work is partly funded by the European Commission under projects GREDIA IST-034363 and CoreGrid IST-2002-004265, and by the related Polish SPUB-M grant.

References

1. Aloisio, G., Cafaro, M., Epicoco, I., Fiore, S., Lezzi, D., Mirto, M., Mocavero, S.: Resource and Service Discovery in the iGrid Information Service. In: Gervasi, O., Gavrilova, M.L., Kumar, V., Laganá, A., Lee, H.P., Mun, Y., Taniar, D., Tan, C.J.K. (eds.) ICCSA 2005. LNCS, vol. 3482, pp. 1–9. Springer, Heidelberg (2005)
2. Astalos, J., Flis, L., Radecki, M., Ziajka, W.: Performance Improvements to BDII – Grid Information Service in EGEE. In: Proc. CGW 2007, Krakow, Poland. ACC CYFRONET AGH (2008)

---

[4] See http://www-unix.mcs.anl.gov/perfvis/software/viewers/index.htm

[5] Gredia project homepage: http://www.gredia.eu

3. Balis, B., Bubak, M., Łabno, B.: GEMINI: Generic Monitoring Infrastructure for Grid Resource and Applications. In: K-WfGrid – The Knowledge-based Workflow System for Grid Applications, Proc. CGW 2006, Krakow, vol. II, pp. 60–73 (2006)
4. Bubak, M., Fahringer, T., Hluchy, L., Hoheisel, A., Kitowski, J., Unger, S., Viano, G., Votis, K.: K-WfGrid Consortium: K-Wf Grid – Knowledge based Workflow system for Grid Applications. In: Proc. CGW 2004, Poland, p. 39. Academic Computer Centre CYFRONET AGH (2005) ISBN 83-915141-4-5
5. Cannataro, M., Talia, D., Tradigo, G., Trunfio, P., Veltri, P.: SIGMCC: a System for Sharing Meta Patient Records in a Peer-to-peer Environment. Future Generation Computer Systems 24(3), 222–234 (2008)
6. Cooke, A., et al.: The Relational Grid Monitoring Architecture: Mediating Information about the Grid. Journal of Grid Computing 2(4) (December 2004)
7. Decandia, G., et al.: Dynamo: Amazon's Highly Available Key-value Store. In: SOSP 2007: Proceedings of twenty-first ACM SIGOPS symposium, pp. 205–220. ACM Press, New York (2007)
8. Fortino, G., Russo, W.: Using P2P, GRID and Agent Technologies for the Development of Content Distribution Networks. Future Generation Computer Systems 24(3), 180–190 (2008)
9. Foster, I.T., Iamnitchi, A.: On Death, Taxes, and the Convergence of Peer-to-Peer and Grid Computing. In: Kaashoek, M.F., Stoica, I. (eds.) IPTPS 2003. LNCS, vol. 2735, pp. 118–128. Springer, Heidelberg (2003)
10. Gubala, T., Harezlak, D., Bubak, M., Malawski, M.: Semantic Composition of Scientific Workflows Based on the Petri Nets Formalism. In: Proc. 2nd IEEE International Conference on e-Science and Grid Computing (Avaialble only on CD-ROM). IEEE Computer Society Press, Los Alamitos (2006)
11. Schopf, J.M., Pearlman, L., Miller, N., Kesselman, C., Foster, I., D'Arcy, M., Chervenak, A.: Monitoring the grid with the Globus Toolkit MDS4. Journal of Physics: Conference Series 46, 521–525 (2006)
12. Schopf, J.M., Raicu, I., Pearlman, L., et al.: Monitoring and discovery in a web services framework: Functionality and performance of Globus Toolkit MDS4. Technical report, Mathematics and Computer Science Division, Argonne National Laboratory (2006)
13. Tierney, B., Aydt, R., Gunter, D., Smith, W., Taylor, V., Wolski, R., Swany, M.: A grid monitoring architecture. Technical Report GWD-PERF-16-2, Global Grid Forum (January 2002)
14. Trunfio, P., Talia, D., Papadakis, H., Fragopoulou, P., Mordacchini, M., Pennanen, M., Popov, K., Vlassov, V., Haridi, S.: Peer-to-Peer resource discovery in Grids: Models and systems. Future Generation Computer Systems 23(7), 864–878 (2007)
15. Zhang, X., Freschl, J.L., Schopf, J.M.: Scalability analysis of three monitoring and information systems: MDS2, R-GMA, and Hawkeye. J. Parallel Distrib. Comput. 67(8), 883–902 (2007)

Transparent Mobile Middleware Integration for Java and .NET Development Environments

Edgar Marques, Luís Veiga, and Paulo Ferreira

Distributed Systems Group at INESC-ID/Technical Univ. of Lisbon,
Rua Alves Redol N. 9, 1000-029 Lisbon, Portugal
emarques@gsd.inesc-id.pt, {luis.veiga,paulo.ferreira}@inesc-id.pt
http://www.gsd.inesc-id.pt

Abstract. Developing a distributed application for mobile resource constrained devices is a difficult and error-prone task that requires awareness of several system-level details (*e.g.*, fault-tolerance, ...).

Several mobile middleware solutions addressing these issues have been proposed. However, they rely on either significant changes in application structure, extensions to the programming language syntax and semantics, domain specific languages, cumbersome development tools, or a combination of the above. The main disadvantages of these approaches are lack of transparency and reduced portability.

In this paper we describe our work on enabling transparent integration between applications and middleware without changing application structure, extending the programming language or otherwise reducing portability. We used the OBIWAN middleware but our solutions are general. To achieve this goal we employ program analysis and transformation techniques for extending application code with hooks for calling middleware services. Application code extension is performed automatically at compile-time by a code extension tool integrated with the development environment tool set. We describe the implementation of our .NET and Java prototypes and discuss evaluation results.

Keywords: distributed mobile applications, fault-tolerance, incremental object replication, transparent middleware integration, program transformation, aspect-oriented programming, integrated development environment.

1 Introduction

Mobile devices like cellular phones and other resource constrained devices are inherently hard to program. CPU power, memory footprint and battery consumption are examples of some of the issues developers must be constantly aware of when developing stand-alone, connectionless applications for such devices.

The development of network applications over mobile networks is even more difficult. In addition to the afore mentioned issues associated with these devices, the developer must also handle issues like loss of connectivity, variable bandwidth (due to variation of link signal quality) and increased battery consumption (while connected). All these issues play an important role on design decisions specific to network applications like fault tolerance, shared data consistency, object location and security.

Over the years, several middleware solutions for developing applications running over fixed and mobile networks have been proposed [2, 3, 15]. Each one of them addresses one or more design issues while exposing the developer to a simpler and higher level view of the system, with the purpose of reducing development effort and allowing him to focus on business logic.

However these solutions suffer from lack of transparency and reduced portability, due to the following reasons: i) inflexible and awkward application structure, ii) employment of domain specific languages or programming language extensions, and iii) cumbersome development tools.

In this paper we describe our work on enabling transparent integration between applications and a research mobile middleware called OBIWAN [7]. The OBIWAN mobile middleware is a platform developed for the purpose of aiding the development of distributed applications running on resource constrained mobile devices. Currently there are two prototypes of the middleware running on the .NET Common Language Runtime and the Java Virtual Machine (both standard and mobile editions). The middleware requires no changes to the underlying virtual machine thus assuring portability among a wide range of devices. The OBIWAN middleware provides several features which have been discussed in previous work [16, 19, 20, 21]. It's important to note that we could have used other middleware instead of OBIWAN as our solutions are general.

The motivation for this work started from the fact that despite the various features provided by OBIWAN, interacting with the middleware was complicated and tedious even for simple tasks. The developer not only had to issue several API calls, but he also had to write additional code and data structures for the sole purpose of interfacing between the application and the middleware.

A first step towards making the interaction with the middleware easier was to write a helper tool for automatically generating some of the required code and data structures. This tool, called *obicomp* [7, 19], made use of reflection in order to perform simple program analysis. However, it was very limited in scope (*e.g.*, it couldn't analyse method bodies) and it imposed an awkward process for building applications (because the tool was based on reflection, the developer had to partially build the application before running the tool and then build it again after including the generated code). Furthermore, the developer still had to manually issue the required API calls.

To overcome these faults, we redesigned and rewrote the *obicomp* tool from scratch to achieve seamless integration with the programming languages (either Java or C#) and integrated development environments (Eclipse [6] or Visual Studio 2005 [22]). The new version employs program analysis and transformation techniques for extending application code with hooks for calling middleware services. The tool runs at compile-time and it directly manipulates application source code. By manipulating source code instead of bytecode, the generated code is not only easier to understand and verify as it is also more portable, running on a wider range of devices. It also makes the tool easier to integrate with existing development tool sets.

The tool currently performs source code analysis and requires the developer only to specify the classes, packages/assemblies or fields whose behaviour is to be extended by the mobile middleware. To ensure maximum portability, we chose not to add any extensions to the programming languages, relying instead on standard language constructs (*attributes* in the case of the C# language and *annotations* in the case of the Java language).

In summary, the contributions of this work are:

- A framework for transparent middleware integration based on automatic code generation and without sacrificing portability, *i.e.*, without requiring any changes to programming languages or underlying virtual machines.
- Measurements of the performance penalty on compilation times introduced by the code generation stage.
- Identification of usability issues associated with our solutions.

The remainder of this paper is organized as follows. Section 2 presents an overview of the middleware integration architecture, including integration with existing tool sets. Section 3 exposes the implementation of the code generation tools for the C# and Java languages and how these were integrated with existing development environments for these languages. Section 4 presents performance results for the code generation tools with respect to possible overhead to regular project/solution compilation and deployment. Current usability issues are also reported. In Sections 5 and 6, we compare our work with others' and draw some conclusions, respectively.

2 Middleware Integration Architecture

As we mentioned earlier, transparent integration in OBIWAN is accomplished through the use of a code generation tool for:

- Automatic generation of middleware service calls.
- Automatic generation of additional auxiliary code and data structures.

Because the nature of the generated code depends mostly on the specific feature being used, a concrete example is necessary for better clarification. For this purpose and without loss of generality we focus on the particular case of incremental object replication.

In the next subsection we give a brief overview of incremental object replication and describe the necessary API calls and data structures that are required for integrating applications and middleware.

We conclude this section with an explanation of the generic code generation architecture of our development tools and how they integrate with existing tool sets.

2.1 Example: Incremental Object Replication

Object replication improves both availability and scalability of distributed applications. By allowing individual nodes to work on local replicas of shared data, network failures and quality of service concerns can be masked from the application, thus permitting uninterrupted execution even in connectionless scenarios.

Due to the resource constrained nature of mobile devices (e.g., limited battery power, scarce available memory, etc.), incremental object replication is employed in OBIWAN. Since only the objects that are actually required by the application are replicated, this technique reduces the total amount of memory used by the application and the bandwidth required for message exchange between processes. Battery power consumption is also reduced because of reduced network usage and the fact that the radio interface is only activated when needed.

Overview of Incremental Object Replication. Incremental object replication allows mobile applications to fetch data from remote processes as they need. When an object is replicated from a remote process, all references that object has to other objects are replaced with references to proxy objects. When the application needs to access an object which is represented by a proxy object, the proxy object fetches a replica of the remote object it represents and replaces itself with that replica. The proxy object is no longer referenced by any other object in the local process and the garbage collection mechanism will reclaim it.

The whole process is transparent from the application's point of view: it is the proxy's responsability to request a new object replica when the application needs it. The application can't tell the difference between a replica and its proxy because they both implement the same interfaces [7, 19]. A thorough discussion of incremental object replication is given in [19].

Integration of Incremental Object Replication. We now describe the data structures and API calls that are automatically generated to add support for incremental object replication in a distributed mobile application. The full generated code is quite extensive so we only show a small subset for explanation purposes. Additional details can be found in [19]. All code examples are written in the C# language and are quite similar to the Java versions. The main difference between the two versions is the usage of *attributes* in C# and of *annotations* in Java.

Consider the following example of a C# class for implementing an incrementally replicatable singly-linked list. We use a singly-linked list for clarity; other more complex data structure would complicate the description. Each node of the list is replicated on demand while it is being traversed. Notice the use of the C# attribute `[Replicatable]` for denoting that support for incremental replication should be added to the class. This annotation must be explicitly specified by the developer since *obicomp* isn't capable of telling replicatable types and non-replicatable ones apart on its own. In Java the equivalent annotation `@Replicatable` would be used instead.

An example C# class implementing an incrementally replicatable singly-linked list.

```
using INESCID.GSD.Obiwan;

[Replicatable]
public class SinglyLinkedList {
  private SinglyLinkedList _next;
  public SinglyLinkedList GetNext() { return _next; }
  public void SetNext(SinglyLinkedList next) { _next = next; }
}
```

obicomp analyses the source code of the class and automatically generates the interface definition for it (which also includes *properties* in the case of the C# language), as shown in the next code snippet. Notice how *obicomp* replaced every type reference to the class with a type reference to its interface.

C# interface generated from the example C# class.

```
public interface ISinglyLinkedList__Obiwan__ {
  public ISinglyLinkedList__Obiwan__ GetNext();
  public void SetNext(ISinglyLinkedList__Obiwan__ next);
}
```

This is necessary so that the application is unable to tell the difference between a replica and a proxy. The same type reference replacement is made throughout the entire application, including the replicatable class itself. The next code snippet shows the class after code extension. Notice how the class now implements not only the newly generated interface but also other auxiliary interfaces (`IObiwanObject`, `IDemander` and `IProvider`) that handle automatic replica creation and proxy replacement.

The same C# class after code extension.

```
using INESCID.GSD.Obiwan;

[Replicatable]
public class SinglyLinkedList : ISinglyLinkedList__Obiwan__,
  IObiwanObject, IDemander, IProvider {
  private ISinglyLinkedList__Obiwan__ _next;
  public ISinglyLinkedList__Obiwan__ GetNext() { return _next; }
  public void SetNext(ISinglyLinkedList__Obiwan__ next) { _next = next; }
  ...
}
```

These auxiliary interfaces define callback methods which are invoked by the middleware during the incremental replication process. Further information on these callbacks is given in [19].

obicomp also generates the corresponding proxy type for the replicatable class. The proxy implements the generated interface and other auxiliary interfaces that allow the middleware to handle association with the actual object and its parent (refering) object.

Generated C# proxy-out class for the example C# class.

```
using INESCID.GSD.Obiwan;

public class SinglyLinkedListProxyOut__Obiwan__ :
  ISinglyLinkedList__Obiwan__, IObiwanObject, IDemandee {
  private ISinglyLinkedList__Obiwan__ _replica;
  public ISinglyLinkedList__Obiwan__ GetNext() {
    _replica = (ISinglyLinkedList__Obiwan__) this.Demand();
    return _replica.GetNext();
  }
  public void SetNext(ISinglyLinkedList__Obiwan__ next) {
    _replica = (ISinglyLinkedList__Obiwan__) this.Demand();
    _replica.SetNext(next);
  }
  ...
}
```

The proxy type implements the object fault mechanism. A proxy object stands in place for an object not replicated yet. When the application invokes a method of a proxy object, it is handled as an object fault, and the proxy object calls the middleware object replication service through its `Demand` method. The method returns the replicated object and the proxy redirects the initial method call to it. Although not shown in the previous examples, the `Demand` method also updates the object reference that points to the proxy object to point instead to the newly replicated object. This is done by calling the callback methods added to the extended C# class.

2.2 Generic Code Generation Architecture

Our approach is based on program transformation techniques that are also commonly employed in the *Aspect-Oriented Programming* (AOP) paradigm [8]. In AOP they are generically known as *aspect weaving*, *i.e.*, the automatic generation and insertion of code relating to non-functional requirements, such as fault-tolerance, security, etc. Aspect weaving can be performed at compile-time or at run-time, at source code level or at bytecode level.

In our work we chose to perform source code generation at compile-time. Source code generation is easier to implement and to check and it's also more portable than bytecode, because many virtual machines running on mobile devices use a different, more compact representation of bytecode that can change between implementations. The main disadvantage of weaving source code is the inability to extend third party components whose source code isn't available. Although run-time code generation is a simpler and more powerfull technique for building highly adaptable applications, it requires run-time services (such as reflection) that aren't available in most virtual machine implementations running on mobile devices.

Application source code is parsed into an *Abstract Syntax Tree* (AST). Code generation is performed by grafting new nodes to the AST and modifying or deleting existing ones. The AST is then translated into temporary source code files (pretty-printing) which are then compiled. The original source code files remain unchanged. The whole process is illustrated in Figure 1.

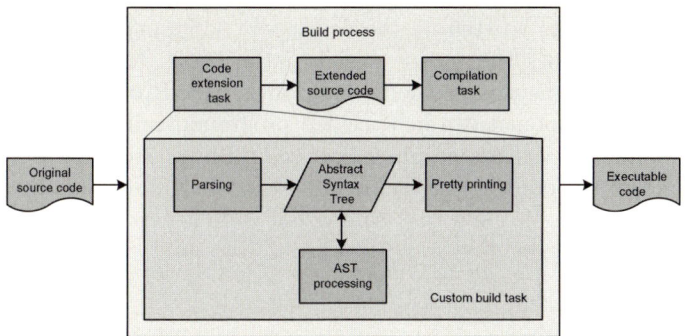

Fig. 1. Code generation flowchart

obicomp is implemented as a custom pre-compilation build tool which can be easily added to existing build tool chains. Seamless integration is achieved by supplying the developer with project templates for developing applications on top of the OBIWAN middleware. These templates include all the middleware libraries, the *obicomp* build tool for automatic code generation and a template project build file which references the libraries and the *obicomp* build tool.

3 Implementation

In this section we discuss the implementation details of the middleware integration framework for the .NET and Java environments.

3.1 .NET

We developed a custom build task for the MSBuild [10] building system used by the .NET Framework 2.0 [11], Visual Studio 2005 [22] and following versions. We took advantage of .NET's CodeDOM framework [4] for implementing our code extension build task. CodeDOM provides a metamodel for representing and transforming .NET application source code written in any .NET language. The namespaces `System.CodeDom` and `System.CodeDom.Compiler` define AST nodes for representing program elements and code generators (pretty-printers) for the

VB.NET and C# languages. We have used an existing C# CodeDOM parser [5] and extended it according to our needs. We also used Visual Studio 2005's built-in support for developing project templates for the OBIWAN middleware.

3.2 Java

We developed a custom build task for the Ant build tool [1] using Spoon [14]. Spoon is a Java program processor fully compliant with the Java Language Specification 3 (JLS3). It provides a Java metamodel for analysing and transforming Java programs. Spoon parses Java programs into an AST that can be read and modified by Spoonlets written by the developer. A Spoonlet is a program processor that implements the *visitor* design pattern [13]. It traverses the entire AST and executes when a specified condition is met. Program transformation performed by the Spoonlet can be specified programatically or through the use of Spoon templates, written as pure Java code. Spoon supplies a custom Ant task for executing Spoonlets during the build process. Our custom build task for Ant is in fact the Spoon build task calling our code generation Spoonlets.

4 Evaluation

We have performed quantitative and qualitative evaluations of the OBIWAN middleware integration with the targeted development environments.

Regarding the quantitative evaluation we calculated the time overhead due to the code extension stage by measuring how long it takes to complete the global building process with code extension disabled and measuring again with code extension enabled. Overhead must be low relative to the global building process time in order to ensure usability and transparency to the developer. Figure 2 shows the time measurements for building projects with a varying number of replicatable types and fields. The test machine used is a Pentium 4 at 3.2 GHz with 1 GB of DDR2 RAM running Windows XP Professional with Service Pack 2. All measurements were taken by running the .NET implementation of the *obicomp* code generation tool with MSBuild on a command line interface.

The building time measurements show that the code generation stage introduce a very high overhead, accounting for about 90% of the global building time. The results also show that code generation time is more sensitive to the variation in the number of fields than the variation in the number of classes. Code generation time increases linearly with an increase in the number of classes and it also increases linearly with an increase in the average number of fields per class. We should note that in most real world applications very few classes have more than 16 fields. In most cases a number of fields higher than that is indicative of a need to refactor the application. In our measurements, the time for building a project with 128 classes with an average number of 16 fields per class was about 8 seconds, which is quite tolerable for the developer. We also draw attention to the fact that the *obicomp* isn't optimized regarding memory usage, and that lower building times might be achieved.

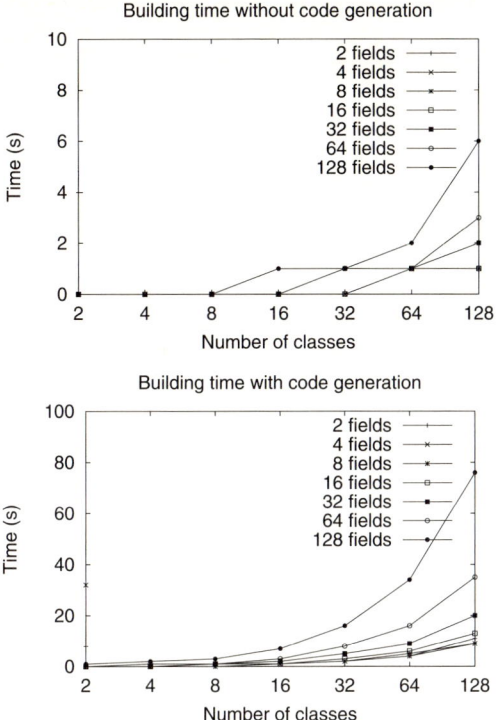

Fig. 2. Project building times with and without code generation

For the qualitative evaluation, we tested the usability of the OBIWAN middleware integrated in the targeted development environments by developing some sample mobile applications. The main usability issues encountered are a lack of support for partial builds, requiring the whole application to be compiled again in each rebuild, the inability to extend third-party components whose source code isn't available and exposure of the generated code to the developer while debugging. The latter can be alleviated by including source code comments in the generated code that leverage existing integrated development environments' ability to selectively hide code snippets (*e.g.*, employing `#region` directives in Visual Studio 2005).

5 Related Work

WrapperAssistant [17] is a code generation tool (aspect weaver) for adding fault-tolerance support to applications targetting the .NET Framework and written in the C# language, which is very similar to our own. It uses C# *attributes* for parameterizing fault-tolerance support for chosen classes and runs at compile-time. However, it manipulates bytecode instead of source code and makes use of unmanaged metadata interfaces, making it less portable between development environments. Also, the developer must directly participate in the aspect weaving process by using the tool's graphical interface, thus lacking the same level of transparency of *obicomp*.

Afpac [18] is a middleware for dynamic adaptation that makes use of a static weaver (Taco) for generating C++ code and integrating the middleware without changes in program structure. Taco offers a very fine grain view of the application code, allowing it to target individual code statements, while *obicomp* currently only handles class declarations, method calls and type references. However, Afpac makes use of an aspect language while OBIWAN requires none, thus making Afpac less transparent to the developer than OBIWAN.

Jarcler [12] is an aspect-oriented middleware for building distributed applications using replicated objects. Just like Afpac, it relies on an aspect language (AspectJ [9]).

6 Conclusions and Future Work

We presented our approach for enabling transparent middleware integration. Our main goals are transparency and portability. Although our main research is in the area of distributed mobile applications, we use generic program transformation techniques that can be applied to any kind of middleware and integrate easily in existing development tool sets.

Our approach requires no language extensions, no special support from the underlying virtual machine running on the device and no modifications to the development tools. The OBIWAN middleware code generation tool fits naturally in the application building process, providing seamless integration from the developer's point of view.

We gave implementation details on prototypes developed for the Java and .NET environments. We showed quantitatively that the additional time overhead for source code extension is tolerable and reported current usability issues.

For future work we plan to address the usability issues discovered during application development with OBIWAN and optimize the code generation process. We are also considering extending OBIWAN's language support to other languages targeting the JVM and the CLR, such as Python, Ruby and VB.NET.

References

1. The Apache Ant Project, http://ant.apache.org
2. Caromel, D.: Toward a method of object-oriented concurrent programming. Commun. ACM 36(9), 90–102 (1993)
3. Caughey, S.J., Hagimont, D., Ingham, D.B.: Deploying distributed objects on the internet. In: Advances in Distributed Systems, Advanced Distributed Computing: From Algorithms to Systems, London, UK, pp. 213–237. Springer, Heidelberg (1999)
4. Using the CodeDOM,
http://msdn2.microsoft.com/en-us/library/y2k85ax6.aspx

5. Ivan Zderadika's C# CodeDOM Parser,
   http://www.codeproject.com/csharp/codedomparser.asp
6. Eclipse.org home, http://www.eclipse.org
7. Ferreira, P., Veiga, L., Ribeiro, C.: Obiwan: design and implementation of a middleware platform. Transactions on Parallel and Distributed Systems 14(11), 1086–1099 (2003)
8. Gray, J., Roychoudhury, S.: A technique for constructing aspect weavers using a program transformation engine. In: AOSD 2004: Proceedings of the 3rd international conference on Aspect-oriented software development, pp. 36–45. ACM, New York (2004)
9. Kiczales, G., Hilsdale, E., Hugunin, J., Kersten, M., Palm, J., Griswold, W.: Getting started with aspectj. Commun. ACM 44(10), 59–65 (2001)
10. MSBuild - MSDN Library,
    http://msdn2.microsoft.com/en-us/library/wea2sca5.aspx
11. NET Framework Developer Center,
    http://msdn2.microsoft.com/en-us/netframework/default.aspx
12. Nishizawa, M., Chiba, S.: Jarcler: Aspect-oriented middleware for distributed software in java. Technical Report C-164, Tokyo Institute of Technology (December 2002)
13. Palsberg, J., Jay, C.B.: The essence of the visitor pattern. In: Proc. 22nd IEEE Int. Computer Software and Applications Conf., COMPSAC, pp. 9–15, 19–21 (1998)
14. Pawlak, R.: Spoon: annotation-driven program transformation — the aop case. In: AOMD 2005: Proceedings of the 1st workshop on Aspect oriented middleware development. ACM Press, New York (2005)
15. Preuveneers, D., Rigole, P., Vandewoude, Y., Berbers, Y.: Middleware support for component-based ubiquitous and mobile computing applications. In: Joolia, A., Jean, S. (eds.) ACM/IFIP/USENIX 6th International Middleware Conference Workshop Proceedings, Demonstrations Extended abstracts, Grenoble/France, pp. 1–4. cd-rom (November 2005)
16. Santos, N., Veiga, L., Ferreira, P.: Transaction policies for mobile networks. In: Fifth IEEE International Workshop on Policies for Distributed Systems and Networks, 2004. POLICY 2004, 7-9 June 2004, pp. 55–64 (2004)
17. Schult, W., Polze, A.: Aspect-oriented programming with c# and.net. In: ISORC 2002: Proceedings of the Fifth IEEE International Symposium on Object-Oriented Real-Time Distributed Computing, Washington, DC, USA, p. 241. IEEE Computer Society Press, Los Alamitos (2002)
18. Vaysse, G., André, F., Buisson, J.: Using aspects for integrating a middleware for dynamic adaptation. In: AOMD 2005: Proceedings of the 1st workshop on Aspect oriented middleware development. ACM Press, New York (2005)
19. Veiga, L., Ferreira, P.: Incremental replication for mobility support in obiwan. In: 22nd International Conference on Distributed Computing Systems, 2002, pp. 249–256 (2002)
20. Veiga, L., Ferreira, P.: Poliper: policies for mobile and pervasive environments. In: ARM 2004: Proceedings of the 3rd workshop on Adaptive and reflective middleware, pp. 238–243. ACM Press, New York (2004)
21. Veiga, L., Santos, N., Lebre, R., Ferreira, P.: Loosely-coupled, mobile replication of objects with transactions. In: ICPADS 2004. Proceedings. Tenth International Conference on Parallel and Distributed Systems, 2004, 7-9 July 2004, pp. 675–682 (2004)
22. Visual Studio 2005 Developer Center,
    http://msdn2.microsoft.com/en-us/vstudio/default.aspx

Providing Non-stop Service for Message-Passing Based Parallel Applications with RADIC

Guna Santos, Angelo Duarte, Dolores Rexachs, and Emilio Luque

Computer Architecture and Operating Systems Department,
University Autonoma of Barcelona, Bellaterra, Barcelona 08193, Spain
{guna,angelo}@caos.uab.es, {dolores.rexachs,emilio.luque}@uab.es

Abstract. The current supercomputers are almost achieving the petaflop level. These machines present a high number of interruptions in a relatively short time interval. Fault tolerance and preventive maintenance are key issues in order to enlarge the MTTI (Mean Time To Interrupt). In this paper we present how RADIC, a architecture for fault tolerance, provides different protection levels able to avoid system interruptions and allows the performance of preventive maintenance tasks. Our experiments show the effectiveness of our solution in order to keep a high availability with a large MTTI.[1]

1 Introduction

The current supercomputers have already reached the teraflop level and the new generation of petascale machines is coming. Recent studies [1] have demonstrated that failures in these machines may occur at the rate of twice a day. In these environments fault tolerance represents a key issue in order to provide high availability.

In order to achieve high availability, a fault-tolerant system must provide automatic and transparent fault detection and recovery. Even in these cases, service interruptions (a complete stop of the program execution) may occur if there are no replacement nodes or the system degradation generated by the faults reaches an unacceptable level. In order to ensure a large MTTI (Mean Time To Interrupt), such solutions must also provide the means to restore the original system configuration (initial number of replacement nodes, or the process per node distribution) without stopping a running application. In addition to reactive fault tolerance, it is also very desirable that it should perform preventive maintenance tasks by, for example, replacing fault-probable machines without system interruptions.

Considering these aspects, we proposed and developed RADIC (Redundant Array of Distributed Independent Fault Tolerance Controllers) [2]. RADIC is an architecture for fault tolerance in message-passing systems providing high availability with transparency, decentralisation, flexibility and scalability.

In order to improve the MTTI of a message-passing based parallel application, we incorporated different protection levels within RADIC, helping to avoid or reduce the number of interruptions during program executions.

---
[1] This work is supported by the MEC-Spain under contracts TIN 2004-03388 and TIN2007-64974.

In this paper, we present the different RADIC protection levels. In the first level, also called basic level, RADIC operates without the need for any passive resource in order to provide its functionalities and is based on the rollback-recovery paradigm, using some active node of the configuration to recover a failed process which could lead to performance degradation. This protection level is well-suited for short-running applications, or applications that may tolerate resource loss, such as the dynamic load balanced ones.

The next protection level fits applications demanding a non-stop behaviour. At this level, RADIC provides a flexible dynamic redundancy through a transparent management of spare nodes. Such functionality allows it to request and to use spare nodes as needed without any user intervention and without keeping any centralised information about them. Moreover, it is possible dynamically to insert new replacement nodes during the program execution, allowing replacement of used spares or failed nodes. Such a feature increases the MTTI of a parallel application once the number of idle spare nodes remains constant. In continuous running applications, preventive maintenance stops are undesirable, so it became necessary to find a mechanism allowing the performance of non-stop maintenance tasks. Actually, RADIC also provides a mechanism for proactive fault tolerance.

Our experiments show the behaviour of RADIC in different situations and its effectiveness in providing high MTTI by using the correct protection level.

The remainder of this paper is organised as follows: The next section presents the basic concepts regarding the RADIC architecture. The section 3 explains the protection levels currently implemented with some experimental results relating to them. More experimental results and the experiment environment are presented in section 4 and in section 5 we present the related work. Finally, in section 6 we present our conclusions and future work.

2 The RADIC Architecture

RADIC is an architecture for fault tolerance in message-passing systems providing high availability for parallel applications with transparency, decentralisation, flexibility and scalability. The RADIC architecture acts as a layer between the fault-probable cluster structure and the message-passing implementation. Such a layer performs fault-masking (message-delivering) and fault tolerance (checkpoint, event logs, fault detection and recovery) tasks.

RADIC is based on rollback-recovery techniques applying a pessimistic event-log approach [3]. Such an approach was chosen because it does not need any coordinated or centralised action in order to provide its tasks, which does not affect its scalability. RADIC considers any absence of expected communication as a fault, and it tolerates short transient faults by retrying the communication.

2.1 Protectors and Observers

The RADIC architecture working is based on two kinds of processes, *protectors* and *observers*. Such processes work together in order to perform a distributed

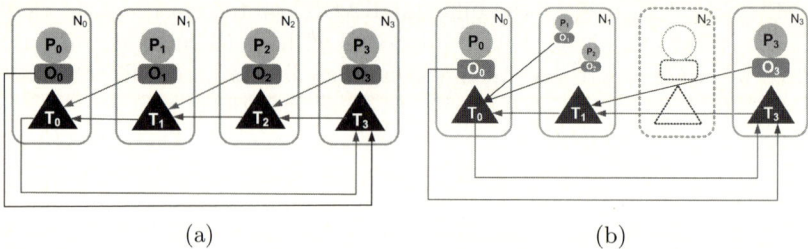

Fig. 1. Basic protection level in 2 situations: (a) before a fault. (b) after recovery.

controller for fault tolerance. Each node of the parallel system runs one protector while each application process has one observer attached to it. Indeed, an observer forms an indissociable pair with the application process, implementing the message-passing mechanism for the parallel application. Moreover, the observers are in charge of performing tasks concerned with fault tolerance, taking checkpoints and event logs of the attached application process and sending them to their respective protectors. The observers also detect communication failures between applications processes and their protectors. The observers maintain a data structure called *radictable* which stores the location of each process and is used in fault-masking tasks. When recovering, the observers are in charge of dealing with the event logs, replaying them in order to achieve a consistent system state [3].

Each execution node runs a protector process, which may be in two states: active, when it forms part of the detection scheme and there are some application processes running on its node, or passive, when it is running in a spare node. An active protector establishes a fault-detection scheme communicating with two other protectors, called predecessor and successor. Such a fault-detection scheme uses a heartbeat/watchdog protocol. The protectors communicate with the observers in a successor node receiving their checkpoints and event logs and storing them on their own node. The protectors also start the recovery of failed processes. The passive protectors do not participate in the fault detection system, but just stay waiting for a connection from any other active protector requesting them to recover a failed process.

3   RADIC Protection Levels

During the program execution, observers look after checkpoints and event logs, while the protectors monitor the cluster nodes. When one of them detects a failure, both perform some tasks in order to reestablish the consistent system state. These tasks depend on the protection level applied, changing the recovery and masking procedures, while the detection and protection procedures remain unchanged. We explain below the levels currently implemented.

3.1 The Basic Protection Level

At this level, RADIC simply demands the application's active resources in order to perform its recovery tasks. Fig. 1a depicts a simple system configuration with this protection level and the relationship between observers and active protectors in a four-nodes cluster ($N_0..N_3$). In this figure, we can see that each observer ($O_0..O_3$) has a connection to a protector (represented by an arrow) in a neighbouring node to which it sends checkpoints and event logs of its attached application process. Each protector ($T_0..T_3$) receives the connection of one or more observers and connects with other protector in the neighbouring node. A protector only communicates with its immediate neighbours. Fig. 2 shows the atomic activities simultaneously taken by the protectors and observers implicated in the failure in order to re-establish the integrity of the RADIC controller's structure.

In such case the system configuration changes after the recovery, and the recovered process will run in the same node as its protector. Fig. 1b shows a RADIC configuration with basic protection level after a recovery process. In this picture we can see that the node N_2 has failed and the process P_2 has recovered in the node of its protector (T_1) and it sends its own checkpoint and log to its new protector. As the figure shows, after the recovery the system configuration has changed and the node N_1 hosts two running processes. Thus, this protection level provides high availability, but it may degrade the performance according to the application type, being well-suited for applications like the dynamic workload-balanced ones.

The charts in Fig. 3a and in Fig. 3b show the results of the execution of an N-Body particle simulation [4] running in a ten-node circular pipeline and observed during a time interval of 50 minutes at the RADIC basic protection level. In these charts, we see two lines representing the throughput (in simulation steps) of the application: the first one (with squares) represents a failure-free execution of the program, and the second line (with circles) represents the execution with fault injection. These situations represent an scenario where: a) 3 faults has occurred in different nodes of the cluster (Fig. 3a) and b) after a long period of execution, 3 faults occurred in an already overloaded node, i.e. a node already used to recover a failed process (Fig. 3b).

In the chart in Fig. 3a we see that after the first fault the failed process recovers in its protector, leaving the node overloaded, generating a slowdown in the entire pipeline. The subsequent faults do not generate more throughput degradation after the recovery process because the first overloaded node masks the effects of the two other overloaded ones. In each failure, the throughput falls quickly owing to the recovery process, varying according to the checkpoint

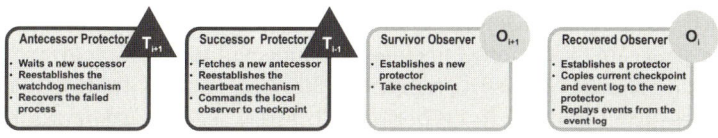

Fig. 2. Recovery activities performed by each element implicated in a failure using the basic protection level

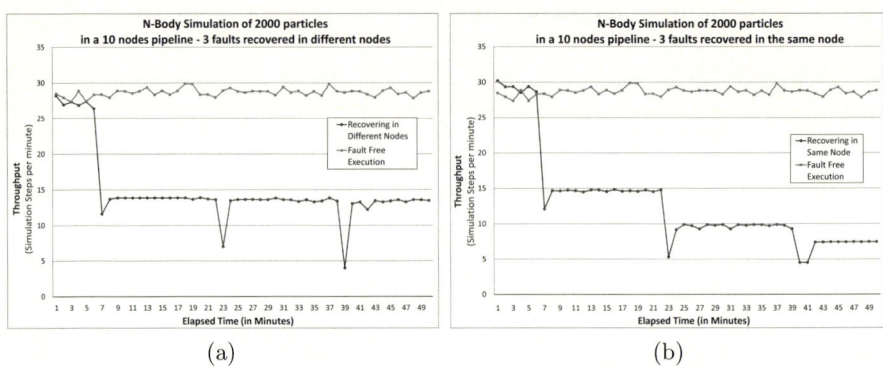

Fig. 3. Results of a N-Body simulation after three faults are recovered in: (a) different nodes and (b) the same node

and message log sizes. Despite the generated slowdown, it should be noted that there is no interruption to the program execution, and all the steps are performed automatically and transparently.

In the chart in Fig. 3b, we can see that the throughput is slowing down at each fault. This occurs because after the faults one node in the pipeline hosts two, then three and finally four processes. Despite the lack of any interruptions, such a phenomenon may lead to very low throughput levels, and a need to restart the application to restore the initial configuration.

3.2 The Resilient Protection Level

The basic protection level can tolerate faults without program interruptions, but it suffers certain performance degradation. After a certain number of tolerated faults such degradation may therefore achieve an unacceptable level, leading to a halt in the processing in order to re-establish the original system configuration. In order to avoid such a situation, we implemented a protection level which provides a flexible dynamic redundancy. At this level, RADIC allows us to restore the system configuration so as to avoid active node losses. We explain below how these functionalities work.

Restoring the System Configuration. In the initial application of the RADIC basic protection level, the mechanism developed for it allows us to re-establish the original process distribution changed by the recovery procedure (described in item 3.1). Such mechanism permits the insertion of a replacement node (N_r) during the program execution. This inserted node will take the recovered process, restoring the original process distribution. Starting at the situation depicted in Fig. 1b, these are the steps to be performed: First, the execution of a protector (T_r) in the replacement node using a special mode. In this mode, T_r connects with any active protector of the system and starts its announcement procedure using a reliable broadcast based on the message forwarding technique [5]. Such procedure

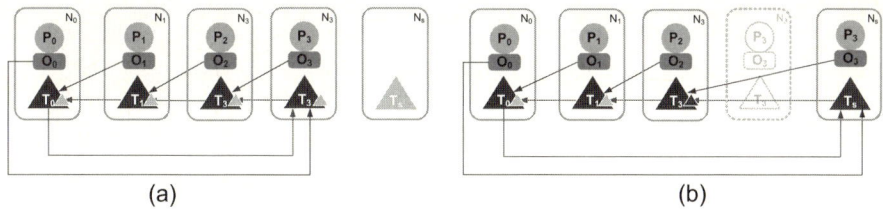

Fig. 4. The resilient protection level in 2 situations: (a) before a fault with an idle spare and (b) after the fault recovery with the allocated spare

continues until the overloaded node is reached, in such case the node N_1. At this point, the protector T_1 requests the usage of the node N_r.

Some other steps form the node usage request: Initially, the protector T_r incorporates itself in a heartbeat/watchdog system establishing two neighbours. In sequence, the protector T_1 will command the observer O_2 to send the application process checkpoint to N_r. After, T_1 then tells to the T_r to spawn the process P_2, and it tells to the process P_2 running at N_1 to commit suicide. Finally, the message forwarding continues carrying the information of the new node as allocated. The mechanism presented above is able to restore the original configuration in a system that was using the basic protection level, but depends on an unpredictable user intervention to start the procedure.

Avoiding System Configuration Changes. The resilient protection level avoids the system configuration change by incorporating a transparent management of spares nodes. Such management allows it to request and to use these spares without administrator intervention. Moreover, there is no centralised information regarding the existence of the spares, keeping faithful to the architecture's main principle of decentralisation. The flexibility of this dynamic redundancy mechanism is given by the ability to start an application with a determined number of spares, or to include them dynamically during the application execution. We explain this mechanism below.

The following procedure may be executed at the application start or during the application execution: Initially we insert a node running a protector in spare mode. When the protector starts, it searches for an active protector running with the application and starts a communication protocol requesting for its addition to a structure existent in the protectors called *spare table* - The *spare table* contains some information about the current spare nodes and their states and it is present in each active protector, keeping the decentralisation. The protector receiving this request confirms whether the new spare data are not already in its *spare table*. If not, it adds the new spare data and forwards this request to its neighbor, passing the new spare information in sequence. Each protector performs the same tasks until it receives the same spare node data, finalising the message forward process. Fig. 4a shows a simple configuration with an idle spare node (T_s), it should be noted that each protector has the information regarding this spare node (the small grey triangle).

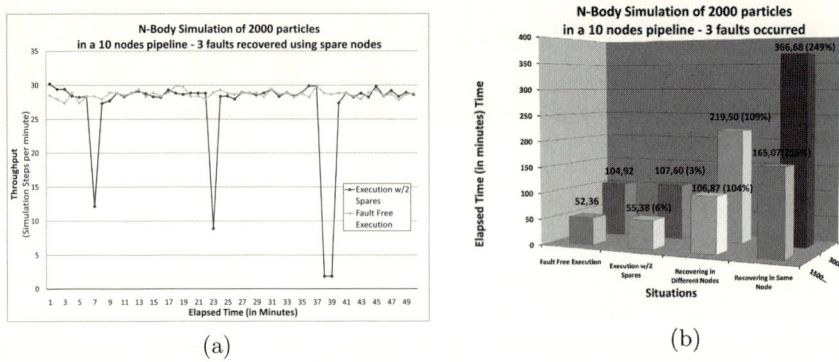

Fig. 5. (a) Results of an N-Body simulation after three faults using spare nodes. (b) Overhead comparison between the four situations.

The Recovery Procedure. At this protection level, every time a fault is detected, the protector responsible for the recovery (generally the predecessor) searches first for spare data in its own spare table. In case of an idle spare node being found, the protector starts the spare use protocol. In such protocol, the protector first confirms the spare node state by asking how many observers are executing on its node, and in sequence it sends a request command to the spare. From this moment the spare will not accept any requests from other protectors. The protector commands the spare to join the heartbeat/watchdog scheme, following which it sends the checkpoint and the log of the failed process to the spare, and finally the protector commands the spare to perform the RADIC basic level recovery procedure. Fig. 4b shows the final system configuration after this procedure. The spare node N_s assumes the failed process P_3 keeping the original system distribution.

Fig. 5a depicts the chart with the result of this execution of the same N-Body simulation using the resilient protection level with two spare nodes initially defined in our configuration and injecting three faults during the program execution. Moreover, we applied the spare nodes dynamic insertion to re-insert a "fixed" failed node between the first fault and the second fault. In the chart there are also two lines representing the failure-free execution (with squares) and the faulty execution (with circles). Following the faulty execution line, we can see that after a quick program throughput fall, the performance returns to its normal level. It should be noted that between the first and the second fault, we re-inserted the failed machine (as a "fixed" one) without generating a noticeable overhead. Thus, using this feature, we theoretically can maintain a continuous execution of the program without permanent slowdowns. The large recovery overhead in the third fault is generated mainly by the large size of the message log to be transmitted and processed (when the fault occurs just before a checkpoint).

Preventive Maintenance. The mechanism used to implement the flexible dynamic redundancy at the resilient protection level is very effective at keeping a high interval between interruptions. Some stoppage may, however, be necessary during preventive maintenance, e.g. replacing some fault-imminent nodes with healthy ones or replacing nodes by upgrade reasons.

The resilient RADIC protection level also allows to perform proactive fault tolerance without the need to stop the entire application. This feature is based on the conjunction of a failure injector, and the mechanism described previously. Using the mechanism presented before we insert a new spare node in order to receive the process running in the fault-imminent node. With the failure injector, we can schedule the appropriate moment to inject a fault in referred node (just after taking its checkpoint, avoiding processing the event log). Hence, by the spare use process previously described, the process running on the fault-imminent node will migrate to the new spare node added. Such a procedure allows a system administrator going replacing cluster machines without interrupt a running application. Some fault-prediction systems may also be used in conjunction with our solution, monitoring the node state, in order to trigger this mechanism when some values are reached.

4 Experiments

In order to validate our proposal, we had modified the RADIC MPI prototype called RADICMPI[6], including the dynamic redundancy functionality. Currently, RADICMPI incorporates basic MPI functions, including the blocking and non-blocking peer-to-peer communications. The experiments were conducted over twelve 1.9GHz Athlon-XP2600+ PC workstations running Linux Fedora Core 4 with kernel 2.6.17. Each workstation had 256MB of RAM and a 40GB local disk. The nodes were interconnected by a 100BaseT Ethernet switch.

We evaluated the behaviour of our distinct approaches when applied in continuous running applications by performing some experiments executing an N-Body particle simulation implemented as a circular pipeline and based on the example presented by Gropp [4]. We modified this program to run continuously, allowing measurement of the throughput of a continuous running application. In these experiments, we executed the N-Body particle simulation in a ten-node pipeline during a time interval performing checkpoints every 120s and injecting three faults at different moments and in different machines, measuring the throughput of the program in simulation steps per minute. We analysed three situations: a) three faults recovered without spare in different nodes (Fig. 3a); b) three faults recovered without spare in the same node (Fig. 3b) and c) three faults recovered with spare (Fig. 5a). In all of these experiments, we compared each result with a failure-free execution. Moreover, we performed a comparison of the overhead generated in the execution time of each case to reach the 1500 and 3000 simulation steps (Fig. 5b).

The chart in Fig. 5b clarifies our visualisation about the behaviour of the RADIC protection levels in the distinct situations shown in this paper, but measuring the execution time of each one to achieve a number of simulation steps (1500 and 3000 steps, injecting all faults at the first 1500 steps). In the horizontal axis are the tested situations: the vertical axis represents the elapsed time (in minutes) to execute each job presented in the depth axis. The fault-free execution is the comparison basis for the remaining situations. Now it is possible to see that the overhead of using the resilient protection level is negligible, achieving only 6% and improving as the program continues, decreasing to 3% at 3000 simulation steps. In the opposite side, when the faults are recovered at the same node, we see a strong overhead of 215% of the execution time getting worse as the program continues, rising to 249% after 3000 simulation steps. Such a situation, or even that recovering in different nodes (achieving overhead of 104% and 109%, respectively), may be considered under the acceptable limit, causing a system restart in order to re-establish the initial configuration.

5 Related Work

There is ongoing research on fault tolerance in message-passing parallel systems. Our solution allows a transparent management of spare nodes, which is able to dynamically to insert new spare nodes. Such mechanisms also may be applied to perform preventive maintenance by making a *hot swap* of machines. Other solutions also use spare nodes or allow performance of preventive activities and we present some of them and their characteristics below.

MPICH-V[7] is a framework that has implemented four rollback-recovery protocols. MPICH-V provides automatic and transparent fault tolerance for MPI applications using a runtime environment formed by certain components. At the recovery process, it uses spare nodes, but its facility for dynamic spares insertion is not mentioned.

FT-Pro[8] is a fault tolerance solution based on a combination of rollback-recovery and failure prediction that takes some action at each decision-point. Such solutions currently support three different preventive actions: process migration, coordinated checkpoint using central checkpoint storages and no action. FT-Pro only works with an static number of spare nodes.

The **Score-D**[9] checkpoint solution uses spare nodes in order to provide fault tolerance through a distributed coordinated checkpoint system. This system uses a parity generation that guarantees the checkpoint reconstitution in cases of failures. These spares nodes are defined at the application start and are consumed until reaching zero. This solution does not have a mechanism to allow dynamic spare node insertion or node replacement. Furthermore, it performs the recovery process based on a central agent.

6 Conclusions and Future Work

In this paper, we have argued that the actual failure rate of the fastest supercomputers makes indispensable the use of fault tolerance solutions in order to achieve a desired MTTI. We also defended our belief that, in order to avoid system interruptions, more than automatic and transparent recovery, a fault tolerant solution must provide mechanisms to avoid system configuration changes.

We presented an architecture with different protection levels which enable it to provide a high MTTI for message-passing program executions. The first protection level provides high availability by simple reliance on the active nodes of the system in order to recover a failed process. Such behaviour generates a system degradation that may leads the application to an unsatisfactory state and a need to interrupt the execution in order to re-establish the initial configuration. We incorporated a new protection level, the resilient protection level, which provides mechanisms that avoid system degradation or allow system configuration re-establishment, and also allow performance of preventive maintenance tasks.

Our experiments showed the effectiveness and benefits of our solution by comparing different situations with or without the new protection level. The results demonstrated that this new protection level could provide a non-stop service for message-passing systems and the overhead of the spare node insertion and management is very low despite the retention of a distributed controller.

Future work will include additional experiments, and closer scrutiny of benchmark applications under different parallel paradigms. Additional research might be address the integration of preventive maintenance mechanism with some fault prediction scheme. It would also be interesting to assess the effects of the RADIC protection levels in large clusters and with different kinds of applications, giving us a real knowledge about the RADIC scalability. Owing to physical difficulties of accessing these machines, the development of a RADIC simulator would be necessary.

References

1. Schroeder, B., Gibson, G.A.: Understanding failures in petascale computers. Journal of Physics: Conference Series 78, 012022, 11 (2007)
2. Duarte, A., Rexachs, D., Luque, E.: Increasing the cluster availability using RADIC. In: IEEE International Conference on Cluster Computing, 2006, pp. 1–8 (2006)
3. Elnozahy, E.N.M., Alvisi, L., Wang, Y.M., Johnson, D.B.: A survey of rollback-recovery protocols in message-passing systems. ACM Computing Surveys 34(3), 375–408 (2002)
4. Gropp, W., Lusk, E., Skjellum, A.: Using MPI: Portable Parallel Programming with the Message-Passing Interface. MIT Press, Cambridge (1999); LCCN: QA76.642 G76 1999
5. Jalote, P.: Reliable, Atomic and Causal Broadcast. In: Fault Tolerance in Distributed Systems, vol. 1, p. 142. P T R Prentice Hall, USA (1994)
6. Duarte, A., Rexachs, D., Luque, E.: An intelligent management of fault tolerance in cluster using radicmpi. In: Mohr, B., Träff, J.L., Worringen, J., Dongarra, J. (eds.) PVM/MPI 2006. LNCS, vol. 4192, pp. 150–157. Springer, Heidelberg (2006)
7. Bouteiller, A., Herault, T., Krawezik, G., Lemarinier, P., Cappello, F.: Mpich-v project: A multiprotocol automatic fault-tolerant mpi. International Journal of High Performance Computing Applications 20(3), 319 (2006)
8. Li, Y., Lan, Z.: Exploit failure prediction for adaptive fault-tolerance in cluster computing. In: Proceedings of the Sixth IEEE International Symposium on Cluster Computing and the Grid (CCGRID 2006), May 16-19, 2006, vol. 1, pp. 531–538 (2006)
9. Kondo, M., Hayashida, T., Imai, M., Nakamura, H., Nanya, T., Hori, A.: Evaluation of checkpointing mechanism on score cluster system. IEICE Transactions on Information and Systems 86(12), 2553–2562 (2003)

On-Line Performance Modeling for MPI Applications[*]

Oleg Morajko, Anna Morajko, Tomàs Margalef, and Emilio Luque

Computer Science Department. Universitat Autònoma de Barcelona
08193 Bellaterra, Spain
olegm@aia.ptv.es, {anna.morajko,tomas.margalef,
emilio.luque}@uab.es

Abstract. To develop an efficient parallel application is not an easy task. Applications rarely achieve a good performance immediately therefore, a careful performance analysis and optimization are crucial. These tasks are difficult and require a thorough understanding of the program's behavior. In this paper, we propose an on-line performance modeling technique, which enables the automated discovery of causal execution flows, composed of communication and computational activities, in MPI parallel programs. Our model reflects an application behavior and is made up of elements correlated with high-level program structures, such as loops and communication operations. Moreover, our approach enables an assortment of on-line diagnosis techniques which may further automate the performance understanding process.

1 Introduction

Although the evolution of hardware is improving at an incredible rate, to develop an efficient parallel application is still a complex task. Parallel applications rarely achieve a good performance immediately therefore, a careful performance analysis and optimization are crucial. These tasks are known to be difficult and costly, and in practice developers must understand both the application and the environment behavior. They must often focus more on the resource usage, communication, synchronization and other low-level issues, than on the real problem being solved.

There are many tools that assist developers in the process of performance analysis. Graphical trace browsers, such as Paraver [1], offer fine-grained performance metrics and visualizations, but their accurate interpretation requires a substantial time and effort from highly-skilled analysts. Other tools automate the identification of performance bottlenecks and their location in a source code. KappaPI 2 [2] and EXPERT [3] perform off-line analysis of event traces searching for patterns that indicate an inefficient behavior. Paradyn [4] uses runtime code instrumentation to find the parts of a program which contribute a significant amount of time to its execution.

Although these tools greatly support developers in understanding *what* is happening, and *when*, they do not automate the inference process in order to find the *root causes* of the problems. Often, the detection of a bottleneck somewhere in the process

---

[*] This work has been supported by the MEC-Spain under contracts TIN 2004-03388 and TIN2007-64974.

does not indicate *why* this happened and developers are left with the need to continue the search manually. The key issues in finding problem causes is not only a high-level understanding of the computational and communication patterns, but also their *causal* interdependency resulting from the sequential execution or message-passing [5]. As an initial attempt to address these issues, we propose an *on-line performance modeling technique* which allows the automated, runtime discovery of causal execution flows, made up of communication and computational activities in message-passing parallel programs.

The reminder of this paper is organized as follows. In Section 2, we present our approach to on-line performance modeling. In Section 3, we describe the prototype tool implementation which can automatically model an arbitrary MPI application during run-time. In Section 4, we present the results of the experimental evaluation of our tool in real-world applications. The related work is reviewed in Section 5. Finally, we conclude our work in Section 6, pointing out directions for future research.

2 On-Line Performance Modeling

The goal of our approach is to reflect application behavior by modeling execution flows through high-level program structures, such as loops and communication operations and to characterize them with statistical execution profiles. We believe that our model can be valuable to both expert and non-experienced users. It could make the performance understanding process easier and shorter, and it could serve as a base for the development of on-line root-cause analysis.

We define two levels of abstraction. First, we arrange the selected primitive events into concepts called activities and then we track flows through these activities. Our model captures the roadmap of the executed flows together with the aggregated performance profiles. It gives a compact view of the application behavior preserving the structure and causality relationships. It enables a quick on-line analysis which determines the parts of the program most relevant to its performance. Second, we may detect desired *causal paths*, i.e. sequences of executed activities which maintain a temporal ordering and carry contextual data. These paths contain the comprehensive detail of tracing, providing the necessary insight for analysis.

Our technique is hybrid, combining features of both static and dynamic analysis methods. We perform off-line analysis of a binary executable, we discover static code structures and we instrument selected loops to detect cycle boundaries. At runtime, we perform selective event tracing and aggregation of executed flows of activities.

2.1 Modeling Individual Tasks

In our approach, we define *Task Activity Graph (TAG)* as a directed graph which abstracts the execution of a single process. The execution is described by units which correspond to different activities and their causal relationship. We distinguish between two types of activities: the *communication activity* reflects some message-passing operation, and the *computation activity* is a group of statements which belong to the same process; none of these activities is a communication operation. The communication activities are modeled as graph nodes, while the computation activities are

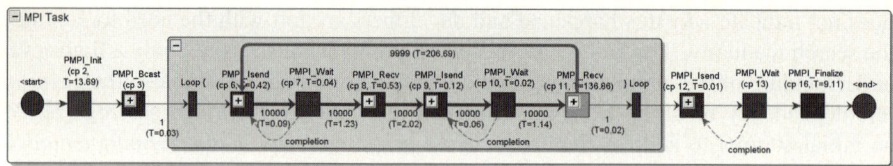

Fig. 1. An example TAG for a single MPI task. We use the rainbow colors spectrum to reflect the relevance of each activity to the total time. The graph has been generated with *yEd* [6].

represented by edges. Additionally, we use marker nodes to model program start/termination events, and entry/exit events of the selected loops.

The execution of a particular communication activity is identified by an ordered pair of events: *entry* and *exit*, for example entry/exit events of an *MPI_Bcast* call. The end of the communication activity and the start of the consecutive one, identify the execution of a computation activity, local to a process. In effect, the sequential flow of a single process execution determines the causal relationship between consecutive activities. Figure 1 shows a TAG model for a single task of a sample MPI application.

Call-path identification: To distinguish the location of the events, we model each communication function considering the *call-path* [7] taken to reach the function. This information is particularly useful as the function behavior in MPI programs often varies widely depending on the caller's chain on the stack. For that reason, an activity invoked from distinct call-paths (E.g. `main/f1/foo/MPI_Isend` and `main/f2/foo/MPI_Isend`) is represented by separate nodes in the graph.

Explicit loop modeling: In many parallel codes, the exhibited behavioral patterns are highly correlated with static program structures such as loops. We explore this feature and we model the execution cycles explicitly. We perform a static code analysis to detect loops and during run-time we can track and model them explicitly in a TAG. We focus only on loops which contain statically determinable invocations of communication activities and we avoid modeling computational loops due to possible high tracing overhead. As a consequence, the multiple executions of a loop are reflected in the TAG just by one loop instance just like in the source code.

Execution profiles: We describe the behavior of the program activities with execution profiles by adding performance data to the nodes and edges. As each activity may be executed multiple times, we aggregate the performance data into statistical metrics. We use two basic metrics for all the nodes and edges: a timer which measures the elapsed virtual time and a counter which counts the number of executions. We also calculate *min*, *max*, and *stddev* metrics to track variations. Additionally, we can add/remove arbitrary performance metrics to/from any activity.

2.2 Modeling MPI Communications

A TAG reflects all the MPI message-passing calls as communication activities. The graph contains a node for each MPI activity (e.g. *MPI_Send* or *MPI_Recv*), and edges between the corresponding send and receive pairs (both for point-to-point and collective operations), as well as between nodes in a consecutive execution order. We refer to the former as *message edges* and to the latter as *process edges*. Message edges reflect the causal relationship between the interacting tasks. Additionally, in order to reflect the semantics of non-blocking operations, we introduce a *completion edge* which connects the start node of the non-blocking operation with its completion node.

To model all the communications, we intercept the MPI communication routines and capture the call attributes, including type, source, destination, message size and others. In order to identify a message edge, we must determine the communicating tasks as well as the particular send and receive activities in them. The key idea is to match on-line a sender call context, represented by a node in the sender TAG, with a receiver call context, represented by a corresponding receive node in the receiver TAG. To accomplish this goal, we piggyback the additional data from sender to receiver(s) in every MPI message. We transmit the current send node identifier and we store it in the matching receive node as the incoming *message edge*. This feature enables us to logically connect TAGs together while maintaining them distributed.

Finally, in order to capture communication profiles, we track the count and time histograms for each message edge individually.

2.3 Parallel Application Modeling

To model the execution of an entire MPI application, we collect TAG snapshots from all the tasks and we merge them into a new global graph we call the *Parallel Task Activity Graph* (PTAG). This process can be performed periodically, upon demand, or at the end of the execution. The merge process is straightforward, as we take advantage of the information stored in the message edges. Each incoming message edge contains data that uniquely identify the sender tasks and the corresponding sending nodes. For point-to-point calls, the edge stores the individual sender data. For collective calls (E.g. *MPI_Gather*, *MPI_Alltoall*) the edge stores a vector of pairs which identifies all the sending tasks and their corresponding node identifiers.

2.4 Causal Paths

To enable lower-level analysis, we introduce *causal paths*: temporary ordered sequences of activities. We take into account two types of causality, based on a happened-before relationship [5]: the sequential execution of the activities within a process and the message passing from one activity to the other. Our approach considers the on-line, upon demand, detection of paths executed between selected activation and deactivation events. Causal paths are in fact recorded event traces which include contextual data (such as sender/receiver rank) and performance profiles. Repeatedly executed paths are subject to on-the-fly aggregation of performance metrics. For example, we may request causal path tracking for a selected loop. Loop entry/exit events determine the path boundaries and each unique sequence of activities is identified as a separate path. Path profiles include counter and total time spent per path, giving insight for analysis.

2.5 Model-Based Analysis Techniques

Our approach enables the assortment of on-line performance analysis techniques. The TAG model allows the distributed reasoning about the behavior of individual processes on-line. The model provides a high-level view of execution and enables the easy detection of performance bottlenecks and their location in each task. As this information is available at runtime, the monitoring could be refined in order to provide more in-depth views on each problem. By merging individual TAGs we gain a global application view, which provides the opportunity to analyze the whole application while it runs. This allows the detection of program phases, the clustering of tasks by their behavior, the detection of a load imbalance by matching loops between tasks and comparing their profiles, and other observations. Some of our model properties, such as the causal relationships between activities and the upon-demand detection of causal paths, can be used to develop tools for root-cause problem diagnosis. Finally, our model can be displayed using visualization tools.

3 Prototype Implementation

In this section we describe the prototype implementation of a tool that is able to build a performance model of an MPI application on-line, in a distributed way, and without access to the application source code. The tool collects and processes the local event traces at runtime in each process, building individual TAGs. Then, it periodically collects the TAG snapshots and merges them into a global graph.

Our tool is made up of three main components: the front-end, the tool daemons (*Dynamic Modeler and Analyzer - DMA*), and the run-time performance modeling library (*RTLib*). The front-end coordinates the tool daemons and collects the TAG snapshots of the individual tasks by merging them into a PTAG model. It is also responsible for processing the model, i.e. behavioral clustering. Finally, the front-end exports the PTAG into an open graph format GraphML [9].

Each *DMA* is a light-weight daemon based on Dyninst [10] that implements the following functionalities: static code analysis, loading of the *RTLib* library into the application process, interception of the MPI routines, instrumentation insertion to trace events and to collect performance metrics, process start, periodical capture of TAG snapshots, while the program is running, and TAG propagation to the front-end.

The *RTLib* library is responsible for the incremental construction of a local TAG. It provides implementation of graph manipulation routines optimized for fast insertion and constant-time look-ups. The graph and the associated performance metrics are stored in a shared memory segment as a compact, pointer-less data structure in order to allow the daemon to take its snapshots periodically without stopping the process.

3.1 Start-Up

Before the application starts, the tool determines the *target functions,* a configurable set of functions which identify program activities. By default, we configure all MPI communication functions as communication activities. However, users may configure their own functions of interest to be reflected in the model. Next, the daemon traverses the program *static call graph* and *control flow graphs* for selected functions in order to select loops which lead to the invocation of target functions.

3.2 Dynamic TAG Construction

Using the *RTLib*, we maintain a local, partial execution graph (TAG) in each process. Starting with an empty graph, we add a new node when a target function is executed for the first time or update its node otherwise. To build the TAG, we instrument the entry and exit points of each target function. This instrumentation captures the record of the executed event. Then, it performs a low-overhead stack walk using *unwind* library [11] to determine the actual call-path and it calculates its signature and looks up a hash table to recover the node identifier. Next, the instrumentation invokes the *RTLib* library routine to process the event record. The library updates the graph structure by adding, if necessary, the node which represents a currently executed activity and the edge from the previous activity. Finally, it updates the execution profile of an affected node/edge by aggregating the desired performance metrics.

3.3 Tracking MPI Communications

In order to model the communications, the tool intercepts the relevant MPI routines to propagate the piggyback data from sender to receiver(s). There are several different solutions to transmit piggyback data over every MPI communication [12]. However, considering the overhead, our observation is that no mechanism outperforms the others in any scenario. Therefore, in order to minimize intrusion, we have developed *a hybrid MPI piggyback technique* which combines the existing mechanisms. For small messages, we take advantage of the data-type wrapping. For large messages, we send an additional message which we found to be much cheaper than wrapping. Moreover, we interleave the original operation with an asynchronous transmission of piggyback data. This optimization partially hides the latency of the additional send and lowers the overall intrusion. Finally, to model non-blocking operations our implementation correlates the start of each blocking operation (E.g. *MPI_Isend*) with its completion operation (E.g. *MPI_Wait* function). For this, we keep track of the opaque MPI request handles to add the appropriate completion edges.

4 Experimental Evaluation

We have conducted experiments with real-world, parallel applications to evaluate our approach. We have run our tests on 32-node clusters at the WCSS[1], made up of dual Itanium 2 processors running Linux and connected via Infiniband network. We have built our prototype tool with the publicly available version of OpenMPI 1.2.2 [13].

In this paper, we present the results using two scientific MPI applications: NAS LU Parallel Benchmark and XFire Simulator. NAS LU [14] is a simulated CFD application benchmark which employs symmetric successive over-relaxation scheme to solve a regular-sparse, lower and upper triangular system. LU is written in Fortran and represents a typical SPMD code. XFire is a forest fire propagation simulator [15] which calculates the next position of the fireline considering the current fireline

---

[1] Experiments were conducted at the Wroclaw Center for Networking and Supercomputing, Poland.

position and a set of different aspects such as weather, vegetation and topography. This application represents a typical master/worker code written in C++.

NAS LU Benchmark: The model of B-class LU benchmark executed on 8 processors is shown in Figure 2. Our tool needed 17±2 seconds at start-up and caused 4%±0.5 of runtime overhead. The exported model size was 274KB (514 nodes, 538 process edges, and 340 message edges). The first observation is that the program exhibits three main phases of execution. In the first phase, task 0 broadcasts initial data to other tasks. Next, a wave-like communication takes place when each task exchanges data with its neighbours. The pattern suggests a 2D decomposition and we can identify border tasks and tasks with all the neighbours. Afterwards, all the tasks synchronize on the barrier. The second phase is the main loop made up of 250 iterations. In each iteration the tasks execute two loops to receive data from the corresponding 2D neighbours, perform local calculations and finally respond back. In the final phase, the application performs a number of reductions and terminates. The performance metrics show a relatively good load balance as most of the time is spent on calculations and there are no signs of communication inefficiencies.

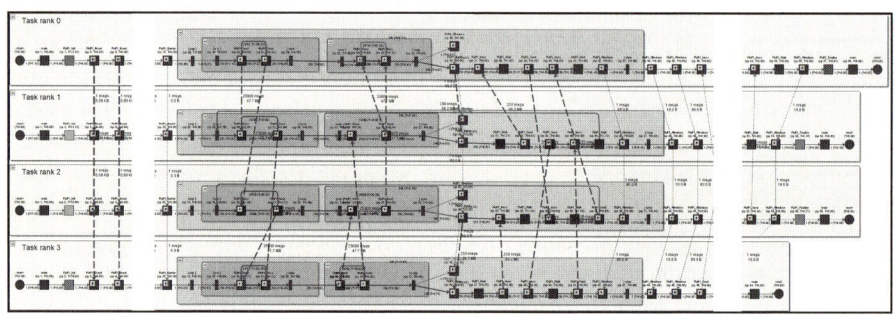

Fig. 2. PTAG visualization of the NAS LU benchmark code

XFire: Figure 3 presents the model of XFire executed on 32 processors (463 nodes, 470 process edges, and 217 message edges). Our tool needed 16±1 seconds at start-up and caused 0.8%±0.2 of runtime overhead. We may observe two types of tasks: task 0 (master) and a set of tasks with similar behaviour (slaves). The model indicates three phases of execution. We can interpret the first phase as an initialization, including synchronization and distribution of 64MB data from master to slaves. The next phase is the main loop. In each iteration, the master sends requests to the slaves, waits for the answers, and finally performs some calculations. Each slave waits for the requests, processes them and responds. Finally, we observe the coordinated termination phase. The performance metrics reveal the existence of severe bottlenecks in the second phase. The red *MPI_Recv* node in the master (77.4% of total time) indicates a bored master waiting for calculating slaves. The green *MPI_Send* nodes in the slaves reveal inefficiency (20.8%) which is caused by master calculations at the end of each iteration. This indicates that potential optimizations could bring significant benefits.

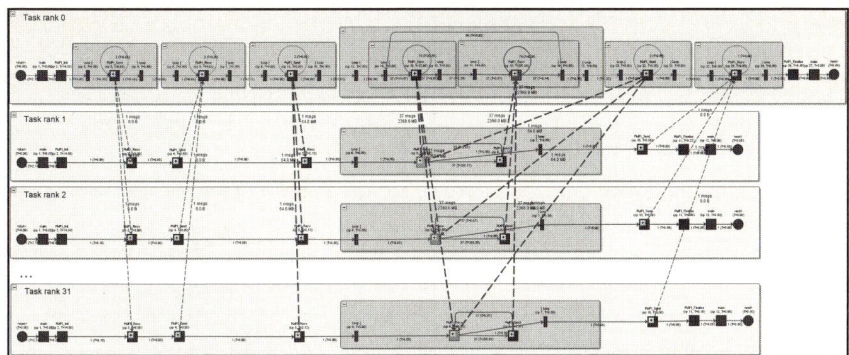

Fig. 3. PTAG visualization of the XFire master/worker code

We have evaluated the overheads caused by our prototype tool in the following way.

Offline start-up overhead: At start-up, each tool daemon performs four actions. First, it connects to the front-end. Second, it parses the program executable using DynInst. The cost of this action depends on the executable size. For 1MB executables, this action took about 4-5 seconds, delaying part of its cost due to lazy parsing. Third, the daemon starts the application process, loads the *RTLib* library (*160KB*), parses it and performs initialization. This took approximately 7-8 seconds. Fourth, it instruments the executable. This includes wrapping selected MPI calls, and inserting instrumentation. This cost depends on the number of used MPI calls and the number of predefined activities and loops. The evaluated applications had from to 6 to 24 calls and the duration varied from 3 to 11 seconds. To summarize, the total start-up cost is constant for a given executable. In our case, the cost varied from 14 to 19 seconds.

On-line TAG construction overhead: Includes the runtime cost of executing event tracing instrumentation, walking the stack, finding a call-path identifier in the hash table, and updating the graph nodes, edges and metrics. The penalty is nearly constant and in our experiments it varied from 4 to 6 μs per instrumented call. The overall cost depends on the number of communication calls and the relevant loops entries/exits.

On-line TAG sampling overhead: Each daemon periodically samples the TAG. In order to take a snapshot, the daemon simply copies a contiguous block of memory shared with the application process to its local memory. The cost of this action depends on the graph size, which in turn reflects the program structure. In our experiments, the sampling overhead was between 40-50 μs per snapshot. Besides that, the cost of a simple TAG traversal was about 1500-1700 μs.

On-line MPI piggyback overhead: This includes the cost of wrapped MPI calls, datatype wrapping overhead for small payloads and the cost of sending an extra message for large payloads. We have compared results of SKaMPI Benchmark [16] for original MPI and MPI with a piggyback mechanism. As illustrated in Figure 4, for point-to-point operations the overhead is nearly constant and it decreases from 10% for messages smaller than 1KB to 2% for 1MB messages. We have observed similar effects for collective operations where the overhead varied from 15% to 0.5%.

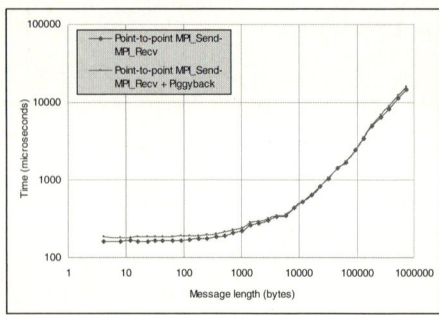 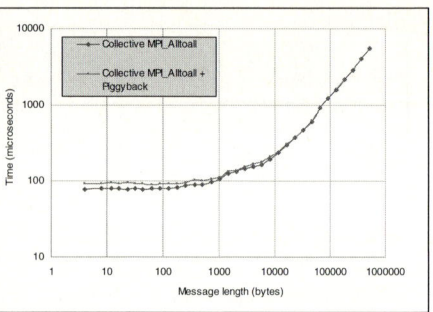

Fig. 4. MPI piggyback overhead for send-receive pattern (left) and all-to-all pattern (right)

5 Related Work

The concept of the detection of causal execution flows for cause-effect inference has been recently studied in an automated problem diagnosis thesis [17]. This approach collects function-level control-flow traces, while our modeling technique aggregates repetitive patterns, yet preserving probabilistic causality. Our work is also related to communication pattern extraction and runtime MPI trace compression techniques [18]. These approaches use pattern matching in order to dynamically discover repeating communication structures in an MPI event graph. This work is different in that it uses statically determined loops in order to find pattern boundaries. Our on-the-fly trace analysis is lossy, as it uses aggregation and builds statistical profiles.

There are also similarities between the techniques presented here and the critical path profiling [8]. This approach builds an execution graph at runtime by tracking communications and piggybacking data over MPI messages. While it focuses only on critical path extraction made up of individual events, our approach differs by capturing all the executed paths together with their statistical execution profiles.

6 Conclusions and Future Work

In this paper, we have presented an on-line performance modeling technique and its prototype implementation, which automates the discovery of causal execution flows, made up of communication and computational activities, for arbitrary message-passing parallel programs. We have demonstrated this ability in two real-world MPI applications. The model of both applications reveals details about their behavior and structure, without requiring an explicit knowledge or a source code.

As a future work, we are planning to improve the scalability of our tool to perform tests thousands of processors. For this purpose, we are planning to replace the global front-end by a tree-based overlay network infrastructure for scalable TAG collection.

Moreover, our approach seems to be a promising technique for the development of new on-line diagnosis techniques, which may further automate the performance understanding process. We will use this modeling technique as the basis of our investigation on automated root-cause performance analysis.

References

1. Pillet, V., Labarta, J., Cortes, T., Girona, S.: Paraver: A Tool to Visualize and Analyze Parallel Code. WoTUG-18, Manchester 44, 17–31 (1995)
2. Jorba, J., Margalef, T., Luque, E.: Performance Analysis of Parallel Applications with KappaPI 2. In: Proc. Parallel Computing Conference, Spain, vol. 33, pp. 155–162 (2006)
3. Wolf, F., Mohr, B.: Automatic performance analysis of hybrid MPI/OpenMP applications. Journal of Systems Architecture 49(10-11), 421–439 (2003)
4. Miller, B.P., Callaghan, M.D., Cargille, J.M., Hollingsworth, J.K., Irvin, R.B., Karavanic, K.L., Kunchithapadam, K., Newhall, T.: The Paradyn Parallel Performance Measurement Tool. IEEE Computer 28, 37–46 (1995)
5. Lamport, L.: Time, clocks and the ordering of events in a distributed system. Communications of the ACM 21(7), 558–565 (1978)
6. yWorks, yEd - Java Graph Editor, http://www.yworks.com/products/yed/
7. Bernat, A.R., Miller, B.P.: Incremental Call-Path Profiling. Concurrency: Practice and Experience 19(11), 1533–1547 (2007)
8. Schulz, M.: Extracting Critical Path Graphs from MPI Applications. In: Cluster Computing 2005, IEEE International, pp. 1–10 (September 2005)
9. Brandes, U., Eiglsperger, M., Herman, I., Himsolt, M., Marshall, M.S.: GraphML Progress Report: Structural Layer Proposal. In: Mutzel, P., Jünger, M., Leipert, S. (eds.) GD 2001. LNCS, vol. 2265, pp. 501–512. Springer, Heidelberg (2002)
10. Buck, B., Hollingsworth, J.K.: An API for Runtime Code Patching. Journal of High Performance Computing Applications 14(4), 317–329 (2000)
11. Unwind Library Project, http://www.nongnu.org/libunwind/
12. Shende, S., Malony, A., Morris, A., Wolf, F.: Performance Profiling Overhead Compensation for MPI Programs. In: Di Martino, B., Kranzlmüller, D., Dongarra, J. (eds.) EuroPVM/MPI 2005. LNCS, vol. 3666, pp. 359–367. Springer, Heidelberg (2005)
13. Graham, R.L., Woodall, T.S., Squyres, J.M.: Open MPI: A flexible high performance MPI. In: Proc. 6th PPAM Conference, pp. 228–239 (2005)
14. Bailey, D.H., Harris, T., Saphir, W., Wijngaart, R., Woo, A., Yarrow, M.: The NAS Parallel Benchmarks 2.0. Report NAS-95-020 (December 1995)
15. Jorba, J., Margalef, T., Luque, E., Andre, J., Viegas, D.X.: Application of Parallel Computing to the Simulation of Forest Fire Propagation. In: Proc. 3rd International Conference in Forest Fire Propagation, Portugal, vol. 1, pp. 891–900 (November 1998)
16. Reussner, R., Sanders, P., Prechelt, L., Muller, M.: SKaMPI: A detailed, accurate MPI benchmark. LNCS, vol. 1497, pp. 52–59. Springer, Heidelberg (1998)
17. Mirgorodskiy, A.V., Maruyama, N., Miller, B.P.: Problem Diagnosis in Large-Scale Computing Environments. In: ACM/IEEE SC 2006 Conference, vol. 11(17) (2006)
18. Noeth, M., Mueller, F., Schulz, M., de Supinski, B.: Scalable Compression and Replay of Communication Traces in Massively Parallel Environments. In: IPDPS 2007, pp. 1–11 (2007)

MPC: A Unified Parallel Runtime for Clusters of NUMA Machines

Marc Pérache[1], Hervé Jourdren[1], and Raymond Namyst[2]

[1] CEA/DAM Île de France Bruyères-le-Châtel F-91297 Arpajon Cedex
[2] Laboratoire Bordelais de Recherche en Informatique 351, cours de la Libération F-33405 Talence cedex

Abstract. Over the last decade, Message Passing Interface (MPI) has become a very successful parallel programming environment for distributed memory architectures such as clusters. However, the architecture of cluster node is currently evolving from small symmetric shared memory multiprocessors towards massively multicore, Non-Uniform Memory Access (NUMA) hardware. Although regular MPI implementations are using numerous optimizations to realize *zero copy* cache-oblivious data transfers within shared-memory nodes, they might prevent applications from achieving most of the hardware's performance simply because the scheduling of heavyweight processes is not flexible enough to dynamically fit the underlying hardware topology. This explains why several research efforts have investigated hybrid approaches mixing message passing between nodes and memory sharing inside nodes, such as MPI+OpenMP solutions [1,2]. However, these approaches require lots of programming efforts in order to adapt/rewrite existing MPI applications.

In this paper, we present the MultiProcessor Communications environnement (MPC), which aims at providing programmers with an efficient runtime system for their existing MPI, POSIX Thread or hybrid MPI+Thread applications. The key idea is to use user-level threads instead of processes over multiprocessor cluster nodes to increase scheduling flexibility, to better control memory allocations and optimize scheduling of the communication flows with other nodes. Most existing MPI applications can run over MPC with no modification. We obtained substantial gains (up to 20%) by using MPC instead of a regular MPI runtime on several scientific applications.

1 Introduction

Over the last decade, Message Passing Interface (MPI) has become a very successful parallel programming environment for distributed memory architectures such as clusters. This is mainly due to its efficiency and its portability. MPI is organized around the concept of a set of communicating tasks (often processes) using send and receive primitives. This feature allows programmers to split their application into several parts in an intuitive way and execute them on different processing nodes, processors or cores. On the top of the basic send/receive procedures, MPI offers a rich set of primitives available from C and Fortran interfaces which makes it possible to build powerful parallel applications. These characteristics led MPI to be adopted by a huge community of users and consequently, there are a lot of MPI applications developed in many different scientific and industrial fields.

Currently, the architecture of cluster nodes is evolving from small symmetric shared memory multiprocessors towards massively multicore, Non-Uniform Memory Access (NUMA) hardware [3]. The emergence of these deeply hierarchical architectures raises the need for a careful distribution of threads and data. Indeed, cache misses and NUMA penalties become more and more important with the complexity of the machine, making these constraints as important as parallelization itself. Parallel programming methods thus have to perfectly match the underling architecture to achieve high performance.

Distributed memory approaches such as MPI do not fully exploit the shared memory underlying architecture and thus may loose some efficiency. Shared memory approaches, based on explicit multithreading or language-generated multithreading (e.g. OpenMP) are more accurate on shared memory architectures. Thus, many hybrid approaches, typically mixing MPI and OpenMP, have been proposed to better exploit cluster of multiprocessors. However, they suffer from many drawbacks, including the fact that they require lots of programming efforts in order to adapt/rewrite existing MPI applications.

In this paper, we propose another approach which consists in a powerful runtime able to run MPI applications using user-level threads. This paper is organized as follows. Section 2 discusses the main parallel programming approaches used over clusters of multiprocessors. We then present our MPC environment in Section 3. Section 4 introduces our experiments and shows the efficiency of the MPC library.

2 Common Approaches for Programming Clusters of NUMA Nodes

To address the problem of programming efficiently clusters of multiprocessor nodes, several programming approaches have been explored.

Advanced MPI Implementations. Many MPI implementations are highly optimized for some specific architectures [4]. Such implementations typically offer specific hardware support for modern network interface cards (Quadrics, Myrinet, ...), *zero copy* data transfers, etc. They exhibit excellent performance regarding latency and bandwidth of communications, but do not fully exploit NUMA node capabilities.

OpenMP Implementations for Clusters. OpenMP is a very convenient way to parallelize existing codes, but it was initially limited to shared memory computing nodes. Nowadays, implementations such as Intel Cluster OpenMP [5] or OpenMPD [6] allow OpenMP applications to run over distributed memory architectures, thanks to the use of software DSM runtime[1]. Obviously, any memory access that triggers the consistency mechanism is much more expensive than an ordinary access to a processor's memory. In fact, a memory access requiring the consistency mechanism can be hundreds to thousands of times slower than an access to any level of cache or hardware memory. That is why this approach is usually not as efficient as expected.

Hybrid MPI + OpenMP Approaches. Mixing MPI and OpenMP looks attractive to benefit from both data sharing on large shared memory nodes (thanks to OpenMP) and multiple processing node usage (thanks to MPI). Nevertheless, MPI and OpenMP implementations aren't very comprehensive to each other [7]. For instance, most MPI implementations use *busy waiting* techniques to increase the performance of communication event detection. Such a policy usually leads to disastrous performance in a multithreaded context. Moreover, MPI implementations are generally not fully thread-safe. Thus, the integration of MPI and OpenMP seems to be a promising approach, but is currently quite difficult to realize in practice.

Process Virtualization. Process virtualization [8] is an efficient way to benefit from shared memory computing nodes. It dissociates tasks and processes. In standard MPI approaches, a task is a process. With this approach, tasks are mapped to threads. Thus, load balancing, *zero copy* method, overloading[2], ... are easier to implement. AMPI [9] and TOMPI [10] are two MPI implementations that use process virtualization. MPC also uses process virtualization to implement its distributed memory API. As emphasized in the remainder of this paper, collective operations and scheduling have been strongly optimized in this context.

3 MPC: MultiProcessor Communications

The purpose of MPC is to provide a single API for programming distributed and shared memory architectures [11]. The MPC library implementation solves the issues of mixing *distributed* and *shared* memory approaches thanks to its unified runtime. The design of MPC follows four objectives. The first one is portability, which is required for most scientific computer codes. The second goal is dynamic workload balancing, which is crucial for example with adaptive mesh refinement. Another important goal is to reach a high level of performance. Last but not least, the fourth goal is to provide an API that allows easy migration from an MPI application, or a multithreaded one, to the MPC unified framework. This section is organized as follows. First of all the MPC execution model is described. Then, we present the specialized MxN thread library. Follows the optimized scheduler that integrates collective communications. The MPC allocator is introduced in the last part.

---

[1] Distributed Shared Memory.
[2] Using more tasks than cores.

The second issue comes with the large number of tasks that may be involved on a single collective communication (see Section 4.1). So, $O(n)$ wakeup methods are prohibited. We need an efficient wakeup method associated with our freeze method, that ideally perform $O(1)$ wakeup and freeze.

The following section is organized as follows: first the collective communication algorithm is described. Then freeze/wakeup methods are introduced. Thread migration is taken into account in the last part.

Collective Communication Algorithm. The algorithm used to perform collective communications is generic[4] and divided into two parts. The first one is the per-core part. At a given time, there is only one executed thread on each core. That is why the first part of this algorithm corresponds to a centralized lock free approach. Its pseudo-code is described in function *contribute_local_core* in Figure 2(a).

The second part of this algorithm performs inter-core collective communications. This part uses a tree based algorithm in order to maximize data locality and scalability. This part of the algorithm allows to synchronize cores where all participating tasks in the collective communication have done their contribution to the collective communication call. The pseudo-code of inter-core collective communications is described in function *contribute_local_group* in Figure 2(b).

```
contribute_local_core (core_rank, data_in,
    data_out,function)
    if (virtual_core[core_rank].nb_tasks == 0)
        copy data_in to vir-
            tual_core[core_rank].data_in
    else
        function (data_in, vir-
            tual_core[core_rank].data_in)
    endif
    virtual_core[core_rank].nb_tasks++
    if (virtual_core[core_rank].nb_tasks ==
        virtual_core[core_rank].nb_tasks_total)
        contribute_local_group(top_level, func-
            tion)
        for i in virtual_core[core_rank].task_list
        do
            copy i.data_out
        done
        wakeup current_task to
            virtual_core[core_rank].task_list
    else
        freeze (current_task,data_out) in
            virtual_core[core_rank].task_list
    endif
```

(a) Per-core contribution.

```
contribute_local_group (level, function)
    if (root == level)
        copy level.data_in to level.data_out
    else
        lock father
        if (level.father.nb_tasks == 0)
            copy level.data_in to
                level.father.data_in
        else
            function (level.data_in,
                level.father.data_in)
        endif
        level.father.nb_tasks++
        if (level.father.nb_tasks ==
            level.father.nb_tasks_total)
            contribute_local_group (level.father,
                function)
            for i in level.task_list do
                copy i.data_out
            done
            wakeup level.task_list
            unlock father
        else
            unlock father
            freeze (current_task,level.data_out)
                in
                level.task_list
        endif
```

(b) Per-group (i.e. between cores) contribution.

Fig. 2. Scheduler-integrated collective communications algorithm (data_in and data_out values are input and output arrays used during reduction and broadcast)

---

[4] The same code is used for barrier, reduction and broadcast.

Freeze/wakeup Methods. All the complexity of efficient collective communications lies in the task freeze and wakeup methods. These methods have been inserted into the thread scheduler in order to provide $O(1)$ complexity. The freeze function allows to insert the calling task into a list that matches the internal scheduler ready thread list structure. This function does not require lock because at a time, there is only one executed thread per core.

Regarding the wakeup function, this function only takes the freezed thread list created within the freeze function. Then, it inserts it directly into the scheduler ready list using a $O(1)$ technique.

Thread Migration. The algorithm presented above assumes that the distribution of tasks among cores is known thanks to the nb_tasks_total variable, whereas MPC allows task migration for load balancing. Thus, we have extended the previous algorithm using a lazy update method to deal with task migration. The aim of the lazy update method is to perform the lowest number of updates. Thus, it does not perform collective communication structure update for each migration. It only requires a check at each collective communication call to determine if the current core used by the calling task is the same than the one used for the previous collective communication call. In migration case, first of all, the calling task is temporary moved to its previous core. Then, it performs the collective communication call. Finally, it schedules a collective communication initialization. This initialization will be performed by all tasks at the next collective communication call. Such a method allows to aggregate all migrations between two collective communication calls.

3.4 Optimized NUMA-Aware and Thread-Aware Allocator

The memory allocator if often a bottleneck for parallel multithreaded programs [14]. It may severely limits program performance and scalability on multiprocessor systems. Allocators suffer from problems that include poor scalability and heap organization leading to false sharing [15]. That is why programmers hoping to achieve performance improvements often use custom memory allocators [16].

The MPC NUMA-aware thread-aware allocator combines a global heap and per-thread heaps. Thus, it avoids false sharing and provides very low synchronization cost in the most common cases. The allocator is linked to the MPC topology module and thread scheduler to maximize data locality on NUMA architectures. The specificity of our allocator mainly resides in the NUMA-aware aspect. The well-known use of multiple local heaps allows to avoid false-sharing, allows scalability, but does not insure data locality. That's why our allocator is linked with the topology module of MPC. This module determines the memory hierarchy and drives the system physical page allocation. This allocation insures that a new allocated page will be local to a thread but does not insure long time data locality. That's why the MPC allocator communicates with the user-level thread scheduler of MPC, in order to move tasks' pages according to thread migration among cores.

Combination of multiple heaps and data locality techniques provides to MPC an efficient and scalable allocator, suited to large multiprocessor NUMA nodes.

4 Experimental Results

Two machines have been used, with very different architectures. The first one is a node of the Bull TERA-10 cluster of CEA/DAM Île-de-France. This node consists of 8 Dual core Itanium2 Montecito processors (16 cores) distributed over four Quad Brick Blocks (QBB). Each QBB has two processors and must be viewed as a NUMA node inside a global shared-memory machine of four QBB and 48 GB of memory. The second machine consists of 2 Quad-core Xeon (8 cores). This machine is a UMA SMP machine.

Experiments reported here are based on two basic numerical kernels. The first one is an *advection* benchmark, corresponding to a 2D upwind *explicit* scheme on a regular Cartesian grid. In SPMD parallel mode, the scheme just requires one point-to-point communication per direction (update of ghost cells), and one reduction for the prediction of the next time step (CFL condition). The second numerical kernel is a *conduction* benchmark, corresponding to a 2D Cartesian grid *implicit* heat conduction solver, based on a a five-point stencil and a Conjugate Gradient method with diagonal preconditionning. In SPMD mode, this kernel can be distinguished from the precedent one due to the conjugate gradient method that involves many reductions at each time step (scalar product).

4.1 Scalability Results with Domain Overloading

Results are given Figure 3. The first part of each curves illustrates the scalability of MPC versus MPI. The MPI Bull implementation is the manufacturer implementation available on TERA-10. This implementation is optimized according to the underlying architecture and thus, it reaches very good performances. The MPI implementation available on Xeon machine is a standard MPICH2 implementation.

Comparison of MPI Bull and MPC shows the rather good performances achieved by MPC. More generally, in scalability terms, MPI and MPC implementations reach similar performances on both architectures.

To cover the whole spectrum, we have performed multi-node execution. The following table presents relative execution time to MPI for the *advection* and *conduction* benchmarks on 32 core Itanium2 Montecito architecture (2 nodes) with $4,000 \times 1,000$ cells.

Benchmark	Number of tasks								
	32	64	128	192	256	320	384	448	512
Advection (50 cycles)	0.99	0.90	0.84	0.80	0.81	0.84	0.86	0.85	0.87
Conduction (25 cycles)	1.02	0.96	0.92	0.89	0.92	0.91	0.93	0.91	0.91

These results illustrate the low overhead of MPC in multi-node context, demonstrating also the benefits of overloading as in single-node context. Let us mention that a large scale run over 4,096 processors of TERA-10 has been

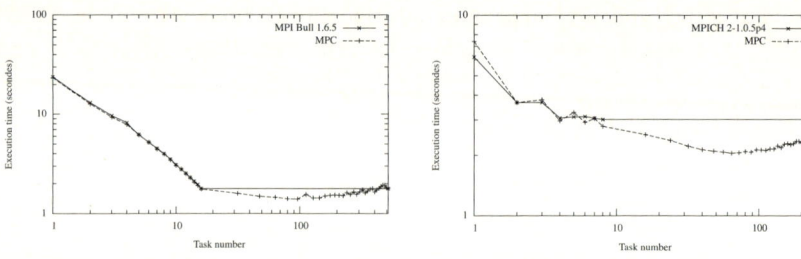
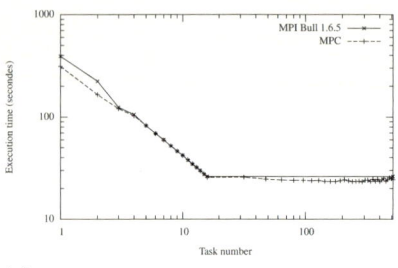
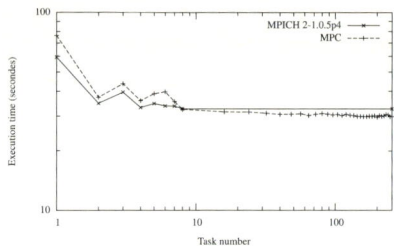

(a) Execution time for the *advection* benchmark on 16 core Itanium2 Montecito architecture with $2,000 \times 1,000$ cells and 50 cycles

(b) Execution time for the *advection* benchmark on 8 core Xeon $1,000 \times 1,000$ cells and 50 cycles

(c) Execution time for the *conduction* benchmark on 16 core Itanium2 Montecito architecture with $4,000 \times 1,000$ cells and 10 cycles

(d) Execution time for the *conduction* benchmark on 8 core Xeon with $2,000 \times 1,000$ cells and 10 cycles

Fig. 3. Evaluation of scalability and overloading method on representative scientific computing 2D code. Parallelization is done via 1D domain decomposition.

performed [17] to check scalability of robustness of the MPC library, along with numerous computations with the HERA AMR platform [18], up to several thousands processors.

These codes have been tested with domain overloading. In this context, MPC allows better execution times thanks to cache effects. This also illustrates the good performances of our scheduler-integrated collective communications, especially with the *conduction* benchmark, that performs a high number of reductions per cycle. Overloading allows to gain more than 10% and up to 20% on the execution time, without *any* modification to the original code.

4.2 Memory Allocation and Data Placement Results

In order to evaluate the MPC NUMA-aware and thread-aware allocator, the *advection* benchmark on TERA-10 has been used. Results are summarized in the following table.

Allocator	Number of tasks							
	1	2	4	6	8	10	12	14	16
Standard	23.47s	12.79s	8.27s	5.44s	4.21s	3.25s	2.66s	2.22s	2.02s
MPC	23.47s	12.64s	7.86s	5.20s	3.95s	3.05s	2.51s	2.08s	1.76s
Gain	0.00%	1.19%	5.22%	4.62%	6.58%	6.57%	5.98%	6.73%	14.77%

A reduction of 14% of the overall execution time is observed in multithread mode, when compared to the standard C library memory allocator. Results with the *conduction* benchmark are similar. Results are similar on the Xeon machine. The MPC allocator strongly contributes to the performances of MPC, performances that would not be achieved without an optimized NUMA-aware and thread-aware allocator.

5 Conclusion and Future Works

In this paper, we have introduced the MPC library. MPC offers a unified runtime for both distributed-memory and shared-memory parallel codes. The MPC internal execution model also insures a good integration of *hybrid* shared- and distributed-memory approaches *via* appropriate *thread scheduling*. To reach a high level of performance from SMP machines to large NUMA nodes, MPC provides a NUMA-aware and thread-aware *allocator* that contributes to the overall scalability and efficiency. The MPC scheduler is optimized to deal with a *very* large number of threads, providing pooling and highly efficient scheduler-integrated collective communications. The scheduler and allocator modules cooperate to preserve data locality, with or without thread migration, a crucial issue when dealing with NUMA nodes. Our experiments have shown that the MPC approach leads to a high level of performance on several HPC parallel codes.

Today, MPC allows an easy migration path for existing MPI parallel codes and multithread codes based on the POSIX thread API. As far as MPI codes are concerned, the main issue is thread safety. Such codes have to be thread safe to be converted to MPC. This limitation will soon disappear using precompilation or embedded virtual machines. Another evolution of MPC will concern a full implementation of the OpenMP standard, with an extension of MPC's scheduling policy to OpenMP-related tasks. With the support of the three most widely used parallel APIs[5], MPC will then be able to address most parallel computer codes, offering efficient scheduling, memory allocation, NUMA locality and loadbalancing on today and tomorrow architectures.

References

1. Cappello, F., Etiemble, D.: MPI versus MPI+OpenMP on the IBM SP for the NAS benchmarks. SuperComputing (2000)
2. Smith, L., Bull, M.: Development of mixed mode MPI/OpenMP applications. Scientific Programming (2001)
3. Van der Steen, A.: Overview of recent supercomputers (2006)
4. Liu, J., Chandrasekaran, B., Jiang, J., Kini, S., Yu, W., Buntinas, D., Wyckoff, P., Panda, D.: Performance comparison of MPI implementations over InfiniBand Myrinet and Quarics (2003)
5. Hoeflinger, J.: Extending OpenMP* to clusters (2006)

---

[5] MPI 1.0, POSIX Thread and (planed) OpenMP 1.0.

6. Lee, J., Sato, M., Boku, T.: Design and implementation of OpenMPD: An OpenMP-like programming language for distributed memory systems. In: Chapman, B.M., Zheng, W., Gao, G.R., Sato, M., Ayguadé, E., Wang, D. (eds.) IWOMP 2007. LNCS, vol. 4935. Springer, Heidelberg (2008)
7. Smith, L., Kent, P.: Development and performances of a mixed OpenMP/MPI quantum monte carlo code. Concurrency: Practice and Experience (2000)
8. Kalé, L.: The virtualization model of parallel programming: runtime optimizations and the state of art. In: LACSI (2002)
9. Huang, C., Lawlor, O., V., K.: Adaptive MPI. In: Proceedings of the 16th International Workshop on Languages and Compilers for Parallel Computing (2003)
10. Demaine, E.: A Threads-Only MPI implementation for the development of parallel programming. In: Proceedings of the 11th International Symposium on High Performance Computing Systems (1997)
11. Pérache, M.: Contribution à l'élaboration d'environnements de programmation dédiés au calcul scientifique hautes performances. PhD thesis, Bordeaux 1 University (2006)
12. Namyst, R.: PM2: un environnement pour une conception portable et une exécution efficace des applications parallèlles irrégulières. PhD thesis, Lille 1 university (1997)
13. Abt, B., Desai, S., Howell, D., Perez-Gonzalet, I., McCraken, D.: Next Generation POSIX Threading Project (2002),
http://www-124.ibm.com/developerworks/oss/pthread
14. Berger, E., McKinley, K., Blumofe, R., Wilson, P.: Hoard: a scalable memory allocator for multithreaded applications. In: International Conference on Architectural Support for Programming Languages and Operating Systems (ASPLOS-IX) (2000)
15. Torrellas, J., Lam, M.S., L., H.J.: False sharing and spatial locality in multiprocessor caches. IEEE Transaction on Computers (1994)
16. Berger, E., Zorn, B., McKinley, K.: Composing high-performance memory allocators. In: Proceedings of the ACM SIGPLAN conferance on Programming Language Design and Implementation (2001)
17. Del Pino, S., Despres, B., Have, P., Jourdren, H., Piserchia, P.F.: 3d finite volume simulation of acoustic waves in the earth atmosphere. Computer and fluids (submitted)
18. Jourdren, H.: HERA: a hydrodynamic AMR platform for multi-physics simulations. In: Adaptive mesh refinement - theory and applications, LNCSE (2005)

Topic 2: Performance Prediction and Evaluation

Francisco Almeida[*], Michael Gerndt[*], Adolfy Hoisie[*], and Martin Schulz[*]

In recent years, a range of performance evaluation methodologies and tools has been developed for evaluating, designing, and modeling of parallel and distributed systems. The aim of Topic 2, Performance Prediction and Evaluation, is to bring together system designers and researchers involved with qualitative and quantitative evaluation of large scale parallel machines, Grids, and, especially, multicore architectures suffering from contention for critical resources. Of particular interest is work forming a bridge between theory and practice as well as reporting on success or failure of current approaches.

The main topics are:

- Performance evaluation of large scale systems
- Performance optimizations
- System measurement and monitoring
- Advanced simulation tools and techniques
- Hybrid models
- Verification and validation
- Scheduling and routing in distributed systems
- Memory analysis and modeling

This year we received over 34 papers from which we selected 13 for presentation at the conference. We would like to thank all the authors for submitting to topic 2. We would also like to thank all the reviewers who did a tremendous work in providing four reviews for each paper. Since we could accept only a small number of papers, we selected, based on the reviews, the best 13 papers. In addition, one of these papers was also selected for the best paper awards of the conference.

---

[*] Topic Chairs.

Directory-Based Metadata Optimizations for Small Files in PVFS

Michael Kuhn, Julian Kunkel, and Thomas Ludwig

Ruprecht-Karls-Universität Heidelberg
Im Neuenheimer Feld 348, 69120 Heidelberg, Germany
michael.kuhn@stud.uni-heidelberg.de
http://pvs.informatik.uni-heidelberg.de/

Abstract. Modern file systems maintain extensive metadata about stored files. While this usually is useful, there are situations when the additional overhead of such a design becomes a problem in terms of performance. This is especially true for parallel and cluster file systems, because due to their design every metadata operation is even more expensive.

In this paper several changes made to the parallel cluster file system PVFS are presented. The changes are targeted at the optimization of workloads with large numbers of small files. To improve metadata performance, PVFS was modified such that unnecessary metadata is not managed anymore.

Several tests with a large quantity of files were done to measure the benefits of these changes. The tests have shown that common file system operations can be sped up by a factor of two even with relatively few changes.

1 Introduction

There are cases when many small files must be stored in a cluster file system. For each file additional metadata like ownership, permissions and timestamps is stored. If these files are accessed frequently, metadata performance plays an important role, therefore a reduction of the number of metadata operations should be considered. Also, if they are only stored temporarily for subsequent processing and deleted afterwards, most metadata is not really important. There are also cases when metadata does not need to be stored, because it is either available somewhere else – for example, in a database, maybe even with extended information – or simply not interesting. This can be used to further increase the performance, because much metadata overhead can be avoided.

Several other approaches can be taken to increase metadata performance, either by focusing on individual file system operations or by trying to improve the overall scalability. One such approach for individual file system operations is presented in [1]. The authors only consider file creation and evaluate multiple strategies to speed up this operation. This includes compound operations and pre-allocation of handles and datafiles. More general approaches are also possible. In [2] a combination of hashing and caching of parent directory permissions is implemented to reduce the communication overhead. On the other hand, in [3] metadata performance is optimized by dynamically partitioning the metadata of the file system tree into subtrees to distribute the load according to the current workload. In contrast, the changes presented in this paper simply remove all metadata. However, for reasons presented in section 3, this effectively makes striping of file data impossible, therefore these optimizations are only useful for small files.

The following sections introduce our concept of the optimizations. Optimizations are done to three basic file system operations, as shown in section 2, that is, only individual file system operations are considered, not the overall metadata design. This section also gives an overview of the internal structure of the file system provided by PVFS. In section 4 the actual impact on performance in terms of execution time is evaluated with a relatively simple benchmark program, which simulates parallel accesses.

2 Current Design of PVFS

PVFS is a parallel cluster file system, which supports multiple data and metadata servers. The whole file system is made up of several objects, each identified by a unique handle. Each server is responsible for a so-called handle range. Because these handle ranges are non-overlapping, each object is managed by exactly one server. To distribute the load, file data is striped across all available data servers with a default stripe size of 64 KByte. On file creation, the first data server is chosen randomly, then a round-robin scheme is used. File metadata however is not distributed. The metadata for any file is managed by exactly one metadata server. To determine which metadata server is responsible a hashing algorithm is employed. For more information on PVFS's internal design, also see [4]. Internally, PVFS distinguishes several different types of physical objects that can be stored and in turn combined to make up logical objects like files and directories. The most important physical objects are introduced here. Because there are physical and logical objects with the same name, the physical objects are always identified by the suffix "object" to ease the differentiation. For example, a (logical) file is made up of a (physical) metafile object and multiple (physical) datafile objects.

Metafile objects represent logical files. They are used to store file metadata like ownership and permissions, but also all handles of the datafile objects associated with this particular file. The total file size is not stored in the metafile object, but computed dynamically by adding up the respective file sizes of all datafile objects. This is done so that the metafile object does not have to be modified with each operation that changes the size of the file. Attributes stored for a metafile object include POSIX metadata, datafile distribution, datafile handles and the datafile count.

Datafile objects are used to store the actual data of files. They are distributed across all data servers. Metadata like ownership and permissions is not stored with each datafile object but rather with the metafile object the datafile object is associated with. This is done because each metafile object can reference multiple datafile objects. Attributes stored for a datafile object include the datafile size, which is implicitly available through the underlying file system.

Directory objects represent logical directories. They store directory metadata like ownership and permissions. They also store the handle of a directory data object, which in turn stores all files within the directory. So-called directory hints can be set on these directory objects. These hints affect all files within the directory. For example the datafile distribution and the number of datafile objects that should be allocated for a newly created file in this directory can be set. Attributes stored for a directory object include POSIX metadata, the directory entry count and directory hints like distribution name (`dist_name`) and parameters (`dist_params`) and datafile count.

The directory hints are currently mostly used to control the distribution of file data across the data servers. For example, the hints `dist_name` and `dist_params` are used to automatically set a distribution function for every new file. Distribution functions control the way file data is striped. For example, one data server could receive twice the amount of data all other data servers receive. This could be used to balance the load if servers of different capacity are used. The `num_dfiles` hint is simply used to assign the number of datafile objects that should be used for a file. Normally one datafile object is created on each data server. This hint can be used to, for example, force that a file is striped only across two data servers. However, directory hints can be used to influence other behavior of objects within the directory they are set on.

Directory data objects store key-value pairs of the form `file_name`: `metafile_handle` to identify all files within the directory the directory data object is associated with. This indicates that the file represented by the metafile object with the handle `metafile_handle` is available as the file called `file_name` within this particular directory. Further information is not stored, because it is already available from the associated directory object. There exists a one-to-one mapping between directory objects and directory data objects, that is, each directory object references exactly one directory data object and each directory data object is associated with exactly one directory object. This separation is done transparently to the client. If a client requests all directory entries, both objects are read by the server and returned as one. Attributes stored for directory data objects include the directory entries.

3 Metadata Optimizations

Based on PVFS's design, we implemented metadata optimizations especially targeted at small files for which striping does not improve performance considerably and can therefore be disabled. The optimizations can still be used for files of any size, but may even degrade performance for larger files. A new directory hint called `no_metafile` was introduced, which can be used to turn the metadata optimizations on and off on a per-directory basis.

The metafile object's purpose is to link together all datafile objects that belong to a particular file. It is obvious that the metafile object can be omitted if only one datafile object exists. For small files it is not really necessary to create multiple datafile objects, so in this particular use case there is no need for a metafile object. If only one datafile object is created for each file, the datafile object's handle can simply be put into the directory data object's list of directory entries. In particular, with these modifications, there now is only one datafile object and no metafile object. As can be seen, these metadata optimizations affect both the actual file and the directory in which it is located. Instead of a metafile object that references several datafile objects there now is only one datafile object that stores all file data. Also, the datafile object's handle is used instead of the metafile object's handle to reference the file in the list of directory entries. It is also worth mentioning that no common metadata is set on the datafile object at all. Common metadata like ownership and permissions could be set on the datafile object itself, since this metadata can be set on every object. At the moment, this is not done for performance reasons, because another message would need to be sent to the appropriate data server to retrieve this information. Another possible approach would be the use of the parent directory's metadata.

With these changes made, however, several problems have to be considered. The limit of one datafile object per file must be enforced, otherwise the file system ends up corrupt: Other datafile objects would not be referenced by any metafile object or directory entry and therefore be lost. The client and server also expect a metafile object to be present. This metafile object stores all metadata of a file, so this information must be faked in some way. On the other hand, the following advantages become apparent. No metadata server has to be contacted if a file needs to be read or written. Only one data server needs to be contacted for each file. Additionally, the total file size is available directly, avoiding expensive computation. This even applies to small files, since the default striping size is only 64 KByte, and therefore even a small file of size 1 MByte is striped across 16 data servers, if available.

This also has impact on the file system semantics, because certain metadata is no longer stored at all. However, since the metadata optimizations are implemented as a directory hint, users must explicitly enable them and therefore should know what to expect. Consequently, if these metadata optimizations are not activated, they do not influence the normal operation of PVFS in any way. Also, file data is now only stored on one data server, which decreases performance for larger files. Since the metadata optimizations are to be used with small files, however, this is to be expected. In theory, if the metadata optimizations are enabled for some files, it could be possible for other users to access and modify these files, because no ownership information and permissions are available, thus rendering permission checks useless. However, an initial analysis shows that PVFS clients can send arbitrary credentials and therefore effectively circumvent all permission checks anyway.

3.1 File System Operations

Three basic file system operations are adapted to make use of these optimizations. Each of these operations is internally split into several smaller steps that are executed consecutively by a state machine. A reduction of the number of these steps increases performance, therefore it is now analyzed which of these steps can be skipped safely. Even though only these three file system operations are adapted and examined here, all other common file system operations – like copying or moving a file – work, too. However, these three are best suited to demonstrate the metadata optimizations, because other file system operations include additional overhead. For example, when copying a file, obviously the actual file data has to be transferred as well.

The following steps are necessary to create a new file in a directory: (i) get the directory's attributes, (ii) create the metafile object, (iii) create the datafile objects, (iv) set the metafile object's attributes, (v) create a directory entry for the file. To implement the metadata optimizations steps two and four are skipped. Also, it is enforced that only one datafile object is created. While creating the directory entry the handle of this single datafile object is used instead of the metafile object's handle.

The following steps are necessary to list the metadata of a file: (i) get the metafile object's attributes, (ii) get the file size of each datafile object. Since there is no metafile object anymore, step one is skipped. Also, only one datafile object exists and therefore only one data server has to be contacted to request the file size. The metadata usually stored as the metafile object's attributes is faked.

The following steps are necessary to remove a file from a directory: (i) remove the file's directory entry, (ii) get the metafile object's attributes, (iii) remove the datafile objects, (iv) remove the metafile object. Again, as there is no metafile object step four is skipped. Step two can not be skipped, because it is needed to determine if a file was created with the `no_metafile` hint set or not.

4 Evaluation

To measure the benefits of the changes described in the previous chapters a relatively simple benchmark program was designed. The program creates, lists and removes a big number of files in a relatively flat directory hierarchy. To simulate several different environments the number of concurrently accessing clients and the underlying storage are varied. Moderate load is simulated by only one client accessing the file system, while operation of five concurrent clients simulates heavy load. The clients are independent instances of the benchmark program. To observe the influence of disk latency, PVFS's storage space is put into a normal directory on an `ext3` partition and in RAM, that is, its own `tmpfs` partition. This is especially important as PVFS – in its default configuration – forces metadata modifications to disk. Consequently, disk latency plays an important role in the overall performance.

4.1 Environment

Five machines from our evaluation cluster are used. Two machines act as data servers, another two as metadata servers and a fifth machine is used for the clients. Each machine is equipped with two Intel Xeon 2.0 GHz, 1 GByte RAM, an ATA disk and a 1 GBit/s network interface.

The numbers shown below represent average values collected over at least five runs of the benchmark program. Apart from setting the no_metafile directory hint all tests were done with an unmodified default configuration of PVFS.

4.2 File Creation

The benchmark program creates 100 child directories in a single parent directory and populates each with 500 files. Only the time needed to create these 50,000 files is measured. To exclude the influence of the io client state machine, files of size 0 are created.

Figure 1a shows the time each client needs to create 50,000 files, once with the no_metafile directory hint set and once without it. PVFS's storage space is put in a normal directory on an ext3 partition. In figure 1b the same values as in the last one are shown, except that PVFS's storage space is put on its own tmpfs partition, thus removing any latencies the disk introduces.

As can be seen in figure 1a, if only one client writes to the file system and the no_metafile directory hint is set, the time needed to create the 50,000 files decreases to about 50% of the time needed to create them without the hint. However, if five clients work concurrently the time decreases to about 40% of the original. The speedup increase is probably due to the fact that metadata writes are by default synchronous. However, these are exactly the operations that are skipped if no_metafile is set and thus the server can process more requests in parallel instead of waiting for the slow disk. Since this time the network is used, it can be seen that disk latency still plays an important role in terms of performance, even with the additional network latency.

As shown in figure 1b the speedup with five concurrent clients is less drastic on tmpfs, because no disk seek times could be avoided.

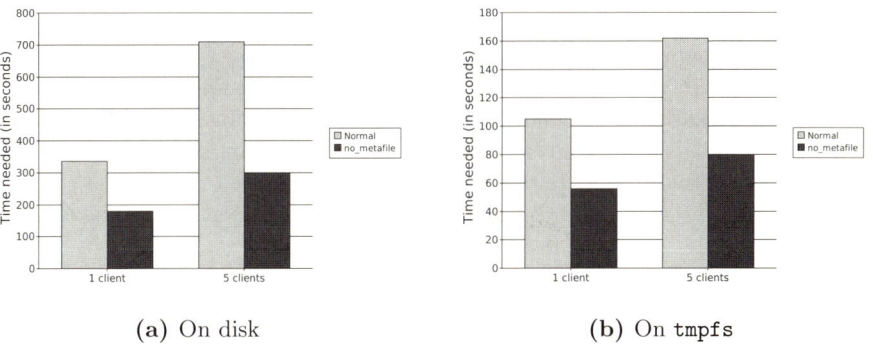

Fig. 1. File creation

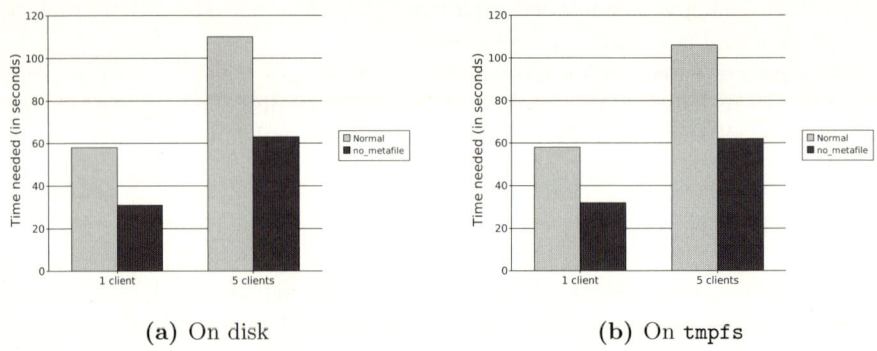

Fig. 2. File listing

4.3 File Listing

The benchmark program lists the files in each directory such that details like permissions, ownership etc. are shown, too. This is done in order to force the client to contact each datafile's server, because otherwise only the names would need to be fetched from the metadata server. In particular the -l flag of pvfs2-ls is used.

Figure 2a shows the time each client needs to list the 50,000 files, once with and once without the no_metafile directory hint set. PVFS's storage space is put in a normal directory on an ext3 partition. In figure 2b the same values as in the last one are shown, except that PVFS's storage space is put on its own tmpfs partition, thus removing any latencies the disk introduces.

As can be seen in figure 2a, if only one client reads from the file system and the no_metafile directory hint is set, the time needed to list the 50,000 files decreases to about 50% of the time needed to list them without the hint. With five concurrent clients the time is slightly higher at about 55% of the original. This is one of the rare cases where an increase in client concurrency does not improve the speedup. Since only metadata reads are needed for this file system operation and therefore no slow metadata writes could be skipped, there are no huge performance gains possible by reducing the impact of disk latency. In contrast to metadata writes, these metadata reads can be sped up by using the file system cache. The optimized version only does one metadata read instead of two metadata reads and since they usually are fast because of caching, network latency outweighs the benefits of the one skipped metadata read.

As shown in figure 2b, the times on tmpfs are nearly identical to the ones on ext3 as presented in figure 2a.

4.4 File Removal

The benchmark program removes all files and directories such that the file system is in the same state as before the benchmark was started. Only the time needed to remove the 50,000 files is measured.

Figure 3a shows the time each client needs to remove the 50,000 files, once with and once without the `no_metafile` directory hint set. PVFS's storage space is put in a normal directory on an `ext3` partition. In figure 3b the same values as in the last one are shown, except that PVFS's storage space is put on its own `tmpfs` partition, thus removing any latencies the disk introduced.

As can be seen in figure 3a, if only one client at a time is running and the `no_metafile` directory hint is set, the time needed to remove the 50,000 files decreases to about 60% of the time needed to remove them without the hint. However, if five clients run concurrently the time decreases to about 40% of the original. The speedup increase is probably due to the fact that metadata writes are by default synchronous. However, these are exactly the operations that are skipped if `no_metafile` is set and thus the server can process more requests in parallel instead of waiting for the slow disk.

As shown in figure 3b the speedup with five concurrent clients is less drastic on `tmpfs`, because no disk seek times could be avoided.

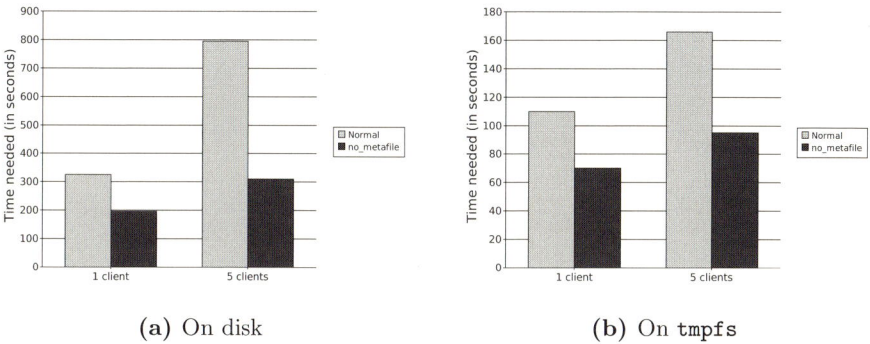

(a) On disk (b) On `tmpfs`

Fig. 3. File removal

4.5 Summary

Figure 4 shows an overview of the efficiency of the metadata optimizations. For each operation – that is, creation, listing and removal – the percentage of time needed for completion with the `no_metafile` hint set is shown in comparison to the time needed without it. Also, for each operation the efficiencies for a varying number of concurrent clients and underlying file systems are shown in detail. For a visualization of the changes caused by the metadata optimizations in the internal workflow of PVFS and more results, also see [5]. For more information on the used visualization environment, see [6].

As can be seen in figure 4, only disk-bound operations benefit from an increase in the concurrency, because of network effects. The benefit is less pronounced on `tmpfs` partitions, since in this case there are no slow synchronous disk operations that could be skipped. As shown in section 2 about half of the work in each of the three file system operations is skipped, therefore the performance gains are within expected boundaries or – as is the case with file removal – even surpass the expectations of doubling the performance.

Figure 4 shows that the metadata optimizations reduce the time needed for any of the affected operations – that is, file creation, listing and removal – to about 50–60%, independent of the underlying file system. The disk-bound operations especially benefit from these optimizations. If the underlying file system is on disk – which should be the normal case – an increase in client concurrency even reduces the time needed to 30–40%. Therefore the optimizations are especially useful for parallel access from multiple clients.

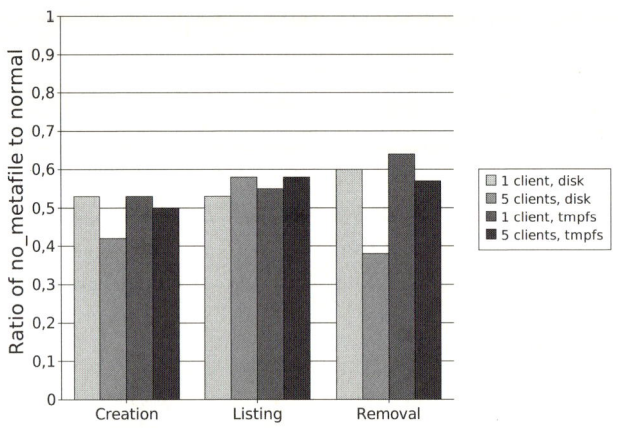

Fig. 4. Efficiency of the optimized file system operations

5 Conclusion and Future Work

While the presented metadata optimizations do not offer a speedup of several orders of magnitude, the time needed for some common file system operations could be reduced to about 50%. This achievement is quite satisfying, considering the relatively small amount of changes made. Also, since about 50% of the work in each affected file system operation is skipped, this improvements are well within expected boundaries. On the other hand, these metadata optimizations change the file system semantics, because certain metadata is simply not stored. However, because the optimizations must be enabled explicitly and do not influence the normal operation of PVFS, this is not much of a concern. The metadata optimizations are not yet ready to be used in production environments, because of several issues with their implementation.

It would be interesting to do benchmarks with even more concurrent clients to see if this increases the efficiency of the optimizations even further. Varying the number of data servers and metadata servers could also prove to be interesting, because the metadata optimizations reduce the load on the metadata servers. This load reduction is simply due to the fact that there are no more metafile objects, which would otherwise be managed by the metadata servers.

Also, the actual implementation is based on the modified version of PVFS from [4], which in turn is based on a development version between versions 2.6.2 and 2.7.0 of PVFS. This version in turn is based on the last official PVFS release version that was available at the time, which is already some months old. The reason for this is that the modified version offers enhanced tracing capabilities used for visualization. To enable wider testing or even integration into PVFS, the implementation would need to be updated to the current development version, which features a significant number of changes.

In the future, it would be useful for file systems to provide some mechanism to allow users to tune file system semantics according to their needs, especially concerning metadata operations and thus metadata performance. One first step in this direction was presented in this paper.

References

1. Devulapalli, A., Wyckoff, P.: File Creation Strategies in a Distributed Metadata File System. In: Proceedings of IPDPS 2007, Long Beach, CA (March 2007)
2. Brandt, S.A., Miller, E.L., Long, D.D.E., Xue, L.: Efficient Metadata Management in Large Distributed Storage Systems. In: Proceedings of the 20th IEEE / 11th NASA Goddard Conference on Mass Storage Systems and Technologies, San Diego, CA (April 2003)
3. Weil, S.A., Pollack, K.T., Brandt, S.A., Miller, E.L.: Dynamic Metadata Management for Petabyte-scale File Systems. In: Proceedings of SC 2004, Pittsburgh, PA (November 2004)
4. Kunkel, J.M.: Towards Automatic Load Balancing of a Parallel File System with Subfile Based Migration. Master's thesis, Ruprecht-Karls-Universität Heidelberg, Institute of Computer Science (July 2007)
5. Kuhn, M.: Directory-Based Metadata Optimizations for Small Files in PVFS. Bachelor's Thesis, Ruprecht-Karls-Universität Heidelberg (September 2007)
6. Ludwig, T., Krempel, S., Kuhn, M., Kunkel, J.M., Lohse, C.: Analysis of the MPI-IO Optimization Levels with the PIOViz Jumpshot Enhancement. In: Cappello, F., Herault, T., Dongarra, J. (eds.) PVM/MPI 2007. LNCS, vol. 4757, pp. 213–222. Springer, Heidelberg (2007)

Caspian: A Tunable Performance Model for Multi-core Systems

Abbas Eslami Kiasari[1,2], Hamid Sarbazi-Azad[2,1], and Shaahin Hessabi[2]

[1] IPM School of Computer Science, Tehran, Iran
[2] Sharif University of Technology, Tehran, Iran
kiasari@ipm.ir, {hessabi,azad}@sharif.edu

Abstract. Performance evaluation is an important engineering tool that provides valuable feedback on design choices in the implementation of multi-core systems such as parallel systems, multicomputers, and Systems-on-Chip (SoCs). The significant advantage of analytical models over simulation is that they can be used to obtain performance results for large systems under different configurations and working conditions which may not be feasible to study using simulation on conventional computers due to the excessive computation demands. We present Caspian[1], a novel analytic performance model, aimed to minimize prediction cost, while providing prediction accuracy. This is accomplished by using a G/G/1 priority queueing model which is used for arbitrary network topology with wormhole routing under arbitrary traffic pattern. The accuracy of this model is examined through extensive simulation results.

Keywords: Performance evaluation, Analytical model, Multi-core systems, G/G/1 queueing model.

1 Introduction

Multi-core system designers are constantly confronted with the challenge of designing high performance system while simultaneously meeting constraints such as communication latency, network throughput and design costs [4]. The problem of identifying multi-core system configurations is further exacerbated for the following reasons. First, multi-core systems are evolving into increasingly complex systems with a large number and type of components such as processors, memories, routers, and queues. As a consequence, designers must deal with a large architectural design space consisting of several interacting parameters. Furthermore, new workloads are composed of a large spectrum of programs with widely differing characteristics. System designers have addressed these problems in the past by exploring the design space using detailed simulations. However, this approach has high simulation costs due to the low speed of cycle-accurate simulators.

---

[1] The Caspian Sea is the largest enclosed body of water on Earth by area, variously classed as the world's largest lake or a full-fledged sea. It lies between the southern areas of the Russian Federation and northern Iran [Wikipedia].

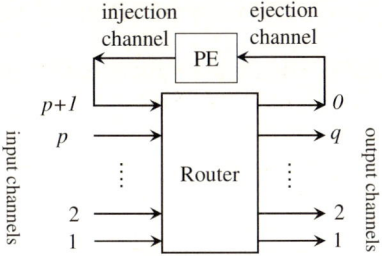

Fig. 1. A general structure for a node in a generic multi-core system

Performance models are frequently employed by multi-core system vendors in their design of future systems. Typically, engineers construct a performance model for one or two key applications, and then compare future technology options based on performance model projections. An analytical model that accurately characterizes the relationship between multi-core system performance and various implementation parameters would, in theory, obviate the need for detailed, expensive, and time consuming simulations. As an alternative to analytical models, in this research a tunable analytical modeling technique for multi-core system performance has been proposed and evaluated. The proposed approach, which is developed for wormhole flow control, provides buffer utilization, channels throughput, achievable throughput of the network, average waiting time for each channel, and average packet latency. These metrics can be conveniently used for design and optimization purposes, as well as obtaining quick performance estimates.

The main contribution of the work is a novel performance model, Caspian, for multi-core systems which can generalize the traditional delay models. Finally, the proposed model provides not only aggregate performance metrics, such as average latency and throughput, but also useful feedback about the network behavior. Hence, it can be invoked in any optimization loop for multi-core systems for fast and accurate performance estimations.

2 Performance Analysis

If the performance is measured in terms of average packet latency, then maximizing the performance is equivalent to minimizing the end-to-end packet latency. In this section, we derive an analytical performance model for multi-core systems using a G/G/1 [2] priority queueing model. It can be used for any arbitrary network topology with wormhole routing under any arbitrary traffic pattern.

2.1 Assumptions and Notations

We consider input buffered routers with $p+1$ input channels, $q+1$ output channels, and target wormhole flow control under deterministic routing algorithm. This form of

Table 1. Parameter notation

Symbol	Description	
t_r	Spent time for packet routing decision (*cycles*)	
t_s	Delay of crossbar switch (*cycles*)	
t_w	Spent time for transmitting a flit between two adjacent router (*cycles*)	
M	The size of a packet (*flits*)	
L	The average packet latency (*cycles*)	*Platform specific parameters*
$\mathcal{R}$	Routing function	
R^N	The router located at address N	
PE^N	The processing element located at address N	
IC_i^N	The ith input channel of router R^N	
OC_j^N	The jth output channel of router R^N	
S_j^N	set of all source nodes for packets which pass through OC_j^N	
D_j^N	set of all destination nodes for packets which pass through OC_j^N	
$P^{S \to D}$	The probability of a packet generated by PE^S to be delivered to PE^D	
α^N	The average packet injection rate of PE^N (*packets/cycle*)	
$\lambda_{i \to j}^N$	The average packet rate from IC_i^N to OC_j^N (*packets/cycle*)	
λ_j^N	The average packet rate to OC_j^N (*packets/cycle*) $\left(\lambda_j^N = \sum_i \lambda_{i \to j}^N\right)$	
μ_j^N	The average service rate of OC_j^N (*packets/cycle*)	*Application specific parameters*
b_j^N	The average service time of OC_j^N (*cycles*) $\left(\overline{b_j^N} = 1/\mu_j^N\right)$	
$\overline{(b_j^N)^2}$	The second moment of the service time of OC_j^N	
$C_{B_j^N}$	The CV (coefficient of variation) for service time of the OC_j^N	
$C_{A_{i \to j}^N}$	The CV for interarrival time of packets from IC_i^N to OC_j^N	
$\rho_{i \to j}^N$	The fraction of time that the OC_j^N is occupied by packets from IC_i^N	
$W_{i \to j}^N$	The average waiting time for a packet from IC_i^N to OC_j^N (*cycles*)	

routing results in a simpler router implementation and has been used in many practical systems [3]. So in this research we use the deterministic routing for deadlock free routing. The structure of a single node is depicted in Fig. 1. Each node contains a router and a Processing Element (PE) capable of generating and/or receiving packets.

Packets are injected into the network on input port $p+1$ (injection channel) and leave the network from output port 0 (ejection channel). Generally, each channel

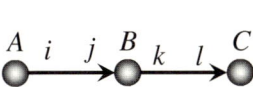
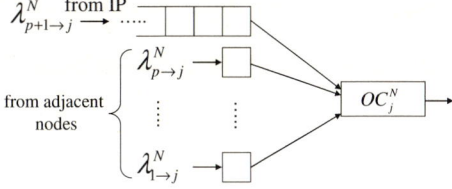

Fig. 2. A two hop packet from node A to node C

Fig. 3. Queueing model of a channel of an arbitrary topology

connects output port j of node N to input port i of node M. So, we denote this channel OC_j^N (jth output channel of router N) or IC_i^M (ith input channel of router M). Messages are broken into some packets of fixed length of M flits, as listed in Table 1 along with other parameters. The routing decision delay for a packet, crossing time of a flit over the crossbar switch, and transfer time of a flit across a wire between two neighboring routers are t_r, t_s, and t_w, respectively. Also the transfer time of a flit across the injection and ejection channels are considered to be t_w.

Let $P^{S \to D}$ be the probability of packet transmission from the source node at router S (R^S) to the destination node at router D (R^D). Likewise, the traffic arrival rate of the header flits from IC_i^N to OC_j^N is given by $\lambda_{i \to j}^N$ packets/cycle. Also we assume that the packet injection process to the router R^N has a general distribution with mean value of α^N packets/cycle. The average packet latency (L) is used as the performance metric. Similar to previous works [1], [7], [8], we assume that the packet latency spans the instant when the packet is created, to the time when the packet is delivered to the destination node, including the queuing time spent at the source. We also assume that the packets are consumed immediately once they reach their destination nodes.

2.2 Analytical Model

In Fig. 2 consider a packet which is generated in IP^A, and reaches its destination (IP^C) after traversing R^A, R^B, and R^C. The latency of this packet ($L^{A \to C}$) consists of two parts: the latency of header flit ($L_h^{A \to C}$) and the latency of body flits (L_b). In other words

$$L^{A \to C} = L_h^{A \to C} + L_b \qquad (1)$$

$L_h^{A \to C}$ is the time from when the packet is created in IP^A, until when the header flit is reached to the IP^C, including the queueing time spent at the source node and intermediate nodes. In Fig. 2, $L_h^{A \to C}$ can be computed as

$$\begin{aligned} L_h^{A \to C} = W_{p+1 \to i}^A + t_w + t_r + t_s \\ + t_w + t_r + W_{j \to k}^B + t_s \\ + t_w + t_r + W_{l \to 0}^C + t_s + t_w \end{aligned} \qquad (2)$$

where $W_{i \to j}^{N}$ is the mean waiting time for a packet from IC_i^N to OC_j^N. Note that in Fig. 2 the channel between B and C can be addressed with OC_k^B or IC_l^C. Since the body flits follow the header flit in a pipelined fashion, L_b is given by

$$L_b = (M-1)(t_s + t_w) \tag{3}$$

The only unknown parameter for computing the latency is $W_{i \to j}^{N}$. This value can be calculated in a straightforward manner using a queuing model. The basic element in the model is a G/G/1 priority queue (the customer interarrival time and server's service time follow general distributions and queues have one server to provide the service). A router is primarily modeled based on nonpreemptive priority queuing system [11]

Now, let us consider, for instance, the jth output channel of R^N (OC_j^N). As can be seen in Fig. 3, this channel is modeled as a server in a priority queueing system with $p+1$ classes (IC_1^N to IC_{p+1}^N), with arrival rates $\lambda_{i \to j}^N$ ($1 \le i \le p+1$), served by one server (OC_j^N) of service rate μ_j^N. Note that since all incoming packets are similar, the service times of all packets are equal. Both interarrival and service times are independent and identically distributed with arbitrary distributions.

Since the input channels (except injection channel) have one flit rooms, we should compute the average waiting time for the head of class i. Using a technique similar to that employed in literature for priority queues [2], [11] we can write

$$W_{i \to j}^{N} = \begin{cases} \overline{R_j^N}/(1-\rho_{i \to j}^N), & i = p+1, \\ \dfrac{1+\rho_{i+1 \to j}^N - \sigma_{i+2 \to j}^N}{1-\sigma_{i+1 \to j}^N} W_{i+1 \to j}^N, & 1 \le i \le p. \end{cases} \tag{4}$$

where $\overline{R_j^N}$ is the residual service time of OC_j^N seen by an incoming header flit and $\sigma_{i \to j}^N = \sum_{k=i}^{p+1} \rho_{i \to j}^N$. In a G/G/1 queueing system, $\overline{R_j^N}$ is approximated by [2]:

$$\overline{R_j^N} \approx \sum_{i=0}^{p} \rho_{i \to j}^N \frac{C_{A_{i \to j}^N}^2 + C_{B_j^N}^2}{2\mu_j^N} \tag{5}$$

Since we do not have enough insight about the first and second moments of interarrival time, we suppose that $C_{A_{i \to j}^N}$ is constant for all input channels in the network and equal to the coefficient of variation (CV) of the arrival process to network ($C_{A_{i \to j}^N} = C_A$). So, we can rewrite Eq. (5) as

$$\overline{R_j^N} \approx \frac{1}{2}\lambda_j^N \left(\overline{b_j^N}\right)^2 \left(C_A^2 + C_{B_j^N}^2\right) \tag{6}$$

Therefore, to compute $W_{i \to j}^{N}$ we must calculate the average arrival rate over OC_{j}^{N} (λ_{j}^{N}), and also first and second moments of the service time of OC_{j}^{N}. Assuming the network is not overloaded, the arrival rate over OC_{j}^{N} can be calculated using the following general equation

$$\lambda_{j}^{N} = \sum_{\forall S} \sum_{\forall D} \alpha^{S} \times P^{S \to D} \times \mathcal{R}\left(S \to D, OC_{j}^{N}\right) \tag{7}$$

In Eq. (7), the routing function $\mathcal{R}\left(S \to D, OC_{j}^{N}\right)$ equals 1 if the packet from PE^{S} to PE^{D} passes through OC_{j}^{N}; it equals 0 otherwise. Note that we assume a deterministic routing algorithm, thus the function of $\mathcal{R}\left(S \to D, OC_{j}^{N}\right)$ can be predetermined.

Although λ_{j}^{N} can be computed exactly for all topologies by Eq. (7), service time moments of the output channels cannot be computed in a direct manner by a general formula for any topology and any routing algorithm. To compute the moments of the service time of the output channels we first divide the channels into some groups based on their routing order and then an index is assigned to the groups opposite of the routing order, from ejection channel to injection channel. Then, we estimate the first two moments of the service time for the output channels. Determination of the channel service time moments starts at the ejection channel and works backward to the source of the packets. Therefore, the contention delay from lower numbered groups can then be thought of as adding to the service time of packets on higher numbered groups. In other words, to determine the waiting time of channels in group k, we must calculate the waiting time of all channels in group $k-1$. This approach is dependent to the topology and routing algorithm. Here we derive an analytical performance model for for e-cube routing [4] in a hypercube network. Due to the popularity of the hypercube network for multicomputer vendors [4], our analysis focuses on this topology but the modeling approach used here can be equally applied for other topologies after few changes in the model.

We consider a system which is composed of 2^n processing cores interconnected by an n dimensional hypercube (H_n). Packets are injected into the network on crossbar input port $n+1$ and leave on output port 0. A dimension-i channel connects output port i of a node to input port i of another node that differs only in the ith bit of its address. (In this paper, the least significant bit is bit 1). The $n+1$ input channels of each router are represented with $n+1$ (injection channel) and 1 to n (dimension 1 to n). Also these channels are assigned to priority classes from index $n+1$ (the highest priority) to 1 (the lowest priority), respectively. It is assumed that a static total ordering of input channel priorities exists. The packet arriving on the higher priority input channel will receive use of the crossbar output first. E-cube routing specifies that a packet sent between two nodes be first routed in the most significant dimension in which the addresses differ, then in the next most significant dimension in which they differ, etc. Finally, it is fed to the destination node via ejection channel. By restricting the order in which the dimensions may be traversed, the possibility of cycles is removed, eliminating deadlock.

We divide the output channels of the hypercube network into $n+2$ groups based on their dimension numbers. Injection and ejection channels are located in group $n+1$ and 0, respectively, and physical channels are located in groups 1 to n. In the ejection channel (group 0) of R^N the header flit and body flits are accepted in t_w and L_b cycles, respectively. So, we can write $\overline{b_0^N} = t_w + L_b$ and since all packets have the same service time, there is not any variation in the service times. In other words $C_{B_0^N} = 0$. Now, we can determine the value of $W_{i \to 0}^N$ where $1 \le i \le n$.

The moments of service time for OC_j^N, $j > 0$, are obtained by tracing each of the 2^{j-1} paths from output j to the network outputs (ejection channels). Since each of these paths is not equally probable, the service time moments are weighted mean of each path service time. If S_j^N and D_j^N be the sets of all possible source and destination nodes for a packet which passes through OC_j^N, respectively, a passing packet through OC_j^N are destined to $M \in D_j^N$ with the probability of $\sum_{\forall S \in S_j^N} P^{S \to M} / \sum_{\forall S \in S_j^N} \sum_{\forall D \in D_j^N} P^{S \to D}$. The contention delays along each path are random variables; however each is only a fraction of the packet length for all packet rates that can be sustained on the hypercube.

For example, consider the output channel in dimension 2 of R^0 (OC_2^0) in an n-dimensional hypercube. One possible path from OC_2^0 to a network output is directly to ejection channel of the adjacent node R^2, for an average service time of $L_1 = t_w + (t_r + W_{2 \to 0}^2 + t_s) + t_w + L_b$ where $W_{2 \to 0}^2$ was already computed. The second path from OC_2^0 to a network output is through dimension 1 of R^2 and ejection channel of R^3, for an average service time of $L_2 = t_w + (t_r + W_{2 \to 1}^2 + t_s) + t_w + (t_r + W_{1 \to 0}^3 + t_s) + t_w + L_b$ where $W_{1 \to 0}^3$ was already computed and $W_{2 \to 1}^2$ can be computed with the same approach. So, the first and second moments of the service time can be estimated as

$$\overline{b_2^0} = \frac{\sum_{\forall S \in S_2^0} P^{S \to 2}}{\sum_{\forall S \in S_2^0} \sum_{\forall D \in D_2^0} P^{S \to D}} L_1 + \frac{\sum_{\forall S \in S_2^0} P^{S \to 3}}{\sum_{\forall S \in S_2^0} \sum_{\forall D \in D_2^0} P^{S \to D}} L_2$$

and

$$\overline{(b_2^0)^2} = \frac{\sum_{\forall S \in S_2^0} P^{S \to 2}}{\sum_{\forall S \in S_2^0} \sum_{\forall D \in D_2^0} P^{S \to D}} L_1^2 + \frac{\sum_{\forall S \in S_2^0} P^{S \to 3}}{\sum_{\forall S \in S_2^0} \sum_{\forall D \in D_2^0} P^{S \to D}} L_2^2$$

Now, we are able to calculate the coefficient of variation of the service time in OC_2^0, $C_{B_2^0}^2 = \overline{(b_2^0)^2} / \overline{(b_2^0)}^2 - 1$, and then the mean waiting time for OC_2^0 seen by other channels ($W_{i \to 2}^0$, $i > 2$) can be computed with Eq. (4). After computing the mean waiting time of all channels in group 2, the mean waiting time for other output channels (channels in groups 3, 4, …, $n+1$) can be calculated using the same approach. Now, we can calculate the packet latency between any two nodes in the network by Eq. (1). The average packet latency is the weighted mean of these latencies as

$$L = \sum_{S=0}^{2^n-1} \sum_{D=0}^{2^n-1} P^{S \to D} \times L^{S \to D} \tag{8}$$

3 Model Validation

The proposed analytical model has been validated through a discrete-event simulator that mimics the behavior of the network at the flit level. To achieve a high accuracy in the simulation results, we use the batch means method [9] for simulation output analysis. There are 10 batches and each batch includes up to 500,000 packets depending on the traffic injection rate and network size. Statistics gathering was inhibited for the first batch to avoid distortions due to the startup transient. The standard deviation of latency measurements is less than 2% of the mean value.

For the destination address of each packet, we have considered the uniform and hotspot traffic patterns [10]. Packets are transferred to the local PE through the ejection channel as soon as they arrive at their destinations. Nodes generate packets independently of each other, and which follows a Poisson process. It means that the time between two successive packet generations in a PE is distributed exponentially, so for the first time we run the model program with $C_A = 1$. The Poisson model simplicity made it widely used in many performance analysis studies, and there are a large number of papers in very diverse application domains that are based on this stochastic assumption [5].

Using the proposed performance model, the CV of the interarrival time (C_A) can be adjusted to account for conformity between model and simulation results. Fig. 4 shows the flow chart used for tuning of the performance model. The model is run with various C_A until the predicted latency by the model is matched to its corresponding simulated value. The tuning procedure is run for the H_8 with $t_r = t_s = t_w = 1$ and $C_A = 1.0498$ is obtained for average packet generation rate of $\lambda = 0.045$ packets/cycle and packet length of $M = 32$ flits. Result of this tuned model has been presented in Fig. 5. The horizontal axis in the figure shows the traffic generation rate (packets/cycle) at each node while the vertical axis shows the mean packet latency (cycles). Tuned C_A is shown to give good quantitative agreement of model to simulation for a wide range of packet generation rate and packet length.

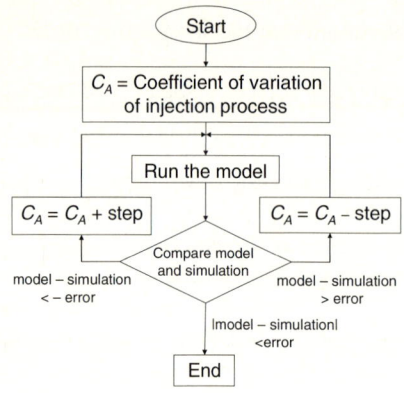
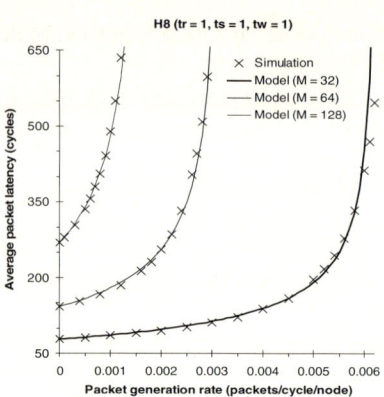

Fig. 4. Flow chart showing the strategy of the performance model tuning to simulation

Fig. 5. The average packet latency predicted by the tuned model against simulation results for an H_8

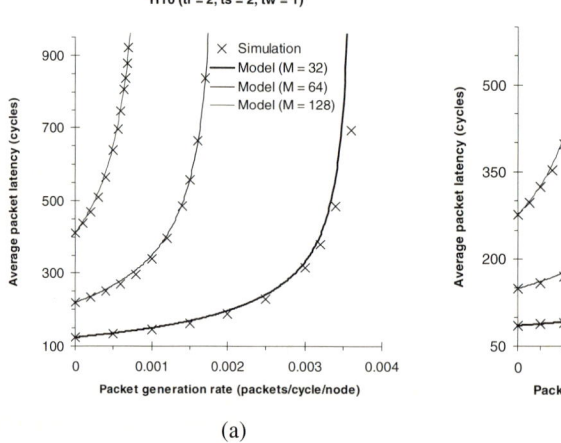
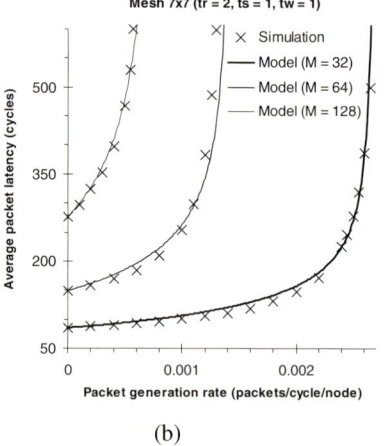

Fig. 6. The average packet latency predicted by the tuned model against simulation results for (a) H_{10}, and (b) 7x7 mesh network with hotspot traffic

Fig. 6(a) illustrates average packet latency predicted by the tuned model, plotted against simulation results for H_{10} network. ($C_A = 1.0035$). Furthermore to verify the model accuracy for other topologies and non-uniform traffic pattern, we have modeled a 7x7 mesh network under hotspot traffic [10]. According to hotspot traffic pattern, there is a hot node in the network to receive the packets. Each node sends packets to the hot node with probability h, and sends packets to other nodes with probability $1-h$. In our experiments, we consider the node 24 in the center of the network as a hot node with hotspot rate $h = 0.1$. The comparison results is shown in Fig. 6(b) ($C_A = 0.8653$).

In [6], we have used Caspian and presented a performance-aware mapping algorithm which maps the IPs onto a generic System-on-Chip architecture such that the average communication delay is minimized.

4 Conclusions and Future Work

A novel methodology for predicting the communication performance of multi-core systems was proposed. The choice of the hypercube and mesh networks as the underlying interconnection architecture serves mostly as an example. In fact, our methodology can be modified to arbitrary topologies by adapting the analytical models accordingly to the target topology. Moreover, although we have evaluated our algorithm only for multi-core systems with dimension order routing, the approach is general enough to be applied to other deterministic and oblivious routing schemes.

We plan to advance this research in several directions. One possible direction is to extend this approach to multi-core systems with realistic workloads. Another important extension is to accommodate interconnection networks that support adaptive routing. The main challenge comes from the difficulty involved in the calculation of the arrival rate for each channel as multiple routing paths are possible in adaptive routing. Finally, we are extending this work for routers with finite size buffers.

References

1. Aljundi, A.C., Dekeyser, J., Kechadi, M.T., Scherson, I.D.: A Universal Performance Factor for Multi-criteria Evaluation of Multistage Interconnection Networks. Future Generation Computer Systems 22(7), 794–804 (2006)
2. Bolch, G., Greiner, S., De Meer, H., Trivedi, K.S.: Queueing Networks and Markov Chains: Modeling and Performance Evaluation with Computer Science Applications, 2nd edn. John Wiley and Sons, Chichester (2006)
3. Duato, J.: Why Commercial Multicomputers Do Not Use Adaptive Routing. IEEE Technical Committee on Computer Architecture Newsletter, pp. 20–22 (1994)
4. Duato, J., Yalamanchili, C., Ni, L.: Interconnection Networks: An Engineering Approach. IEEE Computer Society Press, Los Alamitos (2003)
5. Hu, J., Ogras, U.Y., Marculescu, R.: System-level Buffer Allocation for Application-Specific Networks-on-chip Router Design. IEEE Transactions on Computer-Aided Design of Integrated Circuits and Systems 25(12), 2919–2933 (2006)
6. Kiasari, A.E., Hessabi, S., Sarbazi-Azad, H.: PERMAP: A Performance-Aware Mapping for Application-Specific SoCs. In: Proceedings of the Application-specific Systems, Architectures and Processors (2008)
7. Kiasari, A.E., Rahmati, D., Sarbazi-Azad, H., Hessabi, S.: A Markovian Performance Model for Networks-on-Chip. In: Proceedings of the Euromicro International Conference on Parallel, Distributed and Network-Based Processing, pp. 157–164 (2008)
8. Najafabadi, H.H., Sarbazi-Azad, H., Rajabzadeh, P.: Performance Modelling of Fully Adaptive Wormhole Routing in 2D Mesh-connected Multiprocessors. In: Proceedings of the International Symposium on Modelling, Analysis, and Simulation of Computer and Telecommunication Systems, pp. 528–534 (2004)
9. Pawlikowski, K.: Steady-State Simulation of Queueing Processes: A Survey of Problems and Solutions. ACM Computing Surveys 22(2), 123–170 (1990)
10. Sarbazi-Azad, H., Ould-Khaoua, M., Mackenzie, L.M.: Analytical Modeling of Wormhole-Routed k-Ary n-Cubes in the Presence of Hot-Spot Traffic. IEEE Transaction on Computers 50(7), 623–634 (2001)
11. Takagi, H.: Queueing analysis. Vacation and Priority Systems, vol. 1. North-Holland, Amsterdam (1991)

Performance Model for Parallel Mathematical Libraries Based on Historical Knowledgebase[*]

I. Salawdeh, E. César, A. Morajko, T. Margalef, and E. Luque

Departament d'Arquitectura de Computadors i Ssitemes Operatius, Universitat Autònoma de Barcelona, 08193 Bellaterra, Spain
Ihab.Salawdeh@caos.uab.es, {Eduardo.Cesar,Anna.Morajko, Tomas.Margalef,Emilio.Luque}@uab.es

Abstract. Scientific and mathematical parallel libraries offer a high level of abstraction to programmers. However, it is still difficult to select the proper parameters and algorithms to maximize the application performance. This work proposes a performance model for dynamically adjusting applications written with the PETSc library. This model is based on historical performance information and data mining techniques. Finally, we demonstrate the validity of the proposed model through real experimentations.

Keywords: Performance Model, Mathematical Performance, PETSc Performance, Dynamic mathematical model.

1 Introduction

Parallel processing has become attractive with the increase in processor speed and reduction in cost per computation unit. However, writing applications and developing software to solve mathematical problems using the parallel processing programming techniques, such as MPI[1] and PVM[2] is not easy, because of the complexity of the algorithms required to solve such problems, and the need for an elevated level of experience in writing high performance applications.

Mathematical and scientific libraries are helpful tools that provide many pre-implemented algorithms to solve mathematical problems. However, as there is no unique solution for all linear systems, many algorithms are usually provided to solve different problems. However, the performance of these algorithms depends on the nature of the problem to be solved.

Moreover, this performance may vary dynamically during the execution depending on the input data and the parameters of the solvers. For instance, in a PETSc[3] linear solver application the time needed to solve a tri-diagonal 10000x10000 matrix using the Richardson KSP and the Jacobi PC and a sparse memory data structure is more than 14 minutes, while the time needed to solve the same matrix using the Chevychev KSP, the block jacobi preconditioner, and dense memory data structure needs only 15 seconds. Consequently, the need for dynamic models that can help the developer to

---

[*] This work was supported by MEC under contracts TIN2004-03388 and TIN2007-64974.

choose between this huge set of library parameters and system configuration is in increase, as obtaining the best performance in such application is a key issue.

This work, aims to build intelligent performance models for parallel mathematical applications, based on a historical knowledgebase of performance behavior information, that can switch between the available mathematical algorithms, such as KSP solvers and preconditioners, and system specific parameters, such as the number of processors, automatically in order increase the application's performance.

To achieve this objective, we have developed a performance model for the PETSc mathematical library, which depending on the problem type, input data, and environmental parameters, chooses the most suitable solving parameter set: solving algorithm, preconditioner, and data structure to represent the problem data.

In this paper, we will first analyze PETSc applications in order to highlight the performance problems of this library, then we will discuss the proposed performance model and explain each one of its three components, subsequently we will validate our model by real case experiments followed by the related efforts and conclusions.

2 Performance Analysis for PETSc Applications

Mathematical libraries were developed to provide encapsulated and pre-implemented algorithms for the linear system solvers, which provide high level APIs that let the programmer to reuse these algorithms in the development of scientific applications without concerning neither about the communication policies between the processors nor the inner details of the algorithms.

In particular, PETSc or Portable Extensible Toolkit for Scientific computations is a suite of data structures and routines that provide the building blocks for the implementation of large-scale application codes on parallel (and serial) computers. It uses BLAS[4][5] and LAPACK[6] as a mathematical Kernel and Message Passing Interface (MPI) for the communications between the computation nodes. It is organized hierarchically, as shown in Figure 1-a, and provides an expanded tool for parallel linear equation solvers, nonlinear equation solvers, and time integrators.

PETSc provides many algorithms that could be used to solve parallel problems; for example, it provides a large set of Krylov subspace methods and preconditioners and it has many types of data structures representation, as seen in Figure 1-b, which shows some of PETSc numerical components.

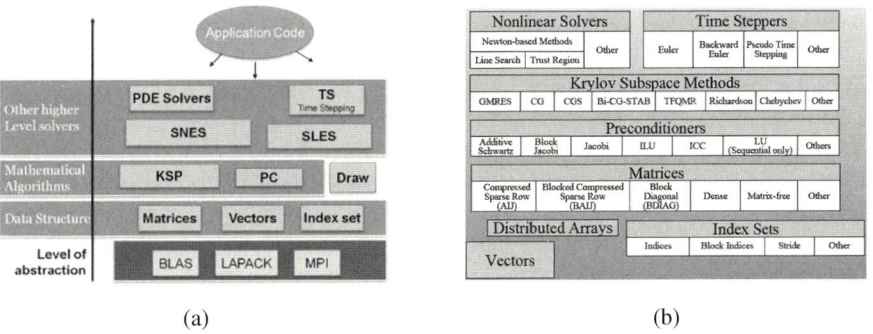

Fig. 1. (a) PETSc level of abstraction. (b) PETSc Numerical Components.

In order to build a performance model for a parallel mathematical library we studied the behavior of applications written with this library and the effects of both the input data provided by the user and the algorithms' parameters provided by the library. Therefore, we executed all the possible cases for different types of input data, using every possible data representation, and solving each case using different Krylov Subspace Solvers and Preconditioners. The results were surprisingly diverse and varied; that means, the time needed to solve a matrix depends on the nature of the matrix, how it was represented in memory, and on both the KSP and the PC used to solve this problem. For instance, Figure 2 shows the execution time in seconds for a 10000x10000 Around-Diagonal matrix that was executed on 12 KSP and three different Preconditioners.

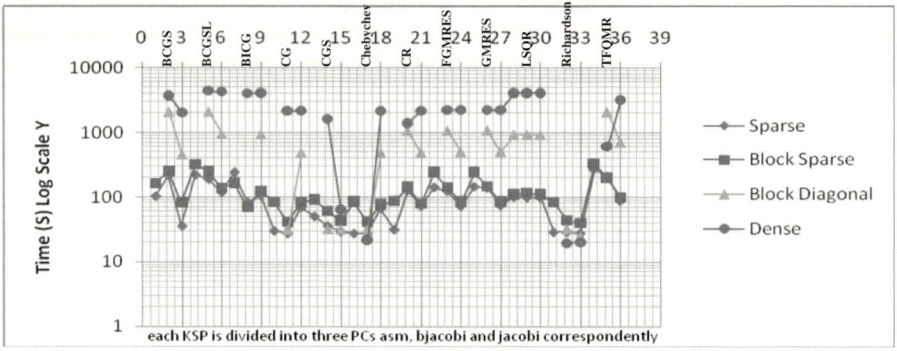

Fig. 2. Around-Diagonal 10000x10000 matrix execution times

From the execution results we can notice that the matrix solving time depends on the way the matrix was stored in memory. It can be seen in the example that the sparse representation had nearly the least execution time, while the dense representation has a very long execution time. Nevertheless, the variance between the KSPs and PCs also affects in a very significant way the problem execution behavior.

3 Performance Model

Implementing and developing a performance model for predicting the performance of an application is not trivial, especially when it considers the application as a black-box and it has to apply tuning actions dynamically for such applications.

To solve an *Ax=b* problem using PETSc a series of steps should be followed when implementing the system. First, a suitable way should be used to represent the data in memory and to decide how to distribute these data across the processors. Then the solver and preconditioner used for solving the problem should be chosen, taking into consideration that these solver and preconditioner should be compatible with each other as well as with the input data category and representation.

The proposed performance model consists of three main modules or parts which cooperate between each other to achieve our goals:

- The **pattern recognition engine** that helps to summarize and categorize the input data characteristics and information.
- The **knowledgebase** that contains information about the historical executions' input data patterns and performance behavior. The pattern recognition engine is responsible for classifying the input data, and comparing between them and the data patterns in the historical knowledgebase.
- The **data mining engine** that collects all the classifications derived by the pattern recognition engine, the input data, and the system environment parameters and behavior in order to find the performance problems and predict the possible best solving algorithms and its correspondent PETSc parameters.

3.1 The Pattern Recognition Engine

Several matrix types exist, depending on the problem nature, and there is no definite way to classify them or to categorize all matrix types. However, several proposals classify matrices depending on the distribution of the nonzero and the main diagonal. Consequently, we have classified the matrices into six main types:

- Diagonal matrix, which has all the nonzero entries in its main diagonal.
- Tri-diagonal matrix, which has all the nonzero entries in its three main diagonals.
- Around-diagonal matrix, which has all, or the majority, of the nonzero entries in and around the main diagonal of the matrix
- Upper triangular matrix, or Lower triangular matrix which has all, or the majority, of the nonzero entries either above or below the main diagonal correspondently.
- Distributed matrix, which have the nonzero entries distributed randomly in the matrix and not only around the diagonal.
- Zero-diagonal matrix, which is a special case where the matrix main diagonal entries are zeros.

The Pattern Recognition Engine functionality is divided into three stages:

- Pattern Creation Stage
- Density Calculation Stage
- Structural Analysis Stage.

3.1.1 Pattern Creation Stage

The pattern has the format of a 10x10 matrix; each entry represents one of the hundred sub matrices that construct the main matrix and contains a structure of statistics that belongs to the corresponding sub-matrix, such as, the number of nonzero entries in the sub-matrix and the percentage of these entries with respect to its total number of values. In order to create the matrix pattern a number of steps should be followed (Figure 3 illustrates the pattern creation process):

- Divide the matrix into sub matrices and calculate the size and the dimension of each sub-matrix which will be 10% of the total dimension and 1% of the total size
- Divide each sub-matrix into four triangular parts that help to clarify the diagonal data and increase the results accuracy.
- Compute the number of nonzero values in each sub-matrix

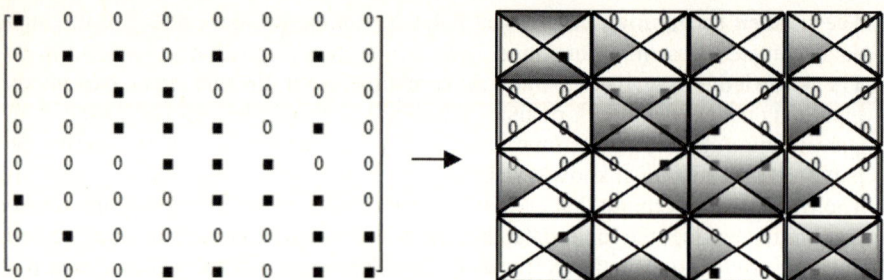

Fig. 3. Pattern creation process for a 4x4 pattern

- Compute the percentage of the nonzero values in each sub-matrix with respect to the sub matrix total size.

The main diagonal is a critical important factor at the time of recognizing the matrix because it has a huge impact on the matrix solving process. Thus, in the pattern creation phase a copy of the main diagonal entries and its related statistics, such as, the number of nonzero entries and their percentage are being saved separately from the matrix Pattern blocks.

3.1.2 Density Calculation Stage
The matrix pattern shows the number and the percentage of the nonzero entries in each of its pattern blocks, these percentages represent the matrix density. The matrix density is a relative characteristic, hence, the computation of such aspect needs techniques which may integrate some image processing and mathematical statistics algorithms. As far as the input matrix and the knowledgebase matrices share the same pattern size of 10x10 blocks each one divided into four triangular parts, the density factor will be the sum of the distances between each triangular part in the input matrix pattern and its equivalent in each knowledgebase pattern.

The distance will be calculated using a special case of the Minkowski Distances[7] of order λ when $\lambda=1$ and it is called the City-Block distance or Manhattan distance, expression 1 shows the Manhattan general case.

$$D_{ij} = \sum_{k=1}^{n} |x_{ik} - x_{jk}| \tag{1}$$

The results should be normalized to values between 0 and 1 according to expression 2, where zero means both matrices share the same density, and one means that they have a very different density.

$$Normalized\ Distance = \frac{Distance}{Max\ Distance} \tag{2}$$

This stage helps in identifying the density and the ratio of the nonzero entries in a matrix, but what happens if two matrices have the same density and a very different data distribution?

3.1.3 The Structural Analysis Stage

The main objective of this stage is to characterize the distribution of the data in the matrix without concerning about the data density or size; the only factor that affects this stage is the presence or the absence of a nonzero entry in the pattern blocks.

The structural analysis phase uses a data masking technique when comparing between matrices, it means that when receiving the input matrix pattern from the pattern creation stage it masks each block in the input pattern with the correspondent block in the knowledgebase patterns, converting its value to 1 if both values are equal or both contain a nonzero entry, and to 0 if one of the values is zero and the other contains at least a nonzero entry. Jaccard's Coefficient[7] (expression 3) is used to calculate the Fitness between the knowledgebase patterns and the input matrix pattern.

$$d_{AB} = 1 - \frac{|A \cap B|}{|A \cup B|} \qquad (3)$$

Consequently, the expression becomes

$$distance\ (\textbf{Fitness}) = 1 - \frac{number\ of\ ones\ in\ the\ masked\ matrix}{400 + 400 - number\ of\ ones\ in\ the\ masked\ matrix} \qquad (4)$$

Matrix similarity value will vary between 0 and 1, zero means both matrices share the same structure while one means they are totally different.

It can be noticed that each of the previous mechanisms classifies the matrix from different perspective, and spotlights different characteristics of the matrix data that cannot be seen by the other. A full image about the data distribution and density is been gotten by combining both pattern recognition strategies

Next, the diagonal density distance is calculated by computing the absolute difference between input matrix diagonal density and the knowledgebase matrices diagonal density.

After combining the three values by an equally likely weight summation where the sum will be a real value between 0 and 3 where zero means both matrices are identical and three represents completely different matrices.

3.2 The Knowledgebase

As the model depends on previous performance knowledge, a historical knowledgebase which contains the performance information about previous executions of linear algebraic problem applications has been built. It contains the behavioral information of a huge number of pre-planned executions of different types of input data with nearly all the possible parameters, providing different data representations, different Krylov subspace solvers, and different Preconditioners, executed on different number of processors.

Then a reference patterns list was built and saved in the historical knowledgebase. These patterns correspond to the matrices which the knowledgebase had been created upon their performance behavior. Table 1 summarizes the input matrices, their sizes and their correspondent patterns and the parameters on which they were executed.

Table 1. The Knowledgebase creating execution parameters

Input Matrix	No. Processors	Matrix Size	Memory Representations	KSP Solvers	Preconditioners
Diagonal Tri-Diagonal Distributed Zero-Diagonal Lower-Triangular Around-Diagonal	1 8 16 32	1000 10000 20000	Sparse Dense Block Sparse Block Diagonal	BiCGStab BiCGStab(L) BiConjugate Gradient Conjugate Gradient Conj. Grad. Squared Chebychev Conjugate Residuals FGMRES GMRES LSQR Richardson TFQMR	Jacobi Bjacobi ASM

3.3 The Data Mining Engine

The pattern recognition engine makes wide steps in finding the most suitable solving parameters by recognizing the data and summarizing its characteristics. After recognizing and classifying the input matrix by the pattern recognition engine, the data mining engine takes the control, and starts searching for the most suitable solving parameter set from the knowledgebase, as the following:

- After receiving the recommended matrix pattern from the pattern recognition engine, the data mining engine starts searching for the solver parameter set from the knowledgebase excluding all the matrix patterns cases, but the recommended one.
- It uses the City-Block (Manhattan) distance algorithms to calculate the distances between the input data factors, and the knowledgebase off-pattern factors such as, the real size of the matrix and the number of processors in the application communication world.
- Then, the solver prediction component chooses the proper configuration according to the distance factors and the least execution time.
- If the solving process did not reach a correct solution within this configuration set, the last step will be repeated until reaching the result excluding the used options.

4 Model Assessment

To examine our model we built a simple linear algebraic solver application based on PETSc library, this application contains only solvers and data related essential PETSc calls. Moreover, we built a tool that controls the application execution, meets the functionality of the model and passes the suitable solver, Preconditioner and data representation to the application by changing the parameters of the PETSc routines calls dynamically.

The experiments were performed on different matrices obtained from Matrix Market[8] web site a component of the NIST project[9], which provides access to a repository of test data for use in comparative studies of algorithms for numerical linear algebra. The SHERMAN5 matrix is an example of the matrices where the model was experimented.

Table 2. SHERMAN5 Pattern Recognition Engine results

Knowledgebase Pattern	City Block (Manhattan) distance	Fitness	Diagonal Density	Overall Distance
Tri-Diagonal	0.14433	0.283262	0	0.427592
Around-Diagonal	0.599593	0.481973	0	1.081566
Lower Triangular	0.35347	0.688525	0.5	1.541994
Distributed	1	0.6733	0	1.6733
Zero-diagonal	0.111314	0.555957	1	1.667271
Diagonal	0.09817	0.4	0	0.49817

The SHERMAN5 is a matrix that represents a fully implicit black oil model from the oil reservoir simulation challenge matrices, it is a 3312x3312 matrix, contains 20793 nonzero entries and 3312 nonzero diagonal entries matrix.

Firstly, we applied the pattern recognition phase which results are shown in Table 2. It can be seen that the most similar matrix in the knowledgebase to the SHERMAN5 matrix was the Tri-Diagonal matrix with a 0.43 overall distance.

At the same time the Data Mining Engine specified the 1000x1000 matrix and the 8 processors execution world as searching criteria for the solving parameter set and the final recommended results were: sparse as memory representation, Jacobi as pre-conditioner, and the chebychev as the recommended Krylov subspace solver.

Upon our proposal both matrices may share similar behavior according to the input parameters. Consequently, to validate these results we made executions of all the possible solution cases for SHAREMAN5 matrix, comparing their solving times to the same cases of the corresponding Tri-diagonal. Accordingly, by looking at the performance behavior for the SHAREMAN5 matrix on 8 processors environment, in Figure 4, it can be found that the model predicted case may not be the most optimal solution, nevertheless, it remains one of the "best" solutions.

At the same time by comparing between SHERMAN5 graph and the Tri-diagonal graph, in Figure 5, it can be noticed that both graphs are not identical; however, most of the Tri-diagonal matrix valid parameters are included in the SHAREMAN5 matrix possible solution, which shows the robustness of the solution predicting process.

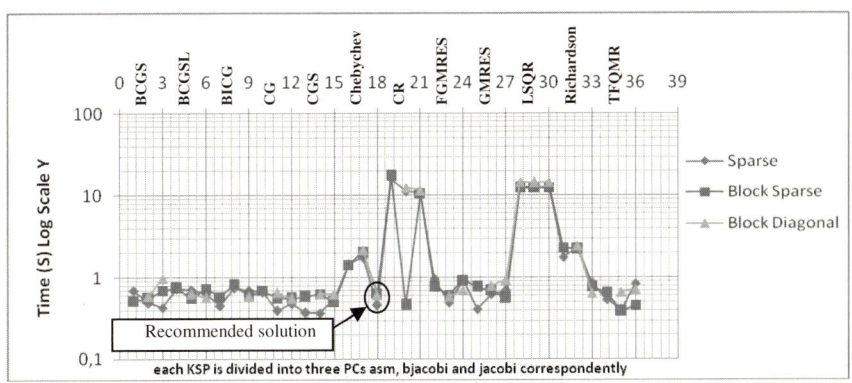

Fig. 4. Execution behavior of SHAREMAN5 3312x3312 matrix on 8 processors

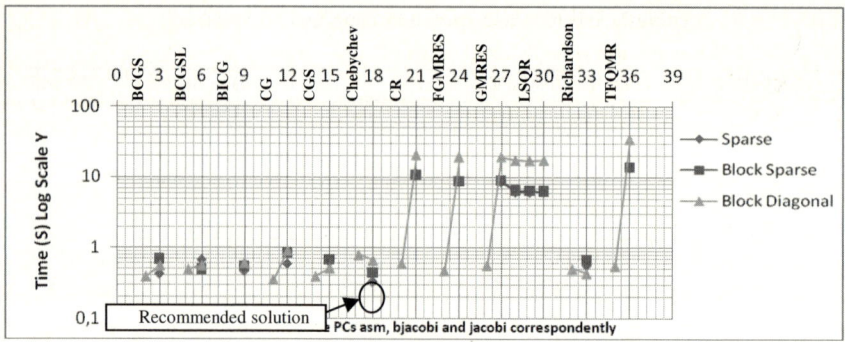

Fig. 5. Execution behavior of Tri-Diagonal 1000x1000 matrix on 8 processors

5 Related Efforts

The importance of parallel programming grew as well as the searching for better performance, a number of investigation lines where lunched to accomplish this objective. ATLAS[10] is an Automatic Tuning Linear Algebra Software project for the automatic generation and optimization of numerical software for processors with deep memory hierarchies and pipelined functional units. It is an implementation of the "Automated Empirical Optimization of Software" AEOS paradigm, that provide many ways of doing a required operation, and uses empirical timing in order to choose the best method for a given operation.

More limited ATLAS like functionality was included in PHiPAC[11], and more dynamic solutions are provided by SANS[12] Self-Adapting Numerical Software and SALSA[13] Self-Adapting Large-scale Solver Architecture. SANS is a collaborative effort between different projects that deals with the optimization of software at different levels in relation to the execution environment and helps to build a common framework on which these projects can possibly coexist. While SALSA aims to assist applications in finding suitable linear and nonlinear system solvers based on analysis of the application-generated data based on a database of performance results that can tune the heuristics over time.

6 Conclusions

From the study of the performance information of the mathematical libraries it was noticed that the performance of the application may vary dynamically according to the input data and the solving environment. In this work we defined a performance model for automatic and dynamic tuning of mathematical applications based on historical performance information.

Thus, we have developed triple component model consisting of: pattern recognition engine that classifies and characterizes the problem, a historical knowledgebase that was filled with plenty of PETSc's library performance information for a wide set of data, and the data mining engine which dives into the knowledgebase in order to get the recommended configuration and tuning points in the application.

Additionally, we planned real case problems in order to validate the model making a full execution for all the possible parameters and the results were optimistic. Moreover, it was noticed that the knowledgebase can be adapted by including more performance information for different types of problems.

References

1. Gropp, W., Lusk, E., Skjellum, A.: Using MPI. In: Portable Parallel Programming with the Message Passing Interface, 2nd edn., Cambridge, London, England. MIT Press in Scientific and Engineering Computation Series (1999)
2. Parallel Virtual Machine, http://www.csm.ornl.gov/pvm/
3. Balay, S., Buschelman, K., Eijkhout, V., Gropp, W.D., Kaushik, D., Knepley, M.G., McInnes, L.C., Smith, B.F., Zhang, H.: PETSc Users Manual. ANL-95/11 - Revision 2.1.5, Argonne National Laboratory (2004)
4. Basic Linear Algebra Subprograms, http://www.netlib.org/blas/
5. Dongarra, J.J., Du Croz, J., Duff, I.S., Hammarling, S.: A set of Level 3 Basic Linear Algebra Subprograms. ACM Transactions on Mathematical Software (TOMS) 16, 1–17 (1990)
6. Anderson, E., Bai, Z., Bischof, C., Blackford, L.S., Demmel, J., Dongarra, J.J., Du Croz, J., Hammarling, S., Greenbaum, A., McKenney, A., Sorensen, D.: LAPACK Users' Guide, 3rd edn. Society for Industrial and Applied Mathematics (1999)
7. Zezula, P., Amato, G., Dohnal, V., Batko, M.: Similarity Search The Metric Space Approach, ch.1, pp. 5–66. Springer, NY (2006)
8. Boisvert, R.F., Pozo, R., Remington, K., Barrett, R., Dongarra, J.J.: The Matrix Market: A web resource for test matrix collections. In: Boisvert, R.F. (ed.) Quality of Numerical Software, Assessment and Enhancement, pp. 125–137. Chapman and Hall, London (1997), http://math.nist.gov/MatrixMarket/
9. Tools for Evaluating Mathematical and Statistical Software, http://math.nist.gov/temss/
10. Whaley, R.C., Petitet, A., Dongarra, J.J.: Automated empirical optimizations of software and the ATLAS project. Parallel Computing 27, 3–35 (2001)
11. Bilmes, J., Asanovic, K., Chin, C., Demmel, J.: Optimizing matrix multiply using PHiPAC: a portable, high-performance, ANSI C coding methodology. In: Proceedings of the 11th International Conference on Supercomputing, pp. 340–347 (1997)
12. Dongarra, J., Bosilca, G., Chen, Z., Eijkhout, V., Fagg, G.E., Fuentes, E., Langou, J., Luszczek, P., Pjesivac-Grbovic, J., Seymour, K., You, H., Vadhiyar, S.S.: Self-adapting numerical software (SANS) effort. IBM J. Res. Dev. 50, 223–238 (2006)
13. Demmel, J., Dongarra, J., Eijkhout, V., Fuentes, E., Petitet, A., Vuduc, R., Whaley, R.C., Yelick, K.: Self Adapting Linear Algebra Algorithms and Software. Proceedings of the IEEE 93(2), 293–312 (2005)

A Performance Model of Dense Matrix Operations on Many-Core Architectures

Guoping Long, Dongrui Fan, Junchao Zhang, Fenglong Song,
Nan Yuan, and Wei Lin

Key Laboratory of Computer System and Architecture,
Institute of Computing Technology, Chinese Academy of Sciences,
100080 Beijing, China
{longguoping,fandr,jczhang,songfenglong,
yuannan,linwei}@ict.ac.cn

Abstract. Current many-core architectures (MCA) have much larger arithmetic to memory bandwidth ratio compared with traditional processors (vector, superscalar, and multi-core, etc). As a result, bandwidth has become an important performance bottleneck of MCA. Previous works have demonstrated promising performance of MCA for dense matrix operations. However, there is still little quantitative understanding of the relationship between performance of matrix computation kernels and the limited memory bandwidth. This paper presents a performance model for dense matrix multiplication (MM), LU and Cholesky decomposition. The input parameters are memory bandwidth B and on-chip SRAM capacity C, while the output is maximum core number P_{max}. We show that $P_{max} = \Theta(B * \sqrt{C})$. P_{max} indicates that when the problem size is large enough, the given memory bandwidth will not be a performance bottleneck as long as the number of cores $P < P_{max}$. The model is validated by a comparison between the theoretical performance and experimental data of previous works.

Keywords: performance model, many-core architecture, dense matrix, memory bandwidth.

1 Introduction

The advancement of semi-conductor technology makes it possible today to integrate large number of processing cores on a single chip to exploit massive parallelism. The many-core architecture (MCA), which meets the demand well, has caught intensive attention and is evaluated extensively by both academia [1,2,4,5] and industry [3] in recent years. An important problem of MCA, as compared with traditional architectures, is the large arithmetic-to-bandwidth ratio. We define the FLOP/Word (64bit) as the ratio between the theoretical peak performance (GFLOPS/s) and peak memory bandwidth (WORDS/s) of the processor. The FLOP/Word ratio of Merrimac [4], IBM C64 [2,8,6] and Godson-T [5] are 50:1, 20:1 and 24:1, respectively. The ratio is an order of magnitude higher than vector processors (1:1) [4] and much larger than conventional microprocessors (between 4:1 and 12:1) [4]. Obviously, memory bandwidth has become an important performance bottleneck of MCA.

Despite the bandwidth limitation, many previous works [2,8,7,6] have demonstrated promising performance potential for many computation kernels. Bibardi et al. [11] explored the optimal partition of chip area between computation and storage for Quantum Chromo Dynamics (QCD). However, there are few quantitative study of the relationship between performance of matrix computation kernels and the limited memory bandwidth. In this paper, we present such a performance model, which studies the impact of bandwidth constraint on the efficiency of cores, and thus on application performance, in a quantitative approach. Specifically we answer the following question: From performance perspective, for the given memory bandwidth (B), on chip SRAM size (C) and the computation structure of an algorithmic kernel, what is the maximum number of cores (P_{max}) that can be supported without sacrifice of efficiency? We choose three typical dense matrix kernels, namely MM, LU and Cholesky to investigate this problem for two reasons. First, all kernels are important in high performance scientific computing and have high data reuse. Second, although related works [6,7] have demonstrated high performance of MM and LU on IBM C64, we are interested to know whether more cores can be supported with each core achieving peak performance.

The main technical idea of this paper is software controlled data orchestration, namely, developing a systematic way to schedule data transfer between the processor and memory in order to overlap the memory latency with computation time as much as possible. The rest of the paper is organized as follows. Section 2 presents an abstract MCA model. Section 3 formalizes the problem into a mathematical model. Section 4 develops the performance model, discusses the implication of the model and compares it with previous experimental results [6,7]. Section 5 concludes this paper.

2 The Abstract Many-Core Architecture

This section presents an abstract MCA, as shown in Fig.1. The basic architecture is enough to represent current typical MCAs [2,3] in that it consists of many processing cores (PE in Fig.1) with limited memory bandwidth. The MESH network topology and additional architectural support for efficient data orchestration (Section 3) are necessary to make quantitative study of bandwidth constraint on performance possible. There are several important features to note.

Each PE is a standard processing core with a floating point unit and a group of scalar functional units. Each core contains a piece of software managed scratch-pad memory (SPM). An important observation is that for MM, LU and Cholesky kernels, if input data are already in SPM, careful scheduling of operations can achieve near theoretical performance on the PE. Let α be theoretical to peak performance ratio, which for Intel Polaris [3], IBM C64 [2], Godson-T [5] and superscalar processors [10] are 0.5, 0.5, 0.5 and 1.0, respectively. We can view α as a metric for measuring the theoretical PE efficiency. In this paper we assume $\alpha = 1$ for MM, LU and Cholesky.

The memory hierarchy consists of three layers: DRAM, global shared memory (SRAM BANK1~4) and SPM of PEs. Global shared memory is also explicitly software managed. The entire memory hierarchy provides programmers with tremendous flexibility for performance optimization.

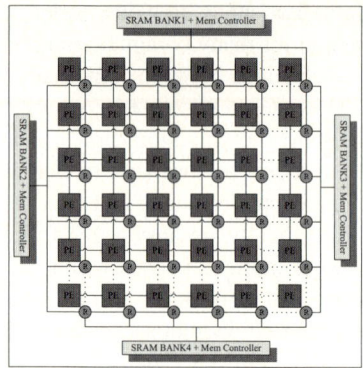

Fig. 1. The abstract many-core architecture

There are logically two on-chip networks, the PE network and the memory network, both of which can be exploited to achieve high performance. The PE network is targeted for fast on chip inter-PE synchronization. And the memory network facilitates highly efficient data orchestration. Each router (denoted as R in Fig.1) has a dedicated programmable data transfer agent (DTA) to move data between PEs and global shared memory efficiently. The DTA includes dedicated architectural support, such as row/column data multicast, gather/scatter, etc, to help programmers improve data locality. The basic operation of DTA is similar with normal DMA controllers.

3 Problem Formulation

In this section, we formulate the problem based on the explicit latency hiding model[1] developed in [8]. We assume the whole program execution can be partitioned into n steps, and each step i consists of three operations: load the input data required by current step of computation, computation, write the result produced by current step back into memory if necessary. We use TM_i, TC_i, and TS_i to denote the time required by loading the input data, computation and storing results back to memory, respectively.

The fundamental concept of explicit latency hiding model is to overlap computation and memory reference in a pipeline manner to hide memory latency, as shown in Fig.2. We assume computation of each step can not start until all required data has been loaded

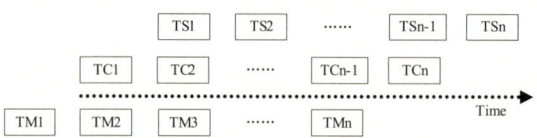

Fig. 2. The explicit latency hiding model

---

[1] The explicit latency hiding model in this paper is also known as double-buffering or triple buffering in this field.

into the SPM of the PE. We define effective latency as the memory latency that could not be overlapped by computation time. Lets first define an operator $d(x, y)$ as follows:

$$d(x, y) = \begin{cases} y - x, & y \geq x \\ 0, & \text{otherwise} \end{cases}$$

Formally, we define the inter-step effective latency of step i ($1 \leq i \leq n$) by function $f(i)$:

$$f(i) = \begin{cases} d(0, TM_1), & i = 1 \\ d(TC_1, TM_2), & i = 2 \\ d(TC_{i-1}, TM_i + TS_{i-2}), & 3 \leq i \leq n \\ d(TC_n, TS_{n-1}), & i = n + 1 \\ d(0, TS_n), & i = n + 2 \end{cases}$$

Each execution step i is performed in parallel by all cores within the processor. Because of inter-core synchronization, there may be memory latency that could not be hidden within the step i. This latency, denoted as $ISEL_i$, is defined as the intra-step effective latency of step i. Note that TC_i is the sum of the computation time and $ISEL_i$. We define memory to computation ratio (MCR) as the ratio between data transfer time and computation time of the program:

$$MCR = \frac{\sum_{i=1}^{n}(TM_i + TS_i)}{\sum_{i=1}^{n} TC_i} \tag{1}$$

MCR is not a direct metric to quantitatively measure the impact of memory bandwidth constraint on PE efficiency, because computation usually overlaps with data transfer to improve performance. We introduce effective memory to computation ratio (EMCR) to meet this purpose. More precisely, we define:

$$EMCR = \frac{\sum_{i=1}^{n}(f(i) + ISEL_i)}{\sum_{i=1}^{n} TC_i} \tag{2}$$

Due to the limited memory bandwidth of MCA, a key challenge for optimizing MM, LU and Cholesky is to schedule data transfer efficiently to minimize $EMCR$. If the PE number is small, the memory bandwidth is high enough that $EMCR \to 0$ for sufficiently large problems. And it is possible that all PEs achieve near theoretical performance through code optimization. This explains why traditional architectures achieve peak performance for dense matrix kernels [10]. Let B, C and P be the memory bandwidth, on-chip memory size and processing core number, respectively. n is a monotonically increasing function of problem size, and TC_i, TM_i, TS_i, $ISEL_i$ all are functions of B and C. The problem can thus be formalized as follows: Finding out the maximum P_{max} such that

$$\lim_{n \to +\infty} EMCR = 0.$$

4 The Performance Model

Table 1 summarizes important parameters of the model. Note that C denote the capacity of the SRAM BANK1~4 in the abstract MCA shown in Fig.1, not including SPM of individual PEs. The memory bandwidth B represents peak load bandwidth which is normalized as maximum number of doubles (64 bits) that can be fetched in to chip per processor cycle on average. Note that B is a compound metric which depends on many factors, including processor/FSB frequency, the number of on chip memory controllers, DRAM access latency, etc. For example, the normalized load bandwidth B for IBM C64 and Itanium2 [10] are 4 and 0.5, respectively. We assume the data path width of both memory network and PE network are the same (W).

Table 1. Key parameters required by the model

Name	Description
C	Capacity of global shared memory (64 bit words)
P	Number of PEs
B	Normalized load bandwidth (words/processor cycle)
W	Data path width of on chip network

4.1 Matrix Multiplication

Blocking is proved to be an efficient way to improve data locality for matrix operations. Previous blocking algorithms generally rely on cache or register tiling to exploit locality [6,7]. This approach is efficient, but is highly empirical. In this paper we propose a systematic data orchestration approach on our abstract MCA. The key idea is to overlap block computation of PEs and data transfer on the memory network explicitly in a rhythmic and manageable way.

The first step is to partition the $N*N$ MM problem into sub-problems small enough ($M*M$) that can be solved entirely on chip. Let $q = \frac{N}{M}$, we have $C_{i,j} = \sum_{k=0}^{q-1} A_{i,k} * B_{k,j}$. Therefore, the $N*N$ MM problem is partitioned into q^3 smaller $M*M$ MM sub-problems. We call each sub-problem an M-step. Since the abstract MCA allows simultaneous operation of PEs (computation) and DTAs (data transfer), it is reasonable to overlap the execution time of previous M-step computation (T_{c-mm}) and the data transfer time (T_{m-2}) of the next M-step. In order to minimize memory traffic, we schedule all M-steps in such a way that each step shares a matrix with each of its adjacent steps. For each M-step i, we have $TC_i = T_{c-mm}$ and $T_{m-2} = TM_i + TS_i$, where TM_i is the time required to load two matrixes to the global shared memory. Note that there are only q^2 resultant matrix blocks. Therefore q^2 of q^3 M-steps need to store a matrix block to memory, otherwise $TS_i = 0$. When the problem size is large, we can ignore the effect of store traffic, and use TM_i to approximate T_{m-2}:

$$T_{m-2} = \frac{2*M^2}{B} \quad (3)$$

At any time, there are at most five $M*M$ matrices on chip, 3 for matrix multiplication and 2 for input data of the next M-step. So we have:

$$5 * M^2 \leq C \tag{4}$$

In Equation (3) the data type of matrix elements are assumed to be double. In Equation (4) C is normalized to the number of matrix elements.

Now it's time to derive T_{c-mm}. Each M-step is performed in parallel by all PEs on chip. Let $p = \sqrt{P}$ and $b = \frac{M}{p}$. We partition each $M * M$ matrix into P blocks of size $b * b$, with each PE responsible for computing one block. There are totally p^3 block multiplications (B-steps), and each PE needs to perform p B-steps. For the same reason with M-steps, it should be reasonable to overlap the execution time of previous B-step computation (T_{c-blk}) and the data transfer time (T_{m-blk}) of the next B-step. It is important to note that for each B-step there is much degree of data sharing between different PEs, that is, a shared block is used by either the same row of all PEs or the same column of all PEs. Recall that DTA has row/column data multicast support for such pattern of data sharing. For the abstract MCA, we have:

$$T_{c-blk} = 2 * b^3 \tag{5}$$

$$T_{m-blk} = \frac{2 * b^2}{W} + p \tag{6}$$

The explicit latency hiding model requires that all data being loaded into private memory of each PE before a B-step starts computation. In our abstract MCA, PEs do not have floating point multiply-add unit. And Each B-step requires b^3 multiply and add operations. We ignore the overhead cycles of control and bookkeeping instructions in Equation (5) for simplicity of the model without sacrificing accuracy.

Equation (6) gives the worst case latency for loading a matrix block from SRAM BANK to PEs' private memory, because the block is shared by either the same row or the same column. The data path width of memory network W is normalized to the number of matrix elements per cycle. A network hop between adjacent PEs is assumed to be one cycle.

Now we derive the effective memory computation ratio of MM ($EMCR_{mm}$). First, we identify the conditions that the MCA must satisfy to make $T_{c-blk} > T_{m-blk}$ hold. The in-equality is equivalent to

$$\frac{2 * M}{p} * \frac{M^2}{p^2} > \frac{2}{W} * \frac{M^2}{p^2} + p \tag{7}$$

We assume $w \geq 1$ (The data path of on-chip network should be at least 64 bit wide). And let $C > 2.5MB$ [2,6,7], by Equation (4) we have $M \geq 256$. It is hard to imagine current memory system technology can support 4096 PEs, thus we assume $p < 32$. It can be easily verified that Equation (7) is true for $W \geq 1, M \geq 256$, and $p < 32$.

This simple analysis justifies two important intuitions: (a) On-chip bandwidth is much higher than off-chip DRAM bandwidth. (b) The on-chip buffer size C should be large enough to hold a reasonably large work set to hide on-chip memory latency. Since assumptions we make of MCA here are well within the reach of current technology, it is safe to ignore the overhead incurred by on-chip memory latency ($ISEL_i = 0$).

The execution time of an M-step can be written as follows

$$T_{c-mm} = T_{c-blk} * p = \frac{2 * M^3}{p^2} \tag{8}$$

Recall the definition of effective memory computation ratio ($EMCR$) in Equation (2), when the problem size N is large enough, we have:

$$EMCR_{mm} = \frac{f(\sum_{i=1}^{q^3} T_{m-2}, \sum_{i=1}^{q^3} T_{c-mm})}{\sum_{i=1}^{q^3} T_{c-mm}}. \tag{9}$$

If p is small, we have $T_{m-2} < T_{c-mm}$, and $EMCR_{mm} = 0$. Otherwise if p is large enough, we have $T_{m-2} > T_{c-mm}$, and $EMCR_{mm} > 0$. The problem is thus to find maximum P_{max} such that when $N \to +\infty$ (which implies $q \to +\infty$):

$$\frac{T_{m-2}}{T_{c-mm}} \to 1. \tag{10}$$

Since $P = p^2$, from Equations (3), (4), (8) and (10) we have:

$$P_{max} = \frac{1}{\sqrt{5}} * B * \sqrt{C}. \tag{11}$$

4.2 LU and Cholesky Decompositon

Since the computation structures of LU and Cholesky are similar, we only discuss LU in this section. The result obtained from LU holds for Cholesky as well. For LU problem, we divide the original $N * N$ matrix into $q * q$ sub-matrixes, partitioning the problem into a series of block matrix operations (M-step) with each operating on $M * M$ ($q = \frac{N}{M}$) matrixes [6]. There are four types of block operations in an M-step: (a) Factor-step. Given matrix A, compute lower triangular matrix L and upper triangular matrix U such that $A = L*U$. (b) Lower-step. Given matrixes A and lower triangular matrix L, compute the matrix $L^{-1} * A$. (c) Upper-step. Given matrixes A and upper triangular matrix U, compute the matrix $A * U^{-1}$. (d) Schur-step. Given matrixes A, B and C, compute the matrix $C - A * B$.

The idea here is same with MM: overlapping the execution time of the previous M-step with the data transfer time of current M-step and parallelizing each M-step among all PEs. The Schur-step is the same with MM and is discussed before. We next derive the execution and data transfer time of other types of M-steps.

The Upper-step is embarrassingly parallel. We partition the $M * M$ matrix A into P blocks of size ($M * \frac{M}{P}$) by column, with each PE responsible for computing one block. All PEs share the same upper triangular matrix U and perform the same operations with different data. Hence, the computation time (T_{c-u}) and the time required to fetch the shared triangular matrix U into the farthest PE's private memory (T_{m-u}) can be written in Equations (12) and (13), respectively.

$$T_{c-u} = M^2 * \frac{M}{P} \tag{12}$$

$$T_{m-u} = \frac{M^2}{2*W} + p \qquad (13)$$

In Equation (12) we ignore the negligible overhead of each core for the same reason with Equation (5). The Lower-step requires less computation than the Upper-step. But they are the same with respect to parallelization. The computation time (T_{c-l}) and the data transfer time (T_{m-l}) of triangular matrix L are given in Equations (14) and (15), respectively.

$$T_{c-l} = (M^2 - M) * \frac{M}{P} \qquad (14)$$

$$T_{m-l} = \frac{M^2}{2*W} + p \qquad (15)$$

For the Factor-step, we partition the $M*M$ matrix into blocks of size $p*p$, with each PE responsible for one block. When a block is finished, the corresponding PE is idle for the rest of the time within current M-step. Although this approach is less optimal than load balanced schemes in [7], it is simple and intuitive. Moreover, as will be shown shortly, a little load imbalance in the Factor-step does not effect the main result of the model. The execution time of Factor-step is given in Equation (16).

$$T_{c-lu} = p * (\sum_{i=1}^{b-1}(2*i^2 + i)) + (p-1)*b^3 \qquad (16)$$

There are p iterations to perform a Fator-step [7]. Data dependences exist between different blocks within iteration and between adjacent iterations as well. We do not overlap computation and data transfer for Factor-step, that is, each PE waits until all required blocks have been transferred to private memory then starts computation. The data transfer time (T_{m-lu}) is thus given in Equation (17):

$$T_{m-lu} = \sum_{i=1}^{p-1} 2*(\frac{b^2}{W} + p - i) \qquad (17)$$

Let T_{m-1} be the time required to transfer one M*M matrix between DRAM and the processor. From Equation (1) and the dependence graph of LU, we have

$$MCR_{lu} = \frac{\sum_{i=1}^{q-1}(T_{m-1} + T_{m-lu} + 2(q-i)*T_{m-1} + (q-i)^2*T_{m-2})}{\sum_{i=1}^{q-1}(T_{c-lu} + (q-i)*(T_{c-l} + T_{c-u}) + (q-i)^2*T_{c-mm})} \qquad (18)$$

Note that $q = \frac{N}{M}$, where M is the maximum problem size that can be hold in on-chip SRAM banks. Hence, $\forall \varepsilon > 0, \exists N_t > 0$, such that $| MCR_{lu} - \frac{T_{m-2}}{T_{c-mm}} | < \varepsilon$ for $N > N_t$. In other words, for sufficiently large problem size N_t, we have $MCR_{lu} = \frac{T_{m-2}}{T_{c-mm}}$ and $EMCR_{lu} = \frac{f(T_{m-2}, T_{c-mm})}{T_{c-mm}}$. From (9) and (10) we know $P_{max} = \frac{1}{\sqrt{5}} * B * \sqrt{C}$.

4.3 Discussion of the Model

The result, $P_{max} = \Theta(B * \sqrt{C})$, is a little surprising and deserves some explanations. First, the same result applies for MM, LU and Cholesky, as long as the problem size is large enough. The reason is that execution time of all computation kernels are dominated by MM for large problems. Second, P_{max} is proportional with respect to B, because all kernels have high degree ($O(N)$) of data reuse.

A direct corollary of the model is that, if $P < P_{max}$, the abstract MCA achieves theoretical performance. This result is justified by the experimental results in [6] for MM problem. Venetis and Gao [7] conduct a series of optimizations for LU on IBM C64 architecture, and the result is that only 50% of efficiency can be achieved for 4096*4096 matrix. According to our model, there are two reasons: (1) Data orchestration based on empirical approach is not effective enough to hide memory latency for MCA; (2) the problem size is not large enough to observe higher efficiency.

A related interesting question to ask is: for dense matrix operations such as MM, LU and Cholesky, how much theoretical potential does current memory system technology provides for MCA? Previous works [2,6,7,8] present IBM C64 design with 5MB of on-chip memory (half is used as global shared memory) and 16GB/s memory bandwidth, thus $P_{max} \approx 1024$. The potential is huge and it is not surprise that 64 thread units can achieve theoretical performance (which is approximately half of the peak performance) [6].

5 Conclusion

Current MCAs have a common problem, that is, the arithmetic-to-bandwidth ratio is larger than conventional processors. In this paper, we present a theoretical analytical model to quantitatively evaluate the impact of memory bandwidth on the performance of dense matrix operations, namely MM, LU and Cholesky. For the given the memory bandwidth B and on-chip SRAM capacity C, we derive the maximum number of cores $P_{max} = \Theta(B * \sqrt{C})$, such that if $P \leq P_{max}$, the limited memory bandwidth is not a performance bottleneck when the problem size is sufficiently large. We validate the model by comparing the theoretical results with previous experiment results.

Although the model implies good potential performance for dense matrix operations, for memory bound computations, bandwidth may still be a bottleneck. Better memory system technologies are expected to solve the problem for coming generations of MCA.

Acknowledgements

This work is supported by the National Grand Fundamental Research 973 Program of China under Grant No. 2005CB321600 and the National Natural Science Foundation of China under Grant No. 60736012. The authors would like to thank anonymous reviewers for their constructive suggestions.

References

1. Asanovic, K., Bodik, R., Catanzaro, B.C., Gebis, J.J., Husbands, P., Keutzer, K., Patterson, D.A., Plishker, W.L., Shalf, J., Williams, S.W., Yelick, K.A.: The Landscape of Parallel Computing Research: A View from Berkeley
2. Zhu, W.R., Sreedhar, V.C., Aang Hu, Z., Gao, G.R.: Synchronization State Buffer: Supporting Efficient Fine-Grain Synchronization for Many-Core Architectures. In: Proceedings of the 34th International Symposium on Computer Architecture (ISCA 2007), San Diego, CA, USA, June 9-13 (2007)
3. Vangal, S., Howard, J., Ruhl, G., Dighe, S., Wilson, H., Tschanz, J., Finan, D., Iyer, P., Singh, A., Jacob, T., Jain, S., Venkataraman, S., Hoskote, Y., Borkar, N.: An 80-Tile 1.28TFLOPS Network-on-Chip in 65nm CMOS. In: Proceedings of IEEE International Solid-State Circuits Conference, February 11-15 (2007)
4. Dally, W.J., Labonte, F., Das, A., Hanrahan, P., Ahn, J.H., Gummaraju, J., Erez, M., Jayasena, N., Buck, I., Knight, T.J., Kapasi, U.J.: Merrimac: Supercomputing with Streams. In: Proceedings of the Supercomputer Conference, November 15-21 (2003)
5. Tan, G., Fan, D., Zhang, J., Russo, A., Gao, G.R.: Experience on Optimizing Irregular Computation for Memory Hierarchy in Manycore Architecture. In: The 13th ACM SIGPLAN Symposium on Principles and Practice of Parallel Programming, February 20-23 (2008)
6. Ang Hu, Z., del Cuvillo, J., Zhu, W., Gao, G.R.: Optimization of Dense Matrix Multiplication on IBM Cyclops-64: Challenges and Experiences. In: The 12th International European Conference on Parallel Processing, 29 August - 1 September (2006)
7. Venetis, I.E., Gao, G.R.: Optimizing the LU Benchmark for the Cyclops-64 Architecture. CAPSL Technical Memo 75 (February 2007)
8. Tan, G.: Locality and Parallelism of Algorithm in Irregular Computation. PH.D. dissertation. Institute of Computing Technology, Chinese Academy of Sciences (6) (2007)
9. Automatically Tuned Linear Algebra Software (ATLAS), http://math-atlas.sourceforge.net/
10. Yotov, K., Roeder, T., Pingali, K., Gunnels, J., Gustavson, F.: An Experimental Comparison of Cache-oblivious and Cache-aware Programs. In: Proceedings of the 19th Annual ACM Symposium on Parallelism in Algorithms and Architectures, June 9-11 (2007)
11. Bilardi, G., Pietracaprina, A., Pucci, G., Schifano, S.F., Tripiccione, R.: The Potential of On-Chip Multiprocessing for QCD Machines. In: Proceedings of the International Conference on High Performance Computing, pp. 386–397 (December 2005)

Empirical Analysis of a Large-Scale Hierarchical Storage System

Weikuan Yu, H. Sarp Oral, R. Shane Canon, Jeffrey S. Vetter,
and Ramanan Sankaran

Oak Ridge National Laboratory
Oak Ridge, TN 37831
{wyu,oralhs,canonrs,vetter,sankaranr}@ornl.gov

Abstract. To prepare for future peta- or exa-scale computing, it is important to gain a good understanding on what impacts a hierarchical storage system would have on the performance of data-intensive applications, and accordingly, how to leverage its strengths and mitigate possible risks. To this aim, this paper adopts a user-level perspective to empirically reveal the implications of storage organization to parallel programs running on Jaguar at the Oak Ridge National Laboratory. We first describe the hierarchical configuration of Jaguar's storage system. Then we evaluate the performance of individual storage components. In addition, we examine the scalability of metadata- and data-intensive benchmarks over Jaguar. We have discovered that the file distribution pattern can impact the aggregated I/O bandwidth. Based on our analysis, we have demonstrated that it is possible to improve the scalability of a representative application S3D by as much as 15%.

1 Introduction

High Performance Computing (HPC) is quickly moving into the peta-scale computing era and beyond [2, 3]. In such large-scale environments, the composition and organization of the I/O system (and its storage hardware) is as complicated as the other system components, such as processor/memory and interconnects. The I/O system often encompasses a combination of software and hardware components such as parallel I/O programming middleware, parallel file systems, storage area networks, and the hardware storage devices. Such complex system presents a steep learning curve for application scientists to realize, appreciate and leverage the performance characteristics of storage systems, and as a result, causing a performance gap between the system deliverable I/O rate and the application achievable bandwidth.

This paper adopts a perspective from user-level programs and applications, and presents a set of experiments that analyze the performance characteristics of the hierarchical storage system on Jaguar [11]. Several earlier studies have measured the performance of different Cray XT platforms using micro-benchmarks [9, 12]. They have included relevant I/O performance information such as peak system throughput and the impact of Lustre file striping patterns. But little has been revealed on the performance implications of the storage hierarchies. Especially that little is pursued on leveraging such information for the performance benefits of scientific applications. In this paper, we focus on the evaluation, tuning and optimization of parallel I/O programs from user applications' point of view, assuming no privileges on re-configuring any system component. We first characterize the hierarchical nature of Jaguar's storage system. Then, we use micro-benchmarks to evaluate the performance of individual storage components, and the scalability of storage system for metadata- and I/O-intensive programs. Moreover, we examine the performance impacts of file distribution over Jaguar's hierarchical storage system. In doing so, we use an open-source MPI-IO library: OPAL (**OP**portunistic and **A**daptive MPI-IO Library over **L**ustre) [15], which allows dynamically-controlled file distribution by a parallel program using the MPI-IO interface [13, 14]. Furthermore, we demonstrate that leveraging the understanding of storage characteristics can directly lead to the I/O performance improvement in a combustion application, S3D [7].

The rest of the paper is organized as follows. In the next section, we provide an overview of Jaguar [11] and the organization of its storage system. Following that, we discuss our experimental analysis of parallel I/O on Jaguar in Sections 3, 4 and 5. In Section 6, we demonstrate the optimization of S3D. Section 7 concludes the paper.

2 Hierarchical Organization of Jaguar's Storage System

Jaguar's storage system is equipped with the Silicon Storage Appliance (*S2A*) from DataDirect Network (DDN), Inc. The S2A family of products has a number of key features for offering reliable, sustaining bandwidth from a large storage pool without going through a switch-based, contention-prone storage area network [5]. The current storage system deployed on Jaguar is DDN S2A 9550, a revision of S2A 9500. Each S2A consists of two Parity Processing Engines (PPEs). These PPEs horizontally parallelize the data streams to its array of Disk Controller Engines (DCE). DCEs in turn commit I/O to tiers of vertically attached SATA disks. Due to page limit, please refer to [5] for further details on the internal hierarchies of S2A.

2.1 Organization of Storage Devices and Lustre File Systems on Jaguar

Jaguar is equipped with 18 S2A storage targets, providing I/O services through Lustre file system. Each S2A target has a capacity of 32TB. We also refer to an S2A target as a *rack* as it forms an entire rack in the machine room. A separate rack is assigned as the storage device for metadata over Jaguar. Each S2A is equipped with 16 tiers of disks. These 16 tiers are organized into 16 LUNs (Logical Unit Number). Each LUN spans two tiers through vertical striping and disks within a single tier are allocated into two LUNs. Each LUN has a capacity of 2TBs and a 4KB block size. The cache is set to 1MB on each DCE.

Lustre [4] is a POSIX-compliant, object-based parallel file system. Lustre separates essential file system activities into three components, often referred to as clients, Meta-Data Servers (MDSes) that manage Lustre metadata, Object Storage Servers (OSSes) that serve clients' object requests, and Object Storage Targets (OSTs) that serve backend storage as objects, respectively. Three Lustre file systems on Jaguar provide the temporary scratch space for experimental data, namely, scr144, scr72a and scr72b. 72 I/O service PEs are configured as OSSes for these file systems. In addition, each file system has its own dedicated MDS service node. Every LUN from S2A 9550 is configured as a single OST for one of three Lustre file systems. For this reason, in the rest of paper we use *OST* and *LUN* interchangeable. We also use the term *rack* to represent all the 8 LUNs in a S2A for a Lustre file system. DDN 9550s are connected to Jaguar service nodes via direct 4Gbps fibre channel (FC) links. Fig. 1 shows the assignment of LUNs to the services nodes and Lustre file systems. The biggest file system, scr144, is equipped with 144 OSTs, i.e. 8 LUNs from every S2A 9550 storage devices, with a storage capacity of 288TBs. The other two, scr72a and scr72b, have 72 OSTs. More information on the network configuration of Jaguar can be found in [6, 11].

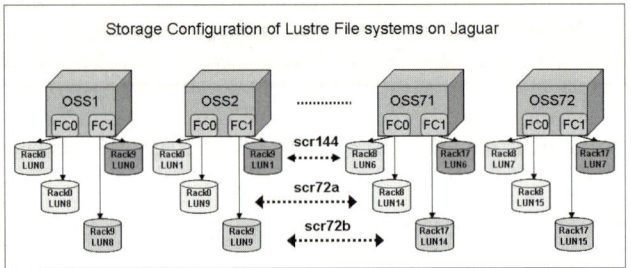

Fig. 1. Storage Organization of Lustre File systems on Jaguar

3 Bandwidth Characterization of Different Hierarchies

We start by examining the characteristics of individual components. The IOR benchmark [1] from Lawrence Livermore National Laboratory is used for these bandwidth measurements. Our experiments were conducted while other jobs were also running on Jaguar. We instructed IOR to run three iterations and reported the peak measurement. Then the same experiment was repeated 10 times. The final result was the average of 10 peak measurements.

Different Mapping of Storage Accesses – As discussed earlier, the storage system on Jaguar is presented to the parallel applications as a hierarchy of components, from individual LUNs, racks, to the entire storage subsystem. When parallel processes

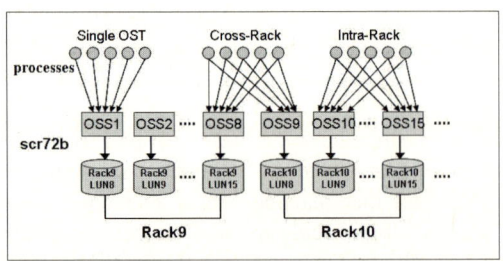

Fig. 2. Mapping Scenarios among Processes, Lustre OSSes and DDN 9550s

access files stored on the storage devices, their I/O requests are mapped to these storage components. We have categorized the scenarios as *single-OST mapping*, *intra-rack mapping* and *cross-rack mapping*. Fig. 2 illustrates these mapping scenarios on the *scr72b* Lustre file system of Jaguar. A file that stripes across all LUNs in the *scr144* file system is an extreme case of cross-rack mapping.

3.1 Single-OST

In the single-OST experiments, a varying number of parallel processes are concurrently reading from or writing to a single OST. The transfer size per client is set to vary between 4MB and 64 MB. Fig. 3(L) shows the results with a shared file. The maximum read or write bandwidths are 406 MB/s, which comes close to the peak of a single OST, with 4Gbps Fibre Channel adaptors. Comparing the read and write performance, it is evident that the performance of writes scales more gracefully under the hot-spot pressure from many processes. As also shown in the figure, the performance of parallel writes is not as sensitive to the changing transfer sizes. In addition, we have measured the performance of single-OST mapping using different Lustre stripe sizes – the unit size of objects in which Lustre stripes data to different OSTs. Not surprisingly, the stripe size does not affect the I/O performance when a file is located within a single OST.

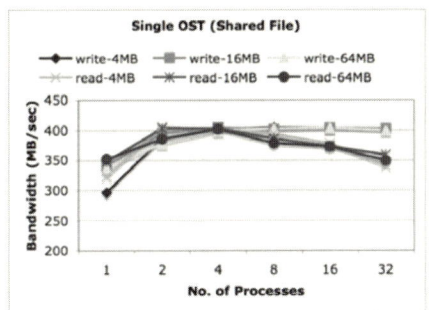
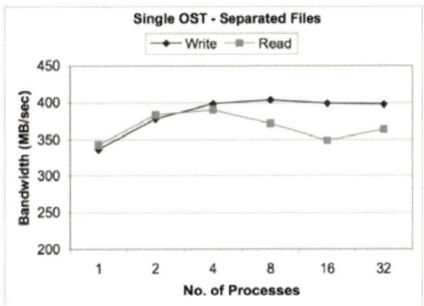

Fig. 3. Performance of Single OST: (L) Shared File; (R) One File per Process

Based on the results of Figure 3(L) (as well as those of Figure 4), we measured the performance of a single OST with separated files using only 16MB and 64MB, using the stripe size of 4MB. Fig. 3(R) shows our measurement results. Again, the performance of writes scales more gracefully to the hot-spot pressure from many processes. In these tests, both reads and writes can achieve the peak performance.

3.2 Single Rack

Single-Rack Bandwidth – We measured the peak performance of a single rack. All files are striped across 8 LUNs, i.e., all 16 tiers in an S2A target. Based on the earlier results, we have chosen the transfer sizes to be 64 MB. Fig. 4(L) shows the performance of a single rack with different Lustre stripe sizes (1MB, 4MB, 16MB and

64MB). Parallel reads provide better peak bandwidth compared to parallel writes. As also shown in the figure, the stripe sizes 1MB and 4MB are able to deliver the best performance, while 4MB is slightly better overall. The aggregated performance of a single rack increases initially with the increasing number of processes. The performance for both reads and writes reaches the peak with 16 processes. However, neither of the two can sustain the same peak performance with a strong scaling on the number of processes. As seen earlier with single OST, reads see more performance degradation due to the increasing number of processes.

We also measured the performance of a single rack with a separated file for each process, using the stripe size of 4MB. Fig. 4(R) shows our measurement results. In contrast to the single OST results, when the number of processes is less than 64, the performance of reads is significantly better than that of writes. However, as the number of processes increases, both reach a plateau at around 2500MB/sec. As shown in the figure, the peak performance is much lower than the peak physical bandwidth (8 LUNs of ~406MB/sec each). This phenomenon suggests that when all the tiers of a rack are mobilized, it does not sustain linear scaling due to potential contentions on shared data paths, such as P3E and DCE.

Intra-Rack Scaling – In this test, the targeted files are striped across multiple LUNs, starting all from the first LUN. Figures 5 and 6 show the performance of intra-rack

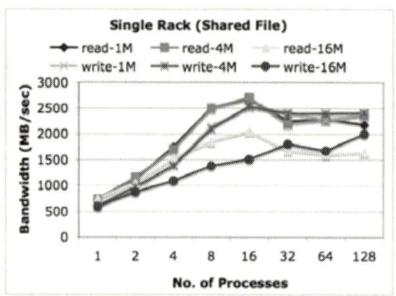
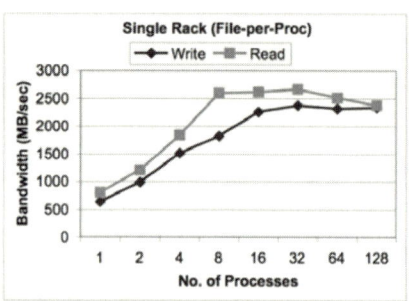

Fig. 4. Performance of a Single Rack: (L) Shared File; (R) One File-Per-Process

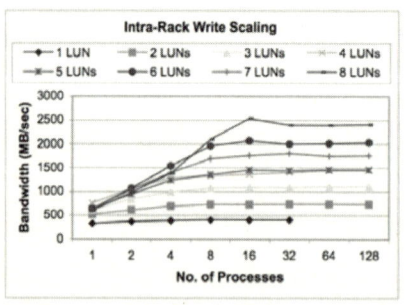
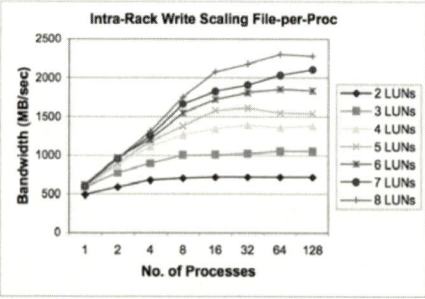

Fig. 5. Performance of Intra-Rack Scaling with Shared File

Fig. 6. Performance of Intra-Rack Scaling with one File per Process

scaling with a shared file or one file-per-processes, respectively. As shown in Figure 5, the performance of 3 LUNs is about the same with that of 4 LUNs, while the performance of 7 LUNs is rather lower than that of 6 LUNs! In contrast, these tests with one file per processes provide a different trend. The aggregated bandwidth is in general increasing along with the number of the LUNs being used. Due to page limit, only the write performance is shown. These results suggest that: (a) contentions among tiers can vary dependent on their physical locations; and (b) one file-per-process mode would help smooth out the achievable data accesses among LUNs. Our purpose for this performance analysis is to examine the performance trend of Jaguar's storage system with various testing scenarios and shed light on what possible strategies to exploit benefits or avoid impacts. The root causes of these problems need further examination of the internal processing of storage and file system. It is not intended in this application-oriented empirical I/O performance analysis.

3.3 Cross-Rack

In view of the results with intra-rack scaling, we consider that it is possible to improve the aggregated bandwidth with 8 LUNs by distributing LUNs across different racks. Without changing the configuration of the existing configuration of Jaguar storage system, it is possible to study this by dividing the stripes of a file into two contiguous racks. We have measured the performance when different LUNs across two racks are used for storage. For example, a file with 2 stripes will utilize one LUN from each rack; a file with 3 stripes will use one LUN from a rack and two from the other, and so on. We used the OPAL library for the cross-rack experiments because it provides the convenience of arbitrary specification of striping pattern on a per-file basis. Figures 7 and 8 show the performance of cross-rack scaling (write only again) with a shared file or one file-per-process, respectively. Interestingly, the earlier situation of reverse scaling in aggregated bandwidth is no longer present. One might argue that the performance difference is solely because of the utilization of more P3E engines from multiple racks. Our further study on the impact of file distribution suggests that this is not the case, because a significant performance improvement is also possible when the same racks are employed for storage, except that the first LUN starts from a different location.

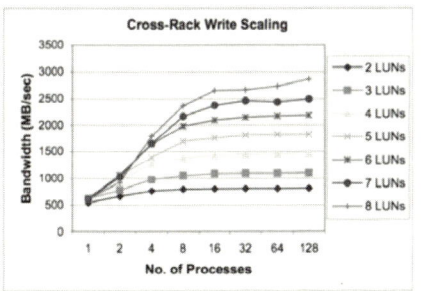
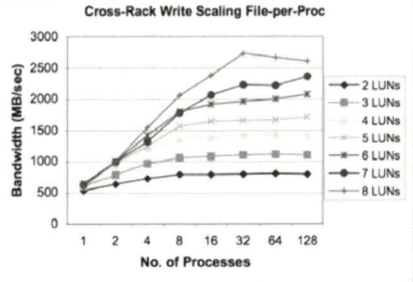

Fig. 7. Performance of Cross-rack Scaling with Shared File

Fig. 8. Performance of Cross-rack Scaling with one File per Process

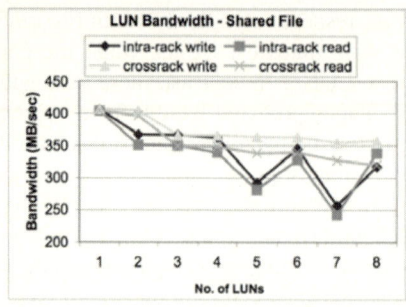 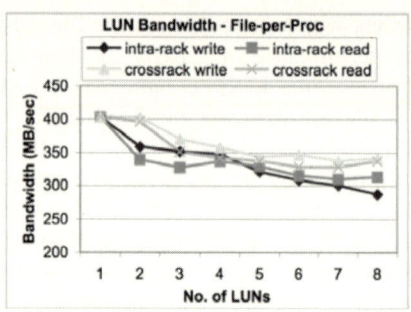

Fig. 9. Bandwidth per LUN for Intra-Rack and Cross-Rack

Achieved I/O Bandwidth per LUN – We also note the aggregated performance with cross-rack mapping rises much faster. So we take the peak bandwidth when different numbers of LUNs are used for intra-rack and cross-rack testing. Fig. 9 shows the achieved bandwidth per LUN under different mapping scenarios. It is evident that cross-rack mapping improves the performance per LUN for both the shared file and one file-per-process cases.

3.4 System Scalability

We have also measured the scalability trends with more racks of storage devices, using the largest file system scr144. Fig. 10 shows the aggregated bandwidth with a shared file. The files are created to stripe across an increasing number of racks. As shown in the figure, the performance of reads seems to scale better compared to that of writes. When files are striped across many racks, the achieved peak bandwidth per LUN is around 300MB/sec for reads, and 250MB/sec for writes. Note that this measurement is done with 1024 processes, base on the fact that too many processes to a fixed number of storage targets can lead to performance drops – a phenomenon we showed in earlier figures and also observed at other sites with similar Cray XT platforms (c.f. Figure 1 and [9]).

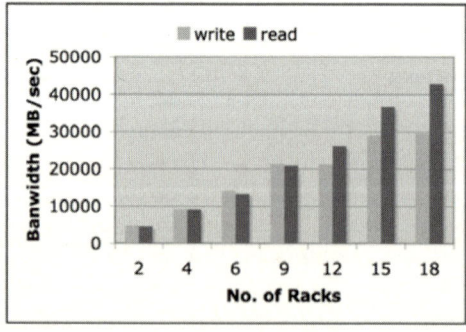

Fig. 10. Bandwidth Scalability across a Varying Number of Racks

4 Parallel File Open

Besides the need for scalable bandwidth, there is also an increasing need on the metadata scalability of Lustre over Jaguar's storage system. In particular, the problem of creating and opening files in parallel across tens of thousands of processes has been a significant scalable challenge [10]. There is also a team from the U.S. Department of Energy laboratories working on extending the current POSIX I/O interface with routines to facilitate scalable implementation of parallel open [8]. Using the scr72b file system over Jaguar, we have measured the scalability of creating/opening files in parallel across an increasing number of racks. Fig. 11 shows the time taken for opening a shared global file across all processes and the same for opening one file per process. In our tests, all files are striped with its first OST corresponds to the first LUN of the first rack. As shown in the figure, for either mode the time increases dramatically with the number of processes, as well as with the increasing racks of storage devices. Note that, besides the drawback of bandwidth scalability shown in Section 3, the one file-per-process mode is also an order of magnitude more costly than the shared-file mode.

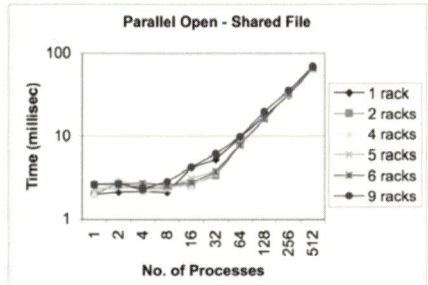 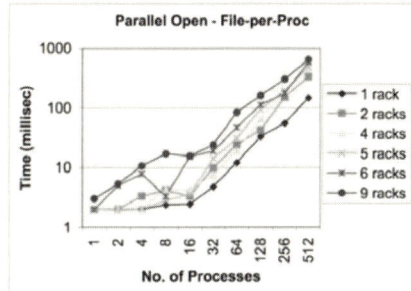

Fig. 11. Scalability of Parallel Open with an Increasing Number of Racks

5 Optimizing File Distribution

The cross-rack results suggest that the I/O performance is dependent on the physical locations of OSTs within a rack. Without changing the configuration of Jaguar's storage system in production, it is possible to examine potential benefits by adjusting the distribution of the files, especially for the one file-per-process mode. To this aim, we have used the OPAL library to create many files, one file per process. To demonstrate the possible performance difference caused by the locations within a rack, files need to be striped across less than 8 LUNs. We chose 4-stripe files in this experiment. All files are evenly distributed across all racks. However, in each test, the *offset index*–the index of a file's first OST inside a DDN rack–is globally controlled. Fig. 12 shows the performance of aggregated bandwidth with different offset indices for the first OST/LUN. Among the eight possible indices, 0 and 4 lead to the lowest performance, while all other indices can improve the aggregated bandwidth to a varying degree between 4% and 10%. The maximum process count in these tests is 256. Also note

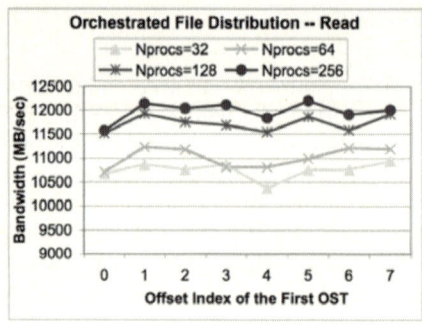
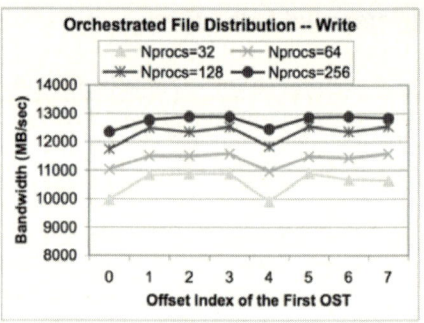

Fig. 12. Benefits of Optimized File Distribution

that in these tests all racks have the same number of LUNs being used. The only difference is on the offset indices. These results suggest that it could be beneficial for the improvement of overall bandwidth if a hierarhical storage system can be configured in a way that LUNs from different racks are interleaved with each other. This will increase the possibility of cross-rack mapping for files with small striping widths.

6 Case Study: Turbulent Combustion Simulation, S3D

Combustion simulation requires an unprecedented computational power to achieve deep understanding and fine-granularity control. S3D is a prominent application for turbulent combustion simulation. It is based on a high-order accurate, non-dissipative numerical scheme and solves the full compressible Navier-Stokes, total energy, species and mass continuity equations coupled with detailed chemistry. S3D is parallelized using a three-dimensional domain decomposition and MPI communication. Each MPI process is in charge of a piece of the three dimensional domain. All MPI processes have the same number of grid points and the same computational load. A complete course of S3D simulation can take millions of computation hours to finish. To save its intermediate simulation results, the original S3D code writes out its output from each process into individual files, periodically at every simulation step, which creates an enormous amount of data for the storage system.

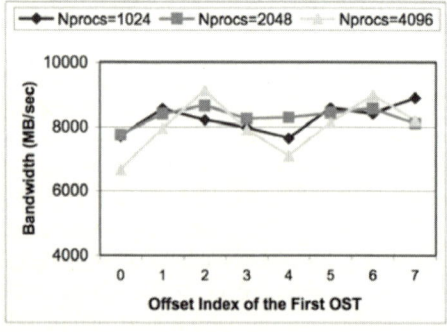

Fig. 13. Benefits of Optimized File Distribution for S3D

We exploited the benefits of optimized file distribution for S3D. With the large number of test cases, we used a smaller file system (scr72b) for this experiment. By globally orchestrating the offset index of the first OST for all files, we have measured the application-level I/O bandwidth for S3D. Fig. 13 shows that the maximum bandwidth can be achieved when the offset index is selected as 2 or 6, for S3D with 4096 processes. The performance difference can be more than 35% compared to the choices of the first OST as 0 or 4. A random choice of the first OST would be closed to the average of the eight different choices, to which the optimized choice of the first OST at 2 (or 4) can still improve an I/O bandwidth by 15%. This case study demonstrates that optimizing file distribution pattern can bring significant returns on I/O performance, especially for applications that have to maintain the one file-per-process pattern.

7 Conclusions

In this paper, we characterized the hierarchical organization of the storage system on Jaguar [11]. With an application-oriented perspective, we empirically analyzed the I/O performance of the different levels of storage components. We also examined the scalability of Jaguar storage system for metadata- and data-intensive parallel programs. We revealed that the file distribution pattern in a large-scale application can impact its aggregated I/O bandwidth. Based on our analysis, we have demonstrated its benefits to the combustion application S3D. It is also possible to optimize file distribution to gain 15% I/O performance improvement compared to the default implementation of S3D. The case study with S3D offers an example for similar optimizations to applications with similar I/O access patterns. Much of our analysis is limited with tuning and optimizations within parallel I/O library and/or user-level programs. A number of questions need to be further addressed by adjusting and reconfiguring the low-level storage hierarchies. We plan to pursue such studies with a similar, yet smaller DDN storage platform. Our empirical study presented herein could lend insights to other system practitioners on how to optimize the configuration of their storage systems.

Acknowledgments

This research is sponsored by the Office of Advanced Scientific Computing Research; U.S. Department of Energy. The work was performed at the Oak Ridge National Laboratory, which is managed by UT-Battelle, LLC under Contract No. DE-AC05-00OR22725.

References

[1] IOR Benchmark, http://www.llnl.gov/asci/purple/benchmarks/limited/ior
[2] TOP 500 Supercomputers, http://www.top500.org/

[3] Simulation and Modeling at the Exascale for Energy, Ecological Sustainability and Global Security (E3SGS), Town Hall Meetings (2007),
http://hpcrd.lbl.gov/E3SGS/main.html
[4] Cluster File System, Lustre: A Scalable, High Performance File System
[5] DataDirect Network, S2A Nearline SATA Solution Overview (2005)
[6] Fahey, M., Larkin, J., Adams, J.: I/O Performance on a Massively Parallel Cray XT3/XT4. In: 22nd IEEE International Parallel & Distributed Processing Symposium (IPDPS 2008), Miami, FL (2008)
[7] Hawkes, E.R., Sankaran, R., Sutherland, J.C., Chen, J.H.: Direct Numerical Simiulation of Turbulent Combustion: Fundamental Insights towards predictive Models. Journal of Physics: Conference Series, 65–79 (2005)
[8] High End Computing Extenstions Working Group (HECEWG), Manpage - openg (group open),
http://www.opengroup.org/platform/hecewg/uploads/40/10899/openg.pdf
[9] Laros, J., Ward, L., Klundt, R., Kelly, S., Tomkins, J., Kellogg, B.: Red Storm IO Performance Analysis, in Cluster, Austin, TX (2007)
[10] Latham, R., Ross, R., Thakur, R.: The Impact of File Systems on MPI-IO Scalability. In: Proceedings of the 11th European PVM/MPI User Group Meeting (Euro PVM/MPI 2004), pp. 87–96 (2004)
[11] National Center for Computational Sciences, http://nccs.gov/computing-resouces/jaguar/
[12] Shan, H., Shalf, J.: Using IOR to Analyze the I/O Performance of XT3, in Cray User Group (CUG), Seattle, WA (2007)
[13] Thakur, R., Gropp, W., Lusk, E.: An Abstract-Device Interface for Implementing Portable Parallel-I/O Interfaces. In: Proceedings of Frontiers 1996: The Sixth Symposium on the Frontiers of Massively Parallel Computation (1996)
[14] Thakur, R., Gropp, W., Lusk, E.: On Implementing MPI-IO Portably and with High Performance. In: Proceedings of the 6th Workshop on I/O in Parallel and Distributed Systems, pp. 23–32 (1999)
[15] Yu, W., Vetter, J.S., Canon, R.S.: OPAL: An Open-Source MPI-IO Library over Cray XT. In: International Workshop on Storage Network Architecture and Parallel I/O (SNAPI 2007), San Diego, CA (2007)

To Snoop or Not to Snoop: Evaluation of Fine-Grain and Coarse-Grain Snoop Filtering Techniques

Jessica Young, Srihari Makineni, Ravishankar Iyer, Don Newell,
and Adrian Moga

Intel Research Labs
2111 NE 25th Avenue
Hillsboro, Oregon, USA
{jessica.c.young,srihari.makineni,ravishankar.iyer,
donald.newell,adrian.c.moga}@intel.com

Abstract. Cache coherency protocols implemented in today's shared memory multiprocessor systems use snooping mechanism to keep the data correct and consistent between the caches and the system memory. This requires a large number of snoops sent out on the system interconnection links. However, published research has been shown that a large percentage of these snoops are not necessary or can be eliminated. To detect and eliminate these unnecessary snoops, several techniques have been proposed. But these techniques have not been evaluated using commercial server benchmarks and large caches that are common on today's server platforms. In this paper, we evaluate three popular snoop filtering techniques, namely Region Scout (RS), Region Coherence Array (RCA) and Directory Cache (DC), using four different commercial server workloads. We compare and contrast these three techniques and show how effective these techniques are in eliminating unnecessary snoops. These techniques differ in implementation approaches and the implementation differences yield accuracy and areas tradeoffs. We show 38% to 98% of the last level cache snoops are unnecessary in major commercial server benchmarks. With the snoop filtering techniques we are able to eliminate 35% to 97% of the unnecessary snoops with 1-3% additional die area.

Keywords: CMP, cache regions, snoop filtering, coarse-grain tracking, fine-grain tracking.

1 Introduction

Dual and Quad processor (socket) systems are very commonly used in the enterprise data centers. These are considered to be the workhorses of enterprise computing. To maintain data coherency and correctness in these multi-processor systems, cache coherency protocols [13,15] have been developed. These coherency protocols use a mechanism called snooping. Using this mechanism, whenever a processor needs an address that is either not stored in its local caches or is not in the right state, it sends out snoop messages to all the other peer nodes. Snoops are broadcast on the system interconnect and every recipient of the snoop message responds back. It has been shown that a large number of snoops get generated during program execution and the number increases with the number of processors in the system. Typically, the requesting processor has to wait for all the snoop responses to come back before deciding whether to fetch the requested address from the memory. While these snoops play a vital role in keeping the data coherent, they can cause delays, take up precious interconnect bandwidth, and consume power. The snoops that miss in all peer caches are therefore unnecessary and should be avoided. To understand the percentages of unnecessary snoops in commercial server workloads on today's server systems, we have run cache simulations using large bus traces collected for four popular commercial server benchmarks: SAP [3], SPECjbb2005 (SJBB) [4], SPECjAppServer2004 (SJAS) [6], and TPC-C [5] (more on this in later sections). Figure 1 shows the percentages of snoops that miss in all peer caches and are therefore unnecessary. The X-axis shows different cache sizes and numbers of LLCs (one LLC per socket). The data shows that for benchmarks with little data and code sharing among program threads (i.e. SAP and SJBB), more than 80% of the snoops are unnecessary. For benchmarks with significant sharing among CPUs (i.e. TPCC and SJAS), the percentage decreases as the cache size increases and as the number of caches increases. However, even for these benchmarks, at least 35% and as much as over 80% of the snoops are unnecessary.

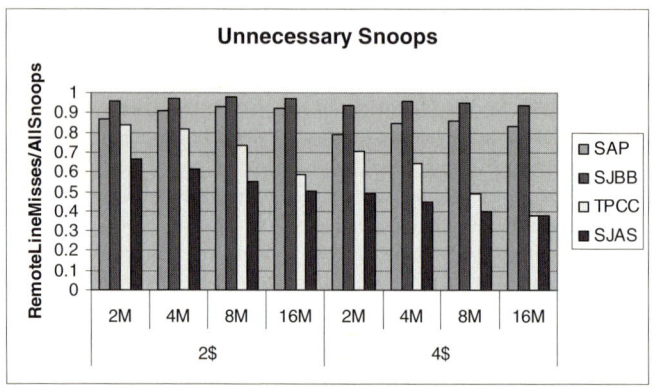

Fig. 1. Unnecessary LLC Snoops in Server Benchmarks

Furthermore, when a line is found to miss in all peer caches, the entire region of that line is also often not stored in any of the peer caches. This is called a region miss. A region is defined as a block of contiguous memory addresses and the region size is pre-defined. We have run simulations for various region sizes and the results are shown in Figure 2. The data shows that a large percentage of lines misses are also region misses even as we increase the defined region size up to 32KB per region. for all the benchmarks except for SJAS, at least 50 to 90% of the unnecessary snoops also result in coarse-grain region misses. The results strongly suggest that we can track and capture line sharing information at much coarser granularities than the line-granularity.

Several techniques have been proposed in the past with the intention of eliminating the unnecessary snoops, in particular Region Scouts (RS) [7, 9], Region Coherence Arrays (RCA) [8, 9], and Directory Cache (DC) [10, 11, 12, 14]. RS and RCA take advantage of the region miss ratios mentioned above and tracks information at a coarse-grain region level. Directory Cache stores information in the granularity of regions but tracks fine-grain sharing information for each line. However, these techniques have been evaluated using non-server workloads and with cache sizes that are far smaller than what are common in today's systems and in future systems. Large caches have potential to reduce the number of misses hence reduce the number of unnecessary snoop messages. Motivated by this, we have evaluated these three snoop reduction techniques using commercial server benchmarks with cache sizes common in today's CMPs. Our main contributions in this paper are to compare and contrast these techniques using commercial server workloads and to make recommendations based on our in-depth analysis.

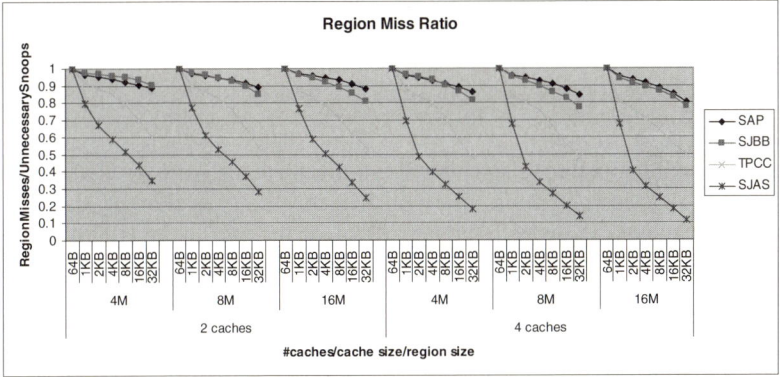

Fig. 2. LLC Region Miss Ratios in Commercial Server Benchmarks

The rest of the paper is organized as follows. In the next section, we provide a brief description of the three techniques. In Section 3, we describe our simulation tools, methodology and configurations. In Section 4, we evaluate each individual technique, analyze its behavior, and discuss its strengths and weaknesses. We also show how these techniques compare in their snoop filtering performance with similar amounts of die area overhead. Section 5 concludes the paper.

2   Overview of Evaluated Techniques

In this section, we provide a brief overview of the three snoop filtering techniques (RS, RCA and DC) by describing each's data structures and operations. For detailed description of these techniques, readers are requested to read the provided references.

RegionScout. RegionScout consists of two data structures, Cached-Region Hash (CRH) and Non-Shared-Region Table (NSRT), in each LLC. The CRH is a hash table with each entry tracking the number of cache lines currently in the local LLC for a certain region. The lower bits of the region address are used as a hashing function to index into CRH. Each entry has a present bit that is set to 1 when the counter value is > 1 (more than 1 cache line is present in the cache) and is reset to 0 whenever the counter is 0. NSRT is a tagged, set associative structure, with each entry tracking regions that are not currently in any other LLCs (i.e., non shared). Each entry has a valid bit when a region is stored in another LLC or the sharing information is unknown. Essentially, CRH indicates what regions are currently in the local LLC and NSRT indicates what regions are in the peer LLCs and determines whether an LLC miss entails snooping as usual. Upon receiving a snoop message, each LLC's CRH is looked up to determine if the region (size predetermined) is present or absent in the local cache. This region response is sent along with the conventional snoop response. If the snoop response indicates that the requested region is absent in all the peer caches, then the region is entered into the requesting node's NSRT and any further requests to that region can be avoided until at least one of the remote caches request for a line in that same region at which time the region is marked non-shared.

Note that the CRH is inclusive (i.e. the total line count in all the counters should add up to be the valid line count in the LLC) but imprecise (i.e. multiple regions can hash into the same entry because the hashing function is only a part of a region address). Therefore the counters can contain false positives.

Region-Coherence Array. RCA keeps track of shared and non-shared regions of memory in a small structure, also called Region Coherence Array (RCA). An RCA is a tagged, set-associative structure in each LLC, each entry containing an address tag for a region, a counter to indicate the number of cache lines in the region currently in the local LLC, a state bit to indicate shared or not shared state of the region, and a valid bit. An RCA entry is allocated for a region when any line in the region is brought to the cache for the first time. Subsequently, any lines in the region brought to the cache will increment the line counter for that region. Conversely, on a line eviction the line counter is decremented for that region. The RCA is accessed on each LLC miss to determine whether a snoop broadcast is necessary and is accessed when snoops requests are received to update the share state bit in the local RCA. If the entry in RCA indicates that the requested region is currently not being shared then no snoops are sent out for that region.

The RCA is inclusive (i.e. all the counters should add up to be the total valid line count in the LLC) and precise. In order to be precise, when an RCA entry is evicted due to either the set conflict or the RCA capacity, all the valid lines in that region need to be back-invalidated. This side effect will be quantified and analyzed further in the Results and Analysis section.

Directory Cache. For all the memory addresses, the information about which LLCs have particular address lines is tracked and stored in the main memory in a directory structure. In this structure, each entry contains a tag per region and an array of N-bit values, one value for each 64-byte line in this region. The full size of the array is therefore the number of lines in a region depending on the region size chosen. The N-bit value for each line tracks which ones of the N LLCs have the line. This directory structure tracks all memory addresses.

Since the entire directory is too large to be kept on the die, each LLC keeps a small tagged and set-associative structure, called a directory cache, to store entries for the most frequently used regions. Whenever there is a line miss in the LLC, we look up the local directory cache to figure out if any peer LLC currently stores the line and send snoops accordingly. If there is a miss in the directory cache (which means we don't have the information about lines in this region including the line that misses in the LLC), the entry is fetched from the main directory. When an entry is evicted from the directory cache, it is written back to the main directory.

Note that the LLCs don't inform the directory caches about line evictions. A directory cache learns that a line is no longer in an LLC when the LLC returns a miss as the result of a snoop, at which time the local directory cache updates the information about the line accordingly. As a result, there are some false positives in the directory cache which affect the efficiency of snoop filtering (but this does not cause any correctness issues).

3 Methodology

We use the CASPER [1, 2] simulator for our simulations. CASPER is a trace-driven functional cache simulator that supports a rich set of features including multiple levels of cache hierarchy based on the MESI coherence protocol. The platform we simulate is an 8-core CMP that contains two or four last level caches (LLC), with four cores sharing a cache in the case of two LLCs and two cores sharing a cache in the case of four LLCs. Since our primary interest is on the performance improvement of these techniques on server benchmarks, we experiment with four multi-threaded commercial server benchmarks:

- SAP SD/2T [3]: SAP SD 2-tier is a sales and distribution benchmark to represent enterprise resource planning (ERP) transactions.
- SPECjbb2005 [4]: SPECjbb2005 models a warehouse company with warehouses that serve a number of districts.
- TPC-C [5]: An online transaction processing benchmark that simulates a complete computing environment where a population of users executes transactions against a database.
- SpecjAppServer2004 [6]: a multi-tier server benchmark that represents J2EE application servers. SJAS models the information flow between an automotive dealership, manufacturing, supply chain and order/inventory. An industry standard benchmark designed to measure the performance of J2EE 1.3 application servers.

We collected long bus traces for these benchmarks on Intel Xeon™ MP Platform with eight hardware processor threads running simultaneously and the hardware LLCs shrunk to a very small size (256KB). The traces collected were then processed by the LLCs simulated in CASPER.

4 Results and Analysis

In this section, we first present the results for each technique with a wide range of configurations and discuss its efficiency as well as its limitations. We then choose a set of similar configuration from each technique and compare the results among them.

4.1 Region Scout Results

The accuracy of RegionScout depends on the sizes of both CRH and NSRT structures. To study the impact of NSRT sizes, we conducted experiments with extremely large CRH structures (e.g. 2M entries) to minimize the CRH size impact and varied the NSRT size from 512 entries to 16K entries with 4-way associativity. We found that 1K entries for NSRT were sufficient (is able to capture most of the region misses) to achieve close to optimal effectiveness. We fixed the NSRT size at 1K entries with 4-way associativity for the rest of our experiments.

To study the impact of the CRH size and the region size on RegionScout's snoop-filtering performance, we ran a set of experiments with a wide range of CRH sizes and region sizes for various LLC sizes (see Figure 3). It shows that benchmarks with little sharing among LLCs such as SAP and SJBB benefit from increasing region sizes since their LLC line misses often result in region misses even for large regions. By contrast, benchmarks with a lot of sharing among LLCs such as TPC-C and SJAS benefits from the region size increases up to a certain point, after which size the region miss ratio and the snoop-filtering opportunity decrease.

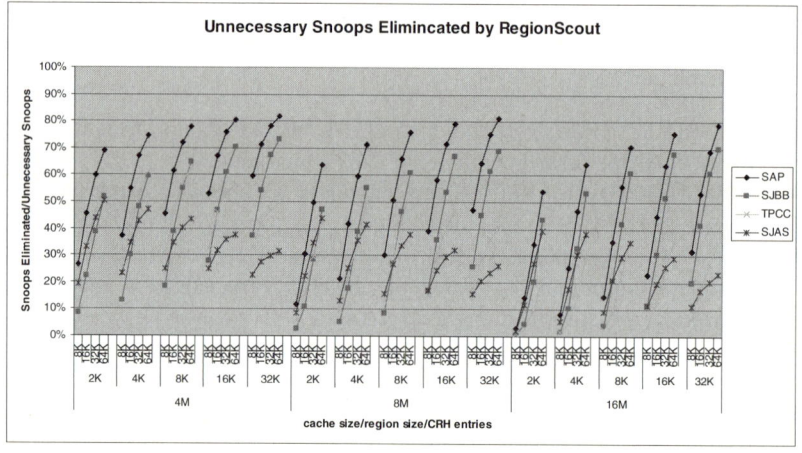

Fig. 3. Snoop Filter Rates by RegionScout

We found that in order to achieve decent performance across the board, both the region and CRH sizes need to be large. Smaller region sizes or smaller CRHs would cause more regions to be hashed into the same CRH entry and therefore higher false positive ratios. This situation aggravates when there are many collisions in the CRH and there are many accesses to the lines in the non-shared region.

To reduce the false positive ratios, we examined the CRH occupancy and collisions with various CRH sizes for all the benchmarks. We found that increasing the CRH size helped reduce collisions only to a certain extent. Due to the memory access patterns of the server benchmarks, many regions still collided into the same entries. For example, when we doubled the number of entries from 32K to 64K, the occupancy of a 64K CRH for these benchmarks was nearly halved because many regions that collide in the 32K CRH still end up colliding in the 64K CRH and nearly half of the entries are empty with no regions mapped to them. 64K entry CRH can generate false positives up to over 50% of the time with 8MB cache and this ratio increases with larger caches.

To reduce hashing collisions, we experimented with alternative hashing functions that could be feasible to implement in hardware. Instead of using the lower address bits of the region tag, we used middle portions of the region tag or even the upper address bits. We also experimented with XOR functions on two different parts of the CRH address tag bits in attempt to randomize the hashing key. However, we did not find a hashing function significantly better than the simple function of using the lower address bits that works across the board. CRH hashing collisions and the resulting false positives remain as the limiting factors in RegionScout's performance.

4.2 RCA Results

We ran sets of experiments to study the impact of various parameters on the efficiency of RCA: the associativity, number of entries, region size, and cache size. The results show very little impact of the RCA associativity (a 16-way RCA yielded up to 7% and often less improvement in eliminating unnecessary snoops over a 4-way RCA). For the rest of the experiments we used 16-way associativity for RCA. The RCA snoop filter rates are shown in Figure 4.

The results show that RCA performs better than RegionScout in general. It is worthwhile to point out that both techniques are limited by the optimal filter rates that can be achieved with coarse-grain tracking (i.e. the region miss ratios inherent in a benchmark), and the optimal filter rates decrease as the region sizes increase. While RCA can be very effective on benchmarks with little sharing, it misses to filter up to 80% of the unnecessary snoops of benchmarks that offer small region miss ratios. This seems to be a limitation of schemes using coarse-grain region-based tracking.

One significant side effect of the RCA technique is cache line back-invalidations, which cause extra cache lookups and extra LLC misses. Since the RCA is a precise

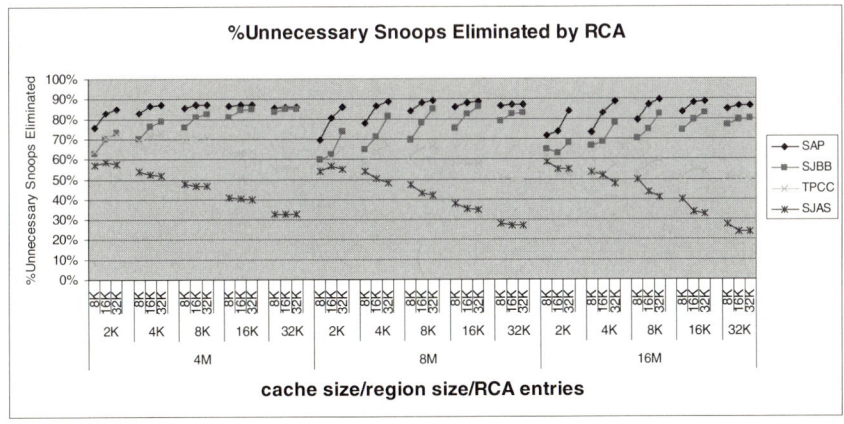

Fig. 4. RCA Snoop Filter Rates

representation of all the cache lines currently in the local LLC, whenever a region needs to be evicted from RCA, all the valid lines in that region also need to be back-invalidated from the cache. As a result, extra LLC misses occur when these lines are needed by the processor later. We ran experiments to quantify this side effect. We found that the extra LLC miss ratios can be as high as 70% even for 16K-entry RCAs and 8KB regions. Increasing the region size and RCA entries helped reducing the extra misses. For example, a 32K-entry RCA with a region size of 16KB resulted in 5% extra LLC misses.

4.3 Directory Cache Results

The directory cache stores information in the granularity of regions but tracks fine-grain sharing information for each line. The directory cache's snoop filter rates are not limited by the region miss ratios as the coarse-grain techniques. The following graph shows the directory cache can achieve very high unnecessary snoop filter rates. The results are the same for different directory cache sizes and region sizes since, if the directory cache does not currently have the sharing information of a region, it will simply fetch the region from the main directory in the memory and decide if snooping is required. However, one import limiting factor of the directory cache is the false positive sharing information on the lines. As mentioned earlier, the directory cache is not informed immediately when a cache line is evicted. Rather, it finds out about this information when a later snoop request of this line is responded with a negative response by the cache. The directory cache can thus contain false positive information on whether a cache has a line. The false positives directly affect the efficiency of the directory cache. Our study showed these false positives 5% to over 20% of the time.

Another important disadvantage of the directory cache is the extra latency of fetching a region from the main memory when there is a directory cache miss. It is important to have enough die areas for the directory caches to ensure a high hit ratio. We have done an extensive study on the hit ratios of various directory cache sizes. A 2K-entry directory cache has hit ratios from 55% to 92%.

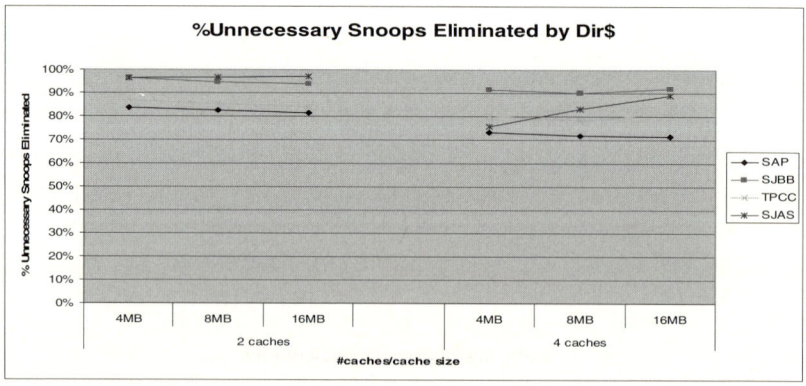

Fig. 5. Directory Cache Snoop Filter Rates

4.4 Comparison

To compare these techniques, we first calculate the die area required by each technique to decide on the numbers of entries that take up similar die areas and compare their snoop filtering effectiveness using these sizes.

For the same region size and cache size, increasing the number of entries for the directory cache drastically increases its die area, taking up much larger die areas than RegionScout and RCA. An RCA is twice as large as a CRH with the same number of entries. Figure 6 shows a comparison of performance of the three techniques and their die area overheads. RCA and the directory cache both perform better than Region-Scout. In some cases, RCA out-performs the directory cache but the directory cache works very well in cases where coarse-grain snoop filters are less effective, i.e. benchmarks with significant sharing and low region miss ratios such as SJAS.

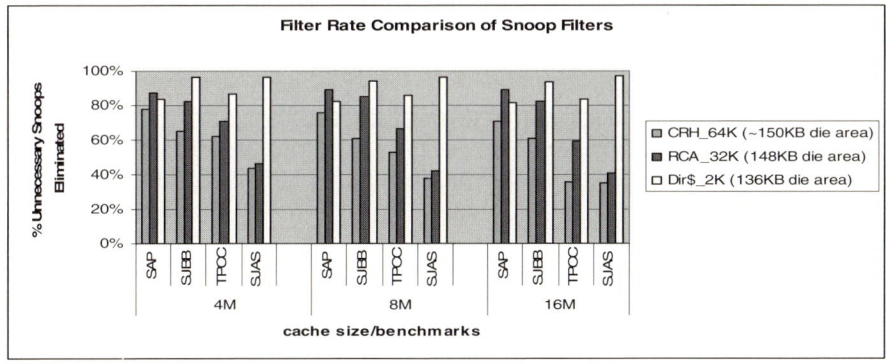

Fig. 6. Comparison in Snoop Filter Rates

5 Conclusion

We have shown high percentages of last level cache snoops are unnecessary in commercial server benchmarks. Eliminating these snoops helps alleviating LLC-to-LLC bus bandwidth demands. We have evaluated and compared three region-based snoop filtering techniques, specifically RegionScout, RCA, and Directory Cache, with major commercial server benchmarks on simulated CMP platforms of current industry standards. We showed that 35%-97% of the unnecessary snoops can be eliminated from the commercial server benchmarks. They dynamically track information to adapt to changing sharing patterns and are transparent to the operation system and software applications.

References

1. Iyer, R.: CASPER: Cache Architecture, Simulation and Performance Exploration using Refstrems. In: Intel's Design and Test Technology Conference (DTTC) (2001)
2. Iyer, R.: On Modeling and Analyzing Cache Hierarchies using CASPER. In: Int'l Symposium on Modeling, Analysis and Simulation of Computer & Telecom Systems (MAS-COTS-11) (2003)

3. Sap America Inc., SAP Standard Benchmarks, http://www.sap.com/solutions/benchmark/index.epx
4. SPECjbb (2005), http://www.spec.org/jbb2005/
5. The TPC-C Benchmark, http://www.tpc.org/tpcc
6. SPECjAppServer2004, http://www.spec.org/jAppServer
7. Moshovos, A.: RegionScout: Exploiting Coarse Grain Sharing in Snoop-Based Coherence. In: Proc. Int'l Symp. Computer Architeccture (ISCA 2005). ACM Press, New York (2005)
8. Cantin, J., Lipasti, M., Smith, J.: Improving Multiprocessor Performance with Coarse-Grain Coherence Tracking. In: Proc. Int'l Symp. Computer Architeccture (ISCA 2005). ACM Press, New York (2005)
9. Cantin, J., Moshovos, A., Falsafi, B., et al.: Coarse-Grain Coherence Tracking: Region-Scout and Region Coherence Arrays. IEEE Micro. (2006)
10. Gupta, A., Weber, W.-D., Mowry, T.: Reducing Memory and Traffic Requirements for Scalable Directory-Based Cache Coherence Schemes. In: Proc. 1990 Int'l Conf. Parallel Processing, pp. 312–321. IEEE Computer Society Press, Los Alamitos (1990)
11. O'Krafka, B.W., Newton, A.R.: An Empirical Evaluation of Two Memory-Efficient Directory Methods. In: Proc. I7th Int'l Symp. Computer Architecture, pp. 138–147. IEEE CS Press, Los Alamitos (1990)
12. Lenoski, et al.: The Stanford DASH. IEEE Computer, Los Alamitos, http://ieeexplore.ieee.org/iel1/2/3459/00121510.pdf
13. Michael, et al.: Coherence Controller Architectures for SMP-Based CC-NUMA Multiprocessors, ISCA 1997
14. Chaiken, D., Kubiatowicz, J., Agarwal, A.: LimitLESS Directories: A Scalable Cache Coherence Scheme. In: Proceedings of the Fourth International Conference on Architectural Support for Programming Languages and Operating Systems (ASPLOS IV), pp. 224–234 (April 1991)
15. Agarwal, A., Simoni, R., Hennessy, J., Horowitz, M.: An Evaluation of Directory Schemes for Cache Coherence. In: Proceedings of the 15th International Symposium on Computer Architecture, New York, June 1988. IEEE, Los Alamitos (1988)

Performance Implications of Cache Affinity on Multicore Processors

Vahid Kazempour, Alexandra Fedorova, and Pouya Alagheband

Simon Fraser University, Vancouver Canada
vahid_kazempour@sfu.ca, fedorova@cs.sfu.ca,
palagheb@cs.sfu.ca

Abstract. Cache affinity between a process and a processor is observed when the processor cache has accumulated some amount of the process state, i.e., data or instructions. Cache affinity is exploited by OS schedulers: they tend to reschedule processes to run on a recently used processor. On conventional (unicore) multiprocessor systems, exploitation of cache affinity improves performance. It is not yet known, however, whether similar performance improvements would be observed on multicore processors. Understanding these effects is crucial for design of efficient multicore scheduling algorithms. Our study analyzes performance effects of cache affinity exploitation on multicore processors. We find that performance improvements on multicore *uniprocessors* are not significant. At the same time, performance improvements on multicore *multiprocessors* are rather pronounced.

Keywords: multicore processors, cache affinity, performance evaluation, scheduling.

1 Introduction

Our study investigates performance effects of cache affinity on multicore processors. Cache affinity between a process and a processor (or a processing core) is observed when the processor cache has accumulated some amount of the process's state, i.e., its data or instructions. Affinity may be high or low depending on how much state has been accumulated. In modern multiprocessor operating systems, schedulers exploit high cache affinity by scheduling a process on a recently used processor whenever this is possible [11]. When a process runs on a high-affinity processor it will find most of its state already in the cache and will thus run more efficiently [14]. While exploitation of cache affinity is known to improve performance on *unicore* multiprocessors, its effect on *multicore* processors has not been studied. Understanding this effect is crucial for building efficient multicore scheduling algorithms. Many of these algorithms (aiming to improve performance [2,6,9,13], reduce energy consumption [8] or improve thermal regulation [4,12]) work via frequent migrations of processes among CPU cores. Frequent migrations prevent the scheduler from exploiting cache affinity and may thus hurt performance. To understand whether performance may in fact suffer, we study how variations in cache affinity affect performance of applications on multicore processors. Specifically, we compare performance of benchmarks when they run in conditions of high and low cache affinity. These data tell us to what extent performance can be improved by exploiting high cache affinity and to what extent performance may suffer if affinity is not exploited. Our results will help multi-core OS designers built better systems.

We analyze performance effects of cache affinity on *multicore uniprocessors* and *multicore multiprocessors* (see Figures 1(a) and 1(b)). The difference between the two is the physical placement of cores with respect to processor caches. In multicore uniprocessors all cores placed on a single chip, typically sharing the L2 cache. In multicore multiprocessors, there are several multicore chips, and the cores on the same chip share a per-chip L2 cache. The importance of studying both kinds of processors is that on the multicore uniprocessor, only the L1 cache affinity may be exploited (because there is only a single L2 cache), so any performance differences would come from L1 affinity. In contrast, on a multicore multiprocessor, both L1 and L2 cache affinity can be exploited because there are multiple L2 caches. Our goal is to understand the impact of both kinds of cache affinity. Processors used in our study are Sun Microsystems UltraSPARC T2000 "Niagara" (a multicore uniprocessor) and Intel Quad-Core E5320 Xeon "Clovertown" that can be configured both as a multicore uniprocessor and a multicore multiprocessor.

In the multicore uniprocessor study, we analyze how performance of applications changes if at each new scheduling quantum they run on a high-affinity core vs. a low-affinity core. Running on a high-affinity core lets the application capitalize on its L1 cache state; running on a low-affinity core requires that the L1 cache state be re-loaded. Reloading the L1 cache state on multicore uniprocessors processors is generally inexpensive, however, because it can be usually restored from the low-latency L2 cache. Therefore, we propose a hypothesis that *failure to exploit L1 cache affinity on multicore uniprocessors has a small effect on performance*.

On multicore multiprocessors, there are two kinds of affinities: affinity to the L1 cache and affinity to the L2 cache. In our multicore multiprocessor study, we focus on the effects of L2 cache affinity, i.e., how the performance of applications changes if they are always scheduled near a high-affinity L2 caches as opposed to being arbitrarily moved between high and low-affinity cores. Here, we are interested in evaluating differences between multicore multiprocessors and conventional (unicore)

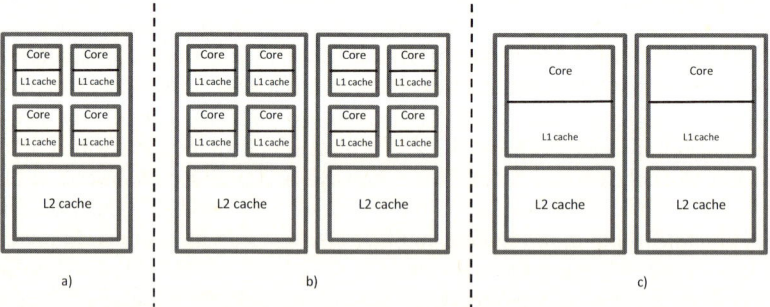

Fig. 1. Schematic view of (a) a multicore uniprocessor consisting of a single chip and four cores, (b) multicore multiprocessor consisting of two multicore chips, and (c) a conventional multiprocessor consisting of two unicore chips

Table 1. Experimental hardware

	Niagara: UltraSPARC T2000	*Clovertown:* Intel Quad-Core Xeon E5320
Clock Frequency	1.2 GHz	1.86 GHz
L2 cache groups, Cores/group	1, 8	2, 2
L1 caches	8KB D-cache, 16KB I-cache per core	32KB D-cache, 32KB I-cache per core
L2 cache	3MB unified	2x4MB unified

multiprocessors (Figure 1(c)). We hypothesize that *performance improvements on multicore multiprocessors will be insignificant in comparison with conventional multiprocessors*. On multicore multiprocessors, L2 caches are shared and competition for them can be high. As a result it is harder to retain cache state across invocations of a process. Since the degree of L2 cache state retention will be small, the benefits of exploiting L2 cache affinity will be insignificant.

Our study confirmed the first hypothesis: exploitation of L1 cache affinity has virtually no effect on performance (4% at most in an isolated case). Our second hypothesis, however, was refuted. Although we do find that L2 cache affinity has a smaller performance impact on multicore multiprocessors than on conventional (unicore) multiprocessors, we still observe that the impact is quite significant, especially for applications with large working sets. Those applications experience as much as 27% performance degradation when L2 cache affinity is not exploited on multicore multiprocessors.

The rest of the paper is organized as follows. In Section 2 we present our study on multicore uniprocessors, and in Section 3 on multicore multiprocessors. In Section 4, we discuss related work. In Section 5 we summarize our findings.

2 Multicore Uniprocessors

2.1 Methodology

In this section we restrict our study to multicore uniprocessors (Figure 1(a)). We use two hardware platforms for our study (Table 1). One is Sun Microsystems UltraSPARC T2000 "Niagara" with eight cores and a shared L2 cache. Although each core is multithreaded, we run only one thread per core. Another system is Intel Quad-core Xeon E5320 "Clovertown". Although this processor is built of two dual-core chips, in the experiments of this section we use only one of the chips for running benchmarks, hence we have a multicore uniprocessor.

We experiment with benchmarks from the SPEC CPU2000 suite [1]. We selected eight benchmarks with varied temporal reuse patterns of cached data, because temporal reuse behaviour determines the impact of cache affinity on performance. Our selected benchmarks are *art, crafty, gap, gcc, gzip, mcf, parser, twolf*. Temporal reuse behaviour of benchmarks like *gzip* and *mcf* is good. This causes them to be sensitive

Table 2. Summary of experiments ran for each benchmark

	Low L1 cache affinity		High L1 cache affinity
	D-cache	I-cache	D-cache or I-cache
High L2 retention	Run benchmark interleaved with BV_L1D;	Run benchmark interleaved with BV_L1I;	Run benchmark interleaved with BV_0;
Low L2 retention	Run benchmark interleaved with BV_L1D; Run BV_L2 concurrently	Run benchmark interleaved with BV_L1I; Run BV_L2 concurrently	Run benchmark interleaved with BV_0; Run BV_L2 concurrently

to their cache states, so cache affinity may play an important role in their performance. On the other hand, benchmarks such as *art* have a poor temporal locality. As a result they are less sensitive to their cache states and cache affinity may not be as important.

We run each benchmark in two experimental scenarios: (1) *low affinity* – when no state is retained in the core's L1 cache at each new scheduling quantum, and (2) *high affinity* – when the benchmark's state is almost entirely retained in the L1 cache at each new scheduling quantum. We measure the instructions per cycle (IPC) completed by the benchmark and its cache miss rate. Comparison of these metrics in the low and high-affinity scenarios allows us to gauge the *upper bound* on potential performance improvements from exploiting cache affinity. As such, this experiment's results tell us whether affinity scheduling would matter under *any* affinity-aware scheduling policy, all else being equal.

Here is how we create low and high cache affinity for this experiment. We run the SPEC benchmark together with a *base vector application* [5]. Base vector (BV) is a simple application that can be configured to use a pre-defined cache footprint. We bind the SPEC benchmark and the base vector to the same virtual processor, so their scheduling quanta are interleaved. Therefore, the base vector may displace the cache state of the SPEC benchmark at each quantum. We use two base vectors, BV_L1 and BV_0. BV_L1 has the cache footprint equal to the size of the L1 cache, so it completely displaces the cache state of the SPEC benchmark at each scheduling quantum. This creates the conditions of low cache affinity. BV_0 has the cache footprint of a negligible size, so it leaves the cache state of the SPEC benchmark almost intact. This creates the conditions of high cache affinity.

In addition to varying the degree of L1 cache affinity, we vary other parameters of the experiment, which are discussed below.

The size of the L1 cache. The larger the L1 cache the longer it takes to rebuild its state. Therefore, performance impact from exploiting cache affinity will be higher on systems with larger caches. To account for that, we experiment on systems with different L1 cache sizes (see Table 1).

Retention of state in the L2 cache. Performance effect of L1 cache affinity will depend on if the process reloads its L1 cache state from the L2 cache or from the main memory. To force the reloading from the L2 cache we run our experiments in conditions of *high L2 cache retention*. To force the reloading from the main memory, we run with *low L2 cache retention*. To create low L2 cache retention we run the SPEC benchmark concurrently with a base vector application configured to have a working set equal to the size of the L2 cache (BV_L2). BV_L2 is run on a different core than the main benchmark, but that core shares the L2 cache with the core on which the SPEC benchmark is run. Therefore, when the SPEC benchmark is de-scheduled, BV_L2 completely displaces its L2 cache state. For high L2 cache retention, we run *no* BV_L2 with the SPEC benchmark.

Type of cache. Performance effects of cache affinity may differ for L1 *data* cache and L1 *instruction* cache. Therefore, we experiment with these caches separately. We vary cache affinity using different base vectors for L1 I-cache and L1 D-cache. BV_L1I is a base vector configured with the I-cache footprint equal to the size of the I-cache and a negligible D-cache footprint. BV_L1D is a base vector configured with the D-cache footprint equal to the size of the D-cache and a negligible I-cache footprint.

Scheduling time quantum. When affinity is not exploited, the process must reload its cache state at each new scheduling quantum. Per-core L1 caches tend to be small, thus reloading them is cheap. So the failure to exploit L1 cache affinity will hurt performance only when the L1 cache state must be reloaded very frequently (i.e., when the scheduling time quantum is small). Therefore, while a large time quantum amortizes the penalty of reloading the cache, a small quantum causes the negative performance effects to be more pronounced. The time quantum assigned to a thread by the scheduler depends on the thread's workload characteristics. I/O intensive or interactive programs will have shorter time quanta (often as short as a few milliseconds), while CPU-bound programs may be assigned time quanta of hundreds of milliseconds [11]. To account for this variation, we used three different scheduling quanta in our experiments: two, ten and 200 milliseconds.

Pipeline architecture. Due to the ability of masking the cache miss latency with dynamically scheduling instructions, deep out-of-order pipelines have a higher tolerance to L1 cache misses than shallow in-order pipelines Therefore, performance effects of cache affinity could vary depending on the pipeline architecture. In our study we consider processors with both deep super-scalar out-of-order pipelines (Clovertown) [10] and shallow in-order single-issue pipelines (Niagara) [7].

For each SPEC benchmark we run six experiments shown in Table 2. Further, we run each experiment from Table 2 with the three scheduling quanta on the two experimental machines. This gives us 288 experiments in total. We run each experiment three times.

2.2 Results

We found that in most cases retaining L1 cache affinity had no measurable impact on performance. There was only a single experimental scenario where exploiting L1 cache affinity resulted in measurable performance difference. This was the case where the cache was large, the scheduling quantum was small, and the L2 cache retention was low. We observed it in the experiment with the Intel system (that has a larger 32KB instruction cache) with low L2 cache retention and a timeslice of 2ms (the experiment from the second row and the second and third columns in Table 2). Figure 2 shows the average IPC and Figure 3 the misses per instruction (MPI) of this

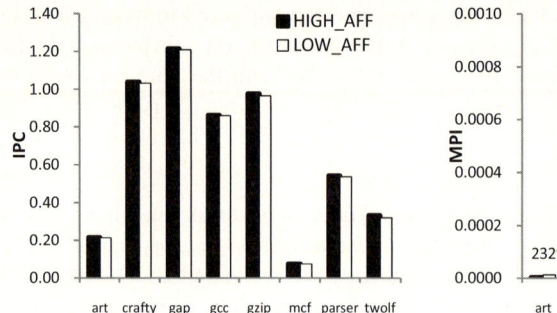 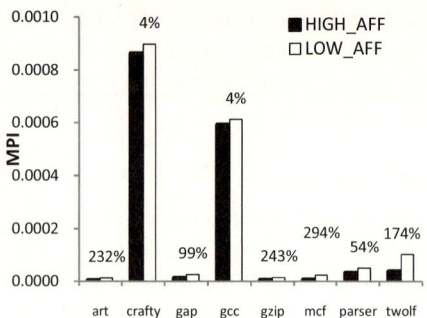

Fig. 2. IPC on the Intel system. Low L2 retention, 2ms time quantum.

Fig. 3. MPI on the Intel system. Low L2 retention, 2ms time quantum.

experiment. Black bars show the high-affinity scenario (the benchmark runs with BV_0), white bars show the low-affinity scenario (the benchmark runs with BV_L1I). *Twolf* is the only benchmark that experienced a statistically significant decrease in the IPC when the cache affinity was low. *Twolf*'s IPC dropped by 4%, accompanied by a 174% increase in the miss rate. All other benchmarks experienced IPC degradation of less than 1%.

Referring now to Figure 3, where the difference in the I-cache miss rates between the low and high-affinity scenarios is shown on top of each pair of bars, we note that although five out of eight benchmarks experienced dramatic increases in miss rates (from 99% for gap to 294% for mcf), their IPC stayed unchanged. The reason is that the cache miss rates of these benchmarks were small in absolute terms, so they had little effect on performance. These benchmarks have a good reuse of their I-cache, and that is why their cache miss rates are low. That is also why their miss rates skyrocket if cache affinity is not exploited – good cache reuse implies sensitivity to variations in the cache affinity. Benchmarks whose cache miss rates are high, such as *crafty* and *gcc*, are not sensitive to variations in the cache affinity, because their cache reuse is low.

As to the rest of our experimental scenarios, on both systems, with all scheduling quanta and L2 retention levels, we observed no statistically significant effect on the IPC as the degree of affinity varied. We did not observe any positive effects on the Intel system due to the ability of its out-of-order pipeline to mask cache latency (Niagara has an in-order pipeline). Both on Intel and Niagara systems cache affinity effects were negligible with the exception of the case reported above.

We have two explanations for these results: in the case when the L1 cache is reloaded from the L2 cache (high L2 retention) reloading the entire L1 cache is cheap, even with a small scheduling timeslice. In the case when the L1 cache is reloaded from the main memory (low L2 cache retention), the performance impact is small as well, because L1 caches tend to be small, and reloading them is cheap. On the Intel platform with larger L1 caches performance penalty is also masked by aggressive prefetching.

These results confirm our hypothesis that exploiting L1 cache affinity has negligible performance effect on multicore uniprocessors.

Table 3. Benchmark combinations

MMP		UMP	
Main	Interfering	Main	Interfering
2x art	crafty	4x art	2x crafty
2x crafty	gap	4x crafty	2x gap
2x gap	gcc	4x gap	2x gcc
2x gcc	gzip	4x gcc	2x gzip
2x gzip	mcf	4x gzip	2x mcf
2x mcf	parser	4x mcf	2x parser
2x parser	twolf	4x parser	2x twolf
2x twolf	art	4x twolf	2x art

3 Multicore Multiprocessors

In this section we study multicore multiprocessors (Figure 1(b)) and compare them to conventional multiprocessors (Figure 1(c)). For a multicore multiprocessor (MMP), we used the Intel system shown in Table 1, but unlike in the previous section, we configured it to use both chips. For a conventional unicore multiprocessor (UMP), we configured the Intel system to use only one core per chip, effectively creating a conventional two-way multiprocessor. We could use Niagara for the experiments in this section, because (by virtue of having only a single chip) it cannot be configured as a multicore multiprocessor.

We compare performance of multiprogram workloads running in conditions of high core/chip affinity and in conditions of low core/chip affinity. To create high-affinity conditions, the measured benchmark is bound to a processing core for the duration of the run. Therefore, it is always rescheduled to run on a high-affinity core. To create low-affinity conditions, the benchmark is not bound to a particular core and may thus be rescheduled to run on any core or chip, including the ones of low affinity. In the low-affinity conditions, we use the Solaris time-sharing scheduler with affinity settings disabled. This experiment thus lets us compare performance achievable by the ideal affinity-aware scheduler with the performance achieved by the affinity-oblivious scheduler. As we learned from the previous section, L1 cache affinity makes no difference for performance, so if there are any performance gains they would be due to L2 cache affinity. Therefore, in the rest of this section we talk about evaluating the effects of L2 cache affinity.

In each experiment, we use two groups of benchmarks: main benchmarks and interfering benchmarks. Main benchmarks are those whose performance we measure. Table 3 shows main and interfering benchmarks for the MMP and UMP experiments. Each benchmark gets to be in the main and in the interfering role. This creates a wide range of experimental scenarios with respect to cache reuse patterns and degrees of contention. We run several copies of the *same* main benchmark, to avoid measuring any effects due to cache contention and isolate the effects of cache affinity only.

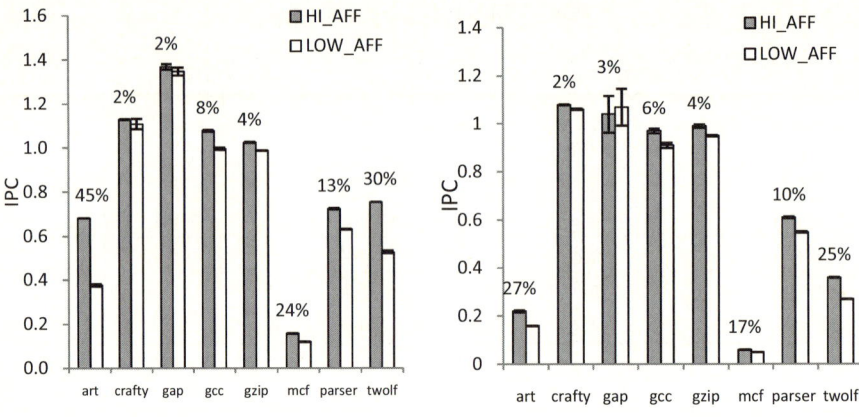

Fig. 4. IPC on UMP   **Fig. 5.** IPC on MMP

An experiment consists of running a group of benchmarks concurrently (from Table 3), on the MMP and on the UMP configuration. For each configuration we run two experiments: the high-affinity experiment, where the main benchmarks are bound each to its own core, and the low-affinity experiments where they are not bound. Interfering benchmarks are not bound to any core in any experiment.

We run the benchmarks with a 2ms scheduling time quantum, because this is where cache affinity has the most impact – our goal is to measure the upper bound. We run each main benchmark three times to measure the IPC and another three times to measure the L2 cache miss rate. (Separate runs were needed because only a single hardware counter was operational on our Intel system.)

Figures 4 and 5 show the IPC of the main benchmarks on UMP and MMP systems with high affinity (HI_AFF) and with low affinity (LOW_AFF). (Note the difference in scale on the Y-axis.) The bars indicate average values, and the whiskers denote two standard deviations. The percent values at the top of each pair of bars show the decrease in performance between the high-affinity and low-affinity scenarios. Figures 6 and 7 show the corresponding L2 cache miss rates. (Again, note the difference in scale on the Y-axis). The percentage values show the difference in misses per instruction between the high-affinity and low-affinity scenarios.

We note three things about the data. First, on both systems performance noticeably degrades when affinity is low. (Even though the *gap* benchmark on MMP appears to run more quickly with low affinity, this result is not statistically significant as indicated by the whiskers). The most significant degradation in performance is experienced by memory bound benchmarks: *art*, *mcf*, *parser* and *twolf*. Those benchmarks are more dependent on good L2 cache performance than the rest of the benchmarks.

Second, the performance impact of low affinity on the UMP system is greater than on the MMP system for all benchmarks without exception. On the UMP system, performance decreases due to low affinity by as much as 45% (for *art*) and by 16% on average for all benchmarks. On the MMP system, corresponding performance degradation is 27% (for *art*) and 11% on average for all benchmarks. This difference is explained by more dramatic increases in the L2 cache miss rates on the UMP system.

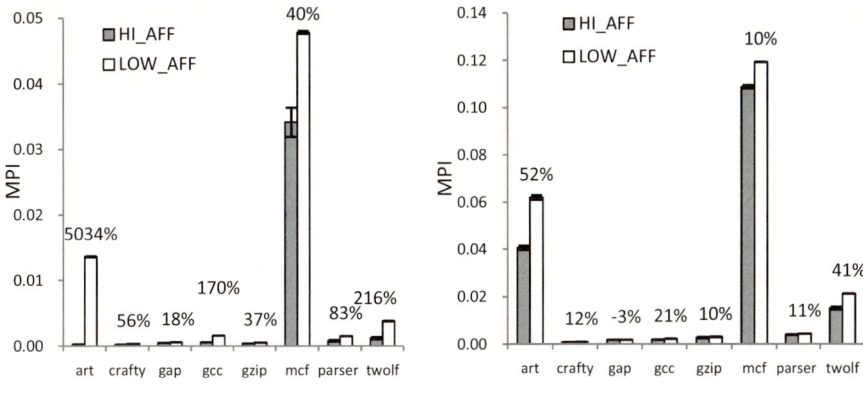

Fig. 6. MPI on UMP   **Fig. 7.** MPI on MMP

Art's miss rate increases by a factor of 51, and *gcc*'s and *twolf*'s miss rates increase by more than a factor of two. On the MMP system, all benchmarks' miss rates increase by less than a factor of two. A smaller impact of cache affinity on the MMP system could be explained by the presence of contention for the L2 cache (in contrast with the UMP system), and thus there is a lower retention of the L2 cache state across process invocations and a smaller cache miss degradation when cache affinity is not preserved. As a result, the benefits from exploiting cache affinity are lower.

Finally, we note that although performance effects of high L2 cache affinity are smaller on the MMP system than on the UMP system, they are still significant to merit inclusion of affinity awareness in multicore scheduling algorithms.

4 Related Work

Torrellas et al. studied performance effects of affinity aware scheduling on conventional (unicore) multiprocessors [14]. Affinity aware scheduling reduced cache miss rates by 7-36% and improved performance by as much as 10%, according to their study. We pursued a similar goal, but targeted multicore processors. In addition, we answered a slightly different question. Unlike the Torrellas's study that measured performance impact of a particular affinity-aware scheduling algorithm, we evaluated the *upper bound* on performance gains achievable by exploiting cache affinity.

Constantinou et al. considered performance effects of migrating a process among cores on a multicore processor [3]. They studied performance effects of warming up L1 instruction and data caches on the new core before migrating the process to that core (as opposed to leaving the caches cold). Warming up the caches creates affinity between the core and the migrated process. Therefore, experiments in the Constantinou's study effectively measured the effects of exploiting L1 cache affinity, which is similar to what we did. The key differences of our study are in the experimental conditions. While Constantinou's study varied cache affinity by warming up the caches using special hardware, we varied it by means of interfering applications in a multi-program workload. Therefore, while Constantinou's study served the purpose of evaluating migration-friendly hardware architectures, our results are applicable to scheduling. Constaninou's study evaluated deep out-of-order pipelines *only*. These pipelines are more tolerant to cache misses than in-order pipelines. We evaluated systems with both a shallow in-order pipeline and a super-scalar out-of-order pipeline. Finally, we also compared performance gains from exploitation of cache affinity on multicore multiprocessors to conventional multiprocessors. To the best of our knowledge, this has not been done in the past.

5 Conclusions

We evaluated performance effects of exploiting cache affinity on multicore processors. We studied both multicore uniprocessors and multicore multiprocessors, and evaluated both the effects of exploiting L1 cache affinity and the effects of exploiting L2 cache affinity. We hypothesized that cache affinity does not affect performance on multicore processors: on multicore uniprocessors — because reloading the L1 cache state is cheap, and on multicore multiprocessors – because L2 cache affinity is generally low due to cache sharing. Our first hypothesis was confirmed. Exploiting cache affinity on multicore uniprocessors has no measurable impact on performance even when the L1 cache is relatively large, scheduling time quantum is small and L2 cache retention is low. Our second hypothesis, on the other hand, was refuted. Even though upper-bound performance improvements from exploiting cache affinity on multicore multiprocessors are lower than on unicore multiprocessors, they are still significant: 11% on average and 27% maximum. This merits consideration of affinity awareness on multicore multiprocessors.

We conclude that affinity awareness in multicore scheduling algorithms will make no difference on multicore uniprocessor systems, but will improve performance on multicore multiprocessors. We hope that our results will help multicore OS designers build better systems.

References

[1] SPEC CPU, web site (2000), http://www.spec.org
[2] Becchi, M., Crowley, P.: Dynamic Thread Assignment on Heterogeneous Multiprocessor Architectures. In: Proceedings of the Conference on Computing Frontiers (2006)
[3] Constantinou, T., Sazeides, Y., Michaud, P., Fetis, D., Seznec, A.: Performance Implications of Single Thread Migration on a Chip MultiCore. In: Proceedings of the Workshop on Design, Architecture and Simulation of Chip Multi-Processors (2005)
[4] Coskun, A., Rosing, T.: Temperature aware task scheduling in MPSoCs. In: Proceedings of the DATE (2007)
[5] Doucette, D., Fedorova, A.: Base Vectors: A Potential Technique for Microarchitectural Classification of Applications. In: Proceedings of the Workshop on the Interaction between Operating Systems and Computer Architecture (WIOSCA), in conjunction with ISCA-34 (2007)
[6] Fedorova, A., Vengerov, D., Doucette, D.: Operating System Scheduling On Heterogeneous Multicore Systems. In: Proceedings of the PACT 2007 Workshop on Operating System Support for Heterogeneous Multicore Architectures (2007)

[7] Kongetira, P.: A 32-way Multithreaded SPARC(R) Processor. In: Proceedings of the 16th Symposium On High Performance Chips (HOTCHIPS) (2004)
[8] Kumar, R., Farkas, K., Jouppi, N., Parthasarathy, R., Tullsen, D.M.: Single-ISA Heterogeneous Multi-Core Architectures: The Potential for Processor Power Reduction. In: Proceedings of the 36th annual IEEE/ACM International Symposium on Microarchitecture (2003)
[9] Kumar, R., Tullsen, D.M., Ranganathan, P., Jouppi, N., Farkas, K.: Single-ISA Heterogeneous Multicore Architectures for Multithreaded Workload Performance. In: Proceedings of the 31st Annual International Symposium on Computer Architecture (2004)
[10] Marr, D.T., Binns, F., Hill, D.L., Hinton, G., Koufaty, D.A., Miller, J.A., Upton, M.: Hyper-threading Technology Architecture and Microarchitecture. Intel Technical Journal 6(1), 4–15 (2002)
[11] McDougall, R., Mauro, J.: Solaris^{TM} Internals: Solaris 10 and OpenSolaris Kernel Architecture. Prentice Hall, Englewood Cliffs (2006)
[12] Powell, M.D., Gomaa, M., Vijaykumar, T.N.: Heat-and-Run: Leveraging SMT and CMP to Manage Power Density Through the Operating System. In: Proceedings of the ASPLOS (2004)
[13] Snavely, A., Tullsen, D.M.: Symbiotic Jobscheduling for a Simultaneous Multithreaded Processor. In: Proceedings of the Ninth International Conference on Architectural Support for Programming Languages and Operating Systems (ASPLOS) (2000)
[14] Torrellas, J., Tucker, A., Gupta, A.: Evaluating the Performance of Cache-Affinity Scheduling in Shared-Memory Multiprocessors. Journal Of Parallel and Distributed Computing 24, 139–151 (1995)

Observing Performance Dynamics Using Parallel Profile Snapshots

Alan Morris, Wyatt Spear, Allen D. Malony, and Sameer Shende

Performance Research Laboratory
Department of Computer and Information Science
University of Oregon, Eugene, OR, USA
{amorris,wspear,malony,sameer}@cs.uoregon.edu

Abstract. Performance analysis tools are only as useful as the data they collect. Not just accuracy of performance data, but accessibility, is necessary for performance analysis tools to be used to their full effect. The diversity of performance analysis and tuning problems calls for more flexible means of storing and representing performance data. The development and maintenance cycles of high performance programs, in particular, stand to benefit from exploration of and expansion of the means used to record and describe program execution behavior. We describe a means of representing program performance data via a time or event delineated series of performance profiles, or profile snapshots, implemented in the TAU performance analysis system. This includes an explanation of the profile snapshot format and means of snapshot analysis.

Keywords: Parallel computing, performance measurement and analysis.

1 Introduction

In the evolution of parallel performance tools, the two general methods of measurement and analysis – *profiling* and *tracing* – have each found their strong advocates and critics, yet both continue to be dominant in performance engineering practice. In fundamental terms, the differences between the two are clear. Profiling methods compute performance statistics at runtime based on measurements of events made either through sampling or direct code instrumentation. Tracing, on the other hand, merely records the measurement information for each event in a trace for future analysis. Whereas the statistics calculated in profiling can be computed by trace analysis, certain performance results can only be generated from traces. These results are best characterized as *time-dependent*. Indeed, tracing is fundamentally distinguished from profiling in that the trace data retains complete event timing information.

If the potential for temporal analysis of performance is tracing's forte, its weakness is the generation of large, sometimes prohibitively large, traces. In general, trace sizes are proportional to both the number of processes in a parallel application and the total execution time. Applications of a thousand processes running several hours can easily produces traces in the hundreds of gigabytes. While tracing systems have made excellent advances in dealing with trace size in measurement and analysis (e.g., the Vampir [1] and Kojak/Scalasca projects [2,3]), the use of profiling methods does not suffer such drastic size concerns.

Unfortunately, profiling also loses track of time, to put it simply. The statistics it produces are summary in nature and do not allow performance to be observed in a time relative manner. At least, this is a reasonable synopsis of what we might call "classical profiling." An interesting question is whether profiling methods could be enhanced to introduce a time reference, in some way, in the performance data to allow time-oriented analysis.

In this paper, we introduce the concept of *parallel profile snapshots* and describe how profile snapshots are implemented in the *TAU performance system*^{TM} [4]. While the approach we describe in Section §2 is simple, it is powerful in that it opens many opportunities for its use and generates a few problems to resolve along the way. Section §3 discusses the TAU implementation of parallel profile snapshots, both the measurement mechanisms and the profile snapshot output. Performance profiles snapshots can also be generated from trace analysis. Section §4 discusses how this is done in the TAU trace-to-profile tool. However, the goal of a profile snapshot capability is to add temporal analysis support to performance profiling, while avoiding resorting to tracing methods. In Section §5 we show results from the application of profile snapshots. We provide background on related work in Section §6 and give final remarks in Section §7.

2 Design

A *parallel profile snapshot* is a recording of the current values of parallel profile measurements during program execution. It is intended that multiple profile snapshots are made, with each snapshot marked by a time value indicating when it took place. In this manner, by analyzing the profile snapshot series, temporal performance dynamics are revealed. Figure 1 shows a high-level view of the performance profile snapshot workflow. For any snapshot, the profile data for each thread of execution is recorded. Depending on the type of parallel system, thread-level (process-level) profiles may be stored in different physical locations during execution. However, analysis of temporal performance dynamics requires all parallel profile snapshots to be merged beforehand.

A *snapshot trigger* determines when a profile snapshot is taken. Triggers are defined with respect to actions that occur during execution, either externally, within the performance measurement system, or at the program level. Timer-based triggers initiate profile snapshots at regular fixed time internals. These intervals can be changed during the execution. Triggers can be conditional, determined by performance or application state. The key issue is where trigger control is located. User-level trigger control allows a profile snapshot to be taken at any point in the program. The performance measurement system can invoke triggers at points where it has gained execution control.

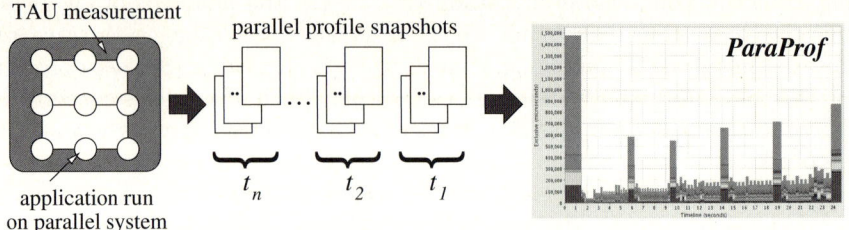

Fig. 1. Profile snapshot architecture

Because the profile snapshots being taken are from parallel executions, the triggers are also executed in parallel. There may be different triggers for different threads of execution and they may be based on different conditions. Thus, it is possible for profile snapshots to be made at different times for different threads for different reasons. Profile snapshots can also record any portion of the parallel profile state by selecting which performance events are of interest and what performance data (e.g., time and counters) should be stored.

A series of parallel profile snapshots is a time-sequence representation of the changing performance measurements of a program's execution. Flexibility in trigger control and profile snapshot selection is important to allow the desired views of temporal performance dynamics to be obtained. For instance, timer-based triggers allow performance frequency and rates to be calculated. However, interpreting the relationship between profile snapshots and between different threads of execution for the same 'logical' snapshot can be tricky, especially when the per thread snapshots are recorded at different time points. One of the challenges of parallel profile snapshots is capturing "synchronized" performance state across the whole parallel execution. As the application scales, this becomes more difficult. In general, by associating profile snapshots (triggers and profile selection) with application semantics (e.g., between computation phases), analysis results can be more meaningfully interpreted.

3 Profile Snapshots in TAU

We have implemented profile snapshot data collection in TAU. The measurement system, API, and analysis tools have all been extended to support this new technique.

We have implemented a new file format in TAU to support scalable profile snapshot data collection. We created an open XML based format with concise data blocks for raw performance data. Identifier information is normalized and separated in definition blocks. Metadata blocks store machine and OS information collected by the measurement system. The format supports streamability for use in online performance monitoring. This is achieved through incremental definition blocks interleaved with performance data blocks such that there is no final index that must be read before data can be interpreted. Additionally, full definition blocks can recur in the stream to support readers that may start reading partway through the stream. Record blocks can be split across multiple files. The measurement system writes the snapshots for each thread of execution in a separate file. This way there is no need for locking between threads and no need for synchronization across process boundaries. The files can be merged by simply appending one to another, or they can be interleaved, which could be done during online monitoring using a tree network such as MRNet [5] or Supermon [6]. Indeed, we have already shown how a performance measurement system can be integrated with a transport layer such as Supermon [7] to transport distributed profiles at runtime from many sources to a single sink. We have also integrated TAU output with MRNet [8], which allows us to utilize data reductions and filters as profiles are collected through the system.

Profile snapshots are created by applications instrumented with TAU using an API call similar to existing calls for exporting profiles to disk. Some identifying information such as a character string and/or integer value can be associated with each snapshot to correlate them with application level events. For example, in many scientific simulations, there is a main iteration or timestep loop. We would instrument this by placing a snapshot call before the loop begins (called the initialization snapshot), then another at the end of the loop, identified with the iteration number. The initialization snapshot is necessary so that the first iteration of the loop is distinguished from the execution of the application before the main loop begins. At the end of execution, a final snapshot is written. The raw data from the final snapshot is the same as what would normally be written as regular profile.

The option to perform snapshot profiling is orthogonal to all of the other profiling options in TAU. It can be combined with callpath profiling, phase profiling, and any other specialized profiling options. We capture both interval events with begin/end semantics (such as timers) as well as atomic user-defined events that are triggered with application specific data values.

We have tested the scalability of this format with hundreds of processors and hundreds of events on long running applications. Depending on the application, creating snapshots at coarse intervals still provides a wealth of useful information. Our profile snapshot format typically requires on the order of 20 bytes per event recorded. In the execution of a 6 minute simulation of FLASH across 128 processors, we generated 320MB of uncompressed data (58MB compressed) with 6.3% overhead above regular profiling (which had a 4.6% overhead) . By comparison, with tracing, the same run generated 397GB of trace data and imposed a 130.3% overhead (13m31s).

We have extended the PerfDMF [9] system to support reading the new snapshot format. For those components that cannot interpret the intermediate snapshot data, such as PerfExplorer [10], the data is interpreted as a single profile representing the entire execution, just as if regular profiling had been done. Other tools, such as ParaProf [11], can take advantage of the full range of snapshot profiles.

ParaProf has been significantly enhanced to support profile snapshots. Each chart and table can display both individual and cumulative data from snapshots, all linked through a separate window with a slider to control snapshot position. Because the snapshots are timestamped, we present it as a timeline and allow automatic playback of the execution.

4 Trace File Conversion

In addition to generating profile snapshots via TAU instrumentation, we have implemented a tool for extracting them from existing trace data. A full program trace implicitly contains all profile data that might have been extracted from the traced application. By converting traces to profile snapshots we open the wealth of data contained in traces to profile and profile snapshot analysis methods.

We developed the trace-to-snapshot functionality by extending an existing trace-to-profile utility in TAU. It operates by reading trace files and maintaining a time-stamped callstack of trace events. From this, it is able to produce profile files through simulation of the original program execution, essentially using the trace data as a script.

Each thread of execution in the trace is assigned an individual callstack which records the inclusive and exclusive time spent in routines as they are entered and exited. The callstack data structure also aggregates any user defined event data contained in the trace. Profile snapshots are produced by periodically finalizing the current callstacks, as if all active routines exited at the current timestamp. The collected profile data is then written to disk. The converter then resumes the simulation with a non-finalized version of the callstack.

The trace-to-profile converter generates snapshots on the basis of specified time intervals by default. However, all collected metrics remain visible to the snapshot logic throughout the conversion process. Wall clock time intervals are merely one special case. Other triggers for snapshot generation, such as inclusive or exclusive time spent in a given routine, the number of calls to a given routine or the value of a given hardware counter can be just as easily designated as triggers for snapshot generation. Because they are driven by program behavior rather than static time increments, snapshots generated by these triggers may reveal more about the program's behavior with respect to certain phases of execution.

The process of converting multi-threaded traces to profile snapshots is embarrassingly parallel. So long as the trace files themselves are not merged, the trace-to-profile converter can be independently invoked on the trace output of distinct processes. No programmatic means of taking advantage of this parallelism, which also exists in merged traces, has been implemented, however.

Because event driven trace files typically share analogous content it is straightforward to extend the converter's format recognition. We leveraged this innate flexibility by separating the trace event processing routines from the trace reader API in use. This makes it fairly simple to extend the converted to support other trace formats.

5 Application of Profile Snapshots

We have applied our profile snapshot technique to the FLASH [12] application from the ASC Flash Center at the University of Chicago.

FLASH is a parallel adaptive-mesh multi-physics simulation code designed to solve nuclear astrophysical problems related to exploding stars. The FLASH code solves the Euler equations for compressible flow and the Poisson equation for self-gravity.

We instrumented FLASH with TAU using PDT [13] for routine level timing information. The instrumentation has been optimized so that not all routines are instrumented (to reduce overhead, small routines which are called with very high frequency are often excluded [14]). We instrumented the main iteration loop for snapshots using the method described in section §3. Each iteration of the loop takes a different amount of time due to a variety of factors. The profile snapshot technique allows us to verify what is happening in the simulation.

Some iterations perform different tasks such as checkpointing and AMR re-gridding. Regular profiling will tell us the aggregate time that these operations take for the entire execution, but the per-iteration snapshots will show how these operations perform within the context of the iteration. Additionally, we find that the amount of work per iteration increases due to the mesh refinement. There are more total leaf blocks in the grid and thus more work to do. We can verify this behavior and its effects with snapshot profiles.

Figure 2 shows a variety of analysis displays from ParaProf showing performance data from each of the profile snapshots. The data shown here is for MPI rank 0 from a 6 minute 128 processor run on LLNL's Atlas machine. Figure 2(a) shows the time taken in each of the top 20 events for each snapshot, across a timeline, as a stacked bar chart. The data here is *differential*, meaning that the snapshots are viewed as the difference between the timing information at the start of the snapshot vs. the end of the snapshot. Alternatively, we can view each chart in cumulative mode. Figure 2(b) shows a line chart of the number of calls for the top 20 routines. The AMR grid used in FLASH is refined as the simulation proceeds, so we expect to see more calls and more time spent in later timesteps. This is verified by the data we see in the profile snapshots.

Figure 2(c) shows the differential per call exclusive time. Because the per call value can decrease between snapshots, the values here can be negative. Here we see that the *MPI_Alltoall()* call has spikes of large per-call values during certain iterations. While the regular snapshot view would show us that more time is spent in this routine, it could be due to more *MPI_Alltoall()* calls being made, however, with this view, we are able to determine that the duration of each call has actually increased.

Figure 2(d) shows the cumulative exclusive percent of time spent in each of the top 20 routines. As expected, the cumulative percentage of time spent in each routine stabilizes as the simulation proceeds.

Each of ParaProf's regular displays can show cumulative or differential snapshot data. A slider is used to select which snapshot is currently viewed across all windows. Additionally, the execution history can be replayed automatically

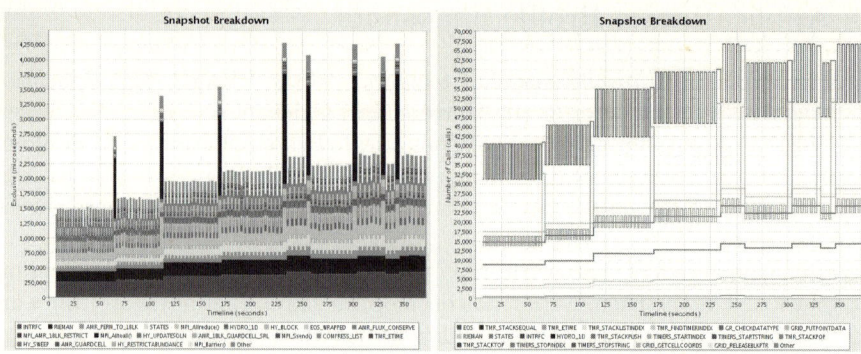

a. Differential exclusive time, stacked   b. Differential number of calls, line chart

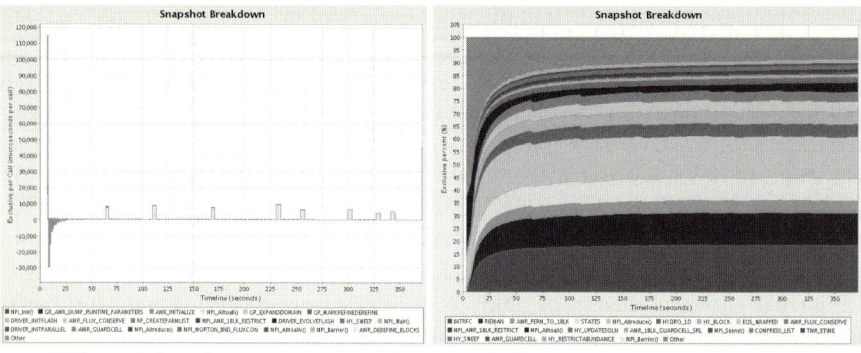

c. Differential exclusive time per call   d. Cumulative exclusive percent

Fig. 2. ParaProf charts of profile snapshots from FLASH

Fig. 3. Three-dimensional scatterplots from cumulative snapshots showing the change in clustering over time

and the user can watch as each window animates through the history of the execution, similar to a saved history of an online monitoring framework.

Figure 3 shows one of the three dimensional charts from ParaProf for two different snapshots. The 3D scatterplot can be used to determine performance data clustering. With a snapshot profile, we can see how the clustering changes over the course of the execution of the application.

Using the new capabilities provided by profile snapshots in TAU, we are able to verify our understanding of the execution of FLASH and look for inconsistent program behavior over time.

6 Related Work

The concept of parallel profile snapshots complements the work by Fürlinger on "incremental profiling" [15,16] of OpenMP parallel programs. Incremental profiling shares the same objectives as TAU's profile snapshot to capture temporal performance dynamics. Fürlinger developed the *ompP* tool and has shown it to be effective at tracking variations in performance properties of OpenMP loops over time, in particular overheads associated with loop imbalance and thread synchronization. Our work on profile snapshots generalizes incremental profiling to operate with any parallel program and at any scale. TAU implements a broader spectrum of snapshot triggers than ompP's regular, fixed-length time triggers. Also, a wider choice of analysis and display is available. We should note that the incremental profile data captured by ompP can be easily converted to the TAU profile snapshot format, making it possible to use ParaProf's performance displays with ompP.

Both TAU and ompP use direct measurement for performance profiling. Other tools use statistical sampling to build profile data. The *Intel Thread Profiler*, part of the *VTune Performance Envionment* [17], and the *Sun Studio Performance Analyzer* [18] both use statistical profiling. In addition, they provide views of performance dynamics. The Intel Thread Profiler has a timeline view that highlights thread state and performance activity. Similarly, the Sun Studio Performance Analyzer captures a profile sample trace for every thread of execution that includes data about call stacks, thread microstate, synchronization delay, memory allocation, and operating system interactions, and then displays this information as a function of time. However, because they are based on statistical sampling, both tools are limited in their support for general parallel programs and profile snapshot points (i.e., triggers) are constrained to sampling events (e.g., timer interrupts). In contrast, TAU performance snapshots are more scalable and flexible in both measurement and analysis.

Statistical profiling systems include those that can externally measure application performance and provide online access to the data. The Digital Continuous Profiling Infrastructure (DPCI) [19], *OProfile* [20], and Sun's *DTrace* [21] all implement infrastructure for gathering a wide variety of application and system statistics, and connecting with daemons to process and store the results. While providing the capability to observe temporal performance dynamics, these technologies are application agnostic and not targeted to parallel applications per se. They lack the generality of the profile snapshot approach in TAU to capture and study performance behavior with respect to application semantics and performance optimization needs.

7 Conclusions and Future Work

Profile snapshots extend the capability of profiling systems with the addition of temporal data analysis without the need for full application tracing. This new capability opens up an area of time-based differential profile analysis that allows us to see how an application's performance changes through the course of its execution.

Our future plans include enhancing the snapshot triggering mechanism of both the runtime measurement system and the trace conversion utility. We would like to be able to specify and create a more rich set of triggers for snapshot creation based on runtime measurements, application level events, and conditionals. Additional enhancements to the trace-to-profile tool will include the option to specify lock step or thread-specific snapshot generation.

Profile snapshots are an ideal vehicle for integration with an online analysis infrastructure. We plan to create a robust, extendable online analysis system. Several key additions to the snapshot infrastructure will be necessary. We will need the capability to perform selective snapshots (e.g. subsets of events, counters), and allow for a reverse control channel for runtime adjustment of this selection. Along these lines, we can also build in mechanisms to buffer snapshot data for those cases where scalable I/O is not available or not necessary, in the case of online data collection.

Acknowledgments

This research is supported by the U.S. Department of Energy, Office of Science, under contracts DE-FG02-05ER25680 (Application-Specific Performance Technology for Productive Parallel Computing) and DE-FG02-07ER25826 (Knowledge-Based Parallel Performance Technology for Scientific Application Competitiveness).

References

1. Brunst, H., Kranzlmüller, D., Nagel, W.E.: Tools for Scalable Parallel Program Analysis - Vampir NG and DeWiz. Distributed and Parallel Systems, Cluster and Grid Computing 777 (2004)
2. Wolf, F., Mohr, B.: Automatic Performance Analysis of Hybrid MPI/OpenMP Applications. Journal of Systems Architecture 49(10-11), 421–439 (2003); Special Issue Evolutions in parallel distributed and network-based processing
3. Geimer, M., Wolf, F., Wylie, B., Mohr, B.: Scalable Parallel Trace-Based Performance Analysis. In: Mohr, B., Träff, J.L., Worringen, J., Dongarra, J. (eds.) PVM/MPI 2006. LNCS, vol. 4192, pp. 303–312. Springer, Heidelberg (2006)

4. Shende, S., Malony, A.D.: The TAU Parallel Performance System. The International Journal of High Performance Computing Applications 20, 287–331 (2006)
5. Roth, P., Arnold, D., Miller, B.: MRNet: A Software-Based Multicast/Reduction Network for Scalable Tools. In: SC 2003: ACM/IEEE conference on Supercomputing (2003)
6. Sottile, M., Minnich, R.: Supermon: A High-Speed Cluster Monitoring System. In: CLUSTER 2002: International Conference on Cluster Computing (2002)
7. Nataraj, A., Sottile, M., Morris, A., Malony, A.D., Shende, S.: TAUoverSupermon: Low-Overhead Online Parallel Performance Monitoring. In: Europar 2007: European Conference on Parallel Processing (2007)
8. Nataraj, A., Morris, A., Malony, A.D., Arnold, D., Miller, B.: Scalable Online Monitoring of Parallel Applications (under submission)
9. Huck, K., Malony, A., Bell, R., Morris, A.: Design and Implementation of a Parallel Performance Data Managment Framework. In: Proceedings of the International Conference on Parallel Computing, 2005 (ICPP 2005), pp. 473–482 (2005)
10. Huck, K.A., Malony, A.D.: Perfexplorer: A Performance Data Mining Framework for Large-Scale Parallel Computing. In: Conference on High Performance Networking and Computing (SC 2005), Washington, DC, USA. IEEE Computer Society, Los Alamitos (2005)
11. Bell, R., et al.: A Portable, Extensible, and Scalable Tool for Parallel Performance Profile Analysis. LNCS, vol. 2790, pp. 17–26. Springer, Heidelberg (2003)
12. Rosner, R., et al.: Flash Code: Studying Astrophysical Thermonuclear Flashes. Computing in Science and Engineering 2, 33–41 (2000)
13. Lindlan, K.A., Cuny, J., Malony, A.D., Shende, S., Mohr, B., Rivenburgh, R., Rasmussen, C.: A Tool Framework for Static and Dynamic Analysis of Object-Oriented Software with Templates. In: Proceedings of SC 2000: High Performance Networking and Computing Conference (2000)
14. Shende, S., Malony, A.D., Morris, A.: Optimization of Instrumentation in Parallel Performance Evaluation Tools. In: Kågström, B., Elmroth, E., Dongarra, J., Waśniewski, J. (eds.) PARA 2006. LNCS, vol. 4699, pp. 440–449. Springer, Heidelberg (2007)
15. Fürlinger, K., Dongarra, J.: On Using Incremental Profiling for the Performance Analysis of Shared Memory Parallel Applications. In: Proceedings of the 13th International Euro-Par Conference on Parallel Processing (Euro-Par 2007) (August 2007) (accepted for publication)
16. Fürlinger, K., Moore, S.: Continuous Runtime Profiling of OpenMP Applications. In: Proceedings of the 2007 Conference on Parallel Computing (PARCO 2007), pp. 677–686 (September 2007)
17. Intel Vtune Performance Analyzer, http://www.intel.com/cd/software/products/asmo-na/eng/vtune/239144.htm
18. Itzkowitz, M.: Sun Studio Performance Analyzer (2007)
19. Anderson, J., et al.: Continuous Profiling: Where Have All the Cycles Gone (July 1997)
20. Oprofile, http://oprofile.sourceforge.net/
21. Cantrill, B., Shapiro, M., Leventhal, A.: Dynamic Instrumentation of Production Systems. In: USENIX Annual Technical Conference (ATEC 2004), p. 2 (2004)

Event Tracing and Visualization for Cell Broadband Engine Systems

Daniel Hackenberg, Holger Brunst, and Wolfgang E. Nagel

Technische Universität Dresden,
Center for Information Services and High Performance Computing (ZIH),
01062 Dresden, Germany
daniel.hackenberg@zih.tu-dresden.de,
{holger.brunst, wolfgang.nagel}@tu-dresden.de

Abstract. Event-based software tracing is a common technique for developing and optimizing parallel applications. It provides valuable information to application designers. This paper discusses software tracing on the Cell Broadband Engine, a heterogeneous multi-core processor, which is widely used in video game consoles, blade servers, and even supercomputer studies. However, the complex design of the Cell architecture poses challenging problems to developers. Our new monitoring approach improves this situation significantly as it visualizes Cell specific events on the SIMD cores that are usually hidden to programmers. We use the Vampir tool suite for visualization. Our design seamlessly integrates with the respective MPI monitor which additionally enables the tracking of large hybrid Cell/MPI applications.

1 Introduction

Today, multi-core technology is available for many processor families. The Cell Broadband Engine (CBE) is one example that has caught the attention of both industry and academia. The first processor generation targets a large volume market being part of the Playstation 3. It is also used in blade servers. The second generation will probably drive the first petaflop supercomputer [1]. Recent publications [2,9] show first promising results to use the CBE for scientific applications. However, the heterogeneous CBE Architecture is sophisticated in many aspects: Similarities with general purpose processors are confined to a common PowerPC core (PPE) that allows conventional software to run without modifications at moderate speeds. It is necessary to use the additional SIMD cores called Synergistic Processor Elements (SPEs) to fully exploit the potential of the processor. This step is attractive but difficult as dealing with parallelization and new architectural concepts is required. Therefore, developers need tool support to deal with the complex on-chip situation that used to be "reserved" to multi-processor systems in the past.

This paper provides a concept for event-based software tracing on the CBE. Software tracing allows to record detailed program log files (traces) at runtime. Thus, important events of the program flow and their corresponding point in time can be displayed in a very helpful way. Conventional tools only cover the PPE which is of limited use. Our approach generates comprehensive program traces of the entire system and thereby supports the complex process of CBE software development. System concepts like the SPE threads, mailbox communication, and memory access via DMA transfers become more transparent. Existing MPI tracing features are retained to display conventional PPE processes communicating via message passing *and* their corresponding SPE threads at the same time. Such hybrid programs are very likely on future HPC systems.

This paper is organized as follows: Section 2 gives background information on the CBE and its already available tools for performance evaluation. Our comprehensive software tracing design for the Cell platform and a reference implementation is explained in Section 3. Section 4 presents the results we obtained. Section 5 concludes this paper and sketches ideas for future work.

2 Background and Related Work

2.1 Cell Broadband Engine

The Cell Broadband Engine is a heterogeneous multi-core processor jointly developed by IBM, Sony, and Toshiba. The processor incorporates one PowerPC Processor Element (PPE), eight Synergistic Processor Elements (SPEs), a memory controller, an I/O interface, and a high-speed bus on one chip (see Fig. 1).

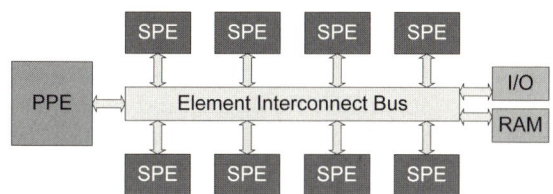

Fig. 1. Cell Broadband Engine

The PPE can be programmed like an ordinary PowerPC. For the SPEs, the programmer needs to write a separate program and pay attention to the characteristics of the CBE Architecture. SPEs have 256 KB of on-chip memory (Local Store, LS) that holds both data and instructions. This memory has its own address space and is *not* a cache. Data from main memory or other resources has to be transferred into the LS using a DMA engine that is associated with the SPE. Furthermore, the LS of each SPE is memory mapped into the virtual address space of the PPE process. Therefore, a DMA command on the SPE may access the main memory as well as the LS of another SPE – the latter resulting in an extremely fast on-chip transfer. DMA transfers are one-sided. Therefore, the partner is unaware of the ongoing communication and the events for both starting and finishing a DMA communication happen on the same unit. For fast short message communication between cores, the CBE Architecture features mailbox channels. They can be used for synchronization and are an interesting target for our tracing as well as DMA transfers.

2.2 Vampir Tool Suite

Vampir [3] is a tool for performance analysis and optimization that enables developers to quickly display program behavior at any level of detail. It converts performance data obtained from a program into different views and supports navigation and zooming within these displays. Vampir thereby helps to identify inefficient code parts that should be improved. A special focus lies on the visualization of communication and synchronization constructs in parallel programs. Huge data volumes can be analyzed with a parallel version of Vampir. Trace files are generated with the performance monitor VampirTrace [7]. Its output files comply with the *Open Trace Format* (OTF) [8]. Both VampirTrace and a reference implementation of OTF are available as Open Source.

2.3 Cell Enabled Software Tracing Tools

To the knowledge of the authors, there are two tracing tools available for Cell systems. *Paraver* [10] can be used to analyze and visualize MPI and OpenMP programs. It supports hardware performance counters and provides a GUI for trace data visualization. An instrumentation package for the Cell platform is included. It supports basic manual instrumentation of SPE code but does not automatically cover SPE communication facilities. A combination with standard MPI tracing is possible. The *Cell BE Performance Debugging Tool* (PDT) [6] is the second tracing representative. It instruments selected functions of the Cell SDK in order to generate trace files. Re-linking and re-compiling the PPE and SPE code are required respectively. Additionally, the PDT kernel module needs to be installed. Tracing of cross-blade applications using MPI is not supported. The Eclipse-based visualization presents the data in a basic timeline view.

3 Design of the Tracing Infrastructure

3.1 Overview

The PPE of the CBE is a conventional PowerPC core. In principle, tracing of PPE events can be carried out with standard monitoring tools. However, the PPE needs to manage several tasks to incorporate the SPEs into the data acquisition. First of all, the SPE thread creation needs to be detected. This includes synchronization of the PPE and all SPE hardware timers. Furthermore, the SPE's Local Store is too small to hold extensive SPE trace data. Therefore, the PPE process also needs to take care of buffers in main memory that can be accessed by the SPEs. Those buffers need to be post-processed and written to trace files by the PPE. Last but not least, CBE features like mailbox communication with the SPEs need to be added to the PPE monitor.

A tracing concept for SPE programs needs to be designed with the overall CBE Architecture in mind. Our approach is shown in Fig. 2. Instrumented SPE programs produce performance events at runtime. These events are stored in a small trace buffer located in Local Store. As soon as the buffer is full the following happens: 1) A DMA transfer is started to copy the buffer to main memory, 2) the SPE program keeps running and uses a second buffer to store the trace information, 3) the monitor switches back to the first buffer when the second buffer is full. Assuming that the DMA transfer of buffer 1 already finished at this point, program perturbation is very small (see Section 4.2). This concept works for one SPE as well as for 16 parallel SPEs on an IBM QS20/QS21 blade with two CBE processors in an SMP configuration. The processing of the SPE trace buffers and the trace file generation is done after the program has finished. This minimizes the overhead on the PPE during the actual program run.

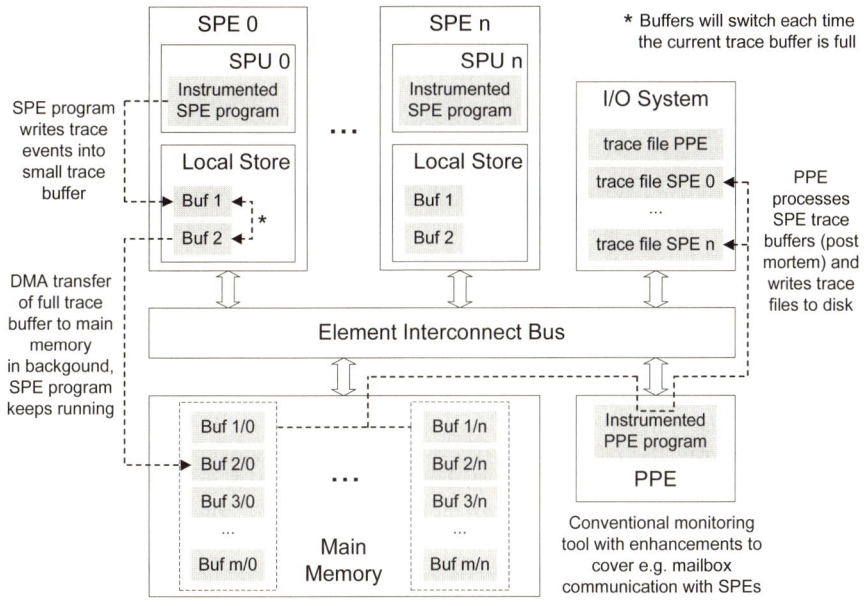

Fig. 2. Trace Design Overview

3.2 Prototype Implementation

We verified our approach in the scope of the trace monitor VampirTrace (see Section 2.2). As stated above, tracing of PPE events works out of the box with manual or compiler instrumentation. To trace a CBE program it needs to be recompiled and linked with special PPE and SPE monitor libraries. Furthermore, "wrapper" header files need to be included to allow tracing of functions provided by Cell SDK headers. Minor source code modifications provide SPE thread registration in VampirTrace, timer synchronization, and SPE trace buffer processing. Moreover, SPE user functions can be instrumented by using the provided macros.

3.3 Event Model

Our implementation enables support of the following CBE specific events:

- Enter and exit of SPE user functions
- Start of a DMA transfer on an SPE: Event information includes address, size, DMA tag, and type (get/put) of the transfer
- Wait for a DMA transfer tag to finish: Resulting in two trace events (before and after the command) to determine the waiting time
- Send and receive mailbox messages between PPE and SPE including markers to determine the waiting time

The address of a DMA transfer is useful during trace buffer post-processing to find out the target of the DMA transfer. We can currently distinguish between main memory and the SPE's Local Store. Support for other memory mapped targets such as I/O buffers can be included easily.

3.4 Visualization

The Vampir tool (see Section 2.2) provides the graphical presentation of our CBE trace files. Some aspects of the Cell architecture need to be examined with respect to visualization. The left illustration in Fig. 3 shows a conventional MPI communication where the send and the receive events occur on different locations. In contrast to this two-sided communication, a DMA transfer on the CBE is one-sided, i.e., starting of transfers and waiting for their completion happens at the same location. Displaying these transfers like MPI communication would mislead users. In case of a DMA get operation, its start event would be visually assigned to a location which was not the trigger. Furthermore, puts and gets would be indistinguishable. We therefore introduce an additional vertical line that helps to identify the active and the passive partner of the transfer. Fig. 3 illustrates the concept for both DMA get and DMA put operations.

DMA transfers on Cell have an asynchronous nature. They are non-blocking and immediately return after the transfer was triggered. The DMA transfer has to be concluded by a proper wait command prior to using its payload. It stalls until the transfer is finished or returns immediately if it has already been finished before. Therefore, we measure the time before (t_1) and after (t_2) the call. Fig. 4 illustrates this concept. If t_1 and t_2 differ by more than one time

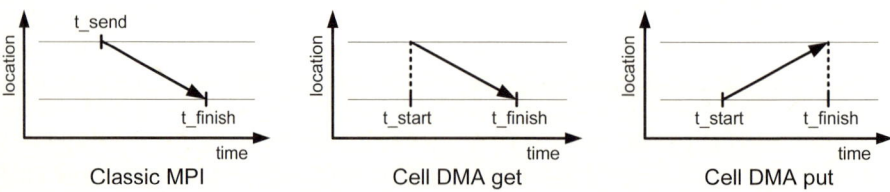

Fig. 3. Conventional two-sided MPI communication (left) vs. one-sided DMA get (center) and put (right) on the Cell Broadband Engine

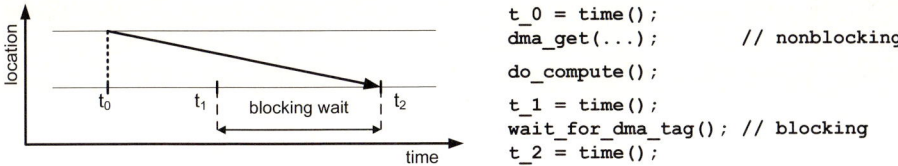

Fig. 4. Asynchronous DMA communication on the Cell Broadband Engine

step, we can conclude that t_2 reflects the transfer finish time. Consequently, a bandwidth calculation based on t_0 and t_2 is correct (unless the wait command refers to multiple DMA transfers). Furthermore, we can introduce a new time period between t_1 and t_2 that represents the actual wait phase. If the wait call returned immediately ($t_2 - t_1 \leq 1$), we can conclude that the DMA transfer most likely finished before t_1. Bandwidth calculations based on those events do only indicate a lower bound of the physical transfer rate.

Our proposal for CBE trace visualization is depicted in Fig. 5. The PPE process and its SPE threads are individually assigned to a horizontal bar, similar to the processes of MPI parallel programs. An important point is to correctly identify the passive partner of a DMA transfer. Triggered on an SPE, it may access the main memory as well as another SPE's Local Store. The latter case can be easily displayed as a line between two SPE bars as illustrated in Phase 4 of Fig. 5. For the former case we introduce an additional horizontal bar that represents the main memory. Consequently, a main memory access of an SPE is illustrated by a line connecting the SPE and the memory bar (Phase 1 of Fig. 5). Lines between a PPE process and an SPE thread refer to mailbox communication between these two partners (Phase 2 and 3 of Fig. 5).

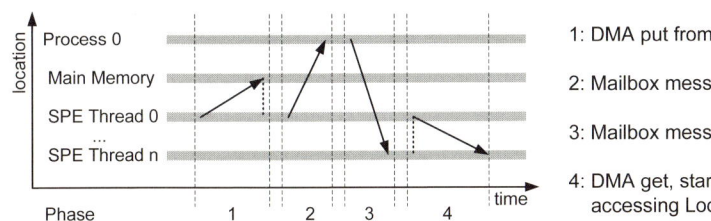

Fig. 5. Visualization of different Cell communication primitives

3.5 Hybrid MPI/Cell Analysis

VampirTrace is able to monitor large-scale MPI applications. This feature is not affected by our extensions for the CBE. Consider an IBM QS20/QS21 blade server with two Cell processors each running an MPI process that starts eight SPE threads. In this case Vampir shows two PPE processes, both with eight SPE threads and their individual main memory bar. MPI communication between the PPE processes is visualized as well. Large Cell clusters using MPI could be effectively analyzed using our extended Vampir framework. Even hybrid systems using CBE as well as x86 processors form no exception in this regard.

4 Results

4.1 Tracing Examples

We generated several traces on an IBM BladeCenter QS20/QS21 to evaluate our prototype implementation. Two examples of SPE main memory access are illustrated in Fig. 6. In the first one, SPE 2 loads data from main memory to its Local Store (DMA get). There is only one active transfer at a time. The SPE waits for the transfer to finish before it starts the next one. In the second example[1], SPE 1 stores data to main memory (DMA put) with interleaved transfers (double buffering).

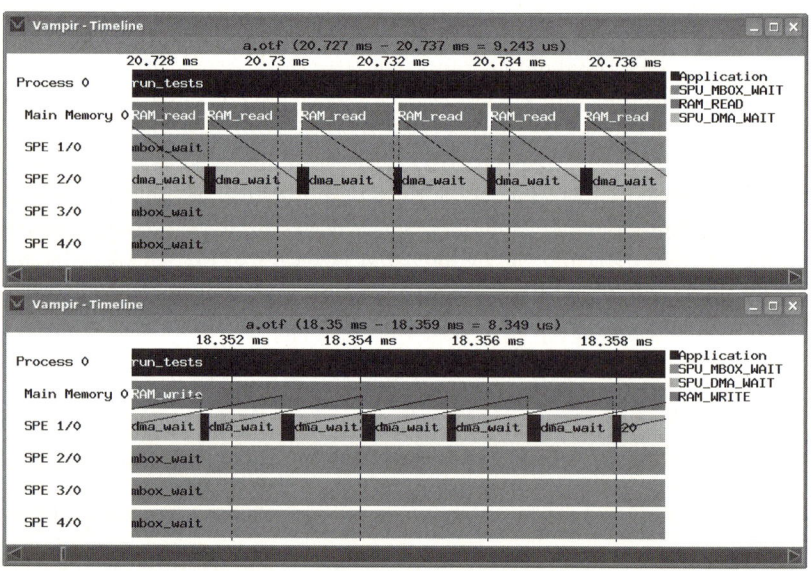

Fig. 6. Top: DMA transfers from main memory to SPE 2 (get). Bottom: Interleaved DMA transfers from SPE 1 to main memory (put).

The example in Fig. 7 shows the difference between two mailbox implementations. On the left, standard send/receive mailbox messages on the PPE are presented. On the very right, its direct problem state implementation [5] is depicted, which is significantly faster.

Local Store to Local Store DMA transfers between two pairs of SPEs are depicted in Fig. 8. Additionally, it illustrates specific message characteristics and

---

[1] Vampir uses numbers as shortcut for region names ("20" instead of "dma_wait").

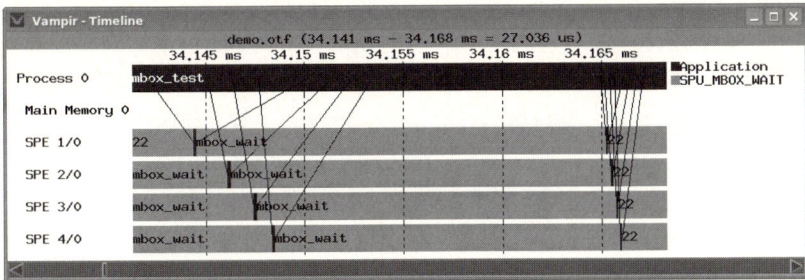

Fig. 7. Mailbox messages between PPE and SPEs: Slow regular (left) vs. fast direct problem state (right) implementation

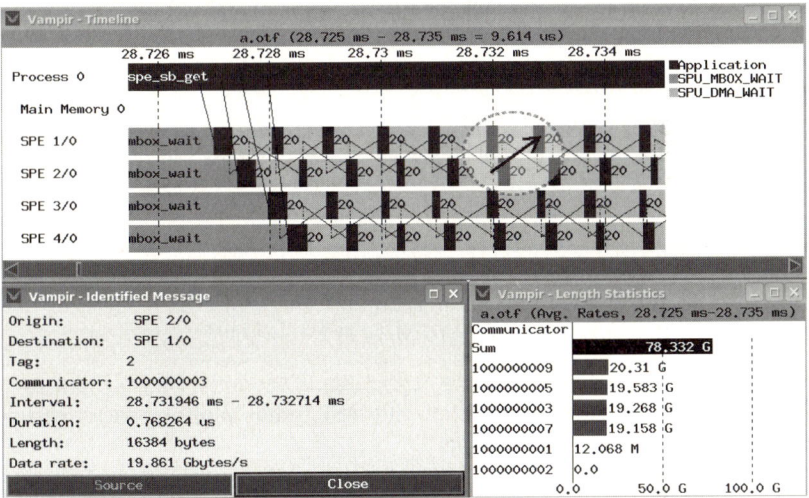

Fig. 8. Top: LS-to-LS DMA transfers between two pairs of SPEs (get). Bottom left: Characteristics of selected transfer. Bottom right: Average transfer rates in GB/s.

transfer rates. The selected message has a size of 16 KB and took 0.77 μs; the corresponding bandwidth is 19.8 GB/s. The displayed tag information (2) reflects the DMA tag of the transfer. It can be used for message filtering and other Vampir features. The bottom right part of Fig. 8 shows average DMA transfer rates per SPE. We use individual communicators to provide a logical separation of the SPEs.

The runtime behavior of IBM's Fast Fourier Transform example implementation is compared for two different page sizes in Fig. 9. The first FFT run used a page size of 64 KB and resulted in 6.13 GFLOPS. Its trace (top) reveals that significant time is spent waiting for DMA transfers. The second trace shows the same situation with huge pages (16 MB). There is much less wait time and the FFT performance raises to 25.25 GFLOPS. Both examples show the same synchronization point. The four SPEs use mailbox communication to report the

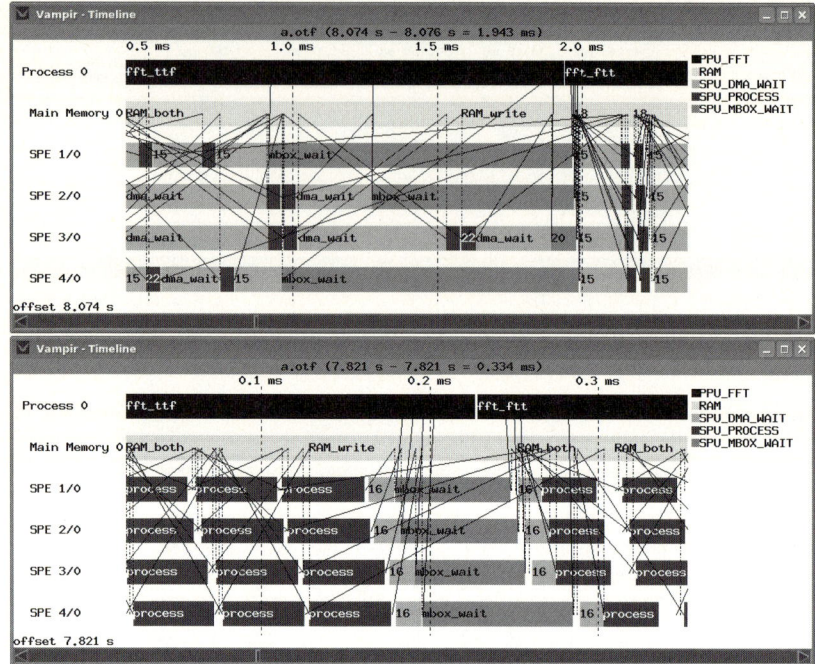

Fig. 9. FFT workload with 4 SPEs at synchronization point; Top: Page size = 64 KB (6.13 GFLOPS); Bottom: Page size = 16 MB (25.25 GFLOPS)

completion to the PPE. Shortly after, the PPE sends mailbox messages to the SPEs that start the next calculation.

4.2 Trace Overhead and Performance Impact

Our software tracing approach introduces certain overhead sources. The transfer of trace buffers from Local Store to main memory consumes memory bandwith which depends on the average trace event rate. Furthermore, the trace buffers and the monitor on an SPE need Local Store memory that cannot be used by the application anymore. Currently, our implementation needs less than 12 KB out of 256 KB. If the trace events occur at a very high rate, trace buffers may not be flushed quickly enough via DMA. In this unlikely case, the SPE program stalls until a buffer is available. Finally, each trace event on an SPE requires a function call into the trace library and the generation of the trace buffer entry.

We conducted several measurements with different Cell applications to quantify the overhead of our trace monitor. All experiments have been carried out using 8 SPEs and a page size of 64 KB. The FFT workload described in Section 4.1 slows down by 0.7% from originally 11.93 GFLOPS to 11.85 GFLOPS with tracing enabled. The fast matrix multiplication described in [4] drops by 1.3% from 203.25 GFLOPS to 200.73 GFLOPS.

The trace monitor also affects the PPE program. However, the overhead for both the SPE thread creation and post-processing the SPE trace data does not affect the runtime behavior of SPE programs.

5 Conclusions and Future Work

We presented a general concept for software tracing on the Cell Broadband Engine Architecture that allows to monitor program behavior and various means of communication, both on-chip and off-chip. We verified our new ideas in the scope of the Vampir tool suite and generated program traces that demonstrate the new possibilities. The visualization allows developers to gain new insights into the runtime behavior of their Cell applications. Furthermore, large hybrid MPI/Cell applications can be studied at a high level of detail. Our new approach generates less than 3% overhead for common applications. Future work will be carried out on even more sophisticated Cell support like automatic alignment checks for optimal DMA performance.

Acknowledgments

We would like to thank Matthias Jurenz for his valuable support with Vampir-Trace and the Jülich Supercomputing Centre for providing access to the Juelich Initiative Cell cluster.

References

1. IBM to build world's first Cell Broadband Engine based supercomputer (2006) http://www03.ibm.com/press/us/en/pressrelease/20210.wss
2. Belletti, F., et al.: QCD on the Cell Broadband Engine. In: Proceedings of The XXV International Symposium on Lattice Field Theory (2007)
3. Brunst, H., Nagel, W.E.: Scalable performance analysis of parallel systems: Concepts and experiences. In: Parallel Computing: Software, Algorithms, Architectures Applications, pp. 737–744 (2003)
4. Hackenberg, D.: Fast matrix multiplication on Cell (SMP) systems (April 2007), http://www.tu-dresden.de/zih/cell/matmul/
5. IBM: SPE Runtime Management Library (2006)
6. IBM: Software Development Kit for Multicore Acceleration Version 3.0: Programmer's Guide (2007)
7. Jurenz, M.: VampirTrace Software and Documentation. ZIH, TU Dresden (2007), http://www.tu-dresden.de/zih/vampirtrace/
8. Knüpfer, A., Brendel, R., Brunst, H., Mix, H., Nagel, W.E.: Introducing the Open Trace Format (OTF). In: Proceedings of the ICCS 2006, part II, pp. 526–533 (2006)
9. Petrini, F., et al.: Multicore surprises: Lessons learned from optimizing Sweep3D on the Cell Broadband Engine. In: IPDPS, pp. 1–10. IEEE, Los Alamitos (2007)
10. Pillet, V., Labarta, J., Cortes, T., Girona, S.: PARAVER: A tool to visualise and analyze parallel code. In: Proceedings of WoTUG-18: Transputer and occam Developments, vol. 44, pp. 17–31. IOS Press, Amsterdam (1995)

Evaluating Heterogeneous Memory Model by Realistic Trace-Driven Hardware/Software Co-simulation

Wei Wang[1,2], Qigang Wang[1], Wei Wei[1], and Dong Liu[1]

[1] Intel Corporation
No.2 Kexueyuan south road, Haidian, Beijing, P.R. China, 100080
{wei.wang,qigang.wang,wei.a.wei,dong.liu}@intel.com
[2] Department of Electronic Engineering
Beijing Institute of Technology, Beijing, P.R. China, 100081
vanvane@gmail.com

Abstract. Traditional DRAM has faced more challenges in the memory subsystem. Meanwhile, more types of memories become available as new technologies have been developed in many areas. In this case, the unified memory architecture should be changed to a heterogeneous one to utilize the new memories and obtain optimal performance in terms of memory access latency and life time. In this paper, a hierarchical model is studied and compared with a flat model. To evaluate our designs, the system bus trace is collected for realistic trace-driven simulation. We use typical server benchmark SPEC jbb2005 and typical desktop benchmarks Quake 3 and SYSmark 2007 as our evaluation workloads. The experimental results show that the performance of proposed hierarchical model is very stable in writing access and its average reading access time is not sensitive to its associativity.

Keywords: Memory architecture, Performance model, Trace-driven simulation.

1 Introduction

The performance growth of CMP processors will result in DRAM disaster [4]. Meanwhile, Phase-Change RAM (PCRAM, PCM), Magneto Resistive RAM (MRAM) and Ferromagnetic RAM (FRAM) are three main contenders in the race for replacing flash, SRAM and DRAM. Twin Transistor RAM (TTRAM) and Zero capacitor RAM (Z-RAM) are considered to compete with SRAM and DRAM in the future. This paper focuses on exploring the potential of heterogeneous memories and evaluating the architectural options in detail.

Different from the predominantly unified main memory system, in this paper we propose and investigate a mixed memory model that may adopt two or more types of memory. Our proposed heterogeneous memory system consists of 2 or more parts, each of which is denoted as M_j, and part M_i has shorter latency than M_{i+1}. Such a memory subsystem brings new opportunities in cutting cost and shrinking size for main memory.

While access to M_1 can be carried out at the fastest speed, access to lower levels has longer latency. The problem addressed here is how to design heterogeneous memory subsystem to organize different memory types so that we get the optimal performance, shorter latency and longer life time.

To simplify the problem without loss of generality, in this study we consider the case when only two different types of memories are available. One type of memory is faster, yet smaller and more expensive, while the other is slower, yet larger and cheaper. We do realistic trace driven experiments to evaluate the performance of heterogeneous memory models.

The rest of the paper is organized as follows. In Section 2 we propose two different memory models, the hierarchical model and the flat one. In Section 3 we present details for our experimental system. We evaluate our models with benchmarks in Section 4. In Section 5 we conclude and present the future work.

2 Heterogeneous Memory Architectures

In this section, we introduce two heterogeneous memory architecture models. Hierarchical model is derived from the traditional cache/memory/storage infrastructure, while flat model was originally used in embedded system including most DSPs and MCU supporting uniform memory addressing and accessing. Fig. 1 illustrates the architectures for hierarchical and flat memory models. We use Average Memory Access Time (*AMAT*) as our performance measurement during our experiments.

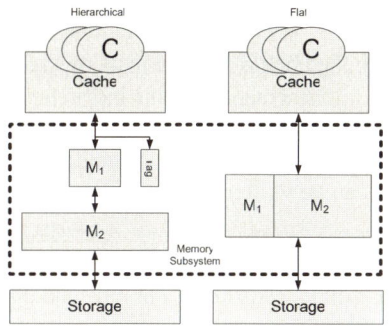

Fig. 1. Two memory models (Hierarchical and Flat)

2.1 Hierarchical Model

The idea of a hierarchical memory model is derived from the traditional memory hierarchy. In a hierarchical architecture, the upper level memory serves as an inclusive memory cache for lower level memory, where level M_i is included in level M_{i+1}. For a two level case, M_2 memory occupies the entire memory address space, while M_1 only occupies the hottest addresses. Tag is also a key consideration of memory hierarchy design. M_1 memory of larger line size and less associativity can reduce tag size. The time to find a victim tag for replacement also contributes to the miss penalty. But when compared with M_2 latency, as long as we keep this penalty low enough, the time to access and update tag could be neglected. In our experiment, SRAM tag is assumed with little overhead in tag comparison and refreshing, thus the tag time is not considered.

Table 1. Hierarchical memory model parameters

$L(atency)_{Mi\_rd}$	Time to read a page from M_i
$L(atency)_{Mi\_wr}$	Time to write a page to M_i
$missrate_{rd}$	Read misses / Read references
$missrate_{wr}$	Write misses / Write references
$dirtyrate_{rd}$	Writebacks occurred in read reference / Read misses
$dirtyrate_{wr}$	Writebacks occurred in write reference / Write misses

Some parameters are defined in Table 1 which will be used later to calculate *AMAT* for the proposed hierarchical model.

Then we can get *AMAT* by the following formula:

$$AMAT_{rd(wr)} = t_{hit\_rd(wr)} \times (1 - missrate_{rd(wr)}) + (t_{miss\_rd(wr)} + t_{dirty} \times dirtyrate_{rd(wr)}) \times missrate_{rd(wr)} \quad (1)$$

Where, $t_{hit\_rd} = L_{M1\_rd}$, $t_{miss\_rd} = \max\{L_{M2\_rd}, L_{M1\_wr}\}$, $t_{hit\_wr} = L_{M1\_wr}$, $t_{miss\_wr} = L_{M1\_wr}$, $t_{dirty} = \max\{L_{M1\_rd}, L_{M2\_wr}\}$. It is reasonable to assume L_{M2_rd} is longer than L_{M1_wr} and L_{M2_wr} is longer than L_{M1_rd}. When there is a reference from system bus to memory, the controller will first check its address in tag to see whether it hits in M_1 or not. A hit in M_1 will shorten the total access time to M_1, while a miss will result in longer reading access time due to loading data from M_2, finding a victim block and then further examining dirty bit in its tag. A dirty block will add extra time t_{dirty} to the access time as to backup the current content of the M_1 block to M_2. The dirty bit is cleared when the bock is brought in M_1 by a read reference and set after a write reference. In our first implementation of this hierarchical model, LRU algorithm is adopted for block replacement policy.

From formula (1), *AMAT* ratio of hierarchical model with different configurations (set associativity, M_1 size) can be written as below:

$$AMAT\frac{hierarchy}{hierarchy'_{rd}} = \frac{(1 - missrate_{rd}) + \lambda(\theta \cdot dirtyrate_{rd} + 1) \cdot missrate_{rd}}{(1 - missrate'_{rd}) + \lambda(\theta \cdot dirtyrate'_{rd} + 1) \cdot missrate'_{rd}}; AMAT\frac{hierarchy_{wr}}{hierarchy'_{wr}} = \frac{(1 - missrate_{wr}) + (\eta \cdot dirtyrate_{wr} + 1) \cdot missrate_{wr}}{(1 - missrate'_{wr}) + (\eta \cdot dirtyrate'_{wr} + 1) \cdot missrate'_{wr}} \quad (2)$$

Different configurations will have different missrate and dirtyrate. An extreme case is when $missrate'_{rd(wr)} = 0$, we get *AMAT* ratio of hierarchical model to entire M_1 memory.

Where, $\lambda = L_{M2\_rd} / L_{M1\_rd}$, $\theta = L_{M2\_wr} / L_{M2\_rd}$, $\eta = L_{M2\_wr} / L_{M1\_wr}$. $\lambda(\eta)$ reflects the reading(writing) access time ratio of level-2 to level-1. θ reflects access time ratio of writing to reading in level-2.

2.2 Flat Model

In this architecture, M_1 and M_2 are both connected to the system bus and each occupies a fixed part of the total physical memory address space. A case for this architecture aims at memory resource QoS. As more threads/cores are enabled on die, the computing capability is exploited by simultaneously executing multiple tasks or applications. It is common that one application requires higher priority than the others, e.g., critical application running get higher priority than common business server application. Under such circumstance, QoS-aware architecture should be designed on

Table 2. Flat memory model parameters

$L(atency)_{Mi\_rd}$	Time to read a page from M_i
$L(atency)_{Mi\_wr}$	Time to write a page to M_i
Ref_{Mi_rd}	Read references to M_i
Ref_{Mi_wr}	Write references to M_i

die. Otherwise OS should manage and schedule the accesses to the two different types of memory. For example, a memory remapping layer may be added to support this. All memory references from the workload with higher priority will be redirected to M_1, and those from lower priority will be redirected to M_2. QoS policies or priority-based policies should be considered in this model [5].

The main issue is similar with hierarchical memory model. To better utilize the speed advantage of M_1, we need to prioritize system bus requests so that we get optimal system performance. As a first implementation of the studied system, we assume only high priority workloads can use M_1 memory and workloads with low priority can only use M_2 memory.

According to such assumption, the memory management module of OS is also the priority manager. It allocates memory in faster memory for higher priority tasks and allocates memory in slower memory for lower priority tasks. High priority tasks can also use slow memory if fast memory overflows, but low priority tasks can't use fast memory. AMAT can be calculated by the following formula and the variables are defined in Table 2.

$$AMAT_{rd(wr)} = \frac{Ref_{M1\_rd(wr)} \times L_{M1\_rd(wr)} + Ref_{M2\_rd(wr)} \times L_{M2\_rd(wr)}}{Ref_{M1\_rd(wr)} + Ref_{M2\_rd(wr)}} \quad (3)$$

From (1) and (3) AMAT ratio of hierarchical model to flat model can be written as below:

$$AMAT \frac{hierarchy}{flat}\bigg|_{rd} = \frac{(1-missrate_{rd}) + \lambda(\theta \cdot dirtyrate_{rd}+1) \cdot missrate_{rd}}{(Ref_{M1\_rd} + \lambda \cdot Ref_{M2\_rd})/(Ref_{M1\_rd} + Ref_{M2\_rd})} ; AMAT\frac{hierarchy}{flat}\bigg|_{wr} = \frac{(1-missrate_{wr}) + (\eta \cdot dirtyrate_{wr}+1) \cdot missrate_{wr}}{(Ref_{M1\_wr} + \eta \cdot Ref_{M2\_wr})/(Ref_{M1\_wr} + Ref_{M2\_wr})} \quad (4)$$

From previous work [1], hierarchical model always performs much better than flat one in $AMAT_{wr}$ and write back ratio, and the $AMAT_{wr}$ of hierarchical one is shorter or longer than flat one (see Fig. 2) when λ, θ parameters change. The black region in Fig. 3 illustrates the scenario when hierarchical should be used to build a heterogeneous architecture. In this paper, we explore the hierarchical architecture in detail.

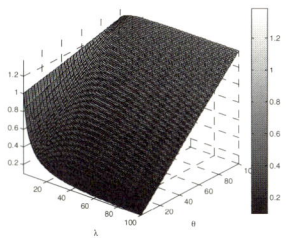

Fig. 2. $AMAT_{rd}$ Ratio

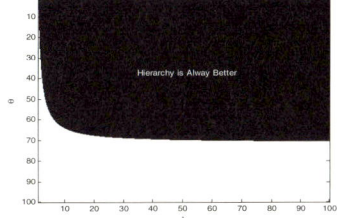

Fig. 3. Hierarchical VS. Flat

3 Research Methodology

To calculate *AMAT* with our formulas, lots of statistical results from trace-driven simulation are needed. In this section, we describe the trace-driven simulation for the proposed architectures.

There are two phases in trace-driven simulation: trace generation and simulation. In our experiment, the trace is collected from the system bus, Front Side Bus (FSB) of a machine which is running the realistic workloads and then analyzed by a simulator CASPER [3] which contains the detailed hierarchical and flat model implementations.

3.1 Physical Environment of the Simulation System

We developed an FSB transaction data collector called DragonHead (DH) 1.1. It is a system for cycle accurate long FSB trace collection and cache simulation. The experiment environment consists of eight main components, as is shown in Fig. 4.

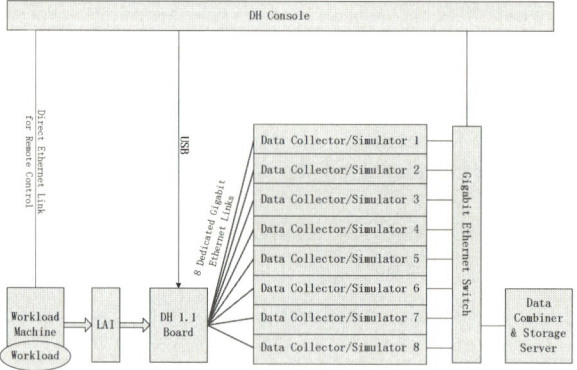

Fig. 4. Simulation System

- Workload Machine: A computer which hosts the workload and the Logic Analyzer Interposer (LAI) connectors. Its FSB traffic is captured by DH 1.1.
- Data Collector Cluster: A cluster employed to receive FSB traffic from DH 1.1 Board over Gigabit Ethernet cables.
- Data Combiner & Storage Server: A server used to receive the raw data from the Data Collection / Simulation Cluster, combine & refine the raw data to a trace file, and store the trace file. It also converts a trace file to CASPER format so that CASPER can do simulation on the converted file.
- Data Simulator Cluster: A cluster employed to run do simulations. It might be the same physical cluster of the DH data collector cluster.
- DH Console: A console which controls the whole system. It connects to the DH 1.1 Board through a USB interface, and connects to the Workload Machine, the Data Collector / Simulator Cluster and the Data Combiner & Storage Server with Ethernet link.

- DH 1.1 Board: A hardware board which collects FSB traffic and transports the collected traffic to DH data collection cluster over Gigabit Ethernet cables.
- Gigabit Ethernet Switch: It internally connects the DH Console, the Data Collection / Simulation Cluster, the Data Combiner & Storage Server, and optionally the Workload Machine;
- LAI: It connects the DH 1.1 board with the workload machine. It accepts the signals from the FSB of the workload machine.

With these components, our simulation system can generate traces from the memory references of workloads, and do simulations on these traces. In our experiment, the traces collected by DH1.1 are converted to a format which CASPER can handle.

3.2 Workload Machine

The workload machine is a dual-core Xeon server (detailed server configurations in Table 3).

Table 3. Server Configuration

CPU type	1.2GB Xeon Paxville (2 Cores with HT disabled)
Northbridge	Intel E7520
FSB frequency	100MHz
L1 Data cache	2 x 16 KBytes, 8-way set associative, 64-byte line size
Trace cache	2 x 12 Kuops, 8-way set associative
L2 cache	2 x 2048 KBytes, 8-way set associative, 64-byte line size
Page size	4096 Bytes
Memory Size	8192 MBytes

3.3 Workload

To evaluate the hierarchical model, we run standard server benchmark SPEC jbb2005 and two desktop benchmark workloads Quake 3 and SYSmark 2007. SPEC jbb2005 is a Java-based multi-threaded server benchmark that models a warehouse company with warehouses that serve a number of districts (much like TPC-C). SPEC jbb2005 is configured with 128 warehouses. Quake 3 is set to replay a DEMO, and SYSmark 2007 runs through all 4 parts: E-learning, Video Creation, Productivity and 3D.

An x86_64 kernel 2.6.18-8.el5 is installed in our workload machine as SPEC jbb2005 with our configuration consumes more than 4GB memory. For Quake 3 and SYSmark 2007, a 32bit Microsoft Windows XP with SP2 is also installed in our workload machine.

4 Experimental Result

In this section, we present the simulation result of the proposed heterogeneous memory architecture. The sensitivity of M_1 size and set associativity is shown with *AMAT* ratio and writeback to M_2 ratio.

4.1 Target Configurations

Various configurations of the studied models can be evaluated by altering parameters of the simulator. For hierarchical model, we evaluate the target systems with 8G M_2 memory and different M_1 memory sizes from 128MB to 4096MB with different associativity configurations, from 1-way to 64-way. The cache configurations of the targeted systems are the same with the workload machine (see Table 3) and configurations of the studied hierarchical memory system are shown in Table 4.

Table 4. Studied System Configurations

	Hierarchical
M_1 Size	128, 256, 512, 1024, 2048, 4096 MB
M_2 Size	8192 MB
Block Size	4096 B
Associativity	1, 2, 4, 8, 16, 32, 64 Way

4.2 Workload Characteristics

As our experimental data comes from the FSB, the 3 workloads have conspicuous differences in their memory reference behavior.

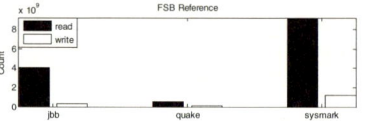

Fig. 5. Memory Reference

Missrate is a key factor in hierarchical *AMAT* model. The following figures show missrates for different M_1 sizes from 128MB to 4096MB while associativity scales from 1-way to 64-way. Read missrate is usually higher than write missrate according to Fig. 6. For most workloads, higher associativity brings much lower missrate than direct mapped when the size of M_1 memory is smaller than the working set.

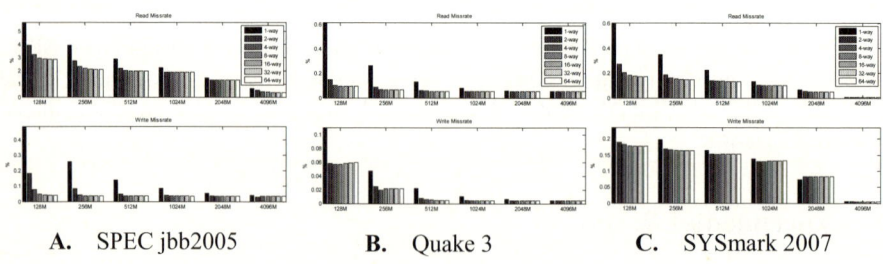

A. SPEC jbb2005   B. Quake 3   C. SYSmark 2007

Fig. 6. Missrate

4.3 Write Reference to M_2

Writeback is a vital indicator of the heterogeneous model when low speed memory has limited write times. From Fig. 7, we can conclude that higher associativity and bigger M_1 size of the hierarchical model help to reduce writebacks to M_2 for most workloads, thus give a longer life to M_2. But the performance will not go up with the growth of its set associativity when M_1 is bigger than 256M.

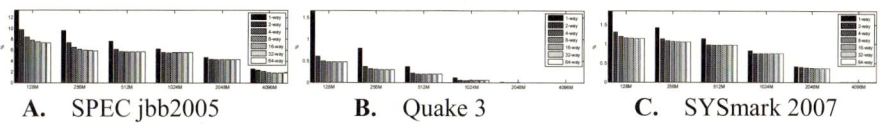

A. SPEC jbb2005   B. Quake 3   C. SYSmark 2007

Fig. 7. Writeback Ratio

4.4 Sensitivity to M_1 Size

AMAT is our major performance measurement. We did experiments for hierarchical architecture with different configurations. It's obvious that larger M_1 will result in higher performance. However, 4x M_1 size doesn't bring back 4x performance. For the best case Quake 3, the minimal $AMAT_{rd}$ ratio is 0.3 according to Fig. 8. And for write access, the performance is not so sensitive to M_1 size.

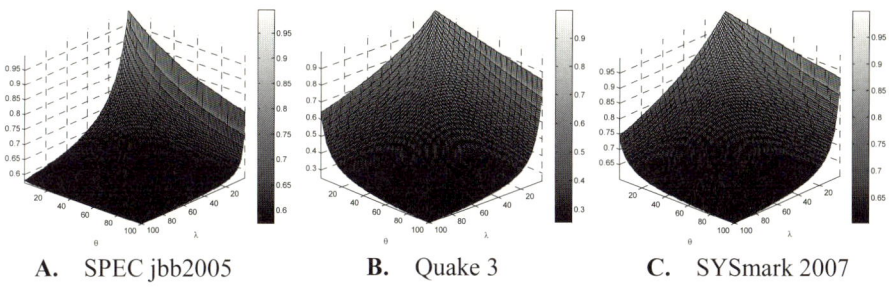

A. SPEC jbb2005   B. Quake 3   C. SYSmark 2007

Fig. 8. $AMAT_{rd}$ Ratio of 512MB M_1 to 128MB M_1 of 1-way set associative

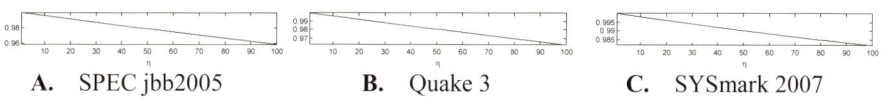

A. SPEC jbb2005   B. Quake 3   C. SYSmark 2007

Fig. 9. $AMAT_{wr}$ Ratio of 512MB M_1 to 128MB M_1 of 1-way set associative

4.5 Sensitivity to Associativity

Associativity helps to reduce the $AMAT_{rd}$. but similar to the performance of writeback ratio, the improvement grow little when M_1 size grows up according to Fig. 10 and Fig. 12.

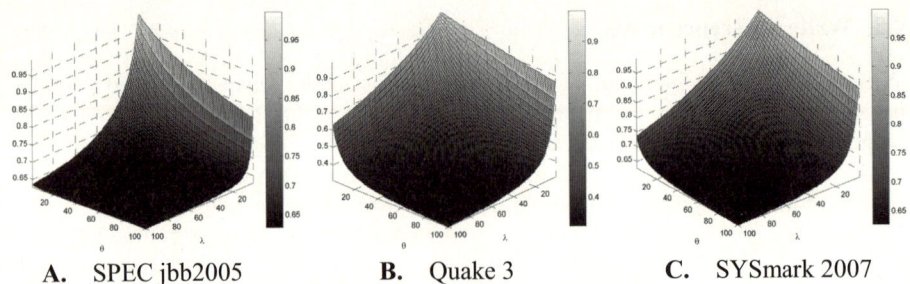

Fig. 10. $AMAT_{rd}$ Ratio of 4-way to 1-way Memory with 128M M_1

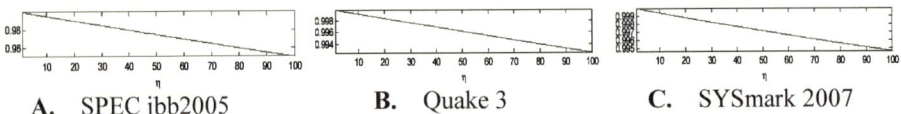

Fig. 11. $AMAT_{wr}$ Ratio of 4-way to 1-way Memory with 128M M_1

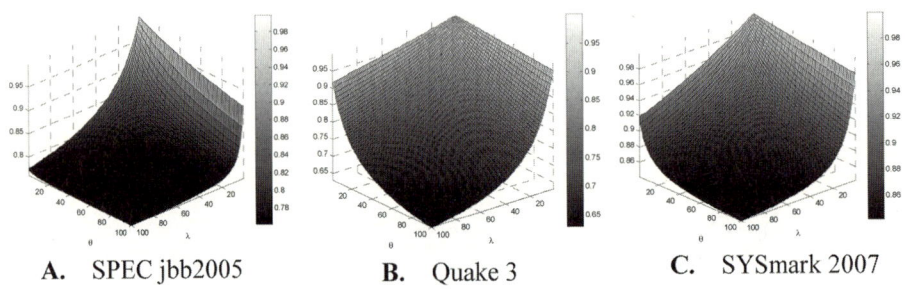

Fig. 12. $AMAT_{rd}$ Ratio of 4-way to 1-way Memory with 512M M_1

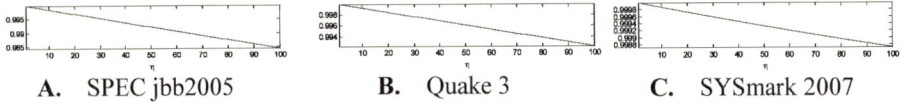

Fig. 13. $AMAT_{wr}$ Ratio of 4-way to 1-way Memory with 512M M_1

From Fig. 11 and Fig. 13, we can see that the write performance is nearly constant in the hierarchical model.

5 Conclusion and Future Work

In this paper, we have studied the performance a two-level hierarchical model where the first level is accessed at fast speed whereas the second level is a magnitude slower. By managing this, hierarchical model treats M_1 as a cache that uses LRU, write allocate and write back policy. We found the write performance is very stable.

And our experimental result suggests the performance of hierarchical model is not sensitive to its set associativity under most circumstances. So we should pay more attention to its size than its associativity when building a memory hierarchy.

Using a heterogeneous memory architecture opens up many opportunities due to cutting memory cost and reducing power consumption in future memory systems. We are doing research to further improve memory hierarchy on the following areas.

- Explore the potential impact of workload machine cache configurations.
- Do research in scheduling memory operation according to the hierarchical model for power saving.
- Consider other opportunities such as compression and intelligent prefetching schemes to optimize the hierarchical architecture.

References

[1] Wang, W., Wang, Q., Wei, W., Liu, D.: Modeling and Evaluating Heterogeneous Memory Architectures by Trace-driven Simulation. In: MAW 2008, Ischia, Italy, May 5 (2008)
[2] Hennessy, J.L., Patterson, D.A.: Computer Architecture – A Quantitative Approach, 4th edn. Morgan Kaufmann, San Francisco (2007)
[3] Iyer, R.: On Modeling and Analyzing Cache Hierarchies using CASPER. In: 11th IEEE/ACM Symposium on Modeling, Analysis and Simulation of Computer and Telecom Systems (October 2003)
[4] Ekman, M., Stenstrom, P.: A case for multi-level main memory. In: Proceedings of the 3rd Workshop on Memory Performance Issues: in Conjunction with the 31st international Symposium on Computer Architecture. WMPI 2004, Munich, Germany, June 20 - 20, 2004, vol. 68 (2004)
[5] Iyer, R., Zhao, L., Guo, F., Illikkal, R., Makineni, S., Newell, D., Solihin, Y., Hsu, L., Reinhardt, S.: QoS policies and architecture for cache/memory in CMP platforms. In: Proceedings of the 2007 ACM SIGMETRICS international Conference on Measurement and Modeling of Computer Systems (SIGMETRICS 2007), San Diego, California, USA, June 12 - 16 (2007)

Mapping Heterogeneous Distributed Applications on Clusters

Sylvain Jubertie, Emmanuel Melin, Jérémie Vautard, and Arnaud Lallouet

Université d'Orléans, LIFO B.P. 6759
F-45067 ORLEANS Cedex 2
{firstname.name}@univ-orleans.fr

Abstract. Performance of distributed applications largely depends on the mapping of their components on the underlying architecture. On one side, component-based approaches provide an abstraction suitable for development, but on the other side, actual hardware becomes every day more complex and heterogeneous. Despite this increasing gap, mapping components to processors and networks is commonly done manually and is mainly a matter of expertise. Worse, the amount of efforts required for this task rarely allows to further consider optimal hardware use or sensitivity analysis of data scaling. In this paper, we rely on a formal and experimentally sound model of performance and propose a constraint programming based framework to find consistent and efficient mappings of an application onto an architecture. Experiments show that an optimal mapping for a medium-sized application can be found in a few seconds.

1 Introduction

Distributed architectures can have very different levels of parallelism. For example a cluster can be composed of an heterogeneous set of nodes where each node owns a set of (possibly multicore) processors sharing a common memory. These nodes can be linked to some others by multiple networks with different topologies and characteristics (bandwidth and latency). To hide the complexity and to foster portability, parallel programming models abstract these difficulties by providing a uniform notion of process. Then it remains to find a suitable placement, which is an assignment of each process to a processor.

Two common solutions are to use parallel libraries, like MPI[1] and PVM[2], or process migration techniques, like openMosix[3]. For some applications, these two solutions have drawbacks. The parallel libraries are not well suited for the creation of heterogeneous applications since the resulting code also contains communication and synchronization schemes. Thus the developer has to modify the application code each time he needs to optimize the application or to take advantage of a different cluster. On the other side, the load balancing provided by

---

[1] http://www.mpi-forum.org/
[2] http://www.csm.ornl.gov/pvm/pvm_home.html
[3] http://openmosix.sourceforge.net

process migration techniques moves both processes and data, which may result in poor performances for some applications.

The FlowVR framework[4] [1,2] was created to address this problem and to ease the development of heterogeneous distributed applications (especially Virtual Reality ones). To build a FlowVR application, the developer first creates the components, called *modules*, which encapsulate codes, and then independently defines a communication and synchronization scheme between them. This is a convenient abstraction level for many applications since it provides a coarse granularity level for the code and an explicit representation of the data-flow.

Classically, the developer has to map modules on cluster nodes and connections on network links by taking care of hardware performance to ensure an efficient mapping. When hardware performance is far beyond the needs of the application, this task is fairly easy to perform. But for handling larger applications, or to be able to ensure a better interaction with the user, resources become quickly scarce and have to be used with care. Moreover, the number of possible mappings dramatically increases when we consider large applications and clusters. The result is that allocation made by human is strongly suboptimal and cannot obtain the best result. For the same reason, it does not seem reasonable to generate all the possible mappings and to test each one.

In this paper, we propose to automatically find a mapping from modules to processors and from communication requirements to network links using Constraint Programming (CP). The optimization capabilities of CP allow to answer questions users were asking, like:

- what is the largest data size allowed for this application on my cluster?
- is it possible to ensure this frequency for this module on my cluster? what is the maximum frequency?
- is it possible to run this application on fewer processors while ensuring the same level of performance?
- is is possible to deploy my application on cluster X?

The search for a suitable allocation uses the performance model of FlowVR introduced in [8]. Some general constraints are defined from the FlowVR model and its performance model and are common to all FlowVR distributed applications. Some constraints are specific to the considered distributed application, like synchronization scheme. Other constraints are derived from the underlying architecture, like hardware limitations, number of processors, network bandwidths and latencies. Finally the developer can also add his own constraints. For example he may need a precise performance on a given application part. This can be useful to restrict mappings to those with expected performance. We propose an implementation in Gecode[5] [9] which takes advantage of the advanced features of the solver and the model (reified constraints, global constraints, symmetry breaking, user-defined heuristics, branch and bound). For the medium-sized application introduced in the experimental section, it yields a problem involving more than 2000 variables.

---

[4] http://flowvr.sourceforge.net
[5] http://www.gecode.org/

2 Performance of FlowVR Applications

The FlowVR framework is an open source middleware used to build distributed applications. A FlowVR application consists of a set of objects which communicate via messages through a data-flow network. Each message is associated with lightweight data, called *stamps*, which contain information used for routing operations. A FlowVR application can be viewed as a multigraph $G(V, E)$, called the *application graph*, where each vertex in V represents a FlowVR object and each directed edge in E a point to point FIFO connection between two objects. Objects can be of three kinds: *modules*, *filters* and *synchronizers*.

Modules are endless iteration which encapsulate tasks. Each module owns a set of I/O ports. It waits until it receives one message on each of its input ports (thus providing an implicit synchronizations between connected modules), then it processes the messages, computes its task and produces new messages that are put on its output ports. Operations on messages like routing, broadcasting, merging or scattering are done by filters, while synchronization and coupling policy are performed by synchronizers. Both filters and synchronizers are placed on connections between modules. A synchronizer only receives stamps emitted by filters or modules, then takes a decision according to its coupling policy and sends new stamps to destination objects. This decision is then performed by the destination object. With the use of synchronizers, it is possible to implement a *greedy* filter, which allows its connected modules to communicate asynchronously. In this case, the destination module always uses the last available message while older messages are discarded. More details on FlowVR can be found in [1].

The performance of a FlowVR application can be described by a formal model, as introduced in [8]. This model takes several inputs :

- a FlowVR application graph $G(V, E)$
- a cluster configuration represented by a multigraph of SMP nodes connected to networks by network links. Each network link l has a maximum bandwidth $BWmax_l$
- a mapping description : the destination node of each FlowVR object and the network links used for each connection
- some information on each module m : its execution time T_m^{exec} and the load $Load_m$ it generates when m is mapped alone on its destination processor
- the amount of data $Vol_m^{o_i}$ sent by each module m through output port o_i

The goal of our model is to determine for each module its frequency F_m and the load $Load_m^c$ it generates on the destination processor. We also need to determine the required bandwidths bw_{nl} on each network link nl to detect possible network contentions. Note that we assume that synchronizers have negligible execution times and loads compared to module ones, and generate only stamps and we choose to ignore them in our study. We also assume that filters generate negligible loads on processors compared to modules since they only perform few memory operations. However the mapping of modules modifies the amount of data sent through network links. Thus we only consider the mapping of modules and filters on nodes and the mapping of connections on network links.

The performance of each module in the whole application depends on synchronization with other modules. We propose in [8] to study the application graph to determine implicit synchronizations between modules. Then, we compute the frequency F_m of modules according to their execution times, implicit synchronizations and explicit ones defined with synchronizers. Note that the processor load required for each module may vary depending on synchronization between modules, thus, we provide in [8] an algorithm to determine for each module the new value of its load, noted $Load_m^c$. At the end of each iteration, each module m sends messages on its output ports, thus we can compute the required bandwidths bw_l for each network link l from F_m and $Vol_m^{o_i}$. Our performance model allows to determine performance of modules for a given mapping but also to detect possible synchronization scheme misconfigurations or network contentions.

In order to be executed on a target architecture, a FlowVR application has to be mapped on available processors and network links. The technique we propose hereafter takes advantage of this formal performance model to find automatically sound and efficient mappings i.e. efficient homomorphisms from the application graph into the architecture multigraph. Thus, for each module m, the developer needs to provide the execution time $T_{m,p}^{exec}$ and the load $Load_{m,p}$ it generates when m is mapped alone on a processor p.

3 Modeling the Problem Using Constraint Programming

We first present the principle of Constraint Programming [3], then we show how to use it to solve our mapping problem.

3.1 Constraint Programming

A Constraint Satisfaction Problem (CSP) is a search problem established by giving a set of variables ranging over finite domains, and a conjunction of constraints i.e. logical relations, mentioning such variables. CSP formulations are naturally suited to model real-world problems, and countless applications exist indeed. For example, given $x \in \{1,2,3\}$, $y \in \{3,4\}$, and $z \in \{4,5,6\}$, the following CSP :
$$x < y \ \wedge \ x + y = z \ \wedge \ z \neq 3x$$
is solved by selecting (if possible) one value for each variable in so as to satisfy the three constraints at once. For example, $x = 1$, $y = 4$, $z = 5$ is a valid solution, while $x = 2$, $y = 4$, $z = 6$ is not.

Formally, a CSP is a 3-tuple (V, D, C) where V is a set of variables $v_1 \ldots v_n$, D a set of finite domains $d_1 \ldots d_n$ for the variables of V, and C a set of constraints $c_1 \ldots c_m$ over the variables of V. Many CSP solvers exists in the literature. The most common way of searching CSP solution is to combine a backtracking algorithm with a constraint propagation algorithm. The first will perform a tree-like search over the domains of all the variables of the CSP since the last will reduce these domains by reasoning on the constraints of the problem. Constraints are generally of limited arity. However, there exist some constraints with arbitrary large arity, called *global constraints*, that usually encapsulate a specific efficient algorithm or give access to a data-structure. For example we make use of the *Element* constraint [6] that links an index and its value in an array.

3.2 Problem Modeling

Modeling the mapping problem into a CSP can be split in three parts : (1) the pure *module and filter placement* problem, (2) taking care of the *FlowVR connection* between objects, and (3) the *traffic* part, where the placement of connections between objects through the available links and networks is done, constrained by the links maximum bandwidth and network paths.

Let us describe this problem by illustrating it with a very simple example : we consider an application composed of three modules, the first sending data to the second, which in turn sends data to the third. We want to run it on a little cluster composed of two dual-processor nodes linked by a single network. Note that there are 4 processors in the cluster (2 per node).

Practically, a boolean variable is implemented as an integer variable ranging from 0 to 1 (0 for False, 1 for True). This will be assumed in this section.

Modules and Filters Placement. Basically, the problem we want to solve is a placement of modules on processors and filters on nodes since we assume that filters generate negligible loads compared to modules. So, we begin with creating variables $Module_i$ for each module in $G(V, E)$ (i going from 0 to the number of modules the application is composed of), which value will be the number of the processor on which the i-th is to be executed. Then we create filter variables $Filter_i$ for each filter in $G(V, E)$ (i going from 0 to the number of filters the application is composed of) which value will be the number of the node on which the i-th is to be executed. In our example, our processors are indexed from 0 to 3, we hence have three variables $Module_1$, $Module_2$ and $Module_3$ ranging on this interval.

The load $Load_{i,j}^c$ put by a module $Module_i$ on a processor p_j is expressed in percents and is determined by our performance model [8]. A first restriction is that a processor cannot be loaded beyond 100%. This restriction can be expressed using arithmetic constraints: first, a matrix M of auxiliary boolean variables is created, each $M_{i,j}$ being constrained to be true if module m_i executes on processor p_j, and false otherwise, using reified equality constraint ($Module_i = j$) $\leftrightarrow M_{i,j}$. Then, for each processor p_j, the constraint $\sum_i M_{i,j} * Load_{i,j}^c \leq 100$ is posted. The consistency between $Module_i$ variables and the M matrix is ensured by this last contraint, plus a set of *Element* constraints enforcing, for each module i, that $M_{i,Module_i} = 1$. In our example, the matrix M is created with a size of $3 * 4$ (three modules, four processors), as well as the $Load_{0,1}^c$ to $Load_{3,4}^c$ variables, ranging from 0 to 100. Then, we post the following constraints for the consistency of the model:

- $M_{0,0} + M_{0,1} + M_{0,2} + M_{0,3} = 1$
- $M_{1,0} + M_{1,1} + M_{1,2} + M_{1,3} = 1$

- $M_{2,0} + M_{2,1} + M_{2,2} + M_{2,3} = 1$
- $M_{0,Module_0} = 1$
- $M_{1,Module_1} = 1$
- $M_{2,Module_2} = 1$

and the following ones to ensure a processor will not be overloaded:

- $M_{0,0} * Load^c_{0,1} + M_{1,0} * Load^c_{1,1} + M_{2,0} * Load^c_{2,1} \leq 100$
- $M_{0,1} * Load^c_{0,2} + M_{1,1} * Load^c_{1,2} + M_{2,1} * Load^c_{2,2} \leq 100$
- $M_{0,2} * Load^c_{0,3} + M_{1,2} * Load^c_{1,3} + M_{2,2} * Load^c_{2,3} \leq 100$
- $M_{0,3} * Load^c_{0,4} + M_{1,3} * Load^c_{1,4} + M_{2,3} * Load^c_{2,4} \leq 100$

Connection Mapping. Several issues occur when modeling communications: first, a connection between two objects must travel through two network links which share the same network. Of course, these links must belong to the nodes the modules are running on. Then, the total amount of communication going through one given link l_i must not exceed its bandwidth $BWmax_i$.

Each FlowVR connection $c_i \in E$ in the graph $G(V,E)$, is represented by two variables c_i^{in} and c_i^{out}, giving respectively the index of its input and output network link. Another variable cn_i indicates the network this connection is traveling through. To solve the first issue, we first build a static array LoN (Links on Network) such that LoN_i is equal to the network to which is connected the link l_i. Then, we post two *Element* constraints to ensure $LoN[c_i^{in}] = cn_i$ and $LoN[c_i^{out}] = cn_i$.

In the example, we have two connections (numbered 0 and 1), and therefore create the c_0^{in}, c_0^{out}, c_1^{in} and c_1^{out}, ranging over the two existing links (one for each node), numbered 0 and 1. Variables cn_0 and cn_1 can also be created, however their domain is already reduced to value 1, as there is only one network available. The array LoN in this case is equal to $[1,1]$, and we then post the *Element* constraints $LoN[c_0^{in}] = cn_0$, $LoN[c_0^{out}] = cn_0$, $LoN[c_1^{in}] = cn_1$ and $LoN[c_1^{out}] = cn_1$.

Traffic. The traffic bw_i generated by a connection c_i is equal to the product of the frequency F_j of the emitter module m_j and the volume emitted by this module at each iteration Vol_{c_i}. This traffic really travels through a link iff the connection is not local (in this case, the connection is ignored). For each connection, Vol_{c_i} is a constant integer, and F_j a variable already defined, so the variable bw_i is created and the constraint $bw_i = F_j * Vol_{c_i}$ is posted. As we will need to know if a connection is local or not, we have to define for each connection c_i a boolean variable Loc_i that will be true iff c_i is local. This is enforced simply by checking that c_i^{in} and c_i^{out} are equal i.e. posting the reified constraint $(c_i^{in} = c_i^{out}) \leftrightarrow Loc_i$.

In our example, we create variables bw_0, bw_1, Loc_0 and Loc_1 and simply post the constraints $bw_0 = F_0 * Vol_0$ and $bw_1 = F_1 * Vol_1$, $(c_0^{in} = c_0^{out}) \leftrightarrow Loc_0$ and $(c_1^{in} = c_1^{out}) \leftrightarrow Loc_1$.

The link bandwidth issue is solved like the processor maximal load one : we create two matrices of boolean variables Cin and $Cout$, $Cin_{i,j}$ (resp. $Cout_{i,j}$) being constrained to be true if and only if the connection c_i input (resp. output) is made via the link l_j. Then, for each link, we sum the traffic of the non-local connections passing through it by posting the constraints $\sum_i Cin_{i,j} * Loc_i * bw_i \leq BWmax_j$ and $\sum_i Cout_{i,j} * Loc_i * bw_i \leq BWmax_j$. Note that we have two distinct sums because the links work in full-duplex mode i.e. that they can emit and receive at their full bandwidth at the same time.

In the example, variables $Cin_{0,0}$ to $Cin_{2,2}$ and $Cout_{0,0}$ to $Cout_{2,2}$ are created, integers $BWmax_0$ and $BWmax_1$ are given, so we post the following constraints:

- $Cin_{0,0} * Loc_0 * bw_0 + Cin_{1,0} * Loc_1 * bw_1 \leq BWmax_0$
- $Cin_{0,1} * Loc_0 * bw_0 + Cin_{1,1} * Loc_1 * bw_1 \leq BWmax_1$
- $Cout_{0,0} * Loc_0 * bw_0 + Cout_{1,0} * Loc_1 * bw_1 \leq BWmax_0$
- $Cout_{0,1} * Loc_0 * bw_0 + Cout_{1,1} * Loc_1 * bw_1 \leq BWmax_1$.

4 Experiments

We have implemented this framework using the constraint solver Gecode[6] [9]. Given descriptions of a distributed application and of a cluster architecture, it generates the CSP translation of the mapping problem using the techniques presented in previous section, plus possibly some user-defined constraints.

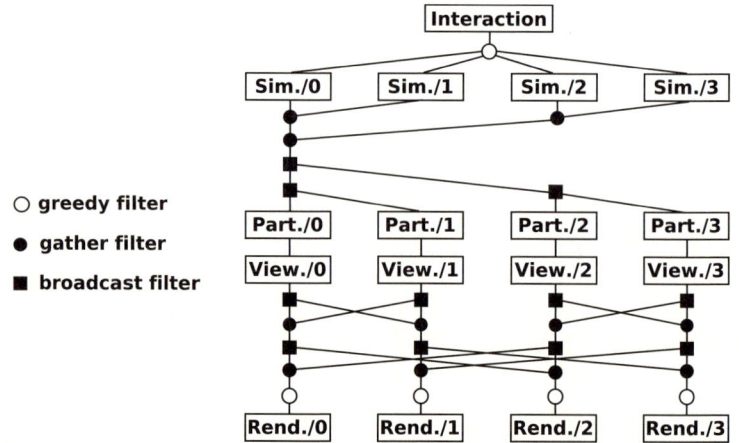

Fig. 1. FluidParticle application graph

In the following, we use the medium-sized FlowVR application *FluidParticle* to benchmark the different mappings found by the solver. We have been able to leverage the hardware power by scaling up the application to a size that was impossible before. The application is composed of the following parts:

---

[6] http://www.gecode.org

- *simulation* : it is a parallel version [4] of the Stam's fluid simulation [10].
- *particles* : it stores a set of particles and moves them according to a force field.
- *viewer* : it converts particle positions into graphic primitives.
- *renderer* : it displays on the screen information provided by the viewer modules.
- *interaction* : it is an interaction module, it converts user interaction into forces.

The graph (without synchroniszers) of our *FluidParticle* application is shown in figure 1. Note that we define multiple instances of some modules to decrease their execution time.

Our tests are performed on our VR platform, described in figure 2. We now show the different possibilities offered by our approach by answering questions of increasing difficulty.

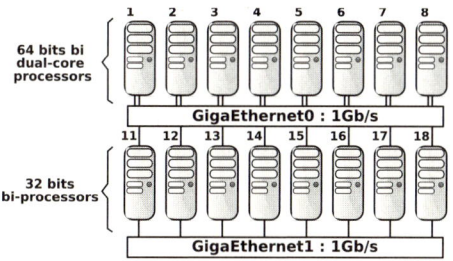

Fig. 2. Our cluster platform

4.1 Validating Mappings

Since our approach integrates our performance model, we can use it to validate mappings. In this case we set the mapping of objects and connections by restricting each variable domain to a given value. Then, we run the solver which only verifies the mapping constraints.

We have validated mappings of our application [7,8] previously obtained after a long trial and error process.

4.2 Generating Mappings

The main interest of our approach is to automatically generate mappings for a given application on a given architecture. Depending on the application, some constraints can be added to the problem. For example, some modules, like the interaction or visualization ones, are hardware dependent. Consequently they must be mapped on a given node or only on a subset of the cluster and we can restrict the domain of the corresponding variables. In our example, we need to map *renderer* modules on nodes 1 to 4 which are connected to our video projectors, thus we add the following constraints :

$$renderer_0 = 1, renderer_1 = 2, renderer_2 = 3, renderer_3 = 4$$

Then we can use the solver to automatically generate pertinent mappings.

When running the solver, we can have two possible results : it produces mappings as it is exploring the search domain, or it ends without giving any mapping. We have tried out different configurations of our application and of our architecture. For example, if we only use a single network link to connect nodes to the gigaEthernet network, then the solver does not find a solution. If we use the three available networks, then the solver provides thousands of solutions. Note that the execution time of our solver may vary from seconds to hours depending on the cluster configuration.

To improve the efficiency of our solver we can add some constraints. In our example, we observe that some mappings are symmetric and provide the same performance. For example, modules $simulation_0$ and $simulation_1$ have the same performance and send the same amount of data. Thus, if we swap them we obtain the same performance. To remove symmetries, we can add lexicographic order constraints [5] on the corresponding modules variables, for example : $simulation_0 < simulation_1$. We can also add constraints to restrict the mapping of filters. Indeed, if a filter is not mapped with one of its source or destination objects, then its input and output messages are sent through a network. Thus, if we map a filter on the same node as one of its source or destination objects, then we avoid a distant communication. To restrict the mapping of filters, we use a disjunctive constraint. For example, to restrict the mapping of the *greedy* filter between *interaction* and *renderer* modules, we define:

$$greedy = interaction || greedy = simulation_0 || greedy = simulation_1$$
$$|| greedy = simulation_2 || greedy = simulation_3.$$

4.3 Testing Application and Hardware Limits

We can also use our solver to find the limits of our application. For example, we can increase the number of particles in our application while the solver finds a least one solution. In our default application, we define a set of 400×400 particles. If we now consider a set of 500×500 particles, our solver still gives some solutions. But when we reach 600×600 particles, then the solver does not provide solutions anymore. Tests confirm these results. Indeed, if we try to run the application with a set of 600×600 particles, then it produces a buffer overflow due to network contention. Thus we have reached the limit of our application on our architecture.

If we want to run our application with a set of 600×600 particles then we need a more powerful cluster. Thus, we modify the current description of our architecture by virtually adding nodes and networks. This way we can determine which choices are to be made to run our application. If we add more nodes then our solver does not provide solutions, but if we virtually replace the common gigaEthernet network with a Myrinet one then we obtain some solutions.

4.4 Optimization of the Cluster Use

Clusters are often used by several users at the same time. However, interactive applications, like the FluidParticle one, require dedicated nodes to ensure performance. We propose to use our solver to find mappings that minimize the number of nodes. Thus we run our solver with different cluster configurations. Results show that it is possible to find mappings using only six nodes with two dual-core processors on our current architecture, for example nodes 1 to 6. It is even possible to use only four nodes if we add a Myrinet network between nodes 1 to 4.

5 Conclusion and Future Work

The approach presented in this paper brings to developers a very useful tool to create and optimize mappings for heterogeneous distributed applications. Its implementation allows to validate mappings and enables to automatically generate mappings which respects constraints from our performance model and those defined by the developer. It is also possible to determine the cluster configuration required to run a given application. Moreover, we have shown that optimization of mappings are possible. For example it is possible to reduce the number of nodes required by distributed applications. This answers to a very important problem since clusters are often shared by several users.

References

1. Allard, J., Gouranton, V., Lecointre, L., Limet, S., Melin, E., Raffin, B., Robert, S.: FlowVR: a Middleware for Large Scale Virtual Reality Applications. In: Danelutto, M., Vanneschi, M., Laforenza, D. (eds.) Euro-Par 2004. LNCS, vol. 3149. Springer, Heidelberg (2004)
2. Allard, J., Ménier, C., Boyer, E., Raffin, B.: Running large VR applications on a PC cluster: the FlowVR experience. In: Proceedings of EGVE/IPT 2005, Denmark (October 2005)
3. Apt, K.: Principles of Constraint Programming. Cambridge University Press, Cambridge (2003)
4. Gaugne, R., Jubertie, S., Robert, S.: Distributed multigrid algorithms for interactive scientific simulations on clusters. In: Online Proceeding of the 13th International Conference on Artificial Reality and Telexistence, ICAT (December 2003)
5. Gent, I.P., Petrie, K.E., Puget, J.-F.: Symmetry in constraint programming. In: Rossi, F., van Beek, P., Walsh, T. (eds.) Handbook of Constraint Programming, ch. 10. Elsevier, Amsterdam (2006)
6. Van Hentenryck, P., Carillon, J.-P.: Generality versus specificity: An experience with ai and or techniques. In: AAAI, pp. 660–664 (1988)
7. Jubertie, S., Melin, E.: Multiple networks for heterogeneous distributed applications. In: Arabnia, H.R. (ed.) Proceedings of PDPTA 2007, pp. 415–424. CSREA Press, Las Vegas (2007)
8. Jubertie, S., Melin, E.: Performance prediction for mappings of distributed applications on PC clusters. In: Proceedings of IFIP International Conference on Network and Parallel Computing, NPC 2007, Dalian, China (September 2007)
9. Schulte, C., Tack, G.: Views and iterators for generic constraint implementations. In: Hnich, B., Carlsson, M., Fages, F., Rossi, F. (eds.) CSCLP 2005. LNCS (LNAI), vol. 3978, pp. 118–132. Springer, Heidelberg (2006)
10. Stam, J.: Real-time fluid dynamics for games. In: Proceedings of the Game Developer Conference (March 2003)

Neural Network-Based Load Prediction for Highly Dynamic Distributed Online Games*

Vlad Nae, Radu Prodan, and Thomas Fahringer

Institute of Computer Science, University of Innsbruck
Technikerstraße 21a, A-6020 Innsbruck, Austria
{vlad,radu,tf}@dps.uibk.ac.at

Abstract. We propose a neural network-based prediction method for the future entity layout in massively multiplayer online games. Our service has the potential to timely foresee critical hot-spots in fast-paced First Person Shooter action games that saturate the game servers which no longer respond to user actions at the required rate. Using our service, proactive load balancing (and redistribution) actions can be triggered.

We show results based on a realistic simulation environment that demonstrate the advantages of our method compared to other conventional ones, especially due to its ability to adapt to different load patterns.

1 Introduction

Online games can be seen as a collection of *game servers* that are concurrently accessed by a number of users that dynamically interact with each other within a *game session*. Clients connect directly to one game server, send their play actions (e.g. movements, collection of items) and receive appropriate responses. The responses must be delivered promptly within a given time interval to ensure a smooth, responsive and fair experience for all players.

For the vast majority of games there is a similar computational model. The game server runs a large loop in which the state of all entities is first computed and then broadcasted to the clients. All entities within a specific avatar's *area of interest* (usually a surrounding zone as shown in Figure 1(a)) are considered to be interacting with it and have an impact on its state. The more populated the entities' areas of interest are and the more interactions between entities exist, the higher the load of the underlying game server is. An overloaded game server delivers state updates to its connected clients (i.e. movements and actions of teammates and opponents) at a significantly lower frequency than required, which makes the overall environment fragmented, unrealistic and unplayable.

First Person Shooter(FPS) action games are considered as the next generation of distributed online games, for which no massively multiplayer support exists yet. Fast-paced online FPS games have very demanding Quality of Service (QoS) requirements in terms of client state computations and updates (i.e. around 35

---

* This work is funded by EU through IST-034601 edutain@grid and IST-004265 Core-Grid projects.

Hertz for a satisfactory experience). To support this need, previous work [1] developed two parallelization schemes that aim to improve the scalability of a game session (i.e. maximum 64 − 128 players for sequential FPS action games) by distributing the user load across multiple processors (see Figure 1(b)).

Zoning is based on data locality which partitions the game world in geographical zones to be handled independently by separate machines. Zones are not necessarily of the same shape and size, but should produce even runtime load distribution. *Mirroring* defines a method of distributing load by replicating the same game world (or zone) on several machines. Each server computes the state for a subset of the entities called *active entities*, while the remaining ones, called *shadow entities* (which are active in the other participating servers), are synchronised across servers. It was proven in previous work that the overhead of synchronising shadow entities is much lower than the overhead of computing the load produced by active entities [1].

Establishing a new zoning or mirroring scheme is an expensive procedure (in the order of seconds) that may introduce a lag in the user experience if not handled appropriately by the runtime middleware environment. To address this requirement, we introduce in this paper a novel approach for estimating the number of entities and their position within a game session. Based on the entity number, position, and area of interest, it is possible to derive analytical models for estimating the load of a game session (comprising processor, memory, and network load) [1]. We will address this aspect in future work, while for the current paper we only focus on the entity distribution prediction. Using our method, one can timely foresee critical hot-spots in FPS games and trigger proactive parallelization actions in a manner that makes the load balancing and entity migration seamless to the end-user.

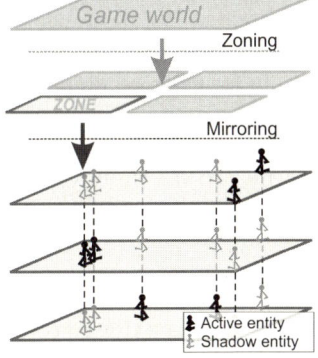

(a) Entity distribution

(b) Zoning and mirroring

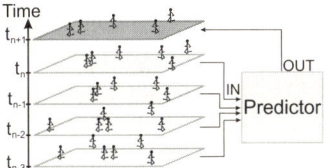

(c) Prediction system overview

Fig. 1.

The paper is organised as follows. In the next section we present the general load prediction strategy we employ, followed by a concrete implementation using neural networks in Section 3. In Section 4 we describe a distributed FPS game simulator for collecting realistic trace information for training, testing, and tuning our neural network (see Section 5). In Section 6 we compare our results against other prediction methods. We finally summarise the related work in Section 7 and conclude in Section 8.

2 Method

The problem of predicting the game load reduces therefore to estimating two fundamental parameters: the number of entities managed by a game server and their spatial distribution within the game world. The challenge in designing such a prediction service is that one physical game zone is in general too big and contains too much information (spatial position of over one hundred entities) for a prediction system to produce an accurate estimation of the future layout in real-time. This is particularly critical for fast-paced FPS action games where the game load can dramatically change within a short time interval and where fast prediction is an absolute requirement. We therefore apply once again the zoning technique (see Figure 1(a)), which partitions one game zone in multiple *subareas* of reasonable size to be given as input to the prediction service. The subareas are small enough to be characterised by their entity count only. The overall entity distribution in the entire game world consists of a map of entity counts for each subarea.

We use a prediction method based on historical information collected by tracing the execution of existing game servers. For each subarea, the prediction service uses as input the entity count at equidistant past time intervals, and delivers as output the entity count at the next time step (see Figure 1(c)).

3 Neural Network-Based Load Prediction

As we already mentioned, fast prediction methods are required for highly dynamic applications like FPS games for being of any real use. At the same time, the (often unpredictable) human factor makes the problem even harder and requires adaptive techniques, which simple methods such as averaging or exponential smoothing fail to achieve. Our solution goes towards neural networks due to a number of reasons which make them appropriate for distributed online games as we will demonstrate in Section 6: they adapt to a wide range of time series, they offer better prediction results than other methods, and they are faster compared to other more sophisticated statistical analysis.

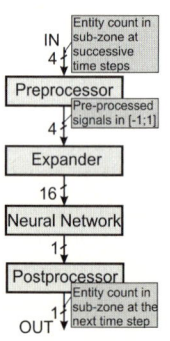

Fig. 2. Neural network-based prediction service

We designed a neural network-based load prediction service consisting of four important components: a preprocessing unit, a signal expanding unit, the actual neural network predictor, and a postprocessing unit (see Figure 2). The signal expander is used to help the neural network extract the relevant information from the preprocessed signal by applying simple transformations to it (distance, squaring, averaging).

In order to utilise the neural network-based prediction, two offline phases are required. First, the *data set collection* phase is a long process in which the game is observed by gathering entity count samples for all subareas at equidistant time steps. The second *training* phase uses most of the previously collected samples as training sets, and the remaining as test sets. The training phase runs for a number of eras, until a convergence criterion is fulfilled. A training era consists of three steps: (1) presenting all the training sets in sequence to the network; (2) adjusting the network's weights to better fit the expected output (the real entity count for the next time step); and (3) testing the network's prediction capability with the different test sets. Separating the training from the test sets is crucial in avoiding memorisation and ensures that the network has enough generalisation potential for delivering good results on new data sets.

4 Distributed FPS Game Simulator

As there is no real online game available which is capable of generating the load patterns required for testing and validating our prediction service, we developed a distributed FPS game simulator supporting the zoning concept and inter-zone migrations of the entities (see Figure 3). We use this simulator for generating realistic load patterns such as entity interaction hot-spots or simply large numbers of entities managed by one game server. The entities in the simulation are driven by several Artificial Intelligence (AI) profiles which determine their behaviour during a simulation: *aggressive* determines the entity to seek and interact with opponents; *team player* causes the entity to act in a group together

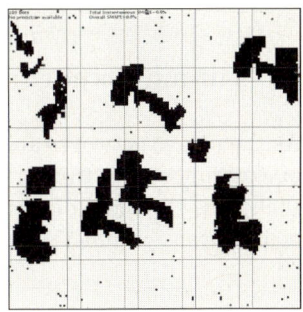

Fig. 3. Game simulator snapshot

with its teammates; *scout* leads the entity for discovering uncharted zones of the game world (not seeking any interaction); and *camper* simulates a well-known tactic in FPS games to hide and wait for the opponent. Each entity is able to dynamically switch between all these AI profiles during the simulation. This emulates the players' behaviour in a real game session (i.e. a player is aggressive at the start of the session, but once wounded he has to change his tactics to a conservative behaviour to avoid being eliminated).

Using this game simulator, we generated eight different trace data sets with different characteristics by running 17 hours of simulations for each set and sampling the game state at every two minutes. In each simulation, we used a different configuration determined by four simulation parameters, which we varied by appropriately setting the predominant entity AI profiles usage (see Table 1). We first modelled peak hours in online gaming such as late afternoons or weekends. Then, we varied the entities' speed and inter-zone migration patterns to mimic two different dynamic profiles: (1) *instantaneous dynamics* (typical to fast-paced FPS games) meaning a large difference in the entity interaction over a short period of time; and (2) *overall dynamics* (typical to slower-paced Massively Multiplayer Online Role Playing Games (MMORPG) [2]) has a much more stable entity interaction load with large variations over a longer period of time. Finally, we model the popularity of a game by setting the maximum peak load to different values.

The validation of these data traces is difficult since currently there are no games capable of providing the needed entity distributions at regular time intervals. To this end, we tried to get as close as possible to real games by importing some of the maps from a very popular FPS game called Counter Strike 1.6 [3].

Table 1. Simulation trace data sets

Data set	Peak hours modelling	Peak load	Overall dynamics(17h)	Instantaneous dynamics(2min)
Set 1	No	+++	+++++	+++
Set 2	No	+	+++	++++
Set 3	No	++++	++++	++++
Set 4	No	++	++++	+++++
Set 5	Yes	++++	++	+++
Set 6	Yes	+++++	+	+
Set 7	Yes	++++	+++++	++
Set 8	Yes	++++	+	+

5 Tuning Experiments

As the neural networks are not deterministic, we carried out a significant number of experiments for tuning the parameters that influence the prediction accuracy: the signal expanding technique, the neural network type and structure, and the neural transfer function [4]. The goal of our experiments is to minimise the prediction error: $PE = \frac{\sum_{i=1}^{N} \left| n_i^{(real)} - n_i^{(pred)} \right|}{\sum_{i=1}^{N} n_i^{(real)}}$, where N is the total number of samples in the trace data set, and $n_i^{(real)}$ and $n_i^{(pred)}$ are the real, respectively predicted entity counts at time step i.

The challenge of the tuning process is caused by the fact that the variation of the accuracy with one parameter is not independent and not even coherent with its variation with another parameter. In conclusion, sequentially finding the best accuracy for every parameter is not possible and a guided exhaustive parameter study is necessary. In the following, we present only the main track of our experimental results, not mentioning the backtracking we have done for assessing the impact of altering one parameter on the others. The experiments presented are independent of each other or, in the worst case, have a very small impact on one another.

Table 2. Experimental results for different network types

Input set	Network set-up			Prediction Error		
	Structure	Transfer Function	Inputs [exp+raw]	MLP	Jordan Elman	Modif. MLP
Set 1	3,2,1	Sigmoid	6+3	34.86%	**34.64%**	36.73%
Set 1	5,2,1	Sigmoid	6+3	35.08%	**34.86%**	37.39%
Set 1	3,2,1	Sigmoid	3+3	34.86%	**34.70%**	40.00%
Set 1	5,2,1	Sigmoid	3+3	34.92%	**34.70%**	36.95%
Set 1	3,2,1	Linear	6+3	34.42%	**33.33%**	35.65%
Set 1	5,2,1	Linear	6+3	**33.11%**	33.77%	35.00%
Set 1	3,2,1	Linear	3+3	34.49%	**33.18%**	40.00%
Set 1	5,2,1	Linear	3+3	**31.23%**	33.83%	37.39%
Set 2	3,2,1	Sigmoid	6+3	**28.90%**	29.24%	29.11%
Set 2	5,2,1	Sigmoid	6+3	**28.93%**	29.24%	31.01%
Set 2	3,2,1	Sigmoid	3+3	**30.15%**	**30.15%**	34.49%
Set 2	5,2,1	Sigmoid	3+3	**30.15%**	30.47%	31.32%
Set 2	3,2,1	Linear	6+3	**29.24%**	29.55%	33.22%
Set 2	5,2,1	Linear	6+3	**28.93%**	**28.93%**	33.54%
Set 2	3,2,1	Linear	3+3	29.52%	**29.20%**	35.12%
Set 2	5,2,1	Linear	3+3	**29.20%**	29.52%	33.22%

5.1 Network Type

The two main neural network types we experimented with are the classical feed-forward networks and the recurrent networks. In feed-forward networks the stimuli propagate only from the input layer towards the output layer, while in the recurrent networks there are also feedback loops towards a separate type of neurons called context neurons. From the feed-forward category, we experimented with a simple *multilayer perceptron (MLP)* and a modified three-layer perceptron, which has a different input layer consisting of fuzzy neurons intended to provide a different type of signal expansion. The recurrent network we use is a Jordan-Elman network [4].

As we previously mentioned, the parameters that influence the prediction accuracy are not independent. As a consequence, for each network type we present eight experiments varying most of the available parameters: the network structure, the transfer function, and the signal expansion technique.

We present in Table 2 the results of these experiments on the input data sets 1 and 2 (see Table 1) since they model best dynamic FPS action games. In the modified MLP case, we used the fuzzy neuron input layer for expanding the input signals by varying their fuzzy domains. The simple MLP and the Jordan-Elman network performed well providing almost identical results, while the modified MLP struggled especially during the experiments with more fuzzy domains. Our conclusion is that the neural networks that best fit our problem are the MLP and Jordan-Elman and, therefore, our next experiments will only take these two types into consideration.

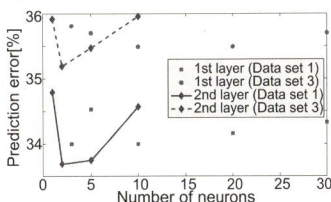

Fig. 4. Prediction error for different first and second layer sizes

5.2 Network Structure

In finding the best suited network structure, we focus on finding the appropriate number of neurons on each layer. We fixed the number of layers to three since the performance of these types of networks hardly improves with more layers.

We carried out a series of experiments using different three-layered network structures while maintaining all other relevant parameters fixed: classic MLP, full signal expanding, and linear transfer function [4]. Table 3 demonstrates that the prediction does not improve when using networks with sizes bigger than 15 − 20 neurons. Figure 4 shows that the minimum prediction error is obtained for around 2 − 4 neurons in the second layer, while for the first layer we cannot make a similar assessment.

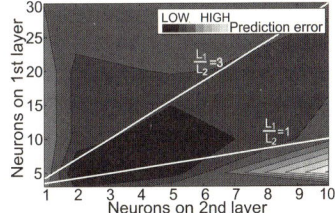

Fig. 5. Error map for variable first and second layer neurons

Representing in Figure 5 the prediction error as a function of the number of neurons in both layers, we observe that the lowest error occurs if the network has twice as many neurons on the first layer than on the second layer. Taking into account these observations, we conclude that the optimal network structure is [6, 3, 1] (representing the number of neurons on each layer). Obviously, similar structures will also produce comparably good results (e.g. [9, 3, 1], [8, 4, 1]).

5.3 Transfer Function and Signal Expanding

The transfer function represents the composition of two functions: the activation function which determines the total stimulus a neuron receives, and the output function which determines the total stimulus a neuron generates. We studied the behaviour of our system by using different transfer functions with three types of output functions: sigmoid, linear, and a modified Gaussian ($G : [-1, 1] \rightarrow [-1, 1]$, $G(x) = 2.1 \cdot e^{\frac{-(x-1)^2}{2 \cdot 0.86^2}} - 1$).

In this batch of experiments, we fixed the previously determined parameters (i.e. network type and structure) at their best values. We used a classic MLP neural network with a [6, 3, 1] structure and ran experiments on input data sets 1, 2, and 3 with variable signal expanding. The results displayed in Table 4 confirm our original assumption that, even though the sigmoid functions give good results in most cases, they are not the best choice for all applications. The linear function performed best for all data sets and is closely followed by the modified Gaussian which performed worse for data sets 1 and 3 characterised by higher overall dynamics. This leads us to the conclusion that, although the modified Gaussian gives good results for signals with high instantaneous dynamics, it cannot follow the overall trend of entity count over long time intervals.

For the signal expanding experiments we used three levels of signal expansion: $EX_i^I = X_{i-1} - X_i$ (1), $EX_i^{II} = \frac{X_{i-2} + X_{i-1} + X_i}{3}$ (2) and $EX_i^{III} = |X_{i-2} - X_i| - |X_{i-1} - X_i|$ (3), where EX_i represents the expanded stimulus and the X_k values represent the preprocessed stimuli. The results for this batch of experiments displayed in Table 5 are not encouraging, the gain in performance being marginal

Table 3. Experimental results for different network structures

Exp.	Network structure	Prediction error Set 1	Set 3
1	3,1,1	34.70%	35.84%
2	5,1,1	34.92%	35.84%
3	15,1,1	34.92%	35.98%
4	20,1,1	34.92%	35.98%
5	30,1,1	34.49%	35.98%
6	3,2,1	33.40%	35.27%
7	5,2,1	32.92%	34.56%
8	15,2,1	33.83%	34.99%
9	20,2,1	33.83%	35.41%
10	30,2,1	34.49%	35.70%
11	3,5,1	34.27%	35.27%
12	5,5,1	33.18%	36.13%
13	15,5,1	32.97%	35.56%
14	20,5,1	34.05%	34.85%
15	30,5,1	34.27%	35.56%
16	3,10,1	33.62%	36.84%
17	5,10,1	37.09%	36.27%
18	15,10,1	34.27%	35.41%
19	20,10,1	33.83%	35.70%
20	30,10,1	34.05%	35.56%

Table 4. Experimental results for different transfer functions

Data set	Inputs [exp+raw]	Prediction error Linear	Sigmoid	Gaussian
Set 1	4+2	**32.53%**	35.14%	32.97%
Set 1	9+3	**32.75%**	34.70%	33.18%
Set 1	12+4	**33.62%**	34.27%	**33.62%**
Set 2	4+2	29.84%	29.84%	**29.52%**
Set 2	9+3	29.37%	30.93%	**29.06%**
Set 2	12+4	**28.61%**	29.55%	29.24%
Set 3	4+2	**32.71%**	37.41%	34.85%
Set 3	9+3	**35.27%**	37.55%	36.41%
Set 3	12+4	36.54%	36.54%	**35.83%**

even with the highest level of expanding. Nevertheless, the network shows some improvement in performance with the first and third levels of expanding.

6 Results

The final step of our experiments represents the evaluation of the quality of the results delivered by the neural network-based prediction compared to other methods. We use the best suited neural network architecture determined in the previous section, which is a standard fully connected MLP with a [6, 3, 1] structure, a linear transfer function, and a three level signal expansion.

We compared our system against other known fast prediction methods like average, moving average, last value, and three levels of exponential smoothing [5] on the input data sets described in Table 1. We selected these statistical methods for comparison since we observed them to be among the most accurate in highly dynamic systems like the Grid [6], while fulfilling the time constraints of FPS games where a high density of prediction intervals is essential.

Table 5. Results for signal expanding using data set 1

Exp level	Inputs [exp+raw]	Prediction error	Avg. error
0	0+2	32.32%	
	0+3	33.77%	33.09%
	0+4	33.18%	
1	2+2	32.10%	
	3+3	32.67%	32.72%
	4+4	33.40%	
2	4+2	32.53%	
	6+3	32.67%	32.94%
	8+4	33.62%	
3	6+2	32.75%	
	9+3	32.23%	32.72%
	12+4	33.18%	

The results in Table 6 show that, apart from producing better or at least equal predictions, the important quality of our system is its ability to adapt to various types of input signals. More precisely, we had in our data sets three major types of signals: (1) signals with high instantaneous dynamics and medium overall dynamics (sets 2, 3, and 4) which were best approximated by average; (2) signals with low instantaneous dynamics (sets 6, 7 and 8) which were best approximated by last value; and (3) signals with medium instantaneous dynamics (sets 1 and 5) which were best fitted by the 50% exponential smoothing and respectively moving average. The drawback of these conventional methods is that it is not universally clear during a game play which of them should be applied as the real-time prediction method for the next time step. Moreover, as the dynamics of the game may change, for example during peak hours, the best prediction method may change too. Our neural network-based prediction successfully manages to adapt to all these types of signals and

Table 6. Comparison with other fast prediction methods

Input data	Neural Network	Prediction Error			Exponential smoothing		
		Avg.	Moving Avg.	Last Val.	25%	50%	75%
Set 1	**32.23%**	39.69%	39.25%	44.51%	40.04%	**37.83%**	39.60%
Set 2	**28.61%**	30.79%	34.60%	40.31%	34.19%	35.78%	36.74%
Set 3	**33.00%**	37.98%	39.40%	47.36%	38.34%	39.06%	41.92%
Set 4	**32.18%**	34.48%	39.78%	48.28%	42.90%	41.55%	43.97%
Set 5	**16.58%**	25.06%	**17.98%**	23.31%	19.85%	19.59%	20.27%
Set 6	**4.94%**	23.55%	8.13%	**5.08%**	10.89%	7.03%	5.66%
Set 7	**11.17%**	48.26%	18.88%	**11.84%**	20.50%	16.06%	12.53%
Set 8	**5.51%**	15.26%	8.45%	**5.66%**	12.96%	8.78%	5.90%

always delivers good prediction results. In addition, since this load prediction service should be part of a generic platform capable of supporting a wide variety of games, adaptability to different types of signal is a key feature.

To compare our results, we calculate the *gain* of our prediction: $Gain = \frac{\min\{PE_{other}\} - PE_{NN}}{\min\{PE_{other}\}}$, where PE_{NN} denotes the prediction error of the neural network and $\min\{PE_{other}\}$ represents the minimum prediction error from the set of other prediction methods (average, moving average, last value, and exponential smoothing). We obtained the highest gains for signals with high instantaneous dynamics (sets 1 through 5) which represents the main characteristic of FPS games (see Figure 6). For data sets 6 through 8, characteristic to

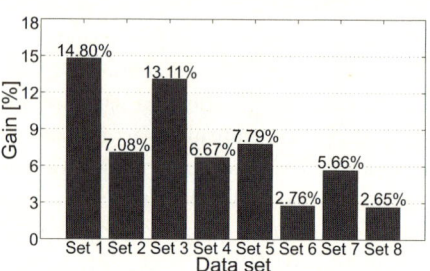

Fig. 6. Neural network gain against next fastest prediction method

slower-paced MMORPGs, the best method other than our service was last value, which performed well leaving little margin for improvement. Nevertheless, our service performed better than the other methods, showing some gain in all cases.

The average prediction time for one subarea using our service is extremely fast of around 0.8 microseconds on a 2.66 Gigahertz Intel Core Duo processor. Even with a few hundreds of subareas, the prediction time remains below one second which, considering a realistic prediction time step of about 30 – 300 seconds, leaves at least 97% of this time to the middleware for load balancing (i.e. creation of a new mirror) and migration decisions.

7 Related Work

Neural networks have been used in distributed systems with the purpose of load balancing, [7] being an example of such usage. However, this approach differs from the one presented here, firstly because it uses winner-take-all neural networks. Secondly, it is realising the load balancing at a generic task level, whereas our system's intended usage is for load balancing for a specific, highly dynamic application class, using internal application information.

The Distributed Interactive Simulation effort funded by the US Government refers to a distributed system capable of managing simulations with a high number of participants and reduced network usage by localising events only within the participants' areas of interest [8]. Our system is designed to support the novel idea of dynamic resource usage for this type of applications by offering load predictions based on which the resources can be timely reserved or freed.

Neural networks-based prediction has been successfully applied to a lot of applications coming from different fields of research: weather forecasting [9], prediction of traffic flow [10].

In the gaming area, prediction is used at the client side in fast-paced games for hiding synchronisation lags generated by network latency limitations [11]. Complementary to these approaches, our prediction service runs at the server side preventing saturation of game servers.

8 Conclusions

In this paper we presented a neural network-based prediction service to support the session management of massively multiplayer online games, especially for next generation massively multiplayer FPS games, but also for state-of-the-art MMORPG games. Our approach to predicting the future game layout is based on distributing the game world in subareas of reasonable size, whose entity count can quickly and accurately be approximated through a well-trained neural network using historical information. We developed a game simulator which uses several AI entity modelling patterns for generating a range of realistic load traces. We showed a series of experiments for tuning the network parameters (e.g. structure, type, transfer function, signal expanding) that were crucial for obtaining good prediction results. We presented experiments which demonstrate the capability of our predictor to adapt to input signals with different characteristics modelling various load patterns, which other conventional prediction methods fail to achieve. As future work, we plan to present experimental results for a load-balancing system and assess the impact using our load prediction method has on its efficiency.

References

[1] Müller, J., Gorlatch, S.: GSM: a game scalability model for multiplayer real-time games. In: Infocom. IEEE Computer Society Press, Los Alamitos (2005)
[2] MMORPG.COM: Your headquarters for massive multiplayer online role-playing games, http://www.mmorpg.com/
[3] GameData, I.: Counter strike, http://www.counter-strike.com
[4] Haykin, S.: Neural Networks: A Comprehensive Foundation, 1st edn. Prentice Hall PTR, Englewood Cliffs (1994)
[5] Makridakis, S., W.S., R., H.: Forecasting Methods and Applications. John Wiley & Sons, Inc., Chichester (1998)
[6] Wolski: Experiences with predicting resource performance on-line in computational grid settings. ACM Sigmetrics Performance Evaluation Review 30, 41–49 (2003)
[7] Aly, E., El-Abd, M.I.E.B.: A neural network approach for dynamic load balancing in homogeneous distributed systems. In: 30th Hawaii International Conference on System Sciences (HICSS), vol. 1, p. 628 (1997)
[8] Macedonia, Zyda, Pratt, Brutzman, Barham: Exploiting reality with multicast groups. IEEE Computer Graphics and Applications 15(5), 38–45 (1995)
[9] Maqsood, I., Khan, M., Abraham, A.: An ensemble of neural networks for weather forecasting. Neural Computing & Applications 13(2), 112–122 (2004)
[10] Huisken, G.: Soft-computing techniques applied to short-term traffic flow forecasting. Systems Analysis Modelling Simulation 43(2), 165–173 (2003)
[11] Bernier, Y.: Latency compensating methods in client/server in-game protocol design and optimization. In: Proceedings of the Game Developers Conference (2001)

Bottleneck Detection in Parallel File Systems with Trace-Based Performance Monitoring

Julian M. Kunkel and Thomas Ludwig

Ruprecht-Karls-Universität Heidelberg
Im Neuenheimer Feld 348, 69120 Heidelberg, Germany
Julian.Kunkel@informatik.uni-heidelberg.de
http://pvs.informatik.uni-heidelberg.de/

Abstract. Today we recognize a high demand for powerful storage. In industry this issue is tackled either with large storage area networks, or by deploying parallel file systems on top of RAID systems or on smaller storage networks. The bigger the system gets the more important is the ability to analyze the performance and to identify bottlenecks in the architecture and the applications.

We extended the performance monitor available in the parallel file system PVFS2 by including statistics of the server process and information of the system. Performance monitor data is available during runtime and the server process was modified to store this data in off-line traces suitable for post-mortem analysis. These values can be used to detect bottlenecks in the system. Some measured results demonstrate how these help to identify bottlenecks and may assists to rank the servers depending on their capabilities.

1 Introduction

Deployed storage systems continuously increase in size: Last year the US Department of Defense linked existing Storage Area Networks (SANs) into a single 17,000-port Meta SAN [1]. Also GPFS [2] and Lustre [3] are deployed over thousands of nodes. High-availability is mandatory for large setups, fail-over mechanisms must be incorporated to deal with defective hardware. Administration of such an environment requires sophisticated tools at least capable to monitor the state of each particular component to detect failures. For cost-effectiveness operators of such a system expect a high utilization of the provided infrastructure. In case the performance of a deployed system stays behind expectations, an on-line analysis of the system is necessary to detect the bottleneck. There are many reasons for performance degraded hardware. In case the components consist of inhomogeneous hardware a setup is likely to result in load-imbalance among the components. The common way to increase cost-effectiveness in big setups is to deploy a hierarchical storage management (HSM). Also, already existing hardware might be combined to improve throughput leading to an inhomogeneous environment.

The performance of disks and RAID systems varies depending on the observed access patterns. Ongoing RAID-rebuilds degrade the capabilities of a server.

A server with more main memory could cache more data leading to performance variation. The question which arises is: how do we determine the inefficient subsystem or component that causes the performance degradation?

To tackle this issue most storage systems implement a performance monitor which measures various metrics like throughput of disk and network. Unfortunately, these metrics are not always suitable to determine if this particular component is the bottleneck or if another component involved in the I/O path causes this problem. While it is easy to determine the recent throughput of a component, it is no easy task to assess the observed performance or even to determine the bottleneck of the current workload. For instance, one component might be twice as fast as another, but the measured performance is at the same level. This paper is structured as follows: In section 2 related work shows an excerpt of the state of monitoring concepts in SANs and parallel file systems. Available and potential useful performance statistics are discussed in section 3. The implemented solution for an extended performance monitoring with PVFS is presented in section 4. Results obtained by a set of experiments with different levels of access in MPI are assessed in section 5. The concept and potential future work is discussed in section 5.

2 State-of-the-Art and Related Work

It is common for network, distributed or parallel and cluster file systems to include a performance monitor. On Linux machines NFS provides access statistics via the `/proc` interface on client and server nodes. The statistics include the total number of observed data- or metadata operations of a given type on this particular machine since startup, e.g. the number of write operations, lookups, created directories. In GPFS a monitoring of client I/O performance is possible with a separate command line application (`mmpmon`, see [4]). The performance statistics provided are quite similar to NFS, but data is monitored on the file system level. In addition, the amount of data read or written is available. Furthermore, the number of requests within a byte range, which took a specific amount of time is maintained in configurable histograms. These histograms contain up to 16 byte ranges and up to 16 latency ranges.

In Lustre more information is available via the `/proc` interface [5]. Lustre is capable to track information per process on the client nodes. This includes statistics about non-sequential accesses as well as total numbers of accesses depending on the amount of data accessed in a histogram, i.e. it is possible to determine that a process has written an amount of data between 0 and 4 KBytes about 10 times. Lustre also monitors the usage of each Object Storage Target (i.e. storage node or SAN disk) including the number of pending and currently active operations. It is also possible to get more information, for instance by enabling the debugging output. See [6] for more information. Recently a new project was started, which collects interesting performance data of the servers using the debugging output and the `/proc` interface to visualize this performance data with the help of Ganglia [7]. Collected data includes the average pending (and currently processed) operations and the processing time of the different VFS calls, which is obtained from the clients. The parallel file system PVFS [8] embeds a performance monitor in the server process which counts the number of metadata and I/O operations, and the amount of data accessed. Statistics are recorded in configurable sampling intervals and can be fetched with the command line tool `pvfs2-perf-mon-example` directly from the server process.

There are some frameworks which allow to monitor the state of a system beyond the state of just the file system. These tools have in common that collected data is used to generate diagrams showing the usage of a given resource within a fixed sampling interval, e.g. the number of NFS opens per second or the CPU usage could be visualized in a diagram. The `collectl` utility [9] uses the proc interface to access Lustre statistics and NFS statistics and shows them in relation to other system parameters like network throughput or load. `Collectd` [10] is built on a plugin concept and can be fed by any source, i.e. by external applications. The already mentioned Ganglia uses a similar module concept.

In a Storage Area Network (SAN) it is possible to measure the performance of a switch, storage I/O response time on SCSI transactions or the average queue depth of the host port. Available performance statistics vary depending on the manufacturer of the storage system.

An off-line performance analysis tool for PVFS2 is PIOviz [11,12]. This tool allows to trace MPI applications in conjunction with all their induced server activities and visualizes them with Jumpshot. However, the level of detail provided by the tool is more than a normal user can cope with. Also, the data only gets available after the application finished. Further system information like observed disk throughput or CPU usage is not traced by the tool. Currently, the University of Dresden works to integrate I/O rates of Lustre for each target device in the visualization tool Vampir [13]. However, compared to the PIOviz approach, no detailed insight into the server activities is given. In contrast to discussed solutions the extensions presented in this paper allow to trace MPI-I/O calls together with several metrics provided by Linux and new PVFS2-internal metrics. These metrics could also be accessed directly to allow a quantitative on-line detection of performance bottlenecks. First, however, interesting performance statistics are discussed.

3 Useful Performance Statistics and Metrics

It is important to detect the bottleneck of the workload to tune or upgrade the system. While it is necessary to detect the machines responsible for a degraded performance, it is also important to detect the component within the particular machine. Basic components are CPU, network and disks. In general, two categories of sampled performance statistics can be differentiated: absolute (but limited) metrics i.e. statistics showing a value, but we do not know how this value corresponds to the maximum possible throughput in the given situation, and relative metrics i.e. values of statistics which directly depend on the capability and usage of the component or subsystem. An example for the absolute metrics is observed throughput. While the value of this metric might reveal a difference in current usage, it does not allow to determine the capability of the monitored system. Imagine data being striped in round-robin-fashion across multiple servers. If we observe that all servers contribute a specific amount of throughput to the aggregated throughput, we can not conclude that one server is faster than another. An instance of this problem is the case where servers are attached to the network with different speeds. However, if we can measure a higher throughput on a subset of servers, we can conclude that these servers are more utilized than the others. As an administrator you might be interested to see a metric like 90% utilization of network and 50% utilization of the disks of a particular machine. Knowing the maximum throughput of a component, these values could be computed easily. Consequently, the administrator could see a relative usage of the component. Unfortunately, even these computed values depend on the requests of the clients. Assume a machine's network is utilized by 50% and another machine's network by 90%. It is no good idea to conclude that the machine with 50% utilization is the bottleneck. The reason might be that the clients simply accessed less data on this machine. However, a load imbalance could be detected with this information.

Sometimes it is not possible to achieve the maximum possible throughput, for instance with random disk access patterns or during a RAID rebuild. Also, just a specific network path between a subset of machines might be slower. Consequently, measured values are inaccurate. On the other hand, metrics showing a value depending on the relative usage help to identify whether a component is overloaded in comparison to other components. An instance is the 60 second kernel load on machines, which depends on the number of currently active processes and indirectly on the capabilities of the system i.e. faster machines finish their jobs earlier, resulting in a lower average load.

In the following, load refers to such a relative metric, in particular the load of a subsystem is the average number of queued and scheduled requests within the sampling interval. Normally, a component must multiplex available capabilities somehow between pending jobs. Consequently, a problem with this kind of relative values is that a measured load of a sampling interval might vary depending on the processing order of short requests within the sampling interval. This problem is demonstrated for a configuration with two clients and two servers in figure 1. While jobs running longer than the length of the sampling interval result in the expected average load (see figure 1(a)), the load of short jobs within a sampling interval is higher if they are processed concurrently (see figure 1(b)). In this example, the time to process both jobs concurrently doubles. Due to statistical effects, the average value should be close to reality. Under the assumption that the component in the first server works twice as fast as the component in server two, the two situations in figure 2 are possible. Jobs running over multiple intervals might finish earlier, resulting in intervals with zero load (see figure 2(a)). Short running jobs lead to a decreased load as shown in figure 2(b). Now one might ask the question whether the load metric is more suitable instead of measuring some absolute metric like throughput?

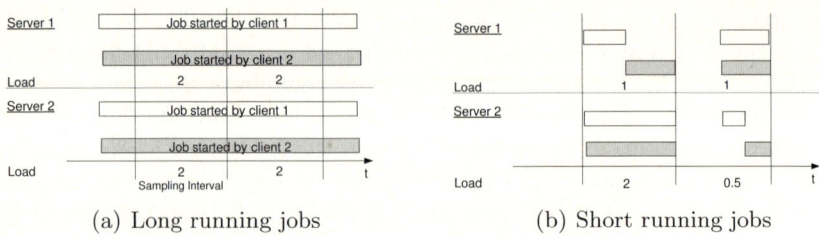

Fig. 1. Example load for homogenous hardware

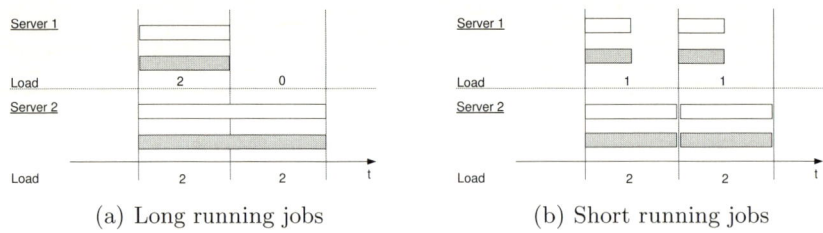

Fig. 2. Example load for inhomogeneous hardware

Considering a file distributed in a round-robin fashion, the average throughput of each server is identical for unbalanced hardware. Therefore, looking at the average throughput does not help to identify the faster (or slower) components, while the load allows to do so.

Another metric which directly depends on the behavior of the clients and the performance of a component is the idle time i.e. the time the component does not serve any jobs at all. The ratio between jobs currently pending on the network and the disk might also help to determine whether the network path or I/O subsystem is the bottleneck. For each physical component (network, disk) of a server, the maximum (best case) value and the current value is important. For physical and virtual components, e.g. different server internal layers, the average number of processed jobs (load) and the idle time are useful.

4 Extended Performance Monitoring with PVFS

This section presents extensions made to PVFS. The modifications include the new statistics and extensions to the PIOviz environment capable to trace the values and to visualize them with Jumpshot. First, to acquire various statistics available by the kernel, pieces of the `atop` [14] source code were incorporated into the PVFS performance monitor. This code uses the proc interface to fetch kernel statistics into a single data structure. The following selection of system wide metrics is incorporated into the performance monitor: average load over

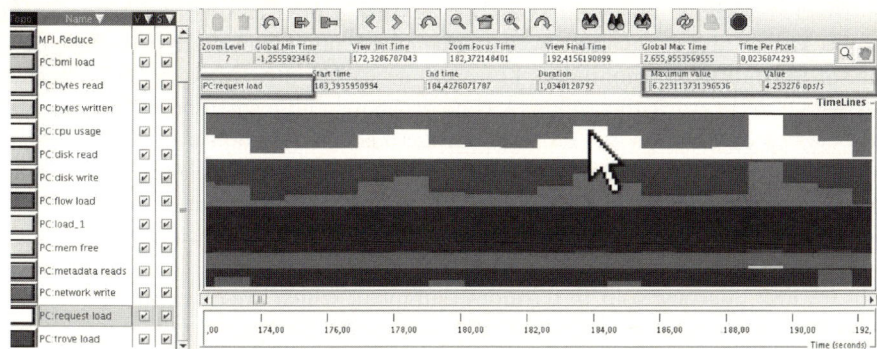

Fig. 3. Screenshot of the enhanced Jumpshot of PIOviz

one minute, free memory (Bytes), memory used for I/O caches (Bytes), CPU usage (Percent), data received from the network (Bytes/s), data sent to the network (Bytes/s), data read from the I/O subsystem (Bytes/s), data written by the I/O subsystem (Bytes/s). Next, a set of server internal metrics and statistics was added to the performance monitor. Modifications to the persistency layer (TROVE), the network layer (BMI), the job layer (glues the other layers together) and the server's main process allow to trace the load (as defined in section 3) of the server, the flow layer, the network and disk subsystems. Additionally, the idle time of the persistency layer was added. Note that in PVFS the persistency layer uses an underlying local file system to store the actual data. For metadata multiple Berkeley databases are used. These layers can use background threads to synchronize modified data with the disks. The statistics are updated in the fixed interval of the performance monitor, which is configurable. All statistics are computed (or fetched from /proc) at the end of each interval. In order to visualize the percentage of a metric's value, Jumpshot must be adapted, because it is not possible to render such a concept with the plain Jumpshot. Figure 3 shows a screenshot of the modified version of Jumpshot included in the extended PIOviz environment. The window on the left contains new categories for the metrics of the performance monitor, while the main window shows different height levels depending on the value of each metric. Modifications of the menu panel are highlighted in the screenshot. For more details refer to [15].

5 Results

The evaluation focuses on the four levels of access in MPI [16]. All experiments are run on our evaluation cluster consisting of 10 Linux machines with the following configuration: Two Intel Xeon 2000 Mhz processors (32-bit architecture), Kernel 2.6.21-rc5, Debian 3.1, MPICH2-1.0.5, 1 GByte memory, Intel 82545EM Gbit Ethernet network card. All nodes are equipped with an IBM IC35L090AVV207-0 hard drive and five nodes contain two additional Maxtor hard drives bundled to a software RAID-0 by a Promise FastTrack TX RAID controller. Specifications from IBM list the disk's read throughput between 29 and 56 MiB/s and an average access time of 8.5 ms. Characteristics of a single Maxtor 6G160E0 (DiamondMax 17 series) as specified by Maxtor are an access time of 8.9 ms, a track-to-track seek time of 2.5 ms and a sustained I/O throughput between 30.8 MiB/s and 58.9 MiB/s. Ext3 is configured as a local file system on top of a 38 GByte partition. The RAID performance was measured by IOzone and for convenience, a sequential throughput of 100 MiB/s can be assumed on the RAID partition and about 50 MiB/s on the local drive. Currently, the nodes use the anticipatory elevator to schedule I/O operations.

In PVFS2, files are split in datafiles (subfiles), which are distributed over the available servers. Instead of placing only a single datafile per server, two datafiles (subfiles) are placed in the experiments. The experiments use the benchmark MPI-IO-level which is an I/O-intensive application designed by the working group to record traces in the PIOviz environment for different access levels. It first writes an amount of data with a strided access pattern into a single file, and once all processes finish, it waits a second, then the data is read back in the same fashion. Non-contiguous operation accesses a number of i contiguous blocks at a time and may repeat this process a couple of times (o times). Contiguous operation accesses a specified block size a number of iterations equal to the total number of accessed blocks by a non-contiguous version ($i * o$). In the following experiments, each client accesses a total of 2000 MByte. With independend access (level 0), a contiguous 10 MByte block is accessed 200 times by each client. In level 2 and 3, each client accesses 500 MByte 4 times with a single call.

Average statistics over the whole run are extracted from the resulting trace files by a script. In the first experiment, an inhomogeneous I/O subsystem is used. While three servers use the local RAID system, one server operates on the single local disk, which runs at almost half the speed of the RAID disks. Screenshots of a few statistics are shown in figure 4. For each server and statistic an individual timeline is given. Note that the first timeline is always the slower server. With independent client I/O in figure 4(a), the actual data accessed during the write and read phase is balanced over all three servers (see statistics IV and VI). However, the Request load (statistic II) and Trove load (statistic IX) show that the operations aggregate on the first server. Consequently, it can be concluded that the first server is slower than the others. Also, the I/O subsystem's idle time on the first server is close to 0, while it is much higher on the others (statistic III). In PVFS2, up to 8 concurrent Trove operations are started per datafile, which leads to the observed Trove load of 80 (five clients use two datafiles). When non-contiguous requests are used, more data is transfered to the servers by each call (see figure 4(b)). Now requests aggregate on the slow server - when the faster servers finish to access data, the first server is still busy to process the data. Then long idle times manifest (statistic III) and can be seen in the access statistics IV and V as well. However, compared to the request load II a look at the write statistic does not reveal performance variation that clearly. The statistics in figure 4(d) were measured with collective non-contiguous calls. With this level of access, the two-phase protocol of MPICH2 is used to access data. Two-phase ships data between the clients leading to more idle time on all machines. In conjunction with the kernel's write behind strategy, the server with the single disk is not slower during the write phase. However, in the read phase the load is higher and the idle time is lower than on the faster machines. This reveals a load-imbalance during reads. For verification a screenshot of a run on homogenous hardware i.e. all servers use the RAID system, is given in figure 4(c). Average statistics of these experiments are shown in table 1. Statistics include values for metadata accesses and observed throughput. In addition, the statistics for homogenous hardware and for only one datafile are listed for the sake of completion. By comparing the average Trove load or Request load, it is possible to identify the slower server in all

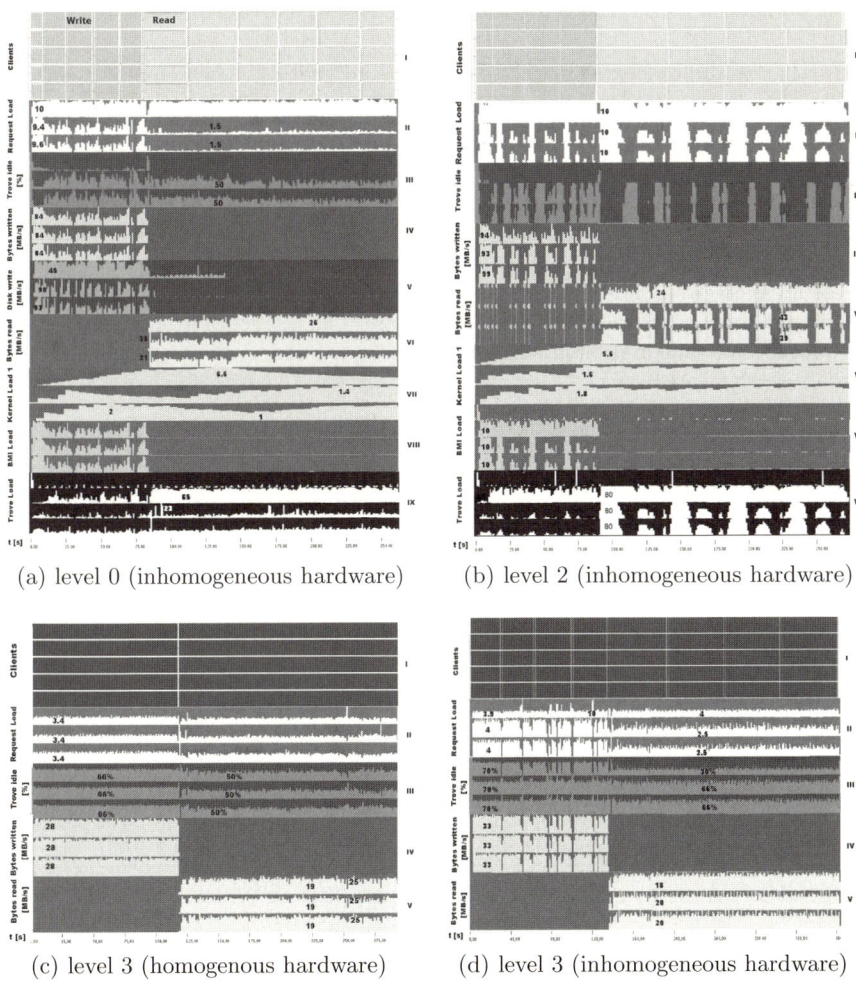

(a) level 0 (inhomogeneous hardware) (b) level 2 (inhomogeneous hardware)

(c) level 3 (homogenous hardware) (d) level 3 (inhomogeneous hardware)

Fig. 4. Jumpshot screenshot montages of three different levels of access

cases. However, there are some abnormalities for homogenous hardware. With level 0 and level 2, one server appears slower than the others i.e. with level 0 the first server has a request load of 7.8, while the other servers have a load of 5.1 and 5.5. The reason for the load variance are short term processing imbalances leading to faster or slower processing on a single server. In average all servers have the same capabilities. However, the I/O subsystem on a server may need slightly longer to reposition the access arm on a disk for a sequence of pending operations. Thus, the operations on the other servers finish earlier. An I/O operation ends when all pending flows are finished, therefore once the slower server finishes, a new I/O operation is started by the client. In the meantime, the other servers have to process less work and potentially finish earlier. In fact, this leads to a congestion on the server which takes a bit longer first. Due to statistical effects the roles of the servers may change. With increasing network and CPU speed compared to the I/O subsystem, the effect of a local congestion gets more likely.

Further evaluated experiments can be found in [15]. These experiments include data for cached I/O, partially cached data, unbalanced access patterns which prefer a server subset, and a static load balancing of inhomogeneous server hardware. With cached access, the network is the bottleneck resulting in a high BMI load compared to the Trove load.

Table 1. Average statistics for five clients and three data-servers. The first two blocks contain data measured on homogeneous hardware. The last set of experiments uses an inhomogeneous configuration in which the first server stores data on a single local disk instead of the faster RAID.

	Request load			BMI load			Trove load			Trove idleness [%]			Metad. reads [op/s]			Metad. writes [op/s]	Write [MiB/s]	Read [MiB/s]
level 0	7.8	5.1	5.5	2.1	2.1	2.1	36.7	17.9	20.6	5.4	9.7	9.8	23.09			0.05	216	80
level 1	5.1	5	5.1	1.7	1.7	1.7	9.2	9	9.2	26.9	27.6	27.3	55.08			0.04	166	64
level 2	8.7	8.8	8.2	2.2	2.3	2.2	54.4	54.9	49.9	3.4	2.1	4.4	1.2			0.05	235	78
level 3	2.9	3	2.9	1.2	1.2	1.2	4.4	4.8	4.6	56.7	54	56.3	34.19			0.03	86	57
level 0 - 1 datafile	3.2	3.1	3.9	1.2	1.2	1.2	14.8	14.5	20.2	15.5	16.9	9.5	12.85			0.03	214	93
level 1 - 1 datafile	2.7	2.5	2.6	1.1	1.1	1.1	8.5	7.6	7.9	30.3	34.9	33.2	30.37			0.02	167	73
level 2 - 1 datafile	4	4.3	4.1	1.2	1.4	1.2	25.7	28.6	26.6	10.1	5.3	8.8	0.64			0.02	198	92
level 3 - 1 datafile	1.5	1.5	1.5	0.9	0.9	0.9	4.1	4.1	4.1	60.8	60.4	60.9	18.3			0.01	83	66
level 0-inh. I/O	8.4	2.3	2.2	1.2	1.3	1.3	44.1	5	4.6	2.6	40.6	42.1	15.2			0.03	120	56
level 1-inh. I/O	5.8	3.5	3.6	1.2	1.3	1.3	11.9	6	6.2	10.1	49.5	49.2	42.08			0.03	119	50
level 2-inh. I/O	9.2	4.1	4.1	2.6	1.1	1.1	65.2	25.6	25	1.6	39.1	39.8	0.76			0.03	114	54
level 3-inh. I/O	3.5	2.3	2.3	0.9	1	0.9	7.2	3.5	3.5	40.4	63.7	64.3	27.61			0.02	75	44

6 Conclusions and Future Work

The presented implementation allows to record system behavior of the servers in conjunction with the activities of the MPI application. Compared to absolute metrics like measured throughput, relative metrics allowed us to identify the limiting server and even the component i.e. disk or network, which might be the bottleneck. This is an important task in inhomogeneous and large environments. In combination with well known maximum values, servers could be identified to perform load balancing in dynamic environments. Also, implemented average statistics support the monitoring of the file system, or they could be used for an automatic on-line bottleneck detection by the administrator.

References

1. Mellor, C.: US defense department builds world's biggest SAN (2006), http://www.techworld.com/news/index.cfm?RSS\&NewsID=6846
2. Schmuck, F., Haskin, R.: GPFS: A Shared-Disk File System for Large Computing Clusters. In: Proc. of the First Conference on File and Storage Technologies (FAST), January 2002, pp. 231–244 (2002)
3. Cluster File Systems Inc: Lustre, http://www.lustre.org
4. IBM: General Parallel File System - Advanced Administration Guide V3.1. (2006), http://publib.boulder.ibm.com/epubs/pdf/bl1adv00.pdf
5. Cluster File Systems Inc: Lustre 1.6 Manual, http://manual.lustre.org/manual/LustreManual16_HTML/DynamicHTML-21-1.html
6. Cluster File Systems Inc: Lustre Debugging (2007), http://wiki.lustre.org/index.php?title=Lustre_Debugging
7. Cluster File Systems Inc: Lustre: Profiling Tools for IO (2007), http://arch.lustre.org/index.php?title=Profiling_Tools_for_IO
8. Ligon, W., Ross, R.: PVFS: Parallel Virtual File System. In: Sterling, T. (ed.) Beowulf Cluster Computing with Linux. Scientific and Engineering Computation, November 2001, pp. 391–430. The MIT Press, Cambridge (2001)
9. Seger, M.: Homepage of collectl, http://collectl.sourceforge.net/
10. Forster, F.: Homepage of collectd, http://collectd.org/
11. Ludwig, T., Krempel, S., Kunkel, J.M., Panse, F., Withanage, D.: Tracing the MPI-IO Calls' Disk Accesses. In: Mohr, B., Träff, J.L., Worringen, J., Dongarra, J. (eds.) PVM/MPI 2006. LNCS, vol. 4192, pp. 322–330. Springer, Heidelberg (2006)
12. Ludwig, T., Krempel, S., Kuhn, M., Kunkel, J.M., Lohse, C.: Analysis of the MPI-IO Optimization Levels with the PIOViz Jumpshot Enhancement. In: Cappello, F., Herault, T., Dongarra, J. (eds.) PVM/MPI 2007. LNCS, vol. 4757, pp. 213–222. Springer, Heidelberg (2007)
13. Juckeland, G.: Vampir and Lustre (2007), http://clusterfs-intra.com/cfscom/images/lustre/LUG2007/lug07-dresden.pdf
14. AT Consultancy bv: Atop, http://www.atcomputing.nl/Tools/atop
15. Kunkel, J.M.: Towards Automatic Load Balancing of a Parallel File System with Subfile Based Migration. Master's thesis, Ruprecht-Karls-Universität Heidelberg, Institute of Computer Science (July 2007)
16. Gropp, W., Thakur, R., Lusk, E.: 3.10.1. In: Using MPI-2: Advanced Features of the Message Passing Interface, pp. 101–105. MIT Press, Cambridge (1999)

Topic 3: Scheduling and Load Balancing

Dieter Kranzlmueller[*], Uwe Schwiegelshohn[*], Yves Robert[*],
and Francisco F. Rivera[*]

The key objective in scheduling and load balancing is to reduce the computing power that remains unusable by planning and distributing tasks among processing elements to achieve the expected performance goals, such as minimizing execution time, minimizing communication delays, or maximizing resource utilization.

Scheduling and load balancing have been the subjects of research and development for decades. They are critical issues for achieving good performance in parallel and distributed systems at different levels. While a variety of parallel and distributed systems are being developed throughout the world, the scheduling and load balancing studies are progressively adapting to this variety.

Nowadays, a vast number of papers, projects and developments are devoted to this topic at different levels related with different parallel architectures: from multithreading processors to Grids, including multi-core processors, SMPs, NUMA systems, clusters, and so on. In addition, they can be applied to a number of resources as the computing devices (processors, computers, FPUs, etc), the communication stages (networks, buses, etc), and the memory (disk, registers, etc). 9 papers selected to be presented in the 14th Euro-Par that cover different examples in this broad spectrum. All of them raised new and exciting challenges from theory to practice.

There were 22 papers submitted to the Topic 3 track. Each paper has been reviewed by 4 reviewers. The 9 selected papers present solutions to different problems like the dynamic scheduling in Grid systems; the use of predictions of execution times or the communication speeds in multicluster systems to guide the scheduling of parallel jobs on clusters; the introduction of data structures for task stealing on multiprocessors; the impact on performance when co-scheduling several jobs on chip multiprocessors; the impact of dynamic page migration in NUMA systems; the scheduling for virtual machine monitors; the replica migration problem; and the processor assignment to pipelines of tasks.

We would like to thank to our colleagues, experts in the field, who helped in the reviewing process.

---

[*]Topic Chairs.

Dynamic Grid Scheduling Using Job Runtime Requirements and Variable Resource Availability

Sam Verboven, Peter Hellinckx, Jan Broeckhove,
and Frans Arickx

CoMP, University of Antwerp, Middelheimlaan 1,
2020 Antwerp, Belgium
Sam.Verboven@ua.ac.be

Abstract. We describe a scheduling technique in which estimated job runtimes and estimated resource availability are used to efficiently distribute workloads across a homogeneous grid of resources with variable availability. The objective is to increase efficiency by minimizing job failure caused by resources becoming unavailable. Optimal scheduling will be accomplished by mapping jobs onto resources with sufficient availability. Both the scheduling technique and the implementation called PGS (*Prediction based Grid Scheduling*) are described in detail. Results are presented for a set of sleep jobs, and compared with a first come, first serve scheduling approach.

1 Introduction

During the last couple of years, the demand for more computational resources within grid systems has grown significantly. This has lead to situations where traditional dedicated grids can no longer satisfy that demand. In an effort to increase the amount of available resources one can turn to the concept of *CPU harvesting* on idle resources. Organizations and private users all over the world have large amounts of user-controlled resources (e.g. workstations, personal computers) that often go unused over long periods of time. These resources could be made available to heavily used grid systems without the need to invest in extra equipment and infrastructure. Some existing grid systems such as Condor [1], Globus [2] and CoBRA [3][4] allow user-controlled resources and dedicated clusters to co-exist within a single grid.

There are some drawbacks that need to be considered. Job failure caused by a resource becoming unavailable becomes an issue when employing large numbers of non-dedicated resources. In [5] a performance analysis of the impact of failures is made for a range of scheduling policies. It concludes that failures have a large impact on the total runtime of failure unaware scheduling policies. The author presents a solution using temporal information in combination with checkpointing [6]. However, this approach requires that users instrument their code to enable the checkpointing. For example, in Condor users have to link their code to a system call library to allow for checkpointing. Such instrumentation is not always possible and, in any case, it represents an additional burden that users have to assume in order to use the grid. Users should be unaware of the scheduling technique being used, and the complexity of distributing a problem needs to be minimized. Since we want the user to have as few specific requirements as possible, a more general solution is proposed. Such implementation however requires more information than a classic grid scheduling technique. The extra information required is time related: how long does it take for a certain jobs to execute on a particular resource and for how long will this resource be available.

Availability of resources can be divided into two categories, *predicted availability* and *planned availability*. Planned availability could be used in the case of workstations that are periodically available e.g. during non-work hours, or dedicated grid resources that are periodically unavailable e.g. during maintenance. Predicted availability presents a more complex problem. Predictions have to be made by monitoring the grid system. Methods have already been developed in specific areas, such as Fine-Grained Cycle Sharing systems [7], as well as more general approaches suitable for both desktop and enterprise environments [8]. In this paper we will concentrate on a scheduling algorithm based on known limited availability information, e.g. resources configured to become (un)available at predetermined times. These situations can be found in large organizations where workstations are available during nights and weekends or even lunch hours. We will use the term *uptime* to define the amount of time a resource is available for distributed computations.

The other crucial element needed to efficiently schedule, is the job runtime. In general one distinguishes three possible techniques to predict job runtimes: *code analysis* [9], *analytical benchmarking/code profiling* [10] and *statistical prediction* [11]. The best method for predicting runtimes depends heavily on the type of application one is distributing.

In this paper will propose a *fault-aware scheduling* mechanism for use with *Bag-of-Tasks* (BoT) applications [12], loosely-coupled parallel applications consisting of mutually independent jobs. Using BoT applications removes inter-job constraints when scheduling. The proposed technique is based on the availability of job runtime estimates and resource availability estimates. Instead of just tolerating failures like *fault-tolerant scheduling* this technique will pro-actively try to prevent failures from occurring. By distributing jobs only to resources available for the full executing time of the job, no CPU cycles are wasted on jobs that will be unable to complete. For the implementation and testing of PGS, the CoBRA [3][4] grid system is used.

The rest of the paper is organized as follows. In section 2 an overview is given of the scheduling technique. We discuss collecting the needed information and the scheduling mechanism. Section 3 presents the implementation of the scheduling technique introduced in section 2. A short introduction is given into CoBRA followed by the implementation details. In section 4 a description is given on the testing technique followed by an overview of the test results. More information on future work can be found in section 5 followed by a conclusion in section 6.

2 Scheduling Technique

The goal is simple, given the available information try to find the optimal job distribution that causes as little job failure as possible while minimizing the total application runtime. This goal can be achieved by insuring no job is scheduled onto a resource that will not be available for the required runtime. To make the scheduling mechanism possible, the required information must first be gathered. This information consists of two main parts, the time needed by a given job to complete itself on a certain resource, and the amount of time this resource will remain available. The way the job runtimes are predicted may depend on the type of jobs. Similarly, the expected uptimes can also be obtained in various different ways depending on the grid configuration. As such, our scheduling technique needs to be independent of the way this information is determined. Care needs be taken when gathering initial data and consequent updates of this data. Each update constitutes data transfer across the network that could form a possible bottleneck slowing down the scheduling process.

2.1 Collecting Job Runtime Information

The first requirement is efficiently obtaining accurate job runtime predictions. Since large amounts of jobs may be available to the scheduler at any given time, the number of network messages required per job needs to be reduced to a minimum. A simple yet elegant solution is proposed: jobs are submitted to the scheduler once a stable runtime prediction is available. By excluding functionality to gather runtime updates, dependent on the prediction method, the number of needed network messages is reduced. There are, however, drawbacks if a prediction method is used that relies on information from previous jobs. In this case, accurate job runtime estimates can not be made from the start and job submission becomes an iterative process. To solve this problem an optional interface is added which allows the prediction component to update job runtimes even after submission to the scheduler. When necessary, this allows updates to be made when new information becomes available.

2.2 Collecting Resource Availability Information

For the second requirement, obtaining accurate resource uptimes, more effort is needed. When a resource becomes available and its uptime is given we cannot assume that this value remains constant. Updates at regular intervals are needed. Between these updates the uptime prediction is estimated using a standard interpolation technique. This is not the only factor that needs to be taken into consideration. The scheduling mechanism will attempt to match job runtimes with the remaining resource uptimes, taking into account the queue of jobs already associated with that resource. These jobs can be found in two locations: on the resource after being submitted and in a local queue on the scheduler after being scheduled for the resource but not yet submitted. This requires information records containing two additional aspects next to the estimated uptime:

1. The predicted runtimes for the jobs that have been scheduled to a particular resource but have not yet been submitted.
2. The predicted runtime of the currently running job and the already elapsed runtime.

With this information it is possible to accurately predict tl, the time a resource has left for computations :

$$tl = ru - (et_{rj} - el_{rj}) - \sum_{i=0}^{qj} et_i$$

With ru the resource uptime, et_{rj} the runtime of the current running job, el_{rj} the elapsed runtime, qj the amount of jobs queued on the scheduler for this resource and et_i the runtime of the i'th job in this queue.

2.3 Scheduling Mechanism

When the required information has been obtained the scheduling mechanism can start mapping jobs onto resources. It requires three lists to be maintained. The list of all available resources, a list of all jobs that need to be run but have not yet been scheduled, and a list of jobs that have already been processed in some way but are still in need of scheduling (e.g. a job failed or no suitable resource was found in a previous mapping attempt). This last list is called the priority queue, and in each scheduling step we first try to map the jobs in this queue to a resource before turning to the regular job queue. In an effort to maximize resource utilization the main scheduling algorithm is split up into two complementing parts.

The first part consists of finding and scheduling a first job for each resource. When there are large amounts of resources in the grid, the time needed by the second part might leave some resources without a job to execute. To prevent this, the scheduler makes sure each resource is given at least one job for its queue before filling all queues with the most appropriate jobs. By taking this first step, as little resources as possible are wasted while running the next scheduling step. The algorithm used in the first step works as follows:

– Select resource R with an empty queue from the available resources.
– Select the first job J so that runtime J < uptime R.

These steps are repeated as long as a resource R is found. In this first part of the scheduling mechanism the mapping is resource oriented so as to increase the throughput.

The second part of the mapping is done by iterating over the jobs and matching them to resources. For this part, two requirements need to be fulfilled. There have to be resources with sufficient uptime left and unfilled queues, and there have to be jobs left to execute. As long as this requirement is met we keep matching jobs to resources and adding them to their queues. After a first job has been put in each resource's queue, all resources are ordered by the amount of computing time they have left. Using this ordered list, jobs are then be placed on the resource with the lowest amount of remaining uptime strictly greater than the required job runtime. This way resources with time to execute longer jobs are available for longer jobs further down the queue.

The jobs that have runtimes that are too long are put on the priority queue. When the resource list is updated and new resources are added with longer available uptimes, these longer jobs will get the first chance to be submitted. This method allows longer jobs to be run as soon as possible while maximizing resource utilization by filling the gaps with smaller jobs. It is important to notice that this second scheduling step is job oriented and tries to minimize the round trip time.

3 Implementation

3.1 CoBRA

The CoBRA grid [3] stands for *Computational Basic Reprogrammable Adaptive grid* and can be defined as:

> A portable generalized plug-in middleware for Desktop computing that allows developers to dynamically adapt and extend the distributed computing components without compromising the functionality, consistency and robustness of the deployed framework.

We have opted for the CoBRA middleware, as it allows to easily extend and dynamically replace available middleware components. This makes it a perfect environment to implement and test a new scheduling mechanism. It also provides a standard scheduler whose functioning can be compared with the newly proposed technique. The standard CoBRA grid scheduler uses a first come, first serve (FCFS) method to distribute jobs across available resources. The only requirement for a job to be scheduled on a resource is that the resource queue is not full. A list of available resources is composed using a resource manager component. A resource proxy, through which jobs can be submitted, is returned. Each job is taken from the queue and submitted to the first resource that has less jobs than the maximum configured queue length. When a resource fails and jobs are rescheduled they are added to the front of the queue.

3.2 Extending the Scheduler

This section gives a short overview of the implementation details. It describes how the CoBRA grid components are extended to obtain the functionality described in section 2. As can be seen in figure 1, the scheduling implementation consists of four main components. The *JobContainer* objects whose main purpose is to provide a local cache for remote information. The *ResourceContainer* objects are also used for caching purposes but, more importantly, maintain the job queues during job scheduling and submission. A separate *JobSubmitter*

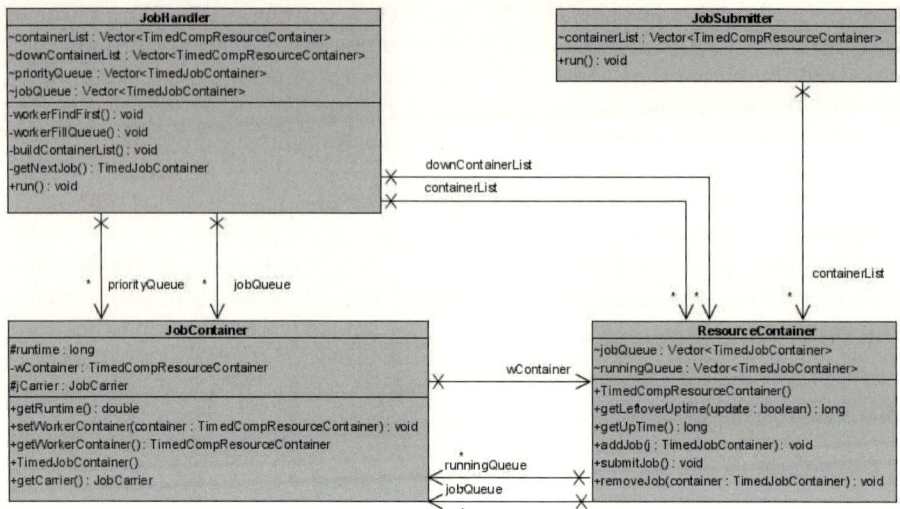

Fig. 1. Simplified scheduling UML diagram

thread is used to continuously submit jobs from the local queues on the scheduler to the resources. Combined with the two step scheduling mechanism this minimizes the delay between deciding where a resource should be submitted and the actual submission. The most important part of the scheduling technique is implemented in the *JobHandler* thread. Here all required information is gathered, organized and subsequently used to distribute each job to its most suitable resource. The JobHandler thread operates in three main steps:

1. Building/updating the list of JobContainer objects encapsulating the currently available resources.
2. Finding a first job for each resource that currently has an empty queue.
3. Filling the queues.

The JobContainer list built in step 1 is made up of two separate parts: the currently available resources and the previously available resources. When a resource becomes unavailable its container is moved to the previously available list and all its queued jobs are added to the *priorityQueue*. The subsequent steps are implemented as previously described in section 2.

4 Testing and Results

4.1 Testing Technique

To facilitate easy, correct and comprehensive testing, we use the "sleep testing technique" to evaluate the implemented scheduling mechanism. This technique was first introduced in [13] and has already been used for testing in CoBRA

[3]. It allows to generate many different simulated workloads using a limited number of parameters. It is also possible to simulate real, recorded workloads by replacing the actual jobs with sleep jobs that occupy the resource for the same amount of time. An additional benefit is that we know the exact job runtime and that it is independent of the machine type the job is executed on.

The next element needed to benchmark the proposed scheduling technique is a set of resources that have to become periodically unavailable. The requirement for these resources is that they become available and go down for predictable amounts of time. A practical solution that takes advantage of the CoBRA grid philosophy is used. All different components of the CoBRA grid consist of pluglets registered in a central lookup service, this includes the worker pluglets deployed on the resources. By encapsulating the existing worker functionality inside a new pluglet responsible for starting and stopping the worker, we can configure the availability of the corresponding worker resource. The encapsulating pluglet reads a startup-configuration file containing pairs of integers. These pairs contain the amount of seconds a resource will be available followed by the amount of seconds the resource will be unavailable. This way we can retain the original worker functionality while still having a reliable and accurate way of obtaining the availability information by simply requesting it from the pluglet. The reuse of the original worker allows for a more accurate comparison between old and new system tests.

4.2 Test Configuration

To test the proposed scheduling technique three different job scenarios are used. Each scenario is composed of a series of increasingly larger sleep jobs totaling 482 minutes. By changing the job duration and the amount of jobs we can test the impact different types of workload have on both the PGS and the original FCFS scheduling approach. Intuitively, in an environment where resources frequently become unavailable, small jobs should have less impact on the total runtime. The test scenarios describe the following job configurations:

1. 960 jobs ranging from 0.25 to 60 seconds in steps of 0.25 seconds (4 of each).
2. 480 jobs ranging from 0.5 to 120 seconds in 0.5 seconds steps (2 of each).
3. 240 jobs ranging from 1 to 240 seconds in 1 second steps.

The grid configuration used consists of three major components: 1 broker (Intel Pentium 4 CPU @ 2.26GHz, 512 MB), 8 resources (Intel Pentium 4 CPU @ 2.26GHz, 512 MB) and 1 scheduler (Intel Core2 CPU 6400 @ 2.13GHz, 1 GB). The resources are configured with the uptimes given in table 1. Each resource

Table 1. Uptime of the resource at restart

Resource	1	2	3	4	5	6	7	8
Uptime (Seconds)	84	117	163	228	318	443	619	864

is restarted after 1 second. On average it takes 1.2 seconds for a resource to become available again, including the time needed for the startup. Taking into account the total problem time of 482 minutes spread over 8 resources, the lower boundary for the total run time is 60 minutes and 15 seconds.

4.3 Results

Each test is run ten times and an average is taken from these runs. For comparison we add a scenario 0, corresponding to scenario 1, in which resources remain available during the full test run. The next three test scenarios use resources with the uptimes described in table 1.

In table 2 and figure 2 we show the test results comparing the standard FCFS approach with the PGS approach. It is observed that PGS is more efficient, with a more pronounced difference as job times (in terms of runtime) increase: for job configuration 1 the difference is 13.31% on average, increasing up to 38.64% for configuration 3. The reason for this lies in job failures that occur more frequently with FCFS. As average job times become longer, the amount of lost CPU cycles increases accordingly when failure occurs. This increases the relative benefit obtained by using PGS. From table 1 we can conclude that the standard deviation remains relatively small which proves the consistincy of the obtained results.

Table 2. Comparison between PGS and FCFS

Scenario	0	1	2	3
PGS (Minutes)	63.54	65.54	68.46	87.88
FCFS (Minutes)	63.21	74.26	87.3	121.83
PGS STDEV	0.19	0.39	073	2.03
FCFC STDEV	0.12	0.63	1.68	2.25
Difference	-0.51%	13.31%	27.51%	38.64%

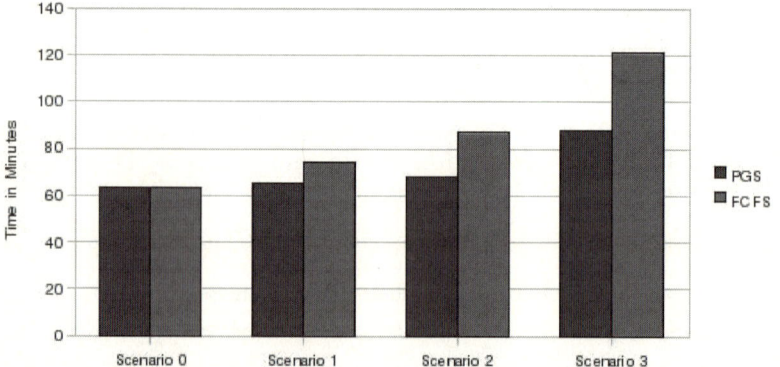

Fig. 2. Test results using the job configurations

5 Future Work

Future work can be performed in two directions, improving the scheduling technique and introducing more realism in the tested grid implementation. For this paper we have chosen to work with sleep jobs, allowing the sole focus of the tests and results to be on the scheduling mechanism. It is however not realistic to assume job runtimes prediction to be 100% accurate. Work is already underway to further extend the CoBRA grid with a system to automatically generate predicted runtimes for parameter sweep applications. The idea is to add a pluglet to the grid which is a front-end for the GIPSy *ModelBuilder* [14] that has already been developed by our research team. This front-end can then be used to generate predictions for jobs contained in a particular application. While runtime data is gathered the ModelBuilder will continuously keep building better models and suggest sets of points for which data is preferably obtained. The newest model is used to update job runtime predictions and reorder the queue of jobs that still need scheduling. This ensures the most valuable runtime data is gathered as soon as possible.

6 Conclusion

In this paper, we proposed a dynamic fault-aware scheduling mechanism that uses job runtime predictions and resource availability predictions to improve performance of BoT applications. This technique was implemented and compared to the FCFS scheduling technique. Empirical results show that large reductions in total runtime can be achieved in situations with variable resource availability. The difference in total runtime increases in favor of the proposed mechanism as job runtime increases. Results also indicate that the scheduling overhead remains the same in situations where resources are continuously available.

References

1. Condor, http://www.cs.wisc.edu/condor/
2. Globus, http://www.globus.org/
3. Hellinckx, P., Arickx, F., Broeckhove, J., Stuer, G.: The CoBRA grid: a highly configurable lightweight grid. International Journal of Web and Grid Services 3(20), 267–286 (2007)
4. Hellinckx, P., Stuer, G., Hendrickx, W., Arickx, F., Broeckhove, J.: Grid-user driven grid research, the CoBRA grid. In: CCGRID 2006: Proceedings of the Sixth IEEE International Symposium on Cluster Computing and the Grid (CCGRID 2006), Washington, DC, USA, p. 49. IEEE Computer Society, Los Alamitos (2006)
5. Zhang, Y., Squillante, M.S., Sivasubramaniam, A., Sahoo, R.K.: Performance implications of failures in large-scale cluster scheduling. LNCS. Springer, Heidelberg (2005)
6. Litzkow, M., Tannenbaum, T., Basney, J., Livny, M.: Checkpoint and migration of UNIX processes in the Condor distributed processing system. Technical Report UW-CS-TR-1346, University of Wisconsin - Madison Computer Sciences Department (April 1997)

7. Ren, X., Lee, S., Eigenmann, R., Bagchi, S.: Resource availability prediction in fine-grained cycle sharing systems. In: Proceedings of the Conference on High Performance Distributed Computing (2006)
8. Brevik, J., Nurmi, D., Wolski, R.: Automatic methods for predicting machine availability in desktop grid and peer-to-peer systems. In: CCGRID 2004: Proceedings of the 2004 IEEE International Symposium on Cluster Computing and the Grid, Washington, DC, USA, pp. 190–199. IEEE Computer Society, Los Alamitos (2004)
9. Reistad, B., Gifford, D.K.: Static dependent costs for estimating execution time. SIGPLAN Lisp Pointers VII(3), 65–78 (1994)
10. Yang, J., Ahmad, I., Ghafoor, A.: Estimation of execution times on heterogeneous supercomputer architectures. In: ICPP 1993: Proceedings of the 1993 International Conference on Parallel Processing, Washington, DC, USA, pp. 219–226. IEEE Computer Society, Los Alamitos (1993)
11. Iverson, M.A., Özgüner, F., Potter, L.C.: Statistical prediction of task execution times through analytic benchmarking for scheduling in a heterogeneous environment. In: HCW 1999: Proceedings of the Eighth Heterogeneous Computing Workshop, Washington, DC, USA, p. 99. IEEE Computer Society, Los Alamitos (1999)
12. Cirne, W., Paranhos, D., Costa, L., Santos-Neto, E., Brasileiro, F., Sauve, J., Silva, F.A.B., Barros, C.O., Silveira, C.: Running bag-of-tasks applications on computational grids: The MyGrid approach. ICPP 00, 407 (2003)
13. Hellinckx, P., Stuer, G., Dewolfs, D., Arickx, F., Broeckhove, J., Dhaene, T.: Dynamic problem-independent metacomputing characterization applied to the condor system. In: Procedings ESM 2003, pp. 262–269 (2003)
14. Hellinckx, P., Verboven, S., Arickx, F., Broeckhove, J.: Scheduling parameter sweeps in desktop grids using runtime prediction. Poster, Grid@Mons (2008)

Enhancing Prediction on Non-dedicated Clusters*

Joseph Ll. Lérida[1], F. Solsona[1], F. Giné[1], J.R. García[2],
M. Hanzich[2], and P. Hernández[2]

[1] Departamento de Informática e Ingeniería Industrial, Universitat de Lleida, Spain
{jlerida,francesc,sisco}@diei.udl.cat
[2] Departamento de Arquitectura y Sistemas Operativos,
Universitat Autònoma de Barcelona, Spain
{jrgarcia,mauricio,porfidio.hernandez}@aomail.uab.es

Abstract. In this paper, we present a scheduling scheme to estimate the turnaround time of parallel jobs on a heterogeneous and non-dedicated cluster or NoW(Network of Workstations). This scheme is based on an analytical prediction model that establishes the processing and communication slowdown of the execution times of the jobs based on the cluster nodes and links powerful and occupancy. Preservation of the local application responsiveness is also a goal.

We address the impact of inaccuracies in these estimates on the overall system performance. Furthermore, we demonstrate that job scheduling benefits from the accuracy of these estimates. The applicability of our proposal has been proved by measuring the efficiency of our method by comparing the predicted deviations of the parallel jobs in a real environment with respect to the most representative ones of the literature.

The additional cost of obtaining these was also evaluated and compared. The present work is implemented within the CISNE project, a previously developed scheduling framework for non-dedicated and heterogeneous cluster environments.

1 Introduction

Several studies [1] have revealed that a high percentage of the computing resources in NoWs and Clusters environments are idle. The possibility of using this computing power to execute parallel jobs without perturbing the performance of the local users applications on each workstation has led to a proposal for new job schedulers [6, 7, 15].

With the aim of taking advantage of the idle computing resources available across the cluster, in a previous work [6], we developed a new scheduling environment, named CISNE. Entering jobs wait in an input queue to be scheduled and mapped into the cluster. The Scheduler supports backfilling and mapping techniques based on prediction of the turnaround time of parallel jobs. The prediction engine is a simulation tool, integrated into the CISNE scheduling system. Estimation of the future state of the NoW/Cluster is a critical component of our scheduling environment. It was also so in other well-known systems, as in [2, 3, 12, 13].

The first step to estimate the future cluster state is to predict the job run times. In this sense, there are a large number of proposals. The most widely used method is based on a

---
* This work was supported by the MEyC-Spain under contract TIN2007-64974.

historical system that records the past executions of an application [4, 5, 12]. The second alternative is to use a *simulation system* based on *analytical models*, which by means of the characterization of the environment and the workloads, allows a future state to be estimated [6, 8, 9]. Finally, another typical approach is the combination of *a simulation system* and a *historical scheme*. In this case, the simulation engine approximates the future cluster state based on the search for similarities in previous cluster states stored in the historical database, thus generally obtaining more accurate estimations [3, 13, 14].

Most of the prediction studies only consider the state of the processing resources without insight into job communication. This also applies in [2, 6, 16]. In [6], Hanzich presented a new analytical model that only considered the number of parallel jobs mapped into a non-dedicated cluster in order to estimate the runtime of a parallel job. Additionally, communication issues where not considered. We extend this model by considering the resource heterogeneity and a real measurement of the parallel and local workload.

In [11], Jones presented an application bandwidth-aware model that measures the impact of the saturation of communication links on the runtime of a parallel workload. Recently, Jones in [10], addressed the impact of inaccuracies in user-provided communication requirement estimates on overall system performance. He showed that underestimating the bandwidth requirements specified in the job arguments, gives worse overall system performance than overestimation due to the fact that network saturation occurs when this is the case. In our proposal we also takes communication into account. We add the Jones model to our scheme, and even extend it by also considering the effect of the local applications communications.

In this paper, we present a new analytical model that predicts the parallel job runtime by considering the future non-dedicated and heterogeneous cluster state of the processing and communicating resources, and models the impact of the local activity on the prediction of the parallel job runtime. Preservation of local workload responsiveness is also a goal. Together these are the contributions of this work. We evaluated the effectiveness of our proposals in relation to various estimation techniques from the literature. In general, in-depth experimentation demonstrates the rigorous and low time-costly estimations without excessively damaging the local workload of our proposal.

The outline of this paper is as follows. Section 2 describes the cluster-scheduling environment used in the present work and our proposal for a new estimation model. Next, we describe the experimental environment and analyze the results in section 3. Finally, the conclusions and future work are explained in section 4.

2   Prediction Model for Non-dedicated Clusters

The CISNE system [6] is a scheduling environment for non-dedicated and heterogeneous clusters. CISNE ensures benefits for the parallel applications, while preserving the user task responsiveness. Fig. 1 shows the architecture of CISNE.

Entering jobs wait to be scheduled and mapped by the *Scheduler* in the *Input Queue*. The *Scheduler* is made up of the *Job* and *Node selection* modules. *Job selection* supports two different policies, namely *FCFS* (First-Come-First-Served) and *Backfilling*. *Backfilling* [3] consists of selecting the job in the queue that does not delay the start of

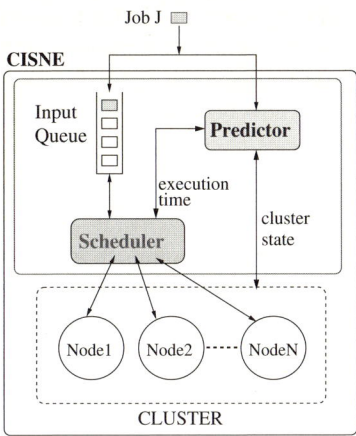

Fig. 1. CISNE architecture

the first job in the Input Queue. To do this, accurate estimations of the job turnaround times must be performed. We implemented two node selection policies, *Normal* and *Uniform*. The *Normal* policy selects the nodes by taking into account only their load. The *Uniform* policy merges CPU and I/O bound parallel applications in the same node as much as possible, with the restriction that nodes should also be evenly loaded.

Estimations of the job turnaround times are performed by the simulator engine (*Predictor*), according to job's priorities (order in the queue), the computational requirements of each parallel job and the cluster *state*. The cluster *state* includes the occupancy of the Memory, CPU and communication links of each cluster resource. The assignment is static, that is, once the job is mapped into a particular set of nodes, no more re-allocations are performed.

The *Predictor* simulates the execution of a parallel job in a non-dedicated cluster. The simulator models a cluster as a collection of heterogeneous and non-dedicated computational resources and allows us to configure several scheduling mechanisms. The input arguments of the simulation engine are the computational resources required by parallel jobs as well as the cluster state and returns the estimated turnaround time. In the present work the *Predictor* was extended with a new analytical model and modified to take more information about the resource nature and their usage into account.

We are interested in arbitrary sized clusters made up of heterogeneous nodes interconnected by means of an internal switch. Formally, a Cluster C is made up by β nodes, this is $C=\{N_1..N_\beta\}$, and a set of β cluster links $\mathscr{L}$, $\mathscr{L}=\{L_1..L_\beta\}$, where L_i denotes the cluster link between node N_i and the switch in Cluster C.

Jobs are not supposed to be malleable. That is, they require the same number of processors (one per task) during their lifetime. The computing and communicating requirements of every job task are very similar. Considering this, we define the job execution time, T^e, as follows:

$$T^e = T^p \cdot SP + T^c \cdot SC, \qquad (1)$$

where T^p and T^c are the processing and communicating times measured in a dedicated environment. In a real situation, due to the heterogeneity and the non-dedicated property of the resources, T^p and T^c may be lengthened by the *SP* and *SC*, the processing and communication slowdowns respectively. We propose a means for obtaining the SP and SC, which are explained below separately.

2.1 Obtaining SP

In a heterogeneous and non-dedicated environment, the processing capabilities of the constituent nodes depend on its computing power and availability.

We define the *relative computing Power* (P^i) of the node i, as the computing power ratio of such a node with regard to the most powerful node in the Cluster. The P^i range is $0 < P^i \leq 1$. $P^i = 1$ means that node i is the most powerful node in the Cluster. The *relative computing Power* of each node can be obtained by averaging samples obtained with different applications.

The *Availability* of the node i (A^i), is defined as the percentage of CPU idleness. $A^i \simeq 0$ when 100% of the CPU is occupied and $0 < A^i \leq 1$ otherwise. We define the *Effective computing power* of node i (Γ^i) as the product between the *relative computing Power* and the *Availability* of such a node. Formally, Γ^i is defined as follows:

$$\Gamma^i = P^i \cdot A^i, \qquad (2)$$

where $0 \leq \Gamma^i \leq 1$. $\Gamma^i = 0$ means that node i is unable to execute any task. $\Gamma^i = 1$ tells us that node i can execute the task at full speed. Therefore, the processing slowdown of such a node (SP^i) is inversely proportional to its *Effective computing power*, $SP^i = (\Gamma^i)^{-1}$.

As we assume that each job task in our model is very similar in size and they are executing separately, the job execution time is defined as the elapsed execution time of the slowest task. Accordingly, we define the processing time slowdown (*SP*) as the maximum obtained by every forming job task. Formally:

$$SP = max\{SP^i, 1 \leq i \leq \rho \leq \beta\}, \qquad (3)$$

where ρ is the number of tasks (nodes) making up the job.

2.2 Obtaining SC

Communication characterization is based on the model described by Jones in [11] for homogeneous and dedicated environments. The communication slowdown of each parallel job (*SC*) is defined as the maximum relation between its required bandwidth (*BW*) and the bandwidth finally assigned to the job by the communication system (BW^{as}). BW^{as} is the bandwidth assigned to the job in each mapped link as a consequence of the bandwidth adjustment to the most saturated link. Formally:

$$SC = \left(\frac{BW}{BW^{as}}\right) \qquad (4)$$

$SC > 1$ means that the job will suffer delays due to saturated links. When $SC = 1$, the parallel application can communicate at full speed.

2.3 Prediction Engine

When a new parallel job enters the system, or the scheduler needs to know the remaining execution time of any existing parallel job in order to take better scheduling decisions, the simulation engine is activated in order to obtain the remaining execution time of such a job (*Target*). The simulation process is detailed in Algorithm 1. First, the simulator is updated with the current cluster state: the *Input Queue*, the *Target*, the *Running List* and for each cluster node i its *Effective computing power* (Γ^i, defined in section 2.1) and its *link bandwidth requirements*. Next, the simulation engine estimates the execution of all the previous jobs in the system until *Target* was executed. Finally, the remaining execution time $T^e_{rem}(Target)$ of *Target* is returned.

Algorithm 1. Simulation process.

1: Input arguments: Input Queue (*IQ*), Running List (*RL*, List of executing jobs), *Target*, Γ^i, Cluster (*C*), *Job_Selection_Policy* and *Node_Selection_Policy*.
2: Set t to the simulation start-time. $J = \phi$.
3: **while** (($RL \neq \{\phi\}$) and ($J \neq Target$)) **do**
4:    **forall** ($j \in RL$) Estimate the execution remaining time $T^e_{rem}(j)$, at time t.
5:    Select the next job $J = min\{T^e_{rem}(j)\}$ to finish. Let $(t + \Delta t)$ the end time of J.
6:    Remove J from RL.
7:    **forall** ($j \in RL$) Obtain its T^p_{rem} and T^c_{rem} at time $(t + \Delta t)$.
8:    **forall** ($j \in IQ$) Increase the estimated *Waiting_Time*(j) in Δt time units.
9:    **while** (($IQ \neq \{\phi\}$) and (available resources in C)) **do**
10:      Select the next job $k \in IQ$ by using the *Job_Selection_Policy*.
11:      Select the C nodes to map k by using the *Node_Selection_Policy*.
12:      Remove k from IQ. Insert k into RL.
13:    **end while**
14:    Set t to $t + \Delta t$.
15: **end while**
16: **return** $T^e_{rem}(J)$ // $J = Target$

In each simulation step, the simulation engine estimates the execution remaining time of each job in the *RL* by means of the equation 5 (line 4). Let t be current simulation time. The estimated remaining execution time of a job J at time t, $T^e_{rem}(J)$, depends on the remaining processing and communicating times, T^p_{rem} and T^c_{rem}, as well as the current processing and communication slowdown, *SP* and *SC*. This gives,

$$T^e_{rem}(J) = T^p_{rem} \cdot SP + T^c_{rem} \cdot SC, \tag{5}$$

Next, the job J with the minimum estimated remaining time ($min\{T^e_{rem}(J)\}$) was selected (line 5). Let $(t + \Delta t)$ be the time at which the selected job J ends. Then, the remaining processing and communicating times of the rest of jobs in the *RL* should be calculated at time $(t + \Delta t)$ by means the equation 6 (line 7).

The remaining processing time at time $(t + \Delta t)$, T^p_{rem}, is calculated by means of the difference between the remaining processing time at time t, T'^p_{rem}, and the processing time spent during Δt time units with its corresponding slowdown SP', that is $\frac{T^p_{\Delta t}}{SP'}$. This is also true for the remaining communicating time T^c_{rem}.

$$T^p_{rem} = T'^p_{rem} - \frac{T^p_{\Delta t}}{SP'}, \quad T^c_{rem} = T'^c_{rem} - \frac{T^c_{\Delta t}}{SC'} \quad (6)$$

The algorithm also obtains the estimated waiting time (*Waiting_Time(j)*, line 8) of the jobs in the *IQ*. This metric will be very useful in the experimentation to understand the behavior of our proposal. If there exist jobs in the *IQ* and available resources, the simulator tries to schedule the next job based on the configured *Job_Selection_Policy* (lines 9..13). Finally, $T^e_{rem}(Target)$ is returned.

3 Experimentation

Our proposal was evaluated in a real non-dedicated cluster made up of sixteen 3-GHz uniprocessor workstations with 1GB of RAM, interconnected by a 1-Gigabit network. We studied the performance of our method with respect to various scheduling strategies and different processing and communication load levels. Likewise, we compared the accuracy and the cost/complexity of our proposal with other estimation methods described in the literature.

In order to carry out the experimentation process, the local and parallel workloads must be defined. The local workload was represented by a synthetic benchmark (named *local_bench*) that can emulate the usage of 3 different resources: CPU, Memory and Network traffic. The use of these resources was parameterized in a real way. According to the samples collected over a couple of weeks in an open laboratory, *local_bench* was modelled to use 15% CPU, 35% Memory and a 0,5KB/sec LAN, in each node where it was executed.

The parallel workload was a mixture of PVM and MPI applications, with a total of 90 NAS parallel jobs (CG, IS, MG, BT), with a size of 2, 4 or 8 tasks (class A and B), which reached the system under a Poisson distribution. These jobs were merged so that the entire parallel workload had a balanced requirement for computation and communication.

This workload was executed with different combinations of job and node selection policies. More specifically, we combined both *FCFS* and *Backfilling* (*BF*) job selection policies with both *Normal* and *Uniform* node selection policies. In order to compare the accuracy of the different estimation methods of the literature, we tested all the estimation methods by varying the MPL (Maximum Parallelism Level) upper bound between 1..4.

3.1 Experimental Results

First, we evaluate the performance of our analytical proposal for predicting the turnaround time (named from here on *SDPN*: SlowDown-Processing-Networking), under different MPL upper bound values. In Figure 2, *SDPN* is compared with the methods proposed by *Li* [13], *Smith* [14], *Hanzich* [6] and *Historical* [4, 5, 12].

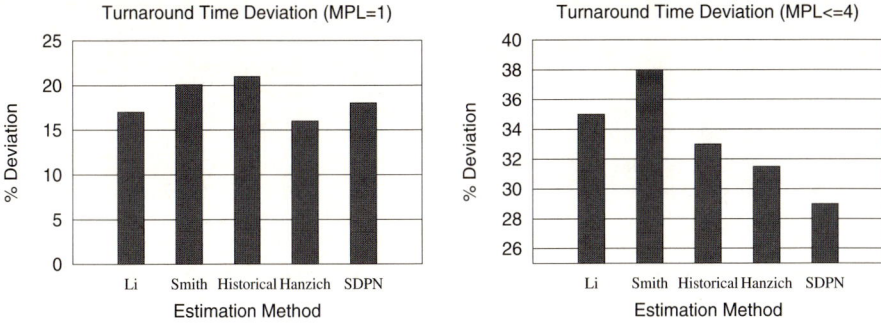

Fig. 2. Turnaround deviation. (left) MPL=1 (right) MPL≤4.

Li and Smith take scheduling decisions by discrete event simulators jointly with the help of a historical database, which only stores information about input parameters and execution time of the previously executed jobs. The *Historical* method tries to infer the future cluster state from a database as a simple replication of the past. *Hanzich* used an analytical model that penalizes the remaining time of the parallel jobs by considering only the degree of parallelism (*MPL*) of the nodes being executed.

The experiments in figure 2 was performed without communication saturation, combining both job selection (FCFS and Backfilling) and node selection (Normal and Uniform) policies. Figure 2 (left) shows the average deviation in estimating the turnaround time of the parallel jobs with a MPL=1 restriction (only one parallel job per node was allowed). The worst behavior belongs for the *Historical* methods. This is so because the waiting queue length increases due to the MPL restriction and the historical repository does not contain enough information to follow the evolution of a job in the waiting queue. Only execution times can be more precisely matched in the database. It can be seen that our proposal, *SDPN*, is slightly worse than *Hanzich*. This means that in dedicated environments the simplest model behaves better. No more sophisticated mechanisms to estimate the future load state, as *SDPN*, are required.

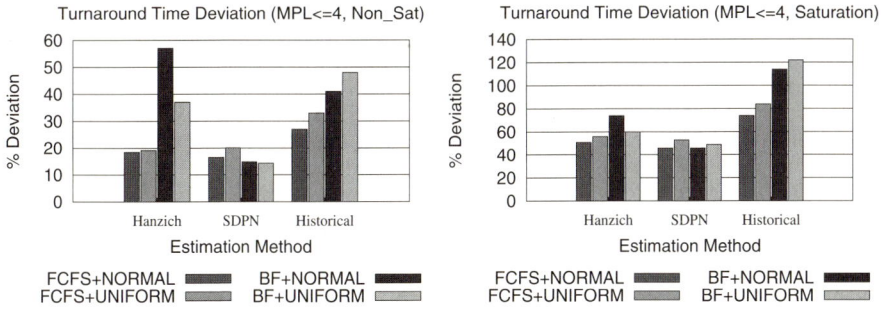

Fig. 3. Turnaround deviation. (left) Non-Saturated links (right) Saturated links.

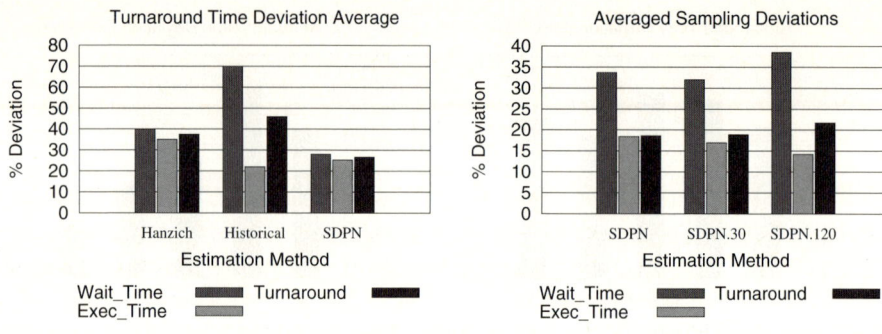

Fig. 4. Waiting and execution time deviations

Figure 2 (right) shows the deviation of the averaged estimated turnaround time with $MPL \leq 4$. In general, the simulation methods based on analytical models, *Hanzich* and *SDPN*, obtained better results than *Li* and *Smith*. This is because, in order to detect the variability in a non-dedicated environment, the analytical models capture more accurate information and detect the workload variability better than Li and Smith's proposals. In this case, *SDPN* obtained in average a 6% gain with respect to *Hanzich*.

Figure 3 shows the behavior of the different estimation methods for different job selection (FCFS and Backfilling), node selection (Normal and Uniform) policies and $MPL \leq 4$. In the figure 3 (right) the local tasks saturated 50% of the mapped links. On the left one, the local workload did not saturate any link at all. *SDPN* presented the highest accuracy in almost all the situations. In general, backfilling policies obtained the worst results, except for *SDPN*. This model captured the workload variations much better than the other ones. Note that the *SDPN* behavior for the FCFS case was very similar to *Hanzich*, but not for the backfilling policies where *SDPN* obtains in average a 80% gain. As figure 3 (right) shows, the prediction deviation grew with the presence of saturation. Differences between the scheduling policies were not significant. Nevertheless, the good behavior of our model even with a high saturation level is remarkable. The gain obtained by the *SDPN* method was 8% higher than with the *Hanzich* proposal.

In figure 4 (left), we compare the waiting and the execution time deviations obtained by the *Historical* and the analytical methods. As can be seen, in the historical case, there is no correlation between the results achieved by both metrics. It means that both passed job executions and recent cluster state information have to be taken into account when looking for similarities in the historical data. In the Historical case, as the cluster state does not vary, all the job execution times are similar, and consequently the predictions are very close to real executions. Waiting time predictions are the poorest because no information about the Input Queue is managed by this method. The analytical models were more accurate in both metrics, especially for the *SDPN* method.

In order to find solutions to increase the accuracy, we implemented a mechanism in the *SDPN* method to obtain an averaged resources state of several samples taken over a period of time. Figure 4 (right), shows average deviations of the waiting and execution times for different windowed mean, instantaneous, 30 and 120 seconds. Samples are taken each second. As we can see, the prediction accuracy of the execution time grows

Table 1. Time cost of our estimation proposals

	Simulation	Historical	Hybrid
Time Cost (milliseconds)	2.8	24	52
Complexity	$O(N_{RL}^2)$	$O(N_{HistDB})$	$O(N_{RL}^2 N_{HistDB})$

by increasing the length of the time period. This situation does not occur for the waiting time. This part of the turnaround time must be investigated in depth because is the main reason for the prediction inaccuracy.

We have measured the time cost spent by the different methods studied in the present work to estimate the turnaround time of a single application. This cost was compared with the complexity associated to each algorithm. The *Simulation* column represents the *Hanzich* and *SDPN* methods and the *Hybrid* column represents the *Li* and *Smith* ones (see table 1). The complexity of the Simulation methods are quadratic with the length of the jobs in the running list (N_{RL}), which is at most 4 jobs, whereas the order of the Historical one is linear with the number of elements in the Historical Repository (N_{HistDB}), which is at least 10^4 times bigger than N_{RL}. Likewise, note that the time cost of the Hybrid one is strongly correlated with its complexity. Finally, we emphasize that the time cost is in the order of milliseconds in all the cases, hardly noticeable with respect to the turnaround time of the parallel jobs.

4 Conclusions and Future Work

In this paper, we presented a prediction scheme to obtain an estimation of the parallel turnaround time in heterogeneous and non-dedicated clusters. Our proposal is based on an analytical model that establishes the processing and communication slowdown of the job's execution time by taking the future cluster state into account.

The model presented was implemented in a prediction engine integrated into the scheduling system of the CISNE platform. We corroborated the usefulness and accuracy of our model in real and widely used and accepted job scheduling policies, such as *Backfilling*. Applicability of our proposal has been proved and compared in a real environment with respect to the most representative models from the literature.

The analytical models gave the best results. In general in situations with no saturation, overtook the *Hanzich* one by a mean average of 40%. In situations with link saturation, our model underestimates the communication slowdown nevertheless the averaged gain was also important, at about 8%. The network parameters and the communication model of the parallel applications must be more deeply analyzed.

Regression models must be developed for obtaining the tendencies in the future cluster state. By doing this, precision can even be increased a bit more, especially in overloaded situations and dynamic load. The elapsed waiting time of the parallel jobs must also be more accurately estimated. The results shows that accurate execution time prediction are not the only factor that determines the accuracy of the waiting time predictions. The variation in the length of the input queue must be reflected in the cluster state at each simulation step. This is a drawback to be solved in future work.

References

1. Acharya, A., Setia, S.: Availability and utility of idle memory in workstation clusters. In: Proceedings of the ACM SIGMETRICS 1999, pp. 35–46 (1999)
2. Buyya, R., Abramson, D., Giddy, J.: Nimrod/G: An Architecture of a Resource Management and Scheduling System in a Global Computational Grid. ArXiv Computer Science e-prints (2000)
3. Etsion, Y., Tsafrir, D., Feitelson, D.G.: Backfilling using system-generated predictions rather than user runtime estimates. IEEE Trans. Parallel & Distributed Syst. 18(6), 789–803 (2007)
4. Downey, A.: Predicting queue times on space-sharing parallel computers. In: 11th Intl. Parallel Processing Symp., pp. 209–218 (1997)
5. Aridor, Y., Yom-Tov, E.: A self-optimized job scheduler for heterogeneous server clusters. In: Frachtenberg, E., Schwiegelshohn, U. (eds.) JSSPP 2007. LNCS, vol. 4942. Springer, Heidelberg (2008)
6. Hanzich, M., Giné, F., Hernández, P., Solsona, F., Luque, E.: Using on-the-fly simulation for estimating the turnaround time on non-dedicated clusters. In: Nagel, W.E., Walter, W.V., Lehner, W. (eds.) Euro Par 2006. LNCS, vol. 4128, pp. 117–187. Springer, Heidelberg (2006)
7. Harchol-Balter, M., Li, C., Osogami, T., Scheller-Wolf, A., Squillante, M.S.: Cycle stealing under immediate dispatch task assignment. In: Proceedings of the fifteenth annual ACM symposium on Parallel algorithms and architectures, pp. 274–285 (2003)
8. Jarvis, S., Spooner, D., Keung, H.L.C., Cao, J., Saini, S., Nudd, G.: Performance prediction and its use in parallel and distributed computing systems. Future Gener. Comput. Syst. 22(7), 745–754 (2006)
9. Javadi, B., Abawajy, J.: Performance analysis of heterogeneous multi-cluster systems. In: Proceedings of the 2005 International Conference on Parallel Processing Workshops (ICPPW 2005), Washington, DC, USA, pp. 493–500 (2005)
10. Jones, W.: The impact of error in user-provided bandwidth estimates on multi-site parallel job scheduling performance. In: The 19th IASTED International Conference on Parallel and Distributed Computing and Systems (PDCS 2007), Cambridge, Massachusetts (November 2007)
11. Jones, W., Ligon, W., Pang, L., Stanzione, D.: Characterization of bandwidth-aware meta-schedulers for co-allocating jobs across multiple clusters. The Journal of Supercomputing 34(2), 135–163 (2005)
12. Lafreniere, B., Sodan, A.: Scopred—scalable user-directed performance prediction using complexity modeling and historical data. In: Feitelson, D.G., Frachtenberg, E., Rudolph, L., Schwiegelshohn, U. (eds.) JSSPP 2005. LNCS, vol. 3834, pp. 62–90. Springer, Heidelberg (2005)
13. Li, H., Groep, D., Templon, J., Wolters, L.: Predicting job start times on clusters. In: 4th IEEE/ACM International Symposium on Cluster Computing and the Grid (CCGrid 2004) (April 2004)
14. Smith, W., Taylor, V., Foster, I.: Using run-time predictions to estimate queue wait times and improve scheduler performance. In: Feitelson, D.G., Rudolph, L. (eds.) JSSPP 1999, IPPS-WS 1999, and SPDP-WS 1999. LNCS, vol. 1659, pp. 202–219. Springer, Heidelberg (1999)
15. Urgaonkar, B., Shenoy, P.: Sharc: Managing cpu and network bandwidth in shared clusters. IEEE Trans. Parallel Distrib. Syst. 15(1), 2–17 (2004)
16. Wolski, R.: Experiences with predicting resource performance on-line in computational grid settings. ACM SIGMETRICS Performance Evaluation Review 30(4), 41–49 (2003)

Co-allocation with Communication Considerations in Multi-cluster Systems

John Ngubiri and Mario van Vliet

Nijmegen Institute for Informatics and Information Science
Radboud University Nijmegen
Toernooiveld 1, 6525 ED, Nijmegen,
The Netherlands
{ngubiri,mario}@cs.ru.nl

Abstract. Processor co-allocation can be of performance benefit. This is because breaking jobs into components reduces overall cluster fragmentation. However, the slower inter-cluster communication links increase job execution times. This leads to performance deterioration which can make co-allocation unviable. We use intra-cluster to inter-cluster communication speed ratio and job communication intensity to model the job execution time penalty due to co-allocation. We then study viability of co-allocation in selected job and system based instances. We also study performance variation with selected job stream parameters. We observe that co-allocation is viable so long as the execution time penalty caused is relatively low. We also observe that the negative performance effect due to co-allocation is felt by the entire job stream rather than only the (few) co-allocated jobs. Finally, we observe that for every value of communication time penalty, there is a job size s^*, where if all jobs whose size is greater than s^* are co-allocated, we get the best performance.

1 Introduction

The load, like the processing power on supercomputers, has been growing fast over the past decade [17]. Supercomputer resources, therefore, remain scarce. This calls for efficient scheduling of competing (job) requests so as to put the resources to optimal utility.

A lot of research has been done in parallel job scheduling [7]. This has mostly been on shared memory computers, distributed memory multi-processors, clusters, multi-cluster systems and the grid. Currently, clusters are the most popular supercomputing platform with over 70% of the top 500 supercomputers [21]. This can be attributed to their cost-effectiveness, scalability and fault tolerance. Multi-cluster systems are set up by combining multiple clusters into a bigger computational infrastructure. Different clusters are connected by wide-area links so that they can collaboratively process large jobs.

Large jobs may be broken into components and each component (simultaneously) processed in a different cluster [4] (co-allocation). Co-allocation is beneficial because it makes use of scattered resources and hence minimizes fragmentation. However, co-allocated components communicate across (slower) inter-cluster links which increase their run times leading to poorer performance. Co-allocation may become unviable.

The negative effect of co-allocation is the extension of the job run time. We use the ratio of intra to inter cluster speed and job communication intensity compute the execution time penalty. We investigate parameter bounds within which co-allocation is beneficial. We investigate optimal parameter combinations for co-allocation as well as their variation with other job stream parameters. We also investigate the effect of dispersion in job communication intensities.

We observe that (i) co-allocation is viable if the execution time penalty caused is low; (ii) the threshold of co-allocation viability is a function of intra/inter-cluster speed ratio and jobs' communication intensity; (iii) entire job stream results are insufficient to deduce co-allocation viability; (iv) for any execution time penalty, there exists a job size $s*$ where if all jobs with size greater than $s*$ are co-allocated, we get best results; and (v) due to possible heterogeneous communication pattern, co-allocation may not be as viable as previously implied.

In the rest of the paper, we discuss related work, the research model and scheduling algorithm used in Sections 2, 3 and 4 respectively. The experimental instances used are discussed in Section 5. We investigate the viability of co-allocation in Section 6 and the effect of selected parameters on performance and viability of co-allocation in Section 7. We study how the dispersion of communication intensity among the jobs affects performance in Section 8 and make conclusions and suggestions for future work in Section 9.

2 Related Work

2.1 Communication and Its Effect on Co-allocation

Ignoring communication is one of the common pitfalls in parallel job scheduling [8]. It leads to artificially good but misleading deductions. In multi-cluster systems, communication is more problematic due to relatively slow wide-area speeds. Parallel jobs consist of tasks that communicate as they execute. Communication may be synchronous or asynchronous. In synchronous communication, the tasks communicate after specific time intervals. Job execution is broken into a sequence of processing and communication steps. In asynchronous communication, tasks process independently but different pairs occasionally communicate.

Bucur and Epema [3] studied an all-to-all synchronous communication model with the First Come First Served (FCFS) scheduler. They focused on the intra/inter cluster speed ratio to determine the execution time penalty. They observed that there exists a communication ratio beyond which co-allocation is unviable. Sonmez et al. [13] considered a case where the penalty is proportional to the number of clusters the job is processed. They proposed placement policies that minimize the effect of communication. Components are placed in such a way that the number of clusters processing a job is minimized. Jones et al. [11][10] studied the effect of communication from a bandwidth point of view. They consider a case where a job needs certain amount of bandwidth to process for the initially allotted time. If within the process of execution the link gets over saturated and the job uses less bandwidth, the job's rate of processing lowers in proportion to the bandwidth shortfall. This leads to a job execution time which is pegged on link states as the job processes.

2.2 Workloads

Using unrealistic workloads leads to unrealistic deductions [8]. Workloads are generated synthetically or from archived logs of existing supercomputers [18, 19]. Synthetically, job characteristics are generated from statistical distributions estimated by workload trace studies. Since they are easy to generate and extrapolate, the stable state can easily be achieved. However, coming up with an accurate distribution is hard; it may therefore be preferable to use archived logs. Workload logs avail job characteristics without necessarily knowing their statistical distribution. However, the job stream may be too short to generate a stable state and extrapolation is hard. The load is also hard to vary. Changing the inter-arrival time for example, as a means of changing load, changes the daily and weekly peaks which is unrepresentative of the real life situation of different traffic. Aspects like communication patterns are not archived. Traces may also contain flurries which highly affect results [20].

2.3 Performance Evaluation

A performance metric used in parallel job scheduling has to put the scheduling scenario into consideration [8]. The deductions made are sometimes more metric than system dependant. The Shortest Job First (SJF) scheduling algorithm, for example, gives an impressive performance when measured by throughput despite obvious starvation of long jobs. Some metrics may have different implications depending on the system studied. Average waiting time (AWT) and average response time (ART) have similar performance implications for dedicated processing but have different implications for time sliced/preemptive cases. Making performance conclusions based on entire job stream metric value may hide internal performance details. Grouping jobs by the characteristics that constrain schedulability provides deeper understanding of performance [5, 14, 15, 16].

3 Research Model

We consider a system of homogeneous clusters $C_1, C_2, \cdots C_n$ that process by pure space slicing. They are connected by wide-area communication links that are slower than intra-cluster links. They are served by one queue and one scheduler.

3.1 Job Stream

We use synthetic online jobs with exponentially distributed inter-arrival and execution times. These distributions have also been used in previous related work [2][9]. Job execution time is finite but unknown to the scheduler. Job sizes are generated from the distribution $D(q)$ $(0 < q < 1)$ where the probability p_i that a job has size i is $(\frac{q^i}{Q})$ $\frac{3q^i}{Q}$ if i is (not) a power of 2. It is defined over an interval $[n_1, n_2]$ $(0 < n_1 < n_2)$. Parameter q varies mean job size while Q is in such a way that p_i sums up to 1. It favors small jobs and those whose size is a power of 2 which is known to be a realistic choice [6].

Jobs with size greater than a threshold $thres$ are broken into components and co-allocated. If a job of size s is broken into k components, one component has width $s - (k-1)\lfloor \frac{s}{k} \rfloor$ while the other $k-1$ has $\lfloor \frac{s}{k} \rfloor$ each.

3.2 Communication

We consider a synchronous communication pattern (like in [3]). The execution time (T_E) of the job is made up of the processing (T_P) and communication (T_C) components. Like in [10][11], we represent the total execution time on one cluster as:

$$T_E = T_C + T_P \quad (1)$$

If $T_C = \alpha T_E$, where α $(0 < \alpha < 1)$ represents the job communication intensity, then (1) can be rewritten as

$$T_E = \alpha T_E + (1-\alpha) T_E \quad (2)$$

If the ratio of the time taken by an inter-cluster packet to an intra-cluster packet is $(1+\lambda)$ $(\lambda > 0)$, then co-allocating a job increases T_C by $(1+\lambda)$. The execution time of a co-allocated job T'_E is therefore given by $T'_E = \alpha(1+\lambda)T_E + (1-\alpha)T_E = (1+\alpha\lambda)T_E$. If we define $\psi = \alpha\lambda$, then;

$$T'_E = (1+\psi)T_E \quad (3)$$

This model is similar to the fixed penalty approach employed in [3] though it considers two aspects instead of one.

4 Scheduling Algorithm and Placement Policy

We use the Fit Processors First Served (FPFS) [1] scheduling algorithm.

In FPFS, jobs are queued in their arrival order. The scheduler starts from the head and searches deeper into the queue for the first job that fits into the system. In case one is found, it jumps all jobs ahead of it and starts processing. If none is found, the scheduler waits either for a job to finish execution or a job to arrive and the search is done again. To avoid possible starvation of some jobs, the scheduler limits (to $maxJumps$) the number of times a job at the head of the queue can be jumped. After being jumped $maxJumps$ times, no other job is allowed to jump it until enough processors have been freed to have it scheduled. We use FPFS (x) to represent FPFS when $maxJumps = x$.

To map components onto clusters, we use the Worst Fit (WFit) policy. In the WFit policy, the kth widest component is processed in the kth freest cluster. It distributes free processors evenly among the clusters.

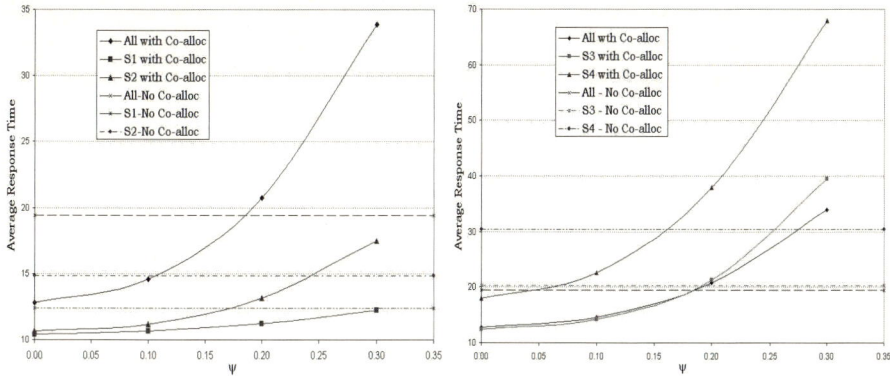

Fig. 1. Comparing co-allocation with no co-allocation

5 Experimental Set Up

We consider a system of 5 homogeneous clusters of 20 nodes each. The jobs are generated from $D(0.85)$ over the interval $[1, 19]$. Jobs have a mean execution and inter-arrival time of 10 and 0.54 respectively. This leads to a load of 0.786 (when $\psi = 0$). ART is used to measure performance. Performance evaluation is done for the entire job stream as well as for job-size based groups. We use four approximately equal size-based groups S_1, S_2, S_3 and S_4. They are bounded by the (size) lower quartile, median and upper quartile. They have a numerical representation of 25.3%, 27.7%, 22.9% and 24.1% and load representation of 6.0%, 27.7%, 23.1% and 57.6% respectively.

6 Viability of Co-allocation

Co-allocation studied without considering communication (like in [12]) is always viable. This is due to the packing advantage of breaking up large jobs but no communication penalty. We now compare performance at different ψ values with a case of no co-allocation. We use $thres = 10$ (effect of $thres$ studied in 7). Where co-allocation is used, jobs where $size > thres$ are broken into 4 components. We present the results in Figure 1.

In Figure 1, we observe that co-allocation is viable for low ψ. We observe that the value of ψ beyond which co-allocation is unviable is different for different job groups. It is 0.185 for the entire job stream, 1.60 for S_4 and over 0.3 for S_1.

Like in [3], we observe that there is a threshold beyond which co-allocation is not viable. However, (i) the threshold is not only dependant on the intra and inter cluster speed ratio. It also depends on the communication intensity of the jobs. Co-allocation is viable for any speed ratio so long as the jobs' communication intensity is low enough. (ii) The (entire) job stream threshold value is practically misleading. This is because large jobs have a lower threshold and they constitute a larger part of the load in the system.

7 The Effect of System and Job Parameters

7.1 The Effect of *Thres* on Performance

We set $\psi = 0.05$ (investigation of ψ in 7.2), vary *thres* from 3 to 19 (Figure 2).

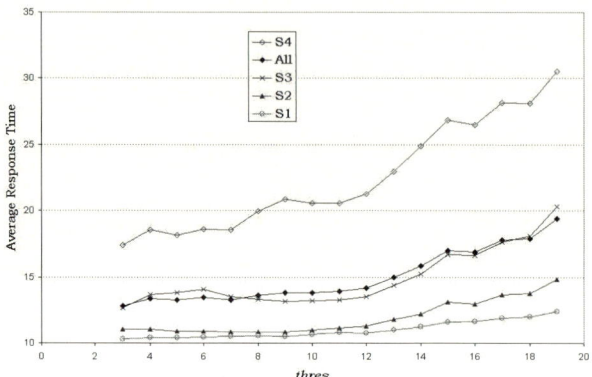

Fig. 2. Performance variation with *thres*

From Figure 2, we observe that increasing *thres* leads to poorer performance. It is therefore better to keep *thres* low. We also observe that all groups take the same trend. The rate of performance deterioration is higher for large jobs. Co-allocation affects both co-allocated and non co-allocated jobs.

7.2 The Effect of ψ on Performance Sensitivity to *Thres*

We now investigate the effect of ψ on the way performance varies with *thres*. Since S_4 jobs perform worst and constitute over half of the load, we consider them more representative. We therefore use S_4 jobs only. We use four values of ψ and summarize the performance trend in Figure 3.

We observe that there exists an optimal value of *thres* for each ψ value. This optimal value increases with ψ. An increase in ψ reduce the *thres* range in which co-allocation is viable.

7.3 The Effect of Load

We now investigate performance trends at different loads. The loads are computed when co-allocation is not employed. Loads are varied by changing the mean inter-arrival time. We consider $\psi = 0.1$ and summarize the performance trends in Figure 4. We observe that an increase in load leads to a poorer performance. Increase in load however does not affect the optimal *thres* value for co-allocation.

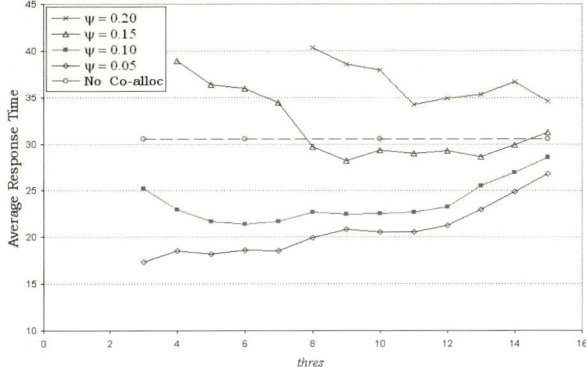

Fig. 3. Performance variations for different ψ values

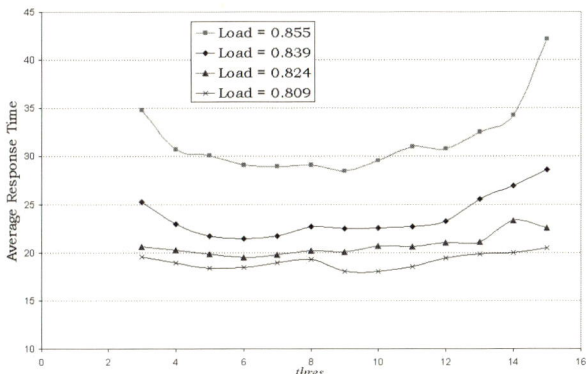

Fig. 4. Performance variation with *thres* for different values of load

7.4 Overall Effect of System/Job Parameters

We now discuss the overall effect of the parameters investigated in 7.1 - 7.3.

First, we observe that at low values of ψ, co-allocation is beneficial. Breaking up of jobs make them easier to pack but the execution time penalty leads to more occupation of processors. If processor hours due to the penalty exceed those saved from reduced fragmentation, then there is no net benefit in co-allocation. Secondly, we observe that there is an optimal *thres* value for any ψ value. It increases with ψ and independent of the load. This is due to the fact that at high ψ, if a lot of jobs are broken into components, a lot of processor hours are lost due to the increased execution time which exceeds those saved from fragmentation. This leads to unnecessary occupation of the processors which leads to jobs over delaying in the queue. This translates into poor performance. This can be solved by breaking fewer jobs (increasing *thres*). If however *thres* is

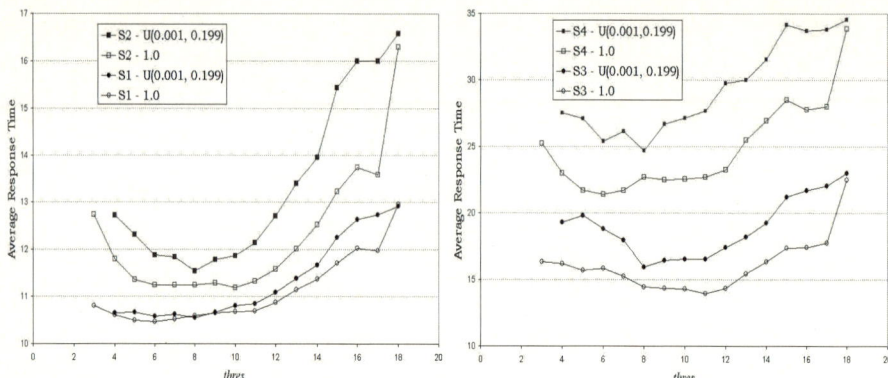

Fig. 5. Group-wise performance for $\psi = 0.1$ and $\psi \sim U[0.001, 0.199]$

too high, the packing problem of unbroken jobs becomes significant. The system suffers fragmentation and hence poor performance.

8 Communication Intensity Distribution

So far, we have considered cases where ψ is fixed. This implies that both α and λ are fixed. As far as we know, there are no documented studies on the extent and distribution of communication intensities in supercomputer workloads. However, we believe that due to the diversity of the sources and applications processed by supercomputers, α (hence ψ) is not fixed. We therefore assume λ to be fixed but α to vary among jobs. We consider a case where $\psi \sim U[0.001, 0.199]$. We compare its performance with a case when $\psi = 0.1$. We also study the relative performance of jobs grouped by ψ.

8.1 The Effect of ψ Distribution

We now compare the performance of S_1, S_2, S_3 and S_4 for the job stream when with $\psi = 0.1$ and $\psi \sim U[0.001, 0.199]$ (Figure 5). We observe that more dispersion in ψ leads to poor performance. Deterioration in performance is felt by both co-allocated and non co-allocated jobs.

8.2 Classification by Communication Intensity

In 8.1, we observed that communication heterogeneity negatively affect performance. We now study group-wise performance of co-allocated jobs grouped by ψ. We create four groups C_1, C_2, C_3 and C_4 consisting jobs whose ψ lies in the ranges $(0.00, 0.05)$, $(0.05, 0.10)$, $(0.10, 0.15)$ and $(0.15, 0.20)$ respectively. We summarize their performance variation with *thres* in Figure 6.

We observe small deviations in performance of the different groups. This implies that the effect of communication is felt in the entire job steam rather than the individual co-allocated jobs.

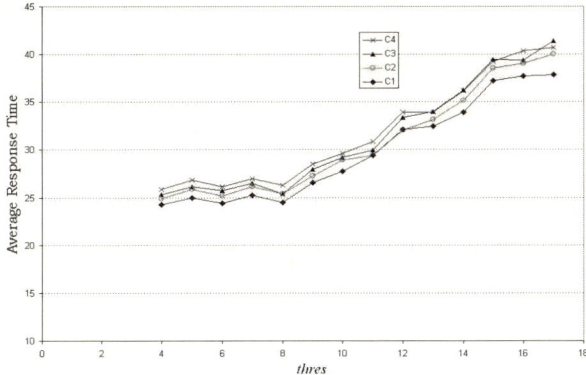

Fig. 6. Performance of communication based groups

9 Conclusion and Future Work

We have used communication intensity and intra to inter cluster speed ratio to represent execution time penalty. The approach is synonymous to the fixed penalty approach but more elaborate. We have also studied the limits of co-allocation viability as a function of ψ, load and *thres*. We have observed that there are parameter limits within which the co-allocation is viable. They depend on both α and λ. We have also observed poorer performance for heterogeneously communicating jobs. This implies that co-allocation is not as viable as depicted in earlier studies that considered fixed penalties.

Our work opens up more avenues for future research. This includes studying asynchronously communicating jobs and communication cognizant scheduling.

Reference

1. Aida, K., Kasahara, K., Narita, S.: Job scheduling scheme for pure space sharing among rigid jobs. In: Feitelson, D.G., Rudolph, L. (eds.) IPPS-WS 1998, SPDP-WS 1998, and JSSPP 1998. LNCS, vol. 1459, pp. 98–121. Springer, Heidelberg (1998)
2. Bucur, A.I.D.: Performance analysis of processor co-allocation in multi-cluster systems. PhD Thesis, Technical University Delft, Delft, The Netherlands (2004)
3. Bucur, A.I.D., Epema, D.H.J.: The influence of communication on the performance of co-allocation. In: Feitelson, D.G., Rudolph, L. (eds.) JSSPP 2001. LNCS, vol. 2221, pp. 66–86. Springer, Heidelberg (2001)
4. Czajkowski, K., Foster, I.T., Kasselman, C.: Resource co-allocation in computational grids. In: Proc. HPDC 1999, pp. 37–47 (1999)
5. Feitelson, D.G.: Metric and workload effects on computer systems evaluation. Computers 36(9), 18–25 (2003)
6. Feitelson, D.G., Rudolph, L.: Towards convergence of job schedulers for parallel supercomputers. In: Feitelson, D.G., Rudolph, L. (eds.) IPPS-WS 1996 and JSSPP 1996. LNCS, vol. 1162, pp. 1–26. Springer, Heidelberg (1996)

7. Feitelson, D.G., Rudolph, L., Schwiegelshohn, U.: Parallel job scheduling: A status report. In: Feitelson, D.G., Rudolph, L., Schwiegelshohn, U. (eds.) JSSPP 2004. LNCS, vol. 3277, pp. 1–16. Springer, Heidelberg (2005)
8. Frachtenberg, E., Feitelson, D.G.: Pitfalls in parallel job scheduling evaluation. In: Feitelson, D.G., Frachtenberg, E., Rudolph, L., Schwiegelshohn, U. (eds.) JSSPP 2005. LNCS, vol. 3834, pp. 257–282. Springer, Heidelberg (2005)
9. Jones, W.M.: Improving parallel job scheduling performance in multi-clusters through selective job co-allocation. PhD dissertation, Clemson University, Clemson, South Carolina, USA (2005)
10. Jones, W.M., Ligon III, W.B., Pang, L.W.: Characterization of bandwidth-aware meta-schedulers for co-allocating jobs across multiple clusters. Journal of Supercomputing 34(2), 135–163 (2005)
11. Jones, W.M., Pang, L.W., Stanzione, D., Ligon III, W.B.: Bandwidth-aware co-allocating meta-schedulers for mini-grid architectures. In: Proc. CLUSTER 2004, pp. 45–54 (2004)
12. Ngubiri, J., van Vliet, M.: Group-wise performance evaluation of processor co-allocation in multi-cluster systems. In: Frachtenberg, E., Schwiegelshohn, U. (eds.) JSSPP 2007. LNCS, vol. 4942, pp. 1–13. Springer, Heidelberg (2008)
13. Sonmez, O., Mohamed, H., Epema, D.H.J.: Communication-aware job placement policies for the KOALA grid scheduler. In: Proc. 2nd IEEE Int. Conf. on e-Science and Grid Comp., pp. 79–87 (2006)
14. Srinivasan, S., Kettimuthu, R., Subramani, V., Sadayappan, P.: Characterization of backfilling strategies for parallel job scheduling. In: Proc. ICPPW 2002, pp. 514–520 (2002)
15. Srinivasan, S., Kettimuthu, R., Subramani, V., Sadayappan, P.: Selective reservation strategies for backfill job scheduling. In: Feitelson, D.G., Rudolph, L., Schwiegelshohn, U. (eds.) JSSPP 2002. LNCS, vol. 2537, pp. 55–71. Springer, Heidelberg (2002)
16. Srinivasan, S., Krishnamoorthy, S., Sadayappan, P.: A robust scheduling technology for moldable scheduling of parallel jobs. In: Proc. CLUSTER 2003, pp. 92–99 (2003)
17. Stromaier, E., Dongarra, J.J., Meuer, H.W., Simon, H.D.: Recent trends in the marketplace of high performance computing. Parallel Computing 31(3,4), 261–273 (2005)
18. The Grid Workloads Archive, http://gwa.ewi.tudelft.nl/
19. The Parallel Workloads Archive, http://www.cs.huji.ac.il/labs/parallel/workload/
20. Tsafrir, D., Feitelson, D.G.: Instability in parallel job scheduling simulation: The role of workload flurries. In: Proc. IPDPS 2006 (2006)
21. Top500 supercomputing sites (Accessed December 20th, 2007), http://www.top500.org

Fine-Grained Task Scheduling Using Adaptive Data Structures

Ralf Hoffmann and Thomas Rauber

Department for Mathematics, Physics and Computer Science
University of Bayreuth, Germany
{ralf.hoffmann,rauber}@uni-bayreuth.de

Abstract. Task pools have been shown to provide efficient load balancing for irregular applications on heterogeneous platforms. Often, distributed data structures are used to store the tasks and the actual load balancing is achieved by task stealing where an idle processor accesses tasks from another processor. In this paper we extent the concept of task pools to adaptive task pools which are able to adapt the number of tasks moved between the processor to the specific execution scenario, thus reducing the overhead for task stealing significantly. We present runtime experiments for different applications on two execution platforms.

1 Introduction

The efficient parallel execution of applications with an unpredictable computational behavior requires the use of sophisticated load balancing methods. In this paper, we consider task-based load balancing methods for platforms with a shared address space. The computations performed by an application are arranged as fine-grained single-processor tasks which can be executed by an arbitrary processor. Tasks can be created dynamically during the execution of the application, and usually there are much more tasks available than processors for execution. Tasks that are ready for execution are stored in specific data structures, so-called task pools, from which they can be accessed by idle processors for execution. The task pool runtime environment schedules these tasks to the available processors on demand using varying strategies. The processors independently fetch new tasks from the task pool as soon as their previous task has been completed. As long as there are enough tasks available for execution the processors remain busy up to the end of the application. Smaller tasks enable a better load balancing but lead to a larger overhead.

A simple implementation of a task pool for storing and scheduling tasks is a central data structure. Since all processors need to access this shared data structure, scalability may be limited due to the synchronization required, especially if the data structure is accessed often. Distributed data structures are often better suited as the synchronization overhead can be reduced, e.g., by using a separate task list for each processor. For load balancing the distributed data structure still needs to be shared in some way so that idle processors can obtain tasks from other processors for execution. Moving tasks from one processor to another is referred to as task stealing.

In previous work we have shown that the task pool overhead can be reduced by improving the synchronization operations [1]. This enables an efficient realization of task-based applications also if fine-grained tasks are used. A small task granularity and therefore many fine-grained tasks enables a good load balancing especially for large parallel systems. But using many fine-grained tasks may increase the number of stealing operations performed, thus increasing the overhead for the load balancing. In this paper we present an adaptive task pool implementation which is especially suited for storing a large number of tasks. The new implementation adapts the number of tasks accessed by a single stealing operation to the total number of tasks stored in the task pool. Experiments with several large applications show that the overhead for task stealing and other operations can be significantly improved by using the adaptive implementation.

The rest of the paper is organized as follows: Section 2 presents the adaptive data structure and Section 3 describes the adaptive task pool. Section 4 presents experimental results. Section 5 discusses related work and Section 6 concludes the paper.

2 Adaptive Data Structure

For fine-grained tasks, an important requirement for the data structure to store the executable tasks is a fast insertion and removal of tasks. To improve the task stealing operation the data structure needs to support the removal of large chunks of tasks in a single operation. Distributed queues implemented as linear lists are often used to store the task, and their performance can be improved by additionally using blocks of tasks for task stealing. A linear list takes constant time for insertion or removal of tasks but each task has to be removed in a separate step. Using blocks of tasks allows to steal several task with one operation but it may limit the parallelism if there are only a few executable tasks available which might be stored in a single block on a single processor.

The data structure described in the following solves this problem by using adaptive blocks of tasks which grow or shrink with the number of tasks available. The tasks are stored in a set of fully balanced trees so that for a tree T_i the length of every path from the root to a leaf is i. Each node of a tree stores a pointer to the first child and a pointer to the next sibling in the same level.

The trees are stored in a forest vector $F[0..w]$ forming a forest of fully balanced trees where w is the depth of the largest tree to be stored. Each entry $F[i]$ is a pointer to a list of trees T_i of depth i, i.e. $F[0]$ only stores fully balanced trees of tasks with one level, $F[1]$ stores trees with two levels and so on. Since all trees are fully balanced, new tasks can only be inserted in the first level $F[0]$ or by combining existing trees with the same depth into a new tree with a larger depth.

Although the use of a list of children does not limit the width of a tree level we still limit the length by a specific criterion. This criterion can be used to control the growing of the individual trees. The limit can be any fixed number of children or even dynamic limits based on the actual work described by each tasks. For simplicity we assume a fixed limit l for the following description of the insertion and removal process.

Insertion of tasks: New tasks are inserted into the forest vector as outlined in Figure 1. Figure 2 illustrates the process of inserting a new task (T) for $l = 2$. Since the first level of F is fully occupied and the first non-full level is 1, the new task becomes the root of a new tree containing all trees of level 0 as children. The new tree now forms a fully balanced tree of level 1 and is therefore inserted into $F[1]$.

```
Create new tree t = new T₀ {
    t → task = new task
    t → child = NULL
    t → sibling = NULL
}
if ( size(F₀) < l ) {
    t → sibling = F₀
    F₀ = t
} else {
    find first i with size(Fᵢ) < l
    t → child = Fᵢ₋₁
    Fᵢ₋₁ = NULL
    t → sibling = Fᵢ
    Fᵢ = t
}
```

Fig. 1. Task insertion

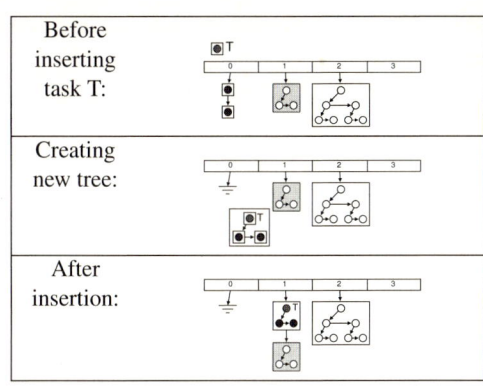

Fig. 2. Example insertion of a new task T

```
Find first i with size(Fᵢ) > 0
t = Fᵢ
Fᵢ = t → sibling
if ( i > 0 ) {
    Fᵢ₋₁ = t → child
}
return t → task
```

Fig. 3. Task removal

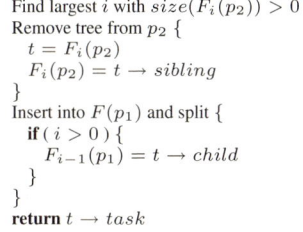

Fig. 4. Task stealing from processor p_1 to p_2

Task removal: The removal is done similarly (in opposite direction) as described in Figure 3 but the ordering is not strictly FIFO (first in, first out). This may have a negative impact on the locality of the executed tasks, but implementing strict FIFO order would definitely have a performance penalty for both task insertion and removal, since the removal operation would need to search for an empty slot and split the following tree into sub-trees to undo the insertion. Especially for a large number of tasks the insertion and removal operations would always work with large trees. On the other hand, the proposed implementation tries to access tasks from the smaller side of the forest making the find operation faster.

Task stealing: The data structure facilitates migration of several task with one operation by moving a tree from $F[0..w]$ from one processor to another. To reduce the total number of stealing operations, we choose to remove the largest tree from another processor using the algorithm described in Figure 4.

Access times and number of tasks: To approximate the number of task stolen in a single operation we consider a completely filled data structure using a fixed limit l. Each tree in level i stores $\frac{l^{i+1}-1}{l-1}$ tasks and a full forest $F[0..w]$ contains

$$t_{sum} = \sum_{i=0}^{w} l * \left(\frac{l^{i+1}-1}{l-1} \right) = \frac{l^{w+3} - (w+2)l^2 + (w+1)l}{(l-1)^2}$$

tasks. The steal operation removes a tree from level i so the fraction of tasks stolen in one operation is

$$f = \frac{l^{i+1} - 1}{l - 1} * \frac{(l-1)^2}{l^{i+3} - (i+2)l^2 + (i+1)l}$$

$$= (l-1) \frac{l^{i+1} - 1}{l^{i+1}} \frac{1}{l^2 - \frac{(i+2)l^2 - (i+1)l}{l^{i+1}}}$$

The largest value for f is $f = 1/l$ for $i = 0$ and the smallest value for f is $f = \frac{l-1}{l^2}$ for $i \to \infty$. For a binary tree ($l = 2$) one steal operation removes between $1/4$ and $1/2$ of all available tasks. The fraction may be higher if the forest is not completely filled but the lower limit still applies. After removing a tree from a processor the task stealer puts the remaining sub-trees into its own data structure so $\approx 1/l$ of these tasks can be stolen by other processors again in a single operation. In a situation where only one processor stores most of the tasks the work can still be redistributed using only a few operations.

Inserting or removing a task takes $O(\log t_{sum})$ steps in the worst case as the number of tasks stored in the forest vector grows exponentially with its length. Typically the operation uses much less steps as the find operation does not need to walk through the whole vector all the time but can stop at the first non-empty entry. Task stealing is also $O(\log t_{sum})$ but is $O(1)$ when storing the largest $i \le w$ with $size(F_i) > 0$.

3 Adaptive Task Pool

The current task pool implementation uses the data structures as described in the previous section with a limit $l = 2$, thus using fully balanced binary trees. Each processor stores its own instance of this data structure. To reduce the synchronization overhead the locks uses hardware operations for mutual exclusion.

If a processors runs out of work, i.e. its forest vector is empty, it will search for new work by task stealing. For this, the processor visits all other processors in a given order for an available tree in their forest vector. The tree is then split into two sub-trees which are stored in the forest vector of the stealing processor for later execution but they are also available for stealing. The root of the stolen tree is the task to be executed next.

Stealing work from other processors may have negative locality effects as the data for the work units is possibly not in the cache of the current processor, so it needs to be transferred from remote memory (especially on NUMA systems there is an additional access cost for remote memory from other processors). But grouped stealing as implemented by the adaptive task pool may reduce this effect. Task created by the same processor in direct succession often solves sub-problems of some part of the whole input problem so they may access the same portion of input data. Each tree in the forest vector can potentially contain such related tasks so stealing it may impose an access penalty for some but not all tasks in this group. Due to the tree combine and split steps in the algorithm some sub-trees might be created by a different processor than some other sub-tree. In rare scenarios a tree may contain tasks created by many different processors but these potentially related tasks will still be grouped in some sub-trees. To additionally reduce the locality problems when stealing tasks, the processors search for available tasks in their neighborhood (based on their IDs). So a processor steals work from the nearest processor with available work.

Since lock contention can be a problem when using a large number of processors, private and public areas are used to reduce the overhead as the data structure owner can access the private area without any locking. The size of the private area is a tradeoff between synchronization overhead and available parallelism. If the private area stores a relatively large number of tasks the parallelism may be limited as these task cannot be stolen by other processors. Smaller private areas on the other hand limit the positive effect of lock-less access for the owner.

We use the forest vector to implement a dynamical resizing of private and public areas. Two parameters are used to control these areas. The forest vector F is divided into a private part $F[0..priv\_length - 1]$ and a public part $F[priv\_length..w]$. The private area is limited to $0 \leq priv\_length \leq MAX\_PRIV\_LENGTH$. As an additional criterion for the size of the private area, we use another variable pub_length with a higher priority than $priv\_length$. The private area is only non-empty if $pub\_length \geq MIN\_PUB\_LENGTH$. This decision is made because exploiting parallelism has a high priority, so there will only be a private area if there are enough trees available in the public area. Limiting the private area to an upper limit also reduces the number of updates of these variables for frequent accesses.

The adaptive task pool implementation takes significant advantage of the existence of a large number of tasks. The trees grow with the number of tasks; therefore the number of tasks stolen also increases. The size of the private area also depends on the number of available tasks, i.e., so creating many tasks actually reduces the overhead for storing and scheduling them.

4 Experimental Results

Runtime experiments are performed on a SGI Altix 4700 machine with 4864 dual-core Itanium2 processors running at 1.6 GHz and an IBM p690 machine with 32 Power4+ processors running at 1.7 GHz. To evaluate the implementation we use several irregular applications. Additionally, the use of a synthetic application makes it possible to directly measure the overhead of the task pool implementation.

4.1 Synthetic Task Application

The synthetic application uses two parameters f for controlling the task size and t for controlling the number of tasks created. The work S of a task with an argument i can be described by the following recursive definition:

$$S(i) = \begin{cases} 100f & \text{for } i \leq 0 \\ 10f + S(i-2) + 50f + S(i-1) + 100f & \text{else} \end{cases}$$

For $i \geq 1$ task $S(i)$ creates two tasks $S(i-1)$ and $S(i-2)$ and simulates some work depending on the parameter f before, between and after the task creation. Initially there is one task $S(i)$ created for each $0 \leq i < t$ so there are t tasks available for execution. For our experiments we use a constant parameter $t = 35$. For comparison

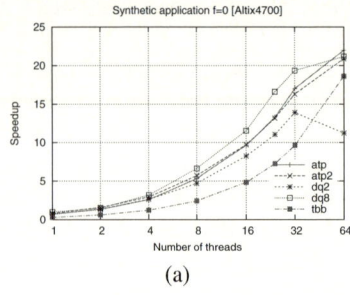
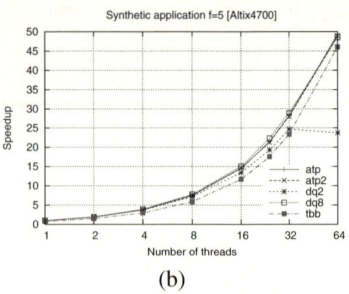

Fig. 5. Speedups for the synthetic application on the Altix4700

we use two different implementations of the adaptive task pool and two non-adaptive task pool implementations. Additionally we also use the TBB [2] library to execute the tasks of the synthetic application. For the comparison with TBB it should be noted that TBB is based on C++ while the adaptive task pool framework is based on C. The non-adaptive task pool *dq2* uses a plain linear list for each processor to store each tasks. The block-oriented implementation *dq8* stores a fixed number (4) of tasks in a single block and stores these blocks in linear lists, one for each processors. Due to the implementation at least one block is always private so it can be accessed without locking. The adaptive task pool implementations *atp* and *atp2* use the data structure as described in the previous sections. The forest is completely public in the *atp* implementation while *atp2* uses private and public areas using the parameters $MIN\_PUB\_LENGTH = 2$ and $MAX\_PRIV\_LENGTH = 3$.

Figure 5 shows the speedups for the implementations based on the best sequential execution for $f = 0$ (Figure 5a) and $f = 5$ (Figure 5b). For empty tasks the speedups do not exceed 22 for a maximum of 64 threads. For up to 32 threads the *dq8* task pool performs best. This is due to the lower overhead in handling the data structure and the availability of enough tasks for execution. In our test with $t = 35$ there are 35 tasks at the beginning distributed round robin over all threads. With more threads even new tasks will still be stored in the private block so some threads have to wait. The adaptive task pools (*atp* and *atp2*) can handle this situation better and are at least as fast as the block-distributed task pool *dq8*. The use of private and public areas does not give an advantage in this case, since the overhead of dynamically adjusting the areas is higher than the benefit from the reduced number of locks required in the private area. The *dq2* implementation with public lists cannot compete and is significantly slower with 64 threads. The alternative implementation of the synthetic application using TBB scales well (almost linearly in respect to sequential execution of the TBB implementation) but is still slower due to the additional overhead in the C++ implementation.

For slightly larger tasks with a factor $f = 5$ (Figure 5b) all implementations can achieve a significantly better scalability reaching a speedup of almost 50. The adaptive task pools and the block-distributed task pool *dq8* achieve similar speedups. Only the *dq2* implementation cannot keep up with the other implementations. This is remarkable as *dq2* as well as *atp* uses a lock to protect access to the data structure and no private

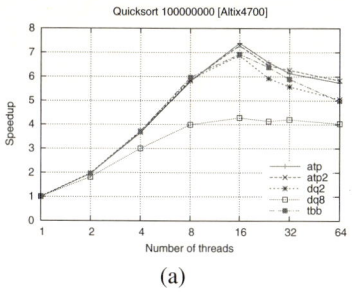 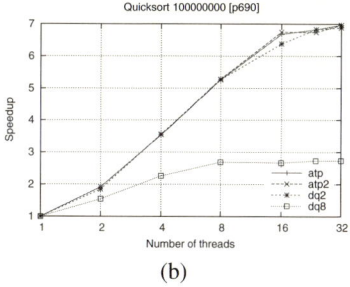

Fig. 6. Speedup for the quicksort application on the Altix4700 (a) and on the p690 (b)

area. The additional benefits for the adaptive task pool, especially task grouping and grouped stealing, actually improve the performance in this case.

4.2 Quicksort

The sequential quicksort creates two sub-arrays based on a pivot element and recursively sorts both arrays. The parallel implementation creates new tasks for sorting the sub-arrays (if the array is large enough based on the fixed limit). As both arrays typically do not have the same size, depending on the pivot element, both tasks created also take different time to complete. Task based execution can cope with this irregularity but the main key is making the existing parallelism available. At the beginning there is only a single task partitioning the whole array. In the next step there exist two tasks, then four and so on. In this implementation the speedup cannot be linear (as described in [1]) and it is important to allow task stealing even for a single task.

Figure 6 shows the speedups for sorting 100,000,000 integers. The best speedup for the Altix4700 machine is 7.39 for 16 threads reached by the adaptive task pool implementation *atp* without private areas and 6.97 for 32 thread on the p690 machine also for the implementation *atp*. The block-distributed task pool dq8 shows bad performance never reaching a speedup above 4.3 and 2.74 respectively. This is however expected as the tasks stored in the private block cannot be stolen by other idle threads. As the parallelism is already limited at the beginning, this significantly reduces the overall speedup. The adaptive task pool implementations can also handle this special situation making all task available if necessary and building large blocks for stealing when possible.

4.3 Ray Tracing and Hierarchical Radiosity

The parallel ray tracing application [3] is a more complex irregular application which creates images from three-dimensional scenes. For each pixel in the image a ray is traced through the geometrical scene. The work associated with a ray depends on the location and complexity of the objects in the scene. We use a modified implementation from the SPLASH-2 suite [4]. As second large application we consider the hierarchical radiosity [5] which computes the light distribution between the objects of a three-dimensional scene. The application uses four different task types to compute the

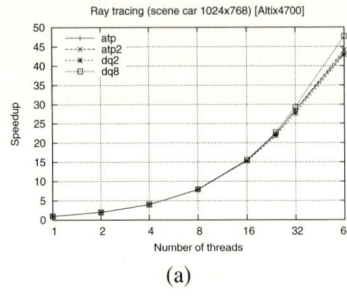
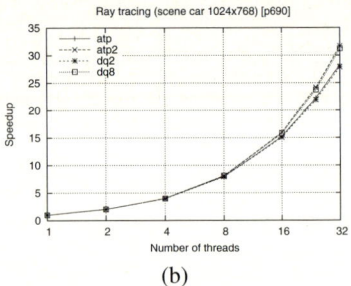

Fig. 7. Speedups for the ray tracing application on the Altix4700 (a) and on the IBM p690 (b)

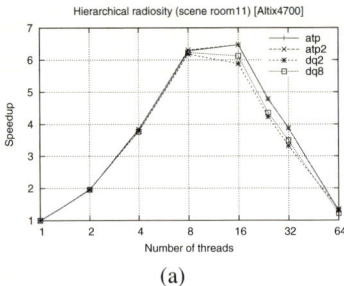
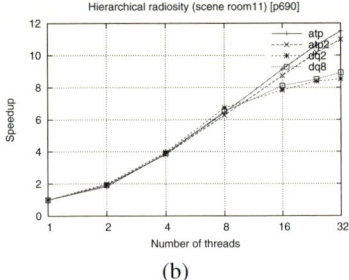

Fig. 8. Speedups for the hierarchical radiosity on the Altix4700 (a) and on the p690 (b)

visibility factors as well as the light distribution between patches. Another task type refines the scenes into smaller patches as required to achieve a specific error bound and a fourth task type performs some post-processing actions. New tasks will be created at runtime to refine the patches so there are read-write accesses from different tasks creating additional dependencies. We use the parallel implementation from the SPLASH-2 suite for evaluation.

Figure 7 shows the results of the ray tracing application on the Altix4700 machine and the p690 machine. The ray tracing application shows good speedups for any task pool implementation. The *dq8* implementation performs best with a speedup of 47.7 for 64 threads on the Altix4700 machine and 31.2 for 32 threads on the p690 system. The low overhead and guaranteed existence of private blocks gives an advantage. However, the adaptive implementations also show good performance and are slightly faster than the *dq2* implementation with very low overhead. In this application the use of private and public areas in the adaptive task pools helps to improve the performance; on the p690 systems the implementation *atp2* is the fastest with a speedup of 31.7.

The speedups for the hierarchical radiosity (Figure 8) are significantly worse than the for the ray tracing due to the additional dependencies and small task sizes. The best speedup is 6.47 for 16 threads for both adaptive task pool implementation on the Altix4700 system while the adaptive task pools can reach a speedup of 11.5 for 32 threads on the p690 machine. The previous results suggested that the non-adaptive implementation *dq8* should be faster because of the lower overhead. But if there are not always enough task available or more task stealing is required the adaptive implementation can outperform the other implementations. Because of this the ray tracing applications works well for *dq8* as all tasks are created at the beginning with no additional task creation. Radiosity on the other hand spawns new tasks so the adaptive task pools can handle this situation better.

5 Related Work

Dynamic load balancing is often used to execute irregular applications efficiently [6]. There are several libraries and programming languages which utilize dynamic load balancing. Charm++ [7] is based on C++ and offers load balancing by using object migration. TBB [2] is a C++ library and allows the use of different programming paradigms. It offers, for example, parallel loops to describe data parallelism but also enables the programmer to explicitly create tasks for a task parallel execution. TBB uses hardware operations to implement synchronization with low overhead, it is however currently available only for a limited number of architectures. Similar approaches are used in language like Fortress [8] or X10 [9] which focus on data parallelism but task parallelism is also supported.

Task based execution becomes more important for modern architectures to keep the growing number of processing units busy. The Cell architecture is well suited for task based execution [10] and CellSs [11] proposes a programming environment using annotations similar to OpenMP to schedule tasks to the available SPEs. [12] proposes a hardware accelerated support for dynamic task scheduling.

Adaptive methods have been used in many applications to handle irregularity. [13] shows the effectiveness of dynamic loop scheduling with adaptive techniques. [14] proposes an adaptive scheduler which uses runtime information to dynamically adapt the number of processors used to execute a job. Data structures to adapt the amount of work stolen for load balancing are proposed in [15] which enables the stealing of about half of the tasks from a given queue but the approach needs dynamically executed balancing steps. The data structure proposed in this paper does not need rebalancing steps and has a lower limit for the number of task stolen but it also takes more time to insert and remove tasks.

6 Conclusions

We have presented an adaptive data structure which is used to implement adaptive task pools. The forest vector storing the trees of tasks introduces a small overhead in contrast to linear lists but it provides advantages for a task based execution. The tasks are stored in larger groups with a growing number of tasks while the groups shrink as the number of tasks shrinks. The size of the private area of tasks also dynamically depends on the number of task available for execution. Creating many fine-grained tasks actually leads to a benefit as the forest vector owner can access parts of it without locks. Also, the cost for task stealing is reduced as a single operation can move a large group of task at once with only one write access to a remote forest vector. The stolen tree contains, to some degree, related tasks which can reduce the penalty for stealing tasks.

Runtime experiments have shown that the adaptive task pool implementation can cope with a large number of fine-grained tasks but is still able to handle situations with a limited degree of parallelism. Non of the previous implementations could handle both situations equally well.

Acknowledgments. We thank the LRZ Munich and NIC Juelich for providing access to their computing systems.

References

1. Hoffmann, R., Korch, M., Rauber, T.: Performance Evaluation of Task Pools Based on Hardware Synchronization. In: Proceedings of the 2004 Supercomputing Conference (SC 2004), Pittsburgh, PA, IEEE/ACM SIGARCH (November 2004)
2. Reinders, J.: Intel Threading Building Blocks: Outfitting C++ for Multi-core Processor Parallelism. O'Reilly, Sebastopol (2007)
3. Singh, J.P., Gupta, A., Levoy, M.: Parallel visualization algorithms: Performance and architectural implications. IEEE Computer 27(7), 45–55 (1994)
4. Woo, S.C., Ohara, M., Torrie, E., Singh, J.P., Gupta, A.: The SPLASH-2 programs: Characterization and methodological considerations. In: Proceedings of the 22nd International Symposium on Computer Architecture, Santa Margherita Ligure, Italy, pp. 24–36 (1995)
5. Hanrahan, P., Salzman, D., Aupperle, L.: A Rapid Hierarchical Radiosity Algorithm. In: Proceedings of SIGGRAPH (1991)
6. Xu, C., Lau, F.C.: Load Balancing in Parallel Computers: Theory and Practice. Kluwer Academic Publishers, Dordrecht (1997)
7. Kale, L.V., Krishnan, S.: CHARM++. In: Wilson, G.V., Lu, P. (eds.) Parallel Programming in C++, pp. 175–214. MIT Press, Cambridge (1996)
8. Allen, E., Chase, D., Hallett, J., Luchangco, V., Maessen, J.W., Ryu Jr., S., Steele G.L., Tobin-Hochstadt, S.: The Fortress Language Specification. version 1.0beta (March 2007)
9. Charles, P., Grothoff, C., Saraswat, V.A., Donawa, C., Kielstra, A., Ebcioglu, K., von Praun, C., Sarkar, V.: X10: an object-oriented approach to non-uniform cluster computing. In: Johnson, R., Gabriel, R.P. (eds.) OOPSLA, pp. 519–538. ACM, New York (2005)
10. IBM developerWorks Power Architecture editors: Unleashing the power of the cell broadband engine. Technical report, IBM Systems Group (2005)
11. Bellens, P., Perez, J.M., Badia, R.M., Labarta, J.: CellSs: a programming model for the Cell BE architecture. In: SC 2006. IEEE, Los Alamitos (2006)
12. Kumar, S., Hughes, C.J., Nguyen, A.: Carbon: Architectural support for fine-grained parallelism on chip multiprocessors. ACM SIGARCH Computer Architecture News 35(2), 162–173 (2007)
13. Banicescu, I., Velusamy, V., Devaprasad, J.: On the scalability of dynamic scheduling scientific applications with adaptive weighted factoring. Cluster Computing, The Journal of Networks, Software Tools and Applications 6, 215–226 (2003)
14. Agrawal, K., He, Y., Leiserson, C.E.: Adaptive work stealing with parallelism feedback. In: Yelick, K.A., Mellor-Crummey, J.M. (eds.) PPOPP, pp. 112–120. ACM Press, New York (2007)
15. Hendler, D., Shavit, N.: Non-blocking steal-half work queues. In: PODC, pp. 280–289 (2002)

Exploration of the Influence of Program Inputs on CMP Co-scheduling*

Yunlian Jiang and Xipeng Shen

Department of Computer Science
The College of William and Mary, Williamsburg, VA, USA 23185
{jiang,xshen}@cs.wm.edu

Abstract. Recent studies have showed the effectiveness of job co-scheduling in alleviating shared-cache contention on Chip Multiprocessors. Although program inputs affect cache usage and thus cache contention significantly, their influence on co-scheduling remains unexplored. In this work, we measure that influence and show that the ability to adapt to program inputs is important for a co-scheduler to work effectively on Chip Multiprocessors. We then conduct an exploration in addressing the influence by constructing cross-input predictive models for some memory behaviors that are critical for a recently proposed co-scheduler. The exploration compares the effectiveness of both linear and non-linear regression techniques in the model building. Finally, we conduct a systematic measurement of the sensitivity of co-scheduling on the errors of the predictive behavior models. The results demonstrate the potential of the predictive models in guiding contention-aware co-scheduling.

1 Introduction

As industry rapidly switches to multi-core processors, on-chip cache sharing is becoming common on modern machines. Although the sharing is good for hiding inter-thread communication latency and permitting flexible cache usage, it results in cache contention on Chip Multiprocessors (CMP), often causing cache thrashing and considerable performance degradation [3,5,6,7,15,17].

Recent studies have shown that co-scheduling—that is, assigning suitable jobs onto the same chip—is beneficial for alleviating cache contention. The previous research on co-scheduling falls into two categories. The first relies on runtime sampling [5,7,15,17]. Symbiotic scheduling, for example, samples program runtime performance under various schedules and picks the best one as the optimal schedule [15]. Although runtime sampling works well for a small number of programs, it may be difficult to scale up because the number of possible schedules is exponential in the number of jobs.

The second category includes profiling-directed techniques. These techniques first conduct a profiling run of the executions and then co-schedule them accordingly [3,6]. Although they showed effectiveness, it is unclear how they would work if the real executions' inputs differ from the training ones.

On a given CMP architecture, cache contention depends on two factors: the programs that run together, called *corunners*, and their inputs. The first factor has been the main

---
* Supported by the National Science Foundation (CNS-0720499) and IBM CAS Fellowship.

focus of previous studies. This work is distinctive in concentrating on the second factor. The goal is to uncover the effects of program inputs on CMP co-scheduling and to explore the solutions.

This study contains two major components. First, we conduct a systematic measurement to the influence of program inputs on corun performance. The experiments employ hardware performance counters in an Intel quad-core machine to measure all possible coruns of a dozen programs on different inputs. The results show that a schedule, although suitable for runs on one set of inputs, may cause 4 times more performance degradation to the runs on a different set of inputs. A CMP co-scheduler, therefore, must have the capability to adapt to different program inputs.

To address the effects of program inputs, in the second part of this work, we explore the construction of cross-input predictive models. We model the relation between program inputs and memory behavior through statistical learning techniques, and compare the effectiveness of both linear and non-linear regression techniques. We use a recently proposed cache-contention-aware proactive scheduler, CAPS [12], to evaluate the predictive models. A broader sensitivity study shows the different effects of various memory behaviors on co-scheduling, suggesting the opportunities for further improvement of the predictive models. The evaluation on CAPS shows an accuracy of over 85% for memory behavior prediction and a 26.3% reduction of the performance degradation that the default coruns cause.

In the rest of the paper, Section 2 uncovers the influence of program inputs on corun performance on CMPs. Section 3, after giving an overview of CAPS, concentrates on the approaches to constructing predictive models for a set of memory behaviors. Section 4 reports the sensitivity of CAPS on the prediction errors of memory behaviors. Section 5 discusses related work, followed by a summary in Section 6.

2 Influence of Program Inputs on Corun Performance

To explore the influence of program inputs on co-scheduling, we measure the coruns of a dozen SPEC CPU2000 programs on their *test*, *train*, and *ref* inputs. The machine we use is a Dell PowerEdge 1850 server with two Intel Xeon 5150 2.66 GHz dual-core processors, each equipped with a 4MB shared L2 cache. The machine runs Fedora Core 5 Linux x86_64 distribution with a Linux kernel of 2.6.17. We use Gcc 4.1 as our compiler. For performance measurement, the Linux kernel is patched to support Performance API (PAPI) version 3.5, which collects performance events by accessing the hardware performance counters on the machine [2].

In the experiment, each time we bind two programs on a dual-core processor and start running them at the same time. To avoid the distraction from the difference between programs' executions, we follow Tuck and Tullsen's method [16], letting each program run 10 times consecutively, and only collecting the behavior of those runs that overlap with the other's execution. In that way, we conduct all possible coruns of the 12 programs for each kind of input, totally 198 coruns. For each corun, PAPI reports, for each of the two programs, the average cycles per instruction (CPI), denoted by *cCPI* (*c* stands for corun). We also measure the CPI of the single run of each program, denoted by *sCPI* (*s* for single-run). Single-runs are subject to no cache contention. We define a program's performance degradation (because of cache contention) as follows:

$$corun\ degradation = \frac{cCPI - sCPI}{sCPI}.$$

The larger a degradation is, the worse the cache sharing affects the program's running speed.

The boxplots in Figure 1 show the results. The differences among the boxplots inside a group reveal the strong influence of program inputs on corun performance. Among the 12 benchmarks, *twolf* and *vpr* are the two that have the largest performance variation across inputs. The *test* runs of both of them have no performance degradation, no matter which program is their corunner. Whereas, their *train* runs show up to 15% and 36% degradations, and their *ref* runs show up to 76% and 64% degradations. For the other programs, the *train* and *ref* runs are 15% to 564% worse than those of their respective *test* runs (in terms of median values). The results demonstrate that program inputs affect corun performance significantly.

The results also show a second phenomenon. Although the working sets of the programs usually increase as input size increases, the corun performance degradation doesn't necessarily increase. For instance, the *ref* runs of *equake*, *mcf*, and *parser* clearly have less degradation than their *train* runs. This phenomenon shows that corun degradation does not necessarily increase when the single-run cache miss rate increases. An extreme case may convey the intuition behind: A program whose single run has no cache hits clearly won't have any more cache misses when it coruns with other programs; hence, its corun performance degradation must be negligible. This observation suggests that in the design of co-scheduler, cache miss rate may not provide the sufficient information.

To see the influence of inputs on corun scheduling, we use CAPS (described next) to find three best schedules, respectively for the *test*, *train*, and *ref* runs of the 12 programs. We then apply the best schedule of *ref* runs to the other two sets of runs. The two sets show up to 4.3 times more performance degradation than their executions under their

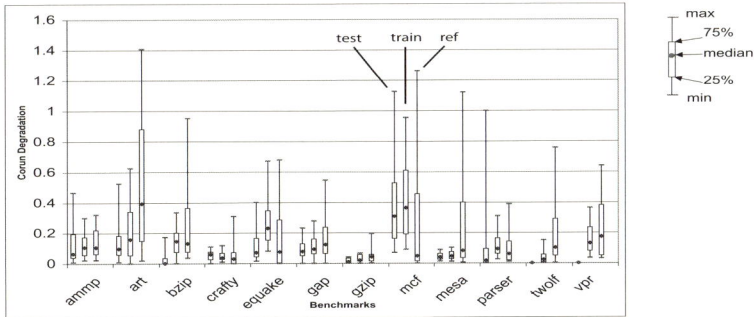

Fig. 1. The boxplot showing the distribution of the performance degradation of each program when it coruns with the other 11 programs. The three boxplots in a group respectively correspond to the executions on *test*, *train*, and *ref* inputs.

own best schedules. These results suggest the great importance for a scheduler to adapt to different program inputs when dealing with cache contention on CMPs.

3 Handling Program Inputs for Co-scheduling

Our approach to addressing the influence of program inputs is to build predictive input-behavior models, which can predict program memory behavior from a given input. Because some co-schedulers can estimate corun performance from single-run memory behavior and then derive the best schedules, we need only the mechanism to accurately predict the memory behavior of a program's single-runs (on arbitrary inputs).

Before describing the model construction, we briefly describe a contention-aware scheduling system, CAPS [12], as it is our underlying framework for evaluation. We choose CAPS for two of its desirable features. First, CAPS is able to efficiently produce the schedule that minimizes the total degradation given the performance of all possible coruns. Thereby, we can easily use the desirable schedule as the baseline to evaluate the schedules produced upon the input-behavior models. Second, some of the memory behaviors (e.g., reuse signatures) used by CAPS have been showed to be cross-input predictable [4], which simplifies some parts of the construction of the input-behavior models.

3.1 Overview of CAPS

CAPS is a system for proactive job-scheduling on CMPs by exploiting the prediction of cache contention. It has two versions, respectively for runtime process scheduling and batch job scheduling. This work uses the version for batch processing, in which case, all jobs to be scheduled are known beforehand.

As depicted in Figure 2, at the heart of CAPS are two components. The first component predicts the performance degradation of each possible corun using the memory behavior of single-runs of each program. The second component maps the corun performance to a fully connected graph, with each vertex representing a program, and each edge having a weight equal to the total performance degradation of the corun of the two vertices. It then applies the minimum-weight perfect matching algorithm to efficiently determine the schedule that minimizes the total of the corun degradation of all the programs.

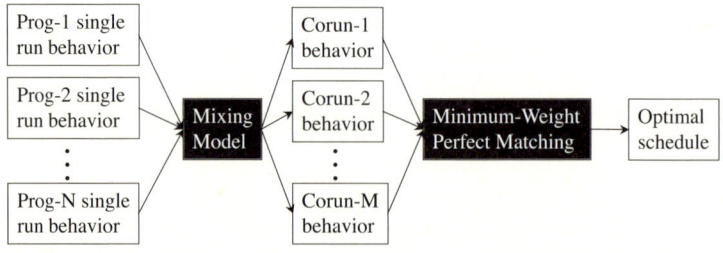

Fig. 2. The key components of the cache-contention-aware proactive scheduler (CAPS)

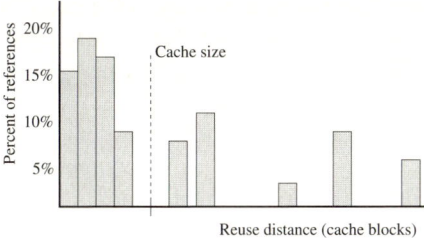

Fig. 3. An example of cache-block reuse signature

CAPS complements previous co-scheduling in that it is proactive, relying on predicted corun performance rather than runtime sampling, and thus overcoming the scalability issue of previous techniques. The details of CAPS are out of the scope of this paper. Here we only describe the single run behaviors used by the mixing model in CAPS; they are the prediction targets of the input-behavior models that are to be built.

- **Reuse Signature:** a histogram showing the distribution of data reuse distances in an execution. **Reuse distance**, also called LRU stack distance, is the number of *distinct* data elements accessed between this and the previous access to the same data element [4]. For the second access to "a" in the reference trace "a b b c d a", the reuse distance is 3 because "b","c" and "d" are accessed in the between. Figure 3 illustrates a reuse signature, with reuse distance on the horizontal axis and the percentage of memory references on the vertical axis. Each bar on the graph shows the percentage of memory references whose reuse distances are in a particular range. If the counting unit for reuse distance is a cache line, a reuse signature can be used to approximate the cache miss rate of the execution for a cache of arbitrary size: All accesses with reuse distance larger than the cache size are simply considered as misses. The approximation has shown an accuracy of over 94% for both fully-associative and set-associative caches [18]. CAPS uses reuse signatures of single runs as the basis to estimate corun cache performance.
- **Accesses per Instruction:** the average number of memory accesses per instruction. This statistic reflects the density of memory references in an execution. It is one of the factors CAPS uses to approximate program performance from memory behaviors (for both single-run and coruns).
- **Distinct Blocks per Cycle:** the average number of distinct memory blocks that are accessed in a CPU cycle. This statistic reflects how aggressive a process competes for caches. CAPS uses it for the prediction of corun cache performance. In CAPS, the counting unit of memory blocks is simply a cache block.

Next, we focus on the construction of the predictive models for each of the three kinds of memory behaviors through statistical learning techniques.

3.2 Constructing Predictive Input-Behavior Models

The memory behavior of a single-run of a program, denoted by B, depends on the running environment E, the program code P, and the input I. In this work, E and P are given, and the goal is to find the function $f()$ mapping from I to B. With such a function, plugging any input into $f()$ will generate the predicted behavior of the program's corresponding single-run execution. We formalize the task as a statistical learning problem. By feeding a program with different inputs, $I_1, I_2, \ldots, I_N$, we observe the corresponding behavior of the program's executions, represented by $B_1, B_2, \ldots, B_N$. The input-behavior pairs, $< I_i, B_i > (i = 1, 2, \ldots, N)$, compose a training set, from which we use regression techniques to approximate function f.

Linear and Non-Linear Regression. Regression techniques are designed to discover the relation between a set of input attributes and a set of outputs. Linear regression assumes that the relation can be expressed by a linear function; non-linear regression permits more sophisticated functions.

Least Mean Squares (LMS) is a commonly used linear regression technique. Suppose f is a linear function mapping input $\vec{I}$ to a behavior B for a given program. Given training data set $< \vec{I_i}, B_i >$ (i=1,2,...,N), the goal of LMS is to find the approximation of function f, represented by $\hat{f}$, such that the mean error squares, $\frac{1}{N} \sum_{i=1}^{N}(B_i - \hat{f}(\vec{I_i}))^2$, is minimized.

LMS is simple and efficient, but applies to only linear functions. For non-linear regression, we choose the k-*Nearest-Neighbor* method. This method is an instance-based learning technique. For a new query instance, it retrieves a set of similar instances from memory and uses them to estimate the new output value. When $k = 1$, the method is named the Nearest-Neighbor method, or *NN* in short. The approximated function $\hat{f}()$ has an implicit and usually non-linear form [8]. The model building is simple, just recording the training instances into a data structure that can be efficiently searched. There are many other statistical learning techniques, such as Regression Trees and Support Vector Machines; they are more complex and costly. We restrain ourselves to a small number of training runs in order to limit the overhead of the offline profiling. Those more complex learning techniques often require a larger training data set.

Besides LMS and NN, we also use a hybrid method. For a given program, it chooses the better one between LMS and NN in terms of *training* errors. (The training error of a model is the prediction error of the model when being applied to the training data.) For each program showed in Figure 1, besides its *test*, *train*, and *ref* inputs included in the SPEC suite, we obtained another input from the collection of additional representative inputs attained by Berube and Amaral [1]. For programs not included in the collection (*ammp*, *art*, *equake*, *mesa*, and *twolf*), we created an input by modifying the corresponding *ref* input. We use *train* inputs for model testing, and the others for training.

Next, we show the effectiveness of the three regression techniques on each of the three kinds of memory behavior that are used in CAPS.

Prediction of Accesses per Instruction. The first question for building a model between program inputs and accesses per instruction is the representation of program inputs. Given the close relation between program data size (i.e., the number of distinct data items) and memory behavior, we adopt the approach proposed by Ding and Zhong, characterizing a program input by the estimated data size that can be obtained through distance-based sampling. Distance-based sampling observes data reuses at the beginning of an execution and estimates data size based on long reuse distances [4]. So, in this and the rest experiments, data size is the I_i in the input-behavior pair $< I_i, B_I >$, whereas the B_i is specific to each experiment; it is the accesses per instruction in this experiment.

The left half of Table 1 reports the accuracy in predicting accesses per instruction. The three methods produce similar accuracies: 86.43% by LMS, 88.27% by NN, and 88.69% by the hybrid method. Program *equake* shows the lowest accuracy (54.58%) mainly because of its more complex relations between inputs and accesses per instruction. More training inputs and more sophisticated models may be helpful.

Table 1. Prediction accuracies of linear (LMS) and non-linear (NN and Hybrid) models

Programs	Accesses per instruction			DPI		
	LMS	NN	Hybrid	LMS	NN	Hybrid
ammp	89.58	98.76	98.76	39.83	86.72	86.72
art	98.86	94.25	98.86	98.96	94.25	98.96
bzip	75.79	78.62	78.62	67.69	64.05	67.69
crafty	99.54	99.24	99.54	76.31	72.50	76.31
equake	54.58	54.42	54.58	82.27	82.13	82.27
gap	74.75	79.35	79.35	79.87	78.08	79.87
gzip	82.76	86.98	86.98	77.85	66.47	77.85
mcf	90.25	92.45	92.45	89.73	88.11	89.73
mesa	96.39	96.98	96.98	89.43	93.33	93.33
parser	96.02	98.61	98.61	89.49	70.42	89.49
twolf	97.11	98.10	98.10	52.12	86.75	86.75
vpr	81.50	81.50	81.50	96.30	95.28	96.30
Average	**86.43**	**88.27**	**88.69**	**78.32**	**81.51**	**85.44**

Prediction of Distinct Blocks per Cycle. The statistic, distinct blocks per cycle, reflects the average cache requirement of a process. It can be regarded as a product of two factors:

$$DPC = DPI * IPC$$

where, DPI is the average number of distinct blocks accessed per instruction, and IPC is the instructions per cycle. DPI is an attribute solely determined by the program; whereas IPC is a runtime behavior, attainable from hardware performance counters. The prediction of DPC therefore can be conducted in two steps. Given a new input, an offline-trained model predicts the DPI of the new execution. During the new execution, the DPC can be obtained by multiplying the predicted DPI with the runtime IPC. Therefore, building a predictive model for DPI is the key to the prediction of distinct blocks per cycle.

Because DPI is an average value for an interval, it is determined by the interval length. For an interval containing nothing except one memory access instruction, the DPI is 1, which is the upper bound of DPI under the assumption that one instruction may conduct at most one memory access. As the interval becomes larger, DPI changes non-monotonically, determined by the ratio of non-memory-access instructions and the frequency in which memory-access instructions access a new object. When the interval length becomes large enough to cover at least one access to all the blocks in the program, DPI decreases as the interval length increases.

The DPI used in CAPS is the average DPI of all the reuse intervals[1], computed in the following formula:

$$w = \frac{\sum_{i=1}^{B} r_i \bar{w}_i}{\sum_{i=1}^{B} r_i}$$

where, B is the number of bars in the reuse signature of the execution, r_i is the number of memory references in bar i, and $\bar{w}_i$ is the average of all the DPIs of the reuse intervals in bar i.

The right half of Table 1 shows that NN is slightly more accurate than LMS, 81.51% versus 78.3%. The hybrid model yields an accuracy of 85.4%.

Reuse Signatures. Previous work has explored the cross-input predictability of reuse signatures. For example, Ding and Zhong have shown an accuracy of over 94% for the prediction of the reuse signatures of 15 complex programs [4]. Their technique is based on a desirable property of reuse signatures: No reuse distance of an execution can be larger than the data size of the execution. (This property comes from the definition of reuse distance.) They therefore test a set of sub-linear functions in training runs and choose the best one as the model for the prediction of reuse signatures. This work adopts their established technique.

4 Influence of Prediction Errors on Co-scheduling

We feed CAPS the predicted memory behaviors to test the influence of the prediction errors on co-scheduling. Figure 4 shows the average performance degradation of the benchmarks included in Figure 1.

The baseline is an *a posteriori* schedule, which is the best over all possible schedules. We obtained it by applying the minimum-weight perfect matching to all real coruns. (Recall that the algorithm minimizes the total degradation.) The *random* bar shows the average result of 100 random schedules. It reflects the performance of the default scheduler in the current CMP system.

The difference between *caps-pred* and *caps-real* shows the influence of the prediction errors of the behavior models—0.28 more degradation. With that influence, *caps-pred* still reduces the performance degradation of the random schedule from 1.99 to 1.46. The extra degradation that *caps-real* has over the *a posteriori* schedule is due to the inaccuracy inside CAPS (e.g., the mixing model).

To achieve a better understanding of the influence from prediction errors, we conducted a broader study to the sensitivity of CAPS on each of the three kinds of memory behaviors. We introduce a range of random errors into the three kinds of memory behavior, one kind per time, and then measure the resulting performance of CAPS.

---

[1] The reuse interval of a data reuse is the interval between the previous and the current access to the same data item.

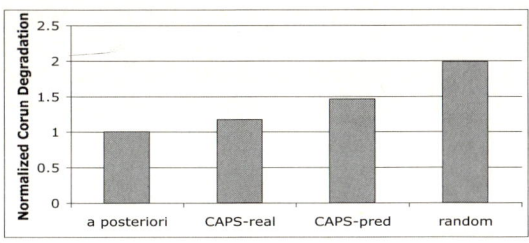

Fig. 4. The average performance degradation under different schedules. The "a posteriori" schedule is the best schedule obtained on all corun information; "CAPS-real" is the schedule by CAPS on real single-run behaviors; "CAPS-pred" is the schedule by CAPS on single-run behaviors predicted by the models described in Section 3.2; "random" reflects the default schedule in the CMP system.

For lack of space, we leave the detailed results in a technical report [9]. As a summary, CAPS is most sensitive to the errors in accesses per instruction and DPIs: an error of 8% in them respectively causes the performance degradation to increase by 12.3% and 17.6%; 16% causes an increase of 18.3% and 18.8%. CAPS is less sensitive to the errors in reuse distance histograms: an error of 8% causes an increase of 3.6%; 16% causes an increase of 12.2%.

To improve the accuracy of the predictive models, more training inputs may help. A combination with hardware performance counters may also be beneficial, especially for accesses per instruction. In addition, it is potentially helpful to characterize program inputs more sophisticatedly [13] rather than only relying on sampled data size. Finally, the combination of CAPS with locality phase analysis [14] can make the scheduler adaptive to runtime program behavior changes.

We emphasize that the main contributions of this paper are the exploration of the influence of program inputs on co-scheduling and cross-input memory behavior modeling. The details on the integration of the models into CAPS and the extension to runtime scheduling (presented in our technical report [12]) are out of the scope.

5 Related Work

We are not aware of any work on the study of program inputs for co-scheduling on CMPs. The closest work on program inputs exists in runtime adaptive optimizations and feed-back directed optimizations behavior (e.g., [1, 10]). Most recent studies on CMP (or SMT) co-scheduling either rely on runtime estimation of cache usage from hardware performance counters [5, 7, 15, 17], or offline profiling [3, 6]. None of them systematically explores the effects of program inputs on co-scheduling. Although runtime techniques implicitly adapt to input changes, they require periodic sampling of many different coruns, making them subject to some scalability or applicability limitations as discussed in Section 1. Architecture extensions, e.g. cache activity vector [11], are complementary to software co-scheduling in offering fine-grained cache behavior.

6 Conclusion

This work focuses on the exploration of the influence of program inputs on corun performance of programs running on CMPs equipped with shared caches. It draws the conclusion that the influence of program inputs is so strong that a cache-contention-aware scheduler has to adapt to them. The second part of the paper describes our practice in constructing cross-input predictive models for a set of memory behaviors that are used in a recently proposed proactive co-scheduling system. The experiments show reasonably accurate prediction through the uses of linear and non-linear regression techniques. The paper then presents a systematic measurement of the influence of the prediction errors on co-scheduling. The results suggest that the cross-input prediction models are able to help the scheduler significantly reduce cache contention on shared caches.

References

1. Berube, P., Amaral, J.N.: Benchmark design for robust profile-directed optimization. In: Standard Performance Evaluation Corporation (SPEC) Workshop (2007)
2. Browne, S., Deane, C., Ho, G., Mucci, P.: Papi: A portable interface to hardware performance counters. In: Proceedings of Department of Defense HPCMP Users Group Conference (1999)
3. Chandra, D., Guo, F., Kim, S., Solihin, Y.: Predicting inter-thread cache contention on a chip multi-processor architecture. In: Proceedings of HPCA (2005)
4. Ding, C., Zhong, Y.: Predicting whole-program locality with reuse distance analysis. In: Proceedings of PLDI (2003)
5. El-Moursy, A., Garg, R., Albonesi, D.H., Dwarkadas, S.: Compatible phase co-scheduling on a cmp of multi-threaded processors. In: Proceedings of IPDPS (2006)
6. Fedorova, A., Seltzer, M., Small, C., Nussbaum, D.: Performance of multithreaded chip multiprocessors and implications for operating system design. In: Proceedings of USENIX Annual Technical Conference (2005)
7. Fedorova, A., Seltzer, M., Smith, M.D.: Improving performance isolation on chip multiprocessors via an operating system scheduler. In: Proceedings of PACT (2007)
8. Hastie, T., Tibshirani, R., Friedman, J.: The elements of statistical learning. Springer, Heidelberg (2001)
9. Jiang, Y., Shen, X.: Study of cross-input predictability of inclusive reuse distance. Technical Report WM-CS-2007-13, Computer Science Department, The College of William and Mary (2007)
10. Li, X., Garzaran, M.J., Padua, D.: A dynamically tuned sorting library. In: Proceedings of CGO (2004)
11. Settle, A., Kihm, J.L., Janiszewski, A., Connors, D.: Architectural support for enhanced smt job scheduling. In: Proceedings of PACT (2004)
12. Shen, X., Jiang, Y., Mao, F.: Caps: Contention-aware proactive scheduling for cmps with shared caches. Technical Report WM-CS-2007-09, Computer Science Department, The College of William and Mary (2007)
13. Shen, X., Mao, F.: Modeling relations between inputs and dynamic behavior for general programs. In: Proceedings of LCPC (2007)
14. Shen, X., Zhong, Y., Ding, C.: Locality phase prediction. In: Proceedings of ASPLOS (2004)
15. Snavely, A., Tullsen, D.: Symbiotic jobscheduling for a simultaneous multithreading processor. In: Proceedings of ASPLOS (2000)

16. Tuck, N., Tullsen, D.M.: Initial observations of the simultaneous multithreading Pentium 4 processor. In: Proceedings of PACT (2003)
17. Zhang, X., Dwarkadas, S., Folkmanis, G., Shen, K.: Processor hardware counter statistics as a first-class system resource. In: Proceedings of HotOS (2007)
18. Zhong, Y., Dropsho, S.G., Shen, X., Studer, A., Ding, C.: Miss rate prediction across program inputs and cache configurations. IEEE Transactions on Computers 56(3) (2007)

Integrating Dynamic Memory Placement with Adaptive Load-Balancing for Parallel Codes on NUMA Multiprocessors

Paul Slavin* and Len Freeman

Centre for Novel Computing, School of Computer Science
The University of Manchester, Manchester, M13 9PL
{slavinp,lfreeman}@cs.man.ac.uk

Abstract. This Paper describes and evaluates a system of dynamic memory migraton for codes executing in a Non-Uniform Memory Access environment. This system of migration applies information about the load-imbalance within a workload in order to determine the affinity between threads of the application and regions of memory. This information then serves as the basis of migration decisions, with the object of minimising the NUMA distance between code and the memory it accesses. Results are presented which demonstrate the effectiveness of this technique in reducing the runtime of a set of representative HPC kernels.

1 Introduction

The Non-Uniform Memory Access (NUMA) environment presents the programmer of parallel HPC applications with a convenient and intuitive representation of memory in the form of a unified global address space comprised of several physically discrete memories which are transparently integrated by the actions of hardware. This layer of abstraction between the physical layout and conceptual presentation of memory in a NUMA system manifests itself in the form of a variable latency that differs according to the region of the address space accessed, as different regions are mapped by the operating system's page tables to different physical banks of memory. An access by a processor to a local bank completes in less time than if the same access were satisfied from a more remote memory to which requests and responses are mediated by an interconnect.

The placement of memory by a parallel program is therefore an important determinant of that program's performance [1] and it is desirable to have as great a proportion as possible of the memory that a process will access during its execution located in the same node of the NUMA machine as the processor executing this process [2]. The data in memory, on which the threads of a parallel program will operate, is termed the *workload* of the program. For applications with a regular and predictable workload, the optimal placement of data within memory

---

* This work was supported by the award of a Doctoral Training Studentship by the EPSRC.

may be specified in advance, by way of source code directives or by the actions of a compiler that is aware of the physical memory layout of the NUMA system in question. A large class of applications have irregular, sparse, or otherwise unpredictable workloads whose optimal placement cannot be determined *a priori*. For these cases, *page migration* techniques have been developed which dynamically relocate memory between the nodes of a NUMA system with the objective of minimising the distance between threads and the data they operate upon.

2 Page Migration

Where the distribution in memory of a workload cannot be determined before runtime, page migration methods must examine the runtime behaviour of the parallel program in order to establish the affinities that exist between its threads and areas of the program's address space that are occupied by the partitioned workload that code will operate upon [3]. Then, having identified the affinity of processors for certain regions of the partitioned workload, these regions are relocated in physical memory to be as close as possible to the processors which access them. The *partition* of the workload in this sense refers to the division of the total of the program's data into a sequence of slices, each of which is allocated to a processor in the system.

As such, the task of a page migration scheme may be decomposed into two principal activities. The first is the gathering of information relating to the affinity of each of a parallel program's threads for certain regions of the workload. The second is the physical relocation of these regions of the workload to memory in the NUMA system that is in proximity to the appropriate threads. This paper deals with the first of these tasks and describes how an extended Feedback-Guided Dynamic Loop-Scheduling (FGDLS) [4] algorithm may be used to create a representation of a parallel program's workload which reveals the affinities of processors for regions of the workload.

Existing page migration schemes determine which of the processors participating in a parallel program exhibit an affinity for which regions of the address space by examining a sample of the accesses made by each thread to each page of virtual memory [5,6,7,8,9]. In such schemes a counter is maintained which records the number of accesses to that page originating from each node of the NUMA machine. When a sufficient number of accesses from a particular remote node are recorded, migration is triggered and the page in question is associated with a physical page frame local to (or at least closer to) the accessing node. We denote this technique as the *sampling/threshold* page migration technique. Although the technique of sampling and thresholds is widely used in migration schemes, there are aspects of real-world HPC applications which can cause the simple perspective on a program's memory accesses which this method offers to diverge from the real pattern of memory accesses that the program will exhibit. Foremost amongst these is the implicit and fundamental assumption of such schemes that observations about the historical behaviour of a program will continue to be relevant to the program's future behaviour. In many cases, the underlying algorithms embodied by a program necessitate that the operations of the program are divided into several distinct "phases", within each of which the behaviour of the program is consistent yet between which behaviour differs considerably. It can be readily envisaged that migration performed in response to a program's behaviour in one phase may not be relevant to a subsequent phase.

The experimental results presented in Sect. 5 indicate that this class of page migration technique is unable to achieve substantial reductions in runtime for representative HPC applications on a commercially available parallel machine. Analysis of the behaviour of this traditional migration scheme with the Speed-Shop profiling environment [10] indicates that, of the two components of the page migration procedure identified above, the physical relocation of memory between the nodes of a system is not time-consuming and does not impose a substantial overhead on code which makes use of page migration. As such, this implies that it is in the domain of the other component task, that of gathering accurate information about a program's affinities for regions of memory, that the sampling/threshold system of migration experiences problems.

This analysis agrees with that described in [3] where problems in tuning the threshold number of remote accesses required to trigger migration are encountered and no ready technique for determining the optimal sensitivity can be determined. Where the appropriate level of sensitivity for an application cannot be established, the sampling/threshold system of page migration will inevitably manifest 'false positives' due to overly-sensitive migration and similar 'missed-opportunities' where the potential to reduce latency by a migration is overlooked due to insufficient sensitivity to remote accesses. In view of this circumstance, we assert that the principal source of poor performance with existing page migration schemes is the problem of accurately determining *what* is to be migrated to *where* on the system, and to do so in a timely manner. The overhead of physically migrating data is minimal when compared to the consequences of making poor decisions as to the memory affinities of the program. This recognition has motivated our attempt to develop a source of information on which page migration decisions may be based that better describes the affinities between threads in a parallel program and the regions of the partitioned workload they operate upon.

3 Feedback-Guided Dynamic Loop Scheduling

Feedback-guided dynamic loop scheduling may be applied to a sequence of nested loops where a parallelised inner loop is contained within a sequential outer loop whose iterations typically represent change with respect to time, as depicted in the following code fragment:

```
DO SEQUENTIAL K = 1, NSTEPS
    DO PARALLEL I = 1, N
        CALL LOOP_BODY(I)
    END DO
END DO
```

In the case of a sparse workload, where equal extents of the workload do not contain equal amounts of work, the task of a FGDLS algorithm is to interrogate the program's historic execution profile to dynamically determine the amount of work that is represented by each partition of the workload.

After the first iteration of a nested loop is performed with an inital equipartition of the workload, the FGDLS algorithm compares the deviation of the execution time of each slice from the mean execution time denoted by $\frac{T}{P}$ and adjusts the boundaries of each slice according to whether it is over or under endowed with work. By this technique of gradual refinement, the FGDLS algorithm converges upon an equal allocation of work to each of the processors.

3.1 Integrating FGDLS with Page Migration

In a standard FGDLS algorithm of the type described in [4], each slice of work is represented by a data structure of the type indicated below. The *start* and *end* values represent the lower and upper boundaries respectively of a subdivision of the program's workload. After each outer loop iteration therefore, an execution time is associated with a region of the workload extending from the *start* to the *end* element, and so recording the execution time that is attributable to this delineated region of the data on which the program will operate.

```
struct slice{
    int start;
    int end;
    int cpuid;
    struct slice *next;
};
```

This load balancing operation results in an updated slice structure in which load imbalance will be reduced relative to the previous iteration. The values within this updated slice structure will be applied to each processor at the beginning of the next outer loop iteration. However, because of the representation of each processor's allocation as a contiguous region of the workload in memory, the *start* and *end* values in conjunction with the *cpuid* value in each slice define the region of the address space that the *cpuid*'th processor will access on the subsequent outer loop iteration.

It is this crucial observation which permits the information contained within the workload's partition to be applied to the placement of memory for the program in question. Because the values in each slice of the partition will dictate which processor operates upon which region of the workload, these same values also indicate the affinity of that processor for certain pages in memory. This is precisely the same information that a page migration scheme requires in order to migrate memory towards the processors which make most frequent use of it. As such, by migrating the region defined between the *start* and *end* boundaries of each slice to the same NUMA node as the *cpuid*'th processor which will access that region, it is possible to enhance the locality of memory placement at each outer loop iteration in the same proportion as the FGDLS algorithm reduces load imbalance.

The following section describes how such a scheme combining load balancing and memory migration may be implemented on a representative shared-memory NUMA machine.

4 Implementation

The technique of page migration described in the sections above was implemented on an SGI Origin 3400 machine with 16 MIPS R12000 processors and 4GB of main memory. This system is comprised of four nodes, each containing four processors, and 1GB of local memory. Each processor has an 8MB level 2 cache consisting of 128 byte cache-lines with a two-way set associative hashing policy. The machine's operating system is IRIX 6.5.

4.1 Exposing Physical Topology to Userlevel Code

The NUMA API of such operating systems expose functions to the programmer which allow the naming and compartmentalisation of regions of the machine, each consisting of one or more nodes comprising processors and memory. This provides a mechanism for informing userlevel code of the physical layout of the machine and provides the conceptual basis that permits regions of the address space of a particular program to be selectively assigned to the physical resources of the NUMA machine of which it runs.

In the terminology of IRIX, these named and demarcated regions of the machine are termed *Memory Locality Domains (MLDs)*. These MLDs are an abstract representation of a machine's resources which are created dynamically at runtime and need not coincide with the physical topology of the NUMA machine. However, by configuring MLDs which coincide with the physical resources of the machine, userlevel applications may be given a method of addressing specific nodes of the machine rather than being restricted to the unified address space abstraction presented by the system's hardware.

As such, our first step is to use the *mld_create()* syscall to configure a MLD for each node in the system. Each MLD so created is provided with a *Resource Affinity List* which specifies its proximity to physical nodes of the system, as identified by the filenames of their corresponding entries in the /hw virtual filesystem. This results in a set of MLDs, each of which represents a physical portion of the machine's hardware.

4.2 Unifying Load Balancing and Page Migration

The computational kernel of the code in question consists of a sequence of nested loops. As described in Sect. 3, the FGDLS algorithm updates its 'map' of the program's workload after each outer loop iteration and modifies the quantity of work allocated to each processor in response to any load imbalance that is identified. The schedule resulting from this reallocation is then applied to the next outer loop iteration. As such, a period exists where the FGDLS algorithm has calculated in advance the allocation of work to processors that will be applied to the $K+1$ outer loop iteration. As described in Sect. 3, this allocation determines the regions of memory which each processor will access, but at this point the workload in memory remains in the state determined by the K allocation. By migrating to the appropriate processor those regions of the address space which the forthcoming $K+1$ schedule will allocate to that processor, each memory access made during the $K+1$ iteration will be satisfied from local memory. The nested loop is modified to the following state by the inclusion of load balancing and subsequent migration:

```
DO SEQUENTIAL K = 1, NSTEPS
   DO PARALLEL I = 1, N
      CALL LOOP_BODY(I)
   END DO
   CALL FGDLS()
   CALL MIGRATE(FGDLS_PARTITION)
END DO
```

Section 5 demonstrates that for some applications, the cost of migrating this contiguous region of memory as a unit is substantially lower than the cost implied by having some proportion of the $K+1$ iteration's memory accesses satisfied from remote memories.

4.3 Migrating Address Ranges between Nodes

Having identified the processors to which regions of the workload will be assigned in the next outer loop iteration, it remains to migrate the address ranges corresponding to these regions to the appropriate processors. The system call which effects this is *migr_range_migrate()* with the signature:

```
int migr_range_migrate(void* base_addr, size_t length,
                       pmo_handle_t pmo_handle)
```

The *base_addr* and *length* parameters specify a region of the virtual address space and the *pmo_handle* object represents a placed MLD. This MLD is the destination to which the designated range of virtual memory will be migrated. To determine whether such a migration is necessary, the *va2pa()* system call is passed a virtual memory address and returns the node of the system on which the physical page frame containing this address is located. In conjunction with the virtual addresses which correspond to the *start* and *end* boundaries that define each slice of the workload, *va2pa()* may be called to determine the current node of residence of the data described by this slice and then *migr_range_migrate()* called to reallocate this region to the node housing the processor that will operate upon this data in the subsequent loop iteration.

The procedure to implement scheduling guided page migration may therefore be summarised as follows:

1. Establish a set of Memory Locality Domains which correspond to the nodes of the NUMA system.
2. Implement an FGDLS algorithm which represents the program's workload as a set of contiguous slices, each associated with one processor.
3. Apply this FGDLS algorithm after each outer loop iteration to create a schedule for the next iteration.
4. According to this schedule, migrate each processor's workload to memory local to that processor.
5. Begin execution of the next outer loop iteration.

5 Experimental Evaluation

5.1 Method

The steps described above were applied to a set of source codes representing typical linear algebraic operations that constitute the computational kernel of real-world HPC applications. The first group of these is a parallel sequence of multiplications of sparse matrices of varying sizes by a dense vector. The second is the Conjugate Gradient benchmark from version 2.3 of the NAS Parallel Benchmark Suite. Trials were performed on a NUMA system as described in Sect. 4.

For each of these trials, the original source code is extended to incorporate the scheduling-guided page migration scheme described above. These extended codes are then compared with the original, unmodified version in terms of the absolute 'wallclock' runtime, and of the proportion of all memory accesses by each program that are made to remote memory. Furthermore, a series of trial are conducted with the inbuilt system of page migration in IRIX 6.5 enabled for each program. This page migration system bases its migration decisions on a sampling/threshold scheme such as that described in Sect. 2. Each trial is executed in the NUMA-aware SpeedShop [10] profiling environment. This utility has been configured to interrogate the Origin's hardware counters in the event of an L2 cache miss and to determine whether this miss is satisfied from local or remote memory.

5.2 Matrix-Vector Multiplication

This experiment consists of a sparse square matrix repeatedly multiplied by a dense vector. The Posix Threads library has been used to parallelise this operation such that each participating processor is assigned a contiguous set of the rows of the matrix.

The matrix is populated with work according to the Gaussian distribution which commonly occurs in statistical applications. The probability of a matrix element being populated with a non-zero value is inversely proportional to the distance of its row coordinate from the central row of the matrix.

At the beginning of the multiplication, the matrix is divided into an equipartition where each division contains $\frac{N}{P}$ elements of the matrix, where P is the number of participating processors. The component calculations of the multiplication are then performed by a nested loop structure, with the allocation of work between each of the participating processors being modified by the FGDLS routine after completion of each outer loop iteration. Migration is then performed following each update to the schedule.

5.3 Conjugate Gradient

The CG application is an iterative solver which is conceptually similar to matrix-vector multiplication in that the CG algorithm is itself dominated by the multiplication of a dense vector by a positive definite sparse matrix.

In this code, the *rowstr* array is used to partition the main matrix and so performs the function in CG that is performed by the *slice* structure in the matrix-vector multiplication. One notable characteristic of the matrix used in this code is that the distribution of data is less regular and more fragmented than in the matrix-vector example. This implies that migration must be performed on a larger number of smaller, less contiguous regions of data. As described in the next section, the repercussions of this are evident in the observed results.

5.4 Results and Analysis

Tables 1 and 2 describe the effects of the inclusion of scheduling-guided migration within each benchmark's source code in terms of the proportion of memory accesses which are to remote memory and of the wallclock runtime for each program. Columns of each table describe these metrics for the case of the unmodified source code ("WithOut migration"), the scheduling-guided migration described in this paper ("SG migration") and the inbuilt operating-system version of sampling/threshold migration ("OS migration"). Matrix-vector multiplication is performed with square matrices of size 8000 and 12000 and sizes 'B' and 'C' of the CG application are evaluated.

The first notable observation from these results is the failure of the operating-system's migration scheme to substantially affect either the proportion of accesses to remote memory or the wallclock runtime. This coincides with the observations made in [1] regarding the efficacy of page migration on this platform for real-world problems, rather than in the simulated environment described in [11].

In contrast, trials featuring a schedule-guided migration scheme show a marked reduction in both the proportion of remote memory accesses and in the overall execution time. While this is the case for both matrix-vector and CG programs, the extent of the reduction in remote memory accesses, and the corollary reduction in runtime, that is achieved by schedule-guided migration is observed to be notably more pronounced for the matrix-vector code than for the

Table 1. Effect of Schedule-Guided Migration on Percentage of Memory Accesses made to Remote Memory

Benchmark	WO Migr %	SG Migr %	OS Migr %
MV 8K	49.98	0.13	49.26
MV 12K	48.54	0.18	48.08
CG.B	38.96	3.24	36.94
CG.C	57.05	31.46	56.94

Table 2. Effect of Schedule-Guided Migration on Runtime

Benchmark	WO Migr (s)	SG Migr (s)	OS Migr (s)
MV 8K	272.66	211.2	271.83
MV 12K	840.66	673.96	837.57
CG.B	1523.73	1060.71	1491.46
CG.C	3789.73	2811.08	3711.66

CG code. Although both applications have a 'sparse' workload, the differences in the contiguity vs. fragmentation of each workload makes itself evident in this respect. The overhead of migrating one large region of the address space is significantly less than that required to migrate many smaller regions, as is the case for the CG application. This overhead is derived both from the cost of calling the *va2pa()* syscall to determine the current physical residency of a virtual memory page, and from the cost of the *migr_range_migrate()* function.

The influence of this characteristic of each workload becomes more evident as problem-size increases. While the matrix-vector trials with schedule-guided migration achieve a consistently high reduction in the proportion of remote memory accesses, essentially eliminating remote accesses for both sizes of matrix, the success of this same technique for the largest size of CG application is seen to decline relative to the results recorded for CG.B. This suggests that there exists a certain 'threshold of fragmentation' in a workload, beyond which the expense of migrating many small regions becomes sufficient to offset the latency that is saved by having these regions local the processor which accesses them. The repercussions of this phenomenon and its relation to the system's virtual memory page size are discussed in the following section.

6 Issues and Extensions

The results presented in the previous section demonstrate that for a workload which is partitioned so that each processor's allocation of work consists of a contiguous region of the address space, memory migration guided by a FGDLS load balancing algorithm is capable of producing a substantial reduction in remote memory accesses, but that this performance declines where the workload is distributed less favourably. This section considers some of the limits on the general applicability of the concept of schedule-guided migration and some of the techniques which may be used to extend it to deal with these challenges.

6.1 Page Level False-Sharing

Of central importance in this respect is the effect that virtual memory page size exerts on the granularity with which data may be migrated between nodes. Where a virtual memory page is large relative to the size of the data elements it contains, many of these elements are likely to coexist on a single page. It is probable however that the boundaries of the workload partition assigned by a FGDLS scheme will not coincide with page boundaries but instead fall within a page. As the smallest unit that may be migrated between two nodes of a NUMA system is a single page, this implies that some portion of the data elements occupying a page are migrated *away* from the appropriate processor as they have the misfortune to share a page with elements which form part of the workload of another processor.

Although this problem affects a small proportion of the data assigned to each processor, its effect becomes progressively more apparent where the workload of a processor is comprised of many small regions of memory for which many separate migration operations are required. For each of these migrations, some portion of the data on each page containing a boundary of the workload's partition will be incorrectly migrated along with that page as a whole. This phenomenon is conceptually similar to the recognised issue of false-sharing that is applicable to coherent caches in a NUMA environment. This observation raises the prospect of whether similar data transformations may be applied to a workload in memory in order to restructure data into a form more amenable to page migration.

7 Related Work

The concept of dynamically relocating memory pages between the nodes of a NUMA machine in response to a program's runtime behaviour is first described in [12]. Other authors have developed this theme whilst continuing to treat page migration as a function of the operating system, for example in [11,9]. The alternative technique of implementing page migration in userspace is advocated in [6] and a related userspace technique employing a software virtual-memory layer is described in [13]. More recent reflections on migration as a solution to the latency problem in distributed shared-memory machines have returned to the theme of operating-system modification, as in [7], and even hardware assistance to migration, as in [14]. A page-migration scheme which employs Solaris' inbuilt migration system calls on a Sun Fire system to improve locality for a particular PDE solving routine is described in [2].

The issue of work scheduling for the NUMA environment has been widely considered, with the FGDLS technique in particular described in [4]. Although the techniques of page migration and load balancing have heretofore been considered in isolation, [1] recognises their separate contributions to the performance of parallel code on a NUMA machine.

References

1. Jiang, D., Singh, J.P.: Scaling application performance on a cache-coherent multiprocessor. In: ISCA 1999: Proceedings of the 26th annual international symposium on Computer architecture, pp. 305–316. IEEE Computer Society, Los Alamitos (1999)
2. Nordén, M., Löf, H., Rantakokko, J., Holmgren, S.: Geographical locality and dynamic data migration for OpenMP implementations of adaptive PDE solvers. In: Müller, M.S., Chapman, B.M., de Supinski, B.R., Malony, A.D., Voss, M. (eds.) IWOMP 2005 and IWOMP 2006. LNCS, vol. 4315. Springer, Heidelberg (2008)
3. Scheurich, C., Dubois, M.: Dynamic page migration in multiprocessors with distributed global memory. IEEE Trans. Comput. 38(8), 1154–1163 (1989)
4. Bull, J.M.: Feedback guided dynamic loop scheduling: Algorithms and experiments. In: Pritchard, D., Reeve, J.S. (eds.) Euro-Par 1998. LNCS, vol. 1470, pp. 377–382. Springer, Heidelberg (1998)
5. Bartal, Y., Charikar, M., Indyk, P.: On page migration and other relaxed task systems. Theoretical Computer Science 268(1), 43–66 (2001)
6. Nikolopoulos, D.S., Papatheodorou, T.S., Polychronopoulos, C.D., Labarta, J., Ayguado, E.: A case for user-level dynamic page migration. In: ICS 2000: Proceedings of the 14th international conference on Supercomputing, pp. 119–130. ACM Press, New York (2000)
7. Corbalan, J., Martorell, X., Labarta, J.: Evaluation of the memory page migration influence in the system performance: the case of the SGI Origin 2000. In: ICS 2003: Proceedings of the 17th annual International Conference on Supercomputing, pp. 121–129. ACM Press, New York (2003)
8. LaRowe Jr., R.P., Wilkes, J.T., Ellis, C.S.: Exploiting operating system support for dynamic page placement on a NUMA shared memory multiprocessor. In: Proceedings of the 3rd ACM SIGPLAN Symposium on Principles & Practice of Parallel Programming, Williamsburg, VA, April 1991, vol. 26(7), pp. 122–132 (1991)
9. Chandra, R., Devine, S., Verghese, B., Gupta, A., Rosenblum, M.: Scheduling and page migration for multiprocessor compute servers. In: ASPLOS-VI: Proceedings of the sixth international conference on Architectural support for programming languages and operating systems, pp. 12–24. ACM Press, New York (1994)
10. SGI Incorporated: Speedshop user's guide. Technical Report 007-3311-003, SGI, Mountain View, CA (2003)
11. Verghese, B., Devine, S., Gupta, A., Rosenblum, M.: Operating system support for improving data locality on ccNUMA compute servers. In: ASPLOS-VII: Proceedings of the seventh international conference on Architectural support for programming languages and operating systems, pp. 279–289. ACM Press, New York (1996)
12. Black, D., Sleator, D.: Competitive algorithms for replication and migration problems. Technical Report CMU-CS-89-201, Department of Computer Science, Carnegie-Mellon University (1989)
13. Petersen, K., Li, K.: An evaluation of multiprocessor cache coherence based on virtual memory support. In: Proceedings of the 8th International Symposium on Parallel Processing, pp. 158–164. IEEE Computer Society, Los Alamitos (1994)
14. Tikir, M.M., Hollingsworth, J.K.: Using hardware counters to automatically improve memory performance. In: SC 2004: Proceedings of the ACM/IEEE SC2004 Conference (SC 2004), p. 46. IEEE Computer Society, Los Alamitos (2004)

Guest-Aware Priority-Based Virtual Machine Scheduling for Highly Consolidated Server*

Dongsung Kim[1], Hwanju Kim[1], Myeongjae Jeon[1],
Euiseong Seo[2], and Joonwon Lee[1]

[1] CS Department, Korea Advanced Institute of Science and Technology
{dskim,hjukim,mjjeon}@camars.kaist.ac.kr,joon@cs.kaist.ac.kr
[2] Pennsylvania State University
euiseong@cse.psu.edu

Abstract. The use of virtualization is rapidly expanding from server consolidation to various computing systems including PC, multimedia set-top box and gaming console. However, different from the server environment, timeliness response for the external input is an essential property for the user-interactive applications. To provide timeliness scheduling of virtual machine this paper presents a priority-based scheduling scheme for virtual machine monitors. The suggested scheduling scheme selects the next task to be scheduled based on the task priorities and the I/O usage stats of the virtual machines. The suggested algorithm was implemented and evaluated on Xen virtual machine monitor. The results showed that the average response time to I/O events is improved by 5~22% for highly consolidated environment.

Keywords: Xen, Credit scheduler, Virtual Machine, Virtualization.

1 Introduction

The operating system virtualization is resurrected as a key technology for server consolidation, which reduces the cost for management and deployment. As blossoming in performance aspects [1,2], the use of virtualization has expanded gradually into various fields such as multimedia, game, and interactive applications [3,4,5]. Although diverse workloads have become feasible in the virtualized environment, contemporary virtual machine monitors (VMMs) generally focus on fairness of VMs and the improvement of I/O throughput. Therefore, latency-sensitive applications would preform poorly in the virtualized environment.

The scheduling turn-around time for each VM could be considerable under highly consolidated environment. Since VMM typically has lack of knowledge about guest-level tasks, the status and priorities of tasks, which run on each guest kernel, can not be considered when VMM chooses the next VM to be

---

* This work was supported by KOSEF grant funded by the Korea government(MOST) (No. R01-2006-000-10724-0) and also partially funded by the MIC, Korea, under the ITRC support program supervised by the IITA.

scheduled. Such CPU allocation mechanism can increase the response time of a latency-sensitive application with a high priority. As more VMs are consolidated on a physical machine, larger performance degradation occurs and consequently results in unsatisfactory quality of service [6].

This paper introduces a priority-based VM scheduling algorithm to reduce scheduling latency of a VM that requires timeliness response. In our scheme, VMM allocates CPU to each VM based on the guest-level task information, which is provided by each guest kernel. VMM prioritizes VMs by using the collected information about priorities and status of guest-level tasks in each VM. Our algorithm preferentially treats the VMs that run latency-sensitive applications in response to I/O by inspecting I/O pending status. The proposed algorithm is implemented and evaluated on Xen, which is a virtualization software widely used by many VM researchers.

The rest of this paper is organized as follows. Section 2 briefly describes related work and Xen architecture especially focusing on credit scheduler and I/O handling mechanism. Section 3 demonstrates the mechanism on how VMM uses information of guest-level tasks and proposes the priority-based VM scheduling algorithm. Section 4 evaluates our mechanism in terms of performance and fairness compared with the credit scheduler. Finally, section 5 summarizes the paper and presents the future work.

2 Related Work

2.1 Xen Virtual Machine Monitor

Xen is an open source virtual machine monitor based on para-virtualization, which makes a guest operating system aware of underlying virtualization layer through kernel modification [2]. The para-virtualization achieves large performance improvement by optimizing a guest operating system to virtualized architecture. In Xen architecture, a VM is referred to as a *domain* and the privileged VM, called *domain0*, controls other guest domains.

Credit scheduler, which is the default scheduler in Xen 3.0, manages CPU allocation for VMs based on *credit* value set by predefined weight of each VM [7]. The calculated credit is assigned to each VM every 30ms and is consumed proportional to the processing time of the VM; this consumption is conducted at the granularity of a tick interval (10ms).

Credit scheduler has three priorities: *BOOST(0)*, *UNDER(-1)*, and *OVER(-2)*. Two priorities (UNDER and OVER) are exclusively determined based on the remaining credit of a virtual CPU, which belongs to a VM. If the remaining credit of a virtual CPU is larger than zero, the virtual CPU has the priority of UNDER; otherwise, the virtual CPU has the priority of OVER. To guarantee fairness, a virtual CPU with UNDER priority is preferentially scheduled than those with OVER priority. When a virtual CPU with UNDER priority is woken by an event such as I/O completion, it acquires BOOST, which is the highest priority; this mechanism makes I/O-bound VMs be scheduled earlier than others. Although credit scheduler guarantees fairness, it results in a large response time of a latency-sensitive task with high priority since credit scheduler does not consider the priorities of individual tasks inside each VM.

Xen introduces *isolated driver domain*(IDD) to allow specific domains to access hardware directly. To do this, IDD includes native device drivers and conducts I/O operations on behalf of all guest domains [8]. A guest domain has virtual device driver, called a *frontend* driver, which communicates with a *backend* driver in an IDD. Xen uses shared I/O descriptor rings and event channels to communicate between an IDD and guest domains. I/O descriptor ring is a circular queue of I/O descriptor with producer/consumer pointers and is shared between an IDD and a guest domain. A virtual interrupt is delivered via an event channel for notification of I/O requests and completions.

2.2 Purpose-Specific Virtual Machine Scheduling

In addition to the fairness support of VM scheduling, there have been researches on VM scheduling optimization for specific workloads.

Govindan et al. [6] proposed a communication-aware scheduling algorithm to deal with the problem of VM scheduler on highly consolidated hosting platform. They showed that current VM schedulers do not consider communication behavior of VMs and thus result in degraded response time. Communication-aware scheduling algorithm takes into account network communication patterns when VMM chooses a VM to be scheduled. This algorithm preferentially schedules I/O-intensive VMs by using heuristic methods on the basis of the amount of I/O operations. This mechanism, however, could not improve the response time of the VM that has latency-sensitive tasks with high priority because it does not consider guest-level priority.

Cherkasova et al. [9,10] analyzed three CPU schedulers of Xen(BVT, sEDF, and credit) by measuring I/O throughput for different scheduling parameters. Their experiments demonstrate the performance impact of CPU allocation for domain0, which hosts I/O on behalf of guest domains. They show that frequent interventions of domain0 degrade I/O throughput because they incurs several domain switches and prevents guest domains from batching I/O requests. This work illustrates challenging issues related to VM scheduling mechanism for varied workloads.

Ongaro et al. [7] has explored the impact of VMM scheduling on I/O performance where different types of applications are run concurrently in multiple domains. Through various experiments, they improved I/O performance of Xen by optimizing the credit scheduler and alleviating the unfairness of event processing mechanism. The optimized credit scheduler sorts domains in run queue based on remaining credits so that short-running I/O domains are preferentially scheduled. It reduces the variance in the delivery of events by preventing the driver domain from tickling the scheduler when an virtual interrupt occurs. Their technique, however, cannot address a mixed domain, which include both I/O- and CPU-bound tasks. Our approach preferentially can schedule the latency-sensitive tasks, which is not even related to I/O or is in the mixed domain, by considering guest-level priority.

3 Guest-Aware Priority-Based Scheduling

3.1 Motivation

Since multiple guest domains share a single underlying hardware, a physical interrupt is not delivered to a corresponding domain immediately. A physical interrupt is received by VMM first and then is delivered to a destination domain. In the case of I/O interrupt, VMM forwards the received interrupt to domain0, which then is scheduled and notifies the target domain of the interrupt. Due to this procedure, the time when the target domain receives an I/O event depends on the status of the run queue of VMM. Domain0 is not guaranteed to be scheduled instantly after an interrupt, and furthermore several domains can be placed on the run queue between domain0 and the target domain. The target domain should wait until preceded domains finish their execution when it runs a latency-sensitive task with CPU-bound tasks simultaneously. Therefore, a latency-sensitive application in the target domain suffers low responsiveness, especially for highly consolidated server system.

This paper addresses the problem where current VM scheduler manages run queue without considering guest-level tasks. We propose the algorithm that assigns effective priority based on guest-level tasks. Our algorithm modifies the original run queue management that is simply sorted by credit-based priority. In our scheme, VMM dynamically re-assigns finer grain priorities than the original credit scheduler to guest domains based on the information about guest-level tasks in the run queue and wait queue. In addition, VMM infers which domain waits for I/O events by using the status of shared I/O descriptor rings in domain0.

3.2 Design

Our priority-based scheduling algorithm adopts an intrusive approach in that guest domains explicitly expose their local information to VMM. In this approach, a guest kernel is modified to inform VMM of the priority and status of its tasks using shared variables. Based on the information, the priority of a

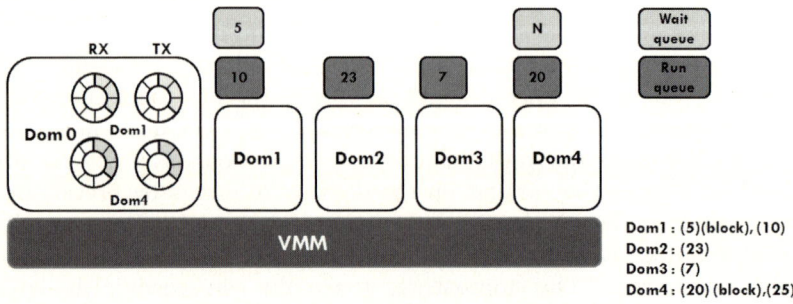

Fig. 1. Xen scheduling scheme

guest domain is simply taken as the highest priority of tasks in the run queue of the guest domain. Figure 1 shows the snapshot of guest domains and tasks of each guest domain in run queue and wait queue; the number in each task shows the priority of the task. First, we just use a simple approach by taking domain's priority as the priority of the highest active task in it. In this figure, dom1's priority is 10, which is the same as the highest priority of tasks in the run queue of dom1, and others are assigned similarly; smaller value is higher priority. Dom3 has the highest priority and will be scheduled first according to the simple approach.

This approach, however, has a limitation because it does not consider the tasks in wait queue. For example, since dom1 has a task with the highest priority, 5, in its wait queue, it should be scheduled earlier than dom3 if the event for which the task waits is pending at that time. To solve the above limitation, we take account of both run queue and wait queue of a guest domain to choose next VM to be scheduled. For this, a guest domain also has to expose the highest priority of the task that is on block state and is not included in run queue. In our approach, VMM inspects the status of shared descriptor rings to check whether I/O is pending with respect to the domain that has the blocked task with the highest priority. Hence, in the case of the above example, our mechanism makes dom1 scheduled in advance of others if corresponding I/O is pending at scheduling time.

The mechanism that inspects pending I/O and blocked tasks induces a problem if the pending I/O is unrelated with the blocked task of a guest domain scheduled by our algorithm. For this reason, it needs to correlate pending I/O with a blocked task exactly. The exact relation, however, can incur significant computational overhead due to the inspection of process-related clues from pending I/O. In case of TCP/IP networking, for example, VMM should examine almost all network packets including control packets such as ICMP or ARP to find a port number. Moreover, a guest domain should export port mapping of blocked tasks.

We propose a probabilistic method to relate pending I/O with the blocked task in the guest domain. This method makes a guest domain inform VMM of the list of recently woken tasks by I/O completion. As with LRU (Least Recently Used) mechanism, the VMM regards these tasks in this list as active tasks, which

Fig. 2. Probabilistic method for relation between I/O and blocked tasks

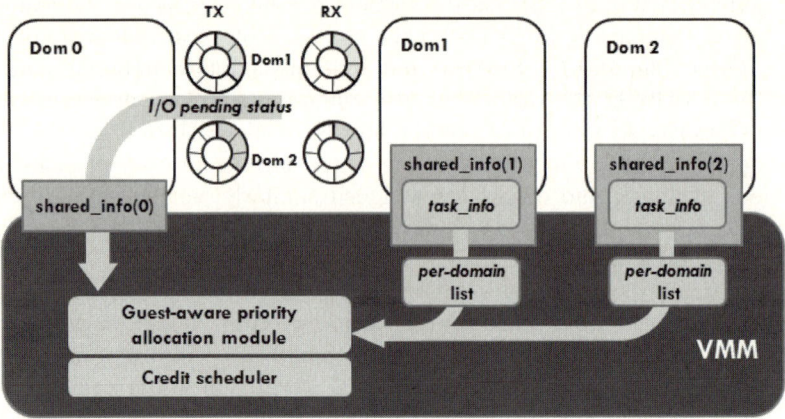

Fig. 3. System design

are likely to be involved with the I/O in near future. Figure 2 shows that two tasks,1 and 5, are recently woken by I/O while five tasks currently reside in wait queue of dom1. The per-domain list of dom1 maintains task 1 and 5 and can be referenced by VMM. When VMM prioritizes a guest domain, it checks both pending I/O and the per-domain list that maintains active I/O tasks. Only if pending I/O exists and the blocked task with high priority is within this list, the priority of blocked task is reflected to the effective priority of the guest domain.

3.3 Assumption

First, we assume that our VM system works in the trusted environment. In other words, there are no malicious users who intentionally raise the priority of its own task. The intentional priority boost can result in the performance degradation of other guest domains. Though VMM can detect and restrict malicious priority boosting, we left this as a policy issue.

Second, the exposed guest-level priorities should be coordinated by the unified scale since each operating system has its own priority system. In this paper, we only propose the way to scale priority systems of three prominent operating systems: Linux, FreeBSD, and Windows XP. The priority translation module have not yet implemented.

3.4 Implementation

Our implementation is based on Xen 3.0.4 and para-virtualized Linux 2.6.16. We modified a Linux kernel to share guest-level task information with VMM via the data structure shared between a guest kernel and VMM. As shown in figure 3, we introduce an additional structure which is called *task_info*. The shared structure contains information about runnable and blocked tasks with the highest five priorities. To relate pending I/O with blocked tasks, the shared structure also stores task IDs, which are recently woken by I/O. Since domain0 can access shared I/O descriptor rings for all guest domains, domain0 exposes pending I/O information to VMM via shared structure. The number of pending I/O is calculated by using producer/consumer pointers in the shared rings.

We use hierarchical priority scheme to support CPU fairness. In this scheme, the scheduler basically manages run queue in the original manner by three priorities of credit scheduler. When the scheduler chooses a guest domain to be scheduled next, an effective priority is decided on the basis of guest-level task information only if the selected guest domain has UNDER priority. Such mechanism prevents a guest domain with the highest priority task from monopolizing CPU resource. More importantly, this mechanism does not compromise CPU fairness of credit scheduler.

4 Evaluation

4.1 Evaluation Environment

We used Xen hosted server with pentium 4 2.4GHz CPU and 1.5G RAM for experiments. A client machine, which is used for measurement of network response time, has Pentium 4 2.4GHz CPU and 1G RAM. We allocated 256MB memory to domain 0, and 128MB to each guest domain. The weights of all domains are equally fixed for fair sharing. In our experiment, the number of domain varies from four to eight. We evaluate our scheduling algorithm in two approaches: *GAPS-RO (Guest-Aware Priority-based Scheduling - Run queue Only)*, a simple method that reflects the highest priority of tasks in run queue only, and *GAPS(Guest-Aware Priority-based Scheduling)*, a method that considers tasks in both run queue and wait queue as well as pending I/O in domain0.

4.2 Scheduling Latency

A physical interrupt is delivered to the target domain through the VMM and domain0 as described in the above background section. Since network or disk I/O is batched and requires I/O processing, it is difficult to measure pure scheduling latency for repeated experiments; scheduling latency means the elapsed time until the target domain is scheduled just after a corresponding interrupt occurs. We implement *vlatdriver*, a simple split driver consisting of frontend and backend, to exactly measure scheduling latency using a virtual interrupt. After generating a virtual interrupt, vlatdriver records timestamps at VMM, the backend driver in domain0, and the frontend driver in the target domain.

We run five guest domains with CPU-intensive tasks; one's priority is higher than others for each experiment. Figure 4 shows the average latency and the lowest 10% latency as worst case for credit scheduler and *GAPS*. The result

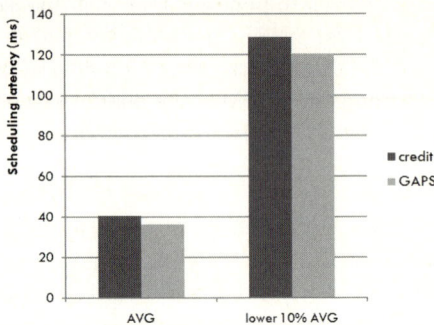

Fig. 4. Scheduling latency

demonstrates that scheduling latency is reduced for both the average and the worst case.

The scheduling latency of GAPS is more reduced compared with credit scheduler in the worst case than the average. Our algorithm preferentially schedules the domain with the highest effective priority when the domain is given UNDER priority; on the other hand, credit scheduler executes each domain in the round-robin manner in case where all domains are CPU-intensive. Therefore, GAPS decreases scheduling latency by reducing the waiting time until scheduling the domain with high priority.

4.3 I/O Response Time

We measure I/O response time through a ping-pong test in simple server/client environments; a client stressfully sends small requests to the server. Each guest domain runs a CPU-intensive task. Only dom1 also contains a server daemon with the highest priority. The priority of the CPU-intensive task in dom2 is higher than those of all CPU-intensive tasks in other domains, but is lower than that of the server daemon in Dom1. The experiment with this configuration evaluates the difference between *GAPS-RO* and *GAPS*. *GAPS-RO* preferentially schedules dom2 because the server daemon in dom1 is I/O-intensive and thus almost resides in wait queue waiting for a client's request. In *GAPS*, on the other hand, dom1 with the server daemon is likely to be scheduled earlier than dom2 by considering pending I/O and blocked tasks.

Figure 5 shows the response time of a client for credit scheduler, *GAPS-RO*, and *GAPS* as the number of guest domains increases. Both *GAPS-RO* and *GAPS* achieve lower response time than credit scheduler. In addition, *GAPS* reduces more response time than *GAPS-RO* since *GAPS* strives to schedule dom1 in advance of others. As the number of guest domains increases, the improvement in response time is larger. Consequently, our scheduler accomplishes low responsiveness of latency-sensitive applications on high consolidated environment.

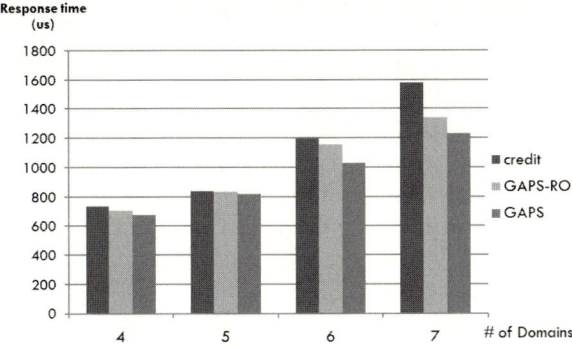

Fig. 5. Average I/O response time

Table 1. CPU fairness: The consumed CPU for each domain is normalized on the basis of dom1

	Dom1	Dom2	Dom3	Dom4
Credit scheduler	1	1	0.999	1
GAPS	1	1	0.998	0.994

4.4 Fairness Guarantee

We evaluate that our scheduling algorithm does not compromise CPU fairness supported by credit scheduler. Four guest domains run CPU-intensive tasks, and only dom1 additionally runs server daemon with the highest priority similar to the above experiment. The dom4's task has the lowest priority to show the possibility of starvation.

Table 1 shows the CPU allocation for each guest domain. The CPU allocation is calculated from the consumed credit of each guest domain during the experiment. All results are normalized by that of dom1. Although dom4 has slightly less CPU allocation than others for our scheduler, this difference is negligible. Our scheduling algorithm, therefore, still guarantees CPU fairness and incurs no starvation of the guest domain including the lowest priority task. However, we do not address I/O fairness, which is not considered in the original credit scheduler.

5 Conclusion and Future Work

Although virtualization technologies have advanced in terms of high degree of consolidation, the absence of support for latency-sensitive workload could be an obstacle to services that need good quality of responsiveness. To address this problem, we introduce a guest-aware priority-based scheduling, which runs on Xen-based system, to preferentially schedule high-priority and latency-sensitive tasks. Our mechanism guarantees CPU fairness because it is implemented over the credit scheduler of Xen.

In this paper, the proposed mechanism is achieved by the intrusive way for VMs to send information of guest-level information to VMM. The intrusive approach has some drawbacks. First, this approach requires guest kernel modifications. This requirement cannot be applied to closed-source operating systems such as Windows. Second, the guest-level information could be untrusted because the information is explicitly informed by guest domains; the intrusive way can impede VM isolation in the untrusted environment.

As future work, we are developing the non-intrusive mechanism for reducing the response time of latency-sensitive tasks. To support responsiveness without kernel modifications, we should determine a VM that has latency-sensitive tasks by inferring from I/O behavior and scheduling pattern. By this approach, we will achieve the responsiveness as well as fairness while preserving VM isolation.

References

1. Sugerman, J., Venkitachalam, G., Lim, B.H.: Virtualizing i/o devices on vmware workstation's hosted virtual machine monitor. In: Proc. of the USENIX Annual Technical Conf., Berkeley, CA, USA, pp. 1–14. USENIX Association (2001)
2. Barham, P., Dragovic, B., Fraser, K., Hand, S., Harris, T., Ho, A., Neugebauer, R., Pratt, I., Warfield, A.: Xen and the art of virtualization. In: SOSP 2003: Proceedings of the nineteenth ACM symposium on Operating systems principles, pp. 164–177. ACM, New York (2003)
3. Neumann, D., Kulkarni, D., Kunze, A., Rogers, G., Verplanke, E.: Intel Virtualization Technology in embedded and communications infrastructure applications. 10(3) (August 2006)
4. VMware: http://www.vmware.com
5. Lin, B., Dinda, P.A.: Vsched: Mixing batch and interactive virtual machines using periodic real-time scheduling. In: SC 2005, p. 8. IEEE Computer Society, Los Alamitos (2005)
6. Govindan, S., Nath, A.R., Das, A., Urgaonkar, B., Sivasubramaniam, A.: Xen and co.: communication-aware cpu scheduling for consolidated xen-based hosting platforms. In: VEE 2007: Proceedings of the 3rd international conference on Virtual execution environments, pp. 126–136. ACM, New York (2007)
7. Ongaro, D., Cox, A.L., Rixner, S.: Scheduling i/o in virtual machine monitors. In: VEE 2008: Proceedings of the fourth ACM SIGPLAN/SIGOPS international conference on Virtual execution environments, pp. 1–10. ACM, New York (2008)
8. Fraser, K., Hand, S., Neugebauer, R., Pratt, A.W.I., Williamson, M.: Safe hardware access with the xen virtual machine monitor. In: Proc. of Workshop on Operating System and Architectural Support for the on demand IT Infrastructure (2004)
9. Cherkasova, L., Gupta, D., Vahdat, A.: Comparison of the three cpu schedulers in xen. SIGMETRICS Perform. Eval. Rev. 35(2), 42–51 (2007)
10. Cherkasova, L., Gupta, D., Vahdat, A.: When virtual is harder than real: Resource allocation challenges in virtual machine based it environments. Technical Report HPL-2007-25 (February 2007)

Dynamic Pipeline Mapping (DPM)*

A. Moreno[1], E. César[2], A. Guevara[2], J. Sorribes[2],
T. Margalef[2], and E. Luque[2]

[1] Escola Universitària Salesiana de Sarrià, Passeig Sant Joan Bosco 74, 08017
Barcelona, Spain
amoreno@euss.es

[2] Departament Arquitectura de Computadors i Sistemes Operatius, Universitat
Autònoma de Barcelona, 08193 Bellaterra, Spain
{eduardo.cesar@,alex.guevara@caos.,joan.sorribes@,
tomas.margalef@,emilio.luque@}uab.es

Abstract. Parallel/distributed application development is an extremely difficult task for non-expert programmers, and support tools are therefore needed for all phases of the development cycle of this kind of applications. In particular, dynamic performance tuning tools can take advantage of the knowledge about the application's structure given by a skeleton based programming tool. This study shows the definition of a strategy for dynamically improving the performance of pipeline applications. This strategy, which has been called Dynamic Pipeline Mapping, improves the application's throughput by gathering the pipe's fastest stages and replicating its slowest ones. We have evaluated the new algorithm by experimentation and simulation, and results show that DPM leads to significant performance improvements.

1 Introduction

Parallel/distributed programming constitutes a highly promising approach to the improvement of the performance of many applications. However, in comparison to sequential programming, several new problems have emerged in all phases of the development cycle. One of the best ways to solve these problems would be to develop tools that support the design, coding, and analysis and/or tuning of parallel/distributed applications.

In the particular case of performance analysis and/or tuning, it is important to note that the best way for analyzing and tuning parallel/distributed applications depends on some of their behavioral characteristics. If the application being tuned behaves in a regular way, then a static analysis will be sufficient. However, if the application changes its behavior from execution to execution, or even within a single execution, then dynamic monitoring and tuning techniques should be used instead.

The key issue in dynamic monitoring and tuning is that decisions must be taken efficiently while minimizing intrusion on the application. We show that this

---

* This work was supported by MEC under contract TIN2007-64974.

is easier to achieve when the tuning tool uses a performance model associated to the structure of the application. Knowing the application's structure is not a problem if a programming tool, based on the use of skeletons or frameworks, is used for its development.

This study, focused on a comprehensive performance model associated to the Pipeline framework, represents a further step to our previous contributions [1], [2] and [3] to the development of performance models associated to the application structure for dynamic performance tuning.

The Pipeline framework is a well-known parallel programming structure used as the most direct way to implement algorithms that consist of performing an orderly sequence of essentially identical calculations on a sequence of inputs. Each of these calculations can be broken down into a certain number of different stages, which can be concurrently applied to different inputs.

The possible inefficiencies of pipelined applications are also well known. At first, the concurrency is limited at the beginning of the computation as the pipe is filled, and at the end of the computation as the pipe is drained. Programmers should deal with this inefficiency at the design phase of the application because the way to avoid it is to assure that the number of calculations the application will perform are substantially higher than the number of stages of the pipe.

Secondly, it is important not to have any significant differences among the computational efforts of the pipe stages, because the application throughput of a pipe is determined by its slowest stage. This is the most important inefficiency of this structure, and the most difficult to overcome because it does not depend exclusively on the application design, but also on run-time conditions. Consequently, our study is focused on dealing with this drawback, which is suitable for being solved dynamically.

This paper is organized in six sections, the first is this introduction, the second reviews some relevant related studies, the third shows the expressions defined in order to model the stages of a pipeline, the fourth describes the Dynamic Pipeline Mapping algorithm we propose in this study, the fifth assesses the algorithm through simulation and synthetic experiments, and finally, the sixth section shows the main conclusions of this study.

2 Related Work

There are several studies about the performance modelling of pipeline applications. Some of them propose highly constrained models, such as Subhlok and Vondram [4] and Lee et al. [5]. The former proposes a mapping algorithm which optimizes latency under some throughput constraints for purely linear pipes, while the latter defines a policy for maximizing the throughput of homogeneous pipelines (those where each stage processes a homogeneous group of tasks).

Nevertheless, there are studies, such as Hoang and Rabey [6], focused on more generic pipeline applications. This work proposes an algorithm for maximizing the throughput that has been improved lately by Yang et al. [7] and Guirado et al. [8] considering that the application performs several iterations.

On the other hand, Almeida et al. [9] have defined an algorithm, based on gathering stages on a processor, to improve the performance of a pipeline application on a cluster of heterogeneous processors. Their model comprehends the whole life of the application, including the filling-in and draining phases of the execution of a pipeline, which they try to minimize.

Another highly relevant study in this area is the Murray Cole's group of the School of Informatics of the University of Edinburgh. They have realized that using skeletons carries with it considerable information about implied scheduling dependences and have decided to use process algebras (specifically PEPA [10]) for modeling them.

All these studies are mainly focused on the static analysis of the pipeline application. This is the main difference regarding our model proposal, which is intended to dynamically tuning the application's performance. Consequently, we consider that filling-in and draining the pipe are transient phases, whose inefficiencies cannot be solved dynamically. On the other hand, we improve the application's performance by gathering fast consecutive stages in the same processor, which leads to lower communication costs, and by replicating the slowest stages in several processors in order to increase their throughput.

3 Modelling the Stages of a Pipeline Application

This section introduces the mathematical expressions defined to model the performance of a replicated stage, as well as those defined to model the performance of a set of stages assigned to the same processor. For these expressions we will use the following terminology:

- P = Number of available processors.
- N = Number of pipeline stages.
- Tr_i = Inverse throughput of stage i, which is the time needed by the stage i to process each task assuming that this stage is not sharing processor with any other. We call this the *independent production time* of stage i.
- Tr_i' = Inverse throughput of stage i when it is sharing processor with other stages. We call this the *grouped production time* of stage i.
- $Tr_{i replica}$ = Inverse throughput of stage i when it has been replicated in several processors. We call this the *replicated production time* of stage i.
- Tp_k = Inverse throughput of processor k, which is the elapsed time from moment a task arrives to the first stage until it leaves the last stage assigned to processor k. We call this the *production time of processor k*.

3.1 Replicated Stage Performance Model

It has been earlier shown [8] that the overall throughput of a pipeline application is determined by slowest stage. Consequently, the performance of the application can be improved by replicating that particular stage. We have chosen a very simple approach for modeling a replicated stage, which consists of dividing the independent production time of the non replicated stage by the number of processors used to replicate it (P_i):

$$Tr_{ireplica} = \frac{Tr_i}{P_i}. \tag{1}$$

This is an oversimplification of the real system because it does not take into consideration the overhead introduced by the extra communications, nor the time needed to manage the replicas. However, it is good enough for our purposes and helps keeping the overall performance model simple.

3.2 Grouped Stages Performance Model

Assembling several fast consecutive stages in the same processor leads to performance improvements because it decreases the communication cost and, even more important, it releases processing resources that can be dedicated to the replication of the slowest stages.

We have modeled a set of grouped stages as the production time of the processor there are assigned to (Tp_k). It is calculated adding up the independent production times (Tr_i) of each gathered stage:

$$Tp_k = \sum Tr_i. \tag{2}$$

We will need the independent production time (Tr_i) of an individual stage in a group in order to evaluate the overall pipeline performance model. However, when a stage is sharing processor with others stages, it is not possible to measure its Tr_i because, as far as we are only inserting instrumentation in the application code, any measure will include the stage execution time plus the time it has spent waiting for the processor while other stages were executing. This is the reason why we have given a different name (Tr'_i) to the grouped production time of a gathered stage. Consequently, we will use this time (Tr'_i) and the total processor production time (Tp_k) to estimate the independent production time of a stage in a group according to Eq. (3), which assigns to a stage a share of the overall group execution time (Tp_k) proportional to its observed weigh ($Tr'_i / \sum Tr'_i$) within the group.

$$Tr_i = Tp_k \frac{Tr'_i}{\sum Tr'_i}. \tag{3}$$

4 Dynamic Pipeline Mapping

A pipeline application will reach its best performance when the processor production times (Tp_k) of every processor holding one or more stages, and the production time of every replicated stage ($Tr_{ireplica}$) are the same, it is, when the workload is balanced among the available processors. Moreover, in any other case the slowest stage will determine the throughput of the application.

We have defined an algorithm called Dynamic Pipeline Mapping with the objective of improving the performance of a pipeline application. The main idea is to gather fast consecutive stages and to replicate slower ones in order to find the best possible mapping leading to the best possible load balancing.

DPM consists of three phases, which are executed iteratively at runtime in order to adapt the mapping to the current conditions of the application:

1. *Measurement or estimation of independent production time (Tr_i).* It is obtained for every pipe stage, including those assembled with other stages in the same processor. In this case Eq. (3) will be used to estimate this value.
2. *Alternative mapping proposal.* Knowing the (Tr_i) of every stage makes it possible to calculate the ideal throughput of the pipe ($\frac{P}{\sum Tr_i}$) and, given the current mapping of the application, it is possible to propose a new distribution of stages that gets as closer as possible to this throughput. We use the term *mean production time*, Tp_{ideal}, as the inverse of the ideal throughput of the pipe.
3. *Proposal evaluation and implementation.* The proposal generated in the second phase is evaluated comparing its predicted throughput with the current one. If the gain is good enough then it will be worth implementing the new mapping.

From the point of view of this study, the second phase is the core of this algorithm. It consists of two steps, in the first one, aimed to release resources, the whole pipe is traversed from its first stage identifying groups of stages whose production times are below the mean, while in the second step the freed resources are used for increasing the throughput of the slowest stages.

In this first step, the pipe is traversed from its first stage. If a replicated, a single or a set of grouped stages are found whose production time is below the mean production time (Tp_{ideal}), some resources will be released according to the following rules:

- *Replicated stage.* The desirable number of replicas (P_i) is calculated using Eq. (4). Then the remaining replicas are proposed for elimination, releasing the processors they were assigned to.

$$P_i = \frac{Tr_i}{Tp_{ideal}} \quad (4)$$

- *Set of single or grouped stages.* Using Eq. (5) a new gathering, including more stages, is proposed in order to release some processors.

$$Tp_{ideal} = \sum Tr_i \quad (5)$$

On the other hand, if the algorithm founds a replicated, single, or a set of grouped stages whose production time is above the mean production time (Tp_{ideal}), it will use some spare processors in order to approach its production time to Tp_{ideal} in the following way:

- *Replicated or single stage.* The desirable number of replicas (P_i) is calculated using Eq. (4) and the needed replicas must be added. However, this process will be performed at the next step of the algorithm when the number of available resources are known.
- *Grouped stages.* The current gathering should be broken up in order to improve its production time. We use Eq. (5) to determine the partition of the gathering.

Finally, in the second step, knowing the available resources and the stages or replicated stages that need processors, the algorithm assigns processors to stages or replicated stages that need them, because these are the ones which have greatest influence on the global performance of the pipeline application.

In order to clarify how this algorithm would work, we propose a particular application example. It is assumed that initially the application state is the one shown in Figure 1(a). There are 5 stages (E1, E2 ... E5) and 6 processors (P1, P2 ... P6). Tr_i is the independent production time of stage i in time units.

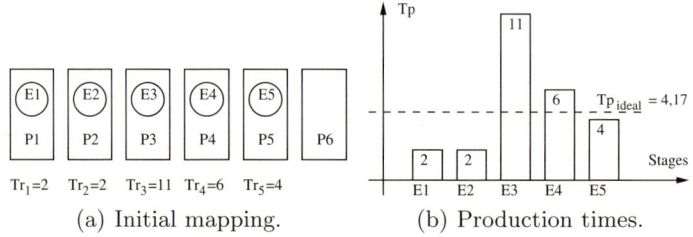

(a) Initial mapping.   (b) Production times.

Fig. 1. Application example, initial mapping of 5 stages and 6 processors

First, the mean production time, Tp_{ideal}, is calculated:

$$Tp_{ideal} = \frac{\sum Tr_i}{P} = 4.17. \qquad (6)$$

The relationship between the mean production time and the independent production of each stage can be seen in Figure 1(b).

Then, the second phase of the algorithm is executed. First we evaluate the Eq. (5) and we see that if we group the stages E1 and E2, the gathering production time will be 2+2=4, a value closer to the ideal production time 4.17. As a consequence processor P2 would be released to be used later.

Next, the stage E3 is above the mean production time stage and its replication with the free resources is proposed. The desirable number of replicas (P_i) is calculated using Eq. (7) and we obtain 2.64 as result. Finally, we round up to 3 processors. Figure 2(a) shows the proposed mapping and Figure 1(b) the respective production times.

$$P_i = \frac{Tr_i}{Tp_{ideal}} = \frac{11}{4.17} = 2.64 \qquad (7)$$

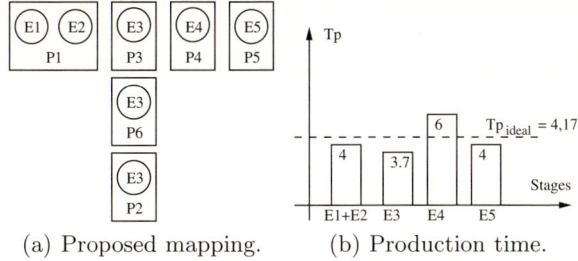

Fig. 2. Application example, mapping proposed by Dynamic Pipeline Mapping algorithm

In the third phase of the algorithm the proposal is evaluated. As the pipeline production time is defined by the maximum production time, with the proposed mapping this value changes from 11 (stage E3 in Figure 1(a)) to 6 (stage E4 in Figure 2(a)). Consequently, the throughput of the pipeline would be improved significantly.

5 Algorithm Assessment

This section describes the evaluation of the Dynamic Pipeline Mapping algorithm through experimentation and simulation. We have used simulation because it allows the systematic evaluation of hundreds of cases with few resources and in a reasonable period of time, and we have validated simulation results executing several scenarios in a cluster of workstations.

The simulation method considers that the independent production time (Tr_i) of each stage can be modeled as a random variable with a normal distribution and with parametric mean (μ) and standard deviation (σ). Therefore, in order to build a particular execution scenario, a sample value of each random variable is generated. Next, the execution time of the application is calculated for a MPI-like mapping (Te_{MPI}) and, finally, the DPM algorithm is applied and the execution time (Te_{DPM}) for its proposed mapping is also calculated.

The simulation examples are shown in Table 1. Independent production time (Tr_i) samples were obtained from a normal distributed random variable with $\mu = 10$ and $\sigma = 8$ time units. Table 1 shows the ratio between execution time

Table 1. Simulation results of 1000 executions scenarios for 32 processors pipeline

Stages	Mean of Te_{MPI}/Te_{DPM}	Standard deviation of Te_{MPI}/Te_{DPM}
16	1.36	0.23
32	1.55	0.26
64	1.24	0.33

of MPI-like mapping (Te_{MPI}) and execution time of DPM algorithm mapping (Te_{MPI}) of 1000 scenarios. Results clearly indicate that for an overwhelming number of cases applying DPM leads to significant improvements in the application performance. Although, the algorithm obviously produces better results when there are more available processors than stages.

In order to validate simulation results we have written a MPI synthetic pipeline program that allows the definition of the number of stages of the pipe, the number and size of data elements to be processed, the computation time associated to each stage, the number of instances of each replicated stage, and the stages included in each grouped stage.

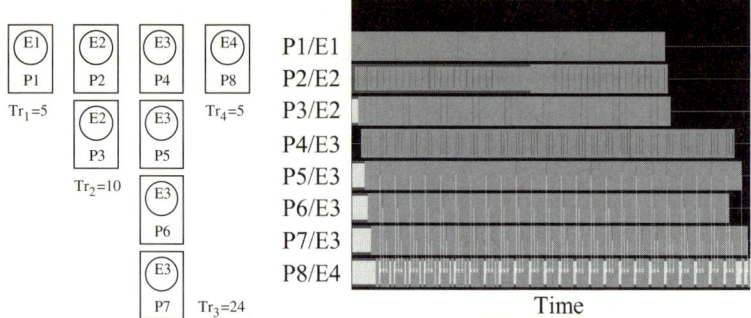

(a) Mapping of 4 stages and 8 processors case.

(b) Execution trace with DPM algorithm.

Fig. 3. First experimental scenario: 4-stage pipe on a cluster of 8 homogeneous workstations (independent production time,Tr, is in ms)

Figure 3 shows the execution trace of a 4-stage pipe on a cluster of 8 homogeneous workstations. The number of data elements processed are 100 and the message size is 100 bytes (low communication cost). In addition, the computation load is 5 ms for stages 1 and 4, 10 ms for stage 2, and 24 ms for stage 4.

We have compared the execution time of the MPI-like mapping against the DPM proposed mapping. In this case DPM has several available processors that can be used for replicating slower stages. Consequently, the algorithm proposes the mapping shown in Figure 3(a), where one extra instance of stage 2 and three new instances of stage 4 are created. The execution time of the application using the MPI-like mapping is 2.43 s, while the one for the DPM proposed mapping is 0.64 s, which is 3.8 times better.

Figure 4 shows the results for a less favorable case, where an 8-stage pipe is executed on the same cluster using the MPI-like mapping and the DPM proposed mapping (Figure 4(a)). The number and size of messages are the same than in the previous example. However, in this case the computation load is 150 ms for

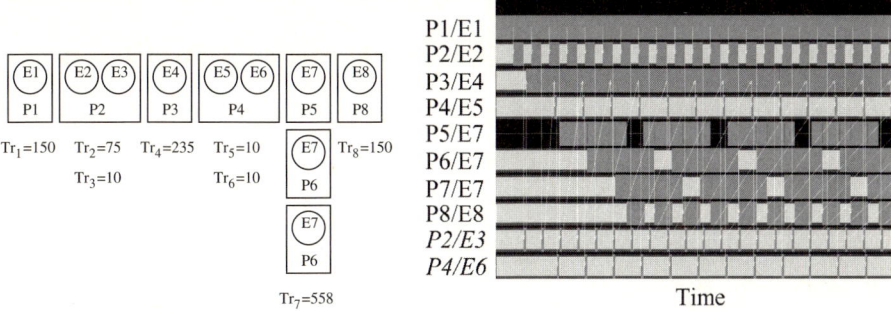

(a) Mapping of 8 stages and 8 processors case.
(b) Execution trace with DPM algorithm.

Fig. 4. Second experimental scenario: 8-stage pipe on a cluster of 8 homogeneous workstations (independent production time,Tr, is in ms)

stages 1 and 8; 75 ms for stage 2; 10 ms for stages 3, 5, and 6; 235 ms for stage 4; and 558 ms for stage 7.

In this case DPM has no spare processors at the beginning, so it proposes to group stages 1 and 2 (grouped production time of 85 ms), and stages 4 and 5 (grouped production time of 20 ms). These actions liberate 2 processors that are used to introduce 2 extra instances of stage 7, leading to the mapping shown in Figure 4(a). The execution time of the application using the MPI-like mapping is 62.03 s, while the one for the DPM proposed mapping is 26.6 s, which is 3.33 times better. These results show that for both cases the DPM proposed mapping led to significant performance gains.

6 Conclusions

We have proposed a strategy for dynamically improving the performance of pipeline applications. The resulting algorithm, which has been called Dynamic Pipeline Mapping, is intended to improve the application's throughput by gathering the pipe's fastest stages and replicating its slowest ones, and it is based on simple analytical models of the pipeline stages behavior.

In addition, we have shown simulated and experimental results that demonstrate that the DPM proposed mappings usually lead to significant performance improvements that justify the effort of dynamically implementing the necessary changes.

Completing the analytical models to include efficient communication management considerations is the next challenge. However, we believe that DPM is a relevant contribution for developing model based dynamic performance tuning tools.

References

1. Cesar, E., Moreno, A., Sorribes, J., Luque, E.: Modeling master/worker applications for automatic performance tuning. Parallel Comput. 32(7), 568–589 (2006)
2. Cesar, E., Sorribes, J., Luque, E.: Modeling pipeline applications in poetries. In: Cunha, J.C., Medeiros, P.D. (eds.) Euro-Par 2005. LNCS, vol. 3648, pp. 83–95. Springer, Heidelberg (2005)
3. Morajko, A., Cesar, E., Caymes-Scutari, P., Margalef, T., Sorribes, J., Luque, E.: Automatic tuning of master/worker applications. In: Cunha, J.C., Medeiros, P.D. (eds.) Euro-Par 2005. LNCS, vol. 3648, pp. 95–103. Springer, Heidelberg (2005)
4. Subhlok, J., Vondran, G.: Optimal use of mixed task and data parallelism for pipelined computations. Journal of Parallel and Distributed Computing 60(3), 297–319 (2000)
5. Lee, M., Liu, W., Prasanna, V.K.: A mapping methodology for designing software task pipelines for embedded signal processing. In: IPPS/SPDP Workshops, pp. 937–944 (1998)
6. Hoang, P.D., Rabaey, J.: Scheduling of dsp programs onto multiprocessors for maximum throughput. IEEE Transactions on Signal Processing 41(6), 2225–2235 (1993)
7. Yang, M.-T., Kasturi, R., Sivasubramaniam, A.: A pipeline-based approach for scheduling video processing algorithms on now. Transactions on Parallel and Distributed Systems 14(2), 119–130 (2003)
8. Guirado, F., Ripoll, A., Roig, C., Luque, E.: Exploitation of parallelism for applications with an input data stream: optimal resource-throughput tradeoffs. In: PDP 2005. 13th Euromicro Conference on Parallel, Distributed and Network-Based Processing, 9-11 February, pp. 170–178 (2005)
9. Almeida, F., González, D., Moreno, L.M., Rodríguez, C.: An analytical model for pipeline algorithms on heterogeneous clusters. In: Proceedings of the 9th European PVM/MPI Users' Group Meeting on Recent Advances in Parallel Virtual Machine and Message Passing Interface, London, UK, pp. 441–449. Springer, Heidelberg (2002)
10. Gilmore, S., Hillston, J., Kloul, L., Ribaudo, M.: Pepa nets: a structured performance modelling formalism. Perform. Eval. 54(2), 79–104 (2003)

Formal Model and Scheduling Heuristics for the Replica Migration Problem

Nikos Tziritas[1], Thanasis Loukopoulos[1], Petros Lampsas[2], and Spyros Lalis[1]

[1] Dept. of Computer and Communication Engineering, University of Thessaly,
Glavani 37, 38221 Volos, Greece
{nitzirit,luke,lalis}@inf.uth.gr
[2] Dept. of Informatics and Computer Technology, Technological Educational Institute (TEI)
of Lamia, 3rd km. Old Ntl. Road Athens, 35100 Lamia, Greece
plam@teilam.gr

Abstract. Replication of the most popular objects is often used in distributed data provision systems to reduce access time and improve availability. In fact, a given replica placement scheme may have to be redefined as object popularity changes. Given two replica placement schemes X^{old} and X^{new}, the Replica Migration Problem (RMP) is to compute a schedule of replica transfers and deletions that lead from X^{old} to X^{new} in the shortest time possible. In this paper, we provide a rigorous problem formulation and prove that even for trivial cases RMP is intractable. We also propose a set of heuristics and evaluate them for different scenarios using simulations.

1 Introduction

Replication is crucial to the performance of distributed data provision systems such as web and video server networks. The issue of defining a replication scheme, i.e. which data objects to replicate on which nodes, was studied extensively under the context of the replica placement problem (RPP) [1], [2], [3], [4]. Equally important, however, is to derive an implementation strategy for obtaining the desired replication scheme. The problem can be briefly stated as: *given two replication schemes X^{old} and X^{new}, find a series of object transfers and deletions that lead from X^{old} to X^{new} in the shortest time possible*. We refer to this as the Replica Migration Problem (RMP).

RMP has been tackled in [5] and [6] with focus primarily on disk farms, while [7] focuses on content distribution networks. In all these cases the aim is to optimize the migration time. More recently the problem has been incorporated in task scheduling over the Grid [3] where the aim is to minimize the final makespan of task executions. The problem is also studied in [8] but with the aim to minimize network usage. In [5] and [7] object sizes are assumed to be equal, while in [5] and [6] hosting nodes are assumed to be fully connected. We differ from the above work both in the scope of the problem assumptions (which are more general) and the heuristics we propose.

Our contributions are as follows: (i) we provide a rigorous formulation of RMP as a mixed integer programming problem with some of the constraints being quadratic; (ii) we prove that even for trivial cases RMP-decision is NP-complete given different object sizes; (iii) we propose and experiment with heuristics capturing different problem parameters such as deletions and the creation of auxiliary replicas. To the best of our knowledge this is the first time RMP is stated and tackled in this way, with the aim of minimizing replica migration time under various important parameters such as object size, network bandwidth and storage space.

The rest of the paper is organized as follows. Section 2 presents the system model, and Section 3 gives the formal problem statement. Then, Section 4 describes our heuristics, which are evaluated via simulations in Section 5.

2 Problem Description

Consider a distributed system with M servers and N data objects. Let S_i and $s(S_i)$ denote the name and the storage capacity (in abstract data units) of the ith server, $1 \leq i \leq M$. Also, let O_k and $s(O_k)$ denote the kth data object and its size, $1 \leq k \leq N$. We say that S_i is a *replicator* of O_k if it holds a replica thereof. Let X be a $M \times N$ *replication matrix* used to encode a replication scheme as follows: $X_{ik}=1$ if S_i is a replicator of O_k, else $X_{ik}=0$. Servers communicate via point-to-point *links*. A link between S_i and S_j, if it exists, is denoted by l_{ij} and has a capacity of c_{ij}, representing the number of data units that can be transferred via the link per (abstract) time unit. Let T_{ikj} denote the transfer of object O_k from source S_i to destination S_j. This involves sending $s(O_k)$ data units along a path from S_i to S_j. The transfer will complete after $s(O_k)/r$ time units, where r is the transfer rate of that path, equal to the available capacity of the bottleneck link. Both c_{ij} and r are integers, denoting multiples of one data unit/time unit. Finally, the deletion of O_k at S_i, denoted by D_{ik}, does not introduce any time penalty.

The problem we tackle is to define a series of transfers and deletions so that starting from the current replication scheme X^{old} we reach a new replication scheme X^{new} in the shortest time. We illustrate it through the example of Figure 1, using a network of 6 servers with 2 objects: A and B. In X^{old}, S_1 and S_2 hold object A whereas S_5 and S_6 hold object B. Objects must be swapped in X^{new}. Assuming object size and server capacity of 4, schedule $\{D_{5B}, T_{1A5}, D_{2A}, T_{6B2}, D_{6B}, T_{1A6}, D_{1A}, T_{2B1}\}$ implements X^{new} in 6 time units. The start and end time of the transfers are listed in the table of Figure 1. Transfers can occur in parallel, even if their paths overlap, provided that there is enough capacity available. Specifically, in this schedule, T_{1A5} via links l_{13}, l_{34} and l_{45} is performed in parallel to T_{6B2} via links l_{64}, l_{34} and l_{32}, with a rate of 4 and 2, respectively. However, if link l_{34} had a capacity of just 5 instead of 8, at least one of these transfers would have been performed at a lower rate, if done in parallel.

It is important to note that it is not always possible to find a schedule, even for valid problem statements where X^{new} respects the server capacity constraints. For example, if two servers with enough storage capacity to hold just one object must exchange their objects, and there are no other servers that can be used as a source for these objects, a deadlock-lie situation occurs, as shown in Figure 2. The investigation of such cases is out of the scope of this paper. Therefore we extend the problem formulation by assuming that there is one *primary replica* for each object O_k that remains fixed on a designated *primary server* P_k in both X^{old} and X^{new}.

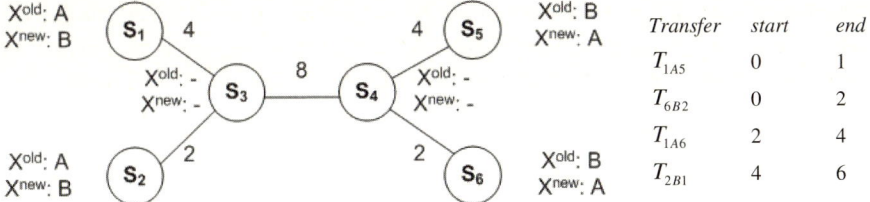

Fig. 1. An example problem instance

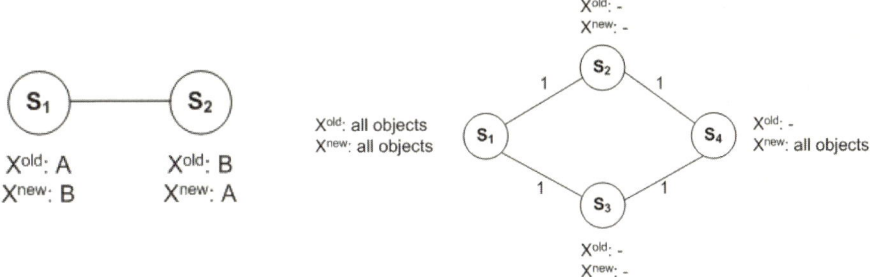

Fig. 2. A deadlock example **Fig. 3.** Network construction for 2-proc reduction

Continuing with the example of Figure 1, one may observe that the aforementioned schedule is not optimal. The optimal schedule is $\{T_{1A4}, T_{5B3}, D_{1A}, D_{2A}, D_{5B}, D_{6B}, T_{4A5}, T_{4A6}, T_{3B1}, T_{3B2}, D_{4A}, D_{3B}\}$ with a makespan of 3 time units. This schedule is non-trivial in the sense that it involves *auxiliary* replicas, i.e., replicas that are not required in X^{new} and will be deleted at some point further in the schedule.

In fact RMP-decision is intractable. Due to space limitations we provide a proof sketch by reducing the 2-processor scheduling problem (2-proc) [9], which is defined as follows: *given a set of tasks N and their execution times, assign them to 2 processors so that the total makespan is minimized*. For each 2-proc instance we construct the network of Figure 3, where N objects exist and their sizes correspond one to one with the execution times of the N tasks. X^{old} consists of primary replicas stored at S_1, while in X^{new} one additional replica per object must be created at S_4. Notice that the two paths connecting S_1 and S_4 play the role of the two processors in 2-proc. As a consequence, there exists a solution to 2-proc if and only if a solution exists for RMP-decision in the problem instance of Figure 3. Thus, RMP-decision is NP-complete.

3 Integer Programming Formulation

We formulate RMP as a mixed integer programming (MIP) problem with some constraints being quadratic. The idea is to consider a schedule of transfers and deletions, similar to the example of Figure 1, and impose the respective validity requirements. Each transfer is modelled using a *transfer-start* and a *transfer-end* event. Deletions correspond to a single *delete* event.

The formulation assumes a known upper bound for the number of events in the optimal schedule, let Z. An additional (dummy) void event is needed at the end of the schedule in order to confirm that the desired replication matrix has been reached after the Zth event. Thus, the total length of the schedule is $Z+1$, its tail comprised of at least one void event (or more if the actual optimal schedule involves fewer than Z events).

For the case where no auxiliary replicas are created, a conservative value for Z is: 2 × *outstanding replicas* + *superfluous replicas* (outstanding are the new replicas that must be created and superfluous are the old replicas that need to be deleted to reach X^{new}). This corresponds to the number of required transfers (2 events per transfer) and deletions (1 event per deletion), which can be trivially determined as a function of X^{old} and X^{new}. In case auxiliary replicas can be created, the upper bound for Z is: 2 × *outstanding replicas* + *superfluous replicas* + 3 × *auxiliary replicas* (for each auxiliary replica, 2 events are needed to create it, and 1 event is needed to delete it). Given that the number of auxiliary replicas for each outstanding replica cannot exceed $(M-2)$ (worst case, an auxiliary replica is created on all servers except the primary server and the server where the outstanding replica is to be created): $Z \leq (3M-4)*outstanding + superfluous$. Note that these bounds do not hold for schedules that may contain deletions and subsequent re-creations of replicas needed in X^{new}.

Table 1 summarizes the variables used to describe the events in the schedule as well as additional problem variables. Unless otherwise stated, the indices in the variables take the following values: $1 \leq k \leq N$, $1 \leq i,j \leq M$, $1 \leq u,v \leq Z$.

Table 1. Problem variables

Variable	Description
ST_{ikj}^{u}	1 iff the uth event is the start of transfer T_{ikj}, 0 otherwise
ET_{ikj}^{uv}	1 iff the uth event is the end of transfer T_{ikj} whose start is the vth event in the schedule ($v<u$), 0 otherwise
D_{ik}^{u}	1 iff the uth event is the deletion of O_k at S_i, 0 otherwise
V^{u}	1 iff the uth event is void, 0 otherwise
X_{ik}^{u}	1 iff S_i has a replica of O_k before the uth event occurs, 0 otherwise
p_{ij}^{u}	1 iff the uth event is a transfer start/end event and link l_{ij} is part of the corresponding transfer path, 0 otherwise
r^{u}	the transfer rate for the uth event (integer$\neq 0$)
t^{u}	the clock time when the uth event takes place (real≥ 0)

The Replica Migration Problem can then be stated as: *minimize t^{Z+1} subject to constraints (1)-(11)*. Constraints (1)-(6) relate event types among themselves and with the current replication matrix, (7)-(9) concern path reservations for transfers, while (10)-(11) tackle bandwidth assignment and time calculation.

$$\sum_{\forall i}\sum_{\forall k}\sum_{\forall j}\sum_{\forall v} ET_{ikj}^{uv} + \sum_{\forall i}\sum_{\forall k}\sum_{\forall j} ST_{ikj}^{u} + \sum_{\forall i}\sum_{\forall k} D_{ik}^{u} + V^{u} = 1 \;\forall u, \; V^{Z+1} = 1. \quad (1)$$

$$X_{ik}^{1} = X_{ik}^{old} \;\forall i,k\,, \; X_{ik}^{Z+1} = X_{ik}^{new} \;\forall i,k\,, \; X_{P_k k}^{u} = 1 \;\forall k\,, \; \sum_{\forall k} X_{ik}^{u} s(O_k) \leq s(S_i) \;\forall i,u. \quad (2)$$

$$X_{jk}^{u+1} = X_{jk}^{u} + \sum_{\forall i}\sum_{\forall v} ET_{ikj}^{uv} - D_{jk}^{u} \;\forall j,k,u. \quad (3)$$

$$ST_{ikj}^{u} \leq X_{ik}^{u} \;\forall i,k,j,u\,, \; ST_{ikj}^{u} \leq 1 - X_{jk}^{u} \;\forall i,k,j,u\,, \; D_{ik}^{u} \leq X_{ik}^{u} \;\forall i,k,u. \quad (4)$$

$$ST_{ikj}^{u} = \sum_{v>u} ET_{ikj}^{vu} \;\forall i,k,j,u\,, \; \sum_{\forall i}\sum_{\forall k}\sum_{\forall j}\sum_{\forall u} ST_{ikj}^{u} = \sum_{\forall i}\sum_{\forall k}\sum_{\forall j}\sum_{\forall u}\sum_{\forall v} ET_{ikj}^{uv}. \quad (5)$$

$$\sum_{\forall j}\sum_{\forall v<u} ST_{ikj}^{v} - \sum_{\forall j}\sum_{\forall v<u}\sum_{\forall x|v<x<u} ET_{ikj}^{xv} \leq 1 - D_{ik}^{u} \;\forall i,k,u. \quad (6)$$

$$p_{si}^{u} = \sum_{\forall k}\sum_{\forall j} ST_{ikj}^{u} + \sum_{\forall k}\sum_{\forall j}\sum_{\forall v<u} ET_{ikj}^{uv} \;\forall i,u. \quad (7)$$

$$p_{jd}^{u} = \sum_{\forall k}\sum_{\forall i} ST_{ikj}^{u} + \sum_{\forall k}\sum_{\forall i}\sum_{\forall v<u} ET_{ikj}^{uv} \;\forall j,u\,, \; \sum_{\forall i} p_{ij}^{u} = \sum_{\forall x} p_{jx}^{u} \;\forall j,u. \quad (8)$$

$$p_{xy}^{u} - p_{xy}^{v} \leq 1 - \sum_{\forall i}\sum_{\forall k}\sum_{\forall j} ET_{ikj}^{uv} \;\forall x,y,u,v\,, \; p_{xy}^{u} \leq 1 - \sum_{\forall i}\sum_{\forall k} D_{ik}^{u} - V^{u} \;\forall x,y,u. \quad (9)$$

$$ET_{ikj}^{uv}(r^{v} + r^{u}) = 0 \;\forall i,k,j,u,v\,, \; r^{u} p_{ij}^{u} + \sum_{v<u} r^{v} p_{ij}^{v} + \sum_{v<u} r^{v} p_{ji}^{v} \leq c_{ij} \;\forall i,j,u. \quad (10)$$

$$t^{u} \leq t^{u+1} \;\forall u\,, \; ET_{ikj}^{uv}(t^{u} - t^{v} - \frac{s(O_k)}{r^{v}}) = 0 \;\forall i,k,j,u,v. \quad (11)$$

Constraints (1) state that each event is either a transfer start, transfer end, deletion or void, and that the last event is void. (2) requires that the replication scheme starts with X^{old} and reaches X^{new} without deleting primary replicas or violating server capacities. (3) captures the bit flips in the replication matrix, i.e. if the uth event is a transfer end, then the resulting matrix should have a value of 1 at the corresponding cell; if it is a deletion it should have a 0, while in all other cases the matrix cell should remain unchanged. Since the variables of (3) are binary, the uth event cannot be a transfer-end if $X_{jk}^{u} = 1$, and similarly it cannot be a deletion if $X_{jk}^{u} = 0$. (4) states that in order for a transfer to start, the source server must have a copy of the object and the destination server must not, while for deletions the server must have the replica to be deleted. (5) states that each start event must have a corresponding end event that occurs later in the schedule, and that the number of end events must be equal to the number of start events, to avoid having orphan end events. (6) ensures that the source of a transfer cannot be deleted before that transfer ends.

Next come constraints related to path reservation (7)-(9). Whenever a transfer start/end event occurs, a path from the source to the destination must be reserved (7)-(8). To do this, we assume that all transfers start from a dummy source (7) and end to a dummy destination (8). These dummy servers are connected through direct links of unlimited capacity to all other servers. To guarantee that a path is not interrupted, (8) requires that if a server (other than the dummies) has an incoming link belonging to the path, it should also have an outgoing. (9) demands that corresponding start and end events have the same path, while deletion and void events do not have a path.

Constraints (10) capture bandwidth management aspects. The first part states that the sum of the rates of corresponding transfer start and end events equals zero, ensuring that bandwidth is properly freed when a transfer completes. The second part requests that the aggregate rates of current and past events do not exceed link capacity. The final set of constraints (11) keeps track of clock time. The first part states that events must be properly ordered in time, while the second part calculates the time of an end event as the sum of the start time and the transfer duration. Note that the rate of a start event must be positive (and thus the rate of an end event must be negative), else the end event would occur prior to the start event in the schedule.

We have implemented this MIP problem in LINDO [10], a commercial optimizer. Unfortunately, we were able to obtain solutions, within acceptable time, only for very small problem sets (around 5 objects and servers).

4 Scheduling Heuristics

Given the computationally intensive nature of RMP, we have designed a set of heuristics that can be used to produce solutions for this problem. These heuristics follow the same generic algorithmic template, described in the following pseudocode:

```
(1)     while (outstanding replicas exist)
(2)        for each outstanding replica
(3)           for each source for this outstanding replica
(4)              select a transfer using <selection criterion>
(5)           end for
(6)           apply cut-off rule
(7)           select source using <selection criterion>
(8)        end for
(9)        choose transfer/s with the earliest completion time
(10)       choose transfer/s that require no deletions, if any
(11)       choose transfer/s with the smallest hop count
(12)       select a single transfer by breaking ties randomly
(13)       if (free storage at destination less-than object size)
(14)          perform deletion(s) according to <deletion rule>
(15)       end if
(16)       schedule the selected transfer
(17)    end while
(18)    delete remaining superfluous replicas
```

In a first phase, for each outstanding replica and possible source for it, one transfer path is chosen subject to a *selection criterion* (lines 2-4). As a result, a set of tuples of the form <outstanding replica; source; path> is produced. Then, a cut-off rule is applied to eliminate some candidates (line 6). Specifically, all transfers are discarded that have paths with an intermediate node that is either a replicator or a host for an outstanding replica of the object to be transferred. The rationale is to favor transfers that do not occupy many links. Then, the same *selection criterion* of line 4 is applied (again) to choose one <source; path> candidate per outstanding replica (line 7).

In a second phase, out of the set of candidate transfers, one per outstanding replica, the ones with the earliest completion time are selected (line 9). Among the remaining candidates, the ones that require no deletions are chosen, and from those, preference is given to transfers having the shortest path hop-wise (line 11). Ties are randomly broken. Before scheduling the chosen transfer, in a third phase, the remaining storage capacity at the destination is checked (lines 12-13). If needed, deletions of superfluous replicas are performed at the server, according to a *deletion rule*.

These three phases are repeated until there are no more outstanding replicas, i.e. all transfers have been scheduled. Finally, the remaining superfluous replicas are deleted (line 18), at no extra cost. Given this template, the additional aspects of our heuristics are introduced below.

Per Object variants *(O-)*: This family of heuristics follows the generic template, but on a per-object basis (imagine an extra outer loop, iterating over all objects added in the generic algorithmic template). This considerably shrinks the search space for selecting a transfer, reducing the running time, at the risk of producing inferior results, compared to the default "across-objects" versions. Still, there is an (indirect) advantage: once the outstanding replicas of the selected object are created, all its superfluous replicas can be safely deleted, knowing that they will never be used as sources for future transfers. Objects are considered in descending size of the respective transfer volume *(outstanding replicas × size)*.

Selection criterion options: The criterion for selecting transfers (in lines 4 and 7) is either "earliest start time" (EST) or "earliest completion time" (ECT), computed based on the transfers that have been scheduled and the available link bandwidth.

Deletion rule options: The default option is to choose randomly among the superfluous replicas. The second option (denoted with *-d*) is to delete them in ascending order of their *benefit/size* ratio. Intuitively, the benefit of a replica indicates its importance as a potential source for future transfers. For each outstanding replica for which the replica in question is the best source according to ECT rule (given an unloaded network), the second-best source is found, and the time difference is computed between completing the transfer from the best and from the second-best source, respectively. The aggregated time differences, give the benefit. If a replica is not the best source for any outstanding replica, its benefit is zero.

Auxiliary Replica Creation operator *(-ARC)*: This can be applied once the transfer to be performed is chosen (right after line 12). It checks the inner nodes of the respective path, assessing whether any of them could be used to create a *useful* superfluous replica, as follows. For each additional outstanding replica, the ECT transfer source and path is defined (given an unloaded network). If a node is found in the path of at least two such transfers, it is considered as a candidate, provided it has sufficient storage. If such nodes exist, the one closest (in terms of hops) to the source of the transfer to be performed is selected (the original transfer is dropped), a transfer is scheduled to create an auxiliary replica on it, and the algorithm continues with a new iteration.

Our heuristics are built as different combinations of the above options. Henceforth, we refer to heuristics via acronyms, e.g., EST refers to the heuristic that uses the default template, EST as the selection criterion and the default deletion rule, while O-ECT-ARC-d refers to the per-object heuristic that uses ECT as the selection criterion, the benefit-driven deletion rule and the auxiliary replica creation operator.

5 Experiments

In a first set of experiments, 5 networks of 25 servers with connectivity 1 (tree network) and 5 networks with connectivity 3 were generated using BRITE [11], under the Barabasi-Albert connectivity model [12]. Link capacities and object sizes were set equal to 1 and the number of objects was set to 100.

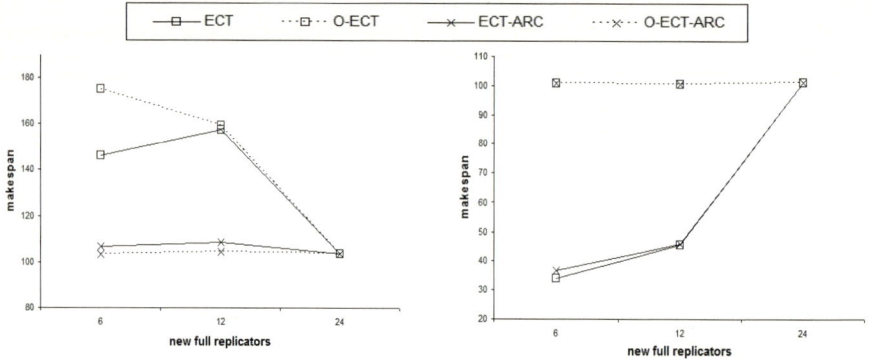

Fig. 4. Replica creations (connectivity 1)   **Fig. 5.** Replica creations (connectivity 3)

Figures 4 and 5 depict the average makespan for the networks with connectivity 1 and 3, respectively, when starting from a single primary server that holds a replica for each object, and creating additional replicas of all objects to 6, 12 and 24 servers (corresponding to 25%, 50% and respectively 100% of the initially empty servers).

As it can be seen in Figure 4, for the tree networks the makespan of ECT and O-ECT drops as more replicas need to be created. This apparently counterintuitive result hints to the merits of creating auxiliary replicas when a limited number of disjoint paths exist, as illustrated by the superior performance of their ARC counterparts. It is also interesting to observe that these variants result in an almost constant makespan, independently of the number of replicas to be created. This indicates that once auxiliary replicas are created at key locations, the creation of even more outstanding replicas can be achieved at a small additional cost. The non-ARC variants have almost equal performance to the ARC variants when replicas must be created on all servers. Indeed, in this particular case, the non-ARC variants unavoidably create (outstanding) replicas on every server, including the locations that are selected by ARC to create the auxiliary replicas for the cases that require a smaller amount of replication.

However, the benefits of the ARC variants diminish for larger connectivity, as illustrated in Figure 5. This is due to the fact that more outstanding replicas can be created with single-hop transfers, reducing the importance of creating auxiliary replicas. It can also be seen that ECT clearly outperforms O-ECT. This is explained by

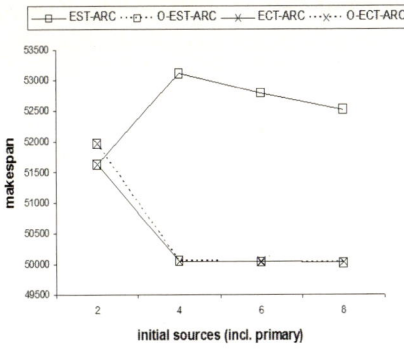
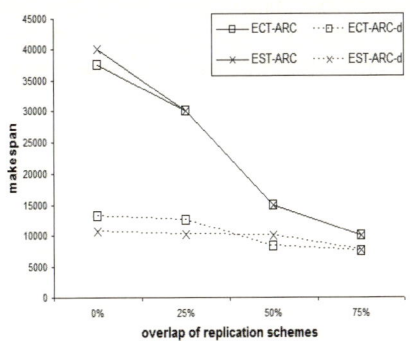

Fig. 6. Replica creations (GÉANT2)   **Fig. 7.** Replica creations+deletions (GÉANT2)

noticing that the makespan of O-ECT is around 100, corresponding to 1 time unit per object, which means that only one object is replicated at a time. On the contrary, ECT aggregates transfers of different objects in each time slot, taking full advantage of alternative paths that exist in the network. This leads to the creation of new replicas that can be used as sources in subsequent time slots, thus maximizing link utilization.

The next set of experiments was performed using a real-world topology, namely the European research and education network GÉANT2 [13]. The relative link capacities were derived from GÉANT2, while the size of objects was set so that a transfer over the fastest link requires 10 time units. Again, the number of objects was 100.

Figure 6 shows the performance of EST-ARC, ECT-ARC and their per-object variants, when starting from a given number of randomly selected servers (in addition to the primary server) that hold replicas of all objects, and creating additional replicas of all objects on 50% of the remaining (initially empty) servers. Results show that ECT-ARC and O-ECT-ARC achieve comparable performance, closely followed by O-EST-ARC. The trends for the first three algorithms are decreasing as the number of initial sources increases, which can be attributed to the increased link utilization when more initial sources are available. EST-ARC is clearly inferior. This is due to the fact that as the potential sources for an object transfer increase, the earliest starting transfer is also more likely to cross a path with relatively limited capacity, thereby increasing the overall makespan.

Last, we assess the performance of the benefit-based deletion criterion. For this purpose we set the capacity of each server to allow the hosting of 10 objects, initially place on each server a replica of 10 randomly selected objects, and vary the replica overlap between X^{old} and X^{new}: an overlap of 0% means that all replicas in X^{new} are stored in different locations compared to X^{old} (except for the primary replicas), while an overlap of 75% means that only 1 out of 4 replicas needs to be relocated in X^{new}. The results are depicted in Figure 7. As it can be seen, benefit-based deletion clearly outperforms random deletion, for both EST-ARC and ECT-ARC, when a large number of deletions need to be performed, i.e., for small replica overlaps. The performance gap shrinks as the number of required deletions drops.

As a conclusion (also based on additional experiments not shown here due to lack of space), the heuristics which create auxiliary replicas and employ the benefit-based deletion rule achieve better overall results. The per-object variants generally perform worse than their counterparts, but have a significantly reduced execution time (5 to 100 times faster, depending on the experiment).

References

1. Khan, S., Ahmad, I.: A Semi-Distributed Axiomatic Game Theoretical Mechanism for Replicating Data Objects in Large Distributed Computing Systems. In: Proc. 21st Int. Parallel and Distributed Processing Symp (IPDPS 2007), Long Beach, California (March 2007)
2. Loukopoulos, T., Lampsas, P., Ahmad, I.: Continuous Replica Placement Schemes in Distributed Systems. In: Proc. 19th ACM International Conference on Supercomputing (ACM ICS), Boston, MA (June 2005)
3. Desprez, F., Vernois, A.: Simultaneous Scheduling of Replication and Computation for Data-Intensive Applications on the Grid. Report RR2005-01, INRIA, France (January 2005)
4. Laoutaris, N., Smaragdakis, G., Bestavros, A., Matta, I., Stavrakakis, I.: Distributed Selfish Replication. In IEEE Trans. on Parallel and Distributed Systems (TPDS) 17(12), 1401–1413 (2006)
5. Hall, J., Hartline, J., Karlin, A., Saia, J., Wilkes, J.: On algorithms for efficient data migration. In: Proc. of the twelfth annual ACM-SIAM Symposium on Discrete algorithms (SODA 2001), Washington D.C., United States, pp. 620–629 (2001)
6. Khuller, S., Kim, Y., Wan, Y.: Algorithms for data migration with cloning. In: Proc. of the twenty-second ACM SIGMOD-SIGACT-SIGART Symposium on Principles of Database Systems (PODS 2004), pp. 448–461 (2004)
7. Killian, C., Vrable, M., Snoeren, A., Vahdat, A., Pasquale, J.: Brief Announcement: The Overlay Network Content Distribution Problem. In: Proc. ACM Symp. on Principles of Distributed Computing (PODC), Las Vegas, NV, July 2005, p. 98 (2005)
8. Loukopoulos, T., Tziritas, N., Lampsas, P., Lalis, S.: Implementing Replica Placements: Feasibility and Cost Minimization. In: Proc. 21st Int. Parallel and Distributed Processing Symp (IPDPS 2007), Long Beach, California (March 2007)
9. Garey, J., Johnson, D.: Computers and Intractability. W. H. Freeman and Co., NY (1979)
10. http://www.lindo.com
11. Medina, A., Lakhina, A., Matta, I., Byers, J.: BRITE: Boston University Representative Internet Topology Generator (March 2001),
    http://cs-pub.bu.edu/brite/index.htm
12. Barabasi, A.L., Albert, R.: Emergence of Scaling in Random Networks. Science 286, 509–512 (1999)
13. GÉANT2, Backbone Network Topology (January 2008),
    http://www.geant2.net/upload/pdf/PUB-07-179_GN2_Topology_Jan_08_final.pdf

Topic 4: High Performance Architectures and Compilers

Koen de Bosschere[*], Ayal Zaks[*], Michael C. Huang[*], and Luis Piñuel[*]

This topic deals with architecture design and compilation for high performance systems – the discovery and support of parallelism at all levels. The areas of interest range from microprocessors to large-scale parallel machines; from general-purpose platforms to specialized hardware (e.g., graphic coprocessors, low-power embedded systems); and from hardware design to compiler technology. On the compilation side, topics of interest include language aspects, program analysis, transformation, automatic extraction of parallelism at all levels, and the interaction between compiler and the rest of the system. On the architecture side, the scope spans system architectures, processor micro-architecture, memory hierarchy, multi-threading, and the impact of emerging trends.

Out of the 23 paper submitted to this topic, 7 were accepted for presentation at the conference.

The paper "Reducing the Number of Bits in the BTB to Attack the Branch Predictor Hot-Spot" by Noel Tomás, Julio Sahuquillo, Salvador Petit, and Pedro Lopez proposes two techniques to store less data in the Branch Target Buffer (BTB): (i) less tag bits and (ii) less target address bits, in order to tackle the power consumption in the BTB. The authors show that up to 35% of power can be saved without performance loss.

The paper "Low-Cost Adaptive Data Prefetching" by Luis Ramos, Jose Briz, Pablo Ibañez and Victor Viñals explores different prefetch distance-degree combinations and very simple, low-cost adaptive policies on a superscalar core with a high bandwidth, high capacity on-chip memory hierarchy. The authors show that sequential prefetching can be tuned to outperform state-of-the-art hardware data prefetchers and complex filtering mechanisms.

The paper "Stream Scheduling: A Framework to Manage Bulk Operations in Multi-level Memory Hierarchies" by Abhishek Das presents an extension to the Sequoia compiler to schedule data transfers and computation kernels on a parallel computer with multiple levels of memory, in such a way that computation and data transfer overlap and performance is maximized. The authors show a performance that is comparable to the best known (hand-tuned) performance; some compute-intensive applications improve by 15%-35%.

The paper "Interprocedural Speculative Optimization of Memory Accesses to Global Variables" by Lars Gesellensetter presents a register promotion technique for global variables. The authors propose a method to speculatively promote global

---

[*] Topic Chairs.

variables to register across function calls by exploiting the Advanced Load Address Table (ALAT) present in Itanium processors.

The paper "Efficiently Building the Gated Single Assignment Form in Codes with Pointers in Modern Optimizing Compilers" by Manuel Arenaz, Pedro Amoedo, and Juan Touriño presents a simple and fast Gated Single Assignment (GSA) construction algorithm that takes advantage of the infrastructure for building the SSA form available in modern optimizing compilers. An implementation on top of the GIMPLE-SSA intermediate representation of GCC is described and evaluated in terms of memory consumption and execution time using the UTDSP, Perfect Club and SPEC CPU2000 benchmark suites.

The paper "Inter-Block Scoreboard Scheduling in a JIT Compiler for VLIW Processors" by Benoit Dupont de Dinechin presents a post-pass instruction scheduling technique suitable for use by Just-In-Time (JIT) compilers targeted to VLIW processors. The technique is implemented in a Common Language Infrastructure JIT compiler for the ST200 VLIW processors and the ARM processors.

The paper "Global Tiling for Communication Minimal Parallelization on Distributed Memory Systems" by Liu Lei presents some strategies to select the matrices for "semi-oblique tiling" considering both iteration space and data space. In addition it proposes a strategy to select among the possible local solutions the optimal ones to achieve a global optimal solution. The experimentations with NPB2.3-serial SP and LU on Qsnet connected cluster achieves an average parallel efficiency of 87% and 73% respectively.

Reducing the Number of Bits in the BTB to Attack the Branch Predictor Hot-Spot

N. Tomás, J. Sahuquillo, S. Petit, and P. López

Dept. of Computing Engineering (DISCA)
Universidad Politécnica de Valencia, Valencia, Spain
ntomas@gap.upv.es,
{jsahuqui,spetit,plopez}@disca.upv.es

Abstract. Current superscalar processors access the BTB early to anticipate the branch/jump target address. This access is frequent and aggressively performed since the BTB is accessed every cycle for all instructions in the ICache line being fetched. This fact increases the power density, which could create hot spots, thus increasing packaging and cooling costs. Power consumption in the BTB comes mostly from its two main fields: the tag and the target address fields. Reducing the length of either of these fields reduces power consumption, silicon area and access time. This paper analyzes at what extent tag and target address lengths could be reduced to benefit both dynamic and static power consumption, silicon area, and access time, while sustaining performance. Experimental results show that the tag length and the target address could be reduced by about a half and one byte, respectively with no performance losses. BTB peak power savings can reach about 35% when both reductions are combined together, thus effectively attacking the hot-spot.

1 Introduction

Traditionally, a key issue to improve microprocessor performance has been the clock frequency. The higher the clock frequency, the faster the processor is able to execute instructions. However, such increase in clock frequency yields to an increase in the processor power consumption. As the frequency has kept rising, the power consumption and the corresponding package and cooling costs have become prohibitive, constraining such trend. It has been estimated [1] that heat dissipation above 30-40 watts increases the total cost of thermal packaging and cooling per chip by more than one dollar per watt. The costs can be as high as those derived from a 130W heat dissipation [2]. Consequently, power consumption has become nowadays a major microprocessor design concern. Power consumption can be reduced by either reducing the static power (i.e., the power consumed due to transistor leakage currents) or dynamic power (i.e., the power consumed due to transistor switching).

Focusing on the average power is important when designing power-limited devices constrained by the power supply such as batteries. However, power is not distributed uniformly across the chip area but on specific structures. In other words, the different microprocessor structures present different power densities [3]. Those structures with highest density may trigger thermal emergencies when working at peak power, and are

Table 1. Increase of temperature per cycle

Component	Area (mm^2)	Peak power (W)	Temp. increase (°C)
Load/Store Queue	0.5	2.7	0.7e-3
Instruction Window	0.9	10.3	3.1e-3
Register File	0.25	5.5	2.6e-3
Branch Predictor	0.35	5.3	5.2e-3
L1 Data Cache	1.0	11.6	2.6e-3
Integer Units	0.5	4.3	2.5e-3
Floating Point Units	0.5	6.7	2.6e-3

referred to as thermal hot-spots. These points are the main responsible for the costs of thermal packaging and cooling solutions, since they must be designed to operate at peak power (even if peak power is rarely reached). That means that, to allow high frequencies while keeping the packaging and cooling costs at a reasonable cost, solutions should address hot spots.

On the other hand, in current microprocessors, deep pipelines have become predominant in order to allow high clock speeds. In these microarchitectures, the fetch stage bandwidth must be high enough to efficiently feed the remaining stages. In this context, fast handling of branch instructions is important because they can stall the fetch stage until their direction (i.e., taken or not taken) and target address are known, thus dropping the performance. To deal with control hazards, branch prediction techniques have been extensively studied during the last decade [4,5,6,7,8].

The branch predictor can be accessed multiple times every cycle. Thus, this structure presents a high power density. Because of this reason, it is one of the scorching hot-spots in the processor. This fact can be appreciated in Table 1, which shows the temperature increase per cycle reached by different main processor structures when working at 1.5Ghz (peak performance). These results are derived from the model detailed in [9] for a processor model similar to the Alpha 21264 using a 100°C baseline temperature. Notice how the branch predictor, despite having one of the smallest areas, is the main heat contributor in the list.

A major structure of the branch predictor is the branch target buffer (BTB), and it constitutes an important percentage of its heat. The BTB has been implemented in modern microprocessors in two different ways. In some processors, the BTB performs both predictions (target address and direction). However, most current microprocessors decouple the target address prediction, which is performed by a BTB table, from the branch direction, which is performed by a branch predictor structure. This decoupled implementation has been the model addressed in this paper.

Different works have been proposed to reduce power consumption in the BTB. In this paper, we study at what extent power consumption might be reduced by merely reducing the tag length, the target address or both. By reducing the power consumption of the BTB without adding any extra hardware, we reduce the peak consumption of a major hot-spot of the processor. The benefits of this reduction are twofold. On one hand, packaging and cooling costs can be decreased, while on the other hand, there are more opportunities for increasing the processor frequency. However, as a side effect, both branch direction and target address misprediction rise, which may negatively impact on performance.

This paper analyzes the effects of reducing the tag and the target address bits of the BTB on power, energy, area, access time, and performance. Experimental results show that the tag length and the target address could be reduced by about a half and one byte, respectively with no performance losses. When both techniques are applied together savings can reach about 35%. Notice that, as we propose a hardwired technique, these benefits consistently apply regardless of whether the BTB is working or not at peak power. Thus, the hot-spot is effectively attacked.

The remaining of this paper is organized as follows. Section 2 discusses some related work. Section 3 summarizes the proposed reduction of the BTB tag and target address length, and its pros and cons. Section 4 analyzes the experimental results and finally, some concluding remarks are drawn.

2 Related Work

Important research work has focused on reducing the BTB power consumption. Some of these works attempt to reduce the power consumption in the BTB by reducing the number of accesses [10,11,12], while other approaches apply at the circuit level [13,14].

Regarding the first approach, Petrov and Orailoglu [10] propose a mechanism that uses control flow information (e.g., basic block lengths), obtained at compile time. This information is stored in a table called the ACBTB (Application Customizable Branch Target Buffer). Two auxiliar registers are used, one to count the number of instructions until the next branch, and other to index the table. When the counter reaches zero, the ACBTB is accessed to read the target address. Then, the counter is updated with a value according to the stored control information.

Deris and Baniasadi [11] propose the Branchless Cycle Prediction (BLCP) that uses a structure to predict which cycles the ICache line has no branch (branchless cycles). Thus, there is no need to access the BTB. To this end, a small Global History Shift Register (GHR) and a Prediction History Table (PHT) are used. The GHR records the history of the branch and the branchless cycles. This table indexes the PHT, which predicts whether a branch instruction will be fetched in the next cycle. If the prediction is false, the BTB is not accessed. The technique proposed by Palermo *et al.* for VLIW architectures [12] uses a branch detector that partially pre-decodes instructions to find possible branches, in order to access the branch prediction block selectively, and thus to the BTB.

Regarding the second approach, Chaver *et al.* [13] propose an adaptive resizing of the BTB. To this end, some portions of the BTB are selectively disabled using dynamic cache resizing techniques.

Hu *et al.* [14] apply decay strategies which, from time to time, switch-off specific entries in the BTB, so reducing leakage energy at the expense of some performance loss.

Unlike these techniques, this paper neither reduces the number of accesses nor disables BTB entries. Instead, we analyze how power consumption can be saved by reducing the number of bits in the BTB, so saving power consumption for every performed access. In this way, we address not only average power savings but also thermal packaging and cooling costs. Nevertheless, notice that the aforementioned techniques are orthogonal to our approach, so they can be applied all together.

3 Proposed Mechanism

The branch target buffer is implemented like a cache structure that has two main fields: the tag and the target address. The tag field is compared with the corresponding bits of the PC of the instruction being fetched. On a hit, if the branch prediction outcome is taken, the stored target address is written to the PC, otherwise, it is discarded. When the real target address is calculated later in the pipeline, it is compared with the predicted one. If the prediction fails, the BTB must be updated with the correct target address.

In modern microprocessors, the BTB is accessed at the same time as the instruction cache. At this point, it is not known whether the instruction being read is a branch or not. A straightforward solution to force that only branches may hit the BTB is to store in the tag field the whole branch address (i.e., its PC). Of course, if some of these bits are used to index the BTB (i.e., implemented as a set-associative table), there is no need to store all of them. In addition, as memory is usually byte addressable but instructions are word aligned, some least significant bits of the instructions address can be discarded since they are always equal to zero.

Another key issue is to analyze the relationship between the target address of a branch and its PC (i.e., how distant they are). In this sense, if both PCs are close enough, they will share some of the most significant bits. In such a case, if the target address field is reduced, the BTB would provide only a fraction of such address, but the final address could be obtained by using the most significant bits of the PC accessing the BTB.

The key issue behind the proposal is to reduce the number of stored bits in the BTB in order to remove static and dynamic power consumed by these bits. As a side effect, area and access time are also reduced. The proposal attacks the two main parts of the BTB (i.e., the tag and the target address).

3.1 Reducing the Number of Tag Bits

Reducing the number of tag bits might affect the hit ratio, because phantom branches and branch aliasing could arise. This section discusses the impact of reducing the tag field on these negative effects.

The problem raises because there could be more than one instruction matching the same tag (of course, only one of them is the correct one), regardless of whether they are branch instructions or not, therefore resulting in BTB misspeculations. This kind of misspeculation is named in two different ways depending on whether the instruction causing it is a branch or not.

A phantom branch is a non-branch instruction that hits the BTB, thus, it is executed as a normal branch. Consequently, if it is predicted taken, the PC is updated with the target address read from the BTB and a wrong inflow of instructions is inserted in the processor pipeline until the misprediction is detected. This is just like a common branch misspeculation, but in this case, it can be detected much earlier, (i.e., when decoding the instruction at the decode stage). Thus, it is not necessary to wait for the branch to be resolved later in the pipeline to recover the machine to a precise state. Notice that only the fetched and not yet decoded instructions are affected. Thus, the only action to be done is to squash those instructions, without affecting instructions from the ROB neither the mapping table.

Branch aliasing refers to different branches that match the same tag in the BTB. The problem is that any of these branches might be predicted with the target address of any other, what would incur a BTB misprediction. This misprediction is detected when the target address is calculated later in the pipeline, and would cause branch misspeculation if the branch is predicted taken. Notice that this case can be handled as a normal branch misspeculation. Thus, to recover from this misspeculation, there is no need to add extra logic.

Reducing the tag length, not only reduces the number of memory cells but also the comparator size (i.e., the number of XOR gates). This fact will positively impact on both static and dynamic power. In addition, the area, the circuit delay and, the BTB access time will be also reduced.

3.2 Reducing the Number of Target Address Bits

The field storing the target address in the BTB may be reduced by removing either of its bits. However, as instructions are stored in continuous memory addresses, they share their most significant bits. Thus, only a subset of the bits might be stored in the BTB and the effective target address could be computed by concatenating the most significant bits of the PC of the instruction accessing the BTB with the fraction of the target address stored in the BTB. In such a case, the problem is that the effective target address might be wrong, thus introducing BTB mispredictions that would result in branch misspeculation if the branch was taken. This kind of misspeculation is handled as a normal branch misspeculation, thus there is no need to add extra logic to detect and recover from it. On the other hand, the benefits of reducing the target address length are similar to those of reducing the tag length, since a reduction in the number of memory cells is applied.

Again, there is a tradeoff between power, area and access time, and performance loss. Thus, a fair analysis should take into account the advantages and shortcomings of reducing the tag and target address lengths. The key issue is to look for how many bits could be removed without hurting the performance.

4 Experimental Results

Experiments were run by using the Multi2Sim simulation framework [15], which was extended to support different tag and target address lengths, detecting phantom branches and branch aliasing, and the SPEC2000 benchmark suite [16] as workload. To measure the energy, area and cycle time of the BTB, the CACTI 4.0 tool [17], a widely used cache timing and power model, has been used.

Table 2. Machine Parameters

Microprocessor core	
Branch predictor	Hybrid gShare/bimodal
gShare	4KB 2-bit counters
Bimodal	4KB 2-bit counters
Choice Predictor	4KB 2-bit counters
BTB	512 sets, 4 ways, 13 cycles misprediction, 3 cycles phantom branch penalty
Decode/Issue/Retire bandwidth	4 instructions/cycle
# of Int ALU's, mult/div	4,1
# of FP ALU's, mult/div	2,1
Memory Hierarchy	
L1 data cache	64KB, 2 way, 64 byte-line
L1 data cache hit latency	1 cycles
L2 data cache	512KB, 4 ways, 64byte-line
L2 data cache hit latency	10 cycles
Memory access latency	200 cycles

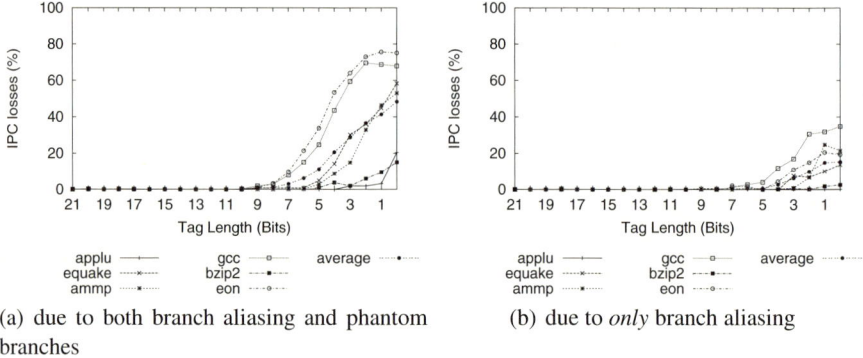

(a) due to both branch aliasing and phantom branches

(b) due to *only* branch aliasing

Fig. 1. IPC losses when reducing the tag length

Experimental results have assumed a 32-bit address microprocessor configuration as shown in Table 2, with a baseline 4-way 512-set BTB implemented using 65 nm silicon process.

4.1 Reducing Tag Bits

First, the effect of reducing the tag length has been evaluated alone (i.e., without reducing the target address length). Note that the length of the tag stored in the BTB, without applying any reduction in baseline processor, must be 21 bits[1]. Thus, the analysis starts assuming a 21-bit tag BTB, and this length is progressively reduced on 1-bit steps, down to zero bits.

Impact on Performance. As far as the tag length is reduced, performance (i.e., IPC) drops as phantom branches and branch aliasing rise. Figure 1(a) shows how phantom branches and branch aliasing impact on the IPC. As observed, if we use less than 9-10

---
[1] 21 = 32 − 2 (4-byte words) − 9 (512 sets).

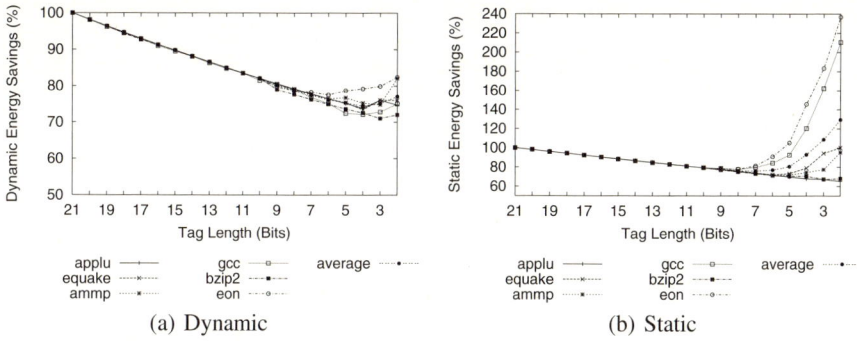

Fig. 2. Energy Savings when Reducing the Tag Length

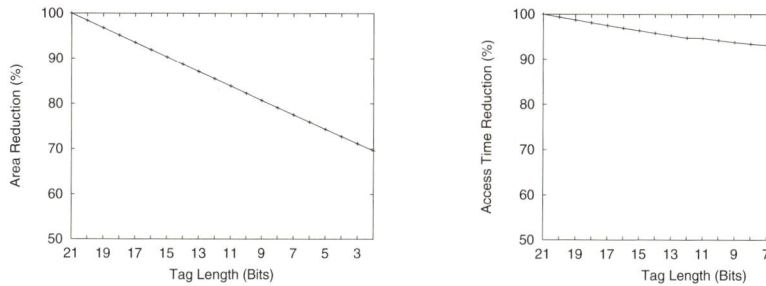

Fig. 3. Area Reduction when Reducing the Tag Length

Fig. 4. Access Time Reduction when Reducing the Tag Length

bits, there is a strong impact on performance, but using just a 10-bit tag (about three times smaller) the performance loss is almost negligible. Figure 1(b) shows the IPC losses due only to branch aliasing (by using branch predecoding). In this case, the tag could be reduced to 6-7 bits without negatively impacting performance. Therefore, the highest fraction of performance losses comes from phantom branches.

Impact on Energy, Area and Access Time. Reducing the tag length also brings hardware benefits, since it reduces the energy consumption, the silicon area and the access time of the BTB. These benefits have been measured ranging the tag size from 21 down to 2 bits. Power savings have been calculated taking into account the whole execution time. For the dynamic power, first CACTI has been used to measure the energy of a single access to the BTB with every tag length. Then, this energy has been multiplied by the number of accesses during the execution time. For the static power, the transistor has been taken as consumption unit and the static energy has been calculated for every tag length. Then, this energy has been multiplied by the number of execution cycles. Notice that under performance loss conditions (higher execution time), this analysis is optimistic because the extra energy consumed by processor structures other than the BTB had not been accounted. Nevertheless, in the absence of performance losses (e.g., a 10-bit tag length) this analysis remains valid.

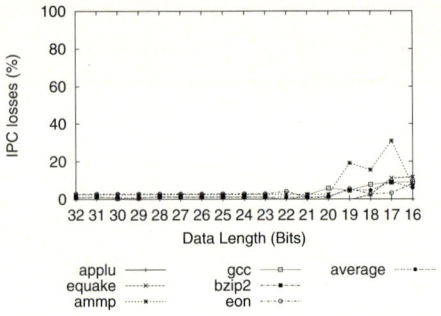

Fig. 5. Combined IPC Losses

Figure 2(a) and Figure 2(b) show the dynamic and static power consumption respectively. As expected, as the tag length is reduced, the BTB power is also decreased. However, notice that, for some applications, a very low tag length gives no further improvements due to increased accesses to the BTB in case of mispredictions. A 9-bit tag length BTB, which has been shown to have no impact on the processor performance, has about 20% less dynamic power consumption and about 20 % less static power consumption.

Finally, Figure 3 and Figure 4 show the results for area and access time. Both of them are reduced as the number of tag bits decrease. Again, a 9-bit tag length gives a good tradeoff, requiring about 20% less silicon area and reducing the access time about 6%.

4.2 Reducing Target Address Bits

This analysis assumes an initial 32-bit target address length, which is progressively reduced down to zero bits while keeping fixed the baseline target address length. Due to space restrictions, results are not plotted but they are discussed.

Impact on Performance. As the target address length is reduced, performance drops due to BTB address mispredictions that, in case of branch predicted as taken, results in a branch misspeculation. Results show that IPC losses rise as the target address length is reduced down to 21 bits for all applications other than applu and bzip2. The explanation is that, in these cases, some BTB mispredictions are hidden due to branches predicted as not taken, thus no branch misspeculation appears. Consequently, there is no negative impact on the IPC.

Impact on Energy, Area and Access Time. Regarding power savings, results show that a good tradeoff value could be a 24-bit target address field, which achieves across the different applications by about 15% and 20% of dynamic and static power savings, respectively. More aggressive target address reduction dramatically impact on performance, and as a consequence, increase the energy budget. Concerning silicon area and access time improvements, results show that a 24-bit target address length achieves about 7% area reduction, decreasing the access time by about 6%.

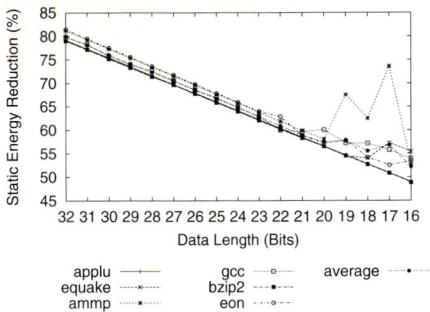

Fig. 6. Combined Static Energy Reduction

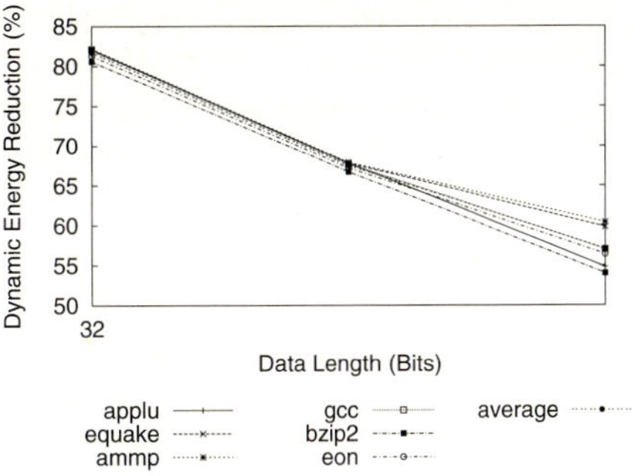

Fig. 7. Combined Dynamic Energy Reduction

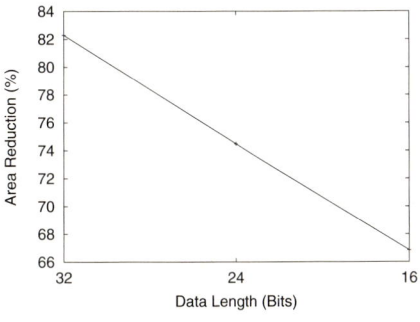

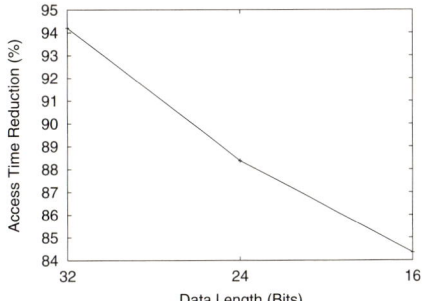

Fig. 8. Combined Area Reduction

Fig. 9. Combined Access Time Reduction

4.3 Combining Tag and Target Address Reduction

This section explores the impact of reducing simultaneously the number of bits in the tag and the target address fields. To this end, we assume a fixed 10-bit tag since, as shown above, it is the smallest size with no performance losses. Figures 5, 6, 7, 8, and 9 plot the results. As expected, when combining both reductions, IPC losses begin to arise for target address lengths shorter than 24 bits. Thus, at this point is when we reach the major benefits without hurting performance, achieving savings of 32%, 35%, 26%, and 12% in dynamic energy, static energy, area, and access time, respectively.

5 Conclusions

The BTB is a key structure of the branch prediction unit, which is aggressively accessed every cycle, and acts as a major hot-spot in current microprocessors. This work has analyzed how both BTB dynamic and static power consumption can be saved by reducing the tag length, the target address length or both. Consequently, silicon area and access time are also reduced. Side effects, such as possible adverse impacts on performance or extra energy due to performance dropping, have been also analyzed.

Results show that a 10-bit tag has no adverse impact on performance while providing important benefits (e.g., by about 17% of power savings). These results can be improved if target address is simultaneously reduced. For instance, using a 10-bit tag length with a 24-bit target address length, power savings grow up 35% with no performance losses.

Acknowledgements

This work was supported by Spanish CICYT under Grant TIN2006-15516-C04-01, CONSOLIDER-INGENIO 2010 under Grant CSD2006-00046 and Universidad Politécnica de Valencia under Grant PAID-06-07-20080029.

References

1. Borkar, S.: Design challenges of technology scaling. IEEE Micro. 19(4), 23–29 (1999)
2. SIA. International Technology Roadmap for Semiconductors (1999)
3. Hamann, H.F., Weger, A., Lacey, J.A., Hu, Z., Bose, P., Cohen, E., Wakil, J.: Hotspot-limited microprocessors: Direct temperature and power distribution measurements. IEEE Journal of Solid-State Circuits 42(1), 56–65 (2007)
4. Evers, M., Yeh, T.Y.: Understanding branches and designing branch predictors for high-performance microprocessors. Proceedings of the IEEE 89(11), 1610–1620 (2001)
5. Lee, C.C., Chen, I.C., Mudge, T.: The bi-mode branch predictor. Micro 0, 4 (1997)
6. Sprangle, E., Chappell, R., Alsup, M., Patt, Y.: The agree predictor: A mechanism for reducing negative branch history interference. In: The 24th Annual International Symposium on Computer Architecture, 1997. Conference Proceedings, 2-4 Jun 1997, pp. 284–291 (1997)
7. Jimenez, D.A., Lin, C.: Dynamic branch prediction with perceptrons. Hpca 00, 0197 (2001)
8. Eden, A., Mudge, T.: The yags branch prediction scheme. Micro 0, 69 (1998)
9. Skadron, K., Abdelzaher, T., Stan, M.R.: Control-theoretic techniques and thermal-rc modeling for accurate and localized dynamic thermal management. In: HPCA 2002: Proceedings of the 8th International Symposium on High-Performance Computer Architecture, Washington, DC, USA, p. 17. IEEE Computer Society, Los Alamitos (2002)
10. Petrov, P., Orailoglu, A.: Low power branch target buffer for application-specific embedded processors. In: Proc. of Euromicro Symposium on Digital System Design, pp. 158–165 (2003)
11. Deris, K.J., Baniasadi, A.: Branchless cycle prediction for embedded processors. In: Proceedings of the 2006 ACM symposium on applied computing (2006)
12. Palermo, G., Sam, M., Silvan, C., Zaccari, V., Zafalo, R.: Branch prediction techniques for low-power vliw processors. In: Proceedings of the 13th ACM Great Lakes symposium on VLSI (2003)
13. Chaver, D., Pinuel, L., Prieto, M., Tirado, F., Huang, M.C.: Branch prediction on demand: an energy efficient solution. In: ISPLED 2003 (2003)
14. Hu, Z., Juang, P., Skadron, K., Clark, D., Martonosi, M.: Applying decay strategies to branch predictors for leakage energy saving. In: Proceedings of IEEE International Conferences on Computers and Processors (2002)
15. Ubal, R., Sahuquillo, J., Petit, S., López, P.: Multi2Sim: A Simulation Framework to Evaluate Multicore-Multithreaded Processors. In: Proc. of the 19th International Symposium on Computer Architecture and High Performance Computing (October 2007)
16. Standard Performance Evaluation Corporation (2000), http://www.spec.org/cpu
17. Tarjan, D., Thoziyoor, S., Jouppi, N.P.: Cacti 4.0. Hewlett-Packard Development Company, L.P. Technical Report (June 2006)

Low-Cost Adaptive Data Prefetching

Luis M. Ramos, José Luis Briz, Pablo E. Ibáñez, and Víctor Viñals

Dpto. Informática e Ing. de Sistemas, Instituto I3A, U. Zaragoza
{luisma,briz,imarin,victor}@unizar.es

Abstract. We explore different prefetch distance-degree combinations and very simple, low-cost adaptive policies on a superscalar core with a high bandwidth, high capacity on-chip memory hierarchy. We show that sequential prefetching aggressiveness can be properly tuned at a very low cost to outperform state-of-the-art hardware data prefetchers and complex filtering mechanisms, avoiding performance losses in hostile applications and keeping the pressure of the prefetching on the cache low, turning it out into a real implementation option for current processors.

1 Introduction

Hardware data prefetching has been largely accepted as an effective way of hiding memory latency. Recent research has lead to very successful proposals like the ones based on a Global History Buffer (GHB) [21], or new stream prefetchers specially focused on servers [12][26]. However, only the simplest mechanisms have been implemented in commercial microprocessors: sequential prefetching in UltraSPARC-IIIcu and SPARC64 VI [17][29], sequential stream buffers in Power4 and Power5 [16][28], and sequential and stride prefetching in the Intel core microarchitecture [8].

Although sequential prefetching can yield the highest speedups, it triggers performance losses in hostile benchmarks and leads to a high pressure on the memory hierarchy. Filtering mechanisms have been recently applied to scheduled region prefetching [3] and sequential (always) prefetching [30]. Both of them call for non negligible hardware.

Losses can also be reduced by tuning prefetching aggressiveness. Let us consider the stream of references a program is going to demand $(a_i, a_{i+1}, a_{i+2}, \ldots)$, where a_i has been just demanded by the program. A prefetcher can dispatch $a_{i+1} \ldots a_{i+n}$, where n is the *prefetch degree*. Alternatively, it could also prefetch only a_{i+n}, and then we say that n is the *prefetch distance*. Increasing the prefetch degree or distance can either boost or ruin performance, causing pollution and exacerbating the pressure on the memory hierarchy. Sequential prefetching with adaptive degree was first proposed in [6], on multiprocessors, focusing on prefetching usefulness. Adaptive stream prefetching is explored in [27], balancing usefulness, timeliness and pollution. Both approaches need far less hardware than the aforementioned filtering proposals.

Our aim is to profit from the simplest hardware prefetcher —sequential tagged— with the smallest hardware investment. We evaluate new and known degree-distance policies along with adaptive mechanisms that can be boiled down to just a few counters, and we compare them with an optimized stride prefetcher [13], a GHB-based prefetcher [21], a correlating prefetcher [22], and a spatial memory stream prefetcher [26]. Prefetched blocks are brought into L2 in all cases. We model in great detail an on-chip memory hierarchy with high bandwidth and capacity that services an aggressive superscalar processor running SPEC CPU 2000 benchmarks. Our best simple adaptive sequential prefetcher reduces execution time 7.6% with respect to a system without prefetching in integer benchmarks (36.6% in floating point benchmarks), whereas the spatial memory stream prefetcher [26] —that performs the best among the others— saves 7.8% (int) and 32.9 % (fp), but issuing 64% more accesses to the second cache level and using a much complex hardware than the adaptive sequential prefetching.

In Sec. 2 we provide essential background and motivate the contribution. Sec. 3 introduces our proposals and all the techniques evaluated. Sec. 4 details the experimental environment. Sec. 5 analyzes the experimental results, including filtering through the Prefetch Address Buffer, and gives some hardware cost estimates. We finally draw some conclusions in the last Section.

2 Background and Motivation

Sequential prefetching prefetches the block or blocks that follow the current demanded block [25]. *Sequential tagged prefetching* does only issue a prefetch upon a cache miss or when a prefetched block is referenced for the first time, and it needs an extra bit per block. These methods tend to issue many prefetches that are not used by the CPU (*useless prefetches*), especially when degree or distance are applied.

Conventional *stride prefetching* uses a Load Table (LT) indexed by the program counter (PC) to identify and predict accesses to memory addresses separated by a constant distance [1]. The size of the table can be much reduced without severe performance losses by applying on-miss insertion in the LT [13]. Stride prefetching can also be implemented by using stream buffers [15].

Correlating prefetchers predict future addresses from tables that record the past memory program behavior. They record the stream of addresses associated either to the load PC or to an address that misses [11][14][18]. Alternatively, differences between consecutive addresses (*deltas*) can be stored. A delta sequence can stand for many miss address sequences, hence it can predict miss addresses that did not occur in the past. A novel table structure (GHB, Global History Buffer) focuses on reducing table sizes, and can be adapted to different prefetching methods with very good results [10][21]. The best performer in the family (PC/DC) uses as index the PC of the loads missing in L2, and consecutive addresses in a linked list are subtracted to calculate deltas. Prefetching is issued when a repeating pattern of deltas is detected. Although the mechanism acts only upon L2 misses, calculating deltas and tracking patterns implies quite a few accesses to the GHB. PDFCM [22] is a more classic correlating prefetcher based on the Differential Finite Context Method (DFCM) [9]. It uses a table indexed by PC, where each entry holds the last value produced by the instruction, and the differences (deltas) between recent values. Deltas are hashed for indexing a second table, to find out the following probable delta. PDFCM performs similarly to GHB with far lower table overhead [22].

SMS (Spatial Memory Streaming) is a hardware prefetcher that identifies code-related spatial access patterns and prefetch into the cache the stream of blocks inside a memory region that are likely to be used [26]. It avoids loading into the cache useless blocks, which is an issue for sequential prefetching and stream buffers, at the cost of using three tables plus some extra logic.

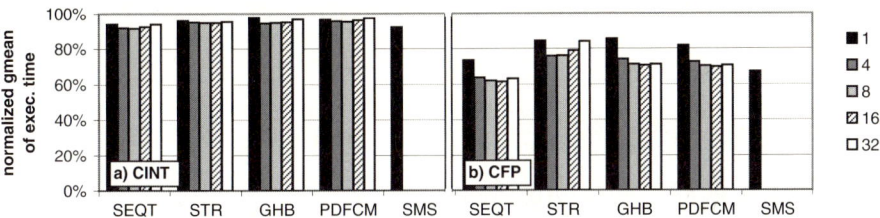

Fig. 1. SEQT, STR, GHB, PDFCM and SMS for a sample of CINT (a) and CFP (b) benchmarks. Degree ranges from 1 to 32 in SEQT, GHB and PDFCM. In STR we vary distance instead. Degree does not apply in the case of SMS.

In Fig. 1 we compare a sequential tagged prefetcher (SEQT) with an optimized stride prefetcher (STR) [13] and three state-of-the-art prefetchers (PC/DC [21], PDFCM [22] and SMS [26]). We vary the prefetching degree from 1 to 32 in all of them but in STR and SMS. We vary distance in STR because it performs better [21]. Concerning SMS, the degree depends on the length of the predicted stream inside a region. Considering the region size selected in [26] and our L2 block size (128 B), the maximum number of prefetched blocks has been set to sixteen. The graph shows the geometric mean of the normalized execution time with respect to a system without prefetching considering the selected programs from SPEC CPU 2000 (see Sec. 4).

Details on the baseline architecture and implementation of the prefetchers are given later in Sec. 4. SEQT with degree 8 yields the best results, with a negligible difference with respect to SMS in the case of integer benchmarks, and reducing the execution time an 8% more than SMS for floating point benchmarks. Fig. 2 reveals that the good performance of the SEQT and SMS implies that they pressure the cache hierarchy a lot more than the selective STR, GHB and PDFCM, concerning the rate of generated prefetch addresses, accesses to L2 and L2 misses. The plot also shows the rate of useful prefetches.

Considering the best two prefetchers (SEQT(8) and SMS), the breakdown per application in Fig. 3 reveals that SEQT degree 8 causes insignificant performance losses in twolf, that become important in ammp. These results show that it is worth looking for mechanisms to cut losses in wrong-case applications and to reduce the pressure on the memory hierarchy caused by sequential prefetchers,

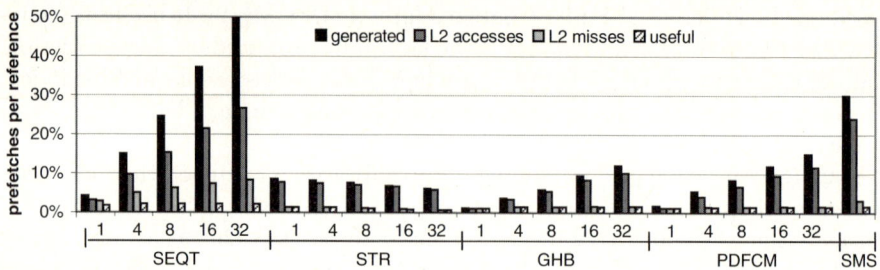

Fig. 2. Pressure on the cache hierarchy made by SEQT, STR, GHB, PDFCM and SMS. Metrics are relative to the number of committed memory references.

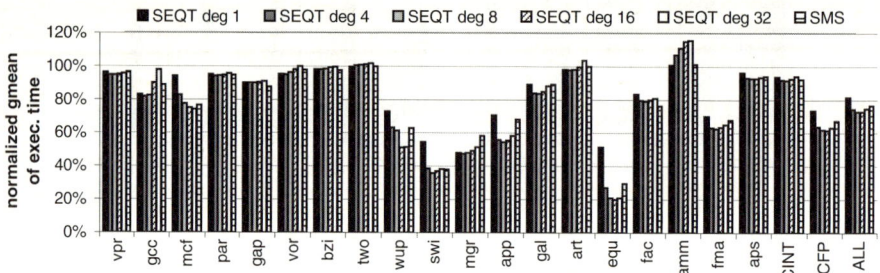

Fig. 3. Breakdown per application for SEQT with degree 1 to 32 and SMS

as long as the hardware needs are kept low. The next section introduces several proposals to handle this problem.

3 Degree-Distance Policies

Table 1 summarizes the options we evaluate in this paper (note that *1st use* refers to a prefetched block). All of them but Deg-dist(x) and Ad5(x) constitute new proposals. Deg(x) and Dist(x) policies are straightforward (see Section 2). Deg-dist(x) and Deg($1-x$) are just as explained in the table. The Deg-dist(x) policy is described in [7], and is quite similar to the stream buffers proposed in [15]. Prefetch performance depends on the *usefulness* and *timeliness* of the prefetched blocks, and on the *pollution* caused by them in the cache. Looking for simplicity, most of our adaptive policies focus only on usefulness. All of them use three counters, *degree*, *up* and *down*. The first one holds the current degree. *Up* increases whenever a prefetched block is demanded for the first time, and when it reaches a threshold *degree* is increased. The *down* counter has the opposite effect and relies on a different threshold. It counts useless prefetches (replacements of tagged blocks). Both the two thresholds determine how many events we let happen before deciding to increase or decrease the degree.

Our Ad1(x) policy prefetches with degree 1 on a demand miss, and with the degree indicated by the counter on the first use of a prefetched block, up to

Table 1. Degree - Distance Policies

	Policy	Description
Fixed	$Deg(x)$	Degree fixed to x
	$Dist(x)$	Distance fixed to x
	$Deg\text{-}dist(x)$	On miss, prefetch with degree x. On 1st use, prefetch with distance x.
	$Deg(1-x)$	On miss, prefetch with degree 1. On 1st use, prefetch with degree x
Adaptive	$Ad1(x)$	On miss, prefetch with degree 1. On 1st use, prefetch with variable degree $[0\ldots x]$
	$Ad2(x)$	On miss, prefetch next and previous block and set their *direction bit*. On 1st use, prefetch with variable degree $[0\ldots x]$ according to the *direction bit* of the block
	$Ad3(x)$	Behaves like $Ad1(x)$, but timeliness and pollution are taken into account
	$Ad4(x,y)$	$Ad2(x)$ applied to y memory regions
	$Ad5(x)$	Follows [6]

a maximum degree x. $Ad2(x)$ prefetches both the next and the previous block on every demand miss, and tags them with the direction they were prefetched (forward or backward). Then, on the first use of a prefetched block *degree* blocks are prefetched following the direction indicated by the block accessed. Therefore, $Ad2(x)$ requires an extra bit per block, besides the one needed by any sequential tagged prefetcher. The $Ad4(x,y)$ policy applies $Ad2(x)$ to y memory regions. It needs 3 counters per memory region to adapt the degree independently.

The $Ad3(x)$ policy takes also into account timeliness and pollution. Here, *up* also increases with *late prefetches* (demand misses on blocks that are being prefetched but that have not reached L2 yet) trying to make up for them. In $Ad3(x)$ the *down* counter also accounts for pollution due to prefetch (demanded blocks replaced by prefetched blocks and causing a demand miss later on). To track this last event we use a Bloom filter like in [27].

$Ad5(x)$ uses a *prefetch* counter, a *useful* counter and a *degree* counter. It closely follows [6] except in that all original counters are four bits long and hence degree range is $[0\ldots 15]$ whereas we let degree increase up to 32.

4 Experimental Environment

The simulation environment is based on SimpleScalar 3.0 using Alpha binaries [2]. SimpleScalar was modified to model in detail a superscalar processor with a three-level on-chip cache memory (Fig. 4). Table 2 shows the baseline architecture parameters. The first-level data cache (L1d) supports up to four loads, one store and up to two loads, or two stores, and includes a store buffer, replicated for supporting four lookups by cycle. Store-load dependences go through a perfect predictor. L2 follows the Itanium 2 model. L2Q holds all data references to the sixteen banks. Refill of the L1d critical block proceeds in parallel with refill in L2. When a load references L1d, its dependent instructions are speculatively issued. L2 tags and L1d are accessed in parallel in the first memory stage.

We run the simple Simpoints, warming caches and branch predictor during 200 million instructions [24]. We selected those SPEC CPU 2000 applications that achieve a speedup greater than 2% with an ideal L2. Table 3 shows the characteristics of the benchmark programs.

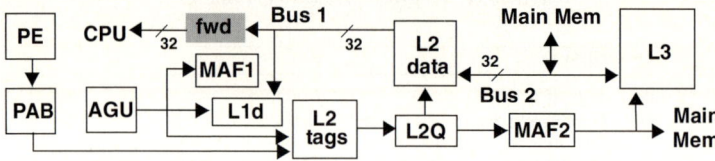

Fig. 4. Main components of the memory hierarchy. AGU: *Address Generation Unit*; L1d: *1st-level data cache*; L2 (tags/data): *2nd-level cache*: MAF1 /MAF2: Miss Address File; L3: 3rd-level cache; fwd: forwarding crossbar; PE: Prefetch Engine; PAB: Prefetch Address Buffer.

Table 2. Baseline architecture: parameters

Fetch & Dec.	8 instructions per cycle
Issue / Retire / ROB	8 int + 4 fp / 16 instructions per cycle / 256 entries
IQ / Exec. Units	64 int + 32 fp / 8 int ALU, 2 int MUL, 4 fp ALU, 4 fp MUL
Store Buffer	128 entries
Branch Pred.	hybrid bi-modal, Gshare (16 bits)
Cache L1 d	16 KB, block 32 B, 2-way, lat. 2 cycles write-through non-allocate, Miss Addr. File (MAF1): 16 entries
Cache L1 i	Ideal
Cache L2	256 KB, block 128 B, 8 way, 16 banks 16B-interleaved. Serial access: tag 1 cycle + data 2 c. (ld/use lat: 8 c.) Write-back alloc., L2Q 32 entries, WB 6 entries, MAF2: 8 entries
Cache L3	4 MB, block 128 B, 16 way; write-back alloc.; WB 2 entries, Serial access: tag 2 cycle pipelined + data 4 c. (ld/use lat: 13 c.)
Memory	Latency 200 cycles; bandwidth 1/20 cycles

Concerning the implementation of the five tested prefetchers, we do not prefetch addresses beyond the physical page limit (8 KB), and data are always brought into L2. We selected optimal table sizes for each prefetching method setting the prefetch degree to one and varying table configuration over a wide range. The number of entries per table are 32 in STR, 256(IT)×256(GHB) in PC/DC, 256(HT)×256(DT) in PDFCM and 32 (Accumulation table) / 64 (FT) / 1024×16 (PHT) in SMS. A Prefetch Address Buffer (PAB) holds addresses issued for prefetching, as many as indicated by the maximum degree. When the prefetch degree is greater than one, the second and following prefetches are issued at a one-per-cycle rate in all prefetchers. Prefetches are not issued if less than 5 free entries are left in MAF2. This precaution dramatically cut losses in all aggressive prefetchers. In STR the LT is read in the address generation stage for every reference. Prefetches are issued in the first memory stage. LT entries are always updated (or assigned) in the Commit stage only for references that hit in LT (or miss in L2). The PC/DC predictor is updated in the first memory stage at a maximum rate of one per cycle. Update and predict activities in PDFCM are also carried out in the memory stage at a maximum rate of one per cycle. SMS matches the implementation given in [26].

Table 3. L1, L2 and L3 miss rates and IPC for the selected benchmarks

		vpr	gcc	mcf	parser	gap	vortex	bzip2	twolf		
CINT	L1 mr	7.2%	2.4%	34.1%	7.6%	1.4%	2.5%	3.1%	12.6%		
	L2 mr	2.5%	0.5%	19.6%	0.8%	0.1%	0.3%	1.2%	4.3%		
	L3 mr	0.3%	0.1%	13.2%	0.0%	0.1%	0.1%	0.0%	0.0%		
	IPC	1.29	5.19	0.24	2.27	1.74	4.72	2.44	1.96		
		wupwise	swim	mgrid	applu	galgel	art	equake	facerec	ammp	fma3d	apsi
CFP	L1 mr	3.3%	23.8%	7.4%	13.8%	15.7%	73.7%	19.3%	4.5%	12.1%	3.0%	1.2%
	L2 mr	0.8%	5.0%	1.8%	3.0%	3.3%	41.5%	3.4%	2.2%	4.6%	0.5%	0.1%
	L3 mr	0.7%	5.0%	0.9%	2.9%	0.2%	0.0%	3.2%	0.2%	0.1%	0.4%	0.1%
	IPC	2.88	0.81	1.94	1.33	3.31	2.22	0.50	2.07	2.74	2.45	4.57

Thresholds for the *up* and *down* counters in the adaptive policies are preset to 100 and 50 events respectively. We experimented with different values, but results were hardly affected as long as the threshold ratio was kept.

5 Results

We have already seen that SMS is the state-of-the-art prefetcher that gives the best results in the preliminary experiments (Sect. 2), and therefore we will use it as the reference for evaluating our proposals.

We do not show the breakdown of results per application for the sake of space. The only benchmarks showing performance losses due to prefetch are ammp — where Deg-dist(x) and Deg(x), on the one hand, and Deg$(1-x)$ and Dist(x), on the other hand, are paired in terms of losses— and art (Deg(32)). No loss shows up in any application for any adaptive method.

Figure 5 gathers the geometric mean of the normalized execution times related to the base system of all the policies we consider in this work (Table 1). In general, the best options for CINT are those with degree $x = \{4, 8\}$, while $x = \{8, 16\}$ yields better results in CFP. Ad5(x) and Dist(x) show the poorest performance in both CINT and CFP groups, hence we will not consider them in which follows. The rest of the techniques perform similar to Deg with $x = \{4, 8\}$ in CINT and to Deg with $x = \{8, 16\}$ in CFP. Among the techniques without losses, the best choice in CINT is Ad4(8, 32) (91.9%) but differences are below 1% with Ad2(4), Ad2(8), Ad4(4, 32), Ad4(16, 32) and SMS. However SMS is widely outperformed in CFP by all the adaptive ones (except Ad5(x)). The best one is now Ad3(x) (62.9%), while SMS amounts to 67.1%), but Ad1(8), Ad2(8), and Ad4(8, 32) are all of them less than 1% above Ad3(x). All in all, Ad4(8, 32) and Ad2(8) seem to be the best tradeoffs on average (INT, CFP).

Figure 6 shows the pressure each technique makes on the memory hierarchy in terms of generated prefetches, lookups in L2, L2 misses and useful prefetches. The difference between the last two bars indicates the percentage of useless prefetches. Ad1(x) and Ad3(x) keep useless prefetches below SMS, whereas Ad2(x) and Ad4(x, y) are a little bit less efficient than SMS concerning this subject.

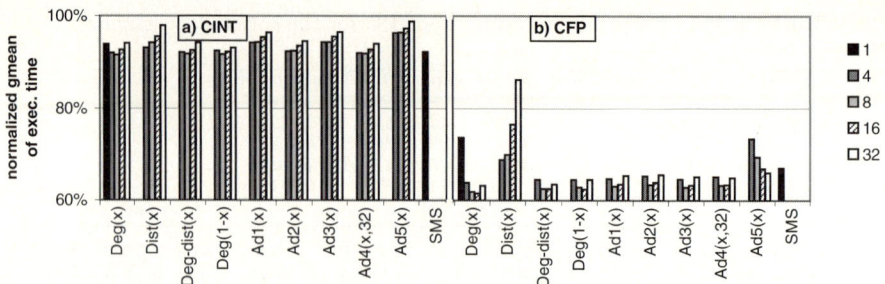

Fig. 5. Comparison of the best adaptive policies in the selected applications

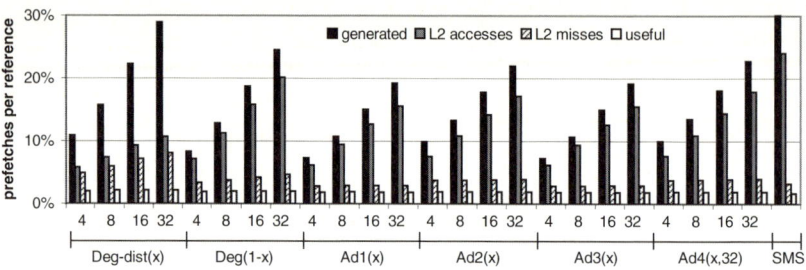

Fig. 6. Pressure on the memory hierarchy. Percentages refer to the number of committed memory references.

Using the Prefetch Address Buffer as a filter. We propose to reduce the pressure on the second cache level (L2) by using the Prefetch Address Buffer (PAB) as a filter. The PAB keeps prefetch requests after they are generated by the PE and until they lookup the L2 tags. Whenever new prefetch addresses are generated, the prefetch unit accesses the PAB to check if they are already on the buffer, to avoid issuing them again. Our proposal maintains the prefetch addresses on the PAB after the lookup on L2 tags, replacing them only when a new PAB entry is needed in FIFO order. New prefetch addresses check all the PAB entries, so they are filtered if they match any of the last N prefetch addresses generated by the PE, where N is the PAB size. Following this strategy, L2 lookups are reduced by 2% for Deg-dist(x), and between 25% and 40% for the rest of policies shown in Fig. 6, leaving performance unaffected. The higher reduction is achieved in SMS (49%), but L2 lookups are still above the figures for the rest of prefetchers. Thus, our best choices in Fig. 5 (Ad4(8, 32) and Ad2(8)) give 7.5%, well below the 12.3% for SMS.

Hardware cost. All the adaptive methods we have proposed require three counters, and an extra bit per cache line –because of the underlying tagged sequential mechanism– accounting for 2Kbit (256 B). Ad2(x) requires another bit to record the direction of the prefetching. Ad3(x) needs a 4 Kbit array (512 B) to implement the Bloom filter. Counters in Ad4(x, y) are per region, hence the best point (8, 32) needs a 64 B table. The approximated table sizes for STR, PC/DC, PDFCM and SMS are respectively 512 B, 4 KB, 5 KB and 33 KB.

6 Conclusions

We have proposed here different simple ways of tuning the aggressiveness of a sequential prefetcher so that it can perform similar to or better than the best state-of-the-art prefetcher, SMS [26]. Among the options we propose, Ad2(8) and Ad4(8, 32) perform the best. Both are adaptive mechanisms that vary the sequential prefetching degree (up and down) according to prefetching usefulness. Ad2(8) prefetches forward and backward with variable degree. Ad4(8, 32) splits memory into 32 regions and keeps separated counters for each region. Both of them equal SMS in CINT and outperform it in CFP, with 60% less lookups in L2. Ad2(8) needs just two bits per cache line and Ad4(8, 32), additionally, a 64 B table. This is far less than the 33 KB needed by SMS tables.

We also propose a simple filtering technique using the Prefetch Address Buffer that helps to reduce significatively the pressure of prefetching on the second level cache. It reduces the L2 lookups generated by Ad2(8) and Ad4(8, 32) in 30%.

Considering the prefetchers implemented by manufacturers so far, ours are a feasible choice showing no losses on typical integer and floating point workloads at a really low hardware cost.

Acknowledgments. Supported by Diputación General Aragón *Grupo Consolidado Investigación*, Spanish MEC TIN2007-66423, and the European HiPEAC-2 (FP7/ICT 217068).

References

1. Baer, J.L., Chen, T.F.: An Effective On-chip Preloading Scheme to Reduce Data Access Penalty. In: ICS, pp. 176–186 (1991)
2. Burger, D., Austin, T.: The SimpleScalar Toolset, v. 3.0, www.simplescalar.org
3. Burger, D., et al.: Filtering Superfluous Prefetches Using Density Vectors. In: ICCD, p. 124 (2001)
4. Charney, M.J., Reeves, A.P.: Generalized correlation-based hardware prefetching. TR EECEG-95-1, School of Electrical Engineering, Cornell Univ. (February 1995)
5. Cooksey, R., et al.: A Stateless, Content-Directed Data Prefetching Mechanism. In: ASPLOS-X, S. Jose, CA, pp. 279–290 (October 2002)
6. Dahlgren, F., et al.: Fixed and Adaptive Sequential Prefetching in Shared-Memory Multiprocessors. In: ICPP, pp. 156–163. CRC Press, Boca Raton (1993)
7. Dahlgren, F., Stenström, P.: Evaluation of Hardware-Based Stride and Sequential Prefetching in Shared-Memory Multiprocessors. IEEE Trans. Parallel and Distributed Systems 7(4), 385–398 (1996)
8. Doweck, J.: Inside Intel Core Microarchitecture and Smart Memory Access. White Paper, Intel Corporation (2006)
9. Goeman, B., et al.: Differential FCM: Increasing Value Prediction Accuracy by Improving Table Usage Efficiency. In: HPCA-7, Monterrey, Mexico, pp. 207–218 (2001)

10. Gracia, D., et al.: MicroLib: A Case for the Quantitative Comparison of Micro-Architecture Mechanisms. MICRO-37, 43–54 (2004)
11. Hu, Z., et al.: TCP Tag Correlating Prefetchers, HPCA-9 (2003)
12. Hur, I., Lin, C.: Memory Prefetching Using Adaptive Stream Detection. MICRO-39, 397–408 (2006)
13. Ibáñez, P., et al.: Characterization and Improvement of Load/Store Cache-based Prefetching. In: ICS, Melbourne, Australia, pp. 369–376 (July 1998)
14. Joseph, D., Grunwald, D.: Prefetching Using Markov Predictors. IEEE Trans. on Computer Systems 48(2), 121–133 (1999)
15. Jouppi, N.: Improving direct-mapped cache performance by addition of a small fully associative cache and prefetch buffers. In: ISCA-17, Seattle, WA (1990)
16. Kalla, R., et al.: IBM Power5 chip: A dual-core multithreaded processor. IEEE Micro. 24(2), 40–47 (2004)
17. Krewell, K.: Fujitsu Makes SPARC See Double. Microproc. Report (November 2003)
18. Lai, A., et al.: Dead-Block Correlating Prefetchers. In: ISCA-28, pp. 144–154 (2001)
19. Lin, W.F., et al.: Filtering superfluous prefetches using density vectors. In: ICCD 2001, Washington D.C., USA, pp. 124–132. IEEE Comp. Society, Los Alamitos (2001)
20. Nesbit, K.J., Smith, J.E.: Data Cache Prefetching Using a Global History Buffer. In: HPCA-10, Madrid, Spain, pp. 96–105 (2004)
21. Nesbit, K.J., Smith, J.E.: Data Cache Prefetching Using a Global History Buffer. IEEE Micro. 25(3), 90–97 (2005)
22. Ramos, L.M., et al.: Data prefetching in a cache hierarchy with high bandwidth and capacity. SIGARCH Comput. Archit. News 35(4), 37–44 (2007), http://doi.acm.org/10.1145/1327312.1327319
23. Sair, S., et al.: A Decoupled Predictor-Directed Stream Prefetching Architecture. IEEE Trans. on Computers 52(3), 260–276 (2003)
24. Sherwood, T., et al.: Automatically Characterizing Large Scale Program Behaviour. In: ASPLOS-X (October 2002)
25. Smith, A.J.: Sequential Program Prefetching in Memory Hierarchies. IEEE Trans. on Computers 11(12), 7–21 (1978)
26. Somogyi, S., et al.: Spatial Memory Streaming. In: ISCA-33, pp. 252–263 (2006)
27. Srinath, S., et al.: Feedback Directed Prefetching: Improving the Performance and Bandwidth-Efficiency of Hardware Prefetchers. In: HPCA-13, pp. 63–74.
28. Tendler, J.M., et al.: Power4 system microarchitecture. IBM Journal of Research and Development 46(1), 5–26 (2002)
29. UltraSPARC III Cu - User's Manual.Sun Microsystems (January 2004), http://www.sun.com/processors/manuals/USIIIv2.pdf
30. Zhuang, X., Lee, H.-H.S.: Reducing Cache Pollution via Dynamic Data Prefetch Filtering. IEEE Trans. on computers 56(1), 18–31 (2007)

Stream Scheduling: A Framework to Manage Bulk Operations in Memory Hierarchies

Abhishek Das and William J. Dally

Computer Systems Laboratory, Stanford University
{abhishek,billd}@cva.stanford.edu

Abstract. With the emergence of streaming and multi-core architectures, there is an increasing demand to map parallel algorithms efficiently across all architectures. This paper describes a platform-independent optimization framework called Stream Scheduling, that orchestrates parallel execution of bulk computations and data transfers, and allocates storage at multiple levels of a memory hierarchy. By adjusting block sizes, and applying software pipelining on bulk operations, it ensures computation-to-communication ratio is maximized on each level. We evaluate our framework on a diverse set of Sequoia applications, targeting systems with different memory hierarchies: a Cell blade, a distributed-memory cluster, and the Cell blade attached to a disk.

Keywords: Stream Scheduling, Bulk Operations, Sequoia, GSOP, Memory Hierarchy, Software Pipelining, Tunables.

1 Introduction

Recently, streaming architectures such as Imagine[1], Storm-1[2], and Cell BE[3] were demonstrated to achieve significantly higher performance and efficiency over traditional architectures by introducing an explicitly managed on-chip storage. This software managed memory serves as a staging area for large amounts of data, making all functional unit memory references short and predictable, and thereby transferring the onus of latency tolerance from hardware to software. Stream programming model[1][6] captured this new paradigm by making computation (kernels) and communication (stream transfers) explicit in a 2-level storage hierarchy for stream processors. Structuring algorithms to explicitly service data from levels of storage residing closer to the functional units applies to modern systems of all scales. Levels of memory hierarchy could include on-die storage, local DRAM, or even remote memory accessed over high-speed interconnect. This often creates a deep memory hierarchy, going beyond the two levels captured in the stream programming model. Sequoia[5] was recently introduced to structure bandwidth-efficient and portable parallel programs by abstracting any machine as a tree of distinct memory modules, and by providing explicit language mechanisms to describe communication and blocking of arrays vertically through the hierarchy. Such programs create a hierarchy of bulk operations, either transfers of data in bulk (arrays) or coarse-grained computations (kernels), either of which take 100s to 1000s of cycles.

With the ubiquity of multi-processor systems and the emergence of multi-core architectures, it has become essential to optimize performance by managing bulk operations explicitly. In addition, programs often need to employ architecture-specific optimizations for high performance. Hence, it is essential to create a platform-independent compilation framework that allows efficient development of parallel algorithms. Stream Scheduling was introduced in [6] to aid compilation for stream processors, which process sequential streams on a 2-level memory hierarchy. The primary contribution of this paper is to show that Stream Scheduling can be extended to schedule bulk operations on any machine with a hierarchy (multiple levels) of memories, as well as to size and allocate blocks of multi-dimensional array data on each level.

- We first map Sequoia programs to a hierarchical graph representation (GSOP graph) that is used as input to the Stream Scheduler, and can represent any hierarchy of bulk operations, along with the mapped memory levels.
- Next, we introduce a recursive operation ordering algorithm that applies the same optimizations on each level of a memory hierarchy, working in an inside-out fashion, thereby making the framework scalable.
- Since software pipelining is critical in maximizing coarse-grained parallelism, we introduce optimizations that enhance it by exploiting slack.
- Finally, we efficiently allocate storage on each memory level, while applying the steepest gradient search to determine sizes of multi-dimension array blocks (*tunables*) that yield maximum performance.

2 Sequoia Programs

Sequoia [5] describes machines as a tree of memories. At any given level in the tree, there is a memory and zero or more parallel sub-machines. Programs are described as hierarchies of *tasks* that include descriptions of data communication and working sets, and are mapped to the memory hierarchy of a target machine. Parameter passing semantics on tasks are used to describe data transfers between different memory levels, while computational kernels are localized to leaf nodes. To optimize working-sets staged in each memory level, and to exploit the parallel processing units, it is essential to break down large computations into smaller sub-tasks. Sequoia provides a family of array blocking functions to facilitate task decompositions, which range from the simplicity of regular blocking to the irregularity of arbitrary array gathers. To make programs portable, blocking is usually expressed in parameterized form. The parameter values (called *tunables*) define the working set size in each memory level. Figure 1 demonstrates Sequoia's task decomposition for matrix multiplication (*matrixmult*) on a Cell BE [3]. The disk acts as the root, parenting the PowerPC (PPE) main memory, while each of the eight software-managed SPE local stores (LSes) correspond to leaves. As shown here, the *matrixmult* task first decomposes large matrices resident in the disk into smaller sub-matrices, such that they can reside in main memory, before dividing them further into LS-sized matrices. All memory levels use same tunable

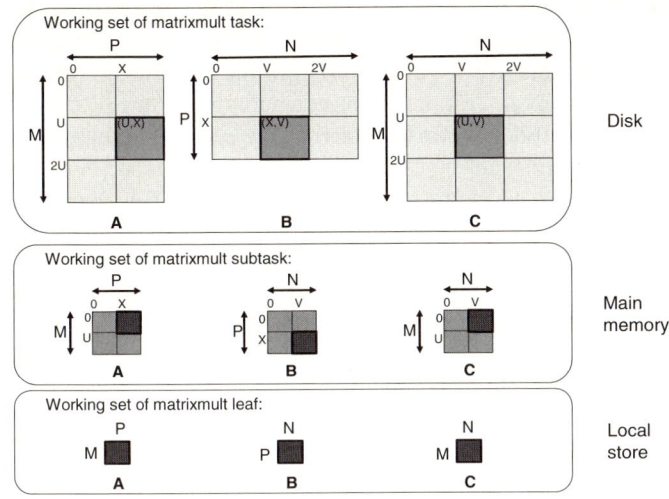

Fig. 1. Task decomposition of *matrixmult* on Cell BE

symbols, U, V and X (dimensions of matrices), but are tailored separately for the respective working-sets.

Knight et al. [4] had presented an intermediate representation (IR) that can describe operational semantics for any Sequoia program. It represents programs as a hierarchy of following operations, each mapped to specific memory level(s): Scalar_M, Kernel_M, Copy_{M_i,M_j}, Exec_M, If_M, For_M, ForAll_M, and $\text{Group}_{M,G}$, where the subscript M symbolizes level(s) of the memory hierarchy on which each operation executes. While Scalar_M corresponds to operations on scalar data only, Kernel_M performs bulk computations on array data. Copy_{M_i,M_j} represents data transfers between memory levels M_i and M_j (bigger indices indicate memories closer to root). Exec_M starts a new SPMD-style execution of tasks on each of its children, whereas If_M, For_M, and ForAll_M are used for control flow, the latter expressing a loop in which iterations can be executed in any order, including in parallel. Finally, $\text{Group}_{M,G}$ assigns a dependence graph G on the operations, giving a partial order of execution.

2.1 GSOP Graph

When introduced in [6], Stream Scheduling was made to accept programs that can be represented as a Stream Operation Precedence (SOP) graph. Each node in the SOP graph represented a coarse-grained stream operation, either a kernel or a memory transfer. The directional edges connecting them were input and output stream(s), representing program data-flow. Control-flow was captured by making the graph hierarchical, much like nested loops. At each nested level, basic blocks get encapsulated in *supernodes* that are connected by control- and data-flow edges. Each supernode essentially is a SOP sub-graph of bulk nodes and nested supernodes, and acts as a coarse-grained operation.

We now describe a more Generalized SOP (GSOP) graph that can represent programs with any hierarchy of operations. We do so by providing a direct mapping of the Sequoia IR to the GSOP graph. Firstly, we observe that the bulk Kernel_M and Copy_{M_i,M_j} operations can substitute for the stream operation nodes in the SOP graph. Similarly, control flow corresponding to If_M, For_M, and ForAll_M operations can be captured by the supernodes. Now we only need to incorporate memory levels into the our graph. Note that Exec_M is the only operation in the IR that traverses memory levels, by spawning task execution on lower levels of the memory hierarchy. Since the hierarchy of a SOP graph is already structured around supernodes, we extend their scope to capture both control and memory hierarchy. A supernode corresponding to an Exec_M contains a sub-graph of operations (nodes and supernodes), that were spawned by it and execute on levels M_{i-1} or below, including supernodes for $\text{Exec}_{M_{i-1}}$ (which in turn spawn operations on levels lower than M_{i-1}). In addition, we also add scalar operation nodes to the GSOP graph.

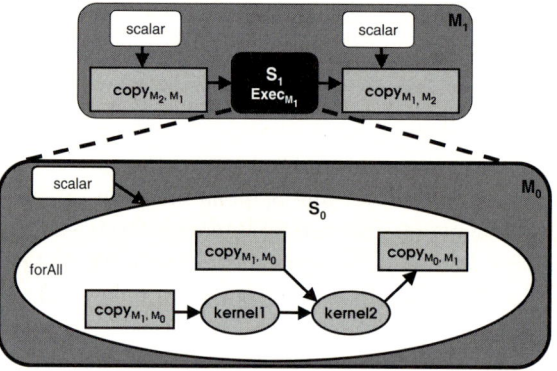

Fig. 2. Hierarchical GSOP graph

Figure 2 illustrates such a GSOP graph on 3 memory levels: a chain of kernels execute in a parallel loop (supernode S_0) on the leaf memories (M_0), which itself is contained within another supernode S_1 spawned from memory level M_1; inputs(outputs) to(from) S_1 require data transfers between levels M_1 and M_2.

3 Stream Scheduling

The primary goal of *Stream Scheduling* is to minimize application execution time. Bulk operations must be coordinated to maximize coarse-grained parallelism and to efficiently utilize memory and computation resources. Use of expensive external (higher levels of memory) bandwidth must be restrained, since spilling an array block could require reading and writing thousands of extra data elements.

3.1 Hierarchical Operation Ordering

Program execution time can be minimized by keeping functional units busy with useful computation, while latency of data transfers can be hidden by performing them in bulk, and by overlapping with computation. Memory systems in modern processors allow such asynchronous bulk transfers using machine primitives such as DMAs and asynchronous I/O (AIO). Before allocating storage, Stream Scheduling determines the best possible assignment of processing units. It creates a resource reservation table and then schedules GSOP operations on these resources using top-down greedy static list scheduling.Priority (criticality) of each operation in achieving the minimum total execution time is determined using topological sort.

Since the GSOP graph is hierarchical, we need to devise a scalable algorithm that can capture both control-flow and memory level hierarchy. Our hierarchical algorithm works in an *inside-out* recursive fashion, applying the same ordering algorithm to increasing levels of hierarchy at a time (*bottom-up* in the tree hierarchy of memories). When applied at level l, all operations in level $l+1$ and above are ignored for scheduling, while operations below level l get encapsulated within supernodes that occupy resources in level $l-1$ and below (determined by the schedule for its corresponding sub-graph). All control-flow supernodes within a given memory level share the same resources, whereas new resources become available on moving up the memory hierarchy (say from M_{i-1} to M_i). These resources can potentially be used for asynchronous data transfers.

To illustrate on Cell, all operations within a SPE (memory level 0) are scheduled first on the respective computation (SPU) and DMA units. When applied at memory level 1, the operations are either asynchronous transfers between main memory and disk (controlled by PPE), or supernodes that execute on SPE

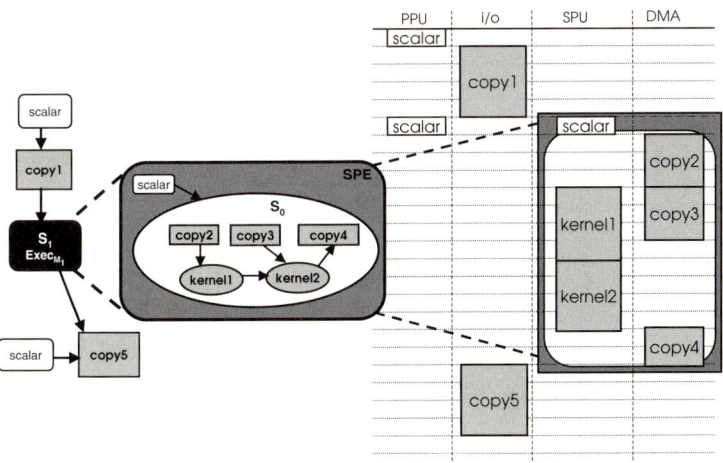

Fig. 3. Hierarchical operation ordering on a Cell processor that is attached to a disk. For ease of illustration, operations are shown to take only a few cycles for execution.

resources. Figure 3 demonstrates this ordering of operations for the earlier shown GSOP graph (Figure 2). Note that multiple iterations of the `ForAll` loop (S_0) execute in parallel on different SPEs, but follow the same schedule.

Controlling Asynchronous Operations: Since hardware mechanisms are not always available to enforce dependencies between asynchronous stream operations, software checks are often required. The control thread running these checks, however, may need to execute on the same unit as that used by an atomic bulk operations. Taking the example of Cell, a single run-time thread on the SPE executes kernels as well as initiates DMA requests. It is essential to account for this conflict during operation ordering. Hence, we not only allocate execution resources to GSOP operations, but also the respective control resources which issue them. The duration of control resource occupancy includes setting up bulk data transfers, such as chopping of multi-dimensional array block transfers into multiple sequential block transfers.

Execution Time Estimation: Stream Scheduling relies on rough execution models to estimate the duration of each GSOP operation, as demonstrated earlier in [6]. Due to the coarse granularity of these operations, and for the use of optimization purposes only, rough execution models suffice. Given a target machine specification, we apply the same models as in [6] to derive bulk operation execution times.

3.2 Software Pipelining

Software pipelining [7] is a popular loop optimization technique that reorders operations to exploit parallelism across successive loop iterations. It can immensely benefit coarse-grained programs by overlapping kernels and data transfers from different iterations, thereby hiding memory latency. These include memory accesses that must occur between a pair of sequential kernels, as well as loads and stores at the start and end of each iteration. Since blocking of data is essential in a memory hierarchy, Sequoia provides mapping primitives (*mappar*) that allows execution on parallel loop iterations without dynamic aliasing.

We perform software pipelining by applying conventional modulo scheduling [7] on the GSOP graph, which selects a (minimum) common schedule for all iterations of a loop. This initiation interval (II) is determined by the most heavily utilized resource and the worst case recurrence for the loop. Each GSOP operation is greedily scheduled on a resource reservation table that spans for time II, occupying it in modulo fashion. Due to the coarse granularity of operations, this is equivalent to searching for a large enough hole (interval) in the table that can fit each bulk operation.

Hole Optimization: On failing to find such a hole within the estimated II, the iteration interval is incremented and the operations are rescheduled. Due to the long execution times of bulk operations (100s to 1000s of cycles), coarse increase in II can significantly hurt performance. Instead, we observe that the currently available holes can themselves be made larger by exploiting *slack* on operations that were scheduled in previous stages. To illustrate on the GSOP graph in Figure 4(a), the schedule on the left shows $Kernel2_{B,C \to C}$ failing to modulo-schedule on the processing element (PE) because $Kernel1_{A \to B}$ was greedily scheduled earlier (immediately following the load A), leaving only smaller holes for $Kernel2_{B,C \to C}$ to fit in. Fortunately, $Kernel1_{A \to B}$ enjoys some slack as its only constraint is to be scheduled before $Kernel2_{B,C \to C}$. We reduce this slack by delaying $Kernel1_{A \to B}$ further, which allows $Kernel2_{B,C \to C}$ to successfully schedule within the original II. By definition, cutting down slack doesn't violate any dependencies. To conclude, the hole optimization creates bigger holes by delaying operations in previous stages, only if the total slack available is long enough to create the required larger hole.

Modulo Variable Expansion (MVE): Lifetime of a data object often overlaps with a subsequent definition of itself during modulo scheduling. Modulo variable expansion (MVE) [7] prevents such cross-iteration overwrites by using different copies of the data object in each conflicting stage. This illustrated in Figure 4(a), where load of C is overlapped with computation on C' (stage 2).

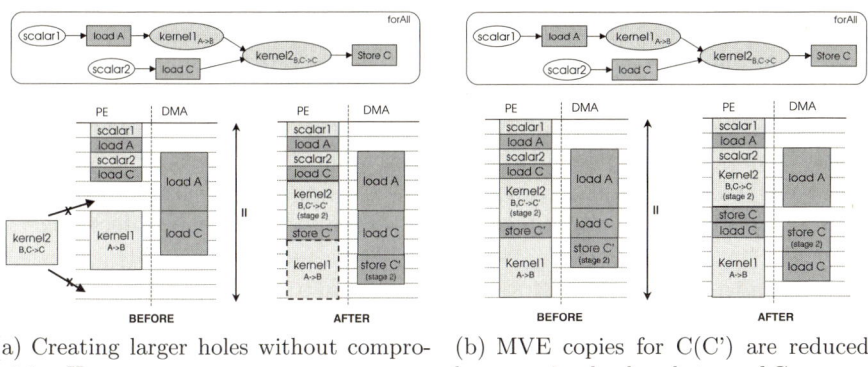

(a) Creating larger holes without compromising II

(b) MVE copies for C(C') are reduced by swapping load and store of C

Fig. 4. Software pipelining optimizations that exploit slack in bulk operations

3.3 Memory Management

Efficient management of memories is essential for high performance since significant portions of program data accesses are staged at each memory level. Prior work in [6] described a static allocation mechanism that reduces use of expensive bandwidth by exploiting producer-consumer locality, while preserving the concurrency exposed through operation ordering. Since similar bandwidth and space constraints exist on machines with even deeper memory hierarchies, we apply the same allocation mechanism on each explicitly managed memory module. Packing fails when data objects try to occupy more space than is available, which is either due to too many data objects subscribing for storage at the same time, or due to the over-estimation of working-set size. While the former is due to excessive concurrency exposed during operation ordering and is addressed below, we discuss the latter in section 3.4.

When storage is over-subscribed, the heuristic applied in [6] sacrifices concurrency, thereby reducing lifetimes and easing storage pressure. Spilling is only used as a last option, preferably for data objects that are accessed after long intervals of time. This heuristic isn't very effective for data objects with MVE copies since each copy is live for entire II duration. We introduce another optimization that exploits slack and reduces MVE copies, without compromising II. Total number of required MVE copies for any data object is derived from its first and last accesses in the schedule:

$$copies = stage_{lastaccess} - stage_{firstaccess} + \lceil (time_{lastaccess} - time_{firstaccess})/II \rceil$$

This implies that copies can be reduced either by delaying the object's definition, or by moving the last accessing operation earlier in time. To illustrate on Figure 4(b), the schedule on the left shows $store_C$ being scheduled after $load_C$ since the DMA unit was busy upon $Kernel_{B,C \to C}$'s completion. This requires two concurrent copies of C: while one is being computed on (stage 2), a new copy is fetched from memory (stage 1). Only one copy is sufficient, however, if $store_C$ can precede $load_C$. We observe that the slack enjoyed by $load_C$ can be reduced to delay it further, thereby allowing $store_C$ to move earlier. As shown on the right, we achieve our desired result by swapping the two operations. Hence, to explore if the last accessed operation can be moved earlier (in modulo fashion), we look for the net slack available in operations scheduled earlier on the same resource. If delaying them doesn't increase MVE copies for other data objects, and opens up a big enough hole to fit the operation, we move the operation earlier. Swapping is continued in this fashion until the number of required MVE copies decrement.

3.4 Tunable Search

To facilitate portability in Sequoia, working-set sizes in each memory level are bounded by symbolic parameters, called *tunables*. These parameters are used with array blocking primitives [8] to decompose a large task into smaller sub-tasks in the memory hierarchy. For maximum performance, Stream Scheduler must select tunable values that optimize the computation-to-communication ratio in each memory level. These tunables essentially are the control knobs to tune performance on a target machine.

With only a single tunable parameter, selection of tunables reduces to finding the best performing strip-size (tunable) in a strip-mined loop [8], which can be addressed using binary search [6]. To illustrate, we have shown on the left of Figure 5 the variation of a typical strip-mined loop's execution time (cost) when strip-size is increased. Performance improves initially since more data (larger strip) becomes available for computation, while software pipelining ensures latency of transfers are hidden. Performance suffers when the increased storage demand requires spilling, or when pipelining stages have to be decreased. This behavior is also representative of programs with multiple tunables, as shown

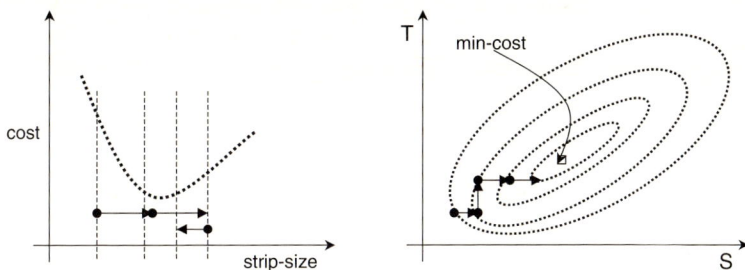

Fig. 5. Binary search and approximate steepest descent search for tunables (dotted plots represent execution times; arrows specify progression of search)

by the 2D plane (tunables S and T) on the right, where contour lines define bounds on the execution time cost. Multiple tunable parameters are usually representative of the different dimensions of array blocks, thereby defining nested strip-mined loops. Though we don't attempt a formal proof, our observation and experimental results suggest that the cost function (execution time) is convex, while the contours are sub-level sets.

This motivates us to adapt the method of steepest descent search [12], using estimated program execution time as cost function. However, due to the lack of a closed-form expression for scheduling cost, we can't determine its gradient. Instead, starting from the initial set of value specified during task mapping, we approach the minimal point by moving along the dimensions of the plane. At every step, relative performance is compared by scaling tunables in each dimension (one at a time). The tunable which reduces the cost most is selected to advance the search, as illustrated with arrows on the contours in Figure 5. A second phase of binary search, similar to the strip-size search algorithm in [6], is required at the end when selecting the best tunable overshoots the minima. Tunable search is also wrapped around the bottom-up hierarchical scheduling discussed earlier.

4 Evaluation

We plug the Stream Scheduler to the back-end of the Sequoia compiler infrastructure [4], and evaluate its performance by executing a suite of Sequoia applications on three different system configurations: a Cell blade, a cluster of workstations, and a Cell blade attached to a parallel ATA disk drive. As discussed before, the Cell broadband engine [3] exposes a two level memory hierarchy. A third level gets added to the hierarchy when a disk is attached. Transfers between disk and external memory are managed by the PowerPC using asynchronous I/O (AIO) routines, while an asynchronous Memory Flow Controller (MFC) DMA unit manages transfers between LS and main memory. The 3.2GHz Cell BE accesses 512MB of system memory, and is attached to a 60GB ATA/100 hard drive.

The cluster setup consists of 16 nodes each with 2.4GHz Intel P4 Xeon processors and 1GB of main memory. It also presents a two level memory hierarchy: at

Table 1. Raw application performance

Application	Arithmetic intensity	Cell (GFLOPS)	Cluster (GFLOPS)	Cell-disk (GFLOPS)
SAXPY	0.16	3.3	1.5	0.003
SGEMV	0.50	12.2	4.1	0.012
SGEMM	85~680	125	90.2	3.9
CONV2D	40.5	88.6	24	0.42
GRAVITY	~2000	96.4	67.6	66

the top is the aggregate cluster memory abstracted as a distributed shared memory (DSM), and at the bottom (leaves) are local memories. This is implemented by partitioning node memories for local and DSM use, and by pre-distributing the input data over DSM in block-cyclic fashion. We ignore lower level caches since the Sequoia run-time system can't manage them currently. Two threads are launched on each node at run-time, one to handle inter-node communication using MPI calls, and another to handle execution of kernels and other compute functions. Remote inter-node communication is performed on an Infiniband interconnect (achieves ~400MB/s).

The applications used in our evaluation are shown in Table 1, kernel implementations for which were tuned using either SSE2 or Cell SPE intrinsics. While the first three are BLAS benchmarks, the latter two include a 9x9 filter convolution and an N-body stellar dynamics simulation on 8192 particles.

4.1 Raw Performance and Resource Utilization

The raw performance achieved for each application is shown in Table 1, which is in close correlation with the inherent arithmetic intensity. To understand the raw numbers better, we show the execution time breakdown for each application in Figure 6, including time spent in kernels, in idle waiting on transfers between different memory levels, and in incurring overheads (such as setting up transfers). On both Cell and cluster, SGEMM, and GRAVITY are compute limited and fully utilize the arithmetic resources, rarely idle waiting on memory. Though CONV2D is compute-limited on Cell, its performance on cluster is limited by network bandwidth as parts of image data need to be read from neighboring nodes. In contrast, SAXPY and SGEMV are memory bandwidth limited; performance on cluster improves slightly due to the higher aggregate intra-node bandwidth (data pre-distribution keeps communication local).

Attaching an order of magnitude slower (~30MB/s) disk to the high performance Cell processor is bound to hurt performance of bandwidth-bound applications. Even SGEMM and CONV2D spend 65%-75% of their time waiting on disk. Though otherwise low, the runtime overheads incurred are also significant for these two. This is due to chopping of multi-dimensional array blocks into multiple sequential transfers, the overhead for which scales with block size. SGEMM suffers more as matrices are traversed in both row- and column-order. GRAVITY is least affected, with performance comparable to cluster version,

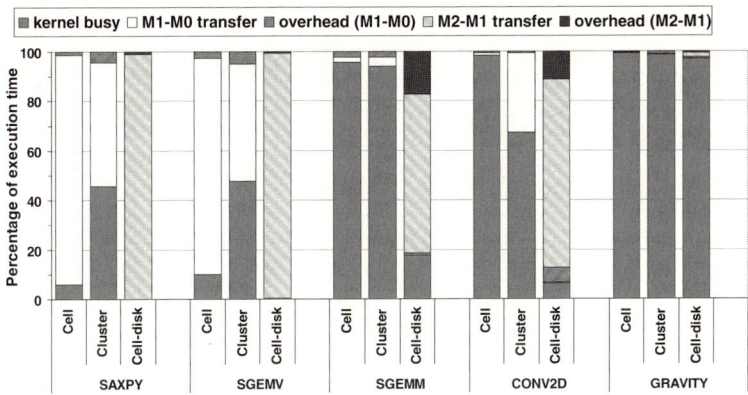

Fig. 6. Execution time breakdown

since updated particles are read from and written to disk only at the start and end of each time step.

To put our performance numbers into perspective, we compare them with those achieved on a custom cell back-end [4] and on a high-level cluster run-time [5]. After accounting for the different clock rates, our performance on Cell matches up for the memory-bound applications, while speeding up CONV2D by 15%. This speedup is due to automatic selection of larger block size tunables, which fit efficiently with MVE copies reduction. In spite of similar optimizations on SGEMM, no noticeable speedup is realized since the custom built IBM environment in [4] minimizes all run-time overheads. This also explains the 13.5% slowdown for GRAVITY, though it still exceeds the GRAPE-6A custom hardware performance [9]. When compared with the cluster run-time, we achieve 35% speedup on GRAVITY from better exploiting producer-consumer locality, while memory-bound applications suffer ~65% slowdown. This slowdown, again, is due to the custom run-time implementation's global knowledge of all program and memory states, thereby using pointer-flips to avoid local memory copies from the DSM layer, and coalescing reads and writes across multiple transfer lists; impact on CONV2D and SGEMM is not very noticeable.

4.2 Software Pipelining

As shown in Figure 7, software pipelining (SWP) achieve 30%-45% speedup for compute intensive applications on Cell. The impact on bandwidth limited applications is marginal since a single kernel can hide only a small fraction of the total communication. Though the main loop in GRAVITY executes a chain of kernels, most transfers are hidden by exploiting coarse-grained parallelism within an iteration; this leaves little to benefit from overlapping of iterations. With the disk attached, we show speedup from applying SWP at the top-level (disk) only. The results are not surprising as applications are limited by disk bandwidth. SGEMM, however, achieves significant benefit as it hides some of the

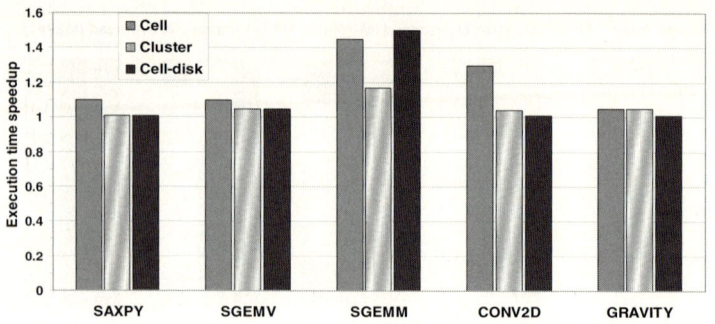

Fig. 7. Speedup from Software Pipelining

overhead of transfer list generation with disk transfers. Both memory levels on the cluster represent large off-chip memories, sizes of which are of the same order of magnitude. This allows staging of large chunks of data, thereby requiring only a few coarse-grained loops iterations to finish the entire data-set. This also leaves little room for improvement using SWP, as numerous iterations are required to amortize the priming and draining overheads.

Since all benchmarks, other than GRAVITY, consist of a single computation kernel, there is little room to exploit producer-consumer locality, or to employ hole optimization. In addition, the working-sets consist of only a few distinct array objects, leaving little flexibility for memory management. On the other hand, only SAXPY and CONV2D benefit from MVE copy reduction on Cell. Since both the disk and the node memories on cluster are orders of magnitude larger than the SPE local stores, they have little trouble in meeting the storage demands of applications. Since the size of on-chip memories, such as L2 caches and SRFs, are of the same order as the SPE local stores, we speculate that multi-core GPPs and stream processors will benefit equally from these optimizations.

5 Conclusions and Related Work

We have described a scheduling framework for managing bulk operations on machines with a hierarchy of explicitly managed memories. Characterizing programs as a GSOP graph allows for same set of optimizations to be applied recursively in a hierarchy. Acknowledging the criticality of software pipelining in hiding communication with computation, we introduced optimizations that exploit slack to enhance modulo scheduling. We also presented an automatic tunable selection algorithm, that adjusts block sizes to get the right computation-to-communication ratio on each memory level. Hence, Stream Scheduling removes the need for machine-specific optimizations.

To the best of our knowledge, this is the only known scalable framework that manages coarse-grained operations to achieve consistent performance across machines with different memory hierarchies. We treat bulk data transfers and computations as atomic operations, differing from the fine-grained techniques used for cache optimizations [8]. Our work complements the machine independent transformations [4] of the Sequoia compiler, which manipulate a hierarchy of bulk operations before mapping them to memory levels. RapidMind [10] Inc. too invokes parallel execution on collections of data (arrays), though using a dynamic compiler, which aggregates operations into bulk computation and distributes them over SPEs at run-time. Taking an alternate approach, the StreamIt compiler [11] optimizes stream programs that are constrained as synchronous data-flow (SDF) graphs.

References

1. Khailany, B., et al.: Imagine: Media processing with streams. IEEE Micro., 35–46 (March/April 2001)
2. Khailany, B., et al.: A Programmable 512 GOPS Stream Processor for Signal, Image, and Video Processing. In ISSCC Digest of Technical Papers (February 2007)
3. Pham, D., et al.: The design and implementation of a first generation cell processor. In ISSCC Digest of Technical Papers, San Francisco, CA (February 2005)
4. Knight, T.J., et al.: Compilation for explicitly managed memory hierarchies. In: Proceedings of PPoPP (2006)
5. Fatahalian, K., et al.: Sequoia: Programming the memory hierarchy. In: Conference on Supercomputing (2006)
6. Das, A., Dally, W.J., Mattson, P.: Compiling for stream processing. In: Proceedings of PACT (2006)
7. Lam, M.: Software pipelining: An effective scheduling technique for vliw machines. In: Proceedings of PLDI (1988)
8. Wolfe, M.: More iteration space tiling. In: Proceedings of the Supercomputing 1989, pp. 655–664 (November 1989)
9. Fukushige, T., Makino, J., Kawai, A.: GRAPE-6A: A Single-Card GRAPE-6 for Parallel PC-GRAPE Cluster Systems. Publications of the Astronomical Society of Japan 57, 1009–1021 (2005)
10. McCool, M.D.: Data-Parallel Programming on the Cell BE and the GPU using the RapidMind Development Platform. In: GSPx Multicore Applications Conference (October 2006)
11. Gordon, M.I., et al.: Exploiting Coarse-Grained Task, Data, and Pipeline Parallelism in Stream Programs. In: Proceedings of ASPLOS (2006)
12. Luenberger, D.G.: Linear and Nonlinear Programming. Addison-Wesley Publishing Company, CA (1984)

Interprocedural Speculative Optimization of Memory Accesses to Global Variables

Lars Gesellensetter and Sabine Glesner

Institute for Software Engineering and Theoretical Computer Science,
Technical University of Berlin, FR 5-6, Franklinstr. 28/29, 10587 Berlin, Germany
{lgeselle,glesner}@cs.tu-berlin.de
http://pes.cs.tu-berlin.de/

Abstract. The discrepancy between processor and memory speed, also known as memory gap, is steadily increasing. This means that execution speed is more and more dominated by memory accesses. We investigate the use of globals, which reside inherently in memory, in standard applications and present an approach to reduce the number of memory accesses, thereby reducing the effect of the memory gap. Our approach can explicitly deal with uncertain information and, hence, optimize more aggressively with the help of speculative techniques while not changing the semantics of the optimized programs. We present an implementation of the proposed optimization in our compiler framework for the Intel Itanium and show that our techniques lead to an increased performance for the SPEC CPU2006 benchmarks, thus showing that the impact of the memory gap can be effectively mitigated with advanced speculative optimization.

1 Introduction

Over the past decade, program performance has been increasingly influenced by memory system performance rather than CPU speed. This phenomenon, termed *memory wall* or *memory gap*, was foreseen in the 1990s [WM95] and is due to the fact that, as technology evolves, CPU speed is increasing faster than memory speed. This can have severe consequences, e.g. modern processors like the Intel Itanium stall up to 50% of the time during program execution. While this effect may not be that drastic for all classes of applications, e.g. for scientific computations on arrays, it poses a challenge for general-purpose applications. This is especially severe if complex data structures on the heap are used, because then the cache cannot mitigate all the effects of the memory system. Novel optimization techniques are therefore required to overcome the memory wall.

In this paper, we consider the class of memory accesses induced by the use of global variables. The concept of globals is widely used across programming languages. In languages with an explicit notion of memory, like C, globals generally lead inherently to memory accesses. Since all functions of a program may read or even change a global, they cannot be safely kept in a register across a call. Our goal is to optimize this class of memory accesses in order to reduce the induced memory traffic and to increase overall program performance. The effect of an optimization for a given program can be measured by the number of issued loads and stores during program run-time on the one hand, and by the overall run-time performance on the other.

Our solution is based on the idea that the memory gap can be reduced if we preload data from memory early enough. While in the classic approach, this idea is constrained by the numerous dependencies between memory accesses, speculative techniques allow for more optimization potential: By speculating about which memory dependencies will be actually present at run-time, irrelevant false dependencies can be neglected. This leads in general to more optimization and to a substantial increase in performance. Certain processors, e.g. the Intel Itanium, offer hardware support for speculatively executing instructions. We have exploited this feature in the work presented here.

In this paper, we present an algorithm to reduce the memory overhead induced by the use of global variables. Our algorithm works in two stages. First, we perform a global program analysis on global usage and use this information to keep globals in registers as long as possible. Secondly, we extend this algorithm by enriching the analysis with results from static branch prediction, and by optimizing more aggressively with the help of speculation, while still strictly preserving program semantics. As a case study, we implemented the optimization in our compiler framework and performed measurements on the Intel Itanium platform using the SPEC 2006 benchmark suite. We show that run-time improves significantly in many cases, and even more with the speculative variant.

The rest of this paper is organized as follows: In Section 2, we present empirical results on the actual use of globals in the SPEC benchmarks and introduce the concept of speculative optimizations. Section 3 presents our global program analysis for the use of global variables. The optimizations based on this information are presented in Section 4. In Section 5, we describe our case study, where we implemented the optimization for the Intel Itanium, and present the results. Related work is reviewed in Section 6, and we end with a conclusion in Section 7.

2 Background

2.1 Globals in the SPEC2006 Suite

We analyzed the use of global variables in the SPEC2006 benchmark suite to investigate the relevance of globals in standard application programs. The number of globals defined in the source programs ranges from a few to over thousand. A significant fraction (up to 75%) thereof is constituted by globals of integer and pointer type. The number of used globals correlates mainly with program size, and is similar for integer and floating-point programs, respectively.

We performed typical program runs using the *train* data of the SPEC benchmarks to measure the dynamic usage of globals at run-time (see Tab. 1). Using the instrumentation tool Pin [LCM+05], we counted all read and write accesses to main memory, resp., and compared them to the total number of issued instructions. We then distinguished between accesses to heap, stack, and global data. The latter were further broken down by different data types. We see that the amount of memory accesses ranges from 10% to almost 40% of all instructions. More specifically, in some cases accesses to globals constitute a significant fraction of all memory accesses (up to 50% for sjeng, over 20% for perlbench, still significant for gcc, gobmk, h264ref, and milc). Especially, integer globals are often the major contributors (sphinx3, milc, sjeng, perlbench, bzip2, gcc).

2.2 Speculation on Data Dependencies

On modern processors, a load can cause the processor to stall up to 200 cycles. To mitigate this problem, loads can be moved upwards to hide their latency, or redundant loads can be eliminated. In doing so, one has to consider the dependencies among the instructions. Speculative techniques can be used to neglect memory dependencies and thus provide more potential for optimization. An example is given in Fig. 1. On the left (Fig. 1(i)), a value is loaded into register $r9$ and then used. The load can entail a long stall. Moving up the load is not safe in general since $r8$ and $r11$ may refer to the same address. However, if we have some evidence that the addresses are different, we can optimize speculatively (see Fig. 1(ii)). We move the load across the store and make it an *advanced* load. Then, after the store, we check whether the loaded value is still valid. If so, we avoided a long stall. Otherwise, we simply reload it again, and the program runtime is similar to the left program. It is important to note that speculation does not sacrifice correctness. If we misspeculate, we only get additional overhead.

In the example, we assumed hardware support for speculation, which allows for efficient checks whether the speculation was correct. On the Itanium, this is done by the *ALAT (Advanced Load Address Table)*, which collects the addresses of advanced loads. Whenever a store conflicts with one of the entries, it is removed from the table. Thus a validity check simply checks whether the corresponding address is still in the ALAT. Alternatively, this can be carried out solely by software. Then, for all intervening stores, additional instructions must check whether the addresses overlap, and recovery code has to be added to reload the

Table 1. Number of executed instructions, fraction of accesses *(reads/writes)* to memory at run-time, split up by accesses to heap, stack and globals, the latter split up again by the different datatypes ('0' close to 0, '–' really 0)

	Benchmark	ins (10^9)	% ins mem	% of memory			% of global				
				heap	stack	global	int	ptr	float	arr	other
INT	perlbench	4.86	8.6/2.1	78/66	1.7/5.1	21/29	26/25	68/68	–/–	2.1/1	4.3/5.3
	bzip2	47.3	14/4.4	85/58	14/42	0.7/0	26/0.1	–/–	–/–	74/100	–/–
	gcc	6.36	13/4.1	82/59	4/9.2	14/33	19/1.6	14/0.2	–/–	50/69	17/30
	mcf	4.77	25/3	98/99	1.6/1.1	0.5/0.1	–/–	–/–	–/–	–/–	100/100
	gobmk	101	15/4.5	76/72	17/28	6.5/0.5	0/0.3	0/0	–/–	94/73	6.4/27
	hmmer	29.2	18/4.2	91/100	8.3/0	0.3/0	0.6/2.6	–/–	–/–	99/97	–/–
	sjeng	26.6	15/3.4	30/9	18/40	52/51	34/38	–/–	0/0	66/62	0/0
	h264ref	142	21/2.3	70/51	24/39	5.9/10	0.2/0.2	35/0	–/–	0.9/0.9	64/99
FP	milc	35.3	27/11	77/52	19/48	3.9/0.01	50/0.1	27/0	0/95	23/4.9	0/0
	lbm	11,0	8.4/5.1	100/100	0/0	0/0	–/–	–/–	–/–	–/–	–/–
	sphinx3	8,96	13/0.9	98/90	1.8/7.5	0.2/2.8	100/100	0/0	–/–	0/0	–/–

```
                        ld.adv r9 = [r11]              ld.adv r9 = [r11]
                        ...                            ...
  st [r8] = r12         st [r8]   = r12                st [r8]   = r12
  ld r9   = [r11]       ld.chk r9 = [r11]              cmp       r8,r11
       STALL                                           beq recovery_code
  ...     = r9          ...       = r9           back: ...       = r9

        (i)                   (ii)                          (iii)
```

Fig. 1. Speculative optimization of memory accesses

value if necessary (see Fig. 1(iii)). This leads to a larger overhead, but can still pay off if the expected gain is sufficiently high. The proposed approach of this paper can be used for both alternatives. It is only reflected in the cost model which way is chosen. We performed a case study on the Intel Itanium, which has hardware support for speculation.

3 Analysis of the Usage of Globals

In this section, we describe the analysis of the usage of globals. The optimization needs to know which pieces of code might use or change the value of a global. While this is directly known for simple instructions, it is not for function calls. We first describe a basic analysis collecting the information which globals are affected by a function. Then we make the analysis more precise and also consider information from static branch prediction. This information will later be used to decide about applicability and profitability in the speculative optimization. Finally, we briefly present the characteristics of the SPEC2006 benchmarks.

3.1 Basic Analysis on Globals

The basic analysis is a straight-forward interprocedural data flow analysis (see e.g. [NNH99]). We first determine for every function, which globals are directly used and modified. Then we propagate this information along the call graph and calculate the fixed point. At the moment, only unaliased globals are considered, hence it is evident whether or not a statement changes a global. If a function call cannot be resolved statically, we assume that all globals are possibly changed by that call. We finally get for every function the list of affected globals.

3.2 Extended Analysis

The analysis presented so far is a quite conservative estimation of the global usage. In this section, we make it more precise. First, we determine which globals definitely must be changed by a function. These are globals that are modified in post-dominators of the start block of a function. This information is propagated across function calls that are definitely (i.e., unconditionally) executed (yielding $MustDef(f)$). Next, we consider potential changes of globals. We have implemented a state of the art static branch predictor, following [WL94]. This yields for every basic block a static estimate of its execution frequency (relative to function invocation). We use this to attach a frequency to every access to a global. Initially, for every function f and every global g, we collect the maximum frequency of g's use and definition within f (*UseFreq(f,g)*, *DefFreq(f,g)*). We also collect the maximum frequency for a function call from f to f' (*CallFreq(f,f')*). In a fixed point iteration over the call graph, we propagate the frequencies: The frequency *UseFreq(f,g)* is updated at a call to a function f' if the resulting frequency *CallFreq(f,f')* × *UseFreq(f',g)* is higher than the previous value.

3.3 Analysis Results

The analysis gives us for every function a list of globals that may be affected by a call to it. For the extended analysis, this information is annotated with the estimated frequency, and we also know which globals are definitely changed. This raises the opportunity for speculation: If a global is *not* definitely changed by a function call, we can speculate that it remains unchanged. The frequency can be used for cost estimation. For the SPEC benchmarks, on average 23 globals may be changed by a function. However, only 1.2 globals are definitely changed. The discrepancy between these numbers constitutes the opportunity for speculation.

4 Optimization

The optimization keeps selected globals in registers throughout a function to reduce memory accesses and to avoid stalls. With the results from the previous section, we know to which extent globals are affected by function calls. This information is required to decide where to insert compensation code (synchronizing the global's value with memory), which influences the profitability.

4.1 Overview

The optimization considers each function in turn, identifies the globals used within the function and estimates the performance gain. Then it selects the best candidates and performs the actual transformation. We present two versions of the optimization: In the basic version, no speculation is used. This optimization can be used on any architecture that can spare registers for optimization. The extended version uses speculation to reload globals only if necessary.

Identify Candidates. Candidates are all globals that are used within the function and have integral data type (i.e. fit in a register).

Rate Candidates. For all candidates in turn, the optimization is performed virtually. We collect the information where compensation code (i.e. loads and stores) has to be placed for a given global (see Sec. 4.2). We then have the following parameters to calculate the estimated gain of the optimization: The number of uses and definitions of the global (*UseCount/DefCount*), which represents the number of loads and stores that could be removed by the optimization, and the number of newly introduced loads and stores (*LoadCount, StoreCount*), which keep the global valid at function call borders. All counts are weighted by the estimated frequency of the corresponding block. The score is then calculated by the following weighted sum (with coefficients $w \in \mathbb{R}$):

$$score = w_{use} \cdot UseCount + w_{def} \cdot DefCount + w_{ld} \cdot LoadCount + w_{st} \cdot StoreCount$$

Since *UseCount* and *DefCount* correspond to the gain, the corresponding coefficients will be positive. On the other hand, *LoadCount* and *StoreCount* indicate the introduced overhead, hence their coefficients will be negative. In case of the speculative optimization, the newly introduced loads will be further broken down into *advanced* and *check* loads (with corresponding weights w_{lda}, w_{ldc}). The score function together with the weights constitutes the cost model.

Select Best Candidates. Only candidates that have a score exceeding a given threshold are considered. Since every selected candidate will eventually require a fixed register, only the best *MaxGlob* candidates are chosen per function.

Perform Optimization. This step actually performs the transformation by replacing all occurences of the global by references to the selected fixed register and by inserting compensation code, as determined before.

4.2 Placement of Compensation Code

The optimization keeps a global in a register throughout the complete function. To ensure correctness, it has to make sure that on the one hand the correct value is in the register whenever it is used internally in the function, and on the other hand that the correct value of the global is in the memory whenever a function is called that may use it. Those two tasks are actually dual to each other, as we see in the following. The optimization uses the results from the analysis presented in the previous section to determine the effects of a statement w.r.t. a global.

Effects of Statements. A statement can have the following effects w.r.t. a given global: The global may be used (*USE*) or defined (*DEF*) directly by the statement. Furthermore, the statement may make a call to a function in which again the global could be used (*XUSE*) or defined (*XDEF*), this time externally.

Compensation Code for Internal Uses. First, for all uses of the considered global in turn, a backwards traversal of the CFG is started. It considers all possible paths leading to the use and stops only on statements that define the global's state, i.e. a *DEF/USE* (in register) or *XDEF* (in memory). The search yields a tree of basic blocks. Fig. 2 gives an example. Starting from a use of *glob*, a tree consisting of all possible paths to this use is constructed, stopping at (internal or external) definitions of *glob*. Functions f and g can possibly change *glob*. Nodes

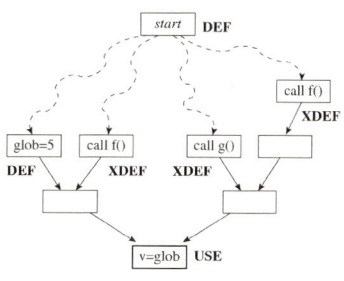

Fig. 2. Constructed Tree

that have an effect on *glob* are annotated correspondingly. Note that the first basic block of a function has always a *DEF* mark since initially the global is loaded from memory. To decide whether the global is available at the use site, we propagate these marks from leaves to root. If all children of a node have the same mark, it is also set for the parent. Otherwise, in all children with *XDEF*, a load instruction is inserted, and they receive now the *DEF* mark, as does the parent. Thus the global is now in a register. If the *XDEF* mark is propagated to the root, a load instruction is inserted direct before the regarded use, and the root node is marked accordingly.

Fig. 3 illustrates the marking algorithm for our example. Left, we see the initially constructed tree with its marks, starting from a use of the global at the root. In the middle, we see an intermediate step. The left child has two children with different marks, hence it is marked with *DEF*, as well as its right child, in which also compensation code is inserted. The right child has only children with *XDEF* marks and hence gets the same mark. The rightmost figure shows the final step. Both children of the root have different marks, hence the root as well as its right child get the *DEF* mark, and compensation code is again inserted in the right child. From now on, the modified nodes will keep their *DEF* marks.

Compensation Code for External Uses. To cope with the dual case, namely to ensure that the correct value of a global is in memory when used by a called function, we proceed almost equally. Now we consider all external uses of the global in turn. We construct a tree of basic blocks as before, and whenever we encounter siblings with different marks, we convert *DEF* nodes to *XDEF* nodes by inserting a store and change the mark of the corresponding parent to *XDEF*. Hence in the end, we receive a tree where the root is marked with *XDEF*.

Aliased Globals. Our approach can be easily extended to aliased globals by treating aliased accesses to the global as $XUSE/XDEF$.

4.3 Speculative Compensation Code

As we have seen before, function calls may affect many globals, but only in very few cases this happens definitely. Hence in many cases, the reload of a global after a function call is not necessary and can be made speculative. On the other hand, the cost of misspeculation has to be considered thoroughly. If p is the probability that a given global was changed by a function call, lat the load latency, and mis

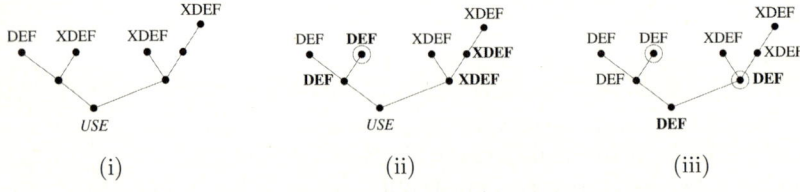

Fig. 3. Example for the different steps of the marking algorithm. Changes are shown boldface, insertion of compensation code is indicated by circles.

the misspeculation penalty, the expected gain will be $gain = (1-p) \cdot lat - p \cdot mis$. We use the previously collected frequencies to approximate p.

The tree is constructed as before, except that we now distinguish between *XDEF* and *XMUSTDEF*. The latter is used to mark external definitions that are definitive or have a frequency above a given threshold *MaxSpecFreq*. *XDEF*, on the other hand, indicates now that speculation should be used. Additionally, the estimated block frequencies are annotated. When a node has only children with *XDEF* and *XMUSTDEF* nodes, it receives the mark for which the sum of the corresponding children's frequencies is maximal. When a node has children both with *DEF* and *XDEF/XMUSTDEF* marks, loads are inserted appropriately as before, but speculation is used only in nodes marked with *XDEF*. All formerly regular loads become *advanced* loads since they initiate the bookkeeping required to check for misspeculation. For speculation, *check* loads are used.

In summary, the results from our analysis can be used for reducing the number of memory accesses induced by globals. We have presented a cost-aware algorithm for the optimization. The cost model allows the algorithm to be applied to different settings, e.g. hardware vs. software supported speculation. Results from a case study are described in the next section.

5 Case Study: Speculation on the Intel Itanium

5.1 Implementation

We implemented the optimization in our compiler framework, which is based on the compiler development system CoSy® by [ACE]. CoSy includes an extensive set of optimizations and the backend generator BEG [ESL89], for which we developed a specification for the Itanium architecture. The Itanium supports speculation by special hardware. A successful *check* load takes one cycle, opposed to 1/5/12 minimum latency for L1/L2/L3 cache accesses (cache size: 16k/256k/1.5M). Misspeculation costs a penalty of 10 cycles extra, plus the time needed to reload the value. Thus speculation has to be used carefully.

5.2 Results

We measured all SPEC CPU2006 C benchmarks[1]. For all measurements, we took the median of three runs. All improvement is compared against the -O4-setting of the CoSy compiler, which includes over 50 standard compiler optimizations.

Fig. 4 shows the results using the reference data of the SPEC CPU2006 benchmarks. At first glance we see that the base optimization leads to an improvement in many cases, and that the speculative variant significantly adds further improvement. For gobmk and hmmer, no speculation is done and the optimization merely leads to prefetching of globals, hence both variants perform equally. In the other cases, the misspeculation rate is low and shows that our cost model worked out well. Concludingly we see that speculative reloading outperforms blind re-loading (as in the base optimization).

---

[1] Except for 462.libquantum since the CoSy frontend is not fully C99 compliant.

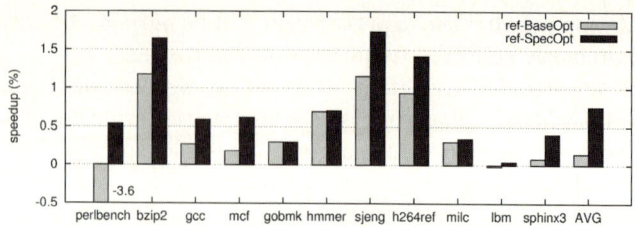

Fig. 4. Results of the SPEC CPU2006 benchmarks

6 Related Work

The presented approach performs register promotion for globals. Much work has been done on register promotion in general. [Wal86] and [CH90] present approaches to global register allocation, which perform register promotion. [CL97] propose register promotion as a separate optimization and focus especially loops. [LCK+98] and [SJ98] exploit partial redundancy to perform register promotion. [BGS99] also focus on eliminating partial redundancy. They investigate how good candidates for register promotion can be statically predicted. The approaches presented so far require conservative, safe information about dependencies, which means especially for memory accesses a very rough overapproximation. This can be solved with speculative techniques. [PGM00] propose a hardware extension that allows to speculate on dependencies and to issue run-time checks to ensure correctness. [LCHY03] present the speculative extension of [CL97]. They report performance improvements for the Intel Itanium. The work discussed so far tries to optimize memory accesses in general. Our presented work, in contrast, tackles a certain class of memory accesses, namely those induced by globals, and therefore can make use of a more precise analysis.

There are also approaches which propose register promotion for global variables. [SO90] consider inter-procedural register allocation and also optimize globals. Results from simulation report a significant improvement, but without regarding cache behavior. [CC02] also examine the effects of promoting globals to registers, mainly focusing on reducing power consumption. They perform an architectural exploration to investigate how many separate registers are required for the optimization, and find that already 4–8 registers are sufficient. Differing from our approach, both works promote a global to a register for the whole program, and they do not consider speculative techniques.

7 Conclusion

As it has been foreseen in the past, the memory gap has become a major limiting factor on general-purpose architectures. Hence novel optimization techniques have to be developed to mitigate this effect. Speculation on data dependencies is required to allow more aggressive optimization, and modern architectures are offering efficient support for it. With the work presented in this paper, we have done a step towards that direction. We tackled a certain class of memory accesses, namely those induced by global variables. In our experiments, we could show that our optimization leads to significant improvement on some benchmarks, and this effect is even stronger for the speculative variant.

For the future, we plan to go one step further and consider a broader class of memory accesses. We think that on the one hand, more precise analyses are required that try to make use of the rich information provided in the intermediate representation and also can yield unsure, or speculative, information, and on the other hand, novel optimizations have to be developed that make use of this information and have a precise, architecture-dependent cost model to achieve an overall performance improvement, while preserving the semantics of the program. We think that this will be the key to sustainably reduce the impact of the memory gap on general-purpose applications.

References

[ACE] Associated Compiler Experts bv., Amsterdam, The Netherlands, http://www.ace.nl
[BGS99] Bodik, R., Gupta, R., Soffa, M.L.: Load-reuse analysis: design and evaluation. In: PLDI (1999)
[CC02] Cilio, A.G.M., Corporaal, H.: Global variable promotion: Using registers to reduce cache power dissipation. In: Horspool, R.N. (ed.) CC 2002. LNCS, vol. 2304. Springer, Heidelberg (2002)
[CH90] Chow, F.C., Hennessy, J.L.: The priority-based coloring approach to register allocation. ACM Trans. Program. Lang. Syst. 12(4) (1990)
[CL97] Cooper, K.D., Lu, J.: Register promotion in C programs. In: PLDI (1997)
[ESL89] Emmelmann, H., Schröer, F.-W., Landwehr, L.: Beg: a generation for efficient back ends. In: PLDI (1989)
[LCHY03] Lin, J., Chen, T., Hsu, W.-C., Yew, P.-C.: Speculative register promotion using advanced load address table (ALAT). In: CGO 2003. IEEE, Los Alamitos (2003)
[LCK+98] Lo, R., Chow, F., Kennedy, R., Liu, S.-M., Tu, P.: Register promotion by sparse partial redundancy elimination of loads and stores. ACM SIGPLAN Notices 33(5) (1998)
[LCM+05] Luk, C.-K., Cohn, R., Muth, R., Patil, H., Klauser, A., Lowney, G., Wallace, S., Reddi, V.J., Hazelwood, K.: Pin: building customized program analysis tools with dynamic instrumentation. In: PLDI (2005)
[NNH99] Nielson, F., Nielson, H.R., Hankin, C.: Principles of Program Analysis. Springer, Heidelberg (1999)
[PGM00] Postiff, M., Greene, D., Mudge, T.: The store-load address table and speculative register promotion. In: Proceedings of ACM/IEEE MICRO (2000)
[SJ98] Sastry, A.V.S., Ju, R.D.C.: A new algorithm for scalar register promotion based on SSA form. In: PLDI (1998)
[SO90] Santhanam, V., Odnert, D.: Register allocation across procedure and module boundaries. In: PLDI (1990)
[Wal86] Wall, D.W.: Global register allocation at link time. SIGPLAN Not. 21(7) (1986)
[WL94] Wu, Y., Larus, J.R.: Static branch frequency and program profile analysis. In: Proceedings of ACM/IEEE MICRO (1994)
[WM95] Wulf, W.A., McKee, S.A.: Hitting the memory wall: implications of the obvious. SIGARCH Comput. Archit. News 23(1) (1995)

Efficiently Building the Gated Single Assignment Form in Codes with Pointers in Modern Optimizing Compilers*

Manuel Arenaz, Pedro Amoedo, and Juan Touriño

Computer Architecture Group
Department of Electronics and Systems
University of A Coruña, A Coruña, Spain
{arenaz,pamoedo,juan}@udc.es

Abstract. Understanding program behavior is at the foundation of program optimization. Techniques for automatic recognition of program constructs characterize the behavior of code fragments, providing compilers with valuable information to guide code optimizations. The XARK compiler framework provides a complete, robust and extensible solution to the automatic recognition problem that was shown to be effective to characterize the behavior of Fortran77 applications. Our goal is to migrate XARK to the GNU GCC compiler in order to widen its scope of application to program constructs (e.g., pointers, objects) supported by other programming languages (e.g., Fortran90/95, C/C++, Java). The first step towards this goal is the translation of the GCC intermediate representation into the Gated Single Assignment (GSA) form, an extension of Static Single Assignment (SSA) that captures data/control dependences and reaching definition information for scalar and array variables. This paper presents a simple and fast GSA construction algorithm that takes advantage of the infrastructure for building the SSA form available in modern optimizing compilers. An implementation on top of the GIMPLE-SSA intermediate representation of GCC is described and evaluated in terms of memory consumption and execution time using the UTDSP, Perfect Club and SPEC CPU2000 benchmark suites.

1   Introduction

Automatic code optimization hinges on advanced symbolic analysis to gather information about the behavior of programs. Compiler techniques for automatic kernel recognition carry out symbolic analysis in order to discover program constructs that are frequently used by software developers (e.g., inductions, scalar

---

* This research was supported by the Ministry of Education and Science of Spain and FEDER funds of the European Union (Projects TIN2004-07797-C02 and TIN2007-67537-C03), and by the Galician Government (Projects PGIDIT05PXIC10504PN and PGIDIT06PXIB105228PR). We gratefully thank the ArTeCS group (Universidad Complutense de Madrid, Spain) for the profile information of the SPEC2000 benchmarks.

reductions, irregular reductions and array recurrences). XARK [7] (first presented in [4]) is an extensible compiler framework for the recognition of a comprehensive collection of kernels that appear in real codes with regular and irregular computations, even in the presence of complex control flows. The framework analyzes the Gated Single Assignment (GSA) form [12] in order to handle data and control dependences, as well as scalar and array variables in a unified manner. XARK was shown to be an effective tool to support parallel code generation [5], compile-time prediction of the cache behavior [3], and program behavior characterization [6].

The current implementation of XARK is built on top of the Polaris compiler [13], which limits its scope of application to the analysis of Fortran77 codes. In order to handle codes written in other programming languages such as Fortran90/95, C/C++ and Java, XARK is being ported to the GIMPLE intermediate representation of the GNU GCC compiler [1]. Advantages of using GCC as a research and development compiler platform is that it is supported by an increasing number of industrial and academic institutions, and that GCC is able to compile codes written in many programming languages for a wide range of computer architectures.

The contribution of this paper is a simple and fast algorithm for the construction of the GSA form taking advantage of the infrastructure for building the Static Single Assignment (SSA) form [9] available in modern optimizing compilers. The key idea is to create artificial scalars that represent the memory regions accessed through both array references and pointer dereferences, and later handle these artificial scalars with the underlying SSA infrastructure. An advantage of this approach is that it enables an optimizing compiler to run GSA-based program transformations in the scope of an SSA-driven compilation process. An implementation in the scope of the GIMPLE-SSA intermediate representation of GCC is presented and evaluated with well-known benchmarks from different application domains, namely, UTDSP, Perfect Club and SPEC CPU2000.

The rest of the paper is organized as follows. Section 2 describes the GSA form and introduces the GSA construction algorithm. Section 3 describes the implementation in the scope of GIMPLE-SSA. Section 4 shows detailed experiments that show the efficiency of the implementation. Finally, Section 5 concludes the paper and outlines future work.

2 Algorithm for the Construction of the GSA Form

Modern optimizing compilers use intermediate representations based on the SSA form in order to facilitate certain code optimizations. GSA is an extension of SSA where the special ϕ operators inserted in the code capture both the reaching definitions of scalar and array variables, and the predicates of the conditional statements of the program. In GSA, different kinds of ϕs are distinguished:

- $\mu(x_{out}, x_{in})$, which appears at loop headers and selects the initial x_{out} and loop-carried x_{in} values of a variable.

```
procedure build_GSA()
{
  1. Build the SSA form
  2. Create pseudoscalars for each array/pointer variable
  3. Replace array references and pointer dereferences with different
     versions of the pseudoscalars
     Replace the statements defining pseudoscalars with α operators
  4. Delete pseudoscalars of read-only variables
  5. Foreach pseudoscalar
     {
           5.1. Run the SSA φ-placement algorithm in order to insert φs
                at the confluence nodes of the Control Flow Graph
           5.2. Run the SSA variable renaming algorithm
     }
  6. Identify φ types at the confluence nodes of the Control Flow Graph
  7. Create predicates for the γ operators
}
```

Fig. 1. Pseudocode of the algorithm for building the GSA form using the infrastructure for the construction of SSA form

- $\gamma(c, x_{false}, x_{true})$, which is located at the confluence node associated with a branch (e.g., if-then-else construct), and captures the condition c for each definition to reach the confluence node: x_{false} if c is not fulfilled; x_{true}, if c is satisfied.
- $\alpha(a_{prev}, s, e)$, which replaces array assignment statements located within basic blocks, and whose semantics is that the s-th element of an array variable a is set to the value e, and the other elements take the values of the previous definition of the array (denoted as a_{prev}).

In general, building the GSA form involves three main tasks: (1) *φ-placement* for the insertion of μs and γs in the points of the program where the control flow merges; (2) *α-placement*, to replace the non-scalar assignment statements (e.g., arrays, pointer dereferences) with αs; and (3) *variable renaming* in order to assure that the left-hand sides of the assignment statements are pairwise disjoint. The key idea that enables the construction of the GSA form by means of the φ-placement and variable renaming algorithms of an existing SSA infrastructure is to replace array references and pointer dereferences with artificial scalar variables (from now on *pseudoscalars*). These variables represent the memory regions that can be accessed through arrays and pointers as a unique entity.

Figure 1 presents the GSA construction algorithm proposed in this paper. The pseudocode consists of seven steps. First, the program is rewritten into SSA form. Second, the symbol table is analyzed in order to create a pseudoscalar for each array variable and each pointer variable declared in the source code. Third, the SSA form is scanned in order to replace each array reference and pointer dereference with a new version of the corresponding pseudoscalar. Whenever a pseudoscalar is inserted in the left-hand side of a statement, the right-hand side is also replaced with an α operator (α-placement). Fourth, the pseudoscalars that represent read-only variables are deleted as they will not lead to the insertion of new φ operators in the fifth step. The fifth step uses the φ-placement and variable renaming algorithms provided by the SSA infrastructure to update the SSA form

```
pB = &B[0];
i = 0;
for (h=0; h<N; h++) {
    if (A[h] != 0) {
        *pB++ = A[h];
        C[i] = h;
        i++;
    }
}
```

Fig. 2. Gather operation implemented with array references and pointer dereferences

with the reaching definitions of the pseudoscalars. Next, the sixth step classifies ϕ operators into μ or γ operators. Finally, for each γ, the control flow of the program that determines the reaching definitions of the γ operator is captured using the algorithm proposed in [10]. As a whole, this algorithm computes a directed acyclic graph that reflects the hierarchy of if-then-else constructs and that computes the set of predicates associated with each reaching definition of the γ operator.

3 Implementation Using the GIMPLE-SSA Infrastructure

The algorithm described in the previous section has been implemented in the scope of the GIMPLE-SSA intermediate representation of the GNU GCC compiler. GIMPLE is a three-address language with no high-level control flow structures (e.g., loops, if-then-else), which are lowered to conditional gotos. Each GIMPLE statement contains no more than three operands and has no implicit side effects. Temporaries are used to hold intermediate values as necessary. Variables that need to live in memory are never used in expressions. They are first loaded into a temporary and the temporary is then used in the expression.

For illustrative purposes, Figure 2 shows an implementation of a gather operation that filters out the elements of an input array A that are equal to zero. Non-zero elements are stored in consecutive entries of an output array B by dereferencing the pointer pB. In addition, the indices of the non-zero elements are stored in the corresponding entries of the output array C. Figure 3(a) shows the GIMPLE-SSA form built by GCC. The beginning of basic blocks is labeled in the figure (e.g., <BB$_0$>). The process of building GIMPLE works recursively, replacing source code statements with sequences of GIMPLE statements. Thus, the source code statement *pB++=A[h] in basic block <BB$_2$> is substituted by five GIMPLE statements that compute: (1) the offset of the element h with respect to the base address of the array A ($D1_1=h_1*4$); (2) the address of the memory location that contains the entry A[h] ($D2_1=A+D1_1$); (3) the value of the array element ($D3_1=*D2_1$); (4) the write operation to store that value in the entry of array B pointed by pB (*pB=$D3_1$); and (5) the increment of pB to point to the next entry of array B ($pB_2=pB_1+4$). Figure 3(a) also shows the variables declared in the program, and indicates the versions of each variable created during the construction of the SSA form.

(a) After step 1.

```
/* Declarations */
pB :: pB_0,pB_1,pB_2,pB_3
A
B
C
i :: i_0,i_1,i_2,i_3
h :: h_0,h_1,h_2,h_3
D1 :: D1_0,D1_1
D2 :: D2_0,D2_1
D3 :: D3_0,D3_1
D4 :: D4_0
D5 :: D5_0
```

```
/* Statements */
<BB_0>:
    pB_0 = B;
    i_0 = 0;
    h_0 = 0;
    goto <BB_4>;

<BB_1>:
    D1_0 = h_1 * 4;
    D2_0 = A + D1_0;
    D3_0 = *D2_0;
    if (D3_0 != 0)
        goto <BB_2>
    else
        goto <BB_3>

<BB_2>:
    D1_1 = h_1 * 4;
    D2_1 = A + D1_1;
    D3_1 = *D2_1;
    *pB = D3_1;
    pB_2 = pB_1+4;
    D4_0 = i_1 * 4;
    D5_0 = C + D4_0;
    *D5_0 = h_1;
    i_2 = i_1+1;

<BB_3>:
    i_3 = φ(i_1,i_2);
    pB_3 = φ(pB_1,pB_2);
    h_2 = h_1+1;

<BB_4>:
    i_1 = φ(i_0,i_3);
    h_1 = φ(h_0,h_2);
    pB_1 = φ(pB_0,pB_3);
    if (h_1<=N) goto <BB_1>;
```

(b) After steps 2 and 3.

```
/* Declarations */
pB :: pB_0,pB_1,pB_2,pB_3
A
B
C
i :: i_0,i_1,i_2,i_3
h :: h_0,h_1,h_2,h_3
D1 :: D1_0,D1_1
D2 :: D2_0,D2_1
D3 :: D3_0,D3_1
D4 :: D4_0
D5 :: D5_0
θpB :: θpB_0, θpB_1
θA :: θA_0,θA_1
θB
θC :: θC_0,θC_1
```

```
/* Statements */
<BB_0>:
    pB_0 = B;
    i_0 = 0;
    h_0 = 0;
    goto <BB_4>;

<BB_1>:
    D1_0 = h_1 * 4;
    D2_0 = A + D1_0;
    D3_0 = θA_0;
    if (D3_0 != 0)
        goto <BB_2>
    else
        goto <BB_3>

<BB_2>:
    D1_1 = h_1 * 4;
    D2_1 = A + D1_1;
    D3_1 = θA_1;
    θpB_0 = α(θpB_1,0,D3_1);
    pB_2 = pB_1+4;
    D4_0 = i_1 * 4;
    θC_0 = α(θC_1,D4_0,h_1);
    i_2 = i_1+1;

<BB_3>:
    i_3 = φ(i_1,i_2);
    pB_3 = φ(pB_1,pB_2);
    h_2 = h_1+1;

<BB_4>:
    i_1 = φ(i_0,i_3);
    h_1 = φ(h_0,h_2);
    pB_1 = φ(pB_0,pB_3);
    if (h_1<=N) goto <BB_1>;
```

(c) After steps 4 to 7.

```
/* Declarations */
pB :: pB_0,pB_1,pB_2,pB_3
A
B
C
i :: i_0,i_1,i_2,i_3
h :: h_0,h_1,h_2,h_3
D1 :: D1_0,D1_1
D2 :: D2_0,D2_1
D3 :: D3_0,D3_1
D4 :: D4_0
D5 :: D5_0
θpB :: θpB_0,θpB_1,θpB_2,θpB_3
θC :: θC_0,θC_1,θC_2,θC_3
```

```
/* Statements */
<BB_0>:
    pB_0 = B;
    i_0 = 0;
    h_0 = 0;
    goto <BB_4>;

<BB_1>:
    D1_0 = h_1 * 4;
    D2_0 = A + D1_0;
    D3_0 = *D2_0;
    if (D3_0 != 0)
        goto <BB_2>
    else
        goto <BB_3>

<BB_2>:
    D1_1 = h_1 * 4;
    D2_1 = A + D1_1;
    D3_1 = *D2_1;
    θpB_2 = α(θpB_1,0,D3_1);
    pB_2 = pB_1+4;
    D4_0 = i_1 * 4;
    θC_2 = α(θC_1,D4_0,h_1);
    i_2 = i_1+1;

<BB_3>:
    i_3 = γ(D3_0!=0,i_1,i_2);
    pB_3 = γ(D3_0!=0,pB_1,pB_2);
    θpB_3 = γ(D3_0!=0,θpB_1,θpB_2);
    θC_3 = γ(D3_0!=0,θC_1,θC_2);
    h_2 = h_1+1;

<BB_4>:
    i_1 = μ(i_0,i_3);
    h_1 = μ(h_0,h_3);
    pB_1 = μ(pB_0,pB_3);
    θpB_1 = μ(θpB_0,θpB_3);
    θC_1 = μ(θC_0,θC_3);
    if (h_1<=N) goto <BB_1>;
```

Fig. 3. Construction of the GSA form on top of GIMPLE-SSA using the algorithm of Figure 1 for the case study of Figure 2

Table 1. Representation of C and Fortran declarations and uses in GIMPLE form

Language	Source code Declaration	Use	GIMPLE form Declaration	Use	Type
C	parameter void f(int A[])	A[i]	int *A	D=A+i*sizeof(int)	2
	parameter void f(int *A)	*(A+i)		*D	
	local int *A	*A	int *A	*A	1
	parameter void f(int A[N][M])	A[i][j]	int[M] *D	D=A+i*sizeof(int)	2
				(*D)[j]	
	local int A[N][M]	A[i][j]	int[N][M] A	A[i][j]	3
Fortran	parameter subroutine f(A) integer A(N)	A(i)	int[N] *A	(*A)[i-1]	3
	parameter subroutine f(A) integer A(*)	A(i)	int[] *A		
	parameter subroutine f(A) integer A(N,M)	A(i,j)	int[N*M] *A	(*A)[(j-1)*N+(i-1)]	3
	local integer A(N)	A(i)	int A[N]	A[i-1]	3
	local integer A(N,M)	A(i,j)	int[N*M] A	A[(j-1)*N+(i-1)]	3

The translation of the GIMPLE-SSA form into GSA starts by creating pseudoscalars for each array variable (A, B and C) and for each pointer variable (pB) declared in the source code of the program. In Figure 3(b), pseudoscalars are denoted by the name of the source code variable prefixed by the symbol θ (θA, θB, θC and θpB). GIMPLE is a common representation for source codes written in different programming languages, and thus array references and pointer dereferences can be represented in many different ways. Table 1 presents the GIMPLE representation of several declarations and uses in C and Fortran. Two scopes are considered: *parameter* for subroutine arguments, and *local* for subroutine local variables. The last column identifies the three types of representations distinguished in the third step of the algorithm of Figure 1 for the creation of new versions of the pseudoscalars:

1. Dereferences of source code pointers, which are substituted by a new version of the pseudoscalar of that pointer (see *pB=D3$_1$ and θpB$_0$=α(θpB$_1$,0,D3$_1$) in basic block <BB2> of Figures 3(a) and 3(b), respectively).
2. Dereferences of temporaries, replaced with a new version of the pseudoscalar associated with the corresponding source array or pointer variable (see *D5$_0$=h$_1$ and θC$_0$=α(θC$_1$,D4$_0$,h$_1$) in basic block <BB2>).
3. Dereferences of array variables and array references, substituted by a new version of the pseudoscalar of the corresponding source array variable.

The third step of the algorithm is completed by replacing with α operators those GIMPLE-SSA statements whose left-hand side has been substituted by a version of a pseudoscalar. The arguments of the α operator are: a new version of the left-hand side pseudoscalar, the offset of the memory location whose value is written during the execution of the statement, and the value assigned to the memory location. The offset is determined as follows. For type one, the offset is zero because the statement writes in the memory location pointed by the source pointer variable (see *pB=D3$_1$ and θpB$_0$ = α(θpB$_1$,0,D3$_1$) in Figures 3(a) and 3(b), respectively). For types two and three, the offset is determined by the subscripts of the GIMPLE array reference or by the offset added to the source pointer variable (see *$D5_0$=h_1 and θC_0=α(θC_1,$D4_0$,h_1)).

The fourth step deletes the pseudoscalars corresponding to read-only variables as they will not lead to the insertion of new ϕ operators. Thus, the implementation of the fifth step is straightforward and consists of running the ϕ-placement and variable renaming algorithms available in the GCC infrastructure. For illustrative purposes, see the versions of the pseudoscalar θA inserted in basic blocks <BB_1> and <BB_2> of Figure 3(b) after step two, which have been removed from the GSA form of Figure 3(c).

Finally, the different types of ϕ operators inserted by the ϕ-placement algorithm are identified. Thus, ϕs located at loop headers are converted into μ operators, and ϕs inserted after if-then-else constructs are converted into γ operators. The GSA form is completed with the computation of the predicate that controls the execution of the if-then-else construct in GIMPLE-SSA form (see predicate ($D3_0$!=0) in Figure 3(c)).

4 Experimental Results

The performance of our GSA construction algorithm was evaluated with the UTDSP [11], Perfect Club [8] and SPEC CPU2000 [2] benchmarks. UTDSP provides routines written in different coding styles (pointer-based and array-based) that are representative of DSP applications (e.g., filters, FFT). The well-known Perfect Club and SPEC CPU2000 benchmarks consist of full-scale applications that have been used extensively in the literature. As a first step towards the analysis of these applications as a whole, the most costly routines in terms of execution time were selected as they would probably be the target of an execution-time-aware optimizing compiler.

In order to characterize the behavior of an application, XARK addresses the recognition of the computational kernels whose results are stored in both scalar and non-scalar variables (e.g., arrays, pointers). As SSA covers scalar variables, the effectiveness of the GSA construction algorithm is measured as the percentage of non-scalar variables (#*non_scalars*) converted into pseudoscalars (#*pseudos*) successfully. Table 2 shows that there are some Fortran routines in Perfect Club and SPEC CPU2000 where #*pseudos* is lower than #*non_scalars*, which means that the GSA form can only be built partially (the effectiveness is less than 100%). The reason for this is that variables (in particular, arrays) declared in Fortran common blocks are represented in GIMPLE as fields of structure data types. This situation can be handled by distinguishing new types of GIMPLE representations in the third step of our algorithm, which is work in progress. Finally, note that the GSA form is built successfully (the effectiveness is 100%) in all the C routines as well as in most of the Fortran routines of Perfect Club and SPEC CPU2000.

Figure 4 compares memory consumption and execution time of the GSA construction algorithm (in white) with respect to the SSA construction algorithm of GCC (in black), the routines being ordered by increasing value of memory

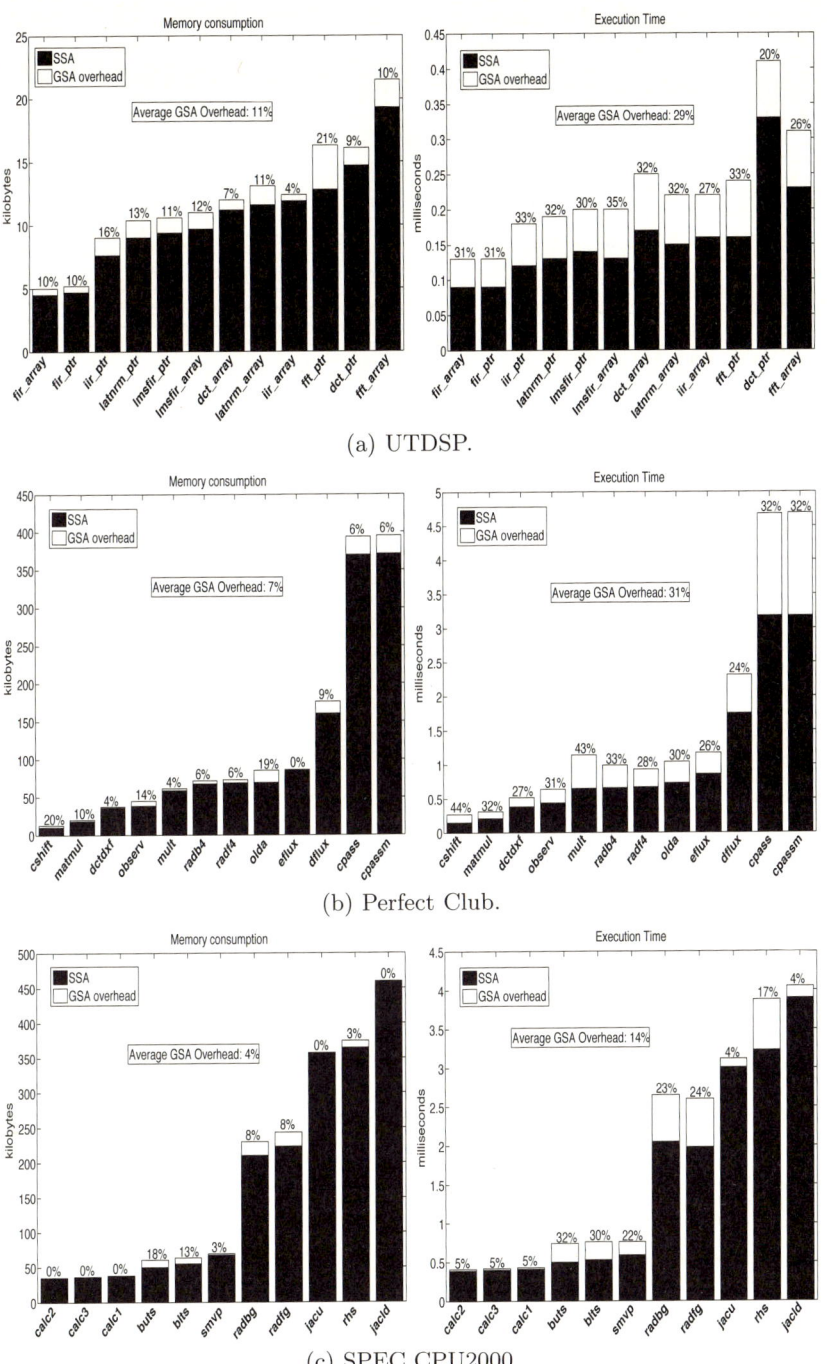

Fig. 4. Memory consumption and execution time of the GSA construction algorithm

Table 2. Effectiveness of the GSA construction algorithm

Benchmark	Application	Routine	Language	#non_scalars	#pseudos	Effectiveness
UTDSP	COMPRESS	dct_array	C	2	2	100%
		dct_ptr	C	2	2	100%
	FFT	fft_array	C	2	2	100%
		fft_ptr	C	4	4	100%
	FIR	fir_array	C	1	1	100%
		fir_ptr	C	1	1	100%
	IIR	iir_array	C	2	2	100%
		iir_ptr	C	2	2	100%
	LATNRM	latnrm_array	C	2	2	100%
		latnrm_ptr	C	2	2	100%
	LMSFIR	lmsfir_array	C	2	2	100%
		lmsfir_ptr	C	2	2	100%
Perfect Club	ADM	dctdxf	Fortran	1	1	100%
		radb4	Fortran	1	1	100%
		radf4	Fortran	1	1	100%
	DYFESM	matmul	Fortran	1	1	100%
	FLO52	dflux	Fortran	7	4	57%
		eflux	Fortran	2	0	0%
	MDG	cshift	Fortran	1	1	100%
	MG3D	cpass	Fortran	2	2	100%
		cpassm	Fortran	2	2	100%
	QCD	mult	Fortran	1	1	100%
		observ	Fortran	2	2	100%
	TRFD	olda	Fortran	7	7	100%
SPEC CPU2000	APPLU	blts	Fortran	2	2	100%
		buts	Fortran	3	3	100%
		jacld	Fortran	4	0	0%
		jacu	Fortran	3	0	0%
		rhs	Fortran	2	1	50%
	APSI	radbg	Fortran	2	2	100%
		radfg	Fortran	2	2	100%
	EQUAKE	smvp	C	3	3	100%
	SWIM	calc1	Fortran	4	0	0%
		calc2	Fortran	3	0	0%
		calc3	Fortran	6	0	0%

consumption of GIMPLE-SSA. Memory consumption is calculated as the sum of the sizes of the symbol table (including the variables declared in the source code as well as the corresponding versions of each variable), the forest of abstract syntax trees, the control flow graph and the data dependence graph. Execution times were measured on an Intel Core2 Duo at 2.4Ghz (4MB of cache and 2GB of RAM). Overall, the results show that our algorithm consumes, on average, between 4% and 11% more memory than the SSA construction algorithm and takes between 14% and 31% longer. The memory overhead varies between 3% and 21%, and the time overhead between 4% and 43%. However, while the time overhead may seem significant, the execution time does not exceed 5ms in the worst case. Thus, the experiments demonstrate that the algorithm is a practical solution for optimizing compilers that require advanced program analysis techniques.

5 Conclusions

This paper has presented a simple algorithm for building the GSA representation using the infrastructure for building SSA available in modern optimizing compilers. The approach based on the concept of pseudoscalar as a representation of references to array and pointer variables was shown to be effective for the analysis of C and Fortran codes from different application domains.

The algorithm has been evaluated in terms of memory consumption and execution time. The experiments have shown that the algorithm introduces an affordable overhead to the underlying SSA implementation. Thus, it provides a practical solution that enables the coexistence of SSA- and GSA-based optimizations. In addition, it provides support for the efficient implementation of advanced analysis techniques targeting pointer- and array-based codes in the scope of widely extended compiler platforms such as GCC.

As future work we intend to analyze applications written in object-oriented programming languages like C++ and Java.

References

1. GNU Compiler Collection (GCC) internals,
   http://gcc.gnu.org/onlinedocs/gccint.pdf [Last accessed June 2008]
2. Standard Performance Evaluation Corporation. SPEC CPU 2000,
   http://www.spec.org/cpu2000 [Last accessed June 2008]
3. Andrade, D., Arenaz, M., Fraguela, B.B., Touriño, J., Doallo, R.: Automated and accurate cache behavior analysis for codes with irregular access patterns. Concurrency and Computation: Practice and Experience 19(18), 2407–2423 (2007)
4. Arenaz, M., Touriño, J., Doallo, R.: A GSA-based compiler infrastructure to extract parallelism from complex loops. In: 17th ACM International Conference on Supercomputing, San Francisco, CA, pp. 193–204 (2003)
5. Arenaz, M., Touriño, J., Doallo, R.: Compiler support for parallel code generation through kernel recognition. In: 18th IEEE International Parallel and Distributed Processing Symposium, Santa Fe, NM (2004)
6. Arenaz, M., Touriño, J., Doallo, R.: Program behavior characterization through advanced kernel recognition. In: 13th International Euro-Par Conference, Rennes, France, pp. 237–247 (2007)
7. Arenaz, M., Touriño, J., Doallo, R.: XARK: An eXtensible framework for Automatic Recognition of computational Kernels. ACM Trans. Program. Lang. Syst. (accepted for publication)
8. Berry, M., et al.: The Perfect Club benchmarks: Effective performance evaluation of supercomputers. Int. J. Supercomputer Apps. 3(3), 5–40 (1989)
9. Cytron, R., Ferrante, J., Rosen, B.K., Wegman, M.N., Zadeck, F.K.: Efficiently computing static single assignment form and the control dependence graph. ACM Trans. Program. Lang. Syst. 13(4), 451–490 (1991)
10. Havlak, P.: Construction of thinned gated single-assignment form. In: 6th International Workshop on Languages and Compilers for Parallel Computing, Portland, OR, pp. 477–499 (1993)
11. Lee, C.G.: UTDSP benchmarks,
    http://www.eecg.toronto.edu/~corinna/DSP/infrastructure/UTDSP.html
    [Last accessed June 2008]
12. Tu, P., Padua, D.A.: Gated SSA-based demand-driven symbolic analysis for parallelizing compilers. In: 9th ACM International Conference on Supercomputing, Barcelona, Spain, pp. 414–423 (1995)
13. Blume, W., Doallo, R., Eigenmann, R., Grout, J., Hoeflinger, J., Lawrence, T., Lee, J., Padua, D.A., Paek, Y., Pottenger, W.M., Rauchwerger, L., Tu, P.: Parallel programming with Polaris. IEEE Computer 29(12), 78–82 (1996)

Inter-block Scoreboard Scheduling in a JIT Compiler for VLIW Processors

Benoît Dupont de Dinechin

STMicroelectronics STS/CEC
12, rue Jules Horowitz - BP 217. F-38019 Grenoble
benoit.dupont-de-dinechin@st.com

Abstract. We present a postpass instruction scheduling technique suitable for Just-In-Time (JIT) compilers targeted to VLIW processors. Its key features are: reduced compilation time and memory requirements; satisfaction of scheduling constraints along all program paths; and the ability to preserve existing prepass schedules, including software pipelines. This is achieved by combining two ideas: instruction scheduling similar to the dynamic scheduler of an out-of-order superscalar processor; the satisfaction of inter-block scheduling constraints by propagating them across the control-flow graph until fixed-point. We implemented this technique in a Common Language Infrastructure JIT compiler for the ST200 VLIW processors and the ARM processors.

1 Introduction

Just-In-Time (JIT) compilation of programs distributed as Java or .NET Common Language Infrastructure (CLI) byte-codes is becoming increasingly relevant for consumer electronics applications. A typical case is a game installed and played by the end-user on a Java-enabled mobile phone. In this case, the JIT compilation produces native code for the host processor of the system-on-chip.

However, systems-on-chip for consumer electronics also contain powerful media processors that could execute software installed by the end-user. Media processing software is usually developed in C or C++ and exposes instruction-level parallelism. Such media processing software can be compiled to CLI byte-codes thanks to the Microsoft Visual Studio .NET compilers or the gcc/st/cli compiler branch contributed by STMicroelectronics [4]. This motivates Just-In-Time compilation for embedded processors like the Texas Instruments C6000 VLIW-DSP family and the STMicroelectronics ST200 VLIW-media family[1].

In the setting of JIT compilation of Java programs, instruction scheduling is already expensive. For instance, the IBM Testarossa JIT team reports that combined prepass and postpass instruction scheduling costs up to 30% of the compilation time [14] for the IBM zSeries 990 and the POWER4 processors. To lower these costs, the IBM Testarossa JIT compiler relies on profiling to identify

---
[1] The ST200 VLIW architecture is based on the Lx technology [7] jointly developed by Hewlett-Packard Laboratories and STMicroelectronics.

the program regions where instruction scheduling is enabled. In addition, the register allocator tracks its changes to the prepass instruction schedules in order to decide where postpass instruction scheduling might be useful.

In the case of JIT compilation of media processing applications for VLIW processors, more ambitious instruction scheduling techniques are required. First, software pipelining may be applied in spite of higher compilation costs, as these applications spend most of their time in inner loops where instruction-level parallelism is available. However, software pipelines implement cyclic schedules that may be destroyed when the code is postpass scheduled using an acyclic scheduler. Second, JIT instruction scheduling techniques should accommodate VLIW processors without interlocking hardware [9,2], such as the TI C6000 VLIW-DSP family or the STMicroelectronics ST210 / Lx [7]. This means that JIT compilation must ensure that no execution path presents scheduling hazards.

To address these issues specific to JIT compilation on VLIW processors, we propose a new postpass instruction scheduling whose main features are:

- Efficiency (code quality) and speed (compilation time). This is possible thanks to *Scoreboard Scheduling*, that is, instruction scheduling by emulating the hardware scheduler of an out-of-order superscalar processor.
- Satisfaction of resource and dependence constraints along all program paths, as required by processors without interlocking hardware. We formulate and solve this *Inter-Block Scheduling* problem by propagating constraints until reaching a fixed-point, in a way reminiscent of forward data-flow analysis.

In addition, we prove our technique preserves the instruction schedules created by prepass scheduling and by software pipelining, provided register allocation and basic block alignment only introduced redundant scheduling constraints.

The presentation is as follows. In Section 2, we review local instruction scheduling heuristics and we propose Scoreboard Scheduling. We then describe an optimized implementation of this technique. In Section 3, we discuss inter-region instruction scheduling and we introduce Inter-Block Scoreboard Scheduling. This technique relies on iterative constraint propagation and we characterize its fixed-points. In Section 4, we provide an experimental evaluation of our contributions, which are implemented in the STMicroelectronics CLI-JIT compiler that targets the ST200 VLIW and the ARM processors.

2 Local Instruction Scheduling

2.1 Acyclic Instruction Scheduling

Acyclic instruction scheduling is the problem of ordering the execution of a set of *operations* on a target processor microarchitecture, so as to minimize the latest completion time. Executions of operations are partially ordered to ensure correct results. Precisely, effects on registers must be ordered in the following cases: Read After Write (RAW), Write After Read (WAR), and Write After Write (WAW). Other dependences arise from the partial ordering of memory accesses and from

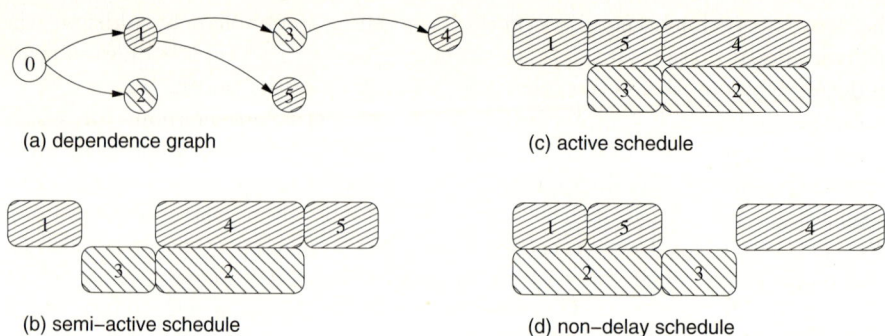

Fig. 1. Sample schedules for a two-resource scheduling problem (horizontal time)

control-flow effects. We assume that the resource requirements of each operation are represented by a *reservation table* [12], where rows correspond to scheduled resources and columns to time steps relative to the operation start date.

Classic instruction scheduling heuristics fall in two main categories [3]:

Cycle Scheduling. Scan time slots in non-decreasing order. For each time slot, order the dependence-ready operations in non-increasing priority and try to schedule each operation in turn, subject to resource availability. Dependence-ready means that execution of the operation predecessors has completed early enough to satisfy the dependences. This is Graham list scheduling.

Operation Scheduling. Consider each operation in non-increasing priority order. Schedule each operation at the earliest time slot where it is dependence-ready and its required resources are available. In order to prevent deadlock, the priority list order must be a topological sort of the dependence graph.

Cycle Scheduling is a time-tested instruction scheduling heuristic that produces high quality code on simple instruction pipelines, given a suitable priority of operations [9]. One such priority is the "critical path" length from any operation to the dependence graph sink node. A refinement is the "backward scheduling" priority that ensures optimal schedules on homogeneous pipelines [8] and on typed pipelines [6] for special classes of dependence graphs.

For the proofs of §2.2, we assume *monotonic reservation tables*, that is, reservation tables whose entries in any row are monotonically non-increasing. Single-column reservation tables, which are virtually always found on modern VLIW processors, are obviously monotonic. Monotonicity enables leverage of classic results from Resource Constrained Project Scheduling Problems (RCPSP) [13]:

Semi-Active Schedule as in Figure 1 b. No operation can be completed earlier without changing some execution sequence. Equivalently, in a semi-active schedule any operation has at least one dependence or resource constraint that is tight, preventing the operation from being locally left shifted.
Active Schedule as in Figure 1 c. No operation can be completed earlier without delaying another operation. The schedule of Figure 1 b is not active,

because operation 5 can be globally left-shifted to time slot 1, without delaying other operations. Operation Scheduling generates active schedules.

Non-Delay Schedule as in Figure 1 d. No execution resources are left idle if there is an operation that could start executing. The schedule of Figure 1 c is not non-delay, because operation 2 could start executing at time slot 0. Cycle Scheduling generates non-delay schedules.

The non-delay schedules are a subset of the active schedules, which are a subset of the semi-active schedules [13]. Active schedules and non-delay schedules are the same in case of operations that require resources for a single time unit.

2.2 Scoreboard Scheduling Principles

The main drawback of the classic scheduling heuristics is their computational cost. In the case of Cycle Scheduling, the time complexity contributions are:

1. constructing the dependence graph is $O(n^2)$ with n the number of operations, but can be lowered to $O(n)$ with conservative memory dependences [15];
2. computing the operation priorities is $O(n + e)$ with e the number of dependences for the critical path, and is as high as $O(n^2 \log n + ne)$ in [8,6];
3. issuing the operations in priority order is $O(n^2)$ according to [9], as each time step has a complexity proportional to m (where m is the number of dependence-ready operations), and m can be $O(n)$.

The complexity of operation issuing results from: sorting the dependence-ready operations in priority order; and matching the resource availabilities of the current cycle with the resource requirements of the dependence-ready operations. The latter motivates the finite-state automata approach of Proebsting & Fraser [11], later generalized to Operation Scheduling by Bala & Rubin [3].

To reduce instruction scheduling costs, we rely on the following principles:

– Verbrugge [15] replaces the dependence graph by an Array of Dependency Lists (ALD), with one list per *dependence record* (see §2.3). We show how Operating Scheduling can avoid the explicit construction of such lists.
– In the setting of JIT postpass scheduling, either basic blocks are prepass scheduled because their performance impact is significant, or their operations are in original program order. In either case, the order operations are presented to the postpass scheduler encodes a priority that is suitable for Operation Scheduling, since it is a topological ordering of the dependences. So (re-)computing the operation priorities is not necessary.
– We limit the number of resource availability checks by restricting the number of time slots considered for issuing the current operation.

Precisely, we define *Scoreboard Scheduling* to be a scheduling algorithm that operates like Operation Scheduling, with the following additional restrictions:

– any operation is scheduled within a time window of constant *window_size*,
– the *window_start* cannot decrease and is lazily increased while scheduling.

```
issue=0     ldb $r23 = 9[$r16]        issue=0     add $r18 = $r18, -12
start=0     | +0 +1 +2 +3 +4 +5 +6 +7 start=0     | +0 +1 +2 +3 +4 +5 +6 +7
----------|-------------------------  ----------|-------------------------
ISSUE     | 1                         ISSUE     | 2
MEM       | 1                         MEM       | 1
CTL       |                           CTL       |
----------|-------------------------  ----------|-------------------------
Control   | a                         Control   | a
$r16      | a                         $r16      | a
          |                           $r18      | aw aw  w  w
$r23      | aw aw  w  w  w  w         $r23      | aw aw  w  w  w  w
Memory    | a  a                      Memory    | a  a
```

Fig. 2. Scoreboard Scheduling within the time window ($window\_size = 4$)

```
issue=4     shl $r24 = $r24, 24       issue=5     add $r15 = $r15, $r24
start=0     | +0 +1 +2 +3 +4 +5 +6 +7 start=1     | +0 +1 +2 +3 +4 +5 +6 +7
----------|-------------------------  ----------|-------------------------
ISSUE     | 3  2  1  3  1             ISSUE     | 2  1  3  1  1
MEM       | 1  1  1  1                MEM       | 1  1  1
CTL       |                           CTL       |
----------|-------------------------  ----------|-------------------------
Control   | a  a  a  a  a             Control   | a  a  a  a  a
          |                           $r15      | aw aw aw aw aw aw  w  w
$r16      | aw aw aw aw aw  w  w      $r16      | aw aw aw aw  w  w
$r18      | aw aw  w  w               $r18      | aw  w  w
$r23      | aw aw aw aw aw  w  w      $r23      | aw aw aw aw  w  w
$r24      | aw aw aw aw aw  w  w      $r24      | aw aw aw aw  w  w
Memory    | a  a                      Memory    | a
```

Fig. 3. Scoreboard Scheduling and moving the time window ($window\_size = 4$)

That is, given an operation to schedule, the earliest date considered is $window\_start$. Moreover, if the earliest feasible schedule date $issue\_date$ of operation is greater than $window\_start + window\_size$, then the Scoreboard Scheduling $window\_start$ value is adjusted to $issue\_date - window\_size$.

Theorem 1. *Scoreboard Scheduling an active schedule yields the same schedule.*

Proof. By contradiction. Scheduling proceeds in non-decreasing time, as the priority list is a schedule. If the current operation can be scheduled earlier than it was, this is a global left shift so the priority list is not an active schedule.

Corollary 1. *Schedules produced by Operation Scheduling or Cycle Scheduling are invariant under Scoreboard Scheduling and Operation Scheduling.*

2.3 Scoreboard Scheduling Implementation

A *dependence record* is the atomic unit of state that needs to be considered for accurate register dependence tracking. Usually these are whole registers, except in cases of register aliasing. If so, registers are partitioned into sub-registers, some of which are shared between registers, and there is one dependence record per sub-register. Three technical records named *Volatile, Memory, Control* are also included in order to track the corresponding dependences.

Let $read\_stage[][]$, $write\_stage[][]$ be processor-specific arrays indexed by operation and by dependence record that tabulate the operand access pipeline stages.

Let $RAW[]$, $WAR[]$, $WAW[]$ be latency tuning parameters indexed by dependence record. For any dependence record r and operations i and j, we generalize the formula of [16] and specify any dependence $latency_{i \to j}$ on r as follows:

RAW Dependence	$latency_{i \to j} \geq write\_stage[i][r] - read\_stage[j][r] + RAW[r]$	(a)
	$latency_{i \to j} \geq RAW[r]$	(b)
WAW Dependence	$latency_{i \to j} \geq write\_stage[i][r] - write\_stage[j][r] + WAW[r]$	(c)
	$latency_{i \to j} \geq WAW[r]$	(d)
WAR Dependence	$latency_{i \to j} \geq read\_stage[i][r] - write\_stage[j][r] + WAR[r]$	(e)
	$latency_{i \to j} \geq WAR[r]$	(f)

Assuming that $write\_stage[i][r] \geq read\_stage[j][r]$ $\forall i, j, r$, that is, operand write is no earlier than operand read in the instruction pipeline for any given r, the dependence inequalities (b) and (e) are redundant. This enables dependence latencies to be tracked by maintaining only two entries per dependence record r: the latest access date and the latest write date. We call *access_actions* and *write_actions* the arrays with those entries indexed by dependence record.

The state of scheduled resources is tracked by a *resource_table*, which serves as the scheduler reservation table. This table has one row per resource and *window_size* + *columns_max* columns, where *columns_max* is the maximum number of columns across the reservation tables of all operations. The first column of the *resource_table* corresponds to the *window_start*. This is just enough state for checking resource conflicts in [*window_start, window_start* + *window_size*].

Scoreboard Scheduling is performed by picking each operation i according to the priority order and by calling $add\_schedule(i, try\_schedule(i))$, defined by:

try_schedule. Given an operation i, return the earliest dependence- and resource-feasible *issue_date* such that *issue_date* $\geq$ *window_start*. For each dependence record r, collect the following constraints on *issue_date*:

Effect	Constraints
Read[r]	$issue\_date \geq write\_actions[r] - read\_stage[i][r] + RAW[r]$
Write[r]	$issue\_date \geq write\_actions[r] - write\_stage[i][r] + WAW[r]$
	$issue\_date \geq access\_actions[r]$

The resulting *issue_date* is then incremented while there exists scheduled resource conflicts with the current contents of the *resource_table*.

add_schedule. Schedule an operation i at a dependence- and resource-feasible *issue_date* previously returned by *try_schedule*. For each dependence record r, update the action arrays as follows:

Effect	Updates
Read[r]	$access\_actions[r] \leftarrow \max(access\_actions[r], issue\_date + WAR[r])$
Write[r]	$access\_actions[r] \leftarrow \max(access\_actions[r], issue\_date + WAW[r])$
	$write\_actions[r] \leftarrow issue\_date + write\_stage[i][r]$

In case *issue_date* > *window_start* + *window_size*, the *window_start* is set to *issue_date* − *window_size* and the *resource_table* is shifted accordingly. The operation reservation table is then added into the *resource_table*.

In Figure 2, we illustrate Scoreboard Scheduling of two ST200 VLIW operations, starting from an empty scoreboard. There are three scheduled resources:

ISSUE, 4 units; MEM, one unit; CTL, one unit. The *window_start* is zero and the two operations are scheduled at *issue_date* zero. We display *access_actions*[r] and *write_actions*[r] as strings of a and w from *window_start* to *actions*[r]. In Figure 3, several other operations have been scheduled since Figure 2, the latest being shl $r24 at *issue_date* 4. Then operation add $r15 is scheduled at *issue_date* 5, due to the RAW dependence on $r24. Because *window_size* is 4, the *window_start* is set to 1 and the *resource_table* rows ISSUE, MEM, CTL are shifted.

Theorem 2. *Scoreboard Scheduling correctly enforces the dependence latencies.*

Proof. Calling $add\_schedule(i, issue\_date_i)$ followed by $try\_schedule(j, issue\_date_i + latency_{i \to j})$ implies that $latency_{i \to j}$ satisfies the inequalities $(a), (c), (d), (f)$.

3 Global Instruction Scheduling

3.1 Postpass Inter-region Scheduling

We define the *inter-region scheduling problem* as scheduling the operations of each scheduling region such that the resource and dependence constraints inherited from the scheduling regions (transitive) predecessors, possibly including self, are satisfied. When the scheduling regions are reduced to basic blocks, we call this problem the *inter-block scheduling problem*. Only inter-region scheduling is allowed to move operations between basic blocks (of the same region).

The basic technique for solving the inter-region scheduling problem is to schedule each region in isolation, then correct the resource and latency constraint violations that may occur along control-flow transfers from one scheduling region to the other by inserting NOP operations. Such *NOP padding* may occur after region entries, before region exits, or both, and this technique is applied after postpass scheduling on state-of-the-art compilers such as the Open64.

Meld Scheduling is a prepass inter-region scheduling technique proposed by Abraham, Kathail, Deitrich [2] that minimizes the amount of NOP padding required after scheduling. This technique is demonstrated using superblocks, which are scheduled from the most frequently executed to the least frequently executed, however it applies to any program partition into acyclic regions.

Consider a dependence whose source operation is inside a scheduling region and whose target operation is outside the scheduling region. Its *latency dangle* is the minimum number of time units required between the exit from the scheduling region and the execution of the target operation to satisfy the dependence. For a dependence whose source operation is outside the scheduling region and whose target operation is inside, its latency dangle is defined in a symmetric way [2].

Meld Scheduling only considers dependence latency dangles, however resource dangles can be similarly defined. Latency dangle constraints originate from predecessor regions or from successor regions, depending on the order the regions are scheduled. Difficulties arise with cycles in the control-flow graph, and also with latency dangles that pass through scheduling regions. These are addressed with conservative assumptions on the dangles.

Meld Scheduling is a prepass technique, so register allocation or basic block alignment may introduce extra code or non-redundant WAR and RAW register dependences. Also with JIT compilation, prepass scheduling is likely to be omitted on cold code regions. On processors without interlocking hardware, compilers must ensure that no execution path presents hazards. In the Open64 compiler, hazards are detected and corrected by a dedicated "instruction bundler".

When focusing on postpass scheduling, the latency and resource dangles of Meld Scheduling are implied by the scoreboard scheduler states at region boundaries. Moreover, we assume that the performance benefits of global code motion are not significant during the postpass scheduling of prepass scheduled regions, so we focus on inter-block scheduling. Last, we would like to avoid duplicate work between an "instruction bundler" and postpass scheduling.

Based on these observations, we propose the *Inter-Block Scoreboard Scheduling* technique to iteratively propagate the dependence and resource constraints of local scheduling across the control-flow graph until fixed-point. As we shall prove, it is possible to ensure this technique converges quickly and preserves prepass schedules, including software pipelines, that are still valid.

3.2 Inter-block Scoreboard Scheduling

We propagate the scoreboard scheduler states at the start and the end of each basic block for all program basic blocks by using a worklist algorithm, like in forward data-flow analysis [10]. This state comprises *window_start*, the action array entries and the *resource_table*. Each basic block extracted from the worklist is processed by Scoreboard Scheduling its operations in non-decreasing order of their previous *issue_date*s (in program order the first time). This updates the operation *issue_date*s and the state at the end of the basic block.

Following this basic block update, the start scoreboard scheduler states of its successor basic blocks are combined through a meet function (described below) with the end scoreboard scheduler state just obtained. If any start scoreboard scheduler state is changed by the meet function, this means new inter-block scheduling constraints need to be propagated so the corresponding basic block is put on the worklist. Initially, all basic blocks are in the worklist and the constraint propagation is iterated until the worklist is empty.

In order to achieve quick convergence of this constraint propagation, we enforce a *non-decrease rule*: **the operation *issue_date*s do not decrease when rescheduling a basic block.** That is, when scheduling an operation, its release date is the *issue_date* computed the last time the basic block was scheduled. This is implemented in *try_schedule*(i) by initializing the search for a feasible *issue_date*$_i$ to the maximum of the previous *issue_date*$_i$ and the *window_start*.

The meet function propagates the scheduling constraints between two basic blocks connected in the control-flow graph. Each control-flow edge is annotated with a *delay* that accounts for the time elapsed along that edge. Delay is zero for fall-through edges and is the minimum branch latency for other edges. Then:

– Advance the scoreboard scheduler state at the end of the origin basic block by elapsing time so *window_start* reaches the *issue_date* of the last operation

plus one (zero if the basic block is empty), plus the *delay* of the connecting control-flow edge (zero if fall-through edge, else the taken branch latency).
- Translate the time of this scoreboard scheduler state so that *window_start* becomes zero. With our implementation, this amounts to subtracting *window_start* from the action array entries and moving the *resource_table*.
- Merge the two scoreboard scheduler states by taking the maximum of the entries of the *resource_table* and of the action arrays.

Theorem 3. *Inter-Block Scoreboard Scheduling converges in bounded time.*

Proof. The latest *issue_date* of a basic block never exceeds the number of operations plus one, times the maximum dependence latency or the maximum span of a reservation table (whichever is larger). The *issue_date*s are also non-decreasing by the non-decrease rule, so they reach a fixed-point in bounded time. The fixed-point of the scoreboard scheduler states follows.

3.3 Characterization of Fixed-Points

Theorem 4. *Any locally scheduled program that satisfies the inter-block scheduling constraints is a fixed-point of Inter-Block Scoreboard Scheduling.*

Proof. By hypothesis, all operations have valid *issue_date*s with respect to basic block instruction scheduling. Also, the inter-block scheduling constraints are satisfied. By the non-decrease rule, each operation previous *issue_date* is the first date tried by Scoreboard Scheduling, and this succeeds.

A first consequence is that any prepass region schedule which satisfies the inter-block scheduling constraints at its boundary basic blocks will be unchanged by Inter-Block Scoreboard Scheduling, provided no non-redundant instruction scheduling constraints are inserted in the region by later compilation steps. Interestingly, this holds for any prepass region scheduling algorithm: superblock scheduling; trace scheduling; wavefront scheduling; and software pipelining.

A second consequence is that Inter-Block Scoreboard Scheduling of a program with enough NOP padding to satisfy the inter-block scheduling constraints will converge with only one Scoreboard Scheduling pass on each basic block. In practice, such explicit NOP padding should be reserved for situations where a high-frequency execution path may suffer from the effects of latency and resource dangles at a control-flow merge with a low-frequency execution path, such as entry to an inner loop header from a loop pre-header.

4 Experimental Results

In the setting of the STMicroelectronics CLI-JIT compiler, we implemented Scoreboard Scheduling as described in Section 2.3 and also a Cycle Scheduling algorithm that closely follows the description of Abraham [1], including reference counting for detecting operations whose predecessors have all been scheduled.

Origin	Size	IPC	RCost	RPerf.	RQuery
mergesort	12	0.92	2.35	1.00	0.60
maxindex	12	2.00	2.52	1.00	0.67
fft32x32s	20	4.00	2.57	1.00	0.50
autcor	21	1.50	3.34	1.00	1.08
d6arith	27	0.87	2.78	1.00	0.60
sfcfilter	29	2.90	3.00	1.00	0.62
strwc	32	3.56	3.17	1.00	0.70
bitonic	34	3.78	3.55	1.00	1.00
floydall	52	1.41	3.62	1.00	0.67
pframe	59	1.59	3.82	1.00	0.63
polysyn	79	2.55	5.95	1.19	1.29
huffdec2	81	0.80	4.23	1.00	0.56
fft32x32s	83	3.61	5.21	1.09	1.00
dbuffer	108	3.18	5.67	1.03	1.00
polysyn	137	3.51	7.29	1.03	1.50
transfo	230	3.59	9.00	1.16	1.04
qplsf5	231	2.96	8.91	1.13	0.11
polysyn	256	1.63	8.79	1.00	0.57
polysyn	297	3.23	9.95	1.04	0.76
radial33	554	3.26	18.78	1.21	1.95

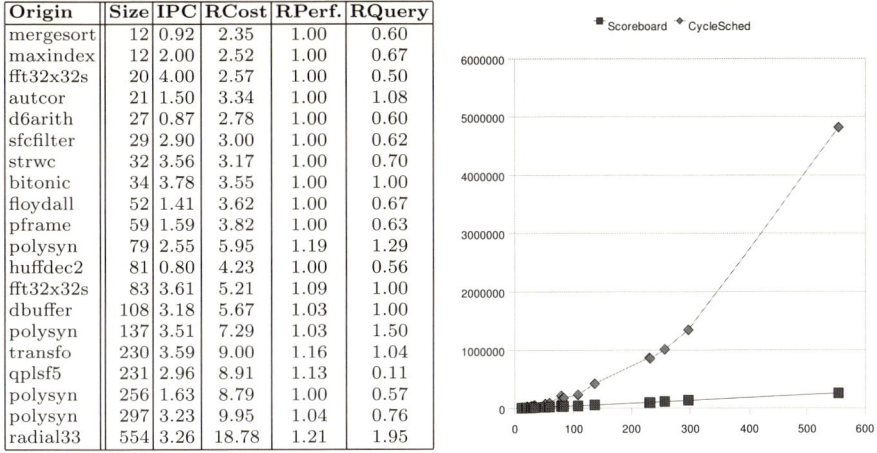

Fig. 4. Benchmark basic blocks and instruction scheduling results

We further optimized this Cycle Scheduling implementation for speed. In particular, we replaced the dependence graph by a variant of the Array of Dependence Lists (ADL) of Verbrugge [15] to ensure a $O(n)$ time complexity of the dependence graph construction. This implies conservative memory dependences, however we assume such a restriction is acceptable for postpass scheduling.

We selected a series of basic blocks from STMicroelectronics media processing application codes and performance kernels compiled at the highest optimization level by the Open64-based production compiler for the ST200 VLIW family [5]. The proposed CLI-JIT postpass scheduler was connected to this compiler.

These benchmarks are listed in the left side of Figure 4. Columns **Size** and **IPC** respectively give the number of instructions and of instructions per cycle after Cycle Scheduling. Column **RCost** is the ratio of compilation time between the cycle scheduler and the scoreboard scheduler at $window\_size = 15$. Column **RPerf** is the relative performance of the two schedulers, as measured by inverse of schedule length. Column **RQuery** is the ratio of compilation time for resource checking between the cycle scheduler and the scoreboard scheduler. In the right side of Figure 4, we plot the compilation time as function of basic block size. Unlike Cycle Scheduling, Scoreboard Scheduling clearly operates in linear-time.

To understand how compilation time is spent, we display in Figure 5 the stacked contributions of the different scheduling phases normalized by the total instruction scheduling time, so their sum is one. We also single out the cumulative time spent in resource checking, yielding the bars above one. For Cycle Scheduling (left side), the cost of computing the dependences **ADL** becomes relatively smaller, as it is linear with basic block size. The **Priority** computing phase is of comparable time complexity yet smaller than the operation **Issuing** phase. For Scoreboard Scheduling (right side), the **Try** schedule phase is consistently slightly more expensive than the **Add** schedule phase.

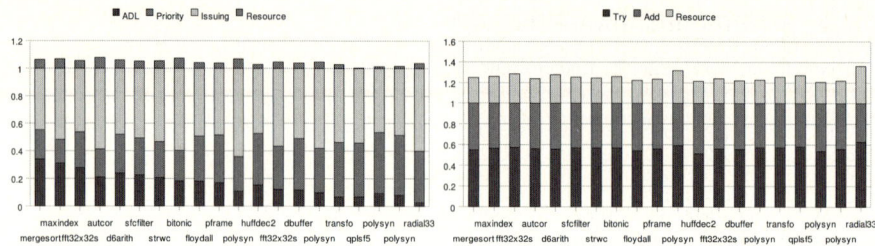

Fig. 5. Time breakdown for Cycle Scheduling and Scoreboard Scheduling

It also appears from Figure 5 that using finite state automata as proposed by Bala & Rubin [3] for speeding up resource checking is not always justified, in particular for processors whose reservation tables are single-cycle. For more complex processors, it would be straightforward to replace the *resource_table* of a Scoreboard Scheduling implementation by such finite state automata.

5 Conclusions

We propose a postpass instruction scheduling technique motivated by Just-In-Time (JIT) compilation for VLIW processors. This technique combines two ideas: Scoreboard Scheduling, a restriction of classic Operation Scheduling that considers only the time slots inside a window that moves forward in time; and Inter-Block Scheduling, an iterative propagation of the scheduling constraints across the control-flow graph, subject to the non-decrease of the schedule dates. This Inter-Block Scoreboard Scheduling technique offers three benefits:

- reducing the instruction scheduling compilation time, compared to classic Cycle Scheduling and Operation Scheduling;
- ensuring that all program paths do not present scheduling hazards, as required by processors without interlocking hardware;
- preserving prepass region schedules that are still valid when postpass scheduling runs, in particular software pipelines without spill code.

Experiments with the STMicroelectronics ST200 VLIW production compiler and the STMicroelectronics CLI-JIT compiler confirm the interest of our approach.

Our results further indicate that compiler instruction schedules produced by Cycle Scheduling and Operation Scheduling are essentially unchanged by the hardware operation scheduler of out-of-order superscalar processors. Indeed active schedules are invariant under Scoreboard Scheduling. Finally, the proposed non-decrease rule provides a simple way of protecting cyclic schedules such as software pipelines from the effects of rescheduling with an acyclic scheduler.

Acknowledgments

Special thanks to Alain Darte for fruitful discussions that improved this paper.

References

1. Abraham, S.G.: Efficient Backtracking Instruction Schedulers. Technical Report HPL- 2000-56, Hewlett-Packard Laboratories (May 2000)
2. Abraham, S.G., Kathail, V., Deitrich, B.L.: Meld Scheduling: Relaxing Scheduling Constraints across Region Boundaries. In: MICRO 29: Proc. of the 29th annual ACM/IEEE int. symp. on Microarchitecture, pp. 308–321 (1996)
3. Bala, V., Rubin, N.: Efficient Instruction Scheduling Using Finite State Automata. In: MICRO 28: Proc. of the 28th annual int. symp. on Microarchitecture, pp. 46–56 (1995)
4. Cornero, M., Costa, R., Pascual, R.F., Ornstein, A., Rohou, E.: An Experimental Environment Validating the Suitability of CLI as an Effective Deployment Format for Embedded Systems. In: 2008 International Conference on High Performance Embedded Architectures and Compilers (2008)
5. Dupont de Dinechin, B.: From Machine Scheduling to VLIW Instruction Scheduling. ST Journal of Research 1(2) (2004)
6. Dupont de Dinechin, B.: Scheduling Monotone Interval Orders on Typed Task Systems. In: 26th Workshop of the UK Planning And Scheduling Special Interest Group (PlanSIG), Prague, Czech Republic (2007)
7. Faraboschi, P., Brown, G., Fisher, J.A., Desoli, G., Homewood, F.: Lx: a Technology Platform for Customizable VLIW Embedded Processing. In: ISCA 2000: Proc. of the 27th annual Int. Symposium on Computer Architecture, pp. 203–213 (2000)
8. Leung, A., Palem, K.V., Pnueli, A.: Scheduling Time-Constrained Instructions on Pipelined Processors. ACM Trans. Program. Lang. Syst. 23(1), 73–103 (2001)
9. Muchnick, S.S., Gibbons, P.B.: Best of PLDI 1979 – 1999: Efficient Instruction Scheduling for a Pipelined Architecture. SIGPLAN Notices 39(4), 167–174 (2004)
10. Nielson, F., Nielson, H.R., Hankin, C.: Principles of Program Analysis. Springer, New York (1999)
11. Proebsting, T.A., Fraser, C.W.: Detecting Pipeline Structural Hazards Quickly. In: POPL 1994: Proceedings of the 21st symposium on Principles of Programming Languages, pp. 280–286. ACM Press, New York (1994)
12. Rau, B.R.: Iterative Modulo Scheduling. International Journal of Parallel Processing 24(1), 3–64 (1996)
13. Sprecher, A., Kolisch, R., Drexl, A.: Semi-Active, Active, and Non-Delay Schedules for the Resource-Constrained Project Scheduling Problem. European Journal of Operational Research 80, 94–102 (1995)
14. Tang, V., Siu, J., Vasilevskiy, A., Mitran, M.: A Framework for Reducing Instruction Scheduling Overhead in Dynamic Compilers. In: CASCON 2006: Proc. of the 2006 Conf. of the Center for Advanced Studies on Collaborative Research, p. 5 (2006)
15. Verbrugge, C.: Fast Local List Scheduling. Technical Report SABLE-TR-2002-5, School of Computer Science, McGill University (March 2002)
16. Wahlen, O., Hohenauer, M., Braun, G., Leupers, R., Ascheid, G., Meyr, H., Nie, X.: Extraction of Efficient Instruction Schedulers from Cycle-True Processor Models. In: Krall, A. (ed.) SCOPES 2003. LNCS, vol. 2826, pp. 167–181. Springer, Heidelberg (2003)

Global Tiling for Communication Minimal Parallelization on Distributed Memory Systems

Lei Liu[1,2], Li Chen[1], ChengYong Wu[1], and Xiao-bing Feng[1]

[1] Key Laboratory of Computer Architecture Institute of Computing Technology, Chinese Academy of Sciences, 100080 Beijing, China
[2] Graduate School of the Chinese Academy of Sciences, 100080 Beijing, China
{liulei,lchen,cwu,fxb}@ict.ac.cn

Abstract. Most previous studies on tiling focus on the division of iteration space. However, on distributed memory parallel systems, the decomposition of computation and the distribution of data must be handled at the same time, in order to attain load balancing and to minimize data migration. In this paper, we formulate a 0-1 integer linear programming for the problem of globally optimal tiling to minimize the total execution time. To simplify the selection of tiling parameters, we restrict the tile shape to semi-oblique shape, and present two effective approaches to decide the tile shape for multi-dimensional semi-oblique shaped tiling. Besides, we present a tile-to-processor mapping scheme based on hyperplanes, which can express diverse parallelism and gain better performance than traditional methods. The experimentations with NPB2.3-serial SP and LU on Qsnet connected cluster achieved the average parallel efficiency of 87% and 73% respectively.

Keywords: compiler, parallelization, tiling, distributed memory systems, tile-to-processor mapping, semi-oblique shaped tile.

1 Introduction and Related Work

Iteration space tiling is one of the most popular transformations used by compiler and automatic parallelizers for improving locality in multi-level memory hierarchies as well as achieving coarse-grain parallelism. In distributed memory parallel computers, iteration space tiling partitions the loop nest into tiles that may be concurrently executed on different processors with a reduced volume and frequency of inter-processor communication [13, 20].

A lot of discussion has been made concerning the selection of an optimal tiling transformation to minimize communication volume and overall execution time in distributed memory machines. Ramanujam and Sadayappan [17], Schreiber [19], Boulet et al [3], and also Xue [20], discussed the problem of the choice of the tiling parameters to solve the communication-minimal tiling optimally, and proved that the communication-minimal tiling can derive from the algorithm's tiling cone. Hodzic and Shang in [9] proposed a method to correlate optimal tile size and shape, and discussed the selection of scheduling-optimal tile shape and size to minimize execution time. Hogstedt et al.[10] studied the idle time associated with parallelepiped tiling.

They defined the rise as a critical parameter to characterize the time processors wait for data from other processors, and gave analytic formulae for the idle time of the program, and also determined the optimal schedule using linear programming.

Despite all these methods for the selection of tiling parameters, general parallelepiped tiling is not applied by commercial and research compilers due to the complexity of implementation. In order to make the tiling optimal problem tractable and without too much performance fluctuating, we restrict the tile shape to semi-oblique, which are hyper-parallelograms with at least one side perpendicular to the coordinate axes.

Andonov et al. [2] addressed the problem of optimal semi-oblique tiling, and determined the optimal tile size, optimal number of processors and also the optimal slope of the oblique tile boundary, based on the BSP model. However, in their paper, the iteration space tiling was restricted to a two-dimensional semi-oblique shaped tile, which is a special case of our multi-dimensional semi-oblique shape tiling.

Previous work, however, addressed only tiling the iteration space for a single nested Do-loop, and did not consider the problem of data layout. But the problem of data layout is a crucial factor for gaining performance on distributed memory systems. If data and computation are not properly partitioned across processors, it may cause heavy inter-processor communication. Such excessive communication will offset the benefit of parallelization, even if each loop nest has selected optimal iteration space tiling. Similar to the iteration space tiling, we introduce the notion of data space tiling to describe the problem of data layout, and synthesize the iteration space tiling and data space tiling to minimize the inter-processor communication.

Traditional program decomposition frameworks use exhaustive search methods for guiding data and computation partitioning [14]. However, in order not to increase the search space, only row-wise and column-wise or other restricted data distribution schemes can be considered in their methods.

Griebl [7] presented an integrated framework for optimizing data placement and parallelism in the use of tiling. However, mainly due to tiling being modeled as a post-processing after space-time mapping, they can not guarantee optimal tiling and minimal remapping communication for the whole program. In technical report [18], the authors developed a tiling approach that can optimize parallelism and locality simultaneously, and used loop fusion to enhance the data locality between loop nests so as to reduce communication between loop nests. However, loop fusion may impact the parallelism, and their framework can not balance between the parallelism gain and benefit from data locality.

In this paper, we present some approaches to calculate multi-dimensional semi-oblique shaped tiling with polynomial time complexity, and develop a unified framework that can be used for computation partitioning and data layout optimization. The central contribution of this paper is a method called global tiling to select the optimal iteration space tiling and data space tiling, in order to improve parallelism as well as to minimize the volume of communication between loop nests for the whole program.

The rest of this paper is organized as follows. Section 2 covers the background of tiling and notation and assumption. In section 3, we describe the tile space selection algorithms and tile-to-processor mapping strategy. Section 4 formulates the 0-1 ILP for global tiling optimization problem. The experimentations with SP and LU applications are illustrated in the section 5, and conclusions are presented in Section 6.

2 Nomenclature and Definitions

2.1 Basic Definitions and Assumptions

The iteration space, denoted J, is the set of all loop iterations bounded by loop limits, which can be viewed as a polytope constrained by loop bounds. Constrained by array bounds, a data space T can also be viewed as a set of polytopes in the same way. The relations between iteration spaces and data spaces can be built via array reference functions. An array reference function is a transformation from iteration space J into data space T, or more exactly, from the iteration vectors to the array elements. We assume that the reference functions are affine. Under this assumption, we can write a reference to an array A as $f(\vec{j}) = F^A \vec{j} + \alpha^A$, where F^A is a linear transformation matrix called access matrix and α^A is the offset vector.

In this paper, the programs considered are limited to a series of perfected nested loops with uniform dependencies, i.e., dependencies that can be described by a finite number of constant dependence distance vectors.

2.2 Iteration Space and Data Space Tiling Transformation

In k-dimensional space, a hyperplane can be defined as a set of tuples $(a_1, a_2, ..., a_k)$, such that $g_1a_1 + g_2a_2 + ... + g_ka_k = q$, where $g_1, g_2 ..., g_k$ are rational numbers called hyperplane coefficients. A hyperplane vector $(g_1, g_2, ..., g_k)$ defines a hyperplane family where each member hyperplane has the same hyperplane vector but different q.

Tiling transformation is defined as k independent families of parallel equidistant hyperplanes that partition the iteration index space into k-dimensional parallelepiped tiles. A square matrix H consists of the k normal vectors as rows, which is a vector orthogonal to the hyperplanes. Similar to matrix H, matrix P contains the side-vectors of a tile as column vector, and $P = H^{-1}$. The tiling hyperplanes defined by matrix H satisfy $HD \geq 0$ (D is the data dependence matrix), i.e., each entry in the product matrix is greater than or equal to zero, which is a sufficient condition for the legal tiling transformation [13, 17, 20].

The entire data space can also be tiled in the similar way that the iteration space is tiled. Therefore, we introduce the notion of data space tiling that defines the data elements accessed by an iteration space tile. An m-by-m nonsingular matrix M is defined as the data tile matrix, and each row of M is a vector perpendicular to a tile boundary. As in the iteration space tiling case, each column of M^{-1} gives the direction vector for a tile boundary. Assuming that F^A is the access matrix of Array A in loop nests x, we have $M = F^A \times H$, which define the relationship between iteration space tiling and data space tiling.

3 Tile Shape Selection and Tile-to-Processor Mapping

3.1 Semi-oblique Shaped Tile

We use the same way as [8] to factorize the tiling transformation matrix. Defining $P = P_u L$, where P_u is a matrix with unit determinant and column vectors in the directions of the corresponding column vectors of the matrix P, L is a $k \times k$ diagonal matrix which defines the size of tile. $H_u = P_u^{-1}$ is a unit determinant with rows in the same direction as rows of matrix H. Matrix H_u and matrix P_u do not include any information about the size of the tile. We call H_u and P_u the tile shape matrix.

The tile parameters selection is a hard, nonlinear optimization problem, and is currently no good solution. So we restrict the tile shape to semi-oblique ones to simplify the tiling parameters selection problem. The semi-oblique shaped tiles are hyper-parallelograms with at least one side that are perpendicular to the coordinate axes. That is, the iteration tiling matrix P has at least one row vector which has exact one non-zero element.

We assume that the data dependence matrix D is a $k \times m$ matrix, and define:

$$D = \begin{bmatrix} d_{1,1} & d_{1,2} & \cdots & d_{1,m} \\ d_{2,1} & d_{2,2} & \cdots & d_{2,m} \\ \vdots & \vdots & \ddots & \vdots \\ d_{k,1} & d_{k,2} & \cdots & d_{k,m} \end{bmatrix}, \text{ a binary operator: } x \div y = \begin{cases} \infty, & \text{if } x \neq 0 \wedge y = 0 \\ 1, & \text{if } x = 0 \wedge y = 0 \\ 0, & \text{if } y = \infty \\ \frac{x}{y} & \text{otherwise} \end{cases}, \text{ and}$$

function: $Min(x, \infty) = x$, $Max(x, \infty) = \infty$. The following algorithms show how to construct a legal semi-oblique tile shape matrix.

Algorithm 1. For data dependence matrix D, a lower triangular matrix P_u is constructed as $P_u = \begin{bmatrix} 1 & 0 & \cdots & 0 \\ p_{2,1} & 1 & \cdots & 0 \\ \vdots & \vdots & \ddots & \vdots \\ p_{k,1} & p_{k,2} & \cdots & 1 \end{bmatrix}$, $p_{i,j} = \begin{cases} Min_{l=1}^m(d_{i,l} \div d_{1,l}) & \text{if } j = 1 \\ Min_{l=1}^m(q_{i,j}^l) & \text{if } j \geq 2 \end{cases}$, where

$i > j$, and $q_{i,j}^l = \begin{cases} \frac{d_{i,l}}{d_{j,l}}, & \text{if } d_{i,l} < 0 \wedge d_{j,l} \neq 0 \\ & \wedge d_{j-1,l} = \ldots = d_{1,l} = 0 \\ 0, & \text{otherwise} \end{cases}$

Theorem 1. Given a Dependence matrix D for loop nest x, the semi-oblique shaped tiling matrix P_u by *Algorithm 1* is a legal loop transformation.

The proof of *Theorem 1* is too long, so we omit this proof due to the space constraints.

When $D \geq 0$, in order to select a better scheduling tile shape, *algorithm 1* can be improved as following:

Algorithm 2. Assuming data dependence matrix D, we define a $(k-1) \times k$ matrix

$P^* = \begin{bmatrix} 0 & 1 & 0 & \cdots & 0 \\ 0 & 0 & 1 & \cdots & 0 \\ \vdots & \vdots & \vdots & \ddots & \vdots \\ 0 & 0 & 0 & \cdots & 1 \end{bmatrix}$. A legal tiling shape matrix $P_u = \begin{bmatrix} \vec{P}_1 \\ P^* \end{bmatrix}$ can be constructed,

where: $\vec{P}_1 = \begin{bmatrix} 1 & 1 \div (Max_{j=1}^m((\sum_{i=2}^k d_{i,j}) \div d_{1,j})) & \cdots & 1 \div (Max_{j=1}^m((\sum_{i=2}^k d_{i,j}) \div d_{1,j})) \end{bmatrix}$.

Theorem 2. If dependence matrix $D \geq 0$ which means that every entry of D is non-negative, and the tile shape matrix P_u by *Algorithm 2* can guarantee a legal tiling transformation.

Proof: Define matrix $Q = H_u D$, for $H_u = P_u^{-1}$, the element of the first row vector in matrix Q is $Q_{1,j} = d_{1,j} - (\sum_{i=2}^{k} d_{i,j}) \div (Max_{j=1}^{m}((\sum_{i=2}^{k} d_{i,j}) \div d_{1,j}))$, the other rows vector in matrix Q is equal to the corresponding rows in matrix D. If $d_{1,j} \neq 0$, then $Q_{1,j} = d_{1,j} \times (1 - (\sum_{i=2}^{k} d_{i,j}) / Max_{j=1}^{m}(\sum_{i=2}^{k} d_{i,j}))$, $\because (\sum_{i=2}^{k} d_{i,j}) / Max_{j=1}^{m}(\sum_{i=2}^{k} d_{i,j}) \leq 1$ $\wedge d_{1,j} > 0$, $\therefore \Rightarrow hd_{1,j} \geq 0$; else $d_{1,j} = 0$, so that $(\sum_{i=2}^{k} d_{i,j}) \div d_{1,j} = \infty$, $\therefore hd_{1,j} = 0 - (\sum_{i=2}^{k} d_{i,j}) / \infty = 0$. Because $D \geq 0$, therefore, the elements of Q are non-negative, that is, $H_u D \geq 0$, P_u is a legal tiling transformation. ∎

3.2 Tile-to-Processor Mapping

On distributed memory systems, we need to allocate both the iteration tiles and data tiles to processors. For k dimensional tiling transformation in loop nest x and k' dimensional processor grid S and $k' \leq k$, the iteration tile-to-processor mapping is defined as: $\vec{s} = G_\theta \times \vec{j}_t$, where G_θ, called iteration tile mapping matrix (mapping matrix for short), is a $k' \times k$ matrix with each row is a hyperplane vector g, $\vec{j}_t$ are the coordinates of tile, and $\vec{s}$ are the coordinates of processor space S. The mapping matrix G_θ also means k' degrees of parallelism in loop nest x.

Taking the semi-oblique shaped tile into account, we only assign the tiles along the hyperplanes that are perpendicular to the coordinate axis of iteration space. The following *algorithm 3* shows how to construct mapping matrix G_θ, giving the tile shape matrix P_u and data dependence D.

Algorithm 3. The tile shape matrix P_u is a $k \times k$ nonsingular matrix, for the data dependence matrix D in loop nest x. If P_u is not a unit matrix, the tile-to-processor mapping matrix G_θ is composed of the row vectors that have exact one non-zero element in P_u. Else if P_u is a unit matrix and the row rank of D is not one, then there are k different mapping matrixes, which are equal to a sub-matrix with k-1 rows of P_u. Otherwise, P_u is a unit matrix and the row rank of dependence matrix D is 1, besides the k different mapping matrix distributing the tile along the coordinate axis of iterations space, another mapping strategy called diagonal tile mapping is produced. Diagonal tile mapping arranges the tile mapping to processors along wrapped diagonals through the axis of iteration space.

For example, considering a two dimensional iteration space, the data dependence matrix $D = \begin{bmatrix} 2 \\ 0 \end{bmatrix}$, thus a semi-oblique shaped tiling $P_u = \begin{bmatrix} 1 & 0 \\ 0 & 1 \end{bmatrix}$ is constructed by *algorithm 2*. Because the row rank of D is 1, there are three different tile mapping schemes according to the *algorithm 3*: in Fig1.a, the mapping matrix $G_\theta = \begin{bmatrix} 1 & 0 \end{bmatrix}$

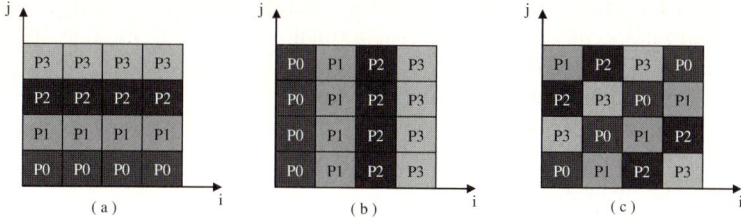

Fig. 1. Three kinds of tile-to-processor mapping strategies for two dimensional tiling

means of allocating the tiles along the axis i in iteration space; in Fig1.b, the mapping matrix $G_\theta = [0\ 1]$ means to allocate the tiles along the axis j, and in Fig1.c, a tile-to-processor mapping $G_\theta = [1\ -1]$ means to assign the tiles along the diagonal.

As for the data tile mapping to processors is considered, for array reference B, F^B is the array access matrix. If F^B is a non-singular matrix, then the data tile mapping matrix is equal to $G_\theta \times (F^B)^{-1}$, where G_θ is the mapping matrix for iteration space tiling. Otherwise we assume that the array is replicated on processors, denoted as $G_\theta = \bot$.

In the case of data tiling mapping strategies, it is possible that two different data tile-to-processor mapping strategies are conflicting, that is, the data tiles are allocated to processors by two ways. If both of the array access matrix F^{B1} and F^{B2} are nonsingular matrixes and $G_\theta^1 \times (F^{B_1})^{-1} = G_\theta^2 \times (F^{B_2})^{-1}$, or F^{B1} and F^{B2} are singular matrixes and $G_\theta^1 = G_\theta^2 = \bot$, then the data tile mapping strategies for array reference B_1 and B_2 are consistent; otherwise, these two data tile mapping strategy are conflicting, where G_θ^1 and G_θ^2 are the corresponding mapping matrixes.

4 Global Tiling Problem

On distributed memory systems, the iteration space tiling and data space tiling should be considered simultaneously. And the optimization of data space tiling is a global problem, because the layout of an array that is determined by a kind of data tiling and data tile mapping strategy should affect other references of that array in the entire program. Conflicting data tile mapping strategies will produce data remapping communications.

In this section, we concentrate on the global tiling optimization problem: that is, optimizing a number of consecutive loop nests simultaneously; and formulate an integer linear programming (ILP) method to solve this problem.

4.1 Local Tiling Candidates

In previous sections we introduced two methods to select a legal semi-oblique tile shape matrix according to the data dependence matrix given in a loop nest. Then we can get the tiling matrix after selecting the corresponding tile mapping matrix through *algorithm 3* and the tile size according to this tile shape. There are a large body of work on determining optimal tile size [1,2,3,5,8,10,16,20], so we will not address the tile size problem in this paper. When working on a global setting which comprises a number of loop nests, however, a local suboptimal solution may be globally optimal or vice versa. This implies that it may not be a good idea to consider only local optimal tiling transformation during global optimization process. In other words, we need to consider a number of local alternatives of tiling transformation per nest in the global optimization. The following algorithms show how to achieve all local tiling candidates for a loop nest.

Algorithm 4. For a loop nest x, the data dependence matrix D, if $D \geq 0$, the corresponding tile shape matrix P_u is constructed by *algorithm 2*; otherwise P_u is constructed by *algorithm 1*. If loop interchange transformation is legal, then we get another data dependence matrix D' and define variable v as the loop depth of the original outermost loop in the new interchanged loop nest. Then for each data dependence matrix D' with different v in loop nest x, we can produce a tiling shape matrix P_u' using *algorithm 1* or *algorithm 2*. Let us interchange the vth row vector of the matrix P_u' with the first row vector, then we get a corresponding candidate tiling matrix P_u^v. Choosing the corresponding tile size and tile mapping matrix for each tile shape P_u^v, then we can get all the tiling candidates for loop nest x.

The following example explains how to get all tiling candidates.

Example 1

```
X₁:    do i =1 to 100
           do j =1 to 200
               a(i,j)=a(i-1,j-1)+a(i-1,j-2)*b(i,j)
```

For loop nest X_1, the data dependence matrix $D = \begin{bmatrix} 1 & 1 \\ 2 & 1 \end{bmatrix}$, and $P_1 = \begin{bmatrix} 1 & \frac{1}{2} \\ 0 & 1 \end{bmatrix}$ is the corresponding tiling matrix constructed through *algorithm 2*. If we interchange the loop i with loop j, then we get a new loop nest X_1'. The dependence matrix of X_1' $D' = \begin{bmatrix} 2 & 1 \\ 1 & 1 \end{bmatrix}$, and tiling matrix $P_2' = \begin{bmatrix} 1 & 1 \\ 0 & 1 \end{bmatrix}$, then $P_2 = \begin{bmatrix} 0 & 1 \\ 1 & 1 \end{bmatrix}$ is the corresponding tiling shape matrix to the original loop nest X_1. Therefore, the tiling matrix P_1 and P_2 are two local tiling candidates for loop next X_1.

4.2 Tile Layout Graph

The basic data structure for the formulation of the ILP model is a graph called Tile Layout Graph (TLG). The nodes in TLG correspond to a local iteration space tiling candidates with different tile mapping strategies. Each node denotes the tile mapping matrix G_θ, the tiling matrix P, and the array access matrixes for all array references in this loop nest. We use the notation $V^x[i]$ to denote the ith iteration tiling candidate of a nest loop x in graph TLG, $E^{xx'}[i,i']$ to denote the remapping edge between the ith iteration tiling candidate of a nest loop x and the i'^{th} iteration tiling candidate of a nest loop x'.

The tiling candidate cost in our problem is the estimation of the total execution time for this tiling candidate and tile-to-processor mapping strategy. This execution time cost is given by $Cost(V^x[i]) = \zeta(T_{comp} + cT_{comm})$, where ζ is the number of synchronization, c is the number of processors that each processor needs to send to, T_{comp} the execution time of a tile, and T_{comm} the communication time. The parameter c depends on the data tile to processor mapping strategy.

If there are conflicting data tile mapping between the ith tiling candidate in loop nest x, and the i'^{th} candidate in loop nest x', then we add a remapping edge $E^{xx'}[i,i']$ to this two nodes in TLG. The value of this edge denoted as $Cost(E^{xx'}[i,i'])$, is the sum of cost of data remapping communications for all conflicting array references between these two loop nests.

4.3 0-1 Integer Programming Problem

After tiling candidates generation for each loop nests, we use the 0-1 integer linear programming (ILP) to solve the global tiling problem optimally. $V^x[i]$ and $E^{xx'}[i,i']$ are the 0-1 integer variables, and if the corresponding node or remapping edge are selected they have a value of 1, otherwise their values are 0.

The objective of the global tiling optimization problem now is to select a tiling candidate from each loop nest in a given TLG and communication edges between pairs of nests that are tile-mapping-conflicting, such that:

$$\sum_{x}\sum_{j=1}^{Num(V^x)}(V^x[j] \times Cost'(V^x[j])) + \sum_{xx'}\sum_{i=1}^{Num(V^x)}\sum_{j=1}^{Num(V^{x'})}(E^{xx'}[i,j] \times Cost(E^{xx'}[i,j]))$$

is minimized, where $Num(V^x)$ is the number of iteration space tiling candidates in loop nest x, and x, x' denotes two nests with remapping edges. This objective is constrained by the following conditions:

For a loop nest x, only one tiling candidate should be selected:

$$\sum_{Num(V^x)} V^x[i] = 1 \quad (c1)$$

An edge $E^{xx'}[i,i']$ will be selected if and only if both $V^x[i]$ and $V^{x'}[i']$ are selected. This condition can be stated as:

$$V^x[i] + V^{x'}[i'] - E^{xx'}[i,i'] \leq 1$$
$$E^{xx'}[i,i'] \leq V^x[i] \quad (c2)$$
$$E^{xx'}[i,i'] \leq V^{x'}[i'].$$

5 Experimental Results

We have implemented a prototype parallelizing compiler based on Open64, except for the code generation part, so that we generate parallelized codes manually, for SP and LU benchmark codes developed by NASA Ames (NPB2.3-serial release). Our experiments were performed on a high performance cluster—DeepComp6800, which is a 4-way SMP cluster with 1.3 GHz Itanium2 processors, connected by Qsnet. In our experiment, we use a noted automatic program decomposition method presented by Kennedy and Kremer [14] to compare with our work.

For the NAS SP class 'B', we compare the parallel efficiency of our global tiling method with two different code versions. One code version is called Doall+Pipelined, which exploits Wavefront parallelism within each sweep in the ADI integration, and the data layout is static. Another code version uses dynamic data remapping communications between different loop nests, and each loop nest can be fully parallelized. The average efficiency of global tiling is 0.87, and that the average efficiency of Doall+Pipelined and doall+Remapping are 0.55 and 0.53 respectively.

And for the experiment with NAS LU class 'B' problem sizes, we compare the parallel efficiency of our global tiling with the method presented by Kremer. The average efficiency of global tiling code version is 0.73, and the average efficiency of the traditional method is 0.62.

6 Conclusion

In this paper, we formulate a 0-1 integer linear programming to solve the global tiling optimization problem, and illustrate how to calculate multi-dimensional semi-oblique shaped tile. Our method differs from previous methods in two aspects: Firstly, our global tiling framework considers the iteration space tiling and data space tiling simultaneously to improve the parallelism and reduce the inter-loop remapping communications. Secondly, our tile mapping scheme can implement different tile distribution strategies, which can yield more efficient parallelism as well as less communication frequency.

References

1. Andonov, R., Rajopadhye, S.: Optimal orthogonal tiling of 2-d iterations. Journal of Parallel and Distributed Computing 45(2), 159–165 (1997)
2. Andonov, R., Balev, S., Rajopadhye, S., Yanev, N.: Optimal semi-oblique tiling. IEEE Trans. Par: & Dist. Sys. 14(9), 944–960 (2003)
3. Boulet, P., Darte, A., Risset, T., Robert, Y. (pen)-ultimate tiling? Intergration. The VLSI journal 17, 33–51 (1994)
4. Desprez, F., Dongarra, J., Rastello, F., Robert, Y.: Determining the idle time of a tiling: new results. In: PACT 1997: Proceedings of the 1997 International Conference on Parallel architectures Compilation Techniques, Washington, DC, USA, p. 307. IEEE Computer Society, Los Alamitos (1997)
5. Desprez, F., Dongarra, J., Rastello, F., Rober, Y.: Determining the idle time of a tiling: new results. Journal of Information Science and Engineering 14, 164–190 (1998)
6. Griebl, M.: On tiling space-time mapped loop nests. In: Proceedings of SPAA 2001, pp. 322–323 (2001)
7. Grieble, M.: Automatic Parallelization of Loop Programs for Distributed Memory Architecture. Univercity of Passau, 2004. Habilitation Thesis (2004)
8. Hodzic, E., Shang, W.: On Supernode Transformation with Minimized Total Running Time. IEEE Trans. Parallel and Distributed Systems 9(5), 417–428 (1998)

9. Hodzic, E., Shang, W.: On time optimal supernode shape. IEEE Trans. On Parallel and Distributed Systems. 13(12), 1220–1233 (2002)
10. Hogstedt, K., Carter, L., Ferrante, J.: Determining the Idle Time of a Tiling. Principles of Programming Languages (January 1997)
11. Hogstedt, K., Carter, L., Ferrante, J.: Selecting Tile Shape for Minial Exectution Time. In: Proc. 11th ACM Symp. Parallel Algorithms and Architectures, pp. 201–211 (June 1999)
12. Högestedt, K., Carter, L., Ferrante, J.: On the parallel execution time of tiled loops. IEEE Trans. Parallel Distrib. Syst. 14(3), 307–321 (2003)
13. Irigoin, F., Troilet, R.: Supernode Partitioning. In: At proc. 15th Ann. ACM Symp. Principles of Programming Languages, pp. 319–329 (1988)
14. Kennedy, K., Kremer, U.: Automatic data layout for distributed memory machines. ACM Trans. Program. Lang. Syst. 20(4), 869–916 (1998)
15. Krishnamoorthy, S., Baskaran, M., Bondhugula, U., Ramanujam, J., Rountev, A., Sadayappan, P.: Effective automatic Parallelization of stencil computations. In: PLDI 2007, pp. 235–244 (2007)
16. Ohta, H., Saito, Y., Kainaga, M., Ono, H.: Optimal tile size adjustment in compiling general doacross loop nests. In: ICS 1995: Proceedings of the 9th international conference on Supercomputing, pp. 270–279. ACM Press, New York (1995)
17. Ramanujam, J., Sadayappan, P.: Tiling Multidimensional Iteration Spaces for Non Shared-Memory Machines. Supercomputing, 111–120 (1991)
18. Bondhuagula, U., Baskaran, M., Krishnamoorthy, S., Ramanujam, J., Rountev, A., Sadayappan, P.: Affine Transformations for Communication Minimal Parallelization and Locality Optimization of Arbitrarily Nested Loop Sequences. OSU CSE Technical Report (2007)
19. Schreiber, R., Dongarra, J.: Automatic blocking of nested loops. Technical report, University of Tennessee, Knoxvile. TN (August 1990)
20. Xue, J.: Communication-minimal tiling of uniform dependence loops. J. Parallel Distrib. Comput. 42(1), 42–59 (1997)

Topic 5: Parallel and Distributed Databases

Domenico Talia*, Josep Lluis Larriba-Pey*, Hillol Kargupta*,
and Esther Pacitti*

Advances in data management, including store, access, query, retrieval, and analysis, are inherent to current and future information systems. Today, accessing very large volumes of information is a reality. Tomorrow data intensive management systems will enable huge user communities to transparently access multiple pre-existing autonomous, distributed and heterogeneous resources (data, documents, images, and services). Existing data management solutions do not provide efficient techniques for exploiting and mining Tera-datasets available in clusters, P2P and Grid architectures. Parallel and distributed file systems, databases, datawarehouses, and digital libraries are a key element for achieving scalable, efficient systems that will both cost-effectively manage and extract knowledge from huge amounts of highly distributed and heterogeneous digital data repositories.

Intensive data oriented applications are running on very large databases (data warehouses, multimedia databases). However, these intensive data consuming applications suffer from performance problems and centralized database sources. Introducing data distribution and parallel processing help to overcome resource bottlenecks and to achieve guaranteed throughput, quality of service, and system scalability. Distributed architectures, cluster systems and P2P systems, supported by high performance networks and intelligent middleware offer parallel and distributed databases a great opportunity to support cost-effective everyday applications. Distribution of data sources and data analysis tasks are key issues are are becoming more and more critical due to the increasing decentralization of human activities and the large availability of network facilities.

This year, 13 papers discussing some the those issues were submitted to this topic. Each paper was reviewed by at least three reviewers and, finally, we were able to select 6 regular papers. The accepted papers discuss very interesting issues about transaction processing and the application of parallelism to web and multimedia content search engines.

In particular, paper "Reducing Transaction Abort Rates with Prioritized Atomic Multicast Protocols" by E. Miedes, F. Muoz and H. Decker, compares a set of classic total order message delivery protocols with their prioritized counterparts. Paper "Fault-Tolerant Partial Replication in Large-Scale Database Systems" by P. Sutra and M. Shapiro, , investigates the use of a decentralized approach to committing transactions in replicated databases. Paper "A Search Engine Index for Multimedia Content", by M. Marín, G. V. Gil-Costa and C. Bonacic, proposes a distributed index structure to support parallel query processing of multimedia content in search engines. Paper "Complex Queries

---

* Topic Chairs.

for Moving Object Databases in DHT-based Systems" by C. Hernández, A. Herández and M. Marín, proposes a distributed indexing method to efficiently support complex spatio/temporal queries. Paper "Exploiting Hybrid Parallelism in Web Search Engines" by C. Bonacic, M. Marín, C. García, M. Prieto and F. Tirado, proposes a hybrid technique devised to take advantage of the multithreading facilities provided by multicore nodes for search engines. Finally, paper "Scheduling Intersection Queries in Term Partitioned Inverted Files", by M. Marín, C. Gómez-Panto, S. González and G. V. Gil-Costa, proposes and compares different scheduling algorithms for load balancing query traffic on distributed inverted files.

We would like to take the opportunity of thanking the authors who submitted a contribution, as well as the Euro-Par Organizing Committee, and the referees with their highly useful comments, whose efforts have made this conference and this topic possible.

Reducing Transaction Abort Rates with Prioritized Atomic Multicast Protocols*

Emili Miedes, Francesc D. Muñoz-Escoí, and Hendrik Decker

Instituto Tecnológico de Informática
Universidad Politécnica de Valencia
Campus de Vera s/n, 46022 Valencia (Spain)
{emiedes,fmunyoz,hendrik}@iti.upv.es

Abstract. Priority atomic multicast is a total-order multicast message delivery service that enables applications to prioritize the sequence by which messages are delivered, while regular total order properties remain invariant. Priority-based message delivery can serve to reduce the abortion rate of transactions. In this study, we compare three classical total order protocols against their corresponding prioritized versions, in the framework of a replication middleware. To this end, we use a test application that broadcasts prioritized messages by these protocols, and measure the effect of the priorization. We show that, under certain conditions, the use of prioritized protocols yields lower abort rates than the corresponding non-prioritized protocols.

1 Introduction

A group communication service (GCS) is a software package that provides a set of building blocks for designing and implementing distributed systems. Atomic (i.e., total-order) multicast message delivery is a standard GCS building block, which enables an application to send messages to a set of destinations such that they are delivered in the same order by each destination. Atomic multicast has been studied for more than thirty years, during which a huge amount of results has been produced [1,2,3,4,5,6]. Some of these services offer an additional feature that enables human or programmed users and agents to prioritize the delivery of certain messages over others [7,8,9].

Such a service can be used in a scenario like the following. Consider an application that runs on top of a database that is transparently replicated over several sites by means of a middleware. Such database systems usually behave according to a *constant interaction* model [10], by which the updates of a transaction are broadcast at its end in total order to all replicas using a single message. The order in which a set of messages are delivered by the replicas determines the final sequence in which those transactions are applied to the database. Different sequences may have different execution properties, such as performance, resource

---

* This work has been partially supported by EU FEDER and the Spanish MEC under grant TIN2006-14738-C02-01 and by IMPIVA under grant IMIDIC/2007/68.

consumption and likelyhood of abortion. In particular, if improperly or unfortunately prioritized, transactions may violate some semantic integrity constraints, and thus must be aborted, but otherwise, they can commit.

A simple example is given by two concurrent transactions which increment and, respectively, decrement a value constrained by some upper and lower thresholds: clearly, prioritization of one transaction over the other may lead to a constraint violation and therefore abortion of the transaction processed first, while the reverse prioritization will cause no such problems.

In general, the idea investigated in this paper is to alter the order in which transactions are committed for achieving a favorable constraint evaluation, thus reducing their abort rate. To this end, the middleware may assign different priorities to different transactions according to some (possibly application-dependent) criteria. Messages sent in the scope of a given transaction can be tagged with the corresponding priority, and a priority-based group communication protocol can be used to broadcast transaction messages. As the protocol prioritizes some messages over others, the respective updates will be prioritized correspondingly. As indicated above, this may be beneficial for reducing the number of abortions due to integrity constraint violations.

As another example, consider a distributed application for controlling critical and non-critical remote systems. Messages sent to critical systems can be prioritized over messages sent to non-critical ones, by means of a priority-based total order protocol.

Non-prioritizing total broadcast policies have been widely studied, while, as far as we know, only a few studies exist for priority-based protocol variants. In [11] (an extension of [9]), a starvation-free priority-based total order protocol is presented. In [8], another priority-based total order protocol is presented. Low priority messages may suffer starvation if too many high priority messages are sent. The problem of message starvation is dealt with specifically in [11]. In [12,13] another common problem of this kind of protocols, known as *priority inversion*, is addressed.

This paper is a follow-up to [14], in which we proposed four ways to extend existing total order broadcast protocols (as classified in [2]), by priority assignment to messages. In this paper we present the results of applying the proposed techniques to an application the transactions of which are subject to semantic integrity constraints. Messages involve requests to modify data that would cause semantic constraints to become violated, so that the modifications are rejected. We show how message prioritization can be used to increase the likelihood of satisfying the semantic constraints of an application.

In Sect. 2 we describe the assumed system model. In Sect. 3 we review the classification of total order broadcast protocols in [2]. In Sect. 4 we briefly sketch several techniques to modify such protocols in order to prioritize messages. Sect. 5 discusses how priorization support can be integrated in a database replication middleware. In Sect. 6, some experimental results of comparing original and modified protocols are exposed. In Sect. 7 we conclude with an outlook to future investigations.

2 System Model

In this section we briefly recapitulate the system model assumed throughout the paper. A complete description can be found in [14].

The considered system is composed of a set of processes that communicate through message passing. Each process has a multilayer structure, whose topmost level is a user application that accesses a replicated DBMS, which in turn uses the services offered by a group communication system (GCS). The latter is composed of one or more group communication protocols (GCP), which use the underlying network's services to send and deliver messages.

The system is partially synchronous. We assume that processes run on different physical nodes and the drift between two different processors is not known. Moreover, the time needed to transmit a message from one node to another can be bounded.

Processes can fail due to several reasons. Also network partitions may occur. However, since we are focusing on the comparison of priorization techniques, we are not going to address failure handling (which can be realized by mechanisms such as group membership services and fault-tolerance protocols).

3 Reviewing Atomic Protocols

A survey of total order protocols is given in [2], where total order protocols are partitioned into five classes.

In a *fixed sequencer* protocol, a single process is in charge of ordering the messages. In a *moving sequencer* protocol, sequencing is also performed by a single agent, but its role is transferred from one process to another.

In a *privilege based* protocol, processes may only send messages when they have permission to do so. If a process has permission to send messages at any time, then the total order can easily be set using a global sequence number.

In a *communication history* protocol, processes use historical information about message sending, reception and delivery to totally order messages. In [2], two different types of *communication history* protocols are identified: *causal history* protocols and *deterministic merge* protocols.

In a *destinations agreement* protocol, some kind of agreement protocol is run to decide the order of one or more messages. In [2], three subclasses of *destinations agreement* protocols are identified, according to the type of agreement performed: (1) on the order (sequence number) of a single message, (2) on the order (sequence numbers) of a set of messages and (3) on the acceptance of an order (sequence numbers) of a set of messages, proposed by one of the processes.

4 Priority Management

In [14], we have identified four basic techniques for adding priority management to total order protocols, including detailed explanations, a cost analysis and pseudo-code outlines. Essentially, they differ mostly with regard to the point in the messages' life-cycle in which priorities are considered.

Priority Sequencing. It can be applied to sequencer-based total ordering protocols like fixed- or moving-sequencer protocols. The idea is to maintain a list of yet unsequenced messages, ordered according to their priority tags. The sequencer then sequences each message in the order of that list. This scheme is quite simple, but low priority messages may suffer starvation [14].

Priority Sending. It applies to privilege-based protocols, some protocols of the *deterministic merge* subclass of the *communication history* protocol class and the first class of *destinations agreement* protocols, as presented in [2]. The idea is to use a priority-ordered list of outgoing messages in each node and send them according to that order. Once sent, messages can finally be treated according to the protocol used to totally order the messages.

Priority Delivering. This technique can be applied to the *causal history* subclass of the *communication history* class of [2]. It consists in ordering concurrent messages (i.e., those that are not causally dependent on each other), taking into account the priorities of the messages before any other criteria. Note that causally dependent messages must still be ordered according to the causal relation imposed by their timestamps, in spite of their priorities, because the modified protocol must still provide the same causal and total order guarantees provided by the original protocol.

Priority-based Consensus. It is applicable to the second and third classes of *destinations agreement* protocols, presented in [2]. The modification, which is actually quite similar to that of the priority delivering technique, consists in taking into account the priorities of the messages, prior to other criteria, to reach the consensus about the order of a set of messages. Nevertheless, both ordering and priorization rely on a consensus among all nodes. This poses additional problems when failures happen. Moreover, these protocols are quite sensitive to delays occurring in a single node, which may end up delaying the operation of the whole system. Therefore, we decided to ban this technique and the corresponding classes of protocols from the experiments outlined in Sect. 6.

5 Integration in Database Replication Systems

Priority assignment mechanisms as outlined in Sect. 4 can be automated modularly in the framework of a replication middleware such as MADIS [15]. Such a module obtains information about declarative constraints (and, in some DBMSs, also about triggers) from the DBMS catalog tables; e.g., in the pg_constraint table of PostgreSQL 8.x. From those, it infers which kind of updates may violate any constraint. For instance, the application described in Sect. 6 depends on CHECK constraints. Such constraints can be found in the table mentioned above with all information (i.e., the constraint expression and the affected columns) needed for adequately prioritizing transactions. In general, the set of all update operations susceptible to integrity violation can be stored in some meta-table, and ordered according to some priority heuristics. The priority module may then scan the operations of each transaction and assign the tabled priority to it.

Instead of preconfiguring priority assignments statically, they may be determined dynamically, by some external component that communicates with our middleware, once the transaction has been started. To this end, specialized operations should be added to the middleware API.

6 Experimental Work

In this section we present some experimental work we have done in order to compare original and modified total order protocols. First, we describe the testbed, then, the parameters and the methodology used to run the tests. Finally, we present and discuss the results.

6.1 Environment

The application uses the services of a total order protocol which in turn uses a reliable transport layer. This layer is our own implementation of the sixth transport protocol presented in [16]. It is based on the services provided by an unreliable transport we built on top of the bare UDP sockets provided by the Java platform.

The experiments have been conducted in a system of four nodes with an Intel Pentium D 925 processor at 3.0 GHz and 2 GB of RAM, running Debian GNU/Linux 4.0 and Sun JDK 1.5.0. The nodes are connected by means of a 22-port 100/1000Mbps DLINK DGS-11224T switch that keeps the nodes isolated from any other node, so no other network traffic can influence the results.

6.2 Test Application

Our test application keeps track of the overall amount of money being processed by all investment brokers of a stock trade enterprise. Each broker runs its own instance (or *node*) of the application, operating on the stock exchange on behalf of the stock owners and a potentially large number of investors.

When a broker decides to perform some operation, the application attempts to apply the requested updates to the global balance. If the operation implies the purchase of shares, the application must check that it can be performed, considering the price of the purchase and the current global balance of the enterprise. The application rejects an operation when the price of the purchase exceeds the global balance.

As there are several brokers working at various sites for the company buying and selling shares concurrently, the global balance is incessantly updated. In order to ensure that the current value of the global balance is consistent among all nodes of the application, a total order protocol is needed. It is used by all nodes to multicast the updates so that all brokers see the same sequence of operations and apply the same sequence of updates to the global balance. That way, consistency among all nodes at each moment is achieved.

Each node creates and broadcasts a number of messages, each one representing a stock trading operation that may update the current balance. Each update carries an integer value. Positive and negative values represent selling and buying operations of stock trading, respectively. To simplify the analysis of the results, we adopted the following convention. The integer values range from -1000 to 1000. The actual value assigned to each message is generated at random.

All messages are multicast to all nodes using a total order protocol, so all messages are delivered by all nodes in the same order. Nodes apply messages in the order as received from the total order protocol. To apply a message means to update the local copy of the global balance, as kept by each node. Since all nodes receive the same update sequence, their corresponding copies of the balance are kept consistent.

Each message carries a second integer value which represents its priority. In real-life stock trading, these priorities are determined by considering a large number of factors, such as the market situation, recent evolutions of shares, some long-term trends, risk analyses, expected benefits, etc.

The priority of each operation is uniquely determined by its type (purchase or sale), as follows. Given the value v of an operation, its priority p is computed as $p = 1000 - v$. Thus, a sale update of the global balance with a value of 1000 obtains the priority value 0, and a purchase update with a value of -1000 obtains priority 2000. Since priority management in the modified total order protocols is implemented according to a *lower value = higher priority* rule, the priority of the first update is higher than that of the second one. So, positive updates (from sales) are prioritized over negative updates (from purchases).

In `BalanceTest`, we implemented the constraint for discarding updates that would overdraw the balance. For each negative update request, the presumptive new balance is computed. If it is greater or equal to zero, then the update is applied. Otherwise, the update is discarded. Thus, the global balance is prevented from ever being in the red. This constraint serves to highlight the benefits that can be obtained using prioritized instead of conventional, non-prioritized total order protocols.

6.3 Methodology

The expected behavior of an execution of `BalanceTest` is different for the conventional and the prioritized protocol versions. For the former, the nodes apply approximately the same number of positive (sale) and negative (purchase) updates. For the latter (prioritized) version, positive updates (i.e., sales transactions) are prioritized, as already stated. This means that the balance is more likely to increase than to decrease, thus less purchase transactions will be discarded.

To test the proposed prioritization techniques, we tested different protocols. For each protocol, we varied two parameters: the number of messages broadcast by each node, and the numeric value of the update request. The values of these parameters and their combination for different test runs are detailed in Sect. 6.4. For each parameter combination, we executed `BalanceTest` and recorded the number of discarded updates.

For obtaining reliable results, each execution of `BalanceTest` has been repeated a statistically relevant number of times. Each execution resulted in a number of discarded updates, so that we could compute the mean and median values of all executions of each test combination. For each total order protocol, the final result was then constituted by comparing the amount of discarded updates of the prioritized and the non-prioritized version.

We took care that the measured results were independent of the sequence of messages sent by each node. We achieved that by having each node send the same sequence of messages, thus obtaining the same distribution of priorities in each test run, with the same parameter combination for each protocol. As said before, each test was run a statistically significant number n of times, but not necessarily with exactly the same sequence of messages (priorities) in each execution series. We have made sure, though, that each node sends the same sequence of messages for each protocol, each parameter vector and each iteration of the test series.

6.4 Parameters

In this section, we describe the values of the test parameters. First, we describe a group of *fixed* parameters, whose values are the same for all tests, and then a group of *variable* parameters.

Each BalanceTest instance is run in a physical node. Each instance creates a sequence of messages, as described above, and sends them by a fixed rate (currently, 50 messages per second). Each message is tagged with a priority value ranging between -1000 and 1000. The initial balance value is set to 0.

The variable parameters are the protocol type, the number of messages sent by each node and the lower bound value for updates.

We have implemented three non-prioritized total order protocols and a prioritized version for each. The *UB* protocol is an implementation of the UB sequenced-based total order algorithm proposed by [17][1]. The *TR* protocol implements a token ring-based algorithm: in essence, it is similar to the ones of [5] and [6]. Finally, the *CH* protocol is an implementation of the causal history algorithm in [2]. The corresponding prioritized versions are *UB_PRIO*, *TR_PRIO* and *CH_PRIO*.

We have executed different tests in which each node receives 400, 2000 and 4000 messages, respectively. For each setting, we have ran 500 executions of the BalanceTest application.

6.5 Results

For each execution of BalanceTest, we recorded the number of discarded messages. Thus, for each of the 500 series of executions, we obtained a number of discarded messages. Then we calculated the mean and median values of each series and displayed the medians graphically.

In Fig. 1a) we represent the medians of the result series. The number of discarded messages is displayed along the Y axis, as a function of the number of messages received by each node (400, 2000 and 4000), on the X axis. The displayed value is the median for each series of 500 executions.

---

[1] UB stands for *Unicast-Broadcast*, as in [2].

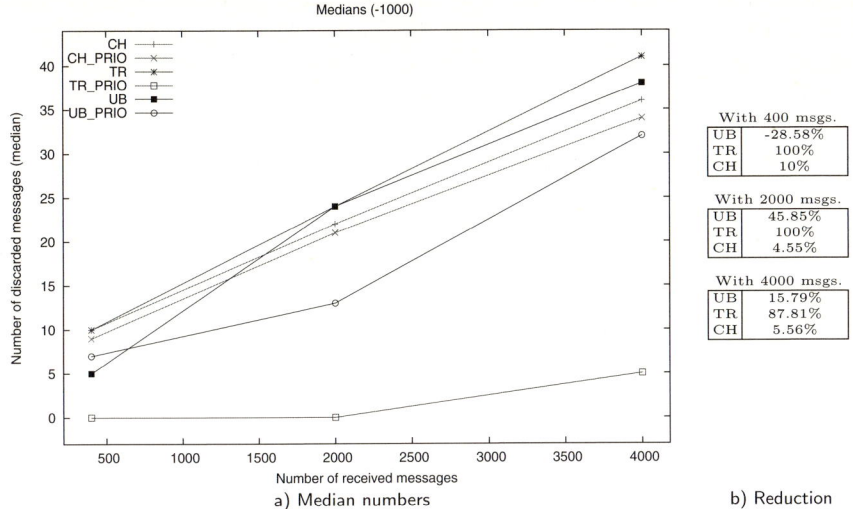

Fig. 1. Discarded messages

6.6 Discussion

The experiments show that the priorization techniques yield good results. The prioritized versions of the *UB* and *TR* protocols offer a significant reduction on the number of discarded messages, with regard to their original counterparts. For the *CH_PRIO* protocol, however, the reduction is lower, with regard to the original *CH* protocol.

Fig. 1b) summarizes the percentages of reduction obtained for each pair of protocols, with different lower bounds of numbers of received messages.

As shown in Fig. 1, the reduction chalked up by the *CH_PRIO* protocol is negligible. This is because the modified protocol must ignore message priorities when reordering and delivering causally dependent messages, as explained in [14]. It can only take into account message priorities for concurrent (causally independent) messages. As the number of causally independent messages is small, the priorization mechanism in the *CH_PRIO* protocol achieves only a very small improvement of the original *CH* protocol.

In [18] we also include the results for a similar set of tests ran with an update lower bound equal to -1200 and show that the lower bound of the balance updates influences the results considerably. When equal to -1000, the number of discarded messages is significantly lower, regardless of the protocol used and the number of messages received per node, when compared to runs with a lower bound of -1200, for the same setting.

When the interval is *[-1200, 1000]*, negative values are more likely than positive ones, so withdrawals are more likely than deposits. Thus, the balance keeps diminishing, so that withdrawals are discarded with increasing likelyhood. When the interval is *[-1000, 1000]*, positive and negative values are equally likely, which is why the number of discarded messages is lower than for the previous interval.

There are other factors to be considered before drawing final conclusions from analyzing the effects of prioritized protocols. The most ponderous factor is probably the application. First of all, an application must send messages by a conscious choice of different priority tags if it wants to benefit from a prioritized total order protocol. Moreover, prioritized protocols are advantageous only if there is a sustained flow of prioritized outgoing messages, sent at a minimum and high sending rate. In conclusion, this means that the benefits of prioritization are highly application-dependent.

7 Conclusions

We have presented an experimental study of different techniques for supporting prioritized messages. We implemented several conventional (non-prioritized) total order protocols and their corresponding prioritized versions, using the techniques discussed in [14] and tested them with a simple application in which a semantic constraint is defined. The results show that the application benefits from using prioritized versions of total order protocols.

Currently existing group communication systems do not include priorization support in their total order protocols. The present results confirm that applications can benefit by making clever use of priority options offered by augmented versions of standard total order protocols. It is likely that existing group communication systems may be improved by adding, to their total order protocols, some priorization support based on our techniques. Our main contribution is to have shown that prioritized total order protocols are beneficial for applications that prioritize their transactions by taking into account their likelyhood of violating given constraints.

As a by-product, the testbed also provides a point of departure for a systematic study of more general comparisons, both between standard total order protocols and prioritization techniques.

A greater challenge for future investigations, however, is given by the goal to design, develop and implement an integrity checking mechanism that automatically assigns priorities to concurrent transactions in order to lower the rate of integrity violations and thus to lower the rate of abortions that are due to integrity violations. For achieving this goal, note that our test scenario is conceptually independent of the question whether integrity is checked by a built-in DBMS module or by some user-defined mechanism. An application-independent solution could be provided by an architecture disposing of a number of parallel processors for checking the preservation of integrity by various alternatives of sequentializable schedules, preferring those that result in less integrity violations and thus in a lower number of aborted transactions.

References

1. Chockler, G., Keidar, I., Vitenberg, R.: Group communication specifications: a comprehensive study. ACM Computing Surveys 33(4), 427–469 (2001)
2. Défago, X., Schiper, A., Urbán, P.: Total order broadcast and multicast algorithms: Taxonomy and survey. ACM Computing Surveys 36(4), 372–421 (2004)
3. Birman, K.P., Joseph, T.A.: Reliable communication in the presence of failures. ACM Transactions on Computer Systems 5(1), 47–76 (1987)
4. Dolev, D., Malki, D.: The Transis approach to high availability cluster communication. Communications of the ACM 39(4), 64–70 (1996)
5. Moser, L.E., Melliar-Smith, P.M., Agarwal, D.A., Budhia, R., Lingley-Papadopoulos, C.: Totem: a fault-tolerant multicast group communication system. Comm. of the ACM 39(4), 54–63 (1996)
6. Amir, Y., Danilov, C., Stanton, J.R.: A low latency, loss tolerant architecture and protocol for wide area group communication. In: DSN, pp. 327–336 (2000)
7. Tully, A., Shrivastava, S.K.: Preventing state divergence in replicated distributed programs. In: 9th Symposium on Reliable Distributed Systems, pp. 104–113 (1990)
8. Rodrigues, L., Veríssimo, P., Casimiro, A.: Priority-based totally ordered multicast. In: 3rd IFAC/IFIP workshop on Algorithms and Architectures for Real-Time Control (1995)
9. Nakamura, A., Takizawa, M.: Priority-based total and semi-total ordering broadcast protocols. In: 12th Intl. Conf. on Dist. Comp. Sys (ICDCS 1992), pp. 178–185 (1992)
10. Wiesmann, M., Schiper, A., Pedone, F., Kemme, B., Alonso, G.: Database replication techniques: A three parameter classification. In: SRDS, pp. 206–215 (2000)
11. Nakamura, A., Takizawa, M.: Starvation-prevented priority based total ordering broadcast protocol on high-speed single channel network. In: 2nd Intl. Symp. on High Performance Dist. Comp., pp. 281–288 (1993)
12. Baker, T.: Stack-based scheduling of real-time processes. Journal of Real-Time Systems 3(1), 67–99 (1991)
13. Wang, Y., Brasileiro, F., Anceaume, E., Greve, F., Hurfin, M.: Avoiding priority inversion on the processing of requests by active replicated servers. In: Dependable Systems and Networks, pp. 97–106. IEEE Computer Society, Los Alamitos (2001)
14. Miedes, E., Muñoz-Escoí, F.D.: Managing priorities in atomic multicast protocols. In: ARES: Intl. Conf. on Availability, Reliability and Security (2008)
15. Irún-Briz, L., Decker, H., de Juan-Marín, R., Castro-Company, F., Armendáriz-Íñigo, J.E., Muñoz-Escoí, F.D.: MADIS: A slim middleware for database replication. In: Euro-Par Conf., August 2005, pp. 349–359 (2005)
16. Tanenbaum, A.S.: Computer Networks. Prentice Hall, Englewood Cliffs (1996)
17. Kaashoek, M.F., Tanenbaum, A.S.: An evaluation of the Amoeba group communication system. In: 16th ICDCS, pp. 436–448. IEEE-CS, Los Alamitos (1996)
18. Miedes, E., Muñoz-Escoí, F.D.: Reducing transaction abort rates with prioritized atomic multicast protocols. Technical Report TR-ITI-ITE-07/22, Instituto Tecnológico de Informática, Universidad Politécnica de Valencia (October 2007)

Fault-Tolerant Partial Replication in Large-Scale Database Systems*

Pierre Sutra and Marc Shapiro

Universit Paris VI and INRIA Rocquencourt, France

Abstract. We investigate a decentralised approach to committing transactions in a replicated database, under partial replication. Previous protocols either reexecute transactions entirely and/or compute a total order of transactions. In contrast, ours applies update values, and generate a partial order between mutually conflicting transactions only. Transactions execute faster, and distributed databases commit in small committees. Both effects contribute to preserve scalability as the number of databases and transactions increase. Our algorithm ensures serializability, and is live and safe in spite of faults.

1 Introduction

Non-trivial consistency problems e.g. file systems, collaborative environments, and databases. are the major challenge of large-scale systems. Recently some architectures have emerged to scale file systems up to thousands of nodes [3, 12, 15], but no practical solution exists for database systems. At the cluster level protocols based on group communication primitives [4, 11, 16] are the most promising solutions to replicate database systems [23] . In this article we extend the group communication approach to large-scale systems.

Highlights of our protocol:

- Replicas do not reexecute transactions, but apply update values only.
- We do not compute a total order over of operations. Instead transactions are partially ordered. Two transactions are ordered only over the data where they conflict.
- For every transaction T we maintain the graph of T's dependencies. T commits locally when T is transitively closed in this graph.

The outline of the paper is the following. Section 2 introduces our model and assumptions. Section 3 presents our algorithm. We conclude in Section 4 after a survey of related work.

2 System Model and Assumptions

We consider a finite set of asynchronous processes or *sites* Π, forming a distributed system. Sites may fail by crashing, and links between sites are asynchronous but reliable. Each site holds a database that we model as some finite set of *data items*. We left

---

* This research is funded in part by the European project Grid4All, and the French project Respire.

unspecified the granularity of a data item. In the relational model, it can be a column, a table, or even a whole relational database. Given a datum x, the replicas of x, noted $replicas(x)$, are the subset of Π whose databases contain x.

We base our algorithm on the three following primitives:[1]

- *Uniform Reliable Multicast* takes as input a unique message m and a *single* group of sites $g \subseteq \Pi$. Uniform reliable multicast consists of the two primitives R-multicast(m) and R-deliver(m). With Uniform Reliable Multicast, all sites in g have the following guarantees:
    - Uniform Integrity: For every message m, every site in g performs R-deliver(m) at most once, and only if some site performed R-multicast(m) previously.
    - Validity: if a correct site in g performs R-multicast(m) then it eventually performs R-deliver(m).
    - Uniform Agreement: if a site in g performs R-deliver(m), then every correct sites in g eventually performs R-deliver(m).

  Uniform Reliable Multicast is solvable in an asynchronous systems with reliable links and crash-prone sites.

- *Uniform Total Order Multicast* takes as input a unique message m and a single group of sites g. Uniform Total Order Multicast consists of the two primitives TO-multicast(m) and TO-deliver(m). This communication primitive ensures Uniform Integrity, Validity, Uniform Agreement and Uniform Total Order in g:
    - Uniform Total Order: if a site in g performs TO-deliver(m) and TO-deliver(m') in this order, then every site in g that performs TO-deliver(m') has performed previously TO-deliver(m).

- *Eventual Weak Leader Service* Given a group of sites g, a site $i \in g$ may call function $WLeader(g)$. $WLeader(g)$ returns a *weak leader* of g:
    - $WLeader(g) \in g$.
    - Let r be a run of Π such that a non-empty subset c of g is correct in r. It exists a site $i \in c$ and a time t such that for any calls of $WLeader(g)$ on i after t, $WLeader(g)$ returns i.

  This service is strictly weaker than the classical eventual leader service Ω [18], since we do not require that every correct site eventually outputs the same leader. An algorithm that returns to every process itself, trivially implements the Eventual Weak Leader Service.

In the following we make two assumptions: during any run, **A1** for any datum x, at least one replica of x is correct, and **A2** Uniform Total Order Multicast is solvable in $replicas(x)$.

2.1 Operations and Locks

Clients of the system (not modeled), access data items by read and write operations. Each operation is uniquely identified, and accesses a single data item. A read operation

---
[1] Our taxonomy comes from [5].

Table 1. Lock conflict table

	R	W	IW
R	1	0	0
W	0	0	0
IW	0	0	1

(lock held across columns; lock requested down rows)

is a singleton: the data item read, a write operation is a couple: the data item written, and the update value.

When an operation accesses a data item on a site, it takes a lock. We consider the three following types of locks: read lock (R), write lock (W), and intention to write lock (IW). Table 1 illustrates how locks conflict with each other; when an operation requests a lock to access a data item, if the lock is already taken and cannot be shared, the request is enqueued in a FIFO queue. In Table 1, 0 means that the request is enqueued, and 1 that the lock is granted.

Given an operation o, we note:

- $item(o)$, the data item operation o accesses,
- $isRead(o)$ (resp. $isWrite(o)$) a boolean indicating whether o is a read (resp. a write),
- and $replicas(o) \triangleq replicas(item(o))$;

We say that two operations o and o' *conflict* if they access the same data item and one of them is a write:

$$conflict(o,o') \triangleq \begin{cases} item(o) = item(o') \\ isWrite(o) \vee isWrite(o') \end{cases}$$

2.2 Transactions

Clients group their operations into *transactions*. A transaction is a uniquely identified set of read and write operations. Given a transaction T,

- for any operation $o \in T$, function $trans(o)$ returns T,
- $ro(T)$ (respectively $wo(T)$) is the subset of read (resp. write) operations,
- $item(T)$ is the set of data items transaction T accesses: $item(T) \triangleq \bigcup_{o \in T} item(o)$.
- and $replicas(T) \triangleq replicas(item(T))$.

Once a site i grants a lock to a transaction T, T holds it until i commits T, i aborts T, or we explicitly say that this lock is released.

3 The Algorithm

As replicas execute transactions, it creates precedence constraints between conflicting transactions. Serializability theory tell us that this relation must be acyclic [2].

One solution to this problem is given a transaction T, (i) to execute T on every replicas of T, (ii) to compute the transitive closure of the precedence constraints linking T to concurrent conflicting transactions, and (iii) if a cycle appears, to abort at least one the transactions involved in this cycle.

Unfortunately as the number of replicas grows, sites may crash, and the network may experience congestion. Consequently to compute (ii) the replicas of T need to agree upon the set of concurrent transactions accessing $item(T)$.

Our solution is to use a TO-multicast protocol per data item.

3.1 Overview

To ease our presentation we consider in the following that a transaction executes initially on a single site. Section 3.9 generalizes our approach to the case where a transaction initially executes on more than one site. We structure our algorithm in five phases:

- In the *initial execution phase*, a transaction T executes at some site i.
- In the *submission phase*, i transmits T to $replicas(T)$.
- In the *certification phase*, a site j aborts T if T has read an outdated value. If T is not aborted, j computes all the precedence constraints linking T to transactions previously received at site j.
- In the *closure phase*, j completes its knowledge about precedence constraints linking T to others transactions.
- Once T is closed at site j, the *commitment phase* takes place. j decides locally whether to commit or abort T. This decision is deterministic, and identical on every site replicating a data item written by T.

3.2 Initial Execution Phase

A site i executes a transaction T coming from a client according to the two-phases locking rule [2], *but* without applying write operations[2]. When site T reaches a commit statement, it is not committed, instead i releases T's read locks, converts T's write locks into intention to write locks, computes T's update values, and then proceeds to the submission phase.

3.3 Submission Phase

In this phase i R-multicasts T to $replicas(T)$. When a site j receives T, j marks all T's operations as pending using variable *pending*. Then if it exists an operation $o \in pending$, such that $j = WLeader(replicas(o))$, j TO-multicasts o to $replicas(o)$.[3]

---

[2] If T writes a datum x then reads it, we suppose some internals to ensure that T sees a consistent value.

[3] If instead of this procedure, i TO-multicasts all the operations, then the system blocks if i crashes. We use a weak leader and a reliable multicast to preserve liveness.

3.4 Certification Phase

When a site i TO-delivers an operation o for the first time[4],i removes o from *pending*, and if o is a read, i certifies o. To certify o, i considers any preceding write operations that conflicts with o. We say that a conflicting operation o' *precedes* o at site i, $o' \rightarrow_i o$, if i TO-delivers o' then i TO-delivers o:

$$o' \rightarrow_i o \triangleq \begin{cases} \text{TO-deliver}_i(o') \prec \text{TO-deliver}_i(o) \\ \text{conflict}(o', o) \end{cases}$$

Where given two events e and e', we note $e \prec e'$ the relation e *happens-before* e', and TO-deliver$_i(o')$ the event: "site i TO-delivers operation o'". If such a conflicting operation o' exists, i sets T's abort flag to 1 (see hereafter).

If now o is a write, i gives an IW lock to o: function *forceWriteLock(o)*. If an operation o' holds a conflicting IW lock, o and o' share the lock (see Table 1); otherwise it means that $trans(o')$ is still executing at site i, and function *forceWriteLock(o)* aborts it.[5]

3.5 Precedence Graph

Our algorithm decides to commit or abort transactions, according to a *precedence graph*. A precedence graph G is a directed graph where each node is a transaction T, and each directed edge $T \rightarrow T'$, models a precedence constraint between an operation of T, and a *write* operation of T':

$$T \rightarrow T' \triangleq \exists (o, o') \in T \times T', \exists i \in \Pi, o' \rightarrow_i o$$

A precedence graph contains also for each vertex T a abort flag indicating whether T is aborted or not: $isAborted(T, G)$, and the subset of T's operations: $op(T, G)$, which contribute to the relations linking T to others transactions in G.

Given a precedence graph G, we note $G.\mathcal{V}$ its vertices set, and $G.\mathcal{E}$ its edges set. Let G and G' be two precedence graphs, the union between G and G', $G \cup G'$, is such that:

- $(G \cup G').\mathcal{V} = G.\mathcal{V} \cup G'.\mathcal{V}$,
- $(G \cup G').\mathcal{E} = G.\mathcal{E} \cup G'.\mathcal{E}$,
- $\forall T \in (G \cup G').\mathcal{V}, isAborted(T, (G \cup G')) = isAborted(T, G) \vee isAborted(T, G')$.
- $\forall T \in (G \cup G').\mathcal{V}, op(T, (G \cup G')) = op(T, G) \cup op(T, G')$.

We say that G is a subset of G', noted $G \subseteq G'$, if:

- $G.\mathcal{V} \subseteq G'.\mathcal{V} \wedge G.\mathcal{E} \subseteq G'.\mathcal{E}$,
- $\forall T \in G.\mathcal{V}, isAborted(T, G) \Rightarrow isAborted(T, G')$,
- $\forall T \in G.\mathcal{V}, op(T, G) \subseteq op(T, G')$.

Let G be a precedence graph, $in(T, G)$ (respectively $out(T, G)$) is the restriction of $G.\mathcal{V}$ to the subset of vertices formed by T and its incoming (resp. outgoing) neighbors. The *predecessors* of T in G: $pred(T, G)$, is the precedence graph representing the transitive closure of the dual of the relation $G.\mathcal{E}$ on $\{T\}$.

---

[4] Recall that the leader is eventual, consequently i may receive o more than one time.
[5] This operation prevents local deadlocks.

Algorithm 1. $decide(T,G)$, code for site i

1: **variable** $G' := (\emptyset, \emptyset)$ ▷ a directed graph
2:
3: **for all** $C \subseteq cycles(G)$ **do**
4:     **if** $\forall T \in C, \neg isAborted(T,G)$ **then**
5:         $G' := G' \cup C$
6: **if** $T \in breakCycles(G')$ **then**
7:     **return** *false*
8: **else**
9:     **return** *true*

3.6 Deciding

Each site i stores its own precedence graph G_i, and decides locally to commit or abort a transaction according to it. More precisely i decides according to the graph $pred(T, G_i)$. For any cycle C in the set of cycles in $pred(T, G_i)$: $cycles(pred(T, G_i))$, i must abort at least one transaction in C. This decision is deterministic, and i tries to minimize the number of transactions aborted.

Formally speaking i solves the minimum feedback vertex set problem over the union of all cycles in $pred(T, G_i)$ containing only non-aborted transactions The minimum feedback vertex set problem is an NP-complete optimization problem, and the literature about this problem is vast [6]. We consequently postulate the existence of an heuristic: *breakCycles()*. *breakCycles()* takes as input a directed graph G, and returns a vertex set S such that $G \setminus S$ is acyclic.

Now considering a transaction $T \in G_i$ such that $G = pred(T, G_i)$, Algorithm 1 returns *false* if i aborts T, or *true* otherwise.

3.7 Closure Phase

In our model sites replicate data partially, and consequently maintain an incomplete view of the precedence constraints linking transactions in the system. Consequently they need to complete their view by exchanging parts of their graphs. This is our closure phase:

- When i TO-delivers an operation $o \in T$, i adds T to its precedence graph, and adds o to $op(T, G_i)$. Then i sends $pred(T, G_i)$ to $replicas(out(T, G_i))$ (line 29).
- When i receives a precedence graph G, if $G \not\subseteq G_i$, for every transaction T in G_i, such that $pred(T, G) \not\subseteq pred(T, G_i)$, i sends $pred(T, G \cup G_i)$ to $replicas(out(T, G_i))$. Then i merges G to G_i (lines 31 to 35).

Once i knows all the precedence constraints linking T to others transactions, we say that T is *closed* at site i. Formally T is closed at site i when the following fixed-point equation is true at site i:

$$closed(T, G_i) = \begin{cases} op(T,G) = T \\ \forall T' \in in(T, G_i). \mathcal{V}, closed(T', G_i) \end{cases}$$

Our closure phase ensures that during every run r, for every correct site i, and every transaction T which is eventually in G_i, T is eventually closed at site i.

3.8 Commitment Phase

If T is a read-only transaction: $wo(T) = \emptyset$, i commits T as soon as T is executed (line 9).

If T is an update, i waits that T is closed and holds all its IW locks: function *holdIWLocks()* (line 35). Once these two conditions hold, i computes $decide(T,)pred(T,G_i)$. If this call returns *true*, i commits T: for each write operation $o \in wo(T)$, with $i \in replicas(o)$, i considers any write operation o' such that $T \rightarrow trans(o') \in G_i \wedge conflict(o,o')$. If $trans(o')$ is already committed at site i, i does nothing; otherwise i applies o to its database.

Algorithm 2 describes our algorithm. This protocol provides serializability for partially replicated database systems: any run of this protocol is equivalent to a run on a single site [2]. The proof of correctness appears in our technical report [22].

3.9 Initial Execution on More Than One Site

When initial execution phase does not take place on a single site we compute the read-from dependencies. More precisely when a site i receives a read operation o accessing a datum it does not replicate, i sends o to some site $j \in replicas(o)$. Upon reception j executes o. At the end of execution, j sends back to i the transitive closure starting from o's read-from dependency.

Once i has executed locally or remotely all the read operations, i checks if the resulting read-from dependancies graph contains a cycle in which T is involved. If this is the case, T will be aborted, and instead of submitting it, i re-executes at least one of T's read operations Otherwise i computes the write set, the update values, and R-multicasts it with the read-from dependancies graph to $replicas(T)$. The dependencies are merged to precedence graphs when sites TO-deliver T's operations. The rest of the algorithm remains the same.

3.10 Performance Analysis

Precedence constraints in a cycle are *not* causally related. Moreover our algorithm handles cycles of size 2 without executing lines 31 to 35. Consequently it is unlikely that closing transactions in a cycle requires additional steps, and we do not suppose it hereafter.

We consider Paxos [14] as a solution to Uniform Total Order Multicast. Algorithm 2 achieves a latency degree[6] of 4: 1 for Uniform Reliable Multicast, and 3 for Uniform Total Order Multicast. Let o be the number of operations per transaction, and d the replication degree, the message complexity of Algorithm 2 is $4od + (od)^2$: od for Uniform Reliable Multicast, o Uniform Total Order Multicasts, each costing $3d$ messages, and od replicas execute line 29, each site sending od messages.

Algorithms totally ordering transactions [11, 17, 19] achieve at least a latency degree of 3, and a message complexity of $3n$. Totally ordering transactions requires to contact $n/2$ sites, whereas our approach needs only to contact od sites; it reduces latency. Moreover in large scale systems we expect $od \ll \sqrt{3n}$, and consequently our algorithm achieves better message complexity than total order based solutions.

---
[6] Maximum length of the causal path to commit a transaction in the best run.

Algorithm 2. code for site i

```
 1: variables G_i := (∅,∅); pending := ∅
 2:
 3: loop                                                              ▷ Initial execution
 4:     let T be a new transaction
 5:     initialExecution(T)
 6:     if wo(T) ≠ ∅ then
 7:         R-multicast(T) to replicas(T)
 8:     else
 9:         commit(T)
10:
11: when R-deliver(T)                                                 ▷ Submission
12:     for all o ∈ T : i ∈ replicas(o) do
13:         pending := pending ∪ {o}
14:
15: when ∃o ∈ pending ∧ i = WLeader(replicas(o))
16:     TO-multicast(o) to replicas(o)
17:
18: when TO-deliver(o) for the first time                             ▷ Certification
19:     pending := pending \ {o}
20:     let T = trans(o)
21:     G_i.𝒱 := G_i.𝒱 ∪ {T}
22:     op(T,G_i) := op(T,G_i) ∪ {o}
23:     if isRead(o) ∧ ∃o', o' →_i o then
24:         setAborted(T,G_i)
25:     else if isWrite(o) then
26:         forceWriteLock(o)
27:         for all o' : o' →_i o do
28:             G_i.ℰ := G_i.ℰ ∪ {(trans(o'),T)}
29:     send(pred(T,G_i)) to replicas(out(T,G_i))
30:
31: when receive(T,G)                                                 ▷ Closure
32:     for all T ∈ G_i do
33:         if pred(T,G) ⊄ pred(T,G_i) then
34:             send(pred(T,G_i ∪ G)) to replicas(out(T,G_i))
35:     G_i := G_i ∪ G
36:
37: when ∃T ∈ G_i, ⎧ i ∈ replicas(wo(T))                              ▷ Commitment
                  ⎨ closed(T,G_i)
                  ⎩ holdIWLocks(T)
38:     if ¬ isAborted(T,G_i) ∧ decide(T,pred(T,G_i)) then
39:         commit(T)
40:     else
41:         abort(T)
42:
```

4 Concluding Remarks

4.1 Related Work

Gray et al. [7] prove that scale traditional eager and lazy replications does not scale: the deadlock rate increase as the cube of the number of sites, and the reconciliation rate increases as the square. Wiesmann and Schiper confirm practically this result [23]. Fritzke et al. [10] propose a replication scheme where sites TO-multicast each operations and execute them upon reception. However they do not prevent global deadlocks with a priority rule; it increases abort rate. Preventive replication [16] considers that a bound on processor speed, and network delay is known. Such assumptions do not hold in a large-scale system. The epidemic algorithm of Holiday et al [9] aborts concurrent conflicting transactions and their protocol is not live in spite of one fault. In all of these replication schemes, each replica execute all the operations accessing the data items it replicates. Alonso proves analytically that it reduces the scale-up of the system [1].

The DataBase State Machine approach [17] applies update values only but in a fully replicated environment. Its extensions [19, 21] to partial replication require a total order over transactions.

Committing transactions using a distributed serialization graph is a well-known technique [20]. Recently Haller et al. have proposed to apply it [8] to large-scale systems, but their solution does not handle replication, nor faults.

4.2 Conclusion

We present an algorithm for replicating database systems in a large-scale system. Our solution is live and safe in presence of non-bizantine faults. Our key idea is to order conflicting transaction per data item, then to break cycles between transactions. Compared to previous existing solutions, ours either achieves lower latency and message cost, or does not unnecessarily abort concurrent conflicting transactions.

The closure of constraints graphs is a classical idea in distributed systems. We may find it in the very first algorithm about State Machine Replication [13], or in a well-known algorithm to solve Total Order Multicast [5][7]. We believe that the closure generalizes to a wider context, where a constraint is a temporal logic formula over sequences of concurrent operations.

References

1. Alonso, G.: Partial database replication and group communication primitives in 2nd European Research Seminar on Advances in Distributed Systems (1997)
2. Bernstein, P.A., Hadzilacos, V., Goodman, N.: Concurrency Control and Recovery in Database Systems. Addison-Wesley, Reading (1987),
http://research.microsoft.com/pubs/ccontrol/

---

[7] In [13] Lamport closes the $\ll$ relation for every request to the critical section. In [5] the total order multicast protocol attributed to Skeen, closes the order over natural numbers to TO-multicast a message.

3. Busca, J.-M., Picconi, F., Sens, P.: Pastis: A highly-scalable multi-user peer-to-peer file system. In: Cunha, J.C., Medeiros, P.D. (eds.) Euro-Par 2005. LNCS, vol. 3648. Springer, Heidelberg (2005)
4. Camargos, L., Pedone, F., Wieloch, M.: Sprint: a middleware for high-performance transaction processing. SIGOPS Oper. Syst. Rev. (2007)
5. Defago, X., Schiper, A., Urban, P.: Totally ordered broadcast and multicast algorithms: a comprehensive survey (2000)
6. Garey, M.R., Johnson, D.S.: Computers and Intractability; A Guide to the Theory of NP-Completeness. W. H. Freeman & Co., New York (1990)
7. Gray, J., Helland, P., O'Neil, P., Shasha, D.: The dangers of replication and a solution. In: Proceedings of the 1996 ACM SIGMOD international conference on Management of data (1996)
8. Haller, K., Schuldt, H., Türker, C.: Decentralized coordination of transactional processes in peer-to-peer environments. In: CIKM 2005: Proceedings of the 14th ACM international conference on Information and knowledge management (2005)
9. Holliday, J., Agrawal, D., Abbadi, A.E.: Partial database replication using epidemic communication. In: ICDCS 2002: Proceedings of the 22 nd International Conference on Distributed Computing Systems (ICDCS 2002), Washington, DC, USA, p. 485. IEEE Computer Society, Los Alamitos (2002)
10. Fritzke Jr., U., Ingels, P.: Transactions on partially replicated data based on reliable and atomic multicasts. In: Proceedings of the The 21st International Conference on Distributed Computing Systems, p. 284. IEEE Computer Society, Los Alamitos (2001)
11. Kemme, B., Alonso, G.: Don't be lazy, be consistent: Postgres-r, a new way to implement database replication. The VLDB Journal, 134–143 (2000)
12. Kubiatowicz, J., Bindel, D., Chen, Y., Eaton, P., Geels, D., Gummadi, R., Rhea, S., Weatherspoon, H., Weimer, W., Wells, C., Zhao, B.: Oceanstore: An architecture for global-scale persistent storage. In: Proceedings of ACM ASPLOS. ACM, New York (2000)
13. Lamport, L.: Time, clocks, and the ordering of events in a distributed system. Commun. ACM 21(7), 558–565 (1978)
14. Lamport, L.: Fast paxos. Distributed Computing 19(2), 79–103 (2006)
15. Muthitacharoen, A., Morris, R., Gil, T.M., Chen, B.: Ivy: A read/write peer-to-peer file system. In: Proceedings of 5th Symposium on Operating Systems Design and Implementation (2002)
16. Pacitti, E., Coulon, C., Valduriez, P., Özsu, M.T.: Preventive replication in a database cluster. Distrib. Parallel Databases 18(3), 223–251 (2005)
17. Pedone, F., Guerraoui, R., Schiper, A.: The database state machine approach. Distrib. Parallel Databases 14(1), 71–98 (2003)
18. Raynal, M.: Eventual leader service in unreliable asynchronous systems: Why? how? In: NCA, pp. 11–24. IEEE Computer Society, Los Alamitos (2007)
19. Schiper, N., Schmidt, R., Pedone, F.: In: 10th International Conference on Principles of Distributed Systems (OPODIS 2006) (2006)
20. Shih, C.-S., Stankovic, J.A.: Survey of deadlock detection in distributed concurrent programming environments and its application to real-time systems. Technical report (1990)
21. Sousa, A., Pedone, F., Oliveira, R., Moura, F.: Partial replication in the database state machine (2001)
22. Sutra, P., Shapiro, M.: Fault-tolerant partial replication in large-scale database systems, Technical report, http://hal.inria.fr/inria-00232662/fr/
23. Wiesmann, M., Schiper, A.: Comparison of database replication techniques based on total order broadcast. IEEE Transactions on Knowledge and Data Engineering 17(4) (2005)

Exploiting Hybrid Parallelism in Web Search Engines

Carolina Bonacic[1], Carlos Garcia[1], Mauricio Marin[2],
Manuel Prieto[1], and Francisco Tirado[1]

[1] Depto. Arquitectura de Computadores y Automática
Universidad Complutense de Madrid
cbonacic@fis.ucm.es, garsanca@dacya.ucm.es,
mpmatias@dacya.ucm.es, ptirado@dacya.ucm.es
[2] Yahoo! Research Santiago of Chile
mmarin@yahoo-inc.com

Abstract. With the emergence of multi-core CPU (or Chip-level Multi-Processor -CMP-), it is essential to develop techniques that capitalize on CMP's advantages to speed up very demanding applications of parallel computing such as Web search engines. In particular, for this application and given the huge amount of computational resources deployed at data centers, it is of paramount importance to come out with strategies able to get the best performance from hardware. This is specially critical when we consider how we organize hardware to cope with sustained periods of very high traffic of user queries. In this paper, we propose an hybrid technique based on *MPI* and *OpenMP* which has been devised to take advantage of the multithreading facilities provided by CMP nodes for search engines under high query traffic.

1 Introduction

Search engines must cope efficiently with dynamic variations in the query traffic generated by users. Most frequent queries are answered quickly by keeping them stored in cache machines. However, queries not found in cache must be directly solved by a set of processors (cluster nodes) forming a cluster. The aim is to determine as fast as possible the top-R results per query and from these results build up the answer web pages presented to the users. For high traffic of queries and given the huge volume of data associated with the web samples kept at each node, this can involve the use of a significant amount of resources – processors utilization, disk and network bandwidth –. Current search engines deal with peaks in traffic by including enough hardware redundancy so that at normal traffic the processors utilization is below 30% or 40%.

Hardware redundancy can be reduced by using query processing strategies that take advantage of the economy of scale present in those situations in which a large number of queries are solved concurrently. Recently, we have found [6,7] that for those high-query traffic scenarios, performing what we call *round-robin query processing* implemented on top of bulk-synchronous parallel (BSP) processing [10], can significantly outperform the standard multi-threaded asynchronous message passing parallel processing employed by current search engines. For low query traffic the opposite holds true, which makes perfect sense since in this case individual queries can be granted as many threads they need, and those threads are kept alive consuming all necessary resources for the time it takes to get the top-R results. This is not harmful since hardware is being under-utilized anyway because of the small number of queries present in the system. In [7] we actually propose switching between both modes of operation depending on the observed query traffic.

In this paper we propose a hybrid parallelization based on a mixed MPI(BSP)-OpenMP programming model to take advantage of the hierarchical structure offered by today's clusters based on CMP processors. On every processor, the document ranking task that select the local top-R results of a query is parallelized using *OpenMP* threads. This is the most costly part of the processing of queries and it is certainly convenient to reduce its total running under high query traffic scenarios. Our aim here is to put T threads to work on the document ranking phase of a group of Q queries being processed all together at the same node in a given period of time with $Q \geq T$ (this is done in parallel across the P nodes available in the system).

The current technology tendency underlines the emergence of the CMP processors. Actually, most systems incorporate these chips discarding the old idea of a multiprocessor system as several nodes mono-processor. Technology trends indicate that the number of cores on a chip will continue to grow as indicates the roadmaps of the most important manufacturers. Nowadays, AMD offers chips with four cores (*Native Quad technology*) and Intel has began to incorporate the Intel Core^{TM} Extreme quad-core Processor in their servers systems. However, there are still studies that evaluate the parallel programming paradigms employed in the context of Web Servers with this technology and whether they are the most appropriated. Taking into account this tendency, the main aim of this paper is to study which is the most efficiently way to exploit this novel technology.

As baseline code we have employed a parallel Web Search Engine based on a bulk-synchronous MPI-based multiple-masters/multiple-slaves scheme previously developed by us, which has been demonstrated to achieve scalable performance on conventional cluster of computers of differing architecture [5,6,7]. One could think that the better way to exploit the new extra thread level parallelism available in today's processors is to extend the number of MPI processes to the cores available (i.e. instead of one MPI process per cluster node, one MPI process per core). However, this would involve an additional partitioning of the inverted file across the cores, resulting in a large number of messages (the query receptionist machine should broadcast the queries to all cores and then collect the answers from all of them). Furthermore, since each core has its own private inverted index, all cores compete with each other for the shared cache space and memory bandwidth. This paper proposes a better method to exploit the additional parallelism provided by cores at each node.

The remaining of this paper is organized as follows. Section 2 describes our general method of parallel query processing for high query traffic and the particular arrangement we make to profit from multicore architectures. Section 3 describes the hardware and databases we used to test the efficiency of our proposal and show performance results. Section 4 presents concluding remarks.

2 Speeding Up Round-Robin Query Processing

2.1 Distributed Inverted File

Web Search Engines use the inverted file data structure to index the text collection and speedup query processing. A number of papers have been published reporting experiments and proposals for efficient parallel query processing upon inverted files which are distributed on a set of P processor-memory pairs [1,2,3,5,8,6,7,11].

An inverted file is composed of a vocabulary table and a set of posting lists. The vocabulary table contains the set of relevant terms found in the collection. Each of these terms is associated with a posting list which contains the document identifiers where the term appears in the collection along with additional data used for ranking purposes. To solve a query, it is necessary to get the set of documents *ids* associated with the query terms and then perform a ranking of these documents so as to select the top-R documents as the query answer.

Current search engines use the document partitioned approach to distributing the inverted file on a set of P processors. In this case, the document collection is evenly distributed at random on the processors and an inverted file is constructed in each processor considering only the documents stored in the processor. Solving a query involves to (a) place a copy of it in each processor, (b) let each processor calculate their local top-R results and (c) make a merge of all results to select the global top-R results.

2.2 Query Processing

At the parallel server side, queries arrive from a receptionist machine that we call the *broker*. The *broker* machine is in charge of routing the queries to the cluster's processors (where for the scope of this paper each processor is a chip-multiprocessor node of the cluster) and receiving the respective answers. It decides to which processor routing a given query by using a load balancing heuristic. The particular heuristic depends on the approach used to partition the inverted file. Overall the *broker* tends to evenly distribute the queries on all processors.

More in detail, the parallel processing of queries is basically composed of a phase in which it is necessary to fetch parts of all of the posting lists associated with each term present in the query, and perform a ranking of documents in order to produce the results. After this, additional processing is required to produce the answer to the user. This paper is concerned with the fetching+ranking part. We are interested in situations where it is relevant to optimize the query throughput.

A relevant issue for this paper is the way we organize query processing upon the piece of inverted file stored in each processor. We basically let queries use of fixed quantum of computation, communication and disk access before granting the resources to another query in a round-robin fashion.

2.3 Iterative Ranking and Round-Robin Query Processing

The processor in which a given query arrives from the broker is called the *ranker* for that query since it is in this processor where the associated document ranking is performed. In fact, all processors are rankers of a subset of queries and as explained below they are also *fetchers* of posting lists in order to let rankers solve their queries. Thus every query is processed iteratively using two major steps:

- **Fetching**. The first one consists on fetching a K-sized piece of every posting list involved in the query and sending them to the *ranker* processor (K= 2R). In essence, the *ranker* sends a copy of every query to all other P nodes. Next, all nodes send K/P pairs (*doc_id, frequency*) of their posting lists to the *ranker* which performs the first iteration of the documents ranking process.
- **Ranking**. In the second step, the *ranker* performs the actual ranking of documents and, if necessary, it asks for additional K-sized pieces of the posting lists in order to produce the K best ranked documents that are passed to the *broker* as the query results. We use the vectorial method for performing the ranking of documents along with the filtering technique proposed in [9]. Consequently, the posting lists are kept sorted by frequency in descending order. Once the *ranker* for a query receives all the required pieces of posting lists, they are merged into a single list and passed throughout the filters. If it happens that the document with the less frequency in one of the arrived pieces of posting lists passes the filter, then it is necessary to perform a new iteration for this term and all others in the same situation.

Thus the ranking process can take one or more iterations to finish. In every iteration a new piece of K pairs (*doc_id, frequency*) from posting lists are sent to the *ranker* for each term involved in the query. This concept of iteration is essential to distribute and allocate system resources to the queries in a round-robin fashion: the quantum comes from the fact that we let queries work on chunks of posting lists of size K and organize document ranking in iterations.

2.4 Hybrid Parallelization

With the irruption of CMPs, it is appropriate to study and review the most appropriate parallelization strategies in our context. The simplest strategy would be to extend the *rankers-fetchers* scheme [6] across CMP. However, we can anticipate this approach which is based on mapping *MPI*-threads in a CMP is not the most suitable approach because it involves an overhead caused by duplication of inverted file and competition of shared resources such as cache memory, main memory access, communication interface, etc..

The way we organize overall computation and communication tries to be more CMP friendly. It is based on the idea of the broker (*master*) continues distributing the queries across the cluster's nodes and having their respective answers [6], but each node, which has to resolve a group of Q queries (query batches), makes the ranking proccess (the most time comsuming phase) in parallel by means of *OpenMP pragmas*.

The idea behind the round-robin query processing approach is that queries are processed in such a way that it properly divides the steps involved in solving each query and interleave these steps whilst processing batches of queries all together. Strict interleaving of steps is possible by ways of bulk-synchronous parallel (BSP) processing. In BSP, the parallel computation is divided in supersteps and in each superstep the P processors are allowed to work on local data and buffer messages to be sent to others in the same cluster. The end of each superstep is marked by the sending of all buffered messages and the barrier synchronization of processors.

In order to make efficient the use of CMP, we arrange the processing of queries as described in the following supersteps which are executed by all processors in parallel. We assume that query traffic is high enough to let the broker place Q queries of t terms in each processor. Each processor is represented by a single *MPI* thread containing T *OpenMP* threads created at the start of the search engine. The algorithm is as follows.

Superstep i (Broadcast). Each processor gets Q$-m$ queries from the broker and m queries already in process requiring a new iteration, and broadcasts them to all processors.

Superstep $i + 1$ (Fetching). Each processor fetches from disk t·Q posting lists of K/P items each, and send them to the requesting processors (rankers).

Superstep $i + 2$ (Ranking)
  Part 1. Each processor receives the arriving t·Q·P posting lists of size K/P and merge posting lists per term and query, to store them in contiguous memory data structures, one per query, each of size t·K.
  Part 2. Each processor uses its T $\leq$ Q *OpenMP* threads to calculate the ranking of each query using the contiguous memory to keep on-going document ranking. Each query is processed sequentially by a single *OpenMP* thread. These threads keep both ownership of the memory and on-going queries during the complete process.
  Part 3. Determine the outcome of on-going queries which can be a request to go back to the logic superstep i (namely superstep $i + 3$) or send the top-R results to the broker.

These steps show the process associated with the solution of queries where ranking does not require all documents to contain all query terms. In this case, all posting lists are kept stored in decreasing in-document frequency. The most costly part of this process which justifies the usage of *OpenMP* threads is the ranking of documents.

In the case of queries requiring intersection of posting lists, that is, systems in which all selected documents must contain all query terms, it is necessary to intersect and rank lists in the superstep $i+1$ above. This may require considering the whole list of each term involved in each query. Thus intersection can be a very expensive operation for which the T *OpenMP* threads can also be employed to compute the intersections.

3 Experiments

Our experimental platform is based on a commodity cluster equipped with shared memory Linux boxes. Each cluster node includes two *Intel's Quad-Xeon* multicore processor, the main features of which are summarized in Table 1.

Table 1. Main features of the target computing platform

Processor	Intel Quad-Xeon (2.66 GHz)	
	L1 Cache (per core)	4x32KB + 4x32KB (inst.+data)
		8-way associative, 64 byte per line
	L2 Unified Cache	2x4MB (4MB shared per 2 procs)
		16-way associative, 64-byte per line
Memory	16 GBytes	
	(4x4GB) 667 MHz FB-DIMM memory	
	1333 MHz system bus	
Operating System	GNU Debian System Linux	
	kernel 2.6.22-SMP for 64 bits	
Intel C/C++ Compiler v10.1 Switches (icc)	-O3 -march=pentium4 -xW -ip -ipo	
	Parallelization with OpenMP: -openmp	
MPI Library	mpich2 v1.0.7 compiled with icc v10.1	
BSPonMPI Library	http://bsponmpi.sourceforge.net	

The exploitation of in-processor thread level parallelism has been performed in this work by means of *OpenMP* directives, which are directly supported by the native Intel C/C++ compiler [4]. It is also worth to mention that we have combined into the same program those directives with the BSPonMPI communication library, which is an implementation of BSP primitives based on MPI.

The results have been obtained using a Chilean Web database sample taken from `www.todocl.cl`. Queries have been selected randomly from a set of 127.000 queries extracted from the `todocl` log.

3.1 Experimental Setting

We executed experiments assuming high and moderate query traffic arriving at the cluster nodes. This traffic is set by the broker machine and is independent of the particular configuration of *MPI* and *OpenMP* threads being used by the search engine.

Let us assume that the broker sends an average of B queries per unit time. The challenge for the search engine is to solve these queries using batches of size B= Q·P where Q queries per processor are solved using T *OpenMP* threads. In the context of the experiments shown in this section the value of P represents the number of *MPI* threads executing the BSP supersteps of the search engine.

Assuming a total of N CPUs across all nodes and cores, the search engine can use all of them provided that N= T·P since in our cluster we observed significant saturation whenever N < T·P. Thus in this section we investigate the practical feasibility of T > 1 for different values of P such that N= T·P. Notice that as B= Q·P a reduction in P produces an increase in Q so for each pair (T,P) we need to set Q properly. To complete our experimental setting we also need to use a practical value of K and actual query log in order to represent precisely the work-load requirements on computation and communication upon the nodes.

We observed by running our parallel program with K= 128 on the nodes that with no exception for any given P the best performance was achieved for the maximum number of *OpenMP* threads such that N= T·P. Thus we only show results for that case. In addition and to better illustrate the comparative performance among the different configurations (P,T) we show results represented as the ratio maximum running time achieved by any (P,T) of the set of experiments, to the running time achieved by the particular (P,T) being shown. All measures were executed 5 times using a very large sequence of queries from our query log and averaged.

We basically performed two set of experiments or runs, the first one indicates a case of high query traffic given by B= 512, whereas the second one represents a moderate traffic given by B= 128. We call these two sets as runs-A and runs-B respectively. These experiments were performed on two nodes. We also investigated the situation in a single node for which we halved the query traffic B/2 and thus we have for this case the counterparts runs-C and runs-D for high and moderate query traffic.

In addition we studied two types of query ranking algorithms, one we call light ranking in which documents are ranked using a small amount of computation time and another one we call heavy ranking which is a method more demanding in computation.

3.2 Performance Results

In this section we attempt to answer those questions raised above about the most suitable configuration for a Web Search engine in a CMP architecture. Let's start this study with performance results obtained on a single node of a cluster which includes two *Intel's Quad-Xeon* multicore processors.

The tables 2.a and 2.b show a comparison in terms of the improvement in speedups between the two parallel programming paradigms (*MPI* vs. *OpenMP*) and their combination for every experiments considered. As a baseline code, we have chosen one which provides the worse throughput for any parallel configurations. It normally corresponds to the naïve parallelization (P=8), so that its speedups respect to itself is 1.00 in the table. The results are quite satisfactory in every situation under study, although they are more impressive for moderate query traffic as a result of significant load imbalance in these cases. Although relative speedups for a more demanding query traffic are not so important, nevertheless, we would like to highlight what provide a higher throughput performance. The table shows better gains for parallelization with *OpenMP* although such parallelization is only applied in the ranking phase. It is worth to remark that the best parallel configuration in a single node corresponds to T=8 in comparison with any possible combination with message passing. The noticeable difference between both paradigms is motivated by the overhead associated with duplication of the inverted file and the saturation involved by its shared memory/disks accesses in *MPI* approaches. This handicap is in part avoided using *OpenMP*, due to positive effects provided from sharing different levels of memory hierarchy between all T threads, which can generate memory-prefetching and important bottlenecks reductions.

Table 2. Improvements in throughput speedups

(a) **Heavy Ranking Single node**

P	T	Runs-C	Runs-D
1	8	1.04	1.16
2	4	1.04	1.16
4	2	1.04	1.12
8	1	1.00	1.00

(b) **Light Ranking Single node**

P	T	Runs-C	Runs-D
1	8	1.09	1.40
2	4	1.10	1.39
4	2	1.10	1.29
8	1	1.00	1.00

(c) **Heavy Ranking Two nodes**

P	T	Runs-A	Runs-B
2	8	1.29	1,76
4	4	1.27	1,72
8	2	1.22	1,54
16	1	1.00	1,00

(d) **Light Ranking Two nodes**

P	T	Runs-A	Runs-B
2	8	1.48	2.15
4	4	1.44	2.08
8	2	1.35	1.76
16	1	1.00	1.00

In tables 2.c and 2.d, we show the speedup improvements achieved in two CMP nodes considering as a base code the poorest throughput one. As can be seen, improvements are bigger than in a single node. Our parallel scheme proposed outperforms any configuration which combine P and T threads. This phenomenon is due mainly to the increment of communications between the P processes and the competition for their shared communications interface. Note that these effects are not so relevant in a single node because the communications are made across the shared memory. For example, taking the most successful configuration (T=8) in Runs-A and Runs-B, there is appreciable detriment in terms of speedups due to communication effects (around 10-35%). However, in such situations and the trend confirm, our hybrid parallelization scheme gets better throughputs in comparison with their counterparts under any traffic and ranking rates which is reflected into impressive improvements from 1.35 to 2.15.

It is also interesting to study the behavior of different parallel configurations when not all cores are available. The figure 1 shows the speedups achieved in the heavy ranking phase for two nodes with high/moderate query traffic [$Speedup = time(P=2, T=1) / time(P,T)$]. As expected, our hybrid parallel scheme based on *OpenMP* again reports better results independently of the number of threads assigned. These encouraging results near to ideal, open future chance of considering the parallelization of a priori cheaper stages as fetching.

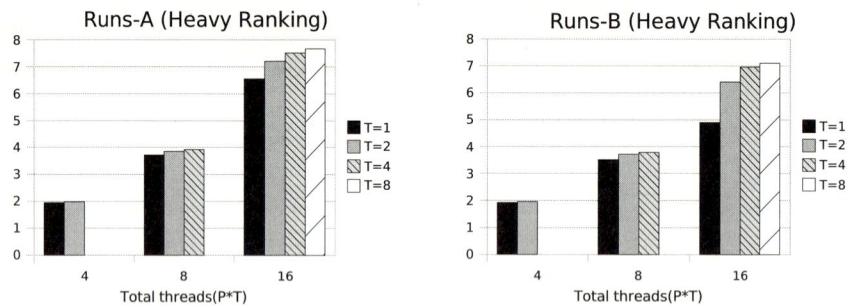

Fig. 1. Speedup achieved in two CMP nodes for high/low traffic

Even though our study has been limited by the availability of two nodes which includes CMP, we have tested the scalability of our method in a bigger cluster in order to extrapolate the results to a more realistic scenario. We were able to prove that it is possible to achieve efficiencies near to 85% [$Efficiency = Tserial / Tparallel * number\ of\ nodes$] in a particular system with 32 nodes.

4 Conclusions

We have described a technique to improve query throughput of Web Search Engines based on the efficient use of parallelism coming from the multithreading hardware available in multi-core processors. Our results on state of the art hardware show significant increment of throughput to process large streams of queries.

As baseline code we have employed a bulk-synchronous realization of the classical document partitioned inverted file used by Web Search Engines as an index to enable very fast solution of user queries. Perhaps, intuitively one could think that the better way to exploit the new extra thread level parallelism available in CMP is to extend the number of logical processors devoted to query processing. However, this implies a division of the inverted file across the cores which can cause serious contention for shared resources, especially cache space and memory bandwidth.

Our proposal tried to minimize these effects by applying a hybrid parallelization in a way that it allows *OpenMP* threads do their job and benefit from positive interactions amongst threads caused by inter-thread temporal locality effects. To the best of our knowledge the feasibility of a hybrid which combines bulk-synchronous parallelism with *OpenMP* multithreading has no been tested so far. We have shown that this scheme can be very effective at increasing throughtput under situations of high and moderate traffic of user queries.

Acknowledgment. This work has been partially supported by the research contracts CICYT-TIN 2005/5619, CYTED-506PI0293, FONDECYT 1060776 and Ingenio 2010 Consolider CSD2007-20811.

References

1. Arusu, A., Cho, J., Garcia-Molina, H., Paepcke, A., Raghavan, S.: Searching the web. ACM Trans. 1(1), 2–43 (2001)
2. Badue, C., Baeza-Yates, R., Ribeiro, B., Ziviani, N.: Distributed query processing using partitioned inverted files. In: Eighth Symposium on String Processing and Information Retrieval (SPIRE 2001), pp. 10–20 (2001)
3. Barroso, A., Dean, J., Olzle, U.H.: Web search for a planet: The google cluster architecture. IEEE Micro. 23(2), 22–28 (2002)
4. Intel Corpation. Intel C/C++ and Intel Fortran Compilers for Linux, http://www.intel.com/software/products/compilers
5. Marin, M., Bonacic, C., Gil-Costa, V., Gomez, C.: A search engine accepting on-line updates. In: Kermarrec, A.-M., Bougé, L., Priol, T. (eds.) Euro-Par 2007. LNCS, vol. 4641, pp. 348–357. Springer, Heidelberg (2007)
6. Marin, M., Costa, G.V.: High Performance Distributed Inverted Files. In: CIKM 2007, Lisboa, Portugal, November 6-9 (2007)
7. Marin, M., Costa, G.V.: (Sync|Async)$^+$ MPI Search Engines. In: EuroPVM/MPI 2007, Paris, France (October 2007)
8. Moffat, W., Webber, J., Zobel, J., Baeza-Yates, R.: A pipelined architecture for distributed text query evaluation. Information Retrieval, published on-line 5 (October 2006)
9. Persin, M., Zobel, J., Sacks-Davis, R.: Filtered document retrieval with frequency-sorted indexes. Journal of the American Society for Information Science 47(10), 749–764 (1996)
10. Valiant, L.G.: A Bridging Model for Parallel Computation. Comm. ACM 33, 103–111 (1990)
11. Zobel, J., Moffat, A.: Inverted files for text search engines. ACM Computing Surveys 38(2) (2006)

Complex Queries for Moving Object Databases in DHT-Based Systems

Cecilia Hernández[1], M. Andrea Rodríguez[1,3], and Mauricio Marin[2,3]

[1] DIICC, University of Concepción, Chile
[2] Yahoo! Research, Santiago, Chile
[3] Center for Web Research, Chile

Abstract. Distributed moving object database servers are a feasible solution to the scalability problem of centralized database systems. In this paper we propose a distributed indexing method, using the Distributed Hash Table (DHT) paradigm, devised to efficiently support complex spatio temporal queries. We assume a setting in which there is a large number of database servers that keep track of events associated with a highly dynamic system of moving objects deployed in a spatial area. We present a technique for properly keeping the index up to date and efficiently processing range and top-k queries for moving object databases. We evaluated our system using event-driven simulators with demanding spatio temporal workloads and the results show good performance in terms of response time and network traffic.

1 Introduction

Spatio-temporal databases use index structures tailored to answering specific types of queries. Among these queries, *time-slice* and *time-interval* queries (also known as range queries) have been usually the focus of investigation. This is also true for distributed spatio-temporal databases, where previous works have solved range queries by using a global and distributed spatio-temporal index that organizes servers in terms of spatial and temporal partitions [4,7,10,12]. These strategies require intensive coordination, which limits their scalability and adaptability.

This work aims at solving not only time-slice and time-interval queries, but also queries about the *current* and *historical* locations of particular objects (i.e., object-location queries), aggregation queries about the number of objects per server, and top-k queries including the top-k servers with largest number of objects and the top-k objects with largest trajectories within a spatial and temporal window. Solving different types of queries imposes particular challenges for large scale and distributed systems, since data distribution needs to accommodate different algorithms for query processing. For example, for solving queries about the location of particular objects, the classical distribution of data based on spatial and temporal data is insufficient.

In this work, we propose to handle distributed spatial-temporal data in a DHT-based network that combines a distribution of objects' trajectories (traces) and spatial partitions, which enables exact and approximated (fast) answers to object-location, range (time slice or time interval), aggregation and top-k queries. In the context of DHT-based distributed systems, such as Chord [13] and Kademlia [9], the paradigm provides hash table semantics, where a DHT interface implements a hash function that maps any given data key to a particular peer through the operations $put(key, data)$ for insertion and $get(k)$ for retrieval. In these systems, lookup is oriented to solve efficiently exact-match queries, usually in $O(\log N)$ hops, where N is the number of peers in the network. However, complex queries like range and top-k are particularly challenging in DHT systems. There have been recent works addressing range [3,11,14] and top-k [1] queries for spatial databases, but as far as we know, spatial-temporal queries have not been proposed using DHT systems.

In our scheme, we have a distributed *meta-index* that contains information about data distributed in several and independent spatial-temporal database servers that register all events associated with the moving objects deployed in the spatial area. The meta-index contains sparse data about the location of particular objects, the geographic extent containing objects stored in servers at different time instants, and statistical information about servers. Peers periodically poll servers to keep properly updated the distributed meta-index, which acts as an entry point to the database servers. Smart polling is esential to keep a good approximation of the real system in the index.

We have reported work on object-location queries and aggregation queries, first for a centralized meta-index in [8], and then for a distributed meta-index on a p2p network in [6]. In this paper we extend the p2p meta-index proposed in [6] to include spatio-temporal range queries and top-k object queries. To do so, we complement the data distribution in [6] and design search algorithms for these queries. In addition, we propose a fully distributed scheme to perform polling by assigning this task to a sub-set of peers. In this way peers forming the crawler (i.e., polling system) can deliver their data to any other peer and clients can submit a richer set of queries to any peer. An advantage of distributing the polling process among several peers is a better use of the collective bandwidth and, consequently, a faster update of the data stored in the meta-index.

The organization of the paper is as follows. Section 2 presents the meta-index distribution. Section 3 describes the full distributed polling strategy for updating the meta-index. Section 4 presents search algorithms for range and top-k objects queries. Evaluation and conclusion follow in sections 5 and 6, respectively.

2 Meta-index Distribution

The meta-index stores partial data about the time-varying location of objects. These data include: the time-varying number of objects per server (statistical or aggregated information), the time-varying geographic extent that contains the location of objects in a server, and the coarse traces of objects' visits across servers. Note that the coarse traces of objects in the meta-index are not "real" sparse trajectories, but lists of locations (database servers) that the objects have visited sorted by the time instant of the data collection performed by the crawler.

With the purpose of answering object-location queries and aggregation queries, we propose in [6] two strategies for distributing the meta-index data with Chord protocol and using the available bandwidth effectively. On one hand, we introduce the concept of *MSB (Most Significant Bits)* to map moving object trace data to Chord keys. The idea of the MSB is that a crawler can compound moving object data in only few *composite objects* by using the most significant bits of object ids. Each composite object contains a set of moving object ids with their respective traces. On the other hand, since the amount of aggregated data per update message is very small, we piggy it back to composite objects. This scheme allows a crawler to send fewer update messages into the peer-to-peer network avoiding overloading the network.

To support range queries (time slice and time interval queries), we also distribute information of the spatial organization of servers using a Z-curve [5]. To do so, a general square grid divides the complete geographic space. We do not impose restrictions on cells in this grid and the dynamic geographic extent associated with each server at different time instants. Thus, the geographic extent may partially cover several cells, or a cell may include the extent of several servers.

The space-filling Z-curve maps a unit line segment to a continuous curve in the unit square. In our case, the Z-code represents the *key* for a range or spatial window, which is used by the Chord protocol to distribute spatial information. The distribution of data based on the dynamic geographic extent handled by servers complements the partial trace information organized into composite objects described above. Whenever a robot (peer) of the crawler informs new updating information (i.e., server, time, number of objects, geographic extent and composite objects), in addition to distributing the composite objects, this robot also sends information to peers whose keys (Z-codes) map to cells in the geographic space overlapping the server's extent. These peers store the server, time, extent, number of objects and composite ids of an inform (Figure 1). Notice

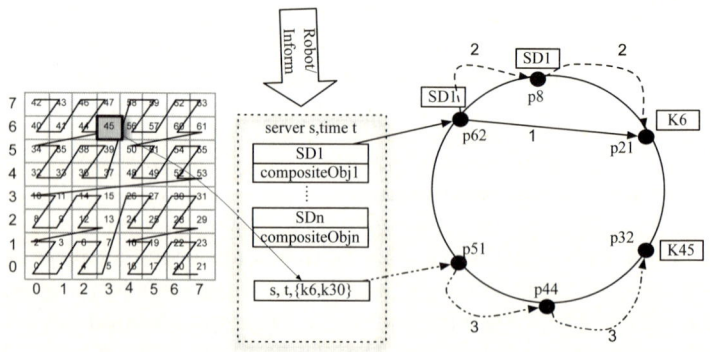

Fig. 1. Spatial and trace distribution on p2p network

that the we do not duplicate the composite, only the composite ids, which are latter used to retrieve objects' ids or traces in approximated answers to range queries.

The meta-index distribution strategy requires the administration of different types of messages. *S-messages* (messages 1 in Figure 1) carry control data in the process of finding the corresponding peers where to store composite objects. S-messages also carry aggregated data about the number of objects per type that were found by the robots at specific servers and time instants, which are stored in all peers crossed until finding the destination peers. The idea behind this strategy is to have an overall view of the global statistics of the system in each peer [6]. *T-messages* (message 2 in Figure 1) transfer composite objects from the entry peers to the destination peers. *R-messages* (message 3 in Figure 1) carry Z-codes together with the server id, crawling time, number of objects in the server, and list of composite ids for the meta-index update.

3 P2P Crawling (Polling)

A centralized crawler, as those devised for Web search engines, is composed of a set of so-called robots that are in charge of contacting servers to download data. In the p2p context, the principle is that machines in a centralized crawler are mapped into clusters of peers that work collaboratively to poll database servers. Thus, we split the work effected by a virtual centralized crawler among several peers per database server. A set of peers plays the role of a set of robots, whereas others peers are coordinators.

We model this problem as a metric space where dimentions are given by restrictions that peers must satisfy in order to guarantee efficient performance. A *metric space* $(\mathbb{X}, d)$ is composed of an universe of valid objects $\mathbb{X}$ and a *distance function* $d : \mathbb{X} \times \mathbb{X} \to \mathbb{R}^+$ defined among them. The distance function determines the similarity between two given objects and satisfies triangle inequality $d(x, z) \leq d(x, y) + d(y, z)$.

In our scheme, the collection of database servers forms a set of centers and crawler peers assign themselves to the sphere of influence (c, r_c) of the center c (server) that is closest to them in terms of the distance function. The value of r_c indicates the number of connections with peer robots the server may accept. This value depends on the relative importance and observed activity in the server with respect to all other servers. Coordinators periodically determine the values of r_c by computing the dynamic ranking of database servers along time, as we proposed for the centralized crawler in [8]. Basically, this method ranks servers considering how active objects are in their domain and what their relative importance is in terms of average number of objects. Server ranking values are between 0 and 1. The value of r_c is $\max\{m, n\}$, where m is the total number of simultaneous connections that servers can accept, and $n = \text{rank}(c) \cdot N$, with N being the average number of moving objects detected in the period.

Peers willing to become crawler robots can get information about servers from selected coordinator peers holding global information about database servers.

A peer robot gets a list of servers IDs from a coordinator peer and calculates its distance to them. Then the peer sends back to the coordinator a request to join one of the k closest servers, and the coordinator decides to accept or reject the peer as robot. The peer q asks joining one of the clusters c based on (1) the increasing order of $d(q, c)$ and (2) whether or not the number of peers assigned to the cluster is less than r_c. Notice that $d(q, c)$ does not only consider the distance between the peer q and the server c measured as the bandwidth between the two, but also a linear combination of the inverse of the sum of all distances between q and a sample of the current peers assigned to the cluster, distances measured in terms of the number of hops required by the DHT to go from q to the sample peer. The objective is to privilege peers which are more distant each other in order to distribute the communication more evenly across the network.

4 Query Processing Algorithms

We propose a two-phase algorithm for processing range and top-k queries (Algorithms 1 and 2, respectively). In the first phase, the query extent is mapped into Z-codes. Peers associated with these Z-codes are then visited to obtain tuples of the form *(server, time, list of composite ids)*. These tuples are obtained by checking the updates of each server in the peer and selecting the closest update in time for each server that overlaps the query extent.

In a second phase, we have two options. For an approximated answer, that is, answers that only use the meta-index, all composite ids selected in the first phase are grouped in a random peer to eliminate duplicates and optimize the visit to peers containing these composites. When visiting these peers, the process retrieves objects whose closest location (server) in time to the query is one of the servers that intersects the query spatial window. For a more accurate answer,

---

Algorithm 1. Algorithm to process *range time slice or time interval* queries using the p2p meta-index.

1: // Query: find all objects os that were in a region R at a time instant t or in a time interval $[t1, t2]$.
2: First Phase
3: QP, the peer where the query starts, gets all Zs that intersect R.
4: **for** z in Zs in parallel **do**
5:    DHT $get(z)$ and returns to QP the list LC of composite objects associated with updates from servers that intersect the query window (time and space).
6: **end for**
7: QP processes LC (combining and eliminating duplication) and determines all Composite Objects to visit (COs).
8: Second Phase
9: **for** co in COs in parallel **do**
10:    DHT $get(co)$
11: **end for**
12: QP assembles the answer and replies to the client

Algorithm 2. Algorithm to process *Top-k time interval* queries using the p2p meta-index.

1: // Query: find Top-k objects os with the longest trajectory found in a region R at a time interval $[t1, t2]$.
2: First Phase
3: QP, the peer where the query starts, gets all Zs that intersect R.
4: **for** z in Zs in parallel **do**
5:     DHT $get(z)$ and returns to QP the list LC of composite objects associated with updates from servers that intersect the query window and the number of times these composite objects form part of updates during the query time interval.
6: **end for**
7: QP ranks Composite Objects to visit based on the number of times they are part of updates for the query time interval and spatial range (COs).
8: Second Phase
9: QP groups composite objects with the same score and create *coSets*
10: **while** there is a *coSet* to visit or the difference of object trace length df < threshold **do**
11:     **for** co in *coSet* in parallel **do**
12:         DHT $get(co)$
13:     **end for**
14:     Compute df
15: **end while**
16: QP assemblies the answer and replies to the client

we only use the meta-index to guide the search to the appropriate servers, which are selected in the first phase. So, in the second phase, we access local servers. For top-k queries about the number of objects per server, we can get good approximated answers by ranking servers in terms of the number of objects stored, as global statistical information, in each peer, or by accessing the number of objects stored with the R-messages in peers organized by the Z-curve.

5 Experimental Evaluation

Our simulation environment used two event-driven simulators. One simulates the database servers and crawling generating the data in the form of the meta-index. The other simulates the Chord protocol to allocate and lookup meta-index data. We also used the network simulator NS-2 (*http://www.isi.edu/nsnam/ns*) in tandem with GT-ITM (*http://www.cc.gatech.edu/projects/gtitm*) to simulate the network topology and environment to measure the performance.

We used workload data generated by a public spatio-temporal dataset generator; the Network-based Generator of Moving Objects (NGMO) [2]. The data set contained 50,000 initial moving objects, existing around 150,000 along the simulation time. We used a network topology in similar way as seen in [14]. We chose peers and clients randomly from stub nodes defined in a transit-stub network of 1168 nodes created with NS-2/GT-ITM.

A first evaluation was a comparison between results with the centralized crawler evaluated in [8] and the results obtained with the p2p crawler proposed in this paper. The differences in speed of crawling depend on the number of peers we deploy to be robots in our simulator. We observed through experimentation that we needed about ten times more peers than central robots, point in which we start to observe idle peers. We also observed that the distributed calculation of the ranking of servers performed by the coordinator was about 10% different from that calculated by the centralized crawler. Overall we observed that the peer robots were evenly distributed across the clusters in a proportion similar to that given by the ranking of servers. Our linear combination factors for distances between peer and servers, and peer and cluster mates, was 0.6 and 0.4 respectively with distances normalized to 1. The NS-2/GT-ITM simulator delivered the following results for the average cost of peer to peer communication during polling.

Number of robot peers	160	320	640
Average Response time (ms)	0.109	0.178	0.258
Number of hops for DHT	4.915	5.058	4.223

Spatio-temporal Distribution. We evaluated the time efficiency of answering queries using the z-curve for the spatial distribution on the p2p network with respect to an ideal scenario where we distribute an R-tree that contains all objects at the query time. Note that the latter simulates a global distributed spatio-temporal indexing structure for the location of objects in every query time, which indeed it is the most time efficient structure, but a very inefficient structure from a storage-cost point of view. Figure 2(a) shows the ratio between the time cost and overhead cost of searching with the R-tree with respect to the z-curve distribution on the p2p network (good values are close to 1.0). We calculated costs in answering 100 random time-slice queries.

For answering both range and object-location queries, our proposal groups composite ids and not object ids in the spatial distribution using the Z-curve. This implies that for range queries we have to access peers where the composite ids

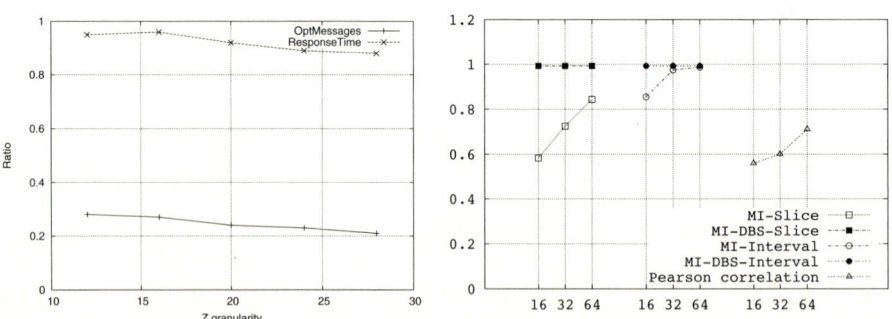

Fig. 2. Distributed meta-index: (a) the distributed meta-index versus a temporal fixed distributed R-tree, (b) quality of approximated answers

are stored to retrieve their corresponding object ids. This disadvantage produces a clear increment in the number of messages of our proposed distribution meta-index. Our proposal, however, competes closely in time cost with the ideal scenario of the distributed R-tree.

Quality of approximated answers. We show experimental results for queries that are solved using only the data stored in the meta-index and establish comparisons with the correct results obtained by visiting all the database servers. Figure 2.b shows the percentage of correct objects in the answers to 100 random time-slice and time-interval queries, and the Pearson correlation when ranking objects by their trajectory length in 100 random time-interval queries (top-k object queries). The values 16, 32 and 64 represent the number of robots used by the crawler. For time slice and time interval, we also show the quality of results when using the meta-index to guide the search to local servers (MI-DBS), results that are almost perfect (over 99%).

Overall, the results show that there are many cases in which the data stored in the meta-index can be used to provide a very fast and good approximated

Area	Message	Time	Interval	Message	Time	TopK	Message	Time
0.25%	21.16	2623.6	5%	25.22	2867.9	10	15.9	2636.3
1%	22.75	2600.8	10%	26.15	2910.7	20	25.2	2882.8
4%	36.14	3047.1	20%	28.04	2861.0	30	29.4	2888.1
	(a)			(b)			(c)	

Fig. 3. Effect of search parameters: (a) spatial window size (b) time interval length and (c) k (*Area* is the percentage of the total geographic region, *Interval* is the percentage of the simulation period, K is the parameter of top-k queries, *Message* is the average number of messages per query, and *Time* in the average time measured in milliseconds)

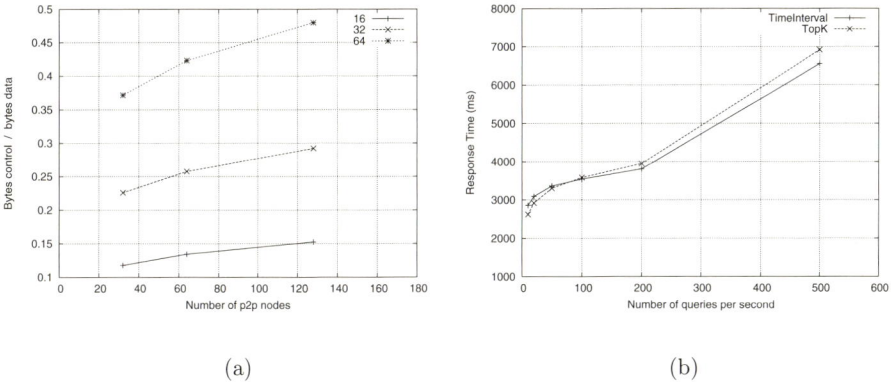

(a) (b)

Fig. 4. Communication overhead and elasticity of using the meta-index: (a) relative number of bytes transmitted in update operations, (b) response time for different query rates given to the system for time interval and top-k queries (MSB=20, 32 robots and 128 peers)

answer to classical queries for this kind of database systems. Users can use this preliminary "hint" to further investigate the system evolution or to refine their subsequent queries.

Update/Search Performance. To measure the performance of the system, we first evaluated the impact of search parameter variations on the type of queries we address in this work. Figure 3 shows the results for search parameter variations in terms of response time and communication cost. The communication cost is measured in terms of the number of messages needed per query. We computed the number of messages using the Chord Protocol. The results show that both metrics increase slightly when increasing the size of the spatial window, time interval and k, being the size of the spatial window the most sensitive. Second, we measured the communication cost to keep the meta-index up to date under different numbers of robots. Figure 4.a shows that 32 robots are enough to collect data for 150,000 moving objects. In this case, MSB was 20, since higher values for the MSB make composite too small and waste bandwidth. Third, we evaluated the elasticity of the system in terms of its ability to scale up when having to respond to concurrent queries. Figure 4.b shows that the system increases its response time with a slightly higher slope over 200 queries per second.

6 Conclusions

In this paper we have presented the design of a p2p index data structure devised to support complex queries in moving objects databases. Our main contributions are: (1) to combine, into the same index location, aggregation and range queries, and (2) to update the index based on a distributed strategy of crawling.

The experimental results show that, at least for the classical range queries based on a spatio-temporal window, our strategy can be as efficient as the well-known RTree, which we set it to work in an extremely convenient setting. To the best of our knowledge, alternative solutions to solve location queries have not been proposed so far by other authors. The use of the p2p index, as a devise to support fast approximated solutions to queries, is also promising. How close the approximated answer is to the exact solution depends on how frequently the index is updated. We have proposed a p2p crawler that performs as efficiently as a centralized crawler. We have found that with 10 peers per robot of a high-performance centralized crawler it is possible to keep the index properly updated along time.

References

1. Akbarinia, R., Pacitti, E., Valduriez, P.: Processing top-k queries in distributed hash tables. In: Kermarrec, A.-M., Bougé, L., Priol, T. (eds.) Euro-Par 2007. LNCS, vol. 4641, pp. 489–502. Springer, Heidelberg (2007)
2. Brinkhoff, T.: A framework for generating network-based moving objects. GeoInformatica 6(2), 153–180 (2002)

3. Chawathe, Y., Ramabhadran, S., Ratnasamy, S., LaMarca, A., Shenker, S., Hellerstein, J.M.: A case study in building layered dht applications. In: Guérin, R., Govindan, R., Minshall, G. (eds.) SIGCOMM, pp. 97–108. ACM, New York (2005)
4. du Mouza, C., Rigaux, P.: Web architectures for scalable moving object servers. In: Proceedings of the 10th ACM international symposium on Advances in geographic information systems, pp. 17–22. ACM Press, New York (2002)
5. Faloutsos, C., Roseman, S.: Fractals for secondary key retrieval. In: PODS, pp. 247–252. ACM Press, New York (1989)
6. Hernández, C., Rodríguez, M.A., Marín, M.: A p2p meta-index for spatio-temporal moving object databases. In: Haritsa, J.R., Kotagiri, R., Pudi, V. (eds.) DASFAA 2008. LNCS, vol. 4947. Springer, Heidelberg (2008)
7. Lee, H., Hwang, J., Lee, J., Park, S., Lee, C., Nah, Y.: Long-term location data management for distributed moving object databases. In: Ninth IEEE International Symposium on Object and Component-Oriented Real-Time Distributed Computing, pp. 451–458. IEEE Press, Los Alamitos (2006)
8. Marín, M., Rodríguez, A., Fincke, T., Román, C.: Searching moving objects in a spatio-temporal distributed database servers system. In: Meersman, R., Tari, Z. (eds.) OTM Conferences (2). LNCS, vol. 4276, pp. 1388–1401. Springer, Heidelberg (2006)
9. Maymounkov, P., Kademlia, D.M.: A peer-to-peer information system based on the xor metric. In: Druschel, P., Kaashoek, M.F., Rowstron, A.I.T. (eds.) IPTPS 2002. LNCS, vol. 2429, pp. 53–65. Springer, Heidelberg (2002)
10. Meka, A., Singh, A.K.: Dist: a distributed spatio-temporal index structure for sensor networks. In: Herzog, O., Schek, H.-J., Fuhr, N., Chowdhury, A., Teiken, W. (eds.) CIKM, pp. 139–146. ACM, New York (2005)
11. Mondal, A., Lifu, Y., Kitsuregawa, M.: P2pr-tree: An r-tree-based spatial index for peer-to-peer environments. In: Lindner, W., Mesiti, M., Türker, C., Tzitzikas, Y., Vakali, A. (eds.) EDBT 2004. LNCS, vol. 3268, pp. 516–525. Springer, Heidelberg (2004)
12. Nah, Y., Lee, J., Lee, W.J., Le, H., Kim, M.H., Han, K.J.: Distributed scalable location data management system based on the GALIS architecture. In: Tenth IEEE International Workshop on Object-Oriented Real Time Dependable Systems, pp. 397–404. IEEE Press, Los Alamitos (2005)
13. Stoica, I., Morris, R., Liben-Nowell, D., Karger, D.R., Kaashoek, M.F., Dabek, F., Balakrishnan, H.: Chord: a scalable peer-to-peer lookup protocol for internet applications. IEEE/ACM Trans. Netw. 11(1), 17–32 (2003)
14. Tanin, E., Harwood, A., Samet, H.: Using a distributed quadtree index in peer-to-peer networks. VLDB J. 16(2), 165–178 (2007)

Scheduling Intersection Queries in Term Partitioned Inverted Files

Mauricio Marin[1], Carlos Gomez-Pantoja[2],
Senen Gonzalez[2], and Veronica Gil-Costa[3]

[1] Yahoo! Research, Santiago, Chile
[2] University of Chile
[3] University of San Luis, Argentina

Abstract. This paper proposes and presents a comparison of scheduling algorithms applied to the context of load balancing the query traffic on distributed inverted files. We put emphasis on queries requiring intersection of posting lists, which is a very demanding case for the term partitioned inverted file and a case in which the document partitioned inverted file used by current search engines can perform very efficiently. We show that with proper scheduling of queries the term partitioned approach can outperform the document partitioned approach.

1 Introduction

Cluster based search engines use distributed inverted files [13] for dealing efficiently with high traffic of user queries. An inverted file is composed of a vocabulary table and a set of posting lists. The vocabulary table contains the set of relevant terms found in the text collection. Each of these terms is associated with a posting list which contains the document identifiers where the term appears in the collection along with additional data used for ranking purposes. To solve a query, it is necessary to get the set of documents associated with the query terms and then perform a ranking of these documents in order to select the top R documents as the query answer.

The approach used by well-known Web search engines to the parallelization of inverted files is pragmatic, namely they use the document partitioned approach. Documents are evenly distributed on P processors and an independent inverted file is constructed for each of the P sets of documents. The disadvantage is that each user query has to be sent to the P processors and it can present imbalance at posting lists level (this increases disk access and interprocessor communication costs). The advantage is that document partitioned indexes are easy to maintain since insertion of new documents can be done locally and this locality is extremely convenient for the posting list intersection operations required to solve the queries (they come for free in terms of communication costs). Intersection of posting lists is necessary to determine the set of documents that contain all of the terms present in a given user query.

Another competing approach is the term partitioned index in which a single inverted file is constructed from the whole text collection to then distribute evenly the terms with their respective posting lists onto the processors. However, the term partitioned inverted file destroys the possibility of computing intersections for free in terms of communication cost and thereby one is compelled to use strategies such as smart distribution of terms onto processors to increase locality for most frequent terms (which can be detrimental to overall load balance) and caching. However, it is not necessary to broadcast queries to all processors (which reduces communication costs) and latency disk costs are smaller as they are paid once per posting list retrieval per query, and it is well-known that in current cluster technology it is faster to transfer blocks of bytes through the interprocessors network than from Ram to Disk. Nevertheless, the load balance is sensitive to queries referring to particular terms with high frequency, making it necessary to use posting lists caching strategies to overcome imbalance in disk accesses.

Both strategies are efficient depending on the method used to perform the final ranking of documents. In particular, the term partitioned index is better suited for methods that do not require performing posting list intersections. For this case we have observed that the balance of disk accesses, that is posting list fetching, and document ranking are the most relevant factors affecting the performance of query processing. The balance of interprocessors communication depends on the balance of these two components. From empirical evidence we have observed that *moderate* imbalance in communication is not detrimental to performance.

The scenario for the term partitioned index is completely different for queries requiring the intersection of posting lists. This can become extremely expensive in communication because it is necessary to send posting lists between processors to let them being intersected. From previous work on implementing search engines on P2P networks we can learn of a number of attempts to reduce the size of the posting lists sent to other processors to be intersected [3, 8, 11]. In addition, work on smart distribution of terms devised to increase the probability of terms appearing very frequently in queries being located in the same processor have been presented in [1, 2, 6, 7, 12]. Other approaches avoid the imbalance effect of frequent terms by just replicating their posting lists in two or more processors [6, 12].

The most recent study on the comparative performance of the term and document partitioned index is the work presented in [6]. They use a realization of the term partitioned index called the *pipelined* approach. In this scheme a query traverses one by one the processors that contain query terms and in each visit it tries to determine the best ranked document that can become part of the top ranked ones to be presented to the user. Since the partial ranking of document is tied to the processors that contain query terms, the imbalance can become significant because of the terms appearing in queries very frequently. Their solution is a combination of posting list replication and the least loaded processor first heuristic for improving load balance. In the experiments they use queries that do not require intersection of posting lists (OR queries). Their study concludes that the term partitioned index cannot outperform the document partitioned index.

However, in [4] we show that for this type of queries the term partitioned index can outperform significantly to the document partitioned index. This because we de-couple document ranking from the processors where the query terms are located and our method of ranking does not require large portions of posting lists to calculate the top R documents. We also show under our method that the most simple heuristics for load balancing leads to running times as good as those achieved by more sophisticated strategies for static and dynamic scheduling of tasks onto processors.

Now the challenge is to consider the more complicated case of queries requiring posting list intersections (AND queries). In this case the amount of communication can be very large and to avoid this one is compelled to consider performing intersection and ranking in the processors holding query terms. Certainly communication can be reduced by using the pruning techniques mentioned in [9], but it is a matter of how big is the text collection to be in the same situation of high cost in communication.

In this paper we deal with this problem and propose solutions based on query scheduling that are able to outperform the document partitioned index under situations of high traffic of queries. A contribution of this paper is also the way in which we model the parallel processing of queries to support scheduling decisions. Queries arrive to the processors from a receptionist machine that we call the *broker*. We study the case in which the broker is responsible for assigning the work to the processors. Jobs badly scheduled onto the processors can result in high imbalance. To this end the broker uses a scheduling algorithm. For example, a simple approach is to distribute the queries uniformly at random onto the processors in a blind manner, namely just as they arrive to the broker they are scheduled in a circular round-robin manner. A more sophisticated scheduling strategy demands more computing power from the broker so in our view this cost should be paid only if load balance improves significantly.

2 Scheduling Framework

The broker simulates the operation of a search engine that is processing the queries as follows. First, it uses bulk-synchronous parallel (BSP) computing to process queries. In BSP [10] the computation is organized as a sequence of *supersteps*. During a superstep, the processors may perform computations on local data and/or send messages to other processors. The messages are available for processing at their destinations by the next superstep, and each superstep is ended with the barrier synchronization of the processors. The underlying communication library ensures that all messages are available at their destinations before starting the next superstep.

Secondly, query processing is divided in "atoms" of size K, where $K = 2R$ where R is the number of documents presented to the user as part of the query answer. These atoms are scheduled in a round-robin manner across supersteps and processors. The asynchronous tasks are given K sized quanta of processor time, communication network and disk accesses. These quanta are granted during supersteps, namely they are processed in a bulk-synchronous manner.

As all atoms are equally sized then the net effect is that no particular task can restrain others from using the resources. This because (**i**) computing the solution to a given query can take the processing of several atoms, (**ii**) the search engine can start the processing of a new query as soon as any query is finished, and (**iii**) the processors are barrier synchronized and all messages are delivered in their destinations at the end of each superstep. It is not difficult to see that this scheme is optimal provided that we find an "atom" packing strategy that produces optimal load balance and minimizes the total number of supersteps required to complete a given set of queries (this is directly related to the critical path for the set of queries). Relevant literature on BSP has shown that BSP computations can simulate well asynchronous computations such as those performed by current search engines. In [5] we show that the difference in performance between these two modes of computation is related to the query traffic.

The simulation assumes that at the beginning of each superstep the processors get into their input message queues both new queries placed there by the broker and messages with pieces of posting lists related to the processing of queries which arrived at previous supersteps. The processing of a given query can take two or more supersteps to be completed. The processor in which a given query arrives is called the *ranker* for that query since it is in this processor where the associated document ranking is performed.

Every query is processed using two major steps: the first one consists on fetching a K-sized piece of every posting list involved in the query and sending them to the ranker processor. In the second step, the ranker performs the actual ranking of documents and, if necessary, it asks for additional K-sized pieces of the posting lists in order to produce the K best ranked documents that are passed to the broker as the query results. We call this *iterations*. Thus the ranking process can take one or more iterations to finish. In every iteration a new piece of K pairs (doc_id, frequency) from posting lists are sent to the ranker for every term involved in the query. At a given interval of time, the ranking of two or more queries can take place in parallel at different processors along with the fetching of K-sized pieces of posting lists associated with new queries. For AND queries it is necessary to first make the intersection of all involved posting lists to determine the document containing all query terms. Then the ranking can proceed as described above by considering only the documents in the intersection.

In figure 1 we illustrate the scheduling problem under this bulk-synchronous framework. The broker performs the scheduling maintaining two windows which account for the processors work-load through the supersteps. One window is for the intersection + ranking operations effected per processor per superstep and the another is for the posting list fetches from disk also per processor per superstep. In each window cell we keep the count of the number of operations of each type. The optimization goal is to achieve an imbalance of about 15%

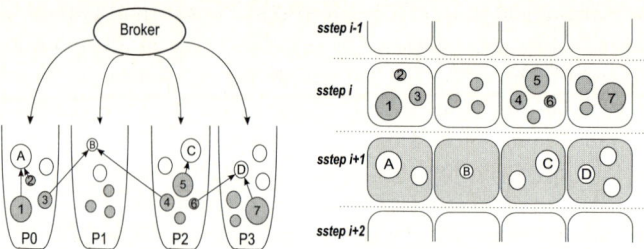

Fig. 1. Scheduling problem in the term partitioned inverted file. Grey balls represent inverted lists of different length and white balls represent the cost of intersecting the posting lists. The abstraction in supersteps allows the broker to consider the temporality of operations and model the cost of the tradeoff involved in decisions such as where to schedule the intersection and ranking, and at index construction time where to place terms onto processors.

across processors. Imbalance is measured via efficiency, which for a measure X is defined by the ratio average(X)/maximum$(X) \leq 1$, over the P processors.

3 Description and Evaluation of Scheduling Algorithms

In the experimental results presented in this section we have used a 12GB sample of the Chilean Web and query log from www.todocl.cl. We use this text collection to explore the effect of load imbalance as we keep fixed the overall size of the inverted file and we increase the number of processors P. We performed experiments by running BSPonMPI programs on a cluster with 32 processors. In every run we process 10,000 queries in *each* processor. That is the total number of queries processed in each experiment reported below is $10{,}000 \times P$. Thus running times are expected to grow with P since the communication hardware has at least $\log P$ scalability. Another parameter used in our experiments is the query traffic Q which indicates the rate of queries per unit time in each processor and superstep.

Thus in the figures shown below the curves for 32 processors are higher in running time than the ones for 4 processors. We have found this useful to see the efficiency of the different strategies in the sense of how well they support the inclusion of more processors to work on a problem of a fixed size N. Given the size of text collection, the case for $P = 32$ becomes a very demanding one in terms of the small slackness N/P available to load balance processors. We show running measures normalized between 0 and 1 by dividing all running times by the maximum running time among the set of strategies being compared in the figure. This makes it easier to see the relative difference in performance of the different strategies. Overall the average running time per query of our programs is less than 1ms for the 12GB sample. Below we refer to the term partitioned index as Global and the document partitioned index as Local.

We have implemented all strategies reported in the literature as the most efficient ones in aspects related to smart term distribution onto processors and replication. We report running times obtained with the ones that behaved best. We also contribute with scheduling algorithms based on the bulk-synchronous abstraction of the scheduling problem described in the previous section. The percentage of replication is 20% which is very similar to the analysis reported in [6]. The strategies tested are the following.

Round-Robin [Circular]: terms are distributed onto machines such that the n-th term goes to machine $n\%P$. Duplication is performed assigning a processor selected at random for the most frequent terms to be replicated.

Correlation-Aware [Corr]: the frequency of each pair of terms is retrieved from the query logs which acts as a training set. Then, all pair-terms are ordered decreasingly according to its frequency. The idea is that two terms highly correlated should be assigned to the same machine. If one of the terms was already distributed, then the other term is assigned in the same machine. If the entire pair has not been distributed, then the pair is assigned to the least loaded machine. We have used two variations: either P or P^2 most frequent terms are distributed –one per machine– before distributing the aforementioned pairs. Note that the initial distribution given as input, only is used to obtain the load of each machine and the processors where is not a certain term. This strategy is similar to the mentioned in [1, 2].

Fill-Smallest: the technique introduced in [6] sorts the terms decreasingly according to the load L_t, defined to be the length of the inverted list of term t times the frequency of t in the query log. In practice, this function produces a big imbalance we considered two variations, one in which the weight of the term is the length of the list, and the other in which the weight is the frequency. The same technique is used for replicating terms.

List-Driven and Node-Driven: these strategies have been developed to properly replicate inverted lists [12]. List-Driven selects first a term to replicate, and then a machine to maximize the benefit associated with this replication. This benefit involves the communication costs associated with the queries of the log. Analogously, the Node-driven approach select in each iteration the machine less loaded, and then finds the term whose allocation to that machine that maximizes the benefit. The input consists of a distribution of terms without replication. For this the authors propose two methods. The first one using a random distribution, and the second guided by a graph partitioning software. Our experiments used the first option. According to them, List-Driven seems to perform better.

Figure 2 shows the normalized running time for the different strategies with $Q = 32$. Note that for the Correlation-aware and Fill-Smallest algorithms there are many variations in performance for different tuning of their operational setting. We have chosen only the versions of each algorithm with the best performance, and these are the ones shown in the figure.

In the figure 3 we show results for the case of posting lists replication. The figure shows poor improvements in running time, thus we do not consider these techniques any further in this paper.

In the term-partitioning approach we can schedule intersections from the broker to improve balance. The plain strategy, called Global, takes into account

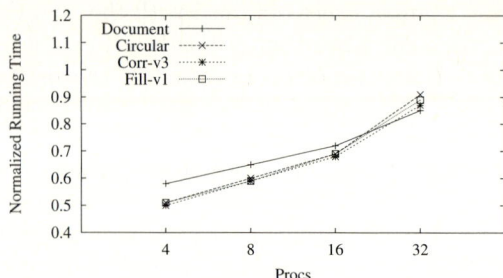

Fig. 2. Comparison of term distribution strategies without replication with Q=32

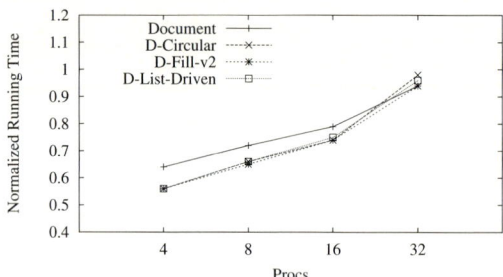

Fig. 3. Comparison of term distribution strategies with replication with Q=32

the communication cost so that to solve a query of two or more terms the broker chooses the machine where the largest term (size of its inverted list) was assigned. In the case of queries with one term, only the ranking operation is assigned to the machine that received the query. We implemented three additional strategies to evaluate different alternatives for this basic scheme.

In the first one (Scheduling-1), we schedule the intersections in a Round-Robin manner, such that in each superstep each machine has the same number of intersection and ranking operations (each ranking operation is performed in the same machine of the intersection to avoid additional communication costs). In the second strategy (Scheduling-2) we select the machines that have the terms involved in the query, then we calculate their load and the query is assigned to the least loaded processor. The load of a machine is determined from the sizes of the terms involved in the solution of the queries assigned to that machine. In the last strategy (Scheduling-3) we give more degrees of freedom to the second strategy, i.e., we mean that the possible candidates to assign a query are all the processors, not only the processors involved in the query. Then, we use a simple heuristic that chooses some queries to be moved to other machines in function of their load. The results are shown in the figure 4.

The previous figure shows clearly that a little effort in assigning intelligently the intersections can be important to reducing overall running time. Moreover when there are a large degree of imbalance we observed that the difference was approximately 30%. The source of this differences is the communication cost.

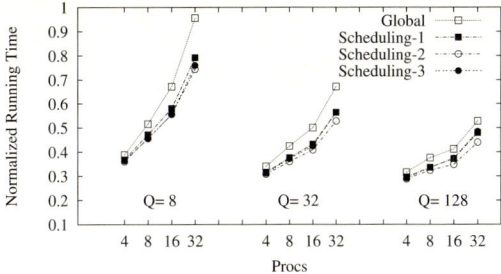

Fig. 4. Scheduling of intersection operations

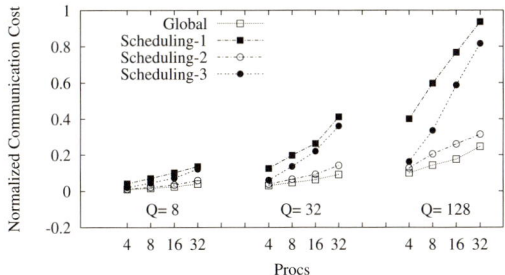

Fig. 5. Communication cost of query scheduling strategies

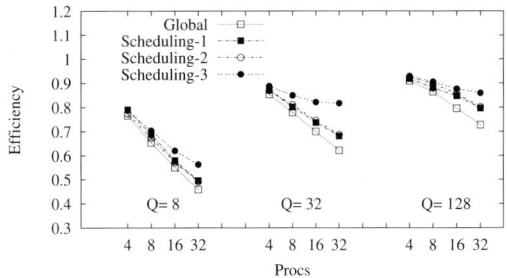

Fig. 6. Efficiency at superstep running time level

The strategy Scheduling-2 could be viewed as an improvement of the Global strategy. The machines involved in the query solution are the same with the exception that Scheduling-2 distributes the intersections to the machines that have minimum load.

In the figure 5 we show the results for the overall cost of communication. Global strategy can be seen as the optimal strategy in terms of communication costs because it only communicates the shortest list related to each query. The Scheduling-2 strategy is very similar in terms of communication.

On the other hand, figure 6 shows the efficiency at computing time level. We measured in each superstep the running time of each machine, but without considering communication overhead. Then we obtained the efficiency measured as the maximum running time at each superstep divided by the average running time. The figure shows that the most balanced strategy is Global with Scheduling 3. However this is not enough to achieve good performance as the effect of communication is relevant for intersection operations.

3.1 Document Versus Best-Term Partitioned Strategies

For the term partitioned approach, we used two schemes for distributing the terms. For the Global strategy explained above, we use the Correlation-Aware distribution in its P^2 version (G-Corr-v3). In addition for the Scheduling-2 (the best of all three) we use the Fill-Smallest partitioning in its *size* version (S-Fill-v1). We also compare with the document partitioning index (Local).

We executed under different traffic conditions (Q) and number of processors. In figure 7 we show the results. There we can observe that when there is low query traffic, the Local strategy outperforms the Global ones. But when we have high traffic of queries, the Global strategies outperform the Local one.

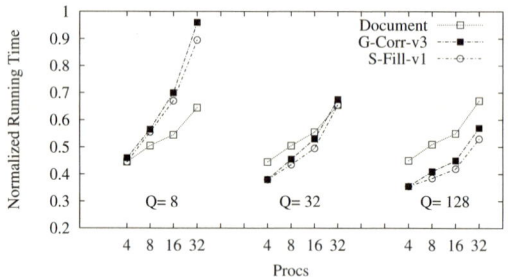

Fig. 7. Normalized running time

4 Conclusions

We have evaluated scheduling strategies which show that the term partitioned inverted file can outperform the document partitioned one under the requirement of posting list intersections. However, this can only occur in situations of high traffic of queries case in which overall load balance is good enough. Nevertheless, for low traffic the cluster resources are not being fully utilized so we think this is not a serious drawback since response times are still small despite of imbalance and high communication.

Notice that we did not resort to techniques for reducing communication such as those based on Bloom filters. Neither we considered compression of posting lists so the results of this paper are pessimistic for the term partitioned index since there is still room for further optimizations. In addition, we have only considered sending the whole posting list in order to perform exhaustive intersection. However, in large scale systems it is certainly possible to avoid this by employing pruning strategies. The rationale is that for each query term we only need to get the top-K documents in the intersection and not the whole set of documents in the intersection set.

Acknowledgment. Partially funded by Millennium Nucleus CWR, Grant P04-067-F, Mideplan, Chile.

References

1. Chaudhuri, S., Church, K., König, A.C., Sui, L.: Heavy-tailed distributions and multi-keyword queries. In: SIGIR 2007: 30th annual international ACM SIGIR conference on Research and development in information retrieval, pp. 663–670. ACM, New York (2007)
2. Falchi, F., Gennaro, C., Rabitti, F., Zezula, P.: Mining query logs to optimize index partitioning in parallel web search engines. In: INFOSCALE 2007: 2nd International Conference on Scalable Information Systems (2007)
3. Li, J., Loo, B., Hellerstein, J., Kaashoek, F., Karger, D., Morris, R.: The feasibility of peer-to-peer web indexing and search (2003)
4. Marin, M., Gomez, C.: Load balancing distributed inverted files. In: WIDM 2007: 9th annual ACM international workshop on Web information and data management, pp. 57–64. ACM, New York (2007)
5. Marin, M., Costa, V.G. (SyncjAsync)$^+$ MPI search engines. In: Cappello, F., Hrault, T., Dongarra, J. (eds.) PVM/MPI 2007. LNCS, vol. 4757, pp. 117–124. Springer, Heidelberg (2007)
6. Moffat, A., Webber, W., Zobel, J.: Load balancing for term-distributed parallel retrieval. In: SIGIR 2006: 29th annual international ACM SIGIR conference on Research and development in information retrieval, pp. 348–355. ACM, New York (2006)
7. Moffat, W., Zobel, J.W., Baeza-Yates, R.: A pipelined architecture for distributed text query evaluation. Information Retrieval (August 2007)
8. Reynolds, P., Vahdat, A.: Efficient peer-to-peer keyword searching. In: Endler, M., Schmidt, D.C. (eds.) Middleware 2003. LNCS, vol. 2672, pp. 21–40. Springer, Heidelberg (2003)
9. Suel, T., Mathur, C., wen Wu, J., Zhang, J., Delis, A., Kharrazi, M., Long, X., Shanmugasundaram, K.: ODISSEA: A peer-to-peer architecture for scalable web search and information retrieval. In: WWW 2003: 12th International World Wide Web Conference (2003)
10. Valiant, L.: A bridging model for parallel computation. Comm. ACM 33, 103–111 (1990)
11. Zhang, J., Long, X., Suel, T.: Performance of compressed inverted list caching in search engines. In: WWW 2008: 17th International World Wide Web Conference (2008)
12. Zhang, J., Suel, T.: Optimized inverted list assignment in distributed search engine architectures. In: IPDPS 2007: 23rd IEEE International Parallel and Distributed Processing Symposium (2007)
13. Zobel, J., Moffat, A.: Inverted files for text search engines. ACM Computing Surveys 38(2) (2006)

Topic 6: Grid and Cluster Computing

Marco Danelutto*, Juan Touriño*, Mark Baker*, Rajkumar Buyya*, Paraskevi Fragopoulou*, Christian Perez*, and Erich Schikuta*

Grid computing has been and continues to be one of the most popular research and development areas in computing science and technology. Much of the research activity in this field has been devoted to grid programming environments, applications, middleware, and system architecture. However, as technology evolves, new emerging challenges are faced, which stimulates further research in this area. Cluster computing is another key technology area, especially when high performance is taken into account.

The Grid and Cluster Computing has been present as a topic in all recent EuroPar conferences. Recently, it has become one of the most popular EuroPar topics, at least if we take into account the number of papers submitted. This year 51 papers have been submitted to the topic; from these 14 have been selected for the program of EuroPar 2008. The final decision has been taken after a high quality review process that produced four reviews per submitted paper, involving a large number of researchers from both the grid and the cluster computing communities. The selected papers present research efforts from nine European countries, USA, Brazil and Japan. The papers have been grouped into five different sessions, according to their research and experimental content. The grid frameworks, scheduling, resource management and performance evaluation sessions host the papers more closely related to grid research, while the cluster computing session hosts the two selected papers that relate to clusters.

Overall, this builds up an interesting program for the Grid and Cluster Computing topic, and we are confident that the conference attendees will be attracted by the topic sessions. As topic Chairs we wish to acknowledge all those that contributed to this effort and in particular the authors of the submitted papers and the reviewers that contributed their valuable time and expertise to the selection process.

---

* Topic Chairs.

Integration of GRID Superscalar and GridWay Metascheduler with the DRMAA OGF Standard*

R.M. Badia[1], D. Du[3], E. Huedo[2], A. Kokossis[3], I.M. Llorente[2], R.S. Montero[2], M. de Palol[1], R. Sirvent[1], and C. Vázquez[2]

[1] Barcelona Supercomputing Center
[2] Universidad Complutense de Madrid
[3] University of Surrey

Abstract. This paper shares the experiences with one of the BEinGRID pilots, BE14, from a technological point of view. The experiment has integrated GRID superscalar (as programming model) with GridWay (as metascheduler) through the DRMAA standard. Additionally, a portal based in GridSphere has been developed. The portal enables the management of the grid and the automatic deployment and monitoring of applications. This environment has been successfully used to speed up an application that enables new processes and products development in the Chemistry sector with considerable success.

Keywords: Grid Computing, DRMAA, GRID superscalar, GridWay Metascheduler.

1 Introduction

Business Experiments in GRID (BEinGRID), is an European Union integrated project funded by the Information Society Technologies (IST) research, part of the EUs sixth research Framework Programme (FP6). The BEinGRID consortium is composed of 75 partners who are running eighteen Business Experiments designed to implement and deploy grid solutions in industrial key sectors.

The main objective of BEinGRID project is to foster the adoption of the so-called Next Generation Grid technologies by the realization of several business experiments and the creation of a toolset repository of grid middleware upper layers. BEinGRID is undertaking a series of targeted business experiment pilots designed to implement and deploy grid solutions in a broad spectrum of European business sectors (entertainment, financial, industrial, chemistry, gaming, retail, textile, etc). Eighteen business experiments are ongoing in the initial stage of the project with a second open call that recently accepted a second bunch of experiments. Secondly, a toolset repository of grid service components and best practise will be created to support European businesses that wish to take-up the

---

* This research was supported by European Union, through BEinGRID project EU contract IST-2005-034702.

grid. To minimise redevelopment of components, BEinGRID will deploy innovative grid solutions using existing grid components from across the European Union and beyond.

The authors of this paper are involved in the Business Experiment 14 (BE14), "New Product and Process Development," that addresses the creation of an integrated environment that enables the automation of new products and processes in the Chemistry sector in a grid environment.

The process industry spends a lot of resources in the development of new products and processes. Nowadays these processes depend heavily on computers and are basically manual and sequential. The objective of this work is to implement a development environment that is able to automate these processes in a computational grid. Grids appear as the ideal venue to enable such an application since they offer tremendous scope to automate studies with virtual access to experts and resources and capabilities to launch integrated experiments.

The added value of the experiment is the increase of the efficiency measured by reductions in development times, systematic accumulation of industrial know-how, and effective use (and re-use) of knowledge and expertise. The application is developed on top of the integration of two powerful grid tools: GRID superscalar (GRIDSs) [1], which provides a grid-unaware programming environment and GridWay [2], a metascheduler which provides reliable execution in heterogeneous grids. The integration of both tools have been performed through the OGF standard DRMAA [3,4], which has also become the first OGF recommendation. This integration give benefits to both GRIDSs and GridWay: GRIDSs is enabled to run now with DRMAA schedulers, like GridWay, being able to rely on their features (fault tolerance, monitoring, migration...) and also with a general view of all the applications run in the grid; and GridWay benefits of a higher level programming environment, that from a sequential application is able to general a graph-dependency graph and exploit the concurrency of the application at task level.

In this work we focus on the technical aspects of the experiment: how GRIDSs and GridWay have been extended and modified to be able to work in cooperation and how an end-user application has been successfully developed on top of this environment. The paper structure is as follows: section 2 presents the Grid Applications Development solution (GridAD) developed in the framework of the BE14. Section 3 gives an overview of the enabling technologies of GridAD: GRIDSs and GridWay. Section 4 describes how GRIDSs and GridWay have been modified to enable their integration through the DRMAA OGF standard. In section 5 we present the early results obtained with the BE application. Finally, section 6 concludes the paper and presents future work.

2 Grid Applications Development Solution (GridAD)

GridAD is the result of the integration through the DRMAA OGF standard of two powerful grid tools: GRIDSs and GridWay Metascheduler. The combination of GRIDSs and GridWay (GridAD) provides a complete and powerful toolset for the development and deployment of applications in the grid. GRIDSs is specially unique for the possibility that it offers to the programmers to make the grid "invisible". On the other hand, GridWay is an efficient metascheduler, worldwide known and used. Additionally, there is no solution equivalent to the combination of both. GridAD can be used for computational grids and also on clusters, by linking to other DRMAA libraries intended for DRMS (Condor, SGE, etc). Figure 1 shows the flow that a GridAD application follows on execution. From a final's user sequential application, GRIDSs is able to find the existing task-level parallelism and schedules the tasks for execution through GridWay. GridWay then performs resource management and monitoring of the application.

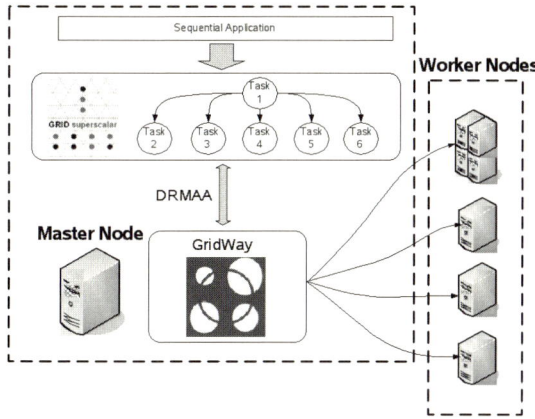

Fig. 1. Execution in GridAD environment

3 Enabling Grid Technologies

3.1 GRID Superscalar

GRID superscalar (GRIDSs) [1,5] is an innovative grid programming framework that enables non-grid experts to develop applications that can be run in a computational grid. GRIDSs provides a very user-friendly programming framework to grid environments. GRIDSs not only provides an abstract layer to program applications in the grid, but also is able to increase the performance of the applications by automatically parallelising parts of the application. Applications that can take advantage of GRIDSs are those composed of one or more coarse grain tasks that are called several times during the application execution. GRIDSs will execute the coarse grain tasks in independent grid servers and will execute sequentially those that have data dependencies. However, when no data dependencies exist between two or more tasks, GRIDSs is able to execute them concurrently.

GRIDSs is composed of:

- User Interface: GRIDSs applications are composed of three parts: main program, tasks' code, and interface of the tasks. A small set of primitives (up to seven) are offered for the main program, and two primitives for the tasks' code. The interface of the tasks is simply an interface specification that includes the direction of the tasks' parameters (input, output or input/output). Expert users can complete their applications by giving resource constraints (memory, disk, OS, ...) and performance costs models of their tasks.
- Automatic code generation: From the interface definition some code is automatically generated by gsstubgen, a tool provided with the GRIDSs distribution. This automatically generates code for stubs and skeletons that will be run on the grid servers and clients.
- Deployment Center: The deployment center is a graphical interface that performs the automatic deployment of the applications in the grid, by transfering the code files, automatic building of the binaries in the servers and configuration file generation.
- GRID superscalar Monitor: The GRID superscalar monitor (GSM) visualizes the task dependence graph (TDG) at run time, so the user can study the structure of the application and track the progress of execution.
- Run-time: The runtime is the more complex component of the system and performs: task dependency maintenance, task scheduling, file renaming (to further exploit the application concurrency), file transfer taking into account shared file systems, checkpointing, and fault tolerance. It is important to emphasize here that the runtime of GRIDSs makes the decision on which grid resource should be used to execute each task. To take this decision, several parameters are considered: location of input files, to reduce file transfers (and therefore exploiting file locality) and resource constraints specified by the user in the constraints interface. Another important feature is file renaming: this technique consists in the generation of several instances of the same file (i.e., several temporal files that are the same in the application, but in fact are different instances) to further increase the application parallelism.

  GRID superscalar run-time handles the renaming, maintaining at each moment for each renamed file the original filename and which is the last renamed filename, and this renaming is taken into account in the data dependence analysis. The run-time also keeps track of the server where each file is located. Files are transferred only on demand and if required. Together with a locality-aware scheduling policy, the number of file transfers is largely reduced.

GRIDSs is distributed as Open Source under Apache v2 license [5].

3.2 GridWay Metascheduler

GridWay [6] provides the end-user with a working environment and functionality similar to those found on local DRM systems, such as SGE, LSF or PBS. The end-user is able to submit, monitor and control his jobs by means of DRM-like commands (gwsubmit, gwwait, gwkill...) or standard programming interfaces.

- Efficient, reliable and unattended execution of jobs: GridWay automatically performs all the job scheduling steps, provides fault recovery mechanisms, and adapts job scheduling and execution to the changing grid conditions
- Broad application scope: GridWay is not bounded to a specific class of application generated by a given programming environment and does not require application deployment on remote hosts, which extends its application range and allows reusing of existing software. GridWay allows Submission of single, array or complex jobs consisting of task dependencies, which may require file transferring and/or database access.
- DRM-like command line interface: The GridWay command line interface is similar to that found on Unix and resource management systems such as PBS or SGE. It allows users to submit, kill, migrate, monitor and synchronize jobs, that could be described using the OGF standard JSDL.
- DRMAA application programming interface: GridWay provides full support for OGF standard DRMAA to develop distributed applications (C, JAVA, Perl, Python and Ruby bindings).

Moreover, GridWay modular architecture (see Figure 2) offers easy deployment, adaptability and extension capabilities, as well as support for site autonomy and dynamic environments. GridWay and the Globus Toolkit support the deployment of enterprise grids, that enable diverse resource sharing to improve internal collaboration and achieve a better return from their information technology investment; partner grids, allowing access to a higher computing performance to satisfy peak demands and also provide support to face collaborative projects; and outsourced grids, managed by dedicated service providers, that supply resources on demand over the Internet.

Since the release of GridWay 4.0, intended for Globus Toolkit 4 components, in January 2005, it is distributed under Apache v2 license [6]. GridWay is a Globus project [7] and, starting with GridWay 5.2.2, it is included in Globus Toolkit [8].

4 Integration

In this section, we discuss about the integration of the technologies explained above by means of DRMAA. The OGF *Distributed Resource Management Application API Working Group* (DRMAA-WG)[1] has developed an API specification for job submission, monitoring and control that provides a high level interface with *Distributed Resource Management Systems* (DRMS) [3]. In this way, DRMAA could aid scientists and engineers to express their computational problems by providing a portable direct interface to DRMS. DRMAA has been the first recommendation proposed by the OGF.

The functional description of the system was devised as follows: GRID superscalar runtime generates tasks that will be submitted to the GridWay metascheduler taking into account data dependencies between the tasks. The GridWay

---

[1] http://www.drmaa.org

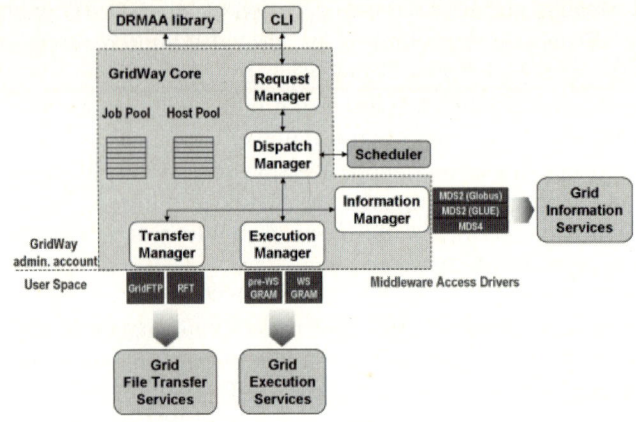

Fig. 2. Architecture of the GridWay Metascheduler

metascheduler receives the tasks submitted by GRID superscalar runtime, following the DRMAA standard, and run them in a remote resource through Globus Toolkit 4. GRIDSs polls GridWay for notifications on job state changes. The application makes several requests to GRIDSs runtime, which derives in the creation of a task in the task-graph. This task, whenever does not have data dependencies with other tasks, is submitted to GridWay for execution in a remote resource.

4.1 DRMAA Implementation in GridWay Metascheduler

In the following list we describe the DRMAA interface routines implemented in GridWay [4]:

- Initialization and finalization routines: drmaa_init and drmaa_exit.
- Job template routines: drmaa_set_attribute, drmaa_allocate_job_template and drmaa_delete_job_template. These routines enable the manipulation of job definition entities (job templates) to set parameters such as the executable, its arguments or the standard input/output streams.
- Job submission routines: drmaa_run_job and drmaa_run_bulk_jobs. GridWay has native support for *bulk* jobs, defined as a group of n similar jobs with a separate job id.
- Job monitoring and control routines: drmaa_control, drmaa_wait, drmaa_ps, drmaa_synchronize... These routines are used for holding, releasing, suspending, resuming and killing jobs, to monitor job status (see Figure 3), to wait for the completion of a job and check its exit status, or to synchronize jobs.
- Auxiliary routines: These routines are needed to obtain a textual representation of errors and other DRMAA implementation-specific information.

GridWay provides both C and Java bindings for DRMAA, as a dynamic library (`libdrmaa.so`), and as a JAR package (`drmaa.jar`), respectively. It also provides binding for scripting languages like Python, Perl and Ruby by using SWIG. Thanks to the use of DRMAA, only slight changes (mainly related to file manipulation) were needed in GridWay.

4.2 DRMAA Usage in GRIDSs

We faced here problems with the job submission with DRMAA and with the direct transfer of files, both of them related to the implementation of the file transfer and resource selection policy in GRIDSs. As explained in section 3.1 originally, GRIDSs decides where to submit a job taking into account the task resource requirements and its own information about file location. With the integration with GridWay, we faced two options: either to delegate GridWay the decision where to execute the tasks, but this would have meant either losing the file-locality exploitation policy or a large reimplementation of GridWay; or to allow GRIDSs to take the resource selection decisions. Current implementation is based on the second option, using GridWay in order to get information regarding the available machines.

Another problem detected is that GRIDSs is event-driven, while DRMAA only provides polling and blocking synchronization routines. This is due to the fact that GRIDSs originally worked with Globus directly, which gives notifications about the change of the jobs status. DRMAA blocking synchronization routines are just about one job status change, and that is when the job status changes to finished. This is not enough for GRIDSs, since it needs to know other changes as well, like from Queued to Running (as seen in Figure 3), to take better advantage of file locality, since then it knows that data needed for one job and that may be useful for another is already present in a particular worker node. To overcome this problem GRIDSs changed the way it waits for events, implementing a proactive polling to GridWay using DRMAA polling routines that enables it to be aware of GridWay jobs state changes.

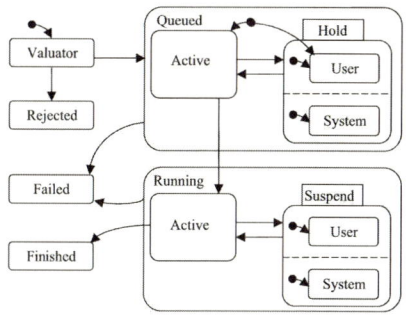

Fig. 3. DRMAA job state transition diagram [3]

4.3 Portal Development

We've implemented a Web Portal for providing the end-users a graphical, easy to use interface for some of the main functionalities of GridAD, these are: File management, uploading and downloading of files, let it be source code files or data files; and binary application deployments to worker nodes. The second functionality requires the portal the ability to deal with source code and being able to send the code to all the machines in the grid as well as compiling that code in the machines and checking the results.

The portal is implemented using GridSphere 2.2.9 [9], which is a portlet based open-source portal framework which supports an interface for working with the Globus Toolkit version 4. The deployment functionality of the portal is based on the GRID superscalar Deployment Center [1], a java based tool, which deploys the code and compiles it in all worker nodes on an execution. This application has been migrated to portlets, which run within the GridSphere framework and we've used the GridSphere grid framework (Gridportlets) to implement the usage of grid services from the portal. With this new grid portlet and MyProxy [10], the user can easily upload the source code of his/her application into the portal, from there select the machines that will run the application, splitting them between workers and a master node and then deploy the code, which will be compiled in a transparent way in each machine, and leave the system ready to be run.

5 Experiences

In the framework of the BE14 experiment, an application is presented that integrates the computation stages of a high-throughput environment for product and process development. The experiment allows the integration of models for optimization and simulation providing a flexible environment on top of GridAD [11,12]. As a result of using the grid, the performance of the experiment is dramatically increased. The high-throughput environment involves generic stages common to a variety of industrial problems, product synthesis applications, process design, materials design, and high-throughput experimentation in specialties, pharmaceuticals, and high-value chemicals. Such problems involve multiple runs, each using availablephysico-chemical and economic data, to target and screen options for products and processes. The combined use of computer and experiments is seen as the future environment for the development of novel products and processes.

In the specific experiment a process and catalyst development problems are modelled mathematically and solved with a combination of stochastic algorithms, deterministic algorithms, and graph-based methods. Among others, the application inputs contain (see Figure 4) superstructure models, kinetic data, configuration seeds and solver controls. The stochastic search takes the form of a Tabu search with parallel steps for intensification and diversification. In each step of the Tabu search, m different initial solutions goes through s slots, and in each slot 4 tasks are executed. Therefore, the number of tasks in one slot is $m \times s \times 4$. The system then updates the solutions with the best results, and the

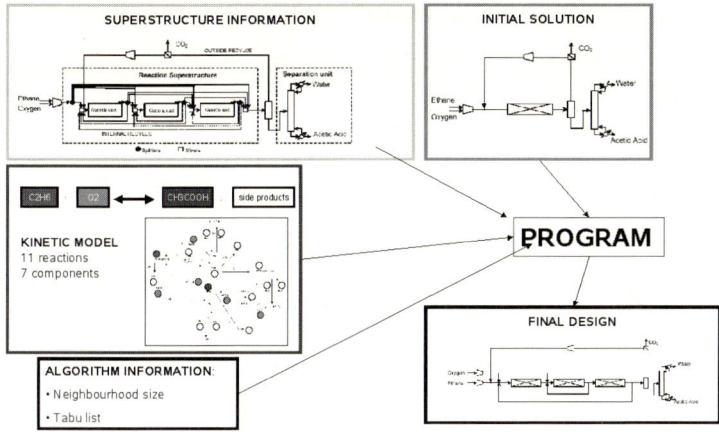

Fig. 4. Application environment

process is repeated i iterations and h times for a neighborhood factor. The total number of simulations is calculated as $m \times s \times 3 \times i \times h$ since one of the 4 initial tasks is very small.

The original sequential code was written in Fortran. Since GRIDSs does not currently support Fortran, the main program of the application, that follows an optimization TABU search scheme, was re-written in C. The computational intensive parts of the application were kept in Fortran and linked to the main program through C wrappers. This new code is still sequential and to adapt it to GRIDSs, a few calls to the GRIDSs API are added in the main program (2 or 3 calls) and the GRIDSs IDL file is written, which includes the interfaces of the computational tasks. The application code is then deployed in the grid using the portal and afterwards run in the grid. At runtime, the GRIDSs runtime exploits the concurrency between the tasks of the application and GridWay manage and monitors the task execution.

Table 1 presents a summary of statistical information for three different processes: a Van de Vusse kinetic scheme, a catalyst design experiment for acetic acid production, and a biotechnology (biocatalytic) process with excessive requirements for computing. The number of tasks and simulations required for each experiment are summarized in table 1. Real-life applications would require multiples of such simulations (typically by 3-5 orders of magnitude).

Main barriers for the adoption of the grid technology have been the differences in the supporting environment: whereas the language bindings offered by GRIDSs are mainly C/C++ (and Java) and GRIDSs can only run on Linux/UNIX based platforms (due to GT4), the user application is in Fortran (as many similar industrial models) and the users' environment is based on Windows OS. The language barrier was overcome by the use of wrappers from C to Fortran. The implementation of the portal subsequently allows now to link Windows OS to a grid based on Linux/UNIX machines.

Table 1. Summary of application cases configuration

Application case	Van de Vusse	Acetic Acid	Biocatalytic
Number of initial solutions (m)	10	6	6
Number of slots (s)	50	20	50
Number of tasks (N)	2,000	480	1,200
Number of iterations per slot (i)	5	5	35
Neighborhood size (h)	7	20	20
Total number of tasks (n)	52,500	36,000	157,500
Sequential execution time	5 hours 22 mins	90 hours	55 hours
Grid execution time	40 mins 45 secs	15 hous 6 mins	7 hours
Speed up	8	6	7.9

GridAD environment has been installed and deployed in a grid composed by 3-site machines (UCM in Madrid, BSC in Barcelona and UniS in Surrey) with up to 20 servers. Preliminary execution results are also shown in Table 1. For these runs, 5 machines were used, with 8 workers. The speedup regarding the initial execution time is given as a reference of the speedup observed by the final user, although this speedup can be missleading: the reference sequential execution time was obtained using a different environment (the original workstation used by the final user) with different Operating System and performance characteristics. In any case, this results have been considered very promising for the final users. The results explain that a computer-based, high-throughput experimentation is now possible and viable. The deployment of a larger network of computers and better automation could further offer much smaller times to handle the actual volume of experiments in real-life problems. Moreover, the authors currently research asynchronous versions of the optimization search to reap additional benefits in the intelligence of the search and a better parallelization of the computing.

6 Conclusions and Future Work

GridAD benefits from its components. From GRIDSs takes the ability to be able to write gridified applications in a really easy way, by just defining which functions we want to execute remotely on an IDL file. GRIDSs then automatically generated the necessary code and in run-time it uses techniques to assure an optimal use of data locality. From GridWay it takes the fault tolerance mechanisms, the ability to dynamically deploy the application, the ability to interoperate with different middlewares (EGEE, TeraGrid, Open Science Grid ,etc) and the resource provisioning among others. Also, there are benefits for their separated components. We can see this in the use of DRMAA for the components communication, how it benefits GRIDSs since now it can be plugged to traditional DRMS and run the application on a local cluster or it can be plugged to GridWay and run it on a grid infrastructure.

The paper presented the application of a high-throughput prototype that would enable the synthesis and design of novel products and processes. The use of grids facilitated the combined deployment of optimization and simulation searches, using problems and data from real-life cases. Grid-enabled computing produces realistic times to complete the experiments and reports a rather promising message for the future of similar applications. Work in progress includes the gridification of the algorithmic stages, the automation of the underlying workflows, and the parallel visualization of the synthesis search, all beyond the scope of our initial effort.

One should note that there exist hundreds of thousands of models in reaction, separation, catalysis, and energy integration. On the basis of the evidence shown in the paper, one could envisage future utility services that could be offered through the grid. Apparently, future models are left with a task to upgrade their communication capabilities, possibly through ontologies and semantics, so that to fully exploit the available computing power and enable their abilities to integrate in similar high-throughput experiments.

References

1. Badia, R.M., Labarta, J., Sirvent, R., Pérez, J.M., Cela, J.M., Grima, R.: Programming grid applications with grid superscalar. Journal of Grid Computing 1(2), 151–170 (2003)
2. Huedo, E., Montero, R.S., Llorente, I.M.: A Framework for Adaptive Execution on Grids. Software - Practice and Experience 34(7), 631–651 (2004)
3. Rajic, H., Brobst, R., Chan, W., Ferstl, F., Gardiner, J., Robarts, J.P., Haas, A., Nitzberg, B., Tollefsrud, J.: Distributed Resource Management Application API Specification 1.0. Technical report, DRMAA Working Group – The Global Grid Forum (2003)
4. Herrera, J., Huedo, E., Montero, R.S., Llorente, I.M.: GridWay DRMAA 1.0 Implementation – Experience Report. Document GFD.E-104, DRMAA Working Group – Open Grid Forum (2007)
5. GRID superscalar website, http://www.bsc.es/grid/gridsuperscalar
6. website, G.: GridWay Metascheduler website, http://www.gridway.org
7. GridWay dev.globus website, http://dev.globus.org/wiki/GridWay
8. Globus Toolkit website, http://www.globus.org
9. Gridsphere website, http://www.gridsphere.org
10. MyProxy website, http://grid.ncsa.uiuc.edu/myproxy
11. Antonopoulos, N., Linke, P., Kokossis, A.: A prototype GRID framework for the Chemical Process Industries. Chemical Engineering Communications 192(10-12), 1258–1271 (2005)
12. A., K.: Modelling power as a utility. White Paper for the future of simulation, optimization, and engineering computing (2005)

Building Hierarchical Grid Storage Using the GFARM Global File System and the JUXMEM Grid Data-Sharing Service

Gabriel Antoniu[1,*], Loïc Cudennec[1], Majd Ghareeb[1], and Osamu Tatebe[2]

[1] INRIA/IRISA, Campus de Beaulieu,
F-35042 Rennes Cedex, Rennes, France
Gabriel.Antoniu@inria.fr
[2] University of Tsukuba, Japan

Abstract. As more and more large-scale applications need to generate and process very large volumes of data, the need for adequate storage facilities is growing. It becomes crucial to efficiently and reliably store and retrieve large sets of data that may be shared at the global scale. Based on previous systems for global data sharing (global file systems, grid data-sharing services), this paper proposes a hierarchical approach for grid storage, which combines the access efficiency of RAM storage with the scalability and persistence of the global file system approach. Our proposal has been validated through a prototype that couples the GFARM file system with the JUXMEM data-sharing service. Experiments on the Grid'5000 testbed confirm the advantages of our approach.

1 Introduction

An increasing number of applications in various fields (such as genetics, nuclear physics, health, environment, cosmology, etc.) are nowadays exploiting large-scale, distributed computing infrastructures for simulation or information processing. This leads to the generation of very large volumes of data. The need to store, manage and process these data in a proper way leads to several important requirements. First, a *large storage capacity* is needed. Second, as these large volumes of data may be produced by (or used as an input for) long and costly computations, *data persistence* is essential. To address these requirements, file-based secondary storage has usually been favored in most grid storage systems. On the other hand, data need to be *efficiently* accessed in a *distributed* way at a large scale. As the cost of disk read/write operations may significantly limit the performance of data accesses, the use of faster-access RAM storage appears as a promising approach. The concept of *grid-data sharing service* [1,2] explores this idea by providing the abstraction of a globally shared memory space, built by aggregating the RAM storage made available by thousands of grid nodes. However, the overall storage capacity is limited to the aggregated RAM storage available.

This paper proposes an architecture for large-scale, distributed grid storage whose goal is to leverage *at the same time* the efficiency of RAM accesses and the larger-capacity, persistent disk storage available on a grid. Our architecture implements a

---

* Corresponding author.

grid-scale memory hierarchy by interconnecting a grid data-sharing service (acting as a grid-scale RAM) and a grid file system.

The remaining of the paper is organized as follows. Section 2 discusses related work. Section 3 briefly describes the two systems on which we rely: the JUXMEM grid data-sharing service and the GFARM grid file system; then, it introduces our hybrid architecture. Section 4 gives details on the interaction between the two systems. An experimental evaluation of our approach is presented in Section 5. Section 6 concludes the paper and discusses future research directions.

2 Related Work

One of the major goals of grid infrastructures is to *transparently* provide access to computational and storage resources, by hiding the details about which resources are used and where they are located, as much as possible. Regarding data storage and management, this goal is still far from being achieved, as most current grid data management systems require *explicit* data transfers before and after the computations. GridFTP [3], Chirp [4] are typical examples of two file transfer tools adapted to grid infrastructures, providing for instance support for parallel streams, authentication, checkpoint/restart in case of failures, etc. Based on such tools, catalogue-based data localization and management services have been built, such as RLS [5], Reptor [6], Optor [6], LDR [7]. Such catalogues allow the user to manually register and characterize data copies, but do not provide any support for transparent access, nor for automatic consistency maintenance.

In contrast, the concept of *grid file system* provides a familiar, file-oriented API allowing to transparently access physically distributed data through globally unique, logical file paths. The applications simply open and access such files as if they were stored on a local file system. A very large distributed storage space is thus made available to existing applications that usually use file storage, with no need for modifications. This approach has been taken by a few projects like GFARM [8], GridNFS [9], LegionFS [10], etc.

The transparent data access model is equally defended by the concept of *grid data-sharing service*, illustrated by the JUXMEM platform (described in detail in the next section). This service provides the grid applications with the abstraction of a globally shared memory in which data can be easily stored and accessed through global identifiers. Compared to the grid file system approach, this approach improves *access efficiency* by totally relying on RAM storage. Besides the fact that a RAM access is more efficient than a disk access, the system can leverage locality-optimization schemes developed within the Distributed Shared Memory (DSM) consistency protocols that serve as a basis for the system's design. However, the system's storage capacity is limited by the overall RAM available on the infrastructure.

3 Combining RAM and Disk Storage to Achieve Scalability, Persistence and Efficiency

As previously shown, grid file systems provide a convenient way to persistently store very large volumes of data into distributed files, whereas memory-based grid data-sharing services provide a more efficient data access. To address all these issues *at the same time*, we propose a hierarchical storage system that combines a data sharing service with a grid file system.

3.1 The JUXMEM Data Sharing Service

Providing a transparent data access model in an efficient way has been one of the major motivations of research efforts on distributed shared memory (DSM) systems [11].

However, the efficiency of traditional DSM consistency protocols has not proved scalable. As the grids brought forward new hypotheses (a larger scale, a dynamic infrastructure with increased failure probability), a new approach to transparent memory-based data sharing was needed. To address this challenge, the concept of *grid data sharing service* has been proposed [1]. The idea is to rely on results from several areas: location-transparent access and consistency protocols of DSM systems; algorithms for fault-tolerant distributed systems; scalability and techniques to support volatility in peer-to-peer (P2P) systems.

From the user's point of view, JUXMEM provides an API inspired by DSM systems allowing to perform memory allocation, data access through global IDs (e.g. pointers), and lock-based synchronization. Users can dynamically allocate shared memory using the juxmem_malloc primitive, which returns a global data ID. This ID can be used by other nodes in order to access existing data, through the use of the juxmem_mmap function. It is the responsibility of the implementation of the grid data-sharing service to localize the data and perform the necessary data transfers based on this ID. This is how a grid data-sharing service provides a *transparent* access to data. Both juxmem_malloc and juxmem_mmap primitives provide a local pointer that can be used to directly access the data. Note that, at the implementation level, the juxmem_mmap primitive does not rely on the mmap call. It will provide the calling client with a full copy of the data, whatever the grain of the subsequent accesses made by that client.

JUXMEM's architecture mirrors a grid consisting of a federation of distributed clusters and it is therefore expressed in terms of *hierarchical* groups of nodes. In order to cope with possible failures that may threaten data persistence, JUXMEM includes automatic replication mechanisms. When allocating a memory block, the client may specify: 1) on how many clusters the data should be replicated; 2) on how many providers in each cluster the data should be replicated; 3) the consistency protocol that should be used to manage the access to this data. As a result of the allocation procedure, a set of distributed replicas are created, called *data group*. This group has a fault-tolerant, self-organizing behavior: failures of its members are automatically detected, and failed nodes are transparently replaced, in order to maintain the replication degrees specified by the user. To do this transparently, while guaranteeing the correctness of the data accesses that may take place during the failures, we rely on fault-tolerant algorithms for group membership and atomic multicast. To favor scalability and take into account the latency hierarchy previously discussed, hierarchical adaptations of these algorithms are implemented (see [2] for details).

From an implementation point of view, the fault-tolerant algorithms used are leader-based.

The main consistency model provided by JUXMEM is *entry consistency*, first introduced in [12]. In this model, which we consider as well-adapted to grid data sharing, processes that need to access data need to properly synchronize by acquiring a lock associated to that data. This is done by calling juxmem_acquire_read (prior to a read access) or juxmem_acquire (prior to a write access). Note that juxmem_acquire_read allows multiple readers to simultaneously access the same data. The juxmem_release primitive must be called after the access, to release the lock. These synchronization primitives allow the implementation to provide consistency guarantees according to the consistency protocol specified by the user at the allocation time.

3.2 The GFARM Distributed File System

GFARM FS is a distributed file system federating local file systems. Typically, it federates local file systems on compute nodes in several clusters. A node that provides a local file system is called a *file system node*.

Physically, files can be replicated and stored on any file system node, but can be accessed transparently by a client. File replicas can be created by a GFARM *replicate* command from a file system node to another file system node. Consistency among file replicas is maintained by a close-to-open consistency like AFS [13] when a file is updated. Every other out-of-date file replicas except an up-to-date replica will be deleted when the updated file is closed.

GFARM FS is designed to achieve scalable file I/O performance in a distributed environment by *putting priority to a local file system*, and *file-affinity scheduling*. When a client is also a file system node, the local file system is a part of a GFARM FS. The data transfer from file system nodes to a client can be reduced by exploiting local file access. When a new file is created, the file is created on the local file system if there is enough disk space. When one of file replicas is stored on a local file system, the local file replica is chosen to be accessed. A file-affinity scheduling is a scheduling policy of a process allocation such that a file system node that has a specified file replica has priority to be scheduled. This increases a chance of a local file access.

GFARM FS consists of a file system metadata server and multiple file system nodes. A file system daemon called *gfsd* runs on every file system node. Client nodes access a GFARM FS by mounting it. It is developed in open source at http://sourceforge.net/projects/gfarm/.

3.3 Our Proposal: A Hybrid Grid Memory Hierarchy

In order to take advantage of the more persistent, larger-capacity storage provided by the GFARM grid file system, while keeping data access efficient (i.e. not impacted by disk access delays), our approach consists in *using* GFARM *as secondary storage for the* JUXMEM *data sharing service*. The main idea is to allow applications to use JUXMEM's more efficient memory-oriented API, while letting JUXMEM to persistently store data on disk files by making calls to GFARM in the background. These calls are internally issued by JUXMEM, so they are totally transparent to the user, as illustrated on Figure 1. Besides, as explained in Section 4, their cost is also generally transparent, as the disk accesses are performed asynchronously in most cases, in order to avoid them to impact the efficiency of the application's data accesses.

With respect to persistence, as seen in the previous section, JUXMEM already enhances data availability in the presence of failures by using data replication strategies. However, every piece of data is stored in physical memory, making this system prone to hard failures of nodes. JUXMEM's consensus algorithm used to implement atomic multicast and group membership operations, supports multiple simultaneous failures within each any group of replicas, as long as a majority of nodes remain correct in the group. However, in a grid, failures of whole clusters may happen (e.g. due to air conditioning problems). This leads to the loss of all data stored exclusively in RAM, if all replicas are stored within the failing cluster. In the context of heavy, long-duration scientific applications, it may be costly (if ever possible) to regenerate the data, e.g. by restarting the computation that produced it. A more efficient approach to ensure data persistence is to use secondary, disk-based storage. Another scenario where disk storage is more appropriate than RAM storage corresponds to situation where data is read and processed a long time after it has been produced (e.g. after several weeks).

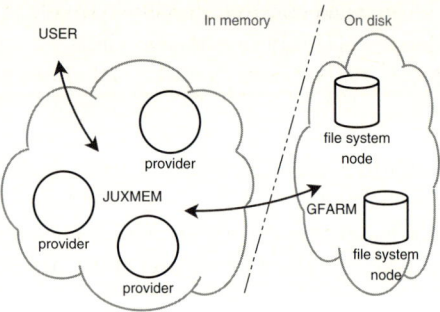

Fig. 1. The JUXMEM- GFARM architecture

Finally, thanks to the use of GFARM, the storage space made available to applications that use JUXMEM's memory-oriented API is significantly increased: JUXMEM can act as a shared cache for actively accessed data, while GFARM ensures a large capacity for long term storage.

4 Implementing the JUXMEM-GFARM Interaction

In the approach presented here, we have chosen to exhibit the memory-oriented API provided by the JUXMEM data-sharing to the grid applications: the user can dynamically allocate memory in the grid storage space, map it to its own address space and access it through local pointers. On the other side, we internally use GFARM's global IDs (i.e. globally shared file names) to persistently store JUXMEM's shared data on physical files, but these IDs, as well as the usage of this file-oriented API are hidden from the user.

We therefore need to define which JUXMEM entities should interact with GFARM, when JUXMEM should flush data to GFARM and when this data should be restored to JUXMEM. In the first version of our hybrid architecture, we decide that, for each data, a single JUXMEM provider should interact with GFARM, as a client: the data group leader. Note that JUXMEM and GFARM storage systems may share (or not!) the same physical nodes for data storage. Setting up physically distinct topologies may however be justified by the different requirements of JUXMEM (size of physical memory) and GFARM (available disk space), but also by the need to enhance fault tolerance.

4.1 Flushing Data from JUXMEM to GFARM

For the sake of simplicity, we have chosen to flush data to GFARM whenever a client updates the corresponding JUXMEM memory providers at the end of a critical section during which the data is modified. According to the *entry consistency* protocol currently implemented within JUXMEM, this happens each time a client releases the lock associated to the data. Using this particular moment enforces the atomicity of the write operation in GFARM: no JUXMEM client can access the data until both shared memory and file system versions are synchronized. (This basic setting can further be refined by tuning the flush frequency as a more complex function of the data modification frequency.)

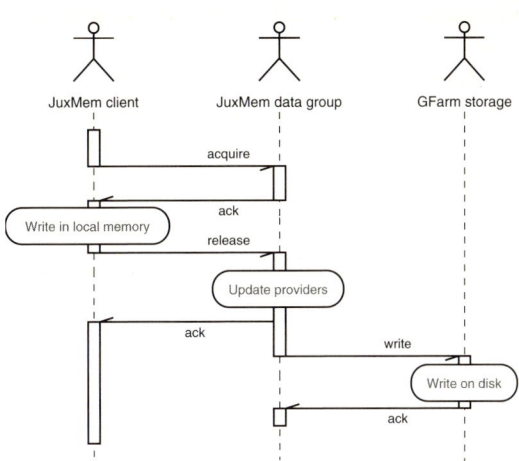

Fig. 2. Sequence diagram of basic JUXMEM-GFARM interactions

Figure 2 describes the interactions needed between the main entities involved in a flush operation, for a basic scenario where the user performs an *acquire-write-release* sequence. Once the user acquires the lock, it gets the data from the corresponding data group; it can then modify the data in its local memory, as exclusive access is guaranteed. When the client releases the lock, the modified data is sent to the data group. All members of the data group update their copy and an acknowledgment is sent to the client to let it continue his computation, while the data group leader flushes the data into a logical GFARM file uniquely identified by a file name identical to the corresponding JuxMem data id. To further improve fault tolerance, this file containing raw data may subsequently be replicated on several GFARM file storage nodes using the dedicated GFARM *replicate* command. This GFARM replication degree can be specified when allocating the memory in JUXMEM for that data.

Note that the acknowledgement to the client is sent before the completion of the flush to GFARM. This asynchronous strategy improves performance on the client side, as it does not need to wait the data to be written in GFARM before proceeding to the next computation. However, in order to maintain data consistency, the associated lock can not be re-assigned until the data has been written in both systems. Any node which subsequently tries to acquire the associated lock in exclusive mode will be blocked until the data flush to GFARM is complete. However, read operations can proceed in parallel with the flush operation. The benefits of our asynchronous scheme are therefore real for write-once data, or if the frequency of writes to the same data does not fall under a threshold where clients have to wait for JUXMEM and GFARM updates. This threshold depends on the data size and on network communication performance.

Data flushing from JUXMEM to GFARM introduces an overhead discussed in section 5. If during a computation step the write frequency to some data is too high, the time needed to flush into GFARM may degrade the user application performances. In that case, it may be assumed that this computation step is short enough to decide a lower frequency for data flushes to GFARM (e.g. one flush every ten modifications instead of one flush after *each* modification). Flush frequency to GFARM should thus be seen as a finely tuned parameter that makes a trade-off between reliability and performance.

4.2 Restoring Data from GFARM to JUXMEM

Restoring data consists in reading a data from the file system in order to store it in the data sharing service. This operation occurs in two cases: 1) a JUXMEM client accesses a data that is no longer in the service, because of failures or because it was produced a long time before; and 2) the user would like to restore a given version of the data within a rollback procedure. As for flushing, one of the simplest way to achieve the restoring operation is to use the data group leader for reading the data from the file system.

When a client requires access to some data, the JUXMEM service is queried to check if the corresponding data group is still present in memory. If not, the corresponding file (if any) is searched for in the GFARM file system, using the *data ID* specified by the client. If the data is found in GFARM, a corresponding JUXMEM data group is created, then the data is sent to the client.

5 Feasibility Study: Evaluation

We have designed and implemented a prototype in which the JUXMEM data-sharing service uses GFARM according to the interaction scheme explained in Section 4. We use our prototype to run a synthetic application simulating producer-consumer access patterns. Each piece of data is written *once* and can be accessed independently. This scenario is inspired by real applications, such as climate (e.g. ocean-atmosphere) modeling applications based on code-coupling [14]. We measure the average time to write (respectively read) a piece of data by performing 20 successive accesses. *The goal of this preliminary evaluation is to show that thanks to our combined approach, the JUXMEM service is enhanced with persistence guarantees provided by* GFARM, *whereas the access cost remains the same (i.e. not impacted by disk access delays) in most cases.*

Evaluations are performed using the Grid'5000 [15] testbed. We use 7 nodes of a Grid'5000 cluster made of Intel Xeon 5148 LV CPUs running at 2.3 GHz, outfitted with 4 GB of RAM each, SATA hard drives (57 MB/s peak throughput) and interconnected by a Gigabit Ethernet network. The theoretical maximum network bandwidth is thus 125 MB/s; however, if we consider the IP and TCP header overhead, this maximum becomes slightly lower: 117.5 MB/s when MTU = 1500 B. GFARM runs on 3 nodes (a metadata server, a cache metadata server, a file system node) and JUXMEM uses 4 nodes (a producer, a consumer, a manager and a memory provider also acting as a GFARM client).

In order to have a reference for our evaluation, we first ran the scenario described above using GFARM only, without JUXMEM. Read and write access times for GFARM for different data sizes, are provided on Figures 3(a) and 3(b). The average read throughput is 69 MB/s and the average write throughput is 42 MB/s. Note that GFARM's read throughput is higher than the peak hard drive throughput (57 MB/s), which indicates that GFARM benefits here from some cache effects. These results are given as reference values for comparison with the access times provided by our hierarchical grid storage system. To evaluate the cost of writing data using our hierarchical grid storage, we consider two scenarios: a common-case scenario and a worst-case scenario.

In the first scenario, we consider that write accesses to a same piece of data are infrequent. In such a case, thanks to our asynchronous scheme, the data flush to GFARM after a write session is complete before the next write to that data into JUXMEM. This is the case of all write accesses for our producer-consumer scenario, because all data are written only once. Figure 3(b) indicates a write throughput of 89 MB/s for our hierarchical storage system, *equal to the pure* JUXMEM *throughput*. This represents an improvement by 112% compared to the pure GFARM throughput (42 MB/s), essentially due to the relative costs of memory accesses compared to disk accesses. Although the data is written to GFARM in both schemes, the improvement is possible thanks to the fact that, once the data is written into JUXMEM, the producer can continue its computation while the data is flushed into GFARM. Note that the JUXMEM write cost includes the cost of synchronization (acquire/release).

In a second scenario, we consider that write accesses to a same piece of data are frequent. In this case, each write (but the first one) has to wait for the previous one to be flushed into GFARM. Basically, the access time is therefore the time to write into JUXMEM plus the time to write into GFARM. This leads to a 26 MB/s write throughput, which is slightly (7%) lower than the theoretical throughput (28.5 MB) that can be estimated based on the separate write throughputs of JUXMEM and GFARM. In this case, as explained at the end of Section 4.1, it may be reasonable to reduce the flush frequency, i.e. to allow several write sessions to JUXMEM to proceed before flushing data to GFARM.

We equally analyze the cost of reading accesses for our hierarchical grid storage using two scenarios. We first consider that the data is present in JUXMEM (i.e. in physical memory). Figure 3(a) shows the time to read a data in such a configuration. The read throughput for our hierarchical prototype is again *equal to* JUXMEM*'s read throughput* and reaches 100 MB/s in this case, i.e. an improvement by 45% compared to an optimized GFARM throughput of 69 MB/s (which already benefits from some cache effects, as explained above). For reference, we remind the reader that, theoretically, the maximum network throughput is 117 MB/s. In this configuration, we can claim that our hierarchical grid storage provides GFARM's persistence guarantees, while the user only "pays" the cost of JUXMEM accesses (which includes, as previously, the synchronization cost, and does not benefit of any specific optimization).

We also consider a reading scenario where the data is not hosted by any JUXMEM provider in physical memory, but remains available in the GFARM file system. The time to read includes the time to retrieve the data from GFARM, to store the data in JUXMEM and to send it to the client. In this configuration, the throughput reaches 39 MB/s. This is a worst-case scenario that only occurs when the data is not present in JUXMEM. Note

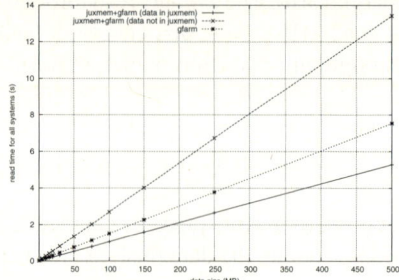 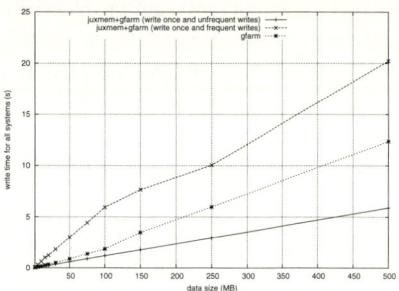

Fig. 3. Cost of read (a) and write (b) operations in JUXMEM and GFARM

that this cost is incurred only once, as subsequent read accesses to the same piece of data benefit from JUXMEM's access cost (100 MB/s).

6 Conclusion and Future Work

While grid file systems provide an elegant solution for *persistent* storage of *large volumes of data* on physically distributed files, the concept of grid data-sharing service offers *efficient* access to globally shared data by relying on RAM storage. We propose a hierarchical grid storage system that simultaneously addresses these issues, based on the JUXMEM *grid-data sharing service* and on the GFARM *grid file system*. The main idea is to allow applications to use JUXMEM's efficient memory-oriented API, while letting JUXMEM persistently and transparently store data on GFARM disk files.

Our experiments performed on the Grid'5000 testbed confirm the advantages of our approach: in most cases the data access cost is not impacted by the cost of disk accesses (100 MB/s read throughput, 89 MB/s write throughput). At the same time, thanks to GFARM, the storage space made available to applications that use JUXMEM's memory-oriented API is significantly increased: JUXMEM can act as a shared cache for actively accessed data, while GFARM ensures a large capacity for long term, persistent storage.

As a future work, we plan to extend our experiments to more complex configurations where replication is used to improve fault tolerance. We plan to evaluate the induced overhead, and to address this issue using parallel data accesses between JUXMEM providers and GFARM storage nodes. We equally intend to develop and compare multiple cache strategies allowing JUXMEM to efficiently act as a cache for actively used data, while GFARM would serve for long-term storage.

Acknowledgment. This work has been supported by the Sakura programme for bilateral Japan-France collaborations, by the AIST (Tsukuba, Japan), by the French National Agency for Research project LEGO (ANR-05-CIGC-11) and by the NEGST France-Japan research collaboration programme. It has been also supported by a grant of Sun Microsystems and a grant from the Regional Council of Brittany, France.

The experiments presented in this paper were carried out using the Grid'5000 experimental testbed, an initiative from the French Ministry of Research through the ACI

GRID incentive action, INRIA, CNRS and RENATER and other contributing partners (see http://www.grid5000.fr/).

References

1. Antoniu, G., Bougé, L., Jan, M.: JuxMem: An adaptive supportive platform for data sharing on the grid. Scalable Computing: Practice and Experience 6(3), 45–55 (2005)
2. Antoniu, G., Deverge, J.F., Monnet, S.: How to bring together fault tolerance and data consistency to enable grid data sharing. Concurrency and Computation: Practice and Experience 18(13), 1705–1723 (2006)
3. Allcock, B., Bester, J., Bresnahan, J., Chervenak, A.L., Foster, I., Kesselman, C., Meder, S., Nefedova, V., Quesnel, D., Tuecke, S.: Data management and transfer in high-performance computational grid environments. Parallel Comput. 28(5), 749–771 (2002)
4. Chirp protocol specification, http://www.cs.wisc.edu/condor/chirp/
5. Dunno, F., Gaido, L., Gishelli, A., Prelz, F., Sgaravatoo, M.: DataGrid prototype 1. EU-DataGrid collaboration. In: Proc. of the TERENA Networking Conf., Limerick, Ireland (June 2002)
6. Kunszt, P.Z., Laure, E., Stockinger, H., Stockinger, K.: File-based replica management. Future Generation Computing Systems 21(1), 115–123 (2005)
7. Lightweight data replicator, http://www.lsc-group.phys.uwm.edu/LDR/
8. Tatebe, O., Morita, Y., Matsuoka, S., Soda, N., Sekiguchi, S.: Grid datafarm architecture for petascale data intensive computing. In: Proc. 2nd IEEE/ACM Intl. Symp. on Cluster Computing and the Grid (Cluster 2002), Washington DC, USA, p. 102. IEEE Computer Society, Los Alamitos (2002)
9. Honeyman, P., Adamson, W.A., McKee, S.: GridNFS: global storage for global collaborations. In: Proc. IEEE Intl. Symp. Global Data Interoperability - Challenges and Technologies, June 2005, pp. 111–115. IEEE Computer Society, Los Alamitos (2005)
10. White, B.S., Walker, M., Humphrey, M., Grimshaw, A.S.: LegionFS: a secure and scalable file system supporting cross-domain high-performance applications. In: Proc. 2001 ACM/IEEE Conf. on Supercomputing (SC 2001), p. 59. ACM Press, New York (2001)
11. Protic, J., Tomasevic, M., Milutinovic, V.: Distributed shared memory: concepts and systems. IEEE Paralel and Distributed Technology 4(2), 63–71 (1996)
12. Bershad, B.N., Zekauskas, M.J., Sawdon, W.A.: The Midway distributed shared memory system. In: Proc. 38th IEEE Intl. Computer Conf (COMPCON Spring 1993), Los Alamitos, CA, February 1993, pp. 528–537 (1993)
13. Kazar, M.L.: Synchronization and caching issues in the andrew file system. In: USENIX Winter, pp. 27–36 (1988)
14. Valcke, S., Caubel, A., Vogelsang, R., Declat, D.: OASIS 3 user's guide. Technical Report TR/CMGC/04/68, CERFACS, Toulouse, France (2004)
15. The Grid'5000 project, http://www.grid5000.org/

Enhancing Grids for Massively Multiplayer Online Computer Games*

Sergei Gorlatch[1], Frank Glinka[1], Alexander Ploss[1], Jens Müller-Iden[1], Radu Prodan[2], Vlad Nae[2], and Thomas Fahringer[2]

[1] University of Münster, Germany
[2] University of Innsbruck, Austria

Abstract. Massively multiplayer online games (MMOG) are an innovative and challenging class of applications for Grid computing that require large amounts of computational resources for providing a responsive and scalable gameplay for concurrently participating players connected via Internet. We present our *Real-Time Framework (RTF)* – a Grid-based middleware for scaling game sessions through a variety of parallelization and distribution techniques. RTF is described within a novel multi-layer service-oriented architecture that comprises three advanced services – monitoring, capacity planning, and runtime steering – that use the potential of Grid computing to provide pervasive access to a potentially unbounded number of resources. We report experimental results on the quality of our capacity planning and scalability of the RTF distribution mechanism.

1 Motivation

Online gaming and applications based on it (training, simulation-driven e-learning, etc.) have recently become a major worldwide trend and are experiencing a tremendous growth. Currently, at any time of the day, more than 250.000 users are online playing *First Person Shooter (FPS)* games on more than 70.000 servers worldwide [9]. The *Steam* platform reports 140.000 servers with more than 2.8 million users monthly for the games on that platform [7].

We consider *Massively Multiplayer Online Games (MMOG)* as an innovative, challenging, and promising application area for Grid computing. Our work aims at using Grid concepts for overcoming the main problems of contemporary online game technology: cumbersome low-level programming, manual hosting, static resource management, and no Quality of Service (QoS) guarantees, which become problematic with a massive number of simultaneous players. At the same time, gaming has a potential to become a "killer application" for Grids and increase its visibility by targeting a huge community of non-expert users who are ready to pay for such services.

In this paper, we present the *Real-Time Framework (RTF)* providing the middleware technology for scaling game sessions through a variety of parallelization

---

* This work is supported by the EU through IST-004265 CoreGRID and IST-034601 edutain@grid projects.

and distribution techniques. RTF is described within a novel multi-layer service-oriented Grid architecture that comprises three advanced services – runtime steering, monitoring, and capacity planning – that provide efficient access to a potentially unbounded number of resources.

Existing Grid-like game infrastructures, as for example *Emergent Server* [8] or *BigWorld* [4], are restricted to so-called role-playing games; furthermore, their servers still reside statically at a particular hoster and there is no option to migrate sessions between data centers for load-balancing reasons and for enabling an open market of MMOG hosting. Our real-time framework and dynamic Grid services together support various distribution concepts (zoning, instancing and replication) especially for challenging action and real-time games, which are very performance- and latency-sensitive. RTF and the supported distribution concepts allow to overcome the saturation of computational and network resources, caused by a growing number or increasing density of online users.

We present our RTF middleware in Sect. 2, followed by the description of the overall Grid architecture with focus on capacity planning in Sect. 3. We report experimental results in Sect. 4 and conclude in Sect. 5.

2 RTF: A Grid-Based Game Middleware

The Real-Time Framework (RTF) [11] provides services for communication and computation within online games. These services allow the developer to realise a portable and scalable game completely independently from the Grid-management infrastructure.

2.1 Middleware Interface

Multiplayer online games typically simulate a spatial virtual world where a particular player moves and acts through an avatar which represents the player within the game. A game implements an endless loop, called *real-time loop*, which repeatedly updates the game state in real time.

Figure 1 shows one iteration of the server real-time loop for multiplayer games based on the client-server architecture. The figure shows one server, but on the Grid, there is usually a group of

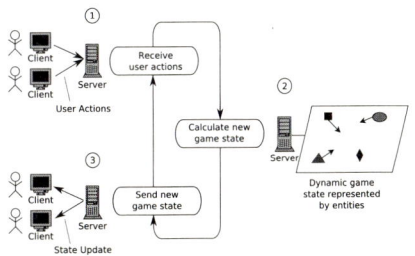

Fig. 1. Server real-time loop

server processes distributed among several machines. A loop iteration consists of three steps: At first, the clients process the users' input and transmit (step ① in the figure) them to the server. The server then calculates a new game state by applying the received user actions and the game logic to the current game state (step ②). As the result of this calculation, the states of several dynamic entities may change. The final step ③ transfers the new game state back to the clients.

From the perspective of the game developer, in steps ① and ③, one has to transfer the data structures realizing user actions and entities over the network. If the server is distributed among multiple machines, then step ② also implies the distribution of the game state and computations for its update. This brings up the task of selecting and implementing appropriate distribution concepts.

2.2 Game State Distribution

RTF supports three basic distribution concepts for multiplayer games within a multi-server architecture: *zoning*, *instancing*, *replication*. The novel feature of RTF is that it allows to combine these three concepts within one game design. Figure 2, explained in the following, shows how the distribution concepts can be combined to adapt to the needs of a particular game.

Zoning partitions the spatial world into disjoint parts, called zones (there are 4 zones in Fig. 2). Clients can move between the zones, but no inter-zone events exist and calculations in the zones are completely independent from each other. RTF enables the developer to specify the partition of the game world; it then automatically does all checks and transfers of the entities and clients as soon as they trigger a movement into another zone. Moreover, adjacent zones can be connected to each other in RTF using a combination of zoning and replication [11].

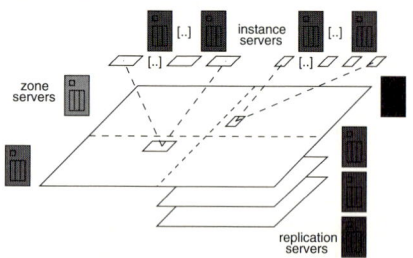

Fig. 2. Combination of zoning, instancing, and replication concepts

Instancing is used to distribute the computational load by creating multiple copies of highly frequented subareas of the spatial world. In Fig. 2 (top), two subareas are copied multiple times and assigned to instance servers. Each copy is processed completely independently of the others. RTF enables the developer to specify instance areas within the game world. Upon request, new instances are created by RTF on the available servers and clients and entities are automatically transferred into these new instances.

Replication uses the calculations for entities as a distribution criteria. The entities are distributed among all servers, such that each server has a list of so-called *active entities* which it owns and is responsible for, and a list of *shadow entities*. The shadow entities are replicated from other servers with only read-access. In Fig. 2, the lower right zone is replicated across multiple servers.

RTF allows the game developer to arbitrarily combine the three distribution approaches depending on the requirements of a particular game design. A common scenario for games includes an overall zoned game world, where dungeons are instanced for each group of players entering a dungeon. Furthermore, crowded hot spots of the game world that can not be split up into smaller zones are dynamically replicated for load-balancing reasons if a certain amount of players move into the same area. RTF provides methods for automatically routing messages to the active entity owner or the server responsible for a particular zone. Furthermore, RTF automatically manages active and shadow entities and changes active and shadow states according to the current distribution. The replication approach is comparatively new and more complex as compared to zoning and instancing, because interactions between active and shadow objects must be specially treated. However, it allows to scale the player density [12], i.e. to place more players in a fixed-sized area by using additional servers. Furthermore, the combination of zoning and replication facilitates a flexible and seamless game world despite of partitioning into zones.

2.3 Modeling and Handling the Game State

When implementing the data structures to model the game state, the developer traditionally has to consider low-level aspects of socket communication and implement individual communication protocols for the entities. Implementing efficient communication protocols for complex data structures is time-consuming, error-prone, and repetitive.

RTF liberates the developer from the details of network programming, by providing support for the transmission of complex data structures. For all transmittable objects like entities, events and messages, RTF provides an automatic serialization mechanism. Since the distribution management and hence the connections between processes are handled within RTF, the network communication is completely transparent to the game developer.

RTF provides automatic and native serialization of the entities and events defined in C++, implements marshalling and unmarshalling of data types and optimizes the bandwidth consumption of the messages. RTF solves this problem for the developer by providing a generic communication protocol implementation for all data structures following a special class hierarchy. All network-transmittable classes inherit from the base class `Serializable` of RTF. The `Serializable` interface can be a) implemented by the developer, or b) automatically implemented using the generic serialization mechanism provided by RTF. This automatic implementation is generated using convenient pre-processor macros provided by RTF. For all entities and events implemented in this manner, RTF automatically generates network-transmittable representations and uses them at runtime according to the distribution mechanisms described in Sect. 2.2.

A Real-World Example: Quake 3. In the popular game *Quake 3* [15], entities are realized as plain C-Structs. To work in the object-oriented manner of RTF, the developer has to rewrite the `playerState_t` struct as a class which inherits from `Local`, as shown in the listing below. Therefore, developers can make use of the advanced RTF-functionality easily, without having to learn a completely new description methodology.

```
class playerState_t : public RTF::Local {
private:
  rtf_int32 _pm_flags; // ducked, jump_held, etc
  // position is now part of RTF::Local, replacing:
  //vec3_t    origin;
  RTF::Vector _velocity;
  rtf_int8  _eventSequence; // index in events
  rtf_int32 _events[MAX_PS_EVENTS];
  rtf_int32 _eventParms[MAX_PS_EVENTS];
  rtf_int8  _damageCount; // health value
  rtf_int32 _weapon;         // ID of weapontype
  rtf_int32 _ammo[MAX_WEAPONS]; // ammo
  [...]};
IMPLEMENT_SERIALIZABLE( playerState_t ,
  ADD_ATTRIBUTE( playerState_t , _pm_flags );
  ADD_ATTRIBUTE( playerState_t , _velocity );
  ADD_ATTRIBUTE( playerState_t , _events, MAX_PS_EVENTS );
[...])
```

Optimized Object Transmission. When parts of the game state are replicated to the clients or the game state is mirrored to other servers, RTF ensures delta updates, i.e. only those attributes of an object are transmitted which have actually changed. This is especially important for games, because in a single tick of the real-time loop only few attributes of a particular entity usually change. Delta updates considerably reduce the amount of data transmitted over the network when the rate of attribute changes per tick is low.

Figure 3 shows how the real-time-loop works in conjunction with RTF. The clients send their user actions as events asynchronously to their server. The events are processed, the game world is updated and the game logic is executed. This finishes the loop iteration, after which the developer calls RTF's onFinishedTick() method, which transfers the updated entities in an asynchronous way to all interested clients and servers. Therefore, the game developer works on a much higher level of abstraction than traditionally (without RTF).

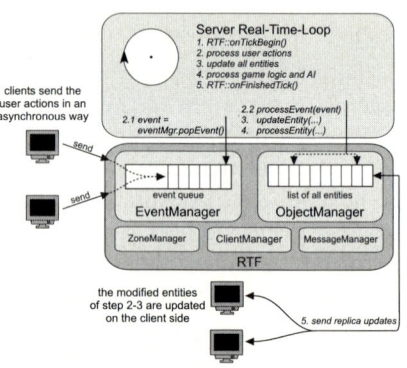

Fig. 3. Data flow in the real-time loop

3   Grid Management Architecture

The RTF middleware described above is built into the bottom layer of a Grid service-oriented architecture (depicted in Fig. 4). This architecture, only briefly introduced in this section due to lack of space, focuses on the development of generic Grid management services, while dealing with the main challenges raised by the main requirements of the targeted Grid application: scalability to thousands of online user connections, optimized allocation of resources, and monitoring and steering to maintain the QoS parameters in dynamic environments like the Grid.

The architecture is based on the interaction of four main actors. (1) *end-user* is the game player that accesses the online game sessions through graphical clients, typically purchased as a DVD; (2) *scheduler* negotiates on behalf of the end-user appropriate game sessions based on the user-centric QoS requirements (e.g. connection latency, game genre, friends, expertise); (3) *hoster* is an organization that provides some computational and network infrastructure for running game servers; (4) *resource broker* provides a mechanism for the actors to find each other in a large-scale Grid environment and negotiate QoS relationships.

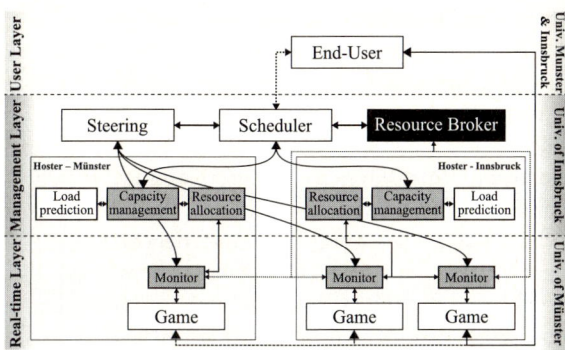

Fig. 4. Grid management architecture for online games

We employ an off-the-shelf resource broker provided by the ASKALON Grid environment [10] and only introduce the scheduling and hoster-specific services in the remainder of this section.

3.1 Scheduler Services

The Scheduler receives QoS requirements from the user which can be performance-related (e.g. maximum latency, minimum bandwidth, minimum throughput) or game-specific (e.g. game genre, minimum number of players, difficulty, tournament planning) and negotiates with existing hosters sessions that best fit these requirements. The result of the negotiation is a *service level agreement (SLA)* that must be preserved for the entire interaction of the end-user with the application.

During the execution of a game session, factors may occur which affect the performance, such that the negotiated SLAs are difficult or impossible to be further maintained. Typical perturbing factors include external load on unreliable Grid resources, or overloaded servers due to an unexpected concentration of users in certain "hot spots". The *steering service* of the scheduler interacts at runtime with the monitoring service of each hoster in the management layer for preserving the negotiated QoS parameters for the entire duration of the game session. Following an event-action paradigm, a QoS violation of an SLA triggers appropriate adaptive steering or load balancing actions using the zoning, instancing or replication APIs provided at the real-time layer.

3.2 Hoster Services

The traditional way of allocating resources in a Grid environment employs opportunistic matchmaking models based on runtime resource requests and offers [13], which are known to converge to local minima as we demonstrated in previous work [10]. From a game point of view, the two main parameters which need to be taken into account for resource allocation are capacity (e.g. memory, number of processors, latency, bandwidth) and time, expressed and negotiated by the hoster as QoS parameters. We improve on the state-of-the-art by designing a *capacity planning* service which uses hoster-specific metrics and heuristic strategies to project new SLAs (typically one or more game session connections) to offer to the scheduler before the actual negotiation takes place. This strategy has the potential to improve the resource allocation in two aspects: (1) enhanced confidence in guaranteeing the fulfillment of global QoS parameters for the entire dis-

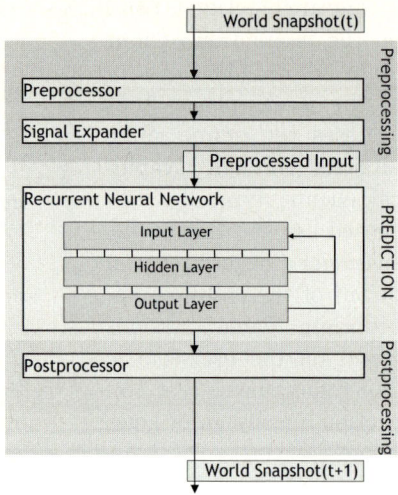

Fig. 5. Neural network for online game capacity planning

tributed game session, like smooth response time or proper load balancing, by avoiding crisis situations through ahead-planning of resource allocation; (2) optimization of local hoster-specific metrics like resource utilization or throughput.

Projecting future load in highly dynamic Grid environments of game players needs to take into account a multitude of metrics such as processor, memory, and network latencies and load. All these metrics can be deterministically expressed as a (game-specific) function of the hardest and the most unpredictable parameter which is the human factor. The load of a game session is typically determined by the concentration of entities within the game world. We therefore reduce the prediction problem to the task of estimating the entity distribution in the game world at several equidistant time intervals.

Of the two existing methods for quantitative predictions, explanatory models and time series prediction, we opted for the latter by employing prediction algorithms that use past values to discover patterns in the historical data, and extrapolate these patterns into the future. Extensive research has been done in this field [6]. As an alternative to the simple (i.e. exponential smoothing, moving average) and to the complex prediction algorithms (i.e. autoregressive models, integrated models), we present the use of neural networks [5],[14]. They are capable of approximating complex, noisy functions, provided that a good input preprocessing is performed.

Our solution is based on the deterministic relationship between the environment and players' actions. For example, an entity can not travel in certain areas of the geographic environment (e.g. mountainous barriers). Another deterministic behaviour example can be identified in team-play based games, where there is a high likelihood of players acting in close proximity groups. We exploit this semi-deterministic game play behavior as a basis for using neural networks for predicting resource demand. Obviously, evaluating and predicting at an entity-level is a difficult and inefficient task; our approach, instead, analyzes this semi-deterministic behavior at the game world level, monitoring the overall actions of entities, mass-movements, without tracking individual entities.

Neural networks are suited for predicting the generated load in such dynamic environments: they can generalize (learn) the aforementioned semi-behavior and they provide very fast predictions. Thus, we employ a neural network for load prediction that has a signal expander as input to ensure a non-linear expansion of the input space fed to the hidden neuron layers, as displayed in Fig. 5. The input fed into the preprocessing layer consists of the positions of the players in the game world at several successive equidistant time intervals (Δt). As output signal, the network provides a similar space representing a prediction of the players' layout in the next time interval ($t + \Delta t$). Because the input is expanded, the expected output will not be a precise estimation of each player's position, but a world of subarea estimations. Each zone of the map is analyzed by dividing it into subareas and providing a local prediction. An interesting aspect is that the edges of the subareas are overlapped to hide latencies upon player transitions.

In order to utilize the neural network-based prediction, two offline phases are required. The *data set collection* phase is a long process in which the game is observed by gathering entity count samples for all subareas at equidistant time steps. The training phase uses most of the previously collected samples as training sets, and the remaining as test sets. The *training phase* runs for a number of eras, until a convergence criterion is fulfilled. A training era consists of three steps: (1) presenting all the training sets in sequence to the network; (2) adjusting the network's weights to better fit the expected output (the real entity count for the next time step); and (3) testing the network's prediction capability with the different test sets.

4 Experimental Results

Grid Management Services

The resource management layer is implemented as a set of WSRF-based services deployed in the Austrian Grid [1] environment that aggregates a large collection of heterogeneous parallel computers distributed across several major cities of Austria. In order to generate demanding load patterns required for testing and validating our prediction method, we developed a distributed FPS game simulator supporting the zoning concept and inter-zone migrations of the entities. The simulator integrates RTF and is capable of generating dynamic load by simulating interaction hot-spots between large numbers of entities managed by one server. The entities in the simulation are driven by several Artificial Intelligence (AI) profiles (aggressive, team player, scout, and camper), which determine their behavior during a game session.

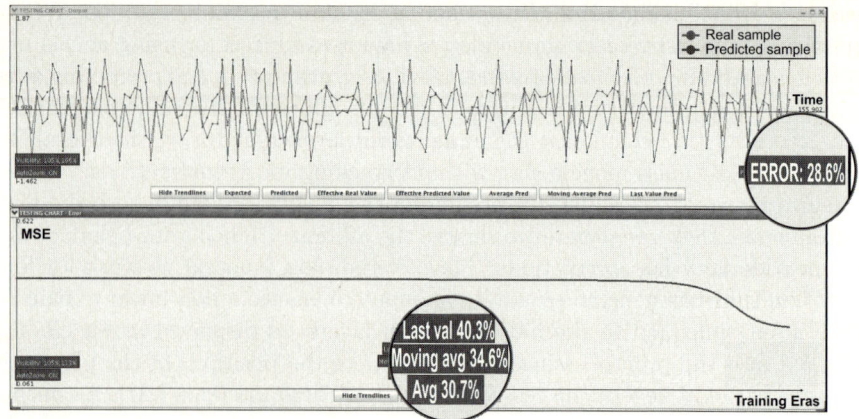

Fig. 6. Neural network prediction testing module

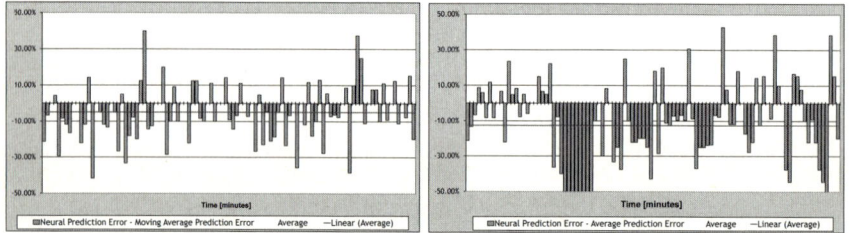

Fig. 7. Neural network prediction result comparison

For testing the load prediction service, we developed a graphical interface which allows the interactive visualization of the network training process (see Fig. 6). The top window displays the real and predicted values at consecutive steps using the training sets and the bottom window displays the error trend (either the mean squared error or the instantaneous error measured on the post-processed values). This tool offers the possibility to stop and resume the training process at any point and allows the visualization of a wide range of signals measured at different locations inside the load prediction module (pre/post-processed inputs, pre/post-processed outputs). Additionally, it offers the possibility to compare the neural prediction against other fast prediction methods such as last value, moving average, or exponential smoothing. An important contribution of this tool is the fact that it helped us analyse the output of the neural network prediction module. We observed that the shape of the output signal was similar to the one of the expected signal, but its amplitude was always smaller. This led us to the introduction of a novel additional phase called *amplitude calibration* at the end of the classical training process that significantly improved our results.

Figure 7 displays the difference between the neural network prediction error and the moving average method (left), respectively average method (right) at subsequent equidistant time intervals during a game session. Even though our method is not always the best at every single prediction step, the average of this difference displayed by the horizontal line is always below zero, which demonstrates the overall superiority of our method. The prediction improvement offered by our neural network method compared to the aforementioned fast prediction methods (moving average, exponential smoothing, etc.) ranges from 5% to 14% (even passing 14% for some data sets). This result is due to the ability of neural networks to adapt to a large variety of user load patterns which the other classical statistical methods fail to achieve.

Real-Time Framework

We also conducted preliminary performance and scalability tests for RTF with a demonstrator application that simulates a 3D world, with clients which can interact and move within this world. The simulation is updated on the server side 25 times per second and the computer-controlled clients continuously send inputs to their server. The scalability test partitions the game world into two, four or eight parts (called zones) and assigns each zone to one dedicated server. The clients are distributed equally between the servers, but can move between the zones. A heterogeneous setup of PCs with 2.66GHz, CoreDuo 2 CPUs and 4GB RAM in a LAN setup was used for servers and clients. As metric for both tests, the average CPU utilization was measured. The results in Fig. 8 show that the RTF prototype implementation already achieves more than 160 clients on a single server machine. The multi-server test-case (Fig. 8) allows to increase the number of participating clients nearly by factor two, four or eight by using the zoning distribution concept of the RTF among multiple servers.

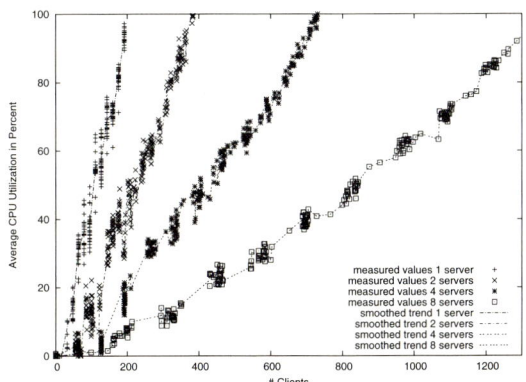

Fig. 8. CPU utilization for different numbers of servers

5 Conclusion and Related Work

We presented a novel, Grid-based approach for massively multiplayer online games. Our comprehensive service-oriented architecture consists of a variety of services that address the specific challenges of online games in comparison to conventional Grid applications, e.g. parameter study or scientific workflows: (1) the application often supports a very large number of concurrent users connecting to a single application instance; (2) the application mediates and responds in real-time to highly frequent user interactions; (3) the applications must deliver and maintain user interactivity; (4) the application is highly dynamic, and adaptive to changing loads and levels of user interaction; (5) the users connect to the application in an ad-hoc manner; (6) users and service providers interact as a community which, in contrast to traditional cooperative Virtual Organizations, compete with (or even try to cheat) each other. We also presented a load prediction system based on neural networks, basis of a load balancing service. Neural networks have been previously used with the final purpose of load balancing [2]. However, this approach differs from our system in two major aspects: (1) it uses winner-take-all neural networks and (2) it realises the load balancing at a generic task level, whereas our system provides real-time load predictions using specific internal application information, which are eventually used for load balancing decisions.

The main novel features of our RTF middleware are as follows: (1) Highly optimized and dynamic real-time communication links adapt to changes in the dynamic Grid environment and can automatically and transparently redirect the communication to new servers; (2) Hidden background mechanisms allow the runtime transfer and redistribution of parts of a game onto additional Grid resources without noticeable interruptions for the users; (3) A high-level interface for the game developer abstracts the game processing from the location of the participating resources; (4) Monitoring data are gathered in the background and used by the management layer for capacity planning. RTF implements novel parallelization concepts, in particular replication in combination with zoning, which allows to scale the density of players inside a zone. These features distinguish RTF, e.g, from [16], where *gamelets* are related to RTF's zones but no extensive support for replication is given and monitoring is currently restricted to CPU load and network metrics of a host for load-balancing decisions. The *Colyseus* [3] system on the other hand has advanced support for the replication concept, but does not integrate instancing and zoning seamlessly into the game development process.

Currently, our real-time framework and grid services are developed in cooperation with game developing companies which test and use RTF for their new game projects. Future work will investigate in which way latency and responsiveness is affected and can potentially improved by various grid-resource usage scenarios, in particular the applicability of geographically distributed servers for zoning and replication.

Acknowledgements

We like to thank the anonymous reviewers, whose comments helped us a lot to improve this paper. The work described in this paper is supported by the EU through IST-004265 CoreGRID and IST-034601 edutain@grid projects.

References

1. The Austrian Grid Consortium, http://www.austriangrid.at
2. El-Bendary, M.I., El-Abd, A.E.: A neural network approach for dynamic load balancing in homogeneous distributed systems. In: HICSS. Software Technology and Architecture, vol. 1, p. 628 (1997)
3. Bharambe, A., Pang, J., Seshan, S.: Colyseus: a distributed architecture for online multiplayer games. In: NSDI 2006, Berkeley, CA, USA, p. 12. USENIX Association (2006)
4. BigWorld. Bigworld Technology, http://www.bigworldtech.com
5. Bishop, C.M.: Neural Networks for Pattern Recognition. Oxford University Press, Oxford (1996)
6. Box, G.E.P., Jenkins, G.M., Reinsel, G.C.: Time Series Analysis, Forecasting and Control. Prentice Hall, Englewood Cliffs (1994)
7. Valve Corporation. Steam platform, http://www.steampowered.com
8. Emergent Game Technologies, http://www.emergent.net
9. IGN Entertainment. Gamespy, http://www.gamespy.com
10. Fahringer, T., Prodan, R., et al.: Askalon: A grid application development and computing environment. In: GRID 2005, Seattle, Washington, USA, pp. 122–131. IEEE Computer Society, Los Alamitos (2005)
11. Glinka, F., Ploss, A., Müller-Iden, J., Gorlatch, S.: RTF: A real-time framework for developing scalable multiplayer online games. In: NetGames 2007, Melbourne, Australia, pp. 81–86 (2007)
12. Müller, J., Gorlatch, S.: Rokkatan: Scaling an RTS game design to the massively multiplayer realm. ACM Computers in Entertainment 4(3), 11 (2006)
13. Raman, R., Livny, M., Solomon, M.H.: Matchmaking: An extensible framework for distributed resource management. Cluster Computing 2(2), 129–138 (1999)
14. Ripley, B.D.: Pattern Recognition and Neural Networks. Cambridge University Press, Cambridge (1996)
15. ID Software. Quake 3, http://www.idsoftware.com/games/quake/quake3-arena
16. Wang, T., Wang, C.-L., Lau, F.C.: An architecture to support scalable distributed virtual environment systems on grid. J. Supercomput. 36(3), 249–264 (2006)

Spectral Clustering Scheduling Techniques for Tasks with Strict QoS Requirements

Nikos Doulamis, Panagiotis Kokkinos, and Emmanouel Varvarigos

Department of Computer Engineering and Informatics, University of Patras and
Research Academic Computer Technology Institute, Patras, Greece
ndoulam@cs.ntua.gr

Abstract. Efficient task scheduling is fundamental for the success of the Grids, since it directly affects the Quality of Service (QoS) offered to the users. Efficient scheduling policies should be evaluated based not only on performance metrics that are of interest to the infrastructure side, such as the Grid resources utilization efficiency, but also on user satisfaction metrics, such as the percentage of tasks served by the Grid without violating their QoS requirements. In this paper, we propose a scheduling algorithm for tasks with strict timing requirements, given in the form of a desired start and finish time. Our algorithm aims at minimizing the violations of the time constraints, while at the same time minimizing the number of processors used. The proposed scheduling method exploits concepts derived from spectral clustering, and groups together for assignment to a computing resource the tasks so to a) minimize the time overlapping of the tasks assigned to a given processor and b) maximize the degree of time overlapping among tasks assigned to different processors. Experimental results show that our proposed strategy outperforms greedy scheduling algorithms for different values of the task load submitted.

1 Introduction

Task scheduling is fundamental for the success of the Grids, especially with regards to its ability to support real-life commercial applications, by directly affecting a) the efficiency with which Grid resources are used and b) the Quality of Service (QoS) offered to the users. Evaluating a task scheduling algorithm should be based not only on resource utilization metrics, but also on user satisfaction factors, such as the percentage of tasks that are served by the Grid without violating their QoS requirements, e.g., their start and finish times [1]. Currently, several open source schedulers have been developed for clusters of servers such as Maui [2] and portable batch system (PBS) [3]. However, the primary objective of most existing approaches is to improve overall system performance (e.g., resource utilization), while the QoS experienced by Grid users is, at best, a secondary consideration [4], [5].

Without QoS guarantees (e.g., given in the form of task deadlines that should not be violated), users may be reluctant to pay for Grid services or contribute resources to the Grid, reducing its economic impact. On the other hand, designing a scheduling algorithm that satisfies only the end-to-end users' QoS, without taking into account Grid utilization efficiency, would result in a wasteful Grid architecture, that uses many more processors than necessary in order to satisfy users' QoS requirements. Equivalently, processor utilization would be relatively small, meaning that only a small percentage of the available resources would be exploited. Therefore, we need scheduling and resource allocation schemes that are able to simultaneously meet these two sometimes contradictory requirements: *optimize Grid utilization efficiency* while *simultaneously guaranteeing the tasks' strict QoS requirements* (e.g., deadlines).

Several computing toolkits and systems have been developed to meet the task QoS requirements in a Grid computing architecture. Globus is probably the most well known [6]. Additionally Condor-G is an enhanced version of Condor that uses the Globus toolkit to manage Grid jobs [7]. The Nimrod-G [8] is a Grid aware version of the Nimrod, which provides a simple declarative parametric modeling language for expressing a parametric experiment. A dynamic Grid resource allocation method is adopted in [9] using market economy notions (the G-commerce architecture). Finally, a new scheduling algorithm developed in the framework of the GrADS (Grid Application Development Software) tool has been proposed in [10]. A survey of state of the art methods for Grid scheduling is presented in [11].

In general, scheduling parallel and distributed applications is a known NP-complete problem. For this reason, several heuristic algorithms have been proposed for task scheduling. Some approaches use genetic algorithms to maximize the overall system performance [12], [13], while others use Directed Acyclic Graphs (DAG) for scheduling on heterogeneous or homogeneous computing environments [14], [15]. Performance evaluation results for these algorithms are presented in [16]. However, all the aforementioned approaches try to maximize overall system performance, (that is, Grid resource utilization), without respecting task deadlines (that is, user's QoS). Advance reservation of resources, which is the ability of the scheduler to guarantee the availability of resources at a particular time in the future, is one mechanism Grid providers may employ in order to offer specific QoS guarantees to the users [4]. However, these algorithms lack scalability, as they are unable to efficiently perform task scheduling in short time for large numbers of Grid resources. Using concepts from computational geometry, [1] solves the scalability problem for task scheduling under a user's satisfaction framework. The scalability problem is also addressed in [17]. Furthermore, fair scheduling algorithms and reservation schemes have been discussed in [5].

The main drawback of the above mentioned approaches is that scheduling is performed either in the direction of maximizing overall system performance (resource utilization efficiency) or minimizing the degradation of user's QoS requirements satisfaction. As mentioned before, a successful Grid scheduling algorithm should actually take into account both directions. This problem is addressed in this paper, by proposing a novel task scheduling algorithm that assigns tasks to processors so that a) *the time overlapping between tasks assigned to the same processor are minimized* (users QoS requirements are met to the degree possible), while simultaneously b) *maximizing overall Grid utilization efficiency.*

As we show in this paper, the two above mentioned objectives can be described by a matrix representation and then the proposed optimal scheduling strategy can be obtained by introducing the notions of generalized eigenvalues through the use of the Ky-Fan theorem [19]. The Ky-Fan theorem states that an optimal schedule that satisfies both aforementioned criteria can be derived as a solution of the largest eigenvectors of the two matrices that represent the two conditions. Therefore, we have a scheduling algorithm of polynomial order with respect to the number of tasks, that simultaneously satisfies the users' QoS and the system's performance conditions.

The paper is organized as follows. Section 2 discusses the proposed scheduling algorithm for jointly optimizing resource utilization efficiency and tasks' QoS requirements. The solution of the joint optimization problem is given in Section 3. In Section 4, we discuss a lower bound on the number of processors required to achieve no task overlapping (no QoS violations) and propose objective criteria for evaluating scheduling efficiency. Experimental results and comparisons with other approaches are given in Section 5, while Section 6 concludes the paper.

2 Joint Optimization of Resource Performance and QoS Requirements

Let us denote by T_i, $i=1,2,...,N$, the tasks that request service in a Grid infrastructure consisting of M processors. Let us also denote by ST_i the desired *Start Time* for Task T_i and by FT_i its desired *Finish Time*. In this paper, we assume that the tasks are scheduled in a *non-preemptable, non-interruptible way*. Under this assumption, if a task has been assigned for execution on a processor and another task requests service on an overlapping time interval, then, the second task should either be assigned to another processor (which is not reserved at the requested time interval) or undergo violation of its QoS, i.e., its start or finish time or both of them.

We denote by σ_{ij} the non-overlapping measure between tasks T_i and T_j. Assuming that the task i Start and Finish Time, ST_i and FT_i, are hard constraints that should not be violated, a proper selection for the non-overlapping measure σ_{ij} is to take zero values when tasks T_i and T_j overlap in time and positive non-zero values when they do not overlap.

$$\sigma_{ij} = \begin{cases} \alpha, & \text{if } T_i, T_j \text{ are non-overlapping in time} \\ 0, & \text{if } T_i, T_j \text{ overlap in time} \end{cases} \quad (1)$$

where $\alpha > 0$.

Let us assume, without loss of generality that the *Start time* ST_i and *Finish time* FT_i for all tasks that are to be scheduled are within a *time horizon T*, which can be considered as the time interval within which one instance of the scheduling algorithm is executed. Let us denote by C_r the set of tasks assigned for execution on processor r.

As stated in Section 1, an efficient scheduling scheme for a commercially successful Grid should assign all the N pending tasks to the M processors so as to a) *minimize the tasks' QoS violations*, while simultaneously b) maximizing the *overall utilization* of the M processors, so that the Grid resources do not stay *idle* most of the time. The first requirement, in terms of the scheduling algorithm, means that the tasks assigned to a *given* processor should present *minimal overlapping*. The second requirement indicates that the task overlapping among *different* processors should be *maximized*, that is, the utilization of all processors in Grid should be as high as possible. These two requirements can be written as

$$Q_r = \frac{\sum_{i \in C_r, j \in C_r} \sigma_{ij}}{\sum_{i \in C_r, j \in V} \sigma_{ij}}, \quad P_r = \frac{\sum_{i \in C_r, j \notin C_r} \sigma_{ij}}{\sum_{i \in C_r, j \in V} \sigma_{ij}}, \quad (2)$$

where $V = \{T_i\}_{i=1,\ldots,N}$ the set of tasks that request service in a Grid infrastructure.

The denominator of equations (2) is used for normalization purposes. Otherwise, optimizing would favor the trivial solution of one task per processor. Parameter Q_r expresses a measure of the overall QoS violation for the tasks assigned to the rth processor. Instead, parameter P_r expresses the Grid utilization. Taking into account all the M processors of the Grid, we can define a measure Q for the total tasks' QoS violation and a measure P for the overall processor utilization as

$$Q = \sum_{r=1}^{M} Q_r, \quad P = \sum_{r=1}^{M} P_r. \quad (3)$$

An efficient scheduler that tries to meet user QoS requirements should maximize Q and simultaneously minimize P. However, it is clear that

$$P + Q = M. \quad (4)$$

Equation (4) shows that the *maximization* of Q simultaneously yields a *minimization* of P and vice versa. Hence, in our problem, the two aforementioned optimization objectives require in fact the use of identical means and they can be met simultaneously. This is intuitively satisfying, since scheduling a set of tasks in a way that makes efficient use of resources is also expected to help meet the QoS requirements of the set of tasks that are scheduled. Therefore, it is enough to optimize (maximize or minimize) only one of the two criteria. In our case, we select to minimize variable P. Thus,

$$\hat{C}_r : \min P = \min \sum_{r=1}^{M} \frac{\sum_{i \in C_r, j \notin C_r} \sigma_{ij}}{\sum_{i \in C_r, j \in V} \sigma_{ij}}, \text{ for all } r=1,\ldots,M, \quad (5)$$

where $\hat{C}_r$ is the set of tasks assigned for execution on processor r.

3 The Proposed Task Scheduling Policy

3.1 Matrix Representation

Optimizing equation (5) is still a NP-complete problem, even for the special case of $M=2$ processors. To overcome this difficulty, we transform the problem of (5) into a matrix based representation. Let us denote by $\Sigma = [\sigma_{ij}]$ a matrix which contains the values of the non-overlapping measures σ_{ij} for all $N \times N$ combinations of tasks T_i and

T_j. Let us now denote as $\mathbf{e}_r = [\cdots e_r^u \cdots]^T$ an $N \times 1$ *indicator vector* whose u-th entry is given by

$$e_r^u = \begin{cases} 1, & \text{if Task } T_u \text{ is assigned to processor } r \\ 0, & \text{otherwise} \end{cases} \quad (6)$$

The indicator vector $\mathbf{e}_r$ points out which of the N tasks are executed on processor r. That is, indices of tasks executed on processor r are marked with one, while the remaining indices take zero values. Since the Grid infrastructure consists of M processors, M different indicator vectors $\mathbf{e}_r$, $r = 1, 2, \ldots, M$ are defined, each indicating the tasks assigned for execution on each processor. This way, we can express the left hand of (5) with respect to vectors $\mathbf{e}_r$, $r = 1, 2, \ldots, M$. However, we also need to express the right hand of (5) as a function of $\mathbf{e}_r$. For this reason, we denote by $\mathbf{L} = diag(\cdots l_i \cdots)$ the diagonal matrix, whose elements l_i express the cumulative non-overlapping degree of task T_i with the remaining tasks. That is,

$$l_i = \sum_j \sigma_{ij}. \quad (7)$$

Using matrices $\mathbf{L}$ and $\mathbf{\Sigma}$, we can express equation (5) as,

$$\hat{\mathbf{e}}_r, \forall r : \min P = \min \sum_{r=1}^{M} \frac{\mathbf{e}_r^T (\mathbf{L} - \mathbf{\Sigma}) \mathbf{e}_r}{\mathbf{e}_r^T \mathbf{L} \mathbf{e}_r}. \quad (8)$$

3.2 Optimization in the Continuous Domain

Let us form the indicator matrix $\mathbf{E} = [\mathbf{e}_1 \cdots \mathbf{e}_M]$, the columns of which correspond to the M processors in the Grid, while the rows to the N tasks, then the rows of $\mathbf{E}$ have only one unit entry and the remaining entries are zero. Optimization of (8) under the discrete representation of matrix $\mathbf{E}$ is still a NP hard problem. However, if we relax the indicator matrix $\mathbf{E}$ to take values in the continuous domain, we can solve the problem in polynomial time. We denote by $\mathbf{E}_R$ the *relaxed version of the indicator matrix* $\mathbf{E}$, i.e. a matrix whose rows take real values instead of binary values as is the case of the indicator matrix $\mathbf{E}$. Then, it can be proven that (8) can be rewritten as

$$P = M - trace(\mathbf{Y}^T \mathbf{L}^{-1/2} \mathbf{\Sigma} \mathbf{L}^{-1/2} \mathbf{Y}), \quad (9a)$$

$$\text{subject to } \mathbf{Y}^T \mathbf{Y} = \mathbf{I}. \quad (9b)$$

$\mathbf{Y}$ is a matrix that is related to the matrix $\mathbf{E}_R$ through

$$\mathbf{L}^{-1/2} \mathbf{Y} = \mathbf{E}_R \mathbf{\Lambda}, \quad (10)$$

where $\mathbf{\Lambda}$ is any $M \times M$ matrix. In this paper, we select $\mathbf{\Lambda}$ to be equal to the identity matrix, $\mathbf{\Lambda} = \mathbf{I}$. Then, the relaxed indicator matrix $\mathbf{E}_R$ is given as

$$\mathbf{E}_R = \mathbf{L}^{-1/2} \mathbf{Y}. \quad (11)$$

Minimization of (11) is obtained through the Ky-Fan theorem [19]. The Ky-Fan theorem states that the maximum value of the $trace(\mathbf{Y}^T\mathbf{L}^{-1/2}\mathbf{\Sigma}\mathbf{L}^{-1/2}\mathbf{Y})$ subject to the constraint of $\mathbf{Y}^T\mathbf{Y}=\mathbf{I}$ is equal to the sum of the M ($M<N$) *largest eigenvalues of matrix* $\mathbf{L}^{-1/2}\mathbf{\Sigma}\mathbf{L}^{-1/2}$. This maximum value is provided for the matrix

$$\mathbf{Y} = \mathbf{U} \cdot \mathbf{R}, \qquad (12)$$

where $\mathbf{U}$ is a $N \times M$ matrix whose columns are the *eigenvectors* corresponding to the M largest eigenvalues of matrix $\mathbf{L}^{-1/2}\mathbf{\Sigma}\mathbf{L}^{-1/2}$ and $\mathbf{R}$ is an *arbitrarily rotation matrix* (i.e., orthogonal with determinant of one). Again, a simple approach is to select matrix $\mathbf{R}$ as the identity matrix, $\mathbf{R}=\mathbf{I}$, that is $\mathbf{Y}=\mathbf{U}$. Therefore, we have that the optimal relaxed indicator matrix $\hat{\mathbf{E}}_R$ in the continuous domain is given as

$$\hat{\mathbf{E}}_R = \mathbf{L}^{-1/2}\mathbf{U}. \qquad (13)$$

3.3 Discrete Approximation

The optimal matrix $\hat{\mathbf{E}}_R$ given by equation (13) does not have the form of the indicator matrix $\mathbf{E}$ since the values of $\hat{\mathbf{E}}_R$ are continuous, while $\mathbf{E}$'s entries are binary. Recall that a unit entry indicates the processor a task is assigned to for execution, under the non-interruptible, non-preemptable assumption. Consequently, the problem is how to round the continuous values of $\hat{\mathbf{E}}_R$ in a discrete form that approximates matrix $\mathbf{E}$.

One simple approach, regarding the rounding process, is to set the maximum value of each row of matrix $\hat{\mathbf{E}}_R$ to be equal to 1 and let the remaining values be equal to 0. However, such an approach yields unsatisfactory performance when there is no dominant maximum value for each row of $\hat{\mathbf{E}}_R$. Furthermore, it handles the rounding process as N (that is the number of tasks) independent problems. An alternative approach, which is adopted in this paper, is to treat the N rows of matrix $\hat{\mathbf{E}}_R$ as M-dimensional feature vectors. Each one of these feature vectors indicates the association degree of each task and the respective M processor of the Grid. Then, we apply the k-means to form the indicator matrix $\mathbf{E}$.

4 Lower Bound - Scheduling Efficiency

An important aspect, which determines the scheduling efficiency is the task granularity g, and the task arrival rate λ defined as

$$\lambda = \frac{N}{T}, \quad g = \frac{D}{T}, \qquad (14)$$

where N is the number of tasks requesting service over the corresponding time interval T and D the average task delay.

Given a granularity g and a rate λ, the *lower bound* of Grid resources required for achieving no task overlapping is given by the following equation

$$B = \frac{ND}{T} = N \cdot g \leq M_{opt}, \qquad (15)$$

where M_{opt} refers to minimum number of processors required for achieving no task overlapping by an optimal (exhaustive search) scheduling algorithm. The lower bound of (15) is achieved in the extreme case that the tasks request execution intervals of a constant duration D that appear one right after the other, completely filling the gaps within the time horizon T. Thus, this lower bound is usually smaller than the M_{opt}.

Given the lower bound B on the number of processors required for no overlapping, the scheduling efficiency is defined as

$$e(A) = \frac{B}{M(A)} \quad \text{or} \quad \varepsilon(A) = \frac{\lceil B \rceil}{M(A)}, \qquad (16)$$

where A refers to the algorithm used to approximate the exhaustive search policy and $M(A)$ is the number of processors required for achieving no task overlapping when algorithm A is used. $e(A)$ is the scheduling efficiency, while $\varepsilon(A)$ is the rounded efficiency for algorithm A. The $\lceil \cdot \rceil$ indicates the ceil operator.

5 Experimental Results

Two different algorithms were implemented in this paper and compared with respect to their scheduling efficiency. The first algorithm is the *proposed scheme,* presented in Section 2. The second scheme is a *greedy approach*, which, for each task, a locally optimum choice is selected. In particular, the algorithm assigns each task to a processor, so that no task overlapping is encountered, by taking into account the current local load of the processors.

Our proposed algorithm is recursively applied assuming different number of processors in Grid. Then, we select the minimum number of processors that provide *no task overlapping* that is no violation of the tasks' QoS. This number M(*Proposed Algorithm*) is used for evaluating the scheduling efficiency. In the greedy algorithm, each time a newly considered task overlaps with the already assigned tasks, then a new resource is activated and this task is assigned to this resource. The number of resources that have been activated after scheduling all tasks, without overlaps, is denoted by M(*Greedy*). We assume that the tasks' *Start and Finish Times* ST_i and FT_i are uniformly distributed within the time horizon T and that the average tasks' duration is constant and equals D. Experiments where the task duration varies significantly from task to task, have also been performed, but are not included here due to space limitations.

Fig. 1(a) presents the efficiency e [see equation (16)] versus the task granularity g for different values of lower bound B. As is observed, the efficiency increases as the granularity decreases for low values of g. However, the ratio of improvement decreases, meaning that the efficiency converges as g increases. We also observe from

Fig. 1 that for values of granularity greater than $g \geq 0.2$ the efficiency also increases as g increases. This is due to singularity issue, since in this case the minimum number of processors required for achieving no task overlapping equals the number of tasks N. In Fig. 1(b), we compare the continuous and rounded efficiency e and ε for the lower bound $B=1$. As expected, the rounded efficiency is a discontinuous function and several peaks are encountered due to the ceiling operator $\lceil \cdot \rceil$ involved in (16). However, in general terms, the overall behavior resembles that of the continuous case.

In Fig. 2(a), we depict the effect of the number of tasks N (equivalently, of the task arrival rate λ, for a given time window T) on the efficiency ε for different values of the granularity g. As we observe, the rounded efficiency presents a periodically discontinuous behavior that depends on the granularity value. This periodicity is due to the ceiling operator involved in the rounded efficiency ε [see equation (16)]. Next, we examined the effect of the number of iterations of the k-means algorithm used for estimating the indicator matrix $\mathbf{E}$ –that is tasks' partitioning– from the relaxed matrix

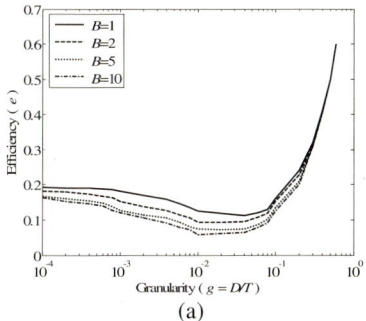
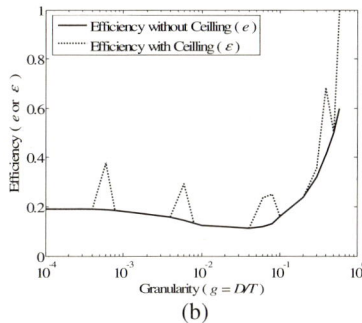

Fig. 1. (a) Efficiency (e) versus granularity (g) for different values of lower bound B in case that the proposed scheduling policy is used. (b) Comparison of the continuous and rounded efficiency (e and ε) for lower bound $B=1$.

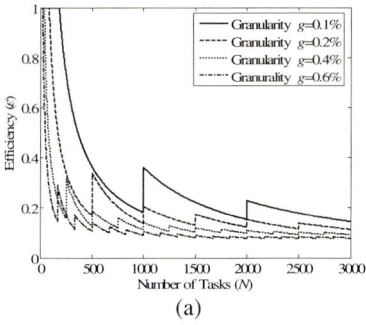
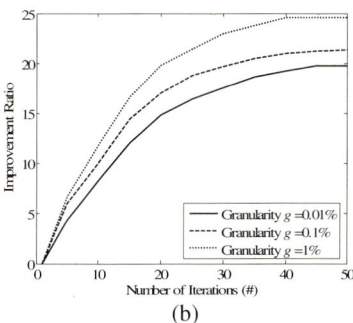

Fig. 2. (a) Efficiency ε versus the number of tasks for different values of granularity in case of $B=1$. (b) Improvement ratio of the efficiency versus the number of iterations of the proposed algorithm.

E_R computing by the Ky-Fan Theorem (see Section 3). In particular, Fig. 2(b) presents the improvement ratio versus the number of iterations for different granularity values, assuming $B=1$. We observe that as the number of iterations increases the scheduling efficiency increases for all granularity values. However, convergent is achieved for large number of iterations.

Fig. 3 presents the comparison results between the proposed algorithm for iterations of 1 and 50 and the greedy scheduling scheme. As we observe, the proposed algorithm exhibits better efficiency at any value of granularity. At low task load (low values of B) the improvement is more evident than for high values of B. Additionally, for low granularity values the improvement is smaller. This is because in this case, task durations are very small compared to the time window and thus both algorithms can schedule more effectively the tasks.

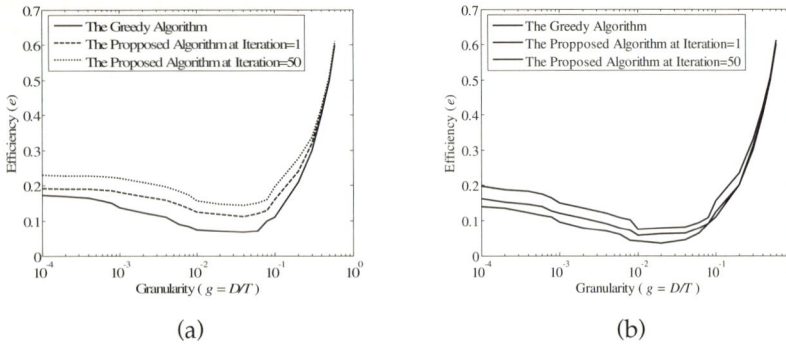

Fig. 3. Comparison of the proposed method for different iterations with the greedy algorithm. (a) $B=1$. (b) $B=10$.

6 Conclusions

We proposed an efficient scheduling strategy that maximizes Grid utilization efficiency, while resulting in a minimal degradation of the QoS offered to the submitted tasks. These two objectives are transformed into a matrix representation and then the scheduling problem is solved by introducing the notions of generalized eigenvalues through the use of the Ky-Fan theorem. Optimization using eigenvectors has the advantage that scheduling is performed in polynomial complexity.

Experimental results and comparisons with a greedy scheduling policy are presented to indicate the efficiency of the proposed scheme. In particular, we investigate the number of processors required for achieving no task overlapping (no QoS violations) under the two scheduling policies. We also define a lower bound on the minimum number of processors required and we estimate the scheduling efficiency of an algorithm as the ratio of the lower bound over the number of processors achieved by the algorithm. Comparison with the greedy scheduling policy demonstrates the efficiency of the proposed scheme for all granularities and different assumptions on the number and durations of the tasks. In addition, as the number of iterations of the proposed algorithm increases better scheduling efficiency is achieved. Algorithm convergence is achieved even for a small number of iterations, e.g., 30. We find that task granularity affects more significantly the scheduling efficiency rather than the task arrival rate. Finally, efficiency is better at low values of granularity, however, convergence is noticed for very low granularities.

Acknowledgment

This work has been supported by the European Commission through the IP Phosphorus project.

References

[1] Castillo, C., Rouskas, G., Harfoush, K.: On the Design of Online Scheduling Algorithms for Advance Reservations and QoS in Grids. In: Int'l Parallel and Distributed Processing Symp., pp. 1–10 (2007)
[2] Jackson, D., Snell, Q., Clement, M.: Core Algorithms of the Maui Scheduler. In: Feitelson, D.G., Rudolph, L. (eds.) JSSPP 2001. LNCS, vol. 2221, pp. 87–102. Springer, Heidelberg (2001)
[3] Bode, B., et al.: The Portable Batch Scheduler and the Maui Scheduler on Linux Clusters. Usenix Conf. (2000)
[4] Al-Ali, R.J., et al.: Analysis and provision of QoS for distributed grid applications. Journal of Grid Computing 2(2), 163–182 (2004)
[5] Doulamis, N., Doulamis, A., Varvarigos, E., Varvarigou, T.: Fair Scheduling Algorithms in Grids. IEEE Trans, on PDS 18(11), 1630–1648 (2007)
[6] Foster, I., Kesselman, C.: Globus: A Metacomputing Infrastructure Toolkit. International Journal of Supercomputer Applications 11(2), 115–128 (1997)
[7] Thain, D., Tannenbaum, T., Livny, M.: Condor and the Grid. In: Berman, F., Hey, A.J.G., Fox, G. (eds.) Grid Computing: Making the Global Infrastructure a Reality. John Wiley & Sons, Chichester (2003)
[8] Abramson, D., Giddy, J., Kotler, L.: High Performance Parametric Modeling with Nimrod/G: Killer Application for the Global Grid. In: Int'l Parallel and Distributed Processing Symp. (2000)
[9] Wolski, R., Plank, J.S., Brevik, J., Bryan, T.: G-commerce: Market Formulations Controlling Resource Allocation on the Computational Grid. In: Int'l Parallel and Distributed Processing Symp. (2001)
[10] K. Cooper et al., "New Grid Scheduling and Rescheduling Methods in the GrADS Project," Int'l Parallel and Distributed Processing Symp., pp. 199-207, 2004.
[11] Maheswaran, M., Krauter, K., Buyya, R.: A taxonomy and survey of grid resource management systems for distributed computing. Software: Practice and Experience 32(2), 135–164 (2002)
[12] Shu, W., et al.: A Grid Computing Task Scheduling Method Based on Target Genetic Algorithm. The Sixth World Congress on Intelligent Control and Automation 1, 3528–3532 (2006)
[13] Ye, G., Rao, R., Li, M.: A Multiobjective Resources Scheduling Approach Based on Genetic Algorithms in Grid Environment. In: Fifth International Conference on Grid and Cooperative Computing Workshops, pp. 504–509 (2006)

[14] Topcuoglu, H., Hariri, S., Wu, M.-Y.: Performance Effective and Low-Complexity Task Scheduling for Heterogeneous Computing. Transactions on Parallel and Distributed Systems 2(13), 260–274 (2002)
[15] Mandal, A., et al.: Scheduling Strategies for Mapping Application Workflows onto the Grid. In: Symp. on High Performance Distributed Computing, pp. 125–134 (2005)
[16] Zhang, Y., Koelbel, C., Kennedy, K.: Relative Performance of Scheduling Algorithms in Grid Environments. In: Int'l Conf. on Cluster Computing and the Grid, pp. 521–528 (2007)
[17] Zhang, Y., et al.: Scalable Grid Application Scheduling via Decoupled Resource Selection and Scheduling. In: Int'l Conf. on Cluster Computing and the Grid, pp. 568–575 (2006)
[18] Varvarigos, E., Doulamis, N., Doulamis, A., Varvarigou, T.: Timed/Advance Reservation Schemes and Scheduling Algorithms for QoS Resource Management in Grids. In: Di Martino, B., Dongarra, J., Hoisie, A., Yang, L.T., Zima, H. (eds.) Engineering the Grid, pp. 355–378. American Scientific Publishers (2006)
[19] Nakic, I., Veselic, K.: Wielandt and Ky-Fan Theorem for Matrix Pairs. Linear Algebra and its Applications 369(17), 73–77 (2003)

QoS-Oriented Reputation-Aware Query Scheduling in Data Grids

Rogério Luís de Carvalho Costa and Pedro Furtado

University of Coimbra - Departamento de Engenharia Informática
Pólo II, Pinhal de Marrocos, 3030, 290, Coimbra, Portugal
rogcosta@dei.uc.pt, pnf@dei.uc.pt

Abstract. In the last few years, the Grid technology has emerged as an important tool for many scientific and commercial global organizations. In grid-based systems, intelligent job scheduling is used to achieve Service Level Objectives (SLOs) and to provide some kind of Quality of Service (QoS) differentiation between users or applications. In data grids, the grid infra-structure is used to provide transparent access to geographically distributed data, which may be replicated in order to increase availability and performance. In this work, we deal with QoS-oriented query scheduling in data grids. Although there exist several works on job scheduling in Grids, QoS-oriented query scheduling in grid-based databases is still an open issue. For instance, how can we provide guarantees against response-time expectations? Our proposal uses a reputation system to answer this problem satisfactorily. We also present experimental results that prove the benefits of proposed strategies.

1 Introduction

In the last few years, the Grid has emerged as the next generation infra-structure technology for distributed computing. It is used by a wide range of applications to provide transparent and coordinated access to distributed shared resources, including servers, workstation clusters, storage systems and databases. For instance, it can be used as basic infra-structure by global (real and virtual) organizations, which are generating huge volumes of distributed data, in order to enable geographically distributed users transparently access the distributed database. Indeed, the term *Data Grid* is commonly used to identify grid-based systems in which data is a major actor [1], including situations on which grid-based tools generate, manage or consume large volumes of data.

Grids are dynamic environments where resource availability and performance may change over time [2]. Besides that, resources are commonly heterogeneous and belong to distinct domains, which may have some degree of autonomy. In fact, local domain controllers may impose constraints on local resource utilization by remote users [2]. Moreover, in grids, job scheduling is usually QoS-oriented, which means that it aims at improving the users' satisfaction by maintaining a good Quality of Service (QoS) [3]. Service Level Objectives (SLO) are commonly specified and used to provide some kind of differentiation between jobs or users.

In this work, we deal with QoS-oriented query scheduling in data grids, where data replication is commonly used to improve availability and performance [4]. Let's consider a situation where a query has an SLO specified in terms of an execution deadline and there are a few data services which already have the data to execute it. How to choose the best data service to execute a user's query according to its SLO and still provide high QoS-levels for other users?

One straightforward approach to schedule one query execution is to choose the data service that would finish the query execution earlier. But this may not be the best strategy. It is important to notice that the user's expectation is related to the fact that the query should be executed by its deadline and not as soon as possible. Then, when a large deadline is specified, a good local resource utilization policy may choose to execute other queries that have tighter deadlines before (or in parallel with) the one with the large deadline, in order to increase the system's SLO fulfillment level. In another scheduling strategy, one may choose to schedule the query for the slowest site between the ones that may accomplish the specified deadline. This approach aims at leaving the faster sites available to execute future queries that may have tighter deadlines than the current one. But predicting a query execution time is not simple, especially when a few queries are executed concurrently. Hence, when the prediction is wrong, the real execution time may be over the predicted time and the deadline requirement may not be achieved.

In this paper, we consider a grid configuration where the community scheduler has no total control over each site's shared resources (like in the hierarchical and decentralized scheduling models commonly used in the grid [5]). Thus, we leave to each site's controller the responsibility to estimate the query execution time at the site and to indicate if the locally available resources can execute the submitted query by the specified deadline. This is the first phase in our scheduling strategy. In the case that more than one data service candidates itself to execute the query, we use a reputation system to choose the one that should execute it. Our strategy aims at choosing the data service that has been more trustworthy in its previous commitments to accomplish specified SLOs. The use of the reputation system is the second phase of our scheduling strategy.

This work is organized as follows: in the next Section we review some related work. In Section 3 we detail the proposed reputation-based query scheduling strategy and identify some performance metrics that can be used to evaluate QoS-oriented scheduling techniques. Experimental results are presented in Section 4. Finally, we draw conclusions and discuss some future work in Section 5.

2 Related Work

In this section we review the concepts and tools involved in grid processing. We also review query scheduling over the grid and reputation systems.

Grid-based applications are commonly deployed over Grid Resource Manager (GRM) Systems, like Globus Toolkit [6] and Legion [7]. Most of the GRM systems enable the use of various job scheduling policies.

The Globus Toolkit is a tools set that can be used as basic infra-structure to deploy grid applications. The available tools are related to different aspects like security, resource reservation, and data replication and movement [8]. Nimrod-G [9] and Condor-G [10] are examples of job schedulers that work over Globus.

Nimrod-G does economic-based job scheduling, scheduling a job execution for the node that has the lowest monetary cost. The GRACE (GRid Architecture for Computational Economy) middleware is used to obtain dynamic information on costs and to do auction-inspired negotiations between the scheduler and other nodes [9]. Condor-G uses the Condor's [11] ClassAds matchmaking mechanism to schedule job execution. In such strategy, jobs' requirements and nodes' capabilities are published in ClassAds (Classified Advertisements). An agent is responsible to do the matchmaking between the job's ClassAds and the available nodes' ClassAds. Globus' GRAM [12] is used to manage remote job execution.

Legion is a GRM system that aims at creating a virtual machine abstraction of the available Grid resources. In Legion, every participant is modeled as an object. Application Class objects are used to instantiate Grid applications. When instantiation an Application Class object, it is possible to specify execution requirements, including the job scheduler that should be used to schedule its execution. Legion has some built-in scheduling mechanisms (e.g. random, and round-robin [13]) but it also supports user-written job schedulers.

There are also some works on query scheduling over the grid. In [14], the authors present a distributed query processor called Polar*, that constructs distributed query execution plans in which distinct plan's operators are executed in distinct nodes. Polar* query processor is used in the OGSA-DQP strategy (Distributed Query Processor based on the Open Grid Services Architecture) [15,16]. In OGSA-DQP, web services are used to enable the use of Polar* in a grid environment. Data movement during query execution is used in order to reduce load imbalance. In [4], the authors argue that doing data movement during grid query execution may reduce performance. Hence, queries should be scheduled to nodes that already the necessary data to execute them and data replication must be done asynchronously with query execution.

The use of reputation systems to schedule job execution in grids is discussed in more recent works. In [17], the authors present generic functions that may be used to define reputation values for issues of interest and for grid service providers. The authors claim that specific equations for each context should be specified by users. In [18], reputation is used in order to detect malicious nodes which may present incomplete results for a task in donation grids. Unreliability and malicious nodes are also considered in works like [19,20].

In this work, we do not consider that a data service can provide an incomplete result for a query execution. But we consider that a local scheduler may fail to predict the necessary time to execute a query (intentionally or not), or even the predicted execution time may not be achieved due to environmental changes. Therefore, our reputation system is used to measure each service's prediction capacity and commitment degree, thus helping the global scheduler to choose the best site to execute a job according to users' expectations.

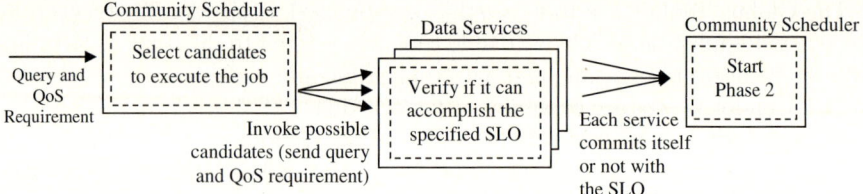

Fig. 1. QoS-oriented Reputation-aware scheduling: phase 1 main steps

3 QoS-Oriented Reputation-Based Scheduling

3.1 System Model

Grid systems may assume different architectures. We consider the existence of a *Community Query Scheduler* that may not have total control over all available shared resources in the Grid, but that is responsible to assign query execution to one of the available *Data Services*.

A Data Service is any computational resource that is capable to execute database queries, like a multi-processor database server or a cluster of workstations. If a local scheduler is used at a site, then all the resources managed by the local scheduler (and the scheduler itself) are considered by the Community Scheduler as a single Data Service. Otherwise, each resource is a Data Service that may directly interact with the Community Scheduler.

3.2 Two-Phase Reputation-Aware Scheduling Model

Our query scheduling model is divided into two phases. Initially, the services that are eligible to execute the query according to its deadline are nominated. In the second phase, a reputation model is used to select the most trustful service to execute the query.

Phase 1: Invoking Candidates

Phase 1 starts with the incoming of a new query and ends when all invoked data services answers to the Community Scheduler if they can or cannot accomplish the SLO. Figure 1 presents the main steps of Phase 1.

Selecting Candidates with the Necessary Requisites: Each submitted query is sent to the Community Scheduler, which should select the Data Services that may execute it (the ones that already have replicas of the necessary data). Such activity is supported by the use of a replica catalog, which is provided by the underlying GRM System (e.g. Globus provides a Replica Local Service that can be used by Globus-based implementations of our scheduler). Then, the Scheduler sends to each selected Data Service the query together with its QoS-requirement.

Each Selected Candidate Declares its Intention to Execute the Job: Each selected Data Service should estimate if the query can be executed with the specified SLO. It should estimate a *Local Query Execution Time* and compare the

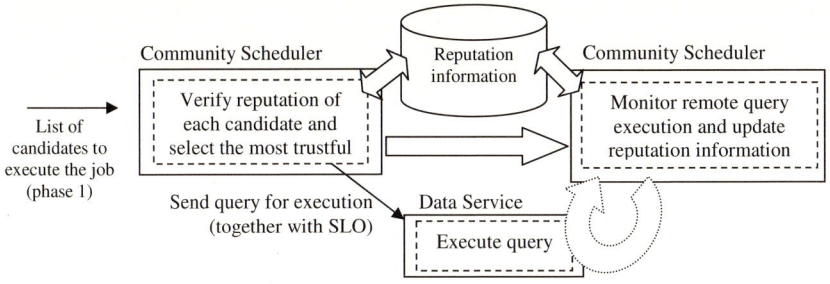

Fig. 2. QoS-oriented Reputation-aware scheduling: phase 2 main steps

foreseen value with the deadline requirement. Usually, the *Local Query Execution Time* includes two main factors: (i) the *Awaiting Queue Time*, which is the time that the new query would wait until other already running queries end up and its execution may begin; and (ii) the *Execution Time*, which is the necessary time to effectively execute the query against the database.

Each Data Service may have its own methods to estimate the *Local Query Execution Time*. For instance, the local query scheduler (or time estimator, when there is no local scheduler) may consider immediately starting the new query, which increases the system's multi-programming level as the new query is executed in parallel to the ones that are already executing. This would reduce the *Awaiting Queue Time* into zero, but would probably increase the *Execution Time* due to multi-query influence. Therefore, the *Execution Time* of each local scheduling alternative should be considered. Such estimation is out of this paper's scope, but some works on estimating query execution time are [21,22,23].

Phase 2: Selecting the Most Trustful Candidate

The Community Scheduler should choose one Data Service to execute the submitted query between those that had agreed to execute it by the specified SLO. In order to do that, we use a reputation system which indicates how much the Community Scheduler may trust in the Data Services' commitment to accomplish the SLO. After scheduling the query execution, the Scheduler must monitor if the query is executed by its deadline in order to update the reputation information about the selected data service. These steps are represented at Figure 2.

The Reputation Model: The reputation value we use for each Data Service is scaled to $[0, 1]$. The larger the value, the greater the confidence that the Community Scheduler has on the Data Service's commitment.

We define a *Success Factor* k ($k \in \{0, 1\}$) as an indicator if a Data Service has accomplished a deadline for a given query ($k = 1 \rightarrow$ the SLO was achieved; $k = 0 \rightarrow$ the node failed to accomplished the SLO). Then, for each Data Service (S), a reputation value R at time j is computed considering the *Success Factor* of each time (i) that the node has executed a query, against the number of times

(t) it has made itself available to execute the job. Equation 1 represents the proposed formula for R.

$$R_{S,j} = \frac{1}{\sum_{i=1}^{t} w_i} \sum_{i=1}^{t} w_i k_i \qquad (1)$$

$$w_i = e^{(-\frac{\Delta t}{\lambda})} \qquad (2)$$

In Equation 1, w is a time discount function used to differentiate old results from newer ones. We intend to consider newer events as more relevant than older ones. For a time window (Δt) between the time t when the query i was executed and the current time, w is computed by Equation 2 (as defined in [24]).

The parameter λ is used to allow the use of different time units and intervals, as it is defined in [24]. For instance, if the time unit used is *minute* and a *twenty minute earlier interval* should have only 10% of the effect than a new *Success Factor* value that was just obtained, then $\lambda = -\frac{20}{\ln(0.1)}$.

Updating Reputation Information: In order to update reputation information, the Community Scheduler must know if each scheduled query was finished by its deadline. Then, it monitors remote schedule execution in order to verify the job finish time. This is done with the aid of the underlying GRM infra-structure (e.g. Globus' GRAM can be used in Globus-based systems).

3.3 Performance Metrics

There are several performance metrics that can be used to describe a system performance (e.g. throughput, scalability and response time). We propose here the use of some intuitive metrics which are specific related to QoS-oriented scheduling. The proposed metrics are used in Section 4 to evaluate our scheduling model.

The first simple metric is the *SLO-Achievement Rate* (AR) of a workload. Such metric is computed considering the number of queries executed by their deadlines (S) and number of queries in the workload (Q). But some queries in the workload may have so tight deadlines that no data service commits itself to execute them by their deadlines. The *Executed Queries Rate* (EQ) is obtained considering the relation between the number of queries that were executed (N) and the number of queries in the workload (Q). The latter metric indicates the rate of queries that had at least one candidate to execute according to the desired QoS levels. The *Breach of Trust Rate* (BTR) is obtained considering the relation between the number of times a commitment to execute a query by its SLO is broken and the number of times a commitment is done (N). Equations 3, 4 and 5 represents AR, EQ and BTR, respectively.

$$AR = \frac{S}{Q} \qquad (3)$$

$$EQ = \frac{N}{Q} \qquad (4)$$

$$BTR = \frac{N-S}{N} \qquad (5)$$

4 Experimental Results

We did several tests to validate our proposals. In this Section we present the most relevant experimental results.

We compare our reputation-aware scheduling model with two other strategies: (i) *Random Scheduling among Candidates* (RS) and (ii) *First Candidate Executes the Job* (FCEJ). RS and FCEJ are two-phase scheduling. In their first phase, a list of candidates is generated (just like it is in our reputation-aware strategy). The main difference is in the scheduling second-phase: in RS, the query executor is randomly selected among the data services that have claimed that can execute the query according to its SLO; in FCEJ, the query is scheduled to the first data service to claim that is capable to finish query execution by its deadline. The second phase decisions of RS and FCEJ are inspired in scheduling strategies used in current GRM systems (e.g. Legion).

Our testbed workload is composed by 100 queries, that are constructed using queries 1, 2, 5, 7, 8, 9, 10, 11, 14 and 18 of TPC-H benchmark [25] with different parameters. We have simulated a data grid with six data replicas of a 1GB TPC-H database. Each replica is stored at a SQL Server 2005 DBMS placed at a different grid site. A data grid with such number of data replicas is already capable to execute a high number of concurrent queries: in our tests, we varied the query submission rate from just a few queries per minute up to 1440 queries per hour. Table 1 briefly describes some relevant hardware parameters of the experimental environment (Site 1 is used by the Community Scheduler). *Local Query Execution Time* at data services is estimated using the method proposed in [23]. Queries that have no candidates to execute them by their deadlines are aborted and do not executed (the user should re-submit the query if it is acceptable to execute the query with a larger deadline).

In the following graphs, we present the measured values for the proposed performance metrics when using the three evaluated scheduling models and different query submission rates. When using low query submission rates, the three evaluated methods achieved high values for AR (Graph 1). With low submission rates, all queries have at least one candidate to execute them (Graph 2) and even not so wise scheduling strategies can lead to high levels of QoS fulfillment. As query submission rates increase, data services start to execute several queries simultaneously

Table 1. Experimental Environment Description

Site	Processor	RAM Memory
1	Pentium IV 1.6Ghz	752MB
2	AMD Duron 1.6Ghz	752MB
3	AMD Athlon 1.5Ghz	480MB
4	AMD Athlon 1.5Ghz	736MB
5	AMD Duron 1.4Ghz	752MB
6	AMD Duron 1.6Ghz	496MB
7	Intel Xeon Dual Processor 2.8Ghz	3.87GB

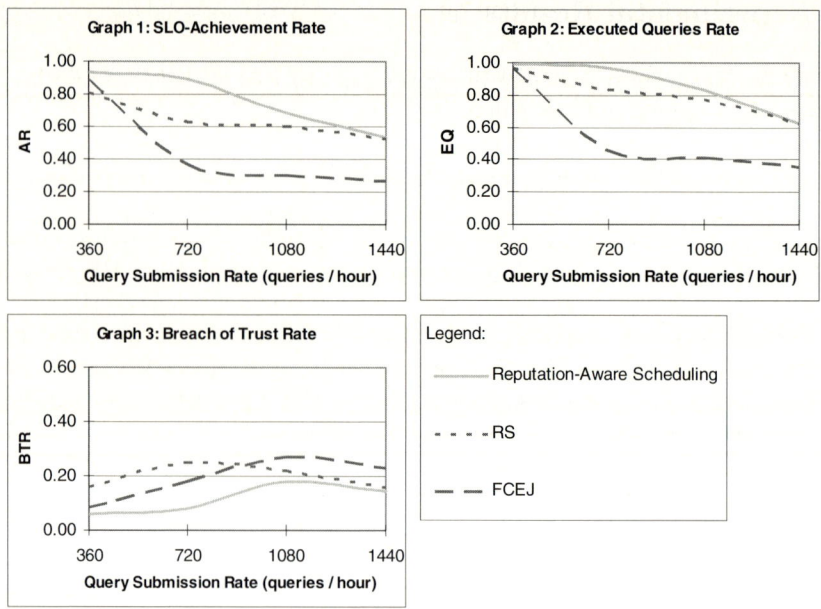

and multi-query influence reduces the service's capacity to foresee the necessary time to execute a query, which leads to higher breach of trust rates (Graph 3).

In fact, the heterogeneity of our system and multi-query influence are the main factors that lead to different BTR values at each node. Multi-query influence affects in different ways the used data services. When a DBMS executes several queries concurrently, the concurrency for RAM memory space increases (especially if the accessed data tables does not fit entirely in available memory), which may lead to performance degradation (I/O performance can also suffer if different locations on disk are accessed). Thus, the smaller the RAM memory available at a data service, the greater the negative impact the service may suffer from multi-query influence.

The benefits of using the reputation-aware scheduling strategy are specially noticed when using incoming query rates between 500 and 1000 queries per hour. With submission rates in such range, the reputation-aware scheduling maintains the BTR values especially low (Graph 3), while a high number of queries is executed (Graph 2), leading to a high deadline achievement rates (Graph 1).

When using submission rates higher than 1000 queries per hour, each data service would have to execute many queries at the same time (the *Awaiting Queue Time* would have to be almost zero in order to achieve specified deadlines), which greatly increases the query execution time of each of them. Therefore, in order to avoid such high number of concurrent queries, data services deny to execute several queries and the number of queries with no candidates to execute them increases (lower values for EQ in Graph 2). This leads to lower deadline achievement rates (Graph 1), but also reduces the BTR values (Graph 3), as a smaller number of concurrent queries are effectively executed at each node (reducing multi-query influence).

Hence, the proposed reputation-aware scheduling model leads to the best deadline achievement and breach of trust rates in all studied situations.

5 Conclusions and Future Work

Globally accessible databases are becoming of great importance to a large number of real and virtual global organizations. Such environment is obtained by the use of a grid-based infra-structure, which provides transparent access to geographically distributed databases. In such Data Grids, database replication is usually done in order to increase availability and performance.

In this work, we present a new query scheduling strategy for the Data Grid. Our two-phase scheduling strategy is QoS-oriented, which means that it aims at maximizing the rate of SLO-achievement. In this work, we used execution deadlines as QoS-requirements, but our strategy may also be used for other types of QoS-requirements. The first phase of our strategy aims at selecting available sites to execute the incoming job maintains site autonomy: each site may deny to the job by the specified deadline. This can be used to implement local-domain rules. In the second phase, a reputation system to choose between the available candidates the one that should execute the query. The use of the reputation system increases the system's QoS level. We present experimental results that prove the validity of our proposals. We also identify some performance metrics that can be used to evaluate QoS-oriented scheduling techniques.

As future work, we plan to experimentally evaluate our scheduling strategy with other types of QoS-requirements and jobs.

References

1. Chervenak, A., Foster, I., Kesselman, C., Salisbury, C., Tuecke, S.: The data grid: Towards an architecture for the distributed management and analysis of large scientific datasets. J. of Network and Computer Applic. 23, 187–200 (2001)
2. Foster, I.T.: The anatomy of the grid: Enabling scalable virtual organizations. In: CCGRID, pp. 6–7 (2001)
3. Roy, A., Sander, V.: Gara: a uniform quality of service architecture. Grid resource management: state of the art and future trends, 377–394 (2004)
4. Ranganathan, K., Foster, I.: Computation scheduling and data replication algorithms for data grids. Grid resource management: state of the art and future trends, 359–373 (2004)
5. Krauter, K., Buyya, R., Maheswaran, M.: A taxonomy and survey of grid resource management systems for distributed computing. Softw. Pract. Exper. 32(2), 135–164 (2002)
6. Foster, I., Kesselman, C.: Globus: A metacomputing infrastructure toolkit. The Internat. Journal of Superc. Appl. and High Perf. Computing 11(2), 115–128 (1997)
7. Grimshaw, A.S., Wulf, W.A., Team, T.L.: The legion vision of a worldwide virtual computer. Commun. ACM 40(1), 39–45 (1997)

8. Foster, I.T.: Globus toolkit version 4: Software for service-oriented systems. J. Comput. Sci. Technol. 21(4), 513–520 (2006)
9. Buyya, R., Abramson, D., Giddy, J.: Nimrod/g: An architecture of a resource management and scheduling system in a global computational grid. CoRR cs.DC/0009021 (2000)
10. Frey, J., Tannenbaum, T., Livny, M., Foster, I., Tuecke, S.: Condor-g: A computation management agent for multi-institutional grids. Cluster Computing 5(3), 237–246 (2002)
11. Tannenbaum, T., Wright, D., Miller, K., Livny, M.: Condor – a distributed job scheduler. In: Beowulf Cluster Computing with Linux. MIT Press, Cambridge (2001)
12. Czajkowski, K., Foster, I.T., Karonis, N.T., Kesselman, C., Martin, S., Smith, W., Tuecke, S.: A resource management architecture for metacomputing systems. In: Proc. of the Work. on Job Scheduling Strat. for Parallel Processing, pp. 62–82 (1998)
13. Natrajan, A., Humphrey, M.A., Grimshaw, A.S.: Grid resource management in legion. Grid resource manag.: state of the art and future trends, 145–160 (2004)
14. Smith, J., Gounaris, A., Watson, P., Paton, N.W., Fernandes, A.A.A., Sakellariou, R.: Distributed query processing on the grid. In: Parashar, M. (ed.) GRID 2002. LNCS, vol. 2536, pp. 279–290. Springer, Heidelberg (2002)
15. Alpdemir, N.M., Mukherjee, A., Gounaris, A., Paton, N.W., Watson, P., Fernandes, A.A., Fitzgerald, D.J.: Ogsa-dqp: A service for distributed querying on the grid. In: Bertino, E., Christodoulakis, S., Plexousakis, D., Christophides, V., Koubarakis, M., Böhm, K., Ferrari, E. (eds.) EDBT 2004. LNCS, vol. 2992, pp. 858–861. Springer, Heidelberg (2004)
16. Gounaris, A., Smith, J., Paton, N.W., Sakellariou, R., Fernandes, A.A.A., Watson, P.: Adapting to changing resource performance in grid query processing. In: DMG, pp. 30–44 (2005)
17. Silaghi, G., Arenas, A., Silva, L.: A utility-based reputation model for service-oriented computing. In: Proc. of the CoreGRID Symposium, pp. 63–72 (2007)
18. Sonnek, J., Nathan, M., Chandra, A., Weissman, J.: Reputation-based scheduling on unreliable distributed infrastructures. In: ICDCS 2006: Proc. of the 26th IEEE Inter. Conf. on Distributed Computing Systems, p. 30 (2006)
19. Kamvar, S.D., Schlosser, M.T., Garcia-Molina, H.: The eigentrust algorithm for reputation management in p2p networks. In: WWW 2003: Proc. of the 12th Inter. Conf. on World Wide Web, pp. 640–651 (2003)
20. Singh, A., Liu, L.: Trustme: Anonymous management of trust relationships in decentralized p2p systems. In: Peer-to-Peer Computing, pp. 142–149 (2003)
21. Spiliopoulou, M., Hatzopoulos, M., Vassilakis, C.: A cost model for the estimation query execution time in a parallel environment supporting pipeline. Computers and Artificial Intelligence (4) (1996)
22. Tomov, N., Dempster, E., Williams, M.H., Burger, A., Taylor, H., King, P.J.B., Broughton, P.: Analytical response time estimation in parallel relational database systems. Parallel Comput. 30(2), 249–283 (2004)
23. de Carvalho Costa, R.L., Furtado, P.: A qos-oriented external scheduler. In: SAC 2008: Proceedings of the 2008 ACM symposium on Applied computing, pp. 1029–1033. ACM, New York (2008)
24. Huynh, T.D., Jennings, N.R., Shadbolt, N.R.: An integrated trust and reputation model for open multi-agent systems. Autonomous Agents and Multi-Agent Systems 13(2), 119–154 (2006)
25. Transaction processing council benchmarks - (Last Visited in January 2008), http://www.tpc.org/

Flying Low: Simple Leases with Workspace Pilot

Timothy Freeman and Katarzyna Keahey

Computation Institute
University of Chicago and
Argonne National Laboratory
{tfreeman,keahey}@uchicago.edu

Abstract. As the use of virtual machines (VMs) for scientific applications becomes more common, we encounter the need to integrate VM provisioning models into the existing resource management infrastructure as seamlessly as possible. To address such requirements, we describe an approach to VM management that uses multi-level scheduling to integrate VM provisioning into batch schedulers such as PBS. We then evaluate our approach on the TeraPort cluster at the University of Chicago.

1 Introduction

Resource leases – allowing a user to request direct access to resources rather than ask for a job to be run on those resources– are emerging as a fundamental abstraction of computing infrastructure. A lease may take the form of a static, long-term agreement with a hosting company, on-demand provisioning of a physical cluster partition with specified configuration as implemented by cluster-on-demand [1], or dynamically deploying a virtual machine for an hour on resources provided by Amazon's EC2 service [2]. A user can adapt such resource to his or her needs in a variety of ways: use it to support an interactive session, run computations requiring an application-specific scheduler, or support portability tests across a variety of environments. The need for resource leases rather than running jobs is exemplified by the widespread popularity of various "pilot job" approaches [3-6] that use batch scheduler installations on sites to deliver a lease rather than submit a job to that scheduler.

Virtual Machines (VMs) represent an ideal vehicle for implementing resource leases because of their isolation and enforcement properties. Among others, a VM configured by an application scientist can be deployed on many different sites without requiring the resource providers to understand the application and its dependencies, or integrate them into the configuration of their site [7, 8]. This makes VM-based resource provisioning attractive to both providers and consumers [9]. However, despite these advantages, VMs have not seen widespread adoption so far due to a relatively high barrier involved in adapting a site infrastructure for VM deployment. A solution is required that would allow sites to experiment with VM adoption without committing themselves to VM-based operations.

In this paper, we use the "pilot jobs" approach, combined with the VM management capabilities of the workspace service [10], to adapt local resource managers (LRMs), such as Torque [11] or SGE [12], for VM deployment. Our "workspace pilot" allows a resource provider to continue making its resources available to run jobs via a batch scheduler within the model of operations prevalent today but also allows for the deployment of VMs as need arises. Further, since the workspace pilot requires no modifications to the LRM it extends, it enables non-invasive, easy adoption. We discuss the advantages and limitations of the proposed approach as well as the implementation details of the relevant parts of the workspace service. The workspace pilot has been deployed at the TeraPort cluster at the University of Chicago [13] using Torque as the LRM: we evaluate and discuss the its performance on that system.

This paper is structured as follows. Section 2 describes our approach and discusses its advantages and limitations. Section 3 describes the relevant implementation details. Section 4 contains the evaluation on the TeraPort cluster. Section 5 discusses the related work and we conclude in Section 6.

2 Approach

We use a multi-level scheduling approach, similar to that employed by Condor [3] glide-ins, to enable resource leasing with VMs. This approach relies on submitting a job to the LRM with a resource allocation request expressed in terms of duration and resources (such as number of nodes or memory). When scheduled, the job request results in the deployment of a "pilot program" that adapts the node for use within its framework and reports the availability of the node to an external framework (e.g. by joining a Condor pool). Our work leverages this mechanism to adapt physical resources for VM deployment, and then reports their availability for VM hosting to the Workspace Service which provisions VMs on it.

2.1 Overview of the Workspace Services

The virtual workspace services (VWS) [10] are a group of WSRF [14] services that allow an authorized remote client to deploy and manage workspaces (implemented as VMs). The *workspace factory* makes available the descriptions of lease types available on a specific site (e.g., what resources can be assigned to a VM). Using the factory, a client can deploy a workspace, which can be represented by a VM, a group of n homogeneous VMs (each associated with the same image and resource allocation -- memory, CPU, etc. available to the VM), or a group of heterogeneous VMs on a specified set of resources [15]. Once the workspace is deployed, the *workspace service* allows the client to access information related to each deployed VM. The client can also subscribe for notifications of events related to the VM lifecycle (e.g., it can be notified when a VM is deployed). The *workspace group* and *workspace ensemble services* allow a client to obtain information about and manage workspaces made up of homogeneous and heterogeneous VMs respectively.

Workspace services are intended to be deployed on a service node of a cluster (i.e., "gatekeeper", or headnode) and rely on a VM manager (workspace back-end) deployed on a set of worker nodes to carry out VM management requests. The workspace tools provide a default implementation of such manager (called "workspace default") that provides a simple, "greedy" mapping of workspaces to nodes. The VM manager back-end could also be implemented by a datacenter technology or by the combination of an LRM and the workspace pilot described here.

2.2 Two-Level Provisioning

The approach described here assumes that VMs will be leased on a cluster equipped with n nodes each of which is configured such that they can serve both as job platform and a VM platform (e.g., Xen [16] nodes that have been booted into domain 0). Each node has access to local disk storage, which we use to store VM images. The nodes are managed by an LRM.

The objective of the "pilot program" submission is to obtain a time-constrained lease of a number of physical cluster nodes and adapt those nodes to make the deployment of VMs possible. We call such lease a *resource slot*. As shown below, a resource slot can support the deployment of potentially multiple VMs (*virtual resources*). We thus operate in a two-level provisioning model: resource slots are provisioned from the resource provider (i.e., the physical clusters) and then virtual resources are provisioned from those slots.

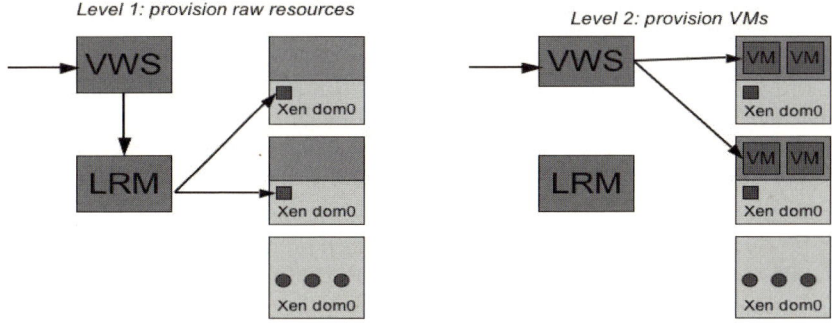

Fig. 1. Two level scheduling: (1) the pilot adjusts the memory to obtain a resource slot, and (2) the obtained slots are used to schedule VMs

The provisioning and deployment of resource slots takes place as follows. First, the workspace service submits a pilot job with requirements defining a resource slot to the LRM. The resource slot is defined in terms of duration, the number of nodes and the number of processors per node. The LRM queues and eventually executes the request. On execution, the pilot job adapts the platform for VM deployment (e.g., adjusts the memory of Xen domain 0 to allow for deployment of user domains). Then, the pilot notifies the workspace service that the resource slot has been obtained. When the resource slot terminates the pilot gracefully terminates the slot collaborating with the workspace service on cleanup actions.

The provisioning of virtual machines (the workspace default) operates as follows. On receiving a client request, the workspace service estimates the amount of physical resource needed to provide the resource allocation requested by the client. If the physical resource is already available (as a result of a prior LRM request) the required resource slot is returned, otherwise a resource slot is requested via the LRM. Once the slot is obtained, the workspace service maps the VMs onto the resource slot using greedy algorithm and the client is notified of the availability of the VM. After the elapsed VM lifetime or upon client request the VMs are terminated.

Note, that the approach described here replaces the assumption that workspace deployment relies on a static set of physical resources with a dynamically provisioned (and dynamically released) set of physical resources. The Workspace Service may implement a variety of policies when requesting/releasing resources via the pilot and mapping VMs onto those resources, e.g. physical resources may be provisioned proactively or in direct response to a request, they may be overprovisioned (e.g., allow for renegotiation of slot duration), or already provisioned resource may be opportunistically used to schedule different workspaces. All these policies balance utilization costs versus flexibility, response time and request priority. The default policy (evaluated in this paper) favors resource utilization: we request exactly as many physical resources as needed to support an incoming workspace request. Further, the default policy always translates the requested resources into the smallest resource slot into which they fit so that it can be provisioned by the LRM, mapping one VM per node.

2.3 Leasing Resources with Workspace Pilot: Client's Viewpoint

Since the workspace pilot relies on the LRM to schedule physical resource leases, the lease semantics it can provide are limited by the LRM. In particular, if our default policy is followed (one physical lease gets requested per virtual lease) the lease semantics will follow the LRM policies exactly. As many sites today do not give users the ability to do advance reservations (even when this functionality is provided by the scheduler) due to policy issues, the leases provided by the workspace pilot are likely to be "best effort" i.e., they will provision the lease as resources become available.

Most scientific computations today are performed on integrated cluster infrastructure where nodes configured to perform specialized services (data access, compute nodes, worker nodes) collaborate on satisfying demands of specific computation. For a functional cluster to be deployed it is necessary to deploy all those nodes at once. Especially when the lease semantics are best-effort (i.e., we cannot time-synchronize that deployment), we need to provide mechanisms that will ensure that the VMs representing cluster nodes are deployed together. This role is fulfilled by the workspace group and ensemble services (see Section 2.1) that allow users to prepare groups of services to be deployed together.

We now describe an example of how various features of the workspace tools are used by a client in a simple deployment case. In order to deploy a complex cluster, e.g. an Open Science Grid (OSG) cluster consisting of a compute element (CE), a storage element (SE) and n worker nodes [17], a client performs the following actions. First, the client requests the creation a workspace (an "ensemble") consisting of n worker node VMs, and a VM representing the SE and CE each. As part of the creation request, the worker nodes request an IP on a private network while each of the service nodes requests a public IP assignment in addition to the private network IP assignment. Since the ensemble workspace is created in one request, the workspace service will allocate resources to host all the members of the ensemble and they all will be deployed at the same time. The final remaining step is to "contextualize" the cluster (i.e., integrate deployment time configuration information into the cluster); this process exceeds the bounds of this paper and is described elsewhere [18].

3 Implementation

To implement the approach described above we developed the workspace pilot program, the workspace control program that integrates the VMs into the network fabric, and a simple LRM adapter.

3.1 The LRM Adapter

The implementation of the LRM adapter is composed of two components. The first is implemented by the workspace service and consists of control and monitoring interfaces to the LRM (e.g., *qsub* and *qdel* commands for Torque). We assume that the LRM may send a courtesy catchable signal before job termination (SIGTERM in Torque) which allows the pilot to implement graceful exit procedures upon receiving the signal. The second component (described in 3.2) is therefore implemented within the pilot program and consists of signal handlers.

3.2 The Workspace Pilot

The actions required to adapt a job platform for VM hosting depends on how much these two platforms differ. Our implementation assumes that the cluster which constitutes a job platform is installed with Xen and booted into domain 0 with maximum amount of memory given to each node. Therefore, to bridge the gap between the job platform and VM hosting platform we only have to reduce domain 0 memory so as to be able to host user VMs.

On deployment, the workspace pilot is given information about the expected duration of the slot and the requested resources. Based on this information the pilot reduces the domain 0 memory using the Xen balloon driver (this is a privileged operation which requires the pilot runs in to have sudo authorization). It is a matter of policy how the memory requirements of a VM are translated into the actual memory reduction: reserving more than absolutely necessary allows us to potentially schedule other VMs in the same slot but on the other hand leaving more memory in domain 0 can favorably impact guest performance [9] (the minimum is currently set to 100 MB). After the memory is adjusted, the pilot notifies the workspace service that the slot is ready. Under a normal set of circumstances the pilot is terminated either by a direct request from the workspace service or because the duration of the slot has expired. It then calls the "release slot" operation that will completely undo the effects of the "reserve slot".

Occasionally the pilot program may receive a catchable signal (SIGTERM) from the LRM, e.g. if it has exceeded its allotted time, is being preempted or removed by the LRM, or due to a reboot action. The workspace pilot catches the warning signal (which in effect offers a "grace period" before hard termination) and implements the following signal handler. It first notifies workspace service that it has received a preemption signal. It then waits for a portion of the "grace period" for the workspace service to clean up any running VMs. If the cleanup does not occur, the pilot destroys the VMs itself, restores the memory, and notifies the workspace service of the performed actions. To address the situation where a system administrator has to manually restore the nodes to a job platform we implemented a standalone "kill all" program (a direct call to the hypervisor to immediately destroy all local VMs and adjust the memory to release all available memory back to domain 0).

The workspace pilot program communicates with the workspace service via a configurable protocol by default relying on HTTP-based notifications (with SSH-based communications also possible). These notifications are time stamped so that they can be tracked by the workspace service for state recovery (e.g., in the event that the service itself recovers from failure).

3.3 The Nuts and Bolts of VM Deployment: Workspace Control Implementation

The workspace control program manages VMs on individual nodes based on commands received from the workspace service. Its primary functions are: (1) to start, stop and pause VMs, (2) to provide VM image reconstruction and management, (3) connect the VMs to the network, and (4) to deliver contextualization information [18].

To carry out VM image management functions, workspace control transfers VM images from a location within the site to the node on which it executes. The workspace service allows clients to request VM image reconstruction from disk partitions cached on the site, e.g. if a large disk partition is frequently used by images deployed on that site. Workspace control orchestrates mounting of the requisite disks and it can also generate blank partitions for images that require extra disk space.

Workspace control connects the deployed VMs to the network via a mechanism that was designed to make the IP assignment process independent of any site DHCP servers while still leveraging this prevalent IP assignment mechanism. It also bootstraps a trusted network for the VMs: the MAC address and the IP address that are chosen for a specific VM are communicated to workspace control by the workspace service. During instantiation, the VM's NICs are each assigned MAC addresses, each connected to a specific bridge port of a Linux bridge in domain 0, and ebtables is configured to recognize the associations and prevent any divergence. The MAC address and IP address association is configured in the DHCP delivery tool which intercepts a VM's boot-up sequence DHCP broadcast, giving the correct IP address to the requests based on the request source's MAC address.

The contextualization information (information allowing the cluster to interpret its context, see Section 6) is currently conveyed by "patching" the deployed image (i.e., mounting the image and copying the information into a well-defined location). Other methods are described in [18].

Workspace control is implemented is a set of lightweight Python programs and shell scripts installed on all the nodes managed by the workspace service. Its main dependencies are a DHCP delivery tool that aids in assigning IP addresses to VMs and the *ebtables* bridging packet filter package for Linux. The workspace service communicates with workspace-control via an SSH-based protocol.

4 Experimental Evaluation

We evaluated the standup and teardown times for the virtual cluster within our system. The experiments were conducted on 16 nodes of the TeraPort cluster [13], managed by Torque 2.2.1 and Maui Cluster Scheduler 3.2.6-19, and consisting of AMD64 IBM Opteron nodes with 4GB RAM each, connected by gigabit ethernet. The nodes were configured with Xen 3.1.0. During the measurements described here only the workspace pilot jobs were submitted to the nodes, such that they could be executed instantly. We measured creation times for differently-sized virtual clusters composed of single CPU nodes with 1GB of RAM. To isolate the performance specific to our service we assumed that images are already available on the nodes (work on coordinating image transfer and deployment can be found in [19]).

The measurements were taken by storing local timestamps of particular events during cluster create/destroy sequences so we synchronized the clocks on all the machines using NTP. The results shown represent a mean taken over 45 measurements for each cluster size (for N>1 we took the mean over the nodes participating in the iteration). While measuring job startup times with Torque we found that in about 20% of the cases job startups for large N (15 and 16) would be delayed in scheduler queue -- this behavior was found to be specific to the site configuration which was outside of our control; we thus discarded those measurements.

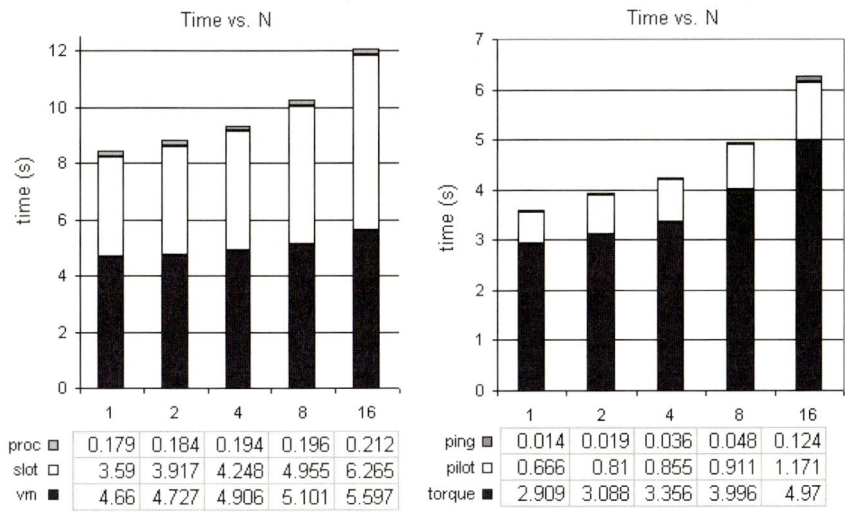

Fig. 2. End to end client time **Fig. 3.** Slot provisioning

We first timed how long it takes to adapt a node for VM deployment using the Xen balloon driver. We used the the xm mem-set command to reduce the memory in domain 0; on average this took 743.6 ms (SD = 100.5). Restoring the memory includes system checks (e.g., for running VMs) and took 1317.2 ms (SD = 96.5). The kill-all command took 2336.27 ms (SD=236.7). Our trials showed no correlation to the size of adjusted memory and the time of the operation; all numbers were computed as arithmetic mean over 100 trials adjusting 1GB of memory.

Figure 2 shows the time elapsed between the time when a client (located on the same node as the workspace service) submits a request and the time when the client receives notification of request completion. We broke the time into three parts: slot provisioning (*slot*), VM provisioning (*vms*), and client-side processing (*proc*). As can be seen, the time increases slightly as the number of nodes is doubled.

We then examined slot provisioning time in detail (Figure 3). The main component responsible for the time increase is the Torque startup time (*torque*) and is caused by the *pbsdsh* program used by Torque to start jobs of more than one process (in general, this component depends on the LRM used). The time increase in the pilot program (*pilot*) was tracked down to the use of *sudo* for invoking the memory reservation process: the cluster's user accounts are backed by an LDAP database and more (virtually simultaneous) memory calls put extra load on the LDAP server. The notification time (*ping*) increases the load on the workspace service as it is required to receive and respond to increasingly more HTTP notifications.

Next, we looked at the time to create a virtual cluster (Figure 4). The invocation of workspace control mechanisms (*invoke*) is currently implemented with SSH and again with increasing N it puts increasing load on the workspace service (the sudo issue also plays a role). Faster messaging mechanisms that implement collective communication will reduce this time by an order of magnitude or more. The bulk of the time is spent in starting the VMs and connecting them to the network (*create*). The slight decreasing tendency with increasing N is deceptive: it is accounted for by significant timing differences between individual nodes (VMs for small N were running on slow nodes hence the higher mean. The time spent in notifications (*post*) is insignificant compared to the other times.

Figure 5 shows the time elapsed during a typical destruction sequence: a client issues an explicit destroy request. In the figure below *destroy* shows the time it takes the workspace service to terminate all VMs, SIGTERM shows the time it takes for the scheduler to post a SIGTERM signal as a result of qdel request generated by the

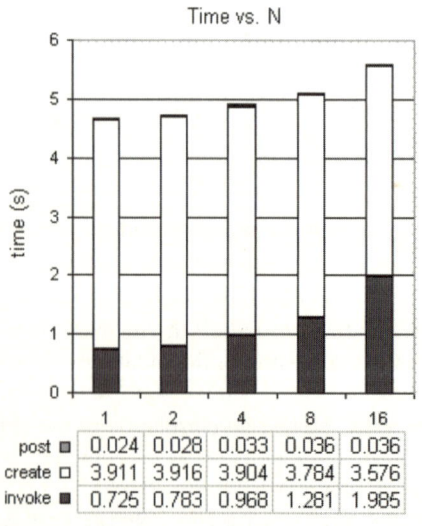 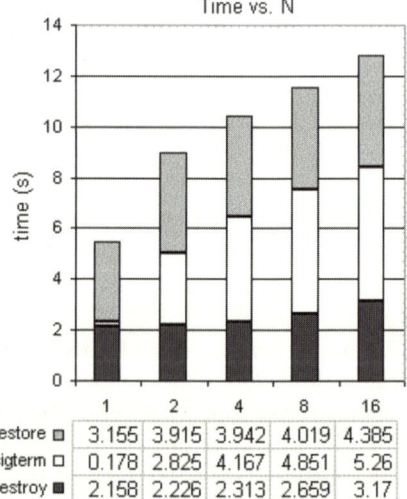

Fig. 4. Service mechanisms without LRM and pilot time

Fig. 5. Destruction overview

workspace service, and *restore* shows the pilot restore operation that includes memory adjustment and a substantial idling period. As in the creation times, the LRM is the least scalable component of the time although the use of sudo in the pilot invocation and SSH request processing also contribute to slowdown for larger N to a lesser degree. The use of *pbsdsh* accounts for the sudden jump of the *sigterm* component. When N is greater than one, *pbsdsh* runs on one node, the SIGTERM signal is sent to the local pilot process, and then only after several seconds is the message propagated to the other nodes in the group.

5 Related Work

Multi-scheduling systems have been proposed before. The Condor glide-in mechanism [3] uses a "pilot program" approach similar to the one described here to provision resources which then join a Condor pool. The MyCluster project [4] uses a similar method to create Condor and Sun Grid Engine (SGE) clusters provisioned on top of TeraGrid resources. The Falkon system [6] provisions local resources to deploy a scheduler optimized for handling fine-grained high-througput tasks. All these approaches use LRMs to dynamically provision local resources on which they then overlay a custom scheduling mechanism. Our approach is different in that we deploy VMs over the dynamically provisioned resources; then the provisioned VMs can be further differentiated (e.g. join different scheduling pools). A cluster provisioned with the workspace pilot does not restrict the client's choice of a scheduler (in fact the client need not use a scheduler at all).

Many groups have also explored the integration of LRMs and virtualization. The Dynamic Virtual Clustering (DVC) system [20] integrates the Moab scheduler [21] with Xen to create virtual clusters on a per-job basis so as to provide a unique software environment for a particular application or a consistent software environment across multiple heterogeneous clusters (similar mechanisms are supported in the production version of the Moab scheduler [22]). Fallenbeck et al. [23] proposed Xen-based extensions to the SGE using two VM images (one representing the environment required for parallel and one for serial jobs) to optimize the scheduling functions of the cluster by suspending and resuming those images. All these approaches assume a priori preparation and vetting of images by the cluster administrator and deploy images on a per-job basis (i.e., the modified scheduler still dispatches and manages jobs running inside the VMs). Our approach is different in that we lease out the provisioned VMs to be used via mechanisms independent of the original scheduler, allow clients to request the deployment of arbitrary images and use the contextualization process to adapt them to a particular deployment.

The leasing approach has also been explored by the Shirako project [24], the Vio-Cluster project [25], the Maestro-VS project [26] and the "cluster on the fly" project [27] all explore a leasing-based mode of cluster provisioning. But whereas our approach in this paper is to provide a leasing environment for VMs within the constraints of an existing scheduling infrastructure, the approaches described above propose new schedulers that could be develop to schedule and deploy VMs.

6 Conclusions

We have described a method that can be used to adapt a job hosting platform to provide a basic VM hosting ability in a non-invasive way. We describe both the implementation of the system and the client's view of provisioning the virtual resources. While this method gives the client limited "terms of service" (constrained by the policies implemented by the batch scheduler), it also provides a simple way for existing resource providers to experiment with VM hosting.

Our evaluation shows that, assuming image availability, virtual clusters can be provisioned reasonably cheaply and scalably using this approach: a 16 node cluster can be provisioned in 12 seconds including VM boot time (as compared to 8 seconds for a cluster of 1). In our experiments, the least scalable component of provisioning proved to be the LRM which took half the time of overall end-to-end deployment.

Acknowledgements

This work was supported by NSF SDCI award #0721867 and, in part, by the Mathematical, Information, and Computational Sciences Division subprogram of the Office of Advanced Scientific Computing Research, SciDAC Program, Office of Science, U.S. Department of Energy, under Contract DE-AC02-06CH11357. We thank Greg Cross and Ti Leggett for discussion of the workspace pilot implementation.

References

1. Chase, J., Grit, L., Irwin, D., Moore, J., Sprenkle, S.: Dynamic Virtual Clusters in a Grid Site Manager. In: HPDC-12 (2003)
2. Amazon Elastic Compute Cloud (EC2), http://www.amazon.com/ec2
3. Frey, J., Tannenbaum, T., Foster, I., Livny, M., Tuecke, S.: A Computation Management Agent for Multi-Institutional Grids. Cluster Computing 5(3), 237–246 (2002)
4. Walker, E., Gardner, J., Litvin, V., Turner, E.: Creating Personal Adaptive Clusters for Managing Scientific Jobs in a Distributed Computing Environment. In: CLADE (2006)
5. Nilsson, P.: Experience from a pilot based system for ATLAS. In: CHEP 2007 (2007)
6. Raicu, I., Zhao, Y., Dumitrescu, C., Foster, I., Wilde, M.: Falkon: a Fast and Light-weight task execution framework. SuperComputing (2007)
7. Agarwal, A., Desmarais, R., Gable, I., Norton, A., Sobie, R., Vanderster, D.: Evaluation of Virtual Machines for HEP Grids. In: CHEP 2006 (2006)
8. Keahey, K., Freeman, T., Lauret, J., Olson, D.: Virtual Workspaces for Scientific Applications. In: SciDAC Conference 2007 (2007)
9. Freeman, T., Keahey, K., Foster, I., Rana, A., Sotomayor, B., Wuerthwein, F.: Division of Labor: Tools for Growth and Scalability of the Grids. In: ICSOC 2006 (2006)
10. Keahey, K., Foster, I., Freeman, T., Zhang, X.: Virtual Workspaces: Achieving Quality of Service and Quality of Life in the Grid. Scientific Programming Journal (2005)
11. Torque, http://www.clusterresources.com/pages/products/torque-resource-manager.php
12. Sun Grid Engine, http://gridengine.sunsource.net

13. The TeraPort Cluster, http://www.ci.uchicago.edu/research/detail_teraport.php
14. Czajkowski, K., Ferguson, D., Foster, I., Frey, J., Graham, S., Sedukhin, I., Snelling, D., Tuecke, S., Vambenepe, W.: The WS-Resource Framework (2004), http://www.globus.org/wsrf
15. Virtual Workspaces, http://workspace.globus.org
16. Barham, P., Dragovic, B., Fraser, K., Hand, S., Harris, T., Ho, A., Neugebar, R., Pratt, I., Warfield, A.: Xen and the Art of Virtualization. In: ACM Symposium on Operating Systems Principles (SOSP)
17. Freeman, T., Keahey, K., Sotomayor, B., Zhang, X., Foster, I., Scheftner, D.: Virtual Clusters for Grid Communities. In: CCGrid (2006)
18. Bradshaw, R., Desai, N., Freeman, T., Keahey, K.: A Scalable Approach to Deploying and Managing Virtual Appliances. In: TeraGrid 2007 (2007)
19. Sotomayor, B., Keahey, K., Foster, I.: Overhead Matters: A Model for Virtual Resource Management. In: 1st International Workshop on Virtualization Technology in Distributed Computing (VTDC) (2006)
20. Emeneker, W., Jackson, D., Butikofer, J., Stanzione, D.: Dynamic Virtual Clustering with Xen and Moab. Workshop on Xen in HPC Cluster and Grid Computing Environments (XHPC) (2006)
21. The MOAB Workload Manager, http://www.clusterresources.com/pages/products/moab-cluster-suite/workload-manager.php
22. MOAB Administrator's Guide: Virtualization and Resource Provisioning, http://www.clusterresources.com/products/mwm/docs/5.6resourceprovisioning.shtml
23. Fallenbeck, N., Picht, H., Smith, M., Freisleben, B.: Xen and the Art of Cluster Scheduling. In: VTDC (2006)
24. Irwin, D., Chase, J., Grit, L., Yunerefendi, A., Decker, D., Yocum, K.: Sharing Networked Resources with Brokered Leases. In: USENIX Technical Conference (2006)
25. Ruth, P., McGachey, P., Xu, D.: VioCluster: Virtualization for Dynamic Computational Domains. In: IEEE Conference on Cluster Computing (2005)
26. Kiyanclar, N., Koenig, G.A., Yurcik, W.: Maestro-VS: A Paravirtualized Execution Environment for Secure On-Demand Cluster Computing. In: CCGrid (2006)
27. Nishimura, H., Maruyama, N., Matsuoka, S.: Virtual Clusers on the Fly – Fast, Scalable and Flexible Installation. In: CCGrid (2007)

Self-configuring Resource Discovery on a Hypercube Grid Overlay

Antonia Gallardo[1], Luis Díaz de Cerio[2], and Kana Sanjeevan[1]

[1] Departament de Arquitectura de Computadors, Universitat Politécnica de Catalunya,
Avda. del Canal Olímpic s/n, 08860 Castelldefels, Barcelona, Spain
[2] Departamento de Automática y Computación, Universidad Pública de Navarra,
Campus Arrosadía s/n, 31006 Pamplona, Spain
{agallard,sanji}@ac.upc.edu, luismanuel.diazdecerio@unavarra.es

Abstract. Grid Resource Discovery Service is a fundamental problem that has been the focus of research in the recent past. We propose a scheme that presents essential characteristics for efficient, self-configuring and fault-tolerant resource discovery and is able to handle dynamic attributes, such as memory capacity. Our approach consists of an overlay network with a hypercube topology connecting the grid nodes and a scalable, fault-tolerant, self-configuring search algorithm. The algorithm improves the probability of reaching all working nodes in the system even in the presence of non-alive nodes (inaccessible, crashed or heavy loaded nodes). We analyze the static resilience of the approach presented, which is the measure of how well the algorithm can discover resources without having to update the routing tables.

Keywords: Static resilience, Fault-tolerance, Grid resource discovery, Hypercube, Self-configuring algorithm.

1 Introduction

The main objective of a Grid is to enable users to solve problems using the available collective resources provided by the often called Virtual Organizations (VO) [1]. In this way, the Grid resource discovery service plays a fundamental role, allowing grid-enabled applications to locate resources based on a given set of requirements. It is a challenging problem since a Grid system includes a large number of heterogeneous and dynamic resources that are geographically distributed.

At present, most implementations of current grids have a centralized or hierarchical architecture. Unfortunately, these types of architectures do not fully address the need for fault-tolerance that a Grid environment requires.

Resource search in Peer-to-Peer (P2P) systems offers an attractive approach to deploy fully distributed fault tolerant grid discovery service. But for the Grid, we have some extra requirements such as the existence of dynamic resource information (e.g. available memory, disk space, etc). In these cases, some of the P2P searching techniques are difficult to apply because they are more suitable for non-dynamic content.

Moreover it is necessary, as pointed out by Ian Foster and Adriana Iamnitchi [2], "to address failure at a fundamental level, using scalable self-configuring protocols in order to have a worldwide computer within which access to resources and services can be negotiated as and when needed".

Motivated by this open research area, we present HGrid as a scalable and decentralized architecture that allows the search of geographically distributed resources while preserving the autonomy of each individual VO. The architecture is based on an overlay network with hypercube topology which interconnects nodes provided by the VOs. We also present a self-configuring resource discovery algorithm that is able to adapt to complex environments where some nodes might be non-alive (crashed, inaccessible, experiencing heavy traffic, etc.) when a resource is required.

One of the challenges of Grid Resource Discovery is to be resilient in the presence of node failures. This resilience has different aspects: *static resilience* and *routing recovery*. As the present work is focused on the resource discovery algorithm this paper only addresses *static resilience*, that is, how well our approach can locate required resources before routing tables are updated by the routing recovery algorithm in order to remove non-alive nodes from the overlay [3]. The other issue, *routing recovery*, deals with the fact that when failures occur, the routing tables are depleted in the remaining nodes. Routing recovery is not addressed in this paper as this issue is related to the building and maintaining of the overlay topology.

The design of the system is driven by its application as part of the resource discovery in grids. Our approach complements current solutions such as MDS-4 (the Monitoring and Discovery System of Globus) by adding a self-configuring and fault-tolerant protocol. Additionally, it improves upon DHT based implementations where for instance, remapping data has very high cost and it is not required in our proposal. A more detailed comparison can be found in section 4.

The rest of the paper is organized as follows: In Section 2 we present an overview of our overlay network architecture. Section 3 describes our resource search algorithm. A brief overview of related work is presented in Section 4. In Section 5, the performance of the algorithm is evaluated. Conclusions and our plans for future work can be found in Section 6.

2 The Hypercube Overlay Architecture

In current Grid environments, the administrative domains do not join or leave the Grid continually but occasionally. Most of the current VOs that form a Grid have powerful servers within their high performance local area networks and maybe they are interconnected by very high speed core networks. The servers seldom fail and they join and leave the system infrequently. Therefore the Grid Resource Management can be organized in a stable and regular topology with low-diameter configurations, efficient searching and routing algorithms that address failures.

Each VO belonging to HGrid provides available resources and makes them accessible through the called Grid Information System (GIS) [4]. Since the Grid is evolving into Grid services we assume the GIS stores a service description [5].

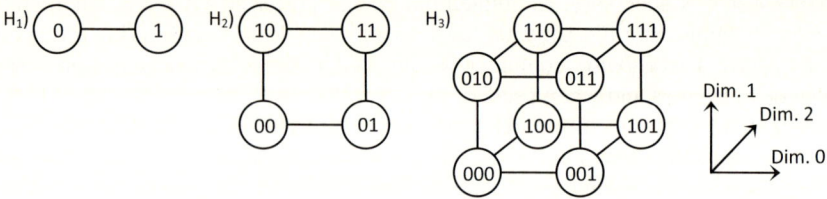

Fig. 1. H_1) The architecture for the interaction among 2 nodes, a one-dimensional hypercube, H_2) 4 nodes, a two-dimensional hypercube and H_3) 8 nodes, three-dimensional hypercube

In HGrid, the interconnections between nodes have the topology of a hypercube. An n-dimensional hypercube (H_n) has $V(H_n) = 2^n$ nodes, where each one represents a GIS. Each node has an identifier from 0 to 2^n-1. Two nodes are said to be neighbors in the m-th dimension if the binary representations of their identifiers differ exactly by the m-th bit. Therefore in a complete hypercube H_n, each node has exactly n neighbors. Figure 1 illustrates the architecture for 2, 4 and 8 nodes respectively.

An overlay network with a hypercube topology connecting each GIS in a grid environment allows each VO to contribute services while assuring their autonomous management. The services offered by a VO (and therefore its resources) can join or leave the system at any time updating its own GIS. Every GIS keeps a small routing table of only n entries ($n = \log_2 N$) corresponding to their n neighbors. Also, each GIS has the responsibility to verify which of its neighbors are still alive. The term alive is applied to a neighbor node that is reachable across the network using a tool such as *ping*. As this tool estimates the round-trip time and rate of packet loss between nodes, a node that has crashed, is inaccessible or is heavily loaded by traffic is considered a non-alive neighbor node.

3 Resource Search Using HGRID

In this section we present a scalable self-configuring resource search algorithm (named Algorithm-H) that is able to adapt to complex environments (where some grid nodes might be non-alive).

In this work, we do not address the building and maintaining of the hypercube topology when a node joins or leaves the overlay. Changes in the overlay network make the routing tables be re-mapped and this does result in some overhead. However, some of the results published regarding the scalability of hypercube overlays used in other environments seem to address this challenge and offer an adequate solution [6], [7], [8]. We assume that in Grid environments, the administrative domains join or leave the Grid occasionally, so the overhead of building and maintaining the hypercube overlay is smaller than in an extremely transient environment (where a significant fraction of the nodes are joining or leaving at any time).

Since an incomplete hypercube could be re-built as a complete hypercube where the void spaces are completed by replicating some of the GIS, we consider the number (N) of GIS is always a power of 2. So all the nodes have n-neighbors (where n is the dimensionality of the hypercube).

```
satisfyRequest =
processRequest(message.request);
IF (NOT satisfyRequest) THEN
    IF (startNode) THEN
        v_d = {0,1,...,n-1};
        v_a = {};
    ELSE
        v_d = message.v_d;
        v_a = message.v_a;
    ENDIF
    n_non-alive = statusNeighbors(v_d)
    IF (n_non-alive > 1) THEN
        v_a2 = addToList(v_a, d_alive);
    ENDIF
    FOR k=0 TO (v_d.size()-n_non-alive-1) DO
        message.v_d = createList(k, v_d);
    ...

        IF (v_d[k] = d_alive) THEN
            message.v_a = v_a2;
        ELSE
            message.v_a = v_a;
        ENDIF
        sendToNeighbor(v_d[k], message);
    ENDFOR
    FOR j=0 TO (v_a.size()-1) DO
        IF (neighbor v_a[j] NOT parent node)
            message.v_d = {};
            message.v_a = {};
            sendToNeighbor([v_a[j], message);
        ENDIF
    ENDFOR
ENDIF
```

Fig. 2. Algorithm-H: Pseudo-code in a node when a new resource request message arrives

In our proposal it is possible to initiate a search request from any of the alive nodes (GIS) of the system and to propagate the request to the rest of nodes. However, for reasons of clarity, all the examples used from now on assume that node 0 is the start node, without a loss of generality.

3.1 The Search Procedure in an H_n Using Algorithm-H

The search procedure starts when a consumer wants to discover a Grid service. The consumer connects to one of the GIS nodes of the system and requests a service (a resource or some resources). The service discovery is tried first inside the own requester's GIS. If there is no provider, then the request is redirected. Figure 2 shows the pseudo-code that is performed at each node when a request message arrives:

1) When a new service request message is received by a node the function *processRequest(message.request)* is called. If the request included in the message cannot be satisfied the node sets the value of *satisfyRequest* to false and the request will be propagated. Otherwise, *satisfyRequest* is set to true and no propagation is performed. The message forwarded is composed of the request (*message.request*) and two vectors of dimensions (*message.v_d* and *message.v_a*).
2) In case the request cannot be satisfied and the node that receives the message is the start node (*startNode* is *true*), the list v_d is initialized to $v_d = \{0, 1, ..., n-1\}$ (the complete set of dimensions) and v_a is initialized to $v_a = \{\}$ (an empty list). Otherwise, v_d and v_a are initialized to the lists received along with the request message. In both cases the lists represent the set of dimensions (neighbors) along which the message must be propagated.
3) The node calls the *statusNeighbors(v_d)* function and reorders the list v_d in such a way that the dimensions corresponding to the non-alive neighbors are located at the last positions of the list. For example if $v_d = \{0,1,2,3\}$ and the neighbor along dimension 1 is not responding, then v_d is reordered to $\{0,2,3,1\}$. The *statusNeighbors(v_d)* also returns two integer values $n_{non-alive}$ and d_{alive}. The integer value $n_{non-alive}$ represents the number of non-alive nodes in the reordered list v_d. The integer value d_{alive} represents the dimension of the last alive neighbor stored in v_d. For

example, if v_d = {2,1,0,3} and its neighbors in dimensions 0 and 3 are non-alive nodes, $n_{non\text{-}alive}$ = 2 and d_{alive} = 1.
4) If the number of non-alive neighbors ($n_{non\text{-}alive}$) is more than one, the node calls the *addToList*(v_a, d_{alive}) function. This function appends d_{alive} to the end of the list v_a and returns the new list (v_{a2}).
5) For each position k in *the* list v_d that represents an alive neighbor node, the node calls the *createList*(k, v_d) function which creates a new list composed of all the dimensions located after position k in the ordered list v_d. In other words, if the number of elements in v_d ($v_d.size()$) is q the function returns {$v_d[k+1]$, ...,$v_d[q-1]$}. For example, if v_d = {0,2,3,1} and k = 1, the call to *createList*(k, v_d) will return {3,1}. Also for each alive neighbor, the v_a list is initialized. The request, v_d, and v_a are sent to the corresponding neighbor in the $v_d[k]$ dimension inside a new message by calling the *sendToNeigbor*($v_d[k]$, *message*) function. See Figure 3 where the start node (0000) sends v_d = {2,1,0} and v_a = {3} to its last alive neighbor (the only one in this case).
6) Finally, the node propagates the request to each of the neighbors along v_a dimensions only if the corresponding neighbor is not its parent node. The request travels inside a message together with v_a and v_d as empty lists. See Figure 3 where the node 1001 send the request to its neighbor 0001 along dimension 3 ($v_a[0]$ = 3) but does not propagate the request to its neighbor in dimension 0 ($v_a[1]$ = 0) because node 1000 is its parent.

Propagating the requests in this way, the effect of non-alive nodes is reduced. Making the rearrangement in the v_d list, non-alive nodes would propagate the request to fewer neighbors than alive ones (in case the propagation were tried). Consequently, the algorithm tries to isolate the nodes that are in a non-alive state so that they become leaf nodes (if it is possible). If, under the circumstances, each node has only one non-alive neighbor, then all alive nodes can be reached. On the other hand, the nodes that are unreachable because of inaccessible or crashed nodes can be reached eventually via other nodes using the v_a list.

3.2 A Complete Example Using Algorithm-H

Figure 3 illustrates a complete example. We transform the hypercube representation to that of a *tree-like* figure in order to illustrate better our search procedure (notice, some *child* nodes could appear more than once during subsequent time steps).

A request for service *P* starts at node 0000 in a four-dimensional hypercube. We assume that none of the nodes has the service requested (note that this is the worst case). In the example, the value of the list v_d at the start node is {0, 1, 2, 3} and the ordering after calling the *statusNeighbors()* function is {3, 2, 1, 0}. In this case 2, 1 and 0 are located at the last three positions of v_d = {3, 2, 1, 0} because we assume that neighbors in dimensions 2 (0100), 1 (0010) and 0 (0001) are non-alive nodes. The neighbor in dimension 3 (1000) is the last alive node (the only one in this case), so v_{a2} = {3} and v_a = {}.

In the first step, the start node's neighbor in dimension 3 (1000) receives the service request *P*, the list v_d = {2, 1, 0} and v_a = {3} since it is the last alive neighbor. The algorithm and try to reach nodes 0110, 0101, 0011 and 0111 (whose parent nodes

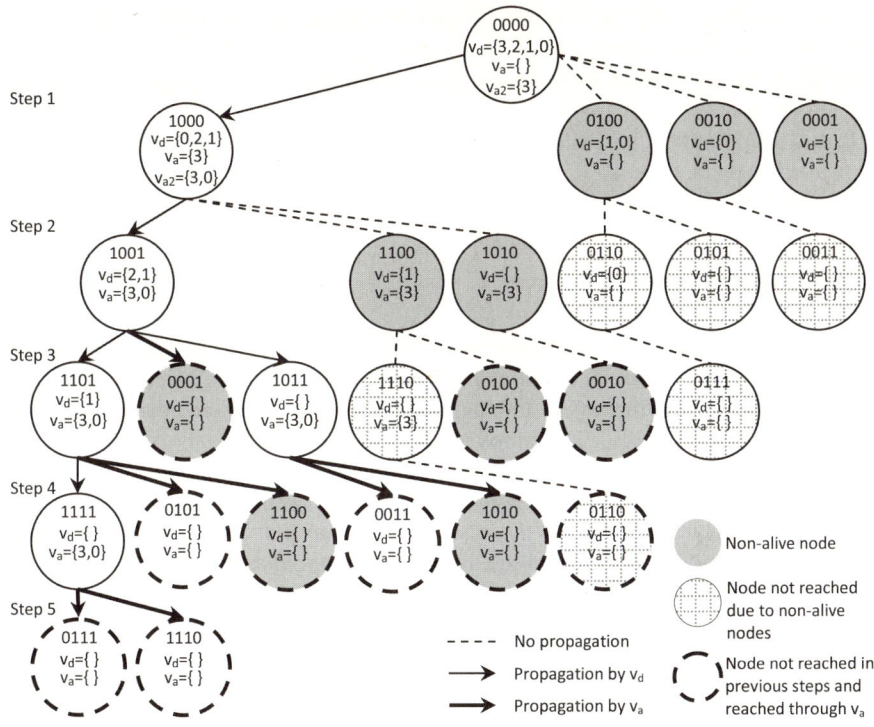

Fig. 3. A complete example using Algorithm-H. A request of resource P started at node 0000 in a four-dimensional hypercube.

are non-alive) by sending the list $v_a = \{3\}$ to node 1000 and reusing dimension 3 in following steps.

In the second step, looking at node 1000, the message composed of the resource request P along with the lists $v_d = \{2, 1, 0\}$ and $v_a = \{3\}$ is received. If the node is unable to satisfy the request (*processRequest()* returns *false*), v_d is sorted as $v_d = \{0, 2, 1\}$ because its neighbor in dimension 2 (1100) and its neighbor in dimension 1 (1010) are non-alive nodes; in this case, the neighbor in dimension 0 (1001) is the last alive node so it receives P, $v_d = \{2, 1\}$ and $v_a = \{3,0\}$. Notice that although $v_a = \{3\}$ is received by the node 1000, it does not propagate the message to its neighbor in dimension 3 (0000) because it is its parent node.

In the third step, looking at node 1001, the message composed of the resource request P along with the lists $v_d = \{2, 1\}$ and $v_a = \{3, 0\}$ is received. If *processRequest()* returns *false*, its neighbor in dimension 2 (1101) receives P, $v_d = \{1\}$ and $v_a = \{3, 0\}$ and its neighbor in dimension 1 (1011) receives P, $v_d = \{\}$ and $v_a = \{3, 0\}$. Besides, its neighbor in dimension 3 (0001) receives P, $v_d = \{\}$ and $v_a = \{\}$ due to the list $v_a = \{3, 0\}$. Notice that the non-alive node 0001 is requested twice, first through the start node and now again through node 1001. During some point between the two requests, its status might have changed from non-alive to alive.

In the fourth step, looking at node 0101, the resource request P is received from node 1101 (0101 is the neighbor in dimension $v_a[0] = 3$). Notice that 0101 was not reached in the second step due to the non-alive node 0100 but it is reached now through the node 1101.

In five steps almost all of the alive nodes inside the four-dimensional hypercube are visited (except node 0110) even when three neighbors of the start node (0100, 0010 and 0001) and two more nodes (1100 and 1010) are presumed to be non-alive.

4 Related Work

The Monitoring and Discovery System (MDS) of Globus Toolkit defines and implements mechanisms for service and resource discovery and monitoring in distributed Grid environments. Vulnerability to single points of failure and adaptation to failures are challenges for MDS-2/3 [9]. Motivated by these issues, recently there have been several studies using the P2P model to build a decentralized architecture of VOs. Most of them adopt Distributed Hash Tables (DHTs), and a few of them introduce unstructured P2P topologies. All these studies indicate that some P2P models could help to overcome the challenges of the dynamic environment in Grids.

Adriana Iamnitchi and Ian Foster [10] suggest a decentralized architecture similar to the Gnutella P2P system. Nevertheless it is not able to guarantee that some required information existing in the system can be found even if all the nodes are accessible.

Several studies have been done by applying DHTs. They handle unexpected node failure through redundancy in the network and some of them also do node lookups asynchronously or periodically, to compensate for disappeared nodes [11]. In HGrid each GIS is responsible for verifying which of its neighbors are still alive. As in DHTs, this causes overhead but keeps the network constantly updated by providing resilience to node failures.

In order to enable efficient searches, a DHT needs to have the data-item distributed across the peers. $O(\log N)$ messages are needed to distribute and searching a data-item. Our approach does not require distributing the data-items but each request sends from 0 to N-1 messages. Keeping the state of highly dynamic data-items updated (such as available memory or CPU processing) require sending a very large amount of messages in DHTs (between distributed peers). So, in the context of a Grid, considering the total number of messages between distributed peers, it is not clear that traditional DHTs are much more efficient than our approach.

In HGrid, changes in the overlay network when a grid node joins or leaves the system do not cause resource information (data-items) to be remapped, whereas in traditional DHTs, it causes both routing tables and data-items to be remapped.

A node in the traditional DHT has no control over the distribution of its data items, and the number of data items belonging to others that it has to store. DGRID [13], a model for supporting GIS over the DHT Chord, maintains the resource information in the originating VO by increasing the total number of DHT nodes. Unlike traditional DHTs, DGRID is by design resilient to node failures without the need to replicate data items. The meaning of resilient to node failures [13] is defined as the ability to locate existing resources whose originating VO is still alive. The approach presented in this paper has the same resiliency to node failures as in DGRID and also guarantees that any data item can be located in O(log N) overlay hops.

Recently, an unstructured topology based on a hypercube has been proposed for Data Grids [15]. The nodes in this work contain pointers to shared data. Data Grids need to improve locality among distributed data (which are stored as pointers in the overlay nodes). In order to improve the locality of data, the paper proposes a hypercube topology of GIS (named DGIS). The goal is to make the peers who always access each other become neighbors in the hypercube. The authors use a broadcast algorithm to send statistic information periodically. However the paper does not address non-alive nodes.

5 Performance Evaluation

As mentioned before, the present work is focused on static resilience. Next we present simulations to evaluate if some required information that exists in the system can be found (lookup guarantees) without resorting to active recovery algorithms.

For this simulation, we have tested static resilience in 14, 17 and 20 dimensional hypercube overlays. All nodes have the same probability P_f of failure. P_f can be seen as the percentage of non-alive nodes that can be found in the overlay. We run the simulation for values of P_f between 0 and 50% because we assume that the Grid environment is not extremely transient. Given a P_f, we start a request for service P at node 0 and count how many alive nodes are not requested (failed paths). We compare our approach (Algorithm-H) with two other search algorithms for hypercube overlays:

1) a non-fault-tolerant search algorithm [15] (HaoRen et al.'s algorithm)
2) a fault-tolerant search algorithm [16] that does not incorporate the v_a list (HGrid Algorithm-P)

The average percentage of failed paths for varying P_f is shown in Figure 4. Our proposal offers substantially better static resilience than the HaoRen et al.'s algorithm. The HGrid algorithm-H works very well in non-extremely transient environments, where a reduced fraction of the nodes are down at any given time (< 50% of failed

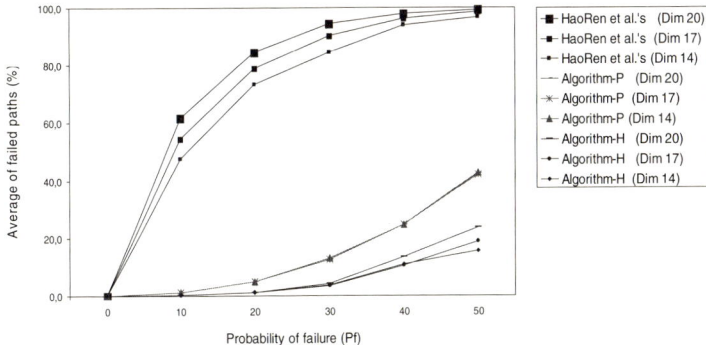

Fig. 4. Percentage of average of failed paths for varying P_f across different search algorithms

nodes in the entire Grid). At the same time, Algorithm-H offers better resilience than Algorithm-P as it can reach more live nodes without using active recovery algorithms.

Algorithm-H is not only scalable in overlay hops (n time steps where n is the dimensionality), but as seen in Figure 4, it is scalable in the number of nodes (2^{14} to 2^{20} from Figure 4)

To summarize, our results confirm that the static resiliency of the approach presented in this paper is very efficient for current Grids (non-extremely transient environments), it offers high lookup guarantees and it is highly scalable with the number of nodes.

6 Conclusions and Future Work

The geometric characteristics of a hypercube determines that the longest path between two nodes is n = $\log_2 N$, that is, the dimension of the hypercube. This property allows us to design search algorithms for resource discovery that require approximately n time steps to cover all N nodes ($N = 2^n$). The proposed algorithm is scalable in terms of time, because it keeps the maximum number of time steps required to resolve a resource request, to a logarithmic scale with respect to the total number of nodes. Moreover, each node has only partial knowledge of the overlay Grid. Nodes do not require having the state information of the whole overlay, but the state of its neighbors only. Therefore, our approach is also scalable in terms of data storage.

The present approach allows the search of geographically distributed resources while preserving the autonomy of each individual VO. Unlike traditional approaches based on DHTs our scheme is suitable for efficiently handling dynamic attributes such as memory capacity without generating overhead across geographically distributed nodes.

In our proposal a search can be initiated from any node (GIS) and propagated in such a way each other alive node is queried only once. This helps to balance the system load and is more efficient than other schemes like flooding. In the worst case, the maximum number of messages propagated through the system is N-1.

Our approach is able to adapt itself to complex environments where nodes could be heavily loaded or even crashed, without requiring any entity (node) to have the global state information. We refer to this property as self-configuring.

In the absence of non-alive nodes, a resource request could reach all nodes in the overlay, in other words, if some node is able to satisfy the request, this node will be found. Therefore the proposed scheme offers lookup guarantees in the absence of faulty nodes.

If non-alive nodes are present, the algorithm also offers lookup guarantees in some cases. More than a half of the nodes can be non-alive and still the totality of live nodes can be reached.

Other efficient DHT properties for Grid resource management have not been evaluated. Completing the comparison with DHT-enabled implementations is a goal for future work.

There are several interesting areas that have opened up as a result of this work and we are presently working on them: a) Design and evaluation of new request forwarding strategies. b) Incorporation of topology construction and maintenance algorithms. c) Evaluation in terms of response time, scalability, etc. by simulation.

Acknowledgements

This work was supported by the Ministry of Science and Technology of Spain and the European Union (TIN2007-68050-C03-01 and TIN2007-68050-C03-02).

References

1. Nabrzyski, J., Schopf, J.M., Weglarz, J.: Grid Resource Management. State of the Art and future Trends. Kluwer Publishing, Academic publishers (2004)
2. Foster, I., Iamnitchi, A.: On Death, Taxes, and the Convergence of Peer-to-Peer and Grid Computing. In: 2nd International Workshop on Peer-to-Peer Systems (2003)
3. Gummadi, K., Gummadi, R., Gribble, S., Ratnasamy, S., Shenker, S., Stoica, I.: The Impact of DHT Routing Geometry on Resilience and Proximity. In: Applications, Technologies, Architectures and Protocols for Computer Communications, pp. 381–394 (2003)
4. Buyya, R., Murshed, M.: GridSim: A Toolkit for the Modeling and Simulation of Distributed Resource Management and Scheduling for Grid Computing. Concurrency and Computation: Practice and Experience 14(13-15), 1175–1220 (2002)
5. Foster, I., et al.: The physiology of the grid: An open grid services architecture for distributed systems integration (2003), http://www.globus.org
6. Bona, L.C.E., Fonseca, K.V.O., Duarte Jr., E.P., Mello, S.L.V.: HyperBone: A Scalable Overlay Network Based on a Virtual Hypercube. In: IEEE International Symposium on Cluster Computing and the Grid, pp. 58–64 (2008)
7. Liebeherr, J., Beam, T.K.: HyperCast: A Protocol for Maintaining Multicast Group Members in a Logical Hypercube Topology. In: Rizzo, L., Fdida, S. (eds.) NGC 1999. LNCS, vol. 1736, pp. 72–89. Springer, Heidelberg (1999)
8. Liebeherr, J., Sethi, B.S.: A Scalable Control Topology for Multicast Communications. In: IEEE Infocom (1998)
9. Czajkowski, K., Fitzgerald, S., Foster, I., Kesselman, C.: Grid Information Services for Distributed Resource Sharing. In: 10th IEEE International Symposium on High Performance Distributed Computing. IEEE Press, Los Alamitos (2001)
10. Iamnitchi, A., Foster, I.: On fully decentralized resource discovery in grid environments. In: International Workshop on Grid Computing, pp. 51–62. Springer, Heidelberg (2001)
11. Kademlia: A Design Specification, http://xlattice.sourceforge.net/components/protocol/kademlia/specs.html
12. March, V., Teo, Y.M., Wang, X.: DGRID: A DHT-Based Resource Indexing and Discovery Scheme for Computational Grids. In: 5th Australasian Symposium on Grid Computing and e-Research, pp. 41–48 (2007)
13. Ren, H., Wang, Z., Liu, Z.: A Hyper-cube based P2P Information Service for Data Grid. In: Conference on Grid and Cooperative Computing, pp. 508–513 (2006)
14. Gallardo, A., Díaz de Cerio, L., Sanjeevan, K., Bona, L.C.E.: HGRID: An Adaptive Grid Resource Discovery. In: International Conference on Complex, Intelligent and Software Intensive Systems. Workshop on Adaptive Systems in Heterogeneous Environments (2008)

Auction Protocols for Resource Allocations in Ad-Hoc Grids

Behnaz Pourebrahimi and Koen Bertels

Computer Engineering Laboratory, Delft University of Technology, The Netherlands
{b.pourebrahimi,k.l.m.bertels}@tudelft.nl

Abstract. Different auction-based approaches have been used to allocate resources in Grids, but none of them provide the design choice for a specific economic model while considering the interest of all participants in the market. In this paper, we implement an auction-based framework for producer and consumer matchmaking in an ad-hoc Grid. In ad-hoc Grids, where the availability of resources and tasks is highly dynamic, the producers and consumers have to compete for providing and employing the resources. The framework is used to assess the usefulness of a particular mechanism using a set of criteria in different network conditions. We present the performance analysis of different auction mechanisms namely First-Price, Vickrey and Double Auctions in a many-to-many manner. The evaluation is performed in terms of throughput, consumer and producer surplus, and uncertainty measure for obtaining required resources in different network conditions.

1 Introduction

Economic-based approaches have been widely studied for resource allocation in Grid [1,2,3]. These approaches mainly focus on efficiency of a particular economic model in the condition where the resources have predefined use and access policy. None of these researches attempts to provide a design choice for a specific economic model while considering the interest of all participants in the market. We propose a meta research on economic-based resource allocation in ad-hoc Grids where resources have different access, use, and cost models and show high variations in their availability patterns. We developed a framework to simulate the Grid components such as Grid users, resource providers and resource allocator(matchmaker) in an ad-hoc Grid. This framework helps to study the impact of different auction models for resource allocation while considering different parameters from Grid owners and Grid users perspectives.

In our implementation of an ad-hoc Grid, every node in the network can act as a consumer or a producer of resources at any time when there is a need for resource or there is a resource available. In such dynamic condition, there is no global information available and decision-making process is distributed across all users and resource owners. We consider many-to-many auctions for matchmaking between these competitive and selfish consumers and producers as these type of auctions support simultaneous participation of producer/consumer, observes resource/request deadlines and can accommodate the variations in resource availability. In our framework, matchmaking model uses three auction protocols (Continuous Double Auction, First Price and Vickrey Auction) in a many-to-many market approach. This paper is not intended to merely compare the efficiency of different auction protocols but intends to provide a design choice in ad hoc Grid by comparing them based on throughput, consumer surplus, producer surplus and uncertainty measure in getting required resources in different conditions of the network.

The paper is structured as follows: we discuss related work in Section 2, Section 3 studies different auction mechanisms and describes the reason for our choice of three specific auction protocols. System implementation is discussed in Section 4. In this section, we present system architecture and pricing algorithm. Experimental setup and results are presented in section 5. In Section 6, we discuss the results and finally we conclude in Section 7.

2 Related Work

In the literature, we can find several computational markets that use auctions for resource allocation such as [4,5,6]. Most of the previous works consider only one type of the auction and compare it with other economic and conventional models. Gomoluch et al [7] investigate that under which circumstances market-based resource allocation by Continuous Double Auction (CDA) and by the proportional share protocol, outperforms a conventional round-robin approach. It is concluded for a cluster of homogeneous resources the Continuous Double Auction will perform best. However, if the load is low, the differences between three protocols are small, and using the computationally less expensive Round-Robin protocol might be sufficient. For a situation where there is a choice of resources with different quality of load - as it is the case in a computational Grid - the results of Round-Robin will be worse than for two market-based protocols [7]. The CDA will perform best in most cases[7]. [8] presents a periodic double auction mechanism with uniform price for resource allocation on Grid. In this work, auction takes place in rounds and all exchanges are performed with the same price. There are few researches that compare different auction models. [9] compares three different variations of Double-Auction protocols from both resource's and user's perspectives. Comparison parameters in [9] are resource utilization, resource profit and consumed budget. It concludes that CDA protocol outperforms the other two variations of DA from both user's and resource's perspectives. In [10], three types of auction protocols are investigated; First-Price Auction, Vickrey Auction and Double Auction. Resource utilization, resource profit and user payment is measured as the parameters for comparing these protocols. Simulation environment consists of limited number of resources with predefined capabilities, reservation price and Risk Averse/Risk Neutral users. Their results show the First-Price Auction is better from resource's perspective while Vickrey Auction is better from user's perspective. Double Auction favors both resources and users [10]. The work in [11] analyzes the different auction models in terms of communication demand for resource allocation in Grid computing environments. The investigation is done on First-Price sealed, English, Dutch and Continuous Double Auctions. Their experiments show that English auction present higher communication requirements while CDA presents least demand of communications.

In above mentioned researches, economic based resource allocation has been done in the context of conventional Grids. In conventional Grid, resources are assumed to be dedicated with a fixed number of nodes which provide services. The main contribution of this paper is to provide a design choice for resource allocation in ad-hoc Grids considering Grid objectives and network conditions. We provide a framework for auction-based resource allocation in ad-hoc Grids, in which every node can be a consumer or a producer of resource at any time according to its current workload and its available resources. The experiments are performed in different network conditions with varying number of resources and tasks available in the network. Three auction protocols are compared based on throughput, consumer surplus, producer surplus and budget and transaction price variation in different network conditions.

3 Economic Price-Based Mechanisms

Microeconomic based resource allocation approaches can be identified in two, *price-directed* and *resource-directed* (non-price based) approaches. Non-price approaches are either selfish or cooperative and they are based on Game theory or cooperative mechanisms[12][13]. In the price directed approaches, consumers and producers interact via market mechanisms for allocating resources. Two main broad of mechanisms for setting prices are: **commodities markets** and **auctions**. In both the mechanisms, the main components are *consumers, producers* and a third party that acts as a *mediator* between consumers and producers. The third party in auction models is auctioneer that determines the sale of an individual resource (or a resource bundle) based on the bids. The basic philosophy behind auctions is that the highest bidder always gets the resources, and the current price for a resource is determined by the bid prices. The third party in commodity market, sets a price for a resource (or a bundle of resources) based on demand and supply. The price is calculated based on tatonnement process [14]. The tatonnement process varies the price of the individual or bundle of resources until an equilibrium is reached. Commodity markets rely on polling aggregate supply and demand repeatedly to calculate the equilibrium price and all allocations are performed in this price. As in ad hoc Grids the resources are not dedicated and supply/demand of resources is very dynamic, the complexity of implementing such centralized market which rely on the aggregate supply/demand of resources becomes infeasible. Therefore, we have selected auction models as the platform for matchmaking of consumer and producer of resources in ad-hoc Grids. In the following section, we study different auction models.

3.1 Auction Mechanisms

Auctions can be classified into *open* or *close* auctions. In open auctions, bidders know the bid value of other bidders. In closed or sealed auctions, the participants' bids are not disclosed to others. Within auction based economic models, pricing is driven by how much value resource owner places on the goods (services) and access to services is won by that consumer whose valuation comes closest to that of the resource owner [15]. In these models, there is no global information available about the supply and demand and buyers and sellers usually are not aware of the other's bids or asks and they decide on their local knowledge. An overview of the most popular auction mechanisms is provided below.

- **English Auction:** In English auction the seller openly announces a minimal price for the good to be sold. It follows a sequential bidding in which buyers take turns publicly to submit increasing bids. Buyers decide a private value depending on their requirements. A bidder stops bidding when its private value is reached. The auction continues until only one potential buyer remains, so that the highest bidder wins the item at the price of its bid.
- **Dutch Auction:** Dutch auction is a sequential auction in which the auctioneer starts with a high price and continuously lowers the price until a sale is confirmed by the first bidder to indicate acceptance of a price. The rate of price reduction is up to auctioneer and it has a reservation price below which not to go. Dutch auction may terminate when the auctioneer reduces the price to reservation price and still there is no buyer.
- **First-price Auction:** The First-price auction is a simultaneous bidding auction in which bidders submit sealed bids. In this auction, each bidder submits only one bid without knowing the others' bids. The highest bidder wins and pays his or her own bid price.
- **Second-price Auction (Vickrey):** In the Vickrey Auction, bidders privately submit sealed-bids simultaneously. It is a single round bidding auction. The winner in Vickrey Auction is the highest bidder but it pays the price of the second-highest bid. If there is no second-highest bidder, then the price of the commodity is the average of the commodity's minimum selling price and the consumer's bid price.
- **Double Auction:** It is a two sided auction in which buyers and sellers are treated symmetrically with buyers submitting requests and sellers submitting offers. There are two types of double auctions, **continuous double auction (CDA)** and **periodic double auction**. Continuous Double Auction matches buyers and sellers immediately on detection of compatible bids. In this type, buy orders(bids) and sell orders(offers) may be submitted at anytime during the trading period. A periodic version of the double auction instead collects bids over a specified interval of time, then clears the market at the expiration of the bidding interval [16]. Pricing policy adopted by auctioneer can be classified into **uniform-price policy** and **discriminatory policy**. In uniform policy, all exchanges occur at the same price determined in auction clearing stage. Whereas in discriminatory policy, the prices are set individually for each matched buyer-seller pair.

For resource allocation in ad-hoc Grids, we need an auction mechanism that supports simultaneous participation of producer/consumer, observes resource/request deadlines and can accommodate the variations in resource availability. English and Dutch auctions are sequential and are based on open-cry where each bid has to be broadcasted to all participants. This becomes a considerable communication overhead in the context of ad-hoc Grids. Moreover their inability to observe time deadlines and no support for the simultaneous participation of producer/consumer are the reasons that make them unsuitable for ad-hoc Grid resource allocation.

First-price auction, Vickrey auction and Double auction are simultaneous and close bid auctions. We implement these three auctions in a many-to-many manner where both consumer and producers can submit their asks or bids at any time. To fulfill the deadline constraints for requests and offers more efficiently, we consider an auctioneer that continuously collects requests and offers from participants, instead of collecting them in a specified time intervals.

4 System Implementation

Design challenge is to develop a test bed that can help one in making the design choices for resource allocation in ad-hoc Grids considering Grid objectives and network conditions. Here we describe system components and pricing algorithms for the developed test bed.

4.1 System Architecture

The model is composed of three agents (see figure-1): **Consumer (buyer)**, **Producer (seller)** and **Auctioneer**. There is one consumer/producer agent per node. This agent controls the process of buying/selling resources by estimating the execution time of the job or availability of the resource. This agent also calculates the price and submits a request/offer for corresponding job/resource to the auctioneer. The consumer/producer agent is also responsible for accepting the offer/request for a matched resource/job from the auctioneer. The auctioneer agent controls the market using either First price or Vickrey Auction or

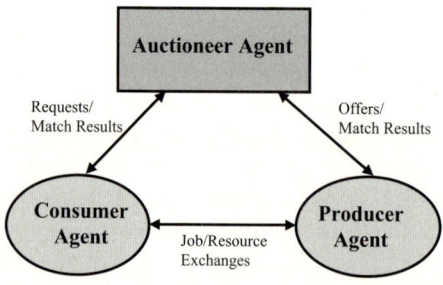

Fig. 1. System Components

Continuous Double Auction Protocol. Auctioneer receives requests and offers continuously and keeps them in its repositories till the time to live (TTL) for them is expired or a match is found. The matching between requests and offers is performed through one of the following protocols:

- **First-price Auction:** In this model, The producers submit their offers for a resource along with a reservation price, the minimum price below which they don't sell. Consumers submit their requests together with a bid price. The consumer agents use a learning mechanism (discussed in section 4.2) to calculate the bid prices. The auctioneer sets up a first price auction for each received offer. The highest bid wins the auction if the bid price is bigger than the offer reservation price and the offered resource satisfies the task's constraints (resource quantity, budget and time frame). In this protocol, transaction price is the bid price.
- **Vickrey Auction:** This model is similar to first price auction, except that the transaction price is the second highest bid price. In fact the winner pays bid price of the first looser. If there is no second highest bidder then the transaction price will be the average of bid and ask prices.
- **Continuous Double Auction:** CDA with discriminatory pricing policy is used as the third protocol for resource allocation in an ad hoc Grid. The buyers and sellers announce their desire to buy or sell computational services to the market. The auctioneer finds the matches between buyers and sellers by matching offers (starting with lowest price and moving up) with requests (starting with highest price and moving down). When a task query arrives at the market place, the protocol searches all available resource offers and returns the best match which satisfies the task's constraints which are resource quantity, time frame and price. When a resource becomes available and several tasks are waiting, the one with the highest price bid is processed first. In this model, consumer and producer agents use the pricing mechanism described in section 4.2 for calculating the bid and ask prices. The transaction price is calculated as the average of ask price and bid price.

4.2 Consumer/Producer Pricing Algorithm

The pricing strategy presented here, defines a logical price by local analysis of the previous trade cases. This bidding mechanism has been introduced in [17]. In the three auction protocols (First Price, Vickrey and CDA), consumer agents calculate their bid prices using this history-based pricing mechanism. Producer agents define their ask prices with this bidding mechanism if CDA is used as the auction mechanism, otherwise their ask price is their minimum price.

The price indicates the price of each unit of resource that consumer and producer agents are willing to buy or sell. Let denote by $p_b(t)$ the bid price of a consumer agent at time t and $p_a(t)$ the ask price for a producer agent at time t. We assume that each consumer agent has a maximum bid price, denoted max_b.

This maximum price is determined by the node's budget. Each producer agent has a minimum ask price. More formally, we have that:

$$\forall t,\ p_a(t) \geq min_a \text{ and } p_b(t) \leq max_b \qquad (1)$$

In our bidding algorithm, agents update their ask (respectively bid) prices using the experience they gained from their previous utilization of the Grid. Informally, the idea is as follows. If an agent has not been successful in buying resources, at current time the agent updates its bid price in a way that tends to increase its chance to buy resources in the future. If an agent has been successful, it conservatively continues to bid in a way that ensures its chance of buying resources in the future. A seller agent behaves in a similar manner. If it has not been successful in selling resources, at current time it updates its ask price in a way that increases its chance of selling its resources in the future. Otherwise, it behaves in a conservative manner. Formally, the ask price of a producer agent at time t is computed according to the assignment in (2), while the bid price for a consumer agent is given by assignment (3).

$$p_a(t) \leftarrow \max\{min_a, p_a(t-1) + \alpha.p_a(t-1)\} \qquad (2)$$

$$p_b(t) \leftarrow \min\{max_b, p_b(t-1) + \beta.p_b(t-1)\} \qquad (3)$$

where α and β are coefficients which determine the rate at which the price is increasing or decreasing. These parameters are set according to variations in task or resource utilization at each individual node over time periods.

For a given node, we define the *task utilization* as the ratio of allocated tasks to all submitted requests and the *resource utilization* as the ratio of allocated resources to all submitted offers. Formally, let $T = [s, e]$ be a time period (length of the history). We shall call s the start of T and e will be called the end of T. Let $ru(T)$ and $tu(T)$ be the resource and task utilization, respectively, over the time period T. For a given time period T, the resource utilization ($ru(t)$) and the task utilization ($tu(t)$) are formally given by Equation (4).

$$ru(T) = \frac{S(T)}{N_o(T)}\ ,\quad tu(T) = \frac{P(T)}{N_r(T)} \qquad (4)$$

where $S(T)$ and $P(T)$ are respectively the total numbers of sold and purchased resources in the time period T. $N_o(T)$ and $N_r(T)$ are respectively the total numbers of offered and requested resources in the time period T. We now define variations in resource and task utilization. To this end, let $T_1 = [s_1, e_1]$ and $T_2 = [s_2, e_2]$ be two consecutive time periods such that $e_1 = s_2$ and e_2 is the current time. We capture variations in resource (respectively task) utilization from period T_1 to T_2 by the following equations:

$$\Delta ru_{(T_1 \to T_2)} = ru(T_2) - ru(T_1)\ ,\quad \Delta tu_{(T_1 \to T_2)} = tu(T_2) - tu(T_1) \qquad (5)$$

We now define the parameters α and β as follows:

$$\alpha = \begin{cases} -(K - (ru(T_2))^2)^2 & if\ \Delta ru_{(T_1 \to T_2)} \leq 0 \\ L * (ru(T_2))^2 & if\ \Delta ru_{(T_1 \to T_2)} > 0 \end{cases} \qquad (6)$$

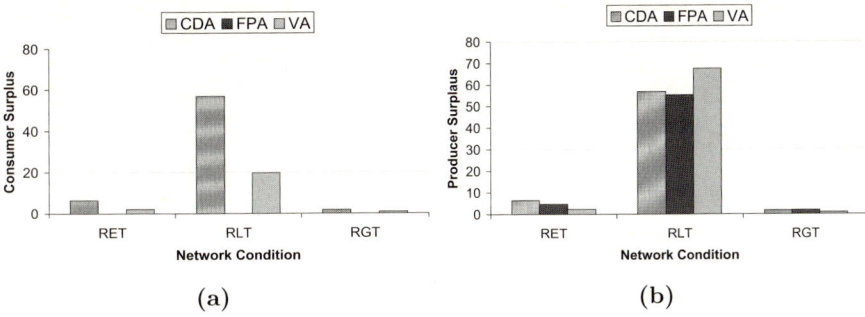

Fig. 2. Task Utilization and Resource Utilization for three protocols in different network conditions

$$\beta = \begin{cases} (K - (tu(T_2))^2)^2 & if\ \Delta tu_{(T_1 \to T_2)} \leq 0 \\ -L * (tu(T_2))^2 & if\ \Delta tu_{(T_1 \to T_2)} > 0 \end{cases} \quad (7)$$

where K and L respectively define the maximum rate of aggressive and conservative bidding (refer to [17]). In our experiments, we have considered $K = 1$ and $L = 0.1$.

5 Performance Evaluation

Throughput, consumer surplus, producer surplus and uncertainty level in obtaining the resources are the criteria to compare the three auction protocols in different network conditions considering availability of tasks and resources. Overall throughput of the system is measured and economic benefit of individual nodes is studied in term of consumer and producer surplus for three auction protocols at different network conditions. The variation in available budget is measured among consumers participating in grid to assess the level of uncertainty for getting the required resources in different auction protocols and in different network conditions.

5.1 Experimental Setup

Our application test-bed is developed using J2EE and Enterprise Java Beans. Auctioneer is deployed on JBoss application server. Consumer and producer of resources are buyers and sellers in the market. There is one consumer and one producer agent per each node. Whenever a node needs computational service for running its tasks, it sends a request to the auctioneer through the consumer agent and whenever a node has some computational service available, it sends an offer through the producer agent. All nodes are assigned equal budget when joining the grid. The limited budget defined for each node can be used to trade for required resources. The nodes earn credits by devoting the idle computational resources

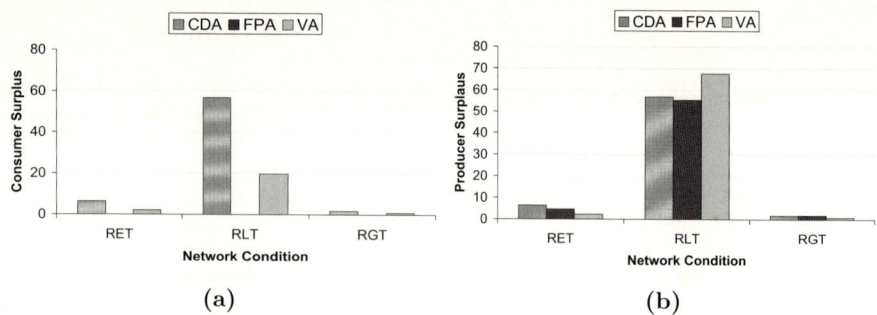

Fig. 3. (a) Consumer Surplus, (b) Producer Surplus for three protocols in different network conditions

for demanding consumers. Each request or offer submitted by consumers or producers has the following specifications:

- Request={ resource type, resource quantity, ttl (time to live for request validity), bid price , budget}
- Offer={ resource type, resource quantity, ttl (time to live for offer validity), ask price }

Cpu time is considered as the resources. Resource request is expressed in the term of cpu time, a ttl (time to live) to determine the time during which the task has to be executed, a price that consumer is able to pay for each unit of resource, and the total amount of the budget that consumer has. An offer includes: a ttl which is the time during which the cpu is available, the type of cpu and a price below which the producer does not sell the resource. In matchmaking between consumers and producers, auctioneer considers not only the price but also the quantity of the resource and ttl constraints. TTLs and task execution times are generated randomly for each request and offer.

The experiments are performed in a local ad hoc Grid with 60 nodes in three different network conditions: **the balanced network** which is the type of the network where there is more or less an equal number of tasks and resources, **the task intensive network** where there are more tasks than resources and **the resource intensive network** where there are more resources than tasks. We provide these different network conditions by creating unbalanced number of tasks and resources in the network. Tasks and resources are generated respectively with probability of 50%-50% in balanced network, 80%-20% in task intensive network and 20%-80% in resource intensive network in a random order. In following section, we study the results obtained from running our simulation using three auction protocols. In all protocols, the starting price for consumers and minimum price for producers has been considered in the same range.

5.2 Experimental Results

The experimental results within different network conditions are presented in following sections. In the figures, balanced network condition is referred to as

RET, resource intensive network condition as RGT, and task intensive network condition as RLT. We also use the abbreviation terms CDA and FPA and VA respectively for Continuous Double Auction, First Price Auction and Vickrey Auction.

5.3 Throughput

Throughput of the system is measured in the terms of task and resource utilization. **Task Utilization** is defined as the ratio of allocated tasks to all submitted requests. **Resource Utilization** is defined as the ratio of allocated resources to all submitted offers in the system. We run the simulation for each model at different conditions and measure the task and resource utilization. As can be seen from the results in Figure 2(a) and 2(b), three mechanisms show more or less the same task/resource utilization in different conditions. In the balanced condition(RET), the Vickrey and First Price auctions auction show around 3% to 4% more throughput over the Continuous Double Auction which can be also the side effect of simulation. We conclude that three auction models are interchangeable concerning the overall throughput of the system in any network condition.

5.4 Consumer Surplus

Consumer surplus is the difference between the price that consumers are willing to pay (bid price) and the actual price (transaction price). The average consumer surplus is calculated for the matched consumers in three protocols within different network conditions. Matched consumers are the consumers which have found matches for their requests. As expected, the consumer surplus for First-Price is equal to zero. As in this auction, the transaction price is equal to consumer price (bid price). In CDA and Vickrey auctions the consumers usually pay less than what they bid, so these auctions favor the consumers. We can see from the figure 3(a) that consumer surplus is higher in CDA than in Vickrey. Higher consumer surplus in CDA is because of the higher difference between the bid prices and transaction prices in CDA compared with the other two auction protocols. In all protocols, consumer surplus has its highest value in task intensive network (RLT) and lowest value in resource intensive network (RGT). As in task intensive networks(RLT), consumers increase the price to outbid their competitors and consequently the difference between transaction and bid price increases. On the other hand, due to abundance of resources in a resource intensive network (RGT) the consumers bid the low prices which are close to ask price. Considering the consumer surplus, CDA provides the highest surplus for consumers in task intensive network (RLT). However, CDA is interchangeable with VA in the balanced (RET) and resource intensive (RGT) networks at this concern.

5.5 Producer Surplus

Producer surplus is the amount that producers benefit by selling a resource at market price that is higher than the price the producer is willing to sell. In

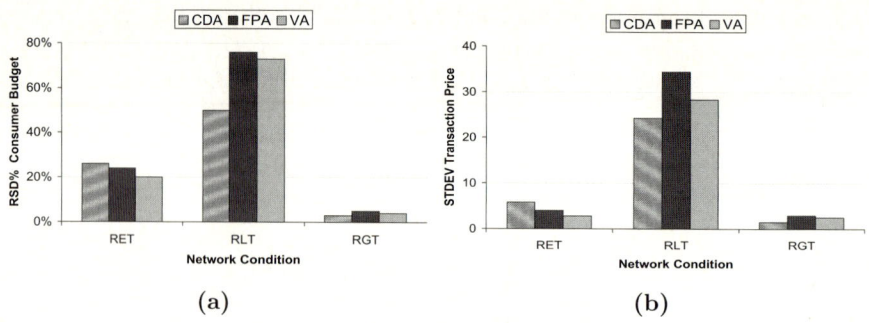

Fig. 4. (a) Variation in Consumers' Budget, (b) Variation in Transaction Prices

fact, the producer surplus is difference between transaction price and ask price. We compute the average producer surplus for the matched producers in three protocols within different network conditions. Matched producers are the producers which have found matches for their offers. The results in figure 3(b) show that the Vickrey auction provides the higher producer surplus as compared to other two auction protocols in task intensive network. Producer surplus is approximately equal for three auction protocols in resource intensive and balanced network conditions. The higher producer surpluses in case of task intensive network and lower producer surplus values in other two network conditions can be explained with the same reasoning as already discussed in section 5.4.

As consumers pay first highest price in First price auction and pay the second highest price in Vickrey auction. So it may be expected that producer surplus will be more in first price auction in comparison with Vickrey auction. This illusion can be clarified with the following explanation in a task intensive network. Consumer pay higher prices in First price auction so they run out of budget more quickly compared with Vickrey auction. We studied the available budget to every node in both protocols at end of simulation and found that some nodes in First price auction got zero budget. As a conclusion where the producer surplus is the selection criterion, the three auction models are interchangeable in the balanced and resource intensive networks. In a task intensive network, VA is the best option.

5.6 Uncertainty Measure

The level of uncertainty for consumers in getting the required resources is indicated by measuring the variation in the available budget among consumer agents. Higher variation in consumers' budget shows lower reliability and higher uncertainty in obtaining the required resources. We measure the budget variation during the trading time for the three auction protocols in different network conditions (see figure 4(a)). The budget variation is presented using relative standard deviation (RSD). RDS% is defined as $RSD = (stdev/mean) * 100\%$, where $mean$ is the average and $stdev$ is standard deviation of consumers' budget. As no

Table 1. Design Choices

Network Condition/Criterion	Throughput	Consumer Surplus	Producer Surplus	Uncertainty Measure
Balanced Network	Interchangeable	CDA, VA	Interchangeable	Interchangable
Task Intensive Network	Interchangeable	CDA	VA	CDA
Resource Intensive Network	Interchangeable	CDA, VA	Interchangeable	interchangeable

budget is injected to the network, the mean of consumers' budget is the initial budget given to the nodes. From the figure 4(a), we can see that task intensive condition has the highest budget variation and resource intensive condition has the lowest. So, uncertainty level is higher in task intensive network than in the two other networks. Whereas, in resource intensive network condition where resources are abundantly available and the transaction prices are low, so probability of getting the required resources is high for consumers. Comparing different protocols, we can see that in the balanced and resource intensive conditions, the budger variation is more or less in the same range in the three protocols. In a task intensive network, CDA shows the lowest variation in budget among three protocols. The budget variation in CDA is around 26% lower than in the FPA and 23% lower than in the VA. It means when resource are scarce, consumer have lower level of uncertainty for getting resources in CDA than the two other protocols. The variations in consumers' budget are consistent with the variation in transaction prices. In our system, the prices are limited by budget(see section 4.2). Higher variation in transaction prices shows higher instability and higher uncertainty. Figure 4(b) shows the standard deviation of transaction prices in different network conditions. We can conclude that considering the uncertainty measure, CDA in the task intensive networks and any protocol can be selected in balanced and resource intensive networks.

6 Results Discussion

This meta-research targets to answer the question: for Grid user/owner, under which network condition, which economic model is suitable? We consider four factors to present Grid and user objectives namely throughput, consumer surplus, producer surplus and the uncertainty measure.

The results show the system throughput in terms of task and resource utilization is approximately the same in the three auction protocols. Therefore, in this regard the protocols are interchangeable. When resources are scarce (task intensive condition) and many resource consumers are waiting for the resources then CDA is an appropriate approach. Because, it increases the economic benefit of the Grid consumers while it gives a promised throughput. However, Vickrey auction favors producers in task intensive condition as it gives higher producer surplus. CDA and Vickrey auction are interchangeable in balanced and in resource intensive conditions regarding consumer surplus. Producer surplus is approximately the same for the three protocols in balanced or resource intensive network.

We observe that any auction protocol can be chosen in a balanced condition and a resource intensive condition while considering the uncertainty level for obtaining resources. In a task intensive network, CDA presents lowest variation in consumers' budget and transaction prices as compared to other two protocols. So, the level of uncertainty is lower for CDA protocol in the task intensive networks. By looking at the results summery presented in table 1, it is observed that CDA can be a design choice in different network conditions regarding the most criteria.

7 Conclusion

In this paper, we provide a framework for auction-based resource allocation in an ad-hoc Grid. We study the impact of choosing a particular economic model in an ad-hoc Grid. The framework enables us to analyze different auction protocols (First Price Auction, Vickrey Auction, Continuous Double Auction) while observing Grid user/owner objectives. The assessment criteria in the framework consider system as well as user preferences. These criteria are throughput, consumer surplus, producer surplus, and uncertainty measure. These parameters are measured in three different network conditions regarding availability of tasks and resources. Based on our experimental results, different design choices are discussed in section 6.

Acknowledgement

We would like to thank Tariq Abdullah from Delft University of Technology, Computer Engineering Laboratory, for his helpful comments on the draft manuscript.

References

1. Wolski, R., Brevik, J., Plank, J.S., Bryan, T.: Grid resource allocation and control using computational economies. In: Grid Computing: Making The Global Infrastructure a Reality. John Wiley & Sons, Chichester (2003)
2. Buyya, R., Abramson, D., Giddy, J., Stockinger, H.: Economic models for resource management and scheduling in grid computing. Concurrency and Computation: Practice and Experience 14(13-15), 1507–1542 (2002)
3. Kurose, J.F., Simha, R.: A microeconomic approach to optimal resource allocation in distributed computer systems. IEEE Transactions on computers, 705–717 (May 1989)
4. Waldspurger, C.A., Hogg, T., Huberman, B.A., Kephart, J.O., Stornetta, W.S.: Spawn: A distributed computational economy. Software Engineering 18(2), 103–117 (1992)
5. Nisan, N., London, S., Regev, O., Camiel, N.: Globally distributed computation over the internet - the popcorn project. In: ICDCS 1998: Proceedings of the The 18th International Conference on Distributed Computing Systems, p. 592. IEEE Computer Society, Los Alamitos (1998)

6. Lalis, S., Karipidis, A.: Jaws: An open market-based framework for distributed computing over the internet. In: GRID, pp. 36–46 (2000)
7. Gomoluch, J., Schroeder, M.: Market-based resource allocation for grid computing: A model and simulation (2003)
8. Weng, C., Lu, X., Xue, G., Deng, Q., Li, M.: A double auction mechanism for resource allocation on grid computing systems. In: Jin, H., Pan, Y., Xiao, N., Sun, J. (eds.) GCC 2004. LNCS, vol. 3252, p. 269. Springer, Heidelberg (2004)
9. Kant, U., Grosu, D.: Double auction protocols for resource allocation in grids. In: Proceedings of the International Conference on Information Technology: Coding and Computing (ITCC 2005), pp. 366–371 (2005)
10. Grosu, D., Das, A.: Auction-based resource allocation protocols in grids. In: Proceedings of the 16th IASTED International Conference on Parallel and Distributed Computing and Systems, pp. 20–27 (November 2004)
11. de Assuncao, M.D., Buyya, R.: An evaluation of communication demand of auction protocols in grid environments. Technical report, Computing and Distributed Systems Laboratory, The University of Melbourne, Australia (2006)
12. Hurwicz, L.: The design of mechanisms for resource allocation. American Economic Review 63(2), 1–30 (1973),
 http://ideas.repec.org/a/aea/aecrev/v63y1973i2p1-30.html
13. Ferguson, D.F., Sairamesh, J., Yemini, Y., Nikolaou, C.: Economic models for allocating resources in computer systems. In: Clearwater, S.H. (ed.) Market-Based Control, pp. 156–183. World Scientific Publishing Co. Pte. Ltd., Singapore (1996)
14. Walras, L.: Elements of pure economics; or, the theory of social wealth. Allen and Unwin (1954)
15. Buyya, R., Abramson, D., Venugopal, S.: The grid economy (2004)
16. Wurman, P., Walsh, W., Wellman, M.: Flexible double auctions for electronic commerce: Theory and implementation. Decision Support Systems 24, 17–27 (1998)
17. Pourebrahimi, B., Bertels, K.: Adaptation to dynamic resource availability in ad-hoc grids through a learning mechanism. In: The 2008 IEEE 11th International Conference on Computational Science and Engineering (July 2008)

GrAMoS: A Flexible Service for WS-Agreement Monitoring in Grid Environments

Glauber Scorsatto and Alba Cristina Magalhaes Alves de Melo

Department of Computer Science, University of Brasilia (UnB)
Campus Universitario – Asa Norte, ICC-Norte, subsolo, 70910-900, Brasilia, Brazil
{scorsatto,albamm}@cic.unb.br

Abstract. In this paper, we propose and evaluate GrAMoS, a low-overhead WS-Agreement monitoring service that runs on Globus 4 and is integrated to JSS. To monitor resources and detect agreement violations, GrAMoS uses the stratified random sampling technique and proposes flexible agreement violation actions. The experimental results collected with a prototype of GrAMoS which monitored CPU reservation WS-Agreements show that the overhead incurred is lower than 2.8%, for grid tasks that take longer than 55s.

1 Introduction

Grid computing has emerged in the mid-1990s as an infrastructure for secure resource sharing among organizations spread over multiple administrative domains [4]. In early grid environments, heterogeneous non-dedicated resources were usually assigned to grid applications in a best effort manner. In this scenario, no guarantees are given that the resource would be available to the grid task during the entire execution. If the resource becomes unavailable, the task either migrates or is stopped until the resource is available again [5]. In both cases, a great slowdown is produced. It was also observed that, for some classes of grid applications, such as time-constrained or synchronous communicating tasks, this type of best effort resource management policy is highly inappropriate.

In grid systems, Quality of Service (QoS) mechanisms would guarantee that the resources are available to the tasks in such a way that the expected service level is attained [5]. Often, QoS requirements are assured by resource reservations. A way to negotiate reservations between grid tasks (consumers) and resources (providers) is by using agreements. An agreement represents clearly a service behavior, which is negotiated and accorded between the parties involved (consumers and providers). WS-Agreement [1] was specified by the Open Grid Forum (OGF) as a language and protocol to establish agreements in a grid environment. WS-Agreements provide a way to inspect the agreement state, which can be fulfilled, violated or not-determined. Nevertheless, deciding if an agreement is violated or not is outside the scope of WS-Agreement, since this decision is domain-specific and needs interaction with lower-level schedulers.

Many recent proposals [6][17][12][3] have focused on offering QoS for grids. Of those, only GrADS (Grid Application Development Software) [17] and JSS (Job

Submission Service) [3] use agreements to negotiate QoS levels. JSS is a quite complete system that negotiates WS-agreements but it does not contain monitoring facilities. Although GrADS does have an agreement monitoring functionality, its agreements are defined in a proprietary way, not following any agreement standard.

The goal of the present paper is to propose and evaluate GrAMoS (Grid Agreement Monitoring Service), which is a WS-Agreement monitoring tool. Its most important characteristics are: a) periodic monitoring of resource usage using the stratified random sampling technique [8]; b) flexible definition of the action to be taken when an agreement is violated; and c) low monitoring overhead. As far as we know, this is the first proposal of a WS-agreement monitoring service that is based upon Globus Toolkit 4.

A prototype of GrAMoS that monitors CPU reservation was implemented and integrated to JSS [3]. The results obtained with this prototype show that, for grid applications that take longer than 1 minute, defining a sampling interval of 5s to measure the number of CPUs introduces an overhead of less than 2.8% in the wallclock execution time. This overhead is reduced to less than 1.3% when the sampling interval is set to 10s.

The remainder of this paper is organized as follows. Section 2 discusses agreement negotiation and monitoring systems for grid computing environments. The design of GrAMoS is presented in section 3. Some experimental results are discussed in section 4. Finally, section 5 concludes the paper and presents future work.

2 QoS in Grid Computing

The term *grid computing* was conceived to denote a new infrastructure of distributed computing for scientists and engineers in a more advanced scope. This name was inspired by the electrical power energy because of its pervasiveness, ease of use and reliability [4].

In developing applications for the grid, it is essential to have an unified middleware to provide a transparent interface to the underlying protocols. The Globus Toolkit [4] emerged in 1998 as an open source project and quickly became a *de facto* standard for grid computing infrastructure. In 2002, the Open Grid Services Architecture (OGSA) [11] was introduced by the Global Grid Forum (GGF). The OGSA provided an architecture based on Web Services in order to achieve interoperability using industry standards.

In its first specification, OGSA was composed by three modules built upon a web services layer. The bottom layer of the OGSA architecture was called OGSI, which defined the infrastructure to manipulate a grid service. OGSI has received many objections from the web service community, mainly because it creates a partial incompatibility with the existing tools for manipulating web services. Therefore, a great effort was made to obtain a new grid service definition that was adjusted to the existing standards. As a result of this effort, the OGSI layer was totally replaced by a new layer, called WSRF (Web Service Resource Framework). WSRF can be seen as the composition of a web service and a stateful resource. Globus Toolkit 4 implements the OGSA/WSRF.

Quality of Service (QoS) is usually defined as a set of quantitative and qualitative assurances that are necessary to attain a certain service level [2]. QoS offers guarantees that suitable resources will be available to the applications, mainly by resource reservation techniques [15]. The term QoS was initially used in the context of networking, but nowadays it is used for a diversity of resources, such as CPU, memory and disk. Clearly, QoS is domain dependent and the guarantees needed by the applications vary a lot. Therefore, the consumer (application) must specify clearly its QoS needs and the provider (service) must agree to provide it. This is usually done by contracts or agreements. Once the agreement is established, it must be monitored and its violation must be reported.

In the context of grid computing, the Open Grid Forum (OGF) has proposed WS-Agreements [1] to standardize the establishment of QoS relations between grid applications and service providers. WS-Agreement specifies an XML-based template to express the dynamic relationship between two parties, defining the rights and obligations of both. Also, it proposes a symmetric negotiation protocol.

At the following paragraphs, some initiatives in QoS for grid computing are discussed.

GARA [14] was one of the first grid architectures that provides mechanisms for reserving different types of resources, such as CPU, memory, disk and network bandwidth. No agreement protocols are supported. GARA was proposed for Globus Toolkit 2 (GT2).

GrADS [17] is a research project that aims to simplify the management of grid applications. In GrADS, an application is encapsulated into an object called Configurable Object Program (COP), which contains the application code, a mapper and a performance model. The output of the resource discovery module is passed to the Performance Modeler, which uses the COP to build an application-specific task-processor mapping. This mapping is transformed into a contract. The execution is monitored by the Contract Monitor component, which can reschedule the application, in the case of contract violation. In [13], a contract monitoring tool based on fuzzy logic is proposed for GrADS. This tool takes into account the great performance variability that is inherent to a grid environment and reacts softly to it. The actions taken on contract violations are defined by the user. GrADS was implemented on top of GT2.

AGMeTs [12] is a framework for adaptive metascheduling. When a grid task is submitted to AGMeTS, the resource discovery module retrieves the characteristics of the resources, including their availability. An appropriate resource is chosen and, once the application starts executing, it is monitored and checkpointed. If the resource is no longer available, the application is migrated. AGMeTS was implemented upon GT3.

A framework to manage QoS in grid environments is proposed in G-QoSm [18]. Its main component is the QoS Grid Service, which deals with reservations. In order to guarantee a reservation, an agreement is generated which is represented by a Resource Service Level Agreement (RSLA) [11]. A protocol is defined for agreement negotiation. Prototypes of G-QoSm were implemented in both GT2 and GT3.

JSS [3] is a task submission service that runs on GT4 and uses grid *de facto* standards such as JSDL, WSRF and WS-Agreements. In JSS, a grid application is described in JSDL (Job Submission Description Language). Tasks and resource reservations are represented by WS-Resources [7]. In order to execute an application, the

Table 1. Comparative summary of the QoS grid projects

Project	Reservation	Agreements	QoS	Middleware	Monitoring
GARA	Yes	No	network,CPU,disk	GT2	No
GrADS	No	Yes	performance	GT2	Contract
AGMeTS	No	No	CPU, disk	GT3	Availability
G-QoSm	Yes	RSLA	CPU	GT2, GT3	No
JSS	Yes	WS-Agreement	CPU	GT4	No

Submitter component receives a JSDL description of the task. The JSS broker selects the appropriate resources for the application execution. The Reserver component can be used for reservations, that are based on WS-Agreements [1].

As can be seen in table 1, three systems (GARA, G-QoSm and JSS) use reservations in order to achieve the required QoS level. GrADS and AGMeTS provide QoS by rescheduling the applications, when the QoS requirements are violated. Agreements are used in GrADS (proprietary format), G-QoSm (RSLA) and JSS (WS-Agreement). All projects discussed provide QoS for at least CPU. Also, all prototype implementations run on top of Globus Toolkit. Nevertheless, JSS is the only one that runs on GT4. Agreement monitoring is only provided by GrADS but, as stated before, GrADS uses a proprietary format to express contracts.

3 Design of GrAMoS

In this section, we propose GrAMoS, a grid service that monitors the resources involved in WS-Agreements. GrAMoS is proposed to achieve three main goals: soft agreement violation detection, flexible violation action and low overhead, that will be detailed in the following paragraphs.

To achieve the first goal, the detection of agreement violations must take into account that, in a grid environment, there are often temporary and dynamic variations on the resource load, that do not imply necessarily QoS violations. To deal with this scenario, we must do our measures in a non-periodical way and the agreement violation action must not always be launched on the first measure outside the established threshold.

This first goal was also considered in [13] and an inference mechanism based on fuzzy logic was proposed. In GrAMoS, we have also a low overhead goal and, for this reason, we propose a simpler mechanism to achieve the same first goal.

In order to monitor the agreements, we opted to use the Stratified Random Sampling technique as defined in [8], which was used, in that case, to monitor network QoS parameters. In this technique [8], periodical intervals are considered as strata and the sampling moment is chosen in a random way, inside the current interval.

In a grid environment, a measure can be taken at the exact moment when an abnormal and temporary load variation occurs. In most cases, this sole measure should not be sufficient for the system to conclude that the agreement was violated. For this reason, we defined the parameter *unfulfillmentTimes*, that determines how many times the measure must be outside the threshold for the system to change the agreement state to *violated*. If the user wishes instantaneous agreement violation detection, the parameter *unfulfillmentTimes* should be set to 1. At most cases, however, it is advisable to set this parameter with a value greater than 1.

In order to achieve the second goal, which is flexible violation action, the action to be taken when an agreement violation is detected must be application-specific and provided by the user. When an agreement is violated, many actions can be taken, concerning the monitored task, such as [5]: kill/suspend/migrate the task, or register the agreement violation on a log file. The action that will actually be taken is obviously dependent of the grid application, the policies of each virtual organization and the grid resource management policies.

For this reason, we designed a generic interface called *AgreementUnaccomplishmentAction*, which exports the methods *agreementStartTimeAction* and *agreementUnfulfillmentAction*, that will be invoked when the monitored task starts execution in a time that is outside the reservation time interval and when the agreement is violated, respectively.

Finally, to achieve our third goal, the monitoring service must use mechanisms that introduce a low overhead. To achieve this goal, a separate thread is used to command the agreement monitoring, that executes concurrently with the monitoring service and the grid task itself. Also, we used the Stratified Random Sampling technique [8], which introduces low overhead.

3.1 Architecture of GrAMos

GrAMos was designed as a web service to be hosted at the Globus Toolkit 4. Figure 1 shows the entities that interact with GrAMos, at both the client and the server side.

At the client node, the application is submitted and the agreement is created. The client part of GrAMoS was integrated to JSS. To do that, a modification was made at the JSS *submitter* component, that will invoke GrAMoS if an agreement is created. At the server site, the application is actually executed. The modules WS-Agreement, GT4, Ganglia [9], Torque [16] and Maui [10] are present, since they are used by JSS. Ganglia interacts with GT4, retrieving resource information. Task execution is controlled by Torque, which uses the scheduling decisions from Maui to place the tasks.

The GrAMoS architecture is illustrated in figure 2. When the Monitoring Service (MS) is activated, a configuration file containing the GrAMoS parameters

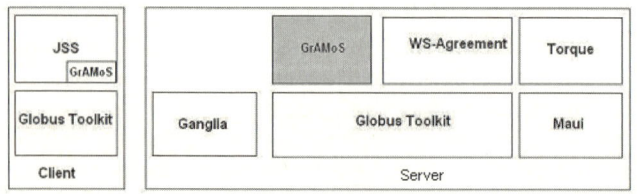

Fig. 1. Interaction between GraMoS and other components

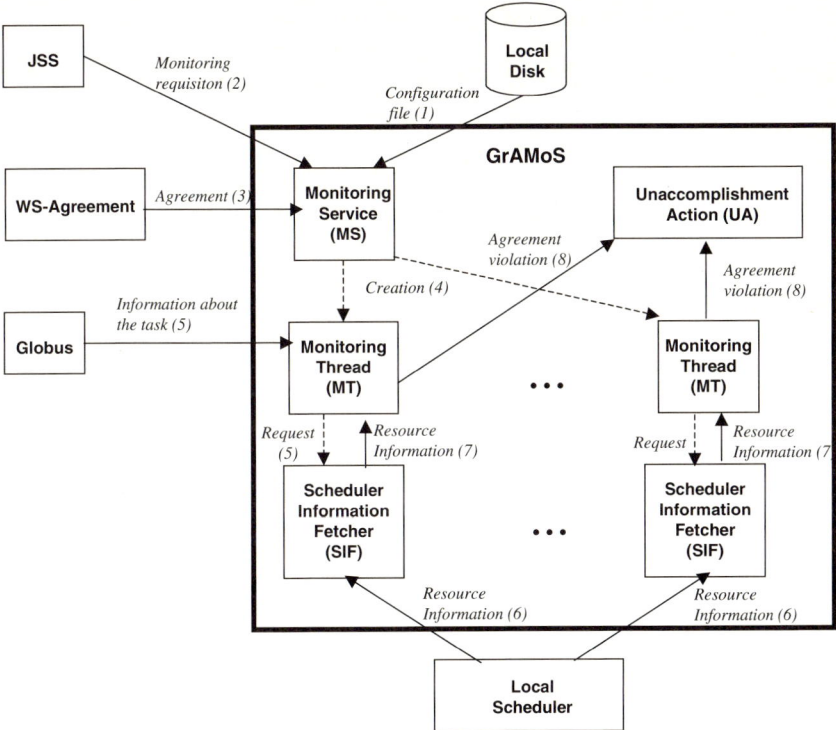

Fig. 2. GrAMoS architecture

(*unfulfillmentTimes*, sampling time interval, name of the agreement violation class and nameof the local scheduler interface class) is read (1). When a task is submitted with an agreement, the client calls the MS method *initiateJobMonitoring* with the task identification (2) and the agreement key (3). Then, the MS creates a Monitoring Thread (4) that will periodically retrieve information about the task. The SIF module is instantiated (5) and it will command the sampling using the stratified random sampling technique (section 3). The local scheduler (in our case, Maui) is the one that actually retrieves resource information (6). By default, the information contained in table 1 is retrieved.

Having the resource information (7), the MT does the following verifications: a) the task start time must be inside the reservation interval; b) the duration of the agreement must be still valid; c) the number of resources defined in the agreement must be available to the grid task. If condition (a) does not hold, the method *agreementStartTimeAction* is invoked. If condition (b) is false, the monitoring thread is terminated, since the agreement is no longer valid. Finally, if condition (c) is false for the last *unfulfillmentTimes*, the module UA is contacted (8), and the class *agreementUnfulfillmentAction* will be executed.

Table 2. Resource information retrieved by default

Information Retrieved	Possible values
task execution status	waiting, executing, terminated
resources allocated	pairs (<resourceName, quantity>)
resources available	pairs (<resourceName, quantity>)
monitoring start time	instant when the monitoring thread started execution
last information retrieval	instant when the last resource information was retrieved

4 Experimental Results

A prototype of GrAMoS was implemented in Java. The test environment used was composed by 2 machines (client and server). The client machine submitted tasks to JSS and the server machine (execution node) was responsible to monitor and execute the grid tasks. After a monitored task is started, monitoring is done exclusively at the server node, without communication with the client. For this reason, the execution times presented in this section are the ones measured at the server node. The client was only used to start the application.

Table 3. Hardware and software configuration of the machines used in the test environment

Machine	Hardware	Software
client	Intel Pentium 4 3.0GHz, 512MB RAM, 80 GB HD	Linux kernel 2.6.17, Globus Toolkit 4.0.4, JDK 1.5.0_08
server	AMD Athlon XP 1.7GHz, 768MB RAM, 40 GB HD	Linux kernel. 2.6.20, Globus Toolkit 4.0.4, JDK 1.5.0_08, Maui Scheduler 3.2.6p13, Torque RM 2.1.7, Ganglia MS 3.0.4

The hardware and software configuration of each machine are shown in table 3.

The grid tasks T1, T5, T10, T15 and T30 were executed. They are compute intensive synthetic tasks that take around 1, 5, 10, 15 and 30 minutes to execute at the server machine. The wallclock execution times present in tables 3 and 4 were collected with the *time* Linux command and the pseudo-random function *random*, from java.util.Random was used to generate the random instants of measure.

The agreement monitored in these tests is the one illustrated in figure 3, where one processor is reserved for 32 minutes.

Table 4 presents the wallclock times to execute the five tasks and the GrAMoS overhead for sampling intervals of 5s and 10s. In table 3, we can see that the overhead generated by GrAMoS when executing task T1 (1 min) is small but slightly higher (2.75%) than the overheads generated for the other tasks. This is due to the overhead of GrAMoS initialization and termination. For the other applications, the overhead remains almost constant, decreasing in small rates for the 10s sampling interval. Since grid tasks are usually long lived, such a small overhead is very appropriate. Also, as expected, the overhead introduced for the 5s interval was almost the double of the one produced for 10s.

```
<wsag:AgreementType ... >

<wsag:Name>Agreement</wsag:Name>
<wsag:Context>
   ...
</wsag:Context>
<wsag:Terms>
    <wsag:All>
       <wsag:ServiceDescriptionTerm
             wsag:Name="numberOfCPUs"
             wsag:ServiceName="Reservation">

       <res:numberOfCPUs>1</res:numberOfCPUs>
           </wsag:ServiceDescriptionTerm>
       <wsag:ServiceDescriptionTerm
             wsag:Name="duration"
             wsag:ServiceName="Reservation">
             <res:duration>1920</res:duration>
       </wsag:ServiceDescriptionTerm>
       ...
    </wsag:All>
</wsag:Terms>

</wsag:AgreementOffer>
```

Fig. 3. Agreement monitored in our tests

Table 4. Wallclock times and monitoring service overheads for five grid tasks

Task	Monitoring service			Overhead (%)	
	without	5s	10s	5s	10s
T1	61.7s	63.4s	62.5s	2.75	1.29
T5	307.4s	314.3s	311.0s	2.24	1.17
T10	611.8s	625.3s	618.8s	2.20	1.14
T15	916.4s	936.4s	927.0s	2.18	1.15
T30	1808.4s	1848.4s	1829.0s	2.21	1.13

Table 5 presents the duration of each resource sampling, from the time when the Monitoring Thread requires the sampling to the moment it receives the resource information (figure 2). It can be noted that the variation between the smallest and the highest resource sampling time is very high. However, this variation is not reflected in the overheads presented in table 3. This probably happens because the grid tasks execute concurrently with the monitoring service. Also, the sampling process involves a separate thread.

Table 5. Sampling duration resource information retrival process

Task	5s			10s		
	lowest	average	highest	lowest	average	highest
T1	0.26s	0.36s	1.39s	0.27s	0.40s	1.50s
T5	0.26s	0.37s	1.39s	0.26s	0.37s	1.40s
T10	0.25s	0.38s	1.58s	0.26s	0.38s	1.30s
T15	0.26s	0.37s	1.38s	0.26s	0.38s	1.37s
T30	0.25s	0.37s	1.42s	0.26s	0.37s	1.45s

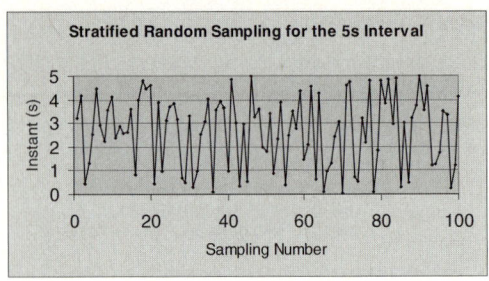

Fig. 4. Sampling instants for 100 measures using the stratified random sampling technique

Figure 4 presents a plot of the sampling instants for 100 measures (5s time interval), illustrating the random behavior of the sampling technique.

In order to verify the behavior of GrAMoS in the case of an agreement violation, we deployed a class that implements the *SchedulerInformationFetcher* interface, informing that the available resources are below the number specified in the agreement, at each 5 samplings. With this class, we can thus simulate the occurrence of violations.

In this case study, the parameter *unfulfillmentTimes* was set to 10 and the class that implements the *AgreementUnfulfillmentAction* interface registers the violation in a log file. Task T5 was used. It was observed that, after the fiftieth sampling, the MT detected the agreement violation and contacted the UA (figure 2), that registered the violation in a log file. This shows that GrAMoS behaves accordingly when an agreement violation occurs.

5 Conclusions and Future Work

In this paper, we proposed and evaluated GrAMoS, a flexible low-overhead WS-Agreement monitoring service. In order to detect agreement violations in grid environments, GrAMoS uses techniques that cope with periodical and instantaneous temporary load variations, making measures in random instants inside time intervals and launching agreement violation actions when more than one measure outside the interval is obtained. A separate thread is used to command the sampling.

The experimental results obtained with a prototype of GrAMoS that was monitoring CPU WS-agreement violations show that overheads that are lower than 2.8% are obtained for grid tasks that take longer or equal to 60s, with a sampling interval of 5s. Also, our results show that GrAMoS behaves accordingly when a WS-Agreement violation is detected.

As future work, we intend to generate a version of GrAMoS that is independent of JSS. Also, we intend to test GrAMoS in a production grid environment and to make GrAMoS deal with more complex agreements.

References

1. Andrieux, A., et al.: Web Services Agreement Specification (WS-Agreement) (2007), http://www.ogf.org/documents/GFD.107.pdf
2. Bochmann, G., et al.: Distributed Multimedia and QoS: A Survey. IEEE Multimedia 2(2), 10–19 (1995)
3. Elmroth, E., Tordsson, J.: An Interoperable, Standards-based Grid Resource Broker and Job Submission Service. In: 1st Int. Conf. on e-Science and Grid Computing, pp. 212–220 (2005)
4. Foster, I., Kesselman, C., Tuecke, S.: The Anatomy of the Grid: Enabling Scalable Virtual Organizations. Journal of High Performance Computing Applications 15, 200–222 (2001)
5. Foster, I., Kesselman, C.: The Grid 2: Blueprint of a New Computing Infrastructure. Morgan Kaufmann, San Francisco (2003)
6. Foster, I., et al.: End-to-End Quality of Service for High-End Application. Elsevier Computer Communications Journal 27(14), 1375–1388 (2004)
7. Foster, I.: Globus Toolkit Version 4: Software for Service-Oriented Systems. Journal of Computer Science and Technology 21(4), 513–520 (2005)
8. Claffy, K., Braun, H., Polyzos, G.: Application of Sampling Methodologies for Network Traffic Characterization: ACM SIGCOMM, pp .194–203 (1993)
9. Massie, M.L., Chun, B.N., Culler, D.E.: The Ganglia Distributed Monitoring System: Design, Implementation and Experience. Parallel Computing 30(7), 817–840 (2004)
10. Maui Cluster Scheduler, http://www.clusterresources.com/pages/products/maui-cluster-scheduler.php
11. Nabrzyski, J., Schopf, J.M., Weglaz, J.: Grid Resource Management: State of the Art and Future Trends. Springer, Heidelberg (2003)
12. Nainwal, K.C., et al.: A Framework for QoS Adaptive Grid Meta Scheduling. In: 16th International Workshop on Database and Expert Systems Applications, pp. 292–296 (2005)
13. Reed, D.A., Mendes, C.L.: Intelligent Monitoring for Adaptation in Grid Applications. Proceedings of the IEEE 93(2), 426–435 (2005)
14. Roy, A.: End-to-End Quality of Service for High-End Applications. PhD Thesis. Department of Computer Science. Chicago University (2001)
15. Siqueira, F., Cahill, V.: Quartz: a QoS architecture for open systems. In: IEEE International Conference on Distributed Computing Systems, Taipei, Taiwan, pp. 197–204 (April 2000)
16. TORQUE R Man, http://www.clusterresources.com/pages/products/torque-resource-manager.php
17. Vadhiyar, S., Dongarra, J.A.: Metascheduler for the Grid. In: 11th IEEE Symposium on High-Performance Distributed Computing, pp. 343–351 (2002)
18. von Laszewski, G.: Analysis and Provision of QoS for Distributed Grid Applications. Journal of Grid Computing 2(2), 163–182 (2004)

Scalability of Grid Simulators: An Evaluation

Wim Depoorter, Nils De Moor, Kurt Vanmechelen, and Jan Broeckhove

University of Antwerp, BE-2020 Antwerp, Belgium
wim.depoorter@ua.ac.be

Abstract. Due to the distributed nature of resources in grids that cover multiple administrative domains, grid resource management cannot be optimally implemented using traditional approaches. In order to investigate new grid resource management systems, researchers utilize simulators which allows them to efficiently evaluate new algorithms on a large scale. We have developed the Grid Economics Simulator (GES) in support of research into grid resource management in general and economic grid resource management in particular. This paper compares GES to SimGrid and GridSim, two established grid simulation frameworks. We demonstrate that GES compares favourably to the other frameworks in terms of scalability, runtime performance and memory requirements. We explain how these differences are related to the simulation paradigm and the threading model used in each simulator.

Keywords: Simulation, Grids, Performance Analysis.

1 Introduction

Conducting research into resource management systems (RMS) on real grids is difficult because of two reasons. Firstly, the costs involved in setting up and maintaining such a system are high. Secondly, there is a need to test a new RMS under a variety of different load patterns and infrastructural arrangements, which is all but impossible to achieve with a real grid system. The large scale on which a grid RMS needs to be studied magnifies the impact of these problems. As a result, the only viable option for researchers is to resort to simulation.

The aim of a grid simulator is to allow easy *comparison* between different resource management approaches and to enable researchers to *focus on the design and implementation* of the chosen approach, while leveraging the strength of the existing framework in *setting up* the grid environment, *running* the simulation and *monitoring* the desired metrics. Because a grid is intrinsically a large scale system, a fundamental requirement for a grid simulator is scalability. An example of such a large scale grid system is the system built by the the European "Enabling Grids for E-sciencE" (EGEE) project. The EGEE infrastructure services over 10 000 users from 45 countries and offers a compute capacity of well over 40 000 CPUs, a figure which is expected to double over the course of the next year. In order to simulate such a vast infrastructure, a simulator has to be able to handle over 10 000 user entities and at least 100 000 computing nodes. In this contribution we evaluate the performance of SimGrid [1], GridSim [2] and GES [3] in light of such large scale simulations.

2 Simulator Overview

Many frameworks have been developed for simulating grid systems [1,2,4]. We have chosen to compare the performance of GES to SimGrid and GridSim because of their maturity, extensive user base and active development status. The main differences between the simulators are the chosen simulation paradigm and threading model. While GES uses single-threaded discrete-time based simulation, both SimGrid and GridSim use massively multi-threaded discrete-event based simulation. Whereas SimGrid offers the choice between the use of `ucontexts` (user space threads) and `pthreads` (native threads), GridSim only supports native threading, a consequence of the threading model used in current JVMs.

The differences in simulation paradigm can be easily explained by the focus and history of the simulators. SimGrid has a strong focus on accurate network simulation. This accuracy can be achieved best using discrete-event simulation. GridSim started out as a framework for testing resource management policies in grids and is built on top of the SimJava discrete-event engine. The addition of a simulated network infrastructure enables the incorporation of network effects in simulations [5]. GES was developed as a tool for studying economic resource management approaches for grids, with a main focus on testing the algorithms and protocols of various economic approaches. Under the assumption that network contention is low there is less need to simulate a network and it is more efficient to use a discrete-time engine.

2.1 SimGrid

SimGrid [6] is an extensive toolkit that provides core functionalities for the simulation of distributed applications. The codebase is written in C. Java bindings that call into the C core using JNI will be provided in future releases. The toolkit started out with a focus on centralized scheduling algorithms and was adapted later on to allow for decentralized scheduling [7]. The simulator takes into account the computational speed of nodes as well as latency and bandwidth of the network links connecting these nodes. SimGrid's network model allows for faster simulation times compared to approaches that use packet-level simulation.

The GRAS layer allows developers to implement distributed services and deploy them in a simulated setting using the Meta-SimGrid (MSG) layer, or in a real world setting using a socket-based communication layer. In the context of our survey on simulation scalability we will evaluate the performance of the MSG layer. This layer provides abstractions for *hosts*, *tasks* and *processes*. A host represents a physical resource with computing capabilities that is able to execute tasks. Hosts are linked to each other through a set of links. Currently, it is not possible to create multi-processor hosts[1]. A process is a piece of logic

---
[1] This might be included as a future extension as communicated to us by the SimGrid developers.

that runs on a specific host and corresponds to a thread. A process can execute tasks on its corresponding host or exchange them with other processes. A task is defined by a computation amount and size.

2.2 GridSim

GridSim is written in Java on top of the SimJava 2.0 basic discrete event infrastructure. The simulator allows for packet-level simulation of the network and provides an output statistics framework. It supports space and time shared allocation policies as well as advance reservation. Contrary to SimGrid it is possible to model clusters as a single entity. GridSim also contains a reusable *GridInformationService* (GIS) which is responsible for the registration, indexing and discovery of resource providers. It is possible to create a single GIS entity in the simulation, but also to organize multiple GIS entities in a hierarchy comparable to a DNS tree. Additionally, GridSim includes components oriented towards data grids, the most important one being the *ReplicaCatalogue* (RC). Like the GIS, a RC can be organized hierarchically. GridSim has also been used to study economic grid resource management [8,9].

Every simulated entity in GridSim extends the `GridSimCore` class which includes both an `Input` and `Output` object to send and receive events. All three of these classes extend the `Sim_entity` class of SimJava. Since every `Sim_entity` is actually a Java thread, this means that every user or resource provider entity requires at least three threads during simulation. GridSim entities use the `sim_pause()`, `sim_get_next()` and `sim_schedule()` primitives of SimJava to pause, receive the next `Sim_event` object or schedule such an event.

2.3 GES

The Grid Economics Simulator (GES) has been developed to study economic grid resource management systems [10,11,12]. The simulator offers a toolkit for analyzing and comparing different economic and traditional resource management algorithms. An overview of the GES core layer is given in figure 1.

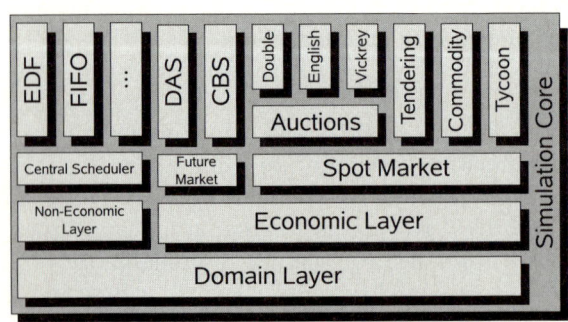

Fig. 1. Overview of the architecture of GES

Two of the key design goals of the architecture are extensibility and reusability. This "extend-and-refine" philosophy can be found throughout the whole `simulation core` and its components. The `domain` layer contains base classes for all domain entities such as `Consumer`, `Provider`, `Job`, `GridResource` and `GridEnvironment`. The `Bank` entity as well as other components supporting economic resource management are located in the `economic` layer. Support for traditional forms of resource management is provided through the `non-economic` layer. Existing components can be easily extended when new RMS algorithms are added to the framework. GES currently has support for a substantial number of spot- and future market mechanisms [3,12].

Simulations can be distributed over multiple processing nodes through the `distribution` layer. This layer interfaces with compute resources that host a Jini-enabled compute service, clusters fronted by a Sun Grid Engine head node, or clusters with a passwordless SSH setup. Currently, distribution is supported at the granularity of a simulated scenario. For a more in depth view of all the capabilities of GES, we refer to [3].

In order to investigate the communication complexity of resource management approaches in more detail, we are planning to extend the simulator with support for simulating the network infrastructure. This will also allow for the development of network-aware scheduling algorithms, market mechanisms for bandwidth pricing, as well as analysis of communication and data transfers.

3 Evaluation

We will test the general scalability of the different simulators and determine whether they are capable of simulating a system on the scale of the EGEE grid. In addition, we will investigate how the three simulators scale in terms of the number of jobs in the system. We use a synthetic scenario that is specifically designed to isolate the different variables which may affect the outcome of our tests. Note that in the following, we will refer to grid users as *consumers* while entities that contribute resources to the infrastructure are referred to as *providers*. All tests use variations of a base scenario with the following parameters:

- Number of consumers $N_c = 1\,000$
- Number of providers $N_p = 100$
- Total number of jobs $N_j = 10\,000$
- Number of jobs per consumer $N_{j_c} = N_j/N_c$
- Job length in processor time slots $L_j \in [7, 13]$
- Total number of CPUs $N_{cpu} = 1\,000$
- Number of cpus per provider $N_{cpu_p} = N_{cpu}/N_p$

Since we want to focus on the performance properties of the simulators' cores, we split up the consumers in groups of 10 and associated each group with a single provider which schedules incoming jobs in a round robin fashion. This simple setup allows us to evaluate the core performance of the different simulators while eliminating unwanted effects caused by complex network configurations or interactions between entities.

For GridSim we performed the tests without a simulated network. For SimGrid we were obliged to use a simple network topology because the network provides the only interaction channel for consumers and providers. Since it is currently not possible to aggregate multiple CPUs in one entity, we have modelled a provider node by combining one forwarding host with N_{cpu_p} CPU hosts. The forwarding host is connected to its CPUs with one link. The consumers are also connected to their provider with one link. Every job is routed over these links from the consumer to the forwarder and then to a CPU node. All links were configured with maximal bandwidth and minimal latency properties. Because of their higher potential scalability and configurability we used ucontexts instead of pthreads. We limited the ucontext stack size to 64 KB.

All tests were performed on the CalcUA cluster at the university of Antwerp which hosts 256 Opteron 250 nodes running a 64-bit Linux distribution. All nodes used in the tests hosted 8 GB of RAM. During testing we measured the simulation time in milliseconds and the maximum memory usage, both real and virtual, by polling the simulation process every second. We used version 1.6.0 of Sun's JVM for the executing of all Java code.

3.1 Test I: General Scaling

This scenario is designed to evaluate the general scaling capabilities of each simulator. We scale N_c from 1 to 10 000 while changing N_p such that $N_c/N_p = 10$. The other parameters maintained their default values. In effect, this test scales up the entire base scenario.

Figure 2 shows the time it took to perform the simulation on a logarithmic scale as a function of the number of simulated consumers.

As shown in the graph, GES scales up better than both GridSim and SimGrid. The difference in simulation time is over two orders of magnitude compared to SimGrid and three orders of magnitude compared to GridSim when simulating

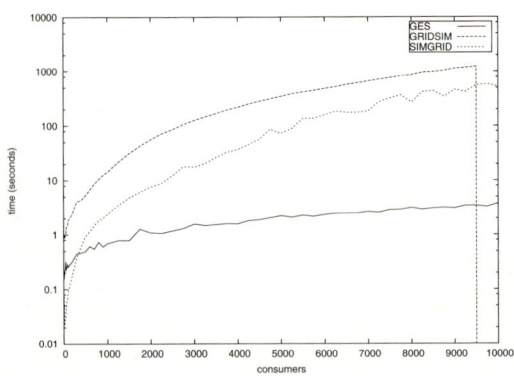

Fig. 2. Simulation time as a function of the number of consumers

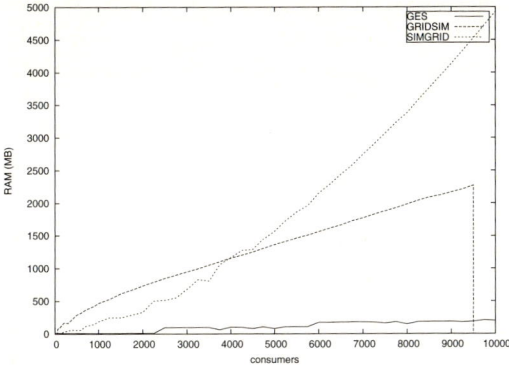

Fig. 3. Real memory requirements as a function of the number of consumers

a grid with 9 000 consumers. GridSim was unable to simulate an environment with 10 000 consumers because it would need to create well over 32 000 threads, more than a normally configured Linux kernel can handle. When scaling up even further we were able to determine that SimGrid could handle a maximum of 12 000 consumers while GES had no problem simulating 100 000 consumers.

Figure 3 shows the actual memory usage in function of the number of consumers. SimGrid does not scale linearly in this regard which can be explained by the fact that it uses a routing table and thus scales quadratically with the number of hosts. While GridSim does scale linearly, its actual memory usage is still substantial and likely related to its heavy use of threading.

3.2 Test II: Job Scaling

This scenario evaluates the influence of the number of jobs on the simulation time. While keeping the total workload per consumer at 100. We scaled N_{j_c} from 1 to 100.

The time it took to perform the tests is plotted in figure 4. We can see that SimGrid handles higher job loads better than GridSim and that GES is virtually unaffected by the amount of jobs. It is clear that when using the discrete event paradigm, the simulation time scales linearly with the number of jobs while this is not the case for the discrete time paradigm. A discrete time paradigm in contrast scales linearly with the size of a job while this has no effect on a discrete event system. The suitability of either paradigm is determined by the resolution at which we wish to model time. While it is interesting to model time in high resolution for the analysis of interaction protocols, it is not necessary to do so for the simulation of job execution.

The choice for discrete-event simulation often leads to a choice for a multi-threaded model as well, because it is logical to think of events being passed between independently running processes. It is not necessary however to use a multi-threaded model in combination with discrete-event simulation as demonstrated by a number of other projects [13,14]. It is clear from the previous test

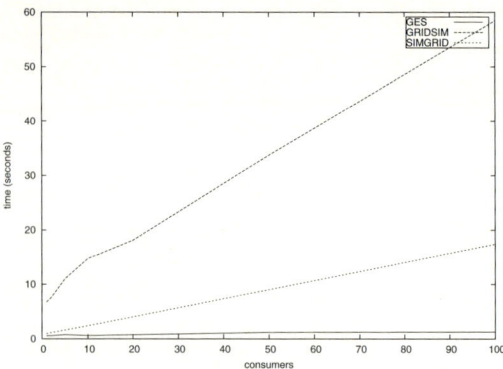

Fig. 4. Simulation time as a function of the number of jobs

that for the simulation of very large systems, a discrete-event simulator may scale up higher when used in combination with a single threaded approach.

4 Threading and Virtual Memory

Both GridSim and SimGrid use threads for each simulated entity. GridSim uses the Java threading model while SimGrid offers a choice between pthreads and ucontexts on Linux. Both Java threads and pthreads are native while ucontexts are user space threads. On a Linux machine with a normally configured kernel, the number of simultaneous native threads is limited to just over 32 000. Since user space threads are not visible to the kernel, they overcome this limitation. Moreover ucontexts offer more tweakable stack sizes than pthreads.

Because the choice of threading model is a key design issue, it is important to understand the consequences and limitations of using a multi-threaded model. One of the most obvious repercussions of using a native multi-threaded model is the overhead caused by context switching. Especially for thread-based discrete-event simulation this overhead can be substantial since a large number of threads will be created. Threads can also be suspended by the scheduler at any time, which may degrade performance unnecessarily. While threads are a good way to develop systems with *actual* concurrent behaviour, it is not necessary to use real threads to *simulate* this concurrency.

Each thread or context will also allocate a stack in virtual memory. This stack will be created in real memory only when it is needed on a per page basis. Therefore, threading does not necessarily have a direct impact on actual *real* memory usage. However there are limits on the amount of *virtual* memory a process can allocate. This limit is 4 GB on any 32-bit architecture of which in general only 3 GB can be used by the process itself on a Linux machine. On 64-bit Linux machines, the practical upper limit of virtual memory available is the sum of the physical memory and the swap size unless oversubscribing is allowed. To mitigate these limitations, it is possible to tweak the size of the

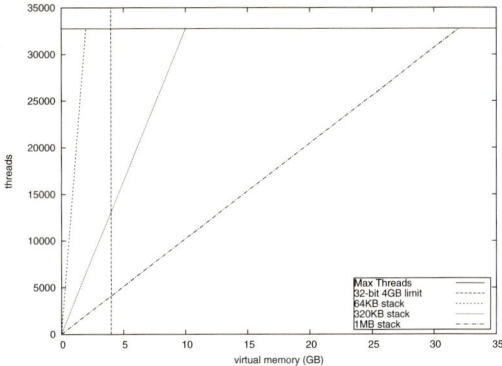

Fig. 5. Number of native threads as a function of available virtual memory

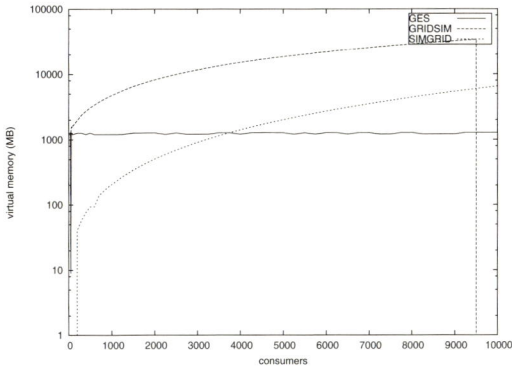

Fig. 6. Virtual memory requirements of the simulators under general scaling scenario

thread stack. The typical thread stack size for Java threads is 320 KB on a 32-bit and 1024 KB on a 64-bit Linux machine. It is possible to reduce this size with a JVM argument to a minimum of 64 KB. For pthreads, the minimum stack size is 56 KB while ucontext stacks can be even smaller. Another advantage of pthreads and ucontexts is their ability to adjust the stack size per thread while Java does not offer this flexibility.

The limitations on the scalability of a threaded approach are depicted in figures 5 and 6. The graph in figure 5 includes both the maximum native thread limit as well as the 32-bit memory wall. It also demontrates the effect of tweaking the stack size on the virtual memory usage. The graph in figure 6 shows the maximal virtual memory allocation of the three simulators as a function of the number of consumers in the general scaling scenario. It shows that the JVM by itself allocates 1 GB of virtual memory. This is used as a code cache which contains the interpreter and code generated by the compilers. Although the size of this cache is adjustable, and future JVMs will default to a more reasonable amount, this will not impact our results as virtual memory is basically free on

64-bit machines. From the graph we can also observe that GridSim is capable of claiming close to 35 GB of virtual memory. The vastness of this allocation is due to the standard thread stack size of 1 MB. SimGrid allocates a significantly smaller amount of virtual memory. When we contrast this with the actual memory usage in figure 3 we can observe that SimGrid uses almost all of its virtual memory while GridSim uses less than a tenth of its allocation.

5 Conclusion

In this contribution we have compared the scalability of GridSim, SimGrid and GES. While both GridSim and SimGrid use a *multi-threaded discrete-event* core, GES uses a *single-threaded discrete-time* core. As we have observed from the results of our tests, both SimGrid and GridSim are unable to scale to the level that would allow them to simulate very large scale grid infrastructures such as EGEE. For GridSim the problem is rather fundamental in that it requires an amount of threads during simulation that reaches the upper limit of threads manageable by a normally configured Linux kernel. While SimGrid can sidestep this issue using `ucontexts`, it still reaches an upper limit of 23 000 simulated entities. These results show that when trying to simulate very large scale grids, a massively multi-threaded simulator is not the best choice.

Depending on the resolution at which time is to be simulated, it is better to choose either the discrete-event or discrete-time simulation paradigm. Whereas a detailed analysis of the impact of communication delays requires a high resolution and thus leans towards discrete-event simulation, a lower resolution discrete-time engine is adequate for simulating the execution and scheduling of jobs in a grid system. Irrespective of the choice for a discrete-time or discrete-event model, one can decide to use a threaded or non-threaded simulation core. We have quantified the impact of these choices through a comparative analysis of GES, SimGrid and GridSim and have shown their effect on simulation performance and scalability.

References

1. Legrand, A., Marchal, L., Casanova, H.: Scheduling distributed applications: the simgrid simulation framework. In: Proceedings of the 3rd IEEE/ACM International Symposium on Cluster Computing and the Grid (CCGRID 2003), pp. 138–145. IEEE Computer Society, Los Alamitos (2003)
2. Buyya, R., Murshed, M.: Gridsim: a toolkit for the modeling and simulation of distributed resource management and scheduling for grid computing. Concurrency and Computat. Pract. Exper. 14(13-15), 1175–1220 (2002)
3. Vanmechelen, K., Depoorter, W., Broeckhove, J.: A simulation framework for studying economic resource management in grids. In: Bubak, M., van Albada, G.D., Dongarra, J., Sloot, P.M.A. (eds.) ICCS 2008, Part I. LNCS, vol. 5101, pp. 226–235. Springer, Heidelberg (2008)

4. Aida, K., Tekefusa, A., Nakada, H., Matsuoka, S., Sekiguchi, S., Nagashima, U.: Performance evaluation model for scheduling in global computing systems. The International Journal of High Performance Computing Applications 14(3), 268–279 (2000)
5. Sulistio, A., Poduval, G., Buyya, R., Tham, C.K.: On incorporating differentiated levels of network service into gridsim. Future Gener. Comput. Syst. 23(4), 606–615 (2007)
6. Casanova, H.: Simgrid: a toolkit for the simulation of application scheduling. In: Proceedings of CCGrid 2001, pp. 430–437. IEEE Computer Society, Los Alamitos (2001)
7. Legrand, A., Lerouge, J.: Metasimgrid: Towards realistic scheduling simulation of distributed applications. Technical Report 2002-28, LIP (2002)
8. Buyya, R.: Economic-based Distributed Resource Management and Scheduling for Grid Computing. PhD thesis, Monash University, Australia (2002)
9. Assuncao, M., Buyya, R.: An evaluation of communication demand of auction protocols in grid environments. In: Proceedings of GECON 2006, pp. 24–33. World Scientific, Singapore (2006)
10. Vanmechelen, K., Broeckhove, J.: A comparative analysis of single-unit vickrey auctions and commodity markets for realizing grid economies with dynamic pricing. In: Altmann, J., Veit, D. (eds.) GECON 2007. LNCS, vol. 4685, pp. 98–111. Springer, Heidelberg (2007)
11. Stuer, G., Vanmechelen, K., Broeckhove, J.: A commodity market algorithm for pricing substitutable grid resources. Future Generation Computer Systems 23(5), 688–701 (2007)
12. Vanmechelen, K., Depoorter, W., Broeckhove, J.: Economic grid resource management for CPU bound applications with hard deadlines. In: Proceedings of CCGrid 2008. IEEE Computer Society, Los Alamitos (in press, 2008)
13. Barr, R., Haas, Z.J., van Renesse, R.: Jist: An efficient approach to simulation using virtual machines. Software Practice and Experience 35, 539–576 (2005)
14. Jacobs, P.H.M., Verbraeck, A.: Single-threaded specification of process-interaction formalism in java. In: Proceedings of the 36th conference on Winter simulation, pp. 1548–1555 (2004)

Performance Evaluation of Data Management Layer by Data Sharing Patterns for Grid RPC Applications*

Yoshihiro Nakajima[2], Yoshiaki Aida[1], Mitsuhisa Sato[1], and Osamu Tatebe[1]

[1] Graduate School of Systems and Information Engineering,
University of Tsukuba, Tsukuba, Japan
{aida,msato,tatebe}@hpcs.cs.tsukuba.ac.jp
[2] NTT Network Innovation Laboratories,
Nippon Telegraph and Telephone Corporation, Tokyo, Japan
nakajima.yoshihiro@lab.ntt.co.jp

Abstract. Grid RPC applications, typically master-slave type of applications, often need to share large size of data among workers. For efficient and flexible data sharing among a master and workers, we have designed and developed a data management layer called OmniStorage. This paper enhances the OmniStorage functionality to accommodate several data transfer methods and to specify a hint for data sharing patterns, and develops a set of synthetic benchmarks based on data sharing patterns required by grid RPC applications to evaluate the performance and characteristics of each data transfer method. The performance evaluation and the hint help to select a suitable data transfer method, which improves the efficiency and also scalability of grid RPC applications that need to share large size of data among a master and workers.

1 Introduction

Grid technology enables integration of the computing resources in the wide-area network and sharing of huge amounts of data geographically distributed in several places. In order to make use of computing resources in a grid environment, an RPC-style system is particularly useful in that it provides an easy-to-use, intuitive programming interface that allows users of the grid system to easily develop grid-enabled applications. Several systems adopt Grid RPC as a basic model of computation, including Ninf [1], NetSolve [2] and DIET [3]. We have developed a grid RPC system called OmniRPC [4] for parallel programming solution in clusters and grid environments.

Grid RPC applications such as parametric search programs and task parallel programs, sometimes require a large amount of shared data among a master and workers. For instance, in some parametric search applications, the workers require a large common initial data and different parameters to execute different computations at remote nodes in parallel. In the RPC model, a master issues a remote procedure call and receives results from the invoked remote procedure. When the master needs to send the same and large initial data to every worker by arguments of the remote procedure call,

---

* This study was supported in part by MEXT KAKENHI (No. 17200002, 17·7324, 19024009), and by the Japan-France collaboration research program (SAKURA) through the JSPS. The study was performed in University of Tsukuba.

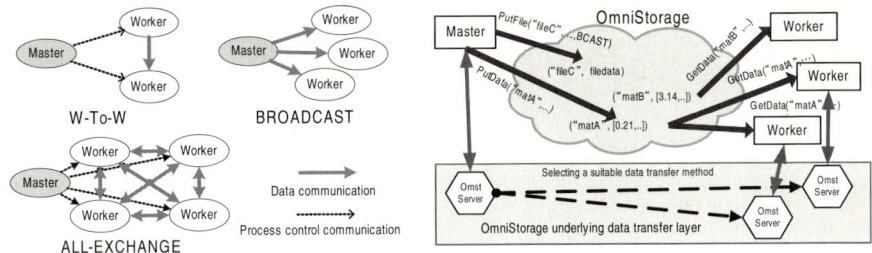

Fig. 1. Synthetic data sharing patterns

Fig. 2. Overview of OmniStorage

the data transfer from the master is wasteful and also causes a bottleneck for scalability. Thus, we proposed a programming model to decouple the data transmission from the RPC model to allow the data to be transferred efficiently by a data management layer [5]. The data management layer provides a temporal storage space that can be shared by both a master and workers, and APIs for data registration and data retrieval to the shared data.

For the data management layer of grid RPC applications, we have designed and developed OmniStorage [5]. OmniStorage provides APIs to access data using an identifier and hides both an internal behavior of data transfer method and a data placement from the application level. In [5], a preliminary design of OmniStorage using tree-topology-aware file broadcasting and the performance results are described. This paper enhances the OmniStorage functionality to exploit several data transfer methods in data transfer layer and to accept a hint for data sharing patterns in order to help to choose a suitable data transfer method.

Several studies on the data management layer gave some performance evaluation using simple benchmarks [6,7], but the lack of synthetic workload benchmarks that model data sharing patterns of grid RPC applications defies the performance comparison between several data management layers. To address this issue, we develop synthetic grid RPC workload models that abstract data sharing patterns typically needed by grid RPC applications, and investigate the performance characteristics of three data transfer methods in OmniStorage. It shows that selecting an appropriate data transfer mechanism promises to solve an inherent inefficiency in Grid RPC regarding data sharing among a master and workers.

Our contributions are as follows:

- Synthetic workload programs for grid RPC applications are developed to investigate the performance characteristics of several data management layers regarding the data sharing pattern among a master and workers.
- We investigate the performance characteristics of different kinds of data transfer methods in a data management layer using the synthetic workload programs so that an optimal data transfer method for each data sharing pattern is examined.
- Through performance evaluation of OmniStorage, we demonstrate the merits of a program model to decouple the data transmission from the RPC.
- We propose an interface which can utilize a hint information for data sharing patterns in order to allow a program to exploit an optimal data transfer method according to the data sharing pattern needed by the application.

```
/* master program */
int main(){
  double initdata[LEN];
  ...
  for(i = 0; i < n; i++)
    req[i] = OmniRpcCallAsync("foo", LEN, initdata, i);
  ...
  OmniRpcWaitAll(n, req);
}
/* worker program */
Define foo(IN int s, IN double data[s], IN int iter){
  /* main calculation */  }
```

Fig. 3. An example of OmniRPC program

```
/* master program */
int main(){
  double initdata[LEN];
  req = OmstPutData("mydat",initdata,
                    sizeof(double)*LEN,OMST_BROADCAST);
  OmstWait(req);
  for(i = 0; i < n; i++)
    req[i] = OmniRpcCallAsync("foo", i);
  OmniRpcWaitAll(n, req);
}
/* worker program */
Define foo(int IN iter){
  double initdata[LEN];
  req = OmstGetData("mydat",initdata, sizeof(double)*LEN);
  OmstWait(req);
  /* main calculation */  }
```

Fig. 4. An example of OmniRPC program with OmniStorage

The remaining of this paper is organized as follows. Section 2 describes data sharing pattern models typically needed by grid RPC applications and benchmark programs. Section 3 describes a design and implementation of the OmniStorage. The performance and the characteristics of OmniStorage are presented in Section 4. A selection policy of data transfer methods depending on data sharing patterns among a master and workers is discussed in Section 5. Section 6 describes previous work related to the present study. Finally, Section 7 concludes the paper.

2 Data Sharing Pattern for Data Management Layer

2.1 Data Sharing Pattern in Grid RPC Applications

Basically RPC mechanism sends arguments and receives results between a master and a worker. However some grid RPC applications need other data sharing patterns such as broadcasting common initial data, and data transmission between workers. Performance issues for each data sharing pattern can be summarized as follows:

Broadcasting initial data: In case of parametric search type parallel applications, workers will receive common initial data and their own parameters from a master to execute their part of computations at remote nodes. In this case, the master has to send both common initial data and different parameters by every RPC. To address this kind of issue, the OmniRPC provides a data persistence mechanism called "automatic-initializing remote module" to hold data specified by an initialization function of a remote executable module [8]. This avoids multiple transmissions of the same initial data. However, the data must be sent directly from a master to each worker when a remote module is invoked. If the initial data is large, or the number of workers increase, the data transfer from a master would be a bottleneck.

Data transfers between workers due to data dependency in RPC's parameters: If an application has data dependency in parameters of RPCs, in other words, several RPCs have data dependency between input and output parameters, which means output of previous RPC becomes the input of the next RPC. A worker communicates to another worker through a master in order to realize the data transfer between the workers. Therefore the communication to the master will disturb application's scalability especially in case of a grid environment due to a long latency and a poor network bandwidth.

Or if an application performs request sequencing of RPC, the efficiency of data sharing will be improved by optimizing the data sharing between workers.

2.2 Data Sharing Pattern

Data sharing patterns required by grid RPC applications are summarized as follows. Figure 1 shows the overview of these patterns.

W-To-W: W-To-W model is seen at a program which an output of a previous RPC becomes the input of the next PC. W-To-W model is used in the concept of RPC request sequencing so that no unnecessary data is transmitted and all necessary data is transferred. In W-To-W, a worker registers its own data to OmniStorage after that another worker retrieves the data from OmniStorage.

BROADCAST: BROADCAST model is observed at a program to broadcast common initial data from a master to workers. The model is used at many parametric search programs. In BROADCAST model, a master sends one common initial file to all workers.

ALL-EXCHANGE: ALL-EXCHANGE models a program that every worker exchanges their own data files each other for subsequent processing. All workers exchange their own data files each other. In other words, each worker registers one file to OmniStorage after that the worker retrieves files which are registered by the other workers. This model is the worst data sharing pattern in case of a black box program which a worker communicates with other workers randomly.

3 OmniStorage: A Data Management Layer for Grid RPC Applications

3.1 Design of OmniStorage

To handle data sharing patterns described in the previous section, we design a data management layer called OmniStorage on wide area networks to realize the efficient data transfers among workers by decoupling the data transmission from conventional RPC model. Decoupling the data transmission form RPC, OmniStorage framework works as a data repository system for grid RPC applications. Figure 2 shows the overview of OmniStorage. A process can register data with a unique identifier and a hint, which indicates a data sharing pattern, to data repository of OmniStorage. In the data repository of OmniStorage, data is managed by a combination of an identifier and a data entity like "(id, value)". A process can retrieve data by specifying an identifier. The data location is transparent to users. In addition, OmniStorage utilizes a hint information of the data in order to choose a suitable data transfer method according to the data sharing pattern.

OmniStorage APIs consist of a data registering function, `OmstPutData(id, data, size, hint)`, data retrieving functions, `OmstGetData(id, data, size)`, request synchronization functions to access a shared data space. Here, Data handling information are given by a logical sum of hints which indicate data sharing patterns, and data transfer methods with `hint` in OmniStorage data registration API. These hints are summarized as follows:

- Attributes of patterns of data transfer
  - OMST_POINT2POINT: Data may be transferred between worker processes.
  - OMST_BROADCAST: Data is supposed to be broadcasted to many processes.
  - OMST_ALL_EXCHANGE: Data is supposed to be exchanged each other by each worker process.
- Attribute to specify a specific data transfer layer.

In the OmniRPC applications with OmniStorage, shared data among workers are managed by OmniStorage, while none-shared data including a parameter in parametric search applications is managed by OmniRPC's parameters.

Figure 3 and Figure 4 show a typical parametric search application with OmniRPC, and the same application with OmniRPC and OmniStorage, respectively. Both of examples, an initial data are broadcasted to all workers. The master program calls OmstPutData() to register data before a worker program accesses the data. Then the worker program calls OmstGetData() to access the data. To identify a data, the same identifier "mydat" in the name space of OmniStorage is used in both a master and workers. Moreover, a hint of data sharing pattern is specified on the data registration API of OmstPutData() so that OmniStorage can select an appropriate data transfer method regarding a data sharing pattern. Here, a hint of broadcast pattern of OMST_BROADCAST is specified.

3.2 Implementations

The data cache in OmniStorage is basically handled as the data file. OmniStorage exploits a data transfer method to transfer a cache data file between processes or to access a cache data file. The cache files will be stored on a remote host so that a program can exploit the data locality.

OmniStorage accommodates several data transfer methods to exploit an suitable data transfer method according to a required data sharing pattern. Although in this paper, OmniStorage employs three middleware as data transfer methods which have different kinds of characteristics for performance evaluations as follows:

Omst/Tree: Omst/Tree exploits our file broadcasting middleware taking network topology into account. Figure 5 shows the overview of Omst/Tree. Omst/Tree uses several relay servers between master and workers so that Omst/Tree can reduce the amount of data communications between a master and workers.

Omst/BT: Omst/BT makes use of BitTorrent to be used as a data transfer method for cache files. BitTorrent [9] is a P2P file sharing protocol in order to distribute a large amount of files to many peers efficiently. Figure 6 shows the overview of Omst/BT. When the number of seeder increases according to the progress of file distribution, the load average of each peer gets lower and BitTorrent can achieve efficient data transfers.

Omst/GF: Omst/GF utilize a grid-enabled distributed file system called Gfarm [10]. Gfarm provides a grid file system that can scale up to petascale storage, and realize scalable I/O bandwidth and scalable parallel processing. Cache files on Omst/GF are managed by Gfarm. These caches are accessed by using the Gfarm remote I/O functions. Omst/GF duplicates the cache files on several nodes in order to improve the scalability of data transfer. For example, if broadcast type data transfer is used in a program, Omst/GF duplicates two more cache files on file system nodes.

4 Performance Evaluation

The basic performance and the characteristics of OmniStorage implementations are investigated using three synthetic benchmark programs by data sharing patterns needed by grid RPC applications. The benchmark programs consist of **W-To-W**, **BROADCAST**, and **ALL-EXCHANGE** based on data sharing patterns as discussed at Section 2. Note, we do not mention the basic performance of the middleware used in OmniStorage, such as BitTorrent and Gfarm. As for these basic performances, refer the reports [11,12,13].

Four clusters connected by different networks are used for performance evaluation. Figure 7 shows cluster configurations and the measured network performance. Each master program of benchmark programs is executed on cTsukuba, and a worker program is assigned per computational node in the clusters. Here, each measured data in the performance evaluations is a mean value of five trials. The software components of OmniRPC 1.2, libtorrent 0.9.1, Azureus 2.5.0.2, Gfarm 1.4, Boost C++ Library 1.33.1, and Java2 SE 1.4.2 are used.

To conduct this performance evaluation, two experimental settings with 16 nodes, where the network configurations between two clusters are different, are configured as follows:

CASE1: Two clusters are in the same network — Using both eight nodes on Dennis cluster and eight nodes on Alice cluster

CASE2: Two clusters are connected by WAN — Using both eight nodes on Dennis cluster and eight nodes on Gfm cluster.

Figure 8 shows the elapsed time of W-To-W benchmark in case of machine configuration of CASE1 and CASE2. In spite of the experimental configuration, Omst/GF achieves better performance than other data transfer methods. In case of Omst/GF and Omst/BT, a worker can directly communicate with another worker so that the efficiency of data transfer between two workers may be improved. On the other hand, to perform W-To-W pattern sharing using only OmniRPC system, two more RPCs, one to send data from a worker to a master, and one to send data from the master to another worker, are required. These sharing patterns cause bottlenecks to improve the performance. Moreover if the necessary number of W-To-W type sharings increases, the efficiency of data transfers would go from bad to worse.

Although Omst/BT could not achieve better performance than using only OmniRPC system. When the number of running workers is small, the BitTorrent protocol cannot perform data transfers efficiently. Moreover, Omst/BT needs pre-procedures, such as creating a torrent file and uploading the torrent file, before the data sharing among a master and workers starts so that the performance of Omst/BT is degraded.

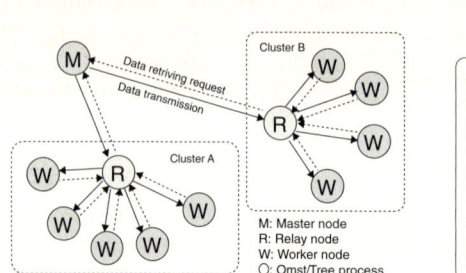
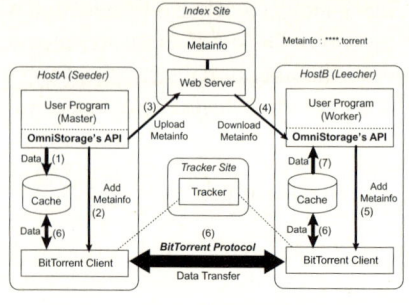

Fig. 5. Omst/Tree implementation

Fig. 6. Omst/BT implementation

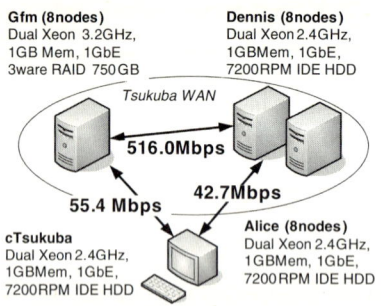
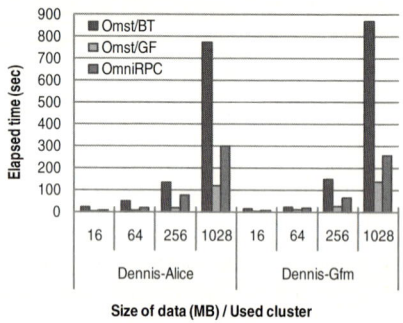

Fig. 7. Experimental platform

Fig. 8. Elapsed time of W-To-W benchmark

Figure 9 shows the elapsed time of BROADCAST on two types of machine configuration. Regardless of the data size, Omst/Tree achieves better performance in most cases. In case of two clusters connected by high speed network, Omst/BT can achieve approximately the same performance on the Omst/Tree. Particularly when the data size is 1024MB, Omst/BT obtains better performance than Omst/Tree does. In Omst/BT, a data file is divided many small pieces, and each piece is transferred in parallel to other processes so that the efficiency of data transfer is improved. Omst/GF performance is degraded because of the increase of number of data communication between a master and a worker by an inadequate scheduling about a host selection in Gfarm.

Figure 10 shows the elapsed time of ALL-EXCHANGE benchmark program in case of CASE1 and CASE2. Omst/GF succeeds twice faster than Omst/BT in all data size and two cluster configurations. In case of the original OmniRPC system, a master sends a large amount of data many times so that the data sharing between the master and a worker becomes a serious bottleneck, as a result, the performance is degraded. Some factors of performance bottleneck on Omst/BT are caused by both inadequate algorithms, such as the way to selection peer on a tracker and choking algorithm on a peer, and parameter configurations of BitTorrent, such as the limit bandwidth and the limit of connections on a data seeder. However there may be an opportunity to improve the performance by optimizing these parameters or replacing the algorithm.

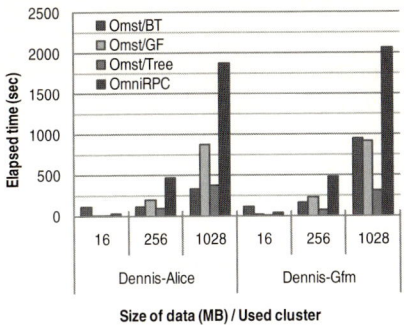 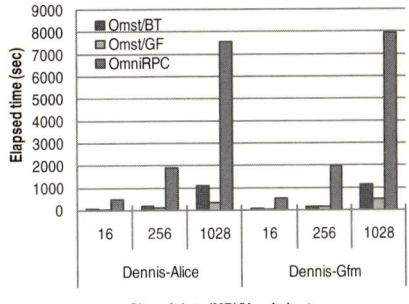

Fig. 9. Elapsed time of BROADCAST benchmark

Fig. 10. Elapsed time of ALL-EXCHANGE benchmark

5 Discussion for an Optimal Data Transfer Method

We discuss for an optimal data transfer method of OmniStorage according to three data sharing patterns from the basic performance evaluation.

- **W-To-W:** Omst/GF is preferred in case of a data sharing pattern of W-To-W. One of reasons may come from the environment in the performance evaluation such that there are too small number of workers to get merits of BitTorrent protocol.
- **BROADCAST:** Omst/Tree is preferred for BROADCAST when the network topology of a grid environment is known. In case that the network topology is not known beforehand, Omst/BT is preferred because the BitTorrent protocol aims to be used in a peer-to-peer environment where the network topology is unknown. In addition, when a user exploits more than 1000 nodes, Omst/Tree requires more complex configurations to run than Omst/BT. Whence Omst/BT is suitable in such case.
- **ALL-EXCHANGE:** A suitable data transfer method is Omst/GF in case of ALL-EXCHANGE. In this evaluation, BitTorrent parameters is not optimized in order to improve the Omst/BT's performance. However, there is a chance to improve the performance of Omst/BT.

We move to discuss the merit of exploiting hint information of data sharing pattern in order to achieve the efficient data sharing. The hint information of the data tells the OmniStorage which data sharing pattern is required and how the data is used in a remote process. Therefore, OmniStorage can select an optimal data transfer method which is the most suitable for the data sharing pattern. In addition, OmniStorage can transfer the data efficiently taking the network topology into account. Suppose that OmniStorage does not handle the data hint information, OmniStorage use W-To-W data sharing pattern, and cannot accomplish the efficient data transfers in case that data broadcasting is required. By exploiting some hint information for data, OmniStorage can exploit an optimal data transfer method depending on data sharing patterns so that it can achieve the efficient data transfer in terms of scalability and performance.

6 Related Work

DIET [14] implemented a data management layer called Data Tree Manager (DTM) to avoid multiple redundant transmissions of the same data from a master to workers using a data cache mechanism, and to provide a persistent data access mechanism without any information of data location by using an identifier. This approach mainly focuses on how to handle the persistent data shared among workers. DTM may reduce the amount of data transfer using the data cache mechanism and finding the shortest path to the data from a consumer. On the other hand, OmniStorage focuses on improving both the efficiency of data transfer among workers and the scalability of grid RPC applications. DIET DTM supports W-To-W data sharing pattern, but it does not support other data sharing models and mechanisms to share the data efficiently. OmniStorage can select an optimal data transfer method from several data transfer methods taking required data sharing pattern into account so that OmniStorage improves the efficiency of data transfer among a master and workers including in case of BROADCAST and ALL-EXCHANGE patterns.

NetSolve [2] integrates Distributed Storage Infrastructure (DSI) named Internet Backplane Protocol [15] to control the placement of data that will be accessed by workers so that a master can reduce the times of the same data transfer to workers. However, data in DSI is still explicitly transferred to/from the storage servers at the application level. That means, a master should know both which node stores the data and which node are closer to the worker before the program runs. On the other hand, OmniStorage can adapt to dynamic environment since OmniStorage provides high-level data access APIs without data location information, such as a node name, and optimizes the data transfer automatically. [6] gave a performance result of NetSolve with DSI using a matrix multiply, but the detailed performance evaluation based on data sharing patterns hasn't been presented yet.

Tanimura el al. proposed a task sequencing which allowed direct data transfer of only file type parameter between RPC workers using Gfarm distributed file system as a data repository on Ninf-G [16]. On the other hand, OmniStorage can handle both file and array data and optimize the data transfer by selecting a suitable data transfer method with hint information.

Batch-Aware Distributed File System (BAD-FS) [17] and Stork [18] aim to orchestrate I/O-intensive batch workloads on remote clusters. They manage data placement, data replication according to job requests submitted to a job scheduler. They statically optimize data transfer beforehand the execution. However, OmniStorage focuses on run-time data transfer instructed by an application.

7 Conclusion and Future Work

OmniStorage is designed and implemented to realize a data management layer that augments functionality of the Grid RPC model in order to decouples the data transmission from RPC mechanism aiming to achieve flexible and efficient data transfer and choose a suitable data transfer method of OmniStorage. The basic performance of three implementations is investigated using synthetic benchmark programs based on data sharing patterns needed by grid RPC applications. OmniStorage achieved better performance than the original OmniRPC system in terms of both scalability and efficiency of data transfer. We have demonstrated the merits of a programming model which decouples the data transmission from the RPC. Moreover, taking a hint information of data sharing patterns into account, OmniStorage accomplishes both high performance and high scalability of applications. As our future work, we will optimize some parameters of OmniStorage especially parameters for Omst/BT.

References

1. Nakada, H., Sato, M., Sekiguchi, S.: Design and Implementations of Ninf: towards a Global Computing Infrastructure. Future Generation Computing Systems 15(5-6), 649–658 (1999)
2. Arnold, D., Agrawal, S., Blackford, S., Dongarra, J., Miller, M., Seymour, K., Sagi, K., Shi, Z., Vadhiyar, S.: Users' Guide to NetSolve V1.4.1. Innovative Computing Dept. Technical Report ICL-UT-02-05, University of Tennessee (June 2002)
3. Caron, E., Desprez, F.: Diet: A scalable toolbox to build network enabled servers on the grid. International Journal of High Performance Computing Applications 20(3), 335–352 (2006)
4. Sato, M., Boku, T., Takahashi, D.: OmniRPC: a Grid RPC system for Parallel Programming in Cluster and Grid Environment. In: Proceedings of the 3st International Symposium on Cluster Computing and the Grid, pp. 206–213 (2003)
5. Aida, Y., Nakajima, Y., Sato, M., Sakurai, T., Takahashi, D., Boku, T.: Performance Improvement by Data Management Layer in a Grid RPC System. In: Proceedings of the First International Conference on Grid and Pervasive Computing, pp. 324–335 (2006)
6. Beck, M., Arnold, D., Bassi, A., Berman, F., Casanova, H., Dongarra, J., Moore, T., Obertelli, G., Plank, J., Swany, M., Vadhiyar, S., Wolski, R.: Middleware for the use of storage in communication. Parallel Comput. 28(12), 1773–1787 (2002)
7. Del-Fabbro, B., Laiymani, D., Nicod, J.-M., Philippe, L.: Dtm: a service for managing data persistency and data replication in network-enabled server environments: Research articles. Concurr. Comput.: Pract. Exper. 19(16), 2125–2140 (2007)
8. Nakajima, Y., Sato, M., et al.: Implementation and performance evaluation of CONFLEX-G: grid-enabled molecular conformational space search program with OmniRPC. In: Proceedings of the 18th Annual International Conference on Supercomputing, pp. 154–163 (2004)
9. BitTorrent, http://www.bittorrent.com/
10. Tatebe, O., Morita, Y., Matsuoka, S., Soda, N., Sekiguchi, S.: Grid datafarm architecture for petascale data intensive computing. In: Proceedings of 2nd IEEE/ACM International Symposium on Cluster Computing and the Grid, pp. 102–109 (2002)
11. Qiu, D., Srikant, R.: Modeling and performance analysis of bittorrent-like peer-to-peer networks. In: Proceedings of The 2004 conference on Applications, technologies, architectures, and protocols for computer communications, pp. 367–378 (2004)
12. Bharambe, A.R., Herley, C., Padmanabhan, V.N.: Some observations on bittorrent performance. In: Proceedings of the 2005 ACM SIGMETRICS international conference on Measurement and modeling of computer systems, pp. 398–399 (2005)
13. Ogura, S., Matsuoka, S., Nakada, H.: Evaluation of the inter-cluster data transfer on Grid environment. In: Protocols of 3rd International Symposium on Cluster Computing and the Grid, pp. 374–381 (2003)
14. Del-Fabbro, B., Laiymani, D., Nicod, J.-M., Philippe, L.: Data management in grid applications providers. In: The First International Conference on Distributed Frameworks for Multimedia Applications (DFMA 2005), pp. 315–322 (2005)

15. Bassi, A., Beck, M., Moore, T., Plank, J.S., Swany, M., Wolski, R., Fagg, G.: The Internet Backplane Protocol: a study in resource sharing. Future Generation Computer Systems 19(4), 551–561 (2003)
16. Tanimura, Y., Nakada, H., Tanaka, Y., Sekiguchi, S.: Design and Implementation of Distributed Task Sequencing on GridRPC. In: Proceedings of the 6th IEEE International Conference on Computer and Information Technology (2006)
17. Bent, J., Thain, D., Arpaci-Dusseau, A.C., Arpaci-Dusseau, R.H., Livny, M.: Explicit control a batch-aware distributed file system. In: Proceedings of the 1st Symposium on Networked Systems Design and Implementation, p. 27 (2004)
18. Kosar, T., Livny, M.: Stork: Making data placement a first class citizen in the grid. In: Proceedings of the 24th IEEE International Conference on Distributed Computing Systems (ICDCS 2004), pp. 342–349 (2004)

The Impact of Clustering on Token-Based Mutual Exclusion Algorithms

Julien Sopena, Luciana Arantes, Fabrice Legond-Aubry, and Pierre Sens

LIP6, Université Pierre et Marie Curie, INRIA, CNRS
{julien.sopena,luciana.arantes,fabrice.legond-aubry,pierre.sens}@lip6.fr

Abstract. We present in this article a theoretical study and performance results about the impact of the Grid architecture on token-based mutual exclusion algorithms. To this end, both the original token-based Naimi-Tréhel's algorithm and a hierarchical approach, suitable to cope with the intrinsic heterogeneity of communication latencies of Grid environments, are studied and evaluated.

1 Introduction

A Grid is usually composed of a large number of machines gathered into small groups called clusters. Nodes within a cluster are linked using local networks (LAN) whereas clusters are connected by wide area network (WAN) links. Therefore, Grids present a hierarchy of communication delays where the latency of sending a message between nodes of different clusters is much higher than sending a message between nodes within the same cluster.

As Grid resources can be shared, applications that run on top of a Grid usually require their processes to get exclusive access to one or more of these shared resources (critical section). Thus, a distributed mutual exclusion algorithm, which ensures that exactly one process can execute the critical section (CS) at any given time (*safety* property) and that all CS requests will eventually be satisfied (*liveness* property), is an important building block for Grid applications. Moreover, the performance of a mutual exclusion algorithm can have a major impact on the overall performance of these applications.

Mutual exclusion algorithms can be divided into two groups: *permission-based* (e.g. Lamport [5], Ricart-Agrawala [11], Maekawa [6], etc.) and *token-based* (Suzuki-Kazami [15], Naimi-Tréhel [8], Raymond [10], etc.). The algorithms of the first group are based on the principle that a node enters a CS only after having received a permission from all the other nodes (or the majority of them [6]). In the second group, a unique system-wide token is shared among all nodes, and its possession gives a node the exclusive right to enter the critical section. Token-based algorithms usually have an average lower message cost than permission-based ones and many of them have a logarithmic message complexity $\mathcal{O}(log(N))$ with regard to the number of nodes N. Hence, they are more suitable for controlling concurrent access to shared resources of Grids since N is often very large.

However, existing token-based algorithms do not take into account the above-mentioned hierarchy of communication latencies. To overcome this problem, we have presented in a previous article [14] a generic composition approach which enables the combination of any two token-based mutual exclusion algorithms: one at *intra-cluster* level and a second one at *inter-cluster* level. By using our composition mechanism, efficient mutual exclusion algorithms for Grids can be built where communication latency heterogeneity is not neglected. Furthermore, they can be easily deployed by just "plugging in" token-based algorithms on each levels of the hierarchy. Performance evaluation tests conducted on a Grid platform have shown that the good choice for an *inter-cluster* mutual exclusion algorithm depends on the frequency with which the distributed processes of the application request for the shared resource, i.e., the degree of parallelism of the application.

We now propose in this article to study the impact of the Grid architecture on token-based mutual exclusion algorithms with and without our composition approach, i.e., *hierarchical* and *flat* mutual exclusion algorithms respectively. Basically, we would like to know if our *hierarchical* approach is more suitable for a Grid platform than the *flat* one when the number of clusters increases, and which is the number of clusters that a Grid platform should have such that the *hierarchical* algorithm presents the highest performance gain when compared to the *flat* one.

In order to answer to the above questions, we did both a theoretical study about the probability of an algorithm's message to be sent over an inter cluster link and we conducted evaluation performance experiments on a Grid emulation cluster platform. For the experiments, we have chosen the Naimi-Trehel's [8] token-based mutual exclusion algorithm, which maintains a dynamic logical tree to transmit processes requests for the execution of the critical section. Thus, the *flat* algorithm consists of the original Naimi-Trehel's algorithm while the *hierarchical* one uses our composition approach with Naimi-Trehel's algorithm at both *intra* and *inter* levels. Our choice can be explained based on the results published in our previously mentioned article [14]: when using Naimi-Trehel's algorithm at *inter-cluster* level, we obtained the smallest delay to get access to the shared resource when compared to other token-based algorithms that use other approaches for transmitting critical section requests such as a logical ring structure or broadcasting. We should also emphasize that we considered applications with different behaviors in our experiments since we also would like to know if the degree of the parallelism of an application has an influence on our study.

The remainder of this paper is organized as follows. Section 2 briefly describes Naimi-Tréhel algorithm. In section 3, we present our compositional approach for mutual exclusion algorithms. Performance evaluation results and a theoretical study about the effect of clustering on token-based algorithms with and without our composition approach are presented in section 4. Some related work is given in section 5. Finally, the last section concludes our work.

2 Naimi-Tréhel's Algorithm

Naimi-Tréhel's algorithm [8] is a token-based algorithm which keeps two datastructures: (1) A logical dynamic tree structure in which the root of the tree is always the last node that will get the token among the current requesting ones. Initially, the root is the token holder, elected among all nodes. This tree is called the *last tree*, since each node i keeps the local variable *last* which points to the *last* probable owner of the token; (2) A distributed queue which keeps critical section requests that have not been satisfied yet. This queue is called the *next queue*, since each node i keeps the variable *next* which points to the *next* node to whom the token will be granted after i leaves the critical section.

When a node i wants to enter the critical section, it sends a request to its *last*. Node i then sets its *last* to itself and waits for the token. It becomes the new root of the tree. Upon receiving i's token request message, node j can take one of the following action depending on its state: (1) j is not the root of the tree. It forwards the request to its *last* and then updates its *last* to i. (2) j is the root of the tree. It updates its *last* to i and if it holds an idle token, it sends the token to i. However, if j holds the token but is in the critical section or is waiting for the token, it just sets its *next* to i. After executing the critical section itself, j will send the token to its *next*.

3 Composition Approach to Mutual Exclusion Algorithms

In this section we present our mutual exclusion composition approach. We consider that there is one process per node, called *application* process.

Our approach consists in a hierarchy of mutual exclusion algorithms: a per cluster token-based mutual exclusion algorithm that controls critical section requests for processes within the same cluster and another algorithm that controls *inter-cluster* requests. The former is called the *intra* algorithm while the latter is called the *inter* algorithm. Each *intra* algorithm controls an *intra* token while the *inter* algorithm controls an *inter* token. An *intra* algorithm of a cluster runs independently from the other *intra* algorithms. An important advantage of our approach is that the original algorithms chosen for both layers do not need to be modified. Furthermore, it is completely transparent for *application* processes which just call the classical mutual exclusion functions *CS_Request()* and *CS_Release()*. Thus, whenever an *application* process wants to access the shared resource, it calls the *CS_Request()* (Figure 1, line 14 of the *intra* algorithm. Upon receiving the *intra* token, the process executes the CS. After executing it, the process calls the *CS_Release()* (line 17 of the same *intra* algorithm to release it.

In order to avoid that *application* processes of different clusters simultaneously access the critical section, we have introduced a special process within each cluster, called the *coordinator*. The *inter* algorithm runs on top of the *coordinators* and allows a *coordinator* to request access to the shared resource on behalf of an *application* process of its own cluster. *Coordinators* are in fact hybrid processes which participate in both the *inter* algorithm with the other *coordinators* and the *intra* algorithm with their cluster's *application* processes. Holding the *intra* token of its cluster is sufficient and necessary for an *application* process to enter the CS since the *intra* token is granted to it only if the *coordinator* of its cluster holds the *inter* token, which is unique for the whole system.

The guiding principle of our approach is described in the pseudo code of Figure 1. The *pendingRequest( )* function (line 21) informs the coordinator if there are token requests of the respective level waiting to be satisfied.

```
 1  Coordinator Algorithm ()                    14  CS_Request ()
 2     /* Initially, it holds the intra-token */ 15     ...
 3     while TRUE do                             16     Wait for Token
 4        if ¬ intra.pendingRequest() then
 5           Wait for intra.pendingRequest()     17  CS_Release ()
 6        inter.CS_Request()                     18     ...
 7        /* Holds inter-token. CS */            19     if pendingRequest() then
 8        intra.CS_Release()                     20        Send Token
 9        if ¬ inter.pendingRequest() then
10           Wait for inter.pendingRequest()
11        intra.CS_Request()                    21  pendingRequest ()
12        /* Holds intra-token CS */            22     return { TRUE   if ∃ pending request
13        inter.CS_Release()                                   FALSE  otherwise
```

Fig. 1. Coordinator algorithm

Initially, every *coordinator* holds the *intra* token of its cluster and only one of them holds the *inter* token. Thus, when an *application* process wants to enter the critical section, it sends a request to its local *intra* algorithm by calling the *Intra.CSRequest()* function. The *coordinator* of the cluster, which is the current holder of the *intra* token in this case, will also receive such a request. However, before granting the *intra* token to the requesting *application* process, the *coordinator* must hold the *inter* token too. The coordinator then calls the *Inter.CSRequest()* function (line 6) in order to request the *inter* token. Upon receiving it, the coordinator gives the *intra* token to the requesting *application* process by calling the *Intra.CSRelease()* function (line 8). After executing the CS, the *application* process calls the *Intra.CSRelease()* function in order to release the *intra* token.

A *coordinator* which holds the *inter* token must also treat *inter* token requests received from the *inter* algorithm. However, it can only grant the *inter* token to another *coordinator* if it holds its local *intra* token too. Holding the token ensures that there is no *application* process within its cluster in the critical section. Thus, before releasing the *inter* token, the *coordinator* sends a request to its *intra* algorithm asking for the *intra* token by calling the *Intra.CSRequest()* function (line 11). Upon obtaining the *intra* token, the *coordinator* can grant the *inter* token to the requesting *coordinator* by calling the *Inter.CSRelease()* function (line 13).

4 Performance Evaluation

Our performance evaluation aims at studying and comparing the influence of the Grid architecture in both the original Naimi-Tréhel mutual exclusion algorithm (*flat* algorithm) and with our composition approach using Naimi-Tréhel at both levels (*hierarchical* algorithm). To this end, the number of nodes of the Grid was set to 120 but the number of clusters varied: 2, 3, 4, 6, 8, 12, 20, 30, 40, 60, and 120. The experiments were conducted on a dedicated cluster of twenty-four Bi-Xeon 2.8 Ghz with 2GB of RAM machines where a Grid environment with 120 virtual nodes was emulated. There is one process per virtual node. For those configurations where the number of virtual clusters is greater than the number of available machines, nodes of the same virtual cluster run on the same machine. This approach prevents side effects of *intra* cluster communication.

Network latencies between clusters were emulated by using the flexible tool DUMMYNET [12] which allows injection of network delay, bandwidth limitation, and packet loss. Hence, for emulating several virtual clusters, every message exchanged between two virtual clusters goes through a dedicated machine, a P4 3Ghz machine, which runs a FreeBSD DUMMYNET. *Intra* cluster communication latency is 0.5ms while *inter* cluster latency is 20ms. Machines are connected by a 140 Gbits/s Ethernet switch.

The mutual exclusion algorithms and the coordinator were written in C using UDP sockets. Each application process that runs on a single virtual node executes 100 critical sections. Each of them lasts 10ms. Every experiment was executed 10 times and the presented results are the average value.

The behavior of an application can be characterized by ρ which expresses the frequency with which the CS is requested. ρ is equal to the ratio β/α, where α is the time taken by a node to execute the CS while β is the mean time interval between the release of the CS by a process and its next request.

We have developed several applications having **low**, **intermediate**, and **high** degrees of parallelism. Considering N as the total number of *application* processes, the three degrees of parallelism can be expressed respectively by:

- **Low Parallelism** ($\rho \leq N$): An application where the majority of *application* processes request the critical section. Thus, almost all *coordinators* wait for the *inter* token in the *inter* algorithm.
- **Intermediate parallelism** ($N < \rho \leq 3N$): A parallel application where some nodes compete to get the CS. Hence, only some *coordinators* wait for the *inter* token.
- **High Parallelism** ($3N \leq \rho$): A highly parallel application where concurrent requests to the CS are rare. The whole number of requesting *application* processes is small and usually distributed over the Grid.

In order to evaluate the *flat* algorithm as well as the *hierarchical* one, two metrics have been considered: (1) the *number of inter-cluster messages* and (2) the *obtaining time*, i.e., the time between the moment a node requests the critical section and the moment it gets it.

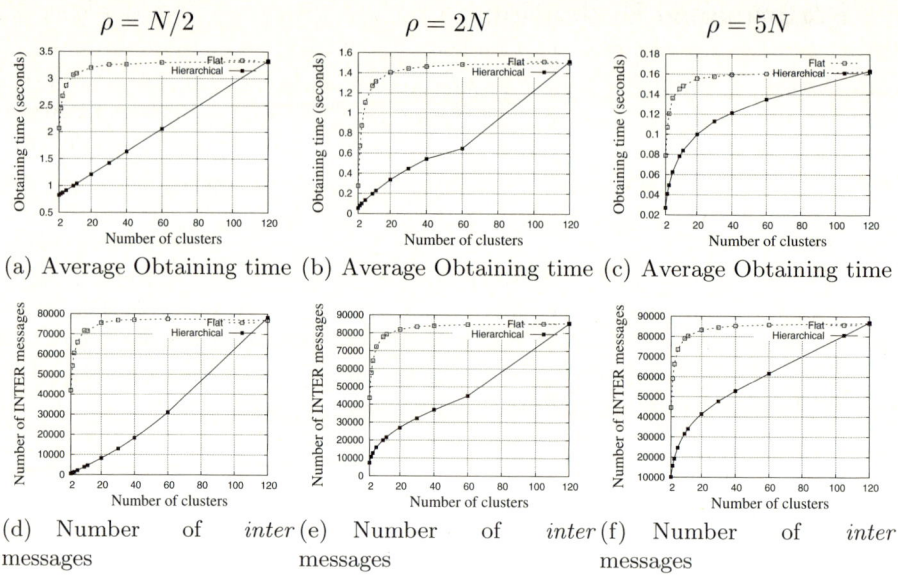

Fig. 2. Impact of the number of clusters

Considering $N = 120$, for each experiment, we have measured the *obtaining time* (Figures 2(a), 2(b), and 2(c)) and the number of *inter* cluster messages (Figures 2(d), 2(e), and 2(f)) for both algorithms when the number of cluster ranges from 2 to 120. Figures 2(a) and 2(d) correspond to a low parallel degree application ($\rho = N/2$); Figures 2(b) and 2(e) correspond to an intermediate parallel degree application ($\rho = 2N$); Figures 2(c) and 2(f) correspond to a high parallel degree application ($\rho = 5N$).

4.1 Flat Algorithm

We start by studying the impact of the number of clusters of the Grid on both the *obtaining time* and the number of *inter* cluster messages in the original *flat* Naimi-Tréhel algorithm. We can observe in Figure 2, that the curves related to this algorithm have a quite similar form. Independently of ρ, all curves present a hyperbolic form: a significant growth when the number of clusters varies from 2 to 12. This growth is then strongly reduced, becoming almost null, when the number of clusters is greater than 40.

In order to explain the form of such curves, we propose to theoretically study the frequency with which a *flat* mutual exclusion algorithm sends an *inter* cluster message, i.e., the probability $\mathcal{P}$ that the destination node of a message does not belong to the same cluster of the message's sender. To this end, we consider a Grid architecture composed of N nodes uniformly distributed over c clusters. Without loss of generality, we also suppose that a node can send a message to itself. This assumption models two successive accesses to the critical section by the same node. Then, we get the following probability $\mathcal{P}$:

$$\mathcal{P} = \frac{N - \frac{N}{c}}{N} = 1 - \frac{1}{c}$$

This equation is totally in accordance with the form of the curves of Figures 2 for the *flat* algorithm. It also shows that such a probability does not depend on the number of nodes N whenever they are uniformly distributed over the Grid, i.e., it depends only on c. A last important conclusion from this equation is that the clustering effect due to the communication latency heterogeneity of a Grid has a negligible impact on the order of CS accesses. In other words, such a heterogeneity does not change the order of priority of the requests in such a way that request from closer nodes would be satisfied before distant ones. In the above equation, any node can be chosen among N with the same probability, independently of the Grid topology. Furthermore, if theoretical curves were drawn from the equation, they would be similar to the ones of Figure 2. Thus, we can deduce that the assumption of equiprobability is reasonable and that the algorithm does not naturally adapt itself to the Grid topology.

Let's come back to the curves in order to study the impact of the number of clusters with respect to the application behavior. The results of Figures 2(a), 2(b), and 2(c) show that the degree of parallelism of an application has an impact on the *obtaining time*. Furthermore, the curves of Figures 2(d), 2(e), and 2(f) show that the parallelism degree of an application has no influence on the number of *inter* cluster messages even if we observe a small reduction of this number for low parallel applications.

4.2 Hierarchical Algorithm

We are now going to study the impact of the Grid architecture on our hierarchical approach. The number of clusters has an influence on the *obtaining time* as well as in the number of *inter* cluster which increase with the number of clusters. However, if we exclude the configuration with one node per cluster where there is in fact no hierarchy of communication at all, our approach always presents a smaller *obtaining time* and number of *inter* cluster messages when compared to the *flat* algorithm. Notice that the benefit of using our composition approach is considerable even for a Grid composed of 60 two-node clusters.

Since the topology of the Grid has not the same impact on our composition approach as on the *flat* algorithm, it would be interesting to study the mean deviation between the *hierarchical* curves and the *flat* ones for both the *obtaining time* and the number of *inter* cluster messages. Thus, based on the curves of Figure 2, Figure 3 shows such mean deviations.

In Figure 3, we can observe that the gain of our composition approach increases when the number of clusters ranges from 2 to 12. This is in accordance with the curves of Figures 2 where the *obtaining time* as well the number of *inter* cluster messages increase sharply for the original algorithm but smoothly

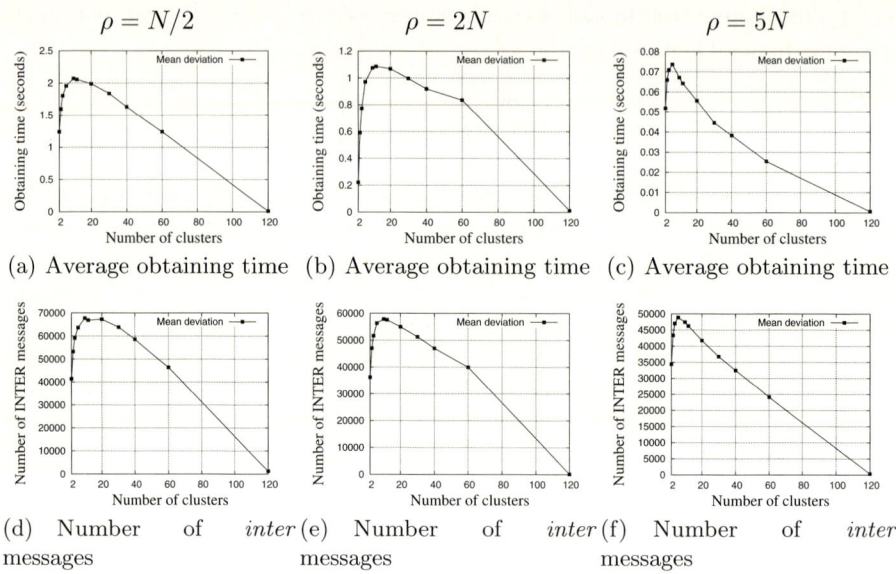

Fig. 3. Mean deviation between the *hierarchical* and *flat* algorithms

for our composition approach. Such a different behavior explains why the maximum mean deviation between the two curves is reached with 12 clusters. Beyond this threshold value, the clustering effect neither has an influence on the *obtaining time* nor on the number of *inter* cluster messages since in our *hierarchical* approach the curves progressively increase while in the curves of the *flat* algorithm remain linear. Thus, the respective mean deviations inversely decrease until they become null for the configuration where each node represents a cluster (120 clusters).

We would like to theoretically evaluate the above threshold in a Grid composed of N nodes uniformly divided into c clusters. Hence, similarly to section 4.1, we need to find the probability $\mathcal{P}$ that a node sends an *inter* cluster message in our own hierarchical approach on top of such a Grid. Without loss of generality, we consider the case where the cluster locality is maximum, i.e., every time a coordinator of a cluster gets the *inter* token, all the N/c nodes of this cluster execute a critical section which corresponds to a low parallel application. Thus, the probability $\mathcal{P}$ is equal to the probability of executing the last of the N/c critical section executions:

$$\mathcal{P} = \frac{1}{\frac{N}{c}} = \frac{c}{N}$$

Therefore, the mean deviation $E(c)$ between our composition approach and the *flat* algorithm in function of the number of clusters c is equal to:

$$E(c) = 1 - \frac{1}{c} - \frac{c}{N}$$

and according to the derivative of E, the mentioned threshold, $c_{threshold}$, is equal to:
$$E'(c) = \frac{1}{c^2} - \frac{1}{N} = 0 \Rightarrow c_{threshold} = \sqrt{N}$$

Such an equation shows that the maximum benefit when using our composition approach is reached for a Grid architecture composed of $\sqrt{N}$ nodes. This result can be verified by the curves of Figure 3 since $\sqrt{120} = 10.95$. Consequently, for $\rho = N/2$ and $\rho = 2N$, the maximum mean deviation is reached between 8 and 12 clusters. It is also worth noting that for low parallel applications ($\rho = 5N$), the Grid architecture corresponding to the highest benefit is equal to 6 clusters.

Finally, contrarily to the *flat* algorithm, the parallelism degree of an application has an influence on our hierarchical approach. Indeed, we can observe in the curves of Figure 2 that it becomes less effective with higher parallel applications when the number of clusters increases, i.e., it does not present a linear behavior anymore as it does with low parallel applications.

5 Related Work

Some works have proposed to adapt existing mutual exclusion algorithms to a hierarchical architecture. In [7], the author presents an extension to Naimi-Tréhel's algorithm, introducing the concept of priority. A token request is associated with a priority and the algorithm first satisfies the requests with the higher priority. Bertier and al. [1] adopt a similar strategy based on the Naimi-Tréhel's algorithm which treats intra-cluster requests before inter-cluster ones.

Several authors have propose hierarchical approaches for combining different mutual exclusion algorithms. Housni and al. [4] and Chang and al. [2] mutual exclusion algorithms gather nodes into groups. Both consider a hybrid approach where the algorithm for intra-group requests is different from the inter-group one. In Housni and al. [4], sites with the same priority are gathered at the same group. Raymond's tree-based token algorithm [10] is used inside a group, while Ricart-Agrawala [11] diffusion-based algorithm is used between groups. Chang and al. [2] algorithm applies diffusion-based algorithms at both levels: Singhal's algorithm [13] locally, and Maekawa's algorithm [6] between groups. The former uses a dynamic information structure while the latter is based on a voting approach. Similarly, Omara et al. [9]'s solution is a hybrid of Maekawa's algorithm and Singhal's modified algorithm which provides fairness. Erciyes [3] proposes an approach based on a ring of clusters where each node in the ring represents a cluster of nodes. The author then adapts Ricart-Agrawala's algorithm to this architecture.

Our work is close to these hybrid algorithms about gathering machines into groups (clusters in our case) which has in influence on the conception of the algorithm. However, none of the articles present an evaluation study of the impact of the number of groups (or clusters) on the performance of the proposed algorithms.

6 Conclusion

Our evaluation results show that clustering induces an important overhead in the *flat* algorithm but does not cause any side effects, i.e., it does not change the order of critical section accesses. Moreover, the impact of the number of clusters on the *flat* algorithm does not depend on the parallelism degree of the application.

In the case of our *hierarchical* algorithm, the number of clusters has an impact on its performance. However, our approach always presents a shorter *obtaining time* and a smaller number of *inter* cluster messages compared to the *flat* algorithm when the number of nodes per cluster is greater than one even for a Grid composed of a large number of clusters. Contrarily to the *flat* algorithm, the parallelism degree of an application has an influence on our hierarchical approach.

Finally, based both on our evaluation experiments and a theoretical study, we can conclude that the optimal number of clusters that a platform should present in order to provide the highest performance gain for the *hierarchical* algorithm is around $\sqrt{N}$, where N is the total number of nodes on the Grid.

References

1. Bertier, M., Arantes, L., Sens, P.: Distributed mutual exclusion algorithms for grid applications: A hierarchical approach. JPDC 66, 128–144 (2006)
2. Chang, I., Singhal, M., Liu, M.: A hybrid approach to mutual exclusion for distributed system. In: IEEE Int. Computer Software and Applications Conf., pp. 289–294 (1990)
3. Erciyes, K.: Distributed mutual exclusion algorithms on a ring of clusters. In: Laganá, A., Gavrilova, M.L., Kumar, V., Mun, Y., Tan, C.J.K., Gervasi, O. (eds.) ICCSA 2004. LNCS, vol. 3045, pp. 518–527. Springer, Heidelberg (2004)
4. Housni, A., Tréhel, M.: Distributed mutual exclusion by groups based on token and permission. In: Int. Conf. on Computational Science and Its Applications, pp. 26–29 (June 2001)
5. Lamport, L.: Time, clocks, and the ordering of events in a distributed system. C. ACM 21(7), 558–564 (1978)
6. Maekawa, M.: A $\sqrt{N}$ algorithm for mutual exclusion in decentralized systems. ACM-Transactions on Computer Systems 3(2), 145–159 (1985)
7. Mueller, F.: Prioritized token-based mutual exclusion for distributed systems. In: Int. Parallel Processing Symp., pp. 791–795 (March 1998)
8. Naimi, M., Trehel, M., Arnold, A.: A log (N) distributed mutual exclusion algorithm based on path reversal. JPDC 34(1), 1–13 (1996)
9. Omara, F., Nabil, M.: A new hybrid algorithm for the mutual exclusion problem in the distributed systems. Int. Journal of Intelligent Computing and Information Sciences 2(2), 94–105 (2002)
10. Raymond, K.: A tree-based algorithm for distributed mutual exclusion. ACM Transactions on Computer Systems 7(1), 61–77 (1989)
11. Ricart, G., Agrawala, A.: An optimal algorithm for mutual exclusion in computer networks. Communications of the ACM 24 (1981)

12. Rizzo, L.: Dummynet: a simple approach to the evaluation of network protocols. ACM Computer Communication Review 27(1), 31–41 (1997)
13. Singhal, M.: A dynamic information structure for mutual exclusion algorithm for distributed systems. Trans. on Parallel and Distributed Systems 3(1), 121–125 (1992)
14. Sopena, J., Legond-Aubry, F., Arantes, L., Sens, P.: A composition approach to mutual exclusion algorithms for grid applications. In: Int. Conf. on Parallel Processing, pp. 65–75 (2007)
15. Suzuki, I., Kasami, T.: A distributed mutual exclusion algorithm. ACM Transactions on Computer Systems 3(4), 344–349 (1985)

Reducing Kernel Development Complexity in Distributed Environments*

Adrien Lèbre[1], Renaud Lottiaux[2], Erich Focht[3], and Christine Morin[1]

[1] IRISA, INRIA Rennes Bretagne Atlantique, France
[2] Kerlabs, Gevezé, France
[3] NEC, Stuttgart, Germany

Abstract. Setting up generic and fully transparent distributed services for clusters implies complex and tedious kernel developments. More flexible approaches such as user-space libraries are usually preferred with the drawback of requiring application recompilation. A second approach consists in using specific kernel modules (such as FUSE in Gnu/Linux system) to transfer kernel complexity into user space.

In this paper, we present a new way to develop kernel distributed services for clusters by using a cluster wide consistent data management service. This system, entitled kDDM for "kernel Distributed Data Management", offers flexible kernel mechanisms to transparently manage remote accesses, cache and coherency. We show how kDDM simplifies distributed kernel developments by presenting the design and the implementation of a service as complex as a fully symmetric distributed file system.

The innovative approach of kDDM has the potential to boost the development of distributed kernel services because it relieves the developers of the burden of dealing with distributed protocols and explicit data transfers.

1 Introduction

Clusters are today a standard computation platform for both research and production. A lot of work has already been done to simplify efficient use of such architectures: batch schedulers, distributed file systems, new programming models, ... and it is likely to continue as cluster constraints are still changing: more cores per CPU socket, faster interconnects, larger scale.

Setting up generic and fully transparent distributed services for clusters implies complex and tedious kernel developments. More flexible approaches such as user-space libraries are usually preferred with the drawback of requiring application recompilations. However a lot of applications are mainly based on standards such as POSIX and recompilation is sometimes not possible (in particular for

---

* The authors from INRIA and NEC carry out this research work in the framework of the XtreemOS project partially funded by the European Commission under contract #FP6-033576.

legacy codes). In such cases, distributed services have to be perfectly transparent, requiring kernel extensions. However, only few kernel mechanisms have been suggested. Current approaches consist in completing major kernel components by modules to bring back kernel complexity to user space. As an example, the FUSE module from the Gnu/Linux system makes distributed file system implementation easier. If such an approach solves the transparency issue, it impacts performance by the multiple copies from user to kernel and symmetrically. On the other side, userland cluster services are designed by levering generic libraries such as MPI making their design and their implementation much easier.

In contrast with userland, only few work has focused on providing generic layers to faciliate distributed kernel services. From our best knowledge, developers are only aware about the remote procedure call protocol. The SUN RPC model [1] is based on a client server where a node (the client) asks for a service delivered by another node (the server). This model offers some flexibility but has several drawbacks. For instance, it only enables point to point communication and is not well designed to share data structures at a fine grain.

In this paper, we present a new way to design and implement kernel distributed services for Gnu/Linux clusters by using a cluster wide consistent data management service. From our point of view, providing such a service is really innovative. First, this system, entitled kDDM for kernel Distributed Data Manager, is built with the purpose to ease the design and the development of more complex distributed services. Second, it provides a real different way to exchange and share kernel data between distinct nodes within a cluster. By using the kDDM mechanism, programmers are able to focus on the real purpose of cluster kernel sevices instead of dealing with distributed protocols. The kDDM infrastructure helps reducing cluster kernel development complexity to a level comparable to the development on a SMP node.

We show how kDDM makes distributed kernel developments easier by presenting the design and the implementation of a service as complex as a fully symmetric distributed file system. This file system, named kDFS enables to:

– Aggregate storage resources available within a cluster,
– Provide a unique cluster wide name-space,
– Provide cooperative cache for both data and meta-data.

More generally, the use of kDDM could be exploited in almost all local kernel services to extend them to cluster scale. Cluster wide IPC, distributed namespaces (such as /proc) or process migration are only a few of the candidates.

The document is organized as follows. Section 2 outlines the kDDM mechanisms. Section 3 is focused on kDFS design and its implementation. Related work is addressed in Section 4. Finally, Section 5 concludes the document and gives some perspectives.

2 Kernel Distributed Data Manager

The Kernel Distributed Data Manager, kDDM [2], allows consistent and transparent data sharing cluster wide. This concept was formerly called *container*

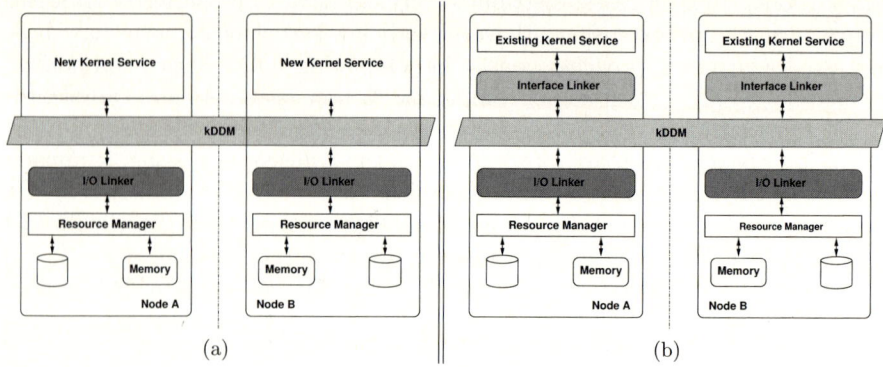

Fig. 1. kDDM overview

and has been renamed to kDDM to avoid confusion with current kernel container mechanisms.

The latest implementation of the kDDM service allows to share at kernel level collections of *objects* between the nodes of a cluster. In kDDM, an object is a set of bytes defined by the kDDM user (data structure, memory page content, etc). Objects of the same kind are stored in a *set*. An object is then identified using a pair (set identifier; object identifier).

The main goal of the kDDM mechanism is to implement distributed kernel services.

Assuming that an OS could be roughly divided into two parts: (1) system services and (2) device managers, developpers could design and implement their own cluster wide services (cf. Figure 1 (a)) or extend the existing ones by using *interface linkers* (cf. Figure 1 (b)). In both cases, kDDM sets are plugged to device managers thanks to *IO linkers*.

2.1 kDDM Sets

A kDDM set is a collection of similar objects a kernel developer wants to share cluster wide. Each set can store up to 2^{32} objects. Objects are managed by the kDDM service without any assumptions on contents and semantics. In other words, developers have the opportunity to share any kind of objects.

For each kind of object to share, a new kDDM set family is created to host this kind of object. It is then possible to create several sets of the same family.

For instance, it is possible to define a kDDM set family to share clusterwide all pages of a system V memory segment. From this kDDM set family, we can create a new set for each system V segment.

Defining a new kDDM set family mainly consists in creating a new IO linker designed to manage the kind of object they are intended to host.

2.2 IO Linkers

Each kDDM set is associated to an *IO linker* depending on the family set it belongs to. For each family there is a different IO linker. During the creation of a new kDDM set, an IO linker is associated to it. Doing this instantiation, the set can be attached to a physical device or simply attached to a dedicated memory allocator (memory pages allocator, specific slab cache allocator, etc). Indeed, the IO linker defines how objects are allocated, freed, transfered from one node to another, etc.

Right after the creation of a kDDM set, the set is completely empty, i.e. it does not contain any data. Memory is allocated on demand during the first access to an object through the IO linker. Similarly, data can be removed from a kDDM set when it is destroyed, when an object is no more in use or in order to decrease the memory pressure when the physical memory of the cluster is saturated. Again, these operations are performed through the IO linker.

2.3 Interface Linkers

Existing kernel services can be extended to a cluster scale thanks to *interface linkers*. An interface linker is the glue between existing services and kDDM sets.

Moreover, it is possible to connect several system services to the same kDDM set by using different interface linkers. For instance, a kDDM set can be used to map pages of a file in the address space of a process P1 on a node A using an interface linker L1, while a process P2 on a node B can access the same kDDM set through a read/write interface using another interface linker L2.

2.4 Manipulation Functions

Objects are handled using manipulation functions which ensure data replication and coherence. These functions can be compared to read/write locking functions. They are mainly used to create *kDDM critical section* enabling to safely access kDDM objects regardless of data location in the cluster.

Objects stored in a kDDM set are handled using a dedicated interface. This interface is quite simple and mainly relies on three functions used to create *kDDM critical sections*: *get*, *grab* and *put*.

The *get* function is close to a *read-lock*: it places a copy of the requested object in local memory and locks it cluster wide. This locking ensures that the object can not be written on any other node in the cluster. However, concurrent read accesses are allowed.

The *grab* function is close to a *write-lock*: it places a copy of the requested object in local memory and locks it cluster wide. No other concurrent access (read or write) is allowed cluster wide (cf. Section 2.5).

The *put* function is used to unlock an object.

In addition to these main functions, a few other ones are used, such as *remove*, *flush* or *sync*. The *remove* function removes an object from the memory cluster wide since the *flush* function only removes an object from local memory and ensures that there is at least one node still hosting a copy.

Finally, the *sync* function synchronizes an object with its attached physical device, if any. This function is useful for instance to write back data to disk.

2.5 Replication and Coherence

During a kDDM critical section, object data is stored in the memory of the node doing a *get* or a *grab* and can be accessed using regular memory operations. Outside a kDDM critical section, there is no guarantee that the object is still present in node local memory. In most cases the data is still present, but the kDDM semantics does not guarantee coherency outside a kDDM critical section.

As suggested in the previous section, objects are moved from one node to another during a *grab* operation and can be replicated on different nodes for efficiency reasons during a *get*. Replication introduces a data coherence issues. Coherency is managed using an invalidation on write protocol, derived from the one presented by Kai Li [3]. The *grab* function, semantically equivalent to a write, is used to catch object modifications. In this case, all the existing remote copies are invalidated before the *grab* returns. During the *grab* critical section, the object is locked on the node (where the *grab* has been done) and cannot be moved or replicated.

3 Kernel Distributed File System

In order to show the interest of generic distributed kernel mechanisms such as the kDDMs, we chose to design and implement a service as complex as a fully symmetric file system. To our knowledge, only few distributed file systems have been designed with fully symmetric constraints [4,5]. The implementation complexity of such systems is generally dissuasive and the current trend consists in setting up distributed file systems composed by one or two meta-data servers and several I/O servers [6,7]. By dividing meta-data and data management, such solutions, entitled

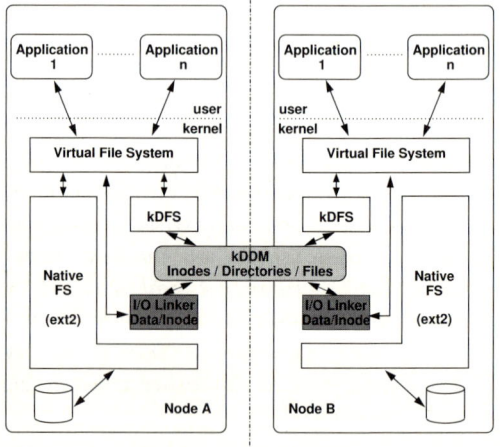

Fig. 2. Overview of the kDFS system

parallel file systems, make the implementation of the client stack easier. However such a model can lead to a non balanced architecture between distinct nodes. For example: the scalability limitation imposed by a single metadata server does not exist in a fully symmetric file system. Thanks to kDDM, we were able to quickly design and implement a symmetric file system, kDFS, providing a cooperative cache for both data and meta-data.

The evaluation of kDFS is behind the scope of this paper. Several parameters have been arbitrarily chosen and advanced mechanisms such as data-striping, redundancy or distributed I/O scheduling are addressed in a more technical document [8]. The innovative work, addressed in this article, consists in setting up such a fully distributed file system at kernel level without dealing with distributed protocols or consistency issues.

The design of kDFS relies on two main concepts:
– Using native file systems available on each node
– Using kDDM sets to provide a consistent cluster wide name space.

The use of kDDM sets facilitates the implementation of a global distributed cache with Posix semantics since kDDM mechanisms directly ensure meta-data and data consistency. Figure 2 illustrates the overall architecture of kDFS.

After describing how kDFS uses native file systems to store data, we present how kDDM mechanisms have helped kDFS be implemented with elegance and simplicity.

3.1 Disk Layout

To avoid block device dependencies and make storage management easier, we have chosen to build kDFS upon native file systems provided by the cluster nodes. As a consequence, each node has to specificy if it takes part in the kDFS storage space or not. Storage space provided by a particular cluster node is considered as a kDFS partition only if it has been kDFS formatted. As kDFS does not directly manipulate block devices, a kDFS partition actually refers to a local directory with a particular hierarchy. This section introduces different sub-directories and different files contained in a kDFS partition.

To format a directory which can be used afterwards in the kDFS storage space, administrators have to use the `mkfs.kdfs` command. This command takes two arguments: `DIR_PATHNAME` and `ROOT_NODEID`. The first one corresponds to the absolute path to store kDFS meta-data and data, the second one is the node identifier for the kDFS root entry (the node that stores the kDFS root inode).

`mkfs.kdfs` creates the kDFS "superblock" file (...) for the node. This file is stored on the local native file system in the given directory. If the current node identifier (last byte of the IP address) equals to the given *id*, `mkfs.kdfs` creates the root entry (the '/' of the file system).

Table 1. kDFS structure creation (two nodes)

On node A: (nodeid = 1)	on node B: (nodeid = 2)
mkfs.kdfs /PATH1 1	mkfs.kdfs /PATH2 1
Create kDFS local '...'	Create kDFS local '...'
Create kDFS root entry	

Table 1 describes the creation of a kDFS structure over two nodes:

For each entry (a directory or a file) of the kDFS hierarchy, a "native" directory is created on one kDFS partition within the cluster. it contains two files:
- *The* `.meta` *file* that stores meta-data associated with the entry (size, timestamp, rights, striping information, ...)
- *The* `.content` that stores real data (directory and file contents).

The name of the "native" directory is defined by the kDFS local inode identifier (each kDFS superblock file contains an identifier bitmap to define the next free inode *id*).

To avoid scalability issues with large directories, we have arbitrarily chosen to sort each kDFS partition in groups of one hundred entries. For instance, when `mkfs.kdfs` creates the kDFS root entry, the command first creates a sub-directory 'DIR_PATHNAME/0-99/'. Then, it creates the corresponding "native" directory which is the DIR_PATHNAME/0-99/1/ directory. Finally, the file '.meta' and the file '.content' are created inside this latest directory.

Every hundred entries, kDFS adds a new sub-directory corresponding to the appropriate range ('DIR_PATHNAME/100-199/', 'DIR_PATHNAME/200-299/', ...).

Once the partition is formatted, users can access the kDFS file system thanks to the mount command: `mount -t kdfs ALLOCATED_DIR|NONE MOUNT_POINT` where ALLOCATED_DIR corresponds to the native file system directory formatted with `mkfs.kdfs` and MOUNT_POINT is the traditional mount point.

Table 2 describes kDFS mounting procedure from two nodes:

Table 2. Mount kDFS partitions

On node A: (nodeid = 1)	on node B: (nodeid = 2)
mount /PATH1 /mnt/kdfs	mount /PATH2 /mnt/kdfs

/mnt/kdfs is now a global kDFS namespace for both nodes

Since files and directories are stored in a distributed way on the whole cluster, we need mechanisms to find the kDFS entry point and thus be able to join the file system. kDFS provides two ways of retrieving the `root` inode. The first one is based on the superblock file stored in the formatted kDFS partition. As mentioned, the kDFS superblock file provides several information including the kDFS root inode id. Thus, when a mount operation is done, the '...' file is read from 'ALLOCATED_DIR' and the root inode *id* is used to retrieve the kDFS root entry. The second mechanism relates to diskless nodes or nodes which do not want to take part in the kDFS physical structure. In such a case, users do not specify a "device" but have to provide the kDFS root inode id as an additional mount parameter.

3.2 File System Architecture

The use of kDDM in our symmetric file system enables to propose a simple design based on two layers. The highest one, in charge of forwarding local requests to the kDDM serivce, is directly plugged under the VFS. The lowest one, composed by the different I/O linkers, applies kDDM requests on proper kDFS partitions previously presented.

Currently, kDFS has been implemented using three families of kDDM sets:
- *Inode kDDM set*, one cluster wide. It provides a cache of inodes recently accessed by processes.
- *Dir kDDM set*, one per directory. Each Dir kDDM set contains directory entries (roughly names of subdirectories and files).
- *File kDDM set*, one per file. It stores data related to the file contents.

Figure 3 depicts the kDDM entities for several kDFS entries. To make reading and understanding easier, we also provide a potential representation of the regular files for each kDFS entry on the native file systems.

Next sections introduce each of these three families of kDDM sets. A fourth kDDM set is depicted in Figure 3: the dentry kDDM set. This unique kDDM set provides a distributed cache to manage all dentry objects. It is currently not implemented and requires deeper investigations.

3.3 kDFS Inode Management

kDFS inode management relies on one global kDDM set. This set exploits a dedicated I/O linker for inserting/removing and maintaining each kDFS entry on the corresponding local file system (sub-directory creation/deletion and updating of the '.meta file'). The inode set is created during the first kDFS *mount* operation within the cluster. At the beginning, it only contains the kDFS root inode. Then, when a process wants to access one file/directory, its corresponding kDFS inode is added into the set (providing by this way a fully distributed inode cache). All file/directory creations are performed locally whenever possible. That means, when a process wants to create a new file or a directory, kDFS looks for a kDFS partition. If there is one directly available on the node, a new inode identifier is obtained from the superblock file. Otherwise, kDFS stores the new entry on the same node as the parent directory.

When a *mount* operation is done, the root inode identifier is used to retrieve the root inode structure directly inside the inode kDDM set (cf. Section 3.1). If the kDDM set already exists, the structure is already cached and the inode is simply returned to the node. Otherwise, the request is forwarded by the kDDM service to the proper I/O linker within the cluster. Finally, the I/O linker exploits the inode *id* to retrieve required information from the hard drive.

KDFS inodes are currently based on 32 bits, the 8 MSB bits provide the node *id* within the cluster and the 24 LSB ones correspond to the local *id*.

3.4 kDFS Content Management

Since kDFS file hierarchy is based on native file systems, both directories and files are stored as regular files. In contrast to traditional file systems, the management of a large kDFS directory containing a huge number of directory entries is similar to the management of a kDFS file content. Regardless of the kDFS entry, its content is stored in its respective '.content' file.

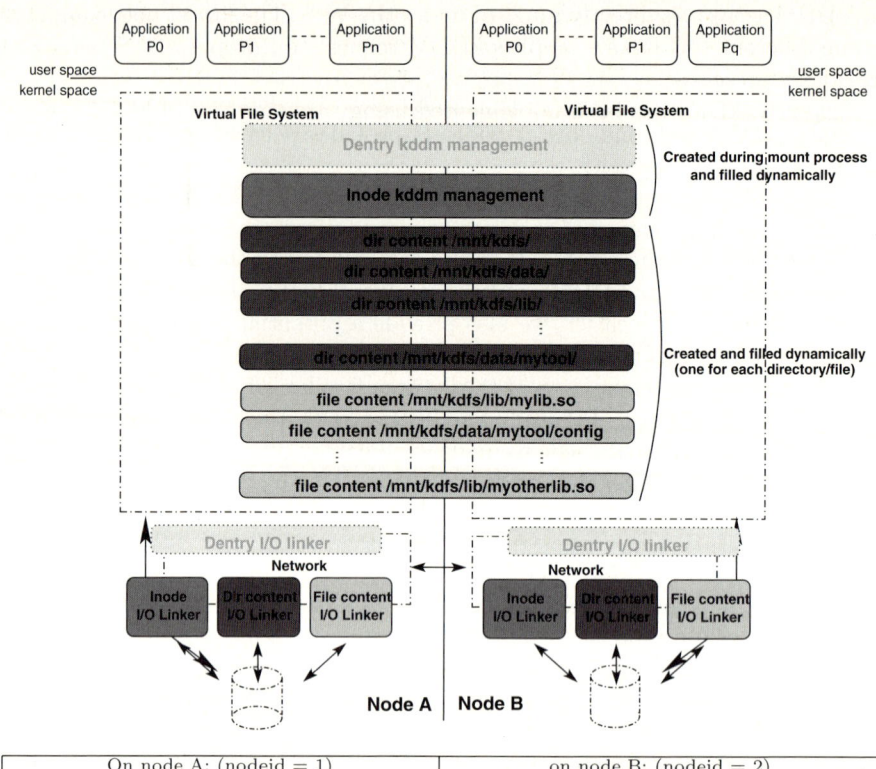

On node A: (nodeid = 1) DIR_PATHNAME: /PATH1	on node B: (nodeid = 2) DIR_PATHNAME: /PATH2
mount /PATH1 /mnt/kdfs	mount /PATH2 /mnt/kdfs
"/mnt/kdfs/" ↪ /PATH1/0-99/1/.meta /PATH1/0-99/1/.content	"/mnt/kdfs/data/" ↪ /PATH2/0-99/1/.meta /PATH2/0-99/1/.content
"/mnt/kdfs/lib" ↪ /PATH1/0-99/2/.meta /PATH1/0-99/2/.content	"/mnt/kdfs/data/mytool/" ↪ /PATH2/100-199/104/.meta /PATH2/100-199/104/.content
"/mnt/kdfs/lib/mylib.so" ↪ /PATH1/200-299/280/.meta /PATH1/200-299/280/.content	"/mnt/kdfs/data/mytool/config" ↪ /PATH2/100-199/105/.meta /PATH2/100-199/105/.content
... ...	"/mnt/kdfs/lib/myotherlib.so" ↪ /PATH2/100-199/180/.meta /PATH2/100-199/180/.content

Fig. 3. Global kDFS namespace distributed on two nodes

kDFS Directory Management. When an application tries to list the contents of a directory stored in the kDFS storage space, kDFS creates a new directory kDDM set. This new set is linked to the inode object stored in the inode kDDM set and caches all directory entries on a page basis. In other words, all file and subdirectory names stored in the directory are loaded in objects of this new kDDM set (one object corresponding to one page). After that, all filename manipulations such as *create*, *rename* and *remove* apply modifications of these pages. The associated dir I/O linker is in charge of propagating changes to the proper hard drive into the '`.content`' file.

kDFS File Management. In this first prototype, kDFS file management is similar to directory management: when an application tries to access a file f, if f is not already "cached", kDFS creates a new file kDDM set. As for directory management, this new set is linked to the corresponding inode object of the file f. The associated file I/O linker is in charge to read/write data from/to the .content file of f and remove/put pages in the set.

4 Related Work

While distributed applications programmers can choose between a multitude of parallelization concepts, libraries and languages, infrastructure extensions for supporting distributed operating systems are rather rare. Most distributed services such as the Linux ones (the global filesystems Redhat GFS and Oracle's OCFS2, the distributed lock manager or the clustered logical volume manager) are each using their own protocols for communicating across nodes and have their own notion and view of what group of nodes they regard as "the cluster".

All these services are implemented on top of the socket interface, with no cluster abstraction or communication layer in between.

A component worth mentioning as piece of infrastructure specially built to ease distributed computing is SunRPC [1]. It is used heavily in the network file-system NFS implementations and offers mechanisms to register, locate and invoke remote procedures, while transfering data in the exchangeable data format XDR, allowing nodes of different architectures to interoperate transparently. Programming with RPCs has been adopted widely in both user and kernel space and has contributed significantly to the development of distributed computing.

A further step towards distributed operating systems is the introduction of cluster aware network stacks like the Transparent Inter Process Communication protocol TIPC [9]. It uses a cluster oriented addressing scheme, implements features like reliable multicast, cluster membership with subscription to membership change notifications, cluster-wide services and name-spaces. TIPC provides a socket interface to ease transition of socket based codes, as well as a raw kernel-only interface which allows full control over all features. kDDM is leveraging TIPC by using it as low level cluster communication infrastructure.

All former solutions are based on the message passing model. Another approach close to the kDDM one has been proposed by the PLURIX project [10]. Built on top of distributed JAVA objects, this system shows that a shared object model can make the design of distributed services easier. The PLURIX object consistency is based on a transactional model whereas kDDM service exploits an invalidation-on-write protocol.

5 Conclusion and Future Work

The paper has introduced kDDM as infrastructure component suitable for building cluster-wide services in a simple and natural way. The symmetric filesystem kDFS was presented as one highly complex distributed service leveraging kDDM functionality. Its implementation shows how the complexity of managing distributed data transfers and protocols can be reduced dramatically by using the kDDM's distributed shared objects concept (no additional network protocol has been required).

The paper also aimed at pointing to a general method of designing and implementing distributed services by extending their well-known non-distributed variants with kDDM functionality. This methodology has been applied in the past years and lead to the Kerrighed single system image system, one of the most complete implementations of SSI. Kerrighed is a distributed operating system where all distributed components are implemented on top of the kDDM infrastructure.

Future work aims at providing kDDM as component loadable as module for normal unpatched Linux kernels, and increasing the number of stand-alone distributed services built on top of kDDM. Work on the symmetric file system kDFS will continue [1], next planned steps being: improvement of stability, evaluation and tuning of performance.

References

1. Sun Microsystems, I.N.W.G.: Rpc: Remote procedure call protocol specification version 2. RFC1057 Internet Request For Comments (June 1988)
2. Lottiaux, R., Morin, C.: Containers: A sound basis for a true single system image. In: Proceeding of IEEE International Symposium on Cluster Computing and the Grid (CCGrid 2001), Brisbane, Australia, May 2001, pp. 66–73 (2001)
3. Li, K.: Shared Virtual Memory on Loosely Coupled Multiprocessors. PhD thesis, Yale University (September 1986)
4. Anderson, T.E., Dahlin, M.D., Neefe, J.M., Patterson, D.A., Roselli, D.S., Wang, R.Y.: Serverless network file systems. Computer Science Division, University of California at Berkeley, CA 94720 (1995)
5. Li, Q., Jing, J., Xie, L.: Bfxm: a parallel file system model based on the mechanism of distributed shared memory. SIGOPS Operating Systems Review 31(4) (1997)
6. Carns, P.H., Ligon III, W.B., Ross, R.B., Thakur, R.: PVFS: A parallel file system for linux clusters. In: Proceedings of the 4th Annual Linux Showcase and Conference, Atlanta, GA, October 2000, pp. 317–327. USENIX Association (2000)
7. Schwan, P.: Lustre: Building a file system for 1,000-node clusters. In: Proceedings of the Linux Symposium, Ottawa (July 2003)
8. XtreemOS consortium: Design and implementation of high performance disk input/output operations in a federation. Deliverable D2.2.5 (November 2007)
9. Maloy, J.: Tipc: Providing communication for linux clusters. In: Proceedings of the Linux Symposium, Ottawa, Ontario, Canada, July 21st-24th, pp. 347–356 (2004)
10. Goeckelmann, R., Schoettner, M., Frenz, S., Schulthess, P.: Plurix, a distributed operating system extending the single system image concept. In: Canadian Conference on Electrical and Computer Engineering, vol. 4, pp. 1985–1988 (2004)

---

[1] The prototype is available at: http://www.kerrighed.org/wiki/index.php/KernelDevelKdFS

A Twofold Distributed Game-Tree Search Approach Using Interconnected Clusters

Kai Himstedt[1], Ulf Lorenz[2], and Dietmar P.F. Möller[1]

[1] University of Hamburg, Department of Informatics,
22527 Hamburg, Germany
{himstedt,dmoeller}@informatik.uni-hamburg.de
[2] Technical University Darmstadt, Department of Mathematics,
64289 Darmstadt, Germany
lorenz@mathematik.tu-darmstadt.de

Abstract. Even sophisticated classical approaches to parallelize game-tree search are restricted to using one single cluster at most. One further idea to speed up the game-tree search is to extend the cluster on the lowest level with specialized hardware components. Two well-known examples for this idea are the FPGA based HYDRA system and IBM's DEEP BLUE. Taking computer chess as an example in this paper a contrasting idea is introduced: A parallelized chess program running on a cluster forms a base component. With a second parallel approach on top several clusters can be used to achieve a further speedup. Results based on benchmarks and on the participation in the latest World Computer-Chess Championship will be presented.

1 Introduction

Our aim was to utilize computing resources at different locations for the highly demanding task of parallelizing the game-tree search, using the domain of computer chess as an example. The technical properties are the following. Two compute clusters at a distance of 500 km, one in the University of Hamburg, one in the University of Paderborn, were available. The inter-cluster latencies of the Internet connections are in the order of milliseconds, while the intra-cluster latencies of the Infiniband interconnections are in the order of microseconds. Our approach takes this into account, resulting in a two-level parallelization. Within a cluster we use the Young Brothers Wait Concept (YBWC) parallelization [1, 2] as is also used e.g. in the very successful chess programs BRUTUS [3] and HYDRA [4]. To be efficient, YBWC requires low-latency interconnections. In order to achieve a further speedup, we use the first Optimistic Pondering ideas, presented in [5], which were concluded to be well suited for distributed environments with high latency interconnections. The results presented in [5] were based on self-play experiments against a single opponent using a maximum of only 4 single processor workstations. The twofold distributed approach presented here shows the suitability for Grid environments in real practice. Furthermore, a major extension of the Optimistic Pondering idea is described and its behavior is investigated.

The paper is organized as follows: At first, the heuristic game-tree search approach and the important factor of computing power for computer chess are sketched. Section 2 describes the combination of Optimistic Pondering with YBWC based on our prototypical GRIDCHESS implementation. Section 3 deals with experimental results. Finally, the major insights are concluded in Section 4, where some future work is also pointed out.

1.1 Heuristic Game-Tree Search

Typically, a game playing program consists of three parts: a move generator, which computes all possible moves in a given position; a heuristic evaluation function which implements a human expert's knowledge about the value of a given position and a search algorithm. This algorithm organizes a forecast: At some level of branching, a so-called horizon is reached and the artificial leaves of the resulting tree are evaluated. These heuristic values are propagated back to the root of the game-tree. The astonishing observation over the last 40 years in many games is: the game-tree acts as an error filter! Usually the tree is examined by the help of the Alpha-Beta [6] or the MTD(f) [7] algorithm. The Alpha-Beta algorithm is used to prune parts of the game-tree without affecting the search result in respect to the Minimax Principle: The MAX player searches for the highest minimum gain and the MIN player for the lowest maximum gain, both in a recursive depth-first manner, when evaluating all possible moves in a given position (a gain G for MAX is $-G$ for MIN). To prune parts of the tree which will not contribute to the final search result, a so called alpha-beta window, initially set to $[-\infty, +\infty]$, is maintained, assuring the final search result will stay within the narrowing window (for pseudocode notations and further details see e.g. [1]). Nowadays, mostly the Negascout [8] variant of the Alpha-Beta algorithm is used to search good ordered game-trees. The basic idea of this variant is to suppose that the first move of a node is the best move and to search from the second move on with so called "null windows", using the evaluation for the best move of the node found so far for both window boundaries. The "null window" search result – determined faster compared to a full window search – is only a bound but usually sufficient for assuring that the move is no improvement or even sufficient to achieve a cutoff. If it is not sufficient for such a decision the window is widened and the child is researched. Several enhancements have been found to improve the search (e.g. [9, 10, 11, 12, 13]).

1.2 Computer Chess and Computing Power

With the invention of von Neumann machines, the idea to build a superior chess machine came up in the 1940s [14]. While early chess programs tried to mimic the human chess playing style, CHESS 4.5 [15] demonstrated in the 1970s that increasing the search speed might be more fruitful. BELLE [16] was a special hardwired chess machine which became a national master in the early 1980s. Beside HITECH [17], another special purpose chess machine, CRAY BLITZ [18], and DEEP BLUE's [19, 20] predecessor DEEP THOUGHT [21] were the top programs in the 1980s. In 1992, a conventional PC program named CHESSMACHINE won the open Computer Chess World Championships for the first time. From that time on, PCs dominated the world of computer chess, with some well-known exceptions like HYDRA and DEEP BLUE.

More recently, "man vs. machine" matches like the one by Wladimir Kramnik against DEEP FRITZ, with a clear win for the chess program, confirm that the end of an era seems to be reached. All top PC programs nowadays support multi core processor mainboards, and even ordinary PCs are now dominating in this discipline. But "computer vs. computer" matches are still suitable to test new game-tree search algorithms, and besides there is a public and commercial interest in such events.

2 Combining Optimistic Pondering with the Young Brothers Wait Concept

Because we had to coordinate resources which do not belong to one site only, used standardized communication interfaces, and coordinated computational power in nontrivial fashion, we have chosen the name GRIDCHESS for our prototypical implementation. This follows the original idea of Grid computing for solving computational problems [22]. Chess programs – so-called chess engines – are usually controlled by graphical user interfaces (GUIs) via standardized engine protocols. One major component of GRIDCHESS is a proxy chess engine, based on Hyatt's well-known CRAFTY open source code. Internal data structures, the protocol handling for the GUI communication and the time control ideas were adopted, whereas the CRAFTY tree search is not used. Workers – controlled by the proxy engine – form another major component and are able to control associated base chess engines. One of the strongest open source engines, Gaksch's TOGA, which is based on Letouzey's FRUIT, was used to implement Feldmann's YBWC at the intra-cluster level. The parallelized base engine is referred to as CLUSTER TOGA in this paper.

2.1 Using YBWC as State of the Art Parallelization at the Intra-cluster Level

The principle of YBWC is to defer the parallelization in each node up to the time when its first child (named eldest brother) has completely been searched. This implicitly avoids non-meaningful parallelization and the related search overhead. The scheduling is implemented based on the Message Passing Interface (MPI) by a work stealing mechanism to balance the load dynamically as follows: The CLUSTER TOGA instance running on processor P_0 is responsible for communicating with its associated worker. When it receives the initial search request it starts its search the same way as the original TOGA would start its Negascout search. At the same time all other CLUSTER TOGA instances, or their associated processors, respectively, permanently send requests for work to other randomly chosen processors. If there is work available, the appropriate information is sent back (i.e. a chess position of a node with the actual alpha-beta window, the move to be searched in parallel for the remaining search depth, etc.). When a processor has finished its work (possibly by the help of other processors), it sends back a result message and requests new work from the next randomly chosen processor.

If a processor detects an evaluation value improvement for a node not leading to a cutoff, either by its own search or by receiving a result message for that node, it sends window update messages to all affected processors still searching for that node. When a processor receives such a message it simply aborts the actual search and restarts with the new window. If a processor detects an evaluation value improvement leading to a cutoff, it adjusts its own search stack appropriately and sends abort messages to all processors also affected by the cutoff.

All processors on the same node share their hash table. The hash table [23] caches search results of already searched positions (e.g. evaluation values, relative search depths, best moves). It dramatically improves the move ordering, especially when iterative deepening is used. Preliminary benchmarks showed a weak performance when only local hash tables were used on each node. For this reason new hash table entries are permanently replicated between all nodes, while the net load may be limited for tuning purposes by only replicating entries from a certain relative minimum search depth. With nowadays easily available hash table sizes of 1 GB main memory per node comparatively few collisions are to be expected when storing new hash table entries during the search. The alternative of implementing a distributed hash table (e.g. used by Feldmann [1]) was not chosen. The potential benefit of memory scalability will probably not counterbalance the additional communication effort to access the entries. TOGA uses history tables to improve the move ordering with the History Heuristic and to avoid searching probably futile parts of the tree with so-called History Pruning. These tables contain increasingly enhanced information about how good or bad a move was statistically in the past. If a next move has to be chosen from the move list, the move generator assumes that a move that worked well in the past is probably good again in the actual position (e.g. produces a cutoff). This is the basic principle of the History Heuristic. The basic principle of History Pruning (also called Late Move Reductions) is to search the first few moves of the move list with the full search depth, and the remaining and probably less good moves with a reduced search depth, assuming that they are probably not better than the best move already found for that node. (The search depth is usually not reduced for tactically interesting moves.) For its History Pruning TOGA also uses the ratio of how often a move was good to how often it was bad in the past and only reduces the search depth if this ratio is below a certain threshold. If a move performed really weak in the past TOGA may even skip the search for that move completely. History Pruning is extensively discussed in internet computer chess forums and used by many top chess programs. It is therefore surprising that there are no publications verifying its effectiveness. This has also been stated e.g. in [24]. Since the history tables information of a processor has a more local character when a subtree is searched, it is neither shared nor replicated.

2.2 Using Optimistic Pondering at the Inter-cluster Level

Searching ahead with the opponent's expected best move is an interesting idea to avoid the processor being idle while the opponent is on move and thinking [25, 26]: The chess program considers the expected move of the opponent (called the ponder move) as already played immediately after its own move. In case the opponent plays the expected move at the end of his thinking time the time so far invested into searching ahead is gained. In case of such a ponder hit the tree search simply continues uninterruptedly until the end of the program's thinking time. The higher the probability (called ponder hit rate) is to "predict" the opponent's next move the more efficient is this method to increase the playing strength of the program.

In the following the term worker is used instead of processor to point out that a worker may already represent a parallel chess program running on a cluster as CLUSTER TOGA in our case. The basic principle of Optimistic Pondering is to start searching speculatively ahead with the expected move not only at the beginning of the opponent's thinking time but already during the own thinking time. This can be done with another worker in parallel to the tree search for the actual move. If a ponder hit is achieved later on, nearly the whole own thinking time can in best case be gained for searching ahead on the next move with this kind of parallelization. This procedure is very similar to a pipeline within a processor using branch prediction.

The principal variation (PV) is a sequence of successive half moves (the move of one player, named a ply), assuming that each player will make the move that best improves his own position. The actual PV is provided by all typical chess programs, as CLUSTER TOGA in our case, during their tree search and contains a forecast for the game. For Optimistic Pondering it is especially advantageous that at least within the first two plies there will often be no change in the PV nearly from the start of the search. Figure 1 shows the Optimistic Pondering method using 3 workers with the example of a few typical opening moves and with a fixed time control of 3 minutes per move. In practice such opening moves are of course played from an opening book, but due to the high degree of popularity, the moves and their associated PVs are very easy to follow. For simplifying the example further, a ponder hit rate of 100% and totally stable PVs right from the start of each new search of a worker for a position are assumed as ideal conditions. During the search for the first three moves the filling of the pipeline becomes apparent. In this fortunate case of permanent ponder hits the maximum of permanently possible time gain is already achieved with the fourth move (4. Bb5). Compared to 6 minutes of conventional pondering for the fourth move with one processor, 18 minutes are available by Optimistic Pondering with 3 workers in the same "sequential sense", i.e. without additional synchronization overheads or redundantly searched nodes. If eventually no ponder hit is achieved, a new tree search is started from the (unexpected) actual position (as for the conventional pondering in that case) and the pipeline has to fill again.

In practice, the PV will vary most frequently at the beginning of a new search and for shallow search depths. The basic scheduling idea is as follows: If there is a change detected in a PV within the first two plies, the actual searching ahead of the according worker is cancelled and a new search for the current PV is started immediately. The method is thereby asynchronous, i.e. at no point in time a worker has to wait for the (partial) result of another worker before it can resume its tree search.

As shown in Figure 1 the idea is applicable to using several workers. But with increasing optimism the chance to finally achieve a ponder hit will decrease. One idea to increase the ponder hit probability for the situations in which the opponent has several equivalent moves at his choice was shortly sketched in [5]. The realization and investigation of this idea is one major extension, presented in the Optimistic Pondering specific parts of our paper: a small set of most recently examined PVs with nearly identical evaluations can be taken into account in parallel. Several good predictions are often produced anyway during the computation for the next move. If the idea is carried out repeatedly in the tree, we can of course not achieve a linear, and thus "efficient" speedup. Nevertheless, we claim that our new pipeline approach is of practical interest, based on the following observation: In the past, when computing

Chess Program (white), chess starting position, fixed time control, no opening book							
1. e4 e5 ...	W 1						
2. Nf3 Nf6 ...	W 2	W 2	W 2				
3. Nc3 Nc6 ...	W 3	W 3	W 3	W 3	W 3		
4. Bb5 Bb4 ...		W 1	W 1	W 1	W 1	W 1	W 1
5. 0-0 0-0 ...				W 2	W 2	W 2	W 2
6. d3 Bxc3 ...						W 3	W 3
Program	e4		Nf3		Nc3		Bb5
Opponent		e5		Nf6		Nc6	
Elapsed Time	3	6	9	12	15	18	21

Fig. 1. Optimistic Pondering with a sequential pipeline of 3 workers (ideal conditions assumed)

resources were rather limited, good efficiency was of major importance, but in Grid environments a highest possible speedup is in the center of interest. Or, in order to stay in the analogy to modern processor-design: using a pipeline based on branch-predictions is certainly better than leaving 90% of the chip area unused.

Following the example above, Figure 2 shows such a tree of workers with their associated pondering pipelines as a snapshot after move 3. Nc3 for some typical opening move variants.

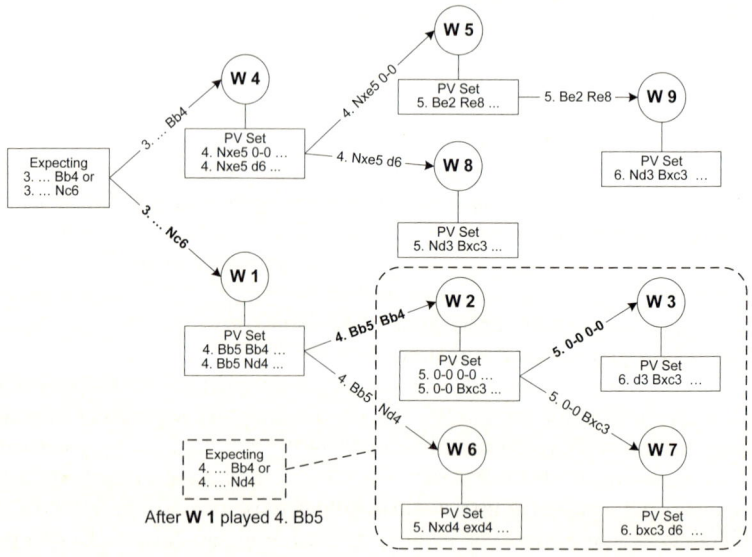

Fig. 2. Optimistic Pondering with 9 workers forming a tree of pipelines (snapshot)

3 Results

The BT2630 test suite was used for benchmarking the YBWC parallelization of CLUSTER TOGA in the two environments located at the Universities of Paderborn and Hamburg. The cluster in Paderborn consists of 2 nodes, each with 2 quad core Intel Xeon CPUs (2.66 GHz) or 16 processors in total. In the cluster in Hamburg 32 nodes each with 2 single core AMD Opteron CPUs (2.4 GHz) or 64 processors in total were available. Due to the nowadays often used multi core CPU architectures, the terms core and processor are used synonymously in this paper.

To benchmark Optimistic Pondering the existence of an opponent as well as taking time control rules into account are necessary conditions. The participation with GRIDCHESS in the 15th World Computer-Chess Championship (WCCC) 2007 was used as an ideal base to show how the new approach performs in real practice.

3.1 Test Suite for Calibration of the Intra-cluster Part of GRIDCHESS

We had only limited access to the high performance clusters. Therefore, the benchmarks were originally used first of all to tune the CLUSTER TOGA base engine using 16 cores – as the most promising configuration – by adjusting internal parameters to control the YBWC behavior (e.g. the granularity of sub-problems, the amount of replicated hash table entries etc.). The hash table size was set to 1 GB shared memory per node.

Benchmarks were run for all 30 BT2630 test positions taking into consideration the ideas presented in [27]. In the following, $CT_{time}(n)$ and $CT_{nodes}(n)$ mean total batch runtime and total nodes searched for all 30 test positions using CLUSTER TOGA with n cores. The values calculated are: $Speedup = CT_{time}(1)/CT_{time}(n)$, $Efficiency = Speedup/n$, $SearchOverhead = CT_{nodes}(n)/CT_{nodes}(1) - 1$, and $npsRatio = Speedup \times (SearchOverhead + 1)$. The searched nodes per second ratio ($npsRatio$), which corresponds to a speedup neglecting the search overhead, indicates the parallelization overheads for synchronization and communication by comparing it to an associated maximum speedup of n. Our 1 core CLUSTER TOGA is a bit slower than the corresponding TOGA executable which was originally downloaded, mainly because of our self-compiled Linux versions. In principle there is only a marginal YBWC-dependent implementation-specific overhead to be expected. For some experiments there were one or two test positions for which the parallel version delivered a different final move than the sequential version. Since the BT2630 test has many alternative solutions, this can happen because of the non deterministic search behavior of the parallel version. These positions were not taken into account for the results shown in Table 1.

In the original sequential depth first search of TOGA the move list of a node is expanded on demand only. Among other optimizations, it is particularly beneficial to fill and access the history tables in a sequential manner. These tables are used to improve the move ordering and, moreover, for the very aggressive History Pruning of TOGA (see Section 2.1). In contrast to this our typical YBWC implementation requires early expanding of the move list to check the requests of other processors if there is work to steal available. Thereby the move ordering deteriorates. Work is also eventually distributed for parts of the tree that would be forwardly pruned with a sequential search.

Table 1. Benchmark results for the YBWC parallelized CLUSTER TOGA (30 test positions)

Cores	Cluster	Nodes x Cores/Node	Hash Table Memory	Speedup	Efficiency	Search Overhead	nps Ratio
8	Paderborn	2 x 4	2 GB	3.74	46.75%	68.90%	6.32
8	Hamburg	4 x 2	4 GB	3.45	43.13%	72.73%	5.96
16	Paderborn	2 x 8	2 GB	5.08	31.75%	129.16%	11.64
16	Hamburg	8 x 2	8 GB	6.32	39.50%	95.46%	12.35
32	Hamburg	16 x 2	16 GB	7.30	22.81%	159.53%	18.95

Preliminary benchmarks showed higher speedups when the History Heuristic and History Pruning optimizations were intentionally disabled. With a recent benchmark (conditions as above) this was verified again: CLUSTER TOGA achieved a regular speedup of 4.19 on a single node with 8 cores, but a speedup of 5.62 when the history tables related optimizations were disabled. But since it is not meaningful for tournament participations to disable any optimizations we present speedups relevant for real practice here.

When 8 cores were used for CLUSTER TOGA, the speedup in Paderborn is higher than in Hamburg. But the speedup in Hamburg is higher than in Paderborn when 16 cores are used. Further investigation is needed to check if the greater totally available hash table memory amount at the cluster in Hamburg and the granularity of the replication are responsible for this effect (table entries with a relative search depth of 3 or less plies are not replicated). Increasing the number of cores from 16 to 32 (not possible in Paderborn, anyway) gives a further speedup but with a considerably lower efficiency. This is also shown by the search overhead of 159.53% and the comparatively small nps ratio of 18.95.

3.2 Tournament Participation Results

For the participation in the 15th WCCC GRIDCHESS was configured to use 5 workers (1 in Paderborn, 4 in Hamburg), each consisting of CLUSTER TOGA using 16 cores. The workers were arranged in a small dynamic tree of pondering pipelines to increase the ponder hit probability by expecting several opponent moves. To support this further, ponder move candidates were explicitly generated while the opponent was on move and thinking. The time control rules in the tournament were defined as a rate of play of 60 moves in 2 hours followed by the rest of the game in 30 minutes and were thereby well suited for Optimistic Pondering. If the rate of play had been substantially faster, as is usual for very fast blitz tournaments, the small communication efforts and the normally short time until a first potentially stable PV is available might have had effects like major overheads for Optimistic Pondering.

Table 2 shows the game result, the total ponder hit rate, and estimated values for speedup and efficiency based on post mortem log file analysis for each opponent of the eleven-round tournament. The log files contain all relevant information for each GRIDCHESS move in a game and all further required information, e.g. opponent thinking times etc. The only assumption made to be able to estimate a fair speedup is that a conventional pondering CLUSTER TOGA engine would *also* have achieved a ponder hit whenever GRIDCHESS achieved a ponder hit for the best expected move. This seems to be justifiable due to the statistical form of the analysis. The differences between the point in time of playing a move with a worker and the point in time when the optimistic pondering had originally been started for that move by the worker can be used to calculate a move related speedup by dividing this amount of time by the amount of time a conventional pondering CLUSTER TOGA engine would have searched for the move. To calculate the "Estimated Speedup" for a game, both amounts of times are first summed up over all moves and than the totals are divided, taking into consideration the ideas presented in [27]. For the averages over all games presented in the last row of Table 2 and for the values in Table 3 each game had the same weight to avoid overweighting outliers which may arise through very long games, if otherwise the thinking times over all moves of all games were added first and after this the sum were divided by the total number of all moves. The speedup values accord to the worker level. This means that under tournament conditions 5 workers are on average (geometric mean) about 1.85 times faster than 1 worker (or a conventional pondering CLUSTER TOGA using 16 cores respectively).

For the sake of completeness, two corresponding average speedups based on the same log file data shall be given: conventional pondering[1] reaches a speedup of 1.65

Table 2. GRIDCHESS (5 workers, each based on CLUSTER TOGA) total ponder hit rates and estimated speedup relative to conventional pondering, based on the 15th WCCC 2007 participation

Game	Opponent	GRIDCHESS Score	Total Ponder Hit Rate		Estimated	
			Optimistic	Conventional	Speedup	Efficiency
1	LOOP	0.5	91.18%	67.65%	1.88	37.60%
2	JONNY	1	84.21%	55.26%	1.68	33.60%
3	ISICHESS	0.5	93.75%	68.75%	1.76	35.20%
4	THE BARON	1	90.91%	58.18%	1.94	38.80%
5	DEEP SJENG	0.5	95.35%	65.12%	1.90	38.00%
6	DIEP	0.5	78.95%	63.16%	2.20	44.00%
7	MICRO-MAX	1	90.00%	60.00%	1.91	38.20%
8	SHREDDER	1	87.88%	57.58%	1.68	33.60%
9	THE KING	1	96.08%	62.75%	1.92	38.40%
10	RYBKA	0	89.29%	57.14%	2.00	40.00%
11	ZAPPA	0	67.92%	34.59%	1.57	31.40%
	Averages	63.64%	87.77%	59.11%	1.85	37.00%

---

[1] When fixed thinking times are defined for each move (which is unusual for tournaments and not the case with the time control rules used for the WCCC) a speedup of 1.59, which directly corresponds to the conventional ponder hit rate would be expected. Log file analysis showed that GRIDCHESS on average moved a bit faster than its opponents in respect to the real chess clock, so ponder hits have a superior beneficial effect. This may explain the slightly higher speedup of 1.65.

and Optimistic Pondering reaches a speedup of 3.05 relative to CLUSTER TOGA using 16 cores but not pondering at all.

Ponder hit rates are shown for expecting several good moves as well as for conventionally expecting the best move only. An optimistic ponder hit is simply a ponder hit achieved by GRIDCHESS, i.e. the opponent has played one of the expected moves. A conventional ponder hit is assumed only when the opponent played *the* best expected move.

Expecting several good moves can increase the ponder hit rate noticeably (90% or more against 6 of 11 opponents). The increase in speedup is moderate, as expected, when only 5 workers are arranged in a tree of pondering pipelines. The total speedup of GRIDCHESS compared to a conventional pondering CLUSTER TOGA using a single core can be estimated by multiplying the speedups achieved with CLUSTER TOGA using 16 cores by the average speedup additionally achieved with Optimistic Pondering. A single core of the cluster in Paderborn is minimally faster in respect to the CLUSTER TOGA application as compared with the cluster in Hamburg, but this is neglected for the sake of simplicity. With the speedup values from Table 1 the total speedup of GRIDCHESS, using our new approach, can be roughly estimated to be in the range between $5.08 \times 1.85 = 9.40$ (worker in Paderborn) and $6.32 \times 1.85 = 11.69$ (worker in Hamburg). This total speedup must be seen in a sequential sense, i.e. all overheads for synchronization or redundantly searched nodes are already taken implicitly into account. – Table 1 shows a relative speedup of $7.30/6.32 = 1.16$ when the number of cores is doubled from 16 to 32 in Hamburg. Without Optimistic Pondering and by running just 1 CLUSTER TOGA using all 64 cores in Hamburg, the speedup will be only slightly above 7.30, assuming legitimately that the relative speedup of 1.16 will further decrease when the number of cores is doubled from 32 to 64. This confirms our decision to use Optimistic Pondering to interconnect both clusters for the tournament participation.

Table 3 shows the detailed averages of the plies ahead at optimistic pondering start. The values for being "exact n Plies Ahead" are written to the log file at the moment a worker has played its move. From a retrospective view this means that the search for the actual position had already been started at a time in the past when the position before n plies was on the real chess board. The corresponding values for being "at least m Plies Ahead" are simply calculated as the sum of the values for being "exact n Plies Ahead" for all n greater or equal to m.

Ponder hits achieved for ponder moves explicitly generated while the opponent was on move and thinking (see this Section above) are shown in the table as being "1 Ply Ahead". With only 5 workers, expecting several good moves will have the greatest effect near the root (e.g. if 3 workers are already used to expect 3 good moves there are only 2 workers left to build deeper sequential pipelines). Being "9 Plies Ahead" is the maximum when 5 workers are used in a purely sequential pondering pipeline. Since several good moves are usually expected, a sequential pipeline will only form if there is a long row of "forced" moves, i.e. if there is exactly one good move in each next position. A ponder hit rate of 0.16% indicates that this rarely happens.

GRIDCHESS reached a score of 7.0 in 11 games and shares the 4th place of 12 with the 12-fold world champion SHREDDER. SHREDDER just won the speed chess tournament discipline and became "World Computer Chess Speed Champion". Beating SHREDDER in the main tournament could impressively show the performance of GRIDCHESS under real tournament conditions.

Table 3. Detailed averaged Ponder Hits Distribution based on the 15th WCCC 2007 participation

	\multicolumn{9}{c}{Plies Ahead at Optimistic Pondering start}
	1	2	3	4	5	6	7	8	9
Exact	24.21%	28.79%	21.01%	8.02%	2.36%	1.98%	0.66%	0.58%	0.16%
at least	87.77%	63.56%	34.77%	13.76%	5.74%	3.38%	1.40%	0.74%	0.16%

4 Conclusions and Future Work

We presented a combination of two distributed game-tree search approaches on different levels and a prototypical implementation of the idea. At the intra-cluster level our CLUSTER TOGA showed a first successful parallelization using YBWC for a very aggressively forward pruning sequential open source chess program. A further speedup was achieved for GRIDCHESS using the Optimistic Pondering ideas as a second parallelization level on top to control several such CLUSTER TOGAs. Results from participating in the 15th WCCC tournament showed the performance and the robustness of the approach in practice.

The asynchronous behavior of Optimistic Pondering is characterized by the event-driven handling of the rather infrequently received principal variations from the base engines containing the actual expected best opponent's move. This made it particularly suited for Grid environments. By expecting several good opponent's moves at a time, the ponder hit rates could be highly increased. So far we have used only 5 workers for GRIDCHESS because we have only limited access to two high performance clusters. How to arrange a larger number of workers in the tree of pondering pipelines to get the best overall performance is a subject of our actual examinations. Last but not least, our results may also be of special interest for pipeline designs in multi core processor architectures.

References

1. Feldmann, R.: Game Tree Search on Massively Parallel Systems. PhD Thesis, University of Paderborn, Paderborn (1993)
2. Feldmann, R., Mysliwietz, M., Monien, B.: Studying Overheads in Massively Parallel Min/Max-Tree Evaluation. In: 6th ACM Annual symposium on parallel algorithms and architectures (SPAA 1994), New York, pp. 94–104 (1994)
3. Donninger, C., Kure, A., Lorenz, U.: Parallel Brutus: The First Distributed, FPGA Accelerated Chess Program. In: Proceedings of the 18th International Parallel and Distributed Processing Symposium (IPDPS 2004), CD-ROM, Santa Fe, p. 44 (2004)
4. Donninger, C., Lorenz, U.: The Chess Monster Hydra. In: Becker, J., Platzner, M., Vernalde, S. (eds.) FPL 2004. LNCS, vol. 3203, pp. 927–932. Springer, Heidelberg (2004)
5. Himstedt, K.: An Optimistic Pondering Approach for Asynchronous Distributed Game-Tree Search. ICGA Journal 28(2), 77–90 (2005)
6. Knuth, D.E., Moore, R.W.: An Analysis of Alpha-Beta Pruning. Artificial Intelligence 6, 293–326 (1975)

7. de Bruin, A., Plaat, A., Schaeffer, J., Pijls, W.: A minimax Algorithm better than SSS*. Artificial Intelligence 87, 255–293 (1999)
8. Reinefeld, A.: Spielbaum-Suchverfahren. Springer, Berlin (1989)
9. Anantharaman, T.S.: Extension heuristics. ICCA Journal 14(2), 47–63 (1991)
10. Beal, D.F.: Experiments with the Null Move. In: Beal, D.F. (ed.) Advances in Computer Chess 5, pp. 65–79. Elsevier Science Publishers B.V., Amsterdam (1989)
11. Donninger, C.: Null Move and Deep Search: Selective-search Heuristics for Obtuse Chess Programs. ICCA Journal 16(3), 137–143 (1993)
12. Björnsson, Y., Marsland, T.A.: Multi-cut $\alpha\beta$-pruning in game-tree search. Theoretical Computer Science 252(1-2), 177–196 (2001)
13. Schaeffer, J.: The History Heuristic and Alpha-Beta Search Enhancements in Practice. IEEE Transactions on Pattern Analysis and Machine Intelligence 11(11), 1203–1212 (1989)
14. Shannon, C.E.: Programming a computer for playing chess. Philosophical Magazine 41, 256–275 (1950)
15. Slate, D.J., Atkin, L.R.: CHESS 4.5 – The Northwestern University chess program. In: Frey, P.W. (ed.) Chess Skill in Man and Machine, pp. 82–118. Springer, Heidelberg (1977)
16. Condon, J.H., Thompson, K.: Belle Chess Hardware. In: Clarke, M.R.B. (ed.) Advances in Computer Chess 3, pp. 45–54. Pergamon Press, Oxford (1982)
17. Berliner, H.: Hitech Chess: From Master to Senior Master with no Hardware Change. In: International Workshop on Industrial Applications of Machine Intelligence and Vision (MIV 1989), Tokyo, pp. 12–21 (1989)
18. Hyatt, R.M., Gower, A.E., Nelson, H.L.: Cray Blitz. In: Beal, D.F. (ed.) Advances in Computer Chess 4, pp. 8–18. Pergamon Press, Oxford (1986)
19. Hsu, F.-H.: IBM's Deep Blue Chess grandmaster chips. IEEE Micro 19(2), 70–81 (1999)
20. Hsu, F.-H.: Behind Deep Blue: Building the Computer that Defeated the World Chess Champion. Princeton University Press, Princeton (2002)
21. Hsu, F.-H., Anantharaman, T.S., Campbell, M.S., Nowatzyk, A.: Deep Thought. In: Marsland, T.A., Schaeffer, J. (eds.) Computers, Chess, and Cognition, pp. 55–78. Springer, Heidelberg (1990)
22. Foster, I., Kesselman, C., Tuecke, S.: The Anatomy of the Grid: Enabling Scalable Virtual Organizations. International Journal of High Performance Computing Applications 15(3), 200–222 (2001)
23. Zobrist, A.L.: A Hashing Method with Applications for Game Playing. Technical Report 88. University of Wisconsin, Computer Sciences Department, Madison (1970)
24. Lim, Y.J.: On Forward Pruning in Game-Tree Search. PhD Thesis, National University of Singapore, Singapore (2007)
25. Hyatt, R.M.: Using Time Wisely. ICCA Journal 7(1), 4–9 (1984)
26. Althöfer, I., Donninger, C., Lorenz, U., Rottmann, V.: On Timing, Permanent Brain and Human Intervention. In: van den Herik, H.J., Herschberg, I.S., Uiterwijk, J.W.H.M. (eds.) Advances in Computer Chess 7, pp. 285–296. University of Limburg, Maastricht (1994)
27. Fleming, P.J., Wallace, J.J.: How not to lie with statistics: the correct way to summarize benchmark results. CACM 29(3), 218–221 (1986)

Topic 7: Peer-to-Peer Computing

Dick Epema[1], Márk Jelasity[2], Josep Jorba[3], and Alberto Montresor[4],*

[1] Delft University of Technology, The Netherlands
[2] Szeged University, Hungary
[3] Universitat Oberta de Catalunya, Spain
[4] University of Trento, Italy

After a decade of intensive investigation, peer-to-peer computing has established itself as an accepted research field in the general area of distributed systems. Peer-to-peer computing can be seen as the democratization of computing—overthrowing the old regime of hierarchies as in client-server systems—largely brought about by last-mile network improvements which have made individual PCs first-class citizens in the computer world. Initially, much of the focus in peer-to-peer systems was on best-effort file sharing. However, over the last few years, research has also been directed at trying to make peer-to-peer systems satisfy properties and have functionality as exhibited by more traditional forms of distributed systems. Examples of such properties and functionality, which in principle run counter to the disorganized nature of peer-to-peer systems, are certain levels of security and providing reliable distributed storage such as required by databases.

Eighteen papers were submitted to this year's Peer-to-Peer Computing track, out of which only four were accepted. Two of these consider problems in the area of security in peer-to-peer systems, one deals with mapping optimization problems to peer-to-peer systems, while the fourth is in the area of query processing in peer-to-peer systems.

In "Scalable Byzantine Fault Tolerant Public Key Authentication for Peer-to-Peer Networks", a group-based scheme for authenticating peers based on public keys is presented that is resilient to Byzantine behavior. When a peer wants to authenticate another peer, it instructs the members of its trusted group to challenge that peer and to send back to it the results of their challenges, based on which it can or cannot authenticate the other peer. An algorithm for maintaining the trusted groups based on a small subset of pre-trusted peers is part of the scheme.

In "Secure Forwarding in DHTs—Is Redundancy the Key to Robustness?", the problem of routing messages to the right node(s) in the presence of malicious peers who may simply drop messages is studied. The two approaches of using reduncancy by having multiple paths and of improving routes by routing messages through selected peers with a high reputation are compared. A new algorithm for either approach is proposed, with a reputation system assumed to be present in the latter case.

In "P2P Evolutionary Algorithms: A Suitable Approach for Tackling Large Instances in Hard Optimization Problems", a population-based method for implementing evolutionary algorithms for solving optimization problems is presented. The population of peers executing the algorithms is structured using a gossiping protocol. With simulations, an assessment is made of such metrics as the computing time of the proposed

---

* Topic Chairs.

method in comparison to that of a sequential genetic algorithm and the required population size.

In "Efficient Processing of Continuous Join Queries Using Distributed Hash Tables", the execution of join queries on continuous data streams flowing into a distributed hash table is studied by means of a newly proposed algorithm, the performance of which is assessed with simulations. The queries are disseminated with a gossiping protocol, the new tuples entering the system are only indexed into the DHT when a query needs them, and the queries are executed by the peers using a distributed sliding window.

Finally, we would like to thank all authors and all reviewers of the papers submitted to this track for their work.

Scalable Byzantine Fault Tolerant Public Key Authentication for Peer-to-Peer Networks

Ruichuan Chen, Wenjia Guo, Liyong Tang, Jianbin Hu, and Zhong Chen

[1] Institute of Software, School of Electronics Engineering and Computer Science, Peking University, China
[2] Key Laboratory of High Confidence Software Technologies (Peking University), Ministry of Education, China
{chenrc,guowj,tly,hjbin,chen}@infosec.pku.edu.cn

Abstract. Peer-to-Peer (P2P) communication model has the potential to harness huge amounts of resources. However, due to the self-organizing and self-maintaining nature, current P2P networks suffer from various kinds of attacks. Public key authentication can provide a fundamental building block for P2P communication security. In this paper, we propose a scalable Byzantine fault tolerant public key authentication scheme for P2P networks, in which each participating peer dynamically maintains a trusted group to perform distributed challenge-response authentication without centralized infrastructure. To guarantee the authentication correctness, we additionally present a complementary trusted group maintenance scheme. The experimental results demonstrate that our authentication scheme can work in various different P2P scenarios effectively and efficiently.

1 Introduction

Peer-to-Peer (P2P) computing has emerged as a popular model aiming at further utilizing Internet resources by having symmetry in roles where a client may also be a server. However, due to the self-organizing and self-maintaining nature of P2P model, each participating peer has to manage the risks involved in the transactions without adequate experience and knowledge about other peers.

In P2P networks, public key authentication is a fundamental issue of communication security. Currently, existing schemes for public key authentication can be grouped into two main categories: *centralized* schemes and *decentralized* schemes.

Centralized schemes, e.g., PKI [1], utilize a trusted third party (TTP) or a collection of TTPs acting as the certification authority to perform public key authentication. Nevertheless, these schemes scale relatively poorly, create a single point of failure, and incur heavy administrative overheads. Moreover, the existence of TTP(s) contradicts the extremely decentralized nature of typical P2P networks, so decentralized authentication schemes should be further considered.

Decentralized schemes avoid the requirement of TTP(s) by distributing the task of public key authentication to all the participants. Two typical decentralized authentication schemes, PGP-like scheme [2] and quorum-based scheme [3], have been proposed. In PGP-like scheme, the participants create a "web of trust" to authenticate public keys based on their acquaintances' opinions. This scheme can perform fully self-organized authentication in a relatively small network; however, when applied to a large network, PGP-like scheme still relies on some kind of centralized infrastructure. Furthermore, the authentication correctness of PGP-like scheme is susceptible to the treachery of even a very few acquaintances. Another decentralized scheme is quorum-based scheme. The essential idea behind quorum-based scheme is to have multiple independent participants replicate public keys for enhancing the availability and reliability of these keys. This scheme works well in decentralized P2P networks where participants may fail benignly; however, it cannot guarantee the consistency of the retrieved public keys when participants suffer Byzantine (i.e., arbitrary) faults.

Given the features of existing public key authentication schemes, in this paper, we propose a scalable Byzantine fault tolerant public key authentication scheme for P2P networks. In our scheme, each participating peer dynamically maintains a trusted group to perform distributed authentication by multiple challenge-response exchanges originating from different trusted group members. Consequently, our scheme can effectively and efficiently defend against Byzantine attacks as well as man-in-the-middle attacks without centralized infrastructure. In addition, to guarantee the authentication correctness, we elaborate a complementary trusted group maintenance scheme. The experimental results indicate that our scheme scales well in various different P2P scenarios.

The rest of this paper is organized as follows. We give an overview of related work in section 2. The notation definition and system model are specified in section 3. We then elaborate the Byzantine fault tolerant public key authentication in section 4. Section 5 presents the simulation methodology and evaluates the system performance. Finally, we conclude and describe future work in section 6.

2 Related Work

Byzantine fault tolerance (BFT) [4] is derived from the Byzantine generals problem which was described in detail by Lamport et al. in [5]. So far, several studies have been focused on introducing BFT mechanisms into various P2P applications. Two P2P file systems, Farsite [6] and OceanStore [7], integrated BFT mechanisms into their storage services for increasing data integrity and reliability. In [8], Rodrigues et al. developed a robust P2P system which is capable of surviving Byzantine faults of its peers. Besides, Castro et al. described several concrete defenses against Byzantine faults in P2P networks [9]. Afterwards, Yoshino et al. in [10] discussed how to design a hierarchical group structure to make a P2P system tolerate Byzantine faults, and Fiat et al. improved upon Chord [11] to provide robustness against Byzantine attacks [12].

Currently, a few Byzantine fault tolerant authentication schemes have been proposed in the context of P2P networks. In [13], Pathak and Iftode presented an authentication scheme which can correctly perform public key authentication in decentralized P2P networks based on Byzantine agreement if the number of honest peers exceeds a certain threshold. However, this scheme is vulnerable to man-in-the-middle attacks during its fourth phase, and its authentication cost is relatively high. Further, Palomar *et al.* integrated Pathak and Iftode's scheme into their authentication framework to propose a content authentication protocol [14] and a certificate-based access control protocol [15] for P2P networks. Compared with these schemes, our scheme can effectively defend against not only Byzantine attacks but also man-in-the-middle attacks; besides, the authentication cost of our scheme is much lower.

3 Notation Definition and System Model

In our public key authentication scheme, we use cryptographic techniques to protect message exchanges. For the sake of simplicity, we define a series of notations as follows:

- ID_A: Identifier of peer A.
- K_A: Public key of peer A.
- K_A^{-1}: Private key of peer A.
- $\{X\} K_A$: A string X encrypted using the public key of peer A.
- $\{X\} K_A^{-1}$: A string X signed by peer A. Note that, we follow the common practice of signing the digest of string X and appending it to the string X rather than signing the full string.
- R_A: A pseudorandom nonce generated by peer A.
- ",": The string concatenation operator.

Since P2P networks are generally lack of admission control, there may be a large number of faulty peers existing in real-world P2P networks at any time. Specifically, a peer is *honest* if and only if the peer executes the protocols elaborated in this paper faithfully; otherwise, the peer is *faulty*, i.e., it can exhibit arbitrary behaviors, such as omitting to act, acting inconsistently and acting in collaboration. A peer can appear to act properly even if it has been compromised, and therefore obtaining an appropriate reply from a peer does not indicate the peer's honesty. In addition, faulty peers do not have sufficient computational power to break cryptographic building blocks, e.g., they cannot forge the signatures of honest peers.

4 Byzantine Fault Tolerant Public Key Authentication

In this section, we first describe the underlying P2P overlay network. Then, we specify the scalable Byzantine fault tolerant public key authentication scheme and the complementary trusted group maintenance scheme.

4.1 Underlying P2P Overlay Network

Current P2P overlay networks can generally be grouped into two categories [16]: *structured* overlay networks, e.g., CAN [17] and Chord [11], that accurately build an underlying topology to support rapid searching, and *unstructured* overlay networks, e.g., Gnutella-like [18] networks, that impose no structure on the topology and typically propagate queries to neighbors for searching. In this paper, we choose a structured P2P overlay network as the underlying structure, since our authentication scheme needs an efficient and reliable distributed information access structure as well as a random peer selection strategy (we will explain this strategy in section 4.3). Without loss of generality, we utilize Chord as the dedicated underlying P2P overlay network; furthermore, we can also conveniently utilize another structured P2P overlay network as an alternative.

4.2 Public Key Authentication

Generally, the classical *challenge-response* protocol can be used to authenticate public keys in P2P networks. Concretely, peer A first makes a key possession claim by informing peer B of its public key K_A. Then, peer B, expecting to authenticate the received public key K_A, sends peer A a nonce (challenge) encrypted using K_A and requires that the subsequent message (response) received from peer A contain the correct nonce value. The protocol is formally described as follows:

$$A \to B : \{ID_A, K_A\} K_A^{-1}$$
$$B \to A : \{R_B\} K_A$$
$$A \to B : \{R_B\} K_A^{-1}$$

Nevertheless, in real-world P2P networks, faulty peers may perform man-in-the-middle attacks. Unfortunately, the simple challenge-response protocol executed by only one challenger cannot effectively defend against such attacks.

In our scalable Byzantine fault tolerant public key authentication scheme, all the participating peers have symmetry in roles and compose a Chord ring. Additionally, each peer dynamically maintains a *trusted group* (TG) to perform distributed challenge-response authentication. Since a TG consists of sufficient randomly selected peers, only a limited number of TG members can, with high probability, be compromised by man-in-the-middle attacks.

The concrete authentication scheme, as informally and formally described in Fig. 1 and Fig. 2 respectively, can be executed in three stages: *claim announcement*, *distributed authentication* and *result generation*. For the sake of clarity, we omit the timestamp information contained in the messages. In particular, a peer (TG *maintainer*) knows all its TG members' correct public keys, and meanwhile, each of its TG members knows the TG maintainer's correct public key (this mutual property will be explained in section 4.3). Therefore, each message transmitted between a peer and its TG member can be signed by the message *sender*, and the *receiver* simply ignores the messages with invalid signatures.

1. **Claim announcement:** The authentication process begins when peer B discovers that peer A claimed to be the owner of an unauthenticated public key K_A. Subsequently, peer B announces the claim to all its TG members and asks them to verify the authenticity of K_A.

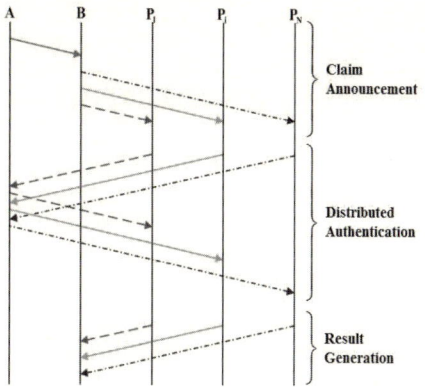

Fig. 1. Informal description of public key authentication scheme, where peer B maintains a trusted group, composed of $P_1, \ldots, P_i, \ldots, P_N$, to perform public key authentication towards peer A

Stage 1: Claim Announcement

$A \rightarrow B: ID_A, ID_B, \{ID_A, K_A\} K_A^{-1}$

For each trusted group member P_i of peer B

$B \rightarrow P_i: \{ID_B, ID_{P_i}, \{ID_A, K_A\} K_A^{-1}\} K_B^{-1}$

Stage 2: Distributed Authentication

For each trusted group member P_i of peer B

$P_i \rightarrow A: ID_{P_i}, ID_A, \{\{R_{P_i}\} K_{P_i}^{-1}\} K_A$

$A \rightarrow P_i: ID_A, ID_{P_i}, \{\{R_{P_i}\} K_{P_i}^{-1}\} K_A^{-1}$

Stage 3: Result Generation

For each trusted group member P_i of peer B

$P_i \rightarrow B: \{ID_{P_i}, ID_B, \{\{R_{P_i}\} K_{P_i}^{-1}\} K_A^{-1}\} K_{P_i}^{-1}$

Peer B generates the authentication result

Fig. 2. Formal description of public key authentication scheme, where peer B maintains a trusted group, composed of $P_1, \ldots, P_i, \ldots, P_N$, to perform public key authentication towards peer A

2. **Distributed authentication:** According to the received identifier ID_A, each TG member P_i of peer B utilizes the underlying Chord overlay network to independently challenge peer A by sending a signed pseudorandom nonce encrypted with the supposed public key of peer A. Peer A has the capacity of recovering the nonce if and only if it holds the corresponding private key K_A^{-1}. Afterwards, peer A utilizes K_A^{-1} to sign the recovered nonce which was formerly signed by P_i, and returns the double-signed nonce to P_i. At the end of this stage, each TG member P_i obtains a proof of peer A's possession of K_A, i.e., the returned double-signed nonce.
3. **Result generation:** Each TG member P_i responds to peer B's authentication request (issued in the stage of claim announcement) with its proof of peer A's possession of K_A. Afterwards, peer B can verify these received proofs using peer A's supposed public key and each TG member's public key. If at least $\lfloor \frac{N-1}{3} \rfloor + 1$ proofs can be successfully verified, peer A indeed possesses the public key K_A; otherwise, peer A is not the genuine owner of K_A. Here, N denotes the total number of peers contained in peer B's TG.

Without loss of generality, we assume that there are f faulty peers existing in the TG. Besides, due to various attacks, t honest TG members may be compromised by faulty peers. That is, $f + t$ members are actually faulty and exhibit Byzantine behaviors. Naturally, these $f + t$ members may not respond. However, it is possible that the $f + t$ members that do not respond are not faulty and, therefore, $f + t$ of those that respond may be faulty. Even so, the honest responses must still be sufficient to outnumber those faulty ones, i.e., $N - 2(f + t) > f + t$. Hence, $N > 3(f + t)$, and the authentication is eventually correct if at least $\lfloor \frac{N-1}{3} \rfloor + 1 \, (> f + t)$ proofs indicate the same result.

4.3 Trusted Group Maintenance

In order to guarantee the authentication correctness and control the authentication cost, each participating peer should carefully maintain its trusted group. Concretely, the trusted group maintenance scheme consists of three kinds of operations: *addition, removing* and *refresh*.

1. **Addition operations:** To defeat man-in-the-middle attacks, each peer should guarantee that its TG members are distributed uniformly in the network. If the TG size of a peer B falls below a predefined threshold N_{min}, peer B randomly generates a distinct identifier ID_C over $[0, 2^{160})$, and utilizes the Chord overlay network to lookup the specific peer C whose identifier is equal to or directly follows ID_C in the identifier space. Then, peer B performs a public key authentication towards peer C, and peer C performs another public key authentication towards peer B simultaneously. If both peer B and peer C authenticate each other as honest, they know each other's correct public keys definitely, and peer B can add peer C into its TG; otherwise, peer B randomly selects another peer C' and performs the process again. The selection-authentication process is repeated until the TG size exceeds the threshold N_{min}.

    To sum up, the addition operations ensure that a TG consists of sufficient randomly selected members which can effectively defend against man-in-the-middle attacks in the public key authentication process; furthermore, these operations can additionally guarantee that a peer (TG maintainer) knows all its TG members' correct public keys, and meanwhile, each of its TG members knows the TG maintainer's correct public key. This mutual property establishes the security relationship between a TG maintainer and its TG members.

2. **Removing operations:** In our scheme, each peer tries to guarantee the honesty of its TG by removing a part of its TG members that exhibited detectable faulty behaviors, and to control the authentication cost by removing some randomly selected TG members.

    Firstly, due to the public key authentication scheme described in section 4.2, the TG members which reply with faulty proofs can be captured and removed; secondly, the TG members that fail to reply with timely responses, or even do not reply at all should also be removed from the TG due to lack of liveness; thirdly, if the number of TG members exceeds a predefined threshold N_{max}, the TG maintainer should repeat removing TG members uniformly at random until the threshold is satisfied; lastly, a TG maintainer removes randomly selected members from its TG periodically.

3. **Refresh (bootstrapping) operations:** As proved in section 4.2, a peer can generate the correct authentication result only if less than one third of its TG members are faulty (or compromised). However, addition operations and removing operations could only guarantee this condition with high probability, because TG membership is granted on public key authentication and does not ensure that these authenticated TG members will not exhibit faulty

behaviors in future. That is, it is possible that a large number of faulty peers masquerade as honest peers to join a TG covertly, and act maliciously when they take up a sufficient fraction of the TG members.

To address this problem, there should be some pre-trusted peers that are known to be honest in the system. For example, the first few peers to join the system are generally known to be honest peers, because these peers, such as system designers and early peers, hardly have any motivation to destroy the system. Thus, each peer has to periodically refresh its TG by replacing all its TG members with M of those well-known honest peers and reestablishing the corresponding mutual security relationship. Generally, $N_{min} < M < N_{max}$. However, if the total number of well-known honest peers is less than N_{min}, extra addition operations need to be performed. In addition, a newcomer of the system should also perform the refresh-like bootstrapping process to build up its initial TG.

5 Evaluation

In this section, we first briefly describe the simulation methodology of our experiments, and then we evaluate the performance of our scheme in various scenarios.

5.1 Simulation Methodology

To evaluate the performance, we need to simulate the authentication scheme in various malicious scenarios. Concretely, we utilize the NS-2 simulator [19] to construct the simulation testbed. With different *trusted group sizes* and *fractions of faulty peers*, we simulate the authentication scheme based on the Chord overlay network consisting of a universe of 5,000 peers. These participating peers are composed of honest peers and faulty peers, both of which are randomly distributed in the overlay network. In addition, each authentication process is performed between two randomly selected peers.

In the following experiments, we characterize the system performance by using one primary performance metric, i.e., *average count of messages per authentication*; each experiment is run 100 times and the results of all runs are averaged. Specifically, all the experiments are simulated on an OpenPower720 with four-way dual-core POWER5 CPUs and 16GB RAM running SuSE Linux 9.1.

5.2 Experiments

As described in section 1, most of existing public key authentication schemes, including centralized schemes and decentralized schemes, cannot work well in real-world P2P networks. Specifically, Pathak and Iftode's scheme [13] (abbr., PI's scheme) is an excellent public key authentication scheme that can be used in P2P networks [14,15]. Therefore, in the following experiments, we compare the system performance between our scheme and PI's scheme, and explore the impact of trusted group size and faulty peers.

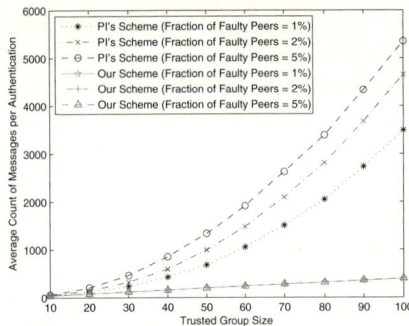 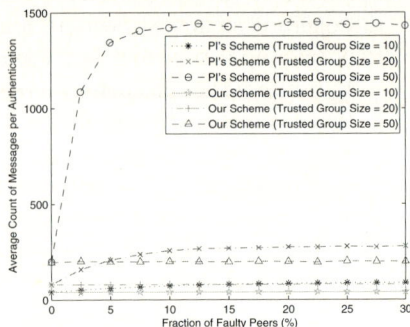

Fig. 3. Average count of messages per authentication vs. trusted group size, with different fractions of faulty peers

Fig. 4. Average count of messages per authentication vs. fraction of faulty peers, with different trusted group sizes

1. **Impact of trusted group size:** With three different fractions of faulty peers, we comparably evaluate the performance of our scheme and PI's scheme by changing the trusted group size from 10 to 100 in steps of 10 for each run of the experiment.

   As shown in Fig. 3, the experimental result demonstrates that PI's scheme scales poorly because its authentication cost (i.e., average count of messages per authentication) increases rapidly with the growth of trusted group size; on the contrary, under our scheme, the authentication cost merely increases with the trusted group size linearly. Moreover, the fraction of faulty peers does not influence the performance of our scheme. A clearer representation of this phenomenon can be found in the next experiment.

2. **Impact of faulty peers:** In this experiment, we investigate the authentication cost incurred by faulty peers. Specifically, with three different trusted group sizes, we compare the performance of our scheme with that of PI's scheme by calculating the average count of messages per authentication in the presence of various fractions of faulty peers.

   The experimental result shown in Fig. 4 indicates that the authentication cost of our scheme is the same as that of PI's scheme in the absence of faulty peers; whereas, in the presence of faulty peers, the cost of our scheme is much lower, and it is independent of the fraction of faulty peers. In particular, since authenticating a faulty peer or being attacked by faulty peers in PI's scheme impose an extra quadratic overhead for the execution of Byzantine agreement protocol, the authentication cost of PI's scheme is drastically influenced by the fraction of faulty peers.

   Somewhat interestingly, when the fraction of faulty peers exceeds 15%, the cost of PI's scheme does not change significantly any more. This phenomenon is due to the fact that if the fraction goes beyond 15%, almost all the authentication processes may be compromised by at least one intermediate faulty peer; that is, PI's scheme needs to perform an additional Byzantine agreement with high probability. Therefore, when faulty peers take up more than 15% of all the peers, the authentication cost of PI's scheme will reach its upper bound, i.e., each authentication initiator should execute the complete authentication process including the expensive Byzantine agreement, which will seriously aggravate the system burden.

6 Conclusion and Future Work

In this paper, we study the existing public key authentication schemes, and propose a scalable Byzantine fault tolerant public key authentication scheme for P2P networks. In our scheme, each participating peer dynamically maintains a trusted group to perform distributed authentication by multiple challenge-response exchanges originating from different trusted group members. Additionally, we specify a complementary trusted group maintenance scheme to guarantee the authentication correctness. The experimental results indicate that our authentication scheme can work in various different P2P scenarios effectively and efficiently.

For future work, we plan to integrate the scalable Byzantine fault tolerant public key authentication scheme with other existing advanced approaches to further improve the system performance, and extend its application field to some other kinds of networks, e.g., sensor networks.

Acknowledgment

This work was supported in part by the National Natural Science Foundation of China under grant No. 60773163.

References

1. Housley, R., Ford, W., Polk, W., Solo, D.: Internet x.509 public key infrastructure certificate and crl profile (rfc2459) (1999),
http://www.ietf.org/rfc/rfc2459.txt
2. Zimmermann, P.R.: The official pgp user's guide. MIT Press, Cambridge (1995)
3. Datta, A., Hauswirth, M., Aberer, K.: Beyond "web of trust": Enabling p2p e-commerce. In: CEC, pp. 303–312 (2003)
4. Castro, M., Liskov, B.: Practical byzantine fault tolerance. In: OSDI, pp. 173–186 (1999)
5. Lamport, L., Shostak, R.E., Pease, M.C.: The byzantine generals problem. ACM Trans. Program. Lang. Syst. 4(3), 382–401 (1982)
6. Adya, A., Bolosky, W.J., Castro, M., Cermak, G., Chaiken, R., Douceur, J.R., Howell, J., Lorch, J.R., Theimer, M., Wattenhofer, R.: Farsite: Federated, available, and reliable storage for an incompletely trusted environment. In: OSDI (2002)
7. Kubiatowicz, J., Bindel, D., Chen, Y., Czerwinski, S.E., Eaton, P.R., Geels, D., Gummadi, R., Rhea, S.C., Weatherspoon, H., Weimer, W., Wells, C., Zhao, B.Y.: Oceanstore: An architecture for global-scale persistent storage. In: ASPLOS, pp. 190–201 (2000)

8. Rodrigues, R., Liskov, B., Shrira, L.: The design of a robust peer-to-peer system. In: ACM SIGOPS European Workshop, pp. 117–124 (2002)
9. Castro, M., Druschel, P., Ganesh, A.J., Rowstron, A.I.T., Wallach, D.S.: Secure routing for structured peer-to-peer overlay networks. In: OSDI (2002)
10. Yoshino, H., Hayashibara, N., Enokido, T., Takizawa, M.: Byzantine agreement protocol using hierarchical groups. In: ICPADS (1), pp. 64–70 (2005)
11. Stoica, I., Morris, R., Karger, D.R., Kaashoek, M.F., Balakrishnan, H.: Chord: A scalable peer-to-peer lookup service for internet applications. In: SIGCOMM, pp. 149–160 (2001)
12. Fiat, A., Saia, J., Young, M.: Making chord robust to byzantine attacks. In: Brodal, G.S., Leonardi, S. (eds.) ESA 2005. LNCS, vol. 3669, pp. 803–814. Springer, Heidelberg (2005)
13. Pathak, V., Iftode, L.: Byzantine fault tolerant public key authentication in peer-to-peer systems. Computer Networks 50(4), 579–596 (2006)
14. Palomar, E., Estévez-Tapiador, J.M., Castro, J.C.H., Ribagorda, A.: A p2p content authentication protocol based on byzantine agreement. In: Müller, G. (ed.) ETRICS 2006. LNCS, vol. 3995, pp. 60–72. Springer, Heidelberg (2006)
15. Palomar, E., Estévez-Tapiador, J.M., Castro, J.C.H., Ribagorda, A.: Certificate-based access control in pure p2p networks. In: Peer-to-Peer Computing, pp. 177–184 (2006)
16. Lua, E.K., Crowcroft, J., Pias, M., Sharma, R., Lim, S.: A survey and comparison of peer-to-peer overlay network schemes. IEEE Communications Surveys and Tutorials 7(2), 72–93 (2005)
17. Ratnasamy, S., Francis, P., Handley, M., Karp, R.M., Shenker, S.: A scalable content-addressable network. In: SIGCOMM, pp. 161–172 (2001)
18. Gnutella, http://www.gnutella.com/
19. NS-2, http://www.isi.edu/nsnam/ns/

Secure Forwarding in DHTs - Is Redundancy the Key to Robustness?*

Marc Sànchez-Artigas[1], Pedro García-López[1], and Antonio G. Skarmeta[2]

[1] Universitat Rovira i Virgili, Catalonia, Spain
{marc.sanchez,pedro.garcia}@urv.cat
[2] Universidad de Murcia, Murcia, Spain
skarmeta@dif.um.es

Abstract. The provisioning of techniques for secure message forwarding over Distributed Hash Tables has been a research concern for a long time. Several techniques have been developed and evaluated, but typically each based on the increase of redundancy as a defense against data forwarding attacks. Although the security vigor of these solutions, they have left the scalability aspect largely unaddressed, as the weak peers may not support the congestion caused by the increase on redundancy. In this article, we take the opposite tack and discuss why improving the quality of delivery paths can achieve a resilience comparable to redundant routing. To prove our intuition, we confront the two strategies and develop a representative algorithm of each category. Further, we validate our work using two other existing protocols that increase redundancy (more independent paths) to fortify routing. Our results reveal that improving the quality of paths can be as effective as increasing redundancy but with minimum overhead.

1 Introduction

Distributed Hash Tables (DHTs) propose a hash table abstraction which provides a scalable indexing service to map keys into peers in a completely decentralized way (e.g. [1], [2]). While early research effort assumed a cooperative environment, security has become a primary concern in order to protect DHTs from malicious attackers, which can join the network and disrupt all operations by intentionally disobeying the protocol specifications.

One critical aspect is message forwarding, the action of delivering a message for a key to the node responsible for that key, since attacks on message forwarding cannot be prevented. For example, a malicious peer may simply drop all messages passing through it, even though these messages are cryptographically secure. To address this issue, all the results we are aware of strengthen message forwarding at the expense of an increase in the number of messages (redundancy). Explicitly, they discard the idea of fortifying routing through the improvement in the quality of delivery paths, or equivalently, the propagation of messages only through those nodes which are apparently more *trustworthy*.

---

* This research was partially funded through project P2PGRID, TIN2007-68050-C03-03, of the Ministry of Education and Science, Spain.

Contributions: The central contribution of this paper is to investigate the extent to which the quality of delivery paths can impact on forwarding attacks. Security never comes for free. When more redundancy is added to routing, in parallel with the increase in security, there is the ever-increasing communication overhead. To address this issue, we make a small step in the opposite direction and prove that, besides redundancy, delivery paths play a decisive role in the quest for a scalable solution to the message forwarding problem. To certify that our thesis is correct, we compare the two opposite viewpoints by proposing two new routing protocols. The first algorithm, called IMR, makes an intensive use of redundancy (in terms of number of messages sent), whereas the second one, called HNS, advocates for increasing the quality of paths in lieu of redundancy. Using these two protocols, we show that no approach is superior to the other in terms of resilience. However, in terms of communication cost, the first approach is by far more expensive.

In addition to clarifying the advantages and disadvantages of both strategies, as a second contribution, we compare our two protocols against Cyclone [3] and Equally-Spaced Replication [4], two existing redundant protocols. Also, we show why they are not asymptotically resilient to forwarding attacks.

1.1 Related Work

For secure forwarding in DHTs, we are not aware of any other work that presents, from the viewpoint of robustness, redundancy as just an alternative with its own advantages and shortcomings; rather, recent results have extensively focused only on its benefits, paying no attention to the role that the quality of the intermediate routers play on delivery paths. For example, [5] proposed first to route normally, and then perform a failure test to decide whether or not routing had gone wrong. If the test failed, routing was retried but this time with a secure routing protocol. A similar idea was adopted in Cyclone [3], but guaranteeing d independent[1] paths between every two nodes in the overlay. Finally, Harvesf and Blough [4] tried to create d disjoint paths by equi-spacing 2^{d-1} replicas on the Chord ring. Querying the 2^{d-1} replicas in parallel, they were able to increase routing robustness. The main shortcoming of using independent paths is the poor asymptotic guarantees it can provide on the success rate without overloading any node (as the value of d increases).

Another interesting work is Myrmic [6]. Myrmic is a secure routing protocol designed to be resilient against adversarial interference. Its distinguishing feature from other DHT implementations is a root verification protocol that authorizes a single node to prove current ownership of a given key. For this purpose, Myrmic introduces an on-line certification authority, called the Neighborhood Authority (NA), which issues certificates binding a node to the range of keys it is responsible for. However, the NA is a central point of trust, so it is rather inappropriate for DHT networks with highly transient population. Note that at every membership change, the NA must re-issue new certificates to the nodes affected by the change.

---

[1] Two paths are said to be *independent* if they share no common node other than the source and the destination.

The work closest to ours was proposed by Marti et. al. [7]. Their idea was to use an external social network to improve the query success rate. Each peer sent its messages through the nodes it knew personally or were friends of friends. So, they implicitly were the first to improve the quality of paths. Compared with us, their system depends on data (social links) that may not be always available.

2 Problem Statement, Model and Assumptions

For this work, we assume the following Threat Model: A DHT network consisting of only honest nodes is infiltrated over a certain period of time by malicious nodes which join the overlay. After some time, the network has $n(1-f)$ honest nodes and nf malicious nodes, where f ($0 \leq f < 1$) denotes the fraction of adversarial nodes in the network. Attackers may collude, but we consider that are uniformly distributed over the DHT namespace, $\tilde{I}$ (e.g., $\tilde{I} = [0, 2^m)$ for Chord). So, we adopt the *random fault model*, in which each peer p is malicious with some probability f, independently of the other nodes. This essentially means that attackers cannot choose their IDs, safeguarding the network against Sybil Attacks [8]. To support this assumption, we make use of Awerbuch and Scheideler's result [9] for keeping honest and adversarial peers well-distributed. In that work, the authors propose a new random ID generator that can keep structured overlay networks in a robust state even under a constant fraction of adversarial peers.

DHT model: We define an abstract model of a DHT network, designed to capture the key concepts common to overlays such as [1][2]. Since throughout this paper, most of the analysis is presented in terms of Chord, we describe its particularities using Chord as a concrete instance. Following convention, we shall use p to refer both to the node and to the ID of the node. The precise meaning should be clear from the context.

For each point $k \in \tilde{I}$, we assume function $root(k)$ returns the node responsible for k. In Chord, $root(k)$ represents the peer, p, whose ID minimizes the clockwise distance between k and p, $d(p, k)$. To tolerate failures, we assume k is replicated at several nodes, called *replica roots*, that in Chord are $root(k)$ and its immediate successors on the ring.

Further, each peer p maintains a *routing table* with $\Theta(\log n)$ pointers to other peers, and a *neighbor set*, consisting of some number of peers with IDs near p in the namespace. For a Chord node p, the routing table contains the nodes (known as *fingers*) that are located ahead of p on the ring at clockwise distances 2^0, 2^1, 2^2, ..., 2^{m-1}, while its neighbor set consists of its $\Theta(\log n)$ immediate successors. For convenience, we will refer to the Chord jump of length 2^i as ϕ_i, $\forall i = 0...m-1$. For a peer p and key k, let $next(p, k)$ denote the finger which minimizes $d(p, k)$. We can now describe the $root()$ operation. Assume that some peer p calls $root(k)$ for some key k. If $next(p, k) = p$, then p already knows the root of k: it is simply the closest clockwise peer to p. The search terminates by returning this peer. If $next(p, k) = p'$ where $p' \neq p$, then p forwards the search request to p'. We will refer to this algorithm as the Chord GREEDY routing protocol.

2.1 The Forwarding Problem

DHTs has been engineered to operate with only a small number of links per node. While this is positive in terms of scalability, it leaves honest nodes vulnerable to attacks that can exploit such limited view of the system (e.g. *forwarding attacks*). This property is what enables attacker nodes to drop and misroute messages at will, since the detection of disruptive actions is certainly complex with no global information. Consequently, we should tackle the following problem:

Definition 1. *(The Forwarding Problem): Develop a secure root() function which ensures that when a honest node sends a message to a key k, the message reaches all legitimate replica roots with high probability (w.h.p.).*

To provide a secure $root()$ primitive, the above problem requires to solve two subproblems: The censor problem, which refers to the impossibility of accessing each honest replica root independently of the others and the forwarding problem we re-interpret as the action of reaching the replica roots. Concerning the censor problem, notice that overlays such as Chord and Pastry suffer from this problem. In Chord, for example, for a given key k, reaching a replica root $r \neq root(k)$ can only be achieved through the predecessor of $root(k)$. As a result, the predecessor node of each key (if compromised) can censor the access to all the other replicas. Formally, the consequence of this is that the probability for a query to succeed is upper bounded by $(1-f)^2$, as both $root(k)$ and its predecessor must be honest. Note that this bound decreases exponentially when f increases. In our protocols, we explicitly address this issue. Specifically, we consider that routing is successful while at least one replica root is legitimate (minimum requirement).

The other challenge is to ensure that each intermediate peer cannot drop and misroute a query message in transit to the set of replica roots. Let ξ_i^h denote the event that an arbitrary query that requires h hops fail at the ith step. Then, for conventional DHTs where there is one optimal path (e.g. Chord), the probability of failure is $Pr[Failure] = 1 - Pr[\bigcap_{i=1}^{h} \bar{\xi}_i^h] = 1-(1-f)^h$, which is asymptotically 1 when $h \to \infty$. The consequence of this result was the birth of a group of works that tried to improve this bound through the use of redundancy. Works such as Cyclone [3] and Equally-Spaced Replication [4] made use of independent paths, the sending of multiple copies of a message over independent routes, to increase the probability of query success. Using d independent paths, they could diminish the probability of query failure by an exponential decay factor:

$$Pr[Failure] \leq B(0, d, (1-f)^h) = (1-(1-f)^h)^d \qquad (1)$$

where $B(0, d, (1-f)^h)$ denotes the probability of obtaining no successes out of d Bernoulli trials (there are d independent routes), where the probability of success is $(1-f)^h$, i.e., all the intermediate nodes on the path are good.

Despite this improvement, which we regard as significant, these solutions are not asymptotically fault-tolerant; they cannot prevent that $Pr[Failure]$ becomes asymptotically high for a fixed d. To see why, consider that, in order to reach the farthest peer in the overlay, $root()$ requires $c \log_b n$ hops. Then, $(1-(1-f)^{c \log_b n})^d$

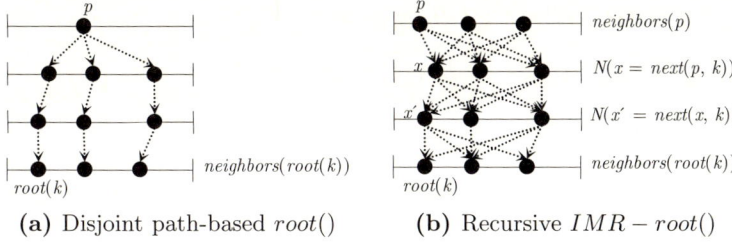

(a) Disjoint path-based $root()$ (b) Recursive $IMR-root()$

Fig. 1. Redundant Routing: The dark arrows represent the paths the query traverses

is approximately $exp(-dn^{c\ln(1-f)/\ln b})$, which implies that to make $Pr[Failure]$ constant, d must be polynomial in n. In particular, if $exp(-dn^{c\ln(1-f)/\ln b}) \leq \varepsilon^2$, d must be at least $\ln(\frac{1}{\varepsilon})n^{-c\ln(1-f)/\ln b}$. Thus, the use of independent paths may lead to traffic overloads (by a factor of d) in the effort of keeping $Pr[Failure] \leq \varepsilon$.

3 Intertwined Multi-path Routing (IMR)

From the preceding analysis, we have seen that independent paths asymptotically provide a low probability of success for a fixed d. In this section, we show how to improve such result through an increase of redundancy. The key idea is illustrated in Fig. 1b. While in independent paths, a query is sent to a single node on each path (see Fig. 1a), in this scheme, it is forwarded to a set of l peers. This way, for a query to fail, an adversary needs to control all the peers in the set; otherwise, some honest peer in this set will correctly forward the query to the next l peers. There is a subtlety here. If all peers in the current set do not forward the request to the same set of peers, more than l peers could receive the query. This growth, if uncontrolled for a sufficient number of steps, could convert $IMR-root()$, our secure $root()$ primitive, into a flooding protocol.

To constraint this growth, we make $IMR-root()$ iterative[3]. Iterative routing incurs just twice the communication cost of recursive routing, but gives the query peer the necessary control to prevent intermediate peers from flooding the DHT network. With iterative routing, the query peer can fabricate a valid set for each step, eliminating the peers that deviate "too much" from the standard path. By standard path we mean the route the request will follow due to a call to $root()$. For instance, in Chord, the standard path from a peer x to a peer y is a sequence of peers $p_0, p_1, ..., p_t$ with the following properties: 1) $p_0 = x$; 2) $\forall i = 0...t-1$, $p_{i+1} = succ(p_i + 2^j)$, where $succ(p)$ returns the successor of peer p on the Chord circle and j is the smallest integer s.t. $p_{i+1} \leq y = p_t$; and 3) $p_t = y$.

Let $N(p_i)$ be the set of the l closest peers to p_i. In order to fabricate a correct $N(p_{i+1})$, a query node p performs two actions: 1) Peer p initially asks each peer in $N(p_i)$ for its l closest peers to p_i; and 2) After collecting the responses, p adds

---

[2] Note that by setting $\varepsilon = n^{-k}$, this bound is a *high probability* bound, as $Pr[Success] = 1 - Pr[Failure]$.

[3] In iterative routing, the query node inquires each node on the path for the next hop.

to $N(p_{i+1})$ only the l closest nodes to point p_{i+1}. This requires in terms of links that each peer maintains l pointers for each entry in the routing table. In Chord, this raises the number of peers any peer links to $\Theta(l \log n)$ with high probability.

Algorithm 3.1: IMR-ROOT(p, k)

$N \leftarrow$ set of l nodes from $neighbors(p)$
if ($\exists p' \in N$ s.t. $neighbors(p')$ has at least 1 legitimate replica r)
  then return (r)
p asks each peer $p' \in N$ for its l closest peers to $(x \leftarrow next(p, k))$
From their responses, p fabricates $N(x)$
$N \leftarrow N(x)$
while not ($\exists p' \in N$ s.t. $neighbors(p')$ has at least 1 good replica r)
do
$\begin{cases} p \text{ asks each peer } p' \in N \text{ for its } l \text{ closest peers to } (x' \leftarrow next(x, k)) \\ \text{After a timeout or after all } l \text{ replies are received, } p \text{ fabricates } N(x') \\ x \leftarrow x' \\ N \leftarrow N(x') \end{cases}$
return (r)

Algorithm 3.1 gives the pseudocode for our robust $root()$ protocol. For a key k and peer p, $IMR - root(k)$ works as follows when called by p. Peer p initially forwards the query for k to the l closest peers in p's neighbors set, $neighbors(p)$. Let x equal the ID of $next(p, k)$. From $neighbors(p)$, p fabricates $N(x)$. Let N be $N(x)$. Until there exists a peer $p' \in N$ such that $neighbors(p')$ contains some legitimate replica root, the following loop repeats: p asks all peers in N for their l closest peers to $x' = next(x, k)$. From the responses of the majority of peers in N, p constructs $N(x')$. The loop now repeats with N set to $N(x')$ and x set to x'. When the loop terminates, p obtains a legitimate response for key k.

Theorem 1. *$IMR - root()$ has the following properties:*
1. *With high probability, a call to $IMR - root()$ retrieves all correct items.*
2. *The lookup takes $O(\log n)$ hops; and requires $O(l \log n)$ messages in total.*

Proof. Statement 2 follows directly from the definition of $IMR - root()$. Hence, we need only to verify that statement 1 is true. Let ξ_i^h be the event that $IMR - root()$ fails at the ith hop of an arbitrary query which requires h hops. Then, we know that $Pr[\xi_i^h] = Pr[\xi_i^h | \bigcap_{j=1}^{i-1} \bar{\xi}_j^h] \leq f^{l+1}$, as for the query to fail, both the ith node and the l candidates for this hop must be malicious. By, the Union Bound, the probability of failure is therefore $Pr[\bigcup_{i=1}^{h} \xi_i^h] \leq f^{l+1} h$. In our abstract model, we assume that the diameter due to the insecure version of $root()$ is $c \log n$. Thus, the probability of failure is at most $f^{l+1} c \log n$, which could be smaller than n^{-k}, for sufficiently small f. It is important to note that for an arbitrary value of f, it is possible to adjust l so that all nodes are reachable from all other nodes w.h.p.

What we want is to determine for which values of l, $f^{l+1} c \log n \leq n^{-k}$ is true for some positive constant k. After taking the logarithm of both sides, it is easy to see that $l \geq (\log c \log n + k \log n) \frac{1}{\log(1/f)} - 1$. □

4 Higher-Reputated Neighbor Selection (HNS)

The idea of HNS routing is to exploit the flexibility of neighbor selection provided by some DHTs such as Chord and Pastry to improve the quality of paths between any pair of nodes. In Chord, for example, it is possible for a node x to select its ith finger from a subset of nodes, called a candidate set, in the range $[x+2^i, x+2^{i+1})$. This enables a node to set up reliable neighbors by selecting the highest reputable node from each candidate set, so that paths are more reliable (which diminishes the amount of redundancy required). The election of the most suitable reputation scheme, however, deserves more attention and has been left as future work. For this work, we assume an hypothetical reputation system which permits detecting honest peers (based on reputation scores) with accuracy $1-\alpha$ and malicious peers with accuracy $1-\beta$. Notice that the probability of a false positive[4] (resp., a false negative) is therefore α (resp., β). The reason of this formalism lies in the idea of having a tool to study the effect of α, β on the quality of paths, i.e., the resistance to forwarding attacks.

Noting that the candidate set may grow too large as i increases, we let HNS sample all nodes whose *ids* are located within a clockwise distance δ_i of the point $x + 2^i$, where $\delta_i = min\{2^i, 2^m C \ln n/n\}$ and C is a small constant depending on our fault-tolerant parameters. Note that this way to select the neighbors requires that all nodes in the network know the values of $\ln n$ and $(\ln n)/n$ exactly. This can be done easily borrowing the ideas in [10]. Albeit the additional overhead to compute $(\ln n)/n$ accurately, using the term $2^m C \ln n/n$ is very convenient, as it certifies that the maximum number of probes per finger will be $O(\ln n)$, while ensuring a certain number of (honest) candidates. The next lemma reflects this.

Lemma 1. *Assume that all peers' points are distributed uniformly at random on the Chord ring. Then, the number of nodes lying in a range of length $2^m \frac{C \ln n}{n}$ is $\Theta(\ln n)$ w.h.p. (at least $(1-\lambda) C \ln n$ w.h.p.) for C sufficiently large but depending on λ, $0 < \lambda < 1$.*

Proof. Consider a generic range I of length $2^m \frac{C \ln n}{n}$. Let X_i be an independent random variable such that $X_i = 1$ if the ith peer belongs to range I or 0 otherwise. Hence, $Pr[X_i = 1] = \frac{C \ln n}{n}$. Let $X = \sum_{i=1}^{n-1} X_i$ and $\mu = E[X] = E[\sum_{i=1}^{n-1} X_i] = \frac{(n-1)C \ln n}{n}$. Using Chernoff Bound [11] and setting $C = 4\lambda^{-2}$, it is easy to see

$$Pr[X \leq (1-\lambda)\mu] = Pr[X \leq C_1 \ln n] \leq e^{-\frac{\lambda^2 \mu}{2}} = e^{-2\frac{\ln n(n-1)}{n}} < \frac{1}{n^2}, \quad (2)$$

with $C_1 = (1-\lambda)\lambda^{-2} \ln n \frac{(n-1)}{n}$. By a similar argument, it can be easily shown that there exists some constant $C_2 > 0$ for which $Pr[X \geq C_2 \ln n] < \frac{1}{n^2}$. Finally, by taking the Union Bound over all possible ranges of length $2^m \frac{C \ln n}{n}$, we have that with probability greater than $1 - \frac{2}{n}$, every range contains $\Theta(\ln n)$ nodes, so the lemma follows. □

---

[4] A false positive is a node considered an attacker when it is honest. Similarly, a false negative is a peer considered to be honest when it is not.

Another obvious requirement is that the communication costs associated with running the reputation scheme are low. Otherwise, it may not be worthy to detect the most reliable fingers through which route queries. For this reason, it is critical that the reputation scheme is local in the sense that each node can evaluate the $O(\ln n)$ candidates according to its personal experience. One way for doing this is to judge a candidate based on the messages this candidate successfully routed in the past. This evaluation is based on the following principle.

Whenever a query successfully reaches a legitimate replica, one expects that this replica responds to the query node within a bounded interval of time. Thus, after a timeout or an answer, the query node obtains a feedback that can use to inform the intermediate peers along the path about the success or failure of the query. To be more specific, the first feedback message is sent immediately by the query node once it has received the answer. Then on, the feedback is forwarded following exactly the same path the query followed until the replica was reached. With this information, each node can gauge their candidates and select the best node by merely doubling the message cost (as in $IMR-root()$).

Of particular importance is the fact that HNS practically does not alter the routing performance of the original protocol. In Chord, for example, it guarantees that each query can be resolved in $O(\log n)$ hops. The basic benefit of this is that HNS increases the resistance to routing attacks with no significant performance degradation. Note that $HNS-root()$ is therefore the result of routing as in the original routing protocol but using the "trustworthy" fingers provided by HNS.

Theorem 2. *In Chord, if the HNS scheme is applied, standard* GREEDY *routing takes $O(\log n)$ hops w.h.p.*

Proof. Suppose that node x wishes to resolve a query for the successor of key y. We analyze the number of hops to reach y. Recall that in Chord a query is sent along only those fingers that diminish the clockwise distance by some power of 2. In other words, at each step, Chord GREEDY routing ensures that the remaining distance between x and y is shortened by at least a factor of 2.

However, if the HNS scheme is applied, the decreasing ratio is lower than $\frac{1}{2}$. Recall that in Chord when a request for a key y reaches a node z, it is forwarded to the node $p = z + \phi_i$ such that $\phi_i \le y - z \le \phi_{1+i}$. As a result of this forwarding, the distance to y is reduced to $\frac{y-p}{y-z}$ times the distance between y and z. Since $\frac{y-p}{y-z} = \frac{y-z-\phi_i}{y-z} = 1 - \frac{\phi_i}{y-x} < 1 - \frac{\phi_i}{\phi_{i+1}}$, the shortening ratio can be upper bounded by $1 - \frac{\phi_i}{\phi_{i+1}}$.

By definition of the HNS scheme, it is easy to see that the maximum spacing (number of *ids*) between these two fingers is $\phi_i < \phi_{i+1} \le 2(1 + d_{i+1})\phi_i$, where $d_{i+1} = \frac{2^{m-(i+1)}C \ln n}{n}$. As before, this result implies that the worst-case distance to y will still be $(y-z)(1 - \frac{1}{2(1+d_{i+1})})$ after forwarding to p. Since this distance attains its maximum for $i+1 = m \log_2(\frac{C \ln n}{n})$, the diminishing ratio will be at least $\frac{1}{d}$, $d = \frac{4}{3}$. Hence, the query will be delivered (within offset ϕ_1) in at most $\log_d(y-x) \le \log_d n$ hops. The number of nodes residing in a interval of length ϕ_1 is $O(\log n)$ w.h.p. Thus, even if the remaining hops advance by only one node at a time, the query will traverse the remaining interval and reach key y within $O(\log n)$ hops, which completes the proof. □

However, compared with other methods such as Cyclone, the maximum *node stress* is higher in this scheme, since the highest-reputable nodes have the highest in-degree as well (notice that node stress can be approximated by the number of nodes pointing to it). The next lemma provides an upper bound for the *maximum node stress* with the HNS scheme.

Lemma 2. *With high probability, the maximum node stress for a node in Chord with the HNS scheme is $2^{m-1}\frac{m(C+1)}{n}\ln n$.*

One detrimental consequence of the above lemma is that if the high in-degree nodes are attackers (they has been chosen by honest nodes for its high reputation scores), the network's overall reachability will be maximally damaged. According to the above lemma, an adversary may compromise all the messages honest peers route through its $2^{m-1}\frac{m(C+1)}{n}\ln n$ immediate predecessors. For each value of α,β, there exists trade-off between the number of nodes within interval $[2^i, \delta_i)$ (which depends on constant C) and the maximum damage the attackers can infringe to the network if they are mistakenly confused with honest nodes. This is the price to pay for an inaccurate reputation system.

Theorem 3. $HNS - root()$ *has the following properties:*

1. *A call to $HNS-root()$ succeeds with probability at least $1-exp(-n^{O(\log(1-p))})$ provided that C is sufficiently large, where $p \approx f\beta/((1-\alpha)(1-f) + f\beta)$.*
2. *An arbitrary query takes $O(\log n)$ hops and $O(\log n)$ messages.*

Proof. By Theorem 2 property 2 follows directly. To demonstrate property 1, we first bound the number of malicious nodes falling in an interval of length $2^m \frac{C\ln n}{n}$. Then, we show that, with probability at least $1 - exp(-n^{O(\log(1-p))})$, $HNS\text{-}root()$ selects no malicious forwarder for all intermediate hops in the delivery path. Let ξ be the event that there is some interval I of length $2^m \frac{C\ln n}{n}$ such that the number of adversarial peers falling in I is greater than $f(1-\lambda)C\ln n$. By Lemma 1, we know that I contains at least $(1-\lambda)C\ln n$ for C sufficiently large. Now we show that ξ holds w.h.p. Applying Chernoff Bounds and then doing the Union Bound over all peers (we only consider those intervals whose counterclockwise endpoint is a malicious peer), it can be shown that no range of size $2^m \frac{C\ln n}{n}$ has more than $f(1-\lambda)C\ln n$ malicious peers, with probability at least $1-n^{-k}$, for C sufficiently large but depending only on k, λ, and some constant λ_0 $(0 < \lambda < f^{-1}\lambda_0)$ that appears as result of the use of Chernoff bounds. This concludes the first part.

Let ξ_M be the event that a peer falling in an range of size $2^m \frac{C\ln n}{n}$ is malicious. Let ξ_S denote the event that some peer in this range is selected by $HNS-root()$. Applying the Bayes Theorem and the above result, we get that $p = Pr[\xi_M|\xi_S] = Pr[\xi_S|\xi_M]Pr[\xi_M]/Pr[\xi_S] \leq \frac{f\beta}{(1-\alpha)(1-f)+f\beta}$, where p denotes the probability that $HNS-root()$ chooses an adversarial forwarder on an interval of length $2^m \frac{C\ln n}{n}$. By Theorem 2, we know there are at most $c\log_b n$ ranges to consider. Hence, the probability of failure is $1 - (1-p)^{c\log_b n} \leq exp(-n^{c\ln(1-p)/\ln b})$, which is smaller than $O(e^{-1})$ for sufficiently small α and β. □

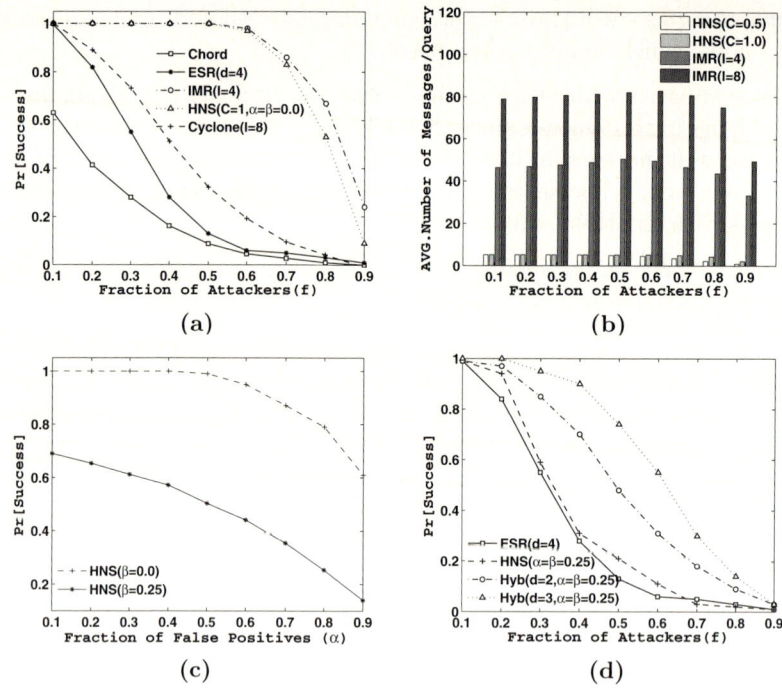

Fig. 2. Experimental Results

5 Simulation Results

In this section, we report the results from the experiments we performed in order to sustain our thesis. In our simulations, we utilized a Chord network comprised of $n = 4000$ peers (the expected number of hops is 7, which we regard as sufficient to verify our hypothesis). Unless otherwise noted, a random $f\%$ of the peers was chosen to behave maliciously in each experiment. We averaged results over 40000 random queries. The number of replicas per key was set to 8.

Figure 2a shows the probability of query success of the four algorithms we study in this work: Cyclone, Equally-Spaced Replication (ESR), IMR, and HNS, for different values of f. To make a fair comparison, the configuration parameters of the first three algorithms were tuned in such a way that the average number of messages per query was approximately 40. For the HNS scheme, we set $C = 1.0$ and $\alpha = \beta = 0.0$. As can be seen from the picture, the curve for IMR has smaller slope than the other curves, signaling that as f increases, the query success rate for IMR is the highest among the four algorithms. However, the key observation is that HNS achieves a success rate over 95% for up to 60% of adversarial nodes with the minimum communication cost. As shown in Fig. 2b, IMR requires in its lightweight version (l set to 4) eight times more messages than HNS, providing the best trade-off relation between communication cost and robustness.

In practice, however, HNS is sensitive to the inaccuracies in reputation values, albeit not significantly. Figure 2c illustrates the success query rate for two values of β as α varies. We set f to 25% for this experiment. For $\beta = 0.0$, the success rate is reduced by 39% in the worst case, which shows that false positives do not thwart significantly HNS. For $\beta = 0.25$, the success rate degrades quickly, which suggests that the reputation system should target its efforts in keeping β low.

To conclude, Fig. 2d depicts the benefits of combining HNS and ESR. With HNS establishing the routes between equally-spaced replicas, $Hyb - root()$, our hybrid protocol, can compensate the inaccuracies in the reputation ratings, while maintaining the cost low: an average of 18 messages for $Hyb(d=3,\alpha=\beta=0.25)$.

6 Conclusions

This paper argues that there is no "one-fit-all" secure forwarding algorithm, but on the contrary to what was early thought, improving the quality of paths using reputation information, albeit the inaccuracies, is a compelling alternative that deserves further attention. Our simulation results confirm that HNS, our routing algorithm targeted at improving the quality of delivery paths, provides the best trade-off relation between communication cost and robustness. To wit, for up to 80% of malicious peers, HNS appears to be as robust as the other three protocols but requiring 8 times less messages.

References

1. Stoica, I., et al.: Chord: a scalable peer-to-peer lookup protocol for internet applications. IEEE/ACM Trans. Netw. 11(1), 17–32 (2003)
2. Rowstron, A., Druschel, P.: Pastry: Scalable, decentralized object location, and routing for large-scale peer-to-peer systems. In: Guerraoui, R. (ed.) Middleware 2001. LNCS, vol. 2218, pp. 329–350. Springer, Heidelberg (2001)
3. Artigas, M., et al.: A novel methodology for constructing secure multipath overlays. IEEE Internet Computing 9(6), 50–57 (2005)
4. Harvesf, C., Blough, D.M.: The effect of replica placement on routing robustness in distributed hash tables. In: P2P 2006, pp. 57–66 (2006)
5. Castro, M., et al.: Secure routing for structured peer-to-peer overlay networks. SIGOPS Oper. Syst. Rev. 36(SI), 299–314 (2002)
6. Wang, P., Osipkov, I., Hopper, N., Kim, Y.: Myrmic: Secure and robust dht routing (submission, 2007)
7. Marti, S., Ganesan, P., Garcia-Molina, H.: Dht routing using social links. In: Voelker, G.M., Shenker, S. (eds.) IPTPS 2004. LNCS, vol. 3279, pp. 100–111. Springer, Heidelberg (2005)
8. Douceur, J.: The sybil attack. In: Druschel, P., Kaashoek, M.F., Rowstron, A. (eds.) IPTPS 2002. LNCS, vol. 2429, pp. 251–260. Springer, Heidelberg (2002)
9. Awerbuch, B., Scheideler, C.: Robust random number generation for peer-to-peer systems. In: Shvartsman, M.M.A.A. (ed.) OPODIS 2006. LNCS, vol. 4305, pp. 275–289. Springer, Heidelberg (2006)
10. King, V., Saia, J.: Choosing a random peer. In: Proceedings of the 23th annual ACM symposium on Principles Of Distributed Computing(PODC 2004), pp. 125–130 (2004)
11. Motwani, R., Raghavan, P.: Randomized Algoritihms. Cambrige Univ. Press, Cambrige (1995)

P2P Evolutionary Algorithms: A Suitable Approach for Tackling Large Instances in Hard Optimization Problems

J.L.J. Laredo[1], A.E. Eiben[2], M. van Steen[2], P.A. Castillo[1], A.M. Mora[1], and J.J. Merelo[1]

[1] Department of Architecture and Computer Technology
University of Granada, Spain
{juanlu,pedro,amorag,jmerelo}@geneura.ugr.es
[2] Department of Computer Science
Vrije Universiteit Amsterdam, The Netherlands
{gusz,steen}@cs.vu.nl

Abstract. In this paper we present a distributed Evolutionary Algorithm (EA) whose population is structured using newscast, a gossiping protocol. This algorithm has been designed to deal with computationally expensive problems via massive scalability; therefore, we analyse the response time of the model using large instances of well-known hard optimization problems that require from EAs a (sometimes exponentially) bigger computational effort as these problems scale. Our approach has been matched against a sequential Genetic Algorithm (sGA) applied to the same set of problems, and we found that it needs less computational effort than the sGA in yielding success. Furthermore, the response time scales logarithmically with respect to the problem size, which makes it suitable to tackle large instances.

1 Introduction

Among the range of techniques used to solve hard optimization problems, *Soft Computing* population-based methods such as Particle Swarm Optimization, Ant Colony Systems, or Evolutionary Algorithms have lately become quite popular [2]. In this paper, we define each individual within the population as an agent which performs a given task and interacts with the rest of individuals. This parallel process leads to the optimization of a problem as a consequence of the iterative convergence of the population to the fittest regions within a search landscape (see e.g. [3] for a survey). Nevertheless, population based methods have been widely approached sequentially despite their intuitively parallel nature. The sequential approach defines by default a *panmictic* way of interaction between individuals, which means that any individual is likely to interact with any other (directly or by means of the environment) sometime. Such an interaction can be visualized as a graph that defines a population structure whose vertices are individuals and edges represent relationships between them.

Therefore, the sequential approach is represented as a complete graph whereas parallel approaches define a richer set of population structures described, for instance, by Tomassini in [16].

Besides, the population size (number of individuals) depends on the population structure and scales according to the given optimization problem. This way, larger instances of a problem require larger populations to be solved and additionally, the computational cost of evaluating the problem also scales depending on its computational order. Hence, large problem instances imply an avalanche effect on the computational cost. Such an effect discourages practitioners since the sequential approach is computationally expensive and not easily scalable for running in a distributed environment.

The challenge of tackling these large instances of a problem and the results regarding small-world structured populations in [6], drove us to analyze in this work the effects of a self-organized population using the gossiping protocol newscast [9,10]. Newscast shares some small-world properties with the Watts-Strogatz model [18], such as a low average path length and a high clustering coefficient, and has been proved to scale to a large number of nodes [17].

Within the whole set of population based paradigms, we consider in this paper Evolutionary Algorithms (EAs) for discrete optimization problems. We describe in Section 2 some related works to our proposal which is detailed in Section 3. In order to assess our approach, we have used three discrete optimization problems proposed by Giacobini et al. in [6] and we have compared the results with a standard Genetic Algorithm (sGA). In addition, we analyse the adequacy of our algorithm for large problem instances by scaling the problems from small to large sizes. For each one of the instances, we fix a lower and upper bound for the population size in which the algorithm works.

We obtain the lower bound using a method based on bisection, which establishes the minimum population size able to solve the problem with a 98% of reliability, such a method is exposed in Section 4.3. Besides, we use an upper bound of 51200 individuals[1] which is reasonably large. For further details, we describe the experimental methodology in Section 4.

The results show in Section 5 that our proposal yields better algorithmic results than the sGA. Meanwhile, the population size scales with polynomial order with respect to the different problem instances as in sequential GAs, whereas the response time does logarithmically. Finally, these results are discussed in Section 6 in which we expose some conclusions.

2 Related Work

The idea of distributed Evolutionary Algorithms has been proposed from early (e.g. the work of Grefenstette in [8]). Recently, in [16], Tomassini makes a good review of the different state of the art models with an special focus in finer grained approaches as the one presented in this paper.

---

[1] In this work, we will refer equally to the terms individual and node, since each individual has its own schedule and could potentially be placed in a different node.

Additionally, the impact on the algorithmic performance has been studied in fine grained approaches for regular lattices [4], and different graph structures such as a toroid [5] or small-world [14].

Nevertheless, P2P EAs are more recent. The DREAM project was one of the pioneers on distributed P2P EAs coming up in [1] with the equally named DREAM framework. The island-based parallelization of DREAM was shown in [13] to be insufficient for tackling large-scale decentralized scenarios. To that end, we proposed in [12] to move the focus into finer grained approaches than the island model. Hence, the key contribution of this paper is showing that our proposal allows massive scalability of a distributed EA.

3 Overall Model Description

The overall architecture of our approach consists of a population of Evolvable Agents (EvAg), described in Section 3.1, whose main design objective is to carry out the main steps of evolutionary computation: selection, variation and evaluation of individuals [3]. Each EvAg is a node within a newscast topology in which the edges define its neighborhood. For the sake of simplicity, we assume a newscast node as a peer. However, a peer could hold several nodes in practice.

3.1 Evolvable Agent

We deliberately leave an open definition for agent under the basic feature of just being an encapsulated processing unit. This way future works could extend easily the EvAg definition (i.e. behavioral learning between agents, self-adaptive population size adjustment on runtime [12,19] or load balancing mechanisms among a real network [1]).

Algorithm 1 shows the pseudo-code of an EvAg where the agent owns an evolving solution (S_t).

Algorithm 1. Evolvable Agent

$S_t \Leftarrow$ Initialize Agent
loop
    Sols $\Leftarrow$ Local Selection(Newscast)   *See algorithm 2*
    $S_{t+1} \Leftarrow$ Recombination(Sols,P_c)
    Evaluate(S_{t+1})
    if S_{t+1} better than S_t **then**
        $S_t \Leftarrow S_{t+1}$
    end if
end loop

The selection takes place locally into a given neighborhood where each agent select other agents' current solutions (S_t). Selected solutions are stored in *Sols* ready to be recombined. Within this process a new solution S_{t+1} is generated. If the newly generated solution S_{t+1} is better than the old one S_t, it replaces the current solution.

3.2 Population Structure

In principle, our method places no restrictions in the choice of population structure, but this choice will have an impact on the dynamics of the algorithm. In this paper, we study the newscast protocol as neighborhood policy and topology builder; however, we intend to assess the impact of other topologies in future works.

Newscast is a gossiping protocol for the maintenance of unstructured P2P overlay networks. Within this section we do not enter on the dynamics but on its procedure (see [10,17] for further details). Algorithm 2 shows the pseudocode of the main tasks in the communication process which build the newscast topology. Each node maintains a cache with one entry per node in the network at most. Each entry provides the following information about a foreign node: Address of the node, timestamp of the entry creation (it allows the replacement of old items), an agent identifier and specific application data.

Algorithm 2. Newscast protocol in node $EvAg_i$

Active Thread
loop
  sleep ΔT
  $EvAg_j \Leftarrow$ Random selected node from $Cache_i$
  send $Cache_i$ to $EvAg_j$
  receive $Cache_j$ from $EvAg_j$
  $Cache_i \Leftarrow$ Aggregate $(Cache_i, Cache_j)$
end loop

Passive Thread
loop
  wait $Cache_j$ from $EvAg_j$
  send $Cache_i$ to $EvAg_j$
  $Cache_i \Leftarrow$ Aggregate $(Cache_i, Cache_j)$
end loop

Local Selection(Newscast)
$[EvAg_j, EvAg_k] \Leftarrow$ Random selected nodes from $Cache_i$

There are two different tasks that the algorithm carries out within each node. The active thread which initiates communications and the passive thread that waits for the answer. In addition, the local selection procedure provides the EvAg with other agents' current solutions (S_t).

After ΔT time each $EvAg_i$ initiates a communication process (active thread). It selects randomly a $EvAg_j$ from $Cache_i$ with uniform probability. Both $EvAg_i$ and $EvAg_j$ exchange their caches and merge them following an aggregation function. In our case, the aggregation consists of picking up the newest item for each cache entry in $Cache_i$, $Cache_j$ and merging them into a single cache that $EvAg_i$ and $EvAg_j$ will share.

The cache size plays an important role in the newscast algorithm. It represents the maximum number of connections (edges) that a node could have. For example, a topology with n nodes and a cache size of n, will lead to a complete graph topology (after the bootstrapping cycles). Therefore, the cache size used needs to be smaller than the number of nodes (typically around logarithm of n) in order to get small-world features. We have fixed the cache size to 20 within the experimental setup.

4 Methodology and Experimental Setup

The focus of the proposed experimentation is to find whether our approach is able to tackle large problem instances on a set of three discrete optimization problems presented in Section 4.1.

Firstly, we compare the EvAg model with a standard GA used as a baseline. To this end, we use a method based on bisection (Section 4.3) to establish the population size in both cases. Such a method guarantees a 98% of Success Rate (SR) on the results. Once the SR is fixed, we consider the Average Evaluations to Solution (AES) metric as a measure of the computational effort to reach success on the problems. Therefore, the more efficient algorithm is the one that guarantees a 98% SR using less computation.

Secondly, we tackle the scalability of the EvAg. We study how the population size and the computational effort (e.g. AES) increase as the problem size scales. Therefore, the response time of the approach will show the algorithm scalability since the computational effort is distributed among the nodes.

4.1 The Benchmark

In this section we present the benchmark problems that we have used to evaluate our proposal. It consists of three discrete optimization problems presented in [6]: The massively multimodal deceptive problem (MMDP), the problem generator P-PEAKS and the deceptive version wP-PEAKS. They represent a set of difficult problems to be solved by an EA with different features such as multimodality, deceptiveness and problem generators.

Massively Multimodal Deceptive Problem (MMDP)
The MMDP [7] is a deceptive problem composed of k subproblems of 6 bits each one (s_i). Depending of the number of ones (unitation) s_i takes the values depicted depicted in Table 1.

The fitness value is defined as the sum of the s_i subproblems with an optimum of k (equation 1). The number of local optima is quite large (22^k), while there are

Table 1. Basic deceptive bipolar function (s_i) for MMDP

Unitation	Subfunction value	Unitation	Subfunction value
0	1.000000	4	0.360384
1	0.000000	5	0.000000
2	0.360384	6	1.000000
3	0.640576		

only 2^k global solutions. We consider several instances from low to high difficulty using $k = 2, 4, 6, 8, 10, 16, 32, 64, 128$.

$$f_{MMDP}(s) = \sum_{i=1}^{k} fitness_{s_i} \qquad (1)$$

Multimodal Problem Generator (P-PEAKS and wP-PEAKS)
The wP-PEAKS and P-PEAKS problems are two multimodal problem generators. The wP-PEAKS is the modified version proposed in [6] of the problem generator P-PEAKS [11]. The idea is to generate P random $N - bit$ strings where the fitness value of a string x is the number of bits that x has in common with the nearest peak divided by N. The modified version consists in adding weights w_i with only $w_1 = 1.0$ and $w_{[2..P]} < 1.0$. Hence, despite P optima solutions as in the P-PEAKS, there is just one optima and $P - 1$ attractors. In P-PEAKS we consider $P = 100$ and $P = 10$ in wP-PEAKS with $w_1 = 1.0$ and $w_{[2..P]} = 0.99$ where the optimum fitness is 1.0. We consider an instance of $P = 10$ with $w_1 = 1.0$ and $w[2..P] = 0.99$ where the optimum fitness is 1.0 (equations 2 and 3).

$$f_{P-PEAKS}(x) = \frac{1}{N} \max_{1 \leq i \leq p} \{N - HammingDistance(x, Peak_i)\} \qquad (2)$$

$$f_{wP-PEAKS}(x) = \frac{1}{N} \max_{1 \leq i \leq p} \{w_i N - HammingDistance(x, Peak_i)\} \qquad (3)$$

In wP-PEAKS we scale the instances by sizing x to $2, 4, 6, 8, 10, 16, 32, 64, 128$. Meanwhile in P-PEAKS the values are $12, 24, 36, 48, 60, 96, 192$.

4.2 Experimental Setup

We have used for the experimentation two similar parametrized algorithms: EvAg with newscast neighborhood and a sGA. The recombination operator is DPX with $p_c = 1.0$ and for the selection of parents we use binary tournament [3]. All results are averaged over 50 independent runs. Finally, we have conducted the experiments in PeerSim Simulator[2]

4.3 A Method for Estimating the Population Size

The Algorithm 3 depicts the method based on bisection [15]. The method begins with a small population size which is doubled until the algorithm ensures a reliable convergence. We define the reliability criterion as the convergence of the algorithm to the optimum 49 out of 50 times (98% of Success Rate). After that, the interval (min, max) is halved several times and the population size adjusted within such a range.

---

[2] Http://peersim.sourceforge.net/. Accessed on January 2008. All source code for the experiments is available from our Subversion repository at https://forja.rediris.es/projects/geneura/

Algorithm 3. Method based on Bisection

P = Initial Population Size
while Algorithm reliability < 98% **do**
    min = P ; max, P = Double (P)
end while
while $\frac{max-min}{min} > \frac{1}{16}$ **do**
    $P = \frac{max+min}{2}$
    (Algorithm reliability < 98%) ? min = P : max = P
end while

5 Results

Results of the first experiment are shown in Table 2, which shows at first glance that our approach needs less computational effort than the sGA to reach success in any of the problems as they scale. Therefore, our algorithm converges faster to a solution than the sGA which is significant in the algorithmic sense. However, such a result provides just an estimation on the algorithm performance since the EvAg is distributed whereas the sGA is not.

Table 2. Computational effort for the different problem instances: sGA vs. EvAg

	MMDP			wPPEAKS			PPEAKS	
Problem Size	sGA (AES)	EvAg (AES)	P. Size	sGA (AES)	EvAg (AES)	P. Size	sGA (AES)	EvAg (AES)
2	1167.3	604.5	2	20	100	12	55.2	128
4	4634.6	1833	4	31.6	120	24	1847.1	669.3
8	12029	6243.8	8	316.2	378	36	9429.8	2838.7
10	17933	8779.5	10	783	551	48	9806.1	5160
16	45186	28796	16	10403	2015	60	21669	10584
32	128310	106290	32	3604480	23037	96	42539	30286
64	562640	518010	64	-	452740	192	131200	125030
128	-	2517300	128	-	2099200	-	-	-

More interesting are the results concerning the scalability of our approach. The analysis of the response time and population size are depicted in Figure 1 for the three problems under study. In any of them, the figures show that the estimated population size scales with polynomial order as the problems scale. Meanwhile, the response time (measured in simulator cycles) scales with logarithmic order showing a good adequacy of the algorithm for large problem instances. Therefore, the necessity of a huge amount of nodes for tackling large problem instances justifies the use of a P2P system in which such an amount would be available.

Finally, we have performed experiments with a network of 51200 nodes independently of the population size estimation. This way, we explore how the redundancy of nodes (individuals) affects the algorithm dynamics. The results show that the response time decreases for small instances and gets closer to the one estimated with the bisection method for large instances. Such a result shows that the algorithm is robust concerning population size. Hence, we will explore the redundancy of nodes as a mechanism for fault tolerance.

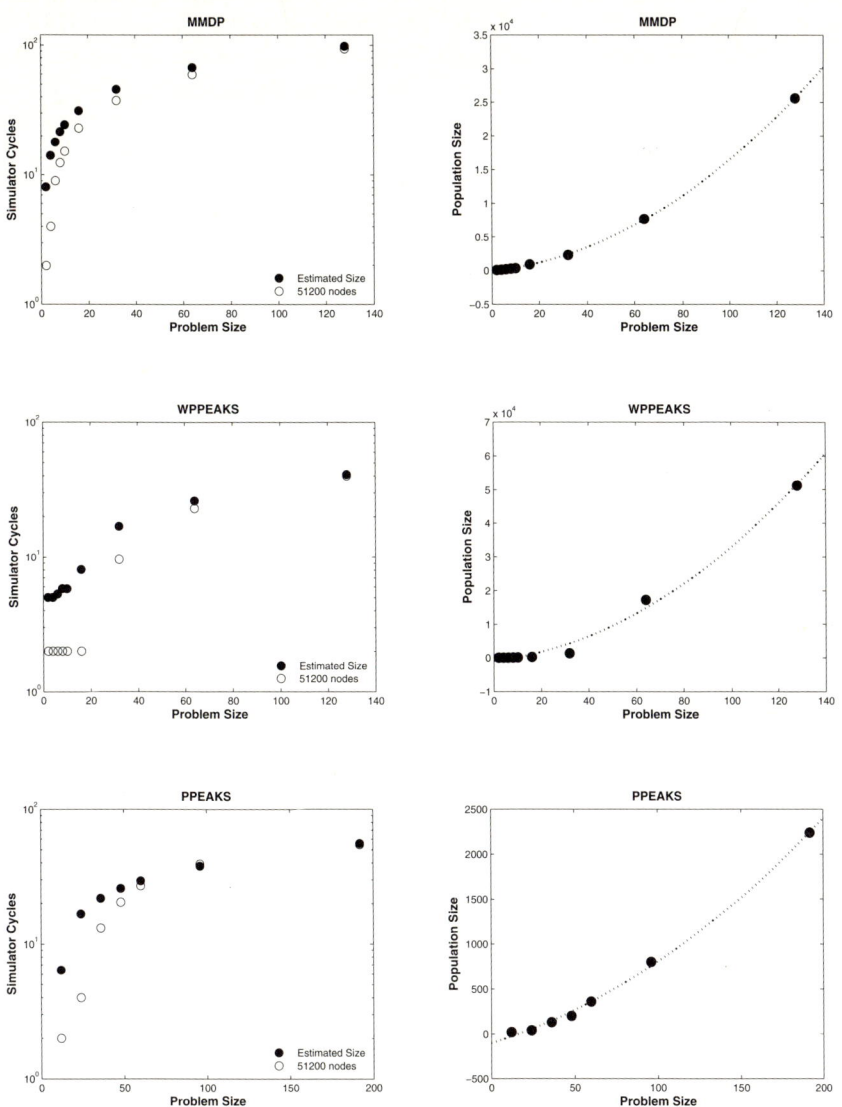

Fig. 1. Scalability analysis for the minimum population size (estimated) and an upper bound of 51200 individuals-nodes *(left)* and the estimated size *(right)* for a 98% of success rate using the method based on bisection

6 Conclusions

In this paper we have presented a P2P Evolutionary Algorithm and proved its adequacy for tackling large problem instances. Specifically, we have studied three discrete optimization problems which have been designed to be difficult for EAs.

Our approach is designed to deal with some P2P features such as decentralization and large-scalability. To this end, the population structure is managed by the gossiping protocol newscast. Through the experimental results we conclude that large instances of hard optimization problems can be tackled in P2P systems using the Evolvable Agent (EvAg) method.

In this paper we have proved that our approach needs less computational effort than a standard GA to reach the same degree of success on the problems under study. Additionally, such a computational effort is distributed whereas in the sGA is not. The population size scales with polynomial order which demands for a big amount of resources. Besides, the expected response time of the algorithm scales logarithmically with respect to the problem size which makes it efficient despite large problem instances. Finally, the algorithm is robust with respect to the population size. Once we estimate the minimum population size that yields success, adding more nodes does not damage the response time.

As future lines of work, we intend to assess the impact of the latency between peers and the use of the gossiping algorithm on the run-time performance. We expect that the idle processing time decreases as the problem instance scales (i.e. bigger instances require a bigger computational time while the communication time can be assumed as fixed). Additionally, we will analyse our approach in several scenarios which take into account arrivals/departures of nodes and heterogeneity conditions.

Acknowledgements

This work has been supported by the Spanish MICYT project TIN2007-68083-C02-01, the Junta de Andalucia CICE project P06-TIC-02025 and the Granada University PIUGR 9/11/06 project.

References

1. Arenas, M.G., Collet, P., Eiben, A.E., Jelasity, M., Merelo, J.J., Paechter, B., Preuss, M., Schoenauer, M.: A framework for distributed evolutionary algorithms. In: Guervós, J.J.M., Adamidis, P.A., Beyer, H.-G., Fernández-Villacañas, J.-L., Schwefel, H.-P. (eds.) PPSN 2002. LNCS, vol. 2439, pp. 665–675. Springer, Heidelberg (2002)
2. Dréo, J., Siarry, P., Pétrowski, A., Taillard, E.: Some Other Metaheuristics. In: Metaheuristics for Hard Optimization, pp. 153–177. Springer, Heidelberg (2006)
3. Eiben, A.E., Smith, J.E.: Introduction to Evolutionary Computing. Springer, Heidelberg (2003)
4. Giacobini, M., Tomassini, M., Tettamanzi, A., Alba, E.: Selection intensity in cellular evolutionary algorithms for regular lattices. IEEE Transactions on Evolutionary Computation 9(5), 489–505 (2005)
5. Giacobini, M., Alba, E., Tettamanzi, A., Tomassini, M.: Modeling selection intensity for toroidal cellular evolutionary algorithms. In: Deb, K., et al. (eds.) GECCO 2004. LNCS, vol. 3103, pp. 1138–1149. Springer, Heidelberg (2004)

6. Giacobini, M., Preuss, M., Tomassini, M.: Effects of scale-free and small-world topologies on binary coded self-adaptive CEA. In: Gottlieb, J., Raidl, G.R. (eds.) EvoCOP 2006. LNCS, vol. 3906, pp. 85–96. Springer, Heidelberg (2006)
7. Goldberg, D.E., Deb, K., Horn, J.: Massive multimodality, deception, and genetic algorithms. In: Parallel Problem Solving from Nature, vol. 2. Elsevier, B. V (1992)
8. Grefenstette, J.J.: Parallel adaptive algorithms for function optimization. Technical Report CS-81-19, Vanderbilt University, Computer Science Department, Nashville (1981)
9. Jelasity, M., Montresor, A., Babaoglu, O.: Gossip-based aggregation in large dynamic networks. ACM Trans. Comput. Syst. 23(3), 219–252 (2005)
10. Jelasity, M., van Steen, M.: Large-scale newscast computing on the Internet. Technical Report IR-503, Vrije Universiteit Amsterdam, Department of Computer Science, Amsterdam, The Netherlands (October 2002)
11. De Jong, K.A., Potter, M.A., Spears, W.M.: Using problem generators to explore the effects of epistasis. In: Bäck, T. (ed.) Proceedings of the Seventh International Conference on Genetic Algorithms (ICGA 1997). Morgan Kaufmann, San Francisco (1997)
12. Laredo, J.L.J., Eiben, E.A., Schoenauer, M., Castillo, P.A., Mora, A.M., Merelo, J.J.: Exploring selection mechanisms for an agent-based distributed evolutionary algorithm. In: GECCO 2007, pp. 2801–2808. ACM Press, New York (2007)
13. Laredo, J.L.J., Castillo, P.A., Paechter, B., Mora, A.M., Alfaro-Cid, E., Esparcia-Alcázar, A., Merelo, J.J.: Empirical validation of a gossiping communication mechanism for parallel EAs. In: Giacobini, M. (ed.) EvoWorkshops 2007. LNCS, vol. 4448, pp. 129–136. Springer, Heidelberg (2007)
14. Preuss, M., Lasarczyk, C.: On the importance of information speed in structured populations. In: Yao, X., Burke, E.K., Lozano, J.A., Smith, J., Merelo-Guervós, J.J., Bullinaria, J.A., Rowe, J.E., Tiňo, P., Kabán, A., Schwefel, H.-P. (eds.) PPSN 2004. LNCS, vol. 3242, pp. 91–100. Springer, Heidelberg (2004)
15. Sastry, K.: Evaluation-relaxation schemes for genetic and evolutionary algorithms. Technical Report 2002004, University of Illinois at Urbana-Champaign, Urbana, IL (2001)
16. Tomassini, M.: Spatially Structured Evolutionary Algorithms: Artificial Evolution in Space and Time (Natural Computing Series). Natural Computing Series. Springer, New York (2005)
17. Voulgaris, S., Jelasity, M., van Steen, M.: A Robust and Scalable Peer-to-Peer Gossiping Protocol. In: Moro, G., Sartori, C., Singh, M.P. (eds.) AP2PC 2003. LNCS (LNAI), vol. 2872, pp. 47–58. Springer, Heidelberg (2004)
18. Watts, D.J., Strogatz, S.H.: Collective dynamics of "small-world" networks. Nature 393, 440–442 (1998)
19. Wickramasinghe, W.R.M.U.K., van Steen, M., Eiben, A.E.: Peer-to-peer evolutionary algorithms with adaptive autonomous selection. In: GECCO 2007, pp. 1460–1467. ACM Press, New York (2007)

Efficient Processing of Continuous Join Queries Using Distributed Hash Tables

Wenceslao Palma[1], Reza Akbarinia[2], Esther Pacitti[1], and Patrick Valduriez[1]

[1] Atlas Team, INRIA and LINA, University of Nantes, France
{FirstName.LastName}@univ-nantes.fr,
{Patrick.Valduriez}@inria.fr
[2] School of Computer Science, University of Waterloo, Canada
rakbarin@cs.uwaterloo.ca

Abstract. This paper addresses the problem of computing approximate answers to continuous join queries. We present a new method, called DHTJoin, which combines hash-based placement of tuples in a Distributed Hash Table (DHT) and dissemination of queries using a gossip style protocol. We provide a performance evaluation of DHTJoin which shows that DHTJoin can achieve significant performance gains in terms of network traffic.

1 Introduction

Recent years have witnessed major research interest in data stream management systems. A data stream is a continuous and unbounded sequence of data items. There are many applications that generate streams of data including financial applications [7], network monitoring [23], telecommunication data management [6], sensor networks [5], etc. Processing a query over a data stream involves running the query continuously over the data stream and generating a new answer each time a new data item arrives. Due to the unbounded nature of data streams, it is not possible to store the data entirely in a bounded memory. This makes difficult the processing of queries that need to compare each new arriving data with past ones. We are interested in systems which have limited main memory but that can tolerate an approximate query result which has a maximum subset of the result. An example of such queries is join queries which are very important for many applications. As an example, consider a network monitoring application that needs to issue a join query over traffic traces from various links, in order to monitor the total traffic that is common among three links L1, L2 and L3 over the last 10 minutes. Each link (stream) contains tuples each one with a packet identifier pid and the packet size. This query can be posed using a declarative language such as CQL [3], which is a relational query language for data streams, as follows:

> Select sum (L1.size)
> From L1[range 10 min], L2[range 10 min], L3[range 10 min]
> Where L1.pid=L2.pid and L2.pid=L3.pid

A common solution to the problem of processing join queries over data streams is to execute the query over a sliding window [11] that maintains a restricted number of recent data items. This allows queries to be executed in a finite memory and in an incremental manner by generating new answers when a new data item arrives.

In this paper, we address the problem of computing approximate answers to windowed stream joins over data streams. Our solution involves a scalable distributed sliding window that takes advantage of the free computing power of DHT networks and can be equivalent to thousands of centralized sliding windows. Then, we propose a method, called DHTJoin, which deals with efficient execution of join queries over all data items which are stored in the distributed sliding window. DHTJoin combines hash-based placement of tuples in the DHT and dissemination of queries using a gossip style protocol. We evaluated the performance of DHTJoin through simulation. The results show the effectiveness of our solution compared with previous work.

The rest of this paper is organized as follows. In Section 2, we introduce our system model and define the problem. In Section 3 we describe DHTJoin. Section 4, describes a performance evaluation of our solution through simulation using Simjava. In Section 5, we discuss related work. Finally, Section 6 concludes.

2 System Model and Problem Definition

In this section we introduce a general system model for processing data streams over DHTs, with a DHT model, a stream processing model and a gossip dissemination system. Then, we state the problem.

2.1 DHT Model

In our system, the nodes of the overlay network are organized using a DHT protocol. While there are significant implementation differences between DHTs [19][22], they all map a given key k onto a peer p using a hash function and can lookup p efficiently, usually in O($log\ n$) routing hops where n is the number of peers. DHTs typically provide two basic operations [22]: *put(k, data)* stores a key k and its associated *data* in the DHT using some hash function; *get(k)* retrieves the data associated with k in the DHT. Tuples and continuous queries are originated at any node of the network. Nodes insert data in the form of relational tuples and each query q is represented in SQL. Tuples and queries are timestamped to represent the time that are inserted in the network by some node. Additionally, each query is associated with a unique key used to identify it in query grouping and to relate it to the node that submitted it.

2.2 Stream Processing Model

A data stream S_i is a sequence of tuples ordered by an increasing timestamp where $i \in [1..m]$ and $m \geq 2$ denotes the number of input streams. At each time unit, a number of tuples of average size l_i arrives to stream S_i. We use λ_i to denote the average arrival rate of a stream S_i in terms of tuples per second.

Many applications are interested in making decisions over recently observed tuples of the streams. This is why we maintain each tuple only for a limited time. This leads to a sliding window W_i over S_i that is defined as follows. Let $T(W_i)$ denotes the size of W_i in terms of seconds, i.e. the maximum time that a tuple is maintained in W_i. Let

$TS(s)$ be a function that denotes the arrival time of a tuple $s \in S$, and t be current time. Then W_i is defined as $W_i = \{s| s \in S_i \wedge t\text{-}TS(s) \leq T(W_i)\}$.

Tuples continuously arrive at each instant and expire after $T(W_i)$ time steps (time units). Thus, the tuples under consideration change over time as new tuples get added and old tuples get deleted. In practice, when arrival rates are high and the memory dedicated to the sliding window is limited, it becomes full rapidly and many tuples must be dropped before they naturally expire. In this case, we need to decide whether to admit or discard the arriving tuples and if admitted, which of the existing tuples to discard. This kind of decision is made using a *load-shedding strategy* [14][21] which yields that only a fraction of the complete result will be produced.

2.3 Gossip Dissemination System

The basic idea behind gossiping [15][26] is to have all nodes collaborating to disseminate information into the entire network using a *partial view* stored in a *local list* of size L. To this end, when a node wishes to disseminate a message or receive it for the first time, it picks k nodes from its *local list* and sends them the message. Initializing and maintaining the local list at each node in face of dynamic changes in the network is done by a *membership protocol*. The number of gossip targets, k, is a typical configuration parameter called *fanout*. The sum of the k links between nodes specifies an overlay network on top of the existing network topology.

If a node receives a message for the second time, it simply discards the message. A relatively inexpensive optimization is to never forward a message back to the node it was just received from. Due to their inherent redundancy, gossip dissemination systems are able to mask network omissions and also node failures. In order to evaluate the performance of gossip dissemination systems, it is essential to define a set of metrics:

- **Hit Ratio:** the number of nodes that receive a sent message. Ideally, a gossip dissemination system should always achieve a hit ratio of 100%, that is, to reach every node in the network.
- **Dissemination Speed:** the time a message requires to reach every node in the network. It depends of network latency and the number of hops a message takes to reach the last node. In our evaluation we focus on the latter factor.
- **Message Overhead:** the number of redundant times that a message is forwarded during its dissemination.

An effective dissemination system assures a high Hit Ratio, a fast dissemination speed, and has a low message overhead.

2.4 Problem Definition

In this paper, we deal with the problem of processing join queries over data streams. A data stream is a sequence of tuples ordered by monotonically increasing timestamps. The timestamps are generated using the KTS service [1] which is a distributed service that deals with generating monotonically increasing timestamps in DHTs. Each tuple and query have a timestamp that may either be implicit, i.e. generated by the system at arrival time, or explicit, i.e. inserted by the source at creation time. However, we do not include the timestamp attribute in the schema of the stream. Formally, the problem can be defined as follows. Let $\Sigma=\{S_1,S_2,......,S_m\}$ be a set of relational data streams, and $Q=\{Q_1,Q_2,....,Q_n\}$ be a set of join queries specified on these data streams. Our goal is to provide an efficient method to execute Q over Σ in terms of network traffic.

3 DHTJoin Method

Using structured overlay P2P networks in data stream processing environments is a novel research topic [13]. We can take advantage of it strengths to support queries over data streams [4]. The main issues for processing continuous queries in DHTs are the following: how to route data and queries to peers in an efficient way; how to provide a data storage mechanism for storing relational data; and how to provide a good approximate answer to join queries.

We describe our solution for continuous join query processing using DHTs. Our method has two steps: indexing of tuples and dissemination of queries. A tuple inserted by a node is indexed, i.e., stored at another node using DHT primitives only if there is a query that requires it. To assure the knowledge of that query to the entire network, it is disseminated using a gossip protocol.

3.1 Indexing Tuples

Existing DHT implementations such as Chord [22] are robust: they use simple algorithms with provable properties even under frequent node failures, departures and rejoins. To answer a query, we consider different kinds of peers. The first kind is Stream Reception Peers (SRP) which are responsible for disseminating queries and indexing tuples to the second kind of peers named Stream Query Peers (SQP). SQPs are responsible for executing queries over the arriving tuples using their local sliding windows, and sending the results to the third kind of node(s) named User Query Peer (UQP). To support dissemination of queries each node is a gossip node and for indexing of tuples each node is a DHT peer. Note that the distribution between SRP, SQP and UQP is functional and the same peer can have all of these functionalities.

The tuples arrive at any SRP and are indexed onto SQPs if there exists a query that requires it. A join processing algorithm is executed at each SQP that receives the tuples sent by an SRP. In our solution, the tuples are indexed in SQPs. Each arriving tuple is entirely indexed in an SQP using a join attribute value as storage key, usually in $O(log\ n)$ routing hops where n is the number of peers.

Let us describe our indexing method for three streams S_1, S_2 and S_3. However, our method is not limited to three streems and works on any number of streams. Let A be the set of attributes of S_1, S_2 and S_3. Let s_1, s_2, and s_3 be tuples belonging to S_1, S_2 and S_3 respectively and $val(s\ a)$ be a function that returns the value of an attribute $a \in A$ in tuple s. Let h be a uniform hash function that hashes its inputs into a DHT key, i.e. a number which can be mapped by the DHT onto a peer. For indexing a tuple s_1 that arrives at a SRP, each tuple obtains an index key computed as $key= h(S_1,val(s_1,a))$ and is then indexed in a SQP using $put(key,s_1)$ only if there exists a query that requires this tuple indexed by using the value of attribute a. For s_2 and s_3 tuples, we proceed in the same way. All tuples of S_1, S_2 and S_3 having the same value in attribute a get indexed at the same SQP. Join operations are performed on the tuples stored within sliding windows. Let W_i denote a sliding window on stream S_i. We use time-based sliding windows where $T(W_i)$ is the size of the window in time units. At time t, a tuple belongs to W_i if it has arrived in the time interval $[t- T(W_i),t]$.

To illustrate, let us consider an equijoin query over three streams S_1, S_2 and S_3. Once a S_1-tuple arrives onto a SRP we verify if a query requires this tuple indexed by some attribute, if so, we index the tuple and execute a Join processing algorithm at each SQP that receives SRP tuples. Processing a join query over timestamp based sliding windows with three input relational streams S_1, S_2 and S_3 is done as follows. Upon each arrival of a new tuple from stream S_1 to W_1, expired tuples in W_2 and W_3 are invalidated, then for each W_2-tuple we evaluate the join of W_3 with the arriving tuple and probe the result set. A load shedding procedure is executed over W_1's buffer if there is not enough memory to insert the tuple. The UQP receives the tuples from SQPs. At any time, a SQP could contain a collection of tuples representing a portion of the join query result. The join query result is inserted into a local queue and sent to the peer that submitted the query. The output of the join sent to that peer (an UQP node) consists of all pairs of tuples $s_1 \in S_1$, $s_2 \in S_2$ and $s_3 \in S_3$ such that $s_1.a= s_2.a=s_3.a$ and, a time t, both $s_1 \in W_1$, $s_2 \in W_2$ and $s_3 \in W_3$.

3.2 Disseminating Queries

A query q can originate at any of the nodes and is disseminated to the whole network. This dissemination allows a global knowledge of queries and to index tuples using an attribute value only if there exists a query that requires it. However, disseminating q can be difficult if nodes have only limited knowledge of the members of the network. This knowledge is stored in a *local list* of size L and we must assure a Hit Ratio of 100%. We assume a network of N nodes. Intuitively, the requirement for assuring a Hit Ratio of 100% is that the components of the *local list* form a strongly connected directed graph over all nodes. For example, if we use the Chord protocol we can build a *local list* of size 1 with an immediate successor pointer from the finger table and disseminate a query in N hops without redundant messages. However, the dissemination speed is very slow. To accelerate the dissemination process we can consider a *local list* composed by an immediate successor pointer from the finger table and the predecessor pointer, used to walk counter clockwise around the Chord ring, maintained by the Chord protocol. In this case, the dissemination speed is reduced to $N/2$ hops with 2 redundant messages. Considering that a tuple can be indexed in $log(N)$ hops we must increase the dissemination speed as high as possible. To this end, we can increase the *fanout* by exploiting the entire finger table and increase the dissemination speed to $log(N)$ hops, i.e., we disseminate a query as fast as a tuple index but that implies redundant messages. Redundancy provides tolerance to dynamic environments but excessive redundancy leads to excessive network traffic.

In addition, with predecessor and successor pointers of the Chord protocol we can form a strongly bidirectional connected directed graph that assures a 100% Hit Ratio and with the entire finger table, we can increase the dissemination speed as fast as a tuple index.

3.3 Optimization

Achieving a dissemination speed of queries equal to *log(N)* hops (taking advantage of the Chord finger table) yields an increase in the number of forwarded messages. We propose an optimization to decrease considerably the number of redundant messages without decreasing the dissemination speed and guaranteeing a 100% Hit Ratio. Our solution is as follows. Each time a node originates a query, it builds a gossip message that consists of the query, its own identifier and its gossip targets: the successor and predecessor pointers and its finger table. Upon reception of a new gossip message, a node builds its gossip targets considering the intersection of the nodes received with the arriving message, its own identifier and its own gossip targets. Thus, we can decrease the number of redundant messages to *1/2log(N)* (see our performance evaluation), while maintaining the same dissemination speed and assuring a 100% of Hit Ratio.

4 Performance Evaluation

To test our DHTJoin method, we implemented a simulator using SimJava [20] running on a Linux PC with a 3.4 Ghz Pentium Processor and 512 megabytes of RAM. Our simulator is based on Chord which is a simple and efficient DHT. To simulate a peer, we use a SimJava entity that performs all tasks that must be done by a peer in the DHT, in the dissemination system and in the stream window-based join processing.

We generate arbitrary input data streams consisting of synthetic asynchronous data items with no tuple-level semantics. We have a schema of 4 relations, each one with 10 attributes. In order to create a new tuple we choose a relation and assign values to all its attributes using a Zipf distribution with a default parameter of 0.9. The max value of the domain of the join attribute is fixed to 1000. Tuples on streams are generated at a constant rate of 30 tuples per second. Queries are generated with a mean arrival rate of 0.02, i.e., a query arrives every 50 seconds on average. The network size is set to 1024 nodes. In all experiments, we use time-based sliding windows of 50 seconds. For each of our tests, we run the simulator for 300 seconds. In order to assess our approach, we compare the network traffic of DHTJoin against a complete implementation of RJoin [13] which is the most relevant related work (see Section 5). RJoin uses incremental evaluation based on tuple indexing and query rewriting over distributed hash tables. In RJoin a new tuple is indexed twice for each attribute it has; wrt the attribute name and wrt the attribute value. A query is indexed waiting for matching tuples. Each arriving tuple that is a match causes the query to be rewritten and reindexed at a different node. The network traffic is the total number of messages needed to index tuples and disseminate a query in DHTJoin or to index tuples and perform query rewriting in RJoin.

In order to show the effectiveness of the dissemination of queries, we use the Hit Ratio, Dissemination Speed and Message Overhead metrics. The fanout parameter is set to 2, $m/2$, m and m_{OPT}, with m equal to $log(N)$. The fanout value m_{OPT} includes the optimization process presented in Section 3.

In the rest of this section, we evaluate network traffic and the effectiveness of gossip dissemination.

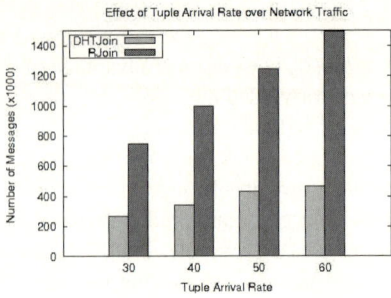

Fig. 1. Effect of Tuples Arrival Rate

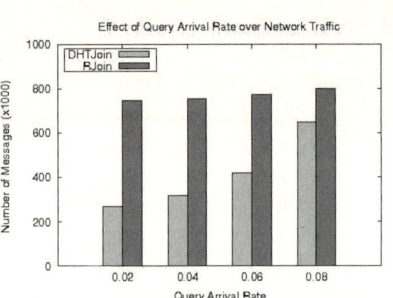

Fig. 2. Effect of Query Arrival Rate

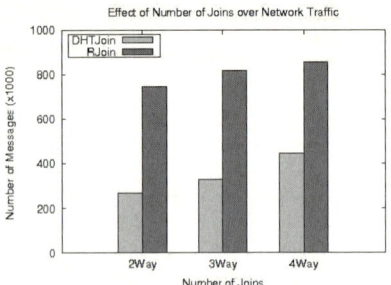

Fig. 3. Effect of Number of Joins

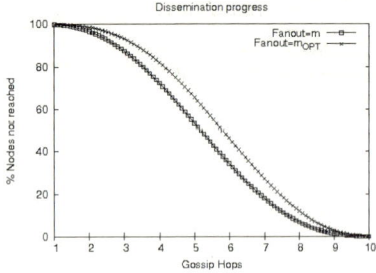

Fig. 4. Dissemination progress

4.1 Network Traffic

In this section, we investigate the effect of tuples' arrival rate, query's arrival rate and number of joins on the network traffic. The network traffic of RJoin and DHTJoin grows as the tuples' arrival rate grows. In RJoin, as more tuples arrive, the number of messages related to the indexing of tuples and query rewriting increases (see Figure 1). As expected, DHTJoin generates significantly less messages because a high tuples' arrival rate does not mean more indexing of tuples. The reason is that before indexing a tuple, DHTJoin checks for the existence of a query that requires it. In Figure 2, we show that, as more queries arrive, RJoin generates more query rewriting messages. However, DHTJoin generates more messages only if new queries related to new different values used in the tuples arrive in the system. Figure 3 shows that more join require more network traffic. RJoin generates more query rewriting when there are more joins in the queries. However, in DHTJoin the network traffic increases only if the arriving queries require of attributes not present in the other queries. The reason is that with the dissemination of queries, DHTJoin can avoid the unnecessary indexing of tuples that are not required by the queries

In summary, due to the integration of query dissemination and hash-based placement of tuples our approach avoids the excessive traffic generated by RJoin which is due to its method of indexing tuples.

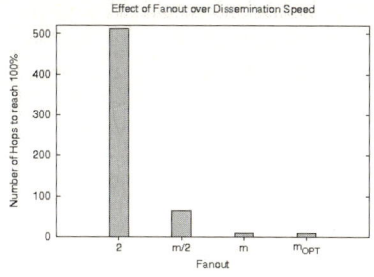
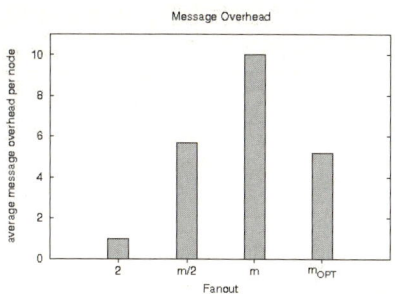

Fig. 5. Speed of dissemination   **Fig. 6.** Message Overhead

4.2 Gossip Dissemination

To evaluate the effectiveness of gossip dissemination of queries, we post a query originated randomly at any node. In this experiment, we show the dissemination speed and look at the evolution of dissemination in terms of the number of nodes that have not yet been contacted as a function of the hops taken. Figure 4 shows that our method yields a complete dissemination, i.e., a Hit Ratio of 100% in $log(N)$ hops. This is because the nodes of the *local list* form a strongly connected directed graph over all nodes. Our proposed optimization to reduce message overhead produces no changes in the speed of the dissemination.

If a query is disseminated as fast as possible we avoid excessive store time of tuples waiting for a query and we can generate join tuples as early as possible. Thus, we state that a query must be disseminated as fast as a tuple. In Figure 5, we confirm this and we can see that the higher the fanout the dissemination speed increases to reach the same speed as a tuple index. However, if we choose a higher fanout, we incur message overhead which overload the network. Conversely, we can choose a lower fanout to obtain a minimal overhead, as shown in Figure 6, but this incurs slower dissemination, as shown in Figure 5. To reduce message overhead we ran experiments to include the optimization proposed in Section 3. In Figure 5, we show that with a fanout m_{OPT}, we obtain a fast dissemination and at the same time, as shown in Figure 6, we reduce the message overhead to $1/2 log(N)$ wrt a fanout m.

5 Related Work

A DHT can serve as the hash table that underlies many parallel hash-based join algorithms. However, our approach provides Internet-level scalability. Our work is related to many studies in the field of centralized and distributed continuous query processing [12][10][24][6][17]. In PIER [12], a query processor is used on top of a DHT to process one-time join queries. Recent work on PIER has been developed to process only continuous aggregation queries. PeerCQ [10] was developed to process continuous queries on top of a DHT, However, PeerCQ does not consider SQL queries and the data is not stored in the DHT. Borealis [24], TelegraphCQ [6] and DCAPE [17] have been developed to process continuous queries in a cluster setting and many of their techniques for load-shedding and load balancing are orthogonal to our work. The most relevant previous work regarding the utilization of a structured overlay P2P network is [13] which proposes RJoin, an algorithm that uses incremental evaluation.

This incremental evaluation is based on tuple indexing and query rewriting over distributed hash tables. A major difference in our work differs is that our tuple index mechanism indexes tuples only if there exists a query that requires it.

Large-scale information dissemination based on gossip protocols are essential for applications such as replicated database maintenance [8], publish/subscribe systems [9] and distributed failure detection [25]. These approaches do not consider a structured overlay setting. The probabilistic dissemination algorithm named Randcast proposed in [15] spreads messages very fast but fails to reach every node in the network. In [18] the authors propose a technique that leverages simple social network principles enabling nodes to select gossip targets intelligently. This work shows experimentally that gossip dissemination on the Chord overlay fails to deliver the messages to every node in the network. Our work instead shows that it is possible to reach every node in the network forming a strongly bidirectional connected directed graph composed by predecessor and successor pointers. In [16] the authors assure a good tradeoff between message overhead and reliability guarantee using a connection graph called a Harary graph. However, its principal drawback is the maintenance of such graph that requires global knowledge of membership. In our work, the structure that supports the membership protocol is supported by the structured overlay and does not require global knowledge of membership for its maintenance. The most relevant previous work regarding dissemination is the hybrid dissemination proposed in [26]. This works uses deterministic links to assure a complete dissemination. However, our work differs in the presence of a structured overlay and a membership protocol based on its routing table.

6 Conclusion

In this paper, we proposed a new method, called DHTJoin, for processing continuous join queries using DHTs. DHTJoin combines hash-based placement of tuples and dissemination of queries using a gossip style protocol. Our performance evaluation shows that DHTJoin obtains significant performance gains due to our schema of global knowledge of queries based on a gossip protocol. This schema has a low message overhead and avoids the excessive traffic produced by the tuple index method and the query rewriting of RJoin. Our results demonstrate that the total number of messages transmitted by DHTJoin is always fewer that RJoin wrt tuple arrival rate, query arrival rate and number of joins.

As future work, we plan to address the problem of efficient execution of top-k join queries over data streams using DHTs taking advantage of the best position algorithms [2] which can be used in many distributed and P2P systems for efficient processing of top-k queries.

References

1. Akbarinia, R., Pacitti, E., Valduriez, P.: Data currency in replicated DHTs. In: ACM Int. Conf. on Management of Data (SIGMOD), pp. 211–222 (2007)
2. Akbarinia, R., Pacitti, E., Valduriez, P.: Best Position Algorithms for Top-k Queries. In: Int. Conf. on Very Large Databases (VLDB), pp. 495–506 (2007)
3. Arasu, A., Babu, S., Widom, J.: An Abstract Semantics and Concrete Language for Continuous Queries over Streams and Relations. Technical Report, DataBase Group, Stanford University (2002)

4. Babcock, B., Babu, S., Datar, M., Motwani, R., Widom, J.: Models and Issues in Data Streams. In: ACM Symp. on Principles of Database Systems (PODS) (2002)
5. Bonnet, P., Gehrke, J., Seshadri, P.: Towards Sensor Database Systems. In: Int. Conf. on Mobile Data Management (2001)
6. Chandrasekaran, S., et al.: TelegraphCQ: Continuous Dataflow Processing for an Uncertain World. Conf. on Innovative Data Systems Research (CIDR) (2003)
7. Chen, J., DeWitt, D., Tian, F., Wang, Y.: NiagaraCQ: A Scalable Continuous Query System for Internet Databases. In: ACM Int. Conf. on Management of Data (SIGMOD) (2000)
8. Demers, A., Greene, D., Hauser, C., Irish, W., Larson, J.: Epidemics Algorithms for Replicated DB Maintenance. In: ACM Int. Conf. on Management of Data (SIGMOD) (1987)
9. Eugster, P., Guerraoui, R., Handurukande, S., Kermarrec, A., Kouznetsov, P.: Lightweight Probabilistic Broadcast. In: Int. Conf. Dependable Systems and Networks (DSN) (2001)
10. Gedik, B., Liu, L.: PeerCQ: A Descentralized a Self-Configuring Peer-to-Peer Information Monitoring System. In: Int. Conf. on Distributed Computing Systems (ICDCS) (2003)
11. Golab, L., Özsu, T.: Processing Sliding Windows Multi-Joins in Continuous Queries over Data Streams. In: Int. Conf. on Very Large Data Bases (VLDB) (2003)
12. Huebsch, R., Hellerstein, J.M., Lanham, N., Loo, B.T., Shenker, S., Stoica, I.: Queying the Internet with PIER. In: Int. Conf. on Very Large Databases (VLDB) (2002)
13. Idreos, S., Liarou, E., Koubarakis, M.: Continuous Multi-Way Joins over Distributed Hash Tables. In: Int. Conf. on Extending Database Technology (EDBT) (to appear, 2008)
14. Kang, J., Naughton, J.F., Viglas, S.: Evaluating windows joins over unbounded streams. In: IEEE Int. Conf. on Data Engineering (ICDE) (2003)
15. Kermarrec, A., Massoulié, L., Ganesh, A.: Probabilistic Realiable Dissemination in Large-Scale Systems. IEEE Trans. Par. Distr. Syst. 14(2), 248–258 (2003)
16. Lin, M.-J., Marzullo, K., Masini, S.: Gossip versus Deterministic Flooding: Low Message Overhead and High-Reliability for Broadcasting on Small Networks. In: Int. Symp. On Distributed Computing (2000)
17. Liu, B., Jbantova, M., Momberger, B., Rundensteiner, E.A.: A dynamically Adaptive Distributed System for Processing Complex Continuous Queries. In: Int. Conf. on Very Large Data Bases (VLDB) (2005)
18. Patel, J.A., Gupta, I., Contractor, N.: JetStream: Achieveing Predictable Gossip Dissemination by Leveraging Social Network Principles. In: IEEE Int. Symp. on Network Computing and Applications (NCA) (2006)
19. Ratnasamy, S., Francis, P., Handley, M., Karp, R.M., Shenker, S.: A Scalable Content-Addressable Network. In: Proc. of SIGCOMM (2001)
20. SimJava, http://www.dcs.ed.ac.uk/home/hase/simjava/
21. Srivastava, U.: Widom J. Memory-limited Execution of Windowed Stream Joins. In: Int. Conf. on Very Large Data Bases (VLDB) (2004)
22. Stoica, I., Morris, R., Karger, D., Kaashoek, M., Balakrishnan, H.: Chord: A Scalable Peer-to-Peer Lookup Service for Internet Applications. In: Proc. of SIGCOMM (2001)
23. Sullivan, M., Heybey, A.: Tribeca: A System for Managing Large Databases of Network Traffic. In: USENIX Annual Technical Conf. (1998)
24. Tatbul, N., Zdonik, S.: Window-Aware Load Shedding for Aggregations Queries over Data Streams. In: Int. Conf. on Very Large Data Bases (VLDB) (2006)
25. Van Renesse, R., Minsky, Y., Hayden, M.: A Gossip-Style Failure Detection Service. In: ACM/IFIP/USENIX Int. Middleware Conf. (1998)
26. Voulgaris, S., Van Steen, M.: Hybrid Dissemination: Adding Determinism to Probabilistic Multicasting in Large-Scale P2P Systems. In: ACM/IFIP/USENIX Int. Middleware Conf. (2007)

Topic 8: Distributed Systems and Algorithms

Elsa María Macías López* and Marc Shapiro**

Fifteen papers were submitted to Topic 8. Each paper was reviewed by four of the topic chairs (a single paper received only three reviews). Three papers were ranked clearly above the others and three others were discussed in more depth between the chairs. As a result, the chairs proposed three papers for acceptance, and two more for discussion, one of which was accepted by the PC meeting.

It is interesting to note that none of the top papers is a "hard-core" distributed systems paper, i.e., this year, there will be no papers on consensus, fault tolerance, or distributed algorithms. Instead all four papers focus on applications of distributed systems. This is not due to any particular bias by the committee, but simply reflects the quality and the spectrum of the submissions we received.

We are proud that a paper in this topic has won a Best Paper award. The article *Automatic Prefetching with Binary Code Rewriting in Object-based DSMs* focuses on reducing the number faults in a Distributed Shared Memory (DSM) system. To achieve this goal, the authors use a profiler that monitors the access behavior of the application, and a dynamic binary rewriter that inserts appropriate prefetch instructions. Evaluation results show an important reduction of the number of messages and high performance gains on the benchmarks. The program committee judged the approach original and well evaluated.

The paper *A PGAS-based Algorithm for the Longest Common Subsequence Problem* focuses on parallelising a well known algorithm. The authors use the Partitioned Global Address Space (PGAS) programming model, to improve data and workload distributions in the Longest Common Subsequence problem.

A practical evaluation of the Cell Broadband Engine running parallel data mining algorithms is presented in the paper *Data Mining Algorithms on the Cell Broadband Engine*.

Finally, the efficient management of striped files and files with complex data structures in active storage is presented in the paper titled *Efficient Management of (Complex) Striped Files in Active Storage*.

---

* Topic 8 Local Chair.
** Topic 8 Global Chair.

Automatic Prefetching with Binary Code Rewriting in Object-Based DSMs

Jean Christophe Beyler[1], Michael Klemm[2], Michael Philippsen[2], and Philippe Clauss[1]

[1] Université Louis-Pasteur de Strasbourg,
ICPS-LSIIT,
Pôle API, Bd Sébastian Brant,
67400 Illkirch, France
{beyler,clauss}@icps.u-strasbg.fr

[2] University of Erlangen-Nuremberg,
Computer Science Department 2,
Martensstr. 3,
91058 Erlangen, Germany
{klemm,philippsen}@cs.fau.de

Abstract. Dynamic optimizers modify the binary code of programs at runtime by profiling and optimizing certain aspects of the execution. We present a completely software-based framework that dynamically optimizes programs for object-based Distributed Shared Memory (DSM) systems. In DSM systems, reducing the number of messages between nodes is crucial. Prefetching transfers data in advance from the storage node to the local node so that communication is minimized. Our framework uses a profiler and a dynamic binary rewriter that monitors the access behavior of the application and places prefetches where they are beneficial to speed up the application. In addition, we adapt the number of prefetches per request to best fit the application's behavior. Evaluation shows that the performance of our system is better than manual prefetching. The number of messages sent decreases by up to 89%. Performance gains of up to 73% can be observed on the benchmarks.

1 Introduction

The high-performance computing landscape is mainly shaped by clusters, which make up 81% of the world's fastest systems [1]. Clusters typically exhibit a distributed memory architecture, i.e., each node of the cluster has its own private memory that is not directly accessible by the other nodes. Software-based Distributed Shared Memory (S-DSM) systems strive to simulate a globally shared address space, alleviating the need to place explicit calls to a message passing library that handles communication (e.g. MPI [6]). Instead, a middleware layer accesses remote memory and ensures memory coherence. Examples of such S-DSM systems are JIAJIA [11], Delphi [14] or Jackal [16].

In addition to registers, L1/L2/L3 caches, and the nodes' local memory, the DSM adds another level (the remote memory) to the memory hierarchy. Remote memory accesses are much more expensive than local accesses, as the high-latency interconnection network has to be crossed. Hence, it is desirable to direct the application's memory accesses to the local memory as often as possible. For applications that do not offer such locality properties, performance drastically drops due to the high-latency remote accesses.

Prefetching provides a solution to this performance problem by requesting data from the storage location before it is actually needed. Most current hardware platforms (e. g. Intel Itanium, IBM POWER) offer prefetch instructions in their instruction sets. Such instructions cause the CPU's prefetching unit to asynchronously load data from main memory into the CPU. Executing the prefetch at the right time, data arrives just-in-time when needed by the program. Based on heuristics, compilers statically add prefetches to the code during compilation.

This paper presents a dynamic software system that automatically profiles and optimizes programs at runtime, outperforming manually optimized prefetching. During compilation, the Jackal DSM compiler [16] adds to the executable monitoring code that profiles memory accesses. A profiler classifies the memory accesses and enables prefetches if beneficial. Dynamic code rewriting keeps the the system's overhead low by interchanging the monitor code and the prefetching code in the executable. If prefetches are unprofitable, calls are completely removed, avoiding a slow-down of the application. However, if profitable, the code rewriter replaces the monitoring calls with prefetcher calls. The Esodyp+ prefetcher [10] is used as an example for our generic optimizer. It predicts memory access patterns and prefetches future memory accesses. While Esodyp+ requires manual placement of calls to its runtime functions, our system automatically inserts these calls if beneficial. Additional performance is gained by adapting the prefetching distance to the application's memory access behavior. For details on the implementation of the Esodyp+ predictor, refer to [10].

2 Implementation of Object-Based DSMs

To understand the requirements for automatic prefetchers in an object-based S-DSM environment, this section first describes the basic DSM features and then explores the design space of DSM implementations.

Instead of using cache lines or memory pages for distributing data, object-based DSMs use objects for data transfers and for memory consistency. The DSM system checks for each object access if the accessed object is already available locally. If not, the DSM system requests the object from its storage location. The programming language's memory consistency model has to be respected, which involves invalidating or updating replicas of objects on other nodes. Testing for object availability can either be implemented in software or hardware.

In general, S-DSMs cannot use specialized hardware for the object access checks, as they should support commodity clusters. Some S-DSMs exploit the Memory Management Unit (MMU) of processors for access checks. The Operating System (OS) can use MMUs to protect memory pages against reading or writing. If a restricted page is accessed, the OS triggers the S-DSM and notifies

```
1         leaq  -1308622848(%r8), %rdi
2         shrq  $5, %rdi
3         movq  %rdi,%rcx
4         movq  %fs:(0), %rdx
5         movq  thread_local_dsm_read_bitmap@TPOFF(%rdx), %rdx
6         bt    %rcx, (%rdx)
7         jc    .L28961
8         movq  %r8,%rdi
9         call  shm_start_read_object@PLT
10        movq  %rax,%r8
11 .L28961:
```

Fig. 1. Example of an access check in assembly code, without prefetching

it about the faulty access. After the S-DSM has loaded the page, the access is re-issued and the application continues. Delphi [14] and others [3,8,11] use this approach to implement a page-based DSM. However, memory protection can only be applied at the page level and, thus, renders this option unusable for object-based S-DSMs, as it causes false faults on local objects that reside on the same page. Hence, for object-based S-DSMs, the access check has to be implemented in software, which is easy to do, because it often requires only a single bit test. Jackal [16], for example, relies on the compiler to prefix each object access with an access check that tests the object's availability on the local node.

We use the Jackal object-based DSM for our prototype implementation. Fig. 1 shows an assembler fragment of a read test as it is emitted by the Jackal compiler (prefetching is switched off). Lines 1–5 compute the object's read bit depending on the relative offset of the object in the heap; lines 6–11 test the bit and call the DSM runtime if the object is not locally available. As the runtime requests the object data from the object's home node and waits until data has arrived, each failing object access has a runtime penalty of roughly two times the latency of a network packet plus additional costs for object serialization and deserialization.

3 Memory Access Profiling and Dynamic Code Rewriting

Using a profiler, our automatic optimizer first needs to classify the access checks into categories to decide which require prefetching. Only a low overhead is acceptable for profiling, as the overhead must be compensated to reduce runtime. In addition, the optimizer adapts the number of prefetches per request message (the so-called *prefetching distance*) to optimally exploit prefetches depending on the application's access behavior. This section first explores the design space of such a dynamic optimizer and the profiler. It then covers the state machine of the profiler and discusses heuristics to adapt the prefetching distance.

3.1 Design Considerations

The main part of our dynamic optimizer is a low-overhead profiler. As prefetching is useless for access checks rarely executed or exhibiting random behavior, a classification by the profiler is crucial for the efficiency of the optimizer. There are several ways such a profiler can be implemented in the dynamic optimizer.

First, the monitoring code and the prefetching code could be accompanied by conditional guards. Implemented by a `switch` statement that decides between monitoring, prefetching, and no prefetching, the guards cause performance losses that result from additional instructions, increase loads on the memory bus, and put a higher pressure on the branch prediction unit of the CPU. Hence, this option is expected to have a high overhead that is difficult to compensate.

With binary rewriting, the compiler prefixes access checks with monitoring code. After profiling, the code is either replaced with prefetching code or removed if prefetching is not beneficial. To remove code, the rewriter has to replace the code with `nops`, as the subsequent binary code cannot replace the to-be-removed code fragment (moving code implies checking and modifying most branch instructions). However, `nops` pollute the instruction cache and pipelines and, thus, cause undesired overheads. In addition, the profiler receives the program's local and remote accesses, as the code is placed in front of the access checks. Hence, the profile represents the general access behavior. Remote and local accesses are interleaved and distinguishing access checks that need prefetching and those that do not is impossible. An additional runtime overhead is caused, as the instrumentation code is always executed, even if only local objects are accessed.

Replacing the original access check code, however, provides low overhead, as only single calls must be changed to implement a state transition. It is possible to dynamically redirect the program's control flow without performance losses that would result from using `switch` statements or `nops`. Furthermore, as a second advantage, access checks can be de-instrumented and replaced by their regular DSM counterparts. Thus, these access checks are executed without any overhead.

Directly integrating the monitor calls and prefetcher calls in access checks has two consequences. First, applications only incur an overhead in case of failing access checks. Therefore, if an application only accesses its local memory, there is no overhead since the prefetcher is never called. Second, as the predictor is only triggered during a failing access check, the created model only represents the application's behavior for accesses into the remote memory instead of modeling the memory references of every accessed object. Hence, the model only predicts the next remote accesses. If the model contained local references as well, they need to be filtered out, which causes an additional overhead when prefetching.

3.2 Profiling State Machine

We distinguish four states that characterize the behavior of an access check. Depending on the state, it may be beneficial to use prefetching (often executed, non-random access behavior) or not. Fig. 2 shows the state machine.

For access checks, the **Monitoring** state is the initial state. If an access check is often executed, it is sent to the *Model Creation* state. This is implemented with

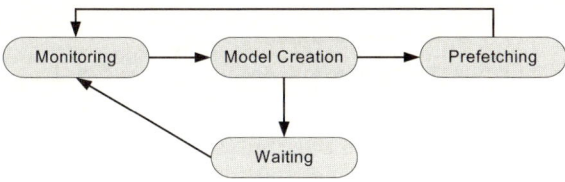

Fig. 2. State evolution of the access checks

a counter per access check and a threshold t. In the **Model Creation** state, a mathematical model (e. g. a Markov model) determines the access behavior of an access check. If its behavior is unpredictable (i. e., random), prefetchers cannot correctly predict the next accesses and the access check state is changed to *Waiting*. If predictable, the access check proceeds to the *Prefetching* state and the prefetcher is enabled for this access check. **Waiting** represents the state in which the original access check code of the DSM is executed. To detect changes in the application's behavior so that the access check might later benefit from prefetching, the access check is periodically re-instrumented by the optimizer. To reduce the overhead and to avoid state thrashing, the time between re-instrumentations is increased at each cycle. **Prefetching** is enabled in the fourth state of an access check. As the access behavior of the access check is predictable, the prefetcher can predict the next accesses with high accuracy and it emits prefetch commands to prematurely request the data needed. If the prefetcher's prediction accuracy drops, the access check falls back to the *Monitoring* state for reassessment.

In the *Model Creation* state and the *Prefetching* state we use the Markov model predictor Esodyp+ [10], which uses past events to predict future events. It relies on the observation that events of the past are likely to repeat. Other Markov model based predictors could have been used as well [2,9].

The profiler needs to efficiently identify access checks, as it profiles them separately. Since Jackal uses function calls for access checks (see Fig. 1), state transitions rewrite these function calls. We use the call's return address as a key into a hash table storing the profiler's data. In other DSM systems, the compiler could mark the access checks with identifying labels. During the *Initial* state, the hash table contains the hit counter for access checks. In the *Model Creation* state, the table stores a buffer collecting the requested memory addresses. Once the buffer overflows, the optimizer selects the most frequent access check, as it is likely to benefit most from prefetching. The addresses are then used to construct a model for which the expected prediction accuracy is calculated. With a high accuracy, the access check enters the *Prefetching* state. If too low, the access check enters the *Waiting* state. In this state, the access check is assigned an age that determines when it will fall back to the *Monitoring* state again.

3.3 Dynamic Adaption of the Prefetching Distance

To reduce the number of messages of an execution, the predictor must emit bulk prefetches that ask for several data items. The number of elements prefetched simultaneously is called the *prefetching distance* N. With an increasing prefetching

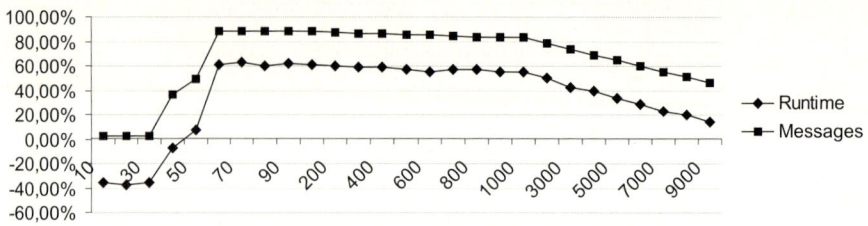

Fig. 3. Effect of the state-transition threshold t on runtime and message count savings

distance the number of messages may be reduced, but the prediction accuracy generally drops and, thus, DSM protocol activity grows due to unused objects or false sharing. Although $N = 10$ turned out in our measurements to be a reasonable trade-off, a static N is not the best prefetching distance for all applications.

Hence, an automatic adjustment of the prefetching distance N is desired. The local node sends out prefetches to remote nodes and counts how many objects are sent back as an answer (mispredictions are possible, causing the remote node to ignore the request). N is doubled if the number of received objects is higher than 75% of the number of requests. It is decreased by two thirds if less than 25% of the objects arrive. Otherwise, the distance remains unchanged. Over time, N stabilizes for applications with stable memory access behavior.

We tested different techniques that generally converged to the same values but not at the same speed. We also have tested the effect of N if adjusted for each individual access check. The proposed solution with N adjusted globally is the one that gave the best results on average for all benchmarks. For brevity, we only present the best solution, but omit benchmarks.

4 Performance

To evaluate the performance of our automatic optimizer, we measured the performance of four benchmarks. They represent classes of applications with different DSM communication patterns. The selection represents applications that use general-purpose DSMs. We evaluate the benchmarks on a cluster of Xeon 3.2 GHz nodes (2 GB memory, Linux kernel 2.6.20.14, Gigabit Ethernet).

The state-transition threshold t represents the number of executions of an access check required before a decision is made. Fig. 3 shows the effect of t on runtimes and message counts, printing relative savings compared to the uninstrumented 4-node execution. For brevity, we only show results for Blur2D. Small thresholds increase message counts and runtimes, as access checks pollute the prediction model when sent to *Prefetching* too early; many transitions also cause runtime penalties. Increasing t, speed-ups are observed as only beneficial access checks are prefetched. Further increases of the threshold deteriorate performance, as the profiler promotes fewer access checks to *Prefetching*. We use $t = 100$ for the evaluation, since it is the best solution.

Table 1. Number of access checks in various states

	Total number of access checks	No. of access checks that once have reached the Model Creation state	No. of access checks that once have reached the Prefetching state	No. of access checks that once have reached the Waiting state
SOR	10	4	4	0
Water	75	32	27	6
Blur2D	9	3	2	1
Ray	6	2	2	0

Table 2. Runtimes and message counts for the benchmarks (best in bold)

	Nodes	Runtime (in seconds)				Messages (in thousands)			
		w/o	manual	DyCo	Dyn. N	w/o	manual	DyCo	Dyn. N
SOR	2	24.3	24.2	25.5	**23.3**	27.6	6.0	10.4	**5.1**
	4	14.4	**13.5**	13.9	13.8	83.6	17.7	31.6	**14.8**
	6	13.1	12.1	11.6	**11.4**	139.7	30.2	53.3	**26.0**
	8	12.0	11.0	11.1	**10.2**	195.8	42.3	74.2	**34.4**
Water	2	122.6	110.4	99.8	**90.4**	1696.1	1024.7	1079.4	**852.4**
	4	73.0	66.82	63.0	**56.9**	2909.3	1748.7	1774.1	**1354.1**
	6	71.7	56.76	55.8	**48.7**	3639.9	2194.8	2147.9	**1567.8**
	8	66.6	53.47	53.2	**46.0**	4248.0	2543.3	2530.7	**1804.5**
Blur2D	2	10.3	**3.5**	4.6	4.7	224.2	**33.5**	129.2	129.2
	4	6.9	4.1	4.6	**2.5**	386.3	100.3	134.9	**46.2**
	6	8.3	5.3	4.1	**2.4**	484.0	166.1	146.5	**51.5**
	8	10.1	8.3	4.8	**2.7**	583.2	233.2	166.0	**60.6**
Ray	2	44.8	45.3	**44.7**	44.9	9.1	5.9	4.7	**3.1**
	4	22.7	22.6	22.7	**22.4**	27.3	17.1	14.1	**9.3**
	6	15.6	**15.4**	15.6	15.8	45.6	28.6	23.6	**15.6**
	8	13.1	13.0	**12.4**	12.9	64.3	46.3	33.5	**22.1**

Table 1 shows how many access checks are in the codes. Only a few of them actually reach the *Prefetching* state, i.e., the profiling code is replaced by prefetches. In two benchmarks, no access checks were sent to *Waiting*, because they were not executed often enough.

Table 2 lists runtimes and message counts. It shows unmodified benchmarks (w/o), with manually added prefetches, with dynamic optimization ($DyCo$), and with automatic distance adjustment ($DynN$). The runtimes of $DynN$ are best in most cases. Otherwise they closely match the results of manual prefetching.

SOR iteratively solves discrete Laplace equations on a 2D grid by averaging four neighboring points for a grid point's new value (5,000×5,000 points, 50 iterations). The threads receive contiguous partitions of grid rows and communicate reading boundary points of another thread, forming a well-formed, regular data access pattern. Although compilers for array-based languages could statically add prefetches to the compiled code, it is instructive to investigate SOR.

SOR's threads access a small working-set; only four of ten access checks qualify for prefetching. Our automatic system roughly saves 82% of the messages for eight nodes and is slightly better than manual prefetching. Because of the small working-set, a prefetcher cannot improve performance much. Comparing to *DyCo*, the dynamic adaptation of the prefetching distance reduces the message count by 50%. Although all three setups reduce the message count by at least 62% compared to the setup without optimization, runtime is not significantly improved. SOR's computation clearly dominates the average message latency, so that saving messages does not actually pay off in a runtime reduction.

Water is part of the SPLASH benchmark suite [17] and was ported to an object-oriented Java version. Water performs an n-body, n-square simulation of 1,728 water molecules, which are represented by objects that hold the velocity and acceleration vectors. The work is divided by assigning molecules to different threads. Threads repeatedly simulate a single time step of ten (by computing new velocity and acceleration vectors for their molecules) and publish new molecule states by means of a simultaneous update at a collective synchronization point.

Our system selects 32 out of 75 access checks for model creation; only 27 are suited for prefetching. The additional messages (manual vs. DyCo) remain mostly unnoticed in the runtimes. When our optimizer automatically selects the prefetching distance ($N = 70$ instead of $N = 10$), the in-transit messages are reduced by roughly 57% on eight nodes, giving a speed-up of almost 31%.

Blur2D softens a picture of 400×400 points over 20 iterations. The picture is stored as a 2D array of `doubles` describing the pixels' gray values. Similar to an SOR stencil, a pixel's value is averaged over the old value and the values of eight neighboring pixels. Prefetching is difficult because the work distribution does not fit the DSM's data distribution scheme. While Jackal favors *row-wise* distribution schemes, Blur2D uses a *column-wise* work distribution. Hence, false sharing and irregular access patterns make Blur2D highly network-bound.

This is directly reflected by Blur2D's poor speed-up behavior. The runtime increases if the node count exceeds four nodes. Blur2D has a very small working-set that makes monitoring access checks difficult. Hence, the manual placement wins for small node counts both in terms of message counts and runtime. For larger node counts the optimizer beats the manual setup. With increasing node counts, Blur2D causes more and more false sharing and the optimizer gathers more data about failing access checks. Thus, it is able to turn off the ones that are too costly. This results in a runtime gain of roughly 73% on eight nodes.

Ray is a simple raytracing application that renders a 3D scene with 2,000 randomly placed spheres. The image is stored as a 2D array of 500×500 RGB values and is divided into distinct areas that are assigned to the threads. As raytracing is embarrassingly parallel, no communication occurs except for the initial distribution of the scenery and the final composition of the finished image. Because of the absence of communication, prefetching should not help much.

Ray's working-set is large enough to allow for message savings. The optimizer identifies two access checks, enabling prefetching for them. This results in a reduction of messages of roughly 65% (48% without adaptation of the prefetching distance). However, this reduction again does not gain any speed-up, as the computational effort completely hides the savings of a few thousands of messages.

5 Related Work

Let us focus dynamic optimizers and prefetching solutions. For brevity, we skip related work in the field of DSM implementation techniques.

Lu et al. [12,13] implemented a dynamic optimizer that inserts prefetching instructions into the instruction stream. Using Itanium performance counters, the system works on available hot trace information and detects delinquent loads in loop nests. Our implementation detects hot traces automatically as it starts from monitoring access checks and only replaces access checks that are likely to benefit from prefetching; explicit hot trace information is not needed.

Dynamic frameworks such as DynamoRIO [4] interpret the application code at runtime, search for hot traces, and optimize the application. UMI [18] uses DynamoRIO to implement a lightweight system that profiles and optimizes programs. DynamoRIO selects program traces and UMI gathers memory reference profiles. The profiles are used to simulate the cache behavior and to selects delinquent loads. UMI also integrates a simple stride prefetching solution into the framework. Since these optimization systems are trace-based systems, an optimization leads to modifications of a set of basic blocks. In contrast, our system handles each access check independently. This enables our system to de-instrument individual access checks that are not profitable and to avoid performance losses due to monitoring single, unprofitable access checks.

Chilimbi/Hirzel's framework [5] samples the program's execution to decide what portions of the code should be optimized. Using the Vulcan [15] editor for IA-32 binaries, it creates two versions of each function. While both contain the original code, one also contains instrumented code and the other is augmented with instrumentation checks. A state machine decides the state of functions at runtime. To lower the overhead, states are globally frozen. We also use state freezing to avoid thrashing of access checks by keeping states fixed over time. We employ state machines to switch between different types of access checks, but we consider each access check independently. This gives finer control over which access checks undergo state transitions and which states are kept fixed.

Finally, being a well-known technique, we only cover a short selection of prefetching techniques for S-DSMs. Adaptive++ [3] and JIAJIA [11] use lists of past memory accesses to predict, while Delphi [14] uses as a prediction table a hash over the last three accesses. An inspector/executor pattern determines future accesses in an OpenMP DSM [8]. These predictors prefetch asynchronously, which gives not enough overlap to hide the high network latencies in object-based DSMs. Stride predictors [7] do not fit either, as they cannot handle the complex memory access patterns of object-based DSMs (which also is a problem for page-based predictors). In contrast to our system, the predictors cannot temporarily be turned off if the prediction accuracy drops.

6 Conclusions

We have shown that it is worthwhile to integrate an automatic dynamic optimizer into object-based S-DSMs. With binary rewriting techniques, superfluous or unprofitable monitoring or prefetching calls can be removed. Measurements show that, on average, performance improves by 18% when binary rewriting based on a state machine is used to automatically place the prefetching access checks; the message count drops by 52%. The dynamic adjustment of the prefetching distance saves 26% of the runtime and decreases the number of messages by 70%. In total, we have achieved runtime improvements of up to 73% on the benchmarks.

We are currently working on an automatic system that automates every prefetching aspect, from the choice of the predictor to the values of the prefetch distance and the threshold value, thus becoming totally transparent to the user.

References

1. TOP500 List (November 2007), http://www.top500.org/
2. Begleiter, R., El-Yaniv, R., Yona, G.: On Prediction Using Variable Order Markov Models. Journal of Artificial Intelligence Research 22, 385–421 (2004)
3. Bianchini, R., Pinto, R., Amorim, C.L.: Data Prefetching for Software DSMs. In: Intl. Conf. on Supercomputing, Melbourne, Australia, pp. 385–392 (July 1998)
4. Bruening, D., Garnett, T., Amarasinghe, S.: An Infrastructure for Adaptive Dynamic Optimization. In: Intl. Symp. on Code Generation and Optimization, San Francisco, CA, pp. 265–275 (March 2003)
5. Chilimbi, T.M., Hirzel, M.: Dynamic Hot Data Stream Prefetching for General-Purpose Programs. In: ACM SIGPLAN 2002 Conf. on Programming Language Design and Implementation, Berlin, Germany, pp. 199–209 (June 2002)
6. MPI Forum. MPI-2: Extensions to the Message-Passing Interface. Technical report, MPI Forum (July 1997)
7. Fu, J.W.C., Patel, J.H., Janssens, B.L.: Stride Directed Prefetching in Scalar Processors. SIGMICRO Newsletter 23(1-2), 102–110 (1992)
8. Jeun, W.-C., Kee, Y.-S., Ha, S.: Improving Performance of OpenMP for SMP Clusters through Overlapping Page Migrations. In: Intl. Workshop on OpenMP, Reims, France, June 2006, CD-ROM (2006)
9. Joseph, D., Grunwald, D.: Prefetching Using Markov Predictors. IEEE Transactions on Computers 48(2), 121–133 (1999)
10. Klemm, M., Beyler, J.C., Lampert, R.T., Philippsen, M., Clauss, P.: Esodyp+: Prefetching in the Jackal Software DSM. In: Kermarrec, A.-M., Bougé, L., Priol, T. (eds.) Euro-Par 2007. LNCS, vol. 4641, pp. 563–573. Springer, Heidelberg (2007)
11. Liu, H., Hu, W.: A Comparison of Two Strategies of Dynamic Data Prefetching in Software DSM. In: 15th Intl. Parallel & Distributed Processing Symp., San Francisco, CA, pp. 62–67 (April 2001)
12. Lu, J., Chen, H., Fu, R., Hsu, W., Othmer, B., Yew, P., Chen, D.: The Performance of Runtime Data Cache Prefetching in a Dynamic Optimization System. In: 36th Ann. IEEE/ACM Intl. Symp. on Microarchitecture, San Diego, CA, pp. 180–190 (December 2003)
13. Lu, J., Chen, H., Yew, P.-C., Hsu, W.-C.: Design and Implementation of a Lightweight Dynamic Optimization System. Journal of Instruction-Level Parallelism 6 (April 2004) (Online)

14. Speight, E., Burtscher, M.: Delphi: Prediction-Based Page Prefetching to Improve the Performance of Shared Virtual Memory Systems. In: Intl. Conf. on Parallel and Distributed Processing Techniques and Applications, Las Vegas, NV, pp. 49–55 (June 2002)
15. Srivastava, A., Edwards, A., Vo, H.: Vulcan: Binary Transformation in a Distributed Environment. Technical Report MSR-TR-2001-50, Microsoft Research (April 2001)
16. Veldema, R., Hofman, R.F.H., Bhoedjang, R.A.F., Bal, H.E.: Runtime Optimizations for a Java DSM Implementation. In: ACM-ISCOPE Conf. on Java Grande, Palo Alto, CA, pp. 153–162 (June 2001)
17. Woo, S.C., Ohara, M., Torrie, E., Singh, J.P., Gupta, A.: The SPLASH-2 Programs: Characterization and Methodological Considerations. In: 22nd Intl. Symp. on Computer Architecture, St. Margherita Ligure, Italy, pp. 24–36 (June 1995)
18. Zhao, Q., Rabbah, R., Amarasinghe, S., Rudolph, L., Wong, W.-F.: Ubiquitous Memory Introspection. In: Intl. Symp. on Code Generation and Optimization, San Jose, CA, pp. 299–311 (March 2007)

A PGAS-Based Algorithm for the Longest Common Subsequence Problem

M. Bakhouya, O. Serres, and T. El-Ghazawi

High Performance Computing Laboratory,
George Washington University
bakhouya@gmail.com

Abstract. Finding the Longest Common Subsequence (LCS) is a traditional and well studied problem in bioinformatics and text editing. In this paper, a customized parallel algorithm based on the Partitioned Global Address Space (PGAS) programming model to compute the LCS is presented. The algorithm is based on two related parameters balancing the communication and the synchronization needs in order to find the best data and workload distributions. The basic design of the algorithm and its complexity analysis are discussed together with experimental results. These results show the impact of those parameters on PGAS algorithm performance.

Keywords: Parallel computing, Longest common subsequence, Partitioned Global Address Space, Unified Parallel C (UPC), Complexity design and analysis.

1 Introduction

Sequences comparison and sequence database searching have played a crucial role in biological research advancements. When biologists discover a new sequence, they are interested in predicting its function, its structure, and its evolutionary history [1], [2]. To do this prediction, a search in a known sequences' database is required to find sequences that are similar. However, today growth of sequences' database makes the search and the sequence comparison a big challenge. Sequence comparison process can be composed into two fundamental phases: the similarity phase and the alignment phase. In the first phase, a metric that measures the syntactic difference between two sequences should be calculated. In the second phase, the cost of additions, deletions, and substitutions required to match one sequence to another is measured. In this paper, we focus on the similarity phase and we consider that one way of detecting the similarity of two or more sequences is to find their LCS (Longest Common Sequence) before starting aligns them.

In the literature, many papers state that this problem can be solved with sequential algorithm in $O(nm)$ computation time using $O(nm)$ memory space by using the dynamic programming technique, where n and m are the size of the considered sequences [3], [4]. For the LCS problem with long sequences, the dynamic programming technique is computationally prohibitive [5]. To reduce this complexity, many parallel algorithms have been proposed [1], [4], [5].

Parallel algorithms, proposed in the literature, can be classified into two categories: fine-grain algorithms and coarse-grain algorithms. Fine grain algorithms are based on PRAM (Parallel Random Access Machine) model as described in [4]. However, in general, PRAM algorithms assume that the number of processors required should be in the same order of the problem size. For example, in [6] a $O(\log m \log n)$ time algorithm using $O(mn/\log m)$ processors is proposed. Another algorithm with a time complexity of $O(\log^2 n + \log m)$ using $O(mn/\log m)$ is proposed in [7]. Unlike fine-grain algorithms, coarse-grain algorithms use BSP/CGM (Bulk Synchronous Parallel/Coarse Grained Multicomputer) model to map very well on existing parallel machines. Coarse-grain algorithms assume that the number of processors p and the size of the problem n are not in the same order, i.e., $p \ll n$, and each processor contains $O(n/p)$ local memory [8], [9]. These processors are connected through any interconnection network and communicate by sending messages in a point-to-point manner. BSP/CGM computational model can be also used to predict the performances of the algorithms when implemented on a distributed memory machine [10]. One of efficient BSP/CGM based parallel dynamic programming algorithm is proposed in [8] for string editing problem with the main goal to minimize the communication complexity. An extension of this algorithm, by the same authors, for biological sequence comparison is proposed in [5]. This extended algorithm, called a *parallel wavefront algorithm*, is based on parameterized scheduling scheme to compromise between the workload of each processor and the number of communication rounds required.

In this paper, customized parallel algorithm based on the Partitioned Global Address Space (PGAS) programming model and inspired by the parallel wavefront algorithm to compute the LCS is presented. Recall that many new PGAS programming languages have recently emerged and are becoming ubiquitously available on almost parallel architectures. PGAS programming languages provide ease-of-use through a global shared address space while emphasizing performance by providing locality awareness and a partition of the address space [11]. Examples of PGAS languages include the Unified Parallel C (UPC), Co-array Fortran, and Titanium languages. PGAS programming model provides two major characteristics namely data partition and the locality that should be used to reduce the communication overhead and get better performance [12], [13]. UPC is one of partitioned global address space programming language based on C and extended with global pointers and data distribution declarations for shared data [11], [14]. The rest of the paper is organized as follows. In section 2, the PGAS-based algorithm to solve the LCS problem is presented together with its complexity analysis. Experimental results are given in section 3. Conclusions and future work are presented in section 4.

2 A PGAS-Based Algorithm

The sequential LCS algorithm takes two input sequences $X(1..m-1)$ and $Y(1..n-1)$, which their elements are in the alphabet Φ that contains s number of symbols (e.g., $\Phi = \{A, C, G, T\}$, s=4) [4], [15]. A common subsequence of X and Y is a sequence which occurs in both sequences X and Y [3], [16]. The longest common subsequence of sequences X and Y, denoted by LCS(X, Y) is a common subsequence of maximal length, denoted by lcs(X,Y). The traditional algorithms for solving the longest common subsequence use a dynamic programming method in two phases. The first phase builds a similarity matrix C by searching all identical pairs. The similarity matrix C is a two-dimensional table of size $m \times n$ and each $C[i][j]$ is computed as follows [3].

$$C[i][j] = \begin{cases} 0 & \text{if } i = 0 \lor j = 0 \\ C[i-1][j-1]+1 & \text{if } X[i] = Y[j] \\ \max\{C[i-1][j], C[i][j-1]\} & \text{if } X[i] \neq Y[j] \end{cases}$$

The function that computes the value of each $C[i][j]$ is named *Compute(C[i][j])* in the rest of this document. The second phase uses a backtracing method to get the lcs(X,Y). The backtracing phase starts from $C[m-1][,n-1]$ and traverse a path through the table until it reaches $C[0][k]$ or $C[k][0]$, where $k \geq 0$, and then the trail indicates the LCS(X, Y).

In this section, a PGAS-based algorithm for computing the similarity between two sequences X and Y, over some alphabet Φ is presented. Alike the sequential algorithm, two phases are considered in the PGAS-based algorithm: the matrix building phase and the backtracing phase as described in next sections.

2.1 The Building Phase

The algorithm that builds the similarity matrix takes two inputs, the sequence X of size $n-1$ and the sequence Y of size $m-1$, where $m \leq n$, and produces as an output the similarity matrix of size $n \times m$. It is worth noting that instead of building a matrix of size $m \times n$, used in the sequential and parallel wavefront algorithm, we use a matrix of size $n \times m$. The data distribution mechanism used in this algorithm is as follows. The sequence Y is local to each thread, i.e., each thread has a copy of the Y. The sequence X is distributed in *round robin manner* to all threads. More precisely, this distribution assigns $\alpha n/T$ elements of X to each threads, where T is the number of threads or processors and α is an adjustment factor that allows the load balancing between threads as described in [5]. The matrix C is distributed in *round robin manner* by block of $\alpha nm/T$ elements. We consider that each thread can be executed in one processor with $O(nm/p)$ memory space, where p is the number of processors. Unlike the algorithm presented in [5] to build the similarity matrix, in this algorithm we use the transpose of this matrix and we add another factor that allows the reduction of the load balancing between threads. Figure 1 shows the general distribution scheme of the workload between threads. In this scheme, we can see for example that in the first steep only the thread T_0 can compute the first sub-matrix. In the second steep, thread T_0 and T_1. In this workload distribution, instead of using a block size of $\alpha nm/p^2$ used in the wavefront algorithm, we have worked with a variable block size of $\alpha \beta nm/T^2$, where T is the number of threads or processors, n and m are the size of the sequences ($m \leq n$).

T_0^0	T_0^1	....	T_0^j	....	$T_0^{T/\beta-1}$
T_1^1	T_1^2	....	T_1^{j+1}	....	$T_0^{T/\beta}$
.	.	.	.	.	.
.	.	.	.	.	.
.	.	.	$m\beta/T$	.	.
T_i^i	T_i^{i+1}	$n\alpha/T$	T_i^{i+j}	....	$T_i^{i+T/\beta-1}$
.	.	.	.	.	.
.	.	.	.	.	.
.	.	.	.	.	.
$T_{T-1}^{T/\alpha-1}$	$T_{T-1}^{T/\alpha}$	....	$T_{T-1}^{T/\alpha+j-1}$	....	$T_{T-1}^{T/\alpha+T/\beta-2}$

Fig. 1. A general distribution scheme of the workload between threads

The PGAS-based algorithm to compute the similarity matrix is as follows:

Computing the similarity matrix

Input: the sequence X of size $n-1$, and the sequence Y of size $m-1$, α and β
Output: the $n \times m$ similarity matrix C
// Initialization process
$nextR_{T_k} \leftarrow T_k \times \alpha n/T$ // the row to be computed by the thread T_k
$C[i][0] \leftarrow 0$, $0 \leq i < m$
$C[0][j] \leftarrow 0$, $0 \leq j < n$
for $i \leftarrow 1$ to n-1, *affinity* parallel do //the elements of C are initialized by threads that have affinity with
    for $j \leftarrow 1$ to m-1 do
        $C[i][j] \leftarrow Nil$
    endfor
endfor
// Computing process
while($nextR_{T_k} < n$) do
    $nextC_{T_k} \leftarrow 0$ // each thread starts at the beginning from the column 0
    while($nextC_{T_k} < m$) do
        for $i \leftarrow nextR_{T_k}$ to $nextR_{T_k} + (\alpha n/T) - 1$ do
            if $i = nextR_{T_k} \wedge i \neq 0$ then
                wait until all $C[i-1][j] \neq Nil$, for all $nextC_{T_k} \leq j < nextC_{T_k} + (\beta m/T)$
            end if
            for $j \leftarrow nextC_{T_k}$ to $(\beta m/T) - 1$ and $j \neq 0$ do
                Compute(C[i][j]) // the function that modifies the value of C[i][j]
            endfor
        endfor
        $lastR_{T_k} \leftarrow nextC_{T_k}$ // used in the backtracing phase
        $nextC_{T_k} \leftarrow nextC_{T_k} + (\beta m/T)$ // the next column from it the thread T_k starts computing
    endwhile
    $nextR_{T_k} \leftarrow nextR_{T_k} + (n/\alpha)$ // the next row from it the thread T_k starts the computation
endwhile
return C

To illustrate this algorithm, let us consider an example that computes the similarity matrix of the sequence $X=$"GAATTCAGTTA" and the sequence $Y=$ "GGATCGA". Let us consider, for example, that the number of threads is equal to 2 ($T=2$), $\alpha = 2$ and $\beta = 2$. In figure 2, the blocks are computed simultaneously, i.e., in the same step. Note also that the elements of this matrix are note necessarily similar to the elements of the matrix used usually in sequential and parallel wavefront algorithm, but the lcs(X, Y) is similar. This matrix is the transpose of the matrix used in the sequential dynamic programming algorithm.

	X\Y			G	G	A	T	C	G	A
			0	1	2	3	4	5	6	7
		0	0	0	0	0	0	0	0	0
T_0	G	1	0	1	1	1	1	1	1	1
	A	2	0	1	1	2	2	2	2	2
	A	3	0	1	1	2	2	2	2	3
T_1	T	4	0	1	1	2	3	3	3	3
	T	5	0	1	1	2	3	3	3	3
	C	6	0	1	1	2	3	4	4	4
T_0	A	7	0	1	1	2	3	4	4	5
	G	8	0	1	2	2	3	4	5	5
	T	9	0	1	2	2	3	4	5	5
T_1	T	10	0	1	2	2	3	4	5	5
	A	11	0	1	2	3	3	4	5	6

Fig. 2. The similarity matrix and the selected path that represents the longest common subsequence of X and Y

In order to calculate the complexity of this algorithm, the complexity model presented in [13] is used. In this algorithm, the number of operations computed by all threads is $O(nm)$. Since the matrix C is distributed equally between the threads, the computation complexity of the algorithm is $O(nm/T)$. According to the data distribution used in the algorithm, at each phase each thread computes two remote memory requests to get the value of $C[i-1][j-1]$, and $C[i-1][j]$ for all j in $\{1..m-1\}$. Then the total communication complexity of the algorithm is $O((T/\alpha - 1)m)$. Since the matrix T is distributed equally between all threads, the communication complexity of each thread is $O((T/\alpha - 1)m/T)$. To calculate the total synchronization complexity of the algorithm, we compute the idle times of all threads. We calculate first the number of operations that the first thread wait before starting the computation, following by that of the second thread and so on. The thread T_0 starts computing immediately without waiting. The thread T_1 starts after the execution of $\alpha\beta nm/T^2$ operations by the thread T_0. The thread T_2 starts after the execution of $2\alpha\beta nm/T^2$ operations by T_0 and T_1,..., and the thread T_{T-1} starts after the execution of $(T-1)\alpha\beta nm/T^2$ operations by T_0, T_1, ..., and T_{T-2}. Therefore, the total of the number operations that represents the idle period that all threads are waiting is $(1+2+...+(T-1))\alpha\beta nm/T^2 = (T-1)\alpha\beta nm/2T$ and this represents the idle time of the thread T_{T-1} since it is the last thread starting the computation. Hence, the synchronization complexity of the algorithm is $O((T-1)\alpha\beta nm/T^2)$. Note that in the other $\alpha-1$ steps (see figure 2), threads can compute without waiting and this represents the main advantage of this load balancing technique. For example, when $\alpha = \beta = 1$ the thread T_{T-1} starts computing after the thread T_0 is almost finishing all its computation. Therefore, this is leads to a poor work balance. To obtain a good work balance, a load balancing scheme that attributes work to each thread as soon as possible is required. This scheme can be obtained by decreasing the values of the parameters α and β. However, according to the communication and the synchronization complexities, decreasing the value α leads to a decrease of the synchronization complexity and an increase of the communication complexity. To illustrate this point, figures 3 (a) and (b) show the number of operations (computation, memory requests) versus α (1/2, 1/4, 1/8, 1/16, 1/32, 1/64, 1/28, 1/256), using 8 threads respectively, where $\beta = 1$, $n=2048$, $m=1024$. The intersection point of the communication curve and the synchronization curve gives the best value of α that minimizes the communication complexity and the synchronization complexity. For example, in figure 3 (a), when the value of β is fixed to 1, the best value of α is 1/16.

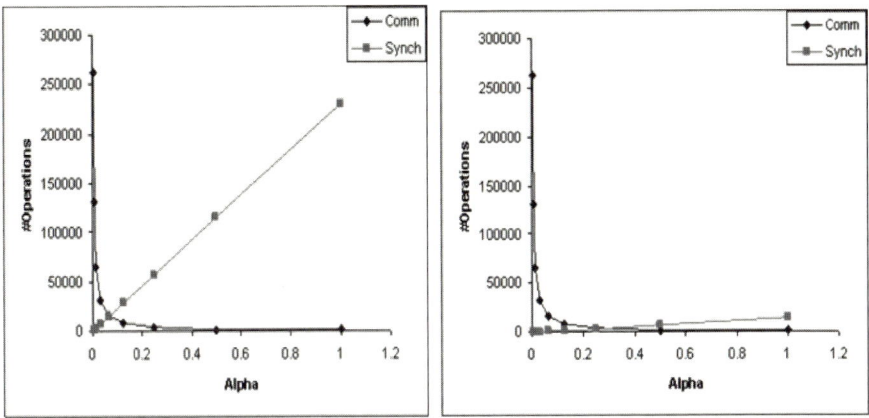

Fig. 3. (a) The number of operations (a) vs. α with fixed value of β ($\beta = 1$), (b) vs., α and the value of beta is equal to 1/16. T is fixed to 8

It should be noted that α and β are not independent. Since both of them influence the synchronization complexity, their values should be chosen simultaneously. To illustrate this point let us consider that the number of threads is equal to 8. Figure 3(b) shows that the best value of α that minimizes simultaneously the communication and the synchronization complexities is 1/4, where the value of β is fixed to 1/16. It is worth noting that small values of α and β allows threads to starts early, but very small value of α will incur a high number of requests to remote shared space.

2.2 The Backtracing Phase

After building the similarity matrix, it is possible to use one thread to compute the LCS. However, using one thread to do that can lead to a bad performance because of the higher number of requests to the remote shared memory required to get all elements that are not local to it. To avoid this problem, all threads can compute a part of the LCS locally but in sequential manner as shown in the algorithm described below. The thread T_{T-1} starts to compute the LCS at $C[n-1][m-1]$ and stops when the row ($lastR_{T_{T-1}} - \alpha n/T$) or the column 0 is reached. In this case, by updating the values of $nextR$ and giving the next column $nextC$ to be computed, the thread T_{T-2} can start to compute from $C[nextR][nextC]$. Note that $nextC$ and $nextR$ are shared variables between threads and by changing their values gives the hand to another thread to start computing on its block. This process is repeated until the LCS is found ($nextR \le 0$). To illustrate this phase, figure 2 shows the path computed and the values of C that represents the matches between the two sequences in bold font. While this matrix is the transpose of the matrix obtained by the dynamic programming technique described above, the result found is similar. Note also that the technique used parallel wavefront algorithm to do the backtracing phase is described [5].

Computing the LCS
Input: the sequences X and Y, and the similarity matrix C
Output: the $LCS(X, Y)$, i.e., the set L. The elements of L are initialized to Nil.
if($T_k = T-1$) then
    $nextR \leftarrow lastR_{T_k}$ // $nextR$ is a shared variable that takes the value of last row computed by
                                   // T_k in the first phase
    $nextC \leftarrow$ m-1 // the next column to be computed
endif
while($nextR > 0$) do
    wait until getting the starting row from the thread T_{k+1}, i.e., $nextR = lastR_{T_k}$
    $j \leftarrow nextC$; $i \leftarrow nextR$
    while ($i \ge (lastR_{T_k} - (\alpha n/T) + 1) \land j > 0$) do
        if($i \ne 0$) then
            Select (i, j) // function allowing the selection of the next cell
        else
            $i \leftarrow$ i-1
        endif
    endwhile
    $nextR \leftarrow i$; $nextC \leftarrow j$
endwhile
$lastR_{T_k} \leftarrow lastR_{T_k} - \alpha n$
return LCS(X, Y)

The total operations computed by all threads is $O(n+m)$. Since the matrix C is distributed equally between the threads, the computation complexity of the LCS algorithm is $O((n+m)/T)$. According to the data distribution used in the algorithm, at each phase, each thread computes two remote memory accesses to get the value of

$C[i-1][j-1]$, and $C[i-1][j]$ for all j in $\{1..m-1\}$. To determine the number of requests to the remote space, we consider the worst case where there is just one match in the given sequences and this match occurs in the last rows computed by the thread T_{T-1}, and more precisely in the row that follows its starting points. In this case, during the backtracing phase, when the thread T_{T-1} encounters this match, it starts computing the first row in the boundary with the thread T_{T-2}. Since there is no match, T_{T-1} goes through this row, by accessing, each time, the row that is local to T_{T-2}, until it reaches the first column. Hence, the worst case communication complexity for this thread is $O(m/T)$. In the same manner, the synchronization complexity is $O(\alpha n/T + m)$. According to the complexities of these two algorithms (the building phase and the backtracing phase), the total computation, communication, and synchronization complexity is $O(nm/T)$, $O(T/\alpha)$, and $O((T-1)\alpha\beta nm/T^2 + \alpha n/T + m)$ respectively. Hence, the PGAS speedup can be expressed as follows:

$$PGAS_{speedup} = O(T/(1 + (1 + 1/\alpha)T/n + (T-1)\alpha\beta/T + \alpha/m)).$$

3 Experimental Results

The PGAS-based algorithm to perform the longest common subsequence is implemented using UPC. More precisely, the experiments were done using the GCC UPC toolset running on Origin 2000 with 16 processors. The GCC UPC toolset provides a compilation and execution environment for programs written in the UPC language. The SGI Origin 2000 platform consists of 16 SGI R10000 processors and 16GB of SDRAM interconnected with a high speed cache coherent Non Uniform Memory Access (ccNUMA) link in hypercube architecture. In the experimentation, two sequences X and Y with size 2048 and 1024 respectively are considered. The elements of these sequences are generated randomly from the alphabet $\phi = \{A, G, C, T\}$. Figure 4 (a) shows the speedup versus several values of α (1, 1/2, 1/4, 1/8, 1/16, 1/32) and a fixed value of β ($\beta = 1$) when running the program using 2, 4, and 8 threads. The result depicted in this figure shows, in one hand, that as we increase the number of threads the program performs better by giving a better speedup. In the other hand, independent of the number of threads used, the highest speedup is obtained with a small value of α. More precisely, the speedup increases when the value of α is very small to reach the higher value when α is equal to a certain threshold and decreases after this threshold. Figure 4 (b) presents the theoretical speedup of this algorithm with several values of α (1, 1/2, 1/4, 1/8, 1/16, 1/32, 1/64, 1/128, 1/256) and by varying the number of threads (2, 4, and 8). In these theoretical results the value of β is fixed to 1. The objective here is to show the similitude between the behavior predicted by the theoretical studies and the behavior from the experimental studies. More precisely, alike the experimental result shown in the figure 4 (a), the speedup increases when the value of α is very small to reach the higher value when α is equal to a certain threshold and decreases after this threshold.

Until now, we only have studied the behavior of α to estimate the optimal block size with the value β fixed to 1. According to the complexity analysis presented above, this value influences only the synchronization complexity. Therefore, the selection of the best value α must be done by also taking into consideration the possible values of β. To illustrate this point, let us consider now a fixed number of threads, 8. Figure 5 (a) presents the variation of the speedup versus α with several values of β (1, 1/2, 1/4, 1/8, 1/16). The same behavior like in figures 4 (a) and (b) is shown, but with different values of higher speedup ((α,β)=(1/4, 1/16)). The objective here is to select the couple (α,β) that gives the highest speedup. From the theoretical result depicted in the figure 5 (b), we show that the best values of (α,β) are (1/4, 1/16).

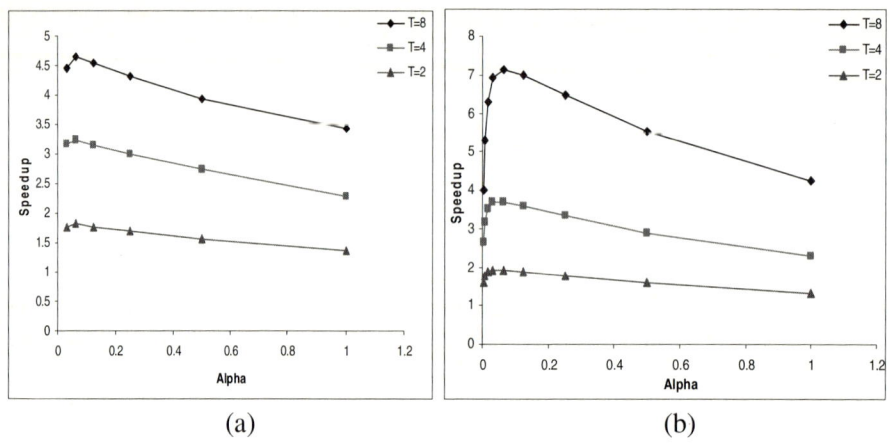

Fig. 4. (a) Experimental, (b) theoretical speedup vs. α using 2, 4, and 8 threads

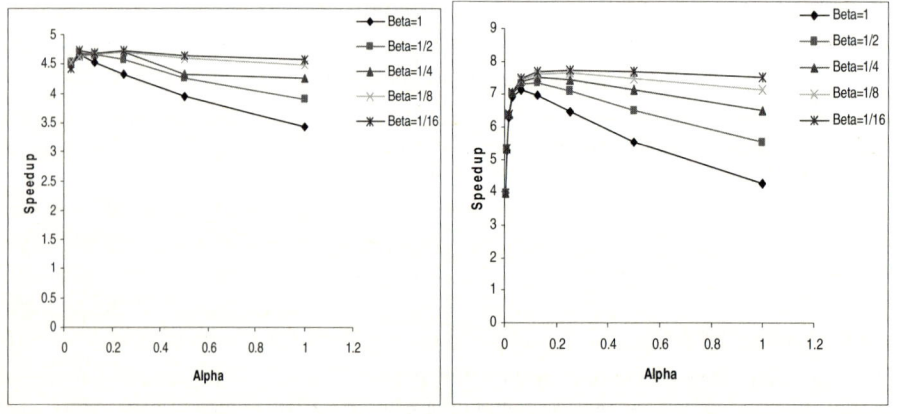

Fig. 5. (a) Experimental, (b) theoretical speedup vs. α by varying β

4 Conclusion and Future Work

In this paper, a PGAS-based algorithm to compute the longest common subsequence is presented. The performance of the algorithm is based on two tuning parameters α and β that can ensure the optimal data and workload distributions. The programmer should select empirically best values for α and β to minimize the communication and the synchronization complexities. Future work addresses an analytical model for the α and β selection issue. In addition, the algorithm will be extended to the LCS computation of multiple sequences together with additional experiments on other platforms.

References

1. Yap, T.K., Frieder, O., Martino, R.L.: Parallel Computation in Biological Sequence Analysis. IEEE Transactions on Parallel and Distributed Systems 9(3), 283–294 (1998)
2. YarKhan, A., Dongarra, J.: Biological Sequence Alignment on the Computational Grid Using the GrADS Framework. Future Generation Computer Systems 21(6), 980–986 (2005)
3. Bergroth, L., Hakonen, H., Raita, T.: A Survey of Longest Common Subsequence Algorithms. In: Proc. 7th Internat. Symp. On String Processing Information Retrieval (SPIRE 2000), pp. 39–48 (2000)
4. Chen, Y., Wan, A., Liu, W.: A fast Parallel Algorithm for Finding the Longest Common Sequence of Multiple Bio-sequences. In: Symposium of Computations in Bioinformatics and Bioscience in conjunction with the International Multi-Symposiums on Computer and Computational Sciences (2006)
5. Alves, C.E.R., Cáceres, E.N., Dehne, F., Song, S.W.: A Parallel Wavefront Algorithm for Efficient Biological Sequence Comparison. In: Kumar, V., Gavrilova, M.L., Tan, C.J.K., L'Ecuyer, P. (eds.) ICCSA 2003. LNCS, vol. 2668, pp. 249–258. Springer, Heidelberg (2003)
6. Apostolico, A., Attalah, M., Lamore, L., Mcfaddin, S.: Efficient Parallel Algorithms for String Editing and Related Problems. SIAM Journal on Computing 19, 968–988 (1990)
7. Lu, M., Lin, H.: Parallel algorithms for the Longest Common Subsequence Problem. IEEE Transaction on Parallel and Distributed System 5, 835–848 (1994)
8. Alves, C.E.R., Cáceres, E.N., Dehne, F.: Parallel Dynamic Programming for Solving the String Editing Problem on a CGM/BSP. In: Proceeding of ACM SPAA, pp. 275–281 (2002)
9. Garcia, T., Myoupo, J.-F., Seme, D.: A Coarse-Grained Multi-computer Algorithm for the Longest Common Subsequence Problem. In: The Euromicro Conference on Parallel Distributed and Network based Processing (PDP 2003) (2003)
10. Valiant, L.G.: A Bridging Model for Parallel Computation. Communication of the ACM 33(8), 103–111 (1990)
11. El-Ghazawi, T., Carlson, W., Sterling, T., Yelick, K.: UPC: Distributed Shared Memory Programming. John Wiley & Sons Inc., New York (2005)
12. Gaber, J.: A Complexity Measure Approach for Partitioned Shared Memory Model, Application to UPC, Research report RR-10-04, Universite de Technologie de Belfort-Montbeliard (2004)

13. Bakhouya, M., Gaber, J., El-Ghazawi, T.: Towards a Complexity Model for Design and Analysis of PGAS-Based Algorithms. In: Perrott, R., Chapman, B.M., Subhlok, J., de Mello, R.F., Yang, L.T. (eds.) HPCC 2007. LNCS, vol. 4782, pp. 672–682. Springer, Heidelberg (2007)
14. Cantonnet, F., El Ghazawi, T., Lorenz, P., Gaber, J.: Fast Address Translation Techniques for Distributed Shared Memory Compilers. In: IPDPS (2006)
15. Pappas, N.P.: Searching Biological Sequence Databases Using Distributed Adaptive Computing. Master of Science in Computer Engineering, Virginia Polytechnic Institute and State University (2003), http://scholar.lib.vt.edu/theses/
16. Wagner, A., Fischer, M.J.: The String-to-String Correction Problem. Journal of the ACM 21(1), 168–173 (1974)

Data Mining Algorithms on the Cell Broadband Engine

Rubing Duan and Alfred Strey

Institute of Computer Science, University of Innsbruck,
Technikerstrasse 21a, A-6020 Innsbruck, Austria
{rubing.duan,alfred.strey}@uibk.ac.at

Abstract. The Cell Broadband Engine (CBE) is a new heterogeneous multi-core processor from IBM, Sony and Toshiba, and provides the potential to achieve an impressive level of performance for data mining algorithms. In this paper, we describe our implementation of three important classes of data mining algorithms: clustering (k-Means), classification (RBF network), and association rule mining (Apriori) on the CBE. We explain our parallelization methodology and describe the exploitation of thread- and data-level parallelism in each of the three algorithms. Finally we present experimental results on the Cell hardware, where we could achieve a high performance of up to 10 GFLOP/s and a speedup of up to 40.

Keywords: Cell Broadband Engine, multi-core, k-Means, RBF, Apriori.

1 Introduction

The rapid evolution in sub-micron process technologies enables the manufacturing of multi-processor system with a large number of processing cores per chip. Such multi-core architectures are mostly built by replicating a standard processor design with its local caches several times and adding an on-chip interconnection network for coupling the cores and the external bus interface. The management of several threads on the available cores is done by the operating system. An alternative solution represents the Cell Processor developed by IBM, Sony and Toshiba [1,2]. Here a simplified PowerPC core (PPU) controls 8 Synergistic Processing Elements (SPEs) that only operate on data read from local stores. The operating system only starts one thread on the PPU; the creation of the SPE threads and all data transfers between PPU and SPEs must be explicitly controlled by the application program. The Cell processor was mainly designed to accelerate multi-media and graphics algorithms, but it is also well suited for various algorithms from other application areas (e.g. digital signal processing, data compression/decompression, data encryption/decryption) [2].

Data mining represents a rather new application area of High Performance Computing (HPC). It mainly deals with the finding of useful patterns in very large data sets. Its algorithms are not only based on standard floating-point calculations, but often operate on simple integer numbers. Three important classes of data mining algorithms exist: classification, clustering and association rule mining. To analyze the suitability of the Cell architecture for such algorithms, a representative algorithm of each of the three classes has been selected and implemented exemplarily on the Cell processor: the k-means algorithm for clustering, a neural network for classification and the Apriori algorithm for association rule mining. The performance of these algorithms on the Cell chip will be analyzed and compared with the performance on Xeon and Opteron.

The rest of this paper is organized as follows: Section 2 describes the architecture of the CBE. In Section 3 we present the data mining algorithms. The optimized algorithms for CBE are presented in Section 4. Experimental results are described in Section 5. We overview the related work in Section 6 and conclusions are drawn in Section 7.

2 The Cell Broadband Engine Architecture

The Cell Broadband Engine architecture was jointly developed by Sony Computer Entertainment, Toshiba, and IBM. Its first commercial application was in Sony's PlayStation 3 game console. The Cell architecture emphasizes efficiency/watt, prioritizes bandwidth over latency, and favors peak computational throughput over simplicity of program code. For these reasons, Cell is widely regarded as a challenging environment for software development.

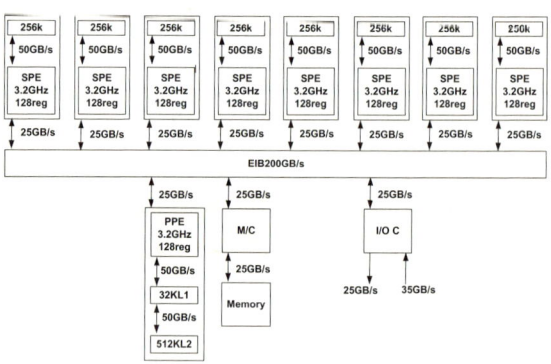

Fig. 1. The architecture of the Cell processor

The Cell processor can be split into four components: external input/output structures, the main processor called the Power Processing Element (PPE) (a two-way simultaneous multithreaded Power ISA v.2.03 compliant core), eight fully-functional co-processors called the Synergistic Processing Elements (SPEs), and a specialized high-bandwidth circular data bus connecting the PPE, input/output elements and the SPEs, called the Element Interconnect Bus (EIB), as depicted in Figure 1. Each SPE can operate in a SIMD-like (Single Instruction, Multiple Data) way on several elements in parallel that are packed into a 128 bit vector. The PPE memory is not shared with the SPEs, all data transfers between SPE and PPE memory are realized by DMA and must be programmed explicitly. The PPE, which is capable of running a conventional operating system, has control over the SPEs and starts, stops, interrupts, and schedules threads running on the SPEs. For the synchronization of threads and for the transfer of short control words a special mailbox system can be used.

Algorithm 1. k-Means

Input: D = Dataset
k = the number of centers
Output: Set of k centroids $c \in C$ representing a good partitioning of D into k clusters

1: Select the initial cluster centroids c
2: **repeat**
3:    changed=0
    // *Find the closest centroid to every data point d ...*
4:    **for all** data point $d_i \in D$ **do**
5:       $assignedCenter = d_i.center$
6:       **for all** center $c_j \in C$ **do**
7:          Compute the squared Euclidean distance $dist = dist(d_i, c_j)$
8:          **if** $dist < d_i.centerDistance$ **then**
9:             $d_i.centerDistance = dist$
10:           $d_i.center = j$
11:          **end if**
12:       **end for**
13:       **if** $d_i.center <> assignedCenter$ **then**
14:          changed++
15:          Recompute $c_j.new$ for next iteration
16:       **end if**
17:    **end for**
18: **until** changed==0

3 Data Mining Algorithms

In this section, we briefly sketch the algorithms under study.

3.1 K-Means Algorithm for Clustering

The k-means algorithm is one of the simplest unsupervised learning algorithms to cluster n objects based on attributes into k partitions, $k < n$. The main idea is to define k centroids, one for each cluster. The next step is to assign each object to the group characterized by the closest centroid. When all objects have been assigned, recalculate the positions of the k centroids. The last steps are repeated until the centroids no longer move. The complete k-means algorithm is presented in Alg. 1.

3.2 RBF Neural Network for Classification

A radial basis function network (RBF) is an artificial neural network model with two layers that is suitable for approximation and classification. It uses neurons with radial basis functions as activation functions in the first (hidden) neuron layer and linear neurons in the output layer. Each RBF neuron j in the hidden layer (see Fig. 2) computes the squared Euclidean distance x_j between an input vector $\mathbf{u}$ and the weight vector c_j (represented by the jth column of a weight matrix C) and applies a radial symmetric output function f (typically a Gaussian function) to x_j. The resulting output $y_j = f(x_j)$ is communicated via weighted links w_{jk} to the linear neurons of the output layer where the sum z_k is calculated.

To achieve good results, the RBF network requires a proper initialization of all weights c_{ij} (e.g. by a clustering algorithm) and of the width σ_j of the Gaussian bells in all RBF neurons (according to the distances between the cluster centers). After the initialization, the network is trained by a gradient descent training algorithm that adapts all wights c_{ij}, w_{ij} and σ_j (the center coordinates, heights and widths of Gaussian bells) according to the error at the network outputs. The complete RBF training algorithm is presented in Alg. 2. Data mining applications can either perform the RBF training itself or a classification of new inputs by an already trained RBF network. In the later case only the forward phase of the algorithm is required.

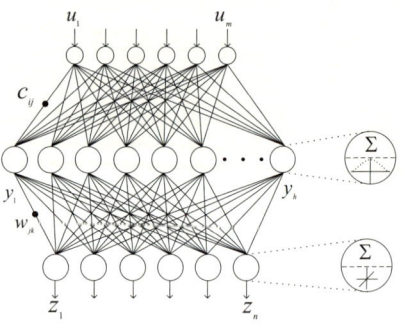

Fig. 2. Architecture of a m–h–n RBF network (with m input nodes, h RBF nodes and n linear outputs nodes)

Algorithm 2. RBF

  Input: Training set of patterns (u, t)
  Output: Trained RBF network with weights c_{ij}, w_{jk} and s_j
1:   Initialize all c_{ij}, w_{jk} and s_j
2:   **for** $loop = 0; loop < max\_iterations$; **do**
3:     Select one pattern u and corresponding output class t
     //Forward phase for classification
4:     $x_j = \sum_{i=1}^{m} (u_i - c_{ij})^2$
5:     $y_j = f(x_j) = e^{-x_j/2\delta^2} = e^{-x_j s_j}$
6:     $z_k = \sum_{j=1}^{h} y_j w_{jk}$
     //Backward phase for training
7:     $\delta_k^z = t_k - z_k$
8:     $\delta_j^y = \sum_{k=1}^{n} \delta_k^z w_{jk}$
9:     $s_j = s_j - \eta_s x_j y_j \delta_j^y$
10:    $w_{jk} = w_{jk} + \eta_w y_j \delta_k^z$
11:    $c_{ij} = c_{ij} + \eta_c (u_i - c_{ij}) \delta_j^y y_j s_j$
12: **end for**

Algorithm 3. Apriori

Input: D: database over the set of items $\jmath$,
Output: F: the set of frequent itemsets
1: $k = 1$; $C_k = \jmath$
2: **while** $C_k \neq 0$ **do**
3:    support_count(D, C_k)
4:    **for all** candidates $c \in C_k$ **do**
5:      **if** $c.support \geq minsup$ **then**
6:        $F_k = c$
7:      **end if**
8:    **end for**
9:    $C_{k+1} = candidate\_generation(F_k)$
10:   $k = k + 1$
11: **end while**
12: $F = \cup_{j=1}^{k} F_j$

3.3 Apriori for Association Mining

Apriori is a classic data mining algorithm for learning association rules. Given a set of itemsets, the algorithm attempts to find subsets of k elements which are common to at least a minimum part $minsup$ of the itemsets. The algorithm uses a bottom-up approach: in each iteration frequent subsets of k elements are extended to subsets of $k + 1$ elements (candidate generation, see Alg. 3), and groups of candidates are tested against the data. The algorithm terminates when no further successful extensions are found. The complete Apriori algorithm is presented in Alg. 3.

4 Optimization on the Cell

We optimized the parallel implementation of the three algorithms using the following methods: (1) SPE thread parallelism. The key is to minimize the communication and the number of synchronization points. (2) SPE data parallelism. Together with SPE thread parallelism, vectorization can be used to reduce the execution time of k-means and RBF (see code snippets in Listings 1.1 and 1.2). This approach was chosen because some data mining algorithms have the following four characteristics: first, inherently parallel; second, wide dynamic range, hence floating-point based; third, regular memory access patterns; last, data independent control flow. Thus the algorithms could be restructured to leverage the SIMD intrinsics available on the Cell. (3) Data overlay. A double buffer scheme is introduced to overlap calculation and transfer. While part i of the data is transferred into one buffer, we concurrently execute the computation on data part $i - 1$ from the other buffer. The performance might be improved if calculation time and transfer time of each part are approximately identical. (4) Elimination of memory consuming parts of the code.

4.1 K-Means on the Cell

It is straightforward to parallelize k-Means. We partition the input datasets such that the number of records on each processor is approximately equal. Note that there are two main constraints to the address and the number of records being passed to a SPE. First, the all addresses must be aligned to 16-byte boundary. Second, the Cell only supports aligned transfer sizes of 1, 2, 4, or 8 byte, and multiples of 16 byte, with a maximum transfer size of 16 kbyte.

Vectorization has the biggest impact in terms of relative gains that can be achieved by calculating distance at once. To take advantage of vectorization, the user must explicitly program the parallel execution in the code by applying special SIMD instructions.

Listing 1.1. Scalar distance calculation

```
1  for(i=0;i<dim;i++)
2      distance = distance+(float)(p[i]-c[i])*(p[i]-c[i]);
```

Listing 1.2. Vectorized distance calculation

```
3  float results[4] __attribute__ ((aligned(16)));
4  vector float *vA = (vector float *) p;
5  vector float *vB = (vector float *) c;
6  vector float *vC = (vector float *) results;
7  vector float vD;
8  for(i=0; i<iter; i++)
9  {
10     vD = spu_sub(vA[i],vB[i]);
11     vC[0] = spu_madd(vD,vD,vC[0]);
12 }
13 for (i = 0; i < 4; ++i)
14     distance = distance + results[i];
```

We include an example showing a snippet of code before and after vectorization in Lsts. 1.1 and 1.2, respectively. Here we make use of two intrinsics, namely *spu_sub* and *spu_madd*. *spu_sub* subtracts corresponding elements of vector vA and vB and stores the result in vD. *spu_madd* multiplies the elements of vD and vD and adds the results to vC. The vectorized code can effective reduce the number of operations, especially when the number of dimensions is much greater than 4. The complete pseudo-code for a SPE is shown in Alg. 4.

4.2 RBF on the Cell

The optimization of RBF is similar to that of k-Means. We need to partition the matrices c_{ij}, w_{jk} and the vectors δ_{zk}, δ_{yj} carefully so that only a part is stored and used in each SPE. Synchronization only occurs at the end of the forward phase for classification (after step 6 in the Alg. 2). Here the local part of vector z needs to be transferred to PPE, where the components z_k from all SPEs are summed up. Each SPE fetches the sum vector z from PPE and resume its calculation. Pseudo-code for RBF has been omitted due to space constraints.

Algorithm 4. k-Means SPE (with data overlay optimization)

    Input: D = Dataset, k = the number of centers, D_p = part of Dataset for one SPU
    Output: Each $d \in D$ is assigned to its closest center $c \in C$
1: GetContext(D_p, k); $totalData = |D_p|$
2: Calculate the available memory m for D_p
3: **while** $message \neq STOP$ **do**
4:     wait for $START$ message from PPE
5:     Fetch centers C into local store via DMA call(s)
6:     Fetch $m/2$ data D_p^1 into local store via DMA call(s)
7:     **while** $totalData > 0$ **do**
8:         Verify all transfers are finished
9:         (a) Fetch $m/2$ data D_p^2 into local store via DMA call(s);
            (b) Concurrently calculate distances and assign center for D_p^1
10:       Put the results of D_p^1 back into system memory
11:       Verify all transfers are finished
12:       (a) Fetch $m/2$ data D_p^1 into local store via DMA call(s);
            (b) Concurrently calculate distances and assign center for D_p^2
13:       Put the results of D_p^2 back into system memory
14:       $totalData = totalData - m$
15:     **end while**
16:     send $COMPLETE$ message to PPE
17: **end while**

4.3 Apriori on the Cell

The optimization of Apriori is a big challenge due to the high complexity of its implementation and the limited local memory on each SPE. Our code is based on the code of Bodon which is known as one of the fastest realizations of Apriori [3]. First, this implementation uses a red-black-tree, and it is a difficult task to parallelize a tree-based algorithm. Second, the algorithm needs C++ STL which invokes some memory consuming functions, e.g. *new* and *delete*. We replaced all *new*/*delete* with *malloc*()/*free*() in both apriori programs and STL implementations, which could help us to obtain additional 60 KByte memory in the local store.

We used the count distribution idea to parallelize Apriori [4]. The count distribution algorithm is a parallel version of Apriori that distributes the data set over all processors. All processors generate the entire candidate k-itemset from the set of frequent $(k-1)$-itemsets. Each SPE can thus independently calculate partial supports of candidates from its local data set partition. Next, the PPE performs the sum reduction to obtain the global support counts that are distributed to all SPEs. Compared to other parallel Apriori implementations, count distribution algorithm has minimum communication, because only count values are exchanged among SPEs. However, in order to exchange count values, it requires that the candidate k-itemsets must be identical on all SPEs, and the entire red-black-tree must be replicated on each SPE.

5 Experimental Results

In this section we present a detailed evaluation of our parallel codes on the Cell chip and present a comparison to implementations on Xeon and Opteron CPUs.

We execute the programs on one Cell chip of a Cell cluster built from IBM BladeCenter QS20 dual-Cell blades; each blade houses two 3.2 GHz Cell BE processors and 1 GB XDRAM (512 MB per processor). With a clock speed of 3.2GHz, the Cell processor has a theoretical peak performance of 204.8 GFLOP/s (single precision). For comparison, we provide execution times for single-threaded reference implementations on the following two processors:

Xeon E5310: 1.6GHz, 4MB L2 cache, Intel C compiler 9.1

Opteron 880: 2.6GHz, 1MB L2 cache, Intel C compiler 9.0

Tab. 1 illustrates the performance advantage of the Cell executing k-Means, RBF and Apriori as compared to two commodity processors. The parameters for k-Means were DataPoints=6K, Dimensions=128, and centers=4. The parameters for RBF were InputNodes=128, RBFNodes=128, and OutputNodes=128. The parameters for Apriori were TransactionNo=2K with transactions from the well-known database T10I4D100K. The Cell outperforms the others a little when only PPE is used, but it scales very well with SPEs. The second best performance was afforded by the Opteron 880, and the Xeon E5310 gave the third.

Table 1. Performance comparison of selected algorithms for various processors

Processor	k-Means (sec.)	RBF (sec.)	Apriori (sec.)
Xeon	2.547792	7.571673	0.059752
Opteron	2.363729	6.456178	0.059523
Cell PPE	2.091699	5.201312	0.055320
Cell 8 SPE with vectorization	0.196709	0.302930	0.023957

In Fig. 3 we present the results of our implementation when using PPE and PPE with vectorization, and when using one or more SPEs with vectorization. All performance data are given for small data sets, but because of the double buffer scheme the performance for large data sets is similar. In our implementation only the centroid data (k-Means), the neural weights (RBF) and the candidate tree (Apriori) must fit into the local stores of the SPE. As shown in the Figs. 3(a) and 3(d), k-Means and RBF hugely benefit from eight SPE. However, Fig. 3(g) shows that Apriori does not benefit a lot from SPE parallelization, since vectorization cannot be used and the 256KB local store limits the problem size. Figs. 3(b) and 3(e) present the speedup of k-Means and RBF which is given against the PPE code. RBF is the most computing intensive application, thus RBF achieves a high speedup of 40.67 when using 6 SPEs and computing

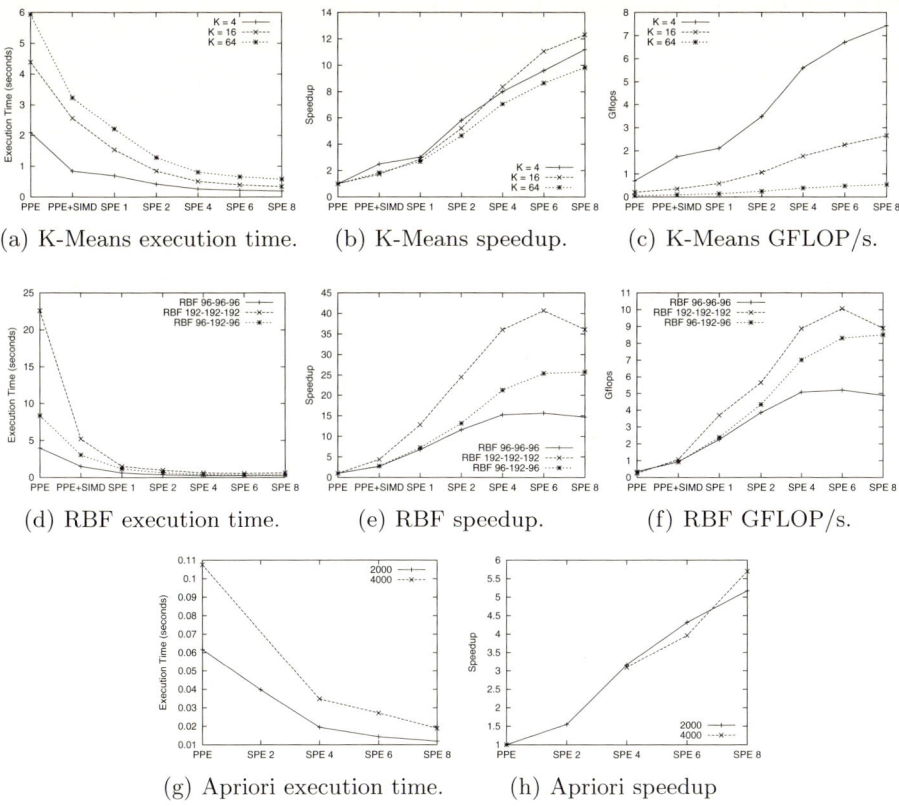

Fig. 3. Experimental results

the largest RBF network 192-192-192. Finally we calculated the GFLOP/s of k-Means and RBF using the total number of arithmetic operations divided by the measured execution time. K-Means attains a single precision performance of 6.8 GFLOP/s, and RBF 10 GFLOP/s.

6 Related Work

The large potential of the Cell architecture for scientific computations is discussed in [5,6]. There are some additional papers in which the performance of data mining algorithms [7] and other computation intensive algorithms [8,9] on the Cell Broadband Engine is investigated. In [7], only the performance of three rather similar algorithms (k-Means, k-Nearest Neighbors, ORCA) is analyzed that are based on the calculation of Euclidean distances. This makes their optimization quite similar and shows less generality. By parallelizing three important classes of data mining algorithms, we proved that data mining algorithms can achieve good performance on the Cell. Additionally we used data overlay to overcome physical limitations, thus enabling larger problem sizes on the Cell. Moreover, no other studies have investigated how effectively the Cell BE can be employed to perform association rules finding and neural network training, and how it compares against the data mining implementations on other architectures in terms of performance. The problem of finding association rules poses difficult challenges. During the parallelization of Apriori, we encountered some problems that were not met by others before, and proposed effective solutions.

7 Conclusion

We have demonstrated that efficient implementations of data mining algorithms are possible on the Cell architecture. Applications with small local memory demand can be implemented without many changes to the code, for example, k-Means and RBF. Nevertheless they can operate on large data sets by applying the data overlay technique. Operations on vectors and matrices can efficiently be vectorized on the SPEs. The implementation of tree-based algorithms like Apriori remains a big challenge because partitioning the tree is difficult. Here we analyzed a parallel version of Apriori in which only the data set is distributed over the SPEs whereas the tree is replicated in each node.

The experimental evaluations have shown that the Cell BE can achieve impressive performance for data mining algorithms. Compared to other processors, a speedup of one order of magnitude is possible. The keys to achieve high performance are a clear understanding of characteristics of the algorithms and, more importantly, a clear understanding of the system and environment limitations. Other data mining algorithms can be implemented on the Cell in a similar way. This will be a topic of our future work.

Acknowledgments

The authors acknowledge Georgia Institute of Technology, its Sony-Toshiba-IBM Center of Competence, and the National Science Foundation, for the use of Cell Broadband Engine resources that have contributed to this research.

References

1. Kahle, J., et al.: Introduction to the Cell multiprocessor. IBM Journal of Research and Development 49(4), 589–604 (2005)
2. IBM Corporation. Cell Broad Band Engine technology,
   http://www.alphaworks.ibm.com/topics/cell
3. Bodon, F.: A fast apriori implementation. In: Proceedings of the IEEE ICDM Workshop on Frequent Itemset Mining Implementations (FIMI 2003) (2003)
4. Zaki, M.: Parallel and Distributed Association Mining: A Survey. IEEE Concurrency 7(4), 14–25 (1999)
5. Williams, S., Shalf, J., Oliker, L., Kamil, S., Husbands, P., Yelick, K.: The potential of the cell processor for scientific computing. In: Proceedings of the 3rd conference on Computing Frontiers (CF 2006), pp. 9–20 (2006)

6. Bader, D., Agarwal, V., Madduriet, K.: On the Design and Analysis of Irregular Algorithms on the Cell Processor: A case study on list ranking. In: 21th IEEE International Parallel and Distributed Processing Symposium (IPDPS) (2007)
7. Buehrer, G., Parthasarathy, S.: The Potential of the Cell Broadband Engine for Data Mining. In: Proceedings of the 33rd Int. Conference on Very Large Data Bases (VLDB) (2007)
8. Bader, D., Agarwal, V.: FFTC: Fastest Fourier Transform for the IBM Cell Broadband Engine. In: Aluru, S., Parashar, M., Badrinath, R., Prasanna, V.K. (eds.) HiPC 2007. LNCS, vol. 4873, pp. 172–184. Springer, Heidelberg (2007)
9. Petrini, F., et al.: Multicore Surprises: Lessons Learned from Optimizing Sweep3D on the Cell Broadband Engine. In: 21th IEEE International Parallel and Distributed Processing Symposium (IPDPS) (2007)

Efficient Management of Complex Striped Files in Active Storage[*]

Juan Piernas[1,2] and Jarek Nieplocha[1]

[1] Pacific Northwest National Laboratory (USA)
[2] Universidad de Murcia (Spain)
piernas@ditec.um.es, jarek.nieplocha@pnl.gov

Abstract. Active Storage provides an opportunity for reducing the bandwidth requirements between the storage and compute elements of current supercomputing systems, and leveraging the processing power of the storage nodes used by some modern file systems. To achieve both objectives, Active Storage allows certain processing tasks to be performed directly on the storage nodes, near the data they manage. However, Active Storage must also support key requirements of scientific applications. In particular, Active Storage must be able to support striped files and files with complex formats (e.g., netCDF). In this paper, we describe how these important requirements can be addressed. The experimental results on a Lustre file system not only show that our proposal can reduce the network traffic to near zero and scale the performance with the number of storage nodes, but also that it provides an efficient treatment of striped files and can manage files with complex data structures.

1 Introduction

Recent improvements in storage technologies in terms of capacity as well as cost effectiveness, and the emergence of high-performance interconnects, have made it possible to build systems of unprecedented power by connecting thousands of compute and storage nodes. However, for large-scale scientific simulations that use these environments, the efficient management of enormous and increasing volumes of data remains a challenging problem.

On the other hand, several parallel/distributed file systems have been recently developed for high-performance and high-data volume computing systems. Some of these file systems, such as Lustre [1] and PVFS [2], use mainstream server computers as storage nodes, that is, computers that contain significant CPU and memory resources, several disks attached to them, and run a general-purpose operating system. Although the combined computing capacity of these nodes can

---

[*] This work was supported by the DoE, Office of Advanced Scientific Computing Research, at the Pacific Northwest National Laboratory (a multiprogram national laboratory operated by Battelle for the U.S. DoE under Contract DE-AC06-76RL01830), and by the Spanish MEC and European Comission FEDER funds under grants "Consolider Ingenio–2010 CSD2006–00046", and "TIN2006–15516–C04–03".

be considerable in many high performance systems, it is exploited for storing and accessing but hardly ever for processing data.

One approach to reduce the bandwidth requirements between the compute and storage elements, and to leverage the processing power of the latter, is to move appropriate processing tasks to the storage nodes. We call this approach **Active Storage** in the context of parallel file systems [3][4]. Active Storage is similar to the *active disk* concept proposed for hard drives [5][6][7][8], but with two important differences: (1) storage devices are now full-fledged computers, and (2) they include a feature-rich environment provided typically by a Linux operating system. These two factors make it possible to run regular application codes on the storage nodes.

In this paper we show how we have enhanced our previous implementation of Active Storage [4] to support several key features which, until the current work, have been lacking in virtually all existing proposals of this technology. Specifically, we focus on striped files with either a simple format (e.g., a list of chunk-aligned records) and a more *complex* format as netCDF, which is very common for data exchange in some scientific applications. In the former case, our implementation provides a framework that makes it possible to transparently run unmodified programs to process the records in a striped file. In the latter case, the program to be run on the storage nodes must be aware of the format and striping of the input file. To address this requirement we enhanced Active Storage by introducing a new component, a *mapper*, to optimize the processing of the striped file.

We have evaluated our implementation of Active Storage by using the Lustre parallel file system and two application kernels. The experimental results show that our design achieves the two main objectives of Active Storage for both striped and non-striped files: it reduces the network traffic to near zero for test workloads, and can take advantage of the extra computing capacity offered by the storage nodes at the same time. Moreover, they prove that Active Storage can efficiently manage striped files, and that high performance can be achieved even for files with complex data structures.

The rest of the paper is organized as follows. Section 2 provides an overview of work related to the *active disks'* concept. Section 3 describes the architecture of our proposal for Active Storage, and the handling of non-striped files. The treatment of (complex) striped files is explained in Section 4. Experimental results are presented in Section 5. Conclusions appear in Section 6.

2 Related Work

The idea of *intelligent storage* was developed by several authors at the end of the 90's, with some similar ideas proposed even earlier in the 80's in the database world [9]. Riedel *et al.* [8] propose a system, called *Active Disks*, which takes advantage of the processing power on individual disk drives to run application-level code. Keeton *et al.* [7] present a computer architecture for decision support database servers that utilizes "intelligent" disks (IDISKs). Acharya *et al.* [5] evaluate the *active disk* architectures, and propose a stream-based programming model for them. Lim *et al.* [10] propose an Active Disk File System (ADFS) where many of the responsibilities of a traditional central file server are offloaded to the active disks. Chiu *et al.* use the previous ideas of Active Disks and IDISKs to design a distributed smart disk architecture [6].

The *object-based storage device* (OSD) [11][12] is another concept which profits the processing power of the disk drives. Schlosser and Iren [13] suggest that, with more processing capability in the storage devices, it would be possible to delegate some database-specific tasks to the OSDs, in an active disk fashion. Du [14] merges the OSD and active disk concepts in order to build the *intelligent storage devices* one. An intelligent storage device is directly attached to the network, supports the OSD concept, and supports the active disk concept.

Felix *et al.* [3] present a first real implementation of *Active Storage* for the Lustre file system. They provides a kernel-space solution with the processing component parts implemented in the user space. Our recent implementation of Active Storage [4], however, offers a solution that is purely in user space. This makes our proposal more flexible, portable, and readily deployable, while it achieves the same or even better performance than Felix's implementation.

None of the previous papers have described a deployable solution that addresses the practical needs of many large scale scientific applications. For example, they have not provided means to deal with striped files. Moreover, the design principles of some approaches also hinder the development of possible enhancements to deal with striped files. The current paper, however, makes a key contribution to the field by showing that, in fact, Active Storage can be implemented efficiently for striped files even for complex data formats of the user data. This is possible by taking advantage of the user-space approach and filesystem-wide data view of our proposal.

3 Active Storage Overview

Figure 1(a) shows a cluster without Active Storage, whereas Figure 1(b) depicts our approach. Without Active Storage, many data-intensive processing tasks are performed on the compute nodes, producing a high network traffic and wasting the processing power of the storage node. Active Storage, however, allows some of those processing tasks to be performed on the storage nodes, reducing the network traffic, and profiting the CPU time of these nodes.

In our proposal, the compute and storage nodes are all clients of the parallel file system. Since the storage nodes are clients, they can access all the files in the file system and, specifically, the files stored locally. One of the clients will run `asmaster`, a program which receives a *rule* describing an Active Storage job and performs the actions contained in it. A rule is an XML file which can specify many actions to perform, but which basically contains the following information: a file pattern specifying the files to process, a program path, and program arguments (if any). In the storage nodes, there also exists an Active Storage Runtime Framework (ASRF), a set of programs which assist `asmaster` in executing a rule, i.e., an Active Storage job.

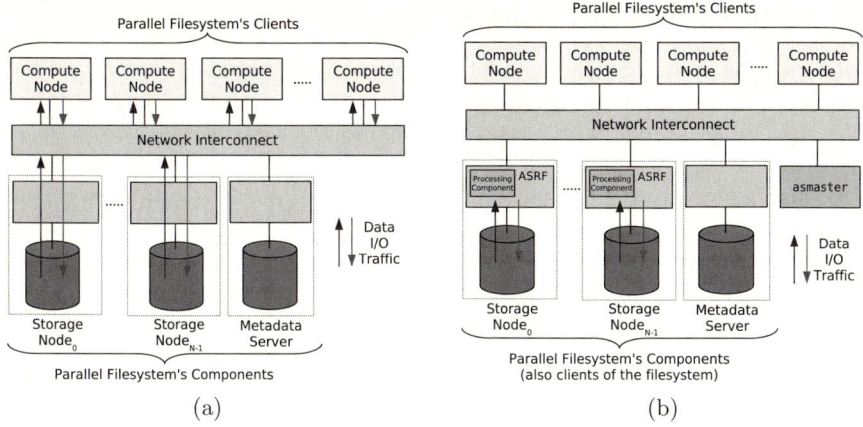

Fig. 1. (a) A traditional system without Active Storage. (b) Overview of the Active Storage architecture.

The files to be processed by an Active Storage job can already exist, or they can be created by a parallel application running on the compute nodes at the same time as the Active Storage job is active. In the latter case, the synchronization between the parallel application in the compute nodes, and the processing components in the storage nodes is important [4]. To simplify the implementation of the processing components, we have built a dynamic library, libas, which contains functions that hide the synchronization details. This library will also play a fundamental role in providing transparent access to striped files.

The processing of non-striped files is simple. For every matching file, asmaster will remotely run the given program as a processing component on the storage node where the file resides. If the processing components create output files, it is possible to instruct a rule to locally create those files. Also, if there are thousands of files which match the pattern, Active Storage will create thousands of processing components, one per file, at the same time.

Note that our Active Storage approach is quite different from running a parallel application on the storage nodes [4]. A major problem for a regular parallel application is that the application should be aware of the file distribution and the properties of the filesystem. Also, the number of files per storage node can change during the course of the time, and files can be unevenly distributed. Therefore, the number of "processing components" of the parallel application per storage node should be variable, and could change from run to run, or during the same run.

4 Management of Complex Striped Files

This section describes extensions to the Active Storage architectures to support striped files. This includes the management of striped files with a simple data format as well as files which have a complex data structure, such as netCDF.

4.1 Striped Files with Chunk-Aligned Records

In the baseline Active Storage model described in the previous section, we have assumed that files to be processed are not striped, i.e., each file is stored in only one storage node. Many parallel applications, however, stripe files across several storage nodes in order to benefit from the increased aggregate bandwidth.

To deal with striped files, our current approach launches a processing component per storage node used by the matching file, and makes every processing component process only the file chunks stored in its own node. If the processing components write to an output file, the output file must be created with the same striping pattern as the input file, and every processing component must write to only the file chunks stored in its corresponding node. Otherwise, the I/O operations would not be entirely local.

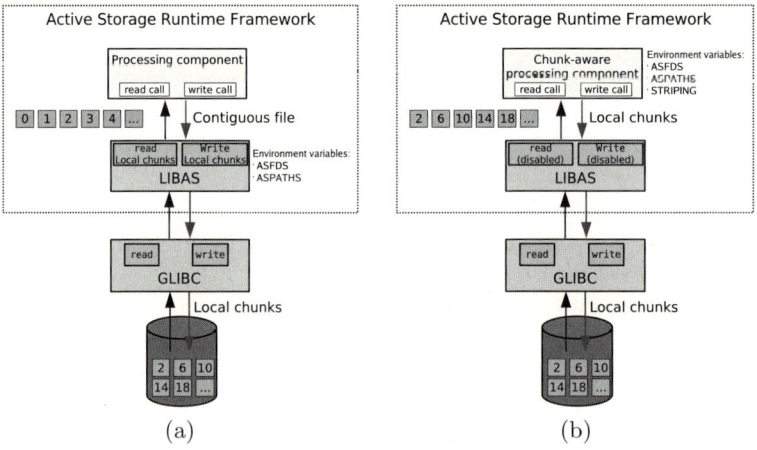

Fig. 2. The libas library. (a) Transparent access, and (b) non-transparent access to striped files.

With fixed-length, chunk-aligned records, Active Storage can provide transparent access to the striped files by exposing the different chunks of a file stored in the same node as a single, contiguous file. Active Storage uses the aforementioned libas dynamic library to provide that transparent access. The mechanism implemented is depicted in Figure 2(a). Using several environment variables, the Active Storage Runtime Framework passes to the libas library striping information about the striped files which must transparently be accessed. When a processing component opens a file, libas checks if the file is one of the files it must manage. If so, libas will intercept any operation on that file in order to only read and write the local chunks of the file.

The single, contiguous file's abstraction provided by Active Storage allows a user to run programs which access files sequentially as processing components, even when the input and output files are striped.

4.2 Striped Files with Unaligned Records

There are cases where the above requirement of fixed-length, chunk-aligned records is not met. In those cases, Active Storage cannot provide a transparent access to the striped files. Instead, our system passes striping information to the processing components (see Fig. 2(b)), which must decide by themselves which data in the local chunks, and other remote chunks, they have to access.

Our design provides a third option to deal with striped files which can not be transparently accessed. In some cases, the amount of output data is much greater or smaller than the amount of input data. Although the input and output files could use the same striping, the output records would not be typically written to the same storage node as their corresponding input records. In those cases, we can run a processing component per chunk of the input file. The output data can then be written to a local non-striped file whose name will have the absolute number of the input chunk. Certainly, there will not be a single "output file" but a set of sub-files, which will be accessed by a subsequent process in the order given by the sequence of chunk numbers. In this way, the write operations will be local, which is one of the primary design objectives for Active Storage.

4.3 Mapper Component for Processing of Complex Data Formats

Until now, we have assumed that all the data in the input files is processed. If Active Storage processing applies only to a part of the data in the files, it becomes necessary to augment the Active Storage architecture with a new element, the *mapper component*, that interacts with `asmaster`. This new component is a program which receives a file and its striping information as arguments, and return a list (a *map*) of the storage nodes which contain the data to process.

The mapper program also allows us to handle files with special data formats. For example, in our project we developed a mapper for netCDF [15] files to deal with climate applications. Our netCDF mapper receives as arguments a file, its striping information and the variable that the processing components will access; then, it reads the netCDF header of the file to locate the variable in the file, and uses the striping information to, finally, build the map of storage nodes. With this approach, the processing is optimized because only the relevant storage nodes run processing components (see Figure 3). Once `asmaster` launches the different processing components, these again read the netCDF header of the file and use its striping information to locate the part of the file that they must process.

5 Evaluation

Our system under test has 17 nodes: 8 compute nodes, 1 MDS/MGS server and 8 OSTs (the storage nodes in Lustre). All the nodes are identical, and their hardware elements are: two Dual Core Intel Xeon 5160 CPUs, 4 GB of RAM, a Dual Port MT25208 NIC, a Seagate ST3250624AS (250 GB) for the OS, and a Seagate ST3500630AS (500 GB) for Lustre. We also use a 24-ports MT47396 Infiniscale-III switch, Lustre 1.6.1 and Linux kernel 2.6.16.42.

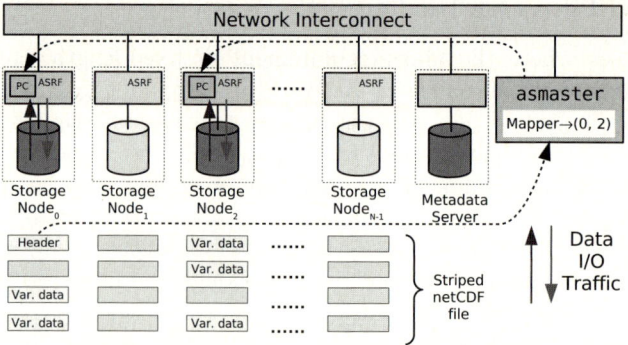

Fig. 3. The *mapper* application for netCDF files

We have compared the performance achieved by Active Storage with that obtained by a system without Active Storage. Our comparison uses two applications. The first ones, DSCAL, reads an input file of doubles in native format (8 bytes), and multiply every number by a scalar. The resulting doubles are written to an output file. In our experiments, this application has to process 16 input files of 1 GB each, and produce 16 output file, also of 1 GB each.

The second application, ClimStat (Climate Statistics), is used to compute the mean of a float variable in a netCDF file. The program receives the netCDF file, the variable and the striping of the file. With the striping information, the program determines which values of the variable are locally stored in its storage node, adds those values, and returns the sum and the number of added values (i.e., the output data is only a couple of numbers). In our experiments, ClimStat has to add the values of a record variable with 13,762,560 float elements (52.5 MB of data) split into 5 records which are spread across a 5.3 GB netCDF file. In total, there are 16 netCDF files and 840 MB of data to process. These files are the output of a Global Cloud Resolving Model simulation [16].

We have evaluated the performance of Active Storage for 1, 2, 4, and 8 storage nodes. Every file is striped across all the OSTs with a stripe size of 1MB. The achieved results have been compared with those obtained by a system without Active Storage and 1, 2, 4, and 8 compute/storage nodes With Active Storage, DSCAL and ClimStat run as processing components on the storage nodes. It is interesting to note that we use the same DSCAL code, and the same ClimStat code, for all the processing components; it does not matter the number of storage nodes. Without Active Storage, the applications run on the compute nodes.

5.1 Experimental Results for DSCAL

Figure 4(a) shows the overall execution time for DSCAL. This is the time to carry out the entire job, either in the compute or storage nodes, and includes the time taken to launch the different processing components, transfer data (when needed), and wait for the completion of the processes.

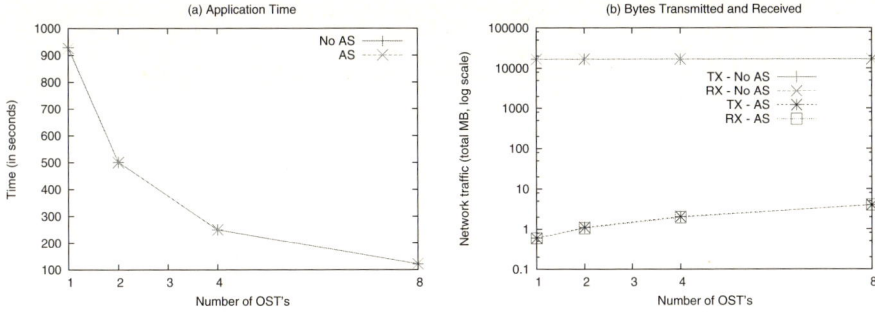

Fig. 4. Results for DSCAL in a non-saturated system

As we can see, there are no noticeable differences between running the application on the compute nodes and on the storage nodes. Since the number of nodes is small, compared to the disk speed our Infiniband interconnect does not become a bottleneck, hence the result. However, the absence of differences is important because it means that the overhead of the processing components on the storage nodes is small, and does not downgrade the performance of Lustre. Another important benefit, is that Active Storage allows to move the processing off the critical path: the application, after initiating the Active Storage processing, can continue instead of waiting for the time consuming I/O operations.

We can also see that the application time is divided by two when the number of OSTs doubles. This proves that Active Storage provides DSCAL with an environment where its performance scales with the number of storage nodes. This also proves that our proposal can handle stripes files efficiently.

Figure 4(b) displays the bytes transmitted and received in DSCAL. Unlike the application time, there is a huge difference between a system with Active Storage and another without it. With Active Storage, the network traffic is very small, while it can be very high without Active Storage, where the interconnect can become a bottleneck if there are hundreds or thousands of nodes. We can also see in the figure that the bytes transmitted and received are roughly the same. This result is expected because the application reads from and writes to files of the same size. Note that the network traffic smoothly increases with the number of nodes. This is mainly due to the meta-data operations (when processing a file, all the nodes have to obtain its meta-data information from the MDS server).

5.2 Experimental Results for ClimStat

In general, the results obtained by ClimStat are quite similar to those achieved by DSCAL, but there are some details to be explained. By coincidence, in our experiments all the storage nodes roughly have the same amount of data of the variable whose mean must be computed. Therefore, all of them take part in the task. With a larger number of storage nodes, other files or a different variable, this might not be true.

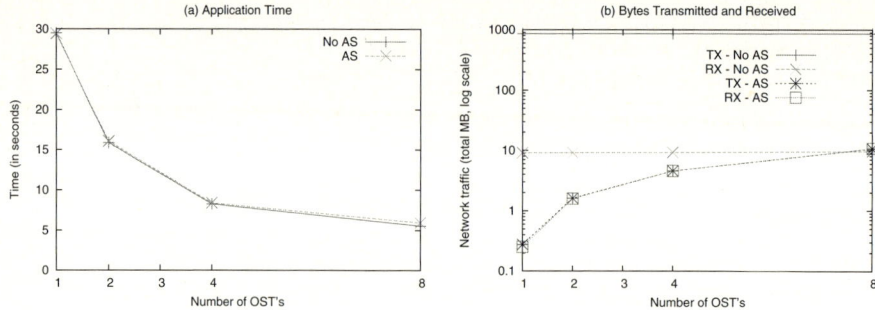

Fig. 5. Results for ClimStat in a non-saturated system

The application time for ClimStat is presented in Figure 5(a). In this case, the application times are much smaller than in DSCAL. However, similarly to DSCAL, there are no noticeable differences between running the application on the compute nodes and running the application on the storage nodes because the Infiniband interconnect does not become a bottleneck.

The network traffic is shown in Figure 5(b). As we can see, the amount of bytes received by every storage node is small, both with and without Active Storage. The reason is, as we have explained before that ClimStat produces only two numbers as output, which represent a few bytes. Therefore, we cannot expect any appreciable difference. The findings are different with respect to the number of bytes transmitted. In a system without Active Storage, the storage nodes have to send the data to the compute nodes. With Active Storage, however, this network traffic is very small.

Figure 5(b) also shows that, with Active Storage, the network traffic smoothly increases with the number of nodes. Like in DSCAL, this is due to the meta-data operations, but, for ClimStat, it is also due to the reading of the netCDF header. This header is small in our case, and is contained in only one storage node which has to send a copy to the other nodes. Without Active Storage, the header must also be sent to all the compute nodes, although its impact is small because of the high network traffic caused by the transmission of the temperature data.

The most important conclusion from the evaluation of the ClimStat application is not only that Active Storage is able to leverage the processing power of the storage nodes and considerably reduce the network traffic at the same time, but also that it can process data stored in files with a given (complex) format, like netCDF, and not evenly distributed among the storage nodes.

6 Conclusions

The current paper addresses two important requirements that were not considered in the previous work on Active Storage: striped files and complex scientific data formats such as netCDF. We have described how these important requirements can be addressed while achieving high performance. The experimental results on a Lustre file system not only show that our approach can reduce the network traffic to near zero, and profit the extra computing capacity offered by the storage nodes at the same time, but also that it provides an efficient treatment of striped files and is able to manage files with complex data structures. We have also improved the usability aspects of Active Storage, providing a scientific-friendly environment to specify, in a simple way, the job to carry out.

References

1. Cluster File Systems Inc.: Lustre: A scalable, high-performance file system (2002), http://www.lustre.org
2. Carns, P.H., Ligon III, W.B., Ross, R.B., Thakur, R.: PVFS: a parallel file system for Linux clusters. In: Proc. of 4th Annual Linux Showcase and Con., pp. 317–327 (2000)
3. Felix, E.J., Fox, K., Regimbal, K., Nieplocha, J.: Active Storage processing in a parallel file system. In: Proc. of the 6th LCI International Conference on Linux Clusters: The HPC Revolution (2006)
4. Piernas, J., Nieplocha, J., Felix, E.J.: Evaluation of Active Storage strategies for the Lustre parallel file system. In: Proc. of 2007 Supercomp. Conf. (SC 2007) (2007)
5. Acharya, A., Uysal, M., Saltz, J.: Active disks: Programming model, algorithms and evaluation. In: Proc. of the ACM ASPLOS Conference, pp. 81–91 (1998)
6. Chiu, S.C., keng Liao, W., Choudhary, A.N.: Design and evaluation of distributed smart disk architecture for I/O-intensive workloads. In: Sloot, P.M.A., Abramson, D., Bogdanov, A.V., Gorbachev, Y.E., Dongarra, J., Zomaya, A.Y. (eds.) ICCS 2003. LNCS, vol. 2660, pp. 230–241. Springer, Heidelberg (2003)
7. Keeton, K., Patterson, D.A., Hellerstein, J.M.: A case for intelligent disks (IDISKs). SIGMOD Record 24(7), 42–52 (1998)
8. Riedel, E., Gibson, G., Faloutsos, C.: Active storage for large-scale data mining and multimedia. In: Proc. of the 24th Int. Conf. on Very Large Data Bases (VLDB), pp. 62–73 (1998)
9. DeWitt, D.J., Hawthorn, P.: A performance evaluation of database machine architectures. In: Proc. of the 7th Int. Conf. on Very Large Data Bases (VLDB), pp. 199–214 (1981)
10. Lim, H., Kapoor, V., Wighe, C., Du, D.H.: Active disk file system: A distributed, scalable file system. In: Proc. of the 18th IEEE Symposium on Mass Storage Systems and Technologies, San Diego, pp. 101–115 (2001)
11. Gibson, G.A., Nagle, D.F., Amiri, K., Chang, F.W., Feinberg, E.M., Gobioff, H., Lee, C., Ozceri, B., Riedel, E., Rochberg, D., Zelenka, J.: File server scaling with network-attached secure disks. In: Proc. of the 1997 ACM SIGMETRICS Intl. Conf. on Measurement and Modeling of Comp. Systems, pp. 272–284 (1997)
12. Mesnier, M., Ganger, G., Riedel, E.: Object-based storage. IEEE Communications Magazine 41(8), 84–90 (2005)
13. Schlosser, S.W., Iren, S.: Database storage management with object-based storage devices. In: Proc. of the First International Workshop on Data Management on New Hardware (DaMoN) (2005)
14. Du, D.H.: Intelligent storage for information retrieval. In: Proc. of the Intl. Conference on Next Generation Web Services Practices (NWeSP 2005), pp. 214–220 (2005)
15. Rew, R.K., Davis, G.P.: NetCDF: An interface for scientific data access. IEEE Computer Graphics and Applications 10(4), 76–82 (1990)
16. Schuchardt, K., Palmer, B., Daily, J., Elsethagen, T., Koontz, A.: IO strategies and data services for petascale data sets from a global cloud resolving model. Journal of Physics: Conference Series 78(012089) (2007)

Topic 9: Parallel and Distributed Programming

José Nelson Amaral[1] and Joaquim Gabarró[2]

[1] Global Chair
Department of Computing Science
University of Alberta, Edmonton, Canada
amaral@cs.ualberta.ca
[2] Local Chair
Universitat Politècnica de Catalunya, Barcelona, Spain
gabarro@lsi.upc.edu

The Parallel and Distributed Programming Topic, Topic 9, is concerned with the development of parallel or distributed applications. Developing such applications is a hard task and it requires advanced algorithms, realistic modeling, efficient design tools, high performance languages and libraries, and experimental evaluation. This topic provides a forum for presentation of new results and practical experience in this domain. It emphasizes research that facilitates the design and development of correct, high-performance, portable, and scalable parallel program. Related to these central needs, this Topic also includes contributions that assess methods for reusability, performance prediction, large-scale deployment, self-adaptivity, and fault-tolerance.

The focus of Topic 9 in 2008 is:

- Innovative languages.
- Development and debugging tools for parallel programs.
- Performance analysis, design and implementation of models for parallelism.
- Parallel program paradigms, their evaluation and their comparison.
- Large-scale experiments and validation of parallel applications.
- Methodological aspects of developing, optimizing and validating parallel programs.
- Domain specific libraries and languages.
- Parallel programming productivity and pattern-based parallel programming.
- Parallel software reusability.

Out of 26 papers submitted to Topic 9, 8 were accepted for presentation at Euro-Par 2008. We thank the authors for submitting papers to this topic, the reviewers for very insightful evaluation of the papers, and we specially thank the five vice-chairs — Luc Bougé, Marcelo Cintra, Marc Feeley, Paul Kelly, and Vivek Sarkar —for coordinating the reviews and for their active participation in the discussions in the Program Committee.

The first paper of Topic 9, "Improving the performance of multiple conjugate gradient solvers by exploiting overlap", describes a new technique to allow overlap of communication and computation in multiple conjugate gradient (CG) solvers. Fast CG solvers are essential for many scientific applications.

The first full session contains three papers. "A software component model with spatial and temporal compositions for grid infrastructures" is concerned with the combination of concerns. Its premise is that both the components and the execution order of tasks are important in models of software. They paper introduces a new programming model based on this premise. The goal in "A design pattern for component oriented development of agent based multithreaded applications" is to develop a design pattern for multithreaded applications that requires little parallel programming expertise from the pattern user. "Advanced concurrency control for transactional memory using transaction commit rate" presents P-only Concurrency Control (PoCC), a new algorithm for concurrency control for software transactional memory. PoCC varies the number o active threads to adapt to the amount of parallelism available in the application.

The common thread in the other full session is the implementation of an application in a specific environment. "Meta-programming applied to automatic SMP parallelization of linear algebra code" presents a Symmetric Multi-Processor (SMP)-aware implementation of a scientific library called NT2. The parallelization of NT2 relies on syntax-tree representation and meta-programming. "Solving dense linear systems on graphics processors" presents multiple algorithms to compute Cholesky and Lower-Upper (LU) factorizations on a Graphic Processing Unit (GPU). These implementations investigate the use of padding, blocking, a hybrid scheme, and an iterative refinement technique. "Radioastronomy image synthesis on the Cell/B.E" proposes an strategy to parallelize convolutional resampling, a data-intensive radioastronomy kernel, on the Cell Broadband Engine.

Finally "Parallel lattice Boltzmann flow simulation on emerging multi-core platforms" presents a parallel implementation of flow simulation based on the Lattice Boltzmann Method (LBM) on multi-core platforms. This paper reports on the author's experience with implementing this application both on a Cell-based cluster and on a GPU card.

Improving the Performance of Multiple Conjugate Gradient Solvers by Exploiting Overlap

José Carlos Sancho and Darren J. Kerbyson

Performance and Architecture Laboratory (PAL),
Los Alamos National Laboratory, NM 87545, USA
{jcsancho,djk}@lanl.gov

Abstract. Conjugate gradient solvers are often being the most time-consuming part of many scientific applications. These solvers exhibit communications operations that can prevent high performance from being achieved at large scale systems. In this paper we present a novel technique to boost the performance of these solvers. In this technique multiple independent solvers that occur in some applications are combined allowing for the overlapping many communications with other communication and computation resulting with increased performance. This work is the first time that combination of CG solvers is exploited and offers performance improvements which may be particularly important in very large-scale systems. Results are presented for the MIMD Lattice (MILC) application and show that the cost of collective communications can be reduced by a factor of 2.5×. Moreover the performance of MILC is significantly improved, by over 10% for typical lattice sizes on a 1,024-processor system.

1 Introduction

Conjugate gradient (CG) solvers [1] are one of the most computationally intensive parts of many scientific simulations [2]. The CG solver is an iterative method for solving a sparse system of linear equations that is found in scientific applications that describe physics problems. For example, this solver can be found in the scientific application *MIMD Lattice Computation* (MILC) that performs large-scale quantum chromodynamics (QCD) calculations [3].

The basic iteration of a CG solver consists of several consecutive computation and communication steps. A communication step consists of one or more collectives, that combines values from every processor and distributes the result back to all processors, and several point-to-point communications that exchange data between logically neighboring processors. Unfortunately, when a CG solver is used in a large-scale application the communication overheads can become a limiting factor to achieve high performance, and thus can limit the scaling of an application to a large number of processors. In a large system, communication costs are generally higher due to increased communication latencies among processors and also to the higher number of steps required to perform a collective which typically scales at the log of the number of processors

Recently there have been efforts to increase the performance of these solvers by overlapping communication with computation [4]. Overlapping allows communication costs to be hidden with other activities of an application such as computation and also other communication operations. Overlapping is an interesting technique to increase the performance of these solvers at large-scale. However, its applicability has been very limited in the CG solver since the potential overlap exhibited in the code is small due to data dependencies between the communication and computation steps. Specifically, the overlap that can be exploited is between communications and between some communication-computation for the point-to-point operations. Collective communications cannot be overlapped in a single CG solver, and thus can dominate the performance at high processor counts.

In this paper we present a novel technique to increase the communication overlap of CG solvers by combining multiple independent instances of a CG solver, we call this approach the *Combined CG (CCG)*. The major advantage of this technique is that it allows for increased overlap of communication with other communication and computation. This is the first time that this type of combination is exploited for collective operations in codes that use multiple CG solvers and may play an important role at very large-scales. Experimental results using the MILC application on a current parallel system have shown that the communication costs of collectives can be reduced by a factor of $2.5\times$. Additionally, the execution time of MILC is significantly reduced by up to 10% on a 1024-processor system for a typical number of lattice sites per processor.

The rest of this paper is organized as follows. In Section 3 we briefly describe the basic algorithm of the CG solver and how it is implemented in the MILC application. Section 4 describes our general technique to combine multiple CG solvers. Section 5 provides an overview of the system used in the evaluation of our technique and includes experimental results. Section 6 summarizes recent work on improving the performance of CG solvers. Finally, conclusions are given in Section 7.

2 MILC

MILC [3] is an important large-scale scientific application sponsored by the Department of Energy (DOE) SciDAC program. It solves the lattice quantum chromodynamics (QCD) described by Lattice Gauge Theory. QCD calculates, on a four-dimensional space-time lattice, the interaction strengths, or coupling, between subatomic particles such as quarks and gluons that compose the internal structure of matter. The understanding of the subatomic scales that MILC provides is currently having a decisive impact on some of the major science goals of the DOE Office of Science. However, the target problems to be solved by this application are very compute intensive requiring large parallel systems. In fact, it is expected that the computational requirements of MILC will easily grow to multiple *Peta-flops* in the near future [11].

A thorough performance analysis of this application performed has revealed that its runtime is dominated by the lattice *Update* function [10]. This is the function that we optimize using the *Combined CG* technique described here. In

Update, the CG solver is called twice to solve the physics of two quark flavors (up and down) with different masses in the QCD problem. This intrinsic duality along with the fact that there are no data dependencies between both quark flavors gave us the incentive to develop the *Combined CG* solver.

Generally speaking there has been a wide adoption of multiple conjugate gradient solvers in scientific applications in the recent years. The causes for this can be diverse: some are driven by the nature of the problem like MILC, while other are driven by the need to increase the number of physical properties being simulated such as in the case of multi-physics applications. The applicability of our approach to these applications is fully dependent on the data dependencies between the solvers. The *Combined CG* solver is targeted to multiple CG solvers where there is no data dependency between them. Additionally, although the *Combined CG* solver is described here in the context of MILC, the technique can also be generalized for other applications.

3 Conjugate Gradient Solvers

Conjugate gradient solvers [1] are a popular iterative method of solving large systems of sparse linear equations of the form, $Ax = b$, where A is the a known, sparse, square, symmetric matrix, b is a known vector, and x is the solution vector. These systems often arise to solve partial differential equations that describe physical problems in many scientific simulations [2]. Basically, the method to solve this equation can be reduced to a minimization problem that tries to find an x that minimizes the quadratic form of the above equation. The method starts at an arbitrary point x_0 and in each iteration calculates how far is from the solution, the error, as well as the next direction, the residual, to get closer to the solution. After a number of iterations x converges to the solution. The domain is usually discretized in four dimensions (x, y, z, t) and the processors are arranged in a logical 4D torus. The global grid is partitioned in a 4D array each containing an equal number of grid points. The number of grid points per dimension per processor varies between dimensions and depends on the number of global grid points per dimension which is specified in the input deck. Processors that are logically neighbors need to exchange sub-grid boundaries in each iteration of the solver. A check for convergence is usually performed when the local error obtained per processor is lower than the pre-desired global error among the processors which usually happens when the solver is near the solution.

Generally, an iteration of the CG solver is composed of a few consecutive communication and computation steps. In particular for MILC this is composed of five steps, that we denoted as S_1, S_2, S_3, S_4, and S_5. The first step is the check for convergence that comprises both computation and communication operations, whereas the second and fourth steps contain only communication operations, and the third and five steps are computation only. Note that overlapping of communication and computation would correspond to overlapping step S_2 and/or S_4 with step S_3 and/or S_5, and the overlapping of communication with communication corresponds to overlapping step S_2 with S_4. Unfortunately, due to data dependencies overlapping both communication-computation and communication-communication is not possible in a single CG solver. An *Allreduce* collective communication operation is performed in the fourth step (S_4) — for MILC this is performed on four double floating-point operands.

In the second step, (S_2), boundary data from neighboring nodes are obtained using two calls to a *Gather* function. This step consists of five sub-steps in which computation and communication operations are performed for the neighbor nodes located in positive and negative directions. Sub-step sS_1 consist of the initiation of the asynchronous point-to-point communications for positive and negative directions, sub-steps sS_2 and sS_4 corresponds to the completion of the communication operations of these directions, respectively. And the remaining sub-steps, sS_3 and sS_5, are computations on the data received. This function allows for overlapping of some communication with computation which is already exploited by MILC. Specifically, the communication costs of the negative direction initiated in sS_1 can be overlapped with the computation of the data received from the positive directions, sub-step sS_3. Other forms of overlap are not possible due to data dependencies.

4 Combining Multiple Conjugate Gradient Solvers

We describe below our novel technique for combining an arbitrary number of instances of a CG solver where there is no data dependencies between them.

Figure 1 illustrates the technique to combine k solver instances and is organized in two parts: on the left is the case of k separate solvers and on the right is the combined solver case. The proposed technique executes the corresponding steps of the CG solver for each individual k solver at the same time in every iteration of the solver before advancing to the next iteration as can be seen in Figure 1. In this way, the communication steps of one solver can be overlapped with the associated communication steps in the others. In particular, steps $S2_1, S2_2, \ldots, S2_k$ can be performed together to maximize overlap, as well as steps $S4_1, S4_2, \ldots, S4_k$; Si_k denotes the ith step of the computation of the kth solver. The computation steps are executed one after the other in the same order as in the initial implementation. When one or more solvers completes before the others, the *Combined CG* proceeds in the same way, but without executing the steps corresponding to the completed solvers.

The mechanisms implemented to allow the overlap between steps $S2_i, \forall\, i, 1 \leq i \leq k$ (corresponding to the gather operations), and the overlap between steps $S4_i, \forall\, i, 1 \leq i \leq k$ (corresponding to the collectives) are described below.

4.1 Overlapping Gather Operations

We combine the separate *Gather* functions (steps $S2_1, S2_2, \ldots, S2_k$) from the k solver instances into a single *Gather* function in order to allow the overlapping

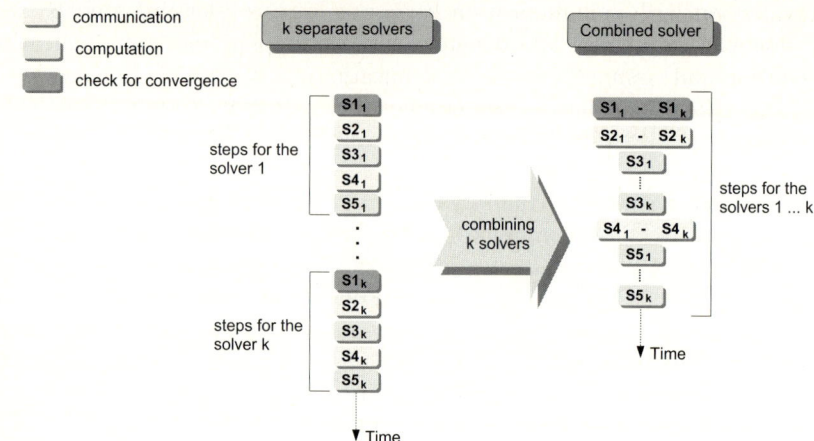

Fig. 1. Steps for the traditional non-combined and the proposed combined of k instances of a CG solver

of all the point-to-point communication operations in these solvers. Figure 2 illustrates the combined function showing the sub-steps required for the case of the traditional non-combined and the proposed combined technique. In the non-combined case the *Gather* functions are performed one after the other preventing the potential communication-communication overlap to be exploited between the k functions. In order to exploit this overlap in the new *Gather* function, sub-steps $sS1_1, sS1_2, \ldots, sS1_k$ are executed together initiating all the asynchronous point-to-point communications for the k solvers at the same time as shown in Figure 2.

On the other hand, the sub-steps that waits for the completion of the previous initiated point-to-point operations $sS2_i, sS4_i \ \forall \ i, 1 \leq i \leq k$ are just performed sequentially when necessary— before they are used for computation— to maximize the communication-computation overlap. This is already exploited in the non-combined version of the *Gather* as previously described in Section 3 where the sub-steps $sS2_i$ and $sS3_i$ are used to overlap the communicating data required in the sub-step $sS5_i$ in each *Gather* function. However, in the combined case this overlap is increased by using the following sub-steps $sS2_j$, $sS3_j, sS4_j, sS5_j \ \forall \ j, 1 \leq j \leq i-1$ of the solvers $1 \ldots i-1$ to overlap the communicating data required in the sub-steps $sS3_i$ and $sS5_i \ \forall \ i, 2 \leq i \leq k$ of the solver i as can be seen in Figure 2. Note that the combined case allows to overlap the communicating data required in the sub-step $sS3_i, \ \forall \ i, 2 \leq i \leq k$ which cannot be overlapped in a single *Gather* function as described in Section 3.

4.2 Overlapping Collective Operations

In the CG solver a collective operation (*Allreduce*) is performed in each iteration of the solver as described in Section 3. In order to overlap this operation among

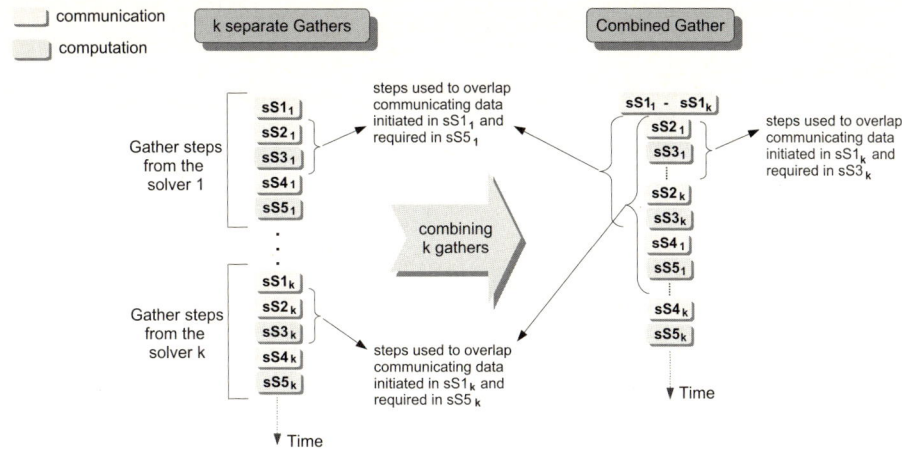

Fig. 2. Steps for the non-combined and the combined of k separate *Gather* functions

k solvers there is no need to use asynchronous operations as with the *Gather* operations described above. This is important because non-blocking collectives are not currently a part of the current MPI standard [12]. The method to allow this overlap is straightforward – to use a single collective with a k operand size, where k is the number of solvers that are combined, so the new collective operation takes operands from the k solvers. In particular for MILC, the overlapped collective operation takes the operands from both solvers resulting in an *Allreduce* of eight double floating-point operands (four for each solver).

5 Evaluation

5.1 Experimental Set-Up

The system used to evaluate the *Combined CG* solver contains 256 compute-nodes interconnected by a Voltaire 288-port InfiniBand 4x SDR switch. Each node contains two dual-core 2.0GHz AMD Opteron processor resulting with a total of 1,024 cores in the system. The MPI message passing library used in the evaluation is Open-MPI version 1.2 [13]. The achievable inter-node latency for small messages is 4 microseconds, and the uni-directional bandwidth is 950 MB/s for large messages on this cluster.

We evaluated the performance of the *Combined CG* solver (called *CCG*) in the *Update* lattice function of MILC. MILC version 7.4 was used in the experiments. The *su3_rmd* code in the MILC suite was used in the evaluation which is the most typical code used in MILC. This code performs simulations with conventional dynamical *Kogut-Susskind* quarks using the R algorithm. For comparison purposes we evaluated the performance of the original implementation of the two CG solvers in MILC which we will refer as *CG*. Timing data presented below are

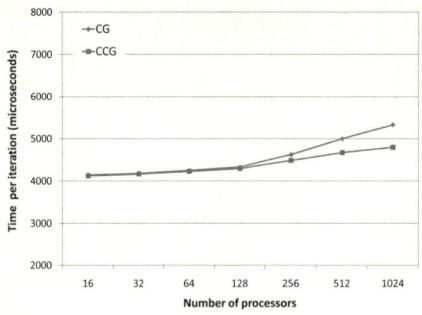 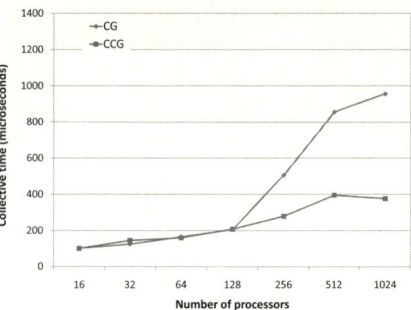

Fig. 3. Execution time per iteration of the CG and CCG solvers

Fig. 4. Collective time for the CG and CCG solvers

averages over multiple executions of both types of CG solvers. The times were filtered in order to discard any network warm up period.

MILC typically runs in a weak scaling mode where the number of grid points or lattice sites per processor is constant while the global problem size grows as the number of processors increases. We perform a scalability study using between 16 and 1,024 processors. The most common number of lattice sites per processor today is 6^4 for MILC [9]. Additionally, scaling studies with 4^4, 8^4, and 10^4 lattice sites per processor are also performed. It is useful to evaluate the effectiveness of our proposed technique with respect to the number of lattice sites. Note that a large number of lattice sites require more memory per processor that might be not fit in the memory available per core (cache or local store) in future multi-core based systems. Memory requirements for the lattice sites of 4^4, 6^4, 8^4, and 10^4 are 300KB, 1.3MB, 4MB, and 9.8MB.

5.2 Results

Figure 3 shows the execution time per iteration of the CG and the CCG solver for various processor counts using 6^4 lattice sites per processor. As can be seen, the CCG achieves a significant reduction of the execution time with respect to the CG solver specially at large processor counts. Reductions of 7% and 10% are achieved on 512 and 1,024 processors. The reason for the higher improvement at large processor counts is expected as the cost of collectives increases with scale and the CCG solver allows the overlap of these between both solvers and hence can hide their costs.

Figure 4 shows the time of just the collectives time per iteration when using the CCG and CG solvers on the same number of processors and number of lattice sites as evaluated before. As can be seen, the CCG solver significantly reduces the collective time with respect to the conventional CG solver. In particular, performance improvements of 1.8×, 2.1×, and 2.5× are achieved for 256, 512, and 1,024 processors. Note that the time to complete a collective in these solvers is actually substantially larger than would be obtained using a typical

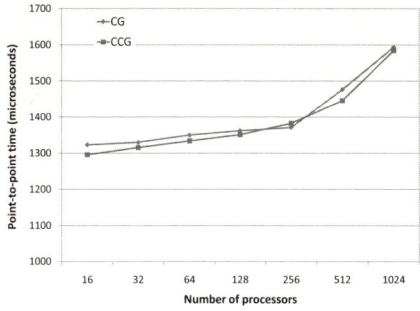 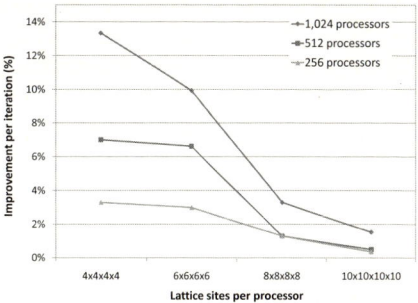

Fig. 5. Time of the point-to-point communications for the CG and CCG solvers

Fig. 6. Performance improvement of the CCG solver with respect to the CG solver for several lattice sites

microbenchmark that measures uniquely the collective time. In the CG solvers there is also point-to-point communication operations that affect the collective performance which are not taken into account in such a microbenchmarks. This is because the completion time of the point-to-point communications may vary from one processor to another, and thus may cause some desynchronization of the processors across the system that negatively affects the collective performance. However, even with this desynchronization occurring in the system, the CCG solver is still providing a substantial improvement with respect to the original CG solver.

On the other hand, the impact on the performance of point-to-point communications is shown in Figure 5 for the CCG and CG solvers and for the same processor counts evaluated above. The performance improvement achieved by CCG is quite negligible, less than 1% when compared with CG, despite allowing for an increased communication-computation overlap. This result exposes the limitations of the underlying current communication library to efficiently exploit communication-communication overlap between point-to-point operations.

Finally, results on scaling the number of lattice sites per processor are shown in Figure 6 showing the performance improvement of the CCG solver with respect to the CG solver for 256, 512, and 1,024 processors. As can be seen, in smaller lattice sites the impact of collectives are more relevant in the overall performance of the solver, and thus larger improvements are experienced, 14% for the lattice site of 4^4 and 1,024 processors. It should also be noted that for the *Peta-scale* use of MILC, the expected sub-grid sizes per processor will be in this range [11]. Conversely, in larger number of lattice sites the performance improvement achieved by CCG gradually diminishes in our testbed system, specially at small number of processors. This is due to the lower impact of the collective with respect to the total execution time which is dominated by computation on a larger number of lattice sites. In particular for 1,024 processors, performance improvements of 3.5% and 1.5% are observed for lattice sites of 8^4 and 10^4.

6 Related Work

Due to the importance of CG solvers in scientific simulations, there has been a lot of research to optimize both their communication and computation requirements.

The work most related to ours on optimizing the communication requirements is based on a particular implementation of the CG solver for solving 3D Poisson equations by overlapping communication with computation [4]. In this work a *MPI_AlltoAll* collective operation is used to gather data from neighbor nodes which is partially overlapped with computation on locally available data. To allow this overlap, the use of non-blocking collective operations [5] were necessary. Our work is different in that it allows for overlapping communication with communication from multiple solver instances while they focus on overlapping only communication with computation in a single solver instance.

Additionally, the scalability of CG solvers has been analyzed on parallel machines with a variety of interconnection network topologies such as meshes and hypercubes [6]. It was found that the scalability of the solver strongly depends on the suitable mapping of the global grid to the processors in the system in order to minimize the point-to-point communication costs. This work complements our own in the sense that these techniques can also be applied to improve the performance of our approach.

Efforts to optimize the computational aspects of CG solvers have included [7] which explored the floating-point efficiency by using a multi-level technique, the cascadic conjugate gradient method, that requires significantly less operations than single-level methods. Moreover, some acceleration techniques have recently been explored to speed up CG computation by using graphics processors (GPUs) e.g. [8]. Although, speeding up the computation of the CG solver is important, since it diminishes the level of parallelism necessary to solve a particular problem and thus indirectly reduces communication costs as well, the major bottleneck in large-scale problems remains as the high communication costs.

7 Conclusions

In this paper we have presented a novel technique to optimize the performance of multiple CG solvers, which we refer to as the Combined CG solver (CCG). CG solvers often limit the performance of scientific applications and the analysis performed in this work provides evidence that the CCG could significantly improve their performance.

CCG is based on combining multiple independent instances of a CG solver allowing for increased overlap of communication with other communication and computation. Two types of communication operations in one instance of a CG solver, namely collective and point-to-point operations, are overlapped with the collective and point-to-point operations in the other instances of the CG solver, respectively. In a general view, this technique can be also applied to combine any other independent computations in which some communication is taking place in order to maximize the overlap of these communications.

The evaluation of this technique has been performed in the context of a large-scale application, MILC, which is expected to have increased processing requirements, to the peta-flop scale, in the near future. MILC contains two independent CG solvers that have been optimized using CCG. A performance evaluation reveals that the CCG solver can reduce the communication costs of the collectives by a factor of 2.5× on a modest size 1,024-processor system. These improvements in the communication costs have a significant impact on the CG solver performance at large-scale. On 1,024 processors the performance is increased by 10% on typical number of lattice sites per processor. These improvements are expected to be significantly larger when using larger systems as the collectives become the dominant factor on the execution time.

References

1. Hestenes, M.R., Stiefel, E.: Methods of Conjugate Gradients for Solving Linear Systems. Journal of Research of the National Bureau of Standards 49(6), 409–436 (1952)
2. Dongarra, J.J., et al.: The Sourcebook of Parallel Computing. Morgan Kaufmann Publishers, San Francisco (2003)
3. MIMD Lattice Computation (MILC) Collaboration, http://www.physics.indiana.edu/sg/milc.html
4. Hoefler, T., Gottschling, P., Rehm, W., Lumsdaine, A.: Optimizing a Conjugate Gradient Solver with Non-Blocking Collective Operations. In: Workshop on ParSim (2006)
5. Hoefler, T., Squyres, J., Rehm, W., Lumsdaine, A.: A Case for Non-Blocking Collective Operations. In: Workshop on Frontier on High Performance Computing and Networking in conjunction with ISPA 2006 (2006)
6. Gupta, A., Kumar, V., Sameh, A.: Performance and Scalability of Preconditioned Conjugate Gradient Methods on Parallel Computers. IEEE Transactions on Parallel and Distributed Systems 06(5), 455–469 (1995)
7. Gottschling, P., Nagel, W.E.: An Efficient Parallel Linear Solver with a Cascadic Conjugate Gradient Method: Experience with Reality. In: Bode, A., Ludwig, T., Karl, W.C., Wismüller, R. (eds.) Euro-Par 2000. LNCS, vol. 1900, p. 784. Springer, Heidelberg (2000)
8. Krüger, J., Westermann, R.: Linear Algebra Operators for GPU Implementation of Numerical Algorithms. In: SIGGRAPH 2005: ACM SIGGRAPH 2005 Courses, p. 234. ACM Press, New York (2005)
9. National Science Foundation, Report of the High Performance Computing Town Hall Meeting: Science, Requirements, and Benchmarks, University of Illinois at Urbana-Champaign (April 2005)
10. Xingfu, W., Taylor, V.: Performance Analysis and Modeling of the SciDAC MILC Code on Four Large-scale Clusters, http://faculty.cs.tamu.edu/wuxf/research/tamu-MILC.pdf
11. Benchmarking Information Referenced in the NSF 05-625 High Performance Computing System Acquisition: Towards a Petascale Computing Environment for Science and Engineering (2006), http://www.nsf.gov/pubs/nsf0605/nsf0605.jsp
12. Snir, M., Otto, S., Huss-Lederman, S., Walker, D., Dongarra, J.J.: MPI: The Complete Reference, 2nd edn., vol. 1. MIT Press, Cambridge (1998)
13. Open-MPI, http://www.open-mpi.org

A Software Component Model with Spatial and Temporal Compositions for Grid Infrastructures*

Hinde Lilia Bouziane, Christian Pérez, and Thierry Priol

INRIA/IRISA
Campus de Beaulieu — F-35042 Rennes Cedex — France
{Hinde.Bouziane,Christian.Perez,Thierry.Priol}@inria.fr

Abstract. Grids are very complex and volatile infrastructures that exhibit parallel and distributed characteristics. To harness their complexity as well as the increasing intricacy of scientific applications, modern software engineering practices are needed. As of today, two major programming models dominate: software component models that are mainly based on a spatial composition and service oriented models with their associated workflow languages promoting a temporal composition. This paper tends to unify these two forms of composition into a coherent spatio-temporal software component model while keeping their benefits. To attest the validity of the proposed approach, we describe how the Grid Component model, as defined by the CoreGRID Network of Excellence, and the Askalon-AGWL workflow language have been adapted.

1 Introduction

Grid infrastructures are undoubtedly the most complex computing infrastructures ever built incorporating both parallel and distributed aspects in their implementations. Although they can provide an unprecedented level of performance, designing and implementing scientific applications for Grids represent challenging tasks for programmers. But this is not only due to the intricacy of the infrastructures. Indeed, numerical simulation applications are also becoming more complex involving the coupling of several numerical simulation codes to better simulate physical systems that require a multidisciplinary approach. To cope with the infrastructure and application complexity, it becomes necessary to design scientific applications with modern software engineering practices. Component-based programming or service-oriented programming are good candidates to design these applications using a modular approach. With a component-based approach, an application can be represented as an assembly of software components connected by a set of ports and described using an Architecture Description Language (ADL) while a service-oriented approach tends to represent an application as an orchestration of several services using a workflow language. In some sense, component programming appears as a spatial composition describing the connection between components while service programming promotes a temporal composition expressing the scheduling and the flow of control between services.

---

* This work was supported by the CoreGRID European Network of Excellence and by the French National Agency for Research project LEGO (ANR-05-CIGC-11).

In the context of Grids, both approaches have been used but in a separate way. In this paper, we show that both spatial and temporal compositions are required in the same programming model. Spatial composition is required to express some specific communication patterns that can be found in multi-physics scientific applications such as in coupled simulation where several simulation codes have to be run simultaneously and have to exchange data at each time step. However, component models do not capture when a given component will communicate with another component it is connected to; consequently all application components have to be deployed in advance on resources and kept until the end of the application. This leads to an inefficient use of resources especially in the context of resource sharing which is one of the aims of the Grid concept. Temporal composition, with respect to resource sharing, is more suitable since the control flow is explicit. It can be used to deploy services only when they are needed allowing thus a better utilization of Grid resources. A programming model, allowing the design of applications using a modular approach, must thus combine spatial and temporal composition to fulfill the programmer's requirements: strong code coupling and efficient use of resources. This paper studies how to combine these two composition schemes together and then it introduces STCM, a spatio-component model, based on the Grid Component Model (GCM) [1] and the ASKALON workflow system [2].

The remainder of this paper is organized as follows. Section 2 introduces and discusses properties of spatial and temporal composition models as well as some related works. Section 3 analyzes some possible designs that combine both compositions into a unique model. In Section 4, we describe STCM, a spatio-temporal component model and an example of application is given in Section 5. Section 6 concludes the paper.

2 Composition in Space and Time: Properties and Discussion

This paper focuses on composition as a mean to describe applications' structure. In general, such a structure reflects a reasoning dimension of the programmer. Our interest is focused on two major but orthogonal dimensions: space and time. Reasoning about space or time appears today as a factor separating two programming model trends for building scientific applications: *software component* and *workflow* models. This section presents their respective properties as well as some works attempting to combine them.

2.1 Composition in Space

Let us define a spatial composition as a relationship between components if and only if components being involved in the relationship are concurrently active during the time this relationship is valid. In general, components interact through adequate and compatible ports often according to a *provides-uses* paradigm. In most spatial composition models, the direction of the interaction is oriented: it is a user that invokes an operation on a provider. However, the interaction frequency is not specified: it is not known whether the user will actually invoke an operation nor the number of invocations. Thus, components are concurrently active during the time the relation is valid, i.e. the components are connected. Therefore, a spatial composition enables to express the architecture of an application, typically captured by UML **component** diagrams [3]. The spatial composition principle is followed by most existing component models like CCA [4], CCM [5], FRACTAL [6], SCA [7] and GCM [1], which we briefly present hereafter.

The Grid Component Model or GCM [1] is a component model being specified within the European *CoreGRID* Network of Excellence. It is based on FRACTAL [6], a hierarchical component model, and extends this latter in order to target Grid applications. GCM defines *primitive* and *composite* components. *Composite* components may contain several (sub-)components that form its *content* as illustrated in Figure 1.

GCM defines also *controllers* to separate non-functional concerns from the computation ones. In particular, *controllers* are used to manage sub-components. GCM supports several kinds of ports such as RMI or data streaming. GCM provides also an Architecture Description Language (ADL) which allows the specification of both components and their composition in a same phase.

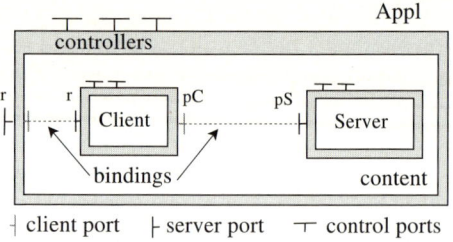

Fig. 1. Example of a GCM component

2.2 Composition in Time

A temporal composition can be defined as a relationship between tasks if and only if it expresses an execution order of the tasks. There are two classical formalisms for describing such a relationship: data flows and control flows. Data flows focus on the dependencies coming from data availability: the outputs of some tasks t_i are inputs of a task T. The execution of T depends on that of all t_i. In control flows, the execution order is given by some control constructs such as sequences, branches or loops. Temporal compositions enable expression of the sequence of actions which typically may be captured by UML **activity** diagrams [3]. There exist many environments [8] that deal with temporal compositions such as workflow systems like ASKALON [2], TRIANA [9], KEPLER [10], BPEL4WS [11], etc. For this paper, let us focus on ASKALON-AGWL.

ASKALON [12] is a Grid environment dedicated to the development and execution of scientific applications, being developed at the University of Innsbruck, Austria. It proposes the *Abstract Grid Workflow Language* (AGWL) [2]. This language is viewed by the designer under an *UML* activity diagram formalism. It offers a hierarchical model made of atomic and composite activities (sub-workflows). A composition is done with respect to both data flow and control flow compositions, as illustrated in Figure 2. A data flow is specified by simply connecting input data port to output data port of dependent activities, while the control flow describes the execution order of activities. AGWL supports several control structures like sequences, branches (*if* and *switch*), loops (*for* and *while*) and parallel structures (*parallelFor* and *parallelForEach*), etc.

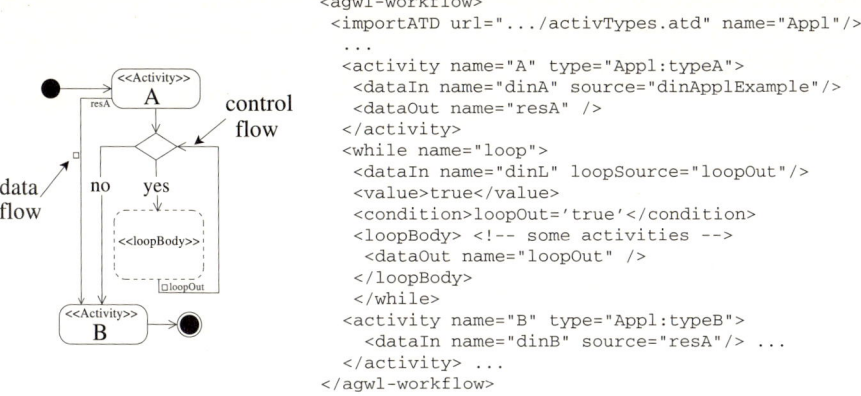

Fig. 2. A composition example in ASKALON-AGWL

2.3 Discussion

Spatial composition is well suited to describe components that must co-exist simultaneously and may communicate. It is the case for strong code coupling simulations such as meteorological simulations. The main limitation of spatial compositions is they do not explicitly capture the temporal dimension. That may lead to an underutilization of the resources because of an overestimation of needed ones. It is possible to embed an orchestration into a component driver. However, any modification on the application structure requires to modify the code. Lazy component instantiation also does not fully solve the problem as it is not known when a component can be safely destroyed.

Temporal composition is able to capture the temporal dimension and hence it enables efficient resource management. Nevertheless, its main limitation is the lack of support to express that two running tasks must communicate, as for example strong code coupling simulations. The solution of externalizing the loop of a code limits the coupling to coarse grained codes with respect to the overhead of launching a task.

Attempts to Merge Spatial and Temporal Compositions. To capture the good properties of the two models, some solutions have been proposed. ICENI [13] describes the internal behavior of a component with a workflow formalism. That helps to compute an optimized *spatial* deployment plan. However, it does not capture temporal relationship *between* components. Workflow models like in TRIANA or ASKALON enable spatial compositions. However, they are often hidden in tasks' implementation. As far as we know, workflow engines are not aware of underlying spatial compositions. Thus, models like in [14] propose specialized tasks dedicated to communications between *communicating* processes. However, that requires to modify codes to extract communications.

To summarize, the limitations seem to mainly come from the fact that the spatial and temporal dimensions are handled at distinct levels of the application structure. Hence, this paper focuses on a model where the two dimensions can co-exist at a same level.

3 Toward a Spatio-temporal Composition Model

3.1 Targeted Properties

Our goal is to define a model that enables the concurrent use of both spatial and temporal composition paradigms at any level of an application structure. First, the model should provide a quite high level of abstraction. In particular, it should abstract the resource infrastructures so that the Grid remains invisible from the programmer point of view. Second, the composition model should be rich enough to support a wide range of composition paradigms like control flow constructs (sequence, conditions, loops, etc.), method invocation, message passing, etc. Third, supporting many kinds of composition paradigms may lead to a complex life-cycle management. Hence, the model should offer a simple life-cycle model for combined spatial and temporal compositions so that the behavior of a whole application is quite easy to determine. Fourth, the model should be *hierarchical* and should provide all composition paradigms at any level of a hierarchy. Hierarchy appears as an important property to structure applications and to improve reusability. Fifth, as we aim at leveraging existing works, it should be possible to specify the model as an extension of some existing ones.

3.2 Analysis of Design Models for a Spatio-temporal Composition Model

Defining a spatio-temporal composition model requires to instantiate the concepts encountered in Section 2 in a coherent model. This section analyzes some design approaches keeping in mind the properties presented in Section 3.1.

There are two kinds of entities that may be embedded into a code: components and tasks. From an architectural point of view, they are very similar: they are black boxes with some communication ports. The main difference is on their life-cycle: a task is implicitly instantiated only at the time of its execution. Hence, we fuse them into the term task-component, which we define as a component supporting the concept of task. Hence, a mechanism is needed to define input and output ports and to bind tasks to components. The term task-component is used to distinguish between components supporting tasks and classical ones. It is just a notation as task-components are components.

As we start from a component model, the concept of ports keeps its usual definition. Spatial composition is thus directly inherited. However, the concept of port has to be extended with input/output ports for temporal compositions. As it consists in associating a piece of data to a port, the basic mechanism looks very similar to event ports.

A third issue is to define the rules governing task-component life-cycle. Such rules should state when a component can and/or must be created/destroyed. For example, the life-cycle of a task-component with only input and output ports can be controlled by its temporal relationship: it can be instantiated when its inputs are ready and destroyed when outputs have been retrieved. However, rules become more complex when a task-component has temporal and spatial ports.

Basing a spatio-temporal composition model on a data flow model is quite straightforward. The composition of input and output ports following the same philosophy as spatial ports, i.e. connections of compatible ports, it seems possible to slightly extend assembly languages of component models – like GCM ADL – to take them into account into an assembly with data flow compositions representing temporal compositions.

Table 1. GCM and AGWL concepts reused for defining a spatio-temporal model

Required concept	Provided concepts	Selected strategy
Task-Component	provided, used operations and tasks	extend GCM with task concept
Ports	spatial: GCM ports temporal: input and output data	extend GCM with temporal ports
Composition	spatial: GCM bindings temporal: data and control flow: AGWL	extend AGWL with GCM components and spatial bindings
Component life-cycle	states and transitions	inferred from composition

It seems also possible to integrate a control flow model. Control flow models are based on "programmable" constructions while component assemblies are based on description languages. Hence, an issue is to deal with the instructions of such a programmable language. There are two classical approaches. The first approach embeds every element of the language into a component, like in TRIANA, which provides a model that is easily extensible by adding new components. However, as components embed the control flow, it turns out that the control flow of the application is not visible: it may restrict optimizations like advance reservation of resources unless using behavioral component models. The second approach distinguishes language instructions from user components, like in many workflow languages. It limits language extensions but it enables runtime optimizations as the language is known.

4 STCM: A Spatio-temporal Model Based on GCM and AGWL

This section presents STCM, a spatio-temporal model based on both GCM and AGWL as well as the objectives presented in Section 3. In particular, the proposal is based on choosing, reusing and potentially merging or extending the specification of components, ports, tasks and the composition model offered by GCM and/or AGWL. Our choices are essentially motivated by keeping the advantages of each model. Table 1 sums up our strategy to reuse GCM and AGWL principal concepts in order to define a spatio-temporal model. The remainder of this section reviews these points in more depth.

4.1 Extending GCM Components with Tasks and Temporal Ports

The type of a component being defined by its ports, a new family of ports is required to define a task-component. Let us call them input and output ports. In contrast to classical client/server ports, that provide a method call semantic, input/output ports are attached to a data type. Hence, STCM provides typed input and output ports. They are provided through an extension of the GCM *TypeFactory* interface dedicated to create types. A *createFcTemporalType* operation creates the definition of an input (*isInput* = *true*) or output (*isInput* = *false*) port named *name* and for which the type is determined by a *data type* argument. As temporal ports are distinguished from classical ones, a component type declaration is also extended to include this new kind of ports.

The next step is to support a task within a task-component. A task can be viewed as a particular operation to be implemented by a user. The definition of such an operation depends on several assumptions. For example, multi-task components required to define a triplet (task, inputs, outputs) for each task, while it may be implicit for single task-component. Because of lack of space, the support of only one task per component is presented here. A task-component is a component which implements a *TaskController* interface which contains only a `void task()` operation which is called when the task needs to be executed. Input data are retrieved through input ports (through getter-like operations) and output data are set through output ports (through setter-like operations).

4.2 Life Cycle Management of Task-Components

Figure 3 presents a proposed state machine diagram with respect to the life-cycle of task-components. Compared to a classical task, where its activation corresponds to its execution, the active state of a task-component may be longer than the task running duration. The duration of the active state depends mainly on both the temporal composition and the requirement of the presence of provided functionality by a component. Hence, a component can be active without any running task like a standard component.

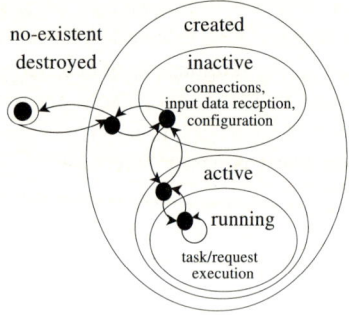

Fig. 3. State diagram

4.3 A Composition Language Based on a Modified AGWL

The STCM composition model is inspired from the AGWL language. The objective is to preserve its algorithmic composition logic but based on a task-component assembly view. Hence, the approach is essentially based on the replacement of the activity concept by a task-component one. Figure 4 presents the main elements of the grammar of the STCM language. Component definition looks like in GCM ADL but with the support of temporal ports as well as the possibility to connect them when being defined. Moreover, the language has dedicated instructions (`setPort` and `unsetPort`) to connect/disconnect ports.

As in AGWL, control flow composition is expressed as the content of composites. Then, it is straightforward to adapt all AGWL control flow constructions. Such instructions can be seen as pre-defined components with a known internal behavior. In STCM ADL, a component instance can be defined in the *declaration* part of a composite assembly or a control flow instruction. It results in distinct behaviors: the former aligns the instance creation and destruction with the composite ones, while the latter enables a dynamic creation and destruction.

The semantics of such a language has yet to be defined as for example with respect to when a component instance can be safely destroyed. We are working on the definition of a semantics able to reflect as much as possible a behavior based on a simple priority system: *if a spatial connection is specified within a control structure body then the temporal dimension is prevailing, otherwise the spatial dimension is to be considered first.*

```
component     ::= <component name=string (extends=string)?>
                      port* content? membrane?
                  </component>
port          ::= clientport | serverport | inport | outport | attribute
clientport    ::= <clientPort name=string type=string (set=string)?/>
serverport    ::= <serverPort name=string type=string/>
inport        ::= <dataIn  name=string type=string (set=string)?/>
outport       ::= <dataOut name=string type=string/>
attribute     ::= <attribute name=string type=string (set=string)?/>

membrane      ::= <controllerDesc desc=string/>
content       ::= primitive | composite
primitive     ::= <impl type=string signature=string/>
composite     ::= <body> stcmassembly </body>
stcmassembly  ::= declaration? instruction?

declaration   ::= <declare> component* instance* configport* </declare>
instance      ::= <instance name=string componentRef=string>
                      content? membrane?
                  </instance>
configport    ::= clientserver | inout
clientserver  ::= <setPort client=string server=string/>
                | <unsetPort client=string (server=string)?/>
inout         ::= <setPort in=string out=string/>
                | <unsetPort in=string (out=string)?/>

instruction   ::= instance | executetask | configport | seq | if | switch | while
                | for | forEach | dag | parallel | parallelFor | parallelForEach
executetask   ::= <exectask nameInstance=string/>

seq           ::= <sequence name=string>port* declaration instruction+</sequence>

if            ::= <if name=string> port* declaration condition then else? </if>
condition     ::= <condition> expr </condition>
then          ::= <then> stcmassembly </then>
else          ::= <else> stcmassembly </else>

parallel      ::= <parallel name=string> port* declaration section+ </parallel>
section       ::= <section> stcmassembly </section>

switch        ::= <switch name=string> port* declaration case+ default? </switch>
case          ::= <case condition=string (break=boolean)?> stcmassembly </case>
default       ::= <default> stcmassembly </default>
boolean       ::= true | false

// Same principle for while, for, forEach, dag, parallelFor and parallelForEach.
// expr represents a logical expression as in AGWL , with the same restrictions.
```

Fig. 4. Overview of the STCM grammar. Keywords are in bold, while strings are in italic.

4.4 Proof-of-Concept Implementation

In order to test the feasibility of the model, we have implemented a proof-of-concept interpreter of the STCM language based on the ANTLR language tool. The interpreter parses the language and generates calls to a GCM extended API so as to manage components, like component creation/destruction, port connection, as well as task invocation. It does not yet support all control flow instructions. A full implementation of the model requires to define a semantic and to implement/adapt a workflow engine.

```
1  <component name ="exApp">                    18  <parallel name="ParallelCtrl">
2   <dataIn name="vectIn"  type="Vect"/>        19   <instance name="a" compRef="A"/>
3   <body><component name="Init">               20   <instance name="b" compRef="B"/>
4     <dataIn  name="ii1" ... set="vectIn"/>    21   <section>
5     <dataOut name="io1" ... />                22    <exectask nameInstance="a"/>
6     <dataOut name="io2" type="double" />      23   </section>
7   </component>                                24   <section>
8   <component name="A">                        25    <while name="LoopCtrl">
9     <dataIn name="inA" ... set="init.io1"/>   26     <dataIn name="c" type="double"
10    <clientPort name="pA" ... set="B.pB"/>    27         set="init.io2"
11  </component>                                28         loopSet="B.outB"/>
12  <component name="B">                        29     <condition> c<0.1 </condition>
13    // in: double inB, out: double outB       30     <loopBody>
14    <serverPort name="pB" type="GetRes"/>     31      <exectask nameInstance="b">
15  </component>                                32       <dataIn name="inB" set="c"/>
16  <sequence name="seq1">                      33      </component>
17    <instance name="init" compRef="Init"      34     </loopBody>
      // lines 18-37 are on the right           35    </while>
38  </sequence></body>                          36   </section>
39 </assembly>                                  37  </parallel>
```

Fig. 6. Main elements of an application description in STCM

5 Example of an Application Description

Figure 5 illustrates a simplified STCM application coming from the French ANR LEGO project. This application contains two coupled codes represented by the spatially connected components a and b. Component a operates on a matrix, initialized according to some initial conditions defined by Component init. The result computed by Component a depends on data provided by Component b, data which depend on the iterative convergence computation which Component b is involved in. It is expected that Component b has a persistent active state for continuous a requesting. Therefore, the integration of b in the loop has to preserve the first created instance during all iterations. For simplicity, the detailed structure of GCM components (membranes, contents, implementations) are not represented in this section.

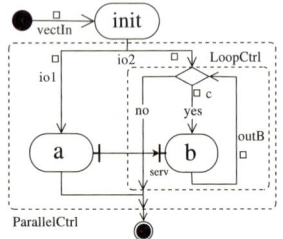

Fig. 5. Application example

Figure 6 shows how this application can be expressed with the STCM language. The expressed execution ordering matched perfectly with the specified requirements. In particular, Instance b of Component B is declared in the header of the parallel section. Hence, it is not destroyed at each iteration of the while loop.

While STCM offers means to explicitly express the specified behavior by the assembly, it is not the case when using separately GCM or AGWL. With STCM, it is usual to hide the temporal logic in a driver component. Depending on the programmer expertise, this component can manage the life-cycle of init, a and b. This management is required to avoid overconsumption of resources, in particular if components are composite/parallel. However, that may be complex to be done by the user. With AGWL, there is no mean to express the spatial dependence between a and b, which is usually hidden in tasks' code. That may limit reusability. In addition, the stateless property of tasks implies the b's state to be saved/reloaded for each iteration. That may lead to inefficient execution. On the contrary, STCM offers a more powerful assembly model in term of behavior expressiveness. This is relevant to ease programing, improve reusability, enable automatic management of an assembly and optimize resources usage.

6 Conclusion and Future Works

In order to harness the programmability of Grids, two major approaches are used to develop applications: software component models mainly used by strongly coupled applications and workflow models mainly used by loosely coupled applications. As both models have benefits and drawbacks with respect to some algorithmic patterns, this paper explores the possibility of designing a model that support both composition models. The paper has analyzed some designs for combining both of them. As a result, the paper describes STCM, a spatio-temporal component model based on two existing models – GCM and ASKALON. Some benefits has been shown through an example.

Future works consist in defining a semantic for the STCM language as well as having a full implementation, either based on a new workflow engine, on the adaptation of an existing one, or on the compilation of STCM to plain AGWL. Though the latter should not lead to the best implementation, it may be enough to validate STCM.

References

1. Institute, P.M.: Basic features of the grid component model. CoreGRID Delivrable D.PM.04, CoreGRID (March 2007)
2. Fahringer, T., Qin, J., Hainzer, S.: Specification of Grid Workflow Applications with AGWL: An Abstract Grid Workflow Language. In: Proceedings of the Fifth IEEE International Symposium on Cluster Computing and Grid 2005 (CCGrid 2005), Cardiff, UK, May 2005, vol. 2, pp. 676–685 (2005)
3. OMG: Unified modeling language. Document formal/2007-02-05 (February 2007)
4. Bernholdt, D.E., Allan, B.A., Armstrong, R., Bertrand, F., Chiu, K., Dahlgren, T.L., Damevski, K., Elwasif, W.R., Epperly, T.G.W., Govindaraju, M., Katz, D.S., Kohl, J.A., Krishnan, M., Kumfert, G., Larson, J.W., Lefantzi, S., Lewis, M.J., Malony, A.D., McInnes, L.C., Nieplocha, J., Norris, B., Parker, S.G., Ray, J., Shende, S., Windus, T.L., Zhou, S.: A component architecture for high-performance scientific computing. International Journal of High Performance Computing Applications 20(2), 163–202 (2006)
5. OMG: CORBA component model, v4.0. Document formal/2006-04-01 (April 2006)
6. Bruneton, E., Coupaye, T., Stefani, J.: The Fractal Component Model, version 2.0-3. Technical report, ObjectWeb consortium (February 2004)
7. Beisiegel, M., Blohm, H., Booz, D., Edwards, M., Hurley, O., Ielceanu, S., Miller, A., Karmarkar, A., Malhotra, A., Marino, J., Nally, M., Newcomer, E., Patil, S., Pavlik, G., Raepple, M., Rowley, M., Tam, K., Vorthmann, S., Walker, P., Waterman, L.: SCA Service Component Architecture - Assembly Model Specification, version 1.0. Technical report, Open Service Oriented Architecture collaboration (OSOA) (March 2007)
8. Yu, J., Buyya, R.: A taxonomy of workflow management systems for grid computing. Journal of Grid Computing 3(3-4), 171–200 (2005)
9. Taylor, I., Shields, M., Wang, I., Harrison, A.: Visual Grid Workflow in Triana. Journal of Grid Computing 3(3-4), 153–169 (2005)

10. Altintas, I., Birnbaum, A., Baldridge, K.K., Sudholt, W., Miller, M., Amoreira, C., Yohann,: A framework for the design and reuse of grid workflows. In: Herrero, P., Pérez, M.S., Robles, V. (eds.) SAG 2004. LNCS, vol. 3458, pp. 120–133. Springer, Heidelberg (2005)
11. Andrews, T., Curbera, F., Dholakia, H., Goland, Y., Klein, J., Leymann, F., Liu, K., Roller, D., Smith, D., Thatte, S., Trickovic, I., Weerawarana, S.: Business process execution language for web services version 1.1. Technical report (May 2003)
12. Thomas, F., Radu, P., Rubing, D., Francesco, N., Stefan, P., Jun, Q., Mumtaz, S., Hong-Linh, T., Alex, V., Marek, W.: ASKALON: A Grid Application Development and Computing Environment. In: Proceedings of the 6th International Workshop on Grid Computing, Seattle, USA, November 2005, pp. 122–131 (2005)
13. Furmento, N., Mayer, A., McGough, S., Newhouse, S., Field, T., Darlington, J.: ICENI: Optimisation of component applications within a grid environment. Journal of Parallel Computing 28(12), 1753–1772 (2002)
14. Pllana, S., Fahringer, T.: Uml based modeling of performance oriented parallel and distributed applications. In: Yucesan, E., Chen, C.H., Snowdon, J., Charnes, J. (eds.) Proc. of the 2002 Winter Simulation Conference, San Diego, California, USA. IEEE, Los Alamitos (2002)

A Design Pattern for Component Oriented Development of Agent Based Multithreaded Applications*

A.L. Rodríguez[1], P.E. López-de-Teruel[1], A. Ruiz[2],
G. García-Mateos[2], and L. Fernández[1]

[1] Dept. Tecnología e Ingeniería de Computadores, University of Murcia
[2] Dept. Informática y Sistemas, University of Murcia
alrl1@alu.um.es, {pedroe,aruiz,ginesgm,lfmaimo}@um.es

Abstract. We present a design pattern which allows for easy multithreaded application development, without requiring parallel programming expertise from potential users. The pattern encourages reusability considering threads as truly independent software components, or agents, while hiding the low level details about safe data sharing and synchronization. Though coarse grained, the solution is perfectly compatible with other more specific multithreading techniques, which could be used in more computationally intensive agents. The approach is based on the classical pipeline pattern, but includes also asynchronous communications and event driven responses, and implements an efficient distributed synchronization and data sharing technique, which minimizes overhead. These features make the pattern specially adequate for real time applications that possibly need to be monitored by an interactive GUI, such as computer vision or signal processing applications, among others.

1 Introduction

As manufacturing processes get near the theoretical minimum semiconductor size in chips, single-threaded processors performance is reaching its natural limit. As a consequence, most technology companies have radically changed their designs in the quest for boosting performance, focusing their efforts in multiplying the number of cores in their architectures [1]. Accordingly, software development will expectedly suffer a revolution in the years to come [2]. Parallel programming will become imperative to take advantage of the computing power unleashed by these new CPUs. But concurrency requires expert knowledge from programmers, so it is not always easy to transform serial applications into parallel programs.

Design patterns, on the other hand, have proven to be useful to manage software complexity, creating specific solutions for recurrent problems and establishing a common language among developers [3]. Recently, some authors have stressed the need for a similar approach to parallel programming [4,5].

---
* This work has been supported by the Spanish MEC and European FEDER funds under grants "TIN2006-15516-C04-03" and Consolider "CSD2006-00046". Special thanks are owed to the referees for their careful reading and very useful suggestions.

In this paper we describe one such pattern in detail. It was initially designed to easily program multicore systems in *QVision* [6] –a software framework for computer vision prototype development–, as many of the potential users would presumably be non-experts in parallel programming. This need for paradigms that ease the migration of traditional software has been acknowledged even in the specific field of image processing [7]. Our pattern, anyway, will prove to be useful also in more general applications, where a set of agents work with several degrees of autonomy, collaborating in order to accomplish a global task.

2 Motivating Example

Computer vision and robotics often imply coordination of multiple perception, control and user interface modules, or agents [8]. The idea of parallelizing those systems is not new, either using dedicated hardware [9], or through middleware based solutions in which each agent independently computes and publish some piece of data through a well defined interface [10]. Multicore CPUs greatly facilitate the implementation of these systems, though also introduce new challenges, such as making them more modular, reusable, maintainable and efficient.

The pattern we propose is a generalization of a *pipeline*, which divides a computation into a sequence of concurrent stages. Though global latency is still the sum of individual computation times of all threads, average throughput is limited only by the slowest one [5]. To make the scheme work correctly, care must be taken to synchronize adjacent threads when sending data from a stage to the next. Data sharing should be thread safe, and we must ensure that a thread does not start processing before every data that it needs is available.

We extend this basic technique by considering more general processing agents, that will not only process data in a fixed order, but will also communicate between them out of the normal data flow, do their job autonomously (while still reading and writing data from/to other agents), and even do event based flow control, adjusting to a wider range of functionality. Figure 1 shows a typical vision application, running on a mobile robot, that follows the described processing scheme. The objective is to guide the robot through an indoor environment using both visual (optical flow and stereo based) and range sensor (laser and ultrasonic based) obstacle detection procedures. The system also uses object recognition techniques to make the robot track previously learned objects.

Details on the involved image processing and control tasks are out of the scope of the paper, so, instead, we focus on the overall task structure and communication pattern. This application fits well to our design pattern, with several semi-independent tasks running in parallel, and *linked* to make their output available for others. Some tasks are *synchronously* linked serially (solid arrows in the figure), much like in a hardware pipeline, with computation clearly divided into consecutive stages: for example, the process of capturing and decoding the input image from both cameras, filtering it, extracting points with the Harris detector, and tracking them to estimate the optical flow. On the contrary, other tasks are simply *asynchronously* connected (dotted arrows) to the corresponding

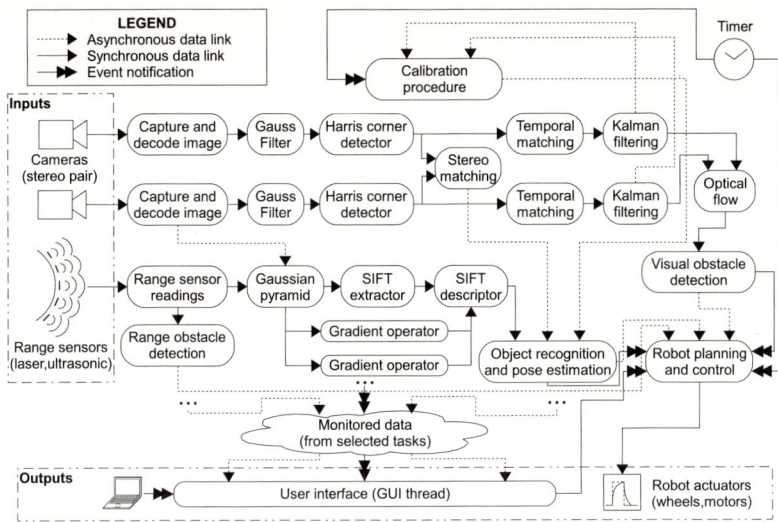

Fig. 1. Example multithreaded application using the proposed pattern

source tasks: for example, the calibration procedure that reads the lists of points produced by the Kalman trackers[1]. *Event notifications* (double arrows) can trigger the activation of these kind of tasks. In our example, robot movement is triggered by one of such events, generated by a periodic timer, by other tasks –such as an obstacle detection or the recognition of a target object–, or even by a direct order of the user, coming from the GUI.

Finally, observe also that simultaneous processing sequences can also run continuously in independent pipeline branches, though at completely different speeds: for example, the object detection branch could run at a noticeably slower rate than the rest of the application, due to the greater cost of the associated Gaussian pyramid, SIFT extractor and descriptor and pose estimation tasks.

3 Pattern Description

Figure 1 shows the flexibility of the global application scheme for which we propose the pattern. The programmer simply creates a directed graph-like structure, where information is processed in the nodes and sent through data links –synchronous or not–, flowing from sources to sinks (from cameras and sensors to user interface and robot actuators, in our case). We will expose a software pattern that directly maps these elements into reusable *worker* objects, with their own encapsulated internal states and well defined interfaces. That is, we will try to build *component oriented* threads, which efficiently communicate data variables of arbitrary type and size among themselves and/or the user interface

---

[1] Calibration does not need to be executed at frame rate, but simply periodically, just to maintain an acceptable estimation of the working parameters of the cameras.

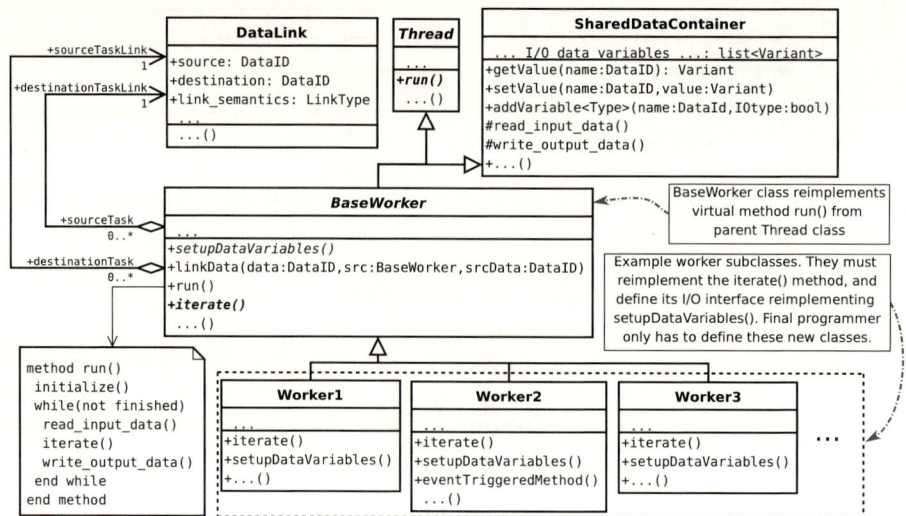

Fig. 2. *Worker pattern* schema

safely, with no need for the programmer to use any kind of low level synchronization primitive. Synchronism will thus be made *explicit* in design, while *implicit* in programming; we could speak of a *declarative synchronism*, rather than classical *imperative synchronism*, much more prone to programming errors, and less scalable, from the software engineering point of view.

As mentioned above, the pattern loosely resembles a *pipeline*, and has also some commonalities with the *event-based coordination* pattern [5]. Figure 2 shows a standard UML schema [11] for it. Processing stages (rounded boxes in figure 1) are modeled by *worker* objects sharing a common superclass `BaseWorker`. The programmer reimplements the virtual method `iterate()` for each specific worker, computing outputs from inputs adequately. The `run()` method of each thread just executes a continuous loop in which, before every call to `iterate()`, every input variable is updated with the latest output values of the source workers. Corresponding output data are written at the end of the iteration.

Input and output parameters are modeled as heterogeneous sets of data variables of any type. The `SharedDataContainer` class offers functionality to add them to new worker objects. In our specific Qt/C++ implementation, this class is programmed using generic templated methods and lists of *variant* objects. `Variant` is a class that acts like a union for any kind of data type. It can hold a single value of a single type at any time [12]. Each data item, independently of its specific type, is always stored in a data container as a variant, and given a name (*DataId* in the diagram). This augments C++ with a powerful generic mechanism, by which the programmer can not only dynamically add data items and access them easily in a type safe manner, but also allows us, the designers of the framework, to work with arbitrary sets of variables without knowing their data types in advance. Programmers should add shared variables to workers before any call to the `iterate()` method, in the `setupDataVariables()` abstract method defined in `BaseWorker`, which in turn will call the corresponding templated `addVariable()` method in `SharedDataContainer`.

Workers can have directed data dependency links between them (arrows between workers in figure 1). The method `linkData()` binds each input variable from the destination worker to a specified output variable from the source. This is the only data sharing mechanism between workers, which are otherwise completely modular and independent. When the pipeline starts its execution, every call to the `iterate()` function is preceded by a call to `read_input_data()`, which performs a thread safe read of output data from any source worker bound to the calling thread. The counterpart `write_output_data()` method saves a copy of every output variable, so that linked threads always have access to the last *coherent output state* generated, while we start working in the next iteration. This way, computation is overlapped with communication with the rest of workers, effectively resembling the behaviour of a classical pipeline.

Due to lack of space, we can not include here any C++ code snippet to illustrate the ease of use of the pattern. Anyway, the reader can consult [6] for some real coding examples.

4 Implementation

The underlying method used to implement both *synchronous* and *asynchronous* links is summarized in Fig. 3. Every input variable is read from the corresponding safe copy -*coherent state*- in the source, protecting the read with a standard read-write lock. This protection is active for both kind of links, synchronous and asynchronous. In reader workers (*B* in the figure), `read_input_data()` just locks the mutex for read, so several simultaneous readings are possible. Whenever a writer worker (*A* in the figure) has to update its output at the end of an iteration, it locks the mutex for write, so that any pending reader temporarily blocks the writer, while any subsequent reading is delayed until writing has been performed. This is a standard procedure in multithreaded access to shared data. Observe that many workers can be simultaneously reading and writing in different zones. The inherent distributed nature of the approach avoids the bottleneck which would occur if we used a centralized *blackboard* architecture (so common in older agent based applications). Observe also that the time that each worker holds the lock is limited to a simple copy operation, which should normally be negligible with respect to the computation time consumed during a worker iteration.

Synchronous links must also enforce a temporal constraint between associated threads. Each *consumer* must wait for the producer to write the corresponding data first. We implement this by waiting on a semaphore associated to each link (`SyncSemOut` in Fig. 3). This semaphore is initialized to zero when the link is created at the start of the application, and subsequently released by the producer (worker *A* in the figure) each time a new coherent state is written, by means of the `write_output_data()` method. The consumer, by calling `read_input_data()`, tries to acquire this semaphore, effectively waiting on it

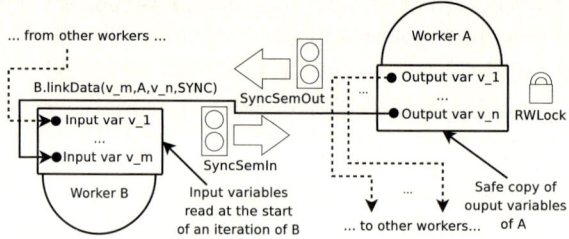

Fig. 3. Implementation of synchronization among workers

until the producer has written some useful data, as required by the semantics of the synchronous link. A completely analogous `SyncSemIn` semaphore also prevents the producer from completing an iteration -that is, writing a new output state- until the corresponding synchronously linked consumers have all read the previous input. This semaphore is this time initialized to one when creating the link, and acquired by the writer and released by the reader, at the end and at the start of their iterations, respectively.

A last important implementation detail regards memory management. Figure 1 showed a set of agents communicated by data flow links. It might seem that the involved communication mechanism resembles more the message passing paradigm than the shared memory approach traditionally used in multithreaded programming. A naive implementation of this message passing would become a serious performance problem, especially regarding large data structures, such as images or long data vectors or matrices, so common in signal and image processing. Expensive copies should be avoided when possible in shared memory architectures, such as the multicore CPUs to which our pattern is targeted. To cope with this, we employ the well known *implicit data sharing* technique [13], which is efficient and thread-safely supported by the Qt library [12] used in our C++ implementation. Every implicitly shared class consists of a pointer to a data block that contains a reference count and the real, possibly large size data. When a shared object is freshly created, its reference count is set to one. The counter is then incremented whenever a new object references the shared data, and decremented when dereferenced. Shared data is deleted only when the counter becomes zero. Making a copy of an object is thus very fast, as it only involves setting a pointer and incrementing the counter. Expensive memory copying occurs only in the (rather uncommon) case that we need to copy an object to immediately modify it. Implicit sharing also avoids unnecessary data duplication and, just as the synchronization procedures exposed before, conveniently occurs behind the scenes, in a completely transparent way for programmers[2].

---

[2] In fact, the technique is just an straightforward adaptation of the *copy on write* method, extensively used by operating system implementers for efficient copying of large pieces of data which are not expected to be immediately modified. The ubiquitous Unix `fork()` system call, that duplicates the memory space of a process, is often implemented this way; filesystems often employ the technique, too.

5 Discussion

There are a number of advantages in our simple approach to task parallelism:

- The proposal fully supports worker reusability. Agents are programmed independently, as isolated processes with a well defined set of input and output parameters. After that, any agent can be efficient and safely used in any application by simply binding their inputs and outputs with the rest of agents of the application, without even needing to recompile any original code. Agents can thus be stored in a reusable, incremental library. Nothing prevents us from even replicating identical tasks in an application, if needed (for example, the stereo pair processing stages, or the sequence of gradient operators on the Gaussian pyramid in Fig. 1). This is truly component oriented software development, applied to the field of multithreaded parallelism.
- The framework ensures thread-safe data sharing in a completely transparent way for the programmer. Application development reduces to reusing preexisting workers from the library, programming some new ones, and communicating them using the desired synchronization semantics on each link. Moreover, deadlocks are not possible, as long as loops in synchronous data links are avoided in the global data path. The inherent distributed approach to data sharing makes the architecture also more scalable (at the cost of multiplying the number of locks and semaphores; but in this way, the chances of performance bottlenecks due to centralized data structures are minimized).
- The pattern is easily *composable*: a worker with a well defined behaviour and interface, while being internally implemented in terms of lighter workers, could be added as a first-class member to the library of agents.
- Reactive agents, that perform actions only as a consequence of internal (application generated) or external events (for example, coming from the GUI), fit perfectly with the pattern. They can be asynchronously linked to other workers, arranging their `iterate()` method to trigger only when conveniently signaled. The well known *signal-slot* mechanism available in many C++ toolkits [12] is perfectly adequate for this kind of agents. Code that updates the GUI, or that communicates with timers, sensors and actuators (see Fig. 1) fits also perfectly with these asynchronous, event-driven links.

But there is no silver bullet for easy and effective parallelism, the approach has also some limitations. Here we will highlight the two most apparent:

- First, there is a clear structural restriction on target applications, which should be clearly modular, repetitive and task oriented.
- Second, load balancing responsibility completely falls on the programmer side. He must take care of adequately dividing the work to be done, study several agent organizations, detect potential bottleneck tasks and dividing them or, ultimately, even parallelizing them using more specific multithreading techniques –for example, data-parallelism based, using OpenMP [14], or a more dynamically oriented nested task parallelism, such as the one used by the *Threading Building Blocks* library from Intel [15].

6 Performance

Independently of the obvious influence of adequate load balancing, it can also be interesting to illustrate the performance impact inherent to the pattern. For example, how much will a perfectly balanced application move away from ideal speedup due to the underlying synchronization mechanisms described in Sect. 4? We performed a series of tests on an eight-core platform[3] to evaluate it. We designed an application with a variable number of threads, all of them executing a dummy, time controlled CPU consumption procedure, combined using increasingly harder types of synchronization and communication patterns:

- *Unlinked*: Ideal case, with all the agents executing independently in parallel.
- *Async*: Agents again execute without temporal dependences, but now they share data in an asynchronous manner. More precisely, $n - 2$ of the total n threads read an output variable from the first, while the last one reads an output variable from each of these $n - 2$.
- *Pipeline*: Classical pipeline, with n agents serially and synchronously linked.
- *Width*: Identical communication pattern to the *async* case, but now using synchronous links. This enforces a sequencing constraint and two clear synchronization bottlenecks (first and last threads).

Figure 4 (left) shows the speedup of two n-threaded applications with 10 and 40 *ms* of approximate CPU consumption per iteration per thread, respectively, against a serial one performing an equivalent CPU work (i.e., $n*10$ and $n*40$ *ms*), for several n values[4]. Note that ideal speedup in continuous operation would be eight in every case, but synchronization overhead will diminish this value, mainly due to agents waiting on the corresponding locks and/or semaphores. Anyway, observe that losses due to synchronization are not very large in almost any case. Only one speedup measure falls below seven, for the worst case *width* test and an individual thread computational load per iteration of 10 *ms*. Note that, the greater the CPU load (40 *ms* vs. 10 *ms* in the example), the less frequency of calls to synchronization primitives, and the smaller impact on the achieved global speedup. The total number of threads, on the other hand, does not seem to have a great influence in the results, possibly due to the fact that, though the number of synchronization points increments accordingly, impact on global performance gets amortized by the greater granularity of the application.

We also studied the impact of memory copying operations. *Implicit sharing* minimizes them, so, in most cases, performance should not noticeably suffer if the non-copy-modify restriction (see Sect. 4) holds. Nevertheless, some applications will contain agents that modify some of their inputs immediately after reading them, forcing real copies. In order to evaluate this somewhat worst case

---

[3] Experiments were performed on a server with two 64 bits Intel Xeon 2GHz CPUs, each one with four cores and 4 MB L2 cache, running a 2.6.22 Linux SMP kernel.

[4] Each measure corresponds to the median value of a set of 10 tests for each configuration. Each of the n workers execute 5000 iterations, which should approximate well the performance on a theoretical stable state of the system.

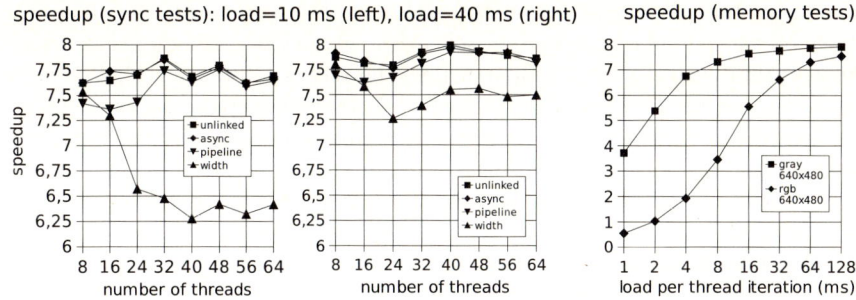

Fig. 4. Speedup for several synchronization and memory tests (see text)

scenario, we designed another testbed application, this time consisting of a simple pipeline of eight threads, with each stage producing a 640×480 output image, which is fed forward to the next stage. Each stage modifies this image, forcing a real memory copy in every data link. Figure 4 (right) illustrates the results for various computational loads per thread iteration (in the same conditions stated in footnotes 3 and 4, and $n = 8$). We study two cases: one channel (~ 300 KB) and three channel images (~ 900 KB). Of course, the bigger the size of data to be copied, the worse the speedup that can be achieved. Performance loss is much more appreciable for excessively light CPU loads per iteration. In these cases the programmer should consider the possibility of joining two or more stages, to avoid the memory copying overhead. Anyway, as computational load grows, relative impact of copying diminishes, with values greater than 128 ms asymptotically approximating ideal values of the speedup.

7 Conclusions

We have proposed a design pattern for easy and efficient programming of task oriented multithreaded applications. The technique is specially adequate in fields such as computer vision and signal processing, but could be used in any application which fits the quite flexible pipeline-like scheme described. The solution encourages reusability by being based on fully component oriented, encapsulated *workers*, which communicate through well defined interfaces. Data links are established declaratively, just before the application starts, hiding the complexities of explicit synchronization programming, thus opening the possibility of fully functional and scalable parallelism to non expert developers.

Our preliminary performance tests indicate that overhead inherent to the pattern (both due to synchronization primitives and possible memory copies) is low. Performance gains, though, still depend strongly on the ability of the programmer to adequately balance the workload among workers. Both heavy loaded agents –which could become a bottleneck– and excessively light ones –whose synchronization and management overhead might be counterproductive– should be avoided. If we follow these recommendations, the static thread planning imposed by the pattern is compensated for by the automatic load balancing performed by the operating system scheduler, given that the application has a sufficient number of threads. In particular, the recent 2.6 linux kernel series include very acceptable support for general multithreaded applications running in SMP systems, balancing the work across available processors while maintaining some CPU affinity for cache efficiency. Threads that are ready to perform useful work are also scheduled while others wait for completion of an I/O operation or in a synchronization point, thus incrementing the probability of maintaining all cores continuously working.

References

1. Sutter, H.: The free lunch is over. Dr. Dobbs Journal 3(30) (2005)
2. Sutter, H., Larus, J.: Software and the concurrency revolution. Queue 3(7) (2005)
3. Gamma, E., Helm, R., Johnson, R., Vlissides, J.: Design Patterns: Elements of Reusable Object-Oriented Software (1994)
4. Anvik, J., Schaeffer, J., Szafron, D., Tan, K.: Why not use a pattern-based parallel programming system? In: Kosch, H., Böszörményi, L., Hellwagner, H. (eds.) Euro-Par 2003. LNCS, vol. 2790. Springer, Heidelberg (2003)
5. Mattson, T., Sanders, B., Massingill, B.: Patterns for Parallel Programming. Addison-Wesley, Reading (2005)
6. Rodriguez, A., Lopez-de-Teruel, P., Ruiz, A., Garcia-Mateos, G., Fernandez, L.: QVision, a development framework for real-time computer vision and image processing research. In: Proceedings of the International Conference on Image Processing, Computer Vision, and Pattern Recognition, IPCV 2008 (2008)
7. Nicolescu, C., Jonker, P.: EASY PIPE: An easy to use parallel image processing environment based on algorithmic skeletons. In: Proceedings of the 15th Parallel and Distributed Processing Symposium (2001)
8. Arkin, R., MacKenzie, D.: Temporal coordination of perceptual algorithms for mobile robot navigation. IEEE Trans. on Robotics and Automation 10(3) (1994)
9. Hu, H., Michael, B.: A parallel processing architecture for sensor based control of intelligent mobile robots. Int. Jou. on Robot. and Autonomous Syst. 17(4) (1996)
10. Farinelli, A., Grisetti, G., Iocchi, L.: Design and implementation of modular software for programming mobile robots. Int. Jou. of Adv. Robotics Syst. 3(1) (2006)
11. Booch, G., Rumbaugh, J., Jacobson, I.: The Unified Modeling Language User Guide. Addison Wesley Longman (1998)
12. Blanchette, J., Summerfield, M.: C++ GUI Programming with Qt 4. P.Hall (2006)
13. Caluwaerts, L., Debacker, J., Peperstraete, J.: Implementing streams on a data flow computer system with paged memory. In: Proceedings of the 10th Annual International Symposium on Computer Architecture (1983)
14. Chapman, B., Jost, G., van der Pas, R.: Using OpenMP. MIT Press, Cambridge (2007)
15. Reinders, J.: Intel Threading Building Blocks. O'Reilly Media, Sebastopol (2007)

Advanced Concurrency Control for Transactional Memory Using Transaction Commit Rate

Mohammad Ansari, Christos Kotselidis, Kim Jarvis, Mikel Luján,
Chris Kirkham, and Ian Watson

The University of Manchester
{ansari,kotselidis,jarvis,mikel,chris,watson}@cs.manchester.ac.uk

Abstract. Concurrency control for Transactional Memory (TM) is investigated as a means for improving resource usage by adjusting dynamically the number of concurrently executing transactions. The proposed control system takes as feedback the measured *Transaction Commit Rate* to adjust the concurrency. Through an extensive evaluation, a new Concurrency Control Algorithm (CCA), called P-only Concurrency Control (PoCC), is shown to perform better than our other four proposed CCAs for a synthetic benchmark, and the STAMP and Lee-TM benchmarks.

1 Introduction

Explicit concurrent programming using fine-grain locks is known to be challenging for developing robust and correct applications. However, the need to simplify concurrent programming has become a priority with the prospect of concurrent programming becoming mainstream to take advantage of multi-core processors. Transactional Memory (TM) [1,2] is a new concurrent programming paradigm that aims to ease the complexity of concurrent programming, yet still offer performance and scalability competitive with fine-grain locking.

TM requires developers to mark code blocks that access shared data structures as *transactions*. A runtime layer manages transactions' concurrent data accesses. Conflicts between any two transactions occur when one attempts to modify data previously modified or read by another active transaction. This conflict for shared data is resolved by a *contention management policy* [3] that decides to *abort* one transaction, and let the other continue. A transaction *commits* if it executes its code block without being aborted, making globally visible its modifications to shared data.

The motivation for this work is the observation that TM applications exhibit fluctuating amounts of *exploitable parallelism*, i.e. the maximum number of transactions that can be committed concurrently, without any aborts, varies over time. We hypothesize that dynamically adjusting the number of transactions allowed to execute concurrently in response to the fluctuating exploitable parallelism should improve resource usage when exploitable parallelism is low, and improve execution time when it is high. *Transaction Commit Rate* (TCR), the percentage of committed transactions out of all executed transactions in a sample period, is investigated as a suitable application-independent measure of exploitable parallelism.

The only previous work is our own proposal of four Concurrency Control Algorithms (CCAs) [4]. This paper evaluates a new CCA, called *P-only Concurrency Controller* (PoCC), against the previously proposed CCAs using a synthetic benchmark and the STAMP [5] and Lee-TM benchmarks [6,7]. The new CCA is called *P-only Concurrency Controller* (PoCC). The evaluation explores the effect of the CCAs on the benchmarks' execution time, resource usage, wasted work, aborts per commit (APC), and responsiveness to changes in TCR. The results show PoCC gives similar or better performance, is more responsive to TCR changes, and more robust to noise in TCR changes, than the previous CCAs.

Section 2 introduces PoCC, and compares it to the other four CCAs. Section 3 details the experimental platform used in the evaluation, and Section 4 presents the results. Finally, Section 5 summarizes the paper.

2 P-only Concurrency Control

Using control theory terminology, the control objective is to maintain the *process variable* TCR at a *set point* desirable value, in spite of *unmeasured disturbance* from fluctuating exploitable parallelism. The *controller output* is to modify the number of transactions executing concurrently in response to changes in TCR. For the purposes of this paper, the maximum number of transactions executed concurrently is controlled by enabling or disabling threads that execute transactions. PoCC is based on a P-only controller [8] and operates as a loop:

1. If currentTime − lastSampleTime < *samplePeriod*, goto Step 1;
2. If numTransactions < *minTransactions*, goto Step 1;
3. TCR ← numCommits / numTransactions × 100;
4. ΔTCR ← TCR − *setPoint*;
5. If (numCurrentThreads= 1) & (TCR > *setPoint*);
   (a) then Δthreads ← 1;
   (b) else Δthreads ← ΔTCR × numCurrentThreads / 100
       (rounded to the closest integer);
6. newThreads ← numCurrentThreads + Δthreads;
7. Adjust *minThreads* ≤ newThreads ≤ *maxThreads*;
8. numCurrentThreads ← newThreads;
9. Set lastSampleTime ← currentTime, go to Step 1;

where the parameters are:

- *samplePeriod* is the sample period (tunable);
- *minTransactions* is the minimum number of transactions required in a sample (tunable);
- *setPoint* is the set point value (tunable);
- *minThreads* is the minimum number of threads, for this paper one; and

– *maxThreads* is the maximum number of threads, for this paper the maximum number of processors, or cores, available.

The *setPoint* determines how conservative PoCC is towards resource usage efficiency. A high *setPoint*, e.g. 90%, is quick to reduce threads when TCR decreases, but slow to adapt to a sudden large increase in TCR, and vice versa. The evaluation in Section 4 shows that maintaining a fairly high *setPoint* of 70% does not result in performance degradation.

PoCC calculates Δthreads using the relative gain formula described in Step 5, which allows *setPoint* to be a value, rather than a range. The other four CCAs (see [4] for their description) use a range of 50-80% to calculate Δthreads with an absolute gain formula, and, thus, a small ΔTCR leads for certain to a modified `numCurrentThreads`. In addition over large thread counts, the range leads to coarse-grain control. In contrast, PoCC, using the relative gain formula (Step 5), allows Δthreads to be zero at low thread counts in response to small ΔTCR, while providing fine-grain control at large thread counts.

Compared with the other four CCAs, PoCC adds a new parameter, *minTransactions*, that acts as a filter against noisy TCR profiles such as in Figure 6. Such noisy samples may occur due to the average transaction execution time being longer than the *samplePeriod*. Few transactions execute every *samplePeriod*, and thus their outcomes (abort/commit) heavily bias TCR. The other CCAs, lacking PoCC's filter, absorbed noise by using a large *samplePeriod*, which is a trade-off with responsiveness, as shown in Section 4.4. However, this may mean that *samplePeriod* needs to be re-tuned for each new application to avoid either slow or noisy responses. In PoCC, *samplePeriod* is determined based on the overhead of executing the control loop. This reduces the application dependence, and makes PoCC suitable for general use.

3 Experimental Platform

3.1 Concurrency Control Parameters

PoCC is implemented in DSTM2, a state-of-the-art Java-based software TM implementation [9]. PoCC's parameters are: *setPoint* is 70%, *minTransactions* is 100. Experimental evaluation found PoCC took on average 2ms to execute its loop, thus *samplePeriod* is set to 1 second to make its overhead negligible.

The other four CCAs (see [4] for more details) are also evaluated, and abbreviated as SA (SimpleAdjust), EI (ExponentialInterval), EA (ExponentialAdjust), and EC (ExponentialCombined). Their configuration is left to their default values.

3.2 Software and Hardware Platform

All popular contention managers [10,11,12] have been used, but only results for the Priority contention manager are presented, as it gives the best execution times when executing without concurrency control. The Priority manager prioritizes transactions by start time, aborting younger transactions on conflict.

The platform used for the evaluation is a 4x dual core (8 core) AMD Opteron 2.4GHz system with 16GB RAM, openSUSE 10.1, and Java 1.6 64-bit using the parameters `-Xms1024m -Xmx14000m`. As the system has a maximum of 8 cores, all benchmarks are executed using 1, 2, 4, and 8 initial threads (except for the synthetic benchmark, see below). We use the term initial threads as concurrency controlled execution may dynamically change at runtime the number of threads (between 1 and 8).

3.3 Benchmarks

One synthetic and seven real, complex benchmark configurations are used. The synthetic benchmark and each complex benchmark configuration is executed five times, and the results averaged. The synthetic benchmark, StepChange, oscillates the TCR from 80% to 20% in steps of 20% every 20 seconds (as seen in Figure 6), and executes for a fixed 300 seconds. StepChange needs to be executed with the maximum 8 threads to allow its TCR oscillation to have impact, as it operates by controlling the number of threads executing committed or aborted transactions.

The complex benchmarks used are Lee's routing algorithm, and the STAMP benchmarks Genome, KMeans, and Vacation, from STAMP version 0.9.5, all ported to execute under DSTM2. All benchmarks, with the exception of Genome, are executed with high and low data contention configurations, as shown in Table 1. Lee's routing algorithm uses early release [3] for its low data contention

Table 1. Benchmark configuration parameters used in the evaluation

Configuration Name	Application	Configuration
StepChange	StepChange	max_tcr:80, min_tcr:20, time:300, step_size:20, step_period:20,
Genome	Genome	gene_length:16384, segment_length:64, num_segments:4194304
KMeansL	KMeans low contention	clusters:40, threshold:0.00001, input_file:random10000_12
KMeansH	KMeans high contention	clusters:20, threshold:0.00001, input_file:random10000_12
VacL	Vacation low contention	relations:65536, percent_of_relations_queried:90, queries_per_transaction:4, number_of_transactions:4194304
VacH	Vacation high contention	relations:65536, percent_of_relations_queried:10, queries_per_transaction:8, number_of_transactions:4194304
Lee-TM-ter	Lee low contention	early_release:true, file:mainboard
Lee-TM-t	Lee high contention	early_release:false, file:mainboard

configuration, which releases unnecessary data from a transaction's read set to reduce false conflicts. This requires application-specific knowledge to determine which data is unnecessary, and manual annotation of the code. The input parameters for the benchmarks are those recommended by their respective providers.

4 Performance Evaluation

In control theory, a controller's performance is primarily measured as its effectiveness to reduce variance in its *output*. This section evaluates the effectiveness of the five CCAs at reducing variance in execution time, resource usage, *wasted work* and *aborts per commit*. Hereafter, *static execution* refers to execution with a fixed number of threads, and *dynamic execution* refers to execution under any CCA.

4.1 Execution Time

For each benchmark, the CCAs should: a) improve execution time over static execution using an initial number of threads that under-exploits the exploitable parallelism, and b) reduce variance in execution time with different numbers of initial threads. Both points are validated in Figure 1. Genome, Lee-TM-ter, and VacH show clear examples of the CCAs improving execution time when the initial number of threads under-exploits the available exploitable parallelism, and reducing variance in execution time irrespective of the initial number of threads. There is little difference in execution time between the CCAs, but only PoCC consistently performs well, whereas SA, EI, EA, and EC all show poor execution times in some benchmark configurations.

Figure 2 presents the execution time standard deviation for each benchmark to compare the effectiveness of the CCAs at reducing execution time variance. The results show PoCC is the best on average, reducing standard deviation by 31% over the next best, EC. Furthermore, averaging speedup of each CCA over static execution for each benchmark configuration, PoCC is second-best with an average speedup of 1.26, and EC is best with a slightly improved speedup of 1.27. Averaging speedup of each CCA over best-case static execution for each benchmark, PoCC is joint-best with EC with an average slowdown of 5%, while EI, EA, and SA suffer an average slowdown of 6%, 7%, and 10%, respectively.

4.2 Resource Usage

Resource usage during a sample is calculated as the duration of the sample multiplied by the number of threads executing during the sample. Resource usage for the entire run is calculated by summing the resource usage of all samples in the run. For each benchmark, the CCAs should improve resource usage over static execution using an initial number of threads that over-exploits the exploitable parallelism.

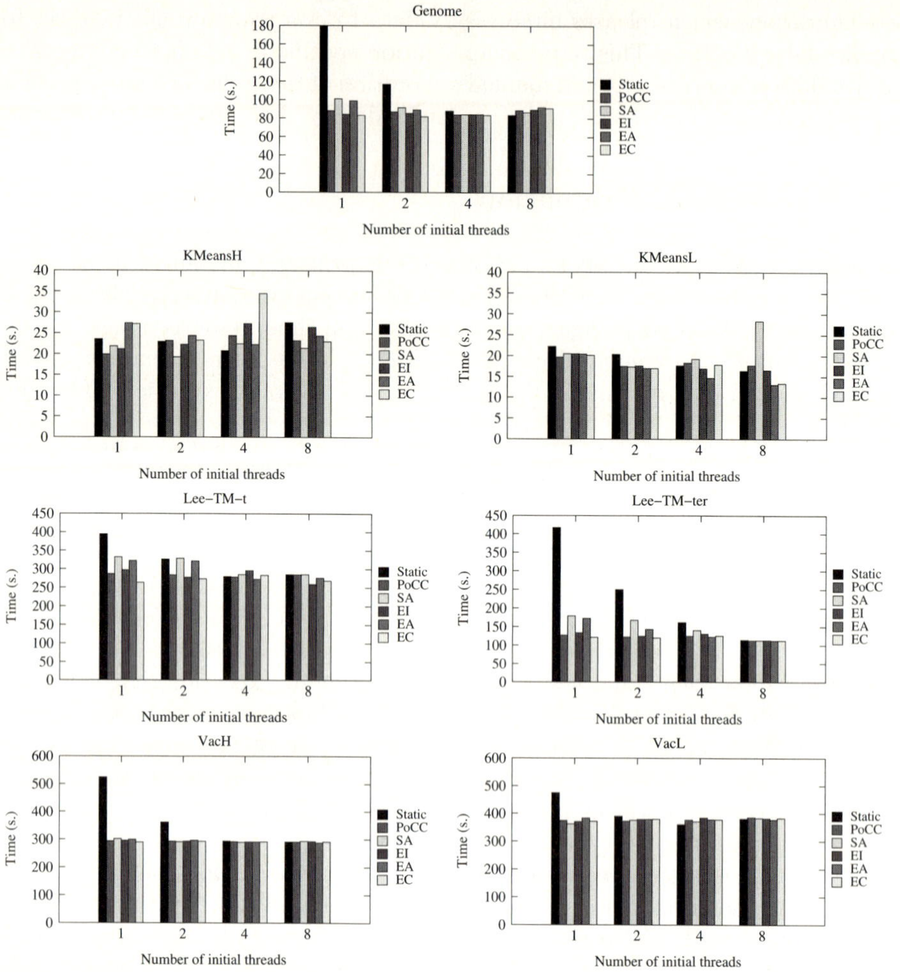

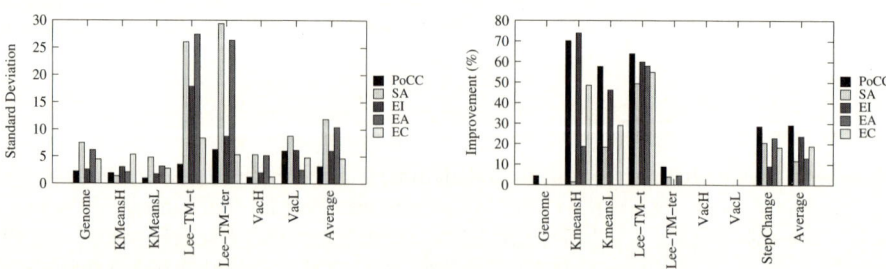

Fig. 1. Execution times for complex benchmarks. StepChange benchmark data is omitted as it executes for a fixed 300 seconds. Less is better.

Fig. 2. Execution time std deviation over all initial threads. Less is better.

Fig. 3. Resource efficiency vs. static execution at 8 initial threads. More is better.

We choose to compare resource usage at 8 initial threads for two reasons: 1) applications that scale past 8 threads should show little resource usage improvement, and 2) applications that do not scale past 8 threads should get maximum resource usage saving at 8 threads with dynamic execution, and thus allow direct comparison between the CCAs. Figure 3 presents the resource usage improvement for each CCA, and shows PoCC is the best on average, improving resource savings by 24% over the next best, EC.

4.3 Transaction Execution Metrics

Two transaction execution metrics are presented: *wasted work* and *aborts per commit* (APC). Wasted work is the proportion of execution time spent in executing transactions that eventually aborted, and APC is the ratio of aborted transactions to committed transactions. Both metrics are a measure of wasted execution, and are thus of interest since concurrency control attempts to reduce variance in TCR, which should result in reduced variance in these metrics.

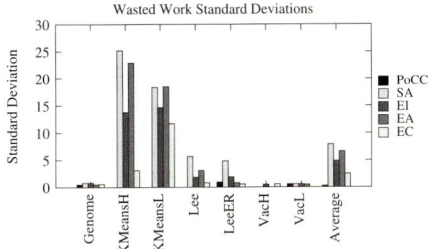

Fig. 4. Wasted work standard deviations for the benchmarks. Less is better.

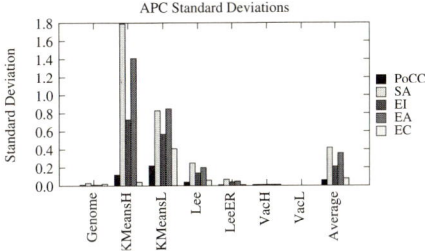

Fig. 5. APC standard deviations for the benchmarks. Less is better.

Figure 4 presents wasted work standard deviations. PoCC significantly reduces variability in wasted work: on average its standard deviation is 88% lower than the next best CCA, which is EC. Figure 5 presents APC, and again PoCC reduces variability: on average its APC standard devation is 26% lower than the next best CCA, which is EC. Furthermore, PoCC reduces average wasted work by 16% over the next best CCA, which is EC, and reduces average APC by 11% over the next best CCA, which is also EC.

4.4 Controller Responsiveness

Controller response is usually measured by three metrics: 1) *response rate*: how fast the number of threads rises when TCR changes, 2) *settle rate*: how quickly the number of threads stops oscillating following the response, and 3) *overshoot*: maximum number of threads above the settled value number of threads.

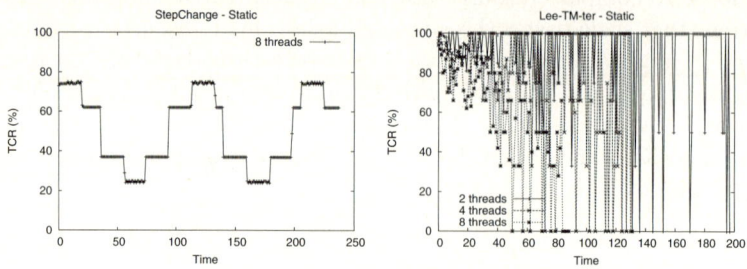

Fig. 6. TCR profiles of StepChange and Lee-TM-ter

The responsiveness analysis is restricted to StepChange and Lee-TM-ter. Both exhibit TCR profiles that stress the CCAs as shown sampled at 1 second intervals in Figure 6. StepChange changes TCR by large amounts at fixed intervals, and Lee-TM-ter has a wildly oscillating TCR due to a fast sample rate.

Figure 7 presents the CCAs' response graphs. PoCC shows good response to both benchmarks: it responds to StepChange quickly due to the 1 second sample rate, but is also robust to noise in Lee-TM-ter due to the *minTransactions* filter. It has no overshoot or settle rate.

The other four CCAs have a slow sample rate, which gives them no overshoot or settle rate, makes them robust to noise in Lee-TM-ter, but respond poorly in StepChange. This is the trade-off for these four CCAs; responsiveness vs. robustness, as mentioned in Section 2.

5 Conclusion

This work has presented a new concurrency control algorithm, called PoCC, and evaluated it against a synthetic benchmark and several complex benchmarks. An extensive evaluation with several complex benchmarks showed PoCC maintains average execution time similar to the best CCA, has the least performance deficit vs. best-case fixed-thread execution, and improves over the other four CCAs by at least 24% average resource usage, 16% average wasted work, and 11% average APC. PoCC improves over the other four CCAs standard deviation by at least 31% in execution time, 24% in resource usage, 88% in wasted work, and 26% in APC. Thus PoCC matches or improves in all benchmark performance metrics analyzed, and improves controller performance by significantly reducing variability in the benchmark performance metrics.

Finally, an analysis of all the CCAs' response characteristics shows PoCC to be more responsive to, and more robust to noise in, changes in TCR. This is due to the new features in PoCC allowing fine-grain response to changes in TCR, and allowing the sample period to be application-independent.

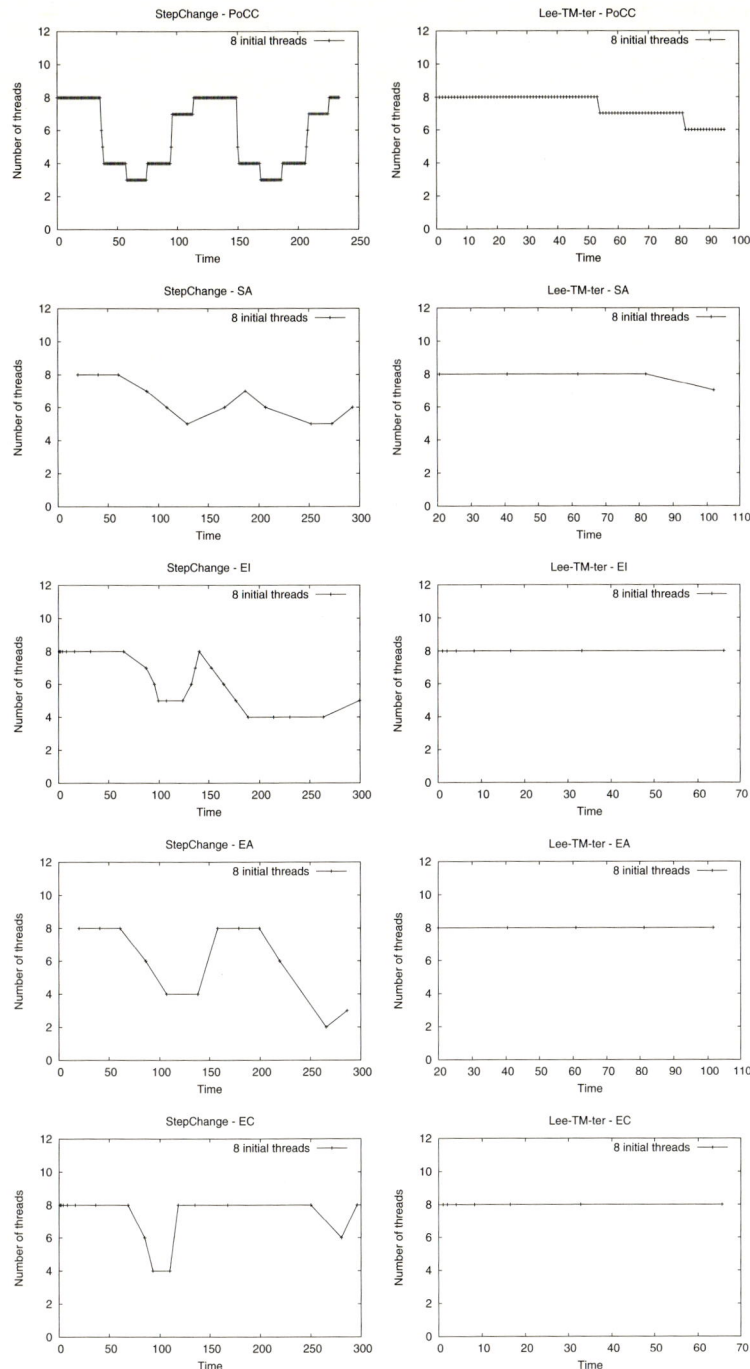

Fig. 7. Number of threads dynamically changing in response to changes in TCR, using all CCAs

References

1. Herlihy, M., Moss, J.E.B.: Transactional memory: Architectural sup-port for lock-free data structures. In: ISCA 1993: Proceedings of the 20th Annual International Symposium on Computer Architecture, pp. 289–300. ACM Press, New York (1993)
2. Shavit, N., Touitou, D.: Software transactional memory. In: PODC 1995: Proceedings of the 14th Annual ACM Symposium on Principles of Distributed Computing, pp. 204–213. ACM Press, New York (1995)
3. Herlihy, M., Luchangco, V., Moir, M., Scherer III, W.N.: Software transactional memory for dynamic-sized data structures. In: PODC 2003: Proceedings of the 22nd Annual Symposium on Principles of Distributed Computing, pp. 92–101. ACM Press, New York (2003)
4. Ansari, M., Kotselidis, C., Jarvis, K., Luján, M., Kirkham, C., Watson, I.: Adaptive concurrency control for transactional memory. In: MULTIPROG 2008: First Workshop on Programmability Issues for MultiCore Computers (January 2008)
5. Minh, C.C., Trautmann, M., Chung, J., McDonald, A., Bronson, N., Casper, J., Kozyrakis, C., Olukotun, K.: An effective hybrid transactional memory system with strong isolation guarantees. In: ISCA 2007: Proceedings of the 34th Annual International Symposium on Computer Architecture, pp. 69–80. ACM Press, New York (2007)
6. Watson, I., Kirkham, C., Luján, M.: A study of a transactional parallel routing algorithm. In: PACT 2007: Proceedings of the 16th International Conference on Parallel Architectures and Compilation Techniques, pp. 388–400. IEEE Computer Society Press, Los Alamitos (2007)
7. Ansari, M., Kotselidis, C., Jarvis, K., Luján, M., Kirkham, C., Watson, I.: Lee-TM: A non-trivial benchmark for transactional memory. In: Bourgeois, A.G., Zheng, S.Q. (eds.) ICA3PP 2008. LNCS, vol. 5022. Springer, Heidelberg (2008)
8. Astrom, K., Hagglund, T.: PID Controllers: Theory, Design, and Tuning. Instrument Society of America (1995)
9. Herlihy, M., Luchangco, V., Moir, M.: A flexible framework for implementing software transactional memory. In: OOPSLA 2006: Proceedings of the 21st Annual Conference on Object-Oriented Programming Systems, Languages, and Applications, pp. 253–262. ACM Press, New York (2006)
10. Guerraoui, R., Herlihy, M., Pochon, B.: Toward a theory of transactional contention managers. In: PODC 2005: Proceedings of the 24th Annual Symposium on Principles of Distributed Computing, pp. 258–264. ACM Press, New York (2005)
11. Scherer III, W., Scott, M.: Contention management in dynamic software transactional memory. In: CSJP 2004: Workshop on Concurrency and Synchronization in Java Programs (July 2004)
12. Scherer III, W., Scott, M.: Advanced contention management for dynamic software transactional memory. In: PODC 2005: Proceedings of the 24th Annual Symposium on Principles of Distributed Computing, pp. 240–248. ACM Press, New York (2005)

Meta-programming Applied to Automatic SMP Parallelization of Linear Algebra Code

Joel Falcou[1], Jocelyn Sérot[2], Lucien Pech[3], and Jean-Thierry Lapresté[2]

[1] IEF, Université Paris Sud, Orsay, France
[2] LASMEA, Université Blaise Pascal,Clermont-Ferrand, France
[3] Ecole Normale Supérieure, Paris, France
falcou@ief.u-psud.fr, lucien.pech@ens.fr
{lapreste,jserot}@lasmea.univ-bpclermont.fr

Abstract. We describe a software solution to the problem of automatic parallelization of linear algebra code on multi-processor and multi-core architectures. This solution relies on the definition of a domain specific language for matrix computations, a performance model for multi-processor architectures and its implementation using C++ template meta-programming. Experimental results asses this model and its implementation on sample computation kernels.

1 Introduction

Scientific computing applications have become more and more demanding in terms of raw computing power. The old and easy solution of waiting for a new generation of processors is no more viable as the rise of CPU power has been slowing down. For a while, building clusters provided a realistic solution for highly demanding applications like particle physics [1], financial modeling or real time vision [2]. However, the multi-core technology [3,4] changed the deal. As time goes, the upcoming **many-core** era will feature ready-to-use, affordable high performance computing platforms in a simple desktop machine [5]. It also becomes clear that a growing audience of developers will have to master these architectures. However, for non-specialists, writing efficient code for such machines is non-trivial, as it usually involves dealing with low level APIs (such as PTHREAD or OPENMP). Such an approach makes code more error-prone, hides domain specific algorithms and increases development cost. Several solutions have been proposed to overcome this problem, ranging from dedicated languages [6], libraries [7] or compiler extensions [8]. Those solutions, however, suffer from various limitations because they have to find an acceptable trade-off between efficiency and expressiveness. Trying to develop a generic tool for parallelizing **any kind of code** on a multi-core machine while providing a high level of expressiveness and efficiency is a daunting task. Instead, we think that such tools can be developed for smaller, **specific domains** of applications, for which accurate performance models and efficient parallelization strategies can be developed. Our work focuses on defining such a domain and providing a user-friendly tool performing automatic SMP parallelization of code, guided by an analytical performance model. This model, similar to the threshold system used by OpenMP[8], is backed up by a high-level interface based on the linear algebra syntax introduced by MATLAB^{TM} [9] as it can be easily parallelized following a simple data-parallel scheme and fuels a large number of applications.. The tool itself is a template-based, object oriented C++ library which is able, at the same time, to provide performances on a par with hand-crafted, low-level C or C++ code on common architectures.

The paper is organized as follow : Section 2 presents our scientific computing library, NT2, and its implementation. Section 3 defines a performance model for SMP architectures, assesses its accuracy and shows how it can be integrated into NT2. Experimental results are provided in Section 4 and we conclude by proposing extensions of this work in Section 5.

2 NT2: A High Performance Linear Algebra Library

NT2 is a C++ template library that aims at providing an efficient implementation of the most common linear algebra functions on multidimensional arrays by using a refinement of E.V.E. [9] code generation engine. It offers an API whose functionalities are close to MATLAB, including template-based wrappers to LAPACK and BLAS and transparent support for a large variety of optimizations : SIMD support for SSE2 and AltiVec, data tiling, loop unrolling, memory management options, copy on write and statically sized matrix.

2.1 A Simple NT2 Use Case

For example, consider the MATLAB code given below, performing a fixed-point RGB to YUV transformation:

```
function [Y,U,V]=rgb2yuv(I)
R=I(:,:,1);
G=I(:,:,2);
B=I(:,:,3);

Y=min(bitshift(abs(2104*R+4130*G+802*B+135168),-13),235);
U=min(bitshift(abs(-1214*R-2384*G+3598*B+1052672),-13),240);
V=min(bitshift(abs(3598*R-3013*G-585*B+1052672),-13),240);
```

The code can be rewritten in a straightforward manner with NT2 as shown below. Most functions are similar, the only difference being the need to declare variables explicitly – the view container being used to prevent unwanted copy of data slices – and to fix some MATLAB syntax specificities – turning : into _ for example. Table 1 reports the performances obtained with MATLAB and NT2 versions, along with those obtained with a direct C version, for several image sizes (from 128 × 128 to 1024 × 1024).

```
void RGB2YUV(const matrix<int>& I, matrix<int>& y,
             matrix<int>& u, matrix<int>& v )
{
view<int> R = I(_,_,1);
view<int> G = I(_,_,2);
view<int> B = I(_,_,3);

y=min(shr(abs(2104*R+4130*G+802*B+135168),13),235);
u=min(shr(abs(-1214*R-2384*G+3598*B+1052672),13),240);
v=min(shr(abs(3598*R-3013*G-585*B+1052672),13),240);
}
```

The relevant information is the speed-up measured between NT2 and MATLAB (Γ_M) and the overhead introduced by NT2 compared to the C implementation (ω_C) on a single core Power PC G5. Results show that NT2 is 40 to 100 times faster than MATLAB in interpreted mode, while the overhead introduced is never greater than 5%.

Table 1. Performance of the RGB to YUV algorithm

N	128	256	512	1024
MATLAB	44.6ms	175.8ms	487.5ms	1521.2ms
C	0.41ms	2.0ms	11.4ms	40.5ms
NT2	0.43ms	2.1ms	11.6ms	40.8ms
Γ_M	103.71	83.7	42.0	37.3
ω_C	4.89%	5%	1.75%	0.74%

2.2 NT2 Implementation

The implementation of NT2 is based upon a meta-programming technique known as *Expression Templates* [10]. As shown above, this mechanism can virtually eliminate the overhead classically associated to object-oriented implementations of matrix and linear algebra libraries (comparable to hand written C or FORTRAN code). In the sequel, we give a short account on the principle of this technique.

Consider for example a simple expression, such as `r=(a+b)/c`, where a, b, c and r are matrices of integers (`matrix<int>`). In an object-oriented setting, the classical approach for evaluating this expression is to overload the + and / operators. However, such an approach produces unnecessary loops and memory copies (see [11,9] for a complete account). The idea of *expression templates* is to overload operators so that they return an object that reflects the structure of the expression in its type. This has the effect of building an expression abstract syntax tree as a first class object at compile-time.

Technically, the leaves of the abstract syntax tree will be matrices and a custom class – `node` – will be used to encode binary operators:

```
template <class O,class L,class R> struct node
{
node(const L& l,const R& r) : l_(l), r_(r) {}
L l_;
R r_;
};
```

This abstract syntax tree is obtained by overloading the classical operators for all combinations of operand types. For example:

```
template<class T,class U> node<Add,matrix<T>,matrix<U> >
operator+( const matrix<T>& l,const matrix<U>& r )
{
return node<Add,matrix<T>,matrix<U> >(l,r);
}
```

With this approach, when evaluating the expression (a+b)*c, the compiler builds a temporary object whose type is:

```
node<Div,node<Add,matrix<int>,matrix<int>>,matrix<int>>
```

where Div and Add are placeholder types encoding the operation associated to a node. Then, we overload the = operator of the matrix class so that it actually evaluates the assignment operator argument. In this operator, a for loop iterates over the elements of each arrays which size are given by the size() method:

```
template<class T> template<class U>
matrix<T>& matrix<T>::operator=( const node<U>& tree )
{
for(int i=0;i<size();i++)
  data[i] = Eval< node<U> >::evalAt(tree,i);
return *this;
}
```

Eval recursively parses the tree argument to produce the corresponding residual code. Depending on the type of tree, it proceeds differently:

– When visiting a leaf, it evaluates the matrix element for the current index:

```
template<class T> struct Eval< matrix<T> >
{
typedef matrix<T> type;
static inline T Do(const type& m, size_t i) { return m[i]; }
};
```

– When visiting a binary node this function first evaluates the values of both node's siblings and passes the results to the embedded operator. The embedded operator itself is a simple functor providing a class method called Do that takes care of the actual computation:

```
template<class O,class L,class R> struct Eval<node<O,L,R>>
{
typedef node<O,L,R> type;
static inline T Do(const type& n,size_t i)
{
   return O::Compute(Eval<L>::Do(n.l_,i),Eval<R>::Do(n.r_,i));
}
};
```

Since all generated functions are candidates for inlining, most compilers are able to optimize call overhead and empty structures so that the result is the same as if we generated the code in place. For the previous example (r=(a+b)/c), the generated code is:

```
for(int i=0;i<size();i++) r[i] = (a[i]+b[i])/c[i];
```

A closer look at the generated assembly code validates this process. This basic technique can be enhanced by using type lists [12] to handle n-ary operators in a seamless fashion and type traits [13] to perform correct return type computation.

3 An SMP-Aware Implementation of NT2

The main motivation for an SMP-aware implementation of NT2 is that many linear algebra operations are regular, exhibit a high potential parallelism and can be easily parallelized by using a simple data-parallel approach in which each core or processor[1] applies the same operation on a subset of the matrix elements.

Parallelization can be beneficial, however, only when the amount of data to be processed is above a certain threshold, because of the overhead of creating and synchronizing threads in an SMP context. It is very easy to observe "negative" speed-ups (i.e. < 1) if data sets are too small and/or overhead is too large on a given architecture. This justifies the need for performance model by which it should possible to evaluate, *thanks to a compile time process*, whether relying on SMP parallelism at run-time is worthwhile or not. In this section, we present such a performance model and show how it can serve parallelization purposes in NT2.

3.1 A Performance Model for SMP Architectures

We propose a simple performance model based on a simple interpretation of SMP speed-up $\Gamma = \frac{\tau_s}{\tau_p}$, where τ_s and τ_p are the sequential and parallel execution times. τ_s can be defined as the sum of the computation time and the memory access time :

$$\tau_s = N \cdot (\psi_c + \psi_m)$$

---

[1] We refer to cores or processors as **processing elements** or **PE**s.

where N is the size of the data to process (the matrix size), ψ_c is the time spent in computation per element and ψ_m the time spent in memory access per element. Similarly, we can define τ_p as

$$\tau_p = N \cdot (\frac{\psi_c}{P} + \psi_m) + \omega$$

where P is the number of **PE**s in the considered architecture and ω the overhead introduced by the parallelization process. In this model, we assume that all **PE**s share a common bus to the main memory, thus forcing the memory access to be serialized and that, for a given architecture, the end user will always use all the **PE**s available, meaning that ω corresponds to the overhead of starting and handling P threads. Hence :

$$\Gamma = \frac{(\psi_c + \psi_m)}{(\frac{\psi_c}{P} + \psi_m) + \omega/N}$$

So we have:

$$\Gamma > 1 \iff N > \frac{P}{P-1} \cdot \frac{\omega}{\psi_c}$$

To check whether it is worthwhile to trigger SMP execution, we therefore only have to compare N to the threshold $N^* = \frac{P}{P-1} \cdot \frac{\omega}{\psi_c}$.

To assess this model, we measured ω once and for all and ψ_c for various basic operations (addition, division, cosinus, ...) and derived a *theoretical* value for N^* (N^*_{theor}) for these operations. Since we do not want the model parameters to depend on cache effects, we performed the measure of ψ_c on a data set whose size was made to fit into the L1 cache of the processor. We then obtained an *experimental* value of N^* (N^*_{exp}) by just running an SMP version of the code and observing when the speed-up got above 1. Results are summarized in table 2, where δ is the relative error between the theoretically and experimentally determined value of the N^* threshold on a dual processor PowerPC G5 ($P = 2$) on which ω has been evaluated to 366000 cycles.

Despite the very simple nature of the model, threshold values are estimated within a 6% error margin, which is fairly acceptable. Moreover, this predicted threshold is always *above* the real one, meaning that the SMP parallelization

Table 2. Comparison of experimental results with our prediction model

ψ_c	N^*_{theor}	N^*_{exp}	δ
Addition			
0.03	24400000	23040000	5.9%
Division			
7	104572	99328	5.2%
Cosinus			
124.74	5869	5632	4.2%

will always be triggered when the resulting speed-up is greater than one. This overestimation is due to the fact that we purposely don't take into account the way compilers may reschedule or optimize instructions within our loop nests.

3.2 Meta-programming the Parallelization Heuristic

To integrate the analytical performance model to the NT2 library, we have

1. to compute, at compile time, ψ_c for any expression, and N^*;
2. to generate sequential or SMP residual code depending on the actual value of N.

The first step is performed by decorating the abstract syntax tree generated by the expression templates with information relative to the cost of operator nodes, so that the total cost ψ_c of an expression can be computed by accumulating costs of basic operations during a simple tree traversal. In practice, the values of ψ_c for every function supported by the library are evaluated and stored into a header file generated by a separate application run off-line. This application proceeds as follow:

- ω is evaluated by timing a group of P threads performing no computation;
- For each operation, the associated ψ_c is evaluated by benchmarking it for each supported numeric types (e.g. char,short,long,float, etc...) on a data block whose size is computed to fit in the CPU L1 cache. This ensures that all estimated ψ_c values are indeed independent of N.
- A header file containing the value of ω and, for each basic operation, a header file containing a structure encoding the value of ψ_c for each supported type [2]. Those constants, for precision purpose, are stored in hundredths. For example, here is a excerpt of the header associated to the cos function specialized for double precision values (whith $\psi_c = 124.74$):

```
template<> struct cost<Cos, double> : int_<12474> {};
```

The second step is performed when expressions are actually evaluated by the overloaded `operator=` of the `matrix` class, as illustrated in the following listing. The various static values needed to decide if parallelization is worth to be triggered are gathered at lines 4-6. A dynamic test is then performed (line 8). As all the required values are static, a single integer comparison is performed at run-time. This test either starts a thread group (line 9) or use a single thread loop (lines 11) to evaluate the expression. The `thread` template class performs boundaries computation, spawns the threads and takes care of threads synchronization using the BOOST::Thread encapsulation of PTHREAD.

---
[2] Technically, these constants are encoded as BOOST::MPL[14,15] static integral constants.

```
1  matrix<T>& operator=( const node<U>& tree )
2  {
3    const size_t proc = config::proc::value;            // Nbr of PEs
4    const size_t num  = proc*config::omega::value;      // P*omega
5    const_size_t den  = (proc-1)*node<U>::cost::value;  // (P-1)*psi_c
6
7    if( tree.size()*den > num )                         // Check if N > P*omega/(P-1)*psi_c
8      thread<proc>::Eval(tree, this);
9    else
10     for(int i=0;i<size();i++) data[i] = tree.eval(i);
11   return *this;
12 }
```

4 Experimental Results

Experimental results for this implementation are given below. We measured the speed-up for SMP implementation of two applications of increasing complexity (the term ψ_c reflects this complexity): image difference and a trigonometric computation involving cos and exponential. The target platforms are:

- a 2x2.5GHz Mac Book Pro with 1 Gb of memory running MAC OS X 10.5;
- a 4x2.4GHz Intel Quad Core Q6600 with 4Gb of memory running Windows XP.

Image difference is performed on 8 bits array. The associated code is:

```
delta = abs(im1 - im2)
```

For this code, our performance predictor evaluates that $\psi_c = 4.75$, $N^*_{dual} = 154106$, $N^*_{quad} = 298443$. Experimental results are given in table 3 in which the rows *Naive speed-up* and *NT2 speed-up* respectively give the the speed-up – compared to single threaded C code – obtained with a hand-coded C multi-threaded version of the application and with the NT2 version of the same application.

For the second application, the associated code is:

```
val = cos(z) - 0.5*( exp(i()*z) + exp(-i()*z) ) )
```

For this code, our performance predictor evaluates that $\psi_c = 660.02$, $N^*_{dual} = 1110$, $N^*_{quad} = 2149$. Experimental results are given in table 4.

Table 3. Speed-up benchmark for the image diffence application

N	2^8	2^{10}	2^{12}	2^{14}	2^{16}	2^{18}	2^{20}
Dual Core							
Naive speed-up	0.003	0.01	0.05	0.19	0.59	1.26	1.74
NT2 speed-up	1.00	1.00	1.00	1.00	1.00	1.24	1.72
Quad Core							
Naive speed-up	0.0011	0.0046	0.02	0.07	0.27	0.91	2.16
NT2 speed-up	1.00	1.00	1.00	1.01	1.00	1.01	2.14

Table 4. Speed-up benchmark for the trigonometric application

N	2^8	2^{10}	2^{12}	2^{14}	2^{16}	2^{18}	2^{20}
Dual Core							
Naive speed-up	0.37	0.96	1.57	1.87	1.97	1.98	1.99
NT2 speed-up	1.01	1.01	1.55	1.85	1.96	1.98	1.99
Quad Core							
Naive speed-up	0.15	0.55	1.55	2.87	3.64	3.90	3.98
NT2 speed-up	1.01	1.00	1.50	2.83	3.62	3.88	3.98

4.1 Discussion

Those results demonstrate the following points:

- The model experimentally scales well with the number of **PE**s;
- The estimated N^* value is correct even for complex expressions;
- For the first application, speed-up is only obtained for large values of N, because of the low ψ_c value. This is detected by NT2, which correctly inhibits SMP parallelization when the actual N value is below this threshold;
- When NT2 triggers SMP parallelization, the measured speed-up is within a 5% margin of the hand-crafted code speed-up.

5 Conclusion

In this paper we introduced the need to provide a SMP-aware scientific computing library. We presented NT2 as a solution to the problem of efficient scientific computing in C++ and exposed the technical challenges to overcome when trying to provide a proper SMP parallelization process for such a library.

Our solution was to define a **performance model for SMP computations** that is able to predict if an expression is worth parallelizing. Then, we proposed an SMP-aware implementation of NT2, taking advantage of its inner meta-programmed core to **statically detect expressions to parallelize**. Experimental results showed that our model, despite its simplicity, was precise enough to trigger parallelization only when needed and provide a significant speed-up for various computation kernels on various multi-core architecture.

Work in progress includes fine tuning the prediction model to target emergent many-core architectures like the IBM/SONY/TOSHIBA CELL processor. Future work could target the TILERA TILE64 or the upcoming Intel Polaris 80. Regarding the cost model, an important issue would be to extend it to deal with situations where complexity depends non-linearly on the data size N. Moreover, in the case of many-core architectures, it can be worth to use only a subset of the available cores for NT2 computations (as several concurrent applications can run on the platform). In this case, a challenging question is whether the cost model can be adapted to predict an optimal size for this subset. Finally, and a on more longer term, we are contemplating the possibility of targeting distributed memory architectures, by providing a message-based implementation model for NT2. Our ultimate goal would be the automatic parallelization of linear algebra code on heterogeneous architectures starting from a single NT2 source, adapted from a MATLAB application.

References

1. Team, T.B.: An overview of the bluegene/l supercomputer. In: Proccedings of ACM Supercomputing Conference (2002)
2. Falcou, J., Sérot, J., Chateau, T., Jurie, F.: A parallel implementation of a 3d reconstruction algorithm for real-time vision. In: PARCO 2005 - ParCo,Parallel Computing, Malaga, Spain (September 2005)
3. Kalla, R., Sinharoy, B., Tendler, J.M.: Ibm power5 chip: A dual-core multithreaded processor. IEEE Micro 24(2), 40–47 (2004)
4. Kahle, J.: The cell processor architecture. In: MICRO 38: Proceedings of the 38th annual IEEE/ACM International Symposium on Microarchitecture, Washington, DC, USA, p. 3. IEEE Computer Society, Los Alamitos (2005)
5. Gepner, P., Kowalik, M.F.: Multi-core processors: New way to achieve high system performance. In: PARELEC 2006: Proceedings of the international symposium on Parallel Computing in Electrical Engineering, Washington, DC, USA, pp. 9–13. IEEE Computer Society, Los Alamitos (2006)
6. El-Ghazawi, T., Smith, L.: Upc: unified parallel c. In: SC 2006, p. 27. ACM, New York (2006)
7. Bischof, H., Gorlatch, S., Leshchinskiy, R.: DatTeL: A data-parallel C++ template library. Parallel Processing Letters 13(3), 461–482 (2003)
8. Clark, D.: Openmp: A parallel standard for the masses. IEEE Concurrency 6(1), 10–12 (1998)
9. Falcou, J., Sérot, J.: E.V.E., An Object Oriented SIMD Library. Scalable Computing: Practice and Experience 6(4), 31–41 (2005)
10. Veldhuizen, T.L.: Expression templates. C++ Report 7(5), 26–31 (1995)
11. Veldhuizen, T.L., Jernigan, M.E.: Will C++ be faster than Fortran? In: Ishikawa, Y., Reynders, J.V.W., Tholburn, M. (eds.) ISCOPE 1997. LNCS, vol. 1343. Springer, Heidelberg (1997)
12. Alexandrescu, A.: Modern C++ Design: Generic Programming and Design Patterns Applied. AW C++ in Depth Series. Addison-Wesley, Reading (2001)
13. Myers, N.: A new and useful template technique: traits. C++ gems 1, 451–457 (1996)
14. Abrahams, D., Gurtovoy, A.: C++ Template Metaprogramming: Concepts, Tools, and Techniques from Boost and Beyond. C++ in Depth Series. Addison-Wesley Professional, Reading (2004)
15. Gregor, D., et al.: The boost c++ library (2003), http://boost.org/

Solving Dense Linear Systems on Graphics Processors*

Sergio Barrachina, Maribel Castillo, Francisco D. Igual,
Rafael Mayo, and Enrique S. Quintana-Ortí

Depto. de Ingeniería y Ciencia de los Computadores,
Universidad Jaume I, 12.071–Castellón, Spain
{barrachi,castillo,figual,mayo,quintana}@icc.uji.es

Abstract. We present several algorithms to compute the solution of a linear system of equations on a GPU, as well as general techniques to improve their performance, such as padding and hybrid GPU-CPU computation. We also show how iterative refinement with mixed-precision can be used to regain full accuracy in the solution of linear systems. Experimental results on a G80 using CUBLAS 1.0, the implementation of BLAS for NVIDIA® GPUs with unified architecture, illustrate the performance of the different algorithms and techniques proposed.

Keywords: Linear systems, Cholesky factorization, LU factorization, graphics processors (GPUs), dense linear algebra, high performance.

1 Introduction

The improvements in performance, functionality, and programmability of the current generation of graphics processors (GPUs) have renewed the interest in this class of hardware for general-purpose computation. These advances also apply to dense linear algebra, with important gains in the performance delivered for basic linear algebra operations. The interest in using GPUs for dense linear algebra is not new. Several earlier studies have evaluated the performance of this type of operations on former generations of GPUs. Some of them were specifically focused in the evaluation of different procedures for solving dense linear systems [1,2].

In this paper we focus on the Cholesky and LU factorizations and update the studies in [1,2], using the current generation of GPUs and the implementation of BLAS optimized for graphics processors with *unified architecture*. In particular, we compare several algorithmic variants of the factorization procedures and evaluate their performance on a G80 graphics processor. In addition, we describe techniques to improve the performance of the basic implementations and, as a result, we obtain optimized routines that outperform the CPU-based implementations. Finally, we also employ an iterative method, which combines single and double-precision arithmetic, to refine the solution of a linear system of equations to achieve full precision accuracy.

The new generation of GPUs, that exhibit a new unified architecture, solves many of the problems that limited the performance of older generations of graphics processors,

---

* This research was supported by the CICYT project TIN2005-09037-C02-02 and FEDER, and project No. P1-1B2007-32 of the *Fundación Caixa-Castellón/Bancaixa* and UJI. Francisco Igual is supported by a research fellowship from the UJI (PREDOC/2006/02).

mainly in terms of memory hierarchy, interconnection buses and programmability. In particular, CUDA has been released by NVIDIA as a general-purpose oriented API for its graphics hardware, with the G80 processor as target platform. In addition, CUBLAS is an optimized version of the BLAS built on top of CUDA, and adapted to the peculiarities of this type of platforms [3,4].

The rest of the paper is structured as follows. Section 2 reviews the algorithms for the Cholesky and LU factorization implemented in our study. Section 3 describes several strategies that are applied to improve the performance of the initial algorithms. The impact of these techniques is evaluated in Section 4. Finally, Section 5 collects the conclusions of this analysis.

2 Overview of the Cholesky and LU Factorization Methods

Let $A \in \mathbb{R}^{n \times n}$ be symmetric positive definite, and consider its Cholesky factorization given by

$$A = LL^T, \tag{1}$$

where L is a lower triangular matrix known as the *Cholesky factor* of A.

There exist three different variants for obtaining the Cholesky factorization [5]. Blocked algorithms for the different variants are given in Figure 1 (left) in a notation that has been developed as part of the FLAME project [6,7]. The thick lines in the figure denote how far the computation of the factorization has proceeded; the notation TRIL (B) refers to the lower triangular part of matrix B, and $n(B)$ stands for the number of columns of B. We believe the rest of the notation to be intuitive. Upon completion, the entries of the Cholesky factor L overwrite the corresponding entries of A. Despite being different from the algorithmic point of view, all variants perform exactly the same operations. However, the performance of the implementations depends on the way and order in which these operations are executed, and also on the specific BLAS implementation employed.

Given a matrix A, the LU factorization with partial pivoting decomposes this matrix into two matrices, L and U, such that

$$PA = LU, \tag{2}$$

where P is a permutation matrix, L is a unit lower triangular matrix, and U is an upper triangular matrix.

Three different variants for obtaining the LU factorization with partial pivoting are given in Figure 1 (right) in FLAME notation. As for the Cholesky factorization, all variants perform the same operations, but in different order, and the triangular factors L and U overwrite the corresponding entries of A upon completion. The notation TRILU(B) stands for the unit lower triangular matrix stored in B.

For each variant shown in Figure 1, we also include the name of the BLAS-3 kernel used to carry out the corresponding operation. For the Cholesky factorization, the performance of the SYRK kernel, invoked to update A_{22}, will determine the final performance of Variant 1 of the blocked algorithm; the TRSM and SYRK kernels, used to

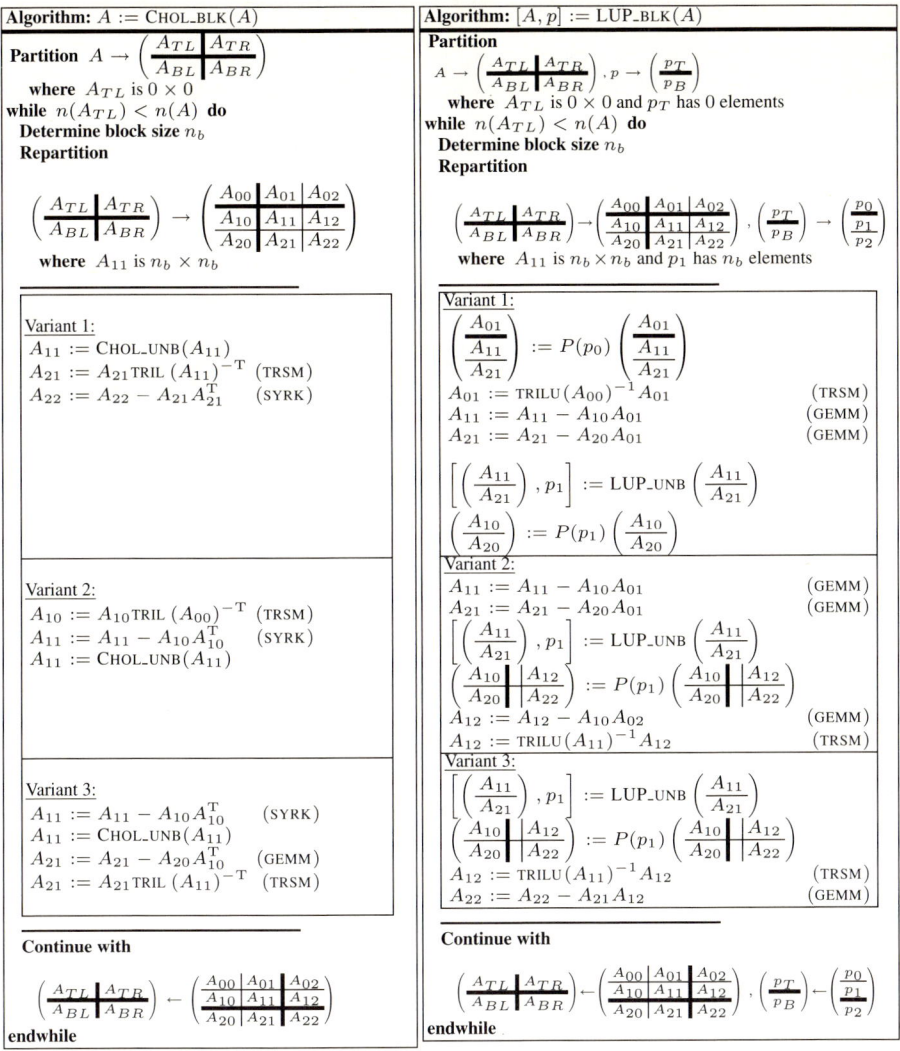

Fig. 1. Multiple blocked variants of the Cholesky factorization (left) and the LU factorization with partial pivoting (right). CHOL_UNB and LUP_UNB refer to the unblocked versions of the Cholesky and the LU factorization procedures.

update A_{10} and A_{11}, are the dominant operations for Variant 2; and the majority of the operations in Variant 3 are performed through the GEMM kernel when updating the submatrix A_{21}. As a result, the performance of these BLAS-3 kernels will determine which of the proposed variants of the Cholesky factorization yields a higher performance.

Similar considerations can be made for the study of the LU factorization variants described in Figure 1 (right).

3 Computing the Cholesky and LU Factorizations on GPUs

Starting from these basic implementations, the following subsections introduce refinements that can be applied simultaneously in order to improve both the performance of the factorization process and the accuracy of the solution of the linear system. These improvements include padding, a hybrid CPU-GPU implementation, a recursive implementation, and an iterative refinement procedure.

3.1 Padding

Experiments in [8] have shown that Level 3 BLAS implementations of CUBLAS (specially the GEMM kernel) deliver much higher performance when operating on matrices with dimensions that are a multiple of 32. This is due to memory alignment issues [3].

Therefore, it is possible to improve the overall performance of the blocked Cholesky factorization (and, similarly, the LU factorization) process by applying the correct pad to the input matrix and selecting the appropriate block sizes. Starting from a block size n_b that is multiple of 32, we pad the $n \times n$ matrix A to compute the factorization

$$\bar{A} = \begin{pmatrix} A & 0 \\ 0 & I_k \end{pmatrix} = \begin{pmatrix} L & 0 \\ 0 & I_k \end{pmatrix} \begin{pmatrix} L & 0 \\ 0 & I_k \end{pmatrix}^T,$$

where I_k denotes the identity matrix of order k, and k is the difference between the matrix size n and the nearest integer multiple of n_b larger than n. By doing this, all BLAS-3 calls operate on submatrices of dimensions that are a multiple of 32, and the overall performance is improved. Moreover, there is no communication overhead associated with padding as only the matrix A and the resulting factor L are transferred between main memory and video memory. On the other hand, we incur in a computation overhead due to useless arithmetic operations which depends on the relation between n and 32.

3.2 Hybrid Algorithm

We have also developed a hybrid version of the blocked algorithm for the Cholesky and LU factorizations which delegates some of the calculations previously performed on the GPU to the CPU. This approach aims to exploit the different abilities of each processor to deal with specific operations. The advantages of the CPU are twofold: it offers higher performance when operating with small matrices, see Figure 2, due to the stream-oriented nature of the GPU, and it delivers higher performance for some fine-grained arithmetic operations, specially the square root calculation, heavily used in the factorization of the diagonal block A_{11}, for which the GPU is not fully optimized.

The hybrid algorithm sends the diagonal block from video memory to main memory, factorizes this block on the CPU and transfers back the results to video memory before the computation on the GPU continues. Whether this technique delivers a performance gain will depend on the overhead introduced by the transference between video memory and main memory.

The same technique has been applied in the LU factorization. In this case, the factorization of the current column panel $\begin{pmatrix} A_{11} \\ A_{21} \end{pmatrix}$ is computed on the CPU.

3.3 Recursive Implementation

It is quite straight-forward to obtain a recursive version of the blocked variants for the Cholesky factorization. The recursive version partitions the matrix into 2×2 square blocks, of similar dimensions, and then factorizes the upper-left block using the same algorithm, which results in a first level of recursion; the procedure is then repeated recursively at each deeper level.

We have implemented recursive implementations of Variants 1 and 2 for the Cholesky and LU factorizations, respectively, which perform a single level of recursion and employ the hybrid algorithm at the bottom stage. Performing several recursive steps did not improve the performance of the algorithm in our experiments.

3.4 Iterative Refinement

The G80 processor only provides single-precision arithmetic. Therefore, computing the Cholesky or LU factorization on the GPU will yield half of the precision that is usually employed in numerical linear algebra. However, iterative refinement can be used to regain full (double-) precision when the factors obtained after the factorization process on the GPU are employed to solve the linear system $A \cdot x = b$, as described next.

This basic procedure for iterative refinement can be modified to use a mixed precision approach following the strategy in [9] for the Cell B.E. The factorization of matrix A is first computed on the GPU (in single-precision arithmetic) using any of the algorithms proposed in previous sections. A first solution is then computed and iteratively refined on the CPU to double-precision arithmetic; see Algorithm 1.1. In this algorithm, the (32) subscript indicates single-precision storage, while the absence of subscript means double-precision format. Thus, only the matrix-vector product $A \cdot x$ is performed in double-precision (kernel GEMV), at a cost of $O(n^2)$ flops (floating-point arithmetic operations), while the rest of the nonnegligible arithmetic operations involve only single-precision operands.

Algorithm 1.1. Solution of a symmetric positive definite system using mixed precision with iterative refinement. The Cholesky factorization is computed on the GPU. A similar strategy can be applied to general systems using the LU factorization.

$A_{(32)}, b_{(32)} \leftarrow A, b$
$L_{(32)} \leftarrow \text{GPU\_CHOL\_BLK}(A_{(32)})$
$x^{(1)}_{(32)} \leftarrow L^{-T}_{(32)} (L^{-1}_{(32)} b_{(32)})$
$x^{(1)} \leftarrow x^{(1)}_{(32)}$
$i \leftarrow 0$
repeat
    $i \leftarrow i + 1$
    $r^{(i)} \leftarrow b - A \cdot x^{(i)}$
    $r^{(i)}_{(32)} \leftarrow r^{(i)}$
    $z^{(i)}_{(32)} \leftarrow L^{-T}_{(32)} (L^{-1}_{(32)} r^{(i)}_{(32)})$
    $z^{(i)} \leftarrow z^{(i)}_{(32)}$
    $x^{(i+1)} \leftarrow x^{(i)} + z^{(i)}$
until $x^{(i+1)}$ is accurate enough

Our implementation of the iterative refinement algorithm iterates until the solution, $x^{(i+1)}$, satisfies the following condition:

$$\frac{\|r^{(i)}\|}{\|x^{(i+1)}\|} < \sqrt{\varepsilon},$$

where ε corresponds to the machine precision of the platform. When this condition is met, the algorithm iterates twice more, and the solution is then considered to be accurate enough [9].

4 Experimental Results

Starting from a basic blocked implementation, we show how the techniques proposed in the previous section (padding, hybrid approaches and recursive implementation) improve the final performance and accuracy of the GPU implementations.

4.1 Experimental Setup

The system used for the performance evaluation is based on an Intel Core2Duo CPU (codename Crusoe E6320) running at 1.86 GHz. On the GPU side, all the implementations have been tested on a Nvidia 8800 Ultra board, with a Nvidia G80 processor. The G80 is a SIMD processor with 128 scalar streaming processors, achieving a peak performance of 345 GFLOPS. The cores are organized in clusters of 8 processors, sharing 16 Kbytes of fast memory; in addition, all cores have access to the video memory.

Based on LAPACK codes, we have developed Fortran 77 implementations of the blocked factorization algorithms linked with CUDA and CUBLAS version 1.0 for the GPU. Thus, the development effort of the implemented codes was not comparable to the complexity of former codes based on OpenGL and Cg.

In the CPU, the algorithms were implemented on top of GotoBLAS 1.19, using LAPACK 3.0 when necessary. The compilers include GNU Fortran Compiler version 3.3.5 and NVCC (NVIDIA compiler) release 1.0, version 0.2.1221.

All the results on the GPU presented hereafter include the time required to transfer the data from the main memory to the GPU memory and retrieve the results back. The kernels for both the CPU and the GPU implementations operate on single-precision real data (except when iterative refinement is considered) and results are reported in terms of GFLOPS. Both cores of the Intel processor were employed in the experiments.

4.2 Basic Blocked Implementations on CPU and GPU

The first set of experiments are based on the basic blocked implementations illustrated in Figure 1, executed on both CPU and GPU. Figure 2 reports the performance of the three variants of the Cholesky and LU factorizations.

On both the CPU and the GPU, the variants of the blocked algorithm deliver a considerable higher performance than their unblocked counterparts; therefore, results for the unblocked implementations are not included in the figures. Due to its stream-oriented architecture, the GPU only outperforms the CPU starting from matrices of large dimension (around $n = 3000$ for Cholesky, and $n = 1500$ for LU). These initial implementations on GPU obtain speedups of 1.91 and 2.10 for Cholesky and the LU, respectively, comparing the best variants on each platform.

The different variants of the blocked algorithm executed on GPU exhibit a much different performance. This can be explained by the different behavior of the underlying CUBLAS kernels, as we argue next. A detailed comparison between the Level 3 CUBLAS routines underlying the Cholesky and LU factorization routines (GEMM, TRSM, and SYRK) can be found in [8]. The results show that the GEMM kernel in CUBLAS is thoroughly tuned, while considerably less attention has been paid to the optimization of SYRK and TRSM. This fact helps to explain the differences in the performance of the three variants of the Cholesky factorization. As noted in Figure 1, SYRK is the dominant operation in Variant 1; the bulk of the computation in Variant 2 is cast in terms of TRSM and SYRK; and the GEMM kernel is the most important in Variant 3.

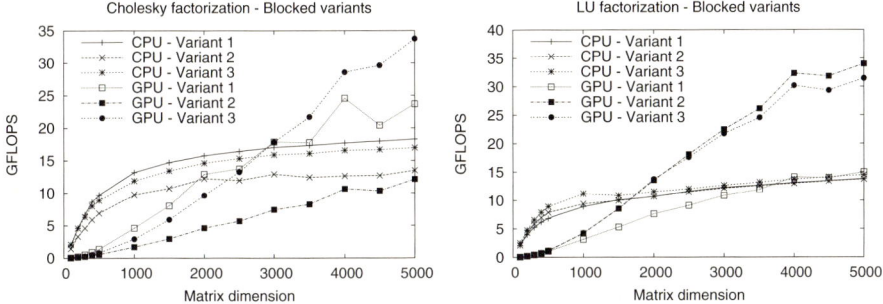

Fig. 2. Performance of the three blocked variants for the Cholesky and LU factorization. Highest performances attained on the GPU are 23.7, 12.2, and 33.7 GFLOPS for Cholesky, and 14.9, 34, and 31.4 GFLOPS for the LU. Peak performances on CPU for the best variants are 17.6 GFLOPS for Cholesky and 14.9 GFLOPS for the LU.

Variant 1 of the LU factorization in Figure 2 obtains a poor performance compared with Variants 2 and 3. As explained before, the underlying BLAS implementation determines the final performance of the LU factorization process. The update of block A_{01} in this variant is implemented on top of the TRSM routine. Through a detailed performance evaluation of the CUBLAS TRSM routine, we have observed that this operation yields worse results when large triangular matrices are involved. The variant implemented suffers from this poor performance of the TRSM implementation of CUBLAS when updating matrices with $m \gg n$.

4.3 Blocked Implementation with Padding

Padding is a simple but effective method for improving the performance of the Level 3 CUBLAS implementations [8]. Our goal here is to exploit the high performance achieved by padding the Level 3 CUBLAS operations (see the difference between GEMM with and without padding in [8] for more details) to improve the overall performance.

Figure 3 shows the results of the three variants of the Cholesky and LU factorizations when the appropriate padding is applied to the input matrices. Comparing the results with those without padding, it is possible to distinguish a small improvement in the final performance of the three variants of both factorizations. In [8] it was noted that the performance gain that is attained when applying padding to the Level 3 BLAS routines in CUBLAS is higher for GEMM than for SYRK. Thus, it is natural that Variant 3 of the Cholesky factorization (based on GEMM) benefits more than the other two variants. In fact, the improvement for Variant 2 is minimal when applying this optimization, as for Variant 1 of the LU factorization, in which TRSM is the main routine.

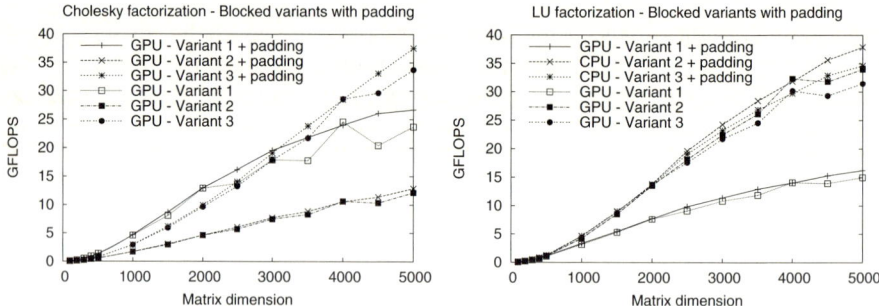

Fig. 3. Performance of the three blocked variants for the Cholesky and LU factorization with padding applied. Highest performances attained on the GPU are 26.7, 12.9, and 37.6 GFLOPS for Cholesky, and 16.2, 37.8, and 34.6 GFLOPS for the LU. Comparing the best CPU and GPU implementations, the achieved speedup is 2.13 for Cholesky, and 2.32 for the LU.

The application of padding masks the irregular behavior of the implementations, when the matrix size is not a multiple of 32 (see Figure 2 for $m = 4000$). In addition, the overall performance is considerably improved: maximum speedups for the Cholesky factorization variants compared with the basic GPU implementations are 1.27, 1.10, and 1.12, while the speedups attained for the LU are 1.09, 1.12, and 1.12, respectively.

4.4 Hybrid and Recursive Implementations

We next evaluate our hybrid and recursive blocked algorithms, including padding, for the Cholesky and LU factorizations based on Variants 1 and 2, respectively. We have chosen these variants because they have obtained the best results for each type of factorization. Figure 4 shows that the hybrid approach delivers notable performance gains compared with the basic implementation for both algorithms. Recursion, however, is only positive when applied to the Cholesky factorization, not to the LU.

Due to the overhead associated with the factorization of the small current diagonal block/column panel on the GPU, the hybrid approach introduces a significant improvement over to the basic implementation of both Cholesky/LU factorization processes. Similar benefits are to be expected for the other two variants. In addition, Figure 4 also shows the improvement attained for a hybrid implementation combined with a recursive

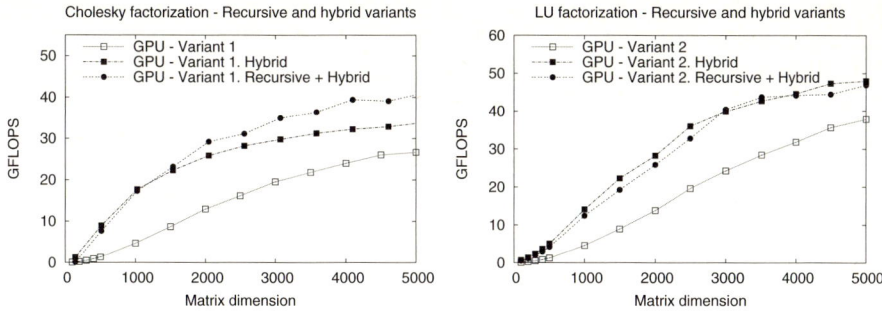

Fig. 4. Left: performance of the implementations of Variant 1 of the blocked algorithm for the Cholesky factorization: basic implementation, hybrid implementation, and a combination of the recursive and hybrid implementations. Highest performances are 27.9, 33.5, and 41.2 GFLOPS, respectively. Right: same implementations for the Variant 2 of the blocked algorithm for the LU factorization. Peak performances are 37.8, 47.9, and 46.9 GFLOPS, respectively.

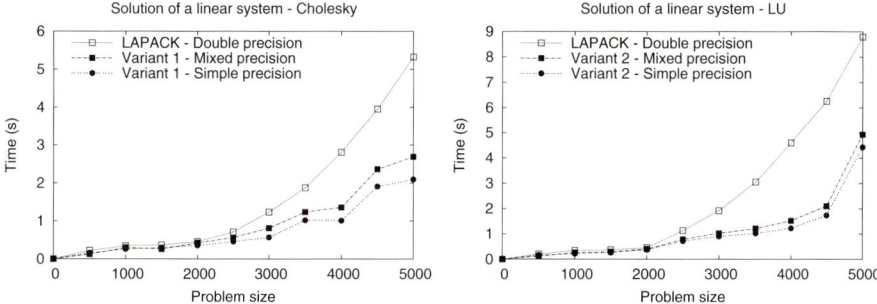

Fig. 5. Execution time of mixed-precision iterative refinement compared with those of a full single-precision solution on the GPU and a full double-precision solution on the CPU. A single right-hand side vector is considered.

approach for the factorization process. The combination of padding, hybrid execution and recursion improves the original blocked implementation on GPU (see Section 4.2), achieving a maximum speedup of 2.34 for the best Cholesky variant, and 3.14 for the LU when comparing the GPU implementations with the CPU ones.

4.5 Iterative Refinement

We next perform a time-based comparison using the basic implementation of Variant 1 for the blocked algorithms. Using the GPU as a general-purpose coprocessor, our mixed-precision implementation first computes a solution using the Cholesky or LU factorization computed on the GPU (single-precision), which is then refined to double-precision accuracy. The overhead of the iterative refinement stage is reported in Figure 5 as the difference between the mixed and single-precision implementations. The figure also includes the time for the corresponding full double-precision routine in LAPACK, executed exclusively on CPU.

Although the mixed-precision version introduces some overhead, the execution time is much lower than that of a full double-precision version executed on the CPU. In fact, the number of iterations required to achieve the desired accuracy was lower than 6 in our experiments. Due to the higher performance of the GPU implementations, the mixed-precision strategy is a good choice to achieve accurate results in less time, as the overhead introduced by the refinement process does not have a significant impact on the overall performance.

5 Conclusions

We have evaluated three blocked variants of the Cholesky and the LU factorizations using tuned implementations of BLAS on a G80 graphics processor and an Intel processor. The study reports that padding, hybrid GPU-CPU computation, and recursion are attractive techniques which deliver important increases in the performance of the implementations. Furthermore, iterative refinement with mixed precision is revealed as an inexpensive technique to regain full accuracy in the solution of a linear system of equations. Similar results and techniques can be expected to apply also to other dense linear algebra factorization procedures, such as the QR factorization, attaining high performance and accuracy on a low cost and widely available hardware platform.

References

1. Galoppo, N., Govindaraju, N.K., Henson, M., Manocha, D.: LU-GPU: Efficient algorithms for solving dense linear systems on graphics hardware. In: SC 2005: Proceedings of the 2005 ACM/IEEE conference on Supercomputing, p. 3. IEEE Computer Society, Los Alamitos (2005)
2. Junk, J.H., O'Leary, D.P.: Cholesky decomposition and linear programming on a GPU. Master's thesis, University of Maryland, College Park
3. NVIDIA: Nvidia CUDA Compute Unified Device Architecture. Programming Guide. NVIDIA (2007)
4. NVIDIA: CUBLAS Library. NVIDIA (2007)
5. Watkins, D.S.: Fundamentals of Matrix Computations, 2nd edn. John Wiley and Sons, Inc., New York (2002)
6. Gunnels, J.A., Gustavson, F.G., Henry, G.M., van de Geijn, R.A.: FLAME: Formal Linear Algebra Methods Environment. ACM Trans. Math. Soft. 27(4), 422–455 (2001)
7. Bientinesi, P., Gunnels, J.A., Myers, M.E., Quintana-Ortí, E.S., van de Geijn, R.A.: The science of deriving dense linear algebra algorithms. ACM Trans. Math. Soft. 31(1), 1–26 (2005)
8. Barrachina, S., Castillo, M., Igual, F.D., Mayo, R., Quintana-Ortí, E.S.: Evaluation and tuning of the level 3 CUBLAS for graphics processors. In: 9th IEEE International Workshop on Parallel and Distributed Scientific and Engineering Computing – PDSEC 2008 (2008)
9. Buttari, A., Dongarra, J., Langou, J., Langou, J., Luszczek, P., Kurzak, J.: Mixed precision iterative refinement techniques for the solution of dense linear systems. Int. J. High Perform. Comput. Appl. 21(4), 457–466 (2007)

Radioastronomy Image Synthesis on the Cell/B.E.*

Ana Lucia Varbanescu[1,4], Alexander S. van Amesfoort[1], Tim Cornwell[2], Andrew Mattingly[3], Bruce G. Elmegreen[4], Rob van Nieuwpoort[5], Ger van Diepen[5], and Henk Sips[1]

[1] Delft University of Technology, The Netherlands
[2] Australia Telescope National Facility
[3] IBM, ST Leonards, NSW Australia
[4] IBM Research, T.J.Watson Research Center, Yorktown Hts, NY, USA
[5] ASTRON, Dwingeloo, The Netherlands

Abstract. Now that large radiotelescopes like SKA, LOFAR, or AS-KAP, become available in different parts of the world, radioastronomers foresee a vast increase in the amount of data to gather, store and process. To keep the processing time bounded, parallelization and execution on (massively) parallel machines are required for the commonly-used radioastronomy software kernels. In this paper, we analyze data gridding and degridding, a very time-consuming kernel of radioastronomy image synthesis. To tackle its its dynamic behavior, we devise and implement a parallelization strategy for the Cell/B.E. multi-core processor, offering a cost-efficient alternative compared to classical supercomputers. Our experiments show that the application running on one Cell/B.E. is more than 20 times faster than the original application running on a commodity machine. Based on scalability experiments, we estimate the hardware requirements for a realistic radio-telescope. We conclude that our parallelization solution exposes an efficient way to deal with dynamic data-intensive applications on heterogeneous multi-core processors.

1 Introduction

High performance computing (HPC) applications can benefit a lot from the emerging multi-core platforms. However, (legacy) sequential code for HPC applications is not re-usable for these architectures, as they require multiple layers of parallelism to be properly exploited to achieve peak performance [1].

On the other hand many large-scale HPC areas, like radioastronomy, have reached a point where computational power and the efficient ways to use it are becoming critical. For example, radioastronomy projects like LOFAR [2], AS-KAP [3], or SKA [4] provide highly accurate astronomical measurements by collecting huge streams of radio synthesis data, which are further processed

---

* This research is partially supported by the AstroSTREAM project, funded by NWO/STARE, and the SCALP project, funded by STW/Progress.

into sky images. For radioastronomy applications, processing power and storage space need to be used with extreme efficiency: whatever is not computed in time, may get stored; whatever does not fit in the storage space gets lost. Therefore, the choice for a suitable parallel hardware platform is essential, and it may come at the price of increased programming effort. For example, on a heterogeneous multi-core platform like the Cell/B.E., three different parallelism classes - multi-processor, multi-core, and core-level - require specific optimization techniques. Most of the "classical" parallel languages (like MPI or OpenMP) fail to adapt automatically to the different hardware scale. The few specific multi-core programming models like RapidMind [5] or Sequoia [6] do not yet provide the full parallelism range that an application should exploit on a Cell-like architecture.

In this work, we present one of the first successful attempts to parallelize radioastronomy kernels on a heterogeneous multi-core platform. Specifically, we focus on the parallelization of *the gridding and degridding* operations on the Cell/B.E.. Both kernels are implemented using convolutional resampling, a dynamic data-intensive radioastronomy kernel which, as a basic building block in many of the data processing phases, dominates the workload of radio synthesis imaging [3]. Optimizing it has a direct impact on the performance and hardware requirements of any of the large radiotelescopes mentioned above. In response to these requirements, our solution leads to a speed-up factor of more than 20 when comparing the Cell/B.E. solution with the reference (sequential) code running on a commodity machine. Based on these results, we provide a scalability analysis for the present solution and show how our solution can be extended to reach the scale of a real application like SKA.

Using our experience with the convolutional resampling, we show a generic scalable solution for parallelizing dynamic data-intensive applications on Cell-like architectures. We claim that efficient execution on heterogeneous multi-cores *requires* identifying and isolating the dynamic behaviour from the parallel computation. Further, using a master-workers model, the parallel processing is assigned to the "worker" cores, while the dynamic, irregular behaviour is assigned to the "master" core. The advantages are threefold: (1) the worker processing can be optimized with generic in-core techniques, (2) data locality decisions can be taken on-the-fly by a master process with better knowledge of the entire application, and (3) overall application scalability is easier to analyze and improve.

The remainder of this paper is organized as follows. Section 2 briefly presents our application, together with a radioastronomy primer. The target platform and the potential parallelization strategies are presented in Section 3. Section 4 discusses our experiments and results, focusing on the increased performance of the parallel version. Scalability analysis is covered in Section 5. We briefly survey existing related work in Section 6. We conclude that although the performance results are good, further research should address more application specific optimizations and different platforms, as presented in Section 7.

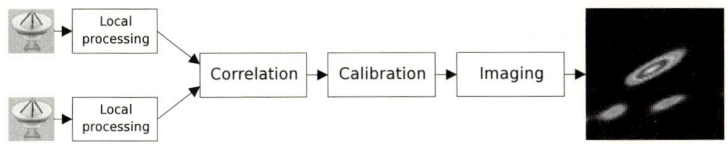

Fig. 1. The software pipeline from antennas to sky images

2 The Gridding and Degridding Kernels

In this section we briefly analyze our application, from its radioastronomy background to its computation and data access patterns.

2.1 Radioastronomy - A Primer

The history of radio astronomy has been one of solving engineering problems to construct radio telescopes of continually increasing angular resolution (i.e., telescopes able to distinguish the finest level of detail in the sky). Very good resolutions require very large antennas. An alternative to building large single-dish radiotelescopes is radio interferometry. This solution enables arrays of connected radiotelescopes (with various antennas types and placement geometries) to collect more signals and, using the aperture synthesis technique [?] to significantly increase the angular resolution of the "combined" telescope. By interfering the signals from different antennas, this technique creates a combined telescope the size of the antennas furthest apart in the array.

The simplified path of the signal from the antenna to a sky image is presented in Figure 1. The signals coming from two antennas forming a *baseline*[1] have to be correlated before they are combined. A correlator reads these (sampled) signals and generates the corresponding set of *complex visibilities*, V, depending on the baseline b, the frequency f, and the sample time t. Increasing the number of baselines in the array (i.e., varying the antennas numbers and/or placement) increases the quality of the generated sky image. The total number of baselines B in an array of A antennas is $B = A \cdot (A+1)/2$, and it is a significant performance parameter of the radiotelescope.

2.2 Building the Sky Image

An image of the sky is a reconstruction of the sky brightness using the measured visibilities. For coplanar baselines, (e.g., for a *narrow field of view*), the visibility function and the sky brightness are a 2D Fourier pair. Thus, in practice, image reconstruction uses the discrete Fourier transform on the observed (sampled) visibilities. For the more general case of non-coplanar baselines (i.e., *wide field*

---

[1] The projected separation between any two individual antennas in the array as seen from the radio source is called *a baseline* and it is described by a set of 3D spatial coordinates, (u, v, w).

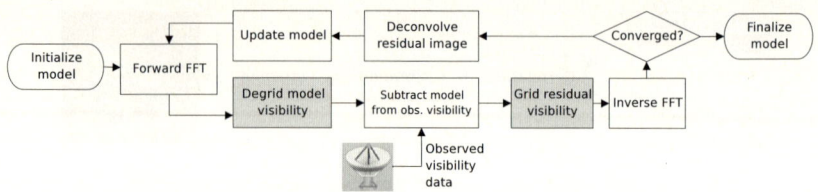

Fig. 2. A diagram of the typical deconvolution process in which a model is iteratively refined by multiple passes. The shaded blocks (gridding and degridding) are both performed by convolutional resampling.

of view), we use the W-projection algorithm [8], which computes one FFT for each projection of the baseline b on P_w parallel planes (usually, betwen 10 and 30), and combines the results.

The practical process of building a sky image has two phases: imaging and deconvolution. The imaging phase generates a *dirty image* directly from the measured visibilities, using FFT. The deconvolution "cleans" the dirty image into a *sky model*. Further, this sky model can be iteratively enhanced by repeating the process using new measured visibilities. A snapshot of this process is presented in Figure 2. Before any FFT operations, data has to be placed in a regularly spaced grid. The operation used to interpolate the original visibility data to a regular grid is called *gridding*. *Degridding* is the "reverse" operation, that projects the regular grid points back to the original tracks; degridding is required when a computed grid is used to refine an existing model.

2.3 Application Analysis

The visibility data is gathered at regular time intervals from each baseline in the system. For a single sample, gridding and degridding are performed by convolution with a function designed to have good properties in the image domain. In practice, all the convolution coefficients are pre-calculated and stored in a large matrix, **C**, and the gridding of the $V(u,v,w)_t$ visibilities into **G**, the $2^g \times 2^g$ regular grid is implemented by convolution with sub-blocks from **C**. Such a sub-block, SK_M, having $M = m \times m$ elements, is called a *support kernel*. Typical values for M are between 15×15 and 129×129, depending on the required accuracy level. Similarly, degridding uses the same support kernels to transform the data from the regular grid back into the visibility domain, generating a new set of $V'(u,v,w)_t$.

The essential application data structures are summarized in Table 2.3. Data is collected from A antennas (i.e., $B = A \cdot (A+1)/2$ baselines); in one observation session, each baseline is sampled at regular intervals, providing $N_{samples}$ for each one of the chosen N_{freq} frequency channels. For example, at a sampling rate of 1 sample/s, $N_{samples} = 28800$ for an 8 hours observation; N_{freq} can vary between tens and thousands of channels.

The computation patterns for gridding and degridding are presented in Listing 1.1. Note that the effective computation is the same: one complex

Listing 1.1. The core of the convolutional resampling kernel. f1 and f2 are two different functions.

```
1    forall (i=0..N_freq; j=0..N_samples-1) // for all samples
2      compute g_index=f1((u,v,w)[j], freq[i]);
3      compute c_index=f2((u,v,w)[j], freq[i]);
4      for (x=0; x<M; x++)    //sweep the convolution kernel
5        if(gridding)   G[g_index+x] += C[c_index+x]*V[i,j];
6        if(degridding) V'[i,j] += G[g_index+x]*C[c_index+x];
```

Table 1. The main data structures of the convolutional resampling and their characteristics

Name	Symbol	Cardinality	Type	Access pattern
Coordinates/baseline	u, v, w	$N_{samples}$	Real	Linear
Visibility data	V	$N_{samples} \cdot N_{freq}$	Complex	Linear
Convolution matrix	$\mathbf{C}$	$M \cdot os^2 \cdot P_w$	Complex	Irregular
Support kernel	SK_M	$M = m \times m$	Complex	Linear
Grid	$\mathbf{G}$	512 x 512	Complex	Irregular
Grid subregion	SG_M	$M = m \times m$	Complex	Linear

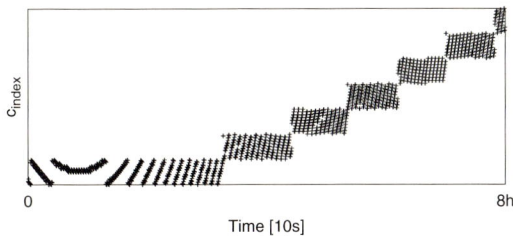

Fig. 3. Irregular access patterns in the **C** matrix for measurements collected by 1 baseline in 8h. The more distant the points are in the Y dimension, the poorer the data locality is.

multiply-add (MADD) operation, i.e., 4 MADD floating point operations. The large execution time of both kernels is caused by (1) the large iteration space ($N_{freq} \times N_{samples} \times M$), and (2) the irregular accesses in both **C** and **G**. Figure 2.3 gives an example of how irregular these accesses are by plotting all the c_index values computed for measurements taken by one baseline in an 8-hour session. A similar graph can be drawn for g_index. These irregular accesses in both **C** and **G** lead to a data-dependent behaviour of the application, which in turn results in poor data locality and requires a non-trivial data layout for parallelization.

3 Parallelization on the Cell/B.E.

In this section we discuss the parallelization solutions used to efficiently implement the gridding and degridding kernels on the Cell/B.E. platform.

3.1 Cell/B.E. Overview

The Cell Broadband Engine (Cell/B.E.) is a heterogeneous multi-core processor, initially designed by Sony, IBM and Toshiba for the Playstation 3 (PS3) game console. Due to its peak performance levels [?], the processor became quickly a popular target for high performance computing applications.

Cell/B.E. has nine cores: one Power Processing Element (PPE), acting as a coordinator for the eight Synergistic Processing Elements (SPEs), which share the main computational load. All cores, the main memory, and the external I/O are connected by a high-bandwidth Element Interconnection Bus (EIB). The theoretical maximum data bandwidth of the EIB is 204.8 GB/s. The PPE contains the Power Processing Unit (PPU) - a two-way multithreaded core, based on the Power Architecture -, separated L1 caches (32KB for data and 32KB for instructions), and 512KB of L2 Cache. The PPE runs the operating system and coordinates the SPEs. An SPE contains a RISC-core (the SPU), a 256KB Local Storage (LS), and a Memory Flow Controller (MFC). The LS is used as local memory for both code and data and is managed *entirely* by the application. All SPU instructions are 128-bit SIMD instructions, and all 128 SPU registers are 128-bit wide. The theoretical peak performance of one SPE is 25.6 single precision GFlops.

The Cell/B.E. cores combine functionality to execute a large spectrum of applications, ranging from scientific kernels [1,10] to image processing applications [11]. The basic Cell/B.E. programming is based on a multi-threading model: the PPE spawns threads that execute asynchronously on the SPEs, until interaction and/or synchronization is required. The SPEs can communicate with the PPE using simple mechanisms like signals and mailboxes for small amounts of data, or DMA transfers via the main memory for larger data.

3.2 Parallelization on the Cell/B.E.

Because both our kernels are data-intensive, the parallelization follows an SPMD model, where all SPEs run the same computation (i.e., the convolution itself) on different sets of data. For an efficient solution, we need to design a balanced data and task distribution, to implement it, and to address the eventual Cell-specific problems that may occur.

Data Distribution. The simplest option for data distribution is to share all data evenly among the SPEs: each core receives a piece of V, **C**, and **G**, and computes its share. This solution could provide linear speed-up when increasing the number of participating cores if a contiguous set of data from V would map uniformly in either **C** or **G**. Of course, this is not the case for the irregular access patterns of convolutional resampling. Choosing **G** or **C** for symmetrical distribution (i.e., each SPE is working *only* with its own subregion, and fetching the other data as needed) leads to overall load-imbalance and extensive communication overhead, as seen in [12]. Finally, we can symmetrically distribute the visibilities $V(u, v, w)_t$. If the data is available offline (i.e., stored in files), a block-based distribution is sufficient for good load-balancing. If the data is streaming in the application, SPE utilization and load balancing are improved by using a cyclic, round-robin-like distribution: each sample fetched by the PPE is distributed to the next SPE in line. The SPE receives the data, fetches $(u, v, w)_t$, computes c_{index_t} and g_{index_t} locally, and then uses DMA to bring the necessary SK_M and SG_M in LS (assuming all these fit!). Although relatively simple, this solution requires excessive SPE-PPE communication, not suitable for the Cell/B.E., where the SPEs are severely underutilized and the overall speed-up (on 16SPEs) is only about a factor of 3.

Implementation. In the end, we opt for a dynamic data distribution, implemented using the master-workers paradigm: the PPE distributes the visibility data samples *on-the-fly*, and stores the share for each SPE in a dedicated queue. In this scenario, the PPE computes the c_{index} and g_{index}, and distributes adjacent values in the same queue. The solution increases per-SPE data locality, at the expense of the extra main memory consumption; the potential load-imbalance (too many work piling up in the same queue) is controlled by limiting the queue size and allowing more queues to focus on the same subregions.

The SPE performs a simple loop: it polls its queue to check if there is work to do; as soon as there is, the SPE fetches the SK_M and SG_M via DMA, computes the new values for SG_M, and does the DMA-out transfer of the new SG_M. To avoid too expensive synchronization mechanisms, we allocate one grid copy for each SPE. The final result, calculated by the PPE, is a simple addition of these individual grids.

We further optimize this solution as follows: if consecutive SPE queue elements have the same c_{index} and g_{index}, the data samples are summed. Once the sequence is over, the convolution is no longer executed for each V_i, but only once, for the entire $\sum(V_i)$. In the case only c_{index} is the same, we can still spare one DMA transfer for the SK_M data. Similarly, if g_{index} is the same, the number of DMA out transfers can be decreased.

Cell-specific Issues. Once the top level parallelization is implemented, we verify the memory footprint of the SPE code: the complete SK_M and SG_M, as well as the local copy of the queue should fit, together with the code, in 256KB of memory. For large values of M, this is not possible. Thus, a slightly more complicated scheme is implemented: for each data sample in the queue, SK_M is fetched entirely in a sequential series of DMA transfers, while SG_M is fetched, updated, and written back line-by-line. Finally, although we only need one SG_M line for the actual computation, we store three such lines - the one being processed, the one ready to be transferred out to the main-memory, and the one being read in for the next computation, thus enabling a simple opportunity for computation/communication overlap Finally, we optimize the core computation of each SPE by partial SIMD-ization and loop unrolling, as well as DMA double buffering [13].

4 Experiments and Results

In this section we present our experiments on two Cell/B.E. platforms and we analyze their results (more detailed experiments and more in-depth explanations are described in [12]).

We run our experiments on two platforms: (1) a PlayStation3 gaming console, and (2) a QS20 Cell blade, a platform for high-performance computing. PS3 has one Cell/B.E. processor, running at 3.2GHz, with six out of the eight SPEs fully available for programming; the QS20 blade has two Cell/B.E. processors, providing (almost) uniform access to 16 SPEs.

Our input data is a collection of samples from a real astronomical measurement. The data is collected from 45 antennas (990 baselines), over a period of 8 hours, with a sampling rate of a one element per 10s. However, all results in this section refer to experiments performed for one baseline only. We discuss the multi-baseline application and its scalability in Section 5.

4.1 Overall Application Performance

The first set of experiments shows the overall performance improvement of the parallelized convolutional resampling. The input data set is a collection of 2880 samples produced by one baseline. The support kernel size varies between $M = 33 \times 33$ and $M = 129 \times 129$ elements. The metric we use is the execution time per operation (i.e., total execution time divided by the number of elementary operations, e.g., the number of grid additions) for both the gridding and degridding kernels. Note that for full utilization and scalability, the values for this metric should be constant (see the Pentium D behavior). We compare the reference code, running on a single core of a 3.4GHz Pentium D machine[2] with the our parallelized version running on different configurations on the two available Cell/B.E. platforms. Figure 4 presents these execution time results, emphasizing the best performance on each Cell platforms and the SPE configuration that generated it.

Note that Cell/B.E. outperforms the sequential machine. Further, the larger the kernel, the better the Cell performance becomes. However, note that for kernels as small as $M = 17 \times 17$, the PentiumD results are somewhat comparable with the Cell ones; also, for $M = 129 \times 129$, where both the PentiumD core and the PS3 hit a memory bottleneck. The case of PS3 is much worse because the total available platform memory is very low. Besides the good speed-up factor (over 20 for $M = 101 \times 101$), these results also signal a significant core underutilization - see the SPEs numbers for each peak performance. This behavior is caused by the small input set: one baseline with 2880×16 data samples does not provide enough computation for a full Cell/B.E.

---

[2] The PentiumD processor is used here as an instance of a general purpose processor; the choice for this machine was only due to availability, and we use the execution time on PentiumD only as a measure of the performance the reference sequential code, not as a measure of the potential performance of the processor.

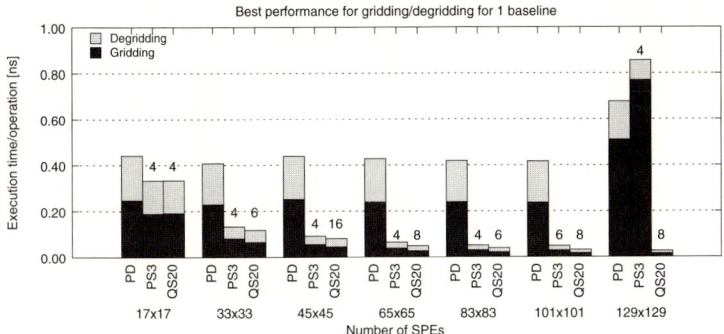

Fig. 4. The overall application performance for the gridding/degridding with different support kernel sizes, running on a PentiumD using 1 core, on the PS3, and on the QS20. The labels inside the graph specify with how many SPEs was each performance peak obtained.

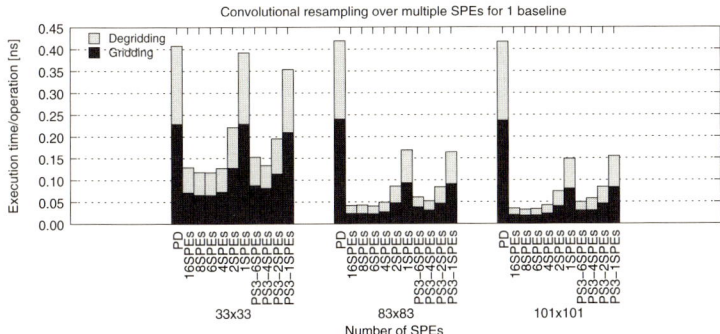

Fig. 5. The performance for the gridding/degridding with different support kernel sizes, running on 6 different hardware configurations

4.2 SPE Utilization

Due to the application low computation-to-communication ratio, we expect the SPEs to be under-utilized. Thus, we show more details on SPE utilization: we measure the execution time for different problem sizes running on different numbers of SPEs (1, 2, 4, 6, 8, and 16). We present the results of these experiments in Figure 5.

Figure 5 shows that for large kernels, i.e., 83x83 elements, the application has good scalability with the number of used SPEs for one Cell/B.E. The best results are indeed obtained for 8 SPEs. The 15% increase in the execution time on 16 SPEs is due to the architecture organization: the 16SPEs are part of two different Cell/B.E. processors, and the "remote" memory accesses from one processor to the other take slightly longer. Thus, for one baseline, one Cell/B.E. (8 SPEs) is sufficient. If a performance penalty of about 10% can be tolerated by the application, using only 6 out of 8 SPEs/Cell provides the hardware cost

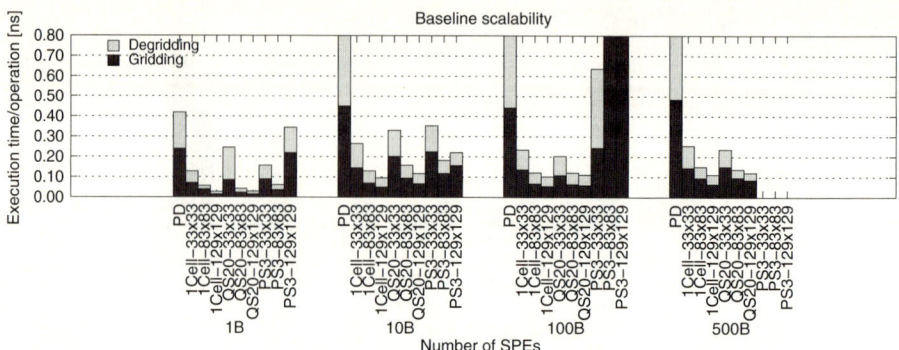

Fig. 6. Baseline scalability: analyzing data from 1, 10, 100, 500 baselines for 4 hardware configurations (PD=1core, PS3=6SPEs, 1Cell=8SPEs, QS20=16SPEs and three different support kernel sizes

advantage (replaces one QS20 with two cheaper PlayStation3). Finally, for smaller support kernels, the SPEs are significantly under-utilized. Ideally, the optimal SPE configuration for a given problem size should be computed by an automated performance predictor. No such tool is available yet for the Cell/B.E.

5 Scalability Analysis

In this section we test the scalability potential of our application, and we evaluate how far off we are from the real system scale.

5.1 Multi-baseline Parallelization

In Section 4, we have discussed the performance results obtained when using the PS3 or QS20 machines to perform the gridding/degridding for a single baseline. To test our solution's scalability, we repeat the experiments for sets of 10, 100 and 500 baselines. To simulate a streaming-like environment, we have used real baseline data, only shuffled such that all data arrives in correct time order, but data coming in the same time interval from different baselines and on different frequency channels has no guaranteed order. We present our results in Figure 6.

Note that the execution time for a single baseline (1B) is better than for a 10 baselines set. This happens because the data locality is decreased by the shuffling. However, as we increase to 100+ baselines, the **G** coverage tends to be more uniform, and the performance is increasing. Also note the differences between the platforms: the sequential version, running on the a single core of a PentiumD, pays some performance penalty only for very large kernel sizes, and only for the gridding operation - probably a cache effect. The PS3 performance drops badly *also* for larger numbers of baselines (about 5-7 times for 100 baselines, and complete crash on 500 baselines), as the processor runs out of main memory. The QS20 - in both 8 and 16 SPEs scales for all test cases.

5.2 The Scale of the Real Application

Radio-telescopes are typically used to gather data during one 8 or 12 hours period (depending on how long the source is above the horizon), and process it later. Data is gathered in a streaming fashion, with a given data rate (e.g, a sample every 10s). For telescopes like SKA, processing is also required to be on-line streaming: gather data, process, move on.

Our goal is to verify whether a collection of X Cell processors can deal with online data processing constraints and, if so, to show how can X be estimated and minimized. Equation 1 shows the upper bound to be enforced on the computation time, T_{sample}^{Cell}, such that data can be processed at a rate of 1 sample/T_{int} [3].

$$\frac{B \times N_{freq}}{T_{int}} \leq \frac{X}{T_{sample}^{multi-Cell}} \quad (1)$$

So, for each data sample (one per baseline per frequency channel) delivered to the X processors in the time T_{int}, there has to be at least one grid addition, which is the time $T_{sample}^{multi-Cell}$. For example, in the case of $B = 1000 baselines$, $N_{freq} = 50000$ frequency channels, and $T_{int} = 10s$, $X = 5.000.000 \times (T_{sample}^{multi-Cell}/1s)$, or the addition time has to be below $200ns$ for a single Cell to be able to handle the data *computation* online.

To further bound $T_{sample}^{multi-Cell}$, we note the following: (1) even if the computation speed may be able to keep-up with streaming requirements for 1000 baselines, the I/O capacity of Cell/B.E. will not: it is impossible to stream data into one single Cell/B.E. at a rate of $(1000 \times 8)B/s$ [14]; (2) streaming at a low rate may decrease the computation performance due to core underutilization; and (3) the application scalability will be different for more Cell/B.E. processors, especially when "packaged" in different machines, thus $T_{sample}^{Cell} \leq T_{sample}^{multi-Cell}$. A more general model, including these new constraints and presented in Equation 2.

$$\frac{B \times N_{freq}}{T_{int}} \leq \frac{X}{\max(T_{sample}^{Cell}, T_{streaming}^{multi-Cell}, T_{IO})} \quad (2)$$

Thus, we conclude that our solution for the parallel implementation of the gridding/degridding kernels scales well with the number of baselines. However, although we seem to be able to deal with more than 500 baselines on a single Cell/B.E. processor, slow I/O and streaming operations may as well impose the use of several Cell/B.E. .

---

[3] B is the number of baselines, $N_f req$ is the number of frequency channels, T_{int} is the time interval for the correlation integral.

6 Related Work

In this section we show how our work can be related with the fields of parallel radio astronomy algorithms and HPC on multi-cores. So far, these two fields have been completely disjoint. Our approach is a first step to high-performance radio astronomy kernels on a high-performance heterogeneous multi-core system.

Astronomers mainly use shared memory and MPI to parallelize their applications. To use MPI on Cell/B.E., a very lightweight implementation is needed and tasks must be stripped down to t in the remaining space of the local store. The only MPI-based programming model for Cell is the MPI microtask model [15], but their prototype is not available for evaluation. OpenMP [16] is not an option as it relies on shared-memory.

Applications like RAxML [17] and Sweep3D [10], have also shown the challenges and results of efficient parallelization of HPC applications on the Cell/B.E. Although we used some of their techniques to optimize the SPE code performance, the higher-level parallelization was too application specific to be reused in our case. Furthermore, typical ports on the Cell, like MarCell [18], or real-time ray tracing are [11] are very computation intensive, so they do not exhibit the unpredictable data access patterns and the low number of compute operations per data byte we have seen in this application.

Currently, efforts are underway to implement other parts of the radio-astronomy software pipeline, such as the correlation and calibration algorithms on Cell and GPUs. Correlation may be very compute-intensive, but it is much easier to parallelize - it has already been implemented very efficiently on Cell and FPGAs [19]. Apart from the general-purpose GPU frameworks like CUDA [20] and RapidMind [5], we are following with interest the work in progress on real-time imaging and calibration [21], which deals with similar applications.

7 Conclusions and Future Work

HPC applications are hard to port efficiently on multi-core processors, due to the multiple levels of parallelism that need to be properly addressed. In this paper, we have presented a significant HPC radioastronomy kernel and we have shown how to efficiently tackle its parallelization on the Cell/B.E. processor. Our approach is based on a locality-enhancing parallelization, which isolates and assigns the lower-level compute intensive blocks to the worker cores, and dedicates master cores to execute the irregular control- and data-flow. Due to its high-level view of the problem, our approach can be easily extended to parallelize dynamic data-intensive applications on heterogeneous multi-cores. We have applied this strategy to the gridding and degridding kernels, one of the very first successful attempts to port radioastronomy kernels on a heterogeneous multi-core processor. The experimental results included in the paper show a 20 times performance improvement of the Cell/B.E. solution over the original sequential code running on a commodity machine, as well as very good scalability. However, due to additional limitations, like the I/O and memory rate, we may still need hundreds of Cell/B.E. to process the LOFAR or SKA data streams on-line.

In the near future, we aim to implement a new series of aggressive, data-dependent optimizations on the current implementation. Further, we aim to test the performance and scalability of the gridding/degridding kernels in a multi-Cell environment. Finally, as data-intensive irregular-access applications like the gridding/degridding kernels are notorious stress-cases for parallel architectures, we plan to make a thorough comparison between parallelization approaches, programming effort and performance pay-off for several multi-core platforms running gridding and degridding.

Acknowledgements. We would like to thank Michael Perrone, Gordon Braudaway, Fabrizzio Petrini and Daniele Scarpazza for their valuable support and ideas during the development of this application. We would also like to thank Jennifer Turner (IBM) for always finding an extra time-slot for us on the QS20 blade.

References

1. Williams, S., Shalf, J., Oliker, L., Kamil, S., Husbands, P., Yelick, K.: The Potential of the Cell Processor for Scientific Computing. In: ACM Computing Frontiers 2006, Italy (May 2006)
2. van der Schaaf, K., Broekema, C., van Diepen, G., van Meijeren, E.: The lofar central processing facility architecture. Experimental Astronomy, special issue on SKA 17, 43–58 (2004)
3. Cornwell, T.J.: SKA and EVLA computing costs for wide field imaging. Experimental Astronomy 17, 329–343 (2004)
4. Schilizzi, R.T., Alexander, P., Cordes, J.M., Dewdney, P.E., Ekers, R.D., Faulkner, A.J., Gaensler, B.M., Hall, P.J., Jonas, J.L.:, Kellermann, K.I.: Preliminary specifications for the square kilometre array. Technical Report v2.4 (November 2007), www.skatelescope.org
5. McCool, M.: Signal processing and general-purpose computing on GPUs. IEEE Signal Processing Magazine, 109–114 (May 2007)
6. Fatahalian, K., Knight, T.J., Houston, M., Erez, M., Horn, D.R., Leem, L., Park, J.Y., Ren, M., Aiken, A., Dally, W.J., Hanrahan, P.: Sequoia: Programming the memory hierarchy. In: Proceedings of the 2006 ACM/IEEE Conference on Supercomputing (November 2006)
7. Thompson, A., Moran, J., Swenson, G.: Interferometry and synthesis in radio astronomy. Wiley, New York (2001)
8. Cornwell, T., Golap, K., Bhatnagar, S.: W projection: A new algorithm for wide field imaging with radio synthesis arrays. In: Astronomical Data Analysis Software and Systems XIV ASP Conference Series, vol. 347, p. 86–95 (2004)
9. Gschwind, M.: The Cell Broadband Engine: Exploiting multiple levels of parallelism in a chip multiprocessor. International Journal of Parallel Programming 35(3), 233–262 (2007)
10. Petrini, F., Fernàndez, J., Kistler, M., Fossum, G., Varbanescu, A.L., Perrone, M.: Multicore Surprises: Lessons Learned from Optimizing Sweep3D on the Cell Broadband Engine. In: IPDPS 2007. IEEE/ACM (March 2007)

11. Benthin, C., Wald, I., Scherbaum, M., Friedrich, H.: Ray tracing on the Cell processor. In: IEEE Symposium on Interactive Ray Tracing 2006, pp. 15–23 (September 2006)
12. Varbanescu, A.L., van Amesfoort, A., Cornwell, T., Elmegreen, B.G., van Nieuwpoort, R., van Diepen, G., Sips, H.: The performance of gridding/degridding on the Cell/B.E. Technical report, Delft University of Technology (January 2008)
13. IBM: Cell Broadband Engine Programming Tutorial. 2.0 edn. (December 2006)
14. Hofstee, P.: Power efficient processor architecture and the cell processor. In: HPCA 2005, pp. 258–262. IEEE Computer Society Press, Los Alamitos (2005)
15. Ohara, M., Inoue, H., Sohda, Y., Komatsu, H., Nakatani, T.: MPI microtask for programming th Cell Broadband Engine processor. IBM Systems Journal 45(1), 85–102 (2006)
16. O'Brien, K., Sura, Z., Chen, T., Zhang, T.: Supporting openmp on the cell. In: International Workshop on OpenMP (2007)
17. Blagojevic, F., Stamatakis, A., Antonopoulos, C., Nikolopoulos, D.S.: RAxML-CELL: Parallel phylogenetic tree construction on the cell broadband engine. In: IPDPS 2007, Long Beach, CA. IEEE/ACM (March 2007)
18. Liu, L.K., Liu, Q., Natsev, A.P., Ross, K.A., Smith, J.R., Varbanescu, A.L.: Digital Media Indexing on the Cell Processor. In: ICME 2007, N/A (July 2007)
19. de Souza, L., Bunton, J.D., Campbell-Wilson, D., Cappallo, R.J., Kincaid, B.: A radio astronomy correlator optimized for the Xilinx Virtex-4 SX FPGA. In: International Conference on Field Programmable Logic and Applications (2007)
20. ***: nVidia CUDA - Compute Unified Device Architecture Programming Guide. nVidia (2007)
21. Wayth, R., Dale, K., Greenhill, L., Mitchell, D., Ord, S., Pfister, H.: Real-time calibration and imaging for the MWA (poster). In: AstroGPU 2007 (November 2007)

Parallel Lattice Boltzmann Flow Simulation on Emerging Multi-core Platforms

Liu Peng, Ken-ichi Nomura, Takehiro Oyakawa, Rajiv K. Kalia, Aiichiro Nakano, and Priya Vashishta

Collaboratory for Advanced Computing and Simulations, Department of Computer Science,
Department of Physics & Astronomy, Department of Chemical
Engineering & Materials Science,
University of Southern California, Los Angeles, CA 90089-0242, USA
{liupeng,knomura,oyakawa,rkalia,anakano,priyav}@usc.edu

Abstract. A parallel Lattice Boltzmann Method (pLBM), which is based on hierarchical spatial decomposition, is designed to perform large-scale flow simulations. The algorithm uses critical section-free, dual representation in order to expose maximal concurrency and data locality. Performances of emerging multi-core platforms—PlayStation3 (Cell Broadband Engine) and Compute Unified Device Architecture (CUDA)—are tested using the pLBM, which is implemented with multi-thread and message-passing programming. The results show that pLBM achieves good performance improvement, 11.02 for Cell over a traditional Xeon cluster and 8.76 for CUDA graphics processing unit (GPU) over a Sempron central processing unit (CPU). The results provide some insights into application design on future many-core platforms.

Keywords: Lattice Boltzmann Method, Flow simulation, Parallel computing, Hybrid thread + message passing programming, Spatial decomposition, Critical section-free, dual representation, PlayStation3 cluster, Cell Broadband Engine architecture, CUDA.

1 Introduction

We are witnessing a dramatic change into a multi-core paradigm, and computer industry is facing a historical shift, in which Moore's law due to ever increasing clock speeds has been subsumed by increasing numbers of cores per microchip [1,2]. While Intel is deploying multi-core processors across key product lines as a pivotal piece [1], AMD begins its multi-core strategy by introducing quad-core processors, and IBM, Sony, and Toshiba provide Cell, which is also an ideal application test bed to prepare for coming many-core revolution [3,4]. The many-core revolution will mark the end of the free-ride era (i.e., legacy software will run faster on newer chips), resulting in a dichotomy—subsiding speed-up of conventional software and exponential speed-up of scalable parallel applications [5]. Recent progresses in high-performance technical computing have identified key technologies for parallel computing with portable scalability. An example is an Embedded Divide-and-Conquer (EDC) algorithmic framework to design linear-scaling algorithms for broad scientific and engineering applications based on spatiotemporal locality principles [6]. The EDC framework maximally exposes concurrency and data locality, thereby achieving reusable "design once, scale on new architectures" (or metascalable) applications. It is expected that such metascalable algorithms will continue to scale on future many-core architectures.

As mentioned above, multi-core processor is the trend for future supercomputers, and how to develop metascalable applications on such platforms is in great need. The Lattice Boltzmann Method (LBM) for fluid simulations—which features robustness, complicated geometry, multiphases, and ease of parallelization—is a representative of this kind of applications. For example, Williams et al. studied performance optimization of the LBM on multi-core platforms [7], while Stuermer implemented the LBM on Cell [8,9] and Li et al. tested the LBM on graphics processing units (GPUs) [10]. In this paper, we present our design of a unified parallel implementation of the LBM on several emerging platforms including a cluster of Cell-based PlayStation3 consoles and Compute Unified Device Architecture (CUDA) based implementations on GPUs. The paper is organized as follows. Section 2 describes the parallelization of the LBM algorithm. The test beds, testing results, and performance analysis are presented in Section 3. Conclusions and future directions are contained in Section 4.

2 Parallel Lattice Boltzmann Flow Simulation Algorithm

2.1 Lattice Boltzmann Method

The essential quantity in the Lattice Boltzmann Method (LBM) [11] is a density function (DF) $f_i(\vec{x},t)$ on a discrete lattice, $\vec{x} = (j\Delta x, k\Delta y, l\Delta z)$ ($j \in [1, N_x], k \in [1, N_y], l \in [1, N_z]$), with discrete velocity values $\vec{e}_i$ ($i \in [0, N_v - 1]$) at time t. Here, each $\vec{e}_i$ points from a lattice site to one of its N_v near-neighbor sites. N_x, N_y, and N_z are the numbers of lattice sites in the x, y, and z directions, respectively, with Δx, Δy and Δz being the corresponding lattice spacings and N_v (= 18) being the number of discrete velocity values. From the DF, we can calculate various physical quantities such as fluid density $\rho(\vec{x},t)$ and velocity $\vec{u}(\vec{x},t)$:

$$\rho(\vec{x},t) = \sum_i f_i(\vec{x},t), \tag{1}$$

$$\rho(\vec{x},t)\vec{u}(\vec{x},t) = \sum_i \vec{e}_i f_i(\vec{x},t). \tag{2}$$

The time evolution of the DF is governed by the Boltzmann equation in the Bhatnagar-Gross-Krook (BGK) model. The LBM simulation thus consists of a time-stepping iteration, in which collision and streaming operations are performed as time is incremented by Δt at each iteration step:
Collision:

$$f_i(\vec{x},t^+) \leftarrow f_i(\vec{x},t) - \frac{1}{\tau}\left(f_i(\vec{x},t) - f_i^{eq}(\rho(\vec{x}),\vec{u}(\vec{x}))\right), \tag{3}$$

Streaming:
$$f_i(\bar{x}+\bar{e}_i, t+\Delta t) \leftarrow f_i(\bar{x},t^+). \quad (4)$$

In Eq. (4), the equilibrium DF is defined as
$$f_i^{eq}(\rho,\bar{u}) = \rho(A + B(\bar{e}_i \cdot \bar{u}) + C(\bar{e}_i \cdot \bar{u})^2 + D\bar{u}^2), \quad (5)$$
where A, B, C and D are constants, and the time constant τ is related to the kinematic viscosity ν through a relation $\nu = (\tau - 1/2)/3$.

It should be noted that the collision step involves a large number of floating-point operations that are strictly local to each lattice site, while the streaming step contains no floating-point operation but solely memory copies between nearest-neighbor lattice sites.

2.2 Parallel LBM Algorithm

Our parallel Lattice Boltzmann Method (pLBM) algorithm consists of three functions: collision, streaming, and communication. The total simulation system Ω is decomposed into several sub-domains Ω_i, where $\Omega = \cup_i \Omega_i$, and each domain is mapped onto a processor (see Fig. 1). The collision and streaming functions update DFs on a single domain, while the communication function is responsible for inter-domain DF migrations. To simplify discussion, Fig. 1 shows a schematic of a 2-dimentional system (the actual implementation is for 3 dimensions). Here, the white squares denote open nodes that have DFs, the black squares denote closed nodes that represent obstacles (and hence no flow), and the gray squares denote buffer nodes that hold buffer DFs for inter-domain communication, which are initialized with the corresponding geometry information (open or closed) in neighbor domains at the beginning of simulation. In the 2-dimensional example, a single domain consists of $N_x \times N_y$ nodes, where N_x and N_y are the numbers of lattice sites in the x and y directions, respectively.

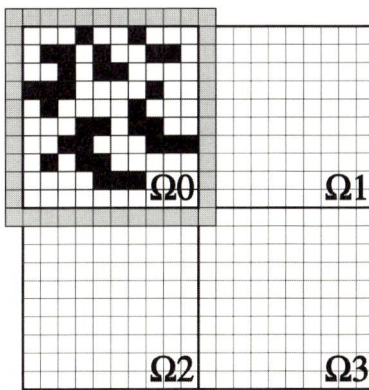

Fig. 1. Schematic of spatial decomposition in 2 dimensions with several (here is 4) domains. White squares are open lattice sites that have the DFs of flow particles. Black squares represent obstacles, where flow does not exist. Gray squares are buffer sites, where some of the DFs move in after streaming function.

Each domain is augmented with a surrounding buffer layer of one lattice spacing, which is used for inter-domain DF migrations. A boundary condition is imposed on DFs propagating toward the closed nodes: reflecting DFs propagation into the closed nodes toward the opposite direction.

2.2.1 Parallel LBM Algorithm on PlayStation3

We use a Linux cluster consisting of PlayStation3 consoles. Within each PlayStation3 console, a main program runs on the Power Processing Element (PPE) and spawns POSIX threads that run on multiple Synergistic Processing Elements (SPEs). Direct Memory Access (DMA) commands are used for data transfer between the main memory of the PPE and the local storage of the SPEs, since there is no access from SPEs to main memory. (Either SPE or PPE can issue DMA commands, which include a get command for retrieving memory contents, and a put command for writing data into memory.) For inter-console message passing, we use the Message Passing Interface (MPI). The hybrid thread + message passing programming thus combines: (1) Inter-console parallelization with spatial decomposition into domains based on message passing; and (2) intra-console parallelization through multi-thread processing of interleaved rows of the lattice within each domain.

Collision

It is a challenging task to design a parallel algorithm due to Cell hardware restrictions. Six SPE programs can be simultaneously performed using POSIX threads on PlayStation3 (only 6 SPEs out of 8 are available for user programming). As mentioned in previous researches, the partitioning of work among the SPEs for load balancing is crucial to high performance [8]. For optimal load balancing, we parallelize by first dividing the simulation problem into a large number (N_x) of chunks, where chunk ID j ($j \in [0, N_x-1]$) processes lattice sites $\bar{x} = ((j+1)\Delta x, k\Delta y, l\Delta z)$ ($k \in [1, N_y]$, $l \in [1, N_z]$). Here, N_x, N_y and N_z denote the numbers of lattice sites *per domain* in the x, y and z directions, respectively. We then interleavingly assign chunks to threads, i.e., chunk ID j is assigned to SPE with thread ID j mod N_{thread}, $j \in [0, N_{thread}-1]$. In our case, the number of threads N_{thread} is 6, so chunk 0 and chunk 6 are assigned to SPE 0, while chunk 1 and chunk 7 are assigned to SPE 1. In Fig. 2(a), the area enclosed by the dotted lines shows the computational task assigned to the first thread with thread ID 0.

One problem in the interleaved thread parallelization is that multiple threads may update a common lattice site. To avoid such a critical section, we have designed a double-layered DF consisting of two floating-point arrays *DF0* and *DF1*, shown in Fig. 2(b). (In Eqs. (3) and (4), $f_i(\bar{x},t)$ and $f_i(\bar{x},t^+)$ denote *DF0* and *DF1*, respectively.) In each LBM loop, the collision subroutine transfers DFs from the array *DF0* to local store on SPE, updates the DFs, and subsequently copies it back to the array *DF1*. The pseudo-code of collision subroutine is given in Table 1, where *fetchAddrData* is the address for a DMA get operation from *DF0* to local store of SPE, *fetchAddrFlag* is the address for DMA get from main memory to local storage of SPE, and *putAddrData* is the address for DMA put from *DF1* to main memory. In the table, *geom(i,j)* denotes the flags (open or closed) of the j-th cell in chunk i. We have not used single instruction multiple data (SIMD) programming in the current implementation.

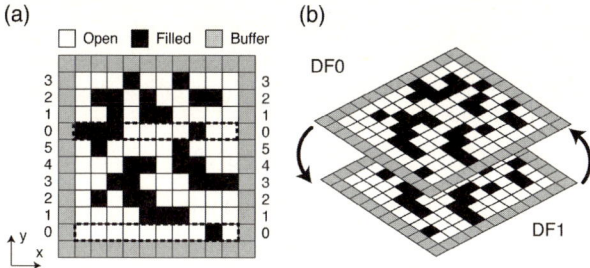

Fig. 2. (a) Schematic of a 2-dimensional system setup for each domain in spatial decomposition. White squares are open lattice sites that have the DF's of flow particles. Black squares represent obstacles in the system, where flow does not exist. Gray squares are buffer sites, where some of the DFs move in after streaming. The simulation system is divided into N_y computational chunks, each of which consists of $N_y N_z$ lattice sites, and the chunks are interleavingly assigned to SPEs. The numerals show thread ID responsible for each chunk. (b) Schematic of a double-layered DF calculation comprising of two floating point arrays *DF0* and *DF1*. The collision function reads DF's from the array *DF0* to do updates, and then store the updated information in the array *DF1*. Subsequently, the streaming function propagates DF's from the array *DF1* to the array *DF0*.

Table 1. Collision calculation algorithm within SPE

Input:
N_x, N_y, N_z
{number of LBM lattice sites in the *x*, *y* and *z* directions}
N_{thread} {number of threads}
tID {thread ID}
array *DF0* in PPE of size *N*
{array of density functions, where $N = N_x N_y N_z$}
array *geom* {array of geometry flags}

Output:
array *DF1* in PPE of size *N* {array of density functions}

Steps:
1 *chunkID* ← *tID*
2 *chunksize* ← N/N_x
3 **while** *chunkID* < N/N_x **do**
4   *fetchAddrData*
    ← address of *DF0* + *chunkID*×*chunksize*
5   *fetchAddrFlag*
    ← address of *geom* + *chunkID*×*chunksize*
6   *putAddrData*
    ← address of *DF1* + *chunkID*×*chunksize*
7   initiate DMA transfers to get data
8   fetch data from *DF0* and *geom*
9   wait for the data

Table 1. (*continued*)

10	**for** $j \leftarrow 0$ to *chunksize*-1
11	$\rho(\vec{x},t) \leftarrow \sum_i f_i(\vec{x},t)$ {see Eq. (1)}
12	$\vec{u}(\vec{x},t) \leftarrow \rho^{-1}(\vec{x},t)\sum_i \vec{e}_i f_i(\vec{x},t)$ {see Eq. (2)}
13	$f_i(\vec{x},t^+) \leftarrow f_i(\vec{x},t) - [f_i(\vec{x},t) - f_i^{eq}(\rho(\vec{x}),\vec{u}(\vec{x}))]/\tau$ {see Eq. (3)}
14	**if** *geom*(*chunkID*, *j*) is open **then** update density functions
15	initiate DMA put for the computed results
16	*chunckID* $\leftarrow$ *chunkID* + N_{thread}
17	synchronize using inter-SPE communication

Streaming

The streaming function propagates the DF according to their flow directions, see Eq. (4). Here the DFs are copied from main memory to main memory, between array *DF1* and array *DF0* in Fig. 2(b). Before propagating DFs, a boundary condition such as reflection rule must be considered according to the simulation geometry. In the case of a static geometry, where the relation between source and destination lattice sites does not change, we avoid repeated computing of boundary condition by defining another array to keep the indices of destination lattice sites for each DF, which significantly speeds up the streaming function. Furthermore, we find that the hardware-supported threads on PPE improve the performance of the complicated memory copy. We use two POSIX threads, each of which is responsible for half of the data transfer. This improves the performance of the streaming computation by 20-30%.

Communication

After the streaming function, some of the DF's move out of their domains. In the communication function, DFs in the buffer lattice sites migrate to proper destination domains. Figure 1 shows a schematic of the domain decomposition consisting of four sub-domains $\Omega 0$-$\Omega 3$. We employ a 6-way dead-lock free communication scheme, in which data transfer is completed in 6 steps. The inter-domain communication is implemented with MPI.

2.2.2 Parallel LBM Algorithm on CUDA

Modern GPUs contain hundreds of arithmetic units to provide tremendous acceleration for numerically intensive scientific applications. The high-level GPU programming language, CUDA, has made this computational power more accessible to computational scientists. We have implemented the pLBM algorithm on GPUs using CUDA.

Specifically, we test NVIDIA's GeForce 8800 GTS that contains 96 stream processors. A block of threads (of which the number of threads per block is user-defined) is processed by each stream processor, and while each block allows its threads to access fast shared memory and communicate with each other, blocks do not have any method of synchronizing with other blocks. Fortunately, the LBM allows each lattice site to be solved independently of all the others during the collision phase, and it only requires knowledge of other subdomains during the streaming phase.

We test the performance of CUDA by implementing both the streaming and collision calculations independent of the CPU, that is, having each time step run entirely on the GPU.

The GPU-based pLBM algorithm consists of two parts as shown in Table 2. First, data is initialized and transferred to the GPU. Then, the collision and streaming computation kernels are executed until the simulation ends. The kernels are designed so that each thread solves one lattice site at a time. Subdomain size (i.e., the number of blocks used) is taken to be the size of the system divided by the block size. Thread management and synchronization, often a potential for major problems in large simulations, is facilitated through CUDA's _syncthreads() function. Because of CUDA's C-like syntax and behavior as well as allowing the GPU to perform the collision and streaming functions entirely, the resulting code strongly resembles that of uniprocessor-based code. Moreover, since the data and programs are small, we put all of them to the memory of GPU.

Table 2. GPU-based pLBM algorithm

Steps:
1 initialize data to send to GPU
2 define block and thread parameters initialized
3 **for** each time step
4   execute collision kernel
5   execute streaming kernel

3 Experiments

3.1 Experimental Test Bed

PlayStation3 Cluster
The Sony Toshiba IBM (STI) Cell processor is the heart of the Sony PlayStation3 (PS3) video game console, whose design is intended to meet the demanding computational requirements of video games. Cell adopts a heterogeneous approach to multi-core, with one conventional processor core (Power Processing Element, PPE) to handle OS and control functions, combined with up to eight simpler SIMD cores (Synergistic Processing Elements, SPEs) for the computationally intensive work [11, 12]. The SPEs differ considerably from conventional core architectures due to their use of a disjoint software-controlled local memory instead of the conventional hardware-managed cache hierarchy employed by the PPE. Rather than using prefetch to hide latency, the SPEs have efficient software-controlled DMA engines that asynchronously fetch data from DRAM into the 256KB local store. This approach allows more efficient use of available memory bandwidth than is possible with standard prefetch schemes on conventional cache hierarchies, but also makes the programming model more complex. In particular, the hardware provides enough concurrency to satisfy Little's law [2] and conflict misses, while potentially eliminating write fills, however capacity misses must be handled in software.

We connect nine PlayStation3 consoles via a Gigabit Ethernet switch, where each PlayStation3 contains: (1) a 3.2 GHz 64-bit RISC PowerPC processor (PPE) with 32KB L1 and 512KB L2 caches and 256MB main memory; and (2) eight 3.2GHz 32-bit SPEs with 256KB of local store (LS) and Memory Flow Controller (MFC). The PPE, SPEs, and main memory are interconnected by a fast internal bus called the Elemental Interface Bus (EIB), with the peak bandwidth of 2,048GB/s, while the memory and I/O interface controller (MIC) supports a peak bandwidth of 25GB/s inbound and 35GB/s outbound. Each PlayStation3 has a Gigabit Ethernet port.

We have installed a Fedora Core 6 Linux OS distribution with libraries and infrastructure to support the IBM Cell Software Development Kit (SDK) version 2.1. The SDK offers an IBM compiler and the GNU Compiler Collection for the Cell processor. Message Passing Interface (MPI) is installed as in a standard Linux cluster. We use the Cell SDK for instruction-level profiling and performance analysis of the code. The code is compiled using GNU C compiler (gcc) with optimization option '-O3' and MPI version 1.2.6.

NVIDIA GPU platform

The GeForce 8800 GTS contains 96 stream processors running at 1.35 GHz. While the memory clock is 800MHz and the memory size is 640MB, the memory interface is 320bit and the memory bandwidth is 64GB/sec.

The system used to run the simulation consists of an AMD Sempron 3500+ CPU with 1 GB of RAM and an NVIDIA GeForce 8800 GTS. The operating system used is Fedora Core 7, kernel version 2.6.23.1-21.fc7. NVIDIA's CUDA is used to develop the application, and nvcc version 1.0 is used to compile the software.

3.2 Performance Test Results

3.2.1 Performance of PlayStation3 Cluster

We first test the intra-processor scalability of pLBM based on multithreading on a single Playstation3 console. Figure 3(a) shows the running time for the collision function as a function of the number of SPEs, S, from 1 to 6 for a simulation system with 64^3 lattice sites. Figure 3(b) shows the corresponding strong-scaling speed-up, i.e., the running time on a single SPE divided by that on S SPEs. The algorithm scales nearly linearly with the number of SPEs. On 6 SPEs, the speed-up is 5.29, and the parallel efficiency (defined as the speed-up divided by S) is 0.882.

Then we implemented our pLBM both on the PlayStation3 cluster as well as on a Xeon cluster to assess the comparative performance of the PlayStation3 cluster and a conventional Linux cluster. The latter is composed of 256 computation nodes, with each node having two processors of 2.8GHz and 512KB L1 cache, where the nodes are connected via 4 Gbit/s Myrinet. (We make comparison using one node.) In Fig. 4(a), the running time of PlayStation3 is compared with that of Xeon for various system sizes from 8^3 to 64^3 lattice points. Figure 4(b) shows the speed-up of PlayStation3 over Xeon.

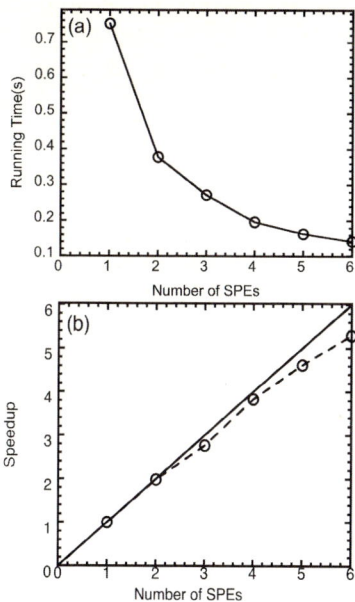

Fig. 3. (a) Running time for the pLBM flow simulation involving 64^3 lattice sites on a single PlayStation3 console as a function of the number of SPEs. (b) Strong-scaling speed-up of the pLBM algorithm (circles) on a single PlayStation3 console as a function of the number of SPEs. The solid line shows the ideal speed-up.

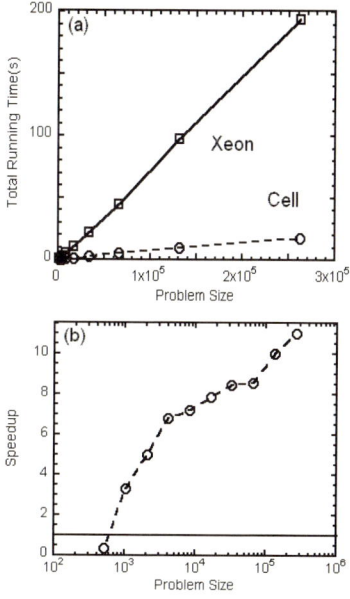

Fig. 4. (a) Total running time of the pLBM flow simulation on Xeon and Cell platforms with different problem sizes. (b) Speed-up of the pLBM flow simulation of Cell over Xeon with different problem sizes.

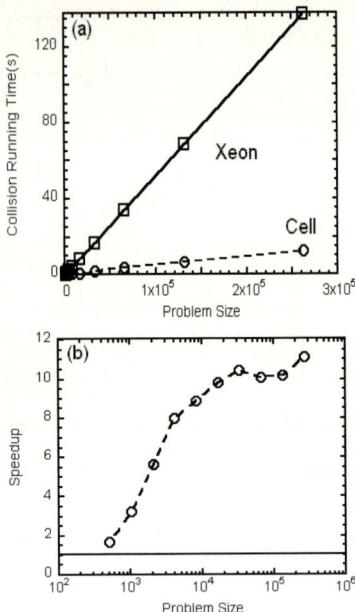

Fig. 5. (a) The running time of the collision function for pLBM flow simulation on Xeon and Cell platforms with different problem sizes. (b) Speed-up of the collision function for pLBM flow simulation of Cell over Xeon with different problem sizes.

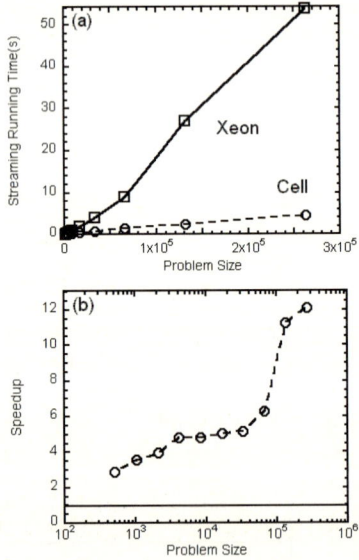

Fig. 6. (a) The running time of the streaming function for pLBM flow simulation on Xeon and Cell platforms with different problem sizes. (b) Speed-up of the streaming function for pLBM flow simulation of Cell over Xeon with different problem sizes.

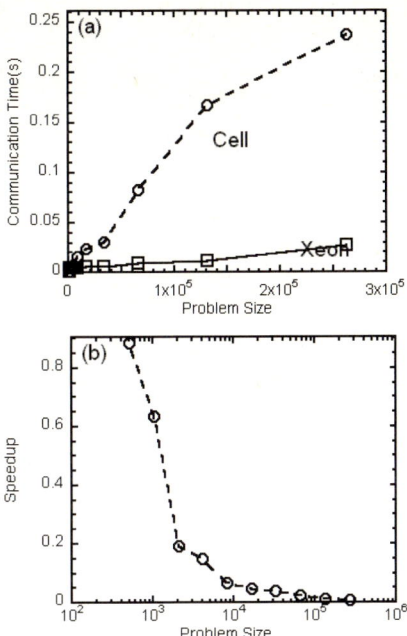

Fig. 7. (a) The running time of the communication part for pLBM flow simulation on Xeon and Cell platforms with different problem sizes. (b) Speed-up of the communication part for pLBM flow simulation of Cell over Xeon with different problem sizes.

To study the performance of individual functions of the pLBM, Figs. 5(a), 6(a) and 7(a) show the running time of the collision function, the streaming function and the communication part on the PlayStation3 cluster and the Xeon cluster for various problem sizes. In addition, Figs. 5(b), 6(b) and 7(b) show the corresponding speed-ups of the PlayStation3 cluster over the Xeon cluster.

3.2.2 Performance of GPU

We have compared the comparative performance of the GPU (NVIDIA 8800 GTS) using CUDA and a conventional CPU (Sempron 3500+) for pLBM. Here, the running time of each function as well as the speed-up of GPU over CPU are measured for various problem sizes from 8^3 to 64^3 lattice points.

Figures 8(a), 9(a) and 10(a) show the running time of the entire program, the collision function, and the streaming function, respectively, on GPU and CPU. In addition, Figs. 8(b), 9(b) and 10(b) show the corresponding speedup of GPU over CPU for the entire program, the collision function, and the streaming function, respectively. Figure 11 shows the running time of the preparation part of pLBM on the two platforms.

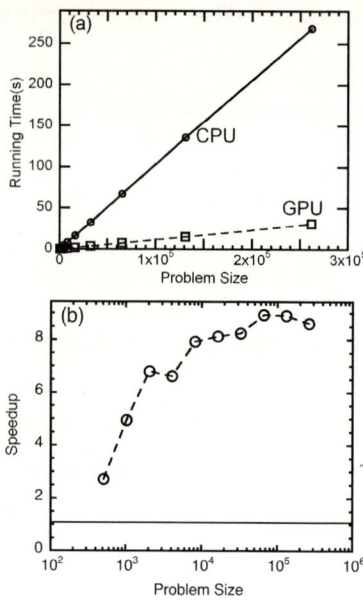

Fig. 8. (a) Total running time of pLBM flow simulation on CPU and GPU with different problem sizes. (b) Speed-up of the total pLBM flow simulation of GPU over CPU with different problem sizes.

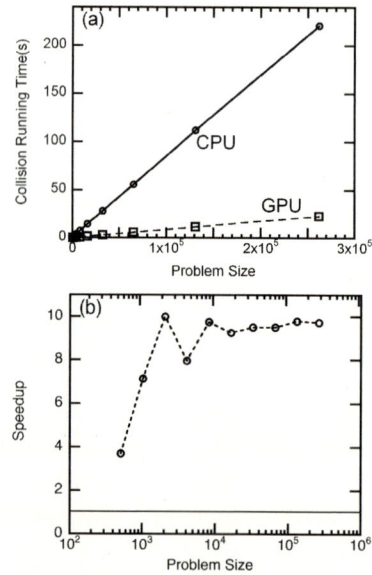

Fig. 9. (a) The running time of the collision function for pLBM flow simulation on CPU and GPU with different problem sizes. (b) Speed-up of the collision function for pLBM flow simulation of GPU over CPU with different problem sizes.

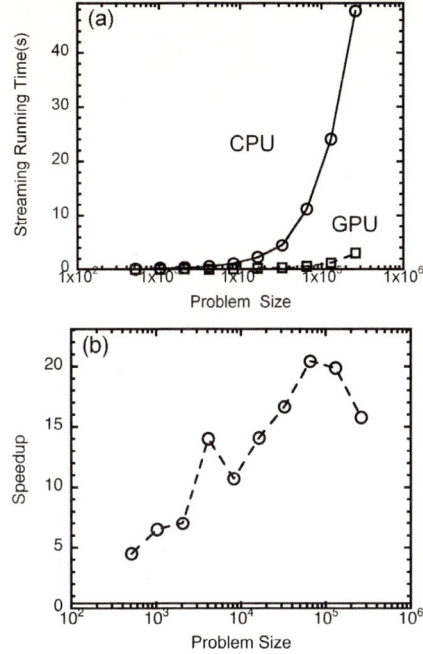

Fig. 10. (a) The running time of the streaming function for pLBM flow simulation on CPU and GPU with different problem sizes. (b) Speed-up of the Streaming function in pLBM flow simulation of GPU over CPU with different problem sizes.

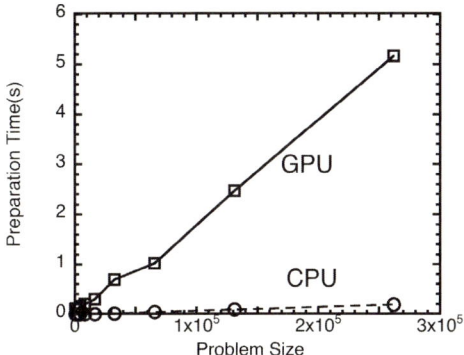

Fig. 11. Preparation time for pLBM flow simulation on CPU and GPU with different problem sizes

4 Conclusions

From the performance test results discussed above, we can draw several conclusions. For the compute-intensive collision part, PlayStation3 outperforms the traditional

Xeon cluster when the problem size is larger than 1024, and the larger the problem size, the better the performance of PlayStation3 over that of Xeon cluster. For the steaming part, which mainly deals with memory access, the performance of PlayStation3 is also better than Xeon when the problem size is larger than 2048, and the speed-up also increases with the problem size. However, for the communication part, the PlayStation3 cluster is not as good as Xeon cluster due to the limited bandwidth of the low-price Ethernet switch.

In general, the PlayStation3 cluster outperforms the Xeon cluster when the problem size is large enough in compute and memory-access intensive applications, and the performance enhancement is an increasing function of the problem size. This indicates that the DMA efficiency increases with the data size. For the largest problem size, the performance enhancement of PlayStation3 over Xeon for pLBM is 11.02.

Regarding GPU using CUDA, the performance of GPU is much better than that of CPU in all problem sizes we have tested, despite the large preparation time of GPU. The best speed-up we obtain is 8.76.

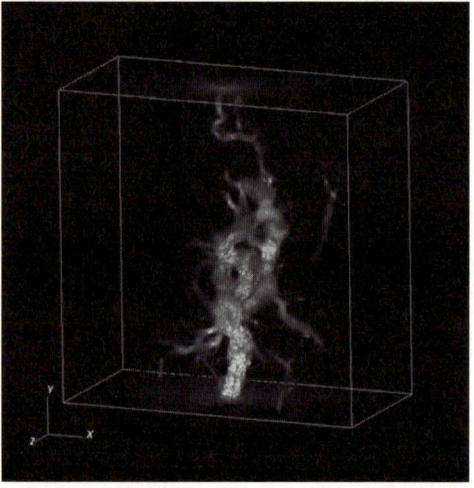

Fig. 12. Visualization of pLBM simulation of fluid flow in fractured silica on the PlayStation3 cluster, where the magnitude of the fluid velocity is color-coded

The pLBM code has been applied to simulate fluid flow in fractured glass. Figure 12 visualizes our pLBM simulation of fluid flow through fractured silica glass, where the fractured surface is prepared through voxelation of atomistic simulation data [13]. Such flow simulation in a complex geometry is important in many areas, e.g., for maximizing oil recovery in petroleum industry.

Acknowledgements

This work was partially supported by Chevron-CiSoft, ARO-MURI, DOE-SciDAC/BES, DTRA, and NSF-ITR/PetaApps/CSR. Numerical tests were performed using a Playstation3 cluster at the Collaboratory for Advanced Computing and Simulations and a CPU-GPU system at the Information Sciences Institute at the University of Southern California. We thank Prof. Robert Lucas and Mr. John Tran for providing access to their CPU-GPU system.

References

[1] Asanovic, K., Bodik, R., Catanzaro, B.C., Gebis, J.J., Husbands, P., Keutzer, K., Patterson, D.A., Pishker, W.L., Shalf, J., Williams, S.W., Yelick, K.A.: The landscape of parallel computing research: a view from Berkeley. University of California, Berkeley (2006)
[2] Shalf, J.: The new landscape of parallel computer architecture. J Phys: Conf Series 78, 012066 (2007)
[3] Buttari, A., Luszczek, P., Kurzak, J., Dongarra, J., Bosilca, G.: SCOP3: A Rough Guide to Scientific Computing On the PlayStation 3. University of Tennessee, Knoxville (2007)
[4] Johns, C.R., Brokenshire, D.A.: Introduction to the cell broadband engine architecture. IBM Journal of Research and Development 51, 503 (2007)
[5] Dongarra, J., Gannon, D., Fox, G., Kennedy, K.: The impact of multicore on computational science software. CTWatch Quarterly 3, 11 (2007)
[6] Nakano, A., Kalia, R.K., Nomura, K., Sharma, A., Vashishta, P., Shimojo, F., van Duin, A.C.T., Goddard, W.A., Biswas, R., Srivastava, D., Yang, L.H.: De novo ultrascale atomistic simulations on high-end parallel supercomputers. International Journal of High Performance Computing Applications 22, 113 (2008)
[7] Williams, S., Carter, J., Oliker, L., Shalf, J., Yelick, K.: Lattice Boltzmann simulation optimization on leading multicore platforms. International Parallel & Distributed Processing Symposium (IPDPS) (to appear, 2008)
[8] Stuermer, M.: Fluid simulation using the Lattice Boltzmann Method on the Cell Processor, Vortrag: Einladung, Zentralinstitut fur Angewandte Mathematik des Forschungszentrum Juelich (11.04.2007)
[9] Stuermer, M.: Optimizing fluid simulation and other scientific applications on the Cell, Vortrag: Einladung vom SFB 716 der Universität Stuttgart, SFB 716, Stuttgart (14.06.2007)
[10] Li, W., Wei, X., Kaufman, A.: Implementing Lattice Boltzmann computation on graphics hardware. The Visual Computer (to appear)
[11] Ladd, A.J.C., Verberg, R.: Lattice-Boltzmann simulations of particle-fluid suspensions. Journal of Statistical Physics 104, 1191 (2001)
[12] Bader, D.A., Agarwal, V.: FFTC: fastest Fourier transform for the IBM Cell Broadband Engine. In: Proceedings of the International Conference on High Performance Computing (HiPC). IEEE, Los Alamitos (2007)
[13] Chen, Y.C., Lu, Z., Nomura, K., Wang, W., Kalia, R.K., Nakano, A., Vashishta, P.: Interaction of voids and nanoductility in silica glass. Physical Review Letters 99, 155506 (2007)

Topic 10: Parallel Numerical Algorithms

H.-J. Bungartz, J.D. Bruguera, P. Arbenz, and B.A. Hendrickson

Since the early days of supercomputing, numerical routines have caused the highest demand for computing power anywhere, making their efficient parallelisation one of the core methodical tasks in high-performance computing. And still, many of today's fastest computers in the world are mostly used for the solution of huge systems of equations as they arise in the simulation of complex large-scale problems in science and engineering. But the scope of numerical algorithms goes far beyond numerical simulation, as their increasing importance in imaging or for search engine algorithmics shows.

Despite this long tradition, parallel numerical algorithms did not lose anything of their relevance. The efficient implementation of existing schemes on state-of-the-art parallel systems (such as clusters or hybrid systems), the scalability challenges resulting from massively parallel systems, the impact of multicore architectures, the design of easy-to-use portable software components, the recent endeavours to tackle optimisation, control, and interactive steering scenarios, too – all this clearly shows that progress in computational science and engineering strongly depends on progress with parallel numerical algorithms. This crucial importance of parallel numerical algorithms certainly justifies to again having devoted a special workshop to this topic at Euro-Par, in addition to the discussion of special aspects of Load Balancing in Topic 3 or Grid and Cluster Computing in Topic 6.

Overall, twelve papers were submitted to our Topic, with authors from Sweden, Switzerland, Germany, Spain, the Netherlands, Greece, UK, Russia, France, Poland, and the United States. Out of these twelve submissions, six were accepted for the conference as regular papers.

Both devising new parallel algorithms for numerical tasks and adapting existing ones to state-of-the-art parallel systems such as multi- or manycore systems or GPU, e.g., are vigorously flourishing and active fields of research. Hence, it is no surprise that the six research papers presented in this section cover a wide range of topics arising in the various subdomains of parallel numerical algorithms. At Euro-Par 2008, the corresponding presentations were arranged in two sessions, one on *Numerical Core Tasks* and one on *Applications*. This substructuring also reflects in the following part of the conference proceedings.

In the *Numerical Core Tasks* section, Robert Granat, Bo Kågström, Isak Jonsson, and Per Andersson address parallel algorithms for triangular periodic Sylvester-type matrix equations, as part of the recently developed HPC library SCASY. Mathieu Luisier, Andreas Schenk, Wolfgang Fichtner, Timothy Boykin, and Gerhard Klimeck deal with kind of an evergreen topic: parallel solvers for sparse linear systems. In their study, they discuss solution strategies for block tridiagonal systems arising from atomistic device simulation based on the nearest-neighbour tight-binding method. Finally, the paper of Michael Bader presents a cache-efficient approach to parallel matrix multiplication, based on a block-wise element layout and an execution order derived from a Peano-type space-filling curve.

The second section with a stronger focus on *Applications* begins with the contribution of Maraike Schellmann, Jürgen Vörding, and Sergei Gorlatch on systematic parallelisation of medical image reconstruction on graphics hardware, combining a non-simulation application of increasing relevance with the more and more attractive GPU as hardware platform. Olivier Hoenen and Eric Violard address aspects of dynamic load balancing for a block-based parallel adaptive 4D Vlasov solver using an adptive meshing of the phase space. Finally, Maciej Patan's paper deals with distributed parameter systems and presents a parallel sensor scheduling approach for fault detection therein.

Altogether, the contributions to Topic 10 at the 2008 Euro-Par in Las Palmas de Gran Canaria show once more the great variety of interesting, challenging, and important issues in the field of parallel numerical algorithms. Thus, we are already looking forward to the new results submitted to and presented at next year's Euro-Par conference.

Parallel Algorithms for Triangular Periodic Sylvester-Type Matrix Equations

Per Andersson, Robert Granat, Isak Jonsson, and Bo Kågström

Department of Computing Science and HPC2N, Umeå University,
SE-901 87 Umeå, Sweden
{c02apr,granat,isak,bokg}@cs.umu.se

Abstract. We present parallel algorithms for triangular periodic Sylvester-type matrix equations, conceptually being the third step of a periodic Bartels–Stewart-like solution method for general periodic Sylvester-type matrix equations based on variants of the periodic Schur decomposition. The presented algorithms are designed and implemented in the framework of the recently developed HPC library SCASY and are based on explicit blocking, 2-dimensional block cyclic data distribution and a wavefront-like traversal of the right hand side matrices. High performance is obtained by rich usage of level 3 BLAS operations. It is also demonstrated how several important key concepts of SCASY regarding communications and the treatment of quasi-triangular coefficient matrices are generalized to the periodic case. Some experimental results from a distributed memory Linux cluster demonstrate are also presented.

Keywords: Periodic Sylvester-type matrix equations, Bartels–Stewart's method, explicit blocking, level-3 BLAS, ScaLAPACK, condition estimation, RECSY, SCASY.

1 Introduction

Consider the periodic continuous-time Sylvester (PSYCT) matrix equation

$$A_k X_k - X_{k+1} B_k = C_k, \ k = 0, 1, \ldots, P-1, \quad (1)$$

where $A_k \in \mathbb{R}^{m \times m}$, $B_k \in \mathbb{R}^{n \times n}$ and $C_k, X_k \in \mathbb{R}^{m \times n}$ are P-cyclic general matrices with real entries. A P-cyclic matrix is characterized by that it repeats itself in a sequence of matrices every Pth time, e.g., $A_P = A_0$, $A_{P+1} = A_1$, etc. Matrix equations of the form (1) have applications in, e.g., computation and condition estimation of *periodic invariant subspaces* of square matrix products of the form

$$\mathcal{A}_{P-1} \cdots \mathcal{A}_1 \mathcal{A}_0 \in \mathbb{R}^{l \times l}, \quad (2)$$

and in periodic systems design and analysis (see, e.g., [28] and the references therein). Matrix products of the form (2) are conceptually studied via the *periodic real Schur form* (PRSF): there exists an orthogonal P-cyclic matrix sequence $\mathcal{Z}_k \in \mathbb{R}^{l \times l}$ such that the sequence

$$\mathcal{Z}_{k+1}^T \mathcal{A}_k \mathcal{Z}_k = \mathcal{T}_k, \ k = 0, 1, \ldots, P-1, \quad (3)$$

consists of $P-1$ upper triangular matrices and one upper quasi-triangular matrix. The products of conforming 1×1 and 2×2 diagonal blocks of the matrix sequence $\mathcal{T}_k$ contain the real and complex conjugate pairs of eigenvalues of the matrix product (2). Similar to the standard case ($P=1$, e.g., see [6]), the PRSF is computed by means of a reduction to periodic Hessenberg form followed by applying a periodic QR algorithm to the resulting sequence [4,15]. The PRSF is an important tool in several applications, including solving periodic Sylvester-type and Riccati matrix equations, see, e.g., [15,27,28].

Periodic matrix equations of the forms (1) is a special case of the periodic Sylvester-like (PSLE) equation

$$\begin{cases} A_k X_k - X_{k+1} B_k = C_k, & \text{for} \quad s_k = 1, \\ A_k X_{k+1} - X_k B_k = C_k, & \text{for} \quad s_k = -1, \end{cases} \quad (4)$$

arising in computing periodic eigenspaces of matrix products of the form

$$\mathcal{A}_{P-1}^{s_{P-1}} \cdots \mathcal{A}_1^{s_1} \mathcal{A}_0^{s_0}, \quad (5)$$

where $s_k \in \{0,1\}$, i.e., matrix products with arbitrary order of the ± 1 exponents, see [13] for details. Another special case of (4) is the periodic continuous-time *generalized coupled* Sylvester (PGCSY) equation

$$\begin{cases} A_k X_k - Y_k B_k = C_k, \\ D_k X_{k+1} - Y_k E_k = F_k, \end{cases} \quad (6)$$

which is considered when computing periodic deflating subspaces of matrix products of the form

$$\mathcal{E}_{P-1}^{-1} \mathcal{A}_{P-1} \cdots \mathcal{E}_1^{-1} \mathcal{A}_1 \mathcal{E}_0^{-1} \mathcal{A}_0, \quad (7)$$

which are conducted via variants of the *generalized* periodic Schur decomposition [4,15]. We refer to [12] for details.

Equation (1) has a unique solution if the matrix products $A_{P-1} \cdots A_1 A_0$ and $B_{P-1} \cdots B_1 B_0$ have no eigenvalues in common. We solve it via periodic variants of Bartels–Stewart's method [2]:

1. Transform the matrix sequences A_k and B_k to PRSFs:

$$T_A^{(k)} = Q_{k+1}^T A_k Q_k, \quad (8)$$
$$T_B^{(k)} = U_{k+1}^T B_k U_k, \quad (9)$$

where Q_k and U_k are P-cyclic orthogonal matrices and $T_A^{(k)}$ and $T_B^{(k)}$ are the periodic real Schur forms, $k = 0, 1, \ldots, P-1$, with quasi-triangular factors $T_A^{(r)}$ and $T_B^{(s)}$, $0 \leq r, s \leq P-1$.

2. Update the matrix sequence C_k with respect to the two periodic Schur decompositions:

$$\tilde{C}_k = Q_{k+1}^T C_k U_k, \quad k = 0, 1, \ldots, P-1. \quad (10)$$

3. Solve the reduced triangular periodic matrix equation:

$$T_A^{(k)} \tilde{X}_k - \tilde{X}_{k+1} T_B^{(k)} = \tilde{C}_k, \ k = 0, 1, \ldots, P-1. \tag{11}$$

4. Transform the sequence $\tilde{X}_k$ back to the original coordinate system:

$$X_k = Q_{k+1} \tilde{X}_k U_k^T, \ k = 0, 1, \ldots, P-1. \tag{12}$$

In step 1, reliable and efficient software for computing the periodic Schur decomposition should be used. Several attempts of implementing such software have been conducted (see, e.g., [15,21,23] and the PEP software library [13]) and the state-of-the-art implementation is implemented in the SLICOT routines MBVH03 (periodic Hessenberg reduction) and MBWS03 (periodic QR iterations). To the best of our knowledge, no parallel implementation exists today.

Steps 2 and 4 above are performed as two series of P *two-sided* matrix-matrix multiplication updates by P pairs of GEMM-operations [22].

In the rest of the paper, we focus on step 3. The reduced triangular problem (11) can be solved via a linear system representation of the corresponding periodic Sylvester operator (see, e.g., [8]):

$$Z_{\text{PSYCT}} \tilde{x} = \tilde{c}, \tag{13}$$

where

$$Z_{\text{PSYCT}} = \begin{bmatrix} -T_B^{(P-1)^T} \otimes I_m & & & I_n \otimes T_A^{(P-1)} \\ I_n \otimes T_A^{(0)} & -T_B^{(0)^T} \otimes I_m & & \\ & \ddots & \ddots & \\ & & I_n \otimes T_A^{(P-2)} & -T_B^{(P-2)^T} \otimes I_m \end{bmatrix} \tag{14}$$

and

$$\tilde{x} = \begin{bmatrix} \text{vec}(\tilde{X}_0) \\ \text{vec}(\tilde{X}_1) \\ \ldots \\ \text{vec}(\tilde{X}_{P-1}) \end{bmatrix}, \quad \tilde{c} = \begin{bmatrix} \text{vec}(\tilde{C}^{(P-1)}) \\ \text{vec}(\tilde{C}^{(0)}) \\ \ldots \\ \text{vec}(\tilde{C}^{(P-2)}) \end{bmatrix}. \tag{15}$$

Only the nonzero blocks of Z_{PSYCT} are displayed explicitly in (14) and by exploiting this structure the system (13) can be solved at the cost of $O(P(m^2 n + mn^2))$ flops by using Gaussian elimination with partial pivoting [8] or structured variants of QR factorization [12,13]; the latter method avoids excessive pivot growth for ill-conditioned problems [5]. By storing only the block main diagonal, the block sub-diagonal and the rightmost block column vector, the storage requirement for Z_{PSYCT} can be kept at $3Pm^2n^2$. Linear systems with this kind of sparsity structure, *Bordered Almost Block Diagonal* (BABD) systems have been studied extensively [5].

The conditioning of (1) is essentially guided by the Sep-function

$$\mathrm{Sep[PSYCT]} = \inf_{\|x\|_2=1} \|Z_{\mathrm{PSYCT}}x\|_2 = \|Z_{\mathrm{PSYCT}}^{-1}\|_2^{-1} = \sigma_{\min}(Z_{\mathrm{PSYCT}}) \quad (16)$$

$$= \inf_{(\sum_{k=0}^{K-1}\|X_k\|_F^2)^{1/2}=1} \left(\sum_{k=0}^{K-1} \|A_k X_k - X_{k+1}B_k\|_F^2\right)^{1/2}.$$

The quantity sep[PSYCT] can be estimated at the cost of solving a few PSYCTs by exploiting the estimation technique for the 1-norm of the inverse of a matrix [14,16,19,20] which was conducted in SCASY for the non-periodic case [10,11].

The Kronecker product representation (13) is only effective to use when m and n are very small, e.g., in kernel solvers for (sub)matrices of dimensions 1–2. Typically, for large-scale triangular matrix equations of the form (11), *recursive matrix blocking* and/or *iterative matrix blocking* of several layers is applied to reformulate the majority of the computational work into level 3 operations.

In [10], parallel algorithms for *non-periodic* Sylvester-type matrix equations were presented, introducing the software library SCASY [11,26]. In this paper, we show how the key concepts of SCASY can be generalized to cover even periodic Sylvester-type matrix equations of the forms (1) and (11). The rest of the paper is organized as follows. In Section 2, we present parallel wavefront algorithms for solving the triangular reduced problem (11). In Section 3, we discuss some implementation issues and before giving a summary and listing some future work in Section 5, we present some real experimental results in Section 4.

2 Parallel Algorithms for Periodic Triangular Matrix Equations

We assume that the cyclic matrix sequences A_k and B_k, $k = 0, 1, \ldots, P-1$, are already in periodic Schur form with quasi-triangular factors A_r and B_s. If A_k and B_k are partitioned by square $m_b \times m_b$ and $n_b \times n_b$ blocks, respectively, we can rewrite (1) in block partitioned form

$$A_{ii}^{(k)} X_{ij}^{(k)} - X_{ij}^{(k+1)} B_{jj}^{(k)} = C_{ij}^{(k)} - \left(\sum_{k=i+1}^{D_A} A_{ik}^{(k)} X_{kj}^{(k)} - \sum_{k=1}^{j-1} X_{ik}^{(k+1)} B_{kj}^{(k)} \right), \quad (17)$$

where $D_A = \lceil m/m_b \rceil$. Summation (17) can be implemented as a serial blocked algorithm using a couple of nested loops, see, e.g., [19,10] and the algorithms in [13] for matrix equations of the form (4). For high performance and portability, level 3 BLAS (mostly GEMM operations) should be utilized for the periodic right hand side updates.

Starting at the South-West corner of X_k, Equation (17) reveals that all subsolutions $X_{ij}^{(k)}$ located on the same block (sub- or super)diagonal, are independent and can be computed in parallel. Moreover, all subsequent updates are internally independent and can be performed in parallel.

Our parallel algorithms adapt to the ScaLAPACK (see, e.g., [3]) conventions of a distributed memory (DM) environment, as follows:

- The parallel processes are organized into a rectangular $P_r \times P_c$ mesh labeled from $(0,0)$ to $(P_r - 1, P_c - 1)$ according to their specific position indices in the mesh.
- The matrices are distributed over the mesh using 2-dimensional (2D) block cyclic mapping with the block sizes m_b and n_b in the row and column dimensions, respectively.

Here we assume that the sequences A_k, B_k and C_k are internally aligned. Then, along the lines of the algorithms in SCASY, we formulate a parallel wavefront algorithm for PSYCT in Algorithm 1.

Algorithm 1. Parallel algorithm for PSYCT.

Input: Matrix sequences A_k, B_k and C_k. A_k and B_k in PRSF. Block sizes m_b and n_b. Process grid configuration P_r, P_c.
Output: Solution matrix sequence X_k (which overwrites C_k).

   for $k = 1, \#$ block diagonals in C_k **do**
      % Solve subsystems on current P block diagonals of $C_{0:P-1}$ in parallel
      if ($mynode$ holds $C_{ij}^{(0:P-1)}$) **then**
         if ($mynode$ does not hold $A_{ii}^{(0:P-1)}$ and/or $B_{jj}^{(0:P-1)}$) **then**
            Communicate for $A_{ii}^{(0:P-1)}$ and/or $B_{jj}^{(0:P-1)}$
         end if
         Solve subsystem $A_{ii}^{(k)} X_{ij}^{(k)} - X_{ij}^{(k+1)} B_{jj}^{(k)} = C_{ij}^{(k)}$, $k = 0, 1, \ldots, P-1$
         Broadcast $X_{ij}^{(0:P-1)}$ to processors holding blocks in block row i or block column j of $C_{0:P-1}$
      else if ($mynode$ needs $X_{ij}^{(0:P-1)}$) **then**
         Receive $X_{ij}^{(0:P-1)}$
      end if
      if ($mynode$ needs block in $A_{0:P-1}$ for updates in block column j of $C_{0:P-1}$) **then**
         Communicate for requested block in $A_{0:P-1}$
      end if
      Update block column j of $C_{0:P-1}$ in parallel
      if ($mynode$ needs block in $B_{0:P-1}$ for updates in block row i) **then**
         Communicate for requested block in $B_{0:P-1}$
      end if
      Update block row i of $C_{0:P-1}$ in parallel
   end for

Notice that the *on-demand* communication scheme from SCASY [10] is generalized to the periodic case by communication of subsequences of the involved matrices. It is also possible to generalize the *matrix block shifts* communication strategy (see [10] and the references therein) to the periodic case.

3 Implementation Issues

Node solvers. As node solvers, we use both the multi-layer blocked periodic solvers from [9] and the recursive blocked periodic solvers from [8] which were developed in the framework of RECSY [17,18]. Both variants are rich in level

3 BLAS operations and apply blocking of each local subsystem to reduce its matrix dimensions down to a level where a kernel solver based on the Kronecker product representation (13) can be efficiently utilized.

Periodic implicit redistribution. To remove 2×2 blocks in A_r and B_s being shared by several blocks (and processors) in the explicit blocking, we generalize the concept of performing an *implicit redistribution* from SCASY [11]. In principle, the implicit redistribution rearranges the data distribution such that all data elements in the quasi-triangular factors are included but the distribution still conforms with ScaLAPACK conventions (see [11] for details). Three main routines from SCASY are used: PDEXTCHK, PDIMPRED and PDBCKRD. The periodic implicit redistribution works as follows:

- PDEXTCHK is used for searching the main diagonals of A_r and B_s for any 2×2 blocks shared by several data layout blocks. The routine returns *redistribution* information which is broadcasted to all processors. PDEXTCHK is only called two times, once for A_r and once for B_s, regardless of the length of the period P.
- PDIMPRED exchanges data between the processors via message passing to build up local arrays of extra elements which are used locally in constructing and decomposing "correct" subsequences from A_k, B_k and C_k (and X_k) on the nodes before invoking local node solvers or performing local GEMM updates. PDIMPRED is called P times, once for each triplet (A_k, B_k, C_k), $k = 0, 1, \ldots, P-1$, using the information from PDEXTCHK.
- PDBCKRD is called right before returning from the corresponding triangular solver and sends back the redistributed parts of a solution matrix sequence to their original owner processes such that the solution matrix sequence is correctly distributed over the process mesh on output. PDBCKRD is called P times, once for each right hand side matrix C_k.

4 Experimental Results

We have implemented Algorithm 1 as the routine PTRPSYCTD in Fortran 77 following the ScaLAPACK coding style. Our target machine is the 64-bit Opteron Linux Cluster *sarek* with 192 dual AMD Opteron nodes (2.2 GHz), 8GB RAM per node and a Myrinet-2000 high-performance interconnect with 250 MB/sec bandwidth. All experiments where conducted using the Portland Group's pgf77 1.2.5 64-bit compiler, the compiler flag -fast and the following software: MPICH-GM 1.5.2 [24], LAPACK 3.0 [22], GOTO-BLAS r0.94 [7], ScaLAPACK 1.7.0 and BLACS 1.1patch3 [3], SCASY 0.10beta and RECSY 0.01alpha [25]. All experiments are conducted in double precision arithmetic ($\epsilon_{mach} \approx 2.2 \times 10^{-16}$).

Our test examples have the non-intersecting spectra: $\lambda(A_{P-1} \cdots A_1 A_0) = \{1, 2, \ldots, m\}$, $\lambda(B_{P-1} \cdots B_1 B_0) = \{-1, -2, \ldots, -n\}$ and we use random right hand sides $C_{ij}^{(k)} \in [-1, 1]$, $i = 1, 2, \ldots, m$, $j = 1, 2, \ldots, n$, $k = 0, 1, \ldots, P-1$.

We present representative results for PSYCT using up to 8×8 processor meshes in Table 1, including following quantities:

- The periodicity and the dimensions of the PSYCT equation: P, m and n.
- Parallel execution time: T_p, in seconds, where $p = P_r \times P_c$ is the number of utilized processor nodes.
- Parallel speedup: $S_p = T_{p_{\min}}/T_p$, where p is the number of utilized processors and $p_{\min}$ is the smallest number of processors for which the data structures of the current problem instance can be stored in the $p_{\min}$ chunks of main memory of the target computer.
- Mflops-rate: Mflops $= P(m^2 n + mn^2) 10^{-6} T_p^{-1}$
- Relative residual (Frobenius) norm:

$$r = \max_k \frac{\epsilon_{\text{mach}}^{-1} \|C_k - A_k \tilde{X}_k - \tilde{X}_{k+1} B_k\|}{\|A_k\| \|\tilde{X}_k\| + \|B_k\| \|\tilde{X}_{k+1}\| + \|C_k\|},$$

where $\tilde{X}_k$, $i = 0, 1, \ldots, P-1$, is the computed solution sequence. This residual norm should be of $O(1)$ for a reliable solution sequence $\tilde{X}_k$ [20], regardless of the conditioning of the underlying problem.

A few remarks regarding Table 1 are in order:

- The parallel execution time increases roughly linearly with the periodicity P, as illustrated in Figure 1.
- The Mflops-rate sometimes decreases with an increasing periodicity P for fixed values of m and n. This can be partly explained by the fact that an increased period leads to new data locality issues, since the blocks involved in the different operations (subsystem solves and GEMM-updates) are located

Table 1. Results of PTRPSYCTD on *sarek* using the block sizes $m_b = n_b = 64$

P	m	n	$P_r \times P_c$	T_p	Mflops	S_p	r
2	3000	3000	1 × 1	63.1	1712	1.0	0.3
2	3000	3000	2 × 2	29.9	3583	2.1	0.3
2	3000	3000	4 × 4	14.8	6993	4.3	0.3
2	3000	3000	8 × 8	7.54	14524	8.4	0.3
4	3000	3000	1 × 1	139	1556	1.0	0.4
4	3000	3000	2 × 2	66.4	3253	2.1	0.4
4	3000	3000	4 × 4	31.9	6771	4.4	0.4
4	3000	3000	8 × 8	15.8	13704	8.8	0.4
8	3000	3000	2 × 2	142	3038	1.0	0.3
8	3000	3000	4 × 4	67.2	6406	2.1	0.3
8	3000	3000	8 × 8	32.0	13505	4.4	0.3
2	6000	6000	2 × 2	195	3658	1.0	0.2
2	6000	6000	4 × 4	90.1	7898	2.2	0.2
2	6000	6000	8 × 8	40.4	17624	4.8	0.2
4	6000	6000	2 × 2	415	3432	1.0	0.4
4	6000	6000	4 × 4	208	6856	2.0	0.4
4	6000	6000	8 × 8	87.4	16278	4.7	0.4
8	6000	6000	4 × 4	429	8047	1.0	0.2
8	6000	6000	8 × 8	167	20736	2.6	0.2

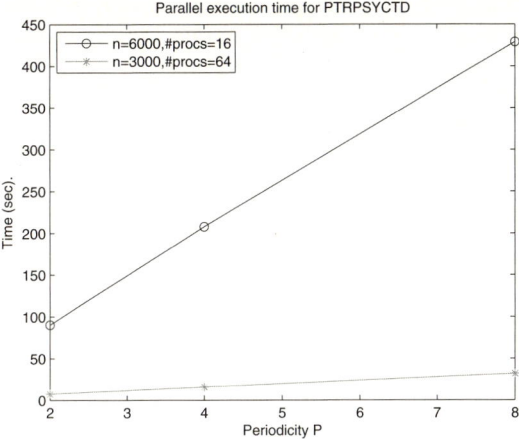

Fig. 1. Execution time results for PTRPSYCTD in relation to the periodicity P solving the PSYCT equation with $m = n = 3000, 6000$ on *sarek* using the block sizes $m_b = n_b = 64$

at far distance from each other, a problem that is amplified with an increasing period (see [8] for a similar observation).
- A main limitation of the possibility of achieving parallel speedup is the limited amount of physical memory on the target machine. For large periods, and when m and n are large enough for motivating the use of a distributed memory parallel computer, there is often not sufficient space to store all P matrices in the main memory unless one uses a huge number of processors.

The execution time information is also displayed in Figure 2. A general observation is that for all but the last results for $n = 6000$ and $p = 8$, an increase of the number of processors by a factor 4 cuts down the parallel execution time

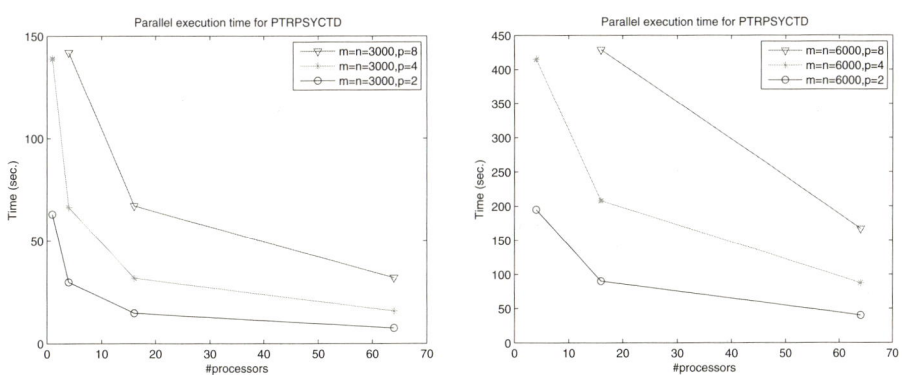

Fig. 2. Execution time results for PTRPSYCTD solving the PSYCT equation with $m = n = 3000, 6000$ on *sarek* using the block sizes $m_b = n_b = 64$

by roughly a factor 2. This is consistent with earlier observations, see, e.g., the performance model of the non-periodic ($P = 1$) SCASY implementations in [10].

5 Summary and Future Work

The work presented in this contribution was based on some preliminary results presented in [1] and can be further generalized to other periodic matrix equations (see, e.g., [8] for a list). In this context, there is a need for developing parallel versions of the periodic QR and QZ algorithms; for serial variants see, e.g., [4,15,21,23] and the references therein.

Acknowledgements

This research was conducted using the resources of the High Performance Computing Center North (HPC2N). Financial support has been provided by the *Swedish Research Council* under grant VR 621-2001-3284 and by the *Swedish Foundation for Strategic Research* under grant A3 02:128.

References

1. Andersson, P.: Parallella algoritmer för periodiska ekvationer av Sylvester-typ. Master's thesis, Tech. report UMNAD 715/07, Department of Computing Science, Umeå University (in Swedish) (2007)
2. Bartels, R.H., Stewart, G.W.: Algorithm 432: The Solution of the Matrix Equation $AX - BX = C$. Communications of the ACM 8, 820–826 (1972)
3. Blackford, L.S., Choi, J., Cleary, A., D'Azevedo, E., Demmel, J.W., Dhillon, I., Dongarra, J.J., Hammarling, S., Henry, G., Petitet, A., Stanley, K., Walker, D., Whaley, R.C.: ScaLAPACK Users' Guide. SIAM, Philadelphia (1997)
4. Bojanczyk, A., Golub, G.H., Van Dooren, P.: The periodic Schur decomposition; algorithm and applications. In: Proc. SPIE Conference, vol. 1770, pp. 31–42 (1992)
5. Fairweather, G., Gladwell, I.: Algorithms for Almost Block Diagonal Linear Systems. SIAM Review 44(1), 49–58 (2004)
6. Golub, G.H., Van Loan, C.F.: Matrix Computations, 3rd edn. Johns Hopkins University Press, Baltimore (1996)
7. GOTO-BLAS - High-Performance BLAS by Kazushige Goto, http://www.cs.utexas.edu/users/flame/goto/
8. Granat, R., Jonsson, I., Kågström, B.: Recursive Blocked Algorithms for Solving Periodic Triangular Sylvester-type Matrix Equations. In: Kågström, B., Elmroth, E., Dongarra, J., Waśniewski, J. (eds.) PARA 2006. LNCS, vol. 4699, pp. 531–539. Springer, Heidelberg (2007)
9. Granat, R., Kågström, B.: Direct eigenvalue reordering in a product of matrices in periodic schur form. SIAM J. Matrix Anal. Appl. 28(1), 285–300 (2006)
10. Granat, R., Kågström, B.: Parallel Solvers for Sylvester-type Matrix Equations with Applications in Condition Estimation, Part I: Theory and Algorithms, Tech. report UMINF-07.15. ACM TOMS (submitted 2007)

11. Granat, R., Kågström, B.: Parallel Solvers for Sylvester-type Matrix Equations with Applications in Condition Estimation, Part II: the SCASY Software, Tech. report UMINF-07.16. ACM TOMS (submitted 2007)
12. Granat, R., Kågström, B., Kressner, D.: Computing Periodic Deflating Subspaces Associated with a Specified Set of Eigenvalues. BIT Numerical Mathematics 47(4), 763–791 (2007)
13. Granat, R., Kågström, B., Kressner, D.: MATLAB tools for Solving Periodic Eigenvalue Problems. In: Proceedings of 3rd IFAC Workshop PSYCO 2007, Saint Petersburg, Russia (2007)
14. Hager, W.W.: Condition estimates. SIAM J. Sci. Statist. Comput. 3, 311–316 (1984)
15. Hench, J.J., Laub, A.J.: Numerical solution of the discrete-time periodic Riccati equation. IEEE Trans. Automat. Control 39(6), 1197–1210 (1994)
16. Higham, N.J.: Fortran codes for estimating the one-norm of a real or complex matrix, with applications to condition estimation. ACM Trans. of Math. Software 14(4), 381–396 (1988)
17. Jonsson, I., Kågström, B.: Recursive blocked algorithms for solving triangular systems. I. One-sided and coupled Sylvester-type matrix equations. ACM Trans. Math. Software 28(4), 392–415 (2002)
18. Jonsson, I., Kågström, B.: RECSY - A High Performance Library for Solving Sylvester-Type Matrix Equations. In: Kosch, H., Böszörményi, L., Hellwagner, H. (eds.) Euro-Par 2003. LNCS, vol. 2790, pp. 810–819. Springer, Heidelberg (2003)
19. Kågström, B., Poromaa, P.: Distributed and shared memory block algorithms for the triangular Sylvester equation with sep^{-1} estimators. SIAM J. Matrix Anal. Appl. 13(1), 90–101 (1992)
20. Kågström, B., Poromaa, P.: LAPACK-style algorithms and software for solving the generalized Sylvester equation and estimating the separation between regular matrix pairs. ACM Trans. Math. Software 22(1), 78–103 (1996)
21. Kressner, D.: An efficient and reliable implementation of the periodic QZ algorithm. In: IFAC Workshop on Periodic Control Systems (2001)
22. LAPACK - Linear Algebra Package, http://www.netlib.org/lapack/
23. Lust, K.: Improved numerical Floquet multipliers. Internat. J. Bifur. Chaos Appl. Sci. Engrg. 11(9), 2389–2410 (2001)
24. MPI - Message Passing Interface, http://www-unix.mcs.anl.gov/mpi/
25. RECSY - High Performance library for Sylvester-type matrix equations, http://www.cs.umu.se/research/parallel/recsy
26. SCASY - ScaLAPACK-style solvers for Sylvester-type matrix equations, http://www.cs.umu.se/granat/scasy.html
27. Varga, A.: Periodic Lyapunov equations: some applications and new algorithms. Internat. J. Control 67(1), 69–87 (1997)
28. Varga, A., Van Dooren, P.: Computational methods for periodic systems - an overview. In: Proc. of IFAC Workshop on Periodic Control Systems, Como, Italy, pp. 171–176 (2001)

A Parallel Sparse Linear Solver for Nearest-Neighbor Tight-Binding Problems

Mathieu Luisier[1], Gerhard Klimeck[1], Andreas Schenk[2], Wolfgang Fichtner[2], and Timothy B. Boykin[3]

[1] Network for Computational Nanotechnology, Purdue University, West Lafayette, Indiana 47907 USA
[2] Integrated Systems Laboratory, ETH Zurich, CH-8092 Zurich, Switzerland
[3] Department of Electrical and Computer Engineering, The University of Alabama in Huntsville, Huntsville, Alabama 35899 USA

Abstract. This paper describes an efficient sparse linear solver for block tri-diagonal systems arising from atomistic device simulation based on the nearest-neighbor tight-binding method. The algorithm is a parallel Gaussian elimination of blocks corresponding to atomic layers instead of single elements. It is known in the physics community as the renormalization method introduced in 1989 by Grosso et al, [Phys. Rev. B **40** 12328 (1989)]. Here, we describe in details the functionality of the algorithm and we show that it is faster than direct sparse linear packages like Pardiso, MUMPS or SuperLU_DIST and that it scales well up to 512 processors.

1 Introduction and Motivation

The simulation of nanoelectronic devices such as ultra-thin-body or nanowire field-effect transistors requires to abandon classical concepts such as drift-diffusion models and to use quantum-mechanical approaches. Furthermore, the strong quantization effects present in aggressively scaled nanostructures can only be captured by models describing the entire bandstructure of a crystal and not only its behavior around some high-symmetry points. The tight-binding approach fulfills these requirements and has become more and more popular among the technology computer aided design (TCAD) community. Each atom of the simulation domain as well as the connection between them are taken into account. They are represented by square blocks whose size depends on the number of atomic orbitals that are kept in the model. For example, in the $sp^3d^5s^*$ nearest-neighbor tight-binding model[1] that is used in this paper, the blocks have a size $N_{tb}=10$ when spin-orbit coupling is not included.

The goal of device simulation is to obtain observable data, such as current characteristics, that can be compared to experimental data. For that purpose the transport properties of electrons and holes must be investigated. Hence, the tight-binding bandstructure model is incorporated into a transport simulator. This is often achieved in the non-equilibrium Green's function formalism[2] which is computationally very intensive. An alternative is to work in the wave function formalism[3] in which sparse linear systems **AC=S** have to be solved. The matrix **A** is block tri-diagonal and of size $(N_A \cdot N_{tb}) \times (N_A \cdot N_{tb})$ where N_A is the number of atoms that the nanostructure contains. The vector **S** describes the injection of states into the device and **C** the resulting wave function coefficients.

The size of the matrix **A** as well as the low memory per processor that is available on high performance machines oblige us to solve the sparse system **AC=S** in parallel. To accomplish this task we have developed an algorithm based on the Gaussian elimination of all the diagonal blocks of **A** till only its first and last blocks are connected[4]. The method is based on a "block cyclic reduction"[5] of the matrix **A** where the off-diagonal blocks are singular. It is known in the physics community as "renormalization method"[6]. When it was introduced in 1989 it was dedicated to very small and one- or two-dimensional problems and it was thought as a sequential algorithm. We have improved it to enable the simulation of realistic three-dimensional nanostructures like nanowire field-effect transistors and to work on massively parallel and/or shared memory computers.

The renormalization algorithm is presented in Section 2. The mathematical structure of the matrix **A** and its advantages are discussed in details. In Section 3 the performances of the algorithm are shown on 1 to 512 processors. It is also compared to other direct sparse linear solvers like PARDISO[7], SuperLU_DIST 2.0[8] and MUMPS 4.6.3[9] on 1 to 16 processors. Apart from a speed-up factor of about 2 or more our renormalization algorithm exhibits better scaling properties than SuperLU and MUMPS.

2 Renormalization Algorithm

The matrix **A** corresponds to the Hamiltonian coming from the Schrödinger equation expressed in the tight-binding basis. It is block tri-diagonal and of size $n \times n$ where $n = N_A \cdot N_{tb}$, the number of atoms in the device (N_A) times the number of orbitals that are kept in the tight-binding model (N_{tb}). A silicon nanowire example is given in Fig. 1 (a). On the left the atoms (black dots) and their connections (four per atom, gray lines) are depicted. The resulting matrix **A** is shown on the right. The sparsity pattern corresponding to the zone delimited by the dashed lines is plotted (layers 1, 2, 3, 4, and 5). Note that each black point is in fact a $N_{tb} \times N_{tb}$ matrix, where $N_{tb}=10$ in our case. Hence, the total system of equations takes the following form

$$\begin{pmatrix} A_{11} & A_{12} & 0 & \cdots & & 0 \\ A_{12}^\dagger & A_{22} & A_{23} & 0 & & \cdots \\ 0 & \ddots & \ddots & \ddots & & 0 \\ \vdots & \cdots & \ddots & \ddots & & A_{N_B-1 N_B} \\ 0 & \cdots & 0 & A_{N_B-1 N_B}^\dagger & & A_{N_B N_B} \end{pmatrix} \cdot \begin{pmatrix} C_1 \\ C_2 \\ \vdots \\ C_{N_B-1} \\ C_{N_B} \end{pmatrix} = \begin{pmatrix} S_1 \\ 0 \\ \vdots \\ \vdots \\ 0 \end{pmatrix}. \qquad (1)$$

The matrix **A** counts N_B diagonal blocks, each of them refers to a specific atomic layer (all the atoms with the same x-coordinate). The diagonal blocks

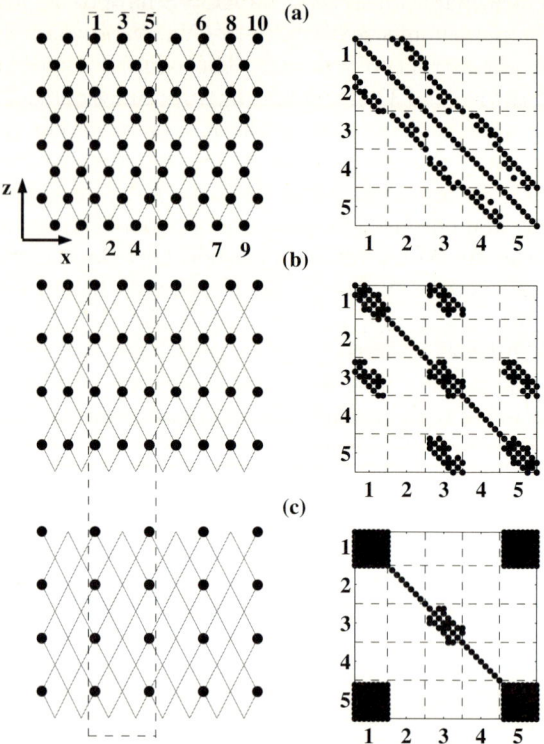

Fig. 1. Nanowire atomic arrangement (left) and corresponding block tri-diagonal matrix (right). Only the $x-z$ face of the nanowire is shown. The black dots depict atoms, the gray lines atomic bonds. The transport direction x is aligned with <100>. The matrices on the right represent the five atomic layers (labeled 1, 2, 3, 4, and 5) surrounded by the dashed lines. Three phases of the renormalization algorithm are represented: (a) initial situation, (b) after the first stage of Gaussian elimination (or layer decoupling), and (c) after the second stage of Gaussian elimination.

A_{mm} represent the on-site energy of the atoms situated in the mth layer of the nanostructure as well as the nearest-neighbor connections of these atoms within the mth layer. The singular off-diagonal blocks A_{mm+1} (A_{mm-1}) describe the connections to the atoms situated in the next (previous) atomic layer. All the blocks are real, sparse, and of size $(n_A \cdot N_{tb}) \times (n_A \cdot N_{tb})$, where n_A is the number of atoms per layer. We have the following properties, (1) $A_{mm-1} = A^\dagger_{m-1m}$, (2) $A_{mm} = A^\dagger_{mm}$, except for A_{11} and $A_{N_B N_B}$ which are complex, full, and do not have any symmetry since they include the open boundary conditions[3]. The vector S_1 represents the incident states.

As it can be observed in the right part of Fig. 1 (a) the diagonal blocks A_{mm} do not contain connections between atoms and are themselves diagonal. Consequently, their inversion is straight forward and the Gaussian elimination of the atomic layers becomes computationally very efficient. This property is verified for all the nanostructures whose transport direction x is aligned with the <100> or <111> crystal axis. However, the renormalization algorithm works well as long as one atomic layer is connected only to its adjacent neighbors. This is the case for x=<110> so that all the important crystal orientations are covered.

The basic process of the renormalization algorithm is the decoupling of an atomic layer from its neighbors which is equivalent to the Gaussian elimination of one atomic layer. To decouple one diagonal block m different from 1 and N_B the matrices $\mathbf{M}_{L,m}$ and $\mathbf{M}_{R,m}$ are introduced. They have the same size as $\mathbf{A}$ and are defined as

$$\mathbf{A} = \mathbf{M}_{L,m}^{-1} \cdot \tilde{\mathbf{A}} \cdot \mathbf{M}_{R,m}^{-1}, \tag{2}$$

$$\mathbf{A} = \begin{pmatrix} \ddots & \ddots & \ddots & & \cdots & \cdots \\ & \ddots & A_{m-1m-1} & A_{m-1m} & 0 & \cdots \\ & 0 & A_{m-1m}^{\dagger} & A_{mm} & A_{mm+1} & \ddots \\ \vdots & & \ddots & A_{mm+1}^{\dagger} & A_{m+1m+1} & \ddots \\ \vdots & & & \ddots & \ddots & \ddots \end{pmatrix}, \tag{3}$$

$$\tilde{\mathbf{A}} = \begin{pmatrix} \ddots & \ddots & \ddots & & \cdots & \cdots \\ & \ddots & \tilde{A}_{m-1m-1} & 0 & \tilde{A}_{m-1m+1} & \cdots \\ & 0 & 0 & A_{mm} & 0 & \ddots \\ \vdots & & \tilde{A}_{m-1m+1}^{\dagger} & 0 & \tilde{A}_{m+1m+1} & \ddots \\ \vdots & & & \ddots & \ddots & \ddots \end{pmatrix}, \tag{4}$$

$$\mathbf{M}_{L,m} = \begin{pmatrix} 1 & 0 & \ddots & \cdots & \cdots \\ & \ddots & 1 & X_m^{\dagger} & 0 & \ddots \\ & \ddots & 0 & 1 & 0 & \ddots \\ \vdots & & 0 & Y_m^{\dagger} & 1 & \ddots \\ \vdots & & \ddots & \ddots & 0 & 1 \end{pmatrix}, \quad \mathbf{M}_{L,m}^{-1} = \begin{pmatrix} 1 & 0 & \ddots & \cdots & \cdots \\ & \ddots & 1 & -X_m^{\dagger} & 0 & \ddots \\ & \ddots & 0 & 1 & 0 & \ddots \\ \vdots & & 0 & -Y_m^{\dagger} & 1 & \ddots \\ \vdots & & \ddots & \ddots & 0 & 1 \end{pmatrix}, \tag{5}$$

$$X_m = A_{mm}^{-1} \cdot A_{m-1m}^{\dagger}, \quad Y_m = A_{mm}^{-1} \cdot A_{mm+1}, \tag{6}$$

$$\tilde{A}_{m-1m+1} = -A_{m-1m} \cdot Y_m, \quad \tilde{A}_{m-1m-1} = A_{m-1m-1} - A_{m-1m} \cdot X_m, \tag{7}$$

$$\tilde{A}_{m+1m+1} = A_{m+1m+1} - A_{mm+1}^{\dagger} \cdot Y_m. \tag{8}$$

The variables carrying a "tilde" are renormalized so that at least one block is decoupled from the others as in Eq. (4). It can be easily proved that $\mathbf{M}_{R,m} = \mathbf{M}_{L,m}^{\dagger}$ and the same relation holds for $\mathbf{M}_{R,m}^{-1}$. Furthermore, by applying the transformation in Eq. (2) only the blocks shown above get modified the other blocks remain unchanged. One solves Eq. (1) by repeatedly decoupling planes until the first layer of $\tilde{\mathbf{A}}$ is connected to its last layer and the rest of the matrix is block diagonal. The last block $\tilde{A}_{N_B N_B}$ is further decoupled by using a modified matrix $\mathbf{M}_{L,N_B}^{-1}$ and $\mathbf{M}_{R,N_B}^{-1}$ where Y_{N_B} is equal to zero. Finally one has

$$\mathbf{A} = \left(\mathbf{M}_{L,N_B}^{-1} \cdot \mathbf{M}_{L,p}^{-1} \cdots \mathbf{M}_{L,q}^{-1} \right) \cdot \hat{\mathbf{A}} \cdot \left(\mathbf{M}_{R,q}^{-1} \cdots \mathbf{M}_{R,p}^{-1} \cdot \mathbf{M}_{R,N_B}^{-1} \right) \qquad (9)$$

where $\hat{\mathbf{A}}$ is block diagonal.

The key point of the renormalization algorithm resides in the ordering of the decoupling process. If one starts by decoupling the second block A_{22} no problem is encountered to compute Eqs. (6) to (8) since all the involved matrices are sparse. For example, inverting the diagonal block A_{22} is obvious. However, the first and the third block are modified by this operation. In particular $\tilde{A}_{33}$ is no more diagonal, but still sparse. If now the third block $\tilde{A}_{33}$ is decoupled, $\tilde{A}_{11}$ and $\tilde{A}_{44}$ becomes renormalized. This is computationally not efficient despite the fact that inverting $\tilde{A}_{33}$ can be achieved by a direct sparse linear solver. In effect $\tilde{A}_{44}$ is now a full matrix and the decoupling of the remaining blocks 4 to N_{B-1} is only possible by inverting full diagonal blocks.

A better approach consists in decoupling alternate interior atomic planes to preserve the sparse nature of the matrix $\mathbf{A}$ as long as possible. In the first renormalization stage the blocks 2, 4, 6, $\cdots$ are eliminated. This can be done by inverting diagonal and multiplying sparse matrices. About $(N_B-2)/2$ blocks are concerned. In the second stage the blocks 3, 7, 11, $\cdots$ are decoupled requiring the inversion of sparse matrices and the multiplication of full and sparse matrices ($\approx N_B/4$ blocks). Finally, only the remaining $\approx N_B/4$ planes require the inversion and the multiplication of full matrices to be decoupled.

This ordering of the decoupling process is illustrated in Fig. 1 (b) and (c). In the first renormalization stage (b) the blocks 2 and 4 are decoupled and the blocks 1, 3, and 5 are renormalized, but keep a sparse pattern. In the second stage (c) the block 3 is decoupled yielding full matrices for the blocks 1 and 5. It is important to note that the decoupling of all the blocks is accomplished in real arithmetic. Only the last step involving the first and the last block is done in complex arithmetic.

Once the matrix $\mathbf{A}$ is fully block-diagonalized by the procedure described in Eq. (9) the vector $\mathbf{C}$ in Eq. (1) is obtained by a simple recursion involving the X_m and Y_m blocks only[4]

$$C_1 = \tilde{A}_{11}^{-1} \cdot S_1, \quad C_{N_B} = -X_{N_B} \cdot C_1 \qquad (10)$$
$$C_m = -X_m \cdot C_{m-p} - Y_m \cdot C_{m+q}. \qquad (11)$$

The recursion proceeds by reverse decoupling order and prior to decoupling the block m was connected to the blocks p and q.

The parallelization of the renormalization algorithm is achieved by simultaneously decoupling alternating planes independently. This is similar to a domain decomposition approach. Two versions of the renormalization algorithm have been implemented, one designed for distributed memory machines and using

MPI to communicate between the processors and one dedicated to shared memory machines and based on OpenMP and thread management. We will restrict the description of the algorithm to its distributed memory variant.

In Fig. 1 it is clear that while a processor is decoupling the blocks (layers) 1 to 5, another processor can proceed to the blocks 6 to 10. The two area are completely independent. Thus, the following parallelization scheme is used if P_{CPU} processors with distributed memory are available. The matrix **A** is divided into P_{CPU} sets of $\approx N_B/P_{CPU}$ subsequent blocks. One and only one set is assigned to each processor P_p. Then the renormalization algorithm is applied until the first block of the processor P_p is only connected to the first block of the processors P_{p-1} and P_{p+1}. To reach this stage no inter-processor communication is required and it remains to decouple P_{CPU} blocks. They are decoupled in $\log_2(P_{CPU})$ steps. In the first step the first blocks of the processors P_2, P_4, P_6, $\cdots$ are decoupled and data are sent via MPI to the processors P_1, P_3, P_5, $\cdots$. In the second step, the first blocks of the processors P_3, P_7, P_{11}, $\cdots$ are decoupled, and so on. At the end the matrix **A** is block-diagonalized.

If we assume that the time to decouple a block is t_0 and is the same for all the blocks, are they diagonal, sparse, or full, we obtain the following factorization time $T(p)$ on p processors and speed-up factor $\lambda = T(1)/T(P_{CPU})$

$$T(p) = [(N_B - 1 - p)/p + \log_2(p) + 1] \times t_0, \tag{12}$$

$$\lambda = \frac{N_B - 1}{(N_B - 1 - P_{CPU})/P_{CPU} + \log_2(P_{CPU}) + 1}. \tag{13}$$

Equation (13) is a theoretical value for the speed-up factor since the time to decouple the first half of the planes is much shorter than the time to decouple the last quarter as explained above. Furthermore, in order for λ to reach its ideal value of $\lambda = P_{CPU}$ the number of blocks N_B should be as large as possible.

3 Results

The performances of the renormalization algorithm are analyzed in four tests run on three machines. The first one is a CRAY XT3 with AMD Opteron CPU running at 2.6 GHz and 2 GB of RAM. It is classified at position #84 in the November 2007 Top 500 list of supercomputers. The second machine is composed of 82 nodes which are Intel Xeon 5140 with 2.33 GHz CPUs and 16 GB of RAM. They are connected with gigabit Ethernet. The last machine is a SUN Opteron with 8 dual-core processors sharing 128 GB of RAM and running at 1.8 GHz.

3.1 Test 1

The first test is conducted on the CRAY machine. It involves two matrices arising from nanowire field-effect transistor simulation with a length of 600 nm and 1200 nm and a cross section of 2.1×2.1 nm². Equation (1) is solved on 16 to 512 processors. The 2GB of RAM per node (1GB per processor) do not allow to consider less than 16 processors. The results of the test 1.a and 1.b as well as the

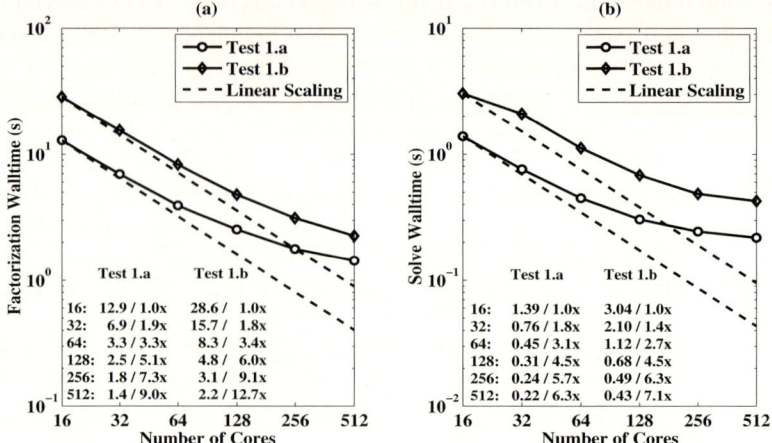

Fig. 2. Strong scaling results of the renormalization algorithm for (a) the factorization and (b) the solve stage on 16 to 512 CPUs. The matrix in the test 1.a is block tri-diagonal with N_B=3684 diagonal blocks of size 320×320 (total size n=1178880), a band b=720, and nnz=37347328 non-zero elements (sparsity of the band 4.4%). The characteristics of the matrix in the test 1.b are: N_B=7656 (size 350×350), n=2679600, b=820, nnz=72865028, sparsity of the band 3.3%. The execution time and the speed-up factor over 16 CPUs are also reported.

characteristics of the matrices are shown in Fig. 2. On the left the factorization time is reproduced, on the right the solve time. The dashed lines represent the ideal linear scaling. The time (in seconds) to factorize and solve the system of equations (values before the "/") and the speed improvement over 16 processors (values after the "/" and followed by a ×) are also reported.

The renormalization algorithm scales well up to 512 processors, where the ideal speed improvement λ over 16 processors should be 32. We have obtained $\lambda_{1.a}$=9.0 and $\lambda_{1.b}$=12.7 for the factorization of the test 1.a and 1.b, respectively. These performances are comparable to those of the "SPIKE" algorithm for "dense in the band" matrices[10]. The λ's estimated by Eq. (13) are larger than the measured λ's since they represent a theoretical limit. However, the measured and the estimated ratio $\lambda_{1.b}/\lambda_{1.a}$ have about the same value of 1.4.

3.2 Test 2

The second test is run on the CRAY XT3 supercomputer for three block tri-diagonal matrices whose size n is linearly proportional to the number of CPUs P_{CPU} that is used to factorize and solve them. Hence, we expect that the factorization and solve time remain constant from 1 to 512 processors. The measured results and the characteristics of the matrices are given in Fig. 3 for the factorization stage. The times are normalized with respect to the time on a single processor. Consequently, in the ideal case, the curves should be close to the constant dashed line $y = 1$. In reality, the factorization time increases as function

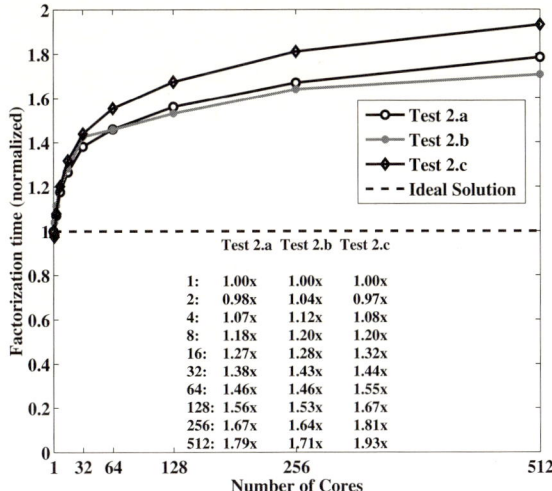

Fig. 3. Weak scaling results for the factorization on 1 to 512 CPUs of three different matrices with the size $n = n_0 \times P_{CPU}$ and the number of diagonal blocks $N_B = N_{B0} \times P_{CPU}$ linearly increasing as function of the number of CPU P_{CPU}. The execution time is normalized with respect to the time on a single processor and is reported in the lower part of the figure. In the test 2.a N_{B0}=16, b=720, and n_0=5120, in the test 2.b N_{B0}=12, b=860, and n_0=5280, and in the test 2.c N_{B0}=12, b=800, and n_0=4200.

of P_{proc}, but on 512 processors less than 2× the time on a single processor is necessary for the tests 2.a, 2.b and 2.c.

3.3 Test 3

The Intel Xeon cluster is used for the third test. We consider 7 block tri-diagonal matrices corresponding to realistic nanowire structures with the same length of 60 nm (=> same number of diagonal blocks N_B), but with a cross section increasing from 2.8×2.8 to 4.1×4.1 nm² (=> increasing band b). The characteristics of these matrices are given in Table 1. The number of blocks N_B of these matrices is too small to factorize them on more than 16 processors.

In Table 2 the performances of the renormalization algorithm (second column) are compared to those of MUMPS 4.6.3[9] (third) and SuperLU_DIST 2.0[8] (fifth) on 1 to 16 processors. The factor λ_M (λ_S) in the fourth (sixth) column is the speed improvement of the renormalization algorithm over MUMPS (SuperLU_DIST). In the second column, the bold values refer to the parallel speed improvement of the renormalization algorithm over 1 processor.

First, we observe that the renormalization algorithm scales well for the tests 3.a to 3.g. A mean speed-up of 1.97× is obtained on 2 processors, 3.63× on 4, 6.27 × on 8, and 9.47 × on 16. Then, we find that the renormalization algorithm is between 1.7× and 2.6× faster than MUMPS and between 3.3× and 4.9 × faster than SuperLU_DIST on a single processor. This is due to the fact that

Table 1. Characteristics of the 7 matrices used for the tests 3.a to 3.g. They have a size n, nnz non-zero elements, a bandwidth b, all the same number of diagonal blocks N_B=440, and the sparsity of the band is given in the last column.

	n	nnz	b	N_B	sparsity %
Test 3.a	243100	8467450	1240	440	2.8
Test 3.b	291500	10374782	1460	440	2.4
Test 3.c	344300	12519854	1720	440	2.1
Test 3.d	371800	13678784	1840	440	2.0
Test 3.e	401500	14911578	1980	440	1.9
Test 3.f	431200	16182212	2120	440	1.8
Test 3.g	495000	18998168	2420	440	1.6

Table 2. Factorization results for the tests 3.a to 3.g. The first column indicates the number of processors that were used to factorize the matrix. In the second column the results of the renormalization matrix are shown with the speed-up factor over 1 processor in bold. The third column contains the results of MUMPS 4.6.3 and the fourth the speed improvement λ_M vs MUMPS obtained with the renormalization algorithm. The fifth and sixth columns are dedicated to the results of SuperLU_DIST 2.0 and the speed improvement λ_S vs SuperLU_DIST obtained with the renormalization algorithm.

3.a	R. (s)	M. (s)	λ_M	S. (s)	λ_S
1	37.7/**1.0x**	95.4	**2.5**	126	**3.3**
2	19.2/**1.96x**	58.4	**3.0**	90.6	**4.7**
4	10.6/**3.55x**	35.6	**3.4**	78.1	**7.3**
8	6.2/**6.08x**	26.2	**4.2**	98	**15.8**
16	4.2/**9.04x**	23.1	**5.5**	364	**87.3**

3.b	R. (s)	M. (s)	λ_M	S. (s)	λ_S
1	63.2/**1.0x**	139.3	**2.2**	259	**4.1**
2	32.0/**1.98x**	85.9	**2.7**	166	**5.2**
4	17.5/**3.61x**	50.8	**2.9**	130	**7.5**
8	10.2/**6.19x**	40.4	**3.9**	158	**15.5**
16	6.9/**9.22x**	30.8	**4.5**	531	**77.6**

3.c	R. (s)	M. (s)	λ_M	S. (s)	λ_S
1	97.1/**1.0x**	256	**2.6**	428	**4.4**
2	49.7/**1.95x**	143	**2.9**	263	**5.3**
4	27.0/**3.6x**	83.9	**3.1**	195	**7.2**
8	15.9/**6.1x**	57.7	**3.6**	226	**14.2**
16	10.6/**9.16x**	50.1	**4.7**	686	**64.7**

3.d	R. (s)	M. (s)	λ_M	S. (s)	λ_S
1	150/**1.0x**	276	**1.8x**	498	**3.3**
2	75.8/**1.98x**	173	**2.3x**	309	**4.1**
4	41/**3.66x**	101	**2.5x**	224	**5.4**
8	23.3/**6.44x**	65.4	**2.8x**	260	**11.2**
16	15.2/**9.88x**	53.5	**3.5x**	795	**52.3**

3.e	R. (s)	M. (s)	λ_M	S. (s)	λ_S
1	153/**1.0x**	396	**2.6**	598	**3.9**
2	77.4/**1.97x**	227	**2.9**	360	**4.6**
4	42/**3.63x**	126	**3.0**	260	**6.2**
8	24.6/**6.2x**	101	**4.1**	307	**12.5**
16	16.4/**9.3x**	73.7	**4.5**	855	**52.1**

3.f	R. (s)	M. (s)	λ_M	S. (s)	λ_S
1	220/**1.0x**	403	**1.8**	902	**4.1**
2	111/**1.98x**	242	**2.2**	597	**5.4**
4	59.5/**3.69x**	138	**2.3**	358	**6.0**
8	34.1/**6.44x**	111	**3.3**	405	**11.9**
16	22.2/**9.9x**	77.5	**3.5**	1021	**46.0**

3.g	R. (s)	M. (s)	λ_M	S. (s)	λ_S
1	330/**1.0x**	568	**1.7**	1604	**4.9**
2	168/**1.97x**	334	**1.99**	919	**5.5**
4	89.5/**3.69x**	181	**2.02**	614	**6.9**
8	51.6/**6.4x**	137	**2.6**	621	**12.0**
16	33.7/**9.8x**	104	**3.1**	1374	**40.8**

Table 3. Factorization results for the test 4. The second column shows the results of the MPI version of the renormalization algorithm (MPIRA). The third column contains the results of the shared memory version of the renormalization method (OMPRA) and the fourth the speed improvement λ_R vs OMPRA obtained with MPIRA. The fifth and sixth columns are dedicated to the results of PARDISO and the speed improvement λ_P vs PARDISO obtained with MPIRA.

4	MPIRA (s)	OMPRA (s)	λ_R	Pardiso. (s)	λ_P
1	610/**1.0x**	631	**1.03**	1202	**1.97**
2	311.3/**1.96x**	321	**1.03**	669	**2.15**
4	169.3/**3.6x**	166.5	**0.98**	328	**1.94**
8	91.5/**6.7x**	94	**1.03**	201	**2.2**
16	68.6/**8.9x**	72.7	**1.06**	135	**1.97**

both MUMPS and SuperLU_DIST work in complex arithmetic while the renormalization algorithm decouples all the blocks in real arithmetic except the first and the last ones that include the complex boundary conditions. Finally, the speed improvement λ_M and λ_S increase with the number of processors showing that the renormalization algorithm scales better than the two other packages.

3.4 Test 4

For the last test the SUN Opteron with 16 shared memory processors is used. The performances of the MPI and OpenMP versions of the renormalization algorithm are compared to those of PARDISO[7] for the same matrix as in the test 3.g. The results are reported in Table 3. First note that the SUN Opteron is about two times slower than the Intel Xeon Cluster. The distributed (second column) and shared (fourth column) memory versions of the renormalization algorithm have very similar performances and are about two times faster than PARDISO. However, the renormalization algorithm does not scale better than PARDISO on the SUN Opteron for this specific test.

4 Conclusion

In this paper we presented a parallel sparse linear solver for block tri-diagonal matrices, the renormalization algorithm. A sequential version was introduced in 1989 in the physics community, but we optimized it to treat larger systems and to work in parallel on distributed and shared memory machines. For matrices with a bandwidth smaller than one thousand and a size larger than one million the renormalization algorithm scales well up to 512 processors. For more realistic structures (bandwidth larger than 1500 and size smaller than 500000) it is faster than the direct sparse linear solvers PARDISO, MUMPS, and SuperLU_DIST and it scales better than the two latter.

As the size of the blocks gets larger it will be useful to use parallel solvers like ScaLAPACK to decouple full diagonal blocks. This improvement will create a second level of parallelism inside of the renormalization algorithm. Then, the factorization of linear systems with a large band and a relative small size will scale on more than 16 processors and require less RAM.

Acknowledgements

This work was supported by the Swiss National Science Foundation (NEQUATTRO SNF 200020-117613/1). Support by the Semiconductor Research Corporation (SRC) is acknowledged. nanohub.org computational resources were used.

References

1. Boykin, T.B., Klimeck, G., Oyafuso, F.: Valence band effective-mass expressions in the sp^{3}d^{5}s* empirical tight-binding model applied to a Si and Ge parametrization. Phys. Rev. B 69, 115201 (2004)
2. Datta, S.: Nanoscale device modeling: the Green's function method. Superlattices Microstruct. 28, 253–278 (2000)
3. Luisier, M., Klimeck, G., Schenk, A., Fichtner, W.: Atomistic Simulation of Nanowires in the $sp^3d^5s^*$ Tight-Binding Formalism: from Boundary Conditions to Strain Calculations. Phys. Rev. B 74, 205323 (2006)
4. Boykin, T.B., Luisier, M., Klimeck, G.: Multi-band transmission calculations for nanowires using an optimized renormalization method. Phys. Rev. B 77, 165318 (2008)
5. Sweet, R.A.: A cyclic reduction algorithm for solving block tridiagonal systems of arbitrary dimension. SIAM J. Numer. Anal. 14, 707–720 (1977)
6. Grosso, G., Moroni, S., Parravicini, G.P.: Electronic structure of the InAs-GaSb superlattice studied by the renormalization method. Phys. Rev. B 40, 12328 (1989)
7. Schenk, O., Gärtner, K.: Solving Unsymmetric Sparse Systems of Linear Equations with PARDISO. Journal of Future Generation Computer Systems 20, 475–487 (2004)
8. Li, X.S., Demmel, J.W.: SuperLU_DIST: A Scalable Distributed Memory Sparse Direct Solver for Unsymmetric Linear Systems. ACM Trans. on Math. Software 29, 110 (2003)
9. Amestoy, P.R., Duff, I.S., L'Excellent, J.-Y.: Multifrontal parallel distributed symmetric and unsymmetric solvers. Comput. Methods in Appl. Mech. Eng. 184, 501 (2000)
10. Polizzi, E., Sameh, A.H.: A parallel hybrid banded system solver: the SPIKE algorithm. Parallel Comp. 32, 177 (2006)

Exploiting the Locality Properties of Peano Curves for Parallel Matrix Multiplication

Michael Bader

Institut für Informatik, Technische Universität München, Germany
bader@in.tum.de

Abstract. The present work studies an approach to exploit the locality properties of an inherently cache-efficient algorithm for matrix multiplication in a parallel implementation. The algorithm is based on a blockwise element layout and an execution order that are derived from a Peano space-filling curve. The strong locality properties induced in the resulting algorithm motivate a parallel algorithm that replicates matrix blocks in local caches that will prefetch remote blocks before they are used. As a consequence, the block size for matrix multiplication and the cache sizes, and hence the granularity of communication, can be chosen independently. The influence of these parameters on parallel efficiency is studied on a compute cluster with 128 processors. Performance studies show that the largest influence on performance stems from the size of the local caches, which makes the algorithm an interesting option for all situations where memory is scarce, or where existing cache hierarchies can be exploited (as in future manycore environments, e.g.).

1 Introduction

Space-filling curves have become a quite well-established tool for parallelisation in scientific computing, which is mainly a result of their strong locality properties. In matrix computations, recursive and block-recursive approaches – which includes approaches based on space-filling curves, Morton order, and similar – can exploit such locality properties to obtain cache-efficient algorithms (see [4] for an overview). In [1,2], we introduced a block-recursive algorithm for matrix multiplication based on Peano space-filling curves, where the Peano curve's locality properties lead to an inherently cache-efficient multiplication scheme with a highly local access pattern to memory. The present paper addresses the question about how these locality properties can be used to obtain an efficient parallel implementation of matrix multiplication. The key idea of the presented approach is to add local software caches to replicate remote matrix blocks on the local processors, and thus turn an inherently cache-efficient algorithm into one that also scales well in a parallel implementation.

Existing parallel algorithms for matrix multiplication, such as PUMMA[3], SUMMA[5], or SRUMMA[7], are typically based on substructuring the involved matrices into smaller blocks. These blocks not only define the distribution of the matrices to several processing units, they also determine the data units that need to be transfered between the processors and, together with the parallel block layout, the resulting communication pattern. Prefetching of remote blocks, however, and overlapping communication with computation is restricted to double-buffering techniques in those approaches.

In contrast, the presented cache-oriented approach exploits the algorithm's strong locality properties for efficient prefetching and communication hiding. The size of the prefetched matrix blocks can be chosen independent of the amount of additional local memory to hold copies of remote matrix blocks, and independent of the dimension of the sequentially executed block multiplications (which also has a strong influence on achievable performance). In addition, the resulting algorithm can be tuned for specific applications – for example when memory is short and the amount of additional local memory is therefore the limiting factor – or for specific hardware, such as for latency and bandwidth of the communication. In a parallel work[6], we showed that a hardware-oriented implementation of our Peano algorithm achieves excellent performance on multicore platforms. Hence, the present study also aims at estimating the capability of the Peano multiplication for future manycore processors with 10–100 cores.

2 Matrix Multiplication Using Peano Curves

To compute the product of two $n \times n$-matrices, as in $C = C + AB$, we need to perform the update $c_{ij} = c_{ij} + a_{ik}b_{kj}$ for all triples $(i,j,k) \in \{1, \ldots, n\}^3$. Due to commutativity, we can execute the updates in any sequence we find appropriate; i.e. we may choose any 3D-traversal of the index space $\{1, \ldots, n\}^3$. Similarly, we may choose any suitable 2D-traversal of the index spaces of the matrices, $\{1, \ldots, n\}^2$, as a storage scheme to map the matrix elements to a contiguous sequence of memory addresses. In [1], we have shown that using a Peano curve for both the 3D- and the 2D-traversal, i.e. the sequence of element updates and the order of the matrix elements, leads to an inherently local scheme for matrix multiplication. For the simple example of multiplying two 3×3-matrices,

$$\begin{pmatrix} a_0 & a_5 & a_6 \\ a_1 & a_4 & a_7 \\ a_2 & a_3 & a_8 \end{pmatrix} \begin{pmatrix} b_0 & b_5 & b_6 \\ b_1 & b_4 & b_7 \\ b_2 & b_3 & b_8 \end{pmatrix} = \begin{pmatrix} c_0 & c_5 & c_6 \\ c_1 & c_4 & c_7 \\ c_2 & c_3 & c_8 \end{pmatrix}, \tag{1}$$

where the element indices indicate the order in which the elements are stored in memory, this leads to the execution order given in figure 1. Note that the update operations on the elements c_r are computed in an inherently local order – from each operation to the next, the involved matrix elements are either reused or one of their direct neighbours in memory is accessed.

Figure 2 illustrates how the Peano element order is extended to store larger matrices. We use 2D *iterations* of a Peano curve, which is described by a nested-recursive scheme of four block-numbering patterns: P, Q, R, and S. Starting from the initial pattern P, the four block patterns are recursively combined and lead to a contiguous storage scheme of matrix blocks. The recursion is stopped once the matrix blocks become smaller than a given block size. On these *atomic*

$$
\begin{array}{ccccc}
c_0 \mathrel{+}= a_0 b_0 & c_3 \mathrel{+}= a_8 b_3 \rightarrow c_4 \mathrel{+}= a_7 b_3 & c_7 \mathrel{+}= a_1 b_6 \rightarrow c_8 \mathrel{+}= a_2 b_6 \\
\downarrow & \uparrow & \downarrow & \uparrow & \downarrow \\
c_1 \mathrel{+}= a_1 b_0 & c_2 \mathrel{+}= a_8 b_2 & c_5 \mathrel{+}= a_6 b_3 & c_6 \mathrel{+}= a_0 b_6 & c_8 \mathrel{+}= a_3 b_7 \\
\downarrow & \uparrow & \downarrow & \uparrow & \downarrow \\
c_2 \mathrel{+}= a_2 b_0 & c_1 \mathrel{+}= a_7 b_2 & c_5 \mathrel{+}= a_5 b_4 & c_5 \mathrel{+}= a_0 b_5 & c_7 \mathrel{+}= a_4 b_7 \\
\downarrow & \uparrow & \downarrow & \uparrow & \downarrow \\
c_2 \mathrel{+}= a_3 b_1 & c_0 \mathrel{+}= a_6 b_2 & c_4 \mathrel{+}= a_4 b_4 & c_4 \mathrel{+}= a_1 b_5 & c_6 \mathrel{+}= a_5 b_7 & c_8 \mathrel{+}= a_8 b_8 \\
\downarrow & \uparrow & \downarrow & \uparrow & \downarrow & \uparrow \\
c_1 \mathrel{+}= a_4 b_1 \rightarrow c_0 \mathrel{+}= a_5 b_1 & c_3 \mathrel{+}= a_3 b_4 \rightarrow c_3 \mathrel{+}= a_2 b_5 & c_6 \mathrel{+}= a_6 b_8 \rightarrow c_7 \mathrel{+}= a_7 b_8
\end{array}
$$

Fig. 1. Optimal execution order for the 3×3-multiplication given in equation (1)

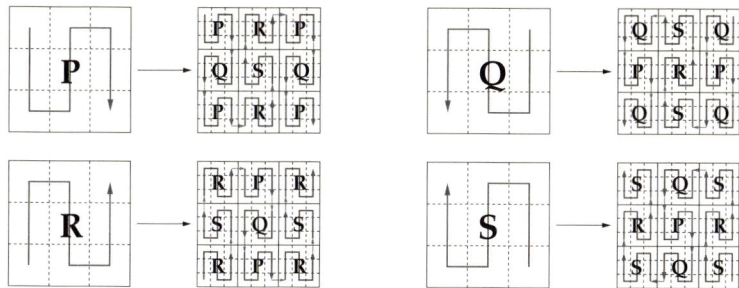

Fig. 2. Recursive construction of the Peano element order

blocks, standard column-major order is used, such that standard library routines (`dgemm`, e.g.) can be used for the sequential atomic block multiplications. Hence, the resulting hybrid numbering scheme is applicable to matrices of arbitrary size, including non-square matrices, if non-square atomic blocks are allowed.

The basic multiplication scheme for 3×3-matrices, as given in figure 1, extends to a block-recursive scheme for larger matrices, if we replace the matrix elements in (1) by matrix blocks numbered according to the Peano order. Equation (2) shows such a blockwise matrix multiplication. Each matrix block is named with respect to its numbering pattern and indexed with the name of the global matrix and the position within the storage scheme:

$$
\begin{pmatrix} P_{A0} & R_{A5} & P_{A6} \\ Q_{A1} & S_{A4} & Q_{A7} \\ P_{A2} & R_{A3} & P_{A8} \end{pmatrix} \begin{pmatrix} P_{B0} & R_{B5} & P_{B6} \\ Q_{B1} & S_{B4} & Q_{B7} \\ P_{B2} & R_{B3} & P_{B8} \end{pmatrix} = \begin{pmatrix} P_{C0} & R_{C5} & P_{C6} \\ Q_{C1} & S_{C4} & Q_{C7} \\ P_{C2} & R_{C3} & P_{C8} \end{pmatrix}. \quad (2)
$$

The block operations are executed following the scheme given in figure 1, starting with $P_{C0} \mathrel{+}= P_{A0} P_{B0}, Q_{C1} \mathrel{+}= Q_{A1} P_{B0}, P_{C2} \mathrel{+}= P_{A2} P_{B0}$, etc. For block multiplications such as $Q_{C1} \mathrel{+}= Q_{A1} P_{B0}$, where matrices are numbered according to alternate numbering patterns, schemes analogous to that in figure 1 are derived, where one, two, or all three of the indices of the three involved matrices are traversed in inverse order. The resulting eight recursive multiplication schemes can thus be combined into a single recursive procedure, where the three index traversal directions are given as parameters – cf. figure 5 in section 4 for a rough sketch or [1] for the full algorithm.

3 Exploiting the Peano Algorithm's Locality Properties

The resulting Peano algorithm for matrix multiplication has excellent locality properties, which are illustrated by its memory access pattern plotted in figure 3. In [1], we quantified these locality features by proving the following properties:

P1. The element traversal of all three involved matrices can be achieved entirely by index increments and decrements: after an element is accessed, the next access will be either to itself or to its direct left or right neighbour.

P2. Any sequence of k^3 floating point operations is executed on only $\mathcal{O}(k^2)$ contiguous elements in each matrix. Vice versa, on any block of k^2 contiguous elements, at least $\mathcal{O}(k^3)$ operations are performed. Hence, we can precisely predict how much computing time is spent on any given block of memory.

P3. As a result, a machine that only operates on a working memory consisting of M lines of L elements each, such as a cache memory or a replicated block of memory within a parallel computer, will require only $\mathcal{O}(n^3/(L\sqrt{M}))$ transfer operations to load matrix elements into the working memory – which is asymptotically optimal.

Property P1 motivates to use the model of a parallel, multi-tape Turing machine to describe the adopted approach to efficiently parallelise the Peano algorithm. Hence, let's consider the model of a parallel Turing machine with three tapes to store the matrices A, B, and C, and with several processing units that simultaneously access the shared Turing tapes via their respective read-write-heads (as illustrated in figure 4). Property P1 then guarantees that all read-write-heads will only move to directly neighbouring elements on the tapes.

To let our Turing machine more closely resemble real-world parallel computers, we allow each Turing unit to replicate a section of each matrix tape in some kind of local memory. Property P2 then guarantees that each Turing unit will spend a guaranteed amount of computing time within these replicated sections of memory. As at least $\mathcal{O}(k^3)$ operations will be executed, the units can precisely estimate when the end of the replicated section will be reached, and can thus issue a timely relocation of the replicated section (i.e. a prefetch of elements).

Finally, property P3 gives an estimate on how often the local copies of the Turing tapes have to be updated. Hence, if the tapes are stored in the distributed memory of a parallel computer, property P3 is a precise estimate of the required number of communication operations.

4 Parallelisation and Implementation

The parallel implementation of the Peano algorithm closely follows this idea of a multi-tape Turing machine. The Global Arrays toolkit [9] and the underlying ARMCI library [8] are used for distributed storage of the matrices and for communication. Each involved matrix is stored as a *global array*, which is evenly distributed to all available processes and takes the role of a Turing tape. Each processor holds a *tape cache* (as in figure 4) that is implemented to replicate a

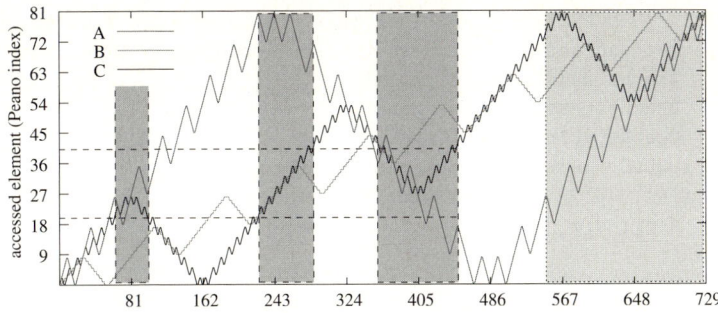

Fig. 3. Locality of data access during the Peano multiplication; the diagram shows the accessed memory locations within matrices A, B, and C throughout the 729 subsequent element operations of a 9×9 matrix multiplication. The grey boxes indicate one parallel partition when using the work-oriented partitioning (dotted box) or the *owner-computes* partitioning (dashed boxes) – see also section 4.

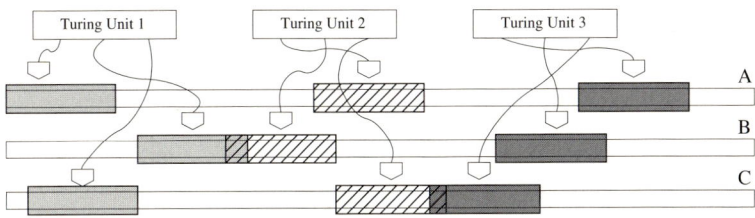

Fig. 4. Parallel Turing machine with several control units; each unit controls three heads that write to the three tapes jointly used to store the matrices. The highlighted parts of the matrix tapes are replicated in some local memory of the Turing units.

part of the global array in local memory. The tape caches are organised into four cache lines that hold a given number of atomic matrix blocks.

Two *read caches* replicate matrix blocks of A and B. The currently accessed cache line and its two (cyclic) neighbours always hold a contiguous section of the respective global array. The fourth block, in the meantime, prefetches one of the adjacent cache lines, using the phsA and phsB parameters to anticipate the next accessed block. As in the SRUMMA approach[7], non-blocking communication ensures that explicit prefetching into the tape cache and block multiplications on other tape cache lines are performed in parallel.

In addition, a *write cache* accumulates block products that have to be added to the result matrix C. A tape cache line that is accessed for the first time is initialised with zeros. At the same time, the least recently used cache line is written back to distributed memory by initiating a non-blocking operation that accumulates the intermediate result to the respective block of the result matrix (using ARMCI's non-blocking accumulate call NGA_NbAcc).

The tape cache mechanism is not only responsible for saving communication operations; it also encapsulates all communication operations and hides them

```
peanomult(int phsA, int phsB, int phsC, int dim) {
  if ((dim <= BLOCKSIZE) && /* block mult. in local task list */ ){
    // manage read and write access to matrix blocks in tape caches:
    Abuf = Acache.readAccess(a, phsA);
    Bbuf = Bcache.readAccess(b, phsB);
    Cbuf = Ccache.writeAccess(c);
    // call BLAS-dgemm for block matrix multiplication:
    dgemm ('n', 'n', dim, dim, dim, 1.0,
           Abuf, dim, Bbuf, dim, 1.0, Cbuf, dim);
  } else {
    /* 27 recursive calls: */
    peanomult( phsA, phsB, phsC, dim/3); a += phsA; c += phsC;
    peanomult( phsA,-phsB, phsC, dim/3); a += phsA; c += phsC;
    peanomult( phsA, phsB, phsC, dim/3); a += phsA; b += phsB;
    /* ... */
  } }
```

Fig. 5. Sketch of the parallelised Peano multiplication: the parameters phsA, phsB, and phsC (values ±1) control which of the eight recursive multiplication schemes is used. Acache, Bcache, and Ccache are the local tape caches for matrices A, B, and C. a, b, and c (here as global variables) are the starting indices of the current matrix blocks. Each processor performs the entire recursion, and decides for each atomic block multiplication whether this is part of its own task list.

from the rest of the implementation. The block recursive algorithm only requires one call for each matrix that requests the next accessed block from the respective tape cache – see figure 5 for the general structure of this algorithm.

For load distribution, the linear sequence of block multiplications generated by the Peano recursion is split into equally sized parts, which are distributed onto the available processors. For sufficiently small atomic blocks, this *task-list oriented* strategy leads to an excellent load balance. For example, three levels of recursion will lead to 27^3 atomic block operations – distributing these to 128 processors results in a load imbalance of less than 1 %. As an alternative approach, an *owner computes* scheme can be used, where each atomic block operation is performed by the processor that owns the respective atomic block of the result matrix C (see illustration in figure 3). This requires considerably smaller atomic block sizes to avoid load imbalances. However, this strategy completely avoids write access conflicts to the matrix C, and is therefore especially suited for multi- and manycore environments with shared cache memories[6].

5 Performance Results

The parallel implementation of the Peano algorithm was tested on an *Infiniband cluster* with 32 Opteron nodes; each node contains four AMD Opteron 850 processors (2.4 GHz) connected to 8 GB of shared memory, and is equipped with one MT23108 InfiniBand Host Channel Adapter card for communication. The atomic block multiplications were executed by the dgemm implementation of

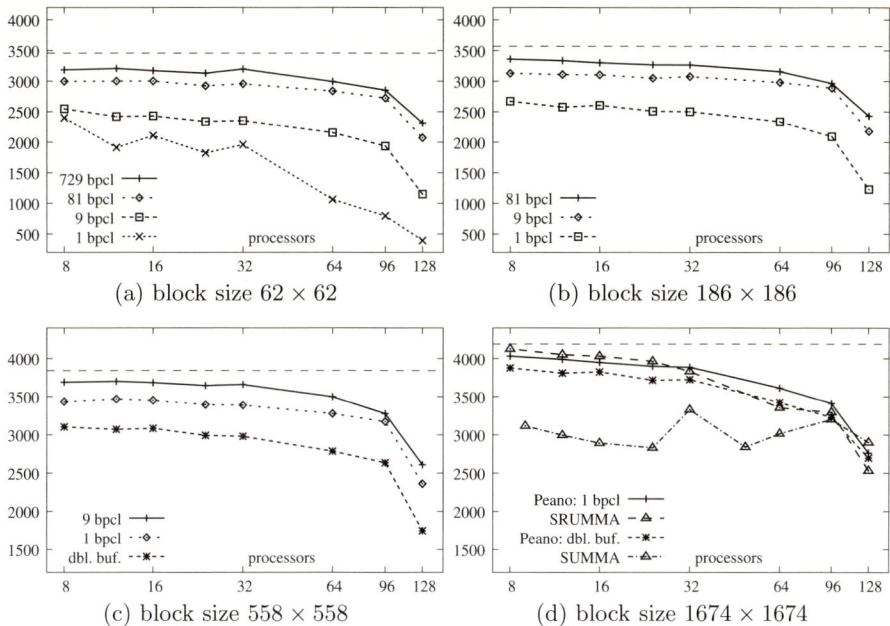

Fig. 6. Parallel efficiency of the parallel Peano algorithm: diagrams (a)–(d) show the achieved MFlop/s per processor for various atomic block sizes. Results are given for different sizes of the tape caches ('bpcl' = 'blocks per cache line') and, in (c) and (d) for double buffering ('dbl. buf.'). The dashed horizontal lines mark the achievable sequential performances for the respective block size. Diagram (d) gives the performance of SRUMMA[7] and ScaLAPACK's SUMMA implementation[5] for comparison.

ACML (AMD Core Math Library, v. 3.6.0). Performance was always evaluated in terms of achieved MFlop/s *per processor* to show the parallel efficiency of the method. The matrix size for all tests was 15066×15066. We used Peano layouts of 243×243, 81×81, 27×27, and 9×9 atomic blocks, starting with 62×62 as the smallest atomic block size (the best size for the level 1 hardware cache[6]).

Figure 6 shows the MFlop/s rates measured for increasing number of processors, and expresses how the parallel efficiency of the Peano algorithm depends on the size of the atomic blocks and of that of the tape caches. At least for up to 32 processors, the Peano implementation scales well for all atomic block sizes. For more processors, efficiency deteriorates, as several processors have to share only one InfiniBand adapter for communication, which noticeably reduces bandwidth and latency, and hence also parallel performance. We also observe a general increase of MFlop/s with growing size of the tape caches. By increasing the cache sizes, the performance can be driven close to the achievable sequential performance, which is determined by ACML's performance for the given block size (dashed lines). Diagram (d) also includes the performance of the SRUMMA implementation in Global Arrays [7,9] and that of ScaLAPACK's implementation of SUMMA[5] to show that the Peano implementation is well competitive

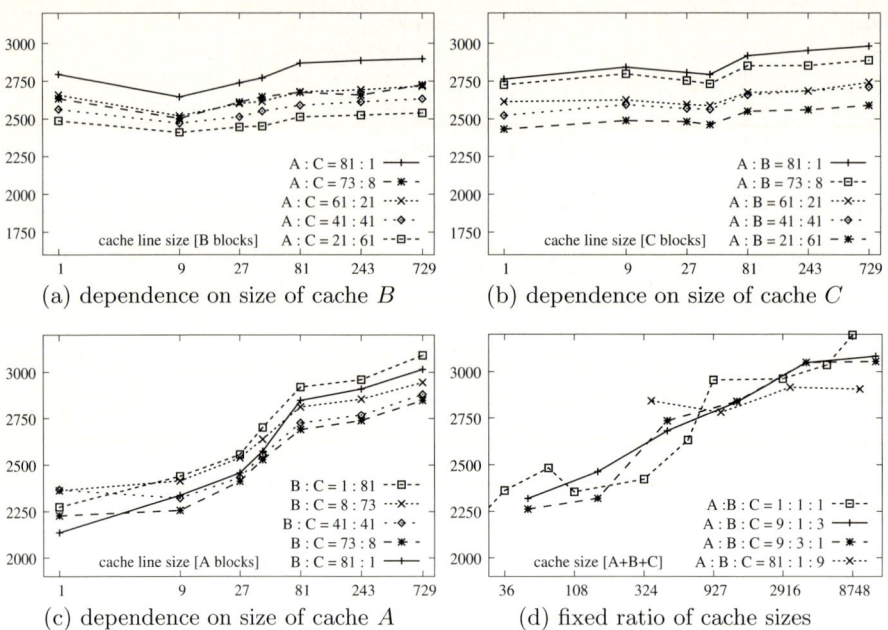

Fig. 7. Parallel efficiency (on 32 processors with uniform block size 62 × 62) for varying sizes of the tape caches for matrices A, B, and C. In plot (d), the given cache size indicates the total number of 62 × 62-blocks cached in all three tape caches.

compared to these established approaches. Apparently, SUMMA falls behind SRUMMA and the Peano algorithm, as long as these can overlap communication and computation. In contrast, SUMMA's minimisation of communication makes it less vulnerable to slow communication when all 128 processors are used.

From the memory access pattern given in figure 3, we can expect that choosing caches of different size for the three involved matrices should be advantageous. For example, the access pattern to B is much more local than that to A, which suggests a smaller cache for B. Judging from the access patterns an optimal cache size ratio of $A : B : C = 9 : 1 : 3$ is to be expected. Performance tests to study this aspect in detail are illustrated in figure 7: diagrams (a), (b), and (c), plot the performance when only one of the three cache sizes is increased while the respective other two cache sizes are kept constant. In addition, different size ratios between the other two caches were tested. Diagrams 7(a) and (b) indeed show a slight increase of performance with growing sizes of B and C; however, the more substantial performance gain seems to result from increasing the cache for A, which is supported by the results in figure 7(c), where an increase of the cache size for A, while keeping the cache sizes for B and C constant, leads to a much stronger performance gain. Figure 7(c) also indicates best performance, when the cache for C is chosen comparably large. Hence, figure 7(d) compares the performance when using different fixed ratios of the cache sizes. As expected, the ratio 9 : 1 : 3 leads to the smoothest increase of performance with growing total

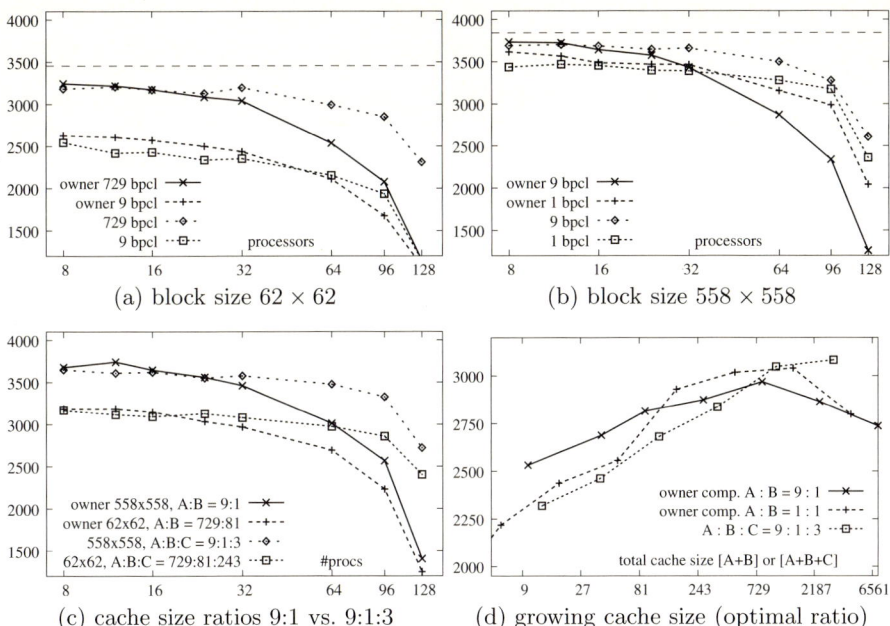

Fig. 8. Performance of the owner-computes scheme ('owner') compared to work-oriented distribution: In (a) and (b), results (in MFlop/s per processor) are given for different sizes of the tape caches (analogous to Fig. 6). In (c), the optimal cache size ratios where used (total cache size identical; two different block sizes). Plot (d) shows the impact of growing cache size (optimal vs. uniform cache size ratio).

cache size, and seems to be the best overall choice. However, the performance differences are small and are overlapped by local performance maxima that occur when a cache line size matches the block size of the Peano layout.

Figure 8 compares the performance when using the *owner computes* approach for load distribution instead of the regular work-oriented approach. The *owner computes* strategy proved to be faster for up to 16 or even 32 processors. For more processors, performance quickly deteriorates, and the work-oriented distribution is clearly the better choice. This slow-down is due to the additional cache misses that occur for the owner computes scheme (note the "splitted" owner-computes partition in figure 3). At such tape cache misses, prefetching of the operand matrices fails, and a blocking call to obtain the required matrix blocks is necessary. This leads to performance penalties for large blocks and especially for large tape cache lines, but also for short task lists (if comparably many processes are used), as then the number or the cost of the tape cache misses grows.

The results for the *owner computes* strategy are especially important for using the Peano algorithm on multi- and manycore platforms[6], because in such a setting the owner computes strategy avoids costly synchronisation of the write accesses to matrix C, and especially of resulting cache coherence conflicts.

6 Conclusion

The present study shows that the inherently cache efficient Peano algorithm can be turned into a competitive parallel implementation of matrix multiplication. The key idea is to include an additional cache level, the *tape caches*, to store and prefetch remote matrix blocks. The performance results show that the size of these caches is the key parameter to achieve optimal parallel efficiency. Thus, the Peano algorithm is especially suitable for situations where memory is scarce and can not easily be invested for replicating large remote matrix blocks.

Our primary aim, however, is to combine the hardware-oriented multicore implementation of our Peano algorithm[6] with the parallelisation approach presented in this paper, which will require the combination of the owner-computes approach with the work-oriented load distribution. In such an algorithm, only two components would need to be hardware-aware: the multiplication kernel for the atomic block multiplications has to be tuned to the specific CPU; and the size of the tape caches has to be adopted to the communication parameters (latency and bandwidth) of the parallel platform. The goal is a both parallel and cache oblivious algorithm that consequently exploits the Peano curve's locality properties on all memory levels, and therefore works well on parallel platforms of all kind – from multi- and manycore CPUs up to parallel compute clusters.

References

1. Bader, M., Zenger, C.: Cache oblivious matrix multiplication using an element ordering based on a Peano curve. Linear Algebra Appl. 417(2–3) (2006)
2. Bader, M., Franz, R., Guenther, S., Heinecke, A.: Hardware-oriented Implementation of Cache Oblivious Matrix Operations Based on Space-filling Curves. In: Wyrzykowski, R., Dongarra, J., Karczewski, K., Waśniewski, J. (eds.) PPAM 2007. LNCS, vol. 4967. Springer, Heidelberg (2008)
3. Choi, J., Dongarra, J.J., Walker, D.W.: PUMMA: Parallel Universal Matrix Multiplication Algorithms on Distributed Memory Concurrent Computers. Concurrency: Practice and Experience 6(7) (1994)
4. Elmroth, E., Gustavson, F., Jonsson, I., Kågström, B.: Recursive Blocked Algorithms and Hybrid Data Structures for Dense Matrix Library Software. SIAM Review 46(1) (2004)
5. van de Geijn, R., Watts, J.: SUMMA: Scalable Universal Matrix Multiplication Algorithm. Concurrency: Practice and Experience 9(4) (1997)
6. Heinecke, A., Bader, M.: Parallel Matrix Multiplication based on Space-filling Curves on Shared Memory Multicore Platforms. In: Proc. 2008 Computing Frontiers Conf. and co-located workshops: MAW 2008 & WREFT 2008, Ischia (2008)
7. Krishnan, M., Nieplocha, J.: SRUMMA: A Matrix Multiplication Algorithm Suitable for Clusters and Scalable Shared Memory Systems. In: Proc. of the 18th Int. Parallel and Distributed Processing Symposium (IPDPS 2004) (2004)
8. Nieplocha, J., Carpenter, B.: ARMCI: A Portable Remote Memory Copy Library for Distributed Array Libraries and Compiler Run-time Systems. In: Proc. of RTSPP IPPS/SDP (1999)
9. Nieplocha, J., Palmer, B., Tipparaju, V., Krishnan, M., Trease, H., Apra, E.: Advances, Applications and Performance of the Global Arrays Shared Memory Programming Toolkit. Int. J. of High Perf. Comp. Appl. 20(2) (2006)

Systematic Parallelization of Medical Image Reconstruction for Graphics Hardware

Maraike Schellmann, Jürgen Vörding, and Sergei Gorlatch

University of Münster, Germany
{schellmann,voerding,gorlatch}@uni-muenster.de

Abstract. Modern Graphics Processing Units (GPUs) consist of several SIMD-processors and thus provide a high degree of parallelism at low cost. We introduce a new approach to systematically develop parallel image reconstruction algorithms for GPUs from their parallel equivalents for distributed-memory machines. We use High-Level Petri Nets (HLPN) to intuitively describe the parallel implementations for distributed-memory machines. By denoting the functions of the HLPN with memory requirements and information about data distribution, we are able to identify parallel functions that can be implemented efficiently on the GPU. For an important iterative medical image reconstruction algorithm —the list-mode OSEM algorithm—we demonstrate the limitations of its distributed-memory implementation and show how our HLPN-based approach leads to a fast implementation on GPUs, reusable across different medical imaging devices.

1 Introduction

In order to achieve good scalability, time-consuming numerical algorithms need to be parallelized on architectures with both a high degree of parallelism and large memory bandwidth. One such architecture is the modern Graphics Processing Unit (GPU) that comprises one or several SIMD (Single Instruction Multiple Data) processors. High-level languages for the general purpose GPU programming like CUDA [3] (Compute Unified Device Architecture) and BrookGPU [1] have emerged recently; they allow developers to write reasonably fast code for the GPU without dealing with the details of the underlying hardware. However, implementing GPU algorithms from scratch is often error-prone and results in implementations that lack modularity and reusability [5].

We focus on the GPU parallelization problem for iterative medical image reconstruction algorithms that solve large, sparse linear systems for a 3D reconstruction image, with a potential to extend our approach to a broader class of numerical algorithms, including iterative linear system solvers. In our approach, we use already existing parallel algorithms for distributed-memory architectures to identify parts that can be re-implemented efficiently in a data-parallel manner on the GPU. We use High-Level Petri Nets (HLPN) to describe parallel algorithms in a simple, intuitive way. We then annotate the HLPN with memory requirements and the type of data distribution that is used in the distributed-memory algorithm. This additional information allows us to identify data-parallelism (which is needed in order to use the SIMD processors efficiently) and memory requirements (which are important due to the comparatively small amount of memory available on the GPU) for the parallel functions.

All iterative medical image reconstruction algorithms share similar computation and communication patterns, because they are usually either multiplicative or additive versions of the Kaczmarz method [4]. Hence, our approach can be applied to all such algorithms. As an example algorithm which we parallelize for GPUs using our Petri Net approach, we use a very accurate, but also quite time-consuming algorithm used in PET (Positron Emission Tomography) reconstruction: the list-mode OSEM (Ordered Subset Expectation Maximization) [7]. We present two parallel strategies for this algorithm on the distributed-memory architecture and show their limitations. By using the Petri Net approach to re-implement these parallel strategies on the GPU, we overcome the limitations of the distributed-memory architecture and, at the same time, facilitate code reusability and modularity.

In medical image reconstruction, the lack of reusability of GPU parallelizations becomes very critical: Previous GPU implementations of the list-mode OSEM algorithm (as shown in [6]), as well as implementations for other iterative reconstruction techniques in medical image reconstruction (see [12]), have focused on the parallelization within the so-called *projection* step. This leads to poor reusability of the code: Different PET devices require different projections, and therefore, for each new device type, a new projection and thus a new GPU parallelization has to be implemented.

The remainder of this paper is structured as follows: we start with an introduction to PET and the list-mode OSEM algorithm in Section 2. We then describe the parallelization of the list-mode OSEM algorithm on distributed-memory computers in Section 3. In Section 4, we introduce our main contribution, the new Petri Net approach, and describe its application to the strategies developed in Section 3. We present experimental results in Section 5 and finally conclude the paper in Section 6.

2 PET and the List-Mode OSEM Algorithm

Positron Emission Tomography (*PET*) is a medical imaging technique that displays metabolic processes in a human or animal body. The data for reconstruction are collected in the PET acquisition process as follows. A slightly radioactive substance which emits positrons is applied to the patient who is placed inside a *scanner*. Each scanner type has a different number of detectors that can be arranged either on rings or banks surrounding the patient. The detectors of a scanner measure so-called *events*: When the emitted positrons of the radioactive substance collide with an electron residing in the surrounding tissue near the decaying spot, they are annihilated. During annihilation, two gamma rays emit from the annihilation spot in opposite directions and form a line, see Fig. 1. For each gamma ray pair, one event, i.e., the two involved detector elements, is saved.

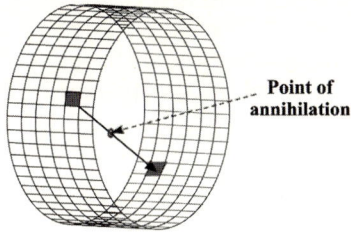

Fig. 1. Detectors register an event in a PET-scanner with 6 detector rings

During one investigation, typically $5 \cdot 10^7$ to $5 \cdot 10^8$ events are registered. From these events, a reconstruction algorithm computes a 3D image of the substance distribution in the body.

We focus in this work on the list-mode OSEM reconstruction algorithm [7] which is an enhanced version of the list-mode Expectation Maximization (EM) algorithm. EM solves the overdetermined linear system $A f = \mathbf{1}$ iteratively for the reconstruction image f, where $\mathbf{1} = (1, ..., 1)$ and A is a matrix with elements $a_{i,j}$ estimating the probability that the emission corresponding to event i has happened in voxel j. The computation of one row A_i of matrix A for event i is called *projection*. In general, for each estimate $a_{i,j} \in A_i$, the amount of intersection of voxel j with the line between the centers of the two detectors of event i is computed on the fly during each iteration. However, more accurate projection algorithms take into account, among others, the detector shape and gamma ray scatter inside the detector. Therefore, for each scanner, there is a different most accurate projection algorithm and it is thus critical for an implementation to be able to easily interchange projection algorithms; such implementations are called *reusable*.

The list-mode OSEM algorithm speeds up the notoriously slow EM algorithm by computing several image updates per iteration: the input dataset—consisting of all measured events—is divided into s equally-sized blocks of events, so-called subsets. The starting image vector is $f_0 = (1, ..., 1) \in \mathbb{R}^N$ (N is the number of voxels in the reconstruction image). For each subset $l \in 0, ..., s-1$, a new, more precise reconstruction image f_{l+1} is computed and used iteratively for the next subset computation as follows:

$$f_{l+1} = f_l c_l; \quad c_l = \frac{1}{A_{norm}^t \mathbf{1}} \sum_{i \in S_l} (A_i)^t \frac{1}{A_i f_l}, \tag{1}$$

where S_l are the indices of events in subset l. The normalization vector $\frac{1}{A_{norm}^t \mathbf{1}}$ is independent of the current subset and can thus be precalculated. After one iteration over all subsets, the reconstruction process can either be stopped, or the result can be improved with further iterations.

3 Distributed-Memory Parallelization

We start with the two strategies for the distributed-memory parallelization of the list-mode OSEM algorithm which we analyzed in [11]:

1. the PSD (Projection Space Decomposition) strategy and
2. the ISD (Image Space Decomposition) strategy.

Since f_{l+1} depends on f_l in (1), both strategies need to parallelize the computations within one subset.

In the PSD (Projection Space Decomposition) strategy, we decompose the input data, i.e., the events of one subset, into p (=number of processors) blocks and compute the forward projection for these blocks simultaneously. The calculations for one subset proceed in five steps, see Fig. 2(a):

- **read:** Every processor reads its part of the subsets' events.
- **proj:** All processors k_j compute simultaneously $c_{l,j} = \sum_{i \in S_{l,j}} (A_i)^t \frac{1}{A_i f_l}$.
- **reduce:** The processors' results $c_{l,j}$ are summed up over the network.
- **update:** $f_{l+1} = f_l c_l$ is computed on one processor.
- **broadcast:** f_{l+1} is sent to all other processors.

In the Image Space Decomposition (ISD) strategy, the output data, i.e., the reconstruction image, is decomposed into p sub-images f^j, $j = 1, ..., p$. The computations proceed as follows, see Fig. 2(b):

- **read:** Every processor reads all the subsets' events.
- **forwproj:** Each processor k_j performs the forward projection for sub-image f^j, i.e., it computes $b_{i,j} = A_i^j f^j$ events $i \in S_l$, where A^j is a sub-matrix of A that is restricted to the voxels in f^j.
- **allreduce:** $b_{i,j}$ are summed up, with the result b_i residing on all processors.
- **update:** Each processor k_j computes $a f^j \sum_{i \in S_l} (A_i^j)^t \frac{1}{b_i}$ for its subimage f^j.

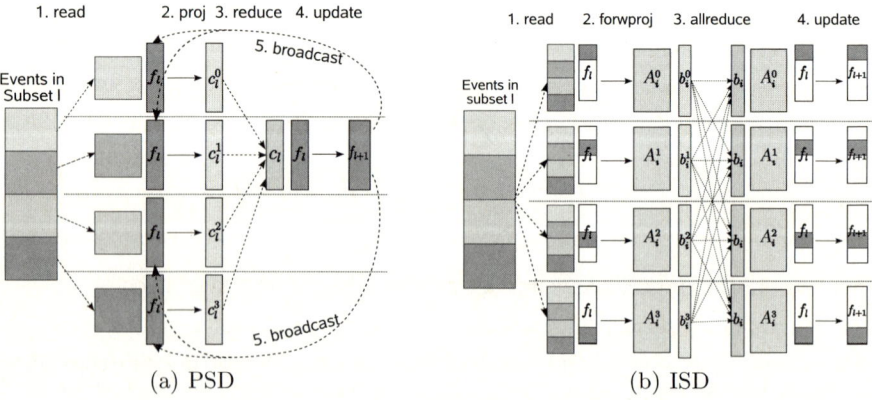

(a) PSD (b) ISD

Fig. 2. Parallel strategies (PSD and ISD) on four distributed-memory processors

On cluster computers, the PSD strategy outperforms the ISD strategy in almost all cases [11], because, in the ISD strategy, large amounts of data have to be read from the remote file system and load imbalances arise from the non-uniform distribution of the radioactive substance inside the reconstruction region. Only in the case of very few events per subset, the ISD strategy is preferable to the PSD strategy.

4 Parallelization: From Distributed-Memory to GPU

4.1 GPU Architecture and Language Support

Modern GPUs (Graphics Processing Units) can be viewed as mathematical co-processors: they add computing power to the CPU. GPUs are primarily designed for the 3D gaming sector, where they support the CPU of commodity PCs to gain better performance, resulting in high-quality graphics at high-screen resolution.

A GPU is a parallel machine (see Fig. 3) that consists of SIMD (Single Instruction Multiple Data) multiprocessors (ranging from 1 to 16). The stream processors of a SIMD multiprocessor are called shader units. The GPU (also called *device*) has its own fast memory with an amount of up to 1.5 GB. On the off-the-shelf main board, one or two GPUs can be installed and used as coprocessors simultaneously. The GeForce 8800 GTX, which we use in our experiments, provides 768 MB device memory and has 16 multiprocessors each with 8 shader units. With CUDA (Compute Unified Device Architecture) [3], the GPU vendor NVIDIA provides a programming interface that introduces the thread-programming concept on GPUs to the C programming language. A block of threads executing the same code fragment, the so-called *kernel* program, runs on one multiprocessor. Each thread of this block runs on one of the shader units of the GPU, each unit executing the kernel on a different data element. All blocks of threads of one application are distributed among the multiprocessors by the *scheduler*. The GPU's device memory is shared among all threads. Among the main features the CUDA programming interface (present version 1.0) lacks, compared to a traditional thread library like pthreads, are mechanisms for mutual

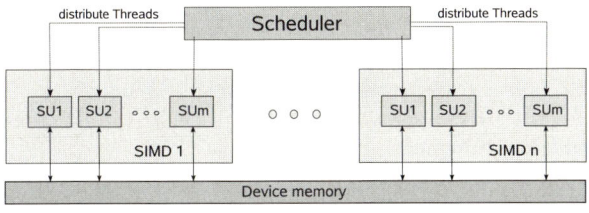

Fig. 3. GPU architecture of modern NVIDIA GPUs: n is the number of multiprocessors, m is the number of shader units. SIMD k denotes the k-th multiprocessor, SU k denotes the k-th shader unit of the multiprocessor.

exclusion like semaphores and monitors. In the next section, we show how the lack of mutual exclusion mechanisms impacts the design and programming of parallel algorithms on the GPU.

4.2 Identification of Data-Parallel Functions Using Petri Nets

Our goal in the Petri Net approach is to systematically develop parallel algorithms for GPUs from HLPN that describe parallel distributed-memory algorithms. HLPN [2] (see Fig. 4 and Fig. 5) consist of places (empty circles), holding data (filled circles), which are linked to transitions (rectangles). If all input places of a transition contain a data element, the transition "fires", i.e., the function corresponding to the transition is executed. The results of the function are placed in one or more output places, which can either be the endpoint of a graph, or again input for preceding transitions. We allow guards for conditional execution of transitions. In order to visualize the parallelism in the Petri Nets, transitions performed on all processors are filled with hatched bars, whereas the fully filled transitions are only computed sequentially on one processor.

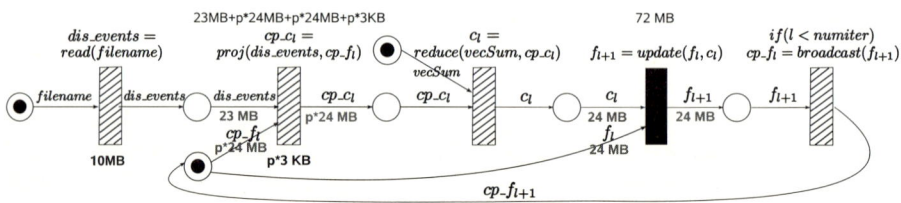

Fig. 4. HLPN for the PSD strategy. The numbers below the different data elements denote their memory requirement.

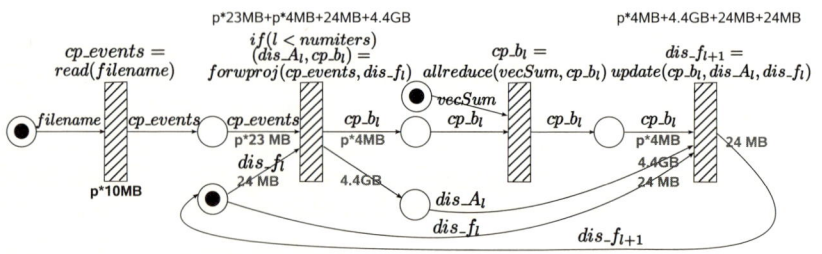

Fig. 5. HLPN for the ISD strategy. The numbers below the different data elements denote their memory requirement.

The idea is to examine two aspects of the parallel algorithm for distributed-memory architectures: 1) the amount of data-parallelism, and 2) the required amount of memory. We start with a HLPN presented in Fig. 4 and Fig. 5. For each of the four steps, we show its application to the parallel PSD and ISD strategy:

1. **Identification of data-parallel functions from parallel transitions:**
The HLPN is annotated with additional information: "*dis_*" prefixes are added to the data elements that are distributed among the processors, whereas the data elements with local copies on each processor are denoted with "*cp_*". The "*dis_*" data elements that are input to a parallel transition now indicate data parallelism for the associated parallel function; i.e., the function can be computed simultaneously on different parts of the data. In Fig. 4 and Fig. 5, we annotated the HLPN for the PSD and the ISD strategy with the two prefixes. Since the "*dis_events*" are input to the parallel *proj* function of the PSD strategy and the "*dis_f_l*" are input to the parallel *forwproj* and the parallel *update* function of the ISD strategy, these three functions can be computed in a data-parallel manner.

2. **Identification of data-parallel functions from sequential transitions:**
Each sequential function is analyzed for data-parallelism that could not be exploited on the distributed-memory architecture, due to the large communication overhead arising from the distribution and collection of data. In the PSD strategy, the *update* function multiplies f_l and c_l element-wise; this can be done in a data-parallel way.

3. **Annotation of data-parallel transitions with memory requirements:**
The data-parallel transitions identified in the two previous steps and their in- and output edges are annotated with their memory requirements. For each data element, the amount of data on the total cluster is annotated; e.g., if one data element takes up k MB on one processor, then the "*cp_*"-prefixed data element takes up p*k MB on the total cluster (p is the number of processors). For each transition, the total memory requirement of the corresponding function is annotated.

4. **Translation and evaluation of memory requirements on the GPU:**
The "*dis_*"-annotated data elements will use the same amount of data on the GPU as on the cluster. For "*cp_*" data elements, it has to be decided if the local copies on all processors are identical; if so, only one copy has to be kept in the device memory from which all GPU processors can read and, thus, requirements are divided by p. The data-parallel functions' memory requirements remain unchanged. Now, for each transition, the total amount of required device memory is added up and is compared to the device memory available on a given GPU. As described in steps 1 and 2, we identified four data-parallel functions: the *proj* and *update* functions of the PSD strategy, and the *forwproj* and *update* function of the ISD strategy.

In CUDA, memory latency is hidden by starting several threads per shader unit [8]. Hence, the identified data-parallel functions should provide fine-grained parallelism in order to obtain a fast GPU implementation. However, the "*dis*" prefix with which we identified data-parallel functions (step 1) implies that one thread can be started for each input data element and, thus, fine granularity of the identified functions is guaranteed.

In general, memory requirements are a function in the algorithm's input parameters and input data size. For our particular algorithm, the memory requirements depend on the reconstruction image size and the number of events per subset. In order to simplify matters in this example, we do not determine memory requirements as a function of parameters, but rather use the particular memory requirements of the reconstruction setup that delivers the most accurate images for our scanner: The image size is $150 \cdot 150 \cdot 280 = 6,300,000$ voxels which take up 24 MB memory and the number of events per subset are 1,000,000 which take up 23 MB memory.

Steps 3 and 4, applied to the *forwproj* function, show that the whole system matrix for each subset $A_l \in \mathbb{R}^{m \times N}$ (m is the number of events per subset), which takes up 4.4 GB memory, has to be kept in the device memory, because it is used again as input to the update function. Thus the memory requirements add up to 24 MB+p*4 MB+4.4 GB≈4.9 GB. With only 768 MB device memory, the ISD strategy is not feasible to be computed on the GPU. The *update* function of the PSD strategy only requires 72 MB device memory (see Fig. 4) and thus can be parallelized on the GPU. The *proj* function also requires 47 MB+p*3 KB+p*24 MB of device memory (see the sum above the *proj* transition in Fig. 4). With the p=128 shader units of our GPU, this adds up to more than 3 GB, with again only 768 MB device memory available. We needed to adapt the original PSD strategy and, therefore, decided not to use separate *proj* and *reduce* steps. Now, each GPU thread writes directly to the shared c_l that resides on the device memory.

One general problem of the CUDA library is its lack of mechanisms for avoiding race conditions (e.g., semaphores). In our case, it would be helpful to protect c_l with a semaphore and thus allow only one thread at a time to write its result. Since this is not supported by CUDA, we decided to allow race conditions due to the following considerations:

- When two threads add one float concurrently to $c_{l,i}$, then, in the worst case, one thread overwrites the result of another; i.e., a small error occurs in $c_{l,i}$.
- The size of c_l is high as compared to the number of parallel writing threads (in our case 6,300,000 voxels vs. 128 threads); therefore, the number of race conditions and thus incorrect voxels is small. We estimated experimentally that only for about 0.04 % of all writes to c_l, a race condition occurs.
- Most importantly: due to the few and very small incorrectnesses in the image, the maximum relative error over all voxels is less than 1 %, which leads to no visual effect on the reconstructed images. However, in order to use the GPU implementation in practice, we will perform a study with many different sets of input data and parameters studied by medical doctors.

With these adjustments to the *proj* function, its memory requirements only add up to 71 MB+p*3 KB≈72 MB for $p = 128$. But even in the best case, where the maximum number of $p = 12288$ threads are started simultaneously, memory requirements only add up to ≈107 MB.

The calculation of one subset on p SIMD processors of the GPU now proceeds as follows:

- **read:** The CPU reads the subsets' events and copies them to the GPU
- **proj:** All processors k_j compute simultaneously $c_{l,j} = \sum_{i \in S_{l,j}} (A_i)^t \frac{1}{A_i f_l}$, $c_{l,j}$ is directly added to c_l.

– **update:** f is divided into sub-images f^j and each processor computes $f^j_{l+1} = f^j_l \, c^j_l$ on its sub-image.

If the target parallel machine has two GPUs available, we have two separate device memories. The computations in this case can proceed as above, with each GPU computing half of the events during the forward-projections and half of the sub-images during the computation of f_{l+1}. After all forward-projections, the two c_ls residing on the device memories are summed up.

The resulting parallel implementation is reusable for different types of PET scanners: a new scanner can be introduced by simply exchanging the sequential projection that computes a_i in the *proj* function. For traditional implementations that parallelize the projection itself, this exchange would require a new, complicated and error-prone parallelization. Furthermore, our implementation is modular, because new functions can be added or interchanged easily; this could be helpful, e.g., when pre- and postprocessing steps are added.

5 Experimental Results (Distributed-Memory vs. GPU)

In our performance experiments, we studied the reconstruction of data collected by the quadHIDAC small-animal PET scanner [10]. We used 10 million events collected during a mouse scan divided in 10 subsets. The reconstruction image has the size $N = (150 \times 150 \times 280)$.

Based on a sequential C++ implementation of the list-mode OSEM algorithm, we used MPI (Message Passing Interface) for our parallelization on a distributed-memory cluster using the two presented decomposition strategies. We performed runtime experiments on the Arminius cluster with 200 Dual INTEL Xeon 3.2 GHZ 64bit nodes, each with 4 GByte main memory, connected by an InfiniBand network. In order to obtain results for the distributed-memory architecture, we used only one of each node's processors. To exploit the fast InfiniBand interconnect, we used the Scali MPI Connect [9] implementation on this machine. In this typical setup, the PSD strategy outperforms the ISD strategy. We measured a minimum runtime of the PSD strategy on 32 processors of

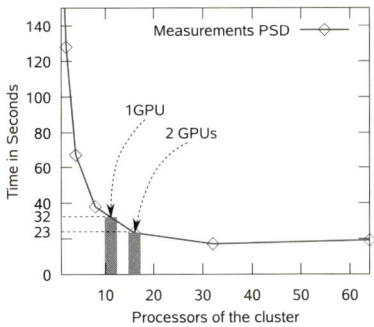

Fig. 6. Runtimes on cluster and GPUs

17.2 seconds (see Fig. 6). With more processors, runtime deteriorates due to the large amounts of data to be communicated per subset. Since sequential runtime measured on one processor of this cluster is about 233 seconds, we achieved a speedup of 13.5 on 32 processors.

For our experiments with graphics processing units, we used two GPUs of the type NVIDIA GeForce 8800 GTX. They have 16 SIMD-multiprocessors, each with 8 shader units running at 1.35 GHz. The device memory is 768 MB. Our CPU is a 2.4 GHz dual-core processor with 2 GB main memory. The average measured runtime is about 32 seconds on one GPU, see Fig. 6. With two GPUs, we achieve a runtime of about 23 seconds. Hence, our parallel GPU parallelization is only about 1.3 times slower than the cluster reconstruction with 32 processors.

We observe similar scalability results for other typical image sizes N on the cluster as well as on the GPU. However, images with $N > 5 \cdot 10^8$ cannot be reconstructed on the GPU because of the small amount of available device memory. This is irrelevant for the quadHIDAC scanner or any other PET scanner at our university hospital, but it could become an issue for future, higher-resolution scanners.

6 Conclusion

We presented a novel approach to systematically develop parallel algorithms for GPUs starting from parallel algorithms for distributed-memory machines. Although we so far limited our considerations to medical imaging, the HLPN approach can be used to analyze data-parallelism and memory requirements for parallel algorithms with the two following properties: First, the distributed-memory implementation has to be made up of separable functions; i.e., each function output is used as input for the subsequent function and no functions are called from within other functions. Second, the memory requirements of the parallel functions can be determined as a function of input parameters and the size of input data. One of the areas where these requirements are fulfilled, are iterative linear system solvers, and, in particular, medical image reconstruction algorithms like the list-mode OSEM algorithm. For the algorithms with data-parallel functions that fulfill the memory requirements, a fast and modular implementation on GPUs can be developed systematically.

For a 3D medical imaging algorithm, we demonstrated in detail how our approach is used to develop a fast, modular and reusable implementation on GPUs. The runtime of the parallel algorithm on two state-of-the-art GPUs is 1.3 times slower than the runtime on 32 processors of a computer cluster. If we take into account the much higher costs for purchase and even more for administration of a distributed-memory cluster, we come to the conclusion that GPU parallelization is a cost-effective choice for list-mode OSEM medical image reconstruction.

Acknowledgments

We thank the NVIDIA corporation for the donation of graphic hardware used in our experiments. We also thank the University of Paderborn for letting us use the

Arminius Cluster. Special thanks go to Dominik Meiländer for his work on the GPU parallelization. This work was partly funded by the Deutsche Forschungsgemeinschaft, SFB 656 MoBil (Project B2). We are grateful to the anonymous referees for their helpful comments.

References

1. Buck, I., Foley, T., Horn, D., Sugerman, J., Fatahalian, K., Houston, M., Hanrahan, P.: Brook for GPUs: Stream Computing in graphics hardware. ACM Trans. Graph. 23(3), 777–786 (2004)
2. Girault, C., Valk, R. (eds.): Petri Nets for System Engineers. Springer, Berlin (2003)
3. NVIDIA. NVIDIA CUDA Compute Unified Device Architecture, http://developer.nvidia.com/object/cuda.html
4. Natterer, F., Wuebbeling, F.: Mathematical Methods in Image Reconstruction. SIAM, Philadelphia (2001)
5. Owens, J.D., Luebke, D., Govindaraju, N., Harris, M., Krüger, J., Lefohn, A.E., Purcell, T.J.: A Survey of General-Purpose Computation on Graphics Hardware. Comp. Graph. Forum 26(1), 80–113 (2007)
6. Pratx, G., Chinn, G., Habte, F., Olcott, P., Levin, C.: Fully 3-D list-mode OSEM accelerated by graphics processing units. In: IEEE Nuclear Science Symposium Conference Record, vol. 4, pp. 2196–2202. IEEE, Los Alamitos (2006)
7. Reader, A.J., Erlandsson, K., Flower, M.A., Ott, R.J.: Fast accurate iterative reconstruction for low-statistics positron volume imaging. Phys. Med. Biol. 43(4), 823–834 (1998)
8. Ryoo, S., Rodrigues, C., Baghsorkhi, S., Stone, S., Kirk, D., Hwu, W.: Optimization principles and application performance evaluation of a multithreaded GPU using CUDA. In: PPoPP 2008: Proc. of the 13th ACM SIGPLAN Symposium, pp. 73–82 (2008)
9. Scali MPI connect, http://www.scali.com/
10. Schäfers, K.P., Reader, A.J., Kriens, M., Knoess, C., Schober, O., Schäfers, M.: Performance evaluation of the 32-module quadHIDAC small-animal PET scanner. Journal Nucl. Med. 46(6), 996–1004 (2005)
11. Schellmann, M., Gorlatch, S.: Comparison of two decomposition strategies for parallelizing the 3D list-mode OSEM algorithm. In: Proceedings Fully 3D Meeting and HPIR Workshop, pp. 37–40 (2007)
12. Xu, F., Mueller, K.: Accelerating popular tomographic reconstruction algorithms on commodity PC graphics hardware. IEEE Trans. Nucl. Sci. 52(3), 654–663 (2005)

Load-Balancing for a Block-Based Parallel Adaptive 4D Vlasov Solver[*]

Olivier Hoenen and Eric Violard

University Louis Pasteur - LSIIT - ICPS, Strasbourg, France
{hoenen,violard}@icps.u-strasbg.fr
http://www-math.u-strasbg.fr/calvi

Abstract. This work is devoted to the numerical resolution of the 4D Vlasov equation using an adaptive mesh of phase space. We previously proposed a parallel algorithm designed for distributed memory architectures. The underlying numerical scheme makes possible a parallelization using a block-based mesh partitioning. Efficiency of this algorithm relies on maintaining a good load balance at a low cost during the whole simulation. In this paper, we propose a dynamic load balancing mechanism based on a geometric partitioning algorithm. This mechanism is deeply integrated into the parallel algorithm in order to minimize overhead. Performance measurements on a PC cluster show the good quality of our load balancing and confirm the pertinence of our approach.

1 Introduction

The Vlasov equation is a non-linear partial differential equation that describes the evolution in time of charged particles under the effects of external and self-consistent electro-magnetic fields. It is used to model important phenomena in plasma physics such as controlled thermonuclear fusion. This equation is defined in the phase space which has 6 dimensions in the real case (one dimension of velocity for each dimension of position).

Amongst the numerical methods for solving the Vlasov equation, recent Eulerian methods (see [1,2]) based on the semi-Lagrangian scheme [3] are of great interest to get an accurate description of the physics. These methods have proven their efficiency on uniform meshes in two dimensional phase space. But when the dimensionality increases, the number of points on a uniform grid becomes very important which makes numerical simulations challenging.

Two approaches have been investigated to simulate four dimensional problems: adaptive methods and parallel algorithms. Adaptive methods decrease computational cost drastically by keeping only a subset of all grid points. Some semi-Lagrangian adaptive methods have been developed, like in [4] and [5,6] where the authors use a moving grid or a multi-resolution analysis based on interpolating wavelets. But, few works use both approaches. A main difficulty in

---

[*] This work was partially supported by a grant from Alsace Region and is part of the french INRIA project CALVI.

developing a time-dependent highly adaptive solver is achieving a good load balancing. At our knowledge, existing parallelized version of these adaptive methods are essentially designed for shared memory architectures [7,8].

In the present work, we investigate another adaptive method for solving the four dimensional Vlasov equation. This scheme is based on a hierarchical finite element decomposition [9] and on a convenient time splitting. It has been designed for targeting distributed memory architectures. This scheme and its parallelization have been introduced in [10]. This previous work tackles load balancing through a static partitioning based on initial function values. In this paper, we address the crucial problem of maintaining a good load balancing during the whole simulation. In order to solve this problem, we developed a suited dynamic load-balancing mechanism based on a geometric partitioning algorithm.

The paper is organized as follows: next section recalls our numerical scheme and parallel algorithm. Section 3 presents our load balancing mechanism and its integration into the algorithm. Section 4 reports performances obtained on a PC cluster before concluding.

2 The Parallel Adaptive Solver

Evolution of particles in the phase space is given by a distribution function $f((\mathbf{x}, \mathbf{v}), t)$ where $(\mathbf{x}, \mathbf{v}) \in \mathbb{R}^d \times \mathbb{R}^d, d = 1, ..., 3$. Value of this function is given by the normalized Vlasov equation,

$$\frac{\partial f}{\partial t} + \mathbf{v}.\nabla_{\mathbf{x}} f + \boldsymbol{E}(\mathbf{x}, t).\nabla_{\mathbf{v}} f = 0 \qquad (1)$$

where the self-consistent electric field $\boldsymbol{E}(\mathbf{x}, t)$ is computed using the Poisson's equation from the charge density $\rho(\mathbf{x}, t)$

$$\rho(\mathbf{x}, t) = \int_{\mathbb{R}^d} f(\mathbf{x}, \mathbf{v}) d\mathbf{v} \qquad (2)$$

In this work we consider the reduced case of a four dimensional phase space ($d = 2$) where $\mathbf{x} = (x, y) \in \mathbb{R}^2$ and $\mathbf{v} = (v_x, v_y) \in \mathbb{R}^2$. We refer the reader to [10] for more details about this numerical resolution scheme and its parallelization.

2.1 Numerical Scheme

Our adaptive mesh is a structured *dyadic mesh*, i.e., a hierarchical mesh with at most J levels, where each cell at level j is a 4-cube that may be subdivided into 16 equal-sized cells at level $j+1$. Coarsest cells (at level 0) belongs to an 4D uniform grid that we call the *coarse grid*.

Our resolution scheme is based on the splitting in time of the Vlasov equation into three transport equations in x, in y and in $\mathbf{v}$. Time is discretized and at each time step $\Delta t = t^{n+1} - t^n$, the three transport equations are solved in turn. The solution of a transport equation is used as initial condition for solving the following one. For any axis direction z, we solve a transport equation in z

by using a semi-Lagrangian scheme based on the conservation property [3] of solution:

$$f((\mathbf{x}, \mathbf{v}), t^{n+1}) = f(\mathcal{A}_{\Delta t}^z(\mathbf{x}, \mathbf{v}), t^n) \tag{3}$$

where $\mathcal{A}_{\Delta t}^z$ is called *advection operator*. This advection operator defines the particles motion along z direction. We have $\mathcal{A}_{\Delta t}^x(\mathbf{x}, \mathbf{v}) = ((x - v_x.\Delta t, y), \mathbf{v})$, $\mathcal{A}_{\Delta t}^y(\mathbf{x}, \mathbf{v}) = ((x, y - v_y.\Delta t), \mathbf{v})$ and $\mathcal{A}_{\Delta t}^{\mathbf{v}}(\mathbf{x}, \mathbf{v}) = (\mathbf{x}, \mathbf{v} - E(\mathbf{x}, t^n).\Delta t)$. The procedure to solve a transport equation in z is called *advection*. It finds a representation (on a dyadic mesh) of the solution at time t^{n+1} from a known representation of the solution at time t^n in three steps:

1. (prediction) We build a new dyadic mesh with enough nodes to get an accurate representation of solution at time t^{n+1}.
2. (valuation) We compute the values at the new mesh nodes from conservation property: each value at point $(\mathbf{x}, \mathbf{v})$ is obtained by a biquadratic Lagrange interpolation from the values at the old mesh nodes close to point $\mathcal{A}_{\Delta t}^z(\mathbf{x}, \mathbf{v})$.
3. (compression) We coarsen some new mesh cells to remove unnecessary nodes that were improperly created during prediction step.

The electric field E is computed on a uniform grid at the finest level J of the 2D position space. We first integrate f to get the discrete charge density ρ at each point of this uniform grid. This is achieved by computing the contribution of every cell of the dyadic mesh and then by computing the sum of all these contributions. Then, we solve the Poisson's equation by using Fourier transforms. Since the value of E is required for performing the advection in $\mathbf{v}$, the computation of E precedes this advection within each time-step iteration.

Figure 1 summarizes our resolution scheme and shows the successive operations within each time-step iteration. For sake of conciseness, specific treatments for diagnostics have been omitted.

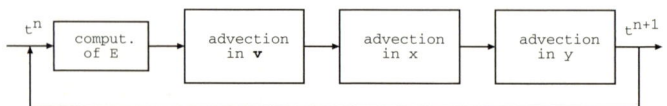

Fig. 1. The time-step iteration of our resolution scheme

2.2 Parallel Algorithm

An important property of our numerical scheme is that each step of an advection (prediction, valuation and compression) can be performed locally within a region of the phase space independently of the others. Therefore, given any partitioning of the phase space, an advection can be performed by applying the same treatment to every partition independently. This is the base of our data-parallel algorithm. Each processor is assigned to one partition. It holds in its local memory all the data within this partition, i.e., the corresponding parts of the old and new meshes. According to the classical owner computes rule, it is in charge of all the computations local to this partition. We define a *partition* as an union of *blocks*, where a block is defined as the 4D cube-shaped phase space area corresponding to a cell of the coarse grid. Our partitioning aims at reducing communication volume and is based on the following dependency analysis.

The data dependencies are defined by the advection operators: value at point $(\mathbf{x}, \mathbf{v})$ depends on the values at a few points close to point $\mathcal{A}_{\Delta t}^z(\mathbf{x}, \mathbf{v})$. Given the advection operator only acts on one particular axis (x, y or $\mathbf{v}$) while letting the other coordinates unchanged, the treatment of any block only requires data within some blocks along the same axis. For example, let us consider a block of integer coordinates $(i_x, i_y, i_{v_x}, i_{v_y})$ within phase space. During any advection in x, the treatment of this block only requires data within some blocks having the same coordinates i_y, i_{v_x}, i_{v_y}.

The block dependencies during an x-advection (similarly during an y-advection) are predictable and linear. Figure 2 shows their projection on the plane (x, v_x) for two distinct values of Δt. Parameters $[xmin, xmax] \times [vxmin, vxmax]$ in the figure define the borders of the domain on which we solve the Vlasov equation. Blocks in light grey are ones needed to compute blocks in dark grey. We observe that provided some assumptions on simulation parameters (for $xmin = -xmax$, $vxmin = -vxmax$, and $\Delta t < \frac{blocksize}{vxmax}$, see the right part of Fig. 2), the treatment of any block only needs the data within two blocks: the block itself and a neighboring block at the left or at the right depending on the v_x sign.

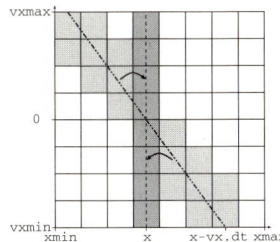 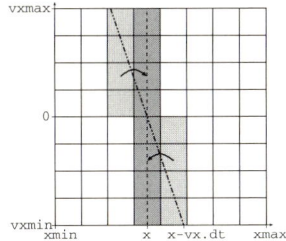

Fig. 2. Dependencies during an advection in x

On the other hand, any $\mathbf{v}$-advection exhibits irregular and unpredictable block dependencies because the advection operator is determined by the self consistent electrostatic field E which depends itself on the values of f. These block dependencies may induce costly communications. Therefore, the partitions we consider are such that all blocks having the same coordinates i_x, i_y in position space (for any coordinates i_{v_x}, i_{v_y} in velocity dimensions) are contained in the same partition. With such a partitioning, any $\mathbf{v}$-advection induces no communication. Let us call *slice* of coordinates (i_x, i_y), the set of all the blocks having the same coordinate i_x, i_y in position dimensions. Each partition is thus a group of slices.

The remaining communications during x- and y-advection are implemented by using *ghost cells* to replicate needed remote data. We also use overlapping

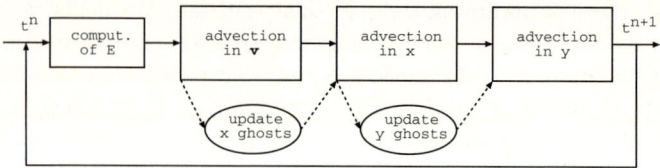

Fig. 3. The time-step iteration of our parallel algorithm including communications/computations overlapping

of communications with computations to reduce the overhead for updating the ghost cells. This update operation is performed one advection ahead in order to maximize computations/communications overlap. Figure 3 shows the location of this update operation within each time step. The computation of electric field E requires one all-to-all communication of ρ contributions.

3 Load-Balancing Mechanism

Our mechanism is based on three issues: a simple cost metric to measure the load of a partition and detect imbalance, a partitioning algorithm and a procedure to map new partitions to processors.

3.1 Imbalance Detection

Our imbalance detection relies on measuring the cost of any partition. Ideally, this cost takes both computations and communications into account [11]. In the scope of this work, we decide to neglect the communications cost. We do this approximation because communications are overlapped with computations and thus their cost is partially hidden. Therefore, the chosen cost metric is time spent in computing one block. The measure is taken dynamically using the processor real time clock. This metric is well adapted to homogeneous architectures where all processors are cadenced at the same frequency. By definition, the cost of any partition is the sum of the costs of all the slices that are contained in this partition. The cost of any slice is the sum of the costs of all the blocks in this slice. Load imbalance is detected when the difference between the greatest partition cost and the lowest one is over a fixed threshold choosen by the user. Note that, for a huge number of processors, it is better to use deviation from average partition cost rather than this difference.

3.2 Partitioning Algorithm

Our partitioning algorithm aims to build partitions having approximately the same cost. We propose a heuristic which is based on the well-known Recursive Coordinate Bisection (RCB) [12]. The RCB technique is a geometric-based partitioning method, which has the advantages of being simple and well suited to Cartesian meshes. The geometric domain that we consider in this variant, is a

2D uniform grid of the position space. Each cell (i, j) of this grid identifies a slice and therefore a sub-domain made of several cells defines a partition. As in the classical algorithm, a divide-and-conquer approach is taken. The domain is first cut in largest dimension to yield two sub-domains. Cuts are then made recursively in the new sub-domains until we have as many sub-domains as processors. Each cut is made so that the two partitions corresponding to sub-domains have approximately the same cost. In the case of our parallel algorithm, we do not want to subdivide a cell: the cut can only be made between adjoining cells.

If we use a straight line cut, then the cost of the two resulting partitions may be too different. We propose an inexpensive optimization with the aim of reducing the difference between the costs of resulting partitions. This optimization consists in using a *zig-zag cut* rather than a straight line cut. This is shown in Fig. 4: on the left, the set of cells is optimally bisected with a straight line cut between two columns. On the right, the optimal bisection (the dotted straight line) passes through a column of cells. In this case we use a zig-zag cut: the orthogonal segment is chosen to better divide the cost.

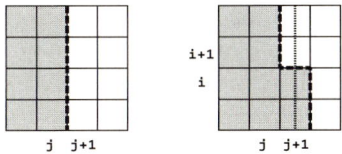

Fig. 4. Bisection of a set of slices

This RCB variant is given in algorithm 1. It uses three local variables : *rank*, the rank of the processor associated to the current partition, *part*, the current partition that corresponds to a sub-domain of the 2D uniform grid, and *nbis*, the number of cuts that have been already made. It could happen that our algorithm generates an empty partition or new partitions such that the imbalance is not better than the previous one. In that case, the new partitioning is considered as not valid and the current one remains unchanged.

3.3 Partitions Re-mapping on Processors

The mapping of the new partitioning onto processors involves communication of slices amongst processors, which may cause a significant overhead. In order to reduce this overhead and not to waste the gain of a better load balance, this redistribution and the other issues of load balancing are mixed up with the successive operations within a time-step iteration. Thus communications can be overlapped with computations which would not be possible if re-mapping was performed in a separate phase. When a load balancing occurs, the time-step iteration given in Fig. 3 is slightly modified as shown in Fig. 5. Load balancing issues (in grey) are integrated into the computation of E and two advection steps. Migration of slices is overlapped with **v**-advection computations.

Algorithm 1. Recursive partitioning function

Data: $nproc$, the number of processors (assumed to be a power of 2)
Initially: $rank = 0$, $part$ is the whole 2D domain and $nbis = 0$
if $2^{nbis} = nproc$ **then**
  | maps partition $part$ to processor $rank$
else
  | compute $(H \times W)$, the height and width extent of the current partition $part$
  | **if** $H > W$ **then**
  | | switch dimensions x and y
  | let $w(n, m)$ be the cost of slice (n, m) if $(n, m) \in part$ (0 otherwise)
  | compute cost $w[n]$ of every column n of partition $part$ ($w[n] = \sum_m w(m, n)$)
  | compute cost sum of the whole partition $part$
  | find column $j = \max\{k \mid S_k \leq sum/2\}$ with $S_k = \sum_{n \leq k} w[n]$
  | **if** $S_j = sum/2$ **then**
  | | the straight line cut is between columns j and $j + 1$
  | **else**
  | | the cut pass through the column $j + 1$
  | | find row i which minimizes $|sum/2 - (S_j + s_i)|$ with $s_i = \sum_{m \leq i} w(m, j)$
  | | the cut is between rows i and $i + 1$
  | let $part_1$ and $part_2$ be the subsets of $part$ defined by bisection
  | call partitioning function with $rank, part_1, nbis + 1$
  | call partitioning function with $rank + nproc/(2^{nbis+1}), part_2, nbis + 1$

Let us describe these changes in details. The cost of each partition is communicated during computation of electric field E within the same message as ρ contribution. These costs are used to perform the imbalance test. If the workload is not sufficiently balanced, then all processors exchange the cost of their slices. This does not penalize solver performance since processors are already synchronized. Then, on each processor, the partitioning algorithm is used to compute new partitions and then, a re-mapping of partitions is planned. For any given processor, say P, let us note P_{old}, its old partition and P_{new}, its new one. During v-advection, processor P computes all the (local) blocks of P_{old}, sends locally computed blocks belonging to the difference $P_{old} \setminus P_{new}$ and receives remote computed blocks belonging to $P_{new} \setminus P_{old}$ (including ghosts cells in x for P_{new}). In order to temporarily store both computed and received data, a new memory space is allocated. Its extent corresponds to the union $P_{tmp} = P_{old} \cup P_{new}$.

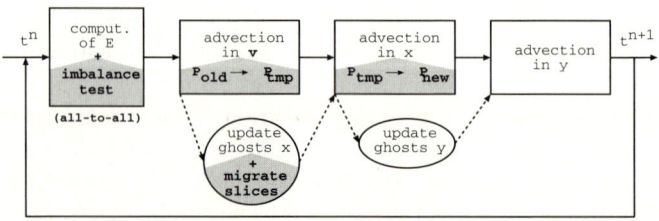

Fig. 5. The time-step iteration including load balancing

During x-advection, the only change made for load balancing issues is to read needed data from the temporary memory space. At the end of the x-advection step, the temporary memory space becomes useless and thus is deallocated. Then the time-step iteration returns to a normal state.

4 Performance Measurements

Our code has been written in C with calls to MPI. Our test case is the uniform magnetic focusing of a semi-Gaussian beam of protons. A detailed description of this test case is given in [10]. We perform 75 time steps. Coordinates **x** and **v** live in $[-6.5, 6.5]^2$. Phase space is split into 16×16 slices of 8×8 blocks each and $J = 2$, which corresponds to maximum grid of $128 \times 128 \times 64 \times 64$ points. Simulation starts with a partitioning determined from the initial distribution function. We test our code on a cluster of 32 Opteron 2.4 GHz bi-processor nodes with 4 GB RAM each, connected through a Myrinet network. Each node holds 2 Myrinet interfaces to achieve a theoretical bandwidth of 495 MB/s.

Impact of load balancing. Figure 6 shows the workload imbalance at each time step of the simulation launched on 16 processors for 3 different load balancing (LB) strategies. We approximate imbalance as the difference between the greatest and the lowest partition cost. Note that for a great number of processors, another measure of imbalance should be used (for example deviation from average partition cost). In this figure, a mark indicates each balancing step and imbalance is given for a simulation without any dynamic load balancing, with dynamic LB based on straight cuts (sDLB) and on zig-zag cuts (zDLB). With zDLB, we can observe that the imbalance cost is always under 1 second.

Figure 7 shows the impact of re-mapping on communications. Light grey columns represent the number of sent blocks, and dark grey ones represent the number of blocks that are waited at the `MPI_Waitall` barrier. We can observe that most of the time, all sent blocks are received before the waiting barrier. But for some re-mapping there is a strong increasing of the number of transferred blocks. When the number of blocks to be sent is over the number of blocks to be computed, communication time can not be entirely overlapped with computation, thus there are some waiting times. This overhead is a drawback of our simple partitioning algorithm that does not take communication cost into account. In order to scale the code on more processors, the partitioning algorithm should be modified to lower the number of transferred blocks during partition re-mapping.

Performance and speedup. We compare the impact of our dynamic load balancing algorithm upon wall-clock time. We run the same simulation with 4 different LB strategies: zDLB, sDLB, and static LB with equal-sized areas (eSLB) and partitioning of a bounding box (bSLB) based on the initial distribution function (as defined in [10]). Figure 8 shows the wall-clock time of the code in each case for an increasing number of processors. We can see that zig-zag cut partitioning always achieves better performance than straight cut one.

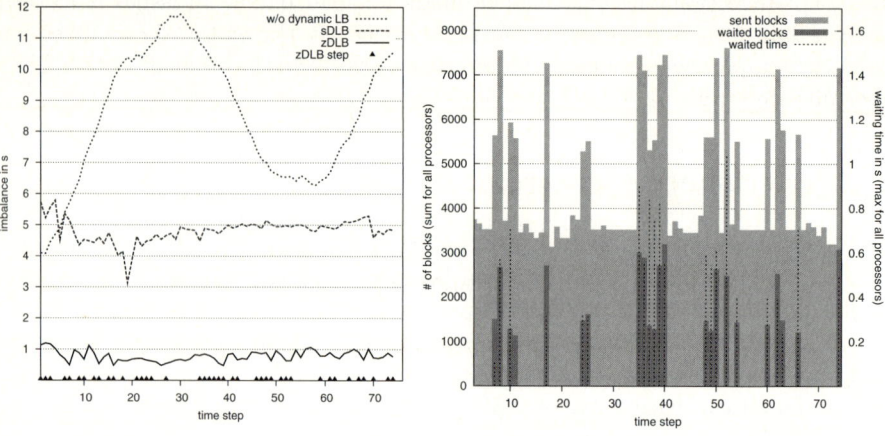

Fig. 6. Imbalance evolution with different dynamic load balancing strategies

Fig. 7. Impact of re-mapping on communications

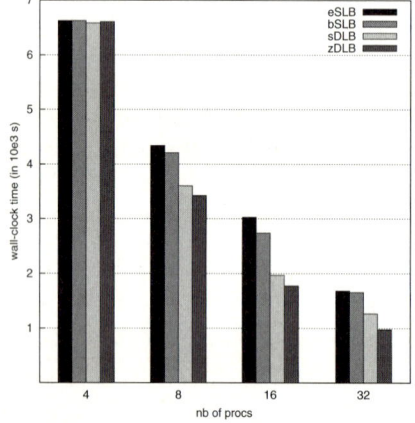

Fig. 8. Wall-clock time with different load balancing strategies

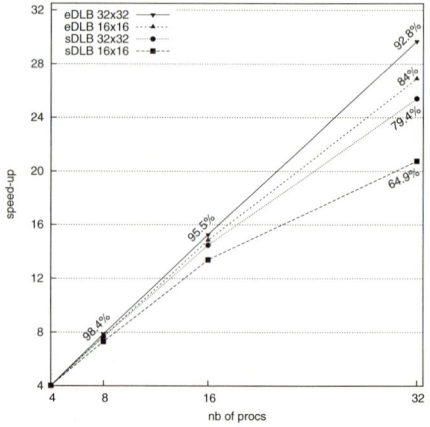

Fig. 9. Speedup and efficiency for 16 × 16 and 32 × 32 slices

Figure 9 shows speedup and efficiency obtained up to 32 processors. We also made a run with 32 × 32 slices instead of 16 × 16. With zig-zag cuts, speedup is quite good for such a highly adaptive 4D non-linear solver, especially since it takes into account the initial step whose imbalance can be penalizing. We can see that a better load balancing is obtained when more slices are used. With 32 × 32 slices, we reach an efficiency over 92%, which is quite good considering that mesh adaptation occurs every time steps and load is frequently balanced.

5 Conclusion

We provided our parallel algorithm presented in [10] with a mechanism to balance the workload. This dynamic load balancing mechanism is based on an improved recursive bisections and gives satisfying results up to 32 processors. This shows that an adaptive 4D Vlasov solver can achieve satisfying efficiency on distributed memory architectures in comparison with shared memory implementations.

Our mechanism may be improved on several points. We have seen that increasing the number of slices gives better load balance. However, this implies to use a smaller Δt because its value is bounded by the size of a block by assumptions on simulation parameters. If we want to use the same Δt then we could increase the number of ghost cells in x and y. This would increase the number of messages but not the volume of transferred data. We also could implement other partitioning algorithms (for example to take communication costs into account) and investigate their advantages for different test cases.

Future works will be devoted to scale the code on more processors. With the multiplication of architectures based on SMP nodes and multicore processors it becomes interesting to use both message passing and shared memory paradigm. A straightforward idea is to distribute blocks within a slice onto several processors sharing the same memory space.

References

1. Filbet, F., Sonnendrücker, E., Bertrand, P.: Conservative Numerical Schemes for the Vlasov Equation. J. Comput. Phys. 172, 166–187 (2000)
2. Filbet, F.: Numerical Methods for the Vlasov Equation. In: Numerical Mathematics and Advanced Applications (2001)
3. Sonnendrücker, E., Roche, J., Bertrand, P., Ghizzo, A.: The Semi-Lagrangian Method for the Numerical Resolution of the Vlasov Equation. J. Comput. Phys. 149, 201–220 (1999)
4. Sonnendrücker, E., Filbet, F., Friedman, A., Oudet, E., Vay, J.L.: Vlasov Simulation of Beams with a Moving Grid. Comput. Phys. Comm. 164, 390–395 (2004)
5. Besse, N., Filbet, F., Gutnic, M., Paun, I., Sonnendrücker, E.: An Adaptive Numerical Method for the Vlasov Equation Based on a Multiresolution Analysis. In: Numerical Mathematics and Advanced Applications, pp. 437–446 (2001)
6. Gutnic, M., Haefele, M., Paun, I., Sonnendrücker, E.: Vlasov Simulations on an Adaptive Phase-Space Grid. Comput. Phys. Commun. 164, 214–219 (2004)
7. Haefele, M., Latu, G., Gutnic, M.: A Parallel Vlasov Solver Using a Wavelet Based Adaptive Mesh Refinement. In: Proceedings of the 2005 International Conference on Parallel Processing Workshops (ICPPW 2005)., pp. 181–188 (2005)
8. Crouseilles, N., Gutnic, M., Latu, G., Sonnendrücker, E.: Comparison of two Eulerian Solvers for the Four Dimensional Vlasov Equation: Part II. In: Proc. of the 2nd international conference of Vlasovia. Communications in Nonlinear Science and Numerical Simulation, vol. 13(1), pp. 94–99 (2008)
9. Campos Pinto, M., Mehrenberger, M.: Adaptive Numerical Resolution of the Vlasov Equation. In: Numerical Methods for Hyperbolic and Kinetic Problems, CEMRACS, pp. 43–58 (2004)

10. Hoenen, O., Violard, E.: A Block-Based Parallel Adaptive Scheme for Solving the 4D Vlasov Equation. In: Wyrzykowski, R., Dongarra, J., Karczewski, K., Waśniewski, J. (eds.) PPAM 2007. LNCS, vol. 4967. Springer, Heidelberg (2008)
11. Teresco, J.D., Devine, K.D., Flaherty, J.E.: Partitioning and Dynamic Load Balancing for the Numerical Solution of Partial Differential Equations. In: Numerical Solution of Partial Differential Equations on Parallel Computers. Springer, Heidelberg (2005)
12. Berger, M.J., Bokhari, S.H.: A Partitioning Strategy for Non-uniform Problems on Multiprocessors. IEEE Transactions on Computers 36(5), 570–580 (1987)

A Parallel Sensor Scheduling Technique for Fault Detection in Distributed Parameter Systems

Maciej Patan

Institute of Control and Computation Engineering
University of Zielona Góra
ul. Podgórna 50, 65–246 Zielona Góra, Poland
M.Patan@issi.uz.zgora.pl

Abstract. The problem under consideration is to determine a scheduling policy for discrete scanning sensors in such a way as to maximize the power of a simple parametric hypothesis test, which verifies the nominal state of the considered distributed system specified over a given multi-dimensional spatial domain. The optimal activation schedule for sensor network is determined based on the D_s-optimality criterion defined on the respective Fisher Information Matrix. A computational scheme based on the branch-and-bound method is provided for the solution of a resulting combinatorial problem. Then, the parallel version of solver is developed in order to overcome the excessively growing computational costs for large-scale problems. The proposed approach is illustrated by simulations on a sensor network scheduling problem for a two-dimensional convective diffusion process.

Keywords: branch-and-bound, distributed parameter systems, fault detection, integer programming, scanning observations, sensor networks.

1 Introduction

Experimental design for spatio-temporal physical systems also called distributed parameter systems (especially, in environmental protection, nuclear energetics, aircraft industry, civil engineering, oil industry etc.) is often related to an optimal choice of measurement conditions in order to obtain the best information for estimating unknown parameters which can then be used in optimal control. The impossibility to observe the system states over the entire spatial domain implies the question of where to locate discrete sensors and how to schedule the observations so as to accurately estimate the unknown system parameters. This question acquires especially vital importance in the context of recent advances in distributed sensor networks.

Over the past years, laborious research on the development of strategies for efficient sensor placement has been conducted (for reviews, see papers [1, 2] and comprehensive monographs [3, 4]). Nevertheless, although the need for systematic methods was widely recognized, most techniques communicated by various authors usually rely on exhaustive search over a predefined set of candidates and the combinatorial nature of the design problem is taken into account very occasionally [2]. Obviously, such an approach is feasible for a relatively small number of possible sensor locations, and becomes useless as the number of possible location candidates increases. Additionally, in spite of the rapid development of fault detection and localization methods for dynamic systems [5], the grave lack of effective methods tailored to spatiotemporal systems can be observed. To fill this gap some successful attempts at exploiting the D_s-optimality criterion were reported in [6, 7].

The main aim of this work is to extend the practical approach to sensor selection for fault detection reported in [8] to the more general case of scanning sensor networks, where the observation system comprises multiple stationary sensors located at already specified locations and it is desired to activate only a subset of them during a given time interval while the other sensors remain dormant. A reason for not using all the available sensors could be the reduction of the observation system complexity and/or the cost of operation and maintenance [2]. In particular, we consider N possible sites at which to locate a sensor, but limitations on the number of sensors at our disposal allow only n of them (typically, n is much smaller than N) to be selected at each time subinterval. Consequently, the problem is to build the sensor time activation schedule so as to maximize the determinant of the Fisher Information Matrix (FIM) associated with the parameters to be estimated. Since selecting the best subset of sites to locate the sensors constitutes an inherently discrete large-scale resource allocation problem whose solution may be time-consuming, an efficient guided search algorithm based on the parallel branch-and-bound method is delineated, which implicitly enumerates all the feasible sensor configurations, using relaxed optimization problems that involve no integer constraints.

2 Sensor Selection for Fault Detection

Consider a bounded spatial domain $\Omega \subset \mathbb{R}^d$ with sufficiently smooth boundary Γ, a bounded time interval $T = (0, t_f]$, and a distributed parameter system (DPS) whose scalar state y at a spatial point $x \in \bar{\Omega} \subset \mathbb{R}^d$ and time instant $t \in \bar{T}$ is governed by the partial differential equation (PDE)

$$\frac{\partial y}{\partial t} = \mathcal{F}(x, t, y, \theta) \quad \text{in } \Omega \times T, \tag{1}$$

where $\mathcal{F}$ is a well-posed, possibly nonlinear, differential operator which involves first- and second-order spatial derivatives and may include terms accounting for forcing inputs specified *a priori*. The PDE (1) is accompanied by the appropriate boundary and initial conditions

$$\mathcal{B}(x, t, y, \theta) = 0 \quad \text{on } \Gamma \times T, \qquad y = y_0 \quad \text{in } \Omega \times \{t = 0\}, \tag{2}$$

respectively, $\mathcal{B}$ being an operator acting on the boundary Γ and $y_0 = y_0(x)$ a given function. We assume that the forms of $\mathcal{F}$ and $\mathcal{B}$ are given explicitly up to an m-dimensional vector of unknown constant parameters θ which must be estimated using observations of the system.

The state y is observed by N pointwise sensors, from among only n are activated at time instants $0 < t_0 < t_1 < \cdots < t_K = t_f$ and will be gather the continuous measurements for the duration of each subinterval $T_k = [t_{k-1}, t_k]$, $k = 1, \ldots, K$. Forming such an arbitrary partition on the time interval T, the considered 'scanning' observation strategy can be formally represented as

$$z_m^\ell(t) = y(x_k^\ell, t; \theta) + \varepsilon(x_k^\ell, t), \quad t \in T_k, \quad \ell = 1, \ldots, n, \quad k = 1, \ldots K \tag{3}$$

where $z_m^\ell(t)$ is the scalar output and $x_k^\ell \in X$ stands for the location of the ℓ-th sensor at time subinterval T_k, X signifies the part of the spatial domain Ω where the measurements can be made and $\varepsilon(x_k^\ell, t)$ denotes the measurement noise, which is customarily assumed to be zero-mean, Gaussian, spatial uncorrelated and white [9].

The most widely used formulation of the parameter estimation problem boils down to estimation θ by $\hat{\theta}$, a global minimizer of the output least-squares error criterion. Then, the basic idea of fault detection is to compare the resulting parameter estimates with the corresponding known nominal values, treating possible differences as residuals which contain information about potential faults. Based on some thresholding techniques, the appropriate decision making system could be constructed to detect abnormal situations in system functioning [7].

Basically, only some parameters can be useful for the diagnosis. This accounts for partitioning the parameter vector into two two subsets. With no loss of generality, we may write

$$\theta = \begin{bmatrix} \theta_1 & \ldots & \theta_s & \theta_{s+1} & \ldots & \theta_m \end{bmatrix}^\mathsf{T} = \begin{bmatrix} \alpha^\mathsf{T} & \beta^\mathsf{T} \end{bmatrix}, \tag{4}$$

where α is a vector of s parameters which are essential for a proper fault detection and β is the vector of some unknown parameters which are a part of the model but are useless for fault detection. Based on the observations, it is possible to test the simple null hypothesis

$$H_0 : \alpha = \alpha^0, \tag{5}$$

where α^0 is the nominal value for the vector α corresponding to the normal system performance.

For a fixed significance level (i.e. fixed probability of rejecting H_0 when it is true), the power of the likelihood ratio test for the alternative hypothesis of the form $H_A : \alpha \neq \alpha^*$ (i.e. 1−the probability of accepting H_0 when H_A is true) can be made large by maximizing the D_s-optimality criterion (see [7] for details)

$$\Psi_s[M] = \log \det[M_{\alpha\alpha} - M_{\alpha\beta} M_{\beta\beta}^{-1} M_{\alpha\beta}^\mathsf{T}], \tag{6}$$

where $M \in \mathbb{R}^{m \times m}$ stands for the so-called *Fisher Information Matrix* (FIM) which is decomposed as

$$M = \begin{bmatrix} M_{\alpha\alpha} & M_{\alpha\beta} \\ M_{\alpha\beta}^\mathsf{T} & M_{\beta\beta} \end{bmatrix}, \tag{7}$$

such that $M_{\alpha\alpha} \in \mathbb{R}^{s \times s}$, $M_{\alpha\beta} \in \mathbb{R}^{s \times (m-s)}$, $M_{\beta\beta} \in \mathbb{R}^{(m-s) \times (m-s)}$. The FIM is widely used in optimum experimental design theory for lumped systems [10, 11]. In our setting, the FIM is given by [9]

$$M = \sum_{\ell=1}^{n} \sum_{k=1}^{K} \frac{1}{t_f} \int_{T_k} g(x_k^\ell, t) g^\mathsf{T}(x_k^\ell, t) \, dt, \tag{8}$$

where

$$g(x,t) = \left[\frac{\partial y(x,t;\vartheta)}{\partial \vartheta_1}, \ldots, \frac{\partial y(x,t;\vartheta)}{\partial \vartheta_m} \right]^\mathsf{T}_{\vartheta=\theta^0} \tag{9}$$

stands for the so-called *sensitivity vector*, θ^0 being the nominal value of the parameter vector θ [3]. Up to a constant scalar multiplier, the inverse of the FIM constitutes a good approximation of $\text{cov}(\hat{\theta})$ provided that the time horizon is large, the nonlinearity of the model with respect to its parameters is mild, and the measurement errors are independently distributed and have small magnitudes [10, 11].

The optimal sensor scheduling problem considered in what follows consist in seeking for each time subinterval T_k the best subset of n locations from among the N given potential ones, so that the problem is then reduced to a combinatorial one. In other words, the problem is to divide for each time subinterval the N available sites between n gauged sites and the remaining $N-n$ ungauged sites so as to maximize the criterion (6) associated with the parameters to be estimated. In order to formulate this mathematically, introduce for each possible location x^i ($i = 1, \ldots, N$) a variable v_k^i which takes the value 1 or 0 depending on whether a sensor is or is not located at x^i at given time T_k, respectively. The FIM in (8) can then be rewritten as

$$M(v_1, \ldots, v_K) = \sum_{i=1}^{N} \sum_{k=1}^{K} v_k^i \frac{1}{t_f} \int_{T_k} g(x^i, t) g^\mathsf{T}(x^i, t) \, dt, \tag{10}$$

where $v_k = (v_k^1, \ldots, v_k^N)$. Then our design problem takes the form:

Problem **P**: Find the sequence $v = (v_1, \ldots, v_K)$ to maximize

$$\mathcal{P}(v) = \Psi\big(M(v)\big), \tag{11}$$

subject to

$$\sum_{i=1}^{N} v_k^i = n, \quad k = 1, \ldots, K \tag{12}$$

$$v_k^i = 0 \text{ or } 1, \quad i = 1, \ldots, N, \quad k = 1, \ldots, K. \tag{13}$$

This constitutes a 0–1 integer programming problem which necessitates an ingenious solution. In [12] a general sequential computational scheme is proposed to solve this problem based on the branch-and-bound method which is a standard technique for such class of tasks. Its brief presentation and development of proper parallel algorithm constitutes the next sections of the paper.

3 Solution Via Branch-and-Bound

The branch-and-bound (BB) constitutes general algorithmic technique for finding optimal solutions of various optimization tasks and stands as a one of classical approach to discrete or combinatorial problems [13, 14, 15]. Its proper application may lead to algorithms of high average performance. The sequential procedure presented in this section is a generalization of the similar algorithm developed in [12] for the stationary sensors selection problem and stand as a basis for the parallel implementation of the algorithm.

Let I denote the set of index pairs $\{(i,k)|\ i = 1, \ldots, N,\ k = 1, \ldots, K\}$ of possible sensor locations at given time intervals. Consider a relaxation of Problem P, which starts by partition of the feasible set

$$V = \left\{ (v_1, \ldots, v_N) \,\Big|\, \sum_{i=1}^{N} v_k^i = n, \forall k\ ;\ v_k^i = 0 \text{ or } 1,\ \forall (i,k) \in I \right\}, \quad (14)$$

into subsets of the form

$$V(I_0, I_1) = \left\{ v \in V \mid v_k^i = 0,\ \forall (i,k) \in I_0,\ v_k^i = 1,\ \forall (i,k) \in I_1 \right\}, \quad (15)$$

where I_0 and I_1 are disjoint subsets of I. Consequently, $V(I_0, I_1)$ is the subset of V such that a sensor is placed at the locations with indices in I_1, no sensor is placed at the locations with indices in I_0, and a sensor may or may not be placed at the remaining locations. Each subset $V(I_0, I_1)$ can be directly identified with a node in the BB tree.

The key assumption in the BB method is that for every nonterminal node $V(I_0, I_1)$, i.e., the node for which $I_0 \cup I_1 \neq I$, there is an algorithm that determines an upper bound $\bar{\mathcal{P}}(I_0, I_1)$ to the maximum criterion value over $V(I_0, I_1)$, and a feasible solution $\underline{v} \in V$ for which $\mathcal{P}(\underline{v})$ can serve as a lower bound to the maximum criterion value over V. The value $\bar{\mathcal{P}}(I_0, I_1)$ can be determined through solution of the following relaxed problem:

Problem $\mathbf{R(I_0, I_1)}$*:* Find a sequence $\bar{v}$ to maximize (11) subject to the constraints

$$\sum_{i=1}^{N} v_k^i = n,\ \forall k, \qquad 0 \leq v_k^i \leq 1,\ (i,k) \in I \setminus (I_0 \cup I_1), \quad (16)$$

$$v_k^i = 0,\ (i,k) \in I_0, \qquad v_k^i = 1,\ (i,k) \in I_1. \quad (17)$$

In Problem R(I_0, I_1) all 0–1 constraints on the variables v_k^i are relaxed by allowing them to take any value in the interval $[0, 1]$, except that the variables $v_k^i,\ i \in I_0 \cup I_1$ are fixed at either 0 or 1.

For a lower bound $\underline{v}$, we can specify it as the best feasible solution (i.e., an element of V) found so far. If no solution has been found yet, we can either set the lower bound to $-\infty$, or use an initial guess about the optimal solution.

The result of solving Problem R(I_0, I_1) can be used to construct a branching rule for the binary BB tree. We adopt here the approach in which the node/subset

$V(I_0, I_1)$ is expanded (i.e., partitioned) by first picking out all fractional values from among the values of the relaxed variables, and then rounding to 0 and 1 a value which is the most distant from both 0 and 1. Specifically, we apply the following steps:

(a) Determine
$$(i_\star, k_\star) = \arg \min_{(i,k) \in I \setminus (I_0 \cup I_1)} |v_k^i - 0.5|. \tag{18}$$

(b) Partition $V(I_0, I_1)$ into $V(I_0 \cup \{(i_\star, k_\star)\}, I_1)$ and $V(I_0, I_1 \cup \{(i_\star, k_\star)\})$.

Combination of this branching rule with a search strategy to incrementally explore all the nodes of the BB tree constitutes the general scheme of the sequential procedure which starts from the root corresponding to $V(\emptyset, \emptyset) = V$ and the fully relaxed problem. Here we use a common depth-first technique [16, 17] which always expands the deepest node in the current fringe of the search tree. A recursive version of the resulting depth-first branch-and-bound is embodied in Algorithm 1. The operators involved in this implementation are as follows:

- SENSOR-NUMBER-TEST(I_0, I_1) returns true only if the constraints (12) on sensor number are violated, i.e. $\exists k, |I_1(k)| > n$ or $|I_0(k)| > N - n$, where $I_1(q)$ and $I_0(q)$ are a subsets of I_1 and I_0, respectively, consisting of pairs with time index fixed at q.
- SINGULAR-FIM(I_0, I_1) returns true only if expansion of the current node will result in a singular FIM. (cf. [12, Prop. 2] for the very simple singularity test for FIM).
- RELAXED-SOLUTION(I_0, I_1) returns a solution to Problem R(I_0, I_1). As for the solution of the relaxed problem a simple and efficient procedure based on the gradient projection technique developed in [8] can be generalized and adopted to the considered setting. As a result of its application, we set $\bar{\mathcal{P}}(I_0, I_1) = \mathcal{P}(\bar{v})$.
- Ds-FIM(v) returns the D_s criterion value for the FIM corresponding to v.
- INTEGRAL-TEST(v) returns true only if the current solution v is integral.
- INDEX-BRANCH(v) returns the index defined by (18).

4 Parallel Realization of Branch and Bound

Branch-and-bound has become a popular method for solving combinatorial problems and until now numerous strategies have been employed for its effective parallelization (for general review of parallel BB methodology see [18]). Two classical approaches are known to accelerate the BB search: node-based and tree-based. This work focus on the latter strategy and in the following we demonstrate how to effectively parallelize the exploration of the BB tree.

The main idea of the parallel implementation of considered computational scheme stems from the dichotomy of branching process suitably splitting the main problem into subproblems which can be solved by different processors [19]. In our implementation, we use a hierarchical Master-Slave configuration applicable on the Message Passing Interface (MPI) in a Windows environment.

Algorithm 1. A sequential recursive version of the depth-first BB method. *LOWER* and *v_best* are the global variables which are respectively the maximal value of the $\mathcal{P}(v)$ over feasible solutions found so far and the solution at which it is attained.

1: **procedure** RECURSIVE-DFBB(I_0, I_1)
2:     **if** SENSOR-NUMBER-TEST(I_0, I_1) **or** SINGULAR-FIM(I_0, I_1) **then**
3:         **return**   ▷ Violation of constraints or singular FIM within whole branch
4:     **end if**
5:     $v\_relaxed \leftarrow$ RELAXED-SOLUTION(I_0, I_1)
6:     $Ds\_relaxed \leftarrow$ DS-FIM$(v\_relaxed)$ ▷ Bounding
7:     **if** $Ds\_relaxed \leq LOWER$ **then**
8:         **return**   ▷ Pruning
9:     **else if** INTEGRAL-TEST$(v\_relaxed)$ **then**
10:        $v\_best \leftarrow v\_relaxed$
11:        $LOWER \leftarrow Ds\_relaxed$
12:        **return**   ▷ Relaxed solution is integral
13:     **else**
14:        $(i_\star, k_\star) \leftarrow$ INDEX-BRANCH$(v\_relaxed)$ ▷ Branching
15:        RECURSIVE-DFBB$(I_0 \cup \{(i_\star, k_\star)\}, I_1)$
16:        RECURSIVE-DFBB$(I_0, I_1 \cup \{(i_\star, k_\star)\})$
17:     **end if**
18: **end procedure**

The Master process takes responsibility for: distribution of jobs to Slave processes, coordination of information interchange among the processes and maintains the progress of computations. The maintenance of job redistribution is based on the busy process queue, idle process queue and a task queue. Each Slave process perform the actual problem solution and fathoming of the nodes in the BB tree, independently working on its part of the subproblem. A depth-and-breadth-first combined strategy is used to explore the BB tree. Slave process always explores the right branch of the subproblem (depth-first approach). The left branch is assigned to another Slave Processes (breadth-first approach) via Master task queue. An extension here is the possibility of updating not only local current best solution and lower bound but also the Master's respective global values, which enhance the pruning process.

Since the complexity of a given subproblem cannot be determined in advance, proper load balancing becomes the key issue of high performance of the parallel BB. Load balancing is a well studied concept, here it is achieved via periodic query and acknowledgments from Slave processes. The general scheme of implementation is given in Algorithms 2 and 3.

5 Computational Results

As a brief illustration of the presented approach to the sensor network design, we consider the problem of sensor activation for fault detection in the transport process of an air pollutant over a given urban area. Within this domain, which

Algorithm 2. MASTER process. It uses IDLE_Q (idle processes queue), BUSY_Q (busy processes queue) and TASK_Q (task queue) for the maintenance of task redistribution. Main vital messages from Master to Slave processes are: new_task (sends I_0, I_1 and $LOWER$ to slave node), update_upper_bound (sends $LOWER$ to slave node) and end_calc (ending the calculations when all slave nodes are done).

1: **procedure** MASTER
2:    SOLVE PDEs   ▷ Solve the underlying PDE system
3:    INITIALIZATION   ▷ Spawn np slaves and broadcast the solution of PDEs
4:    **repeat**
5:       **if** (LENGTH(IDLE_Q)> 0) **and** (LENGTH(TASK_Q)> 0) **then**
6:          SEND new_task TO IDLE NODE   ▷ Pop subproblem from the TASK_Q
7:       **end if**
8:       WAIT FOR A MESSAGE FROM BUSY NODES
9:       EXECUTE THE MESSAGE REQUEST   ▷ Action depending on message type
10:   **until** (LENGTH(IDLE_Q)$=np$) **and** (LENGTH(TASK_Q)$=0$)
11:   FINALIZATION   ▷ Broadcast end_calc and gather the results
12: **end procedure**

has been normalized to the unit square $\Omega = (0,1)^2$, an active source of pollution is present, which influence the pollutant spatial concentration $y = y(x,t)$. The evolution of y over the normalized observation interval $T = (0,1]$ is described by the following advection-diffusion equation:

$$\frac{\partial y(x,t)}{\partial t} + \nabla \cdot \big(v(x)y(x,t)\big) = \nabla \cdot \big(a(x)\nabla y(x,t)\big) + f(x), \quad x \in \Omega \qquad (19)$$

subject to the boundary and initial conditions:

$$\frac{\partial y(x,t)}{\partial n} = 0, \quad \text{on } \Gamma \times T, \qquad y(x,0) = y_0, \quad \text{in } \Omega, \qquad (20)$$

where term $f(x) = 50\exp\big(-50\|x-c\|^2\big)$ represents a source of pollutant located at point $c = (0.3, 0.3)$, and $\partial y/\partial n$ stands for the partial derivative of y with respect to the outward normal to the boundary Γ. The mean spatio-temporal changes of the wind velocity field over the area were approximated by $v = \big(2(x_1+x_2-t); x_2-x_1+t\big)$. The assumed functional form of the spatial-varying diffusion coefficient is $a(x) = \theta_1 + \theta_2 x_1 x_2 + \theta_3 x_1^2 + \theta_4 x_2^2$.

The subject of interest here is a detection of significant increase in the intensity of the pollutant emission from the source. As the symptom of this abrupt fault an excessive deviation of the parameters θ_1 and θ_2 from their nominal values was assumed. Therefore, these parameters need estimation based on measurement data from monitoring stations.

In our simulation studies, the described bound-and-branch technique was applied to determine the D_s-optimal activation schedule for different numbers of activated sensors to maximize the reliability of the detection. In order to determine the elements of sensitivity vector required to calculate FIM the direct-differentiation method [3] was applied assuming the nominal values of the parameters $\theta_1^0 = 0.02$, $\theta_2^0 = 0.01$ and $\theta_3^0 = \theta_4^0 = 0.005$. We solved the resulting

Algorithm 3. SLAVE process. Uses local_stack to explore the right branch of subproblem. Main vital messages from Slave to Master process are: task_results (sends I_0, I_1 and v_best to master node), new_task (sends I_0, I_1 to master node) and im_idle (if slave is done working on a subproblem).

1: **procedure** SLAVE
2:     Read the PDEs solution
3:     **while** (RECEIVEMESSAGE()=end_calc) **do**
4:         RECEIVE THE DATA ▷ Update local bound and/or push the new task to the local_stack
5:         **while** LENGTH(local_stack)> 0 **do**
6:             RUN SEQUENTIAL BB   ▷ lines 2–12 of Algorithm 1
7:             $(i_\star, k_\star) \leftarrow$ INDEX-BRANCH($v\_relaxed$)   ▷ Branching
8:             SEND $(I_0 \cup \{(i_\star, k_\star)\}, I_1)$ TO MASTER   ▷ Left branch to another node
9:             PUSH $(I_0, I_1 \cup \{(i_\star, k_\star)\})$ TO local_stack   ▷ Right branch fathomed
10:        **end while**
11:        REQUEST THE MASTER FOR NEW DATA
12:     **end while**
13:     FINALIZATION   ▷ Send the results to master node
14: **end procedure**

system of PDEs using routines of the MATLAB PDE toolbox for a spatial mesh composed of 682 triangles and 378 nodes.

In considered scenario, the observation grid was assumed to be created at locations selected from among those elements of mentioned above 378-point triangulation mesh which do not lie on the outer boundary (there were 312 such nodes, which are indicated with dots in Fig. 1). The time interval was divided into 13 equal subintervals (this gives the total number of 4056 variables). A Matlab program was written to implement the components of parallel version of the BB procedure embodied by Algorithms 2 and 3 and the mpich-1.2.6 implementation of the MPI was used to call Matlab scripts by parallel processes. Computations were performed on the homogenous local network of workstations equipped with Pentium IV 3.0GHz processors each, running under control of Windows XP system. The connection between nodes is realized via Gigabit Ethernet.

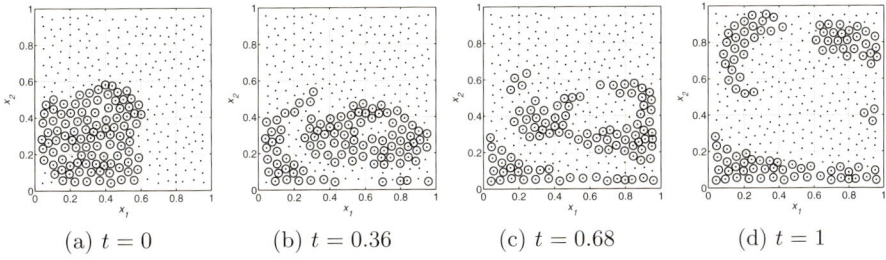

(a) $t = 0$ (b) $t = 0.36$ (c) $t = 0.68$ (d) $t = 1$

Fig. 1. Consecutive D_s-optimal activation configurations for 100 sensors

Exemplary D_s-optimal sensor configurations for chosen time moments are shown in Fig. 1. It is clear that the complexity of the system dynamics makes the proper prediction of the observation locations rather difficult and nonintuitive. The sensors tend to form the pattern reflecting the areas of greatest changes in the pollutant concentration but the observations are averaged over time and it is not trivial to follow the dynamics of the observation strategy. Surprisingly, the measurements in the closest vicinity of the pollution source turned out to be not very attractive for the considered fault detection.

The execution times and speedups concerning the algorithm performance are gathered in Tab. 1.

Table 1. Comparison of algorithm performance (time (h:m:s) vs speedups) for different settings

No. of sensors	Number of slave nodes									
	1		2		4		6		10	
10	17:28:08.5	1.00	8:54:45.9	1.96	4:38:45.7	3.76	3:17:23.4	5.31	1:57:38.2	8.91
30	11:33:46.3	1.00	6:07:04.5	1.89	3:08:00.8	3.69	2:19:35.5	4.97	1:18:50.3	8.80
60	1:48:54.9	1.00	0:59:50.6	1.82	0:30:40.8	3.55	0:24:12.2	4.50	0:12:32.0	8.69
80	1:27:02.5	1.00	0:48:37.6	1.79	0:24:43.7	3.52	0:20:52.4	4.17	0:10:35.3	8.22
100	0:18:36.4	1.00	0:11:24.9	1.63	0:05:22.6	3.46	0:04:15.5	4.37	0:02:19.4	8.01
150	0:08:19.9	1.00	0:05:35.5	1.49	0:02:29.2	3.35	0:01:58.4	4.22	0:01:02.7	7.97

6 Conclusions

The results contained in this paper show that some methods of optimum experimental design and discrete optimization can be extended to the setting of sensor scheduling problem for proper diagnostic of the state of distributed parameter system. Moreover, the efficient parallelization is achieved without complex modifications. Consequently, powerful approach is developed which is capable of solving scheduling tasks for large-scale sensor networks. The current ongoing work is related to an extension of the proposed approach in the direction of full exploitation of the node-based parallelization strategy based on the proper implementation of the algorithm used for solving relaxed problems at each node of BB tree on a grid of computers.

Acknowledgments. The work was supported by the Polish Ministry of Science and Higher Education under Grant N N519 2971 33.

References

1. Uciński, D.: Optimal selection of measurement locations for parameter estimation in distributed processes. International Journal of Applied Mathematics and Computer Science 10(2), 357–379 (2000)
2. van de Wal, M., de Jager, B.: A review of methods for input/output selection. Automatica 37, 487–510 (2001)

3. Uciński, D.: Optimal Measurement Methods for Distributed-Parameter System Identification. CRC Press, Boca Raton (2005)
4. Patan, M.: Optimal Observation Strategies for Parameter Estimation of Distributed Systems. University Press, Zielona Góra (2004), http://www.zbc.zgora.pl
5. Korbicz, J., Kościelny, J., Kowalczuk, Z., Cholewa, W.: Fault Diagnosis. Models, Artificial Intelligence, Applications. Springer, Berlin (2004)
6. Patan, M., Uciński, D.: Optimal activation strategy of discrete scanning sensors for fault detection in distributed-parameter systems. In: Proc. 16th IFAC World Congress, Prague, Czech Republic, 4–8 July (2005); Published on CD-ROM
7. Patan, M., Patan, K.: Optimal observation strategies for model-based fault detection in distributed systems. International Journal of Control 78(18), 1497–1510 (2005)
8. Patan, M., Uciński, D.: Configuring a sensor network for fault detection in distributed parameter systems. International Journal of Applied Mathematics and Computer Science (to appear, 2008)
9. Quereshi, Z.H., Ng, T.S., Goodwin, G.C.: Optimum experimental design for identification of distributed parameter systems. International Journal of Control 31(1), 21–29 (1980)
10. Fedorov, V.V., Hackl, P.: Model-Oriented Design of Experiments. Lecture Notes in Statistics. Springer, New York (1997)
11. Walter, É., Pronzato, L.: Identification of Parametric Models from Experimental Data. In: Communications and Control Engineering. Springer, Berlin (1997)
12. Uciński, D., Patan, M.: D-optimal design of a monitoring network for parameter estimation of distributed systems. Journal of Global Optimization 39, 291–322 (2007)
13. Floudas, C.A.: Mixed integer nonlinear programming, MINLP. In: Floudas, C.A., Pardalos, P.M. (eds.) Encyclopedia of Optimization, vol. 3, pp. 401–414. Kluwer Academic Publishers, Dordrecht (2001)
14. Bertsekas, D.P.: Nonlinear Programming, 2nd edn. Optimization and Computation Series. Athena Scientific, Belmont (1999)
15. Eckstein, J.: Massively Parallel Mixed-Integer Programming: Algorithms and Applications. In: Heroux, M.A., Raghavan, P., Simon, H.D. (eds.) Parallel Processing for Scientific Computing, pp. 323–340. SIAM Books, Philadelphia (2006)
16. Russell, S.J., Norvig, P.: Artificial Intelligence: A Modern Approach, 2nd edn. Pearson Education International, Upper Saddle River (2003)
17. Gerdts, M.: Solving mixed-integer optimal control problems by branch&bound: A case study from automobile test-driving with gear shift. Journal of Optimization Theory and Applications 26, 1–18 (2005)
18. Gendron, B., Crainic, T.: Parallel branch-and-bound algorithms: Survey and synthesis. Operational Research 42(6), 1042–1066 (1994)
19. Lakshmi, S., Aronson, J.: A parallel branch-and-bound method for cluster analysis. Annals of Operation Research 90, 65–86 (1999)

Topic 11: Distributed and High-Performance Multimedia

Frank Seinstra*, Nicolás Guil*, Zoltan Juhasz*, and Simon Wilson*

In recent years, the world has seen a tremendous increase in the capability to create, share and store *multimedia items*, i.e. a combination of pictorial, textual, and auditory data. Moreover, in emerging multimedia applications, generation, processing, storage, indexing, querying, retrieval, delivery, shielding, and visualization of multimedia content are integrated issues, all taking place at the same time and - potentially - at different administrative domains.

As a result of these trends, a number of novel and hard research questions arise, which can be answered only by applying techniques of parallel, distributed, and Grid computing. The scope of this topic embraces issues from high-performance processing, coding, indexing, and retrieval of multimedia data over parallel architectures for multimedia servers, databases and information systems, up to highly distributed architectures in heterogeneous, wired and wireless networks.

This year 3 papers were submitted to this topic area. All the papers were reviewed by 4 referees, and 2 papers were ultimately selected. A third paper, which was initially submitted to Topic 5 (on Parallel and Distributed Databases), has been included as well, as its contents perfectly fit into the current topic.

The first paper, by S. Khanfir and M. Jemni, presents two new parallel FPGA-based implementation schemes for the lifting-based Discrete Wavelet Transform. The first algorithm uses pipelining, parallel processing, and data reuse for increased execution speed. The second algorithm uses a dynamically reconfigurable controller that determines the optimal number of clones of the first algorithm to be deployed for fastest execution. The authors show the two approaches to allow for real-time processing of large and multi-framed images.

The second paper, by R. Godoi, X. Yang, and P. Hernández, gives an extensive analysis of the requirements of the control subsystem of a peer-to-peer (P2P) multicast architecture for Large Video on Demand (LVoD) service provisioning. The analysis, performed by means of a set of analytical models, considers many different control system design schemes. The results indicate that the control modules in LVoD infrastructures are becoming increasingly important for reasons of scalability, load balance, and server resource utilization.

The third paper, by M. Marin, V. Gil-Costa, and C. Bonacic, presents a novel distributed index data structure, as well as a set of related algorithms, devised to support parallel query processing of multimedia content in high-performance search engines. The presented methodology offers high locality in terms of data accesses, thus allowing for a friendly use of secondary memory, and a high

---

* Topic Chairs.

potential for exploiting multithreading. Results obtained on a 32-node compute cluster show superior results in comparison with existing approaches.

To conclude, we would like to express our gratitude to the people whose contributions made the Distributed and High-Performance Multimedia track possible. Above all, we thank the authors who submitted a paper, the Euro-Par Organization Committee, and the numerous referees, whose excellent work was an invaluable help for the topic committee.

On a Novel Dynamic Parallel Hardware Architecture for Lifting-Based DWT

Sami Khanfir and Mohamed Jemni

UTIC – Research Unit of Technology of Information and Communication,
Ecole Supérieure des Sciences et Techniques de Tunis, Tunis, Tunisia
sami.khanfir@esstt.rnu.tn, mohamed.jemni@fst.rnu.tn

Abstract. A novel fast scheme for Discrete Wavelet Transform (DWT) was introduced in last years under the name of lifting scheme [4, 7]. This new scheme presents many advantages over the convolution-based approach [3, 7]. For instance it is very suitable for parallelization. In this paper we present two new parallel FPGA-based implementations of the lifting-based DWT scheme. The first implementation uses pipelining, parallel processing and data reuse to increase the speed up of the algorithm. In the second architecture a controller is introduced to dynamically deploy a suitable number of clones accordingly to the available hardware resources on a targeted environment. These two architectures are able of processing large size incoming images or multi-framed images in real-time. The simulations driven on a Xilinx Virtex-5 FPGA environment has proven the practical efficiency of our contribution: the first architecture has given an operating frequency of 289 MHz, and the second demonstrated the controller's capabilities of deploying the maximum number of clones from the available resources, over a targeted FPGA environment and processing the task in parallel.

Keywords: parallel, reconfigurable, DWT, lifting, FPGA.

1 Introduction

Software implementations of the discrete wavelet transform, though greatly flexible, lead to performance bottlenecks in real-time systems. Hardware implementations, in contrast, offer high-performance but poor flexibility [3, 5]. For these reasons, the use of reconfigurable hardware to implement this technology may be considered as a good solution for real-time processing systems. First implementations of the wavelet transform were based on filters' convolution algorithms. A relatively recent approach [4, 7] uses the lifting scheme for the implementation of the DWT. The lifting-based DWT scheme presents many advantages over the convolution-based approach, particularly the possibility of parallelizing the algorithm. In this context, this paper introduces two new parallel approaches for the lifting-based wavelet transform implemented by using FPGA technology. Several accelerating techniques are used to achieve our goals such as the use of pipelining techniques and data reusability. The first approach proposes an architecture composed of two units for the prediction and the update of the wavelet coefficients. The two units communicate via FIFO queues.

The second approach proposes a dynamically reconfigurable parallel architecture capable of dynamically deploying, clones of the first architecture unit on a given FPGA environment. A controller is implemented in order to determine the necessary available resources allowing the successful deployment of these replicates. The simulation of these two architectures over a Xilinx Virtex-5 FPGA environment has given a maximum operating frequency of 289 MHz, for the first architecture. For the second, the controller has made a successful demonstration of its capabilities of deploying the maximum number of clones from the available resources on a given FPGA environment. The use of these two architectures may be extremely helpful for real-time image processing systems over large size or multi-framed images.

The remainder of the paper is organized as follows. In section 2 the theoretical basis of lifting-based DWT is briefly presented. The description of the lifting-based algorithm of the DWT is presented in section 3. In section 4 we present the details of our proposed approach for the hardware implementation of the lifting-based DWT algorithm. The hardware resources utilization and the performance evaluation of the two architectures are presented in section 5. A conclusion for this paper is drawn in section 6.

2 The Lifting-Based DWT

The basic idea behind the lifting scheme is to use the data correlation for removing redundancy. The lifting algorithm involves three main phases, namely: the Split phase, the Predict phase and the Update phase.

In the split phase, a data set $\lambda_{0,k}$ is split into two subsets to separate the even samples from the odd ones:

$$\lambda_{-1,k} = \lambda_{0,2k} \; ; \qquad \gamma_{-1,k} = \lambda_{0,2k+1} \qquad (1)$$

This decomposition in even and odd samples may also be referred as the lazy wavelet transform [7] since this procedure does not decorrelate the processed data.

At this point, we will use the even subset $\lambda_{-1,k}$ to predict the odd subset $\gamma_{-1,k}$ using a prediction function $P(\lambda_{-1,k})$. This procedure is called the prediction phase [4, 7].

$$\gamma_{-1,k} = \lambda_{0,2k+1} - P(\lambda_{-1,k}) \qquad (2)$$

Afterwards, the coefficient $\lambda_{-1,k}$ is lifted with the help of the neighboring wavelet coefficients. This phase is referred as the primal lifting phase or update phase [4, 7], where U is the update operator.:

$$\lambda_{-1,k} = \lambda_{-1,k} + U(\gamma_{-1,k}) \qquad (3)$$

The inverse lifting-based DWT can be derived by traversing the above steps in the reverse direction with switching the sign between additions and subtractions, applying the dual and primal lifting steps and finally applying the inverse lazy transform.

3 DWT Lifting-Based Algorithm

For clarity purpose, we will illustrate the DWT lifting-based algorithm assuming the use of a set of data with $L = 8$ components and a filter with $N = 2$ dual vanishing moments and $\widetilde{N} = 2$ real vanishing moments. Remark that our design approach is scalable and can be implemented for arbitrary signal lengths and different number of filter coefficients.

During the prediction phase, to compute the $\gamma_{j-1,k}$ coefficients, the following relation has to be implemented:

$$\forall k \in \left[0..\frac{L}{2} - 1\right], \gamma_{j-1,k} = \lambda_{j,2k+1} - \sum_{i=0}^{N-1} \lambda_{j,2(k+i)} * \alpha_{k,i} \quad (4)$$

$\alpha_{k,i}$ are the predict filter coefficients. This implementation is depicted in Fig. 1a.

During the update process, each previously calculated γ will update the λs. This procedure can be illustrated with the following relation:

$$\forall k \in \left[0..\frac{L}{2} - 1\right], \lambda_{j-1,k} = \lambda_{j,2k} + \gamma_{j-1,i} * \beta_{k,i} \quad (5)$$

$\beta_{k,i}$ are the update filter coefficients. This implementation is illustrated through Fig.1b.

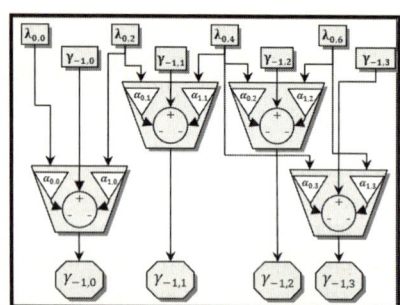

Fig. 1. (a) Prediction phase implementation **(b)** Update phase implementation

4 Hardware Architecture for DWT Lifting-Based Algorithm

The goal of this work is to propose a high memory throughput architecture to treat large size images as well as real-time DWT processing for video treatment.

4.1 The Prediction Unit

Our implementation of the prediction phase of the DWT lifting-base algorithm is based on a pipelined architecture as illustrated in Fig. 2, with $L = 8$ and $N = 2$.

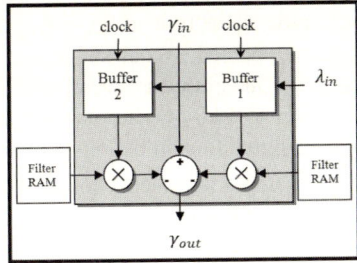

Fig. 2. Parallel prediction unit architecture

Our approach exploits the fact that when processing two consecutive values of λ, some of the coefficients λ are commonly reused during the calculation (Fig. 1a), thus for the processing of the next γ coefficient, only one new λ coefficient is read from the memory, the preceding λ coefficients, involved during the previous calculations, have to be temporarily stored in the buffer for reuse. In this context, the use of the pipelining technique would be of great value for this problem. As a matter of fact, we have implemented a pipeline of N stages for the λ inputs coefficients. $N-1$ cycles would be needed to fill-in the pipeline during the initialization process followed by the parallel processing of $N * \lambda$ coefficients driven to the multiplier. To ensure concurrent access to N filter coefficients, we used separate RAM banks to store the filter coefficients. To ensure the parallel processing of the unit, we have to process the reading of both λ and γ input coefficients at the same time. This means that we have to access different locations of the storage memory of the image at the same time. We have used for this purpose true dual port memories with separate undependably addressable input/output ports configured directly in the Xilinx FPGA processing core [9, 10]. After processing the predicted γ coefficient, we have to write it back at the same initial memory location, rather than at another memory location, to ensure good efficiency and speed up of this architecture. In fact, the reading of the inputs data, λ and γ, from the memory, has to be done at the same time as the writing of the outputs into the memory. This is quite difficult since both ports of the dual ports of the RAM are already involved in the reading process. To counterpart this difficultly, we imposed to the RAM to operate at twice the frequency of the entire design. Finally, when considering the treatments over the boundaries, the processing unit has to stop when attending the signal boundaries and consider only the corresponding filter coefficients and the associated coefficient of γ. For this purpose we have added some enabling signals into the pipeline process.

4.2 The Update Unit

Our parallel approach is based on a pipelined architecture as described in Fig. 3. We will use the same example given in section 3 ($L = 8$ and $\widetilde{N} = 2$). In the update phase the treatment starts by an initialization step to fill the pipeline register with the initial data. Afterwards, the content of the λ registers has to be shifted to the left-hand side; at the same time the acquisition of the data, from the RAM, has to continue. The filter coefficients, corresponding to the last λ with the first γ, have to be loaded, via the update coefficient, with the λ_{in} inputs at the same time as the filling of the last λ. At the adder's output, after being processed, the updated λ coefficients are ready to be stored. While performing all these operations, we have used a special configuration for processing the considered γ coefficients in order to take into account the exceptions of the boundary treatments. We have used a reset signal to stop the pipeline and freeze the λ coefficients from being shifting. The output sample is issued via λ_{out}. When the λ coefficients are available at the output, they are written back in the memory.

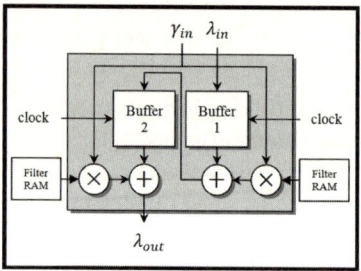

Fig. 3. Parallel update unit architecture

4.3 Inverse Prediction and Update Implementation

The same prediction and update units will be used for both forward and inverse transform by selectively alternating a control signal to set the scheme to forward or inverse processing. This signal applies a control after the multiple-inputs adder for performing either addition or subscription in both units.

4.4 Unified Unit for DWT Lifting-Based Prediction and Update Processing

To conceive a unified unit for both prediction and update DWT lifting based processing phases, we have used a FIFO (First-In First-Out) buffer to synchronize communications between the two units. In fact, a simple parallel implementation of both prediction and update units would overload the memory bandwidth. Indeed, the parallel execution of both units implies six memory accesses per cycle (three accesses for the prediction units and three others for the update unit). We used a FIFO buffer, between the two units, in order to have only four concurrent accesses to memory (two accesses for the prediction module, one access for the outputs and one access for the update). Fig. 4 illustrates this unified unit based on a FIFO buffer use. The input of the update unit uses the same input λ coefficient, of the prediction unit, at a different time rate. It is indeed obvious that we cannot connect the RAM to both inputs of the prediction unit and update unit. The insertion of a *B1*, before the λ input of the update module, allows this latter to reuse the λs that has been involved in the production phase. *B2* absorbs the unequal delivery and compensation rates of data at the beginning and at the end of the prediction and update phases. When considering the inverse transform, the synchronization scheme implies to reverse the above described synchronization process by providing data to the inputs of the prediction unit from the FIFO's and receiving data from the RAM for the update unit.

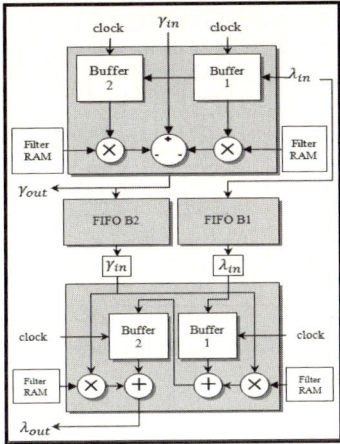

Fig. 4. Parallel unified unit architecture

4.5 Dynamic Parallel Hardware Architecture for Lifting-Based DWT Algorithm

To increase the performance of our implementation, we have used the unified unit, in a dynamic and parallel architecture. Our approach is based on a dynamic reconfiguration in order to use the available resources at the deployment step. In other words, our system verifies the amount of the available resources present in the hardware in question, before any deployment, and then clones the unified unit, described above, following the connection architecture depicted in Fig. 5. Depending on the acquired parameters, the system calculates the maximum number of clones, of the DWT lifting-based unified unit, and builds the adequate connection architecture. For this purpose, we have designed a global controller to insure the synchronization and the communication (if needed) between the different units. Afterward, the controller builds the connection architecture following the parameters that it acquired from the hardware. The final step of the deployment is the building of the different clones at the tail of each created connection. Each clone will have its own memory, based on the cascading asynchronous dual-port block RAM. For our implementation we have used adjacent combined block RAMs memory [9, 10]. Fig. 5 depicts a fully deployed cloned architecture with the connection architecture. After the successful deployment, each clone will work independently from the others. In fact, the controller assigns different tiles to each clone (their size is dynamically fixed by the controller depending on the size of the initial image and the number of deployed clones). Due to the diversity of content of the processed image and therefore the diversity content of each processed tile, a given clone can finish its processing before another. We have used the "First-Finished First-Served" strategy to distribute the jobs over the clones. When two clones finish their job at exactly the same time, the first served one would be the nearest to the controller.

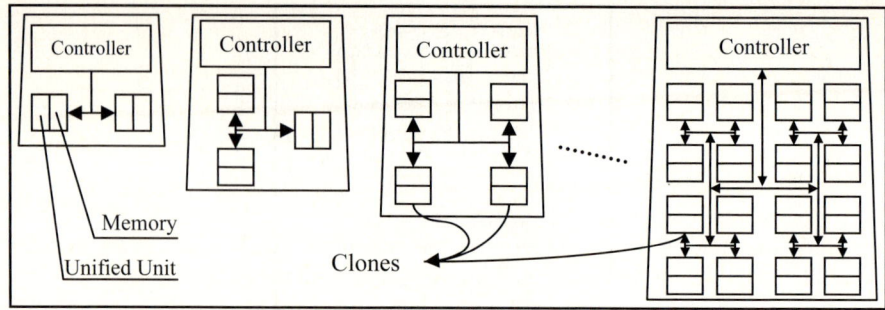

Fig. 5. Dynamic parallel deployment of the DWT lifting-based clones

5 Experimental Results

5.1 Hardware Resources Utilization

We have implemented the above described architectures using VHDL description language and schematic-based design. The synthesis of these architectures was performed using ISE foundation design tool (version 9.1i). We have used a Xilinx ML501 evaluation platform based on the Xilinx Virtex-5 FPGA, XC5VLX50T core to implement our architectures. Fig. 6 illustrates the hardware resources utilization considering the use of an image with 128x64 pixels size and an eight bits gray-scale. We have used the (9/7) wavelet filter used in the JPEG2000 standard. This implementation has given a maximum operating frequency of 289 MHz for one single unified unit.

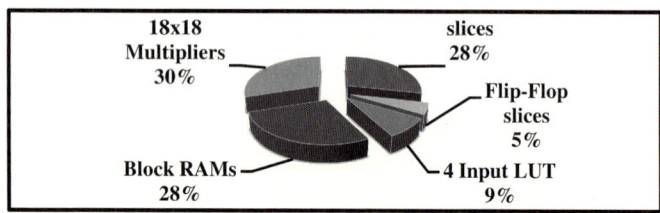

Fig. 6. Hardware resources utilization

From the experimental simulations, we could remark that the implementation of one single unit consumed only 849 slices of the 7200 available ones, 607 Flip-Flop slices and 1046 4-Input LUTs from the 28800 available ones, 14 BRAMs from the 120 available ones and 6 18x18 Multipliers from the 48 available ones. All the statistics, shown in Fig. 6, are also exactly preserved for larger images processing except for the Bank RAMs that are dynamically modified accordingly to the image and filter size.

5.2 Performance Evaluation

Our evaluation is based on the following criteria: the number of cycles per pixel, the number of images per second in the transform time (in clock cycles and in microseconds respectively). We measured the time to perform the discrete wavelet transform on an entire image including all the required data transfers.

Single-unit based implementation evaluation. We have used two evaluation scenarii:
- Diversifying the degree of the polynomial filters, and fixing the image size. Fig. 7 presents the performance results obtained with different polynomial degrees of filtering and an image of 1024x768 pixels size. We can notice that the more the polynomial degree of the used filters increases, the more the transform time increases and the more the number of treated images per second decreases.
- Diversifying the image sizes and maintaining fixed the polynomial degree of the used filter. Fig. 8 presents the performance results using a 2-2 polynomial filter. We can notice that the more the image size increases, the more the FPGA cycles/pixel decreases.

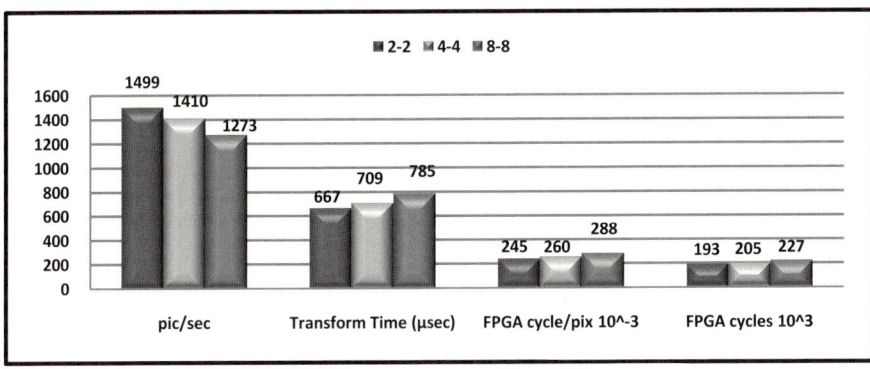

Fig. 7. Single-unit based implementation evaluation for different degrees of polynomial filters

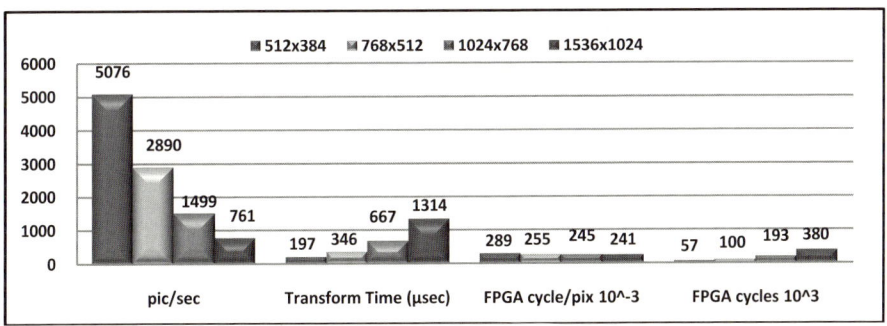

Fig. 8. Single-unit based implementation evaluation for different image's sizes

Table 1 illustrates a comparison with other related works such as [1, 2, 6, 8]. These results show the efficiency of our implementation from hardware resources and maximum operating frequency point of view.

Table 1. Performance comparison with existing FPGA implementations

Ref. to related works	FPGA core	Decomposition Levels	Slices	Freq (MHz)
[6]	4052XL	2	785	85.49
[1]	XCV300	2	853	89.1
[8]	XCVE2000	2	1402	159.51
[2]	XCV2P20	2	1907	201.09
Our work	XC5VLX50T	2	849	289

Dynamic parallel hardware architecture performance evaluation. We have considered three cases for the performance evaluation: the first case where the hardware has completely all its resources fully available for the implementation. The second case where the hardware has an already running application consuming 37% of the available hardware resources in order to prove the controller's capability of adapting the deployment in terms of the available material resources. And finally the third case where the hardware has one running job consuming only 24% of the resources. This job consumes a lot of memory banks allowing the deployment of just one unique clone in order to check the controller's capability of recognizing that the available memory resources are not sufficient for more than one clone deployment even if there are remaining free resources (i.e. case 3 in table 2). These results show that the controller is able to determine the necessary number of clones that can be possibly deployed into a targeted architecture. Table 2 illustrates the different results concerning this implementation.

Table 2. Clones' deployment statistics for different cases of resources availabilities

	Case 1	Case 2	Case 3
Available resources	100%	63%	76%
slices	7200	4536	5472
Flip-Flop slices	28800	18144	21888
4 Input LUT	28800	18144	21888
Block RAMs	120	75	22
18x18 Multipliers	48	30	36
Number of clones	8	5	1

6 Conclusion

We have introduced in this paper two novel hardware implementations of the discrete wavelet transform based on the lifting scheme. We have used several accelerating techniques such as pipelining, parallel module operation and data reuse to implement a unified unit. This latter is composed of one prediction based processing unit and one update based processing unit connected through FIFO blocks. We have also conceived a dynamically reconfigurable parallel hardware architecture capable of dynamically deploying clones of the unified unit on an FPGA environment by determining the necessary available resources allowing a successful deployment of these clones. The performance evaluation has proven the efficiency of our approach. In fact, the simulation of a single processing unit on a Xilinx Virtex-5 FPGA environment has given an operating frequency of 289MHz. The implementation of the parallel reconfigurable version of the DWT lifting-based processing unit demonstrated the controller's capabilities of determining the true available resources needed for a successful deployment over a given FPGA environment. Finally the use of these two architectures could be extremely helpful for real-time image processing systems of large size images.

References

1. Al-Haj, A.: Fast Discrete Wavelet Transformation Using FPGAs and Distributed Arithmetic. International Journal of Applied Science and Engineering, 160–171 (2003)
2. Bishop, S.L., Rai, S., Gunturk, B., Trahan, J.L., Vaidyanathan, R.: Reconfigurable Implementation of Wavelet Integer Lifting Transforms for Image Compression. In: IEEE International Conference on Reconfigurable Computing and FPGAapos, 2006. ReConFig 2006, September 2006, pp. 1–9 (2006)
3. Calderbank, R., Daubechies, I., Sweldens, W., Yeo, B.-L.: Losless image compression using integer to integer wavelet transforms. In: International Conference on Image Processing (ICIP), vol. I, pp. 596–599. IEEE Press, Los Alamitos (1997)
4. Daubechies, I., Sweldens, W.: Factoring wavelet transforms into lifting schemes. J. Fourier Anal. Appl. 4(3), 247–269 (1998)
5. Grapes, A.: An introduction to wavelets. IEEE Computational Science and Engineering 2(2) (Summer 1995)
6. Masud, S., McCanny, J.V.: Rapid design of biorthogonal wavelet transforms. IEE Proceedings of Circuits, Devices and Systems 147(5), 293–296 (2000)
7. Sweldens, W.: The lifting scheme: a custom-design construction of biorthogonal wavelets. Applied and Computaional Harmonic Analysis 3(15), 186–200 (1996)
8. Uzun, I., Amira, A.: Design and FPGA implementation of high-speed discrete biorthogonal wavelet transforms. In: 13th European signal processing conference EUSIPCO 2005 (September 2005)
9. Virtex-5 Family Overview, DS100 (v3.4), December 18 (2007)
10. Xilinx ML501 Evaluation Platform User Guide, UG226 (v1.2), November 26 (2007)

Analytical Evaluation of Clients' Failures in a LVoD Architecture Based on P2P and Multicast Paradigms[*]

Rodrigo Godoi[1], Xiaoyuan Yang[2], and Porfidio Hernández[1]

[1] Computer Architecture and Operating Systems Department
Universitat Autònoma de Barcelona, UAB
Edifici Q, 08193 Barcelona, Spain
`rodrigo@aomail.uab.es, porfidio.hernandez@uab.es`
[2] Telefonica Research
Via Augusta, 177, 08021 Barcelona, Spain
`yxiao@tid.es`

Abstract. Peer-to-peer (P2P), multicast or hybrid paradigms are used nowadays as the main strategies in order to improve performance and scalability of Large Video on Demand (LVoD) systems. Using P2P and multicast supposes facing situations like how often peers connect and disconnect from the system or reconfiguration of multicast delivery trees. Therefore, such distributed designs require a complex control mechanism that can involve huge volume of network messages as well as computational requirements. Nevertheless, the control schemes are neglected in the LVoD design, which is rather focused on the application level logic for video data transmission. In this paper we analyze extensively, by mean of analytical models, the requirement of the control subsystem of a P2P multicast architecture named PCM/MCDB. In our analysis, we consider different designs schemes and the results show an increasing importance of the control module in the LVoD infrastructure.

Keywords: LVoD systems, Peer-to-Peer, Multicast, Control mechanisms.

1 Introduction

The term Large Video on Demand (LVoD) refers to services where many clients, geographically distributed, can request multimedia content at any given moment. LVoD systems are basically made up of three kinds of elements: servers, clients and communications networks. Providing acceptable Quality of Service (Qos) for all the system's client is a key concept in any video service; it involves different aspects, such as image quality or audio and video synchronization. In order to improve LVoD system performance and scalability, the P2P collaborations and multicast communications have been used as the main strategies. P2P architectures allow the use of clients' available resources to decentralize the system load and provide system scalability. The multicast technique consists of the information flow from a source to a group of

---

[*] This work was supported by the MEC-Spain under contracts TIN 2004-03388 and TIN 2007-64974.

users who requested the same content. These allow clients to share resources and decrease the server and network requirements.

Recent advances provide multicast scheme application on real networks. The patching multicast policy [01], for example, dynamically assigns clients to join ongoing multicast channels and patches the missing portion of video into a unicast channel. Many local networks on today's Internet are already multicast-capable. In order to achieve global multicast, Application Level Multicast (ALM) has been proposed, where group members form an overlay network and data packets are relayed from one member to another via unicast. Most recently, the P2P paradigm has been proposed to decentralize the delivery process to all clients. The P2Cast P2P delivery scheme [02] creates a delivery multicast tree and is able to combine the Patching and Chaining policies. P2VoD [03] introduces the concept of generation, which groups a set of clients to distribute information.

In VoD architectures proposed in previous works by our research group [04] [05], we applied P2P collaboration beyond content sharing, extending this concept to resource sharing, e.g. bandwidth and buffer capacity. The PCM/MCDB [04] handles P2P and multicast paradigms substituting on-going server channels with collaboration channels. DynaPeer [05] also applies both paradigms and even considers the heterogeneous bandwidth available in real environments like Internet. Nevertheless, no current LVoD architecture that uses P2P and multicast concepts takes into account, for all phases of a failure process, the control load imposed on the system by a client disruption or a multicast tree reconstruction. In this paper we define as background a *Failure Management Process* (FMP), made up by three components: detection, recovery and maintenance of system information. We apply the FMP to the PCM/MCDB delivery scheme to analyze the control load that implies clients' failures in a system that applies P2P and multicast. We are considering multicast islands, i.e. networks having routers with IP multicast capability [6]. We develop analytical models according to server, network and clients parameters to represent the control costs. Our evaluation is based on the number of control messages interchanged by the elements in an FMP. Centralized and distributed FMPs are analyzed to evaluate system performance in terms of resources consumption, scalability and load balance.

The remainder of this paper is structured as follows. Section 2 presents the key ideas behind PCM/MCDB delivery scheme. The Failure Management Process and analytical models are introduced in Section 3. Performance evaluation is shown in Section 4. In Section 5, we indicate our main conclusions and future studies.

2 P2P Multicast Delivery Scheme Overview

In a VoD service, video information is sent by the server through the network to the clients. The clients receive, decode and display the video information. The clients' design includes buffers that temporarily cache information for three purposes: 1) a portion of this buffer is used to achieve smooth playback. We call this portion the cushion buffer. The size of this portion is invariable and is mainly dependant on the video format and variations in network bandwidth. 2) The client caches video information from the delivery channels (delivery buffer). The size of the delivery buffer changes according to the delivery policy. 3) All the client buffer that is not used for the previous two purposes will be utilized in the client collaboration. We call this portion "collaborative buffer" and it is able to cache video information for sending to another client.

Clients are connected to the VoD server through the network. In our design, we assume that the network is segmented and each client is able to maintain communication with other clients. We also assume that the local client is able to deliver video information to the local network using the multicast technique (IP multicast islands). Video information is assumed to be encoded with a Constant Bit-Rate (CBR). The video information is delivered in network packets and the packet size is invariable. We call a network block a video block. We enumerate the blocks of a video from 1 to L; L being the size of a video in video blocks.

The delivery scheme decides how the video information is sent to clients. Our delivery scheme is designed based on two policies: *Patch Collaboration Manager* (PCM) and *Multicast Channel Distributed Branching* (MCDB).

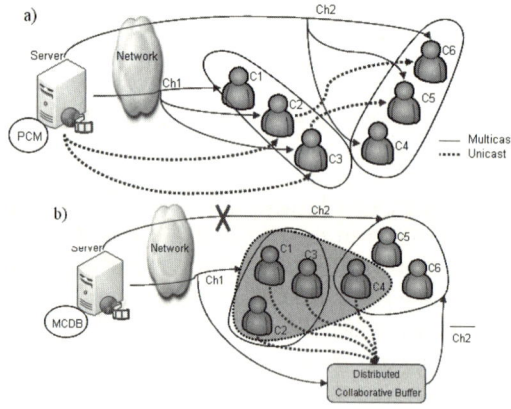

Fig. 1. P2P Delivery Scheme: a) PCM delivery policy and b) MCDB Collaboration policy

The PCM mechanism has the aim of creating multicast channels to service groups of clients, and allows clients to collaborate with the server to deliver portions of video in the admission process. With PCM, clients receive video information from both multicast and unicast channels. The multicast channels are created by the server, whereas the unicast channels could be created either by the server or the clients. Figure 1 a) shows the PCM scheme. The multicast channels deliver every block of a video while the unicast channels only send a portion of a video. The objective of MCDB, however, is to eliminate multicast channels so as to reduce server load. The policy replaces an on-going multicast channel with a local multicast channel. A group of collaborative clients is synchronized to form a Distributed Collaborative Buffer. The clients in this group use their buffers to cache video blocks from another multicasting channel. The cached blocks are delivered by the collaborating clients in order to generate the local multicast channel; figure 1b) illustrate the MCDB mechanism.

3 The Failure Management Process: Description and Models

The PCM/MCDB mechanism takes advantage of clients' collaborations to improve system performance. Nevertheless, users come and go freely in this kind of system, which can degrade the QoS due to interruptions to the video information flow. We propose an FMP as a way to represent the dynamic involved in solving client failures in the PCM/MCDB. It is based on three components: *detection, recovery* and *maintenance of information*. We steer our study towards the number of control messages involved in centralized and distributed FMP, once the volume of messages indicates the control load injected into the network. A centralized FMP approach means a simple design and can represent an adequate and efficient solution for a range of applications. However, a centralized architecture has obvious implications, such as server load or the fact that a central controller represents a single point for managing all failure operations, and if it crashes, the whole fault tolerance scheme is lost. On the other hand, a distributed scheme provides an autonomous FMP, where peers are responsible for managing failures.

Table 1. Parameters used in the analytic models

$C_{detection}$	Network load injected by the detection phase.
$C_{recovery}$	Network load injected by the recovery phase.
C_{maint}	Network load injected by the maintenance phase.
N_C	Number of active clients in the system.
H	Number of clients that trigger a recovery process.
G	Total number of multicast groups.
$HOPS_{g(i)}$	Number of hops for each multicast group G.
p_s	Probability of finding a collaborator.
f_{HB}	Heartbeat message frequency.
f_e	Client failure frequency.
f_{CI}	Client communication messages frequency.
f_{TI}	Router communication messages frequency.
β	Number of messages required for the detection protocol.
σ	Number of messages required between clients for the recovery protocol.
γ	Number of messages required between routers for the recovery protocol.
ω	Number of messages required between clients for the maintenance protocol.
α	Number of messages required between routers for the maintenance protocol.

3.1 Failure Detection

The FMP supposes that a collaborator suddenly leaves the system, so for detection, we assume a heartbeat mechanism, which is widely applied by the community [03] [04]. The heartbeat strategy consists of the exchange of control messages; these messages mean that a client is alive in the system and suitable for collaborative functions. Whenever heartbeat is not received by the manager element, query messages are sent for a limited number of attempts. If there is no answer, the recovery phase is triggered. In case of a centralized detection, a server receives heartbeats from all collaborators and is responsible for sending query messages and starting recovery. In the same way, if detection is distributed, clients organized in a communication topology interchange heartbeat/query messages and trigger the recovery stage. The centralized and distributed detection are described below. For convenience, all parameters used in the analysis are defined in table 1.

Centralized: This scheme supposes all clients send heartbeat messages to a central server. Therefore the model represents the total number of collaborators (N_C) sending β messages to the server in a f_{HB} frequency. This cost is given by equation 1.

Distributed: In the distributed approach, we define a *Manager Node* (MN) per multicast group, which is responsible for keeping information about the group members. The selection of MN is performed based on its history in the system and its capabilities, such as buffer size, processing capacity and available bandwidth. A hierarchy is established in the group in order to enable the MN function for another client in a set of nodes in case the current MN fails. So, heartbeat messages must be sent by all clients in a group ($N_{C\_g(i)}$), for the respective MN. Message interchange is also necessary between MNs in order to detect failures in this kind of element. Thus, the distributed detection cost is expressed by equation 2.

$$C_{\det ection} = f_{HB} \cdot \beta \cdot N_C . \tag{1}$$

$$C_{\det ection} = f_{HB} \cdot \beta \cdot \left[\sum_{i=1}^{G} N_{C\_g(i)} + G^2 \right] . \tag{2}$$

3.2 Failure Recovery

When a failure is detected, corrective actions must be taken respecting a deadline, in order to avoid a loss of QoS. The aim of the recovery phase is find an adequate client (or collaboration group) to substitute the crashed one. This substitution implies that the new collaborator must contribute with satisfactory resources (e.g. buffer capacity). Whenever a substitute peer is not found, the recovery process must contact the server and verify the possibility of it taking on the service of the failed client.

In the MCDB P2P delivery process, a collaborative client can be in 4 states: 1) Client is delivering video information. 2) A client could be waiting to start the delivery process. 3) A client in the group caches the video information from another multicast channel. 4) Clients could be waiting to start the caching process. The collaborators in PCM scheme are always in state 1. In figure 2, C1 is delivering video information, C2 is completely buffered and waiting to start delivery, C3 is caching and C4 is waiting to start caching. Once C1 finishes, C2 must start the delivery, C3 will be full buffered, C4 will start caching and finally, C1 will wait for caching. Clients in a collaboration group interchange messages in order to synchronize their actions, thus guaranteeing the correct information flow. All clients assume a specific state each time, forming a cycle. Clients failed in different states generate distinct actions.

State 1 Delivering: The replacement collaborator has to have the same collaborative buffer capacity. If the new collaborator does not have video information, the server must take over the delivery process temporarily. Since the client failure detection mechanism needs a period of time to trigger the recovery, clients of the disrupted channel will not receive any information before the recovery process. The QoS is guaranteed in this case by the cushion buffer that receivers' clients build through a

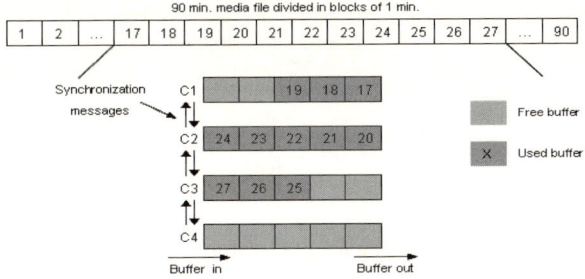

Fig. 2. Buffering states in collaboration process

start-up delay. This cushion buffer provides video information until the end of the recovery process. For example, if C1 in Figure 3 fails, and the recovery process is unable to find a new collaborator that has blocks 17, 18 and 19, the server must send the respectively blocks, until the cycle can be reestablished.

State 2 Waiting for delivering: The recovery action for this state is similar to the case for state 1. However, the new collaborator or server has to send all the video blocks that were cached by the failed client.

State 3 Caching: The new collaborator must continue with caching process of the failed client. The video blocks that are already cached by the failed client will be delivered by the new collaborator or server. For example, in Figure 3, C3 fails and the new collaborator will cache blocks 28 and 29. Blocks 25, 26 and 27 will be sent by the server or the new collaborator.

State 4 Waiting for Caching: The failed client has no useful information in its buffer, so the recovery process only needs to find a new collaborator to replace it.

In a general sense, the recovery depends on the failure frequency (f_e) and client communications. On the other hand, communication between IP multicast routers is also necessary to rearrange the distribution trees. Below, we introduce the centralized and distributed recovery mechanisms.

Centralized: This approach supposes that the recovery process triggers the server, which is responsible for performing a search based on the clients' information. The search should select the most suitable collaborator to substitute the failed one. After selecting an adequate candidate, the server contacts the nodes which have requested recovery and the new(s) collaborator(s), to perform the link. The cost, considering communication to delivery tree restructuring, is given by equation 3.

Distributed: The distributed scheme assume that the recovery process is managed autonomously by own nodes. The MN searches in a list for a substitute collaborator, with the necessary characteristics to substitute the failed peer. If there is a node available in the group, the linking process is performed. Otherwise, the MN contacts the MN of another group, and asks for a qualified candidate to replace the failed peer. This process is repeated for all the groups, until a new collaborator be found, always respecting the deadline in order to maintain the QoS. The cost for this case is given by expression 4.

$$C_{recovery} = f_{e.} \cdot \left[\sigma \cdot H + \sum_{i=1}^{G} \gamma \cdot Hops_{g(i)} \right]. \tag{3}$$

$$C_{recovery} = f_{e.} \cdot \left(\frac{H}{p_s} + \sigma \cdot H + \sum_{i=1}^{G} \gamma \cdot Hops_{g(i)} \right). \tag{4}$$

3.3 Maintenance of System Information Coherence

The search process for a substitute node is done by accessing a list. It implies that clients must send information messages, with a certain frequency, to a determined system element, depending on the scheme adopted (i.e. centralized or distributed). The status information for all clients shall be organized and kept up to date to produce the list that will be used to find a new collaborator in a recovery process. The system must know the state of clients with certain precision; whether they are available or not and all the resource information needed to perform a set of possible collaborators. This is the maintenance of the information coherence phase. The process also needs communication between the routers that implement the IP Multicast to maintain or rearrange the distribution trees. The centralized and distributed maintenance schemes are shown below.

Centralized: In this mechanism, clients send periodic messages to the server to inform about their status. The server analyses the information and creates lists with a set of possible collaborators. Thus, the cost of this stage, including router communications to maintain distribution trees, is represented by expression 5.

Distributed: This approach supposes that clients inside a group exchange messages periodically to inform about their characteristics. In this case, there is no central point that contains the entire system information. All peers in a group send messages to the MN, who creates a list. Also, there are communications between the MNs from different groups in order to know who is necessary to establish contact with in an eventual recovery. The distributed cost is given by equation 6.

$$C_{maint} = f_{CI} \cdot \omega \cdot N_C + f_{TI} \sum_{i=1}^{G} \alpha \cdot Hops_{g(i)}. \tag{5}$$

$$C_{maint} = f_{CI} \cdot \left(\sum_{i=1}^{G} \omega \cdot N_{C\_g(i)} + G^2 \right) + f_{TI} \cdot \sum_{i=1}^{G} \alpha \cdot Hops_{g(i)} \tag{6}$$

4 Performance Evaluation

In this section, we assess the developed models. GT-ITM [07] is used to generate a router topology that represents an IP multicast island. The applied topology has two levels, each made up of six stub-domains and one transit-domain. The six stub-domains are formed by a total of 54 routers, where each one has associated networks that are limited to connecting a maximum of 200 clients. The transit-domain comprises 3 routers that have no clients directly associated; the video server is connected to one of the transit routers. The total number of possible active clients in the system is 10800 (54 routers x 200 clients/router). We consider that the server has sufficient resources to provide service for all the requests and control management. A single recovery request is considered each time (i.e. $H = 1$) and the probability of finding a collaborator (p_s), in the distributed mechanism depends on the size of the multicast groups. We are considering the PIM-SM protocol for IP multicast implementation because, nowadays, it is widely used. The number of messages in the detection, recovery and maintenance protocols is assumed to be *one* (β), *two* (γ, ω, α) and *three* (σ). We consider that the status messages are sent with frequencies f_{CI} and f_{TI} of 1 every 15 seconds [08] [09] [10] [11]. The router tables must support the evaluation structure proposed; so we took [12] [13] as a base and verified that the 57-router topology represents an acceptable memory consumption, as commercial routers today are available with 128MB - 1GB memories [14].

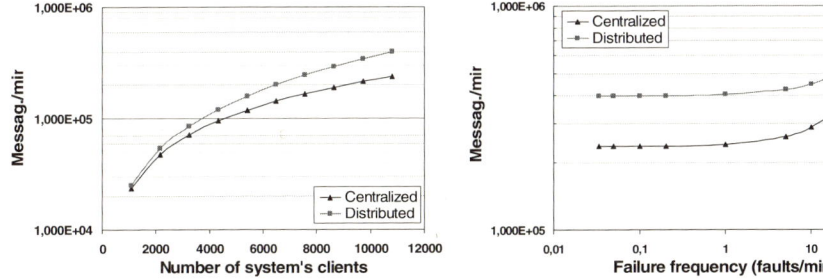

Fig. 3. Influence of the number of clients   **Fig. 4.** Influence of failure frequency

We evaluate the control cost in different aspects. Analyzing the number of clients in the system and the failure frequency, we assess the increase that the distributed scheme represents over the centralized one ({distr.cost–centr.cost}/centr.cost). Bandwidth consumption is evaluated by comparing the control traffic with the content traffic that flows through the system (control traffic/video traffic). For all evaluations we only vary one parameter, attributing fixed values to the others. First, we consider the number of active clients in the system. This varies from 1080 to 10800. The number of multicast groups varies according to the number of clients once the number of clients per group is fixed. In figure 3 is possible to verify a crescent difference between the centralized and distributed approaches, reaching 67.5%. It occurs due to the number of messages interchanged by the multicast groups. Clients dispersed in a few multicast groups generate non-representative communications between each other. Nevertheless, when the higher the number of multicast groups is, the more important the messages originated from MNs. Figure 4 shows the influence of the failure frequency [09]. Each failure triggers a recovery process, which increases the network load cost. The difference between the centralized and distributed schemes decreases with high failure frequency, reaching 37.6%. This occurs because p_s becomes less influential on the number of messages inserted by the recovery process.

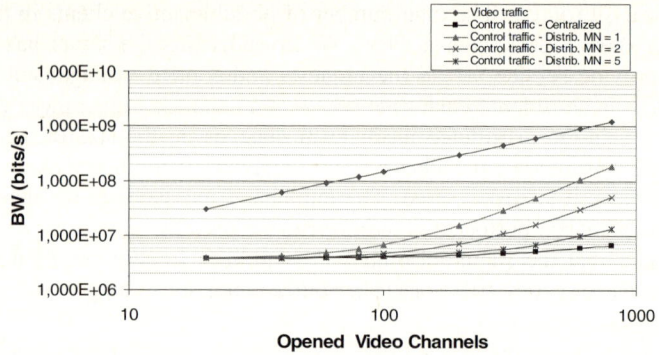

Fig. 5. Video and control resource consumption

In next evaluation, we express the extra load that the control messages represent for the system. Thus, the messages are assumed to have an average length of 128B [15]. The total number of clients is fixed this time. We assume that few members per multicast group imply a larger number of groups, demonstrating that clients arrive at different times or present heterogeneous behaviour in content request. On the other hand, whenever the multicast can group many clients, the total number of groups is lower. Clients arriving close in time and the most popular content being requested provide more users in a server channel and more P2P collaboration. Each multicast group is responsible for one communication channel with a video rate of 1.5Mbps. When the number of multicast groups grows, the total video traffic also rises (No. of multicast channels x video rate). The control message traffic also increases with more multicast groups (No. of messages/sec. x 128B x 8b). Different MNs assignments are considered to the distributed scheme. We evaluate three scenarios that drastically change the dynamics of communications; we consider one MN responsible for managing 1, 2 and 5 multicast groups, reducing the total number of MNs. In figure 5 is possible to verify for a low number of video channels, all schemes represent almost the same when compared to video traffic, around 12%. Nevertheless, when video channels are in the order of hundred, the differences can be noticed between the schemes. The control traffic of the distributed approach considering one MN for each multicast group reaches 15%, compared to video traffic. It makes the influence of the policy adopted at time to provide control mechanisms clear.

5 Conclusions

The application of IP multicast and P2P paradigms on LVoD improve system performance, although they suppose some implications. The results show that the distributed FMP causes an inherent increment in the network load when compared to a centralized approach. However, distributed schemes seem more adequate for LVoD since provide more scalability, network load balance and save server resources. In addition, the distributed approach is more reliable due to it not presenting a single point of failure. We verified that the control messages can consume quite amount of resources that could be applied to delivering content. Therefore, the control mechanism requires careful development and its impact must be considered when we discuss system performance, mainly when paradigms that request a lot of communication and synchronization are applied.

We have started several future research projects. First, our objective is to simulate systems with client disruptions and compare the results against the analytical models. We are studying communication protocols, topologies and hierarchies between clients to achieve an efficient distributed control approach. Finally, we are working on designing a whole LVoD structure, composed of policies and protocols that provide control and delivery content functions to servers and users.

References

1. Hua, K.A., Cai, Y., Sheu, S.: Patching: A Multicast Technique for True Video-on-Demand Services. In: ACM Multimedia Conf., pp. 191–200 (1998)
2. Guo, Y., Suh, K., Kurose, J., Towsley, D.: P2Cast: P2P Patching Scheme for VoD Service. In: WWW 2003, pp. 301–309 (2003)
3. Do, T., Hua, K., Tantaoui, M.: P2VoD: providing fault tolerant video-on-demand streaming in peer-to-peer environment. In: IEEE ICC 2004, vol. 3, pp. 1467–1472 (2004)
4. Yang, X., Hernández, P., Cores, F., Ripoll, A., Suppi, R., Luque, E.: Dynamic Distributed Collaborative Merging Policy to Optimize the Multicasting Delivery Scheme. In: Euro-Par Conference, pp. 879–889 (2005)
5. Souza, L., Cores, F., Yang, X., Ripoll, A.: DynaPeer: A Dynamic Peer-to-Peer Based Delivery Scheme for VoD Systems. In: Euro-Par Conference, pp. 769–781 (2007)
6. Cheng, K.-L., Cheuk, K.-W., Gary Chan, S.-H.: Implementation and Performance Measurement of an Island Multicast Protocol. In: IEEE ICC 2005, vol. 2, pp. 1299–1303 (2005)
7. Zegura, E., Calvert, K., Bhattacharjee, S.: How to Model an Internetwork. In: IEEE INFOCOM 1996, vol. 2, pp. 594–602 (1996)
8. Wang, X., Yu, C., Schulzrinne, H., Stirpe, P., Wu, W.: IP Multicast fault recovery in PIM over OSPF. In: IEEE ICNP 2000, pp. 166–125 (2000)
9. Silverston, T., Fourmaux, O.: Measuring P2P IPTV Systems. In: ACM NOSSDAV (2007)
10. Cicic, T., Gjessing, S., Kure, O.: Tree Recovery in PIM Sparse Mode. Telecommunication Systems 19(3-4), 443–460 (2002)
11. The International Computer Science Institute Center of Internet Research, http://www.icir.org/models/linkmodel.html
12. Billhartz, T., Cain, J.B., Farrey-Goudreau, E., Fieg, D., Batsell., S.: Performance and Resource Cost Comparisons for the CBT and PIM Multicast Routing Protocols. IEEE Journal on Selected Areas in Communications 15(3), 304–315 (1997)
13. Newman, P., Minshall, G., Lyon, T., Huston, L.: IP Switching and Gigabit Routers. IEEE Communications Magazine, 64–69 (1997)
14. Juniper Networks J2300/J4300/J6300 Services Router datasheet (2006)
15. Li, D., Wu, J., Xu, K., Cui, Y., Liu, Y., Zhang, X.: Performance Analysis of Multicast Routing Protocol PIM-SM. In: IEEE AICT/SAPIR/ELETE 2005, pp. 157–162 (2005)

A Search Engine Index for Multimedia Content

Mauricio Marin[1,2], Veronica Gil-Costa[3], and Carolina Bonacic[4]

[1] Yahoo! Research, Santiago, Chile
[2] University of Santiago of Chile
[3] DCC, University of San Luis, Argentina
[4] ArTeCS, Complutense University of Madrid, Spain

Abstract. We present a distributed index data structure and algorithms devised to support parallel query processing of multimedia content in search engines. We present a comparative study with a number of data structures used as indexes for metric space databases. Our optimization criteria are based on requirements for high-performance search engines. The main advantages of our proposal are efficient performance with respect to other approaches (sequentially and in parallel), suitable treatment of secondary memory, and support for OpenMP multithreading. We presents experiments for the asynchronous (MPI) and bulk-synchronous (BSP) message passing models of parallel computing showing that in both models our approach outperforms others consistently.

1 Introduction

Dealing efficiently with multiple user queries, each potentially at a different stage of execution at any given instant of time, is a central issue in large-scale plain-text based search engines. Here the use of suitable parallel computing techniques devised to grant, among other optimizations, all queries an even share of the computational resources is crucial to reduce response time and avoid unstable behavior caused by dynamic variations of the query traffic. At the core of a plain-text search engine is a data structure used as an index that allows fast solution of queries.

New applications demand the use of data more complex than plain text. As such, it is reasonable to expect that in the near future search engines will be compelled to include facilities to handle metric space databases. Metric spaces are useful to model complex data objects such as images or audio. In this case queries are represented by an object of the same type to those in the database wherein, for example, one is interested in retrieving the top-R objects which are most similar to the query. The degree of similarity between two objects is calculated by an application-dependent function called the *distance function*.

A number of data structures and algorithms for metric spaces have been proposed so far [4] and papers on parallelization of some of these strategies have been presented in [5, 8, 9]. In this paper we propose a new strategy which satisfies demanding requirements from high-performance search engines. In the following we describe the two main principles we have identified as the ones leading to efficient performance in plain-text based search engines which we apply in the context of this paper.

Sync/Async search engines. This is about the specific way we organize the parallel processing of queries [7]. For plain text, we have observed that for low query traffic it is efficient to use the standard asynchronous message passing approach to parallel computing whereas for high traffic we can take advantage of bulk-synchronous parallel processing of queries. In this paper we show that this also holds for the metric-space context. Our proposal is openMP friendly in the sense that it can allow in-core threads to efficiently cooperate in the solution of queries. For the Sync and Async modes of operation the communication among nodes is performed by using MPI and BSPonMPI respectively whereas within nodes openMP is used to speed-up the processing of queries.

Round-Robin query processing. This assigns every query a similar share of key resources such as processors time and disk and network bandwidth [6]. In plain-text query processing we can decompose query solution in K-sized quanta of CPU, disk and network traffic where R is a fraction of K such as $1/2$. In this paper we show how to apply this strategy in the metric-space context. This requires careful consideration of the most costly parts of the solution to queries in very large distributed metric-space databases which are secondary memory management and load balance of distance calculations across processors.

The remainder of this paper is organized as follows. In section 2 we describe two basic data structures for metric-space databases which we combine and refine to propose our index data structure in section 3. Section 4 gives details on the parallel realization of the proposed index. We made similar implementations on top of other data structures for comparison purposes. Section 5 presents a comparative evaluation of our proposal including results from sequential and parallel executions. Section 6 presents concluding remarks.

2 Metric Spaces and Indexing Strategies

A *metric space* $(\mathbb{X}, d)$ is composed of an universe of valid objects $\mathbb{X}$ and a *distance function* $d : \mathbb{X} \times \mathbb{X} \to \mathbb{R}^+$ defined among them. The distance function determines the similarity between two given objects. The goal is, given a set of objects and a query, to retrieve all objects close enough to the query. This function holds several properties: strict positiveness ($d(x, y) > 0$ and if $d(x, y) = 0$ then $x = y$), symmetry ($d(x, y) = d(y, x)$), and the triangle inequality ($d(x, z) \leq d(x, y) + d(y, z)$). The finite subset $\mathbb{U} \subset \mathbb{X}$ with size $n = |\mathbb{U}|$, is called the database and represents the collection of objects. There are three main queries,

- *range search:* that retrieves all the objects $u \in \mathbb{U}$ within a radius r of the query q, that is: $(q, r)_d = \{u \in \mathbb{U} / d(q, u) \leq r\}$;
- *nearest neighbor search:* that retrieves the most similar object to the query q, that is $NN(q) = \{u \in \mathbb{U} / \forall v \in \mathbb{U}, d(q, u) \leq d(q, v)\}$;

– *k-nearest neighbors search:* a generalization of the nearest neighbor search, retrieving the set $kNN(q) \subseteq \mathbb{U}$ such that $|kNN(q)| = k$ and $\forall u \in kNN(q), v \in \mathbb{U} - kNN(q), d(q, u) \leq d(q, v)$.

In the following we describe two indexing strategies which we combine into a single one to build up our search engine index.

2.1 List of Clusters (LC)

This strategy [3] builds the index by choosing a set of centers $c \in \mathbb{U}$ with radius r_c where each center maintains a bucket that keep all objects that are within the extension of the ball (c, r_c). Each bucket contains the k objects that are the closet ones to the respective center c. Thus the radius r_c is the maximum distance between the center c and the k-nearest neighbor.

The buckets are filled up as the centers are created and thereby a given element i located in the intersection of two or more center balls is assigned to the first center. The first center is randomly chosen from the set of objects. The next ones are selected so that they maximize the sum of the distances to all previous centers.

A range query q with radius r is solved by scanning in order of creation the centers. At each center we compute $d(q, c)$ and in the case that $d(q, c) \leq r$ all objects in the bucket associated with c are compared against the query. This can end up at the first center found to hold $d(q, c) + r < c_r$, mining that the query ball (q, r) is totally contained in the center ball (c, r_c), or when all centers have been considered.

2.2 Sparse Spatial Selection (SSS)

During construction, this pivot-based strategy [2] selects some objects as *pivots* from the collection and then computes the distance between the pivots and the objects of the database. The result is a table of distances where columns are the pivots and rows the objects. Each cell in the table contains the distance between the object and the respective pivot. These distances are used to solve queries as follows. For a range query (q, r) the distances between the query and all pivots are computed. An object x from the collection can be discarded if there exists a pivot p_i for which the condition $|d(p_i, x) - d(p_i, q)| > r$ does not hold. The objects that pass this test are considered as potential members of the final set of objects that form part of the solution for the query and therefore they are directly compared against the query by applying the condition $d(x, q) \leq r$. The gain in performance comes from the fact that it is much cheaper to effect the calculations for discarding objects using the table than computing the distance between the candidate objects and the query.

A key issue for efficiency is the method employed to calculate the pivots, which must be effective enough to drastically reduce total number of distance computations between the objects and the query. To select the pivots set, let $(\mathbb{X}, d)$ be a metric space, $U \subset \mathbb{X}$ an object collection, and M the maximum distance between any pair of objects, $M = \max\{d(x, y)/x, y \in \mathbb{X}\}$. The set of pivots contains initially only the first object of the collection. Then, for each element $x_i \in \mathbb{U}$, x_i is chosen as a new pivot if its distance to every pivot in the current set of pivots is equal or greater than αM, being α a constant parameter. Therefore, an object in the collection becomes a new pivot if it is located at more than a fraction of the maximum distance with respect to all the current pivots.

3 LC-SSS Combination and Refinements

We propose a combination between the List of Clusters (LC) and Sparse Spatial Selection (SSS) indexing strategies. In this case we both compute the LC centers and SSS pivots independently. We form the clusters of LC and within each cluster we build a SSS table using the global pivots and organization of columns and rows described above. We emphasize on *global* SSS pivots because intuition tells that in each cluster of LC one should calculate pivots with the objects located in the respective cluster. However, we have found that the quality of SSS pivots degrades significantly when they are restricted to a subset of the database, and also the total number of them tends to be unnecessarily large. We call this strategy *hybrid*.

We increase the performance of the SSS index as follows. During construction of the table of distances we compute the cumulative sum of the distances among all objects and the respective pivots. We then sort the pivots by these values in increasing order and define the final order of pivots as follows. Assume that the sorted sequence of pivots is p_1, p_2, ..., p_n. Our first pivot is p_1, the second is p_n, the third p_2, the fourth p_{n-1} and so on. We also keep the rows in the table sorted by the values of the first pivot so that upon reception of a range query q with radius r we can quickly (binary search) determine between what rows are located the objects that can be selected as candidates to be part of the answer. This because objects o_i being part of the answer can only be located between the rows that satisfies $d(p_1, o_i) \geq d(q, p_1) - r$ and $d(p_1, o_i) \leq d(q, p_1) + r$. We have observed that this re-organization of pivots produces a SSS which is between 5 to 10 times faster than the original proposal in [2].

In practice, during query processing and after the two binary searches on the first column of the table, we can take advantage of the column × rows organization of the table of distances by first performing a few, say v, vertical wise applications of the triangular inequality on the objects located in the rows delimited by the results of the binary searches, followed by horizontal wise applications of the triangular inequality to discard as soon as possible all objects that are not potential candidates to be part of the query answer. See figure 1 which shows the case of two queries being processed concurrently.

For secondary memory the combination of these strategies have the advantage of increasing the locality of accesses to disk and the processor can keep in main memory the first v columns of the table. In the experiments performed in this paper we observed that with $v = n/4$ we achieved competitive running times.

This scheme of a table of distances per cluster can have two possible organizations based on a set of blocks stored in several contiguous disk pages. The first

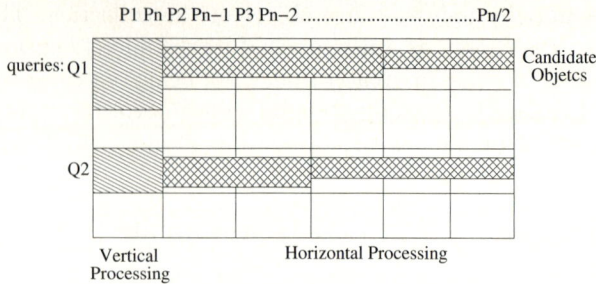

Fig. 1. Optimization to the SSS distance table

one is for the case in which we start with an existing collection of objects and requires sorting of the first pivot (column) across several blocks. In the second one we can insert new objects in an on-line manner. In this case blocks can contain objects as they were inserted with first columns sorted locally. Here sorting is spread across a few blocks, a number given by the amount of blocks that can be hold in main memory. In section 5 we show that both strategies are efficient in terms of total number accesses to disk.

4 Parallelism

In this section we describe the parallel algorithms we have devised to build the different index data structures and to process queries considering the two efficiency principles we enumerated in the introduction section of this paper, namely Sync/Async and Round-Robin parallel query processing.

For the Sync mode of operation we use the bulk-synchronous model of parallel computing (BSP) [11]. In BSP the parallel computer is seen as composed of a set of P processor local-memory components which communicate with each other through messages. The computation is organized as a sequence of supersteps. During a superstep, the processors may perform sequential computations on local data and/or send message to others processors. The messages are available for processing at their destination by the next superstep, and each superstep is ended with the barrier synchronization of processors. In our experiments we use a realization of BSP built on top of the MPI communication library. For the Async mode of operation we use the standard asynchronous message passing model of parallel computing implemented using the same MPI communication library.

The switching between the two modes of operation is effected in accordance with the observed query traffic. Our results show that in situations of low traffic it is more efficient to operate in the Async mode because the barrier synchronization of processors performed by the Sync mode under the same low traffic becomes too detrimental to performance as load balance degrades significantly. On the other hand, when query traffic is high we have a situation in which the

Sync mode can profit from economy of scale by performing optimizations such as bulk sending of messages among processors and proper load balancing of bulk query processing.

Queries are assumed to be received by a broker machine which in turn routes queries to processors. In our case, as we explain below, all queries are sent to all processors (broadcast). The broker can measure traffic to decide in which mode of operation the current queries can be processed. The arrival time of queries is unpredictable and the departure time of queries is also unpredictable along time. Thus the broker needs to estimate the average number of queries being processed during a fixed period of time and use this information to decide the mode of operation for the next period of time. The average number of queries can be determined as we propose in [7] which basically models the system as a $G/G/\infty$ queuing model where service time is given by the response time to queries.

The Round-Robin principle is achieved by assigning to each query being processed a similar amount of the resources. We explain it in the context of BSP. In each superstep, each query is granted a fixed number of distance calculations and in the case of SSS a fixed number of computations on the distance table. This also fixes the amount of communication effected at the end of the superstep and the number of disk accesses. Thus a given query can require several supersteps to be completed.

The database objects are uniformly distributed at random on the set of P processors. This marks the starting point to the design of our index construction and query processing algorithms. Query processing is effected by broadcasting each query to all processors and then each processor works on the partial solution of the query. Then a selected processor is in charge of collecting the partial solutions to integrate them and return the top-R results to the broker. In this case each processor sends its best R results. As we can have several queries being processed and the integrator processor for each query is chosen circularly among all processors, we can achieve a high degree of parallelism during query processing. Notice that both centers/pivots are the same at each processor so we can avoid distance recalculations among the queries and centers/pivots.

Constructing the LC-SSS index is effected as follows. For the List of Clusters (LC) strategy each processor selects its candidate centers using its local objects. Then, these lists of candidates are broadcast to all processors. After receiving the candidate list each processor computes the distance among the local centers and selects the ones maximizing the sum of distance. From this point no communication is required, and each processor can build its local index using the same global centers to organize into buckets its local objects.

In the Sparse Spatial Selection (SSS) strategy we do the same. Namely each processor selects the pivots candidates from the local object collection and broadcast them to all processors. Each processor receives the local pivots computed previously and then they refine these set of pivots selecting only the ones that satisfy the condition $d(p_i, p_j) \geq \alpha M$, $\forall i \neq j$. After that, each processor has the same set of pivots and can build the local distance table for each bucket.

5 Experimental Results

We performed experiments using a 32-processors cluster and different data sets and queries. We use two multimedia data sets. The first one is a collection of 47,000 images extracted from the NASA photo and video archives, each of them transformed into a 20-dimensional vector. The Euclidean distance is the distance function used in this data set. The second one is a large set of 900,000 words taken from documents crawled from the Chilean Web. In this case the number of characters required to make identical two words is the distance function. Using these collections of data we can study the behavior of the algorithm in spaces of different intrinsic dimensionality.

Figures 2 below have been drawn with the following convention. The Y-axis shows the total running time. The X-axis shows different cases for the query traffic, ranging from A (low traffic) to D (high traffic). The curves are divided into two areas, results for the Sync (BSP) and Async (MPI) modes of parallel computation. In each area we show results for the different strategies. For each strategy we show results for $P=$ 4, 8, 16, and 32 processors. Notice that running time increases as we increase the number of processors. This is because we keep constant the total number of queries processed by each processor. That is, every time we double the number of processors we also double the overall number of queries that are processed. The total running time cannot be constant under this scenario since the communication hardware has at least $\log P$ latency.

Figures 2.a and 2.b show results for two MPI realizations of the parallel strategies explained in this paper. The first one is based on the asynchronous message passing (Async) approach and the second one is a bulk-synchronous MPI (Sync) realization. Figure 2.a shows results for the NASA collection whereas figure 2.b shows results for words space data set. In both cases, the results shows that the Hybrid algorithm (combining the LC and the improved SSS strategies) outperforms the others parallel strategies. The curves for SSS and LC alone were obtained with our modified SSS and LC running as a single strategy respectively.

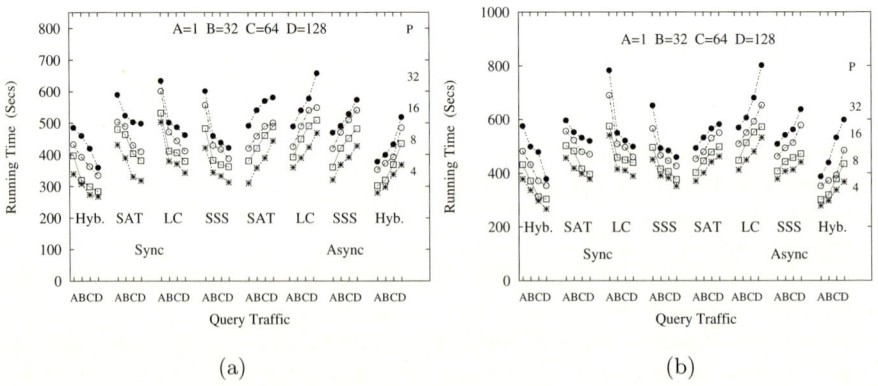

Fig. 2. Running time obtained using two data collections

These results also show that for high query traffic it is more efficient to process queries in bulk and for low traffic it is more efficient to process them individually in an asynchronous manner.

Computing the distance between two complex objects is known to be very expensive in terms of running time in metric-space databases. This produces an implementation independent base upon which comparing different strategies. The load balance achieved during parallel processing is a clear indication of good use of resources. We measure load balance by using the efficiency metric which for the BSP model and for a given measure X we define as the average taken over all supersteps of the ratios $\text{avg}(X)/\text{max}(X)$ observed in each superstep and considering all processors. In figure 3.a we show results for this metric obtained by counting the number of distance evaluations effected in each superstep and processor. The optimum indicating perfect load balance is shown by efficiency equal to 1. The results show that all strategies achieve good load balance, which is evidence that the better performance of our Hybrid index comes from factors such as reduction in the total number of distance computations and small overheads.

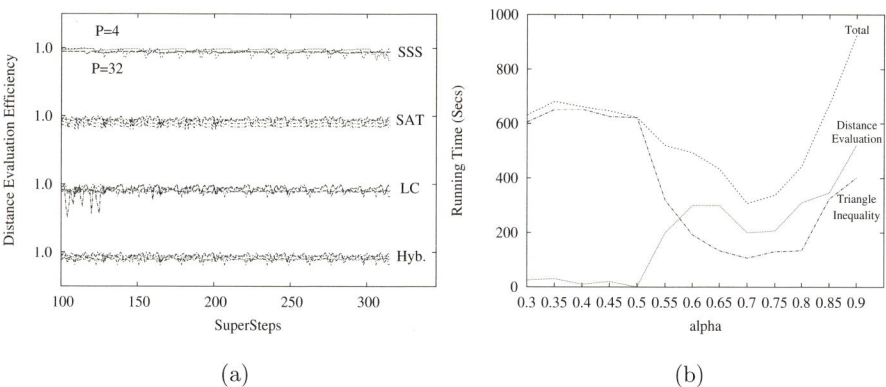

Fig. 3. Running time obtained using two data collections

In figure 3.b we show the effect of the α parameter in the total running time of the SSS strategy and thereby also in our Hybrid index. The results are for the words data set. The figure shows three curves, the one labeled *total* is the sum of the running time of the other two curves. The curve labeled *distance evaluation* is the total time spent computing distance evaluations between two objects and the third curve is the time spent computing on the distances table to reduce the number of candidate objects to be compared against the query object. Clearly for large data sets like the words one there is a value of $\alpha \approx 0.7$ that can reduce total running time significantly.

In the following we review previous studies in sequential computing on comparison of a number of metric-space index data structures and then we compare the best performers against our proposal. Figure 4.a shows results for the distance evaluation metric for different data structures proposed so far. Namely

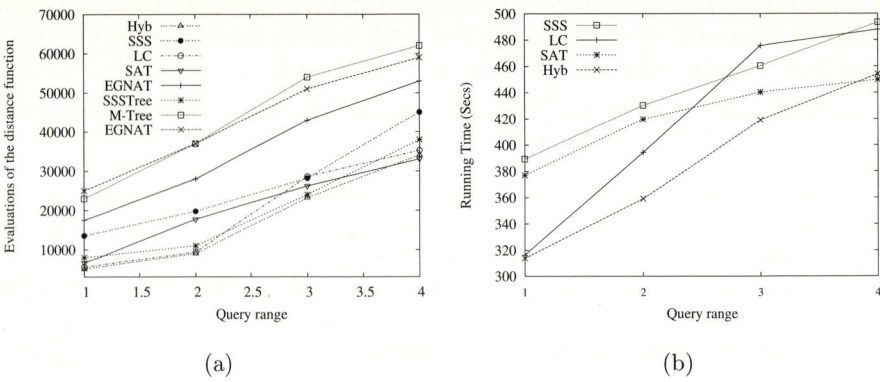

Fig. 4. Sequential computing: results for a 80,000 words Spanish dictionary data set

the M-Tree [4], GNAT [1], EGNAT [9] and SAT [10]. We also included in the comparison the SSS [2] and LC [3] strategies. To make this figure we took results reported by the authors on the same data set. The Hybrid strategy proposed in this paper achieves the best performance in terms of this metric though very similar to the LC strategy. Figure 4.b shows running time results for the best performers (using our own implementation of those strategies). The results are consistent with those of figure 4.a.

Finally we show results for an openMP optimization of the Hybrid index. As suggested in figure 1 we can take advantage of the contiguous memory realization of the index data structure which makes it suitable to run on it a team of openMP threads for vertical and horizontal traversals in each superstep. The openMP threads can also be used in the sequential implementation of the Hybrid index. We made experiments using openMP as implemented in g++ version 4.1.2 and BSPonMPI (http://bsponmpi.sourceforge.net/). In table 1 we show the gain in performance by using T openMP threads on a *Intel's Quad-Xeon* machine (2 nodes, 16 CPUs in total). The second row in the table show results for the ratio sequential running time ($T = 1$) in one CPU to running time with $T \geq 1$ threads and query traffic 64. We process batches of 64 queries using T threads, and once all threads finish we process the next batch.

Table 1. Decreasing running times per node with openMP threads

T	1	2	4	6	8	10	12	14	16
$(T=1)/(T \geq 1)$	1.00	1.76	2.12	2.81	4.07	3.52	2.01	0.88	0.93

6 Conclusions

We have proposed a distributed index data structure devised to support the efficient processing of queries in metric-space databases. Our index is suitable for search engines dealing with multi-media data. We have implemented it by using parallel computing techniques devised to achieve high-performance in multiple-queries processing. We performed experiments on actual data sets upon a cluster of computers.

Our results show that our Hybrid index which is a combination of the List of Clusters (LC) and Sparse Spatial Selection (SSS) indexing methods, which we have optimized and tailored to our setting, is the strategy which achieves the best performance. We have verified that this efficient performance also holds for sequential computing. An important advantage of our proposal over all other alternative indexing methods is that our particular realization of the SSS index is friendly to secondary memory and multithreading (e.g., openMP) because it contains high locality in terms of data accesses.

References

1. Brin, S.: Near neighbor search in large metric spaces. In: 21st conference on Very Large Databases (1995)
2. Brisaboa, N.R., Pedreira, O.: Spatial selection of sparse pivots for similarity search in metric spaces. In: van Leeuwen, J., Italiano, G.F., van der Hoek, W., Meinel, C., Sack, H., Plášil, F. (eds.) SOFSEM 2007. LNCS, vol. 4362, pp. 434–445. Springer, Heidelberg (2007)
3. Chávez, E., Navarro, G.: A compact space decomposition for effective metric indexing. Pattern Recognition Letters 26(9), 1363–1376 (2005)
4. Chavez, E., Navarro, G., Baeza-Yates, R., Marroquin, J.L.: Searching in metric spaces. ACM Computing Surveys 3(33), 273–321 (2001)
5. Costa, G.V., Marin, M.: Distributed sparse spatial selection indexes. In: PDP 2008, Toulouse, France, February 13-15 (2008)
6. Marin, M., Gil Costa, V.: High-performance distributed inverted files. In: CIKM 2007, pp. 935–938. ACM, New York (2007)
7. Marin, M., Gil-Costa, V. (Sync|Async)$^+$ MPI Search Engines. In: Cappello, F., Herault, T., Dongarra, J. (eds.) PVM/MPI 2007. LNCS, vol. 4757. Springer, Heidelberg (2007)
8. Marin, M., Reyes, N.: Efficient Parallelization of Spatial Approximation Trees. In: Sunderam, V.S., van Albada, G.D., Sloot, P.M.A., Dongarra, J. (eds.) ICCS 2005. LNCS, vol. 3514, pp. 1003–1010. Springer, Heidelberg (2005)
9. Marin, M., Uribe, R., Barrientos, R.J.: Searching and updating metric space databases using the parallel EGNAT. In: Shi, Y., van Albada, G.D., Dongarra, J., Sloot, P.M.A. (eds.) ICCS 2007. LNCS, vol. 4487, pp. 229–236. Springer, Heidelberg (2007)
10. Navarro, G.: Searching in metric spaces by spatial approximation. The Very Large Databases Journal (VLDBJ) 711(1) (2002)
11. Valiant, L.G.: A bridging model for parallel computation. Comm. ACM 33, 103–111 (1990)

Topic 12: Theory and Algorithms for Parallel Computation

Geppino Pucci*, Coromoto Leon**,
Ioannis Caragiannis, and Kieran T. Herley***

Parallelism permeates all levels of current computing systems, from single CPU machines to large server farms. Effective use of parallelism relies crucially on the availability of suitable models of computation for algorithm design and analysis, and of efficient strategies for the solution of key computational problems on prominent classes of platforms, as well as of good models of the way the different components are interconnected. With the advent of multicore parallel machines, new models and paradigms are needed to allow parallel programming to advance into mainstream computing. Topic 12 focuses on contibutions providing new results on foundational issues of parallelism in computing and/or proposing improved approaches for the solution of specific algorithmic problems.

This year, six papers were submitted to the topic, investigating algorithmic and modeling problems for parallel computation and communication. Among all submissions, two papers were accepted as full papers for the conference, resulting in a 33% acceptance rate.

The first paper, *Bi-Objective Approximation Scheme for Makespan and Reliability Optimization on Uniform Parallel Machines*, by Jeannot, Saule, and Trystram, focuses on the scheduling of independent tasks on unreliable processors, and aims at devising strategies for the bi-objective problem of optimizing both makespan and reliability. The second paper, *Deque-Free Work-Optimal Parallel STL Algorithms*, by Bernard, Gautier, Maillard, Roch, and Traoré, presents an efficient (deque-free) variant of the well-known decentralized thread-scheduling strategy based on work-stealing, and gives a theoretical analysis of its performance. The resulting dynamic scheduler is then exercised for the parallelization of most of the Standard Template Library (STL) algorithms for containers with random iterator.

---

* Global Chair.
** Local Chair.
*** Vice Chairs.

Bi-objective Approximation Scheme for Makespan and Reliability Optimization on Uniform Parallel Machines

Emmanuel Jeannot[1], Erik Saule[2], and Denis Trystram[2]

[1] INRIA-Lorraine
emmanuel.jeannot@loria.fr
[2] INPG, LIG(MOAIS)
firstname.lastname@imag.fr

Abstract. We study the problem of scheduling independent tasks on a set of related processors which have a probability of failure governed by an exponential law. We are interested in the bi-objective analysis, namely simultaneous optimization of the makespan and the reliability. We show that this problem can not be approximated by a single schedule. A similar problem has already been studied leading to a $\langle \overline{2}, 1 \rangle$-approximation algorithm (*i.e.* for any fixed value of the makespan, the obtained solution is optimal on the reliability and no more than twice the given makespan). We provide an algorithm which has a much lower complexity. This solution is finally used to derive a $(2 + \epsilon, 1)$-approximation of the Pareto set of the problem, for any $\epsilon > 0$.

1 Introduction

With the recent development of large parallel and distributed systems (computational grids, cluster of clusters, peer-to-peer networks, etc.), it is difficult to ensure that the resources are always available for a long period of time. Indeed, hardware failures, software faults, power breakdown or resources removal often occur when using a very large number of machines. Hence, in this context, taking into account new problems like reliability and fault-tolerance is a major issue. Several approaches have been proposed to tackle the problem of faults. One approach is based on duplication. The idea is that if one resource fails, the other resources can continue to correctly execute the application (thanks to redundancy). However, the main drawback of this approach is a possible waste of resources. Another solution consists in check-pointing the application from time to time and, in case of failure, to restart it from the last check-point [1]. However, check-pointing an application is costly and may require to modify it. Furthermore, restarting an application slows it down. Therefore, in order to minimize the cost of the check-point/restart mechanism, it is necessary to provide a reliable execution that minimizes the probability of failure of this application. Scheduling an application correspond to determine which resources will execute the tasks and when they will start. Thus, the scheduling algorithm is responsible of minimizing the probability of failure of the application by choosing the set of resources that enables a fast and reliable execution.

In this paper, we consider an application modeled by a set of independent tasks to be scheduled on a set of heterogeneous machines that are characterized by their speed and their error rate. The goal of the scheduling algorithm is then to minimize the makespan of the application (its run-time) and to minimize the probability of failure of the execution. As no hypothesis is made on the relationship between the speed and the error rate of the resources, there is no correlation between minimizing the makespan and optimizing the reliability of a schedule(the most reliable schedule is not necessarily the fastest one). Moreover, it has been shown that minimizing the schedule length is NP-hard even in the case of two homogeneous machine and independent tasks [2]. Therefore, unless P=NP it is not possible to find the set of optimal trade-off in polynomial time ; *i.e.* to answer the question *"find the shortest schedule that has a probability of success greater than a given value p"*. Moreover, we show that approximating the problem within a constant ratio for both objectives at the same time is impossible. Therefore, in order to solve the problem, we first propose a $\langle \bar{2}, 1 \rangle$-approximation algorithm *i.e.* an algorithm which finds a schedule which length is at most twice as long as a guess value (given by the user), if such a schedule exists, and the reliability is optimal among the schedules that are shorter than this guess value. Based on this algorithm, we are able to construct a set of solutions that approximates the Pareto set (*i.e.* the set of Pareto optimal[1] solutions) by a factor of $2+\epsilon$ for the makespan and 1 for the reliability. For constructing this set, ϵ can be chosen arbitrarily small at the cost of a larger number of solutions.

The paper is organized as follows. In Section 2, we formally define the problem and briefly discuss the related works. Then, we show that the problem cannot be approximated within a constant ratio. We discuss the most reasonable way to approximate the Pareto set. Section 3 reports the main result which is the design and analysis of the $\langle \bar{2}, 1 \rangle$-approximation algorithm. In Section 4 we derive the Pareto set approximation algorithm.

2 Problem

Let T be a set of n tasks and Q be a set of m uniform processors as described in [3]. p_i denotes the processing requirement of task i. Processor j computes $1/\tau_j$ operations by time unit and has a constant failure rate of λ_j. $p_{ij} = p_i \tau_j$ denotes the running time of task i on processor j. In the remainer of the paper, i will be the task index and j will be the processor index.

A schedule is a function $\pi : T \to Q$ that maps a task to the processor that executes it. Let $T(j, \pi) = \{i \mid \pi(i) = j\}$ be the set of tasks mapped to processor j. The completion time of a processor j is $C_j(\pi) = \sum_{i \in T(j,\pi)} p_i \tau_j$. The makespan of a schedule $C_{max}(\pi) = max_j C_j(\pi)$ is the first time where all tasks are completed. The probability that a processor j executes all its tasks successfully is given by an exponential law: $p^j_{\text{succ}}(\pi) = e^{-\lambda_j C_j(\pi)}$. We assume that faults are independent, therefore, the probability that schedule π finished

---

[1] Intuitively, a solution is said *Pareto optimal* if no improvement on every objective can be made.

correctly is: $p_{\text{succ}} = \Pi_j p_{\text{succ}}^j(\pi) = e^{-\sum_j C_j(\pi)\lambda_j}$. The reliability index is defined by $rel(\pi) = \sum_j C_j(\pi)\lambda_j$. When no confusion is possible, π will be omitted.

We are interested in minimizing both C_{max} and rel simultaneously (*i.e.* minimizing the makespan and maximizing the probability of success of the whole schedule).

2.1 Related Works

We now discuss briefly how each single-objective problem has been studied in the literature.

Optimizing the makespan: Scheduling independent tasks on uniform processors in less than K units of time is a NP-complete problem because it contains PARTITION as a sub-problem which is NP-complete [2]. For the makespan optimization problem, a $(2 - \frac{1}{m+1})$-approximation algorithm has been proposed by [4]. It consists of classical list scheduling where the longest task of the list is iteratively mapped on the processor that will complete it the soonest. [5] proposes a PTAS based on the bin packing problem with variable bin sizes. However, the PTAS is only of theoretical interest because its runtime complexity is far too high.

Optimizing the reliability: Minimizing the objective function rel is equivalent to maximizing the probability of success of the schedule on a parallel system subject to failure. More precisely, if processor j can fail with a constant failure rate λ_j and if we assume that faults are statistically independent, the probability of success of a schedule is $p_{\text{succ}} = e^{-rel}$. It has been shown in [6] that a ρ-approximation on rel is a ρ-approximation on $1 - p_{\text{succ}}$. The minimal rel is obtained by scheduling all tasks on the processors j having the smallest $\lambda_j \tau_j$. Indeed, if a task t was scheduled on another processor j', migrating it to j will result in changing rel by the negative value $p_t \lambda_j \tau_j - p_t \lambda_{j'} \tau_{j'}$.

In [7,8] several heuristics have been proposed to solve the bi-objective problem. However, none of the proposed heuristics have a guaranteed approximation ratio.

In [9], Shmoys and Tardos studied the problem of optimizing the makespan and the sum of costs of a schedule on unrelated machines. In their model, the cost is induced by scheduling a task on a processor and the cost function is given by a cost matrix. They proposed an algorithm that receives two parameters, namely, a target value M for the makespan and C for the cost and returns a schedule whose makespan lower than $2M$ with a cost better than C. This model can be directly used to solve our problem. However, their method is difficult to implement as it relies on Linear Programming and its complexity is high: $O(mn^2 \log n)$.

2.2 On the Approximability

Proposition 1. *The bi-objective problem of minimizing C_{max} and rel cannot be approximated within a constant factor with a single solution.*

Proof. Consider the instance of the problem with two machines such that $\tau_1 = 1$, $\tau_2 = 1/k$ and $\lambda_1 = 1$, $\lambda_2 = k^2$ (for a fixed $k \in \mathbb{R}^{+*}$). Consider a single task t_1 with $p_1 = 1$. There are only two feasible schedules, namely, π_1 in which t_1 is

scheduled on processor 1 and π_2 in which it is scheduled on processor 2. Remark that π_2 is optimal for C_{max} and that π_1 is optimal for rel.
$C_{max}(\pi_1) = 1$ and $C_{max}(\pi_2) = 1/k$. This leads to $C_{max}(\pi_1)/C_{max}(\pi_2) = k$. This ratio goes to infinity when k goes to infinity. Similarly, $rel(\pi_1) = 1$ and $rel(\pi_2) = \frac{k^2}{k} = k$ which leads to $rel(\pi_2)/rel(\pi_1) = k$. This ratio goes to infinity with k.

None of both feasible schedules can approximate both objectives within a constant factor.

2.3 Solving the Bi-objective Problem

As we proved in the last section in Proposition 1, the bi-objective problem cannot be approximated with a single schedule. For such problems, several approaches can be used such as optimizing a linear (or convex) combination of objectives [10], or optimizing the objectives one after the other [11]. However, these methods usually do not provide all interesting solutions. We would like to obtain all the best compromise solutions and leave the final choice to a decision maker.

The notion of Pareto dominance [12] allows to formalize the best compromise solutions in multi-objective optimization. A solution is said to be **Pareto optimal** if no solution is as good as it is on all objective values and better on at least one. The **Pareto set** (denoted by Pc^*) of a problem is the set of all Pareto optimal solutions.

Unfortunately, on our problem deciding if a solution is Pareto optimal or not is an NP-complete problem (as the makespan decision problem is NP-complete[2]). Thus, computing the whole set is impossible in polynomial time unless P=NP. Like in standard single-objective optimization, we are interested in obtaining approximate solutions.

Pc is a (ρ_1, ρ_2)-**approximation** of the Pareto set Pc^* if each solution $\pi^* \in Pc^*$ is (ρ_1, ρ_2) approximated by a solution $\pi \in Pc$: $\forall \pi^* \in Pc^*, \exists \pi \in Pc, C_{max}(\pi) \le \rho_1 C_{max}(\pi^*)$ and $rel(\pi) \le \rho_2 rel(\pi^*)$. Figure 1 illustrates this concept. Crosses are solutions of the scheduling problem represented in the $(C_{max}; rel)$ space. The bold crosses are an approximated Pareto set. Each solution $(x; y)$ in this set (ρ_1, ρ_2)-dominates a quadrant delimited in bold whose origin is at $(x/\rho_1; y/\rho_2)$. All solutions are dominated by a solution of the approximated Pareto set as they are included into a (ρ_1, ρ_2)-dominated quadrant.

In [14], Papadimitriou and Yannakakis give a generic method to obtain an approximated Pareto set. The idea is to partition the solution space into rectangles of geometric increasing size of common ratio $(1+\epsilon)$ among all objectives. The set formed by taking one solution in each rectangle (if any) is a $(1+\epsilon)$-approximation of the Pareto set of the problem. We will use an adaptation of this method for designing a Pareto set approximation algorithm. A similar approach has been used in [15] for a single machine scheduling problem.

---

[2] The argument is straightforward in our context. The reader should be aware that the bi-objective decision problem could be NP-complete while both single-objective decision problems are polynomial [13].

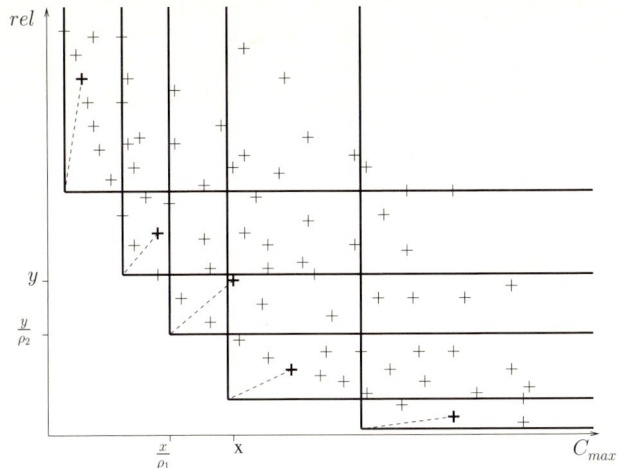

Fig. 1. Bold crosses are a (ρ_1, ρ_2)-approximation of the Pareto set

2.4 $\langle \bar{\rho_1}, \rho_2 \rangle$-Approximation Algorithm

Because it is impossible to get a solution approximating both objectives at the same time (Proposition 1), we are looking for the minimum reliability index among schedules whose makespan are greater than an arbitrary threshold.

Most existing algorithms that solve a bi-objective problem construct a ρ_2-approximation of the second objective constrained by a threshold on the first one. The threshold can be exceeded no more than a constant factor ρ_1. Such an algorithm is said to be a $\langle \bar{\rho_1}, \rho_2 \rangle$-approximation algorithm. More formally,

Definition 1. *Given ω a threshold value of the makespan, a $\langle \bar{\rho_1}, \rho_2 \rangle$-approximation algorithm delivers a solution whose $C_{max} \leq \rho_1 \omega$ and $rel \leq \rho_2 rel^{*,\omega-}$ where $rel^{*,\omega-}$ is the best possible value of rel in schedules whose makespan is less than ω.*

3 A Dual Approximation Algorithm

In this section, we present a $\langle \bar{2}, 1 \rangle$-approximation algorithm called CMLT (for ConstrainedMinLambdaTau) which has a better complexity and which is easier to implement than the general algorithm presented in [9].

Let ω be the guess value of the optimum makespan. Let $M(i) = \{j \mid p_{ij} \leq \omega\}$ be the set of processors able to execute task i in less than ω units of time. It is obvious that if i is executed on $j \notin M(i)$ then, the makespan will be greater than ω.

The following proposition states that if task i has less operations than task i', then all machines able to schedule i' in less than ω time units can also schedule i in the same time. The proof is directly derived from the definition of M and is omitted.

Proposition 2. $\forall i, i' \in T$ such that $p_i \leq p_{i'}$, $M(i') \subseteq M(i)$

The ConstrainedMinLambdaTau algorithm (CMLT) is presented as follows: for each task i considered in non-increasing number of operations, schedule i on the processor j of $M(i)$ that minimizes $\lambda_j \tau_j$ with $C_j \leq \omega$ (or it returns no schedule if there is no processor j). Sorting tasks by non-increasing number of operations implies that more and more processors are used over time.

The principle of the algorithm is rather simple. However several properties should be checked to ensure that it is always possible to schedule all the tasks this way.

Lemma 1. *CMLT returns a schedule whose makespan is lower than 2ω or ensures that no schedule whose makespan is lower than ω exist.*

Proof. We need first to remark that if the algorithm returns a schedule, then its makespan is lower than 2ω (task i is executed on processor $j \in M(i)$ only when $C_j \leq \omega$). It remains to prove that if the algorithm does not return a schedule then there is no schedule whose a makespan lower than ω.

Suppose that task i cannot be scheduled on any processor of $M(i)$. Then all processors of $M(i)$ execute tasks during more than ω units of time, $\forall j \in M(i), C_j > \omega$.

Moreover, due to Proposition 2, each task $i' \leq i$ such that $p_{i'} > p_i$ could not have been scheduled on a processor not belonging to $M(i)$. Thus, in a schedule with a makespan lower than ω, all the tasks $i' \leq i$ must be scheduled on $M(i)$.

There is more operations in the set of tasks $\{i' \leq i\}$ than processors in $M(i)$ can execute in ω units of time.

Lemma 2. *CMLT generates a schedule such that $rel \leq rel^{*,\omega^-}$*

Proof. We first need to construct a (non feasible) schedule π^* whose reliability is a lower bound of rel^{*,ω^-}. Then, we will show that $rel(CMLT) \leq rel(\pi^*)$.

From Theorem 2 of [6] it is known that the optimal reliability under the makespan constraint for unitary tasks and homogeneous processors is obtained by adding tasks to processors in the $\lambda \tau$ increasing order up to reaching the ω constraint. For our problem we can construct a schedule π^* where we apply a similar method. Task i is allocated to the processor of $M(i)$ that minimizes the $\lambda \tau$ product. But if i finishes after ω, the exceeding quantity is scheduled on the next processor belonging to $M(i)$ in $\lambda \tau$ order. Note that such a schedule exists because CMLT returns a solution. Of course this schedule is not always feasible as the same task can be required to be executed on more than one processor at the same time. However, it is easy to adapt the proof of Theorem 2 of [6] and show that $rel(\pi^*) \leq rel^{*,\omega^-}$.

The schedule generated by CMLT is similar to π^*. The only difference is that some operations are scheduled after ω. In π^*, these operations are scheduled on less reliable processors. Thus, the schedule generated by CMLT has a better reliability than π^*.

Finally, we have $rel(CMLT) \leq rel(\pi^*) \leq rel^{*,\omega^-}$ which concludes the proof.

Algorithm 1. CMLT

begin
    sort tasks in non-increasing p_i order
    sort processors in non-decreasing τ_j order
    Let H be an empty heap
    $j = 1$
    for $i = 1$ *to* n **do**
        while $P_j \in M(i)$ **do**
            Add P_j to H with key $\lambda_j \tau_j$
            $j = j + 1$
        if H.empty() **then**
            Return *no solution*
        schedule i on $j' = H.\min()$
        $C_{j'} = C_{j'} + p_i \tau_{j'}$
        if $C_{j'} > \omega$ **then**
            Remove j' from H
end

Lemma 3. *The time complexity of CMLT is in $O(n \log n + m \log m)$.*

Proof. In fact, the algorithm should be implemented using a heap in the manner presented in Algorithm 1. The cost of sorting tasks is in $O(n \log n)$ and the cost of sorting processors is in $O(m \log m)$. Adding (and removing) a processor to (from) the heap costs $O(\log m)$ and such operations are done m times. Heap operations cost $O(m \log m)$. Scheduling the tasks and all complementary tests are done in constant time, and there are n tasks to schedule. Scheduling operations cost is in $O(n)$.

Theorem 1. *CMLT is a $\langle \bar{2}, 1 \rangle$-approximation algorithm of complexity $O(n \log n + m \log m)$.*

4 Pareto Set Approximation Algorithm

Algorithm 2 described below constructs an approximation of the Pareto set of the problem by applying the $\langle \bar{2}, 1 \rangle$-approximation algorithm on a geometric sequence of makespan thresholds which requires a lower bound and an upper bound.

The lower bound $C_{max}^{min} = \frac{\sum_i p_i}{\sum_j \frac{1}{\tau_j}}$ is obtained by considering that a single processor is given the computational power of all the processors of the instance.

The upper bound $C_{max}^{max} = \sum_i p_i \max_j \tau_j$ is the makespan obtained by scheduling all tasks on the slowest processor. No solution can have a worse makespan without inserting idle times which are harmful for both objective functions. Note that C_{max}^{max} can be achieved by a Pareto optimal solution if the slowest processor is also the most reliable one.

Algorithm 2. Pareto set approximation algorithm

Data: ϵ a positive real number
Result: S a set of solutions
begin
$\quad i = 0$
$\quad S = \emptyset$
$\quad$ **while** $i \leq \lceil \log_{1+\epsilon/2}(\frac{C_{max}^{max}}{C_{max}^{min}}) \rceil$ **do**
$\quad\quad \omega_i = (1+\frac{\epsilon}{2})^i C_{max}^{min}$
$\quad\quad \pi_i = CMLT(\omega_i)$
$\quad\quad S = S \cup \pi_i$
$\quad\quad i = i+1$
$\quad$ **return** S
end

Proposition 3. *Algorithm 2 is a $(2+\epsilon, 1)$ approximation algorithm of the Pareto set.*

Proof. Let π^* be a Pareto-optimal schedule. Then, there exists $k \in \mathbb{N}$ such that $(1+\frac{\epsilon}{2})^k C_{max}^{min} \leq C_{max}(\pi^*) \leq (1+\frac{\epsilon}{2})^{k+1} C_{max}^{min}$. We show that π_{k+1} is an $(2+\epsilon, 1)$-approximation of π^*. This is illustrated in Figure 2.

- Reliability. $rel(\pi_{k+1}) \leq rel^*((1+\frac{\epsilon}{2})^{k+1} C_{max}^{min})$ (by Theorem 1). π^* is Pareto optimal, hence $rel(\pi^*) = rel^*(C_{max}(\pi^*))$. But, $C_{max}(\pi^*) \leq (1+\frac{\epsilon}{2})^{k+1} C_{max}^{min}$. Since rel^* is a decreasing function, we have: $rel(\pi_{k+1}) \leq rel(\pi^*)$.
- Makespan. $C_{max}(\pi_{k+1}) \leq 2(1+\frac{\epsilon}{2})^{k+1} C_{max}^{min} = (2+\epsilon)(1+\frac{\epsilon}{2})^k C_{max}^{min}$ (by Theorem 1) and $C_{max}(\pi^*) \geq (1+\frac{\epsilon}{2})^k C_{max}^{min}$.
Thus, $C_{max}(\pi_{k+1}) \leq (2+\epsilon) C_{max}(\pi^*)$.

Remark that $CMLT(\omega_i)$ may not return a solution. However, this is not a problem. It means that no solution has a makespan lower than ω_i. $CMLT(\omega_i)$ approximates Pareto optimal solutions whose makespan is lower than ω_i. Hence, there is no forgotten solution.

The last points to answer are about the cardinality of the generated set and the complexity of the algorithm.

- Cardinality: The algorithm generates less than $\lceil \log_{1+\frac{\epsilon}{2}} \frac{C_{max}^{max}}{C_{max}^{min}} \rceil$ $\leq \lceil \log_{1+\frac{\epsilon}{2}} max_i \tau_i \sum_j 1/\tau_j \rceil \leq \lceil \log_{1+\frac{\epsilon}{2}} m \frac{max_i \tau_i}{min_i \tau_i} \rceil$ solutions which is polynomial in $1/\epsilon$ and in the size of the instance.
- Complexity: We can remark that CMLT sorts the tasks in an order which is independent of ω. Thus, this sorting can be done once for all.
Thus, the complexity of the pareto set approximation algorithm is $O(n \log n + \lceil \log_{1+\epsilon/2}(\frac{C_{max}^{max}}{C_{max}^{min}}) \rceil (n + m \log m))$.

In Section 2.1 we briefly recalled the work of Shmoys and Tardos which can be used in our context [9]. We can derive from it a $\langle 2, 1 \rangle$-approximation algorithm whose time-complexity is in $O(mn^2 \log n)$. This time-complexity is larger than the time-complexity of CMLT in $O(n \log n + m \log m)$. Moreover, in the

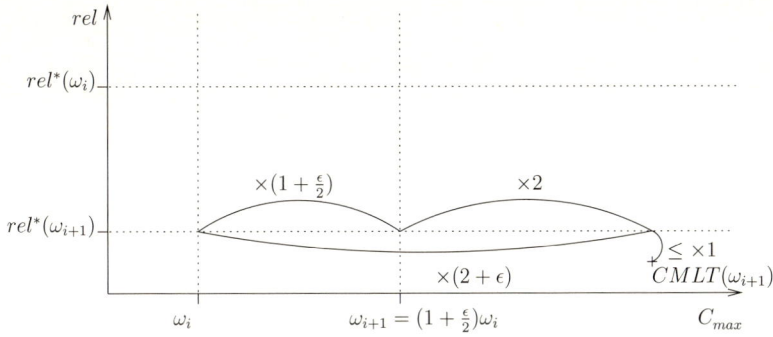

Fig. 2. $CMLT(\omega_{i+1})$ is a $(2+\epsilon, 1)$ approximation of Pareto optimal solutions whose makespan is between ω_i and ω_{i+1}. There is at most a factor of 1 in reliability between $CMLT(\omega_{i+1})$ and $rel^*(\omega_{i+1})$. The ratio in makespan between $CMLT(\omega_{i+1})$ and ω_{i+1} is less than 2 and $\omega_{i+1} = (1 + \frac{\epsilon}{2})\omega_i$. Thus, $CMLT(\omega_{i+1})$ is a $(2+\epsilon, 1)$-approximation of $(\omega_i, rel^*(\omega_{i+1}))$.

perspective of approximating the Pareto set of the problem with the method previously presented; the algorithm derived from [9] will have a time-complexity of $\lceil \log_{1+\epsilon/2}(\frac{C_{max}^{max}}{C_{max}^{min}}) \rceil (mn^2 \log n)$. Unlike CMLT, their algorithm cannot be easily tuned to avoid a significant part of computations when the algorithm is called several time. Thus, CMLT is significantly better than the algorithm presented in [9] which has been established in a more general setting on unrelated processors.

5 Conclusion

As larger and larger infrastructures are available to execute distributed applications, reliability becomes a crucial issue. However, optimizing both the reliability and the length of the schedule is not always possible as they are often conflicting objectives. In this work, we have analyzed how to schedule independent tasks on uniform processors for optimizing both makespan and reliability. It has been proven that the problem cannot be approximated within a constant factor by a single solution. We designed the CMLT algorithm and proved that it is a $\langle \bar{2}, 1 \rangle$-approximation. Finally, we derived a $(2+\epsilon, 1)$-approximation of the Pareto set of the problem. This bound is very good and will be hard to improve. Some previous work could have been used. However, it will have lead to a far worse complexity.

The natural continuation of this work is to address the problem of the reliability with precedence constraints. However, this problem is much more difficult. Firstly, no constant approximation algorithm for the makespan is known. Secondly, the reliability model is much more complex in presence of idle times.

References

1. Bouteiller, A., Herault, T., Krawezik, G., Lemarinier, P., Cappello, F.: Mpich-v: a multiprotocol fault tolerant mpi. International Journal of High Performance Computing and Applications (2005)
2. Garey, M.R., Johnson, D.S.: Computers and Intractability. Freeman, San Francisco (1979)
3. Graham, R., Lawler, E., Lenstra, J., Kan, A.R.: Optimization and approximation in deterministic sequencing and scheduling: a survey. Ann. Discrete Math. 5, 287–326 (1979)
4. Gonzalez, T., Ibarra, O., Sahni, S.: Bounds for LPT schedules on uniform processors. SIAM Journal of Computing 6, 155–166 (1977)
5. Hochbaum, D.S., Shmoys, D.B.: A polynomial approximation scheme for scheduling on uniform processors: Using the dual approximation approach. SIAM Journal on Computing 17(3), 539–551 (1988)
6. Dongarra, J.J., Jeannot, E., Saule, E., Shi, Z.: Bi-objective scheduling algorithms for optimizing makespan and reliability on heterogeneous systems. In: Proc. of SPAA, pp. 280–288 (2007)
7. Dogan, A., Ozgüner, F.: Matching and Scheduling Algorithms for Minimizing Execution Time and Failure Probability of Applications in Heterogeneous Computing. IEEE Trans. Parallel Distrib. Syst. 13(3), 308–323 (2002)
8. Dogan, A., Ozgüner, F.: Bi-objective Scheduling Algorithms for Execution Time-Reliability Trade-off in Heterogeneous Computing Systems. Comput. J. 48(3), 300–314 (2005)
9. Shmoys, D.B., Tardos, E.: Scheduling unrelated machines with costs. In: Proceedings of the Fourth Annual ACM/SIGACT-SIAM Symposium on Discrete Algorithms, pp. 448–454 (1993)
10. Albers, S., Fujiwara, H.: Energy-efficient algorithms for flow time minimization. In: Durand, B., Thomas, W. (eds.) STACS 2006. LNCS, vol. 3884, pp. 621–633. Springer, Heidelberg (2006)
11. Ho, K.: Dual criteria optimization problems for imprecise computation tasks. In: Leung, J.Y.T. (ed.) Handbook of Scheduling (2004)
12. Voorneveld, M.: Characterization of pareto dominance. Operations Research Letters 31, 7–11 (2003)
13. Agnetis, A., Mirchandani, P.B., Pacciarelli, D., Pacifici, A.: Scheduling problems with two competing agents. Operations Research 52(2), 229–242 (2004)
14. Papadimitriou, C., Yannakakis, M.: On the approximability of trade-offs and optimal access of web sources. In: Proc. of FOCS, pp. 86–92 (2000)
15. Angel, E., Bampis, E., Gourvès, L.: Approximation results for a bicriteria job scheduling problem on a single machine without preemption. Information processing letters 94 (2005)

Deque-Free Work-Optimal Parallel STL Algorithms

Daouda Traoré[1], Jean-Louis Roch[1], Nicolas Maillard[2], Thierry Gautier[1], and Julien Bernard[1]

[1] INRIA Moais research team, CNRS LIG lab., Grenoble University, France
Fristname.Lastname@imag.fr
[2] Instituto de Informática, Univ. Federal Rio Grande do Sul, Porto Alegre, Brazil
nicolas@inf.ufrgs.br

Abstract. This paper presents provable work-optimal parallelizations of STL (Standard Template Library) algorithms based on the work-stealing technique. Unlike previous approaches where a deque for each processor is typically used to locally store ready tasks and where a processor that runs out of work steals a ready task from the deque of a randomly selected processor, the current paper instead presents an original implementation of work-stealing without using any deque but a distributed list in order to bound overhead for task creations. The paper contains both theoretical and experimental results bounding the work/running time.

1 Introduction

The expansion of multicore computers, including from two to dozens of processors, has recently led to a new surge of research on the parallelization of commonly used algorithms with special attention to the C++ *Standard Template Library* STL [1, 2, 3, 4, 5]. Most STL algorithms admit fine grain recursive parallelism (see Sect. 2); also implementations [3, 4, 5, 6] commonly rely on *Work Stealing*, a decentralized thread scheduler: whenever a processor runs out of work, it steals work from a randomly chosen processor.

Yet, Work Stealing achieves provably good performances [1, 8, 9, 10]. In the sequel, let W be the parallel work, *i.e.* the number of unit operations; let D be the parallel depth, often denoted T_∞ too since it corresponds to the theoretical time on an unbound number of processors. Then, the following classical bounds hold: with high probability (denoted w.h.p.), the number of steals is $\mathcal{O}\left(p.D\right)$ and the execution time of a recursive computation on p processors is $T_p \leq \frac{W}{p} + \mathcal{O}\left(D\right)$, a similar bound being achieved in multiprogrammed environments [8].

However, work W and depth D are antagonist criteria that often cannot simultaneously be minimized. Let W_{seq} be the minimal sequential work. For some problems, any parallel algorithm with $D = o(W)$ has a work $W = W_{seq} + \Omega(W_{seq})$. For instance, any prefix computation – *i.e.* STL's `partial_sum`– with depth $D = o(W_{seq})$ requires asymptotically a work $W \geq 2W_{seq}$ [11]. Thus, divide&conquer parallel prefix with depth $D = \log^{\mathcal{O}\left(1\right)} W_{seq}$, – e.g. Ladner-Fisher algorithm – takes a time greater than $\frac{2W_{seq}}{p}$. This compares unfavorably to the tight lower bound $\frac{2W_{seq}}{p+1}$ when p is small, up to 4. Similar lower bounds occur for STL unique_copy and remove_copy_if [12].

To minimize the work while preserving the depth, we propose in Sect. 3 an implementation of Work Stealing that performs the recursive on-line coupling of two distinct algorithms: one is sequential, that enforces a minimal work overhead; the other one is parallel, and minimizes the depth on an unbound number of processors. Differently from classical implementations of Work Stealing [7, 9, 10], our scheme does not rely on a deque of tasks but on a list of successful steals, so it is called *deque-free*. It relies on two operations on the work, called extract_par and extract_seq; extending previous works on parallelism extraction [4, 13].

In Sect. 4, we state that, based on a processor on online tuning of the chunk sizes in the loops, the list is managed with work overhead $\mathcal{O}\left(pD\log^{\mathcal{O}(1)} W\right)$. This result is used in Sect. 5 to provide parallel STL algorithms for partial_sum, unique_copy, remove_copy_if, find_if, partition, and Sort that all asymptotically achieve the tight lower bound, *e.g.* $\frac{2W_{seq}}{p+1}$ for partial_sum. The deque free algorithm has been implemented on top of Kaapi [9]. Experimentations on a 16-core computer, presented in Sect. 6, confirm this theoretical result, outperforming Intel TBB [3] and MCSTL [5].

2 Related Work: Parallel STL and Work Stealing

Among the works related to the parallelization of STL (see [5] for a survey), we focus on parallelizations based on recursive range partitioning with random access iterators and Work Stealing. In [2], a one-dimensional structure (a range) is converted into a two-dimensional structure (a collection of subranges) each subrange being processed sequentially by a given thread. Additional merge operations, possibly parallel, may be involved to complete the work. Threading Building Blocks (TBB) [3] and the Multi-Core Standard Template Library (MCSTL) [5] are both dedicated to multicore computers and based on Cilk's [7] Work Stealing implementation. TBB and MCSTL use recursive range partitioning: each subrange is recursively split in order to balance the load by Work Stealing up to a given sequential threshold. In TBB, this threshold may be adapted by the runtime – default *ideal strategy* – or tuned by the user. In MCSTL, a fixed threshold is used; additionally a partitioning in p subranges is implemented with OpenMP. Finally, although its main concern was cryptography, the paper [4] has introduced basic techniques also developed here but was restricted to only few STL algorithms.

Then, using Work Stealing, those libraries provide asymptotic optimal provable performances when recursive range splitting is work optimal: this is the case for instance for STL for_each and accumulate. However, recursive parallelism may introduce an arithmetic overhead, as seen in the introduction for partial_sum, implemented in TBB by the Ladner-Fisher algorithm with a non optimal work $2W_{seq}$. To reach the optimal work $\frac{2p}{p+1}W_{seq}$, MCSTL implements partial_sum by static partitioning in $p+1$ subranges at the price of poor performances on a multiprogrammed environment. A similar implementation is provided for unique_copy. None of these libraries provide a parallel remove_copy_if. The next section presents an implementation of Work Stealing which deals with work optimality.

3 The Deque-Free Work Stealing Algorithm

Implementations of Work Stealing enforce the optimization of the sequential execution of the parallel algorithm according to the *work-first* principle [7]. Potentially parallel tasks are pushed on a local deque according to some sequential order; when a processor completes a task, it just pops the next one from the head of its deque if ready, thus following the sequential order. When the deque is empty, the processor becomes a thief, stealing a ready task from a randomly chosen victim. Although it is based on the work first principle, the deque-free Work Stealing presented in Algorithm 1 replaces the sequential execution of the parallel algorithm by the execution of a work optimal sequential algorithm from which, at any time, a fraction of the work may be extracted.

As is common, the computation is modeled by a DAG that unfolds dynamically as the computation proceeds. However, the unfolding is performed by the scheduling operations, which occur at each stealing attempt. Each node in the DAG corresponds to a work stream $[I_1, \ldots, I_\perp[$ of sequential instructions. For some STL algorithms – *e.g.* transform, for_each – it may correspond to a range of indexes, but not in the general case.

At any time and for any node, it is assumed possible to extract some work from the computation in progress through an operation, named extract_par in the sequel, without blocking the victim. Indeed, on a steal by P_s, let $w = [I_f, I_\perp[$ the instructions that the victim P_m has yet to perform. Then extract_par extracts from w a subrange $[I_k, I_\perp[$ with $k > f$ and creates a new node which range $w' = [I'_{k'}, I'_{\perp'}[$. The thief P_s processes w' while the victim P_m keeps on the sequential execution of w, now restricted to $[I_f, I_k[$. P_s starts the execution of w' behaving as P_m with its own thieves. Note that w' is different from the range $[I_k, I_\perp]$, since it encompasses the parallel work necessary to process what would have been a sequential work in the initial range.

The execution of the deque-free algorithm performed by P_m is described in Algorithm 1. It is structured in two loops: the inner nano-loop corresponds to the computation of the work. The outer micro-loop corresponds to the course of P_m's thieves according to the sequential order in w. Braces indicate critical sections. The figure on the right shows the synchronization scheme between P_m and P_s, similar to the distributed list homomorphism skeleton DH [13] but in an on-line context. Synchronizations are nested and the DAG of nodes corresponding to a given execution matches a Cilk strict multithreaded computation [7].

Generally, the extracted work w' of P_s differs from the stolen range $[I_k, I_\perp]$. Moreover, a subsequent merge operation may be required to complete the result r of $[I_1, I_\perp[$ from the ones of both $[I_1, I_k[$ and $[I'_{k'}, I'_{\perp'}[$. This merge operation may be empty, *e.g.* for_each. However, in general, it consists into non-blocking completion of $[I_1, I_k[$ –resp. $[I'_{k'}, I'_{\perp'}[$– based on a merge_m– resp. merge_s – operation by P_m –resp. P_s –. Each of both operations corresponds to a sequential stream of instructions, that can be executed in sequential in a non-blocking way if no steal occurs. Both streams are parallel; the scheme is similar to the distributed list homomorphism skeleton DH [13].

The merge_m and merge_s instructions to perform depend on the state of the last thief P_s of P_m when P_m completes I_{k-1}. Two cases arise. Either P_s has previously completed w_s; then the results from both P_s and P_m can be merged by P_m to complete r; in this case merge_s= $\emptyset$. Or the thief has completed I'_{l-1} with $k' < l < \perp'$ and is currently processing I'_l, head of $w' = [I'_l, I'_{\perp'}[$. Then, P_m preempts P_s after I'_l; after synchronization, both perform their part of the distributed merge, respectively merge_m and merge_s. Also, the deque of tasks is replaced by a list of stolen computations managed locally on each victim P_m: at extract_par, P_m inserts at the head of P_m's list a pointer to the stolen work. After completion of merge_m P_m accesses the head of its thief list that corresponds to its next instruction, previously stolen by a thief P'_s; and proceeds to a new distributed merge instruction now between P_m and P'_s. P_m is then only interrupted when it performs a preemption on a stealer process, then waiting at most the completion of the current run-seq on P_s.

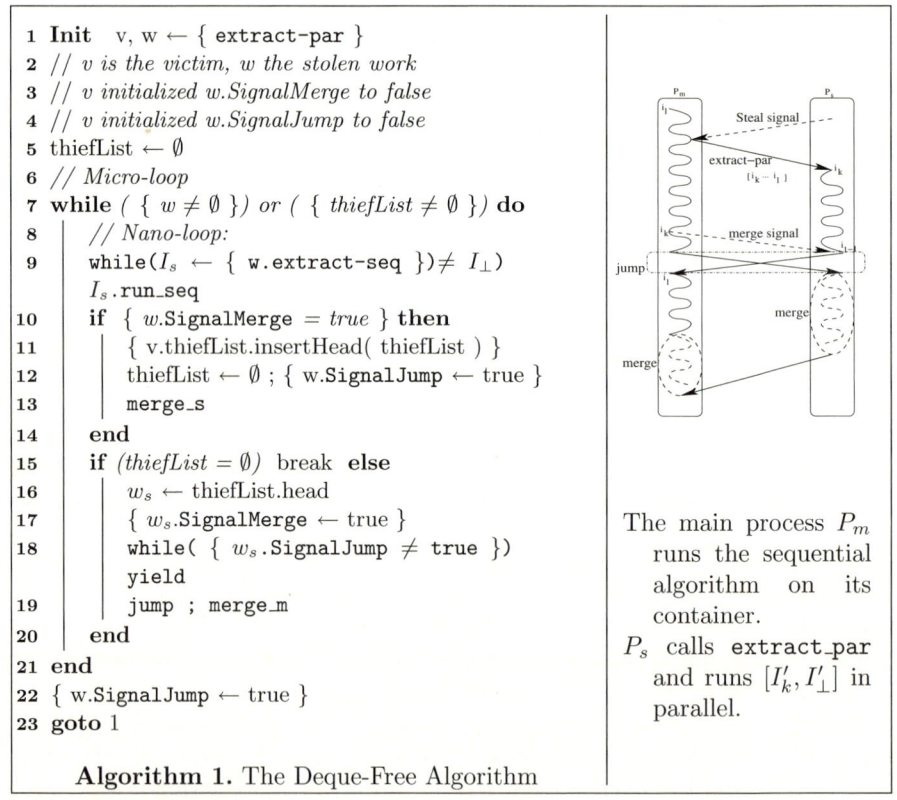

```
 1  Init   v, w ← { extract-par }
 2  // v is the victim, w the stolen work
 3  // v initialized w.SignalMerge to false
 4  // v initialized w.SignalJump to false
 5  thiefList ← ∅
 6  // Micro-loop
 7  while ( { w ≠ ∅ }) or ( { thiefList ≠ ∅ }) do
 8      // Nano-loop:
 9      while(I_s ← { w.extract-seq })≠ I_⊥ )
        I_s.run_seq
10      if { w.SignalMerge = true } then
11          { v.thiefList.insertHead( thiefList ) }
12          thiefList ← ∅ ; { w.SignalJump ← true }
13          merge_s
14      end
15      if (thiefList = ∅) break else
16          w_s ← thiefList.head
17          { w_s.SignalMerge ← true }
18          while( { w_s.SignalJump ≠ true })
            yield
19          jump ; merge_m
20      end
21  end
22  { w.SignalJump ← true }
23  goto 1
```

The main process P_m runs the sequential algorithm on its container.

P_s calls extract_par and runs $[I'_k, I'_\perp]$ in parallel.

Algorithm 1. The Deque-Free Algorithm

The arithmetic work is processed in the nano-loop. To amortize overhead, at each step, P_m extracts from w its next sequential chunk I_s of instructions by `extract_seq` and runs the sequential algorithm on it. It stops only when preempting a thief, thus few times if the depth is small. The next section states some choices for the `extract_seq` chunks in order to achieve optimal work for STL algorithms.

4 Theoretical Bounds for Online Granularity

Let $w = [I_k, I_\perp[$ be the stream of instructions that an arbitrary process P_m is processing at a given top. Let $W_{seq}(w)$ – resp. $D(w)$ – be the work – resp. *potential depth* – in number of unit time instructions to complete w in sequential – resp. in parallel with an unbounded number of steal operations –. The next theorem states that extracting blocks of $D(w)$ operations with `extract_seq` achieves an optimal asymptotic sequential work while not increasing the potential depth on an unbounded number of processors,

Theorem 1. *If the following two hypothesis hold:*
(1) $D(w) \geq \log_2 W_{seq}(w)$, (2) $\forall \epsilon > 0$, $\lim_{W_{seq}(w) \to \infty} \frac{D(w)}{W_{seq}^\epsilon(w)} = 0$,   and if each `extract_seq` *operation returns $D(w)$ unit time instructions, then for all $\delta > 0$, the number of calls to* `extract_seq` *is bounded by* $(1+\delta)\frac{W_{seq}(w)}{\log_2 W_{seq}(w)}$ *when $|w|$ tends to infinity.*

Proof. From hypothesis 2, $\forall \delta, \exists w_0, \forall W_{seq}(w) \geq w_0, D(w) < \frac{\delta}{2} W_{seq}^{\frac{\delta}{2+\delta}}$; and then, $W_{seq}^{\frac{2}{2+\delta}} < \frac{\delta}{2}\frac{W_{seq}}{D(w)}$. Now, let the interval of iterations be split in two parts: (1) For the iterations such that there remain more than $W_{seq}^{\frac{2}{2+\delta}}$ operations: there are at least $D(W_{seq}^{\frac{2}{2+\delta}})$ operations to be extracted at each call to `extract_seq`, which, by hypothesis 1, is larger than $\log\left(W_{seq}^{\frac{2}{2+\delta}}\right) = \frac{2}{2+\delta}\log W_{seq}(w)$. Therefore, there are at most $W_{seq}(w)$ divided by this number calls to `extract_seq`, i.e. $(1+\frac{\delta}{2})\frac{W_{seq}(w)}{\log W_{seq}(w)}$. (2) For the next (fine-grained) iterations, there are at most $W_{seq}^{\frac{2}{2+\delta}} < \frac{\delta}{2}\frac{W_{seq}(w)}{D(w)}$ operations to be performed (for any $W_{seq}(w) \geq w_0$), and therefore at most this number of `extract_seq` calls (if each one includes only one operation). Therefore, and with hypothesis 1, the number of calls to `extract_seq` is, in this phase, less than $\frac{\delta}{2}\frac{W_{seq}(w)}{\log W_{seq}(w)}$. Adding the two bounds, one gets that the number of `extract_seq` calls is at most $\left(1+\frac{\delta}{2}+\frac{\delta}{2}\right)\frac{W_{seq}(w)}{\log W_{seq}(w)}$, hence the expected result.

Thus, the overhead induced by `extract_seq` operations in the nano-loop is asymptotically upper bounded by $\frac{W_{seq}}{\log W_{seq}}$ while the micro/nano loops does not increase the initial potential depth D. This bound is similar to direct recursive partitioning by Work Stealing when recursivity is halved at a grain $\Omega(D)$, but then at the price of an increase of the depth by a factor $\rho > 1$. The first hypothesis seems reasonable, since $\log_2 W_{seq}(w)$ is a lower bound on the potential depth if $W_{seq}(w)$ is optimal. The second means that the work to be performed is much larger than the critical path, which is verified for STL algorithms with polylog depth. Yet, the order of $W_{seq}(w)$ may be unknown, *e.g.* for STL **find_if**. In order to extract either $\log_2(W_{seq}(w))$ (by **extract_seq**) or a fraction (by **extract_par**) of w, a third level of control of the instruction flow is used, called the *macro-loop* [4]. It consists in spanning an *a-priori* unknown set of instructions in steps (or chunks) of size $s_1, s_2, \ldots s_m$, analogously to Floyd's algorithm. The macro-step i of size s_i may start only after completion of step $i - 1$. Eventually, the i-th chunk will contain extra instructions, besides $I_\perp$. But, to obtain $\sum_{i=1,m} s_i \simeq W_{seq}(w)$, in the sequel $s_i = \frac{\sum_{j=1,i-1} s_j}{\log \sum_{j=1,i-1} s_j}$ (with s_1 being some constant value). Then the macro-loop preserves asympt. the work $W_{seq}(w)$ while increasing the potential depth by a factor at most $\log W_{seq}(w)$. Embedding the micro-nano loop in the macro-loop is straight-forward and leads to the final deque-free Work Stealing algorithm, whose performance is stated in the next theorem:

Theorem 2. *If the parallel execution of $w = [I_1, \ldots, I_\perp[$ on an unbounded number of processors performs $(1+\alpha)W_{seq}(w)$ operations with $\alpha \geq 0$, then, w.h.p., the [macro-micro-nano] deque-free algorithm completes w on p processors in time:*

$$T_p(w) = \frac{\alpha+1}{\alpha+p} W_{seq}(w) + \mathcal{O}\left(D(w) \log^2 W_{seq}(w)\right), \text{ when } W_{seq}(w) \to \infty.$$

Proof. Using macro-steps only increases the number of instructions from W_{seq} to $W_{seq}(w) + \mathcal{O}(\log W_{seq}(w))$. From theorem 1, this number is increased by the nano-loop up to $W_{seq}(w) \left(1 + \mathcal{O}\left(\frac{\log W_{seq}(w)}{W_{seq}(w)}\right) + \mathcal{O}\left(\frac{1}{\log W_{seq}(w)}\right)\right) = W_{seq}$ asymptotically. If only one processor P_m runs the program, it will never be preempted and will simply run the sequential algorithm, *i.e.* W_{seq} operations. On $p \geq 2$ processors, $p-1$ perform **extract_par** operations, completing at most $W_{par}(m) = (1+\alpha)W_{seq}(m)$ operations where m is the instructions stream corresponding to those $p-1$ thefts; while P_m completes $W_{seq} - W_{seq}(m)$ operations. Since each call to **extract_par** extracts a fraction of the work, the victim whole number of **extract_par** operations in the macro-loop is $\mathcal{O}\left(\log^2 W_{seq}(w)\right)$ w.h.p; then the sequential process waits $\mathcal{O}\left(D(w) \log^2 W_{seq}(w)\right)$ for all preemption operations. Since P_m is never idle, except when preempting a theft or eventually during the last macro-step of size at most $\frac{W_{seq}(w)}{\log W_{seq}(w)}$: $T_p(w) = W_{seq}(w) - W_{seq}(m) + \mathcal{O}\left(D(w) \log^2 W_{seq}(w)\right)$ (1). Besides, due to Work Stealing, w.h.p. $T_p(w) \leq \frac{\alpha+1}{p-1} W_{seq}(m) + \mathcal{O}\left(D(w) \log^2 W_{seq}(w)\right)$ (2). Elimination of $W_{seq}(m)$ in (2) from (1) leads to $T_p = \frac{\alpha+1}{\alpha+p} W_{seq}(w) + \mathcal{O}\left(D(w) \log^2 W_{seq}(w)\right)$.

This parallel coupling of two algorithms is totally adaptive, without any overhead when run on a single processor. The next section illustrates its optimality on a few STL algorithms.

5 Application to the STL

The generic three loops deque-free worksteaking is specialized here to the STL.

for_each, transform, accumulate, inner_product: the deque-free implementation is direct since $\alpha = 0$: the work is defined by a subrange [f,l[of indexes; `extract_par` extracts the last half of the victim range; `run-seq` performs the call to the native sequential STL. In `for_each` and `transform`, there is no merge (nop). In `accumulate` and `inner_product`, `merge_m` sums the local result with the result of the thief, while `merge_s` is nop. An optimal parallel time $T_p(w) = \frac{W_{seq}(w)}{p}$ is asymp. reached. However, by halving recursive calls at a depth $\log W_{seq}(w)$, the sequential execution of the recursive partitioning algorithm is asympt. optimal. Then, here, our scheme does not improve recursive partitioning by Work Stealing. The parallel time is $T_p = \frac{W_{seq}}{p} + \mathcal{O}\left(\log^2 W_{seq}\right)$ which asymp. reaches the lower bound.

partial_sum. The macroloop splits the range in $\mathcal{O}(\log W_{seq})$ subranges of size $s_i = \frac{\sum_{j=1,i-1} s_j}{\log \sum_{j=1,i-1} s_j}$ computed consecutively. Each macrostep is parallelized as follows: the work and `extract_par` are identical to `transform`. Only one process P_M follows the macrostep and preempts thieves, while other processes never preempt similarly to `transform`; `run-seq` performs a sequential `partial_sum`. `merge_m` gets from the thief the last computed prefix in its subrange and jumps to the first index after this subrange. `merge_s` gets from P_M the last computed prefix and apply a parallel `transform` to compute the final prefix of its subrange. Due to merge, the depth of a macrostep is $\mathcal{O}\left(\log^2 W_{seq}\right)$. Since $\alpha = 1$, the parallel time is $T_p = \frac{2W_{seq}}{p+1} + \mathcal{O}\left(\log^3 W_{seq}\right)$ which asympt. reaches the lower bound.

unique_copy, remove_copy_if. For both, our implementation is similar to `partial_sum` and achieves the similar lower bounds as for stream computations [12].

find, find_if: Our implementation relies on the macroloop: the macrostep i is here of size $s_i = \frac{\sum_{j=1,i-1} s_j}{\log \sum_{j=1,i-1} s_j}$. Each macrostep is processed as follows; `run-seq` is a sequential `find`; `extract_par` is identical to `transform`; `merge_s` is nop; `merge_m` compares the local index found (if any) with the one of the thief, possibly preempted, to take the minimum index. Parallel `find` performs early termination within a macrostep: if a process finds the first iterator N in `run-seq`, then it empties its work. Due to the microloop, all the other processes, when they try to merge with it, or to steal part of its work, terminate. This is also true as soon as one process – in particular the main process – reaches the upper bound r. The algorithm runs in time $T_p = \frac{W_{seq}}{p} + \mathcal{O}\left(\log^3 W_{seq}\right)$

partition and sort: Our implementation of `partition` (on which the Sort is based) [14] performs a parallel, in-place partition. The work corresponds to two subranges S_L and S_R and maintains pointers on the left-most (resp. right-most) block b_L in S_L (resp b_R in S_R); `run-seq` performs a specific partition on the distributed container $[b_L, b_R]$ to partition it, performing in average the same number of swap operations than a sequential partition of a contiguous container. Thus, it follows the STL partition scheme. `extract_par` splits S_L and S_R into two halves, the thief partitioning the right-most half of the left block, and the left-most half of the right block. Special care has to be taken when one whole half of the elements has already been partitioned, since the thieves always try to steal two blocks of elements. In this case, the remaining blocks of elements to be partitioned must be re-ordered, so that the algorithm may proceed. The algorithm runs in time $T_p = \frac{W_{seq}}{p} + \mathcal{O}\left(\log^2 W_{seq}\right)$.

Sort is based on introspective sorting [14] which is based on quicksort. When the size n of input array is lower than a fixed tuned threshold g, the sequential partition algorithm is applied. Else, the previous deque-free partition is performed. When completed, the two parts of the array are sorted in parallel with workstealing. It runs in expected time $T_p = \frac{W_{seq}}{p} + \mathcal{O}\left(\log^3 n\right)$.

6 Experimentations

We have implemented the deque-free Work Stealing algorithm on top of Kaapi [9] and specialized it to implement the previous algorithms: this implementation is referred as DFW below. Experimentations have been performed on an AMD Opteron NUMA machine (8 dual-core, 2.2 GHz, Lunix 2.6.23-1-amd64, architecture x86_64). All tests were run at least 10 times: the average, the fastest and the slowest execution time of the 10 executions are presented. We have used MCSTL_0.8.0-beta and the TBB 20_014 stable version. All programs (MCSTL, TBB, DFW) were compiled with the same gcc 4.2.3 and the same option -O2. All input data follow uniform distributions on an array of n doubles.

partial_sum. Figure 1 compares, for $n = 10^8$, DFW partial_sum to MCSTL [5] partial_sum which is based on a static splitting into $p + 1$ parts. The STL partial_sum average time of this experiment is 1.24s: the sequential execution with DFW exhibits no overhead. DFW outperforms MCSTL, and the runtimes are more stable. We argue that this is due to possible perturbations by system processes since, while Work Stealing is stable, static splitting is sensitive to any perturbation due to intermediate barriers. For this fine grain and memory intensive operation, performances do no scale above 4 processors, but when we have augmented the unit operation, the speedup has augmented. Figure 2 compares with the TBB implementation, which is recursive and depends on the chosen granularity. DFW yet reaches the theoretical bound $\frac{2W_{seq}}{p+1}$ with high stability; while TBB seems to scale and reaches the $T_p = \frac{2W_{seq}}{p}$ for some p.

unique_copy. Figure 3 compares the runtime of DFW unique_copy to MCSTL on $n = 10^8$ double. MCSTL implements a static partitioning in $p+1$ parts. The sequential STL execution time for this experiment is 0.61s. DFW performs much better than MCSTL and appears more stable. For this fine grain and memory intensive operation, performances do no scale above 4 processors.

remove_copy_if. Figure 4 shows the execution times obtained with DFW remove_copy_if with a predicate of $16\mu s$ and $n = 10^6$. At this larger grain, performances scales up to 16 core, reaching the $\frac{W_{seq}}{p}$ lower bound [12].

find_if. The experimentations consist in three measures with $n = 10^6$ where the position k of the first element to find is $10^2, 10^4, 10^6$. The time to compute pred is $\tau_{pred} = 35\mu s$. In table 2 DFW Find_if provides speed up from $k = 10^6$, scaling up to 12 processors. In any case no speed down is observed with respect to the STL sequential time. This illustrates the DFW macroloop scheme in which one among the p processors always follows the sequential order.

sort. Table 1 shows the speed-up for sort w.r.t. sequential STL for $n = 6.410^5$ and $n = 3.2710^8$ and with 2, 8 and 16 threads. Threshold is $g = 10000$. DFW performs better than the two other ones for large n; this is not the case for small values even if close.

Table 1. Sort: speed-up w.r.t. STL

Speed-Up w.r.t. STL sequential	Sort: input size n					
	$n = 6.410^5$			$n = 3.2710^8$		
	p=2	p=8	p=16	p=2	p=8	p=16
DFW	1.6	2.3	1.3	1.9	6.9	8.1
TBB	1.9	3.4	1.8	1.9	4.9	5.1
MCSTL	1.7	2.1	2.0	1.8	5.1	7.1

Table 2. Find_if: speed-up w.r.t. STL

DFW find_if: $n = 10^6$ elements; first matching is at position k				
k	p=2	p=8	p=12	p=16
$k=10^2$	0.99	0.99	0.99	0.99
$k=10^4$	1.92	5.51	6.02	6.35
$k=10^6$	1.99	7.89	11.4	13.1

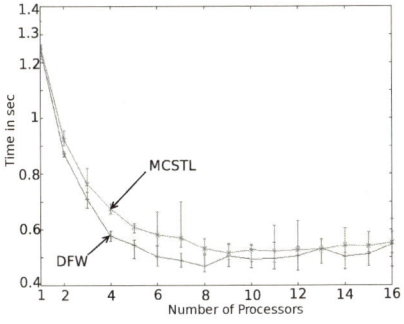

Fig. 1. Partial_sum: runtime of DFW and MCSTL *vs.* number of processors, on $n = 10^8$ double

Fig. 2. Partial_sum: runtime of DFW and TBB with $n = 3.10^4$ objects (unitary operation time $\tau_{op} = 1.5ms$)

7 Conclusions

We have introduced a generic deque-free work-stealing implementation that we have used to parallelize 80% of the STL algorithms for containers with random iterators. The proposed STL algorithms all achieve polylog potential depth on an unbounded number of processors, while the size of the scheme adapts automatically to the available resources and their speeds.

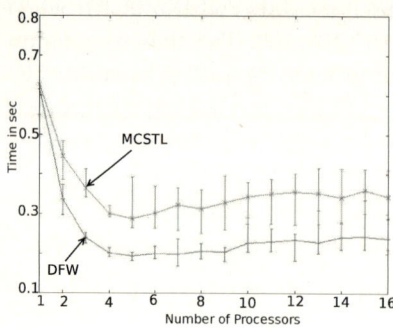 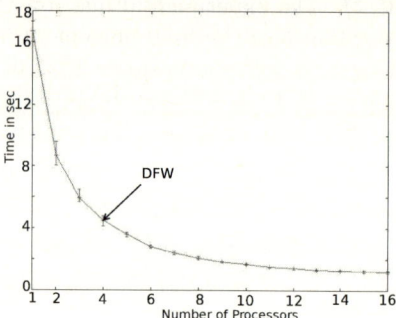

Fig. 3. Unique_copy: runtime of DFW vs. MCSTL on of $n = 10^8$ double

Fig. 4. Remove_copy_if: runtime of DFW (predicate time $\tau_{pred} = 16\mu s$)

A theoretical analysis is provided which proves work optimality for the STL presented algorithms with asymptotic ratio 1 w.r.t. to the lower bound on p identical processors, while this lower bound increases with p. In particular, the partial sum (prefix) computation is performed in asymptotic optimal work $\frac{2p}{p+1}W_{seq}$ without reference to the number of processors in the code, except inside the implementation of Work Stealing. To our knowledge, it provides the first provably work optimal parallel implementations of partial_sum, unique_copy and remove_copy_if. When compared to TBB and MCSTL, the experimentations exhibit good performances and stability w.r.t. static partitioning and direct recursive Work Stealing.

Since it achieves provable optimal performance, we think that this scheme is a basis to design of algorithms that obliviously adapt to the number of processor and their respective speeds. The considered algorithms (except sort) are related to a sequential linear traversal of the container; they are both processor and cache-oblivious on the CO-model. A perspective is then to extend this distributed scheme to algorithms with non-linear complexity in the input/output on distributed memory architectures.

References

1. Musser, D.R., Derge, G.J., Saini, A.: STL tutorial and reference guide, 2nd edn. Addison-Wesley, Boston (2001)
2. Austern, M.H., Towle, R.A., Stepanov, A.A.: Range partition adaptors: a mechanism for parallelizing stl. SIGAPP Appl. Comput. Rev. 4(1), 5–6 (1996)
3. Reinders, J.: Intel Threading Building Blocks - Outfitting C++ for Multi-core Processor Parallelism. O'Reilly, Sebastopol (2007)
4. Danjean, V., Gillard, R., Guelton, S., Roch, J.L., Roche, T.: Adaptive loops with kaapi on multicore and grid: Applications in symmetric cryptography. In: ACM PASCO 2007, London, Canada (2007)
5. Singler, J., Sanders, P., Putze, F.: The multi-core standard template library. In: Kermarrec, A.-M., Bougé, L., Priol, T. (eds.) Euro-Par 2007. LNCS, vol. 4641. Springer, Heidelberg (2007)

6. Yu, H., Rauchwerger, L.: An adaptive algorithm selection framework for reduction parallelization. IEEE Trans. Par. Dist. Syst. 17(10), 1084–1096 (2006)
7. Frigo, M., Leiserson, C., Randall, K.: The implementation of the cilk-5 multi-threaded language. In: SIGPLAN Conf. PLDI, pp. 212–223 (1998)
8. Arora, N.S., Blumofe, R.D., Plaxton, C.G.: Thread scheduling for multiprogrammed multiprocessors. Theory Comput. Syst. 34(2), 115–144 (2001)
9. Gautier, T., Besseron, X., Pigeon, L.: Kaapi: A thread scheduling runtime system for data flow computations on cluster of multi-processors. In: ACM PASCO, London, Canada, pp. 15–23 (2007)
10. Chowdhury, R.A., Ramachandran, V., Blelloch, G.E., Gibbons, P., Chen, S., Kozuch, M.: Provably good multicore cache performance for divide-and-conquer algorithms. In: SIAM/ACM Symposium on Discrete Algorithms (SODA) (2008)
11. Ladner, R.E., Fischer, M.J.: Parallel prefix computation. Journal of the ACM 27(4), 831–838 (1980)
12. Bernard, J., Roch, J.L., Traore, D.: Processor-oblivious parallel stream computations. In: 16th Euromicro Conf. PDP, Toulouse, France (2007)
13. Bischof, H., Gorlatch, S., Leshchinskiy, R.: Generic parallel programming using c++ templates and skeletons. In: Lengauer, C., Batory, D., Consel, C., Odersky, M. (eds.) Domain-Specific Program Generation. LNCS, vol. 3016, pp. 107–126. Springer, Heidelberg (2004)
14. Traoré, D., Roch, J.L., Cérin, C.: Algorithmes adaptatifs de tri parallèle. In: RenPar'18 / SympA 2008 / CFSE'6, Fribourg, Switzerland (2008)

Topic 13: High-Performance Networks

Tor Skeie*, Daniel Ortega*, José Flich*, and Raimir Holanda*

The communication network is the key component of every parallel and distributed system. The trend of always aiming at bigger and more complex cores has shifted towards having many simpler cores, sharing yet another complex communication layer at the chip level. Moreover, advancements on scaling out at the cluster level have pushed communication and storage networks to new limits. All these technological opportunities bring out new and exciting research challenges.

This topic is devoted to communication issues in scalable compute and storage systems, such as parallel computers, networks of workstations, and clusters. In total, 10 papers were submitted to this topic out of which we have selected the six strongest ones. The quality of this years submissions has been extraordinary, resulting in one of the best papers of the conference.

Two of the accepted papers explore some of the problems that networks on chip are bringing to current research. In "Reducing Packet Dropping in a Bufferless NoC", the authors assume the lack of intermediate buffers in NoCs (which has been proven to allow for higher frequencies) and present mechanisms to avoid penalties imposed by packet dropping in a very elegant way. The other paper dealing with NoCs is "A Communication-Aware Topological Mapping Technique for NoCs" where an offline topological mapping based on communication patterns is shown to be an effective replacement for current experimental validations.

Optical network switching costs are discussed in "Approximating the Traffic Grooming Problem with respect to ADMs and OADMs", where the authors present a polynomial approximation to the NP complete problem of determining the minimum cost of switching when combinations of optical and electronic-optical add-drop-multiplexers are used. The paper "On the Influence of the Packet Marking and Injection Control Schemes in Congestion Management for MINs" focuses on congestion management mechanisms and analyses the impact of combining the different alternatives with respect to performance.

In "Deadlock-Free Dynamic Network Reconfiguration Based on Close Up*/Down* Graphs" the authors show how, without the need for additional resources they can dynamically reconfigure networks when new nodes are added or failures prevent certain nodes from correctly functioning. Last, but definitely not least, the paper "HITP: A Transmission Protocol for Scalable High-Performance Distributed Storage" presents a new communication protocol that provides high throughput regardless of network latencies, and compares it favourably to other more common protocols.

---

* Topic Chairs.

Reducing Packet Dropping in a Bufferless NoC*

Crispín Gómez, María E. Gómez, Pedro López, and José Duato

Dept. of Computer Engineering, Universidad Politécnica de Valencia, Camino de Vera, s/n,
46071–Valencia, Spain
crigore@gap.upv.es, {megomez,plopez,jduato}@disca.upv.es

Abstract. Networks on chip (NoCs) has a strong impact on overall chip performance. Interconnection bandwidth is limited by the critical path delay. Recent works show that the critical path includes the switch input buffer control logic. As a consequence, by removing buffers, switch clock frequency can be doubled. Recently, a new switching technique for NoCs called Blind Packet Switching (BPS) has been proposed. It is based on replacing the buffers of the switch ports by simple latches. Since buffers consume a high percentage of switch power and area, BPS not only improves performance but also helps in reducing power and area. In BPS there are no buffers at the switch ports, so packets can not be stopped. If the required output port is busy, the packet will be dropped. In order to prevent packet dropping, some techniques based on resource replication has been proposed. In this paper, we propose some alternative and complementary techniques that does not rely on resource replication. By using these techniques, packet dropping and its negative effects are highly reduced. In particular, packet dropping is completely removed for a very wide network traffic range. The first dropped packet appears at a 11.6 higher traffic load. As a consequence, network throughput is increased and the packet latency is kept almost constant.

1 Introduction

Current high performance microprocessors contain several processing cores on a single chip. Recently, Intel has announced a TeraFLOP processor containing 80 cores on a single chip connected by a NoC [17]. Also, Tilera Corporation [16] has developed the Tile64[TM] processor, which implements 64 general–purpose processors inside the chip. In these chip multiprocessors (CMPs), shared buses and dedicated wires can serve a limited number of processing elements, thus being unable to keep up with the rapidly growing demands for high communication performance. Packet switched NoCs provides the bandwidth required for on-chip communications. NoCs adopt concepts and design methodologies inherited from off-chip interconnection networks. However, NoCs have very different characteristics. While many designs for off–chip networks are mainly performance–driven, power and area consumption are also two important constraints in NoCs. As an example, buffer size should be limited since they consume a lot of area and power [4,5]. On the contrary, wires are an abundant available resource. These differences lead to explore new approaches for NoCs.

---

* This work was supported by the Spanish MEC under Grant TIN2006-15516-C04-01, by CONSOLIDER-INGENIO 2010 under Grant CSD2006-00046, and by the European Commission in the context of the SCALA integrated project #27648 (FP6).

2 Motivation

The growing number of processing elements inside a chip increases the on–chip communication demands. There are several ways to increase NoC performance, most of them inherited from the off-chip networks. Another interesting approach, inherited from the VLSI design, is to increase the network clock frequency. The network clock frequency is determined by the switch critical path delay. Some recent works [12, 13] show that as the switch buffer size is decreased, the clock frequency can be increased. In particular, by eliminating the buffers at the switch ports and replacing them by one–flit latches, the switch frequency can be increased from 1GHz up to more than 2GHz [12, 13] (a 2X increase). This is due to the fact that the critical path is reduced, since the buffering architecture at the switch ports requires some control logic whose delay adds up to data–path delay.

Other works [4, 5] show that a high percentage of both, area and power, is consumed by the switch port buffers, so reducing buffer size can mitigate or even compensate the power consumption increase due to working at higher frequencies. Therefore, reducing the buffer size is an objective in NoCs as it has a positive impact on area and power and enables improving performance.

On the other hand, the high wiring capability of NoCs has led to networks with very wide links. For instance, in [4, 15], two different NoCs are proposed with link widths of 80 and 256 bits, respectively. Moreover, 512–bit wires are considered feasible in the near future [1]. These wide links provide low latency communication, because it decreases the number of *phits* that compose a packet.

Network topology also plays a key role, since it has a high impact on the overall performance and power consumption. The current trend is to use low dimensional networks such as meshes and tori. Meshes are the preferred choice because they allow exploiting the locality of communication, they are scalable, regular and are very energy–efficient [10].

These two facts could lead to use meshes with wide links. This will benefit systems that can take advantage of wide links, such as transmitting large packets or streaming communication networks. However, there are some systems that can not take advantage of these wide links, because they generate small packets that cannot fill the link width. An example of small packets are cache coherence messages, where most of the packets are just composed of a little header and a memory address. For current systems, link widths around 64–bit should be enough.

Nevertheless, there are other options to take advantage of the huge wiring capabilities of NoCs. For instance, splitting the wide links into narrower links that better fit packet size, allowing in this way multiple parallel channels in the same direction [7], known as Space Division Multiplexing (SDM).

In [8], we took advantage of these ideas to propose a new switching technique for NoCs called BPS, based on replacing the switch port buffers by simple latches, with the aim of increasing the system performance and, at the same time saving area and power. The main drawback of BPS is that some packets may be dropped when contention arises. These dropped packets are reinjected later from their source node. In [8], some techniques based on resource replication were proposed to reduce the number of dropped packets, since it affects to the network performance.

In this paper, we are going to propose some complementary techniques to reduce the number of dropped packets that are not based on resource replication. For this purpose, we will summarize BPS in Section 4 to make this paper as self–contained as possible. Following, we will present the proposed techniques in Section 4.1. These techniques are going to be applied to BPS, but they could be used to prevent packet dropping in any other NoC that allows packet dropping. They will be evaluated in Section 5. Finally, some conclusions and future work will be drawn in Section 6.

3 Related Work

In NoCs, performance and saving power and area are equally important in most cases [2, 5]. Among all the traditional switching techniques, wormhole is the most appropriate for NoCs [3, 4], because it relies on small size buffers [10]. Some works [9] even propose to return to previous switching techniques such as circuit switching to completely remove buffers. The problem is that it wastes network resources due to the need of resource reservation. We believe that a new switching technique that fits into the limitations of NoCs must be developed, efficiently taking advantage of their singular characteristics. There are some recent works that progress in this direction. For instance, in [3] the authors propose to use the link repeaters in order to provide additional buffering resources, also defining a new flow control mechanism. In [14], the authors propose to retake the *hot potato routing*, or deflection routing, with the aim of using small buffer networks [11], that also work at higher frequencies. However, deflection limits are not guaranteed to prevent livelocks, and the huge wiring capability of NoCs is not exploited.

4 Blind Packet Switching

As buffers are the most consuming part in terms of power and area, BPS remove them from switch ports. Additionally, this allows to achieve a higher network performance, since it is possible to increase the network frequency. Figure 1.(a) shows a switch with input and output buffers. Only one input and one output port of the switch are shown. Buffers are composed by multiple latches serially connected plus some control logic. Every latch can store a flit. Figure 1.(b) represents our switch. Input and output queues have been reduced to just one flit latch per port and, therefore, buffer control logic has been removed. These latches actually work as repeaters, they do not store the flits while packets are blocked. They only store a flit during a clock cycle. As stated in Section 2 and according to [12, 13], this switch can work approximately at least at twice the frequency of the buffered switch.

As there are no buffers, when a packet can not get the resources it requires to go on through the network, it is dropped. The switch that drops the packet sends a Negative Acknowledgment (nack) to the corresponding source node, which will reinject the packet. Dropped packets introduce additional traffic load due to the nack packet and the reinjection of the packet, and also increase the packet latency. To avoid packet dropping, packets must advance through the network like a never-stopping flow. In [8], we proposed several solutions to reduce packet dropping.

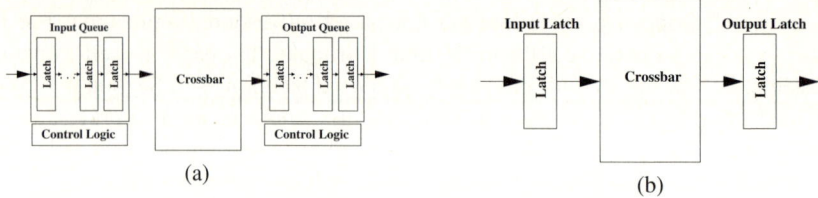

Fig. 1. (a) A traditional buffered switch. (b) A BPS switch.

We proposed to replicate the conflicting resources such as network links, ejection channels and routing circuits.

Concerning network links, we proposed to use fully adaptive routing to increase the number of routing options. To increase even more the routing options, we use multiple parallel links in the same direction (SDM). In the same way, we propose to provide multiple ejection channels between switches and nodes to relax the ejection bottleneck due to SDM. Routing availability can be easily increased by replicating the routing circuit, or by using a single routing circuit that can handle multiple packets at once.

Nevertheless, there are still some scenarios where a packet still may be dropped. In order to prevent packet losing, nack packets are used. When a packet is dropped in a switch, that switch is responsible of forwarding the corresponding nack packet to the source node. Once the nack has reached the source of the packet, it is reinjected into the network. Nack packets are given priority over data packets and can not be dropped. Therefore, if there is not an available output port to send the nack, they are ejected from the network and are stored in a small queue (unique per switch).

Notice that in BPS, deadlocks can not occur since packets are never stopped, so virtual channels are not required [6] even for adaptive routing. On the contrary, in a buffered wormhole network, at least two virtual channels per direction are required to prevent deadlocks. Hence, with BPS all the hardware related to virtual channel multiplexing is removed and the crossbar complexity is reduced to the quarter. Furthermore, no link level flow control mechanism is required. Packets move blindly as switches do not use buffer availability to route packets. As there is neither a link level flow control mechanism, nor a deadlock avoidance mechanism, the switch control logic is expected to be less complex.

In [8], we showed that BPS can outperform wormhole in most of the cases. However, the number of parallel links has a great impact on BPS throughput. In particular, throughput was strongly increased with 4 and 8 parallel links (a 8×8 mesh achieved a 50% higher throughput than wormhole). Finally, BPS latency did not depend on traffic for low and medium network loads and was approximately half the latency of the corresponding buffered network. The percentage of reinjected packets was negligible at low and medium traffic loads for 4 and 8 parallel links. Moreover, for high traffic loads before saturation point, the highest percentage of reinjected packets for a 8×8 mesh was close to a 5%. Nack queue size did not exceed 4 packets for the aforementioned networks.

However, dropping packets and reinjecting them from the source nodes not only requires the burden of nacks but also it may introduce out of order delivery of packets.

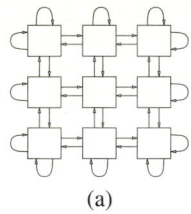 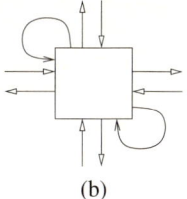

Fig. 2. (a) A closed 3×3 mesh, external output ports are connected to their corresponding input port. (b) A switch with two extra loopback channels.

Therefore, some additional techniques to reduce the percentage of reinjected packets are required. What is actually needed is that there will not be any reinjected packet for an extended range of network traffic. In this way, a technique that expands this traffic range is welcomed.

4.1 Reducing Packet Dropping by Misrouting and Loopback Channels

In this section, we propose some techniques to reduce packet dropping and its consequences. All the proposed techniques provide a second chance to packets that should be dropped. We propose using misrouting, external misrouting and loopback channels. Misrouting consists of forwarding the packet through any free output port that provides a non–minimal path towards its destination and is well–known in interconnection networks [6, 11]. We also propose two variants of misrouting specially designed for NoCs. All these techniques can be used on their own or combined, and can be applied to any network that has a reduced amount of buffers like [11] or that allows packet dropping, like BPS.

External Misrouting. External misrouting is an extension of the common misrouting. When misrouting a packet, its latency is increased. However, when compared with dropping the packet, the increase of packet latency is clearly smaller than the reinjection time.

The novelty of external misrouting comes from the following idea. External links of the mesh–border switches are not used. We propose to connect these unconnected switch output ports to their corresponding input port, forming a loopback channel (Figure 2.(a)). This loopback channel will act as a false buffer to store one flit during one clock cycle, providing an additional chance to the packet. The switch provides an extra buffer at almost no cost (a very short link).

When a packet should be dropped in a switch that belongs to the border of the mesh, external misrouting is first tried, misrouting the packet through the loopback channels instead of misrouting it through other network links, thus avoiding the use of network links. If the loopback link is busy, then traditional misrouting is used.

Notice that when using external misrouting, the packet is kept at the same switch. Furthermore, when a packet is misrouted though a loopback channel, its route is increased by only one hop, whereas traditional misrouted packets suffer a packet route length increase of two hops, as they are misrouted out of their minimal path (one hop) and then back to their minimal path (another hop). Nevertheless, packets may still be dropped if there is not any available output port, or if the number of misroutings has reached its maximum value, since the number of misroutings must be limited to avoid livelocks.

BPS preserves in-order packet delivery for all the packets that are not dropped. Non-dropped packets use minimal path routing, and there is no packet blocking, therefore all the paths between a source and a destination take the same time. Dropped packets can be delivered out-of-order because a new packet can be injected into the network from the same source to the same destination in the elapsed time between the first injection of the dropped packet and its reinjection. Misrouting steps up packet in-order delivery, since it strongly reduces this elapsed time, as the reinjection takes longer than the misrouting.

Extra Loopback Channels. We propose extending the loopback channels of the mesh border switches to all network switches, thus allowing additional buffering resources at each switch to prevent packet dropping. In Figure 2.(b), we show a central switch of the mesh with two extra loopback channels. Switch degree is increased, but the number of wires out of the switch is the same, as loopbacks are a switch internal connection.

The extra loopback channels can be added by using new wires or not. By using new wires, the total number of switch ports will be increased. This approach provides the best performance. On the other hand, if the number of switch ports can not be increased, we can sacrifice some ports used to connect to other switches to implement the loopback channels. In this case, it is expected that network throughput will be reduced. An analysis of the tradeoff between loopback and network links will be performed in the next section.

5 Evaluation

5.1 Simulation Environment

A detailed event-driven simulator that implements BPS has been developed. The simulator models a mesh with multiple parallel point-to-point bidirectional links in the same dimension. Packets are adaptively routed. Additionally, processing nodes have as injection and ejection channels as parallel links in the network. Routing, link and crossbar delay are supposed to be equal to one clock cycle. We assume that the packet generation rate is constant and the same for all the nodes. The destination of a packet is randomly chosen. Packet sizes and percentage of short packets are set to model a cache coherence system and were used in [1,7,8] to simulate a CMP system. Short packet size is 32 bits and correspond to command packets such as requests and invalidations. Large packet size is 544 bits and correspond to response packets that contain cache lines. The percentage of short packets is 60%. A 32–bit header is attached to all the packets. Link width will be fixed to 64 bits, because that is the total size of short packets. Packet latency is the difference between the first packet injection and its ejection from the network at its destination, including all the packet reinjections.

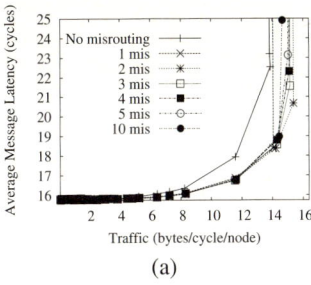
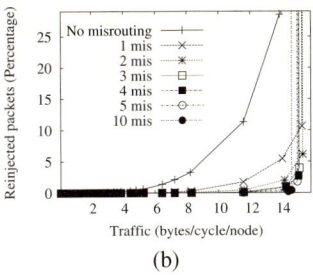

Fig. 3. Impact of misrouting on performance. 4×4 mesh with 4 parallel links per dimension.

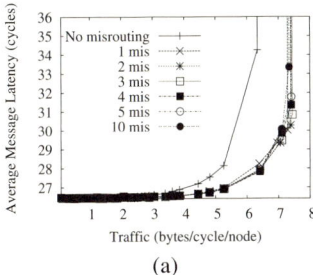
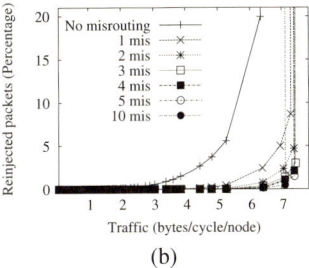

Fig. 4. Impact of misrouting on performance. 8×8 mesh with 4 parallel links per dimension.

5.2 Evaluation Results

In this section, we will analyze the impact of the proposed techniques in the reduction of the number of dropped (and reinjected) packets. As the number of dropped packets is reduced, the throughput is expected to be increased and the packet latency reduced. First, we study the impact of misrouting combined with external misrouting on BPS. Next, we analyze the impact of having extra loopback channels at any switch, both by adding new switch ports and by sacrificing network links to implement loopbacks. Finally, we analyze the impact of using both techniques simultaneously.

Misrouting Plus External Misrouting. In Figures 3 and 4, we show results for a 4×4 mesh and a 8×8 mesh with 4 parallel links per dimension varying the number of maximum misroutes[1]. Misrouting increases the network throughput by 1.5% in the small network and by 15% in the large network (Figures 3.(a) and 4.(a), respectively). The throughput increase is proportional to the network size.

Only the first misroute seems to be significant in both networks. The influence of the additional misroutes seems negligible. As we can see in Figures 3.(b) and 4.(b), the first misroute reduces the percentage of dropped packets from 28% to 5.2%, in the small network, and from 20.1% to 3%, in the large network. In the original BPS the first dropped packet appears when the network throughput is 0.27 bytes/cycle/node. By

---

[1] Eventhough more network sizes were studied, as the results are similar to the ones presented in here, we do not show them due to lack of space.

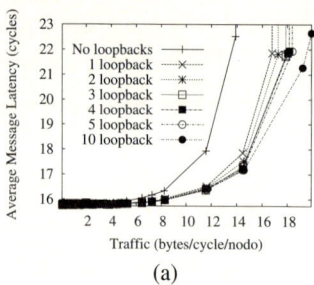 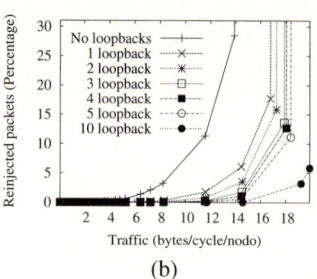

Fig. 5. Impact of loopbacks on performance. 8×8 mesh with 4 parallel links per dimension.

using one misrouting, the first dropped packet appears at 0.86 bytes/cycle/node. The network has to drop the first packet at a 2.2 higher network traffic.

Extra Loopback Channels. In Figures 5 and 6, we show results for the same networks, varying the number of extra loopback channels without using misrouting. In Figures 5.(a) and 6.(a), we can see that just by adding one extra loopback channel per switch, the network throughput is increased by 21% and by 13% for the small and the large network, respectively. On the contrary to misroute, each additional loopback significantly increases the network throughput. For instance, it is increased by 18.4% and by 34% for the small and the large network, when the number of loopbacks is ten instead of one. As the network size is increased, the influence of each additional loopback is also increased. A single loopback provides the packet with another opportunity before dropping it, but the packet is kept in the same switch that was going to drop it. If this switch was suffering a high network traffic load, it is highly probable that the packet can not find a suitable output port in only one clock cycle. It is well-known that the network congestion tends to increase with the network size in a mesh. Hence, as the network size is increased, the percentage of packets that can be saved from dropping is increased by each additional opportunity.

In Figures 5.(b) and 6.(b), we can see that the percentage of dropped packets is strongly reduced as we add loopback channels. Notice that it is negligible till the network saturation when the large network is using ten loopback channels. The first dropped packet appears when the network traffic is 0.58, 1.14, 2.89 and 6.41 bytes/cycle/node when the switches have 1, 2, 5 and 10 extra loopback channels, respectively.

Figure 7 shows the obtained results when the loopback channels are implemented at the expense of network channels. There are two ways of doing this: taking out one of the 4 data links, resulting in three data links and one loopback channel per direction, or reducing the width of every network link to free the number of switch outwards wires required to form a loopback channel, having four narrower data links and one loopback channel per direction. Results show that, when loopback channels are implemented by sacrificing network links, the network performance is similar to the one obtained without loopback channels. Although the use of a loopback channel does not improve the throughput, the number of wires between the switches has been reduced by a 25%, which helps in simplifying the physical wiring and reducing the number of required link

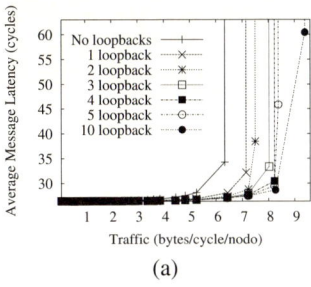
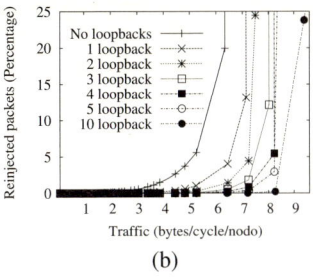

Fig. 6. mpact of loopbacks on performance. 8×8 mesh with 4 parallel links per dimension.

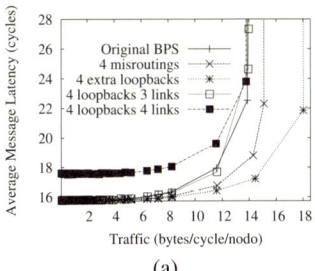
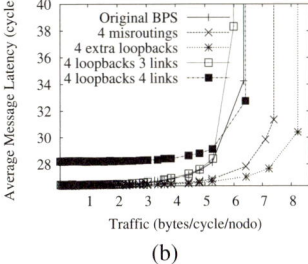

Fig. 7. Comparison of misrouting and loopbacks. 4 parallel links per dimension. (a) 4×4 mesh. (b) 8×8 mesh.

repeaters. Notice that using narrower links is not a good approach because it increases the packet latency.

Misrouting Combined with Loopback Channels. Finally, we evaluate both proposed techniques working together. Figure 8 show the obtained results. In Figure 8.(a), we can see the performance for one maximum misroute, one extra loopback channel, and one maximum misroute and one extra loopback. By combining both techniques, the throughput is increased by 10.6% over one misrouting, and by 12.8% over only one loopback. The first dropped packet appears when the network traffic is 2.51 bytes/cycle/node, a 8.3 higher traffic load.

In Figure 8.(b), we evaluate four different configurations in order to identify the most interesting technique to replicate when combining them. For this purpose, we compare the following combinations: two maximum misroutes, two loopback channels, two misroutes and one loopback, and one misroute and two loopbacks. As it was expected, the best performance is obtained for one misroute and two loopback channels, since, as it was shown, only the first misroute actually improves network performance. So, it is more interesting to have additional loopback channels than increasing the maximum number of misroutings. In this case, with 1 misrouting and 2 loopback channels, the first dropped packet appears at 3.40 bytes/cycle/node. The network traffic when the first packet is dropped is 11.6 times higher.

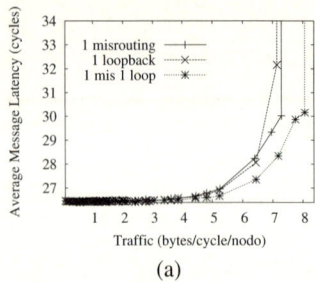 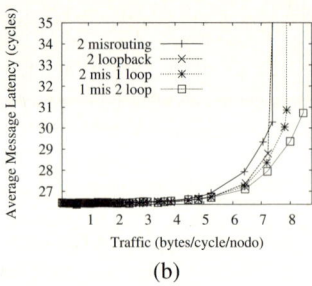

Fig. 8. Impact of combining misrouting and loopback channels on performance. 8×8 mesh with 4 parallel links per dimension.

6 Conclusions and Future Work

We have proposed some techniques to improve the performance of a bufferless NoC with packet dropping. These techniques are focused on reducing the number of dropped packets by using misrouting and loopback channels. The results show that both techniques are able to strongly reduce the number of dropped packets, thus allowing a higher network performance, and reducing the negative effects of packet dropping: nack-related issues and out-of-order delivery of packets. In particular, when combining all the techniques, the first dropped packet appears at a 11.6 times higher traffic; up to this point the network does neither need any nack queue, nor memory in the end nodes to reinject the packets.

Only one misrouting is required to improve performance. Concerning loopback channels, the performance is improved as loopback channels are added, especially in large networks. Furthermore, we have shown that loopbacks can help in reducing wiring requirements in the network. The best option is to combine both techniques, providing one misroute and as many loopback channels as possible.

For future work, we want to make a power and area model of the loopbacks channels in order to evaluate their influence over the total NoC consumption.

References

1. Balfour, J., Dally, W.J.: Design Tradeoffs for Tiled CMP On-chip Networks. In: 20th Annual International Conference on Supercomputing, pp. 187–198 (2006)
2. Benini, L., De Micheli, G.: Networks on Chips: A New SoC Paradigm. Computer 35(1), 70–78 (2002)
3. Bertozzi, D., Benini, L.: Xpipes: a Network-on-chip Architecture for Gigascale Systems-on-chip. IEEE Circuits and Systems Magazine 4(2) (2004)
4. Dally, W.J., Towles, B.: Route Packets, Not Wires: On-chip Interconnection Networks. In: 38th Conf. on Design Automation, pp. 684–689 (2001)
5. De Michelli, G., Benini, L.: Network on Chips. Morgan Kaufmann, San Francisco (2006)
6. Duato, J., Yalamanchili, S., Ni, L.: Interconnection Networks. An Engineering Approach. Morgan Kaufmann, San Francisco (2004)
7. Gómez, C., Gómez, M.E., López, P., Duato, J.: Exploiting Wiring Resources on Interconnection Network: Increasing Path Diversity. In: 16th Euromicro International Conference on Parallel, Distributed and Network-Based Processing, pp. 20–29 (2008)

8. Gómez, C., Gómez, M.E., López, P., Duato, J.: An Efficient Switching Technique for NoCs with Reduced Buffer Requirements. In: International Conference for High Performance Computing, Networking, Storage and Analysis (SC 2008) (submitted, 2008)
9. Goossens, K., Dielissen, J., van Meerbergen, J., Poplavko, P., Radulescu, A., Rijpkema, E., Waterlander, E., Wielage, P.: Guaranteeing the Quality of Services in Networks on Chip. In: Nurmi, J., Tenhunen, H., Isoaho, J., Jantsch, A. (eds.) Networks on Chip, ch. 4, Kluwer, Dordrecht (2003)
10. Kavaldjiev, N.K., Smit, G.J.M.: A Survey of Efficient On-Chip Communications for SoC. In: PROGRESS Symp. on Embedded Systems (2003)
11. Lu, Z., Zhong, M., Jantsch, A.: Evaluation of On-chip Networks Using Deflection Routing. In: 16th ACM Great Lakes Symposium on VLSI, pp. 296–301 (2006)
12. Martini, F., Bertozzi, D., Benini, L.: Assessing the Impact of Flow Control and Switching Techniques on Switch Performance for Low Latency NoC Design. In: 1st Workshop on Interconnection Network Architectures: On-Chip, Multi-Chip (2007)
13. Medardoni, S., Bertozzi, D., Benini, L., Macii, E.: Control and Datapath Decoupling in the Design of a NoC Switch: Area, Power and Performance Implications. In: International Symposium on System-on-Chip, pp. 1–4 (2007)
14. Millberg, M., Nilsson, E., Thid, R., Jantsch, A.: Guaranteed Bandwidth Using Looped Containers in Temporally Disjoint Networks within the Nostrum Network on Chip. In: Conf. on Design, Automation and Test in Europe (2004)
15. Mullins, R., West, A., Moore, S.: The Design and Implementation of a Low-latency On-chip Network. In: Asia and South Pacific Design Automation Conference, pp. 164–169 (2006)
16. Tilera Corporation, http://www.tilera.com/
17. Vangal, S., Howard, J., Ruhl, G., Dighe, S., Wilson, H., Tschanz, J., Finan, D., Iyer, P., Singh, A., Jacob, T., Jain, S., Venkataraman, S., Hoskote, Y., Borkar, N.: An 80-tile 1.28TFLOPS network-on-chip in 65nm CMOS. In: International Solid-State Circuits Conference (2007)

A Communication-Aware Topological Mapping Technique for NoCs*

Rafael Tornero[1], Juan M. Orduña[1], Maurizio Palesi[2], and José Duato[3]

[1] Departamento de Informática - Universidad de Valencia - Spain
Juan.Orduna@uv.es
[2] DIIT - University of Catania - Italy
mpalesi@diit.unict.it
[3] DISCA - Universidad Politécnica de Valencia - Spain
jduato@gap.upv.es

Abstract. Networks–on–Chip (NoCs) have been proposed as a promising solution to the complex on-chip communication problems derived from the increasing number of processor cores. The design of NoCs involves several key issues, being the topological mapping (the mapping of the Intellectual Properties (IPs) to network nodes) one of them. Several proposals have been focused on topological mapping last years, but they require the experimental validation of each mapping considered.

In this paper, we propose a communication-aware topological mapping technique for NoCs. This technique is based on the experimental correlation of the network model with the actual network performance, thus avoiding the need to experimentally evaluate each mapping explored. The evaluation results show that the proposed technique can provide better performance than the currently existing techniques (in terms of both network latency and energy consumption). Additionally, it can be used for both regular and irregular topologies.

1 Introduction

Network-on-Chip (NoC) architectures [1] have been proposed as a promising solution to the complex on-chip communication problems derived from the increasing number of processor cores. In these architectures, each tile of the network contains a resource and a switch. Each switch is connected to a resource (a processor, a memory, or any other Intelectual Property (IP) compatible with the NoC interface specifications) and to some adjacent switches, depending on the NoC topology. The design flow for this architecture involves several steps. First, the application has to be split up into a set of concurrent communicating tasks. Then, the IPs are selected from the IP portfolio and the tasks are assigned and scheduled. Finally, the IPs have to be mapped onto the mesh in such a way that

---

* This work has been jointly supported by the Spanish MEC, the European Commission FEDER funds, the HiPEAC network of excellence, and the University of Valencia under grants Consolider-Ingenio 2010 CSD2006-00046, TIN2006-15516-C04-04, HiPEAC cluster 1169, and UV-BVSPIE-07-1884.

the considered performance metrics are optimized. Different mapping techniques have been proposed last years [2,3,4], since the final mapping onto the mesh has a strong impact on typical performance metrics and the mapping problem is known to be NP-hard [5].

Some of the proposed techniques uses heuristic methods to search a mapping that optimizes the desired performance metrics (latency, power consumption, quality of service, etc.) with a reasonable computational cost [2]. Unfortunately, they require the experimental validation of each solution provided, making the design process very costly. Additionally, the mapping for NoCs with irregular topology like [6,7] is still an open issue.

In order to provide an efficient mapping technique, the experimental validation of each mapping considered should be avoided. On other hand, since the task scheduling is already performed in a prior step, exclusively a communication-based mapping technique should be used. In this paper, we propose a communication-aware topological mapping technique for NoCs. This technique is based on a task mapping technique that was proposed for irregular networks [8], and it consists on globally matching the communication requirements of the application(s) tasks running on the IPs with the existing network resources. Unlike other mapping techniques, the proposed method is based on correlating the model of network resources with the actual network performance. Since the correlation is high, the model is used to estimate the quality of each assignment. The evaluation results show that the proposed technique can provide better performance than other mapping techniques that require the experimental validation of each mapping considered.

The rest of the paper is organized as follows: Section 2 describes the proposed topological mapping technique, including the model of the NoC resources. Next, Section 3 shows the experimental correlation of the network model with the actual network performance. Section 4 shows the performance evaluation of the proposed technique. Finally, Section 5 concludes the paper and draw some directions for future developments.

2   A New Topological Mapping Technique

During the NoC design process, tasks mapping and tasks scheduling are carried out in order to properly balance the computational requirements of the application with the available resources in the existing IPs. These procedures are beyond the scope of this paper, since they have been addressed in the area of hardware/software co-design and IP-reuse [3,9]. However, after these steps, each IP should contain one (or more) task(s) that can exchange information with another tasks assigned to another IPs, generating a given network traffic pattern (due to one or more applications). The topological mapping (assigning each IP to a network node) should exclusively focus on this pattern. We propose a topological mapping technique that near-optimally fits the communication requirements of the IPs with the available network bandwidth in the different parts of the network. This technique consists of several steps:

first, the available network resources must be modeled. Second, the communication requirements of the tasks running on the different IPs must be modeled. Third, a criterion that measures the suitability of each mapping is needed. This criterion should use the model of the network resources and also the communication requirements of the tasks. Finally, some mapping technique that tries to minimize/maximize the previous criterion should be developed.

In order to model the network resources, we have defined a metric that is based exclusively on the internode distances provided by the routing algorithm, since this metric is in turn inversely related with the amount of resources necessary for communicating two nodes. Concretely, our model proposes a simple metric, the *equivalent distance* between each pair of nodes (in what follows we will refer to a network router as a node). A *table of equivalent distances* can be obtained by computing the equivalent distance between each pair of nodes in the network. As a first approach, we assume that the link bandwidth is the same for all the links in the network. Therefore, we assign the unit cost for each link, but this limitation can be removed if necessary by assigning different link costs to different links. The equivalent distance for a pair of nodes is computed taking into account all the shortest paths between them supplied by the routing algorithm. The name of the metric is derived from the analogy to the electrical equivalent resistance. Indeed, we use the same rules as for electrical circuits to compute the total communication cost between nodes, applying Kirchoff's laws. The reason for using these rules is that the alternative paths increase the available network bandwidth between a pair of nodes, but the length of each path increases the number of nodes that share that path. The model of equivalent resistances properly reflects that situation, and it allows to model the network irregularities by containing different values in the table of distances.

Concretely, in order to compute the equivalent distance between each pair of nodes, the following method is used: if the routing algorithm provides only one shortest path between a given pair of nodes, then the equivalent distance is the sum of the costs of the links that form the path. This case is similar to computing the equivalent resistance of an electrical circuit consisting of serially arranged resistors. We have chosen only the shortest paths because usually NoCs work below the saturation point, and therefore it is not likely to use non-minimal paths. However, this model can be modified to take into account all the possible paths. If there exists more than one shortest path between a given pair of nodes, then the communication cost between them is computed similarly to the electrical equivalent resistance between two points of an electrical circuit, replacing each link in a shortest path with a unit resistor and applying Kirchoff's laws. The paths not supplied by the routing algorithm are not considered. As an example, let us consider the 2-D mesh network topology shown in Figure 1 a), and let us assume that the routing algorithm can provide two different paths for going from node 0 to node 6: 0-1-6 and 0-5-6. In this case, all the paths supplied by the routing algorithm are shortest paths.

Therefore, in order to compute the equivalent distance between nodes 0 and 6, the source and destination nodes must be considered as the V_{cc} and GND

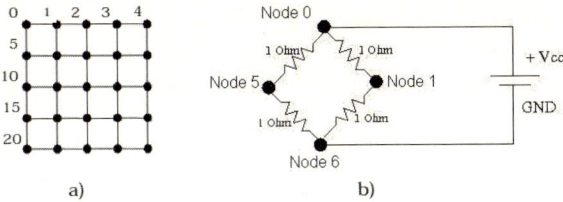

Fig. 1. a) A 2-D network topology b) Equivalent circuit for going from Node 0 to Node 6

points of an electric circuit. Nodes 1 and 5 must be considered as two different intermediate points, and each link must be considered as a resistor with unit resistance,as Figure 1 b) shows. This results in a circuit with two parallel branches, each one composed of two unit resistors serially arranged. Applying Kirchoff's laws to this circuit, an equivalent resistance of 1 Ohm is obtained. Thus, the equivalent distance from node 0 to node 6 would be set to 1. The elements in the table of distances should be computed in this way. If a given element in this table is located at row i and column j $(i,j \in [0..N\text{-}1]$, where N is the number of rows and columns of the table, that is, the number of network nodes), then we will denote that element as d_{ij}. It represents the cost for communicating node i with node j.

The communication requirements of the tasks running on the different IPs can be estimated by measuring the number of bytes exchanged by the tasks being executed on each IP. Although this estimation can vary due to the existence of hotspots, the bandwidth required by two given tasks within a given period is related to the number of bytes exchanged between them. Particularly, this estimation is valid for those applications whose communication patterns do not significantly change in different executions with different input data. For example, self-similar traffic has been observed in the bursty traffic between on-chip modules in typical MPEG-2 video applications [10]. Therefore, the proposed technique also computes a table of communications between IPs. If the application(s) tasks are mapped on N IPs, then this table will consist of $N \times N$ elements. We have denoted each element (i,j) in this table as com_{ij}. This value represents the number of bytes that the task(s) mapped onto IP i send(s) to the task(s) mapped onto IP j. These values can be measured from different executions of the application.

Also, we need a quality function to measure the suitability of each mapping. We will represent a given mapping of IPs (hosting one or more tasks) to network nodes as an array of N elements. We will denote each element i of this mapping array as m_i. This value means that IP i is assigned to the network node m_i. Thus, for example, if the second element of this mapping array contains the value 5, this will mean that the IP 1 (if they are numbered from 0 to $N-1$, or IP 2 if they are numbered from 1 to N) should be located at the network node 5. The quality function is denoted as the *mapping coefficient* M_c, and it is defined as

$$M_c = \sum_{i=1}^{N}\sum_{j=1}^{N} com_{ij} \cdot d_{m_i m_j}$$

where $d_{m_i m_j}$ is the element in the table of equivalent distances in the m_i row and in the m_j column. M_c represents the sum of all the bytes exchanged between the existing tasks, weighted by their corresponding cost of sending these bytes across the network according to the mapping array.

In order to match the communication requirements of the applications with the existing resources in the network, we propose a heuristic search method. In this case, the target function is M_c. If the heuristic search minimizes this function, then the overall cost for transmitting all the application messages will be minimized. The purpose of the proposed mapping technique is to search the best mapping array for a given network topology and for a given communication pattern. Since the communication cost is defined as inversely proportional to network bandwidth [11], we are actually mapping the IPs hosting the tasks that communicate more frequently to the network nodes with the higher network bandwidth between them. By doing so, we fully exploit the existing network resources, delaying network saturation as much as possible. We have tested different heuristic techniques for implementing the search method, including Genetic Algorithms (GA) [12], Simulated Annealing (SA) [13] , and Greedy Randomized Adaptive Search Procedures (GRASP) [14]. However, due to the global nature of the optimization problem, we have obtained the best results with the a random search method. This random search method starts with a random mapping array. Each iteration consists of exchanging two randomly selected values of the mapping array. If the resulting mapping array shows a better mapping coefficient, then this permutation is saved. If not, then it is discarded. The stop condition for the algorithm is to perform a given number of consecutive permutations without decreasing the resulting mapping coefficient. At this point, the minimum reached mapping coefficient and its corresponding mapping array are saved, and another seed (random mapping array) is tried. The algorithm stops when a number of different seeds has been explored. The result of this algorithm is the mapping array with the lowest mapping coefficient reached until that moment. In order to keep diversity, different seeds can be swept.

3 Correlation of the Model of Network Resources

In order to validate the model of network resources, we propose the correlation of the model with actual network performance. Since the quality function M_c uses this model, if the correlation is high then the experimental validation of each mapping will be no longer needed.

For correlation purposes, we have considered a 2-D mesh network topology with X-Y routing and wormhole switching. The table of equivalent distances for that network is computed as described above. We have studied the correlation between each distance in the table of distances and the average latency of the messages exchanged between the corresponding pair of nodes. The performance evaluation methodology used is based on the one proposed in [15].

We have considered different network sizes. However, for the sake of shortness, we show here the correlation results for a 64x64 2-D mesh, since this size is large enough to be representative of the NoCs sizes expected for next years. The correlation results obtained for other network sizes were very similar. We have used different patterns for message generation (uniform, bit reversal, perfect, shuffle, etc). We have considered a fixed packet size of 8 flits. Each router has an input buffer capable of allocating 3 flits. We have made simulations with different injection rates, in order to simulate the network with different workloads (ranging from low load to saturation). The simulator provides the global average latency value obtained for each simulation. This value is computed as the average latency value obtained of all messages transmitted through the network during a given simulation. Additionally, the simulator provides the average latency value for each source-destination pair in the network. From these measurements, we have computed the correlation between the table of distances and network latency.

Figure 2 a) shows the performance evaluation results. This figure shows on the X-axis the traffic injected to the network, measured in packets per cycle and per node. On the Y-axis, it shows the global average message latency. Also, average message latencies for each pair of nodes were computed. However, they are not shown here due to space limitations. Each value in this Figure was computed as the average value of fifty different simulations. Figure 2 a) shows the typical behavior expected for an interconnection network [15]. While the injected traffic is kept below the saturation point, the average latency slightly increases (points $S1$ to $S7$). However, when the injected traffic makes the network to reach saturation (from point $S8$ up) the average latency starts to greatly increase with the traffic rate.

In order to establish the correlation between the table of distances and these performance evaluation results, we have first computed the least square linear adjustment for each point in Figure 2 a). Although they are not shown here due to space limitations, the correlation index was above 85% for the first eight simulation points. From that point up, the correlation coefficient highly

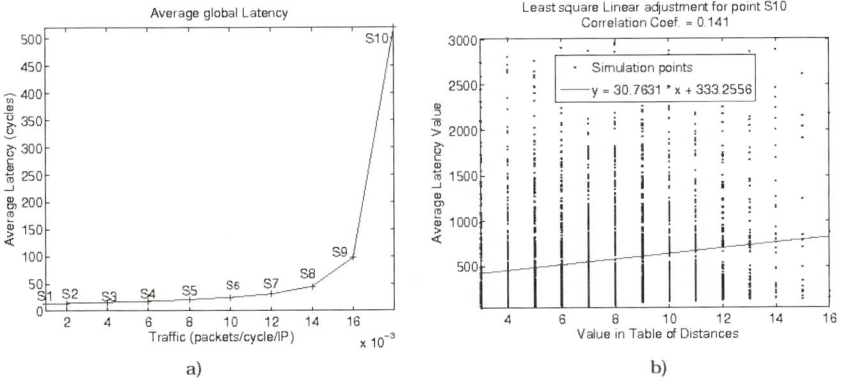

Fig. 2. a) Global performance results for a 8x8 topology b) Correlation for simulation point S1

decreased. For illustrative purposes, Figure 2 b) shows the regression curve for point S10. In this figure, the X-axis shows the values in the table of distance, while the specific latencies obtained by the simulator for each pair of nodes are shown in the Y-axis. The correlation index is 14% in this case, showing that (as it could be expected) when the network is under deep saturation then the contention prevents the network performance to correlate with inter-node distance.

Nevertheless, in order to study the practical correlation of the proposed metric with real performance, when different values are obtained in different simulations (as it is the case) then we should also consider the long-term network behavior. Therefore, we have also studied the correlation between the equivalent distances and the mean values of the average latencies supplied by the simulator. Figure 3 a) shows the corresponding regression curve for the simulation point $S10$. In this figure, there is a point for each different value in the table of distances. These values are represented on the X-axis. For information purposes, the number of occurrences for each value in the table of distances is shown on the right side of the figure. For example, point P4 represents value 6 in the table of distances and appears 552 times in the table of distances. Thus, the long-term network behavior for this value in the table of distances is much more stable than the network behavior for point P12, whose mean value is computed only with 40 different average latencies. As shown in Figure 3 a), the mean values of the average latencies show a much higher correlation with the table of distances (96%) than the average latencies (Figure 2 b), corr. coef. of 14%). The reason for this behavior is that network contention cannot affect this performance metric as it can do to the average latencies.

In order to show the correlation results in a unified way, Figure 3 b) shows the correlation coefficients provided for each of the points shown in Figure 2 a). The correlation COEFFICIENTS for latency values remain about about 86–99% when the network is under a low and a medium load (points $S1$ to $S8$).

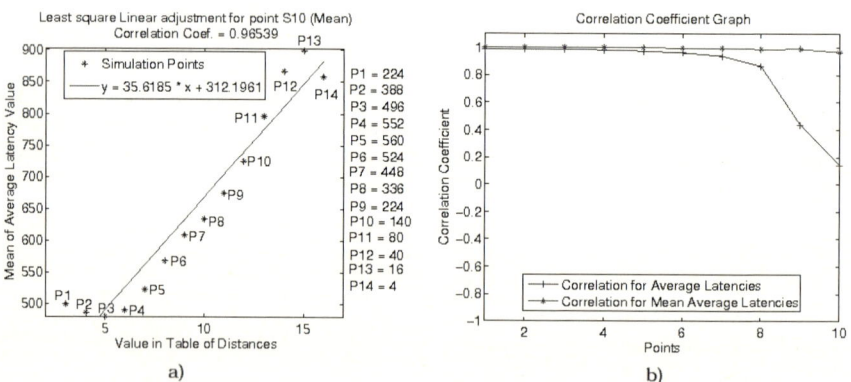

Fig. 3. a) Least square linear adjustment for averages value of average latencies values (point S10) b) Correlation of average latencies values and average values of average latencies for all the points

However, when the network enters deep saturation, the correlation coefficients decrease to values about 40%, and even reaching values of 15%. However, the average values of average latencies obtain a correlation coefficient of about 95% even the network is under a deep saturation, showing that actually the network model properly correlates with the actual network performance.

4 Performance Evaluation

We propose the evaluation of the proposed technique by simulation. For comparison purposes, we have also evaluated the performance of a currently proposed mapping technique based on Genetic Algorithm [2], since to our knowledge this is the mapping technique for NoCs that provide the best performance results (we have denoted this technique as the GA-based technique). Thus, as the application running on the machine we have considered the generic Multi-Media System (MMS). We started from the Communication Task Graph (CTG) of the MMS [2]. From this CTG, that contains 40 different tasks assigned and scheduled onto 25 IPs, we have computed the table of communication requirements (that is, the 40 original tasks are finally grouped in 25 IPs). Concretely, we have simply taken the communication bandwidth required between each pair of processing nodes as the number of messages exchanged between that pair of processing nodes.

Using the local search method described in the previous section, we have obtained a near-optimal mapping of IPs to network nodes. Using the same NoC simulator used for evaluating the GA-based mapping technique [2], we have evaluated the performance of the mapping provided by the proposed mapping technique and also the mapping provided by the GA-based technique. Additionally, for comparison purposes we have evaluated the performance provided by a random mapping as well as the sequential mapping of the MMS.

Figures 4 a) and b) show the comparative results for the MMS application mapped onto a 5x5 mesh. Each point in these figures has been computed as the average value of 50 different simulations. The plots corresponding to the mapping provided by the communication-aware mapping technique have been labeled as "Analytical mapping", while the plots corresponding to the mapping provided by the GA-based technique [2] have been labeled as "GA-Based mapping". Figures 4 a) and b) show on the X-axis the packet injection rates. These values are the scale factor of the different communications which form the MMS. These communications have been equally scaled up to analyze the network behaviour at different traffic loads. On the Y-axis, Figure 4 a) shows the average message latencies obtained during the simulations, while Figure 4 b) shows the power consumption required by the NoC when using each of the mappings for executing the MMS.

Figure 4 a) shows that the mapping provided by the proposed technique obtains the lowest latencies. Although the improvement achieved is not significant if compared with the GA-based mapping, the main advantage of the proposed technique is that it is capable of obtaining better latencies without testing each mapping explored. Figure 4 b) shows that the mappings provided by the

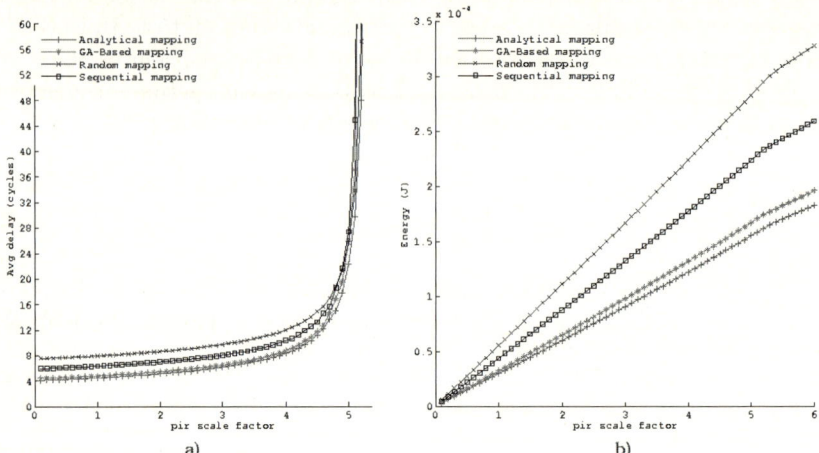

Fig. 4. a) Average latencies b) Energy consumption provided by the mapping techniques

proposed technique require the lowest power consumption. The differences among the considered mapping increase as the traffic injection rates are higher. This behavior is due to the fact that the proposed mapping technique maps closer those tasks that communicate more frequently. As the traffic generated by the tasks increases, the energy saving with respect to other techniques is greater.

These results show that the communication-aware topological mapping can significantly improve the network performance, particularly in terms of energy consumption. Moreover, the proposed technique does not need to test each mapping considered, thus requiring a much lower computational effort than the GA-based method. Additionally, this communication-aware mapping technique can be applied to NoCs with adaptive routing algorithms.

5 Conclusions and Future Work

In this paper, we have proposed a communication-aware topological mapping technique for NoCs. This technique consists of globally matching the communication requirements of the application(s) tasks running on the IPs with the existing network resources. Unlike other mapping techniques, the proposed method does not need to experimentally validate each mapping considered, thus requiring a much lower computational effort.

The evaluation results show that the proposed technique can improve the network performance in regard to other mapping techniques that require experimental validation. Additionally, the proposed technique can be applied to both regular and irregular network topologies.

As a future work to be done, we plan to study the application of this technique to irregular NoC topologies. Also, we plan to analyze the joint application of the proposed technique with recently proposed adaptive routing algorithms.

References

1. Dally, W.J., Towles, B.: Route packets, not wires: On-chip interconnection networks. In: Proceedings of Design Automation Conference, pp. 684–689 (2001)
2. Ascia, G., Catania, V., Palesi, M.: Mapping cores on network–on–chip. International Journal of Computational Intelligence Research 1(1–2), 109–126 (2005)
3. Lei, T., Kumar, S.: A two–step genetic algorithm for mapping task graphs to a netword on chip architecture. In: Proceedings of the Euromicro Symposium on Digital System Design (DSD 2003), IEEE Computer Society Press, Los Alamitos (2003)
4. Hu, J., Marculescu, R.: Energy-and-performance-aware mapping for regular noc architectures. IEEE Trans. on Computer-Aided Design of Integrated Circuits and Systems 24(4), 551–562 (2005)
5. Garey, M.R., Johnson, D.S.: Computers and intractability: a guide to the theory of NP-completeness. Freeman and Company, New York (1979)
6. Schafer, M., Hollstein, T., Zimmer, H., Glesner, M.: Deadlock-free routing and component placement for irregular mesh-based networks-on-chip. In: Proceedings of IEEE/ACM International Conference on Computer-Aided Design, 2005 (ICCAD 2005), pp. 238–245 (2005)
7. Bolotin, E., Cidon, I., Ginosar, R., Kolodny, A.: Routing table minimization for irregular mesh nocs. In: Proceedings of Design, Automation & Test in Europe Conference & Exhibition (DATE 2007), pp. 1–6 (2007)
8. Orduña, J., Silla, F., Duato, J.: On the development of a communication-aware task mapping technique. Journal of Systems Architecture 50(4), 207–220 (2004)
9. Chang, J.M., Pedram, M.: Codex-dp: Co-design of communicating systems using dynamic programming. IEEE Transactions on Computer-Aided Design of Integrated Circuits and Systems 19(7), 732–744 (2002)
10. Varatkar, G., Marculescu, R.: Traffic analysis for on-chip networks design of multimedia applications. In: ACM/IEEE Design Automation Conference, June 2002, pp. 510–517 (2002)
11. Arnau, V., Orduña, J., Ruiz, A., Duato, J.: On the characterization of interconnection networks with irregular topology: A new model of communication cost. In: Proceedings of IASTED International Conference on Parallel and Distributed Computing and Systems (PDCS 1999), pp. 1–6 (1999)
12. Haupt, R.L., Haupt, S.E.: Practical Genetic Algorithms. Willey (1997)
13. Laarhoven, P.J., Aarts, E.: Simulated Annealing: Theory and Applications. Mathematics and its Applications, vol. 37. Springer, Heidelberg (1987)
14. Festa, P., Resende, M.: Grasp: An annotated bibliography. In: Hansen, P., Ribeiro, C. (eds.) Essays and Surveys on Metaheuristics, pp. 325–367. Kluwer Academic Publishers, Dordrecht (2002)
15. Duato, J., Yalamanchili, S., Ni, L.: Interconnection Networks: An Engineering Approach. IEEE Computer Society Press, Los Alamitos (1997)

Approximating the Traffic Grooming Problem with Respect to ADMs and OADMs*

(Extended Abstract)

Michele Flammini[1], Gianpiero Monaco[1], Luca Moscardelli[1,2], Mordechai Shalom[3], and Shmuel Zaks[4]

[1] Dipartmento di Informatica, Università degli Studi dell'Aquila, L'Aquila, Italy
{flammini,gianpiero.monaco,moscardelli}@di.univaq.it
[2] Dipartimento di Informatica ed Applicazioni "R. M. Capocelli",
Università degli Studi di Salerno, Italy
moscardelli@dia.unisa.it
[3] Tel Hai Academic College, Upper Galilee, Israel
cmshalom@telhai.ac.il
[4] Department of Computer Science, Technion, Haifa, Israel
zaks@cs.technion.ac.il

Abstract. We consider the problem of switching cost in optical networks, where messages are sent along lightpaths. Given lightpaths, we have to assign them colors, so that at most g lightpaths of the same color can share any edge (g is the grooming factor). The switching of the lightpaths is performed by electronic ADMs (Add-Drop-Multiplexers) at their endpoints and optical ADMs (OADMs) at their intermediate nodes. The saving in the switching components becomes possible when lightpaths of the same color can use the same switches. Whereas previous studies concentrated on the number of ADMs, we consider the cost function - incurred also by the number of OADMs - of $f(\alpha) = \alpha|OADMs| + (1-\alpha)|ADMs|$, where $0 \leq \alpha \leq 1$. We concentrate on chain networks, but our technique can be directly extended to ring networks. We show that finding a coloring which will minimize this cost function is NP-complete, even when the network is a chain and the grooming factor is $g = 2$, for any value of α. We then present a general technique that, given an r-approximation algorithm working on particular instances of our problem, i.e. instances in which all requests share a common edge of the chain, builds a new algorithm for general instances having approximation ratio $r\lceil \log n \rceil$. This technique is used in order to obtain two polynomial time approximation algorithms for our problem: the first one minimizes the number of OADMs (the case of $\alpha = 1$), and its approximation ratio is $2\lceil \log n \rceil$; the second one minimizes the combined cost $f(\alpha)$ for $0 \leq \alpha < 1$, and its approximation ratio is $2\sqrt{g} \lceil \log n \rceil$.

Keywords: Optical Networks, Wavelength Division Multiplexing(WDM), Add-Drop Multiplexer(ADM), Optical Add-Drop Multiplexer(OADM), Traffic Grooming, Path and Ring Networks.

---

* This research was partly supported by the European Union under Project "Graphs and Algorithms in Communication Networks (GRAAL)" - COST Action TIST 293 and under IST FET Integrated Project AEOLUS (IST-015964).

1 Introduction

1.1 Background

All-optical networks have been largely investigated in recent years due to the promise of data transmission rates several orders of magnitudes higher than current networks [5,19,20]. Major applications are in video conferencing, scientific visualization and real-time medical imaging, high-speed supercomputing and distributed computing [12,19].

The key to high speeds in all-optical networks is to maintain the signal in optical form, thereby avoiding the prohibitive overhead of conversion to and from the electrical form at the intermediate nodes. The high bandwidth of the optical fiber is utilized through *wavelength-division multiplexing*: two signals connecting different source-destination pairs may share a link, provided they are transmitted on carriers having different wavelengths (or colors) of light. The optical spectrum being a scarce resource, communication patterns are often designed for different topologies so as to minimize the total number of used colors, also as a comparison with the trivial lower bound provided by maximum load, that is the maximum number of connection paths sharing a same physical edge (see [2] for a survey of the main related results).

When the various parameters comprising the switching mechanism in these networks became clearer, the focus of studies shifted, and today a large portion of research concentrates with the total hardware cost. This is modelled by considering the basic electronic switching units of the electronic Add-Drop Multiplexer (ADM) and the optical Add-Drop Multiplexer (OADM), and focusing on the total number of these hardware components. Concerning ADMs the key point here is that each lightpath uses two ADMs, one at each endpoint. If two adjacent lightpaths are assigned the same wavelength, then they can use the same ADM. An ADM may be shared by at most two lightpaths. Concerning OADMs, a lightpaths needs an OADM at each intermediate node.

Moreover, in studying the hardware cost, the issue of *grooming* became central. This problem stems from the fact that the network usually supports traffic that is at rates which are lower than the full wavelength capacity, and therefore the network operator has to be able to put together (= groom) low-capacity demands into the high capacity fibers. In graph-theoretic terms, this can be viewed as assigning colors to the lightpaths so that at most g of them (g being the *grooming factor*) can share one edge. In terms of ADMs, in case g lightpaths of the same wavelength enter through the same edge to one node, they can all use the same ADM (thus saving $g-1$ ADMs). Moreover, all the same colored paths ending at the node through two given incident edges can share the same ADM. In terms of OADMs, if g lightpaths of the same wavelength need such a component at the same node, they can share a unique OADM (thus saving $g-1$ OADMs).

The goal is to minimize the linear combination of the total number of ADMs and OADMs $\alpha \cdot |OADMs| + (1-\alpha) \cdot |ADMs|$, for any value $0 \leq \alpha \leq 1$. Therefore, letting $\alpha = 0$ and $\alpha = 1$, our approximation results directly apply respectively to the classical ADMs minimization problem largely investigated in the literature, and to the pure OADMs minimization one.

1.2 Previous Works

The problem of minimizing the number of ADMs for the case $g = 1$ was introduced in [17] for ring networks. For such a topology it was shown to be NP-complete in [13] and an approximation algorithm with approximation ratio 3/2 was presented in [10] and improved in [14,22] to $10/7 + \epsilon$ and 10/7 respectively. For general topologies [13] describes an algorithm with approximation ratio 8/5. The same problem was studied in [9], and an algorithm with approximation ratio $3/2 + \epsilon$ was presented.

The notion of traffic grooming ($g > 1$) was introduced in [18] for ring topologies. In such a setting, the ADMs minimization problem was shown to be NP-complete in [8] for rings and for general g, i.e., with g being part of the input instance. In [21] it is shown that the NP-completeness is in the strong sense. An algorithm with approximation ratio of $2 \ln g$ for any g in a ring topology has been given in [16], whose running time is exponential in g. This algorithm is extended in [15] for directed trees, and undirected trees with bounded degree, with similar provable performance. Such a problem for ring and path networks has been also studied in [1], where the authors show that the problem is APX-complete for fixed values of g and provide an approximation algorithm with guaranteed ratio $O(n^{1/3} \log^2 n)$, where n is the number of nodes of the network.

The all-to-all traffic case, in which there is the same demand between each pair of nodes, has been studied in [4,8] for various values of g, and an optimal construction for the case $g = 2$ in chain networks was given in [3].

In a different scenario, the problem of minimizing hardware components in optical networks using grooming in order to exploit large bandwidth has been studied in [7] for ring networks and in [6] for stars networks.

1.3 Our Contribution

In this paper we first prove that even the problem of minimizing the number of OADMs is NP-complete. More precisely, we prove the hardness of minimizing every linear combination of the total number of ADMs and OADMs, i.e. the cost function $f(\alpha) = \alpha|OADMs| + (1 - \alpha)|ADMs|$ for every fixed α such that $0 < \alpha \leq 1$. Such an intractability result holds even for chains with $g = 2$ (for $g = 1$ the problem on chains can be trivially solved in polynomial time). Then we provide an approximation algorithm for the problem of minimizing $f(\alpha)$ in chains for every α such that $0 \leq \alpha \leq 1$, polynomial in g and having an approximation ratio $2\sqrt{g} \lceil \log n \rceil$. To the best of our knowledge, in the literature there are no results concerning the problem of minimizing the number of OADMs (and any linear combination with the number of ADMs). Moreover, it is the first algorithm with such an approximation ratio having a running time polynomial in g, even for the basic ADMs minimization problem. As a last remark, multi-sets of requests, i.e. multiple requests between a some couple of nodes, are allowed in our model.

The paper is organized as follows. In the next section, we describe the problem and introduce some useful definitions. In Section 3 we describe the NP-completeness proof for the minimization of any linear combination of ADMs

2 Problem Definition

An instance of the *combined traffic grooming problem* is a quadruple (V, P, g, α) where V, $|V| = n$, is the node set of an undirected chain, P is a (multi-)set of simple paths in the chain, g is a positive integer, namely the grooming factor, and $\alpha \in [0, 1]$ is a real number.

A coloring (or wavelength assignment) of (V, P) is a function $w : P \mapsto \mathbb{N}^+ = \{1, 2, \ldots\}$. A proper coloring (or wavelength assignment) w of (V, P, g, α) is a coloring of P in which for any edge e at most g paths using e are colored with the same color. Every colored path $p = \{u, v\} \in P$ from node u to node v of length $l(p)$ needs an ADM operating at wavelength $w(p)$ at each of its endpoint nodes, and an OADM operating at wavelength $w(p)$ at each of its intermediate ones, i.e. 2 ADMs and $l(p) - 1$ OADMs. Given a grooming factor g, at most g paths, colored with the same color c, incident to a node through the same edge can use the same ADM, and such an ADM can be shared also by the at most g path colored with c incident to the same node through another incident edge; Moreover, in a similar way, at most g paths, colored with the same color c, needing an OADM at a node i can use the same one. Given a coloring w, let $|ADMs^w|$ and $|OADMs^w|$ the minimum total number of ADMs and OADMs in the network, respectively. We are interested in finding a proper coloring w of (V, P, g, α) that minimizes $COST(w) = \alpha \cdot |OADMs^w| + (1 - \alpha) \cdot |ADMs^w|$.

3 NP-Completeness

In this section we prove that the corresponding decision problem is NP-complete on a chain even if $g = 2$.

Theorem 1. *Given an instance of the combined traffic grooming problem $(V, P, 2, \alpha)$ and a real value x, the problem of deciding whether there exists a solution of cost at most x is NP-Complete for any $\alpha > 0$.*

Proof. It is easy to check that the decision problem belongs to NP; in order to prove the NP-completeness, we provide a polynomial reduction from the $TRIPART$ problem, known to be NP-complete (see [11]).

An instance of the $TRIPART$ problem is a graph $G = (V_G, E_G)$. The question is whether or not there is a partition of E_G into triangles. Let $V_G = \{v_G^1, v_G^2, \ldots, v_G^n\}$ and $E_G = \{e_G^1, e_G^2, \ldots, e_G^{3q}\}$ (note that if $|E_G|$ is not an multiple of 3, a partition does not exist and the answer is obviously NO). From the above instance $G = (V_G, E_G)$ of $TRIPART$ we build the following instance $I = (V, P, 2, \alpha)$ of the combined traffic grooming problem. For each $v_G^i \in V_G$, we

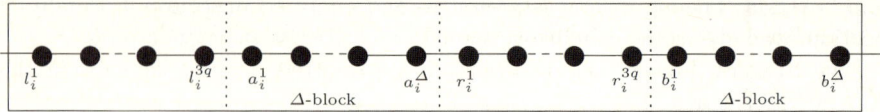

Fig. 1. The subchain C_i associated to node v_G^i

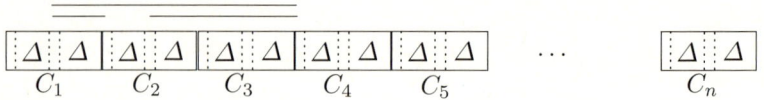

Fig. 2. The chain V with three paths corresponding to the edges of a triangle in the original graph G

build a subchain of nodes $C_i = \{l_i^1, \ldots, l_i^{3q}, a_i^1, \ldots, a_i^\Delta, r_i^1, \ldots, r_i^{3q}, b_i^1, \ldots, b_i^\Delta, \}$ (see Figure 1), where Δ is a sufficiently large value to be determined later. The chain V of our instance is obtained by linking all the subchains C_i, $1 \leq i \leq n$ (see Figure 2). In order to complete our instance, we have the define the path set P; with some abuse of notation, let $(u,v) \in V \times V$ denote the path between u and v in V. For each $e_G^i = \{v_G^{h_i}, v_G^{k_i}\} \in E_G$ with $h_i < k_i$ we add the path $p^i = (r_{h_i}^i, l_{k_i}^i)$ to P.

First of all, notice that each node of the chain is an endpoint of at most a request in P. Therefore, each solution uses exactly $6q$ ADMs. For this reason, we can focus on the minimization of OADMs. More precisely, let $x = \alpha \cdot K + (1 - \alpha) \cdot 6q$. There is a solution with cost at most x if and only if there is a solution using at most K OADMs.

We call a solution a t-solution if it uses $\Delta \cdot t$ OADMs located at the sequences of Δ nodes, i.e. the a and b nodes, in the following Δ-blocks. Δ is determined as a sufficiently high value such that the cost of a solution is mainly determined by the number of OADMs located at such blocks, i.e. every t-solution uses a total number of OADMs lower than the one used by any $t+1$-solution. This value turns out to be $\Delta = 36q^2n + 1$ (i.e. polynomial in the size of the instance), this detail is omitted in this extended abstract. Therefore, a t-solution uses a total number of OADMs between $\Delta \cdot t$ and $\Delta \cdot t + \Delta - 1$.

For each $p^i = (r_{h_i}^i, l_{k_i}^i) \in P$, $h_i < k_i$, the number of crossed Δ-blocks is $blocks(i) = 2(k_i - h_i) - 1$. Let $B = \left\lfloor \sum_{i=1}^{3q} \left(\frac{blocks(i)}{2} + \frac{1}{6} \right) \right\rfloor$ and $K = \Delta B + \Delta - 1$.

In order to complete the proof, it remains to show that a solution using at most K OADMs exists for I if and only if E_G can be partitioned into triangles.

If E_G can be partitioned into triangles, for each triangle composed by edges e_G^i, e_G^j, e_G^k, consider the set of paths $\{p^i, p^j, p^k\}$, assign them the same color and without loss of generality assume that p_k is the longest path of the set. Since $g = 2$, it can be easily checked that such a set is 1-colorable. Moreover, the number of OADMs used at Δ-blocks is $\Delta \cdot blocks(k) = \frac{\Delta}{2}(blocks(i) + blocks(j) + blocks(k) + 1)$. By summing over the sets induced by all the triangles, we obtain that the total number of OADMs used at Δ-blocks is $\frac{\Delta}{2}\sum_{i=1}^{3q}\left(blocks(i)+\frac{1}{3}\right) = \Delta \cdot B$; thus, we have a B-solution that can use at most K OADMs.

On the other side, let us assume that a solution S for I using at most K OADMs exists. We show that S is a B-solution and that in a B-solution every component is of the form $\{(r_i^{\beta_1}, l_j^{\beta_1}), (r_j^{\beta_2}, l_k^{\beta_2}), (r_i^{\beta_3}, l_k^{\beta_3})\}$ with $i < j < k$. Let us assume without loss of generality that S is using the maximum possible number of colors, i.e. no set of paths colored with the same color exists such that it can be split in two sets using two different colors without increasing the number of used OADMs. We call a *component* a set of paths colored with the same color. Since $g = 2$, each component is composed of at most two levels of requests and every OADMs can be used by at most two requests. For each component C using q blocks of OADMs, we want to distribute q among the requests belonging to C such that each request $\beta \in C$ is charged with $\frac{blocks(\beta)}{2} + f(C)$, with $f(C) = \frac{q - \sum_{\beta' \in C} \frac{blocks(\beta')}{2}}{|C|}$ being the *surplus* of component C.

The proof proceeds by cases. We are interested in determining $f(C)$ for a generic component C.

- If a component is of the form $\{(r_i^{\beta_1}, l_j^{\beta_1}), (r_j^{\beta_2}, l_k^{\beta_2}), (r_i^{\beta_3}, l_k^{\beta_3})\}$ with $i < j < k$, it uses $\frac{blocks(\beta_1)+blocks(\beta_2)+blocks(\beta_3)+1}{2}$ Δ-blocks, thus $f(C) = \frac{1}{6}$.
- Let us assume that 3 requests belong to a component, β_1 on the first level and β_2 and β_3 on the second one. If the ones on the second level do not correspond to consecutive edges in G, or β_1 corresponds to an edge of G that is not consecutive to both edges corresponding to the requests on the second level, C uses at least $\frac{blocks(\beta_1)}{2} + \frac{blocks(\beta_2)}{2} + \frac{blocks(\beta_3)}{2} + \frac{3}{2}$ Δ-blocks. Therefore, $f(C) \geq \frac{1}{2}$.
- If a component uses only one level of requests (for our assumption about the maximality of colors, in this case it can contain only a request β), it is using $blocks(\beta) \geq 1$ Δ-blocks. Therefore, $f(C) \geq \frac{1}{2}$.
- If 2 requests β_1 and β_2 belong to a component C, one for each level, C uses at least $\frac{blocks(\beta_1)}{2} + \frac{blocks(\beta_2)}{2} + 1$ Δ-blocks. Thus, $f(C) \geq \frac{1}{2}$.
- If $|C| \geq 4$ requests belong to a component, at least $\frac{|C|-2}{2} + \sum_{\beta \in C} \frac{blocks(\beta)}{2}$ Δ-blocks are needed. Therefore, $f(C) \geq \frac{|C|-2}{2|C|} \geq \frac{1}{4}$.

Since S uses at most K OADMs, by recalling the definitions of B and K, S is a t-solution with $t \leq B$. Moreover, if a component C exists such that $f(C) > \frac{1}{6}$, it is easy to check that S would be a t-solution with $t > B$: a contradiction. Thus, it holds that every component is such that $f(C) = \frac{1}{6}$ and therefore is of the form $\{(r_i^{\beta_1}, l_j^{\beta_1}), (r_j^{\beta_2}, l_k^{\beta_2}), (r_i^{\beta_3}, l_k^{\beta_3})\}$ with $i < j < k$. □

4 Approximation Algorithms

In this section we present and analyze the approximation algorithms for chain topologies.

We first present a general technique that, given an r-approximation algorithm (which will be termed an *edge-algorithm*) for particular instances of our problem, namely for instances in which all requests share a common edge of the chain, builds an $r\lceil \log n \rceil$-approximation algorithm for general instances. In the remaining of the section, we give two edge-algorithms: the first one focuses on the minimization of $OADMs$ and its approximation ratio is 2, and the second one works for any linear combination of $ADMs$ and $OADMs$, guaranteeing an approximation ratio $2\sqrt{g}\lceil \log n \rceil$.

4.1 The $MERGE(EA)$ Algorithm

Let EA be a polynomial r-approximation edge-algorithm.

Given a chain $\{i,\ldots,j\}$, let its *median* edge be the edge $\{\lfloor \frac{i+j}{2} \rfloor, \lfloor \frac{i+j}{2} \rfloor + 1\}$. Consider the following algorithm $MERGE$, composed by a sequence of steps.

At the first step, the set P_1 of all requests sharing the median edge of the chain are given in input to EA, and the requests are colored according to its output. Now the algorithm splits the chain into two subchains by removing the median edge and all the requests using it (i.e. in P_1), and recursively proceeds on the subchains.

At each level of the recursion, the coloring returned by EA is modified so that, colors used in previous levels are not used in the current level. Namely, if max_{i-1} is the highest color used in levels $1,\ldots,i-1$, we add max_{i-1} to the colors returned by EA.

Theorem 2. *Given a polynomial edge-algorithm EA having approximation ratio r, $MERGE(EA)$ is an approximation algorithm for the combined traffic grooming problem guaranteeing an approximation ratio equal to $r\lceil \log n \rceil$.*

4.2 $GROOM - OADM$: An Edge-Algorithm for the Minimization of OADMs

Let $Q = \{p_1,\ldots,p_m\}$ the set of input requests sharing a same edge of the chain; without loss of generality, let us assume $l(p_1) \geq l(p_2) \geq \ldots l(p_m)$, i.e. the requests are first sorted by the algorithm in non increasing order of length.

The algorithm partitions the ordered requests into $k = \lceil \frac{m}{g} \rceil$ sets of g requests (the last set may contain less than g requests) and for each $i = 1,\ldots,k$ assigns to $p_{(i-1)g+1},\ldots,p_{\min\{i\cdot g,m\}}$ a same color, different from the one assigned to the requests belonging to other sets of the partition.

Lemma 1. *$GROOM$-$OADM$ is a 2-approximation edge-algorithm for the minimization of $OADMs$.*

Proof. Since at most g request are assigned the same color, the algorithm is correct; its running time is given by the one of a sorting algorithm and thus is polynomial in the size of the instance.

Since all the requests share a same edge of the chain, any 1-colorable set can contain at most g of them. For this reason, the optimal solution has cost

$m^* \geq \sum_{i=1}^{k}(l(p_{(i-1)g+1}-1))$. On the other hand, the algorithm is using for each set of the partition having its longest request of length L at most $2(L-1)$ OADMs, thus achieving a solution of cost $m \leq \sum_{i=1}^{k}(2(l(p_{(i-1)g+1}-1)))$. Therefore, $\frac{m}{m^*} \leq 2$. □

By combining the previous lemma with Theorem 2, the following theorem holds.

Theorem 3. *MERGE(GROOM-OADM) is a $2\lceil \log n \rceil$-approximation algorithm for the combined traffic grooming problem with $\alpha = 1$, i.e. for the problem of minimizing the number of OADMs.*

4.3 GROOM: An Edge-Algorithm for the Combined Traffic Grooming Problem

Algorithm *GROOM* is obtained from *GROOM−OADM* with a slight modification. In the sort phase, in which the paths are sorted by their lengths, *GROOM* keeps sets of identical paths together. As a set of identical paths have in particular the same length, a set of identical paths will appear together in the order.

Lemma 2. *GROOM is a $2\sqrt{g}$-approximation edge-algorithm for the combined traffic grooming problem.*

Proof. Any execution of *GROOM* is obviously an execution of *GROOM − OADM*. Therefore *GROOM* is a 2-approximation edge-algorithm for the OADM minimization problem. We will show that *GROOM* is a $2\sqrt{g}$-approximation algorithm for the ADM minimization problem. As the combined cost is a linear combination of ADM and OADM costs, this implies the Lemma.

Let W^* be the number of colors used by some optimal solution. For $1 \leq \lambda \leq W^*$, let P_λ^* be the set of paths colored λ by this solution. Then $P = \uplus_{\lambda=1}^{W^*} P_\lambda^*$. Let $\overline{P_\lambda^*} \subseteq P_\lambda^*$ be such that from each (maximal) set of identical paths, exactly one path is in $\overline{P_\lambda^*}$. Let also $\overline{P^*} = \uplus_{\lambda=1}^{W^*} \overline{P_\lambda^*}$.

Recall that we consider edge instances, in which all the paths share a common edge e. All the paths have one endpoint at each side of e. Then any subset of paths can be considered as the edge set of a bipartite graph. A simple bipartite graph (U, V, E) satisfies $|E| \leq |U||V|$. For fixed $|U \cup V|$ this is maximized when $|U| = |V| = \frac{|U \cup V|}{2}$. As $\overline{P_\lambda^*}$ does not contain identical paths, it induces a simple bipartite graph. Therefore, the number ADM_λ^* of ADMs colored λ used by this solution satisfies $|\overline{P_\lambda^*}| \leq \left(\frac{ADM_\lambda^*}{2}\right)^2$. Then $ADM_\lambda^* \geq 2\sqrt{|\overline{P_\lambda^*}|} = 2\frac{|P_\lambda^*|}{\sqrt{|\overline{P_\lambda^*}|}} \geq 2\frac{|P_\lambda^*|}{\sqrt{g}}$.

By summing over all colors, we obtain $ADM^* \geq \frac{2|\overline{P^*}|}{\sqrt{g}}$.

Let W be the number of colors used by the solution returned by *GROOM*. For $1 \leq \lambda \leq W$, let P_λ be the set of paths colored λ by this solution. Then $P = \uplus_{\lambda=1}^{W} P_\lambda$. Let $\overline{P_\lambda} \subseteq P_\lambda$ be such that from each (maximal) set of identical paths, exactly one path is in $\overline{P_\lambda}$. Let also $\overline{P} = \uplus_{\lambda=1}^{W} \overline{P_\lambda}$.

Consider a maximal nonempty set X of identical paths. Any solution, must use at least $\left\lceil \frac{|X|}{g} \right\rceil$ different colors for these paths. In particular, this is true for our optimal solution. In other words $|X \cap \overline{P^*}| \geq \left\lceil \frac{|X|}{g} \right\rceil$. *GROOM* divides X into subsets of size g, except possibly the first and last sets. Therefore $|X \cap \overline{P}| \leq \left\lceil \frac{|X|}{g} \right\rceil + 1 \leq 2 \left\lceil \frac{|X|}{g} \right\rceil \leq 2 |X \cap \overline{P^*}|$. Summing up for all such sets X we get $|\overline{P}| \leq 2 |\overline{P^*}|$. On the other hand a solution returned by $GROOM$, uses at most 2 ADMs per each path in $\overline{P}$. The remaining paths use these ADMs at no additional cost. Therefore the number of ADMs used by GROOM satisfy $ADM \leq 2|\overline{P}| \leq 4|\overline{P^*}| \leq 2\sqrt{g}ADM^*$. □

The following theorem is a direct consequence of the previous Lemma and Theorem 2.

Theorem 4. ***MERGE(GROOM)*** *is a* $2\sqrt{g}\lceil \log n \rceil$*-approximation algorithm for the combined traffic grooming problem.*

5 Summary

Our approximation ratios of $2\lceil \log n \rceil$ and $2\sqrt{g} \lceil \log n \rceil$ are better than the trivial ones (which have a $2g$ factor) in case $g > \lceil \log n \rceil$ in the first case and $g > \lceil \log n \rceil^2$ in the second one.

Notice that our algorithm has the following interesting property: the returned solution achieves the claimed approximation ratio simultaneously with respect to every fixed value of α. Moreover it can be directly extended to ring topologies simply by considering a first initial further edge-algorithm execution, considering all the lightpaths crossing a given edge, thus inducing a remaining chain topology instance. Details will be shown in the full version of the paper.

Some interesting remaining problems are improving the achieved approximation ratio for chain topologies, extending the algorithm and the analysis to other topologies and considering the online version of the problem in which lightpath requests are not given in advance and arrive over time.

References

1. Amini, O., Pérennes, S., Sau, I.: Hardness and approximation of traffic grooming. In: Tokuyama, T. (ed.) ISAAC 2007. LNCS, vol. 4835, pp. 561–573. Springer, Heidelberg (2007)
2. Beauquier, B., Bermond, J.-C., Gargano, L., Hell, P., Perennes, S., Vaccaro, U.: Graph Problems Arising from wavelength-routing in all- optical networks. In: Proc. 2nd Workshop on Optics and Computer Science, WOCS 1997 (April 1997)
3. Bérmond, J.-C., Braud, L., Coudert, D.: Traffic grooming on the path. In: 12 th Colloqium on Structural Information and Communication Complexity, Le Mont Saint-Michel, France (May 2005)
4. Bermond, J.-C., Coudert, D.: Traffic grooming in unidirectional WDM ring networks using design theory. In: IEEE ICC, Anchorage, Alaska (May 2003)
5. Brackett, C.A.: Dense wavelength division multiplexing networks: principles and applications. IEEE Journal on Selected Areas in Communications 8, 948–964 (1990)
6. Chen, B., Rouskas, G.N., Dutta, R.: Traffic grooming in star networks. In: Broadnets (2004)

7. Chen, B., Rouskas, G.N., Dutta, R.: Traffic grooming in wdm ring networks with the min-max objective. In: NETWORKING, pp. 174–185 (2004)
8. Chiu, A.L., Modiano, E.H.: Traffic grooming algorithms for reducing electronic multiplexing costs in wdm ring networks. Journal of Lightwave Technology 18(1), 2–12 (2000)
9. Călinescu, G., Frieder, O., Wan, P.-J.: Minimizing electronic line terminals for automatic ring protection in general wdm optical networks. IEEE Journal of Selected Area on Communications 20(1), 183–189 (2002)
10. Călinescu, G., Wan, P.-J.: Traffic partition in wdm/sonet rings to minimize sonet adms. Journal of Combinatorial Optimization 6(4), 425–453 (2002)
11. Dor, D., Tarsi, M.: Graph decomposition is np-complete: A complete proof of holyer's conjecture. SIAM Journal on Computing 26(4), 1166–1187 (1997)
12. Du, D.H.C., Vetter, R.J.: Distributed computing with high-speed optical networks. In: Proceeding of IEEE Computer, vol. 26, pp. 8–18 (1993)
13. Eilam, T., Moran, S., Zaks, S.: Lightpath arrangement in survivable rings to minimize the switching cost. IEEE Journal of Selected Area on Communications 20(1), 172–182 (2002)
14. Epstein, L., Levin, A.: Better bounds for minimizing sonet adms. In: 2nd Workshop on Approximation and Online Algorithms, Bergen, Norway (September 2004)
15. Flammini, M., Monaco, G., Moscardelli, L., Shalom, M., Zaks, S.: Approximating the traffic grooming problem in tree and star neetworks. Journal of Parallel and Distributed Computing (to appear, 2008)
16. Flammini, M., Moscardelli, L., Shalom, M., Zaks, S.: Approximating the traffic grooming problem. In: Deng, X., Du, D. (eds.) ISAAC 2005. LNCS, vol. 3827, pp. 915–924. Springer, Heidelberg (2005)
17. Gerstel, O., Lin, P., Sasaki, G.: Wavelength assignment in a wdm ring to minimize cost of embedded sonet rings. In: INFOCOM 1998, Seventeenth Annual Joint Conference of the IEEE Computer and Communications Societies (1998)
18. Gerstel, O., Ramaswami, R., Sasaki, G.: Cost effective traffic grooming in wdm rings. In: INFOCOM 1998, Seventeenth Annual Joint Conference of the IEEE Computer and Communications Societies (1998)
19. Green, P.E.: Fiber-Optic Communication Networks. Prentice Hall, Englewood Cliffs (1992)
20. Klasing, R.: Methods and problems of wavelength-routing in all-optical networks. In: Proceeding of the MFCS 1998 Workshop on Communication, August 24-25, Brno, Czech Republic, pp. 1–9 (1998)
21. Shalom, M., Unger, W., Zaks, S.: On the complexity of the traffic grooming problem in optical networks. In: Fun with Algorithms, 4th International Conference, Castiglioncello, Italy, pp. 262–271 (June 2007)
22. Shalom, M., Zaks, S.: A $10/7 + \epsilon$ approximation scheme for minimizing the number of adms in sonet rings. In: First Annual International Conference on Broadband Networks, San-José, California, USA (October 2004)

On the Influence of the Packet Marking and Injection Control Schemes in Congestion Management for MINs[*]

Joan-LLuís Ferrer, Elvira Baydal, Antonio Robles,
Pedro López, and José Duato

Parallel Architecture Group
Universidad Politécnica de Valencia
Camino de Vera s/n, 46022 Valencia, Spain
juaferpe@doctor.upv.es, {elvira,arobles,plopez,jduato}@disca.upv.es

Abstract. Several Congestion Management Mechanisms (CMMs) have been proposed for Multistage Interconnection Networks (MINs) in order to avoid the degradation of network performance when congestion appears. Most of them are based on Explicit Congestion Notification (ECN). For this purpose, switches detect congestion and, depending on the applied mechanism, some flags are marked to warn the source hosts. In response, source hosts apply corrective actions to adjust their packet injection rate. These mechanisms have been evaluated by analyzing whether they are able to manage a congestion situation but there is not a comparison study among them. Moreover, marking effects are not separately analyzed from corrective actions. In this paper, we analyze the current proposals for CMMs, showing the impact of the applied packet marking techniques as well as the corrective actions they apply.

Keywords: Interconnection networks, congestion management, message throttling.

1 Introduction

MINs have become very popular in clusters interconnects because they are feasible topologies able to meet the needs of new comunication-intensive applications and the increasing demand of new services. Usually, the communication model assumes a loosless network, so they cannot drop packets to deal with congestion. Hence, in congestion situations, buffers fill up blocking downstream switches, affecting also flows that are not responsible for congestion and reducing throughput on all switches in which buffers fill up. Congestion occurs when one or more links remain saturated during enough time. An output link becomes

---

[*] This work was supported by the Spanish program CONSOLIDER-INGENIO 2010 under Grant CSD2006-00046, by the Spanish CICYT under Grant TIN2006-15516-C04-01, by Junta de Comunidades de Castilla-La Mancha under Grant PCC08-0078, and by the European Commission in the context of the SARC integrated project #27648 (FP6).

saturated when it is demanded by several packets comming simultaneously from different input links during a certain period of time. If this situation remains for long, packets start to be accumulated at the queues of the affected switches. As a consequence of the back pressure actions performed by the flow control mechanism, packet advance in the previous switches is also delayed, generating Head-Of-Line (HOL) blocking, which prevents the advance of packets addressed to non-congested links. Notice that, if some of the packets that have to cross the saturated links (packets responsible for congestion) were stopped at their origin hosts, HOL could be avoided and, as a consequence, the throughput network would improve. Therefore, it is necessary to detect early the beginning of congestion, as well as the nodes responsible for that situation, applying corrective actions only over them. Over the years, this critical problem has been widely studied [2] and has promoted a lot of research proposing different mechanisms to manage congestion. Most of them are works based on *detection & recovery* strategies [1,4,5,6,7,8]. CMM proposals for MINs based on detection and recovery strategies carry out three simple actions: detection, notification, and correction. Usually, to detect a congestion situation, switch buffer occupancy is checked. If the occupancy at any buffer overcomes a predefined threshold, then packets crossing the switch will be marked. This way, switches are able to detect and identify packets which are contributing to congestion, setting one or more bits in its header to indicate the occurrence of congestion. After detecting congestion, the source hosts that are injecting too much traffic have to be warned. This can be carried out by taking advantage of the acknowledgment (ACK) sent back to the source when a packet has reached its destination. In ACK packets, a set of bits are used to notify congestion to the source. This way of notifying congestion is commonly denominated as Explicit Congestion Notification (ECN). Once the ACK arrives to the source, the origin host will apply message throttling to adjust its packet injection rate. Some of the current proposals have been evaluated by comparing them with respect to the behaviour of the network in absence of any congestion control [5,6,8], thus hindering a comparison with alternative proposals. Also, results do not separately analyze marking from corrective actions effects. Therefore, it is necessary an exhaustive study comparing the current proposals under the same network scenario and traffic load, analyzing to what extend the CMM behaviour is caused by marking effects or, on the contrary, it is due to the corrective actions. The results of a comparative study of three current proposals are shown in this paper and a set of conclusions are listed: Renato's proposal[5], Pfister's implementation[6], and MVCM[8] proposal. The rest of the paper is organized as follows. Section 2 describes the current CMMs evaluated in this paper. The simulation scenario and the evaluation results are presented in Section 3. Finally, in Section 4 some conclusions are drawn.

2 Current CMMs Approaches

In this section, we briefly describe the packet marking techniques and the limitation strategies applied, as well as the CMMs analyzed and evaluated.

Packet marking techniques vary depending on the place where packets are marked, that is, input buffers[5], output buffers[6] or both [8]. Basically, if packet marking is carried out at the input or output buffers, then packets in transit will be marked by setting a single bit in the packet header. On the other hand, if two bits are dedicated, a more refined packet marking technique can be carried out at the input and at the output buffers. When data packets marked arrive to their destination, hosts send an ACK packet to the origin hosts, carrying also the congestion information. If an origin host is informed about a congestion situation, it can apply some of the following techniques to limit the injection rate:

Static Window (SW)[5]. Basically, it defines a window with a fixed size that defines the maximum number of outstanding packets[1] per origin-destination pair. The value of the window size depends on the vendor criteria and it is kept fixed regardless of the resulting network performance.

Dynamic Window (DW)[8]. In this case, the window size is dynamic, allowing to fluctuate between one and a defined maximum value (DWmax), depending on the congestion situation in the network. Initially, the window size is fixed to DWmax value but if congestion appears, the window size is reduced, reaching the value of one if this situation persists. When congestion disappears, the window size will be progressively increased till DWmax. DWmax also depends on the vendor criteria. A technique based on a DW is also used in TCP congestion control [3] but with a more complex management that the one used in MINs.

Waiting Period Insertion (WP)[5,6,8]. Inserting WPs allows to reduce the injection rate in a progressive way. Depending on the severity of congestion, the elapsed time between the injection of two consecutive packets will be increased or decreased. As long as the congestion vanishes, waiting interval will be decreased until it disappears. The technique works as follows. When an origin host receives a marked ACK packet, it waits a WP before injecting a new packet. If more marked ACK packets are received, then more WPs will be inserted. Later, when unmarked ACK packets are received, the number of waiting periods between message injection will be decreased.

Regardless of the corrective actions applied to palliate the congestion, when these actions have to be removed because congestion begins to disappear, there are two possibilities: a total and *immediate elimination* of all the corrective actions immediately, allowing the maximum injection rate, or removing them in a *progressive way*, that is, maintaining preventive actions just in case the congestion has not entirely disappeared.

2.1 Renato's Proposal

This CMM [5] was defined for InfiniBand. It is based on an ECN mechanism that uses a single bit in the packet header to detect and warn congestion. Source limitation mechanism is based on a SW combined with a WPs insertion technique.

---

[1] Oustanding packets are those that have not been acknowledged yet.

Packet Marking: The mechanism operates in three steps. First, a switch input buffer triggers packet marking each time it becomes full. Second, any output link that is requested for at least one packet in such a full buffer, is classified as a congested link. Third, all packets stored in any input buffer at the switch that are destined to an output link classified as congested, will be marked.

Warning the Sources: In response to the reception of a marked packet, destinations set a single bit in ACK packets to warn the sources about congestion.

Corrective and Recovery Actions: This proposal evaluates the possibility of using a window-based congestion management to limit the injection rate. In this way, the number of outstanding packets for a flow is adjusted by using a SW. However, they justify that a window size greater than one completely saturates the network. So, they propose a fixed window size of one at any situation. In addition, an injection rate control based on inserting WPs is used. For rate control, they evaluate and compare different reduction functions.

2.2 Pfister's Implementation

InfiniBand specs v1.2 [1] define a quite general proposal for congestion management where values for thresholds and other variables are left free to the vendor criteria. Pfister's implementation [6] is targeted to this scenario.

Packet Marking: InfiniBand switches have shared input buffers with virtual output queuing. The threshold is defined at the output queues. So, the packet marking actions depend on the output buffers occupancy. Congestion is detected when a relative threshold has been exceeded. The threshold is specified for each port, initializing it with a value between 0 and 15; 0 indicates that the switch is not going to mark any packet, 1 indicates a high value of threshold so there is a high probability that congestion spreads, values 2 to 15 indicate a uniform distribution of decreasing threshold values. The exact meaning of a particular threshold setting is left to the switch manufacturer. When congestion is detected, a bit called Forward Explicit Congestion Notification (FECN) is set.

Warning the Sources: Once a packet with the FECN bit set is received at the destination host, it responds back to the source with an ACK packet having a different bit set called Backward Explicit Congestion Notification (BECN).

Corrective Actions: When the source receives a packet with the BECN bit set, the injection rate of the flow is reduced by inserting WPs. The WP size is based on Inter-Packet Delay (IPD) value. The amount of reduction is controlled using a table called Congestion Control Table (CCT). Each time a BECN is received, an index into the table is incremented.

Recovery Actions: Each Host Channel Adapter contains a timer; if no more BECNs arrive during a defined interval, a timeout occurs and the index into the table (CCT) is reduced. The timeout and the reduction amount is set by the Congestion Control Manager (CCM). Eventually, if no more BECNs are received, the index reaches zero value and no more delays are inserted.

Table 1.
Corrective Actions for MVCM

Ack bits		Actions
MB	VB	
0	0	No Actions
0	1	Not possible
1	0	Moderate (DW)
1	1	Imminent (DW+WP)

Table 2.
Evaluated Traffic Pattern

Bidi.Perf.Shuffle 4-ary 5-fly	
#Srcs.	Destination
448	Uniform.
64	Hot-Spot

2.3 MVCM Proposal

This mechanism has not been proposed for any standard in particular, but for MINs [8]. Switches need to have buffers associated to both their input and output ports. The strategy of this mechanism is to combine a packet marking at input buffers with a packet validation at output buffers.

Packet Marking: The mechanism operates in two steps. First, packets arriving to an input buffer are marked if the number of stored packets in the buffer exceeds a certain threshold. This is performed by activating the Marking Bit (MB) in the packet header. Next, when a marked packet is forwarded through a saturated output link, we proceed to validate it by activating a second bit, the Validation Bit (VB). We assume that an output link is saturated when the number of packets stored in its buffer exceeds another threshold.

Warning the Sources: Once congestion has been detected, destination hosts use two bits to warn origin hosts about the congestion situation. A copy of the MB and VB status is sent in each ACK packet.

Corrective Actions: Two levels of corrective actions are proposed. Table 1 relates them with the status bits of the received ACK packet headers. The first level is based on adjusting the packet injection rate of each flow by using a DW. If congestion persists, a second level will reduce even more the injection rate. It consists of inserting WPs between the injection of packets meanwhile the maximum window size is kept to 1. Preventive actions only can reduce DW value whereas imminent actions can reduce DW value and after insert WPs. Initially, the maximum window size is set to some value DWmax, and several packets can be injected without interruption (WP=0). Preventive actions involve only a reduction over the DWmax size, by subtracting one per each marked ACK packet received till the minimum value (one). In the same way, imminent actions carry out a reduction in the DWmax size as moderate actions do. But if this reduction is not enough to stop the growing of the saturation tree and validated packets (VB=1) continue arriving, heavier actions will be applied intended to reduce even more the injection rate. This second level of actions starts when the DW size becomes equal to one. Then, WPs will be inserted between the injected packets. The WP size is based on the Round-Trip Transmission delay (RTT).

Recovery Actions: When the first non-validated (VB=0) ACK packet is received, if WPs were being applied to that flow before, they will be immediately eliminated thus allowing for a fast recovering but keeping the window size equal to one. Later on, if more non-marked (MB=0) ACK packets arrive, the size will be increased till the DWmax by adding one for each not marked packet received. In this way, recovery technique is progressively applied. On the other hand, to ensure a quick recovery when congestion has dissapeared, if an origin host injects a packet into an empty injection queue, the host will completely remove the corrective actions being applied.

3 Performance Evaluation

3.1 Network Configurations

The proposed CMMs have been evaluated by using an interconnection network simulator. A generic switch-based cut-through network with point-to-point links and buffered credit-based flow control with a link bandwidth of 1 byte/cycle. Packets will be transmitted over the link if there is enough buffer space (measured in credits of 64 bytes) to store the entire packet. We have evaluated several network configurations with different values of switch radix and number of network stages: Perfect Shuffle MINs with bidirectional links (4-ary 3-fly, 8-ary 3-fly, 4-ary 5-fly) and some configurations for Butterfly MINs with unidirectional links. However, for the sake of brevity, we only show the results for a bidirectional Perfect Shuffle 4-ary 5-fly network (512 hosts and 640 switches). A Full Virtual Output Queuing (VOQ) is used at source hosts. Thus, we eliminate HOL blocking at origins. A deterministic routing algorithm is used to forward packets in the network. Data packets (278 bytes) have a payload of 256 bytes plus 22 bytes of control. ACK packet size is 22 bytes. Switches have 1KByte buffers associated at both their input and output ports. We first generate packets according to a uniform distribution of message destinations. Then, we create a hot-spot in the network and analyze what happens with both flows of packets. In particular, hosts that send uniform traffic remain injecting packets during the whole simulation. Hosts that generate hot-spot traffic remain inactive until the first 50,000 packets have been received. Then, they start injecting 1,000 packets with the same injection rate as that of the other hosts, but addressed to only one destination host (the hot-spot). They stop generating packets when each one has injected 1,000 packets. This scenario has been simulated with the traffic pattern shown in table 2. We present two different types of results. First, Figures 1 to 3 compare different CMMs working with several injection rates from low load till saturation. Then, Figures 4 to 7 compare the behaviour of the flows not responsible for the congestion with a medium network load that refers to an injection rate of 58 bytes/cycle, which corresponds to an average injection rate of 0,45 bytes/cycle/injecting sw[2] Qualitatively, similar results are obtained for other injection rates (i.e. 98 bytes/cycle and 32 bytes/cycle for high and low injection rate respectively).

---

[2] Injecting sw refers to the switches with source hosts connected to them (i.e. the switches of the first stage).

3.2 Evaluation Results

First of all, a comparison of the proposals such as they have been originally proposed is performed. Figure 1 shows the average packet latency versus traffic for the different CMMs analyzed in this paper. Renato's proposal shows the worst results. It is because this proposal defines an SW with a fixed size equal to one. So, in absence of congestion, it cannot take advantage of the free bandwidth because packets have to wait at origins meanwhile channels are idle. Moreover, marking packets only at input buffers is not enough to identify in all the situations the flows responsible for congestion. In the same way, although the Pfister's implementation achieves better results than the Renato's proposal, it is not the best one because it uses a packet marking technique only at output buffers with a subsequent simple recovery technique. Marking packets only at output buffers is neither enough to identify the flows responsible for congestion in all the situations. Indeed, this proposal uses only a WPs insertion technique in a progressive way. So, if a hard congestion situation is suddenly reached and many WPs have been inserted, it cannot recover the initial parameters in a short time, while network is getting idle. Since this proposal does not use any window control, it allows to inject packets while no congestion is detected, so it works well with a low injection rate. However, when traffic load approaches to the saturation point and marked packets begin to arrive to the origin hosts, they insert directly WPs that limit excessively the accepted traffic, decreasing network performance. On the contrary, mechanism MVCM obtains the best results since it combines a more refined packet marking based on a DW and WPs insertion. The DW carries out a first injection control if the congestion situation is not so severe. If this situation persists, it starts inserting WPs between generated packets.

Second, in order to analyze the actual impact of the different packet marking schemes described in Section 1.1, Figure 2 shows a comparison between the analyzed CMMs but applying the same corrective actions scheme. In particular, the scheme applied by the MVCM mechanism has been used, since it achieved the best results in Figure 1. The aim is to evaluate to what extend the behaviour of the CMM is influenced by the applied packet marking scheme. Thus, all curves in Figure 2 apply the same corrective actions scheme but with different marking techniques. As it can be seen, all the mechanisms provide similar results,

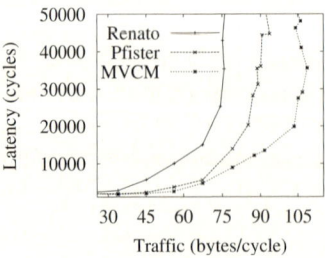

Fig. 1. Latency vs. traffic for different CMMs

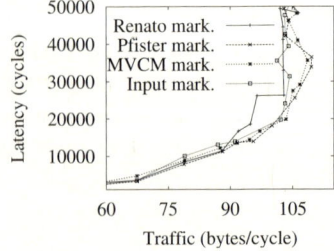

Fig. 2. Impact of the marking technique

although the ones based only on marking at input buffers (i.e. *Renato and Input*) do not achieve the bests results. The best behaviour is achieved by *MVCM*. Anyway, if a mechanism based on a combination of a DW and WPs insertion is applied, results are quite satisfactory, independently of the marking technique.

Next, we are going to analyze the impact of the window management scheme, Figure 3(a) shows the results. Curves $SW=1,2,4$, and 8 show network performance with a SW technique and without applying any other corrective mechanism. On the other hand, curves $DW=2$ and 4 are based on a DW and also without applying any other corrective mechanism. In all the cases, the MVCM packet marking technique has been applied. As it can be appreciated, the worst results are obtained if a CMM is based on an SW. In particular, a fixed value of one restricts too much the injection rate, because not enough traffic is injected although channels are idle. In the same way, although the size of the SW increases, it will never achieve similar results as DW does. The best SW value is two. Higher values decrease network performance until SW=8. From this window size upwards, larger values of SW do not change results (curves not shown). The best results are achieved when applying a DW technique with an initial value of two. If a larger value is used, we continue to obtain better results than with an SW, but worse than with DW=2. That is because with a value of four, too many packets continue to be injected while ACKs are not received. As a consequence, ACKs take more time to reach origin hosts. In this situation, a larger DW is not useful when network begins to be congested. So, the best value for this network is two. In fact, that value depends on the RTT of the network, and it has to be previously calculated applying a uniform distribution near the saturation point [8]. In the analized network, when network is near the saturation point, the RTT is equal to the time needed to inject 1.45 packets. This is the ideal size of the window, as it is the minimum size that is big enough to avoid bubbles in packet sending. Therefore, a value of 2 is the nearest integer. Figure 3(b) shows the effects of using a DW combined with WPs techniques in MVCM mechanism. Results show that performance improves significantly when a combination of DW and WPs insertion technique is used instead of a DW or WP technique alone. Finally, Figure 3(c) shows how an immediate recovery of the initial values (DW=2 and WP=0) can improve network throughput if this corrective action is applied when a packet is injected in an empty injection queue. To conclude,

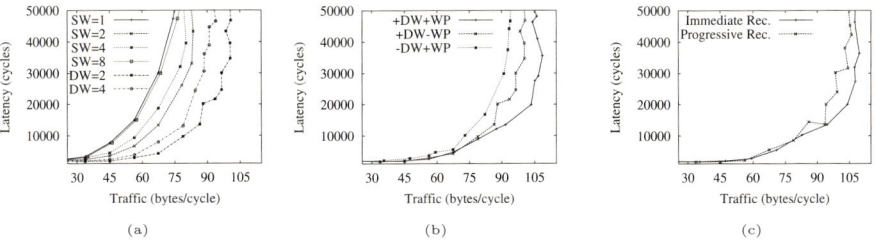

Fig. 3. Impact of (a) window management scheme, (b) applying DW and/or WP, and (c) Immediate vs. progressive recovery, with MVCM marking mechanism

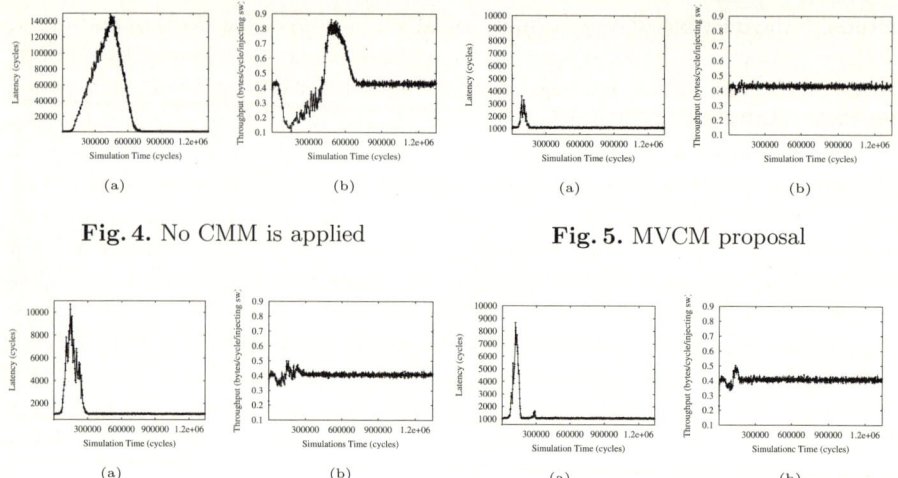

Fig. 4. No CMM is applied

Fig. 5. MVCM proposal

Fig. 6. Renato's proposal

Fig. 7. Pfister's implementation

despite the fact that a DW is an effective mechanism against congestion, able to achieve good results regardless of applied packet marking technique, it is not the best solution if it works alone. In other words, a window control scheme or a reduction and recovery function are not enough on their own to manage congestion. On the contrary, a combination of the four techniques (MVCM Marking + DW + WPs Insertion + Immediate Recovery of the initial values) is the best solution. Once the current proposals have been compared, and the different proposed techniques to detect and recover congestion have been evaluated, it is interesting to check the behaviour of the flows not responsible for congestion when applying the analyzed CMMs in the same scenario and under the same traffic load and destination distribution (see Section 3.1), to confirm the previously obtained results. Figures 4 to 7 show the results. Figure 4 shows the case when no CMM is applied, so during the congestion situation latency increases up to more than 140,000 cycles and a throughput drop is produced. Figures 5 to 7 show the results for the different CMMs analyzed. The best results for latency and throughput have been achieved with the MVCM proposal. If we compare the results for Renato's proposal in Figure 6 with Pfister's implementation in Figure 7, we can observe that marking packets at output buffers allows to detect sooner the beginning of a congestion situation. That is because, in a congestion situation based on a true hot-spot (our traffic load), output buffers fill up earlier than input buffers do, so Pfister's implementation warns early the origins, so then they can react against congestion faster.

4 Conclusions

In this paper, we have evaluated and compared a set of CMMs, based on a *detection & recovery* strategy. The study has been carried out under the same scenario and traffic load, identifying the actual impact of the different marking techniques and the recovery actions proposed by each mechanism.

First, the proposals have been globally evaluated and compared. The results show that mechanism MVCM provides the best results for congestion management because its more efficient recovery actions based on a DW, WPs insertion, and Immediate Recovery of the initial parameters. The other two proposals, Pfister and Renato, obtain worse results because they limit the injection rate too much, specially Renato's proposal due to the fact that a SW is applied whatever the network behaviour is. On the other hand, Pfister's implementation applies a simple recovery technique based on WPs insertion, and if this technique works alone, it is not able to react as fast as the combination of DW and WPs.

Second, we have isolately analyzed the dessign issues that make different these mechanisms: packet marking and recovery technique. Four marking techniques have been compared and results show that the packet marking election is not the most critical issue in the CMM. The strategy that is based on input buffer marking combined with output buffer validation has obtained the best results. Marking only at input buffers achieves lower performance. Concerning recovery techniques, results show that a SW, restricts too much the injection rate and it never achieves the results of a DW. Moreover, using a DW as a preventive action, minimizes the penalization on the flows not responsible for the congestion. Graphs reveal that a simple DW technique, can achieve better results because the DW better tunes injection limitation. Finally, an immediate recovery of the initial values of the injection rate when congestion is not longer detected is much better than a progressive recovery.

To conclude, it becomes necessary to combine an effective packet marking with a fair recovery technique based on a DW, WPs insertion, and Immediate Recovery to achieve the best results.

References

1. InfiniBand, http://www.infinibandta.org
2. Pfister, G., Norton, V.A.: Hot Spot Contention and Combining in Multistage Interconnection Networks. IEEE Trans. on Computers (1985)
3. Allman, M., Paxsm, V., Stevens, W.: TCP Congestion Control (1999), http://www.rfc-editor.org/rfc/rfc2581.txt
4. Thottetodi, M., Lebeck, A.R., Mukherjee, S.S.: Self-Tuned Congestion Control for Multiprocessor Networks. In: Proc. on Int.Sym. on HPCA (2001)
5. Renato, J., Turner, Y., Janakiraman, G.: End-to-End Congestion Control for InfiniBand. In: IEEE INFOCOM (2003)
6. Pfister, G., et al.: Solving Hot Spot Contention Using InfiniBand Architecture Congestion Control. Ion HPI-DC (2005)
7. Duato, J., Johnson, I., Flich, J., Naven, F., Garcia, P., Nachiondo, T.: A New Scalable and Cost-Effective Congestion Management Strategy for Lossless Multistage Interconnection Networks. In: Proc. on Int.Sym. on HPCA (2005)
8. Ferrer, J., Baydal, E., Robles, A., Lopez, P., Duato, J.: Congestion Management in MINs through Marked & Validated Packets. In: Proc. on 15th Int. Conf. Euromicro (2007)

Deadlock-Free Dynamic Network Reconfiguration Based on Close Up*/Down* Graphs[†]

Antonio Robles-Gómez[1], Aurelio Bermúdez[1],
Rafael Casado[1], and Åshild Grønstad Solheim[2,3]

[1] Instituto de Investigación en Informática de Albacete (I³A)
Universidad de Castilla-La Mancha, Spain
{arobles,abermu,rcasado}@dsi.uclm.es
[2] Networks and Distributed Systems Group
Simula Research Laboratory, Norway
aashig@simula.no
[3] Department of Informatics
University of Oslo, Norway

Abstract. Current high-performance distributed systems use a switch-based interconnection network. After the occurrence of a topological change, a management mechanism must reestablish connectivity between network devices. This mechanism discovers the new topology, calculates a new set of routing paths, and updates the routing tables within the network. The main challenge related to network reconfiguration (the change-over from one routing function to another) is avoiding deadlocks. Former reconfiguration techniques significantly reduce network service. In addition, most recent proposals either need extra network resources (such as virtual channels) or their computation complexities are prohibitive. For up*/down* routed networks we propose a new reconfiguration method that supports a virtually unaffected network service at a minor computational cost. This method is suitable for both source and distributed routing networks, and does neither restrict the injection of packets nor the updating of routing tables during the topology-change assimilation.

1 Introduction

The communication subsystem of most modern high-performance distributed systems includes a switch-based interconnection network. In recent years, several different interconnect technologies have been proposed, some based on source routing (Myrinet 2000 [8], Advanced Switching [1]), and others based on distributed routing (InfiniBand [5]).

In this kind of interconnects, after the occurrence of a fault or after the removal or insertion of a component in the network, a new routing function must be calculated based on the new topology that results from the change. For the purpose of

---

[†] This work has been jointly supported by the Spanish MEC and European Comission FEDER funds under grants Consolider Ingenio-2010 CSD2006-00046 and TIN2006-15516-C04-02, and a FPI grant under TIC2003-08154-C06-02; by JCCM under grant PBC05-007-1; by UCLM under grant TC20070061.

path-computation the interconnection network is usually represented as a directed graph. The tasks of discovering the network topology and computing the new routing function are typically performed by a centralized management entity which is called *mapper* in Myrinet, *subnet manager* in InfiniBand, and *fabric manager* in Advanced Switching.

In the literature, the process of replacing one routing function with another is traditionally referred to as *network reconfiguration*. It is well-known that, although both routing functions are by themselves deadlock-free, updating fabric paths in an uncontrolled way may lead to deadlock situations since packets that belong to one of the routing functions may take turns that are not allowed in the other routing function.

Early reconfiguration mechanisms (designed for Autonet [15] and Myrinet [2] networks) solved this problem by emptying the network of packets before replacing the routing function. Such a simple approach is referred to as *static reconfiguration*, and has a negative impact on the network service availability since for a period of time the network cannot accept packets.

Recently, several schemes have been proposed for distributed routing systems in order to increase network availability during the change-over from one routing function to another. These mechanisms allow injection of data traffic while the routing function is being updated, and are known as *dynamic reconfiguration* techniques. In order to guarantee deadlock-freedom the dynamic reconfiguration schemes are, in general, more advanced than the static reconfiguration schemes are.

In this paper we propose a new dynamic reconfiguration strategy which is based on the up*/down* routing algorithm [15] and is applicable to both source and distributed routing networks. The main idea behind the proposed strategy is to transform an invalid up*/down* graph (that results from a topological change) into a valid up*/down* graph, while ensuring that turns that are prohibited by one of the routing functions are not allowed by the other routing function. Section 2 provides background information on the up*/down* routing algorithm and on previous studies of reconfiguration of up*/down* routing networks. Section 3 formally introduces the concept of a close graph and presents the new reconfiguration strategy in detail. In Section 4 the performance of the proposed reconfiguration strategy is evaluated, before we conclude in Section 5.

2 Network Reconfiguration in Up*/Down*-Based Interconnects

Our new reconfiguration scheme is based on up*/down* [15], a popular deadlock-free routing algorithm suitable for regular and irregular topologies. This algorithm is based on a cycle-free assignment of direction to the operational links in the network. This assignment is always possible, regardless of network topology. For each link, a direction is named *up* and the opposite one is named *down*. To avoid deadlocks, legal routes never use a link in the *up* direction after having used one in the *down* direction. Messages can cross zero or more links in the *up* direction, followed by zero or more links in the *down* direction. In this way, cycles in the channel dependency graph [4] are avoided, thus preventing deadlock.

A *sink node* [3] is a node in a directed graph that is not the source of any link –that is, all of its links are labeled as *down*–. The up*/down* routing algorithm requires the existence of a single sink node in the graph. The reason is that there are no legal routes between two sink nodes because each possible route would require *down* to *up* transitions. This restriction is required for network connectivity.

A *break node* is a node that is the source of two or more links –labeled as *up*–. In the up*/down* routing algorithm, these nodes prevent certain connections (input port - output port) from being used by the messages crossing them. These restrictions are necessary for deadlock freedom. There must exist one break node in every cycle, but its position is unrestricted.

In up*/down* routing, the associated directed graph will contain one and only one sink node. Additionally, that graph will be acyclic. A directed graph that is acyclic and contains a single sink node is called a *correct graph*. A correct graph may include several break nodes within its topology, as many as necessary to break all the cycles.

Obviously, an *incorrect graph* is one that does not meet the restrictions imposed in the previous definition. This implies the absence of a sink node, the existence of more than one sink node, or the existence of cycles. If there is no sink node, then the graph will contain one or more cycles and up*/down* routing cannot guarantee deadlock freedom. If there are several sink nodes, then up*/down* routing cannot guarantee network connectivity. There is always at least one false break node between two sink nodes. A *false break node* is a break node in which two links with the *down* end connected to it do not belong to the same cycle in the undirected graph of the network. A false break node splits the network into two unreachable regions. Obviously, a correct graph contains no false break nodes.

Several alternative algorithms for building an up*/down* directed graph have been proposed in the literature. Traditional proposals are based on the computation of a network spanning tree rooted in one of the nodes, by using a breadth-first search (BSF) [15], a depth-first search (DFS) [14], or a propagation-order (POST) [13] strategy.

With respect to the network reconfiguration, deadlock is not an issue when a static reconfiguration scheme is used since packets that are routed according to the old routing function and packets that are routed according to the new routing function are not simultaneously present in the network. Updating the routing function while the network remains up and running, on the other hand, requires more advanced reconfiguration schemes. Next, we briefly depict some dynamic reconfiguration techniques proposed for networks that use distributed routing.

The Partial Progressive Reconfiguration (PPR) [3] and Skyline [6] approaches aim to repair an uncorrected up*/down* graph which includes several sink nodes. PPR computes the new graph in a distributed way, where an invalid up*/down* graph is transformed into valid sub-regions that constitutes a valid up*/down* graph. Skyline is a technique to identify the region of the network that must be reconfigured after the change. Then, any connection method –for example PPR– can be applied over that part of the graph. On the other hand, Double Scheme [10] and Simple Reconfiguration [7] can be used by any routing algorithm, including up*/down*. Double Scheme requires two disjoint sets of virtual channels to separate packets routed according to the old routing function from packets routed according to the new routing function. Simple Reconfiguration introduces a special packet (called a *token*) to govern the transition from one routing function to another. Deadlock is avoided by ensuring that each link first transmits packets that belong to the old routing function, then the token, and finally packets that belong to the new one.

3 A Dynamic Reconfiguration Scheme Based on Close Graphs

This section presents our new reconfiguration method that, after a topology-change, calculates a new routing function which ensures that packets that belong to the new routing function cannot take turns that are prohibited in the old routing function, and vice versa. This guarantees that packets that belong to the old and new routing functions can unrestrictedly coexist in the network without causing deadlocks. The method is based on the concept of close up*/down graphs, which will be defined shortly. This section also presents lemmas to support that, when an up*/down* graph for the new topology is designed close to the up*/down* graph for the previous topology, the routing function can be updated without the risk of transient deadlocks.

Definition 1. Assume that two up*/down* directed graphs, G_1 and G_2, are associated to same network topology. Then, G_1 and G_2 are *close* iff each cycle in G_1 and G_2 is broken in the same node or in neighboring nodes.

Lemma 1. Assume that an up*/down* directed graph G_1 is incorrect due to the presence of several sinks. Then, it is always possible to obtain a correct graph G_2 which is close to G_1.

Proof. In a correct up*/down* graph, each possible cycle must contain at least one node with two incoming up-links and at least one node with two outgoing up-links. For each possible cycle in G_2, we have three options with respect to break node placement (in the same node as in G_1, or in one of the two neighboring nodes). Thus, it is always possible to construct a correct graph G_2 which is close to G_1.

Lemma 2. Assume that a correct up*/down* directed graph G includes a break node $n \in G$. Then, after the suppression of one of the outgoing up-links of n, G remains correct and connected.

Proof. It is not possible to generate a new cycle by suppressing one of the outgoing up-links of a break node. Also, it is not possible to generate a new sink node by suppressing one of the outgoing up-links of a break node (by definition a break node has more than one outgoing up-link).

Lemma 3. Assume that two up*/down* directed graphs G_{old} and G_{new} exist, where G_{new} is correct and close to G_{old}. Then, it is possible to obtain an up*/down* routing function R that satisfies the routing-restrictions (prohibited down-link to up-link transitions) imposed by both G_{old} and G_{new}.

Proof. Assume that G_{sub} is a subgraph of G_{new} in which each link that connects a break node in G_{old} with the corresponding break node in G_{new} is suppressed, and that G_{new} is a correct up*/down* graph. Then, according to lemma 2, we can guarantee that G_{sub} is also a correct up*/down* graph.

Thus, it is possible to define a fully connected deadlock-free routing function R_{sub} over G_{sub}. R_{sub} satisfies the routing-restrictions of both G_{old} and G_{new} since all the break nodes either have the same locations or have been removed.

Construction of G_{new} Close to G_{old}
We have shown above that a new up*/down* graph G_{new} for the current topology can always be constructed close to the previous up*/down* graph G_{old} such that deadlocks

cannot form during the routing function update. This section presents an algorithm for the construction of G_{new} close to G_{old}, but first we define some concepts.

Definition 2. An *exploration process* is the procedure in which the manager goes through the network to discover the links between nodes and the direction assigned to them.

Definition 3. Assume that the exploration process from a node n_1 reaches another node n_2. Then, this link is explored in *downward direction* (from the point of view of the exploration process) if its up*/down* direction is $n_1 \leftarrow n_2$. Similarly, the link is explored in *upward direction* if the direction is $n_1 \rightarrow n_2$. These cases will be referred to as $l^{downward}$ and l^{upward}, respectively.

Definition 4. A *frontier link* is a link currently under evaluation by the exploration process (such as the link from n_1 to n_2 above).

Definition 5. Two directed links are *partners* if they have the same source node.

Definition 6. Assume that the exploration process has reached a node n, that l is a link connected to n, and that l has not been processed from a previously visited node. Then, a *neighboring link* of l is another link connected to n which has not been processed from a previously visited node.

Algorithm.
Let X be the set of frontier links and let l denote a link between two nodes in the network. To construct G_{new} the manager starts an exploration process in one of the sink nodes of G_{old}:
$\forall l$ connected to the start node of the exploration process, evaluate inclusion of l in X *(see below)*.
While X is not empty do:
- If $\exists l \in X$ explored in downward direction, then
    - Remove l from X.
    - $\forall l_1$ which neighboring link of l evaluate inclusion of l_1 in X.
- Else the following invariant applies: $\exists l_1 \in X$ explored in upward direction which guarantees that $!(\exists l_2 \in X)$ such that
    - l_1 is partner of l_2.
    - The destination of l_1 is ancestor node of l_2.
    - With l_1 do:
        - Remove l_1 from X.
        - $\forall l_3$ which is neighboring link of l_1, evaluate inclusion of l_3 in X.
        - If $\exists l_2$ which is partner of l_1 and relative to $l_3 \in X$, then remove l_3 from X.
        - Change the direction of l_1.

Evaluation before inclusion of a link in X.

Before including a link l in X we need to do the following evaluation:
- If l has previously belonged to X, then discard l.
- Else if $l^{upward} \in X$ and l is now explored in downward direction, then update the direction of the link such that $l^{downward} \in X$.
- Else if $!(l \in X)$, then
    - If there is no direction assigned to l, then assign the downward direction to l.
        - If l contributes to form a cycle, that is, the source of l is also its ancestor node, then change the direction of l.
    - Else l is included in X with the direction found by the exploration process.

Definition 7. A node is *ancestor node* of a link if, starting from that link, the node can be reached by traversing only up-links.

Definition 8. Two links are *relatives* if they have common ancestor nodes.

4 Performance Evaluation

In this section we present the simulation study that was undertaken to evaluate our novel dynamic reconfiguration scheme, presented in the previous section. For performance assessment this scheme was compared to an earlier static reconfiguration scheme, proposed in [12] for source routing networks based on the Advanced Switching technology. We compare the time required by each scheme to completely assimilate a topology change, and also their impact on the network service. Before presenting the simulation results, the experiment setup is described.

4.1 Experiment Setup

The simulation model [11] used for this work was developed with the OPNET Modeler [9], and embodies the physical and link layers of Advanced Switching, allowing the simulation of several network designs. The model implements 16-port multiplexed virtual cut-through switches, where each port uses a 1x lane (2.5 Gbps), and endpoints are connected with a single port. This model provides the necessary support to design fabric management mechanisms as defined in the Advanced Switching specification [1]: management entities, device capabilities, and management packets. In addition, it considers the time required by the manager and devices to process incoming management packets and perform the tasks associated.

We evaluated several regular fabric topologies, including meshes, tori, and fixed-arity fat-trees. Although the management mechanisms analyzed do not require the use of several VCs, we used four virtual channels (VCs) per fabric port. According to the Advanced Switching specification, a minimum of two VCs per port must be in place, where one VC is dedicated to management traffic, and the remainder to data traffic [1]. Management traffic gets higher scheduling priority than data traffic in switches and therefore it will always take a similar time to assimilate a topological change, independently of the amount of data packets in the network. The size of the input and output buffers associated with each VC is 8 Kbytes.

For all simulations, the data packet length was fixed at 512 bytes. The traffic load that was applied was dependent on the fabric topology and the number (and size) of available VCs, representing 50% of the saturation rate in each case. The packet generation rate was uniform. The *perfect shuffle*, *bit reversal*, *matrix transpose*, and *uniform* traffic patterns were applied to obtain packet destination endpoints. The results for the different traffic patterns were very similar, and the results for the uniform traffic pattern were selected for presentation.

For each simulation there is an initial transient period in which fabric devices are activated, the manager gathers the original topology, and the fabric operation approaches its steady state. Later, a topological change (either the addition or removal of a randomly chosen fabric switch) is scheduled at time 2.0 seconds (after the fabric starts up). In order to increase the accuracy of the results, each experiment was repeated several times for each fabric topology. The number of simulation runs for each

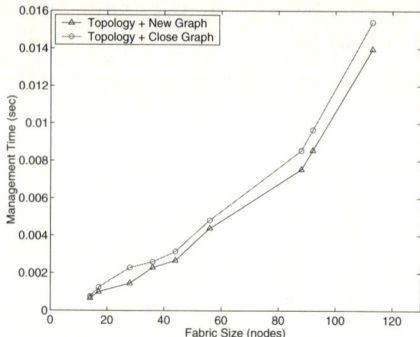

Fig. 1. The time required by the manager to build a new up*/down* graph for our dynamic reconfiguration scheme (Topology + Close Graph) and the static reconfiguration scheme (Topology + New Graph) as a function of fabric size

topology is about 15% of the number of physical nodes (both switches and endpoints) for both switch additions and removals, and averages have been drawn from the solution set and presented.

4.2 Impact on the Management Time

We first analyze the time required to calculate the new up*/down* graph after a topology change (Fig. 1). For the proposed dynamic reconfiguration scheme we measure the time spent in the "Topology + Close Graph" phase, whereas for the static reconfiguration scheme the time spent in the "Topology + New Graph" phase is measured. Both schemes first discover the new fabric topology that results from the topology change. In the next step, the static scheme assigns new link directions without taking the previous up*/down* graph into account, whereas the dynamic scheme transforms the old graph into a close graph by following the algorithm described in the previous section. We compare the duration of the topology discovery and graph calculation phases for the two schemes. Fig. 1 confirms that the overhead of our proposed dynamic scheme is small when compared to the static scheme. In addition, the duration of the topology discovery and graph calculation phases is short when compared to the path computation and reconfiguration phases (Fig. 2).

As a function of the fabric size, Fig. 2 shows the time required by the static and dynamic reconfiguration schemes to discover the new topology and build the new routing graph, compute the new set of routes, and update the routing tables after a topology change (both switch removal and addition are included). We observe that the "Dynamic Reconfiguration" phase spends less time updating the routing tables than the "Static Reconfiguration" phase does. The "Static Reconfiguration" phase comprises four steps: deactivation of the fabric ports to only allow management packets into the network, removal of the information stored at endpoint routing tables, distribution of the new routing paths to the endpoints and, finally, the reactivation of the fabric ports to allow data packets into the network. Routing tables are inactive during a certain period in the path distribution step. The "Dynamic Reconfiguration" phase, on the other hand, only comprises the distribution of the new set of routes. This also

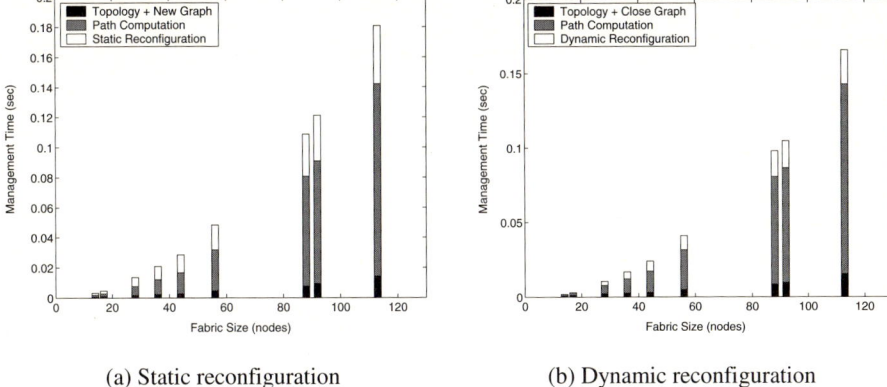

(a) Static reconfiguration (b) Dynamic reconfiguration

Fig. 2. The time required by the static and dynamic reconfiguration schemes to completely assimilate a topology change (both switch removal and addition are included)

explains why the "Dynamic Reconfiguration" phase uses significantly fewer management packets than the "Static Reconfiguration" phase does (these results are not shown here due to lack of space).

4.3 Impact on the Network Service

The number of data packets that are discarded during the topology change assimilation process gives an indication of the level of service a network can provide to applications. As a function of the fabric size, Fig. 3 compares the amount of packets that are discarded due to a switch removal for the static and dynamic reconfiguration schemes. The bars in this figure represent the quantities that relate to three different reasons for packets being discarded. They are labelled "Protected Ports", "Inactive Ports" and "Inactive Tables". The "Protected Ports" label quantifies packets that are discarded when they reach (logically) inactive ports (i.e., in the *DL_Protected* state in which ports can only receive and transmit management packets) [1]. The "Inactive Ports"

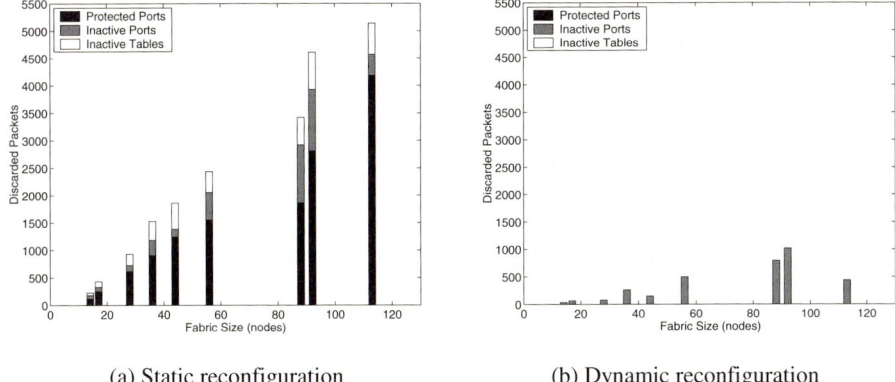

(a) Static reconfiguration (b) Dynamic reconfiguration

Fig. 3. The amount of application packets discarded as a consequence of a switch removal

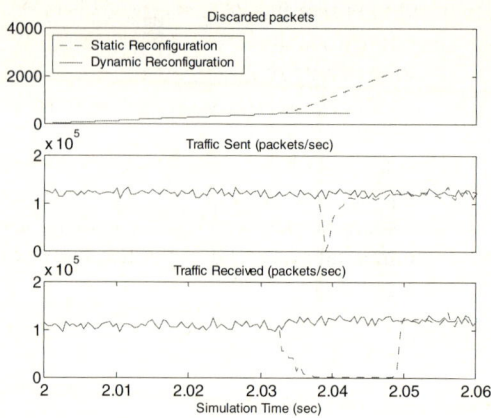

Fig. 4. The impact of a switch removal on application traffic (instantaneous results)

label refers to packets that attempt to cross the switch that has been removed from the network, in order to reach their destination. Finally, the "Inactive Tables" label refers to the packets that can not be injected into the network due to the endpoint routing tables are empty.

The results in Fig. 3 show that the rate at which data packets are discarded is notably lower for the new dynamic reconfiguration scheme than for the static reconfiguration scheme. The explanation is that whereas all three possible reasons for discarding packets apply for the static scheme, for the dynamic scheme packets are only discarded when they attempt to cross the removed switch. On the other hand, in the case of a switch addition (results not shown here due to lack of space), no packets are discarded due to inactive ports because no old routes include the switch that was just added. Moreover, in this case, there is no packet discarding when using the dynamic reconfiguration scheme. The reason is that it does not require deactivating fabric ports and routing tables.

To conclude the evaluation, Fig. 4 illustrates the instantaneous behavior of both the static and dynamic schemes. For both schemes, we have scheduled a removal of a switch in a 6×6 mesh at time 2.0 sec. For all plots, the x-axis represents the simulation time. The top plot shows the aggregate amount of data packets discarded during the assimilation process. The bottom two plots show instantaneous network throughput, represented by the number of data packets sent/received per second in the whole fabric.

The static reconfiguration scheme has a detrimental effect on the network service, and we observe a gap in the instantaneous throughput plots coinciding to the reconfiguration phase. This gap is completely eliminated by using our dynamic reconfiguration scheme. This demonstrates that the introduction of the dynamic reconfiguration scheme enables an uninterrupted network service during the topology change assimilation.

5 Conclusions

We have proposed and evaluated a new deadlock-free dynamic reconfiguration mechanism for updating the routing function after a topological change in a network that applies the up*/down* routing algorithm. At a minor computational cost, the new routing function is designed to ensure that packets routed according to the old and the new routing functions can unrestrictedly coexist in the network, without the risk of forming deadlocks. Simulation results show that this significantly reduces the amount of packets that are discarded during the topology-change assimilation. From the point of view of upper-level applications, our new reconfiguration strategy virtually eliminates the problem of reduced network service availability, which is characteristic of traditional reconfiguration proposals. In addition, our proposed strategy does not require additional fabric resources such as virtual channels, and it could easily be implemented in current commercial systems using either source or distributed routing.

References

1. Advanced Switching Interconnect Special Interest Group, Advanced Switching Core Architecture Specification Revision 1.0 (December 2003), http://www.picmg.org
2. Boden, N.J., et al.: Myrinet: A gigabit per second LAN. IEEE Micro. (February 1995)
3. Casado, R., Bermúdez, A., Quiles, F.J., Sánchez, J.L., Duato, J.: A protocol for deadlock-free dynamic reconfiguration in high-speed local area networks. IEEE Transactions on Parallel and Distributed Systems 12(2) (February 2001)
4. Dally, W.J., Seitz, C.L.: Deadlock-free message routing in multiprocessor interconnection networks. IEEE Transactions on Computers 36(5) (1987)
5. InfiniBand Architecture Specification (1.2) (November 2002), http://www.infinibandta.com/
6. Lysne, O., Duato, J.: Fast dynamic reconfiguration in Irregular networks. In: Proc. Int. Conference on Parallel Processing (August 2000)
7. Lysne, O., Montañana, J.M., Pinkston, T.M., Duato, J., Skeie, T., Flich, J.: Simple deadlock-free dynamic network reconfiguration. In: Proc. of the International Conference on High Performance Computing (December 2004)
8. Myrinet, Inc.: Guide to Myrinet-, Switches and Switch Networks (2000), http://www.myri.com/
9. OPNET Technologies, Inc., http://www.opnet.com/
10. Pinkston, T.M., Pang, R., Duato, J.: Deadlock-free dynamic reconfiguration schemes for increased network dependability. IEEE Transactions on Parallel and Distributed Systems 14(6) (June 2003)
11. Robles-Gómez, A., García, E.M., Bermúdez, A., Casado, R., Quiles, F.J.: A Model for the Development of ASI Fabric Management Protocols. In: Nagel, W.E., Walter, W.V., Lehner, W. (eds.) Euro-Par 2006. LNCS, vol. 4128. Springer, Heidelberg (2006)
12. Robles-Gómez, A., Bermúdez, A., Casado, R., Quiles, F.J., Skeie, T., Duato, J.: A proposal for managing ASI fabrics. Journal of System Architecture (JSA) (to appear, 2008)
13. Rodeheffer, T.L., Schroeder, M.D.: Automatic reconfiguration in Autonet. In: SRC Research Report 77 of the ACM Symposium on Operating Systems Principles (October 1991)
14. Sancho, J.C., Robles, A., Duato, J.: A new methodology to compute deadlock-free routing tables for irregular networks. In: Proc. the 4th Workshop on Communication, Architecture, and Applications for Network-based Parallel Computing (January 2000)
15. Schroeder, M.D., Birrell, A.D., Burrows, M., Murray, H., Needham, R.M., Rodeheffer, T.L., Satterthwate, E.H., Thacker, C.P.: Autonet: a high-speed, self-configuring local area network using point-to-point links. IEEE Journal on Selected Areas in Communications 9(8) (October 1991)

HITP: A Transmission Protocol for Scalable High-Performance Distributed Storage

P. Giacomin[1,2,3], A. Bassi[1], F.J. Seinstra[2], T. Kielmann[2], and H.E. Bal[2]

[1] Hitachi Sophia Antipolis Laboratory - Immeuble Le Thélème
1503 Route de Dolines, 06560 Valbonne, France
alessandro.bassi@hitach-eu.com
[2] Department of Computer Science, Vrije Universiteit
De Boelelaan 1081A, 1081 HV Amsterdam, The Netherlands
{fjseins,kielmann,bal}@cs.vu.nl
[3] giacomin@few.vu.nl

Abstract. In many application and research areas there is a trend towards *petascale* processing and archiving of scientific measurement results and derived data structures. As a consequence, there is an urgent need for disruptive technologies that revolutionize the manner in which we integrate, coordinate, and distribute computing and storage of vast amounts of data. This paper discusses the INCA architecture, a system that aims at providing a sustainable solution to the management problem of *data storage* in very large-scale distributed systems. INCA provides a solution where 'intelligence' in a globally scalable system is put in the middleware, where the lower level deals with local problems only, while all other properties are taken care of at the upper layers. In particular, we focus on a new, efficient transport protocol (referred to as HITP) that is specifically designed for bulk data transfer over high-speed (optical) network connections. We present performance results for basic transmission functionality, and show that HITP is capable of achieving higher throughput and lower latency than existing transport protocols.

1 Introduction

In many scientific research areas, applications are becoming more and more *data intensive* [3]. As an example, with the increasing storage and connectivity of image and video data, emerging applications in *multimedia content analysis* are rapidly approaching the petascale range [16]. For applications of this kind, solutions must be obtained by applying techniques of large-scale distributed storage and computing. From a storage perspective, coordinated handling of *distributed* and *replicated* data collections becomes a complex issue. As an example, we must deal with problems of (1) concurrent access to, (2) high-speed indexing of, and (3) rapid retrieval from, data sets that may be updated continuously.

In our opinion, any sustainable solution to the management problem of distributed data must follow a layered approach, including a new generation of network controllers, novel middleware, and transparent interfaces to applications. To reach the requirements of scalability, security, versatility, location independence, and delivering a Quality-of-Experience driven performance over existing network infrastructures, we are developing a solution (called *INCA*, or *Intelligent Network Caching Architecture*) where 'intelligence' in a globally scalable system is put in the middleware, where the lower level deals with local problems only, while all other properties are taken care of at the upper layers.

Today, network devices such as routers have transparent storage capabilities: when IP packets reach a router, they are stored in a queue, waiting to be processed. An *active network caching* scheme can take advantage of such storage, and buffer streams to be released only at a later stage. To achieve this, the network nodes should expose in some way the underlying storage, thus separating the basic forwarding functions from higher control capabilities. Furthermore, a middleware layer should provide interfaces to these advanced data management properties, to be available to Grid services and applications.

In this paper we focus on the network layer. We introduce a new, efficient transport protocol, capable of taking advantage of the storage capabilities of network devices. We present the protocol definition, and discuss performance results for basic transmission functionality as obtained on Fast Ethernet and Gigabit Ethernet links. Our results indicate that our new protocol is capable of achieving higher throughput and lower latency than existing transport protocols.

This paper is organized as follows. Section 2 presents a general introduction to active network caching and the INCA system, and signals the need for a new transport protocol. In Section 3 we present an overview of transport protocols, and indicate problems and drawbacks with respect to our purposes. Section 4 presents our new transport protocol, referred to as HITP. Section 5 discusses our performance results. Concluding remarks are given in Section 6.

2 Active Network Caching and the INCA System

An active, intelligent network caching scheme aims at taking advantage of otherwise transparent storage capabilities of network devices (such as routers), by buffering streams that are to be released only at a later stage. To achieve this, the network nodes should expose their underlying storage, thus separating the basic forwarding functions from higher control capabilities. This idea was first explored in the Internet Backplane Protocol (IBP) [12], which allows data to be stored at one location while en route from sender to receiver. Active network caching in this manner can improve application performance by allowing files to be staged near where they will be used, or data to be collected near their source.

Our work, as part of the Intelligent Network Caching Architecture (INCA) [2], aims at *exposing* and *expanding* the storage capabilities of network equipment. As an example, the INCA architecture aims to support files that can be replicated and scattered over the network, potentially at a world-wide scale. The INCA system follows a layered approach, ranging from the control of network equipment, up to the interface to applications and services.

This paper focuses on the lowest level of data transmission protocols, in particular at the IP level. At this level we need new mechanisms and protocols to make data storage available *inside* the network boundaries. Above all, this particular storage should be *efficient*, *secure*, and *reliable*. In addition, it should support very simple failure modes, to allow for maximum scalability. The middleware above, which is not the focus of this paper, will then act as the transport layer in networking; it provides all those properties that allow the framework to be useful to services and applications.

The following section gives a brief overview of state-of-the-art network transmission protocols, and indicates problems and drawbacks with respect to our purpose of efficient, secure, and reliable network caching.

3 State-of-the-Art Transmission Protocols

The Transmission Control Protocol (TCP) is one of the core protocols of the Internet protocol suite [14]. TCP provides reliable, in-order delivery of data streams, making it suitable for applications like file transfer and e-mail. Despite its importance, TCP has many drawbacks. The most significant problem is that TCP does not perform well on broadband high latency networks. This is because the maximal bandwidth usable by TCP is an inverse function of the latency [11]. With the recent uptake of high bandwidth delay networks much effort is being put in the circumvention of TCP deficiencies, mostly in three directions: alternative congestion controls algorithms (e.g. Vegas [4], Westwood+ [6], TCP Hybla [5], Scalable TCP [10], and CUBIC-TCP [15]), tuning techniques [18], and smart application level approaches that attempt to deal with TCP's window-size problems by using parallel streams (e.g., Psockets [17]).

An alternative to TCP is the User Datagram Protocol (UDP) [13]. Using UDP, networked computers can send short messages (known as datagrams) to one another. UDP does not guarantee reliability or ordering in the way that TCP does. Datagrams may arrive out of order, appear duplicated, or go missing without notice. Avoiding the overhead of checking whether every packet actually arrived makes UDP faster and more efficient, at least for applications that do not need guaranteed delivery. Despite this increased performance potential, the lack of reliability and congestion control makes UDP less suitable for our purposes.

The problems of UDP have been acknowledged in the field, and have led to many extended and adapted transfer protocols [1]. Two important research efforts in this direction are UDT (or UDP-based Data Transfer Protocol) [8], and RBUDP (or Reliable Blast UDP) [9]. Both protocols have been designed to effectively utilize the rapidly emerging high-speed wide area optical networks, and have been built on top of UDP with reliability and congestion control.

Another reliable data delivery protocol, that proxy TCP connections over UDP, is Airhook [7]. Unlike TCP, Airhook gracefully handles intermittent, unreliable, or delayed networks. In particular, Airhook continuously transmits small status packets to keep both endpoints aware of connection status; lost data packets are transmitted immediately when their absence is reported. Despite the impressive results obtained with UDT, RBUDP, and Airhook, none of these protocols can exploit network storage capabilities. As there is not a straightforward manner to integrate such capabilities (efficiently) within existing protocols, it is essential to define a new transport protocol for our purposes. Our proposed protocol will be introduced in the following section.

4 HITP: High-Volume INCA Transport Protocol

In this section we introduce our new transport protocol, called HITP, or High-volume INCA Transport Protocol. The aim of HITP is to transfer very large volumes of data in the most efficient way. The protocol is connectionless, such that it can deal with multiple peers easily, and get easily proxied.

A natural way to optimize data transport is to minimize overhead. To this end, HITP tries to identify the minimal amount of information needed to transfer a byte-sequence across the network successfully. In addition, HITP is made generic and extensible to allow it to deal with underlying heterogeneous network infrastructures and overlying applications. For these reasons, we have chosen the scheme as shown in Table 1 as the packet header of our protocol implementation. A very important role is played by the most significant bits (msb) of the fields 'rid', 'length', and 'offset', that enable message sizes to be extended for as long as needed. A more detailed explanation of the header fields is available in [2]. We believe that, using this strategy, we are able to keep the protocol extremely expandable. Each extension field is placed after the checksum in the same order as the basic fields. Each extension field of the same type is placed contiguously.

All HITP packets carry from a sender to a receiver, identified by their IP addresses in the IP protocol header, the amount of data specified by the HITP length field. When the packets arrive at the receiver the data are stored in a buffer specified by the rid (receiver identifier) and offset fields in the HITP header.

4.1 A Simplified Header

A simplified header, which is more targeted to current network infrastructures, could be considered as an alternative. For such a simplified header definition, we apply the following basic assumptions: (1) 64 KB is sufficiently large as a single packet size, (2) a peer will never have to handle more than 65536 incoming memory buffers at a time, and (3) a single dataset is limited to 256 TB. Under these assumptions our HITP header would look as in Table 2. This simplified header definition incorporates two new field definitions: **m block**, minor block, and **M block**, major block. Not very different from the offset fields, these fields allows one to address blocks of 64 KB and 4 GB respectively.

With this simplified definition, the implementation performance is expected to increase significantly due to the fixed header size, and (thus) a reduced complexity of packet analysis. Still it is important to note that, even though a 256 TB addressing space is not perceived as a limit today, this may (and probably will) change in the future. Hereinafter we will refer to this simplified version as HITP.

Table 1. Original HITP header

0	1-15	16	17-31
mo	offset	mr	rid
ml	length	\multicolumn{2}{c	}{checksum}
\multicolumn{4}{	c	}{payload...}

Table 2. Simplified HITP header

0-15	16-31
offset	rid
length	checksum
mblock	Mblock
\multicolumn{2}{|c|}{payload...}

4.2 HITP Control

To control the channels carrying HITP packets, we have defined an additional control scheme, which we refer as the *High-volume INCA Control Protocol* (HICP). This protocol assumes that a reliable transport protocol is used as the underlying protocol (e.g., TCP, T/TCP, or even SSL over TCP). HICP is employed in parallel to the HITP channel, and is used directly by the INCA middleware, or between peers.

HICP defines three basic concepts, i.e.: Input Channel, Output Channel, and Missing Table. The Input Channel is the receiver's view of an HITP transfer session. It is characterized by a receiver identifier (rid), pointers to a temporary and final storage facility, each having a negotiated quantity of free memory, a timer, a missing table, a list of linked nodes, and an identifier denoting the applied acknowledge strategy. The Output Channel represents the sender's view of an HITP transfer session. It is characterized by a pointer to the target node, the rid, pointers to temporary and final storage facilities, a missing table, and a list of other characteristics such as the optional rate limit, the MTU, and the send sequence rationale. The Missing Table represents the core concept of HICP/HITP. It consists of a list of tuples <offset, length>, representing data blocks that still need to be transferred.

A HICP session takes place as follows (ignoring error handling, for reasons of simplicity, see also Figure 1): Each HICP command is composed of an opcode of four characters, followed by a variable number of arguments. Once the output channel is initialized at the sender (using the *load* command) and the input channel is initialized at the receiver (using *bind*) the HITP session is ready to start. Subsequently, the receiver sends a *cont* command to remount the Missing Table. Then, the senders start to send HITP packets to the receiver according to their *send sequence rationale* (e.g., 'mask', 'sequential', 'random'). When a sender has finished sending packets it issues a *fini* command. Once this command is obtained by the receiver, it sends another *cont* command ro remount the missing table of the sender. This continues until the Missing Table is empty.

In our experiments, described in the following sections, we have applied the described session using a single sender and a sequential send rationale.

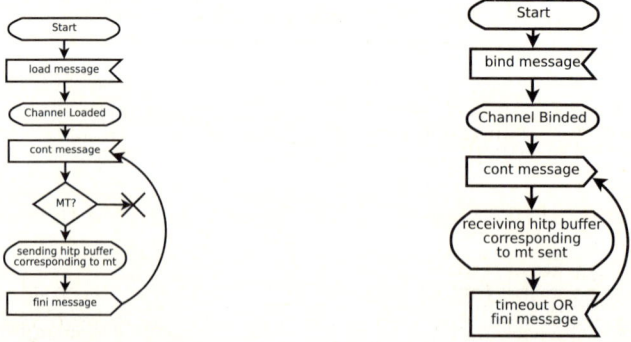

Fig. 1. HITP State Machine (without error handling and security)

5 Performance Evaluation

The following section presents the results obtained with our new protocol using a basic sender-receiver scenario. We will first give a description of two different measurement setups, one based on very old machines having a Fast Ethernet link, and one based on modern machines with Gigabit Ethernet. Based on these setups, we will describe a set of theoretical and real-world transmission scenarios. Subsequently, for each of these scenarios we will present our measurements, and provide a thorough analysis of our results.

Testbed 1: We performed our first measurements on an old testbed system comprising of three standard desktop PCs running Debian GNU/Linux "etch", with Linux kernel 2.6.18 and the Debian set of patches version 4. The first machine, i.e. the 'sender', is a DELL Dimension 4400 with a Pentium 4 1.7 Mhz processor and 512 MB of RAM. The second machine, i.e. the 'receiver', is a DELL Dimension 4500 with a Pentium 4 2.4 Mhz processor and 512 MB of RAM. The traffic between these two hosts, or 'peers', is entirely routed through the third machine, a DELL PowerEdge 600SC, hereafter referred to as the 'gateway/router'. We have performed measurements using several Fast Ethernet network cards, each giving similar performance results.

Testbed 2: Secondly, we have validated our protocol on a set of three modern machines with Broadcom NetXtreme II BCM5708 Gigabit Ethernet interfaces on PCI Express lanes. These machines, each having 4Gbyte of RAM, incorporate a quad-core Intel Xeon clocked at 2.00Ghz. As PCI Express is structured around lanes (i.e. separated point-to-point full duplex serial links), the bus bandwidth is no longer a limiting part of our measurement setup, neither for the gateway, nor for the peers. The MTU of the network adapters was fixed at 9000 bytes.

5.1 Emulation Methodology

In our testbed systems the gateway/router machine is of essential importance, as it is used to introduce controlled packet loss, latency, and packet reordering in a transparent way. These variations in network and transmission behavior have been incorporated using the 'netem' network emulation suite, which consists of a kernel component and a user space extension to iproute2. Hence, all applied software components are either open source, or developed by ourselves. It is also important to notice that in the gateway the bandwidth is not reduced and apart from the variations explicitly cited no traffic shaping is applied.

5.2 Execution Scenarios

To test the TCP protocol for comparison purposes, we have used a simple program that performs a 'sendfile'. This is the prefered — and most often used — way of using TCP to transfer a file. Simililarly, to test UDT we have used udt_sendfile and udt_recvfile, as part of the UDTv4 distribution.

For evaluating our own protocol, we note that it is difficult, if not impossible, to compare protocols acting on such different layers. It is, however, sufficient to simply transfer a static buffer and to see under which protocol the highest throughput is obtained. For this reason, in the case of the Fast Ethernet network, we generated our own static buffer, consisting of the first 100 Mbytes of the Linux kernel 2.6.18 tar archive. In the case of the Gigabit network we choose to transfer a buffer of 400 Mbytes containing some random bulk data. On both networks, the buffers have been transmitted under varying circumstances to evaluate the behavior of our system in comparison with other protocols.

In our evaluation we followed two alternative approaches. In the first approach we have studied the behavior of our protocol under variations in emulated network latency (ranging from no additional emulated latency up to 700 ms of emulated latency), and variations in packet loss (in the range of 0% to 12%). In the second approach we have recreated a real-world scenario with all sorts of concurrent "network perturbations": i.e. variable latency and packet loss. We ignore issues such as packet duplication and packet corruption, as these have no significant effect on performance.

5.3 Throughput Measurements

In our evaluation, we measure the time between the arrival of the first packet and that of the last. As we focus on throughput, we do not need to incorporate the one way latency of transmitting the first packet by the sender. Of course, we do take into account the internal HICP negotiation (i.e. *fini* and *cont*).

In our first measurement (see Figure 2), we compare HITP, TCP and UDP on the full Gigabit testbed (Testbed 2). Our experiments have been performed under variations in emulated latency (i.e. with round trip latencies ranging from 0 ms to 1400 ms with a close-up on the 0 ms to 200 ms part), but without any emulated packet loss or emulated packet reordering. In the experiment we intended to also compare the RBUDP protocol [9], but we have been unable to compile and run the QUANTA distribution on the testbed. Essentially, we should also add a small value representing real network latency. As this value is generally very small (i.e. in the order of 0.5 ms), however, it does not affect throughput results in any significant way. For this reason we ignore this value in this evaluation.

In Figure 2, when considering the results below 200 ms, we immediately see that TCP throughput is significantly and negatively affected by increased latency, which is a well-known TCP problem. Similarly, we see that UDT suffers from reduced bandwidth, which is found to be less than 700 mbps. We assume that this is due to packet size, which is less than 1500 bytes. Alternatively, this issue may be due to the way udt_sendfile reads the file from disk. Both these issues may cause a bottleneck in a Gigabit Ethernet environment. Apart from the total bandwidth, we can see that UDT performs better than TCP. However, even though UDT is designed to deal with high latencies, it is still significantly influenced by it. In contrast, HITP is largely unaffected by latency.

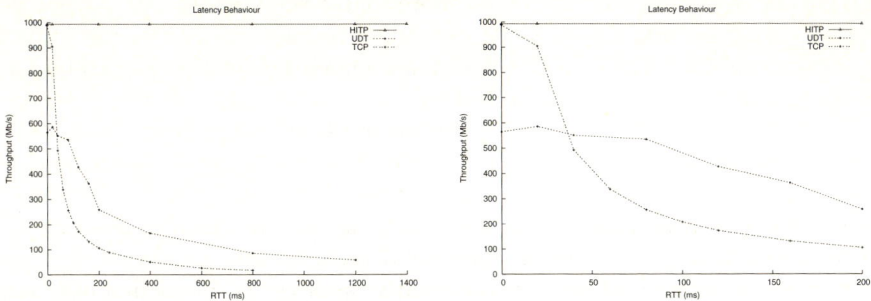

Fig. 2. Throughput under varying latency conditions (Testbed 2)

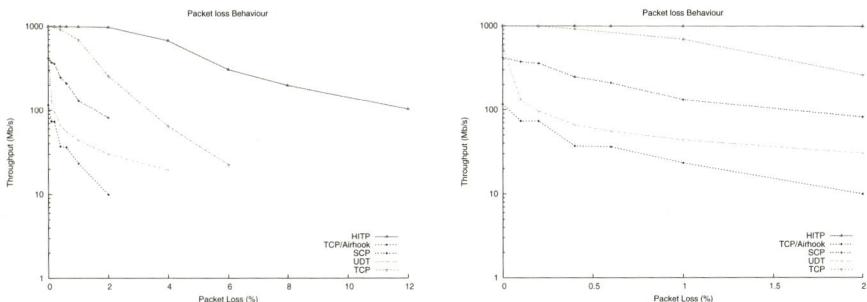

Fig. 3. Throughput under packet loss conditions (Testbed 2)

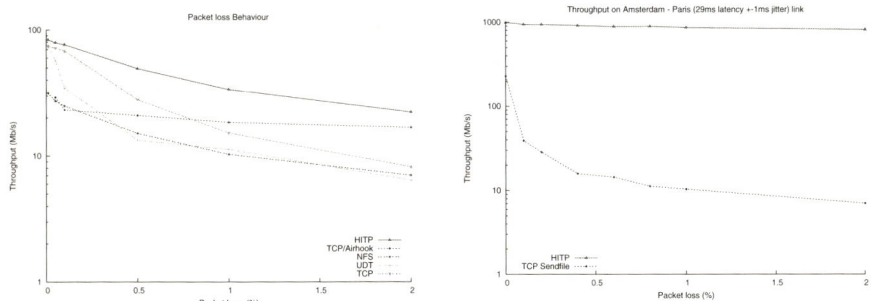

Fig. 4. Throughput under packet loss conditions (Testbed 1)

Fig. 5. Throughput over an Amsterdam - Paris link (Testbed 2)

In our second set of measurements (see Figure 3) we compare the throughput performance of HITP, UDT, SCP, TCP Sendfile, and TCP Sendfile on top of Airhook using a link without latency (or less than 1 ms, as stated above), and no packet reordering, under variations in packet loss ranging from 0% to 12%. As can be seen in Figure 3, in this emulated scenario HITP again performs better than all other protocols. If we look at the more detailed graph on the right, showing the first 2%, and compare these results with the measurements obtained on our initial testbed (Testbed 1, see Figure 4), it shows that HITP has become much more stable. This is due to the fact that, since we performed our measurements on Testbed 1, we have made slight changes to the HITP protocol implementation (in this case, the introduction of a 'request for acknowledge' at the end of a send). More importantly, when comparing these two graphs, Airhook shows significantly different behavior on the two different testbeds. In particular, Airhook seems to suffer much more from packet loss influences in the Gigabit Ethernet environment. Further, whereas Figure 4 gives the impression that Airhook results may become better than those of HITP in case of packet loss ratios of over 2%, our implementation improvements combined with an upgrade to a Gigabit Ethernet environment shows that this is certainly not the case. As in the UDT case, we assume that the inferior Airhook results are partially due to packet size, and partially due to protocol overhead.

In our final evaluation (see Figure 5) we reconstruct a real world scenario, as can be expected on a link between Amsterdam and Paris. On such a link, the latency for http traffic is around 29 ms, with a variation of $+/-$ 1 ms. As a consequence, packet reordering is a realistic and common phenomenon. Hence, for real-world scenarios we must evaluate how the different protocols react to packet reordering as well. In the Fast Ethernet environment (i.e. Testbed 1), UDT and TCP sometimes performed better under at least a certain amount of packet loss (i.e., around 0.5%). This is because an increased packet loss results in an increased number of HITP acknowledge messages, and hence and increased sensitivity to packet reordering. In Figure 5 we see that no such problems exist in our final measurements on Testbed 2. Figure 5 also clearly shows that HITP is not at all influenced by packet reordering. This finding is also supported by yet another measurement (not shown in any of the graphs), in which — with a latency of 160 ms and a jitter varying from 0 ms to 80 ms on a normal distribution — we see almost no perturbations on HITP throughput. This is because the HITP buffer at the receiver side is addressed directly from the packet.

Based on all our measurements we conclude that HITP is only marginally influenced by increased network latency, and not at all affected by packet reordering. HITP is still vulnerable to packet loss, but this is a condition which is rather unusual in high-speed optical Grid network links.

6 Conclusions

In this paper we have presented a new transport protocol (HITP) which is initially conceived for INCA, an active network caching system that aims at taking advantage of transparent storage capabilities of network devices. We have given an overview of state-of-the-art transport protocols, and have indicated problems and drawbacks with respect to our purposes, mostly from an end-user application and integration perspective. We have presented the new protocol, referred to as HITP, or High-volume INCA Transport Protocol, focusing on its ability of addressing, potentially, unlimited buffers in a simple manner. We have performed an extensive set of measurements using our new protocol on two testbed environments (one of which comprising of a Gigabit link), and compared our results with those obtained with other protocols.

Our main conclusions are that HITP performs better than existing protocols, under many realistic variations in transmission and network behavior. Most importantly, HITP is only marginally influenced by increased network latency, and not at all affected by packet reordering. HITP is still vulnerable to packet loss, but this is a condition which is rather unusual in high-speed optical Grid network links. As a result, we conclude that HITP constitutes the necessary, and efficient, low level transport layer that is to serve as a basis for all our further work on the INCA active network caching system.

Acknowledgements

This research is carried out under the FP6 *CoreGRID* Network of Excellence funded by the European Commission (Contract IST-2002-004265). This paper's first author is supported via CoreGRID's Industrial Fellowship Programme under grant no. CIFP-4/06. The authors would like to thank the Università del Piemonte Orientale, and Matteo Angelino, Massimo Canonico, Cosimo Anglano, and Darko Pancev for their valuable contributions to this research.

References

1. Anglano, C., Canonico, M.: Performance Analysis of High-Performance File Transfer Systems for Grid Applications. Concur. Comput.: Pract. Exp. 18(8), 807–816 (2006)
2. Bassi, A., Denazis, S., Giacomin, P.: Towards a Noah's Ark for the Upcoming Data Deluge. In: 3rd VLDB Workshop on Data Management in Grids (September 2007)
3. Bell, G., Gray, J., Szalay, A.: Petascale Computational Systems. IEEE Computer 39(1), 110–112 (2006)
4. Brakmo, L.S., O'Malley, S.W., Peterson, L.L.: TCP Vegas: New Techniques for Congestion Detection and Avoidance. In: SIGCOMM, pp. 24–35 (1994)
5. Caini, C., Firrincieli, R.: TCP Hybla: A TCP Enhancement for Heterogeneous Networks (2004)
6. Dell'Aera, A., et al.: Linux 2.4 Implementation of Westwood+ TCP with Rate-Halving: A Performance Evaluation over the Internet. In: Proc. ICC 2004 (June 2004)
7. Egnor, D.: Airhook: Reliable, Efficient Transmission Control for Networks that Suck, http://airhook.ofb.net/
8. Gu, Y., Grossman, R.: UDT: UDP-based Data Transfer for High-Speed Wide Area Networks. Computer Networks 51(7), 1777–1799 (2007)
9. He, E., et al.: Reliable Blast UDP: Predictable High Performance Bulk Data Transfer. In: Proc. IEEE International Conference on Cluster Computing (September 2002)
10. Kelly, T.: Scalable TCP: Improving Performance in HighSpeed Wide Area Networks (February 2003)

11. Padhye, J., et al.: Modeling TCP Throughput: A Simple Model and its Empirical Validation. In: ACM SIGCOMM 1998, Vancouver, CA, pp. 303–314 (1998)
12. Plank, J., Bassi, A., Beck, M., Moore, T., Swany, M., Wolski, R.: Managing Data Storage in the Network. IEEE Internet Computing 6(5), 50–58 (2001)
13. Postel, J.: User Datagram Protocol, Internet standard RFC 768 (August 1980)
14. Postel, J.: Transmission Control Protocol, Internet standard RFC 793 (September 1981)
15. Rhee, I., et al.: CUBIC: A New TCP-Friendly High-Speed TCP Variant (February 2005)
16. Seinstra, F., et al.: High-Performance Distributed Video Content Analysis with Parallel-Horus. IEEE Multimedia 15(4), 64–75 (2007)
17. Sivakumar, H., et al.: PSockets: The Case for Application-level Network Striping for Data Intensive Applications. In: Supercomputing (SC 2000) (November 2000)
18. Tierney, B.L., et al.: TCP Tuning Guide (January 2008)

Author Index

Aida, Yoshiaki   554
Akbarinia, Reza   632
Alagheband, Pouya   151
Almeida, Francisco   89
Amaral, José Nelson   686
Amoedo, Pedro   360
Andersson, Per   780
Ansari, Mohammad   719
Antoniu, Gabriel   456
Arantes, Luciana   565
Arbenz, P.   778
Arenaz, Manuel   360
Arickx, Frans   223

Bader, Michael   801
Badia, R.M.   445
Baker, Mark   444
Bakhouya, M.   654
Bal, H.E.   950
Baliś, Bartosz   37
Barrachina, Sergio   739
Bassi, A.   950
Baydal, Elvira   930
Bermúdez, Aurelio   940
Bernard, Julien   887
Bertels, Koen   520
Beyler, Jean Christophe   643
Biberstein, Marina   3
Bonacic, Carolina   414, 866
Bouziane, Hinde Lilia   698
Boykin, Timothy B.   790
Briz, José Luis   327
Broeckhove, Jan   223, 544
Bruguera, J.D.   778
Brunst, Holger   172
Bubak, Marian   37
Bungartz, H.-J.   778
Buyya, Rajkumar   444

Canon, R. Shane   130
Caragiannis, Ioannis   876
Casado, Rafael   940
Castillo, Maribel   739
Castillo, P.A.   622
César, E.   110, 295

Chen, Li   382
Chen, Ruichuan   601
Chen, Zhong   601
Clauss, Philippe   643
Cornwell, Tim   749
Costa, Rogério Luís de Carvalho   489
Cudennec, Loïc   456

Dally, William J.   337
Danelutto, Marco   444
Das, Abhishek   337
de Bosschere, Koen   315
de Melo, Alba Cristina Magalhaes Alves   534
De Moor, Nils   544
de Palol, M.   445
Decker, Hendrik   394
Depoorter, Wim   544
Díaz de Cerio, Luis   510
Dikaiakos, Marios   1
Doulamis, Nikos   478
Du, D.   445
Duan, Rubing   665
Duarte, Angelo   58
Duato, José   899, 910, 930
Dupont de Dinechin, Benoît   370

Eiben, A.E.   622
El-Ghazawi, T.   654
Elmegreen, Bruce G.   749
Epema, Dick   13, 599

Fahringer, Thomas   26, 202, 466
Falcou, Joel   729
Fan, Dongrui   120
Fedorova, Alexandra   151
Feng, Xiao-bing   382
Fernández, L.   709
Ferreira, Paulo   47
Ferrer, Joan-LLuís   930
Fichtner, Wolfgang   790
Flammini, Michele   920
Flich, José   898

Focht, Erich 576
Fragopoulou, Paraskevi 444
Freeman, Len 274
Freeman, Timothy 499
Furtado, Pedro 489

Gabarró, Joaquim 686
Gallardo, Antonia 510
García-Mateos, G. 709
García, J.R. 233
García-López, Pedro 611
Garcia, Carlos 414
Gautier, Thierry 887
Gerndt, Michael 89
Gesellensetter, Lars 350
Ghareeb, Majd 456
Giacomin, P. 950
Gil-Costa, Veronica 434, 866
Giné, F. 233
Glesner, Sabine 350
Glinka, Frank 466
Godoi, Rodrigo 856
Gómez, Crispín 899
Gómez, María E. 899
Gomez-Pantoja, Carlos 434
Gonzalez, Senen 434
Gorlatch, Sergei 466, 811
Granat, Robert 780
Guevara, A. 295
Guil, Nicolás 844
Guo, Wenjia 601

Hackenberg, Daniel 172
Hanzich, M. 233
Harel, Yuval 3
Heilper, Andre 3
Hellinckx, Peter 223
Hendrickson, B.A. 778
Herley, Kieran T. 876
Hernández, Cecilia 424
Hernández, Porfidio 233, 856
Hessabi, Shaahin 100
Himstedt, Kai 587
Hoenen, Olivier 822
Hofer, Jürgen 26
Hoffmann, Ralf 253
Hoisie, Adolfy 89
Holanda, Raimir 898
Hu, Jianbin 601

Huang, Michael C. 315
Huedo, E. 445

Ibáñez, Pablo E. 327
Igual, Francisco D. 739
Iosup, Alexandru 13
Iyer, Ravishankar 141

Jarvis, Kim 719
Jeannot, Emmanuel 877
Jelasity, Márk 599
Jemni, Mohamed 846
Jeon, Myeongjae 285
Jiang, Yunlian 263
Jonsson, Isak 780
Jorba, Josep 599
Jourdren, Hervé 78
Jubertie, Sylvain 192
Juhasz, Zoltan 844

Kågström, Bo 780
Kalia, Rajiv K. 763
Kargupta, Hillol 392
Kazempour, Vahid 151
Keahey, Katarzyna 499
Kerbyson, Darren J. 688
Khanfir, Sami 846
Kiasari, Abbas Eslami 100
Kielmann, T. 950
Kim, Dongsung 285
Kim, Hwanju 285
Kirkham, Chris 719
Klemm, Michael 643
Klimeck, Gerhard 790
Kokkinos, Panagiotis 478
Kokossis, A. 445
Kotselidis, Christos 719
Kranzlmueller, Dieter 222
Kuhn, Michael 90
Kunkel, Julian M. 90, 212

Łabno, Bartłomiej 37
Lalis, Spyros 305
Lallouet, Arnaud 192
Lampsas, Petros 305
Lapresté, Jean-Thierry 729
Laredo, J.L.J. 622
Larriba-Pey, Josep Lluis 392
Lèbre, Adrien 576
Lee, Joonwon 285
Legond-Aubry, Fabrice 565

Leon, Coromoto 876
Lérida, J.Ll. 233
Lin, Wei 120
Liu, Dong 182
Liu, Lei 382
Llorente, I.M. 445
Long, Guoping 120
López, Pedro 317, 899, 930
López-de-Teruel, P.E. 709
Lorenz, Ulf 587
Lottiaux, Renaud 576
Loukopoulos, Thanasis 305
Lourenço, Joao 1
Ludwig, Thomas 90, 212
Luisier, Mathieu 790
Luján, Mikel 719
Luque, Emilio 58, 68, 110, 295

Macías López, Elsa María 642
Maillard, Nicolas 887
Makineni, Srihari 141
Malony, Allen D. 162
Margalef, Tomàs 68, 110, 295
Marin, Mauricio 414, 424, 434, 866
Marques, Edgar 47
Mattingly, Andrew 749
Mayo, Rafael 739
Melin, Emmanuel 192
Merelo, J.J. 622
Miedes, Emili 394
Moga, Adrian 141
Möller, Dietmar P.F. 587
Monaco, Gianpiero 920
Montero, R.S. 445
Montresor, Alberto 599
Mora, A.M. 622
Morajko, Anna 68, 110
Morajko, Oleg 68
Moreno, A. 295
Morin, Christine 576
Morris, Alan 162
Moscardelli, Luca 920
Müller-Iden, Jens 466
Muñoz-Escoí, Francesc D. 394

Nae, Vlad 202, 466
Nagel, Wolfgang E. 172
Nakajima, Yoshihiro 554
Nakano, Aiichiro 763
Namyst, Raymond 78

Newell, Don 141
Ngubiri, John 243
Nieplocha, Jarek 676
Nomura, Ken-ichi 763

Oral, H. Sarp 130
Orduña, Juan M. 910
Ortega, Daniel 898
Oyakawa, Takehiro 763

Pacitti, Esther 392, 632
Palesi, Maurizio 910
Palma, Wenceslao 632
Patan, Maciej 833
Pech, Lucien 729
Peng, Liu 763
Pérache, Marc 78
Pérez, Christian 444, 698
Petit, S. 317
Philippsen, Michael 643
Piernas, Juan 676
Piñuel, Luis 315
Ploss, Alexander 466
Pourebrahimi, Behnaz 520
Prieto, Manuel 414
Priol, Thierry 698
Prodan, Radu 202, 466
Pucci, Geppino 876

Quintana-Ortí, Enrique S. 739

Ramos, Luis M. 327
Rana, Omer 1
Rauber, Thomas 253
Rexachs, Dolores 58
Rivera, Francisco F. 222
Robert, Yves 222
Robles, Antonio 930
Robles-Gómez, Antonio 940
Roch, Jean-Louis 887
Rodríguez, A.L. 709
Rodríguez, M. Andrea 424
Ruiz, A. 709

Sahuquillo, J. 317
Salawdeh, I. 110
Sànchez-Artigas, Marc 611
Sancho, José Carlos 688
Sanjeevan, Kana 510
Sankaran, Ramanan 130

Author Index

Santos, Guna 58
Sarbazi-Azad, Hamid 100
Sato, Mitsuhisa 554
Saule, Erik 877
Schellmann, Maraike 811
Schenk, Andreas 790
Schikuta, Erich 444
Schulz, Martin 89
Schwiegelshohn, Uwe 222
Scorsatto, Glauber 534
Seinstra, Frank 844, 950
Sens, Pierre 565
Seo, Euiseong 285
Sérot, Jocelyn 729
Serres, O. 654
Shalom, Mordechai 920
Shapiro, Marc 404, 642
Shen, Xipeng 263
Shende, Sameer 162
Sips, Henk 749
Sirvent, R. 445
Skarmeta, Antonio G. 611
Skeie, Tor 898
Slavin, Paul 274
Solheim, Åshild Grønstad 940
Solsona, F. 233
Song, Fenglong 120
Sonmez, Ozan 13
Sopena, Julien 565
Sorribes, J. 295
Spear, Wyatt 162
Strey, Alfred 665
Sutra, Pierre 404

Talia, Domenico 392
Tang, Liyong 601
Tatebe, Osamu 456, 554
Tirado, Francisco 414
Tomás, N. 317
Tornero, Rafael 910

Touriño, Juan 360, 444
Traoré, Daouda 887
Trystram, Denis 877
Tziritas, Nikos 305

Ur, Shmuel 1

Valduriez, Patrick 632
van Amesfoort, Alexander S. 749
van Diepen, Ger 749
van Nieuwpoort, Rob 749
van Steen, M. 622
van Vliet, Mario 243
Vanmechelen, Kurt 544
Varbanescu, Ana Lucia 749
Varvarigos, Emmanouel 478
Vashishta, Priya 763
Vautard, Jérémie 192
Vázquez, C. 445
Veiga, Luís 47
Verboven, Sam 223
Vetter, Jeffrey S. 130
Viñals, Víctor 327
Violard, Eric 822
Vörding, Jürgen 811

Wang, Qigang 182
Wang, Wei 182
Watson, Ian 719
Wei, Wei 182
Wilson, Simon 844
Wu, ChengYong 382

Yang, Xiaoyuan 856
Young, Jessica 141
Yu, Weikuan 130
Yuan, Nan 120

Zaks, Ayal 315
Zaks, Shmuel 920
Zhang, Junchao 120

Printing: Mercedes-Druck, Berlin
Binding: Stein+Lehmann, Berlin

Lecture Notes in Computer Science

Sublibrary 1: Theoretical Computer Science and General Issues

For information about Vols. 1– 4921
please contact your bookseller or Springer

Vol. 5234: V. Adve, M.J. Garzarán, P. Petersen (Eds.), Languages and Compilers for Parallel Computing. XV, 354 pages. 2008.

Vol. 5204: C.S. Calude, J.F. Costa, R. Freund, M. Oswald, G. Rozenberg (Eds.), Unconventional Computing. X, 259 pages. 2008.

Vol. 5201: F. van Breugel, M. Chechik (Eds.), CONCUR 2008 - Concurrency Theory. XIII, 524 pages. 2008.

Vol. 5191: H. Umeo, S. Morishita, K. Nishinari, T. Komatsuzaki, S. Bandini (Eds.), Cellular Automata. XVI, 577 pages. 2008.

Vol. 5172: S. Dolev, T. Haist, M. Oltean (Eds.), Optical SuperComputing. IX, 129 pages. 2008.

Vol. 5171: A. Goel, K. Jansen, J.D.P. Rolim, R. Rubinfeld (Eds.), Approximation, Randomization and Combinatorial Optimization. XII, 604 pages. 2008.

Vol. 5170: O.A. Mohamed, C. Muñoz, S. Tahar (Eds.), Theorem Proving in Higher Order Logics. X, 321 pages. 2008.

Vol. 5169: J. Fong, R. Kwan, F.L. Wang (Eds.), Hybrid Learning and Education. XII, 474 pages. 2008.

Vol. 5168: E. Luque, T. Margalef, D. Benítez (Eds.), Euro-Par 2008 – Parallel Processing. XXVIII, 964 pages. 2008.

Vol. 5165: B. Yang, D.-Z. Du, C.A. Wang (Eds.), Combinatorial Optimization and Applications. XII, 480 pages. 2008.

Vol. 5162: E. Ochmański, J. Tyszkiewicz (Eds.), Mathematical Foundations of Computer Science 2008. XIV, 626 pages. 2008.

Vol. 5156: K. Havelund, R. Majumdar, J. Palsberg (Eds.), Model Checking Software. X, 343 pages. 2008.

Vol. 5148: O. Ibarra, B. Ravikumar (Eds.), Implementation and Applications of Automata. XII, 289 pages. 2008.

Vol. 5147: K. Horimoto, G. Regensburger, M. Rosenkranz, H. Yoshida (Eds.), Algebraic Biology. XII, 245 pages. 2008.

Vol. 5133: P. Audebaud, C. Paulin-Mohring (Eds.), Mathematics of Program Construction. X, 423 pages. 2008.

Vol. 5132: P.J. Bentley, D. Lee, S. Jung (Eds.), Artificial Immune Systems. XIV, 436 pages. 2008.

Vol. 5130: J. von zur Gathen, J.L. Imaña, Ç.K. Koç (Eds.), Arithmetic of Finite Fields. X, 205 pages. 2008.

Vol. 5126: L. Aceto, I. Damgård, L.A. Goldberg, M.M. Halldórsson, A. Ingólfsdóttir, I. Walukiewicz (Eds.), Automata, Languages and Programming, Part II. XXII, 730 pages. 2008.

Vol. 5125: L. Aceto, I. Damgård, L.A. Goldberg, M.M. Halldórsson, A. Ingólfsdóttir, I. Walukiewicz (Eds.), Automata, Languages and Programming, Part I. XXIII, 896 pages. 2008.

Vol. 5124: J. Gudmundsson (Ed.), Algorithm Theory – SWAT 2008. XIII, 438 pages. 2008.

Vol. 5123: A. Gupta, S. Malik (Eds.), Computer Aided Verification. XVII, 558 pages. 2008.

Vol. 5117: A. Voronkov (Ed.), Rewriting Techniques and Applications. XIII, 457 pages. 2008.

Vol. 5114: M. Bereković, N. Dimopoulos, S. Wong (Eds.), Embedded Computer Systems: Architectures, Modeling, and Simulation. XVI, 300 pages. 2008.

Vol. 5104: F. Bello, E. Edwards (Eds.), Biomedical Simulation. XI, 228 pages. 2008.

Vol. 5103: M. Bubak, G.D. van Albada, J. Dongarra, P.M.A. Sloot (Eds.), Computational Science – ICCS 2008, Part III. XXVIII, 758 pages. 2008.

Vol. 5102: M. Bubak, G.D. van Albada, J. Dongarra, P.M.A. Sloot (Eds.), Computational Science – ICCS 2008, Part II. XXVIII, 752 pages. 2008.

Vol. 5101: M. Bubak, G.D. van Albada, J. Dongarra, P.M.A. Sloot (Eds.), Computational Science – ICCS 2008, Part I. XLVI, 1058 pages. 2008.

Vol. 5092: X. Hu, J. Wang (Eds.), Computing and Combinatorics. XIV, 680 pages. 2008.

Vol. 5090: R.T. Mittermeir, M.M. Sysło (Eds.), Informatics Education - Supporting Computational Thinking. XV, 357 pages. 2008.

Vol. 5084: J.F. Peters, A. Skowron (Eds.), Transactions on Rough Sets VIII. X, 521 pages. 2008.

Vol. 5083: O. Chitil, Z. Horváth, V. Zsók (Eds.), Implementation and Application of Functional Languages. XI, 272 pages. 2008.

Vol. 5073: O. Gervasi, B. Murgante, A. Laganà, D. Taniar, Y. Mun, M.L. Gavrilova (Eds.), Computational Science and Its Applications – ICCSA 2008, Part II. XXIX, 1280 pages. 2008.

Vol. 5072: O. Gervasi, B. Murgante, A. Laganà, D. Taniar, Y. Mun, M.L. Gavrilova (Eds.), Computational Science and Its Applications – ICCSA 2008, Part I. XXIX, 1266 pages. 2008.

Vol. 5065: P. Degano, R. De Nicola, J. Meseguer (Eds.), Concurrency, Graphs and Models. XV, 810 pages. 2008.

Vol. 5062: K.M. van Hee, R. Valk (Eds.), Applications and Theory of Petri Nets. XIII, 429 pages. 2008.

Vol. 5059: F.P. Preparata, X. Wu, J. Yin (Eds.), Frontiers in Algorithmics. XI, 350 pages. 2008.

Vol. 5058: A.A. Shvartsman, P. Felber (Eds.), Structural Information and Communication Complexity. X, 307 pages. 2008.

Vol. 5050: J.M. Zurada, G.G. Yen, J. Wang (Eds.), Computational Intelligence: Research Frontiers. XVI, 389 pages. 2008.

Vol. 5045: P. Hertling, C.M. Hoffmann, W. Luther, N. Revol (Eds.), Reliable Implementation of Real Number Algorithms: Theory and Practice. XI, 239 pages. 2008.

Vol. 5038: C.C. McGeoch (Ed.), Experimental Algorithms. X, 363 pages. 2008.

Vol. 5036: S. Wu, L.T. Yang, T.L. Xu (Eds.), Advances in Grid and Pervasive Computing. XV, 518 pages. 2008.

Vol. 5035: A. Lodi, A. Panconesi, G. Rinaldi (Eds.), Integer Programming and Combinatorial Optimization. XI, 477 pages. 2008.

Vol. 5029: P. Ferragina, G.M. Landau (Eds.), Combinatorial Pattern Matching. XIII, 317 pages. 2008.

Vol. 5028: A. Beckmann, C. Dimitracopoulos, B. Löwe (Eds.), Logic and Theory of Algorithms. XIX, 596 pages. 2008.

Vol. 5022: A.G. Bourgeois, S.Q. Zheng (Eds.), Algorithms and Architectures for Parallel Processing. XIII, 336 pages. 2008.

Vol. 5018: M. Grohe, R. Niedermeier (Eds.), Parameterized and Exact Computation. X, 227 pages. 2008.

Vol. 5015: L. Perron, M.A. Trick (Eds.), Integration of AI and OR Techniques in Constraint Programming for Combinatorial Optimization Problems. XII, 394 pages. 2008.

Vol. 5011: A.J. van der Poorten, A. Stein (Eds.), Algorithmic Number Theory. IX, 455 pages. 2008.

Vol. 5010: E.A. Hirsch, A.A. Razborov, A. Semenov, A. Slissenko (Eds.), Computer Science – Theory and Applications. XIII, 411 pages. 2008.

Vol. 5008: A. Gasteratos, M. Vincze, J.K. Tsotsos (Eds.), Computer Vision Systems. XV, 560 pages. 2008.

Vol. 5004: R. Eigenmann, B.R. de Supinski (Eds.), OpenMP in a New Era of Parallelism. X, 191 pages. 2008.

Vol. 5000: O. Grumberg, H. Veith (Eds.), 25 Years of Model Checking. VII, 231 pages. 2008.

Vol. 4996: H. Kleine Büning, X. Zhao (Eds.), Theory and Applications of Satisfiability Testing – SAT 2008. X, 305 pages. 2008.

Vol. 4988: R. Berghammer, B. Möller, G. Struth (Eds.), Relations and Kleene Algebra in Computer Science. X, 397 pages. 2008.

Vol. 4985: M. Ishikawa, K. Doya, H. Miyamoto, T. Yamakawa (Eds.), Neural Information Processing, Part II. XXX, 1091 pages. 2008.

Vol. 4984: M. Ishikawa, K. Doya, H. Miyamoto, T. Yamakawa (Eds.), Neural Information Processing, Part I. XXX, 1147 pages. 2008.

Vol. 4981: M. Egerstedt, B. Mishra (Eds.), Hybrid Systems: Computation and Control. XV, 680 pages. 2008.

Vol. 4978: M. Agrawal, D.-Z. Du, Z. Duan, A. Li (Eds.), Theory and Applications of Models of Computation. XII, 598 pages. 2008.

Vol. 4975: F. Chen, B. Jüttler (Eds.), Advances in Geometric Modeling and Processing. XV, 606 pages. 2008.

Vol. 4974: M. Giacobini, A. Brabazon, S. Cagnoni, G.A. Di Caro, R. Drechsler, A. Ekárt, A.I. Esparcia-Alcázar, M. Farooq, A. Fink, J. McCormack, M. O'Neill, J. Romero, F. Rothlauf, G. Squillero, A.Ş. Uyar, S. Yang (Eds.), Applications of Evolutionary Computing. XXV, 701 pages. 2008.

Vol. 4973: E. Marchiori, J.H. Moore (Eds.), Evolutionary Computation, Machine Learning and Data Mining in Bioinformatics. X, 213 pages. 2008.

Vol. 4972: J. van Hemert, C. Cotta (Eds.), Evolutionary Computation in Combinatorial Optimization. XII, 289 pages. 2008.

Vol. 4971: M. O'Neill, L. Vanneschi, S. Gustafson, A.I. Esparcia Alcázar, I. De Falco, A. Della Cioppa, E. Tarantino (Eds.), Genetic Programming. XI, 375 pages. 2008.

Vol. 4967: R. Wyrzykowski, J. Dongarra, K. Karczewski, J. Wasniewski (Eds.), Parallel Processing and Applied Mathematics. XXIII, 1414 pages. 2008.

Vol. 4963: C.R. Ramakrishnan, J. Rehof (Eds.), Tools and Algorithms for the Construction and Analysis of Systems. XVI, 518 pages. 2008.

Vol. 4962: R. Amadio (Ed.), Foundations of Software Science and Computational Structures. XV, 505 pages. 2008.

Vol. 4961: J.L. Fiadeiro, P. Inverardi (Eds.), Fundamental Approaches to Software Engineering. XIII, 430 pages. 2008.

Vol. 4960: S. Drossopoulou (Ed.), Programming Languages and Systems. XIII, 399 pages. 2008.

Vol. 4959: L. Hendren (Ed.), Compiler Construction. XII, 307 pages. 2008.

Vol. 4957: E.S. Laber, C. Bornstein, L.T. Nogueira, L. Faria (Eds.), LATIN 2008: Theoretical Informatics. XVII, 794 pages. 2008.

Vol. 4943: R. Woods, K. Compton, C. Bouganis, P.C. Diniz (Eds.), Reconfigurable Computing: Architectures, Tools and Applications. XIV, 344 pages. 2008.

Vol. 4942: E. Frachtenberg, U. Schwiegelshohn (Eds.), Job Scheduling Strategies for Parallel Processing. VII, 189 pages. 2008.

Vol. 4941: M. Miculan, I. Scagnetto, F. Honsell (Eds.), Types for Proofs and Programs. VII, 203 pages. 2008.

Vol. 4935: B. Chapman, W. Zheng, G.R. Gao, M. Sato, E. Ayguadé, D. Wang (Eds.), A Practical Programming Model for the Multi-Core Era. VI, 208 pages. 2008.

Vol. 4934: U. Brinkschulte, T. Ungerer, C. Hochberger, R.G. Spallek (Eds.), Architecture of Computing Systems – ARCS 2008. XI, 287 pages. 2008.

Vol. 4927: C. Kaklamanis, M. Skutella (Eds.), Approximation and Online Algorithms. X, 289 pages. 2008.

Vol. 4926: N. Monmarché, E.-G. Talbi, P. Collet, M. Schoenauer, E. Lutton (Eds.), Artificial Evolution. XIII, 327 pages. 2008.